T0344994

DATA MINING AND MACHINE LEARNING

The fundamental algorithms in data mining and machine learning form the basis of data science, utilizing automated methods to analyze patterns and models for all kinds of data in applications ranging from scientific discovery to business analytics. This textbook for senior undergraduate and graduate courses provides a comprehensive, in-depth overview of data mining, machine learning and statistics, offering solid guidance for students, researchers, and practitioners. The book lays the foundations of data analysis, pattern mining, clustering, classification and regression, with a focus on the algorithms and the underlying algebraic, geometric, and probabilistic concepts. New to this second edition is an entire part devoted to regression methods, including neural networks and deep learning.

Mohammed J. Zaki is Professor of Computer Science at Rensselaer Polytechnic Institute, where he also serves as Associate Department Head and Graduate Program Director. He has more than 250 publications and is an Associate Editor for the journal Data Mining and Knowledge Discovery. He is on the Board of Directors for ACM SIGKDD. He has received the National Science Foundation CAREER Award, and the Department of Energy Early Career Principal Investigator Award. He is an ACM Distinguished Member, and IEEE Fellow.

Wagner Meira, Jr. is Professor of Computer Science at Universidade Federal de Minas Gerais, Brazil, where he is currently the chair of the department. He has published more than 230 papers on data mining and parallel and distributed systems. He was leader of the Knowledge Discovery research track of InWeb and is currently Vice-chair of INCT-Cyber. He is on the editorial board of the journal Data Mining and Knowledge Discovery and was the program chair of SDM'16 and ACM WebSci'19. He has been a CNPq researcher since 2002. He has received an IBM Faculty Award and several Google Faculty Research Awards.

DATA MINING AND MACHINE LEARNING

Fundamental Concepts and Algorithms

MOHAMMED J. ZAKI
Rensselaer Polytechnic Institute

WAGNER MEIRA, JR.
Universidade Federal de Minas Gerais

CAMBRIDGE
UNIVERSITY PRESS

CAMBRIDGE
UNIVERSITY PRESS

University Printing House, Cambridge CB2 8BS, United Kingdom

One Liberty Plaza, 20th Floor, New York, NY 10006, USA

477 Williamstown Road, Port Melbourne, VIC 3207, Australia

314–321, 3rd Floor, Plot 3, Splendor Forum, Jasola District Centre, New Delhi – 110025, India

79 Anson Road, #06–04/06, Singapore 079906

Cambridge University Press is part of the University of Cambridge.

It furthers the University's mission by disseminating knowledge in the pursuit of education, learning, and research at the highest international levels of excellence.

www.cambridge.org
Information on this title: www.cambridge.org/9781108473989
DOI: 10.1017/9781108564175

First edition published 2014, second edition published 2020

A catalog record for this publication is available from the British Library.

Library of Congress Cataloging in Publication Data
Names: Zaki, Mohammed J., 1971- author. | Meira, Wagner, 1967- author.
Title: Data mining and machine learning : fundamental concepts and algorithms / Mohammed J. Zaki, Wagner Meira, Jr.
Other titles: Data mining and analysis
Description: Cambridge, United Kingdom ; New York, NY : Cambridge University Press, 2020. | Revised edition of: Data mining and analysis. 2014. | Includes bibliographical references and index.
Identifiers: LCCN 2019037293 (print) | LCCN 2019037294 (ebook) | ISBN 9781108473989 (hardback) | ISBN 9781108564175 (epub)
Subjects: LCSH: Data mining.
Classification: LCC QA76.9.D343 Z36 2020 (print) | LCC QA76.9.D343 (ebook) | DDC 006.3/12–dc23
LC record available at https://lccn.loc.gov/2019037293
LC ebook record available at https://lccn.loc.gov/2019037294

ISBN 978-1-108-47398-9 Hardback

Contents

Contents

Preface

Data mining and machine learning enable one to gain fundamental insights and knowledge from data. They allow the discovery of insightful, interesting, and novel patterns, as well as descriptive, understandable, and predictive models from large-scale data.

There are several good books in this area, but many of them are either too high-level or too advanced. This book is an introductory text that lays the foundations for the fundamental concepts and algorithms in machine learning and data mining. Important concepts are explained when first encountered, with detailed steps and derivations. A key goal of the book is to build the intuition behind the formulas via the interplay of geometric, (linear) algebraic and probabilistic interpretations of the data and the methods.

This second edition adds a whole new part on regression, including linear and logistic regression, neural networks, and deep learning. Content has also been updated in several other chapters and known errata have been fixed. The main parts of the book include data analysis foundations, frequent pattern mining, clustering, classification, and regression. These cover the core methods as well as cutting-edge topics such as deep learning, kernel methods, high-dimensional data analysis, and graph analysis.

The book includes many examples to illustrate the concepts and algorithms. It also has end-of-chapter exercises, which have been used in class. All of the algorithms in the book have been implemented by the authors. To aid practical understanding, we suggest that readers implement these algorithms on their own (using, for example, Python or R). Supplementary resources like slides, datasets and videos are available online at the book's companion site:

http://dataminingbook.info

The book can be used for both undergraduate and graduate courses in data mining, machine learning, and data science. A brief overview of the chapters is presented at the start of each part of the book. The chapters are mainly self contained (with important equations highlighted), but introductory courses would benefit by covering the basic foundations of data analysis in part one. For example, the kernel methods chapter in part one should be covered before other kernel-based algorithms that appear in later parts. The different parts can be covered in a different order based on the emphasis of the course or the interest of the reader. Finally, we encourage you to contact us about errata or other suggestions via the book companion site.

Mohammed J. Zaki and Wagner Meira, Jr.

DATA ANALYSIS FOUNDATIONS

This part lays the algebraic and probabilistic foundations for data analysis. It begins with basic statistical analysis of univariate and multivariate numeric data in Chapter 2. We describe measures of central tendency such as mean, median, and mode, and then we consider measures of dispersion such as range, variance, and covariance. We emphasize the dual algebraic and probabilistic views, and highlight the geometric interpretation of the various measures. We especially focus on the multivariate normal distribution, which is widely used as the default parametric model for data in both classification and clustering. In Chapter 3 we show how categorical data can be modeled via the multivariate binomial and the multinomial distributions. We describe the contingency table analysis approach to test for dependence between categorical attributes.

In Chapter 4, we show how to analyze graph data in terms of the topological structure, with special focus on various graph centrality measures such as closeness, betweenness, prestige, PageRank, and so on. We also study basic topological properties of real-world networks such as the *small world property*, which states that real graphs have small average path length between pairs of nodes, the *clustering effect*, which indicates local clustering around nodes, and the *scale-free property*, which manifests itself in a *power-law* degree distribution. We describe models that can explain some of these characteristics of real-world graphs; these include the Erdös–Rényi random graph model, the Watts–Strogatz model, and the Barabási–Albert model.

Kernel methods are introduced in Chapter 5, which provides new insights and connections between linear, nonlinear, graph, and complex data mining tasks. We briefly highlight the theory behind kernel functions, with the key concept being that a positive semidefinite kernel corresponds to a dot product in some high-dimensional feature space, and thus we can use familiar numeric analysis methods for nonlinear or complex object analysis, provided we can compute the pairwise kernel matrix of similarities between object instances. We describe various kernels for numeric or vector data, as well as sequence and graph data.

In Chapter 6, we consider the peculiarities of high-dimensional space, colorfully referred to as *the curse of dimensionality*. In particular, we study the scattering effect, that is, the fact that data points lie along the boundaries and corners in high dimensions, with the "center" of the space being virtually empty. We show the proliferation of orthogonal axes and also the behavior of the multivariate normal distribution in high dimensions. Finally, in Chapter 7, we describe widely used dimensionality reduction methods such as principal component analysis (PCA) and singular value decomposition (SVD). PCA finds the optimal k-dimensional subspace that captures most of the variance in the data. We also show how kernel PCA can be used to find nonlinear directions that capture the most variance. We conclude with the powerful SVD spectral decomposition method, studying its geometry, and its relationship to PCA.

CHAPTER 1

Data Matrix

We begin this chapter by looking at basic properties of data modeled as a data matrix. We emphasize the geometric and algebraic views, as well as the probabilistic interpretation of data, which play a key role in machine learning and data mining.

1.1 DATA MATRIX

Data can often be represented or abstracted as an $n \times d$ *data matrix*, with n rows and d columns, where rows correspond to entities in the dataset, and columns represent attributes or properties of interest. Each row in the data matrix records the observed attribute values for a given entity. The $n \times d$ data matrix is given as

$$
\mathbf{D} = \begin{pmatrix}
 & X_1 & X_2 & \cdots & X_d \\
\mathbf{x}_1 & x_{11} & x_{12} & \cdots & x_{1d} \\
\mathbf{x}_2 & x_{21} & x_{22} & \cdots & x_{2d} \\
\vdots & \vdots & \vdots & \ddots & \vdots \\
\mathbf{x}_n & x_{n1} & x_{n2} & \cdots & x_{nd}
\end{pmatrix}
$$

where $\mathbf{x}_i$ denotes the ith row, which is a d-tuple given as

$$
\mathbf{x}_i = (x_{i1}, x_{i2}, \ldots, x_{id})
$$

and X_j denotes the jth column, which is an n-tuple given as

$$
X_j = (x_{1j}, x_{2j}, \ldots, x_{nj})
$$

Depending on the application domain, rows may also be referred to as *entities, instances, examples, records, transactions, objects, points, feature-vectors, tuples,* and so on. Likewise, columns may also be called *attributes, properties, features, dimensions, variables, fields,* and so on. The number of instances n is referred to as the *size* of the data, whereas the number of attributes d is called the *dimensionality* of the data. The analysis of a single attribute is referred to as *univariate analysis,* whereas the simultaneous analysis of two attributes is called *bivariate analysis* and the simultaneous analysis of more than two attributes is called *multivariate analysis.*

Table 1.1. Extract from the Iris dataset

	Sepal length X_1	Sepal width X_2	Petal length X_3	Petal width X_4	Class X_5
$\mathbf{x}_1$	5.9	3.0	4.2	1.5	Iris-versicolor
$\mathbf{x}_2$	6.9	3.1	4.9	1.5	Iris-versicolor
$\mathbf{x}_3$	6.6	2.9	4.6	1.3	Iris-versicolor
$\mathbf{x}_4$	4.6	3.2	1.4	0.2	Iris-setosa
$\mathbf{x}_5$	6.0	2.2	4.0	1.0	Iris-versicolor
$\mathbf{x}_6$	4.7	3.2	1.3	0.2	Iris-setosa
$\mathbf{x}_7$	6.5	3.0	5.8	2.2	Iris-virginica
$\mathbf{x}_8$	5.8	2.7	5.1	1.9	Iris-virginica
$\vdots$	$\vdots$	$\vdots$	$\vdots$	$\vdots$	$\vdots$
$\mathbf{x}_{149}$	7.7	3.8	6.7	2.2	Iris-virginica
$\mathbf{x}_{150}$	5.1	3.4	1.5	0.2	Iris-setosa

Example 1.1. Table 1.1 shows an extract of the Iris dataset; the complete data forms a 150×5 data matrix. Each entity is an Iris flower, and the attributes include sepal length, sepal width, petal length, and petal width in centimeters, and the type or class of the Iris flower. The first row is given as the 5-tuple

$$\mathbf{x}_1 = (5.9, 3.0, 4.2, 1.5, \texttt{Iris-versicolor})$$

Not all datasets are in the form of a data matrix. For instance, more complex datasets can be in the form of sequences (e.g., DNA and protein sequences), text, time-series, images, audio, video, and so on, which may need special techniques for analysis. However, in many cases even if the raw data is not a data matrix it can usually be transformed into that form via feature extraction. For example, given a database of images, we can create a data matrix in which rows represent images and columns correspond to image features such as color, texture, and so on. Sometimes, certain attributes may have special semantics associated with them requiring special treatment. For instance, temporal or spatial attributes are often treated differently. It is also worth noting that traditional data analysis assumes that each entity or instance is independent. However, given the interconnected nature of the world we live in, this assumption may not always hold. Instances may be connected to other instances via various kinds of relationships, giving rise to a *data graph*, where a node represents an entity and an edge represents the relationship between two entities.

1.2 ATTRIBUTES

Attributes may be classified into two main types depending on their domain, that is, depending on the types of values they take on.

Numeric Attributes

A *numeric* attribute is one that has a real-valued or integer-valued domain. For example, `Age` with $domain(\texttt{Age}) = \mathbb{N}$, where $\mathbb{N}$ denotes the set of natural numbers (non-negative integers), is numeric, and so is `petal length` in Table 1.1, with $domain(\texttt{petal length}) = \mathbb{R}^+$ (the set of all positive real numbers). Numeric attributes that take on a finite or countably infinite set of values are called *discrete*, whereas those that can take on any real value are called *continuous*. As a special case of discrete, if an attribute has as its domain the set $\{0, 1\}$, it is called a *binary* attribute. Numeric attributes can be classified further into two types:

- *Interval-scaled*: For these kinds of attributes only differences (addition or subtraction) make sense. For example, attribute `temperature` measured in °C or °F is interval-scaled. If it is 20 °C on one day and 10 °C on the following day, it is meaningful to talk about a temperature drop of 10 °C, but it is not meaningful to say that it is twice as cold as the previous day.
- *Ratio-scaled*: Here one can compute both differences as well as ratios between values. For example, for attribute `Age`, we can say that someone who is 20 years old is twice as old as someone who is 10 years old.

Categorical Attributes

A *categorical* attribute is one that has a set-valued domain composed of a set of symbols. For example, `Sex` and `Education` could be categorical attributes with their domains given as

$$domain(\texttt{Sex}) = \{\texttt{M}, \texttt{F}\}$$

$$domain(\texttt{Education}) = \{\texttt{HighSchool}, \texttt{BS}, \texttt{MS}, \texttt{PhD}\}$$

Categorical attributes may be of two types:

- *Nominal*: The attribute values in the domain are unordered, and thus only equality comparisons are meaningful. That is, we can check only whether the value of the attribute for two given instances is the same or not. For example, `Sex` is a nominal attribute. Also `class` in Table 1.1 is a nominal attribute with $domain(\texttt{class}) = \{\texttt{iris-setosa}, \texttt{iris-versicolor}, \texttt{iris-virginica}\}$.
- *Ordinal*: The attribute values are ordered, and thus both equality comparisons (is one value equal to another?) and inequality comparisons (is one value less than or greater than another?) are allowed, though it may not be possible to quantify the difference between values. For example, `Education` is an ordinal attribute because its domain values are ordered by increasing educational qualification.

1.3 DATA: ALGEBRAIC AND GEOMETRIC VIEW

If the d attributes or dimensions in the data matrix **D** are all numeric, then each row can be considered as a d-dimensional point:

$$\mathbf{x}_i = (x_{i1}, x_{i2}, \ldots, x_{id}) \in \mathbb{R}^d$$

or equivalently, each row may be considered as a d-dimensional column vector (all vectors are assumed to be column vectors by default):

$$\mathbf{x}_i = \begin{pmatrix} x_{i1} \\ x_{i2} \\ \vdots \\ x_{id} \end{pmatrix} = \begin{pmatrix} x_{i1} & x_{i2} & \cdots & x_{id} \end{pmatrix}^T \in \mathbb{R}^d$$

where T is the *(matrix) transpose* operator.

The d-dimensional Cartesian coordinate space is specified via the d unit vectors, called the standard basis vectors, along each of the axes. The jth *standard basis vector* $\mathbf{e}_j$ is the d-dimensional unit vector whose jth component is 1 and the rest of the components are 0

$$\mathbf{e}_j = (0, \ldots, 1_j, \ldots, 0)^T$$

Any other vector in $\mathbb{R}^d$ can be written as a *linear combination* of the standard basis vectors. For example, each of the points $\mathbf{x}_i$ can be written as the linear combination

$$\mathbf{x}_i = x_{i1}\mathbf{e}_1 + x_{i2}\mathbf{e}_2 + \cdots + x_{id}\mathbf{e}_d = \sum_{j=1}^{d} x_{ij}\mathbf{e}_j$$

where the scalar value x_{ij} is the coordinate value along the jth axis or attribute.

Example 1.2. Consider the Iris data in Table 1.1. If we *project* the entire data onto the first two attributes, then each row can be considered as a point or a vector in 2-dimensional space. For example, the projection of the 5-tuple $\mathbf{x}_1 = (5.9, 3.0, 4.2, 1.5, \texttt{Iris-versicolor})$ on the first two attributes is shown in Figure 1.1(a). Figure 1.2 shows the scatterplot of all the $n = 150$ points in the 2-dimensional space spanned by the first two attributes. Likewise, Figure 1.1(b) shows $\mathbf{x}_1$ as a point and vector in 3-dimensional space, by projecting the data onto the first three attributes. The point $(5.9, 3.0, 4.2)$ can be seen as specifying the coefficients in the linear combination of the standard basis vectors in $\mathbb{R}^3$:

$$\mathbf{x}_1 = 5.9\mathbf{e}_1 + 3.0\mathbf{e}_2 + 4.2\mathbf{e}_3 = 5.9\begin{pmatrix} 1 \\ 0 \\ 0 \end{pmatrix} + 3.0\begin{pmatrix} 0 \\ 1 \\ 0 \end{pmatrix} + 4.2\begin{pmatrix} 0 \\ 0 \\ 1 \end{pmatrix} = \begin{pmatrix} 5.9 \\ 3.0 \\ 4.2 \end{pmatrix}$$

Each numeric column or attribute can also be treated as a vector in an n-dimensional space $\mathbb{R}^n$:

$$X_j = \begin{pmatrix} x_{1j} \\ x_{2j} \\ \vdots \\ x_{nj} \end{pmatrix}$$

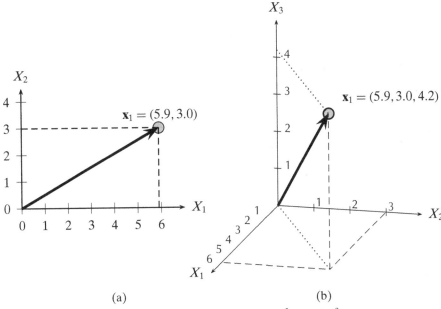

(a)   (b)

Figure 1.1. Row $\mathbf{x}_1$ as a point and vector in (a) $\mathbb{R}^2$ and (b) $\mathbb{R}^3$.

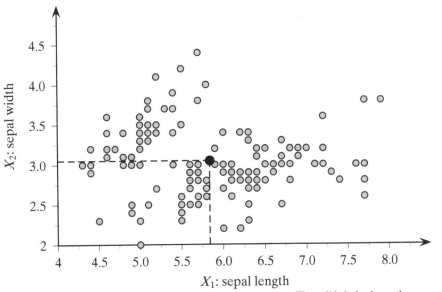

Figure 1.2. Scatterplot: sepal length versus sepal width. The solid circle shows the mean point.

If all attributes are numeric, then the data matrix $\mathbf{D}$ is in fact an $n \times d$ matrix, also written as $\mathbf{D} \in \mathbb{R}^{n \times d}$, given as

$$\mathbf{D} = \begin{pmatrix} x_{11} & x_{12} & \cdots & x_{1d} \\ x_{21} & x_{22} & \cdots & x_{2d} \\ \vdots & \vdots & \ddots & \vdots \\ x_{n1} & x_{n2} & \cdots & x_{nd} \end{pmatrix} = \begin{pmatrix} -\mathbf{x}_1^T- \\ -\mathbf{x}_2^T- \\ \vdots \\ -\mathbf{x}_n^T- \end{pmatrix} = \begin{pmatrix} | & | & & | \\ X_1 & X_2 & \cdots & X_d \\ | & | & & | \end{pmatrix}$$

As we can see, we can consider the entire dataset as an $n \times d$ matrix, or equivalently as a set of n row vectors $\mathbf{x}_i^T \in \mathbb{R}^d$ or as a set of d column vectors $X_j \in \mathbb{R}^n$.

1.3.1 Distance and Angle

Treating data instances and attributes as vectors, and the entire dataset as a matrix, enables one to apply both geometric and algebraic methods to aid in the data mining and analysis tasks.

Let $\mathbf{a}, \mathbf{b} \in \mathbb{R}^m$ be two m-dimensional vectors given as

$$\mathbf{a} = \begin{pmatrix} a_1 \\ a_2 \\ \vdots \\ a_m \end{pmatrix} \qquad\qquad \mathbf{b} = \begin{pmatrix} b_1 \\ b_2 \\ \vdots \\ b_m \end{pmatrix}$$

Dot Product

The *dot product* between $\mathbf{a}$ and $\mathbf{b}$ is defined as the scalar value

$$\mathbf{a}^T\mathbf{b} = \begin{pmatrix} a_1 & a_2 & \cdots & a_m \end{pmatrix} \times \begin{pmatrix} b_1 \\ b_2 \\ \vdots \\ b_m \end{pmatrix} = a_1 b_1 + a_2 b_2 + \cdots + a_m b_m = \sum_{i=1}^{m} a_i b_i \tag{1.1}$$

Length

The *Euclidean norm* or *length* of a vector $\mathbf{a} \in \mathbb{R}^m$ is defined as

$$\|\mathbf{a}\| = \sqrt{\mathbf{a}^T\mathbf{a}} = \sqrt{a_1^2 + a_2^2 + \cdots + a_m^2} = \sqrt{\sum_{i=1}^{m} a_i^2} \tag{1.2}$$

The *unit vector* in the direction of $\mathbf{a}$ is given as

$$\mathbf{u} = \frac{\mathbf{a}}{\|\mathbf{a}\|} = \left(\frac{1}{\|\mathbf{a}\|}\right)\mathbf{a}$$

By definition $\mathbf{u}$ has length $\|\mathbf{u}\| = 1$, and it is also called a *normalized* vector, which can be used in lieu of $\mathbf{a}$ in some analysis tasks.

The Euclidean norm is a special case of a general class of norms, known as L_p-*norm*, defined as

$$\|\mathbf{a}\|_p = \left(|a_1|^p + |a_2|^p + \cdots + |a_m|^p\right)^{\frac{1}{p}} = \left(\sum_{i=1}^{m} |a_i|^p\right)^{\frac{1}{p}} \tag{1.3}$$

for any $p \neq 0$. Thus, the Euclidean norm corresponds to the case when $p = 2$; it is also called the L_2-norm.

Distance

From the Euclidean norm we can define the *Euclidean distance* between **a** and **b**, as follows

$$\|\mathbf{a} - \mathbf{b}\| = \sqrt{(\mathbf{a} - \mathbf{b})^T(\mathbf{a} - \mathbf{b})} = \sqrt{\sum_{i=1}^{m}(a_i - b_i)^2} \tag{1.4}$$

Thus, the length of a vector is simply its distance from the zero vector **0**, all of whose elements are 0, that is, $\|\mathbf{a}\| = \|\mathbf{a} - \mathbf{0}\|$.

From the general L_p-norm we can define the corresponding L_p-distance function, given as follows

$$\|\mathbf{a} - \mathbf{b}\|_p = \left(\sum_{i=1}^{m}|a_i - b_i|^p\right)^{\frac{1}{p}} \tag{1.5}$$

If p is unspecified, as in Eq. (1.4), it is assumed to be $p = 2$ by default.

Angle

The cosine of the smallest angle between vectors **a** and **b**, also called the *cosine similarity*, is given as

$$\cos\theta = \frac{\mathbf{a}^T\mathbf{b}}{\|\mathbf{a}\|\|\mathbf{b}\|} = \left(\frac{\mathbf{a}}{\|\mathbf{a}\|}\right)^T\left(\frac{\mathbf{b}}{\|\mathbf{b}\|}\right) \tag{1.6}$$

Thus, the cosine of the angle between **a** and **b** is given as the dot product of the unit vectors $\frac{\mathbf{a}}{\|\mathbf{a}\|}$ and $\frac{\mathbf{b}}{\|\mathbf{b}\|}$.

The *Cauchy–Schwartz* inequality states that for any vectors **a** and **b** in $\mathbb{R}^m$

$$|\mathbf{a}^T\mathbf{b}| \leq \|\mathbf{a}\| \cdot \|\mathbf{b}\|$$

It follows immediately from the Cauchy–Schwartz inequality that

$$-1 \leq \cos\theta \leq 1$$

Because the smallest angle $\theta \in [0°, 180°]$ and because $\cos\theta \in [-1, 1]$, the cosine similarity value ranges from $+1$, corresponding to an angle of $0°$, to -1, corresponding to an angle of $180°$ (or π radians).

Orthogonality

Two vectors **a** and **b** are said to be *orthogonal* if and only if $\mathbf{a}^T\mathbf{b} = 0$, which in turn implies that $\cos\theta = 0$, that is, the angle between them is $90°$ or $\frac{\pi}{2}$ radians. In this case, we say that they have no similarity.

Example 1.3 (Distance and Angle). Figure 1.3 shows the two vectors

$$\mathbf{a} = \begin{pmatrix} 5 \\ 3 \end{pmatrix} \text{ and } \mathbf{b} = \begin{pmatrix} 1 \\ 4 \end{pmatrix}$$

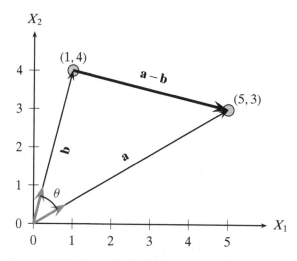

Figure 1.3. Distance and angle. Unit vectors are shown in gray.

Using Eq. (1.4), the Euclidean distance between them is given as

$$\|\mathbf{a}-\mathbf{b}\| = \sqrt{(5-1)^2+(3-4)^2} = \sqrt{16+1} = \sqrt{17} = 4.12$$

The distance can also be computed as the magnitude of the vector:

$$\mathbf{a}-\mathbf{b} = \begin{pmatrix}5\\3\end{pmatrix} - \begin{pmatrix}1\\4\end{pmatrix} = \begin{pmatrix}4\\-1\end{pmatrix}$$

because $\|\mathbf{a}-\mathbf{b}\| = \sqrt{4^2+(-1)^2} = \sqrt{17} = 4.12$.

The unit vector in the direction of $\mathbf{a}$ is given as

$$\mathbf{u}_a = \frac{\mathbf{a}}{\|\mathbf{a}\|} = \frac{1}{\sqrt{5^2+3^2}}\begin{pmatrix}5\\3\end{pmatrix} = \frac{1}{\sqrt{34}}\begin{pmatrix}5\\3\end{pmatrix} = \begin{pmatrix}0.86\\0.51\end{pmatrix}$$

The unit vector in the direction of $\mathbf{b}$ can be computed similarly:

$$\mathbf{u}_b = \begin{pmatrix}0.24\\0.97\end{pmatrix}$$

These unit vectors are also shown in gray in Figure 1.3.

By Eq. (1.6) the cosine of the angle between $\mathbf{a}$ and $\mathbf{b}$ is given as

$$\cos\theta = \frac{\begin{pmatrix}5\\3\end{pmatrix}^T\begin{pmatrix}1\\4\end{pmatrix}}{\sqrt{5^2+3^2}\sqrt{1^2+4^2}} = \frac{17}{\sqrt{34\times17}} = \frac{1}{\sqrt{2}}$$

We can get the angle by computing the inverse of the cosine:

$$\theta = \cos^{-1}(1/\sqrt{2}) = 45°$$

Let us consider the L_p-norm for $\mathbf{a}$ with $p=3$; we get

$$\|\mathbf{a}\|_3 = (5^3+3^3)^{1/3} = (152)^{1/3} = 5.34$$

The distance between **a** and **b** using Eq. (1.5) for the L_p-norm with $p = 3$ is given as

$$\|\mathbf{a} - \mathbf{b}\|_3 = \|(4, -1)^T\|_3 = \left(4^3 + |-1|^3\right)^{1/3} = (65)^{1/3} = 4.02$$

1.3.2 Mean and Total Variance

Mean

The *mean* of the data matrix **D** is the vector obtained as the average of all the points:

$$mean(\mathbf{D}) = \boldsymbol{\mu} = \frac{1}{n} \sum_{i=1}^{n} \mathbf{x}_i \tag{1.7}$$

Total Variance

The *total variance* of the data matrix **D** is the average squared distance of each point from the mean:

$$var(\mathbf{D}) = \frac{1}{n} \sum_{i=1}^{n} \|\mathbf{x}_i - \boldsymbol{\mu}\|^2 \tag{1.8}$$

Simplifying Eq. (1.8) we obtain

$$var(\mathbf{D}) = \frac{1}{n} \sum_{i=1}^{n} \left(\|\mathbf{x}_i\|^2 - 2\mathbf{x}_i^T \boldsymbol{\mu} + \|\boldsymbol{\mu}\|^2 \right)$$

$$= \frac{1}{n} \left(\sum_{i=1}^{n} \|\mathbf{x}_i\|^2 - 2n\boldsymbol{\mu}^T \left(\frac{1}{n} \sum_{i=1}^{n} \mathbf{x}_i \right) + n\|\boldsymbol{\mu}\|^2 \right)$$

$$= \frac{1}{n} \left(\sum_{i=1}^{n} \|\mathbf{x}_i\|^2 - 2n\boldsymbol{\mu}^T \boldsymbol{\mu} + n\|\boldsymbol{\mu}\|^2 \right)$$

$$= \frac{1}{n} \left(\sum_{i=1}^{n} \|\mathbf{x}_i\|^2 \right) - \|\boldsymbol{\mu}\|^2$$

The total variance is thus the difference between the average of the squared magnitude of the data points and the squared magnitude of the mean (average of the points).

Centered Data Matrix

Often we need to center the data matrix by making the mean coincide with the origin of the data space. The *centered data matrix* is obtained by subtracting the mean from all the points:

$$\boxed{\bar{\mathbf{D}} = \mathbf{D} - \mathbf{1} \cdot \boldsymbol{\mu}^T} = \begin{pmatrix} \mathbf{x}_1^T \\ \mathbf{x}_2^T \\ \vdots \\ \mathbf{x}_n^T \end{pmatrix} - \begin{pmatrix} \boldsymbol{\mu}^T \\ \boldsymbol{\mu}^T \\ \vdots \\ \boldsymbol{\mu}^T \end{pmatrix} = \begin{pmatrix} \mathbf{x}_1^T - \boldsymbol{\mu}^T \\ \mathbf{x}_2^T - \boldsymbol{\mu}^T \\ \vdots \\ \mathbf{x}_n^T - \boldsymbol{\mu}^T \end{pmatrix} = \begin{pmatrix} \bar{\mathbf{x}}_1^T \\ \bar{\mathbf{x}}_2^T \\ \vdots \\ \bar{\mathbf{x}}_n^T \end{pmatrix} \qquad (1.9)$$

where $\bar{\mathbf{x}}_i = \mathbf{x}_i - \boldsymbol{\mu}$ represents the centered point corresponding to $\mathbf{x}_i$, and $\mathbf{1} \in \mathbb{R}^n$ is the n-dimensional vector all of whose elements have value 1. The mean of the centered data matrix $\bar{\mathbf{D}}$ is $\mathbf{0} \in \mathbb{R}^d$, because we have subtracted the mean $\boldsymbol{\mu}$ from all the points $\mathbf{x}_i$.

1.3.3 Orthogonal Projection

Often in data mining we need to project a point or vector onto another vector, for example, to obtain a new point after a change of the basis vectors. Let $\mathbf{a}, \mathbf{b} \in \mathbb{R}^m$ be two m-dimensional vectors. An *orthogonal decomposition* of the vector $\mathbf{b}$ in the direction of another vector $\mathbf{a}$, illustrated in Figure 1.4, is given as

$$\mathbf{b} = \mathbf{b}_\| + \mathbf{b}_\perp = \mathbf{p} + \mathbf{r} \qquad (1.10)$$

where $\mathbf{p} = \mathbf{b}_\|$ is parallel to $\mathbf{a}$, and $\mathbf{r} = \mathbf{b}_\perp$ is perpendicular or orthogonal to $\mathbf{a}$. The vector $\mathbf{p}$ is called the *orthogonal projection* or simply projection of $\mathbf{b}$ on the vector $\mathbf{a}$. Note that the point $\mathbf{p} \in \mathbb{R}^m$ is the point closest to $\mathbf{b}$ on the line passing through $\mathbf{a}$. Thus, the magnitude of the vector $\mathbf{r} = \mathbf{b} - \mathbf{p}$ gives the *perpendicular distance* between $\mathbf{b}$ and $\mathbf{a}$, which is often interpreted as the residual or error between the points $\mathbf{b}$ and $\mathbf{p}$. The vector $\mathbf{r}$ is also called the *error vector*.

We can derive an expression for $\mathbf{p}$ by noting that $\mathbf{p} = c\mathbf{a}$ for some scalar c, as $\mathbf{p}$ is parallel to $\mathbf{a}$. Thus, $\mathbf{r} = \mathbf{b} - \mathbf{p} = \mathbf{b} - c\mathbf{a}$. Because $\mathbf{p}$ and $\mathbf{r}$ are orthogonal, we have

$$\mathbf{p}^T\mathbf{r} = (c\mathbf{a})^T(\mathbf{b} - c\mathbf{a}) = c\mathbf{a}^T\mathbf{b} - c^2\mathbf{a}^T\mathbf{a} = 0$$

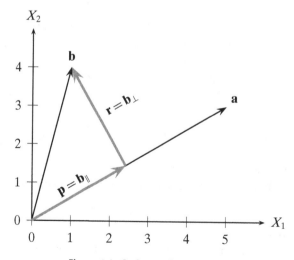

Figure 1.4. Orthogonal projection.

which implies that

$$c = \frac{\mathbf{a}^T\mathbf{b}}{\mathbf{a}^T\mathbf{a}}$$

Therefore, the projection of **b** on **a** is given as

$$\mathbf{p} = c\mathbf{a} = \left(\frac{\mathbf{a}^T\mathbf{b}}{\mathbf{a}^T\mathbf{a}}\right)\mathbf{a} \tag{1.11}$$

The scalar offset c along **a** is also called the *scalar projection* of **b** on **a**, denoted as

$$\text{proj}_{\mathbf{a}}(\mathbf{b}) = \left(\frac{\mathbf{b}^T\mathbf{a}}{\mathbf{a}^T\mathbf{a}}\right) \tag{1.12}$$

Therefore, the projection of **b** on **a** can also be written as

$$\mathbf{p} = \text{proj}_{\mathbf{a}}(\mathbf{b}) \cdot \mathbf{a}$$

Example 1.4. Restricting the Iris dataset to the first two dimensions, sepal length and sepal width, the mean point is given as

$$mean(\mathbf{D}) = \begin{pmatrix} 5.843 \\ 3.054 \end{pmatrix}$$

which is shown as the black circle in Figure 1.2. The corresponding centered data is shown in Figure 1.5, and the total variance is var$(\mathbf{D}) = 0.868$ (centering does not change this value).

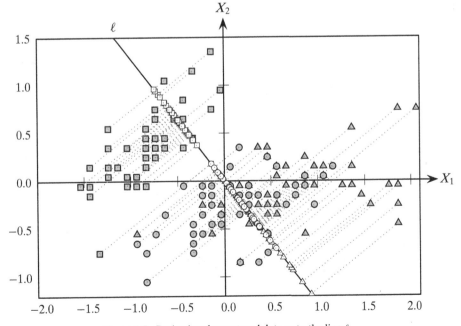

Figure 1.5. Projecting the centered data onto the line ℓ.

Figure 1.5 shows the projection of each point onto the line ℓ, which is the line that maximizes the separation between the class `iris-setosa` (squares) from the other two classes, namely `iris-versicolor` (circles) and `iris-virginica` (triangles). The line ℓ is given as the set of all the points $(x_1, x_2)^T$ satisfying the constraint $\begin{pmatrix} x_1 \\ x_2 \end{pmatrix} = c \begin{pmatrix} -2.15 \\ 2.75 \end{pmatrix}$ for all scalars $c \in \mathbb{R}$.

1.3.4 Linear Independence and Dimensionality

Given the data matrix

$$\mathbf{D} = \begin{pmatrix} \mathbf{x}_1 & \mathbf{x}_2 & \cdots & \mathbf{x}_n \end{pmatrix}^T = \begin{pmatrix} X_1 & X_2 & \cdots & X_d \end{pmatrix}$$

we are often interested in the linear combinations of the rows (points) or the columns (attributes). For instance, different linear combinations of the original d attributes yield new derived attributes, which play a key role in feature extraction and dimensionality reduction.

Given any set of vectors $\mathbf{v}_1, \mathbf{v}_2, \ldots, \mathbf{v}_k$ in an m-dimensional vector space $\mathbb{R}^m$, their *linear combination* is given as

$$c_1 \mathbf{v}_1 + c_2 \mathbf{v}_2 + \cdots + c_k \mathbf{v}_k$$

where $c_i \in \mathbb{R}$ are scalar values. The set of all possible linear combinations of the k vectors is called the *span*, denoted as $span(\mathbf{v}_1, \ldots, \mathbf{v}_k)$, which is itself a vector space being a *subspace* of $\mathbb{R}^m$. If $span(\mathbf{v}_1, \ldots, \mathbf{v}_k) = \mathbb{R}^m$, then we say that $\mathbf{v}_1, \ldots, \mathbf{v}_k$ is a *spanning set* for $\mathbb{R}^m$.

Row and Column Space

There are several interesting vector spaces associated with the data matrix $\mathbf{D}$, two of which are the column space and row space of $\mathbf{D}$. The *column space* of $\mathbf{D}$, denoted $col(\mathbf{D})$, is the set of all linear combinations of the d attributes $X_j \in \mathbb{R}^n$, that is,

$$col(\mathbf{D}) = span(X_1, X_2, \ldots, X_d)$$

By definition $col(\mathbf{D})$ is a subspace of $\mathbb{R}^n$. The *row space* of $\mathbf{D}$, denoted $row(\mathbf{D})$, is the set of all linear combinations of the n points $\mathbf{x}_i \in \mathbb{R}^d$, that is,

$$row(\mathbf{D}) = span(\mathbf{x}_1, \mathbf{x}_2, \ldots, \mathbf{x}_n)$$

By definition $row(\mathbf{D})$ is a subspace of $\mathbb{R}^d$. Note also that the row space of $\mathbf{D}$ is the column space of $\mathbf{D}^T$:

$$row(\mathbf{D}) = col(\mathbf{D}^T)$$

Linear Independence

We say that the vectors $\mathbf{v}_1, \ldots, \mathbf{v}_k$ are *linearly dependent* if at least one vector can be written as a linear combination of the others. Alternatively, the k vectors are linearly dependent if there are scalars $c_1, c_2, \ldots, c_k$, at least one of which is not zero, such that

$$c_1\mathbf{v}_1 + c_2\mathbf{v}_2 + \cdots + c_k\mathbf{v}_k = \mathbf{0}$$

On the other hand, $\mathbf{v}_1, \cdots, \mathbf{v}_k$ are *linearly independent* if and only if

$$c_1\mathbf{v}_1 + c_2\mathbf{v}_2 + \cdots + c_k\mathbf{v}_k = \mathbf{0} \text{ implies } c_1 = c_2 = \cdots = c_k = 0$$

Simply put, a set of vectors is linearly independent if none of them can be written as a linear combination of the other vectors in the set.

Dimension and Rank

Let S be a subspace of $\mathbb{R}^m$. A *basis* for S is a set of vectors in S, say $\mathbf{v}_1, \ldots, \mathbf{v}_k$, that are linearly independent and they span S, that is, $span(\mathbf{v}_1, \ldots, \mathbf{v}_k) = S$. In fact, a basis is a minimal spanning set. If the vectors in the basis are pairwise orthogonal, they are said to form an *orthogonal basis* for S. If, in addition, they are also normalized to be unit vectors, then they make up an *orthonormal basis* for S. For instance, the *standard basis* for $\mathbb{R}^m$ is an orthonormal basis consisting of the vectors

$$\mathbf{e}_1 = \begin{pmatrix} 1 \\ 0 \\ \vdots \\ 0 \end{pmatrix} \quad \mathbf{e}_2 = \begin{pmatrix} 0 \\ 1 \\ \vdots \\ 0 \end{pmatrix} \quad \cdots \quad \mathbf{e}_m = \begin{pmatrix} 0 \\ 0 \\ \vdots \\ 1 \end{pmatrix}$$

Any two bases for S must have the same number of vectors, and the number of vectors in a basis for S is called the *dimension* of S, denoted as $dim(S)$. Because S is a subspace of $\mathbb{R}^m$, we must have $dim(S) \le m$.

It is a remarkable fact that, for any matrix, the dimension of its row and column space is the same, and this dimension is also called the *rank* of the matrix. For the data matrix $\mathbf{D} \in \mathbb{R}^{n \times d}$, we have $rank(\mathbf{D}) \le \min(n, d)$, which follows from the fact that the column space can have dimension at most d, and the row space can have dimension at most n. Thus, even though the data points are ostensibly in a d dimensional attribute space (the *extrinsic dimensionality*), if $rank(\mathbf{D}) < d$, then the data points reside in a lower dimensional subspace of $\mathbb{R}^d$, and in this case $rank(\mathbf{D})$ gives an indication about the *intrinsic* dimensionality of the data. In fact, with dimensionality reduction methods it is often possible to approximate $\mathbf{D} \in \mathbb{R}^{n \times d}$ with a derived data matrix $\mathbf{D}' \in \mathbb{R}^{n \times k}$, which has much lower dimensionality, that is, $k \ll d$. In this case k may reflect the "true" intrinsic dimensionality of the data.

Example 1.5. The line ℓ in Figure 1.5 is given as $\ell = span\left((-2.15 \quad 2.75)^T \right)$, with $dim(\ell) = 1$. After normalization, we obtain the orthonormal basis for ℓ as the unit vector

$$\frac{1}{\sqrt{12.19}} \begin{pmatrix} -2.15 \\ 2.75 \end{pmatrix} = \begin{pmatrix} -0.615 \\ 0.788 \end{pmatrix}$$

1.4 DATA: PROBABILISTIC VIEW

The probabilistic view of the data assumes that each numeric attribute X is a *random variable*, defined as a function that assigns a real number to each outcome of an experiment (i.e., some process of observation or measurement). Formally, X is a function $X: \mathcal{O} \to \mathbb{R}$, where $\mathcal{O}$, the domain of X, is the set of all possible outcomes of the experiment, also called the *sample space*, and $\mathbb{R}$, the *range* of X, is the set of real numbers. If the outcomes are numeric, and represent the observed values of the random variable, then $X: \mathcal{O} \to \mathcal{O}$ is simply the identity function: $X(v) = v$ for all $v \in \mathcal{O}$. The distinction between an outcome and a value of a random variable is important, as we may want to treat the observed values differently depending on the context, as seen in Example 1.6.

A random variable X is called a *discrete random variable* if it takes on only a finite or countably infinite number of values in its range, whereas X is called a *continuous random variable* if it can take on any value in its range.

Example 1.6. Consider the `sepal length` attribute (X_1) for the Iris dataset in Table 1.1. All $n = 150$ values of this attribute are shown in Table 1.2, which lie in the range $[4.3, 7.9]$, with centimeters as the unit of measurement. Let us assume that these constitute the set of all possible outcomes $\mathcal{O}$.

By default, we can consider the attribute X_1 to be a continuous random variable, given as the identity function $X_1(v) = v$, because the outcomes (sepal length values) are all numeric.

On the other hand, if we want to distinguish between Iris flowers with short and long sepal lengths, with long being, say, a length of 7 cm or more, we can define a discrete random variable A as follows:

$$A(v) = \begin{cases} 0 & \text{if } v < 7 \\ 1 & \text{if } v \geq 7 \end{cases}$$

In this case the domain of A is $[4.3, 7.9]$, and its range is $\{0, 1\}$. Thus, A assumes nonzero probability only at the discrete values 0 and 1.

Probability Mass Function
If X is discrete, the *probability mass function* of X is defined as

$$\boxed{f(x) = P(X = x) \qquad \text{for all } x \in \mathbb{R}} \tag{1.13}$$

In other words, the function f gives the probability $P(X = x)$ that the random variable X has the exact value x. The name "probability mass function" intuitively conveys the fact that the probability is concentrated or massed at only discrete values in the range of X, and is zero for all other values. f must also obey the basic rules of probability. That is, f must be non-negative:

$$f(x) \geq 0$$

Table 1.2. Iris dataset: sepal length (in centimeters).

5.9	6.9	6.6	4.6	6.0	4.7	6.5	5.8	6.7	6.7	5.1	5.1	5.7	6.1	4.9
5.0	5.0	5.7	5.0	7.2	5.9	6.5	5.7	5.5	4.9	5.0	5.5	4.6	7.2	6.8
5.4	5.0	5.7	5.8	5.1	5.6	5.8	5.1	6.3	6.3	5.6	6.1	6.8	7.3	5.6
4.8	7.1	5.7	5.3	5.7	5.7	5.6	4.4	6.3	5.4	6.3	6.9	7.7	6.1	5.6
6.1	6.4	5.0	5.1	5.6	5.4	5.8	4.9	4.6	5.2	7.9	7.7	6.1	5.5	4.6
4.7	4.4	6.2	4.8	6.0	6.2	5.0	6.4	6.3	6.7	5.0	5.9	6.7	5.4	6.3
4.8	4.4	6.4	6.2	6.0	7.4	4.9	7.0	5.5	6.3	6.8	6.1	6.5	6.7	6.7
4.8	4.9	6.9	4.5	4.3	5.2	5.0	6.4	5.2	5.8	5.5	7.6	6.3	6.4	6.3
5.8	5.0	6.7	6.0	5.1	4.8	5.7	5.1	6.6	6.4	5.2	6.4	7.7	5.8	4.9
5.4	5.1	6.0	6.5	5.5	7.2	6.9	6.2	6.5	6.0	5.4	5.5	6.7	7.7	5.1

and the sum of all probabilities should add to 1:

$$\sum_x f(x) = 1$$

Example 1.7 (Bernoulli and Binomial Distribution). In Example 1.6, A was defined as a discrete random variable representing long sepal length. From the sepal length data in Table 1.2 we find that only 13 Irises have sepal length of at least 7 cm. We can thus estimate the probability mass function of A as follows:

$$f(1) = P(A = 1) = \frac{13}{150} = 0.087 = p$$

and

$$f(0) = P(A = 0) = \frac{137}{150} = 0.913 = 1 - p$$

In this case we say that A has a *Bernoulli distribution* with parameter $p \in [0, 1]$, which denotes the probability of a *success*, that is, the probability of picking an Iris with a long sepal length at random from the set of all points. On the other hand, $1 - p$ is the probability of a *failure*, that is, of not picking an Iris with long sepal length.

Let us consider another discrete random variable B, denoting the number of Irises with long sepal length in m independent Bernoulli trials with probability of success p. In this case, B takes on the discrete values $[0, m]$, and its probability mass function is given by the *binomial distribution*

$$f(k) = P(B = k) = \binom{m}{k} p^k (1 - p)^{m-k}$$

The formula can be understood as follows. There are $\binom{m}{k}$ ways of picking k long sepal length Irises out of the m trials. For each selection of k long sepal length Irises, the total probability of the k successes is p^k, and the total probability of $m - k$ failures is $(1 - p)^{m-k}$. For example, because $p = 0.087$ from above, the probability of observing exactly $k = 2$ Irises with long sepal length in $m = 10$ trials is given as

$$f(2) = P(B = 2) = \binom{10}{2} (0.087)^2 (0.913)^8 = 0.164$$

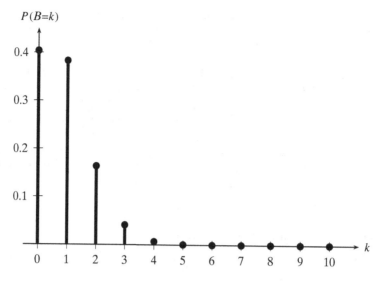

Figure 1.6. Binomial distribution: probability mass function ($m = 10, p = 0.087$).

Figure 1.6 shows the full probability mass function for different values of k for $m = 10$. Because p is quite small, the probability of k successes in so few a trials falls off rapidly as k increases, becoming practically zero for values of $k \geq 6$.

Probability Density Function

If X is continuous, its range is the entire set of real numbers $\mathbb{R}$. The probability of any specific value x is only one out of the infinitely many possible values in the range of X, which means that $P(X = x) = 0$ for all $x \in \mathbb{R}$. However, this does not mean that the value x is impossible, because in that case we would conclude that all values are impossible! What it means is that the probability mass is spread so thinly over the range of values that it can be measured only over intervals $[a, b] \subset \mathbb{R}$, rather than at specific points. Thus, instead of the probability mass function, we define the *probability density function*, which specifies the probability that the variable X takes on values in any interval $[a, b] \subset \mathbb{R}$:

$$P\big(X \in [a, b]\big) = \int_{a}^{b} f(x)\, dx \tag{1.14}$$

As before, the density function f must satisfy the basic laws of probability:

$$f(x) \geq 0, \qquad \text{for all } x \in \mathbb{R}$$

and

$$\int_{-\infty}^{\infty} f(x)\, dx = 1$$

We can get an intuitive understanding of the density function f by considering the probability density over a small interval of width $2\epsilon > 0$, centered at x, namely

$[x - \epsilon, x + \epsilon]$:

$$P\left(X \in [x - \epsilon, x + \epsilon]\right) = \int\limits_{x-\epsilon}^{x+\epsilon} f(x)\, dx \simeq 2\epsilon \cdot f(x)$$

$$f(x) \simeq \frac{P\left(X \in [x - \epsilon, x + \epsilon]\right)}{2\epsilon} \tag{1.15}$$

$f(x)$ thus gives the probability density at x, given as the ratio of the probability mass to the width of the interval, that is, the probability mass per unit distance. Thus, it is important to note that $P(X = x) \neq f(x)$.

Even though the probability density function $f(x)$ does not specify the probability $P(X = x)$, it can be used to obtain the relative probability of one value x_1 over another x_2 because for a given $\epsilon > 0$, by Eq. (1.15), we have

$$\frac{P(X \in [x_1 - \epsilon, x_1 + \epsilon])}{P(X \in [x_2 - \epsilon, x_2 + \epsilon])} \simeq \frac{2\epsilon \cdot f(x_1)}{2\epsilon \cdot f(x_2)} = \frac{f(x_1)}{f(x_2)} \tag{1.16}$$

Thus, if $f(x_1)$ is larger than $f(x_2)$, then values of X close to x_1 are more probable than values close to x_2, and vice versa.

Example 1.8 (Normal Distribution). Consider again the sepal length values from the Iris dataset, as shown in Table 1.2. Let us assume that these values follow a *Gaussian* or *normal* density function, given as

$$f(x) = \frac{1}{\sqrt{2\pi\sigma^2}} \exp\left\{ \frac{-(x - \mu)^2}{2\sigma^2} \right\}$$

There are two parameters of the normal density distribution, namely, μ, which represents the mean value, and σ^2, which represents the variance of the values (these parameters are discussed in Chapter 2). Figure 1.7 shows the characteristic "bell" shape plot of the normal distribution. The parameters, $\mu = 5.84$ and $\sigma^2 = 0.681$, were estimated directly from the data for sepal length in Table 1.2.

Whereas $f(x = \mu) = f(5.84) = \dfrac{1}{\sqrt{2\pi \cdot 0.681}} \exp\{0\} = 0.483$, we emphasize that the probability of observing $X = \mu$ is zero, that is, $P(X = \mu) = 0$. Thus, $P(X = x)$ is not given by $f(x)$, rather, $P(X = x)$ is given as the area under the curve for an infinitesimally small interval $[x - \epsilon, x + \epsilon]$ centered at x, with $\epsilon > 0$. Figure 1.7 illustrates this with the shaded region centered at $\mu = 5.84$. From Eq. (1.15), we have

$$P(X = \mu) \simeq 2\epsilon \cdot f(\mu) = 2\epsilon \cdot 0.483 = 0.967\epsilon$$

As $\epsilon \to 0$, we get $P(X = \mu) \to 0$. However, based on Eq. (1.16) we can claim that the probability of observing values close to the mean value $\mu = 5.84$ is 2.69 times the probability of observing values close to $x = 7$, as

$$\frac{f(5.84)}{f(7)} = \frac{0.483}{0.18} = 2.69$$

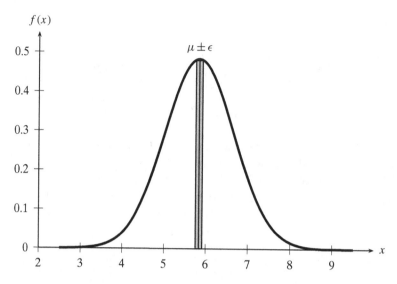

Figure 1.7. Normal distribution: probability density function ($\mu = 5.84$, $\sigma^2 = 0.681$).

Cumulative Distribution Function

For any random variable X, whether discrete or continuous, we can define the *cumulative distribution function (CDF)* $F : \mathbb{R} \to [0, 1]$, which gives the probability of observing a value at most some given value x:

$$F(x) = P(X \le x) \qquad \text{for all } -\infty < x < \infty \tag{1.17}$$

When X is discrete, F is given as

$$F(x) = P(X \le x) = \sum_{u \le x} f(u)$$

and when X is continuous, F is given as

$$F(x) = P(X \le x) = \int_{-\infty}^{x} f(u)\, du$$

Example 1.9 (Cumulative Distribution Function). Figure 1.8 shows the cumulative distribution function for the binomial distribution in Figure 1.6. It has the characteristic step shape (right continuous, non-decreasing), as expected for a discrete random variable. $F(x)$ has the same value $F(k)$ for all $x \in [k, k+1)$ with $0 \le k < m$, where m is the number of trials and k is the number of successes. The closed (filled) and open circles demarcate the corresponding closed and open interval $[k, k+1)$. For instance, $F(x) = 0.404 = F(0)$ for all $x \in [0, 1)$.

Figure 1.9 shows the cumulative distribution function for the normal density function shown in Figure 1.7. As expected, for a continuous random variable, the CDF is also continuous, and non-decreasing. Because the normal distribution is symmetric about the mean, we have $F(\mu) = P(X \le \mu) = 0.5$.

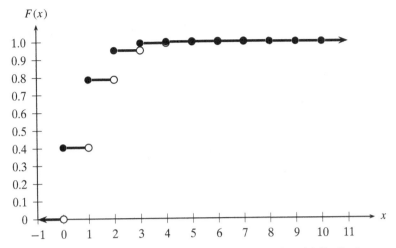

Figure 1.8. Cumulative distribution function for the binomial distribution.

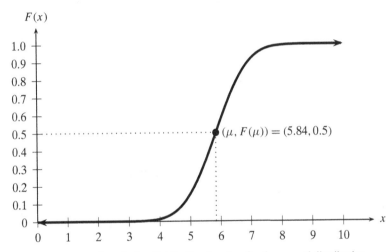

Figure 1.9. Cumulative distribution function for the normal distribution.

1.4.1 Bivariate Random Variables

Instead of considering each attribute as a random variable, we can also perform pair-wise analysis by considering a pair of attributes, X_1 and X_2, as a *bivariate random variable*:

$$\mathbf{X} = \begin{pmatrix} X_1 \\ X_2 \end{pmatrix}$$

$\mathbf{X} : \mathcal{O} \to \mathbb{R}^2$ is a function that assigns to each outcome in the sample space, a pair of real numbers, that is, a 2-dimensional vector $\begin{pmatrix} x_1 \\ x_2 \end{pmatrix} \in \mathbb{R}^2$. As in the univariate case, if the outcomes are numeric, then the default is to assume $\mathbf{X}$ to be the identity function.

Joint Probability Mass Function

If X_1 and X_2 are both discrete random variables then $\mathbf{X}$ has a *joint probability mass function* given as follows:

$$f(\mathbf{x}) = f(x_1, x_2) = P(X_1 = x_1, X_2 = x_2) = P(\mathbf{X} = \mathbf{x})$$

f must satisfy the following two conditions:

$$f(\mathbf{x}) = f(x_1, x_2) \geq 0 \qquad \text{for all } -\infty < x_1, x_2 < \infty$$

$$\sum_{\mathbf{x}} f(\mathbf{x}) = \sum_{x_1} \sum_{x_2} f(x_1, x_2) = 1$$

Joint Probability Density Function

If X_1 and X_2 are both continuous random variables then $\mathbf{X}$ has a *joint probability density function* f given as follows:

$$P(\mathbf{X} \in W) = \iint_{\mathbf{x} \in W} f(\mathbf{x}) \, d\mathbf{x} = \iint_{(x_1, x_2)^T \in W} f(x_1, x_2) \, dx_1 \, dx_2$$

where $W \subset \mathbb{R}^2$ is some subset of the 2-dimensional space of reals. f must also satisfy the following two conditions:

$$f(\mathbf{x}) = f(x_1, x_2) \geq 0 \qquad \text{for all } -\infty < x_1, x_2 < \infty$$

$$\int_{\mathbb{R}^2} f(\mathbf{x}) \, d\mathbf{x} = \int_{-\infty}^{\infty} \int_{-\infty}^{\infty} f(x_1, x_2) \, dx_1 \, dx_2 = 1$$

As in the univariate case, the probability mass $P(\mathbf{x}) = P\big((x_1, x_2)^T\big) = 0$ for any particular point $\mathbf{x}$. However, we can use f to compute the probability density at $\mathbf{x}$. Consider the square region $W = \big([x_1 - \epsilon, x_1 + \epsilon], [x_2 - \epsilon, x_2 + \epsilon]\big)$, that is, a 2-dimensional window of width 2ϵ centered at $\mathbf{x} = (x_1, x_2)^T$. The probability density at $\mathbf{x}$ can be approximated as

$$P(\mathbf{X} \in W) = P\Big(\mathbf{X} \in \big([x_1 - \epsilon, x_1 + \epsilon], [x_2 - \epsilon, x_2 + \epsilon]\big)\Big)$$

$$= \int_{x_1 - \epsilon}^{x_1 + \epsilon} \int_{x_2 - \epsilon}^{x_2 + \epsilon} f(x_1, x_2) \, dx_1 \, dx_2$$

$$\simeq 2\epsilon \cdot 2\epsilon \cdot f(x_1, x_2)$$

which implies that

$$f(x_1, x_2) = \frac{P(\mathbf{X} \in W)}{(2\epsilon)^2}$$

The relative probability of one value (a_1, a_2) versus another (b_1, b_2) can therefore be computed via the probability density function:

$$\frac{P(\mathbf{X} \in \big([a_1 - \epsilon, a_1 + \epsilon], [a_2 - \epsilon, a_2 + \epsilon]\big))}{P(\mathbf{X} \in \big([b_1 - \epsilon, b_1 + \epsilon], [b_2 - \epsilon, b_2 + \epsilon]\big))} \simeq \frac{(2\epsilon)^2 \cdot f(a_1, a_2)}{(2\epsilon)^2 \cdot f(b_1, b_2)} = \frac{f(a_1, a_2)}{f(b_1, b_2)}$$

Example 1.10 (Bivariate Distributions). Consider the sepal length and sepal width attributes in the Iris dataset, plotted in Figure 1.2. Let A denote the Bernoulli random variable corresponding to long sepal length (at least 7 cm), as defined in Example 1.7.

Define another Bernoulli random variable B corresponding to long sepal width, say, at least 3.5 cm. Let $\mathbf{X} = \begin{pmatrix} A \\ B \end{pmatrix}$ be a discrete bivariate random variable; then the joint probability mass function of $\mathbf{X}$ can be estimated from the data as follows:

$$f(0,0) = P(A=0, B=0) = \frac{116}{150} = 0.773$$

$$f(0,1) = P(A=0, B=1) = \frac{21}{150} = 0.140$$

$$f(1,0) = P(A=1, B=0) = \frac{10}{150} = 0.067$$

$$f(1,1) = P(A=1, B=1) = \frac{3}{150} = 0.020$$

Figure 1.10 shows a plot of this probability mass function.

Treating attributes X_1 and X_2 in the Iris dataset (see Table 1.1) as continuous random variables, we can define a continuous bivariate random variable $\mathbf{X} = \begin{pmatrix} X_1 \\ X_2 \end{pmatrix}$. Assuming that $\mathbf{X}$ follows a *bivariate normal distribution*, its joint probability density function is given as

$$f(\mathbf{x}|\boldsymbol{\mu}, \boldsymbol{\Sigma}) = \frac{1}{2\pi\sqrt{|\boldsymbol{\Sigma}|}} \exp\left\{ -\frac{(\mathbf{x}-\boldsymbol{\mu})^T \boldsymbol{\Sigma}^{-1} (\mathbf{x}-\boldsymbol{\mu})}{2} \right\}$$

Here $\boldsymbol{\mu}$ and $\boldsymbol{\Sigma}$ are the parameters of the bivariate normal distribution, representing the 2-dimensional mean vector and covariance matrix, which are discussed in detail

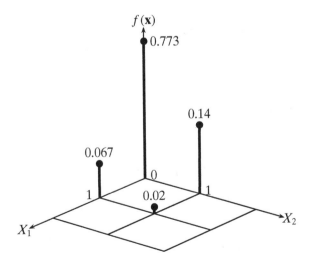

Figure 1.10. Joint probability mass function: X_1 (long sepal length), X_2 (long sepal width).

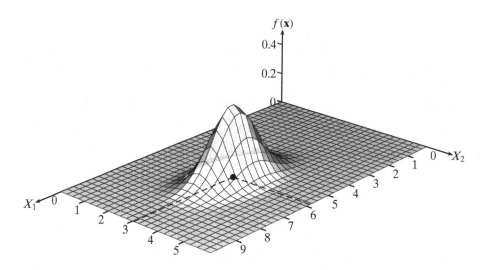

Figure 1.11. Bivariate normal density: $\boldsymbol{\mu} = (5.843, 3.054)^T$ (solid circle).

in Chapter 2. Further, $|\boldsymbol{\Sigma}|$ denotes the determinant of $\boldsymbol{\Sigma}$. The plot of the bivariate normal density is given in Figure 1.11, with mean

$$\boldsymbol{\mu} = (5.843, 3.054)^T$$

and covariance matrix

$$\boldsymbol{\Sigma} = \begin{pmatrix} 0.681 & -0.039 \\ -0.039 & 0.187 \end{pmatrix}$$

It is important to emphasize that the function $f(\mathbf{x})$ specifies only the probability density at $\mathbf{x}$, and $f(\mathbf{x}) \neq P(\mathbf{X} = \mathbf{x})$. As before, we have $P(\mathbf{X} = \mathbf{x}) = 0$.

Joint Cumulative Distribution Function

The *joint cumulative distribution function* for two random variables X_1 and X_2 is defined as the function F, such that for all values $x_1, x_2 \in (-\infty, \infty)$,

$$F(\mathbf{x}) = F(x_1, x_2) = P(X_1 \leq x_1 \text{ and } X_2 \leq x_2) = P(\mathbf{X} \leq \mathbf{x})$$

Statistical Independence

Two random variables X_1 and X_2 are said to be (statistically) *independent* if, for every $W_1 \subset \mathbb{R}$ and $W_2 \subset \mathbb{R}$, we have

$$P(X_1 \in W_1 \text{ and } X_2 \in W_2) = P(X_1 \in W_1) \cdot P(X_2 \in W_2)$$

Furthermore, if X_1 and X_2 are independent, then the following two conditions are also satisfied:

$$F(\mathbf{x}) = F(x_1, x_2) = F_1(x_1) \cdot F_2(x_2)$$
$$f(\mathbf{x}) = f(x_1, x_2) = f_1(x_1) \cdot f_2(x_2)$$

where F_i is the cumulative distribution function, and f_i is the probability mass or density function for random variable X_i.

1.4.2 Multivariate Random Variable

A d-dimensional *multivariate random variable* $\mathbf{X} = (X_1, X_2, \ldots, X_d)^T$, also called a *vector random variable*, is defined as a function that assigns a vector of real numbers to each outcome in the sample space, that is, $\mathbf{X} : \mathcal{O} \rightarrow \mathbb{R}^d$. The range of $\mathbf{X}$ can be denoted as a vector $\mathbf{x} = (x_1, x_2, \ldots, x_d)^T$. In case all X_j are numeric, then $\mathbf{X}$ is by default assumed to be the identity function. In other words, if all attributes are numeric, we can treat each outcome in the sample space (i.e., each point in the data matrix) as a vector random variable. On the other hand, if the attributes are not all numeric, then $\mathbf{X}$ maps the outcomes to numeric vectors in its range.

If all X_j are discrete, then $\mathbf{X}$ is jointly discrete and its joint probability mass function f is given as

$$f(\mathbf{x}) = P(\mathbf{X} = \mathbf{x})$$

$$f(x_1, x_2, \ldots, x_d) = P(X_1 = x_1, X_2 = x_2, \ldots, X_d = x_d)$$

If all X_j are continuous, then $\mathbf{X}$ is jointly continuous and its joint probability density function is given as

$$P(\mathbf{X} \in W) = \int \cdots \int_{\mathbf{x} \in W} f(\mathbf{x}) \, d\mathbf{x}$$

$$P\left((X_1, X_2, \ldots, X_d)^T \in W\right) = \int \cdots \int_{(x_1, x_2, \ldots, x_d)^T \in W} f(x_1, x_2, \ldots, x_d) \, dx_1 \, dx_2 \ldots dx_d$$

for any d-dimensional region $W \subseteq \mathbb{R}^d$.

The laws of probability must be obeyed as usual, that is, $f(\mathbf{x}) \geq 0$ and sum of f over all $\mathbf{x}$ in the range of $\mathbf{X}$ must be 1. The joint cumulative distribution function of $\mathbf{X} = (X_1, \ldots, X_d)^T$ is given as

$$F(\mathbf{x}) = P(\mathbf{X} \leq \mathbf{x})$$

$$F(x_1, x_2, \ldots, x_d) = P(X_1 \leq x_1, X_2 \leq x_2, \ldots, X_d \leq x_d)$$

for every point $\mathbf{x} \in \mathbb{R}^d$.

We say that $X_1, X_2, \ldots, X_d$ are independent random variables if and only if, for every region $W_i \subset \mathbb{R}$, we have

$$P(X_1 \in W_1 \text{ and } X_2 \in W_2 \cdots \text{ and } X_d \in W_d)$$
$$= P(X_1 \in W_1) \cdot P(X_2 \in W_2) \cdot \ldots \cdot P(X_d \in W_d) \quad (1.18)$$

If $X_1, X_2, \ldots, X_d$ are independent then the following conditions are also satisfied

$$F(\mathbf{x}) = F(x_1, \ldots, x_d) = F_1(x_1) \cdot F_2(x_2) \cdot \ldots \cdot F_d(x_d)$$

$$f(\mathbf{x}) = f(x_1, \ldots, x_d) = f_1(x_1) \cdot f_2(x_2) \cdot \ldots \cdot f_d(x_d) \quad (1.19)$$

where F_i is the cumulative distribution function, and f_i is the probability mass or density function for random variable X_i.

1.4.3 Random Sample and Statistics

The probability mass or density function of a random variable X may follow some known form, or as is often the case in data analysis, it may be unknown. When the probability function is not known, it may still be convenient to assume that the values follow some known distribution, based on the characteristics of the data. However, even in this case, the parameters of the distribution may still be unknown. Thus, in general, either the parameters, or the entire distribution, may have to be estimated from the data.

In statistics, the word *population* is used to refer to the set or universe of all entities under study. Usually we are interested in certain characteristics or parameters of the entire population (e.g., the mean age of all computer science students in the United States). However, looking at the entire population may not be feasible or may be too expensive. Instead, we try to make inferences about the population parameters by drawing a random sample from the population, and by computing appropriate *statistics* from the sample that give estimates of the corresponding population parameters of interest.

Univariate Sample

Given a random variable X, a *random sample* of size n from X is defined as a set of n *independent and identically distributed (IID)* random variables $S_1, S_2, \ldots, S_n$, that is, all of the S_i's are statistically independent of each other, and follow the same probability mass or density function as X.

If we treat attribute X as a random variable, then each of the observed values of X, namely, x_i ($1 \le i \le n$), are themselves treated as identity random variables, and the observed data is assumed to be a random sample drawn from X. That is, all x_i are considered to be mutually independent and identically distributed as X. By Eq. (1.19) their joint probability function is given as

$$f(x_1, \ldots, x_n) = \prod_{i=1}^{n} f_X(x_i) \tag{1.20}$$

where f_X is the probability mass or density function for X.

Multivariate Sample

For multivariate parameter estimation, the n data points $\mathbf{x}_i$ (with $1 \le i \le n$) constitute a d-dimensional multivariate random sample drawn from the vector random variable $\mathbf{X} = (X_1, X_2, \ldots, X_d)$. That is, $\mathbf{x}_i$ are assumed to be independent and identically distributed, and thus their joint distribution is given as

$$f(\mathbf{x}_1, \mathbf{x}_2, \ldots, \mathbf{x}_n) = \prod_{i=1}^{n} f_{\mathbf{X}}(\mathbf{x}_i) \tag{1.21}$$

where $f_{\mathbf{X}}$ is the probability mass or density function for $\mathbf{X}$.

Estimating the parameters of a multivariate joint probability distribution is usually difficult and computationally intensive. One simplifying assumption that is typically made is that the d attributes $X_1, X_2, \ldots, X_d$ are statistically independent. However, we do not assume that they are identically distributed, because that is almost never justified. Under the attribute independence assumption Eq. (1.21) can be rewritten as

$$f(\mathbf{x}_1, \mathbf{x}_2, \ldots, \mathbf{x}_n) = \prod_{i=1}^{n} f(\mathbf{x}_i) = \prod_{i=1}^{n} \prod_{j=1}^{d} f_{X_j}(x_{ij})$$

Statistic

We can estimate a parameter of the population by defining an appropriate sample *statistic*, which is defined as a function of the sample. More precisely, let $\{\mathbf{S}_i\}_{i=1}^{m}$ denote a random sample of size m drawn from a (multivariate) random variable $\mathbf{X}$. A statistic $\hat{\theta}$ is some function over the random sample, given as

$$\hat{\theta} : (\mathbf{S}_1, \mathbf{S}_2, \ldots, \mathbf{S}_m) \rightarrow \mathbb{R}$$

The statistic $\hat{\theta}$ is an estimate of the corresponding population parameter θ. As such, the statistic $\hat{\theta}$ is itself a random variable. If we use the value of a statistic to estimate a population parameter, this value is called a *point estimate* of the parameter, and the statistic is called an *estimator* of the parameter. In Chapter 2 we will study different estimators for population parameters that reflect the location (or centrality) and dispersion of values.

Example 1.11 (Sample Mean). Consider attribute sepal length (X_1) in the Iris dataset, whose values are shown in Table 1.2. Assume that the mean value of X_1 is not known. Let us assume that the observed values $\{x_i\}_{i=1}^{n}$ constitute a random sample drawn from X_1.

The *sample mean* is a statistic, defined as the average

$$\hat{\mu} = \frac{1}{n} \sum_{i=1}^{n} x_i$$

Plugging in values from Table 1.2, we obtain

$$\hat{\mu} = \frac{1}{150}(5.9 + 6.9 + \cdots + 7.7 + 5.1) = \frac{876.5}{150} = 5.84$$

The value $\hat{\mu} = 5.84$ is a point estimate for the unknown population parameter μ, the (true) mean value of variable X_1.

1.5 FURTHER READING

For a review of the linear algebra concepts see Strang (2006) and Poole (2010), and for the probabilistic view see Evans and Rosenthal (2011). There are several good books on data mining, and machine and statistical learning; these include Hand, Mannila, and Smyth (2001), Han, Kamber, and Pei (2006), Witten, Frank, and Hall (2011), Tan, Steinbach, and Kumar (2013), and Bishop (2006) and Hastie, Tibshirani, and Friedman (2009).

Bishop, C. (2006). *Pattern Recognition and Machine Learning.* Information Science and Statistics. New York: Springer Science + Business Media.

Evans, M. and Rosenthal, J. (2011). *Probability and Statistics: The Science of Uncertainty.* 2nd ed. New York: W. H. Freeman.

Han, J., Kamber, M., and Pei, J. (2006). *Data Mining: Concepts and Techniques.* 2nd ed. The Morgan Kaufmann Series in Data Management Systems. Philadelphia: Elsevier Science.

Hand, D., Mannila, H., and Smyth, P. (2001). *Principles of Data Mining.* Adaptative Computation and Machine Learning Series. Cambridge, MA: MIT Press.

Hastie, T., Tibshirani, R., and Friedman, J. (2009). *The Elements of Statistical Learning.* 2nd ed. Springer Series in Statistics. New York: Springer Science + Business Media.

Poole, D. (2010). *Linear Algebra: A Modern Introduction.* 3rd ed. Independence, KY: Cengage Learning.

Strang, G. (2006). *Linear Algebra and Its Applications.* 4th ed. Independence, KY: Thomson Brooks/Cole, Cengage learning.

Tan, P., Steinbach, M., and Kumar, V. (2013). *Introduction to Data Mining.* 2nd ed. Upper Saddle River, NJ: Prentice Hall.

Witten, I., Frank, E., and Hall, M. (2011). *Data Mining: Practical Machine Learning Tools and Techniques.* 3rd ed. The Morgan Kaufmann Series in Data Management Systems. Philadelphia: Elsevier Science.

1.6 EXERCISES

Q1. Show that the mean of the centered data matrix $\overline{\mathbf{D}}$ in Eq. (1.9) is $\mathbf{0}$.

Q2. Prove that for the L_p-distance in Eq. (1.5), for $\mathbf{x}, \mathbf{y} \in \mathbb{R}^d$, we have

$$\|\mathbf{x} - \mathbf{y}\|_\infty = \lim_{p \to \infty} \|\mathbf{x} - \mathbf{y}\|_p = \max_{i=1}^{d}\big\{|x_i - y_i|\big\}$$

CHAPTER 2

Numeric Attributes

In this chapter, we discuss basic statistical methods for exploratory data analysis of numeric attributes. We look at measures of central tendency or location, measures of dispersion, and measures of linear dependence or association between attributes. We emphasize the connection between the probabilistic and the geometric and algebraic views of the data matrix.

2.1 UNIVARIATE ANALYSIS

Univariate analysis focuses on a single attribute at a time; thus the data matrix $\mathbf{D}$ can be thought of as an $n \times 1$ matrix, or simply a column vector, given as

$$\mathbf{D} = \begin{pmatrix} X \\ x_1 \\ x_2 \\ \vdots \\ x_n \end{pmatrix}$$

where X is the numeric attribute of interest, with $x_i \in \mathbb{R}$. X is assumed to be a random variable, with each point x_i $(1 \leq i \leq n)$ itself treated as an identity random variable. We assume that the observed data is a random sample drawn from X, that is, each variable x_i is independent and identically distributed as X. In the vector view, we treat the sample as an n-dimensional vector, and write $X \in \mathbb{R}^n$.

In general, the probability density or mass function $f(x)$ and the cumulative distribution function $F(x)$, for attribute X, are both unknown. However, we can estimate these distributions directly from the data sample, which also allow us to compute statistics to estimate several important population parameters.

Empirical Cumulative Distribution Function
The *empirical cumulative distribution function (CDF)* of X is given as

$$\hat{F}(x) = \frac{1}{n} \sum_{i=1}^{n} I(x_i \leq x) \tag{2.1}$$

where

$$I(x_i \leq x) = \begin{cases} 1 & \text{if } x_i \leq x \\ 0 & \text{if } x_i > x \end{cases}$$

is a binary *indicator variable* that indicates whether the given condition is satisfied or not. Intuitively, to obtain the empirical CDF we compute, for each value $x \in \mathbb{R}$, how many points in the sample are less than or equal to x. The empirical CDF puts a probability mass of $\frac{1}{n}$ at each point x_i. Note that we use the notation $\hat{F}$ to denote the fact that the empirical CDF is an estimate for the unknown population CDF F.

Inverse Cumulative Distribution Function

Define the *inverse cumulative distribution function* or *quantile function* for a random variable X as follows:

$$F^{-1}(q) = \min\{x \mid F(x) \geq q\} \qquad \text{for } q \in [0,1] \tag{2.2}$$

That is, the inverse CDF gives the least value of X, for which q fraction of the values are lower, and $1 - q$ fraction of the values are higher. The *empirical inverse cumulative distribution function* $\hat{F}^{-1}$ can be obtained from Eq. (2.1).

Empirical Probability Mass Function

The *empirical probability mass function (PMF)* of X is given as

$$\hat{f}(x) = P(X = x) = \frac{1}{n} \sum_{i=1}^{n} I(x_i = x) \tag{2.3}$$

where

$$I(x_i = x) = \begin{cases} 1 & \text{if } x_i = x \\ 0 & \text{if } x_i \neq x \end{cases}$$

The empirical PMF also puts a probability mass of $\frac{1}{n}$ at each point x_i.

2.1.1 Measures of Central Tendency

These measures given an indication about the concentration of the probability mass, the "middle" values, and so on.

Mean

The *mean*, also called the *expected value*, of a random variable X is the arithmetic average of the values of X. It provides a one-number summary of the *location* or *central tendency* for the distribution of X.

The mean or expected value of a discrete random variable X is defined as

$$\mu = E[X] = \sum_{x} x \cdot f(x) \tag{2.4}$$

where $f(x)$ is the probability mass function of X.

The expected value of a continuous random variable X is defined as

$$\mu = E[X] = \int_{-\infty}^{\infty} x \cdot f(x)\,dx \tag{2.5}$$

where $f(x)$ is the probability density function of X.

Sample Mean   The *sample mean* is a statistic, that is, a function $\hat{\mu} : \{x_1, x_2, \ldots, x_n\} \rightarrow \mathbb{R}$, defined as the average value of x_i's:

$$\hat{\mu} = \frac{1}{n} \sum_{i=1}^{n} x_i \tag{2.6}$$

It serves as an estimator for the unknown mean value μ of X. It can be derived by plugging in the empirical PMF $\hat{f}(x)$ in Eq. (2.4):

$$\hat{\mu} = \sum_{x} x \cdot \hat{f}(x) = \sum_{x} x \left(\frac{1}{n} \sum_{i=1}^{n} I(x_i = x) \right) = \frac{1}{n} \sum_{i=1}^{n} x_i$$

Sample Mean Is Unbiased   An estimator $\hat{\theta}$ is called an *unbiased estimator* for parameter θ if $E[\hat{\theta}] = \theta$ for every possible value of θ. The sample mean $\hat{\mu}$ is an unbiased estimator for the population mean μ, as

$$E[\hat{\mu}] = E\left[\frac{1}{n} \sum_{i=1}^{n} x_i \right] = \frac{1}{n} \sum_{i=1}^{n} E[x_i] = \frac{1}{n} \sum_{i=1}^{n} \mu = \mu \tag{2.7}$$

where we use the fact that the random variables x_i are IID according to X, which implies that they have the same mean μ as X, that is, $E[x_i] = \mu$ for all x_i. We also used the fact that the expectation function E is a *linear operator*, that is, for any two random variables X and Y, and real numbers a and b, we have $E[aX + bY] = aE[X] + bE[Y]$.

Robustness   We say that a statistic is *robust* if it is not affected by extreme values (such as outliers) in the data. The sample mean is unfortunately not robust because a single large value (an outlier) can skew the average. A more robust measure is the *trimmed mean* obtained after discarding a small fraction of extreme values on one or both ends. Furthermore, the mean can be somewhat misleading in that it is typically not a value that occurs in the sample, and it may not even be a value that the random variable can actually assume (for a discrete random variable). For example, the number of cars per capita is an integer-valued random variable, but according to the US Bureau of Transportation Studies, the average number of passenger cars in the United States was 0.45 in 2008 (137.1 million cars, with a population size of 304.4 million). Obviously, one cannot own 0.45 cars; it can be interpreted as saying that on average there are 45 cars per 100 people.

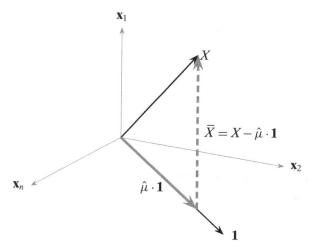

Figure 2.1. Geometric interpretation of mean and variance. The vectors are shown in the (conceptual) n-dimensional space $\mathbb{R}^n$ spanned by the n points.

Geometric Interpretation of Sample Mean Treating the data sample for attribute X as a vector in n-dimensional space, where n is the sample size, we write $X = (x_1, x_2, \cdots, x_n)^T \in \mathbb{R}^n$. Further, let $\mathbf{1} = (1, 1, \cdots, 1)^T \in \mathbb{R}^n$ be the vector all of whose elements are 1, which is also called the *ones vector*. Consider the projection of X onto the vector $\mathbf{1}$, we have

$$\mathbf{p} = \left(\frac{X^T \mathbf{1}}{\mathbf{1}^T \mathbf{1}} \right) \cdot \mathbf{1} = \left(\frac{\sum_{i=1}^n x_i}{n} \right) \cdot \mathbf{1} = \hat{\mu} \cdot \mathbf{1}$$

Thus, the sample mean is simply the offset or the scalar projection of X on the vector $\mathbf{1}$ (see Eq. (1.12)), as shown in Figure 2.1:

$$\hat{\mu} = \text{proj}_{\mathbf{1}}(X) = \left(\frac{X^T \mathbf{1}}{\mathbf{1}^T \mathbf{1}} \right) \tag{2.8}$$

The sample mean can be used to center the attribute X. Define the *centered attribute vector*, $\bar{X}$, as follows:

$$\bar{X} = X - \hat{\mu} \cdot \mathbf{1} = \begin{pmatrix} x_1 - \hat{\mu} \\ x_2 - \hat{\mu} \\ \vdots \\ x_n - \hat{\mu} \end{pmatrix} \tag{2.9}$$

From Figure 2.1 we can observe that $\hat{\mu} \cdot \mathbf{1}$ is the parallel component and $\bar{X}$ is the perpendicular component of the projection of X onto $\mathbf{1}$. We can also see that $\mathbf{1}$ and $\bar{X}$ are orthogonal to each other, since

$$\mathbf{1}^T \bar{X} = \mathbf{1}^T (X - \hat{\mu} \cdot \mathbf{1}) = \mathbf{1}^T X - \left(\frac{X^T \mathbf{1}}{\mathbf{1}^T \mathbf{1}} \right) \cdot \mathbf{1}^T \mathbf{1} = 0$$

In fact, the subspace containing $\bar{X}$ is an *orthogonal complement* of the space spanned by $\mathbf{1}$.

Median

The *median* of a random variable is defined as the value m such that

$$P(X \leq m) \geq \frac{1}{2} \text{ and } P(X \geq m) \geq \frac{1}{2}$$

In other words, the median m is the "middle-most" value; half of the values of X are less and half of the values of X are more than m. In terms of the (inverse) cumulative distribution function, the median is therefore the value m for which

$$F(m) = 0.5 \text{ or } m = F^{-1}(0.5)$$

The *sample median* can be obtained from the empirical CDF [Eq. (2.1)] or the empirical inverse CDF [Eq. (2.2)] by computing

$$\hat{F}(m) = 0.5 \text{ or } m = \hat{F}^{-1}(0.5)$$

A simpler approach to compute the sample median is to first sort all the values x_i ($i \in [1, n]$) in increasing order. If n is odd, the median is the value at position $\frac{n+1}{2}$. If n is even, the values at positions $\frac{n}{2}$ and $\frac{n}{2} + 1$ are both medians.

Unlike the mean, median is robust, as it is not affected very much by extreme values. Also, it is a value that occurs in the sample and a value the random variable can actually assume.

Mode

The *mode* of a random variable X is the value at which the probability mass function or the probability density function attains its maximum value, depending on whether X is discrete or continuous, respectively.

The *sample mode* is a value for which the empirical probability mass function [Eq. (2.3)] attains its maximum, given as

$$\text{mode}(X) = \arg\max_x \hat{f}(x)$$

The mode may not be a very useful measure of central tendency for a sample because by chance an unrepresentative element may be the most frequent element. Furthermore, if all values in the sample are distinct, each of them will be the mode.

Example 2.1 (Sample Mean, Median, and Mode). Consider the attribute sepal length (X_1) in the Iris dataset, whose values are shown in Table 1.2. The sample mean is given as follows:

$$\hat{\mu} = \frac{1}{150}(5.9 + 6.9 + \cdots + 7.7 + 5.1) = \frac{876.5}{150} = 5.843$$

Figure 2.2 shows all 150 values of sepal length, and the sample mean. Figure 2.3(a) shows the empirical CDF and Figure 2.3(b) shows the empirical inverse CDF for sepal length.

Because $n = 150$ is even, the sample median is the value at positions $\frac{n}{2} = 75$ and $\frac{n}{2} + 1 = 76$ in sorted order. For sepal length both these values are 5.8; thus the sample median is 5.8. From the inverse CDF in Figure 2.3(b), we can see that

$$\hat{F}(5.8) = 0.5 \text{ or } 5.8 = \hat{F}^{-1}(0.5)$$

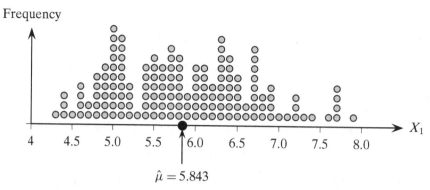

Figure 2.2. Sample mean for sepal length. Multiple occurrences of the same value are shown stacked.

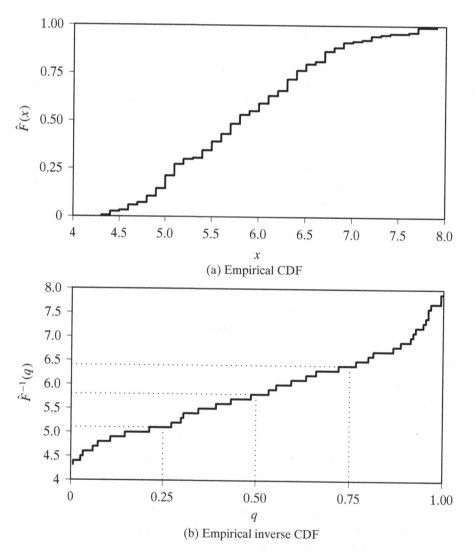

(a) Empirical CDF

(b) Empirical inverse CDF

Figure 2.3. Empirical CDF and inverse CDF: sepal length.

The sample mode for sepal length is 5, which can be observed from the frequency of 5 in Figure 2.2. The empirical probability mass at $x = 5$ is

$$\hat{f}(5) = \frac{10}{150} = 0.067$$

2.1.2 Measures of Dispersion

The measures of dispersion give an indication about the spread or variation in the values of a random variable.

Range

The *value range* or simply *range* of a random variable X is the difference between the maximum and minimum values of X, given as

$$r = \max\{X\} - \min\{X\}$$

The (value) range of X is a population parameter, not to be confused with the range of the function X, which is the set of all the values X can assume. Which range is being used should be clear from the context.

The *sample range* is a statistic, given as

$$\hat{r} = \max_{i=1}^{n}\{x_i\} - \min_{i=1}^{n}\{x_i\}$$

By definition, range is sensitive to extreme values, and thus is not robust.

Interquartile Range

Quartiles are special values of the quantile function [Eq. (2.2)] that divide the data into four equal parts. That is, quartiles correspond to the quantile values of 0.25, 0.5, 0.75, and 1.0. The *first quartile* is the value $q_1 = F^{-1}(0.25)$, to the left of which 25% of the points lie; the *second quartile* is the same as the median value $q_2 = F^{-1}(0.5)$, to the left of which 50% of the points lie; the *third quartile* $q_3 = F^{-1}(0.75)$ is the value to the left of which 75% of the points lie; and the *fourth quartile* is the maximum value of X, to the left of which 100% of the points lie.

A more robust measure of the dispersion of X is the *interquartile range (IQR)*, defined as

$$IQR = q_3 - q_1 = F^{-1}(0.75) - F^{-1}(0.25) \tag{2.10}$$

IQR can also be thought of as a *trimmed range*, where we discard 25% of the low and high values of X. Or put differently, it is the range for the middle 50% of the values of X. IQR is robust by definition.

The *sample IQR* can be obtained by plugging in the empirical inverse CDF in Eq. (2.10):

$$\widehat{IQR} = \hat{q}_3 - \hat{q}_1 = \hat{F}^{-1}(0.75) - \hat{F}^{-1}(0.25)$$

Variance and Standard Deviation

The *variance* of a random variable X provides a measure of how much the values of X deviate from the mean or expected value of X. More formally, variance is the expected value of the squared deviation from the mean, defined as

$$\sigma^2 = \text{var}(X) = E[(X-\mu)^2] = \begin{cases} \sum_x (x-\mu)^2 \, f(x) & \text{if } X \text{ is discrete} \\ \\ \int_{-\infty}^{\infty} (x-\mu)^2 \, f(x)\,dx & \text{if } X \text{ is continuous} \end{cases} \tag{2.11}$$

The *standard deviation*, σ, is defined as the positive square root of the variance, σ^2.

We can also write the variance as the difference between the expectation of X^2 and the square of the expectation of X:

$$\begin{aligned} \sigma^2 = \text{var}(X) = E[(X-\mu)^2] &= E[X^2 - 2\mu X + \mu^2] \\ &= E[X^2] - 2\mu E[X] + \mu^2 = E[X^2] - 2\mu^2 + \mu^2 \\ &= E[X^2] - (E[X])^2 \end{aligned} \tag{2.12}$$

It is worth noting that variance is in fact the *second moment about the mean*, corresponding to $r = 2$, which is a special case of the *rth moment about the mean* for a random variable X, defined as $E[(X-\mu)^r]$.

Sample Variance   The *sample variance* is defined as

$$\hat{\sigma}^2 = \frac{1}{n} \sum_{i=1}^{n} (x_i - \hat{\mu})^2 \tag{2.13}$$

It is the average squared deviation of the data values x_i from the sample mean $\hat{\mu}$, and can be derived by plugging in the empirical probability function $\hat{f}$ from Eq. (2.3) into Eq. (2.11), as

$$\hat{\sigma}^2 = \sum_x (x - \hat{\mu})^2 \hat{f}(x) = \sum_x (x - \hat{\mu})^2 \left(\frac{1}{n} \sum_{i=1}^{n} I(x_i = x) \right) = \frac{1}{n} \sum_{i=1}^{n} (x_i - \hat{\mu})^2$$

The *sample standard deviation* is given as the positive square root of the sample variance:

$$\hat{\sigma} = \sqrt{ \frac{1}{n} \sum_{i=1}^{n} (x_i - \hat{\mu})^2 }$$

The *standard score*, also called the *z-score*, of a sample value x_i is the number of standard deviations the value is away from the mean:

$$z_i = \frac{x_i - \hat{\mu}}{\hat{\sigma}} \tag{2.14}$$

Put differently, the z-score of x_i measures the deviation of x_i from the mean value $\hat{\mu}$, in units of $\hat{\sigma}$.

Example 2.2. Consider the data sample for `sepal length` shown in Figure 2.2. We can see that the sample range is given as

$$\max_i \{x_i\} - \min_i \{x_i\} = 7.9 - 4.3 = 3.6$$

From the inverse CDF for `sepal length` in Figure 2.3(b), we can find the sample IQR as follows:

$$\hat{q}_1 = \hat{F}^{-1}(0.25) = 5.1$$

$$\hat{q}_3 = \hat{F}^{-1}(0.75) = 6.4$$

$$\widehat{IQR} = \hat{q}_3 - \hat{q}_1 = 6.4 - 5.1 = 1.3$$

The sample variance is given as

$$\hat{\sigma}^2 = \frac{1}{n}\sum_{i=1}^{n}(x_i - \hat{\mu})^2 = 102.168/150 = 0.681$$

The sample standard deviation is then

$$\hat{\sigma} = \sqrt{0.681} = 0.825$$

Variance of the Sample Mean Because the sample mean $\hat{\mu}$ is itself a statistic, we can compute its mean value and variance. The expected value of the sample mean is simply μ, as we saw in Eq. (2.7). To derive an expression for the variance of the sample mean, we utilize the fact that the random variables x_i are all independent, and thus

$$\text{var}\left(\sum_{i=1}^{n} x_i\right) = \sum_{i=1}^{n} \text{var}(x_i)$$

Further, because all the x_i's are identically distributed as X, they have the same variance as X, that is,

$$\text{var}(x_i) = \sigma^2 \text{ for all } i$$

Combining the above two facts, we get

$$\text{var}\left(\sum_{i=1}^{n} x_i\right) = \sum_{i=1}^{n} \text{var}(x_i) = \sum_{i=1}^{n} \sigma^2 = n\sigma^2 \tag{2.15}$$

Further, note that

$$E\left[\sum_{i=1}^{n} x_i\right] = n\mu \tag{2.16}$$

Using Eqs. (2.12), (2.15), and (2.16), the variance of the sample mean $\hat{\mu}$ can be computed as

$$\text{var}(\hat{\mu}) = E[(\hat{\mu} - \mu)^2] = E[\hat{\mu}^2] - \mu^2 = E\left[\left(\frac{1}{n}\sum_{i=1}^{n}x_i\right)^2\right] - \frac{1}{n^2}E\left[\sum_{i=1}^{n}x_i\right]^2$$

$$= \frac{1}{n^2}\left(E\left[\left(\sum_{i=1}^{n}x_i\right)^2\right] - E\left[\sum_{i=1}^{n}x_i\right]^2\right) = \frac{1}{n^2}\text{var}\left(\sum_{i=1}^{n}x_i\right)$$

$$= \frac{\sigma^2}{n} \tag{2.17}$$

In other words, the sample mean $\hat{\mu}$ varies or deviates from the mean μ in proportion to the population variance σ^2. However, the deviation can be made smaller by considering larger sample size n.

Bias of Sample Variance   The sample variance in Eq. (2.13) is a *biased estimator* for the true population variance, σ^2, that is, $E[\hat{\sigma}^2] \neq \sigma^2$. To show this we make use of the identity

$$\sum_{i=1}^{n}(x_i - \mu)^2 = n(\hat{\mu} - \mu)^2 + \sum_{i=1}^{n}(x_i - \hat{\mu})^2 \tag{2.18}$$

Computing the expectation of $\hat{\sigma}^2$ by using Eq. (2.18) in the first step, we get

$$E[\hat{\sigma}^2] = E\left[\frac{1}{n}\sum_{i=1}^{n}(x_i - \hat{\mu})^2\right] = E\left[\frac{1}{n}\sum_{i=1}^{n}(x_i - \mu)^2\right] - E[(\hat{\mu} - \mu)^2] \tag{2.19}$$

Recall that the random variables x_i are IID according to X, which means that they have the same mean μ and variance σ^2 as X. This means that

$$E[(x_i - \mu)^2] = \sigma^2$$

Further, from Eq. (2.17) the sample mean $\hat{\mu}$ has variance $E[(\hat{\mu} - \mu)^2] = \frac{\sigma^2}{n}$. Plugging these into the Eq. (2.19) we get

$$E[\hat{\sigma}^2] = \frac{1}{n}n\sigma^2 - \frac{\sigma^2}{n}$$

$$= \left(\frac{n-1}{n}\right)\sigma^2$$

The sample variance $\hat{\sigma}^2$ is a biased estimator of σ^2, as its expected value differs from the population variance by a factor of $\frac{n-1}{n}$. However, it is *asymptotically unbiased*, that is, the bias vanishes as $n \to \infty$ because

$$\lim_{n\to\infty}\frac{n-1}{n} = \lim_{n\to\infty}1 - \frac{1}{n} = 1$$

Put differently, as the sample size increases, we have

$$E[\hat{\sigma}^2] \to \sigma^2 \qquad \text{as } n \to \infty$$

The discussion above makes it clear that if we want an unbiased estimate of the sample variance, denoted $\hat{\sigma}_u^2$, we must divide by $n-1$ instead of n:

$$\hat{\sigma}_u^2 = \frac{1}{n-1} \sum_{i=1}^{n} (x_i - \hat{\mu})^2$$

We can verify that the expected value of $\hat{\sigma}_u^2$ is given as

$$E[\hat{\sigma}_u^2] = E\left[\frac{1}{n-1} \sum_{i=1}^{n} (x_i - \hat{\mu})^2 \right] = \frac{1}{n-1} \cdot E\left[\sum_{i=1}^{n} (x_i - \mu)^2 \right] - \frac{n}{n-1} \cdot E[(\hat{\mu} - \mu)^2]$$

$$= \frac{n}{n-1} \sigma^2 - \frac{n}{n-1} \cdot \frac{\sigma^2}{n}$$

$$= \frac{n}{n-1} \sigma^2 - \frac{1}{n-1} \sigma^2 = \sigma^2$$

Geometric Interpretation of Sample Variance   Let the data sample for attribute X denote a vector in n-dimensional space, where n is the sample size, and let $\overline{X}$ denote the centered attribute vector (see Eq. (2.9))

$$\overline{X} = X - \hat{\mu} \cdot \mathbf{1} = \begin{pmatrix} x_1 - \hat{\mu} \\ x_2 - \hat{\mu} \\ \vdots \\ x_n - \hat{\mu} \end{pmatrix}$$

We can then rewrite Eq. (2.13) in terms of the magnitude of $\overline{X}$, that is, the dot product of $\overline{X}$ with itself:

$$\boxed{\hat{\sigma}^2 = \frac{1}{n} \left\| \overline{X} \right\|^2} = \frac{1}{n} \overline{X}^T \overline{X} = \frac{1}{n} \sum_{i=1}^{n} (x_i - \hat{\mu})^2 \qquad (2.20)$$

The sample variance can thus be interpreted as the squared magnitude of the centered attribute vector, or the dot product of the centered attribute vector with itself, normalized by the sample size.

The geometric interpretation make it clear why dividing by $n-1$ make sense to obtain an unbiased estimate for the sample variance. Define the *degrees of freedom* (dof) of a statistical vector as the dimensionality of the subspace that contains the vector. In Figure 2.1 notice that the centered attribute vector $\overline{X} = X - \hat{\mu} \cdot \mathbf{1}$ lies in a $n-1$ dimensional subspace that is an orthogonal complement of the 1 dimensional subspace spanned by the ones vector $\mathbf{1}$. Thus, the vector $\overline{X}$ has only $n-1$ degrees of freedom, and the unbiased sample variance is simply the mean or expected squared length of $\overline{X}$ per dimension

$$\sigma_u^2 = \frac{\left\| \overline{X} \right\|^2}{n-1} = \frac{\overline{X}^T \overline{X}}{n-1} = \frac{1}{n-1} \cdot \sum_{i=1}^{n} (x_i - \hat{\mu})^2$$

2.2 BIVARIATE ANALYSIS

In bivariate analysis, we consider two attributes at the same time. We are specifically interested in understanding the association or dependence between them, if any. We thus restrict our attention to the two numeric attributes of interest, say X_1 and X_2, with the data $\mathbf{D}$ represented as an $n \times 2$ matrix:

$$\mathbf{D} = \begin{pmatrix} X_1 & X_2 \\ x_{11} & x_{12} \\ x_{21} & x_{22} \\ \vdots & \vdots \\ x_{n1} & x_{n2} \end{pmatrix}$$

Geometrically, we can think of $\mathbf{D}$ in two ways. It can be viewed as n points or vectors in 2-dimensional space over the attributes X_1 and X_2, that is, $\mathbf{x}_i = (x_{i1}, x_{i2})^T \in \mathbb{R}^2$. Alternatively, it can be viewed as two points or vectors in an n-dimensional space comprising the points, that is, each column is a vector in $\mathbb{R}^n$, as follows:

$$X_1 = (x_{11}, x_{21}, \ldots, x_{n1})^T$$
$$X_2 = (x_{12}, x_{22}, \ldots, x_{n2})^T$$

In the probabilistic view, the column vector $\mathbf{X} = (X_1, X_2)^T$ is considered a bivariate vector random variable, and the points $\mathbf{x}_i$ $(1 \le i \le n)$ are treated as a random sample drawn from $\mathbf{X}$, that is, $\mathbf{x}_i$'s are considered independent and identically distributed as $\mathbf{X}$.

Empirical Joint Probability Mass Function
The *empirical joint probability mass function* for $\mathbf{X}$ is given as

$$\hat{f}(\mathbf{x}) = P(\mathbf{X} = \mathbf{x}) = \frac{1}{n} \sum_{i=1}^{n} I(\mathbf{x}_i = \mathbf{x}) \qquad (2.21)$$

$$\hat{f}(x_1, x_2) = P(X_1 = x_1, X_2 = x_2) = \frac{1}{n} \sum_{i=1}^{n} I(x_{i1} = x_1, x_{i2} = x_2)$$

where $\mathbf{x} = (x_1, x_2)^T$ and I is a indicator variable that takes on the value 1 only when its argument is true:

$$I(\mathbf{x}_i = \mathbf{x}) = \begin{cases} 1 & \text{if } x_{i1} = x_1 \text{ and } x_{i2} = x_2 \\ 0 & \text{otherwise} \end{cases}$$

As in the univariate case, the probability function puts a probability mass of $\frac{1}{n}$ at each point in the data sample.

2.2.1 Measures of Location and Dispersion

Mean

The bivariate mean is defined as the expected value of the vector random variable $\mathbf{X}$, defined as follows:

$$\boldsymbol{\mu} = E[\mathbf{X}] = E\left[\begin{pmatrix} X_1 \\ X_2 \end{pmatrix}\right] = \begin{pmatrix} E[X_1] \\ E[X_2] \end{pmatrix} = \begin{pmatrix} \mu_1 \\ \mu_2 \end{pmatrix} \tag{2.22}$$

In other words, the bivariate mean vector is simply the vector of expected values along each attribute.

The sample mean vector can be obtained from $\hat{f}_{X_1}$ and $\hat{f}_{X_2}$, the empirical probability mass functions of X_1 and X_2, respectively, using Eq. (2.6). It can also be computed from the joint empirical PMF in Eq. (2.21)

$$\hat{\boldsymbol{\mu}} = \sum_{\mathbf{x}} \mathbf{x} \hat{f}(\mathbf{x}) = \sum_{\mathbf{x}} \mathbf{x}\left(\frac{1}{n}\sum_{i=1}^{n} I(\mathbf{x}_i = \mathbf{x})\right) = \frac{1}{n}\sum_{i=1}^{n} \mathbf{x}_i \tag{2.23}$$

Variance

We can compute the variance along each attribute, namely σ_1^2 for X_1 and σ_2^2 for X_2 using Eq. (2.11). The *total variance* is given as

$$\sigma_1^2 + \sigma_2^2$$

The sample variances $\hat{\sigma}_1^2$ and $\hat{\sigma}_2^2$ can be estimated using Eq. (2.13), and the *sample total variance* [Eq. (1.8)] is simply

$$\text{var}(\mathbf{D}) = \hat{\sigma}_1^2 + \hat{\sigma}_2^2$$

2.2.2 Measures of Association

Covariance

The *covariance* between two attributes X_1 and X_2 provides a measure of the association or linear dependence between them, and is defined as

$$\sigma_{12} = E[(X_1 - \mu_1)(X_2 - \mu_2)] \tag{2.24}$$

By linearity of expectation, we have

$$\sigma_{12} = E[(X_1 - \mu_1)(X_2 - \mu_2)] = E[X_1 X_2 - X_1 \mu_2 - X_2 \mu_1 + \mu_1 \mu_2]$$
$$= E[X_1 X_2] - \mu_2 E[X_1] - \mu_1 E[X_2] + \mu_1 \mu_2 = E[X_1 X_2] - \mu_1 \mu_2$$

which implies

$$\sigma_{12} = E[X_1 X_2] - E[X_1]E[X_2] \tag{2.25}$$

Eq. (2.25) can be seen as a generalization of the univariate variance [Eq. (2.12)] to the bivariate case.

If X_1 and X_2 are independent random variables, then we conclude that their covariance is zero. This is because if X_1 and X_2 are independent, then we have

$$E[X_1 X_2] = E[X_1] \cdot E[X_2]$$

which in turn implies that

$$\sigma_{12} = 0$$

However, the converse is not true. That is, if $\sigma_{12} = 0$, one cannot claim that X_1 and X_2 are independent. All we can say is that there is no linear dependence between them, but we cannot rule out that there might be a higher order relationship or dependence between the two attributes.

The *sample covariance* between X_1 and X_2 is given as

$$\hat{\sigma}_{12} = \frac{1}{n} \sum_{i=1}^{n} (x_{i1} - \hat{\mu}_1)(x_{i2} - \hat{\mu}_2) \tag{2.26}$$

It can be derived by substituting the empirical joint probability mass function $\hat{f}(x_1, x_2)$ from Eq. (2.21) into Eq. (2.24), as follows:

$$
\begin{aligned}
\hat{\sigma}_{12} &= E[(X_1 - \hat{\mu}_1)(X_2 - \hat{\mu}_2)] \\
&= \sum_{\mathbf{x}=(x_1, x_2)^T} (x_1 - \hat{\mu}_1)(x_2 - \hat{\mu}_2) \hat{f}(x_1, x_2) \\
&= \frac{1}{n} \sum_{\mathbf{x}=(x_1, x_2)^T} \sum_{i=1}^{n} (x_1 - \hat{\mu}_1) \cdot (x_2 - \hat{\mu}_2) \cdot I(x_{i1} = x_1, x_{i2} = x_2) \\
&= \frac{1}{n} \sum_{i=1}^{n} (x_{i1} - \hat{\mu}_1)(x_{i2} - \hat{\mu}_2)
\end{aligned}
$$

Notice that sample covariance is a generalization of the sample variance [Eq. (2.13)] because

$$\hat{\sigma}_{11} = \frac{1}{n} \sum_{i=1}^{n} (x_i - \mu_1)(x_i - \mu_1) = \frac{1}{n} \sum_{i=1}^{n} (x_i - \mu_1)^2 = \hat{\sigma}_1^2$$

and similarly, $\hat{\sigma}_{22} = \hat{\sigma}_2^2$.

Correlation

The *correlation* between variables X_1 and X_2 is the *standardized covariance*, obtained by normalizing the covariance with the standard deviation of each variable, given as

$$\rho_{12} = \frac{\sigma_{12}}{\sigma_1 \sigma_2} = \frac{\sigma_{12}}{\sqrt{\sigma_1^2 \sigma_2^2}} \tag{2.27}$$

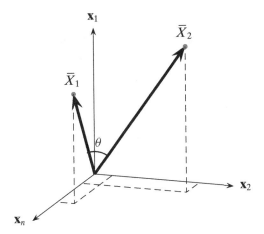

Figure 2.4. Geometric interpretation of covariance and correlation. The two centered attribute vectors are shown in the (conceptual) n-dimensional space $\mathbb{R}^n$ spanned by the n points.

The *sample correlation* for attributes X_1 and X_2 is given as

$$\hat{\rho}_{12} = \frac{\hat{\sigma}_{12}}{\hat{\sigma}_1 \hat{\sigma}_2} = \frac{\sum_{i=1}^{n}(x_{i1} - \hat{\mu}_1)(x_{i2} - \hat{\mu}_2)}{\sqrt{\sum_{i=1}^{n}(x_{i1} - \hat{\mu}_1)^2 \sum_{i=1}^{n}(x_{i2} - \hat{\mu}_2)^2}} \tag{2.28}$$

Geometric Interpretation of Sample Covariance and Correlation

Let $\bar{X}_1$ and $\bar{X}_2$ denote the centered attribute vectors in $\mathbb{R}^n$, given as follows:

$$\bar{X}_1 = X_1 - \hat{\mu}_1 \cdot \mathbf{1} = \begin{pmatrix} x_{11} - \hat{\mu}_1 \\ x_{21} - \hat{\mu}_1 \\ \vdots \\ x_{n1} - \hat{\mu}_1 \end{pmatrix} \qquad \bar{X}_2 = X_2 - \hat{\mu}_2 \cdot \mathbf{1} = \begin{pmatrix} x_{12} - \hat{\mu}_2 \\ x_{22} - \hat{\mu}_2 \\ \vdots \\ x_{n2} - \hat{\mu}_2 \end{pmatrix}$$

The sample covariance [Eq. (2.26)] can then be written as

$$\hat{\sigma}_{12} = \frac{\bar{X}_1^T \bar{X}_2}{n} \tag{2.29}$$

In other words, the covariance between the two attributes is simply the dot product between the two centered attribute vectors, normalized by the sample size. The above can be seen as a generalization of the univariate sample variance given in Eq. (2.20).

The sample correlation [Eq. (2.28)] can be written as

$$\hat{\rho}_{12} = \frac{\bar{X}_1^T \bar{X}_2}{\sqrt{\bar{X}_1^T \bar{X}_1} \sqrt{\bar{X}_2^T \bar{X}_2}} = \frac{\bar{X}_1^T \bar{X}_2}{\|\bar{X}_1\| \|\bar{X}_2\|} = \left(\frac{\bar{X}_1}{\|\bar{X}_1\|}\right)^T \left(\frac{\bar{X}_2}{\|\bar{X}_2\|}\right) = \cos\theta \tag{2.30}$$

Thus, the correlation coefficient is simply the cosine of the angle [Eq. (1.6)] between the two centered attribute vectors, as illustrated in Figure 2.4.

Covariance Matrix

The variance–covariance information for the two attributes X_1 and X_2 can be summarized in the square 2×2 *covariance matrix*, given as

$$\mathbf{\Sigma} = E[(\mathbf{X} - \boldsymbol{\mu})(\mathbf{X} - \boldsymbol{\mu})^T]$$

$$= E\left[\begin{pmatrix} X_1 - \mu_1 \\ X_2 - \mu_2 \end{pmatrix} (X_1 - \mu_1 \quad X_2 - \mu_2) \right]$$

$$= \begin{pmatrix} E[(X_1 - \mu_1)(X_1 - \mu_1)] & E[(X_1 - \mu_1)(X_2 - \mu_2)] \\ E[(X_2 - \mu_2)(X_1 - \mu_1)] & E[(X_2 - \mu_2)(X_2 - \mu_2)] \end{pmatrix}$$

$$= \begin{pmatrix} \sigma_1^2 & \sigma_{12} \\ \sigma_{21} & \sigma_2^2 \end{pmatrix} \tag{2.31}$$

Because $\sigma_{12} = \sigma_{21}$, $\mathbf{\Sigma}$ is a *symmetric* matrix. The covariance matrix records the attribute specific variances on the main diagonal, and the covariance information on the off-diagonal elements.

The *total variance* of the two attributes is given as the sum of the diagonal elements of $\mathbf{\Sigma}$, which is also called the *trace* of $\mathbf{\Sigma}$, given as

$$tr(\mathbf{\Sigma}) = \sigma_1^2 + \sigma_2^2$$

We immediately have $tr(\mathbf{\Sigma}) \geq 0$.

The *generalized variance* of the two attributes also considers the covariance, in addition to the attribute variances, and is given as the *determinant* of the covariance matrix $\mathbf{\Sigma}$, denoted as $|\mathbf{\Sigma}|$ or $\det(\mathbf{\Sigma})$. The generalized covariance is non-negative, because

$$|\mathbf{\Sigma}| = \det(\mathbf{\Sigma}) = \sigma_1^2 \sigma_2^2 - \sigma_{12}^2 = \sigma_1^2 \sigma_2^2 - \rho_{12}^2 \sigma_1^2 \sigma_2^2 = (1 - \rho_{12}^2) \sigma_1^2 \sigma_2^2$$

where we used Eq. (2.27), that is, $\sigma_{12} = \rho_{12} \sigma_1 \sigma_2$. Note that $|\rho_{12}| \leq 1$ implies that $\rho_{12}^2 \leq 1$, which in turn implies that $\det(\mathbf{\Sigma}) \geq 0$, that is, the determinant is non-negative.

The *sample covariance matrix* is given as

$$\widehat{\mathbf{\Sigma}} = \begin{pmatrix} \hat{\sigma}_1^2 & \hat{\sigma}_{12} \\ \hat{\sigma}_{12} & \hat{\sigma}_2^2 \end{pmatrix} \tag{2.32}$$

The sample covariance matrix $\widehat{\mathbf{\Sigma}}$ shares the same properties as $\mathbf{\Sigma}$, that is, it is symmetric and $|\widehat{\mathbf{\Sigma}}| \geq 0$, and it can be used to easily obtain the sample generalized variance, given as $|\widehat{\mathbf{\Sigma}}|$, and the sample total variance, given as

$$\text{var}(\mathbf{D}) = tr(\widehat{\mathbf{\Sigma}}) = \hat{\sigma}_1^2 + \hat{\sigma}_2^2 \tag{2.33}$$

Example 2.3 (Sample Mean and Covariance). Consider the `sepal length` and `sepal width` attributes for the Iris dataset, plotted in Figure 2.5. There are $n = 150$ points in the $d = 2$ dimensional attribute space. The sample mean vector is given as

$$\hat{\boldsymbol{\mu}} = \begin{pmatrix} 5.843 \\ 3.054 \end{pmatrix}$$

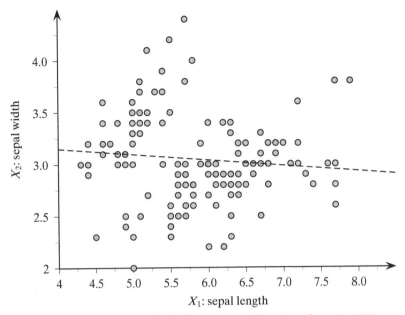

Figure 2.5. Correlation between sepal length and sepal width.

The sample covariance matrix is given as

$$\widehat{\mathbf{\Sigma}} = \begin{pmatrix} 0.681 & -0.039 \\ -0.039 & 0.187 \end{pmatrix}$$

The variance for sepal length is $\hat{\sigma}_1^2 = 0.681$, and that for sepal width is $\hat{\sigma}_2^2 = 0.187$. The covariance between the two attributes is $\hat{\sigma}_{12} = -0.039$, and the correlation between them is

$$\hat{\rho}_{12} = \frac{-0.039}{\sqrt{0.681 \cdot 0.187}} = -0.109$$

Thus, there is a very weak negative correlation between these two attributes, as evidenced by the best linear fit line in Figure 2.5. Alternatively, we can consider the attributes sepal length and sepal width as two points in $\mathbb{R}^n$. The correlation is then the cosine of the angle between them; we have

$$\hat{\rho}_{12} = \cos\theta = -0.109, \text{ which implies that } \theta = \cos^{-1}(-0.109) = 96.26°$$

The angle is close to 90°, that is, the two attribute vectors are almost orthogonal, indicating weak correlation. Further, the angle being greater than 90° indicates negative correlation.

The sample total variance is given as

$$tr(\widehat{\mathbf{\Sigma}}) = 0.681 + 0.187 = 0.868$$

and the sample generalized variance is given as

$$|\widehat{\mathbf{\Sigma}}| = \det(\widehat{\mathbf{\Sigma}}) = 0.681 \cdot 0.187 - (-0.039)^2 = 0.126$$

2.3 MULTIVARIATE ANALYSIS

In multivariate analysis, we consider all the d numeric attributes $X_1, X_2, \ldots, X_d$. The full data is an $n \times d$ matrix, given as

$$
\mathbf{D} = \begin{pmatrix} X_1 & X_2 & \cdots & X_d \\ \hline x_{11} & x_{12} & \cdots & x_{1d} \\ x_{21} & x_{22} & \cdots & x_{2d} \\ \vdots & \vdots & \ddots & \vdots \\ x_{n1} & x_{n2} & \cdots & x_{nd} \end{pmatrix} = \begin{pmatrix} | & | & & | \\ X_1 & X_2 & \cdots & X_d \\ | & | & & | \end{pmatrix} = \begin{pmatrix} - & \mathbf{x}_1^T & - \\ - & \mathbf{x}_2^T & - \\ & \vdots & \\ - & \mathbf{x}_n^T & - \end{pmatrix}
$$

In the row view, the data can be considered as a set of n points or vectors in the d-dimensional attribute space

$$
\mathbf{x}_i = (x_{i1}, x_{i2}, \ldots, x_{id})^T \in \mathbb{R}^d
$$

In the column view, the data can be considered as a set of d points or vectors in the n-dimensional space spanned by the data points

$$
X_j = (x_{1j}, x_{2j}, \ldots, x_{nj})^T \in \mathbb{R}^n
$$

In the probabilistic view, the d attributes are modeled as a vector random variable, $\mathbf{X} = (X_1, X_2, \ldots, X_d)^T$, and the points $\mathbf{x}_i$ are considered to be a random sample drawn from $\mathbf{X}$, that is, they are independent and identically distributed as $\mathbf{X}$.

Mean

Generalizing Eq. (2.22), the *multivariate mean vector* is obtained by taking the mean of each attribute, given as

$$
\boldsymbol{\mu} = E[\mathbf{X}] = \begin{pmatrix} E[X_1] \\ E[X_2] \\ \vdots \\ E[X_d] \end{pmatrix} = \begin{pmatrix} \mu_1 \\ \mu_2 \\ \vdots \\ \mu_d \end{pmatrix}
$$

Generalizing Eq. (2.23), the *sample mean* is given as

$$
\hat{\boldsymbol{\mu}} = \frac{1}{n} \sum_{i=1}^{n} \mathbf{x}_i \tag{2.34}
$$

We can also obtain the sample mean by projecting each attribute vector X_i on the ones vector $\mathbf{1}$, which can be written compactly as

$$
\hat{\boldsymbol{\mu}} = \frac{1}{n} \mathbf{D}^T \mathbf{1}
$$

Covariance Matrix

Generalizing Eq. (2.31) to d dimensions, the multivariate covariance information is captured by the $d \times d$ (square) symmetric *covariance matrix* that gives the covariance for each pair of attributes:

$$\boldsymbol{\Sigma} = E[(\mathbf{X}-\boldsymbol{\mu})(\mathbf{X}-\boldsymbol{\mu})^T] = \begin{pmatrix} \sigma_1^2 & \sigma_{12} & \cdots & \sigma_{1d} \\ \sigma_{21} & \sigma_2^2 & \cdots & \sigma_{2d} \\ \cdots & \cdots & \cdots & \cdots \\ \sigma_{d1} & \sigma_{d2} & \cdots & \sigma_d^2 \end{pmatrix}$$

The diagonal element σ_i^2 specifies the attribute variance for X_i, whereas the off-diagonal elements $\sigma_{ij} = \sigma_{ji}$ represent the covariance between attribute pairs X_i and X_j.

Covariance Matrix Is Positive Semidefinite
It is worth noting that $\boldsymbol{\Sigma}$ is a *positive semidefinite* matrix, that is,

$$\mathbf{a}^T \boldsymbol{\Sigma} \mathbf{a} \geq 0 \text{ for any } d\text{-dimensional vector } \mathbf{a}$$

To see this, observe that

$$\begin{aligned} \mathbf{a}^T \boldsymbol{\Sigma} \mathbf{a} &= \mathbf{a}^T E[(\mathbf{X}-\boldsymbol{\mu})(\mathbf{X}-\boldsymbol{\mu})^T]\mathbf{a} \\ &= E[\mathbf{a}^T(\mathbf{X}-\boldsymbol{\mu})(\mathbf{X}-\boldsymbol{\mu})^T\mathbf{a}] \\ &= E[Y^2] \\ &\geq 0 \end{aligned}$$

where Y is the random variable $Y = \mathbf{a}^T(\mathbf{X}-\boldsymbol{\mu}) = \sum_{i=1}^d a_i(X_i - \mu_i)$, and we use the fact that the expectation of a squared random variable is non-negative.

Because $\boldsymbol{\Sigma}$ is also symmetric, this implies that all the eigenvalues of $\boldsymbol{\Sigma}$ are real and non-negative. In other words the d eigenvalues of $\boldsymbol{\Sigma}$ can be arranged from the largest to the smallest as follows: $\lambda_1 \geq \lambda_2 \geq \cdots \geq \lambda_d \geq 0$.

Total and Generalized Variance
The total variance is given as the trace of the covariance matrix:

$$tr(\boldsymbol{\Sigma}) = \sigma_1^2 + \sigma_2^2 + \cdots + \sigma_d^2 \tag{2.35}$$

Being a sum of squares, the total variance must be non-negative.

The generalized variance is defined as the determinant of the covariance matrix, $\det(\boldsymbol{\Sigma})$, also denoted as $|\boldsymbol{\Sigma}|$; it gives a single value for the overall multivariate scatter:

$$\det(\boldsymbol{\Sigma}) = |\boldsymbol{\Sigma}| = \prod_{i=1}^d \lambda_i \tag{2.36}$$

Since all the eigenvalues of $\boldsymbol{\Sigma}$ are non-negative ($\lambda_i \geq 0$), it follows that $\det(\boldsymbol{\Sigma}) \geq 0$.

Sample Covariance Matrix

The *sample covariance matrix* is given as

$$\widehat{\boldsymbol{\Sigma}} = E[(\mathbf{X} - \hat{\boldsymbol{\mu}})(\mathbf{X} - \hat{\boldsymbol{\mu}})^T] = \begin{pmatrix} \hat{\sigma}_1^2 & \hat{\sigma}_{12} & \cdots & \hat{\sigma}_{1d} \\ \hat{\sigma}_{21} & \hat{\sigma}_2^2 & \cdots & \hat{\sigma}_{2d} \\ \cdots & \cdots & \cdots & \cdots \\ \hat{\sigma}_{d1} & \hat{\sigma}_{d2} & \cdots & \hat{\sigma}_d^2 \end{pmatrix} \tag{2.37}$$

Instead of computing the sample covariance matrix element-by-element, we can obtain it via matrix operations. Let $\overline{\mathbf{D}}$ represent the centered data matrix, given as the matrix of centered attribute vectors $\overline{X}_i = X_i - \hat{\mu}_i \cdot \mathbf{1}$, where $\mathbf{1} \in \mathbb{R}^n$:

$$\overline{\mathbf{D}} = \mathbf{D} - \mathbf{1} \cdot \hat{\boldsymbol{\mu}}^T = \begin{pmatrix} | & | & & | \\ \overline{X}_1 & \overline{X}_2 & \cdots & \overline{X}_d \\ | & | & & | \end{pmatrix}$$

Alternatively, the centered data matrix can also be written in terms of the centered points $\bar{\mathbf{x}}_i = \mathbf{x}_i - \hat{\boldsymbol{\mu}}$:

$$\overline{\mathbf{D}} = \mathbf{D} - \mathbf{1} \cdot \hat{\boldsymbol{\mu}}^T = \begin{pmatrix} \mathbf{x}_1^T - \hat{\boldsymbol{\mu}}^T \\ \mathbf{x}_2^T - \hat{\boldsymbol{\mu}}^T \\ \vdots \\ \mathbf{x}_n^T - \hat{\boldsymbol{\mu}}^T \end{pmatrix} = \begin{pmatrix} - & \bar{\mathbf{x}}_1^T & - \\ - & \bar{\mathbf{x}}_2^T & - \\ & \vdots & \\ - & \bar{\mathbf{x}}_n^T & - \end{pmatrix}$$

In matrix notation, the sample covariance matrix can be written as

$$\widehat{\boldsymbol{\Sigma}} = \frac{1}{n}\left(\overline{\mathbf{D}}^T\,\overline{\mathbf{D}}\right) = \frac{1}{n} \begin{pmatrix} \overline{X}_1^T\overline{X}_1 & \overline{X}_1^T\overline{X}_2 & \cdots & \overline{X}_1^T\overline{X}_d \\ \overline{X}_2^T\overline{X}_1 & \overline{X}_2^T\overline{X}_2 & \cdots & \overline{X}_2^T\overline{X}_d \\ \vdots & \vdots & \ddots & \vdots \\ \overline{X}_d^T\overline{X}_1 & \overline{X}_d^T\overline{X}_2 & \cdots & \overline{X}_d^T\overline{X}_d \end{pmatrix} \tag{2.38}$$

The sample covariance matrix is thus given as the pairwise *inner or dot products* of the centered attribute vectors, normalized by the sample size.

In terms of the centered points $\bar{\mathbf{x}}_i$, the sample covariance matrix can also be written as a sum of rank-one matrices obtained as the *outer product* of each centered point:

$$\widehat{\boldsymbol{\Sigma}} = \frac{1}{n}\sum_{i=1}^n \bar{\mathbf{x}}_i \cdot \bar{\mathbf{x}}_i^T \tag{2.39}$$

Also, the sample total variance is given as

$$\mathrm{var}(\mathbf{D}) = tr(\widehat{\boldsymbol{\Sigma}}) = \hat{\sigma}_1^2 + \hat{\sigma}_2^2 + \cdots + \hat{\sigma}_d^2$$

and the sample generalized variance as $|\widehat{\boldsymbol{\Sigma}}| = \det(\widehat{\boldsymbol{\Sigma}})$.

Sample Scatter Matrix

The *sample scatter matrix* is the $d \times d$ positive semi-definite matrix defined as

$$\mathbf{S} = \overline{\mathbf{D}}^T \overline{\mathbf{D}} = \sum_{i=1}^{n} \overline{\mathbf{x}}_i \cdot \overline{\mathbf{x}}_i^T$$

It is simply the un-normalized sample covariance matrix, since $\mathbf{S} = n \cdot \widehat{\boldsymbol{\Sigma}}$.

Example 2.4 (Sample Mean and Covariance Matrix). Let us consider all four numeric attributes for the Iris dataset, namely sepal length, sepal width, petal length, and petal width. The multivariate sample mean vector is given as

$$\hat{\mu} = \begin{pmatrix} 5.843 & 3.054 & 3.759 & 1.199 \end{pmatrix}^T$$

and the sample covariance matrix is given as

$$\widehat{\boldsymbol{\Sigma}} = \begin{pmatrix} 0.681 & -0.039 & 1.265 & 0.513 \\ -0.039 & 0.187 & -0.320 & -0.117 \\ 1.265 & -0.320 & 3.092 & 1.288 \\ 0.513 & -0.117 & 1.288 & 0.579 \end{pmatrix}$$

The sample total variance is

$$var(\mathbf{D}) = tr(\widehat{\boldsymbol{\Sigma}}) = 0.681 + 0.187 + 3.092 + 0.579 = 4.539$$

and the generalized variance is

$$det(\widehat{\boldsymbol{\Sigma}}) = 1.853 \times 10^{-3}$$

Example 2.5 (Inner and Outer Product). To illustrate the inner and outer product–based computation of the sample covariance matrix, consider the 2-dimensional dataset

$$\mathbf{D} = \begin{pmatrix} A_1 & A_2 \\ 1 & 0.8 \\ 5 & 2.4 \\ 9 & 5.5 \end{pmatrix}$$

The mean vector is as follows:

$$\hat{\mu} = \begin{pmatrix} \hat{\mu}_1 \\ \hat{\mu}_2 \end{pmatrix} = \begin{pmatrix} 15/3 \\ 8.7/3 \end{pmatrix} = \begin{pmatrix} 5 \\ 2.9 \end{pmatrix}$$

and the centered data matrix is then given as

$$\overline{\mathbf{D}} = \mathbf{D} - \mathbf{1} \cdot \mu^T = \begin{pmatrix} 1 & 0.8 \\ 5 & 2.4 \\ 9 & 5.5 \end{pmatrix} - \begin{pmatrix} 1 \\ 1 \\ 1 \end{pmatrix} \begin{pmatrix} 5 & 2.9 \end{pmatrix} = \begin{pmatrix} -4 & -2.1 \\ 0 & -0.5 \\ 4 & 2.6 \end{pmatrix}$$

The inner-product approach [Eq. (2.38)] to compute the sample covariance matrix gives

$$\widehat{\Sigma} = \frac{1}{n}\overline{\mathbf{D}}^T\overline{\mathbf{D}} = \frac{1}{3}\begin{pmatrix} -4 & 0 & 4 \\ -2.1 & -0.5 & 2.6 \end{pmatrix} \cdot \begin{pmatrix} -4 & -2.1 \\ 0 & -0.5 \\ 4 & 2.6 \end{pmatrix}$$

$$= \frac{1}{3}\begin{pmatrix} 32 & 18.8 \\ 18.8 & 11.42 \end{pmatrix} = \begin{pmatrix} 10.67 & 6.27 \\ 6.27 & 3.81 \end{pmatrix}$$

Alternatively, the outer-product approach [Eq. (2.39)] gives

$$\widehat{\Sigma} = \frac{1}{n}\sum_{i=1}^{n}\overline{\mathbf{x}}_i \cdot \overline{\mathbf{x}}_i^T$$

$$= \frac{1}{3}\left[\begin{pmatrix} -4 \\ -2.1 \end{pmatrix}\cdot(-4 \quad -2.1) + \begin{pmatrix} 0 \\ -0.5 \end{pmatrix}\cdot(0 \quad -0.5) + \begin{pmatrix} 4 \\ 2.6 \end{pmatrix}\cdot(4 \quad 2.6)\right]$$

$$= \frac{1}{3}\left[\begin{pmatrix} 16.0 & 8.4 \\ 8.4 & 4.41 \end{pmatrix} + \begin{pmatrix} 0.0 & 0.0 \\ 0.0 & 0.25 \end{pmatrix} + \begin{pmatrix} 16.0 & 10.4 \\ 10.4 & 6.76 \end{pmatrix}\right]$$

$$= \frac{1}{3}\begin{pmatrix} 32.0 & 18.8 \\ 18.8 & 11.42 \end{pmatrix} = \begin{pmatrix} 10.67 & 6.27 \\ 6.27 & 3.81 \end{pmatrix}$$

where the centered points $\overline{\mathbf{x}}_i$ are the rows of $\overline{\mathbf{D}}$. We can see that both the inner and outer product approaches yield the same sample covariance matrix.

2.4 DATA NORMALIZATION

When analyzing two or more attributes it is often necessary to normalize the values of the attributes, especially in those cases where the values are vastly different in scale.

Range Normalization
Let X be an attribute and let $x_1, x_2, \ldots, x_n$ be a random sample drawn from X. In *range normalization* each value is scaled by the sample range $\hat{r}$ of X:

$$x_i' = \frac{x_i - \min_i\{x_i\}}{\hat{r}} = \frac{x_i - \min_i\{x_i\}}{\max_i\{x_i\} - \min_i\{x_i\}}$$

After transformation the new attribute takes on values in the range $[0, 1]$.

Standard Score Normalization
In *standard score normalization*, also called z-normalization, each value is replaced by its z-score:

$$x_i' = \frac{x_i - \hat{\mu}}{\hat{\sigma}}$$

where $\hat{\mu}$ is the sample mean and $\hat{\sigma}^2$ is the sample variance of X. After transformation, the new attribute has mean $\hat{\mu}' = 0$, and standard deviation $\hat{\sigma}' = 1$.

Example 2.6. Consider the example dataset shown in Table 2.1. The attributes Age and Income have very different scales, with the latter having much larger values. Consider the distance between $\mathbf{x}_1$ and $\mathbf{x}_2$:

$$\|\mathbf{x}_1 - \mathbf{x}_2\| = \|(2, 200)^T\| = \sqrt{2^2 + 200^2} = \sqrt{40004} = 200.01$$

As we can observe, the contribution of Age is overshadowed by the value of Income.

The sample range for Age is $\hat{r} = 40 - 12 = 28$, with the minimum value 12. After range normalization, the new attribute is given as

$$\text{Age}' = (0, 0.071, 0.214, 0.393, 0.536, 0.571, 0.786, 0.893, 0.964, 1)^T$$

For example, for the point $\mathbf{x}_2 = (x_{21}, x_{22}) = (14, 500)$, the value $x_{21} = 14$ is transformed into

$$x_{21}' = \frac{14 - 12}{28} = \frac{2}{28} = 0.071$$

Likewise, the sample range for Income is $6000 - 300 = 5700$, with a minimum value of 300; Income is therefore transformed into

$$\text{Income}' = (0, 0.035, 0.123, 0.298, 0.561, 0.649, 0.702, 1, 0.386, 0.421)^T$$

so that $x_{22} = 0.035$. The distance between $\mathbf{x}_1$ and $\mathbf{x}_2$ after range normalization is given as

$$\|\mathbf{x}_1' - \mathbf{x}_2'\| = \|(0, 0)^T - (0.071, 0.035)^T\| = \|(-0.071, -0.035)^T\| = 0.079$$

We can observe that Income no longer skews the distance.

For z-normalization, we first compute the mean and standard deviation of both attributes:

	Age	Income
$\hat{\mu}$	27.2	2680
$\hat{\sigma}$	9.77	1726.15

Age is transformed into

$$\text{Age}' = (-1.56, -1.35, -0.94, -0.43, -0.02, 0.08, 0.70, 1.0, 1.21, 1.31)^T$$

For instance, the value $x_{21} = 14$, for the point $\mathbf{x}_2 = (x_{21}, x_{22}) = (14, 500)$, is transformed as

$$x_{21}' = \frac{14 - 27.2}{9.77} = -1.35$$

Likewise, Income is transformed into

$$\text{Income}' = (-1.38, -1.26, -0.97, -0.39, 0.48, 0.77, 0.94, 1.92, -0.10, 0.01)^T$$

so that $x_{22} = -1.26$. The distance between $\mathbf{x}_1$ and $\mathbf{x}_2$ after z-normalization is given as

$$\|\mathbf{x}_1' - \mathbf{x}_2'\| = \|(-1.56, -1.38)^T - (1.35, -1.26)^T\| = \|(-0.18, -0.12)^T\| = 0.216$$

Table 2.1. Dataset for normalization

$\mathbf{x}_i$	Age (X_1)	Income (X_2)
$\mathbf{x}_1$	12	300
$\mathbf{x}_2$	14	500
$\mathbf{x}_3$	18	1000
$\mathbf{x}_4$	23	2000
$\mathbf{x}_5$	27	3500
$\mathbf{x}_6$	28	4000
$\mathbf{x}_7$	34	4300
$\mathbf{x}_8$	37	6000
$\mathbf{x}_9$	39	2500
$\mathbf{x}_{10}$	40	2700

2.5 NORMAL DISTRIBUTION

The normal distribution is one of the most important probability density functions, especially because many physically observed variables follow an approximately normal distribution. Furthermore, the sampling distribution of the mean of any arbitrary probability distribution follows a normal distribution. The normal distribution also plays an important role as the parametric distribution of choice in clustering, density estimation, and classification.

2.5.1 Univariate Normal Distribution

A random variable X has a normal distribution, with the parameters mean μ and variance σ^2, if the probability density function of X is given as follows:

$$f(x|\mu,\sigma^2) = \frac{1}{\sqrt{2\pi\sigma^2}} \exp\left\{-\frac{(x-\mu)^2}{2\sigma^2}\right\} \tag{2.40}$$

The term $(x-\mu)^2$ measures the distance of a value x from the mean μ of the distribution, and thus the probability density decreases exponentially as a function of the distance from the mean. The maximum value of the density occurs at the mean value $x = \mu$, given as $f(\mu) = \frac{1}{\sqrt{2\pi\sigma^2}}$, which is inversely proportional to the standard deviation σ of the distribution.

Example 2.7. Figure 2.6 plots the standard normal distribution, which has the parameters $\mu = 0$ and $\sigma^2 = 1$. The normal distribution has a characteristic *bell* shape, and it is symmetric about the mean. The figure also shows the effect of different values of standard deviation on the shape of the distribution. A smaller value (e.g., $\sigma = 0.5$) results in a more "peaked" distribution that decays faster, whereas a larger value (e.g., $\sigma = 2$) results in a flatter distribution that decays slower. Because the normal distribution is symmetric, the mean μ is also the median, as well as the mode, of the distribution.

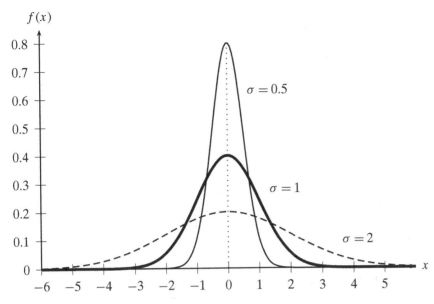

Figure 2.6. Normal distribution: $\mu = 0$, and different variances.

Probability Mass

Given an interval $[a, b]$ the probability mass of the normal distribution within that interval is given as

$$P(a \le x \le b) = \int_a^b f(x \mid \mu, \sigma^2) \, dx$$

In particular, we are often interested in the probability mass concentrated within k standard deviations from the mean, that is, for the interval $[\mu - k\sigma, \mu + k\sigma]$, which can be computed as

$$P\left(\mu - k\sigma \le x \le \mu + k\sigma\right) = \frac{1}{\sqrt{2\pi}\sigma} \int_{\mu - k\sigma}^{\mu + k\sigma} \exp\left\{-\frac{(x - \mu)^2}{2\sigma^2}\right\} dx$$

Via a change of variable $z = \frac{x - \mu}{\sigma}$, we get an equivalent formulation in terms of the standard normal distribution:

$$P(-k \le z \le k) = \frac{1}{\sqrt{2\pi}} \int_{-k}^{k} e^{-\frac{1}{2}z^2} dz = \frac{2}{\sqrt{2\pi}} \int_{0}^{k} e^{-\frac{1}{2}z^2} dz$$

The last step follows from the fact that $e^{-\frac{1}{2}z^2}$ is symmetric, and thus the integral over the range $[-k, k]$ is equivalent to 2 times the integral over the range $[0, k]$. Finally, via another change of variable $t = \frac{z}{\sqrt{2}}$, we get

$$P(-k \le z \le k) = 2 \cdot P\left(0 \le t \le k/\sqrt{2}\right) = \frac{2}{\sqrt{\pi}} \int_{0}^{k/\sqrt{2}} e^{-t^2} dt = \mathrm{erf}\left(k/\sqrt{2}\right) \qquad (2.41)$$

where erf is the *Gauss error function*, defined as

$$\text{erf}(x) = \frac{2}{\sqrt{\pi}} \int_0^x e^{-t^2} dt$$

Using Eq. (2.41) we can compute the probability mass within k standard deviations of the mean. In particular, for $k = 1$, we have

$$P(\mu - \sigma \leq x \leq \mu + \sigma) = \text{erf}(1/\sqrt{2}) = 0.6827$$

which means that 68.27% of all points lie within 1 standard deviation from the mean. For $k = 2$, we have $\text{erf}(2/\sqrt{2}) = 0.9545$, and for $k = 3$ we have $\text{erf}(3/\sqrt{2}) = 0.9973$. Thus, almost the entire probability mass (i.e., 99.73%) of a normal distribution is within $\pm 3\sigma$ from the mean μ.

2.5.2 Multivariate Normal Distribution

Given the d-dimensional vector random variable $\mathbf{X} = (X_1, X_2, \ldots, X_d)^T$, we say that $\mathbf{X}$ has a multivariate normal distribution, with the parameters mean $\boldsymbol{\mu}$ and covariance matrix $\boldsymbol{\Sigma}$, if its joint multivariate probability density function is given as follows:

$$f(\mathbf{x}|\boldsymbol{\mu}, \boldsymbol{\Sigma}) = \frac{1}{(\sqrt{2\pi})^d \sqrt{|\boldsymbol{\Sigma}|}} \exp\left\{-\frac{(\mathbf{x} - \boldsymbol{\mu})^T \boldsymbol{\Sigma}^{-1} (\mathbf{x} - \boldsymbol{\mu})}{2}\right\} \tag{2.42}$$

where $|\boldsymbol{\Sigma}|$ is the determinant of the covariance matrix. As in the univariate case, the term

$$(\mathbf{x} - \boldsymbol{\mu})^T \boldsymbol{\Sigma}^{-1} (\mathbf{x} - \boldsymbol{\mu}) \tag{2.43}$$

measures the distance, called the *Mahalanobis distance*, of the point $\mathbf{x}$ from the mean $\boldsymbol{\mu}$ of the distribution, taking into account all of the variance–covariance information between the attributes. The Mahalanobis distance is a generalization of Euclidean distance because if we set $\boldsymbol{\Sigma} = \mathbf{I}$, where $\mathbf{I}$ is the $d \times d$ identity matrix (with diagonal elements as 1's and off-diagonal elements as 0's), we get

$$(\mathbf{x} - \boldsymbol{\mu})^T \mathbf{I}^{-1} (\mathbf{x} - \boldsymbol{\mu}) = \|\mathbf{x} - \boldsymbol{\mu}\|^2$$

The Euclidean distance thus ignores the covariance information between the attributes, whereas the Mahalanobis distance explicitly takes it into consideration.

The *standard multivariate normal distribution* has parameters $\boldsymbol{\mu} = \mathbf{0}$ and $\boldsymbol{\Sigma} = \mathbf{I}$. Figure 2.7(a) plots the probability density of the standard bivariate $(d = 2)$ normal distribution, with parameters

$$\boldsymbol{\mu} = \mathbf{0} = \begin{pmatrix} 0 \\ 0 \end{pmatrix}$$

and

$$\boldsymbol{\Sigma} = \mathbf{I} = \begin{pmatrix} 1 & 0 \\ 0 & 1 \end{pmatrix}$$

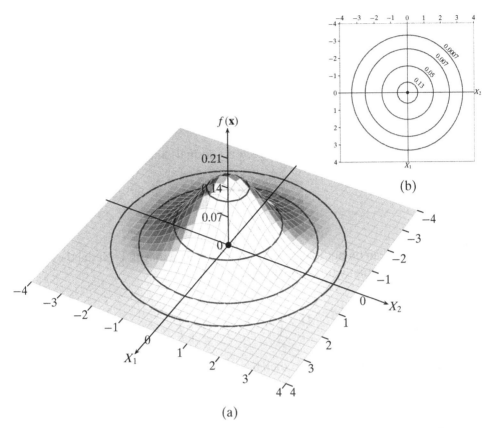

(b)

(a)

Figure 2.7. (a) Standard bivariate normal density and (b) its contour plot. Parameters: $\boldsymbol{\mu} = (0,0)^T$, $\boldsymbol{\Sigma} = \mathbf{I}$.

This corresponds to the case where the two attributes are independent, and both follow the standard normal distribution. The symmetric nature of the standard normal distribution can be clearly seen in the contour plot shown in Figure 2.7(b). Each level curve represents the set of points $\mathbf{x}$ with a fixed density value $f(\mathbf{x})$.

Geometry of the Multivariate Normal

Let us consider the geometry of the multivariate normal distribution for an arbitrary mean $\boldsymbol{\mu}$ and covariance matrix $\boldsymbol{\Sigma}$. Compared to the standard normal distribution, we can expect the density contours to be shifted, scaled, and rotated. The shift or translation comes from the fact that the mean $\boldsymbol{\mu}$ is not necessarily the origin $\mathbf{0}$. The scaling or skewing is a result of the attribute variances, and the rotation is a result of the covariances.

The shape or geometry of the normal distribution becomes clear by considering the eigen-decomposition of the covariance matrix. Recall that $\boldsymbol{\Sigma}$ is a $d \times d$ symmetric positive semidefinite matrix. The eigenvector equation for $\boldsymbol{\Sigma}$ is given as

$$\boldsymbol{\Sigma}\mathbf{u}_i = \lambda_i \mathbf{u}_i$$

Here λ_i is an eigenvalue of $\boldsymbol{\Sigma}$ and the vector $\mathbf{u}_i \in \mathbb{R}^d$ is the eigenvector corresponding to λ_i. Because $\boldsymbol{\Sigma}$ is symmetric and positive semidefinite it has d real and non-negative eigenvalues, which can be arranged in order from the largest to the smallest as follows: $\lambda_1 \geq \lambda_2 \geq \ldots \lambda_d \geq 0$. The diagonal matrix $\mathbf{\Lambda}$ is used to record these eigenvalues:

$$\mathbf{\Lambda} = \begin{pmatrix} \lambda_1 & 0 & \cdots & 0 \\ 0 & \lambda_2 & \cdots & 0 \\ \vdots & \vdots & \ddots & \vdots \\ 0 & 0 & \cdots & \lambda_d \end{pmatrix}$$

Further, the eigenvectors are unit vectors (normal) and are mutually orthogonal, that is, they are orthonormal:

$$\mathbf{u}_i^T \mathbf{u}_i = 1 \quad \text{for all } i$$

$$\mathbf{u}_i^T \mathbf{u}_j = 0 \quad \text{for all } i \neq j$$

The eigenvectors can be put together into an orthogonal matrix $\mathbf{U}$, defined as a matrix with normal and mutually orthogonal columns:

$$\mathbf{U} = \begin{pmatrix} | & | & & | \\ \mathbf{u}_1 & \mathbf{u}_2 & \cdots & \mathbf{u}_d \\ | & | & & | \end{pmatrix}$$

The eigen-decomposition of $\mathbf{\Sigma}$ can then be expressed compactly as follows:

$$\mathbf{\Sigma} = \mathbf{U} \mathbf{\Lambda} \mathbf{U}^T$$

This equation can be interpreted geometrically as a change in basis vectors. From the original d dimensions corresponding to the d attributes X_j, we derive d new dimensions $\mathbf{u}_i$. $\mathbf{\Sigma}$ is the covariance matrix in the original space, whereas $\mathbf{\Lambda}$ is the covariance matrix in the new coordinate space. Because $\mathbf{\Lambda}$ is a diagonal matrix, we can immediately conclude that after the transformation, each new dimension $\mathbf{u}_i$ has variance λ_i, and further that all covariances are zero. In other words, in the new space, the normal distribution is axis aligned (has no rotation component), but is skewed in each axis proportional to the eigenvalue λ_i, which represents the variance along that dimension (further details are given in Section 7.2.4).

Total and Generalized Variance

The determinant of the covariance matrix is is given as $\det(\mathbf{\Sigma}) = \prod_{i=1}^{d} \lambda_i$. Thus, the generalized variance of $\mathbf{\Sigma}$ is the product of its eigenvalues.

Given the fact that the trace of a square matrix is invariant to similarity transformation, such as a change of basis, we conclude that the total variance var($\mathbf{D}$) for a dataset $\mathbf{D}$ is invariant, that is,

$$\text{var}(\mathbf{D}) = tr(\mathbf{\Sigma}) = \sum_{i=1}^{d} \sigma_i^2 = \sum_{i=1}^{d} \lambda_i = tr(\mathbf{\Lambda})$$

In other words $\sigma_1^2 + \cdots + \sigma_d^2 = \lambda_1 + \cdots + \lambda_d$.

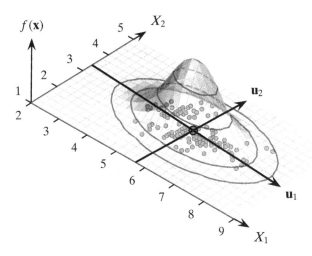

Figure 2.8. Iris: sepal length and sepal width, bivariate normal density and contours.

Example 2.8 (Bivariate Normal Density). Treating attributes sepal length (X_1) and sepal width (X_2) in the Iris dataset (see Table 1.1) as continuous random variables, we can define a continuous bivariate random variable $\mathbf{X} = \begin{pmatrix} X_1 \\ X_2 \end{pmatrix}$. Assuming that $\mathbf{X}$ follows a bivariate normal distribution, we can estimate its parameters from the sample. The sample mean is given as

$$\hat{\mu} = (5.843, 3.054)^T$$

and the sample covariance matrix is given as

$$\widehat{\Sigma} = \begin{pmatrix} 0.681 & -0.039 \\ -0.039 & 0.187 \end{pmatrix}$$

The plot of the bivariate normal density for the two attributes is shown in Figure 2.8. The figure also shows the contour lines and the data points.

Consider the point $\mathbf{x}_2 = (6.9, 3.1)^T$. We have

$$\mathbf{x}_2 - \hat{\mu} = \begin{pmatrix} 6.9 \\ 3.1 \end{pmatrix} - \begin{pmatrix} 5.843 \\ 3.054 \end{pmatrix} = \begin{pmatrix} 1.057 \\ 0.046 \end{pmatrix}$$

The Mahalanobis distance between $\mathbf{x}_2$ and $\hat{\mu}$ is

$$(\mathbf{x}_i - \hat{\mu})^T \widehat{\Sigma}^{-1} (\mathbf{x}_i - \hat{\mu}) = \begin{pmatrix} 1.057 & 0.046 \end{pmatrix} \begin{pmatrix} 0.681 & -0.039 \\ -0.039 & 0.187 \end{pmatrix}^{-1} \begin{pmatrix} 1.057 \\ 0.046 \end{pmatrix}$$

$$= \begin{pmatrix} 1.057 & 0.046 \end{pmatrix} \begin{pmatrix} 1.486 & 0.31 \\ 0.31 & 5.42 \end{pmatrix} \begin{pmatrix} 1.057 \\ 0.046 \end{pmatrix}$$

$$= 1.701$$

whereas the squared Euclidean distance between them is

$$\|(\mathbf{x}_2 - \hat{\boldsymbol{\mu}})\|^2 = \begin{pmatrix} 1.057 & 0.046 \end{pmatrix} \begin{pmatrix} 1.057 \\ 0.046 \end{pmatrix} = 1.119$$

The eigenvalues and the corresponding eigenvectors of $\widehat{\boldsymbol{\Sigma}}$ are as follows:

$$\lambda_1 = 0.684 \qquad\qquad \mathbf{u}_1 = (-0.997, 0.078)^T$$
$$\lambda_2 = 0.184 \qquad\qquad \mathbf{u}_2 = (-0.078, -0.997)^T$$

These two eigenvectors define the new axes in which the covariance matrix is given as

$$\boldsymbol{\Lambda} = \begin{pmatrix} 0.684 & 0 \\ 0 & 0.184 \end{pmatrix}$$

The angle between the original axes $\mathbf{e}_1 = (1, 0)^T$ and $\mathbf{u}_1$ specifies the rotation angle for the multivariate normal:

$$\cos\theta = \mathbf{e}_1^T \mathbf{u}_1 = -0.997$$
$$\theta = \cos^{-1}(-0.997) = 175.5°$$

Figure 2.8 illustrates the new coordinate axes and the new variances. We can see that in the original axes, the contours are only slightly rotated by angle 175.5° (or −4.5°).

2.6 FURTHER READING

There are several good textbooks that cover the topics discussed in this chapter in more depth; see Evans and Rosenthal (2011) and Wasserman (2004) and Rencher and Christensen (2012).

Evans, M. and Rosenthal, J. (2011). *Probability and Statistics: The Science of Uncertainty.* 2nd ed. New York: W. H. Freeman.

Rencher, A. C. and Christensen, W. F. (2012). *Methods of Multivariate Analysis.* 3rd ed. Hoboken, NJ: John Wiley & Sons.

Wasserman, L. (2004). *All of Statistics: A Concise Course in Statistical Inference.* New York: Springer Science + Business Media.

2.7 EXERCISES

Q1. True or False:
  (a) Mean is robust against outliers.
  (b) Median is robust against outliers.
  (c) Standard deviation is robust against outliers.

Q2. Let X and Y be two random variables, denoting age and weight, respectively. Consider a random sample of size $n = 20$ from these two variables

$$X = (69, 74, 68, 70, 72, 67, 66, 70, 76, 68, 72, 79, 74, 67, 66, 71, 74, 75, 75, 76)$$

$$Y = (153, 175, 155, 135, 172, 150, 115, 137, 200, 130, 140, 265, 185, 112, 140,$$

$$150, 165, 185, 210, 220)$$

(a) Find the mean, median, and mode for X.
(b) What is the variance for Y?
(c) Plot the normal distribution for X.
(d) What is the probability of observing an age of 80 or higher?
(e) Find the 2-dimensional mean $\hat{\mu}$ and the covariance matrix $\hat{\Sigma}$ for these two variables.
(f) What is the correlation between age and weight?
(g) Draw a scatterplot to show the relationship between age and weight.

Q3. Show that the identity in Eq. (2.18) holds, that is,

$$\sum_{i=1}^{n}(x_i - \mu)^2 = n(\hat{\mu} - \mu)^2 + \sum_{i=1}^{n}(x_i - \hat{\mu})^2$$

Q4. Prove that if x_i are independent random variables, then

$$\text{var}\left(\sum_{i=1}^{n} x_i\right) = \sum_{i=1}^{n}\text{var}(x_i)$$

This fact was used in Eq. (2.15).

Q5. Define a measure of deviation called *mean absolute deviation* for a random variable X as follows:

$$\frac{1}{n}\sum_{i=1}^{n}|x_i - \mu|$$

Is this measure robust? Why or why not?

Q6. Prove that the expected value of a vector random variable $\mathbf{X} = (X_1, X_2)^T$ is simply the vector of the expected value of the individual random variables X_1 and X_2 as given in Eq. (2.22).

Q7. Show that the correlation [Eq. (2.27)] between any two random variables X_1 and X_2 lies in the range $[-1, 1]$.

Q8. Given the dataset in Table 2.2, compute the covariance matrix and the generalized variance.

Table 2.2. Dataset for Q8

	X_1	X_2	X_3
$\mathbf{x}_1^T$	17	17	12
$\mathbf{x}_2^T$	11	9	13
$\mathbf{x}_3^T$	11	8	19

Q9. Consider Table 2.3. Assume that both the attributes X and Y are numeric, and the table represents the entire population. If we know that the correlation between X and Y is zero, what can you infer about the values of Y?

Table 2.3. Dataset for Q9

X	Y
1	a
0	b
1	c
0	a
0	c

Q10. Show that the outer-product in Eq. (2.39) for the sample covariance matrix is equivalent to Eq. (2.37).

Q11. Assume that we are given two univariate normal distributions, N_A and N_B, and let their mean and standard deviation be as follows: $\mu_A = 4$, $\sigma_A = 1$ and $\mu_B = 8$, $\sigma_B = 2$.
   (a) For each of the following values $x_i \in \{5, 6, 7\}$ find out which is the more likely normal distribution to have produced it.
   (b) Derive an expression for the point for which the probability of having been produced by both the normals is the same.

Q12. Under what conditions will the covariance matrix Σ be identical to the correlation matrix, whose (i, j) entry gives the correlation between attributes X_i and X_j? What can you conclude about the two variables?

Q13. Show that the total variance of a dataset $\mathbf{D}$ is given as the trace of the sample covariance matrix $\widehat{\Sigma}$. That is, show that $var(\mathbf{D}) = tr(\widehat{\Sigma})$.

CHAPTER 3

Categorical Attributes

In this chapter we present methods to analyze categorical attributes. Because categorical attributes have only symbolic values, many of the arithmetic operations cannot be performed directly on the symbolic values. However, we can compute the frequencies of these values and use them to analyze the attributes.

3.1 UNIVARIATE ANALYSIS

We assume that the data consists of values for a single categorical attribute, X. Let the domain of X consist of m symbolic values $dom(X) = \{a_1, a_2, \ldots, a_m\}$. The data $\mathbf{D}$ is thus an $n \times 1$ symbolic data matrix given as

$$\mathbf{D} = \begin{pmatrix} X \\ \hline x_1 \\ x_2 \\ \vdots \\ x_n \end{pmatrix}$$

where each point $x_i \in dom(X)$.

3.1.1 Bernoulli Variable

Let us first consider the case when the categorical attribute X has domain $\{a_1, a_2\}$, with $m = 2$. We can model X as a Bernoulli random variable, which takes on two distinct values, 1 and 0, according to the mapping

$$X(v) = \begin{cases} 1 & \text{if } v = a_1 \\ 0 & \text{if } v = a_2 \end{cases}$$

The probability mass function (PMF) of X is given as

$$P(X = x) = f(x) = \begin{cases} p_1 & \text{if } x = 1 \\ p_0 & \text{if } x = 0 \end{cases}$$

where p_1 and p_0 are the parameters of the distribution, which must satisfy the condition

$$p_1 + p_0 = 1$$

Because there is only one free parameter, it is customary to denote $p_1 = p$, from which it follows that $p_0 = 1 - p$. The PMF of Bernoulli random variable X can then be written compactly as

$$P(X = x) = f(x) = p^x (1-p)^{1-x} \tag{3.1}$$

We can see that $P(X = 1) = p^1 (1-p)^0 = p$ and $P(X = 0) = p^0 (1-p)^1 = 1 - p$, as desired.

Mean and Variance

The expected value of X is given as

$$\mu = E[X] = 1 \cdot p + 0 \cdot (1-p) = p \tag{3.2}$$

and the variance of X is given as

$$\sigma^2 = \text{var}(X) = E[X^2] - (E[X])^2 = (1^2 \cdot p + 0^2 \cdot (1-p)) - p^2 = p - p^2$$

which implies

$$\sigma^2 = p(1-p) \tag{3.3}$$

Sample Mean and Variance

To estimate the parameters of the Bernoulli variable X, we assume that each symbolic point has been mapped to its binary value. Thus, the set $\{x_1, x_2, \ldots, x_n\}$ is assumed to be a random sample drawn from X (i.e., each x_i is IID with X).

The sample mean is given as

$$\hat{\mu} = \frac{1}{n} \sum_{i=1}^{n} x_i = \frac{n_1}{n} = \hat{p} \tag{3.4}$$

where n_1 is the number of points with $x_i = 1$ in the random sample (equal to the number of occurrences of symbol a_1).

Let $n_0 = n - n_1$ denote the number of points with $x_i = 0$ in the random sample. The sample variance is given as

$$\hat{\sigma}^2 = \frac{1}{n} \sum_{i=1}^{n} (x_i - \hat{\mu})^2$$

$$= \frac{n_1}{n}(1 - \hat{p})^2 + \frac{n - n_1}{n}(0 - \hat{p})^2 = \hat{p}(1 - \hat{p})^2 + (1 - \hat{p})\hat{p}^2$$

$$= \hat{p}(1 - \hat{p})(1 - \hat{p} + \hat{p}) = \hat{p}(1 - \hat{p})$$

The sample variance could also have been obtained directly from Eq. (3.3), by substituting $\hat{p}$ for p.

Example 3.1. Consider the sepal length attribute (X_1) for the Iris dataset in Table 1.1. Let us define an Iris flower as Long if its sepal length is in the range $[7, \infty]$, and Short if its sepal length is in the range $[-\infty, 7)$. Then X_1 can be treated as a categorical attribute with domain {Long, Short}. From the observed sample of size $n = 150$, we find 13 long Irises. The sample mean of X_1 is

$$\hat{\mu} = \hat{p} = 13/150 = 0.087$$

and its variance is

$$\hat{\sigma}^2 = \hat{p}(1 - \hat{p}) = 0.087(1 - 0.087) = 0.087 \cdot 0.913 = 0.079$$

Binomial Distribution: Number of Occurrences

Given the Bernoulli variable X, let $\{x_1, x_2, \ldots, x_n\}$ denote a random sample of size n drawn from X. Let N be the random variable denoting the number of occurrences of the symbol a_1 (value $X = 1$) in the sample. N has a binomial distribution, given as

$$f(N = n_1 \mid n, p) = \binom{n}{n_1} p^{n_1} (1 - p)^{n - n_1} \tag{3.5}$$

In fact, N is the sum of the n independent Bernoulli random variables x_i IID with X, that is, $N = \sum_{i=1}^{n} x_i$. By linearity of expectation, the mean or expected number of occurrences of symbol a_1 is given as

$$\mu_N = E[N] = E\left[\sum_{i=1}^{n} x_i\right] = \sum_{i=1}^{n} E[x_i] = \sum_{i=1}^{n} p = np \tag{3.6}$$

Because x_i are all independent, the variance of N is given as

$$\sigma_N^2 = \text{var}(N) = \sum_{i=1}^{n} \text{var}(x_i) = \sum_{i=1}^{n} p(1 - p) = np(1 - p) \tag{3.7}$$

Example 3.2. Continuing with Example 3.1, we can use the estimated parameter $\hat{p} = 0.087$ to compute the expected number of occurrences N of Long sepal length Irises via the binomial distribution:

$$E[N] = n\hat{p} = 150 \cdot 0.087 = 13$$

In this case, because p is estimated from the sample via $\hat{p}$, it is not surprising that the expected number of occurrences of long Irises coincides with the actual occurrences.

However, what is more interesting is that we can compute the variance in the number of occurrences:

$$\text{var}(N) = n\hat{p}(1 - \hat{p}) = 150 \cdot 0.079 = 11.9$$

As the sample size increases, the binomial distribution given in Eq. 3.5 tends to a normal distribution with $\mu = 13$ and $\sigma = \sqrt{11.9} = 3.45$ for our example. Thus, with confidence greater than 95% we can claim that the number of occurrences of a_1 will lie in the range $\mu \pm 2\sigma = [9.55, 16.45]$, which follows from the fact that for a normal distribution 95.45% of the probability mass lies within two standard deviations from the mean (see Section 2.5.1).

3.1.2 Multivariate Bernoulli Variable

We now consider the general case when X is a categorical attribute with domain $\{a_1, a_2, \dots, a_m\}$. We can model X as an m-dimensional Bernoulli random variable $\mathbf{X} = (A_1, A_2, \dots, A_m)^T$, where each A_i is a Bernoulli variable with parameter p_i denoting the probability of observing symbol a_i. However, because X can assume only one of the symbolic values at any one time, if $X = a_i$, then $A_i = 1$, and $A_j = 0$ for all $j \neq i$. The range of the random variable $\mathbf{X}$ is thus the set $\{0, 1\}^m$, with the further restriction that if $X = a_i$, then $\mathbf{X} = \mathbf{e}_i$, where $\mathbf{e}_i$ is the ith standard basis vector $\mathbf{e}_i \in \mathbb{R}^m$, given as

$$\mathbf{e}_i = (\overbrace{0, \dots, 0}^{i-1}, 1, \overbrace{0, \dots, 0}^{m-i})^T$$

In $\mathbf{e}_i$, only the ith element is 1 ($e_{ii} = 1$), whereas all other elements are zero ($e_{ij} = 0, \forall j \neq i$).

This is precisely the definition of a *multivariate Bernoulli variable*, which is a generalization of a Bernoulli variable from two outcomes to m outcomes. We thus model the categorical attribute X as a multivariate Bernoulli variable $\mathbf{X}$ defined as

$$\mathbf{X}(v) = \mathbf{e}_i \text{ if } v = a_i$$

This is also referred to as a *one-hot encoding* of the variable X. The range of $\mathbf{X}$ consists of m distinct vector values $\{\mathbf{e}_1, \mathbf{e}_2, \dots, \mathbf{e}_m\}$, with the PMF of $\mathbf{X}$ given as

$$P(\mathbf{X} = \mathbf{e}_i) = f(\mathbf{e}_i) = p_i$$

where p_i is the probability of observing value a_i. These parameters must satisfy the condition

$$\sum_{i=1}^{m} p_i = 1$$

Table 3.1. Discretized `sepal length` attribute

Bins	Domain	Counts
[4.3, 5.2]	Very Short (a_1)	$n_1 = 45$
(5.2, 6.1]	Short (a_2)	$n_2 = 50$
(6.1, 7.0]	Long (a_3)	$n_3 = 43$
(7.0, 7.9]	Very Long (a_4)	$n_4 = 12$

The PMF can be written compactly as follows:

$$P(\mathbf{X} = \mathbf{e}_i) = f(\mathbf{e}_i) = \prod_{j=1}^{m} p_j^{e_{ij}} \tag{3.8}$$

Because $e_{ii} = 1$, and $e_{ij} = 0$ for $j \neq i$, we can see that, as expected, we have

$$f(\mathbf{e}_i) = \prod_{j=1}^{m} p_j^{e_{ij}} = p_1^{e_{i0}} \times \cdots p_i^{e_{ii}} \cdots \times p_m^{e_{im}} = p_1^0 \times \cdots p_i^1 \cdots \times p_m^0 = p_i$$

Example 3.3. Let us consider the `sepal length` attribute (X_1) for the Iris dataset shown in Table 1.2. We divide the sepal length into four equal-width intervals, and give each interval a name as shown in Table 3.1. We consider X_1 as a categorical attribute with domain

$$\{a_1 = \text{VeryShort}, a_2 = \text{Short}, a_3 = \text{Long}, a_4 = \text{VeryLong}\}$$

We model the categorical attribute X_1 as a multivariate Bernoulli variable $\mathbf{X}$, defined as

$$\mathbf{X}(v) = \begin{cases} \mathbf{e}_1 = (1, 0, 0, 0) & \text{if } v = a_1 \\ \mathbf{e}_2 = (0, 1, 0, 0) & \text{if } v = a_2 \\ \mathbf{e}_3 = (0, 0, 1, 0) & \text{if } v = a_3 \\ \mathbf{e}_4 = (0, 0, 0, 1) & \text{if } v = a_4 \end{cases}$$

For example, the symbolic point $x_1 = \text{Short} = a_2$ is represented as the vector $(0, 1, 0, 0)^T = \mathbf{e}_2$. In essence, each value a_i is encoded via the corresponding one-hot vector $\mathbf{e}_i$ (one-hot refers to the fact that only one entry of $\mathbf{e}_i$ is hot or one, and the rest are all zeros).

Mean

The mean or expected value of $\mathbf{X}$ can be obtained as

$$\mu = E[\mathbf{X}] = \sum_{i=1}^{m} \mathbf{e}_i f(\mathbf{e}_i) = \sum_{i=1}^{m} \mathbf{e}_i p_i = \begin{pmatrix} 1 \\ 0 \\ \vdots \\ 0 \end{pmatrix} p_1 + \cdots + \begin{pmatrix} 0 \\ 0 \\ \vdots \\ 1 \end{pmatrix} p_m = \begin{pmatrix} p_1 \\ p_2 \\ \vdots \\ p_m \end{pmatrix} = \mathbf{p} \tag{3.9}$$

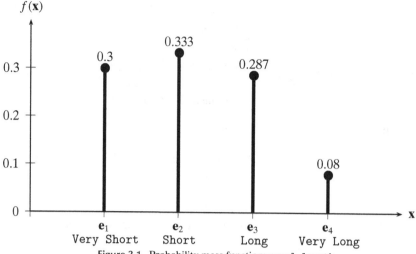

Figure 3.1. Probability mass function: sepal length.

Sample Mean

Assume that each symbolic point $x_i \in \mathbf{D}$ is mapped to the variable $\mathbf{x}_i = \mathbf{X}(x_i)$. The mapped dataset $\mathbf{x}_1, \mathbf{x}_2, \ldots, \mathbf{x}_n$ is then assumed to be a random sample IID with $\mathbf{X}$. We can compute the sample mean by placing a probability mass of $\frac{1}{n}$ at each point

$$\hat{\boldsymbol{\mu}} = \frac{1}{n} \sum_{i=1}^{n} \mathbf{x}_i = \sum_{i=1}^{m} \frac{n_i}{n} \mathbf{e}_i = \begin{pmatrix} n_1/n \\ n_2/n \\ \vdots \\ n_m/n \end{pmatrix} = \begin{pmatrix} \hat{p}_1 \\ \hat{p}_2 \\ \vdots \\ \hat{p}_m \end{pmatrix} = \hat{\mathbf{p}} \qquad (3.10)$$

where n_i is the number of occurrences of the vector value $\mathbf{e}_i$ in the sample, which is equivalent to the number of occurrences of the symbol a_i. Furthermore, we have $\sum_{i=1}^{m} n_i = n$, which follows from the fact that $\mathbf{X}$ can take on only m distinct values $\mathbf{e}_i$, and the counts for each value must add up to the sample size n.

Example 3.4 (Sample Mean). Consider the observed counts n_i for each of the values a_i ($\mathbf{e}_i$) of the discretized sepal length attribute, shown in Table 3.1. Because the total sample size is $n = 150$, from these we can obtain the estimates $\hat{p}_i$ as follows:

$$\hat{p}_1 = 45/150 = 0.3$$
$$\hat{p}_2 = 50/150 = 0.333$$
$$\hat{p}_3 = 43/150 = 0.287$$
$$\hat{p}_4 = 12/150 = 0.08$$

The PMF for $\mathbf{X}$ is plotted in Figure 3.1, and the sample mean for $\mathbf{X}$ is given as

$$\hat{\boldsymbol{\mu}} = \hat{\mathbf{p}} = \begin{pmatrix} 0.3 \\ 0.333 \\ 0.287 \\ 0.08 \end{pmatrix}$$

Covariance Matrix

Recall that an m-dimensional multivariate Bernoulli variable is simply a vector of m Bernoulli variables. For instance, $\mathbf{X} = (A_1, A_2, \ldots, A_m)^T$, where A_i is the Bernoulli variable corresponding to symbol a_i. The variance–covariance information between the constituent Bernoulli variables yields a covariance matrix for $\mathbf{X}$.

Let us first consider the variance along each Bernoulli variable A_i. By Eq. (3.3), we immediately have

$$\sigma_i^2 = \text{var}(A_i) = p_i(1 - p_i) \tag{3.11}$$

Next consider the covariance between A_i and A_j. Utilizing the identity in Eq. (2.25), we have

$$\sigma_{ij} = E[A_i A_j] - E[A_i] \cdot E[A_j] = 0 - p_i p_j = -p_i p_j \tag{3.12}$$

which follows from the fact that $E[A_i A_j] = 0$, as A_i and A_j cannot both be 1 at the same time, and thus their product $A_i A_j = 0$. This same fact leads to the negative relationship between A_i and A_j. What is interesting is that the degree of negative association is proportional to the product of the mean values for A_i and A_j.

From the preceding expressions for variance and covariance, the $m \times m$ covariance matrix for $\mathbf{X}$ is given as

$$\mathbf{\Sigma} = \begin{pmatrix} \sigma_1^2 & \sigma_{12} & \cdots & \sigma_{1m} \\ \sigma_{12} & \sigma_2^2 & \cdots & \sigma_{2m} \\ \vdots & \vdots & \ddots & \vdots \\ \sigma_{1m} & \sigma_{2m} & \cdots & \sigma_m^2 \end{pmatrix} = \begin{pmatrix} p_1(1-p_1) & -p_1 p_2 & \cdots & -p_1 p_m \\ -p_1 p_2 & p_2(1-p_2) & \cdots & -p_2 p_m \\ \vdots & \vdots & \ddots & \vdots \\ -p_1 p_m & -p_2 p_m & \cdots & p_m(1-p_m) \end{pmatrix}$$

Notice how each row in $\mathbf{\Sigma}$ sums to zero. For example, for row i, we have

$$-p_i p_1 - p_i p_2 - \cdots + p_i(1 - p_i) - \cdots - p_i p_m = p_i - p_i \sum_{j=1}^{m} p_j = p_i - p_i = 0 \tag{3.13}$$

Because $\mathbf{\Sigma}$ is symmetric, it follows that each column also sums to zero.

Define $\mathbf{P}$ as the $m \times m$ diagonal matrix:

$$\mathbf{P} = \text{diag}(\mathbf{p}) = \text{diag}(p_1, p_2, \ldots, p_m) = \begin{pmatrix} p_1 & 0 & \cdots & 0 \\ 0 & p_2 & \cdots & 0 \\ \vdots & \vdots & \ddots & \vdots \\ 0 & 0 & \cdots & p_m \end{pmatrix}$$

We can compactly write the covariance matrix of $\mathbf{X}$ as

$$\mathbf{\Sigma} = \mathbf{P} - \mathbf{p} \cdot \mathbf{p}^T \tag{3.14}$$

Sample Covariance Matrix

The sample covariance matrix can be obtained from Eq. (3.14) in a straightforward manner:

$$\widehat{\mathbf{\Sigma}} = \widehat{\mathbf{P}} - \hat{\mathbf{p}} \cdot \hat{\mathbf{p}}^T \tag{3.15}$$

where $\widehat{\mathbf{P}} = \text{diag}(\hat{\mathbf{p}})$, and $\hat{\mathbf{p}} = \hat{\mu} = (\hat{p}_1, \hat{p}_2, \ldots, \hat{p}_m)^T$ denotes the empirical probability mass function for $\mathbf{X}$.

Example 3.5. Returning to the discretized `sepal length` attribute in Example 3.4, we have $\hat{\mu} = \hat{\mathbf{p}} = (0.3, 0.333, 0.287, 0.08)^T$. The sample covariance matrix is given as

$$\widehat{\Sigma} = \widehat{\mathbf{P}} - \hat{\mathbf{p}} \cdot \hat{\mathbf{p}}^T$$

$$= \begin{pmatrix} 0.3 & 0 & 0 & 0 \\ 0 & 0.333 & 0 & 0 \\ 0 & 0 & 0.287 & 0 \\ 0 & 0 & 0 & 0.08 \end{pmatrix} - \begin{pmatrix} 0.3 \\ 0.333 \\ 0.287 \\ 0.08 \end{pmatrix} (0.3 \quad 0.333 \quad 0.287 \quad 0.08)$$

$$= \begin{pmatrix} 0.3 & 0 & 0 & 0 \\ 0 & 0.333 & 0 & 0 \\ 0 & 0 & 0.287 & 0 \\ 0 & 0 & 0 & 0.08 \end{pmatrix} - \begin{pmatrix} 0.09 & 0.1 & 0.086 & 0.024 \\ 0.1 & 0.111 & 0.096 & 0.027 \\ 0.086 & 0.096 & 0.082 & 0.023 \\ 0.024 & 0.027 & 0.023 & 0.006 \end{pmatrix}$$

$$= \begin{pmatrix} 0.21 & -0.1 & -0.086 & -0.024 \\ -0.1 & 0.222 & -0.096 & -0.027 \\ -0.086 & -0.096 & 0.204 & -0.023 \\ -0.024 & -0.027 & -0.023 & 0.074 \end{pmatrix}$$

One can verify that each row (and column) in $\widehat{\Sigma}$ sums to zero.

It is worth emphasizing that whereas the modeling of categorical attribute X as a multivariate Bernoulli variable, $\mathbf{X} = (A_1, A_2, \ldots, A_m)^T$, makes the structure of the mean and covariance matrix explicit, the same results would be obtained if we simply treat the mapped values $\mathbf{X}(x_i)$ as a new $n \times m$ binary data matrix, and apply the standard definitions of the mean and covariance matrix from multivariate numeric attribute analysis (see Section 2.3). In essence, the mapping from symbols a_i to binary vectors $\mathbf{e}_i$ is the key idea in categorical attribute analysis.

Example 3.6. Consider the sample $\mathbf{D}$ of size $n = 5$ for the `sepal length` attribute X_1 in the Iris dataset, shown in Table 3.2a. As in Example 3.1, we assume that X_1 has

Table 3.2. (a) Categorical dataset. (b) Mapped binary dataset. (c) Centered dataset.

	(a) X		(b) A_1	A_2		(c) $\bar{A}_1$	$\bar{A}_2$
x_1	Short	$\mathbf{x}_1$	0	1	$\mathbf{z}_1$	−0.4	0.4
x_2	Short	$\mathbf{x}_2$	0	1	$\mathbf{z}_2$	−0.4	0.4
x_3	Long	$\mathbf{x}_3$	1	0	$\mathbf{z}_3$	0.6	−0.6
x_4	Short	$\mathbf{x}_4$	0	1	$\mathbf{z}_4$	−0.4	0.4
x_5	Long	$\mathbf{x}_5$	1	0	$\mathbf{z}_5$	0.6	−0.6

only two categorical values {Long, Short}. We model X_1 as the multivariate Bernoulli variable $\mathbf{X}_1$ defined as

$$\mathbf{X}_1(v) = \begin{cases} \mathbf{e}_1 = (1,0)^T & \text{if } v = \text{Long}(a_1) \\ \mathbf{e}_2 = (0,1)^T & \text{if } v = \text{Short}(a_2) \end{cases}$$

The sample mean [Eq. (3.10)] is

$$\hat{\mu} = \hat{\mathbf{p}} = (2/5, 3/5)^T = (0.4, 0.6)^T$$

and the sample covariance matrix [Eq. (3.15)] is

$$\widehat{\Sigma} = \widehat{\mathbf{P}} - \hat{\mathbf{p}}\hat{\mathbf{p}}^T = \begin{pmatrix} 0.4 & 0 \\ 0 & 0.6 \end{pmatrix} - \begin{pmatrix} 0.4 \\ 0.6 \end{pmatrix} (0.4 \quad 0.6)$$

$$= \begin{pmatrix} 0.4 & 0 \\ 0 & 0.6 \end{pmatrix} - \begin{pmatrix} 0.16 & 0.24 \\ 0.24 & 0.36 \end{pmatrix} = \begin{pmatrix} 0.24 & -0.24 \\ -0.24 & 0.24 \end{pmatrix}$$

To show that the same result would be obtained via standard numeric analysis, we map the categorical attribute X to the two Bernoulli attributes A_1 and A_2 corresponding to symbols Long and Short, respectively. The mapped dataset is shown in Table 3.2b. The sample mean is simply

$$\hat{\mu} = \frac{1}{5} \sum_{i=1}^{5} \mathbf{x}_i = \frac{1}{5}(2,3)^T = (0.4, 0.6)^T$$

Next, we center the dataset by subtracting the mean value from each attribute. After centering, the mapped dataset is as shown in Table 3.2c, with attribute $\bar{A}_i$ as the centered attribute A_i. We can compute the covariance matrix using the inner-product form [Eq. (2.38)] on the centered column vectors. We have

$$\sigma_1^2 = \frac{1}{5}\bar{A}_1^T \bar{A}_1 = 1.2/5 = 0.24$$

$$\sigma_2^2 = \frac{1}{5}\bar{A}_2^T \bar{A}_2 = 1.2/5 = 0.24$$

$$\sigma_{12} = \frac{1}{5}\bar{A}_1^T \bar{A}_2 = -1.2/5 = -0.24$$

Thus, the sample covariance matrix is given as

$$\widehat{\Sigma} = \begin{pmatrix} 0.24 & -0.24 \\ -0.24 & 0.24 \end{pmatrix}$$

which matches the result obtained by using the multivariate Bernoulli modeling approach.

Multinomial Distribution: Number of Occurrences

Given a multivariate Bernoulli variable $\mathbf{X}$ and a random sample $\{\mathbf{x}_1, \mathbf{x}_2, \ldots, \mathbf{x}_n\}$ drawn from $\mathbf{X}$. Let N_i be the random variable corresponding to the number of occurrences of symbol a_i in the sample, and let $\mathbf{N} = (N_1, N_2, \ldots, N_m)^T$ denote the vector random variable corresponding to the joint distribution of the number of occurrences over all the symbols. Then $\mathbf{N}$ has a multinomial distribution, given as

$$
f\left(\mathbf{N} = (n_1, n_2, \ldots, n_m) \mid \mathbf{p}\right) = \binom{n}{n_1 n_2 \ldots n_m} \prod_{i=1}^{m} p_i^{n_i} \tag{3.16}
$$

We can see that this is a direct generalization of the binomial distribution in Eq. (3.5). The term

$$
\binom{n}{n_1 n_2 \ldots n_m} = \frac{n!}{n_1! n_2! \ldots n_m!}
$$

denotes the number of ways of choosing n_i occurrences of each symbol a_i from a sample of size n, with $\sum_{i=1}^{m} n_i = n$.

The mean and covariance matrix of $\mathbf{N}$ are given as n times the mean and covariance matrix of $\mathbf{X}$. That is, the mean of $\mathbf{N}$ is given as

$$
\boldsymbol{\mu}_{\mathbf{N}} = E[\mathbf{N}] = nE[\mathbf{X}] = n \cdot \boldsymbol{\mu} = n \cdot \mathbf{p} = \begin{pmatrix} np_1 \\ \vdots \\ np_m \end{pmatrix}
$$

and its covariance matrix is given as

$$
\boldsymbol{\Sigma}_{\mathbf{N}} = n \cdot (\mathbf{P} - \mathbf{p}\mathbf{p}^T) = \begin{pmatrix} np_1(1-p_1) & -np_1 p_2 & \cdots & -np_1 p_m \\ -np_1 p_2 & np_2(1-p_2) & \cdots & -np_2 p_m \\ \vdots & \vdots & \ddots & \vdots \\ -np_1 p_m & -np_2 p_m & \cdots & np_m(1-p_m) \end{pmatrix}
$$

Likewise the sample mean and covariance matrix for $\mathbf{N}$ are given as

$$
\hat{\boldsymbol{\mu}}_{\mathbf{N}} = n\hat{\mathbf{p}} \qquad\qquad \widehat{\boldsymbol{\Sigma}}_{\mathbf{N}} = n\left(\widehat{\mathbf{P}} - \hat{\mathbf{p}}\hat{\mathbf{p}}^T\right)
$$

3.2 BIVARIATE ANALYSIS

Assume that the data comprises two categorical attributes, X_1 and X_2, with

$$
dom(X_1) = \{a_{11}, a_{12}, \ldots, a_{1m_1}\}
$$
$$
dom(X_2) = \{a_{21}, a_{22}, \ldots, a_{2m_2}\}
$$

We are given n categorical points of the form $\mathbf{x}_i = (x_{i1}, x_{i2})^T$ with $x_{i1} \in dom(X_1)$ and $x_{i2} \in dom(X_2)$. The dataset is thus an $n \times 2$ symbolic data matrix:

$$\mathbf{D} = \begin{pmatrix} X_1 & X_2 \\ \hline x_{11} & x_{12} \\ x_{21} & x_{22} \\ \vdots & \vdots \\ x_{n1} & x_{n2} \end{pmatrix}$$

We can model X_1 and X_2 as multivariate Bernoulli variables $\mathbf{X}_1$ and $\mathbf{X}_2$ with dimensions m_1 and m_2, respectively. The probability mass functions for $\mathbf{X}_1$ and $\mathbf{X}_2$ are given according to Eq. (3.8):

$$P(\mathbf{X}_1 = \mathbf{e}_{1i}) = f_1(\mathbf{e}_{1i}) = p_i^1 = \prod_{k=1}^{m_1} (p_i^1)^{e_{ik}^1}$$

$$P(\mathbf{X}_2 = \mathbf{e}_{2j}) = f_2(\mathbf{e}_{2j}) = p_j^2 = \prod_{k=1}^{m_2} (p_j^2)^{e_{jk}^2}$$

where $\mathbf{e}_{1i}$ is the ith standard basis vector in $\mathbb{R}^{m_1}$ (for attribute X_1) whose kth component is e_{ik}^1, and $\mathbf{e}_{2j}$ is the jth standard basis vector in $\mathbb{R}^{m_2}$ (for attribute X_2) whose kth component is e_{jk}^2. Further, the parameter p_i^1 denotes the probability of observing symbol a_{1i}, and p_j^2 denotes the probability of observing symbol a_{2j}. Together they must satisfy the conditions: $\sum_{i=1}^{m_1} p_i^1 = 1$ and $\sum_{j=1}^{m_2} p_j^2 = 1$.

The joint distribution of $\mathbf{X}_1$ and $\mathbf{X}_2$ is modeled as the $d' = m_1 + m_2$ dimensional vector variable $\mathbf{X} = \begin{pmatrix} \mathbf{X}_1 \\ \mathbf{X}_2 \end{pmatrix}$, specified by the mapping

$$\mathbf{X}\big((v_1, v_2)^T\big) = \begin{pmatrix} \mathbf{X}_1(v_1) \\ \mathbf{X}_2(v_2) \end{pmatrix} = \begin{pmatrix} \mathbf{e}_{1i} \\ \mathbf{e}_{2j} \end{pmatrix}$$

provided that $v_1 = a_{1i}$ and $v_2 = a_{2j}$. The range of $\mathbf{X}$ thus consists of $m_1 \times m_2$ distinct pairs of vector values $\{(\mathbf{e}_{1i}, \mathbf{e}_{2j})^T\}$, with $1 \le i \le m_1$ and $1 \le j \le m_2$. The joint PMF of $\mathbf{X}$ is given as

$$P\big(\mathbf{X} = (\mathbf{e}_{1i}, \mathbf{e}_{2j})^T\big) = f(\mathbf{e}_{1i}, \mathbf{e}_{2j}) = p_{ij} = \prod_{r=1}^{m_1} \prod_{s=1}^{m_2} p_{ij}^{e_{ir}^1 \cdot e_{js}^2}$$

where p_{ij} the probability of observing the symbol pair (a_{1i}, a_{2j}). These probability parameters must satisfy the condition $\sum_{i=1}^{m_1} \sum_{j=1}^{m_2} p_{ij} = 1$. The joint PMF for $\mathbf{X}$ can be expressed as the $m_1 \times m_2$ matrix

$$\mathbf{P}_{12} = \begin{pmatrix} p_{11} & p_{12} & \cdots & p_{1m_2} \\ p_{21} & p_{22} & \cdots & p_{2m_2} \\ \vdots & \vdots & \ddots & \vdots \\ p_{m_1 1} & p_{m_1 2} & \cdots & p_{m_1 m_2} \end{pmatrix} \tag{3.17}$$

Table 3.3. Discretized sepal width attribute

Bins	Domain	Counts
[2.0, 2.8]	Short (a_1)	47
(2.8, 3.6]	Medium (a_2)	88
(3.6, 4.4]	Long (a_3)	15

Example 3.7. Consider the discretized sepal length attribute (X_1) in Table 3.1. We also discretize the sepal width attribute (X_2) into three values as shown in Table 3.3. We thus have

$$dom(X_1) = \{a_{11} = \text{VeryShort}, a_{12} = \text{Short}, a_{13} = \text{Long}, a_{14} = \text{VeryLong}\}$$
$$dom(X_2) = \{a_{21} = \text{Short}, a_{22} = \text{Medium}, a_{23} = \text{Long}\}$$

The symbolic point $\mathbf{x} = (\text{Short}, \text{Long}) = (a_{12}, a_{23})$, is mapped to the vector

$$\mathbf{X}(\mathbf{x}) = \begin{pmatrix} \mathbf{e}_{12} \\ \mathbf{e}_{23} \end{pmatrix} = (0, 1, 0, 0 \mid 0, 0, 1)^T \in \mathbb{R}^7$$

where we use | to demarcate the two (one-hot) subvectors $\mathbf{e}_{12} = (0, 1, 0, 0)^T \in \mathbb{R}^4$ and $\mathbf{e}_{23} = (0, 0, 1)^T \in \mathbb{R}^3$, corresponding to symbolic attributes sepal length and sepal width, respectively. Note that $\mathbf{e}_{12}$ is the second standard basis vector in $\mathbb{R}^4$ for $\mathbf{X}_1$, and $\mathbf{e}_{23}$ is the third standard basis vector in $\mathbb{R}^3$ for $\mathbf{X}_2$.

Mean

The bivariate mean can easily be generalized from Eq. (3.9), as follows:

$$\boldsymbol{\mu} = E[\mathbf{X}] = E\left[\begin{pmatrix} \mathbf{X}_1 \\ \mathbf{X}_2 \end{pmatrix}\right] = \begin{pmatrix} E[\mathbf{X}_1] \\ E[\mathbf{X}_2] \end{pmatrix} = \begin{pmatrix} \boldsymbol{\mu}_1 \\ \boldsymbol{\mu}_2 \end{pmatrix} = \begin{pmatrix} \mathbf{p}_1 \\ \mathbf{p}_2 \end{pmatrix}$$

where $\boldsymbol{\mu}_1 = \mathbf{p}_1 = (p_1^1, \ldots, p_{m_1}^1)^T$ and $\boldsymbol{\mu}_2 = \mathbf{p}_2 = (p_1^2, \ldots, p_{m_2}^2)^T$ are the mean vectors for $\mathbf{X}_1$ and $\mathbf{X}_2$. The vectors $\mathbf{p}_1$ and $\mathbf{p}_2$ also represent the probability mass functions for $\mathbf{X}_1$ and $\mathbf{X}_2$, respectively.

Sample Mean

The sample mean can also be generalized from Eq. (3.10), by placing a probability mass of $\frac{1}{n}$ at each point:

$$\hat{\boldsymbol{\mu}} = \frac{1}{n} \sum_{i=1}^{n} \mathbf{x}_i = \frac{1}{n} \begin{pmatrix} \sum_{i=1}^{m_1} n_i^1 \mathbf{e}_{1i} \\ \sum_{j=1}^{m_2} n_j^2 \mathbf{e}_{2j} \end{pmatrix} = \frac{1}{n} \begin{pmatrix} n_1^1 \\ \vdots \\ n_{m_1}^1 \\ n_1^2 \\ \vdots \\ n_{m_2}^2 \end{pmatrix} = \begin{pmatrix} \hat{p}_1^1 \\ \vdots \\ \hat{p}_{m_1}^1 \\ \hat{p}_1^2 \\ \vdots \\ \hat{p}_{m_2}^2 \end{pmatrix} = \begin{pmatrix} \hat{\mathbf{p}}_1 \\ \hat{\mathbf{p}}_2 \end{pmatrix} = \begin{pmatrix} \hat{\boldsymbol{\mu}}_1 \\ \hat{\boldsymbol{\mu}}_2 \end{pmatrix}$$

where n_j^i is the observed frequency of symbol a_{ij} in the sample of size n, and $\hat{\mu}_i = \hat{\mathbf{p}}_i = (p_1^i, p_2^i, \ldots, p_{m_i}^i)^T$ is the sample mean vector for $\mathbf{X}_i$, which is also the empirical PMF for attribute $\mathbf{X}_i$.

Covariance Matrix

The covariance matrix for $\mathbf{X}$ is the $d' \times d' = (m_1 + m_2) \times (m_1 + m_2)$ matrix given as

$$\Sigma = \begin{pmatrix} \Sigma_{11} & \Sigma_{12} \\ \Sigma_{12}^T & \Sigma_{22} \end{pmatrix} \tag{3.18}$$

where Σ_{11} is the $m_1 \times m_1$ covariance matrix for $\mathbf{X}_1$, and Σ_{22} is the $m_2 \times m_2$ covariance matrix for $\mathbf{X}_2$, which can be computed using Eq. (3.14). That is,

$$\Sigma_{11} = \mathbf{P}_1 - \mathbf{p}_1 \mathbf{p}_1^T$$
$$\Sigma_{22} = \mathbf{P}_2 - \mathbf{p}_2 \mathbf{p}_2^T$$

where $\mathbf{P}_1 = \mathrm{diag}(\mathbf{p}_1)$ and $\mathbf{P}_2 = \mathrm{diag}(\mathbf{p}_2)$. Further, Σ_{12} is the $m_1 \times m_2$ covariance matrix between variables $\mathbf{X}_1$ and $\mathbf{X}_2$, given as

$$
\begin{aligned}
\Sigma_{12} &= E[(\mathbf{X}_1 - \mu_1)(\mathbf{X}_2 - \mu_2)^T] \\
&= E[\mathbf{X}_1 \mathbf{X}_2^T] - E[\mathbf{X}_1]E[\mathbf{X}_2]^T \\
&= \mathbf{P}_{12} - \mu_1 \mu_2^T \\
&= \mathbf{P}_{12} - \mathbf{p}_1 \mathbf{p}_2^T \\
&= \begin{pmatrix}
p_{11} - p_1^1 p_1^2 & p_{12} - p_1^1 p_2^2 & \cdots & p_{1m_2} - p_1^1 p_{m_2}^2 \\
p_{21} - p_2^1 p_1^2 & p_{22} - p_2^1 p_2^2 & \cdots & p_{2m_2} - p_2^1 p_{m_2}^2 \\
\vdots & \vdots & \ddots & \vdots \\
p_{m_1 1} - p_{m_1}^1 p_1^2 & p_{m_1 2} - p_{m_1}^1 p_2^2 & \cdots & p_{m_1 m_2} - p_{m_1}^1 p_{m_2}^2
\end{pmatrix}
\end{aligned}
$$

where $\mathbf{P}_{12}$ represents the joint PMF for $\mathbf{X}$ given in Eq. (3.17).

Incidentally, each row and each column of Σ_{12} sums to zero. For example, consider row i and column j:

$$\sum_{k=1}^{m_2}(p_{ik} - p_i^1 p_k^2) = \left(\sum_{k=1}^{m_2} p_{ik}\right) - p_i^1 = p_i^1 - p_i^1 = 0$$

$$\sum_{k=1}^{m_1}(p_{kj} - p_k^1 p_j^2) = \left(\sum_{k=1}^{m_1} p_{kj}\right) - p_j^2 = p_j^2 - p_j^2 = 0$$

which follows from the fact that summing the joint mass function over all values of $\mathbf{X}_2$, yields the marginal distribution of $\mathbf{X}_1$, and summing it over all values of $\mathbf{X}_1$ yields the marginal distribution for $\mathbf{X}_2$. Note that p_j^2 is the probability of observing symbol a_{2j}; it should not be confused with the square of p_j. Combined with the fact that Σ_{11} and Σ_{22} also have row and column sums equal to zero via Eq. (3.13), the full covariance matrix Σ has rows and columns that sum up to zero.

Sample Covariance Matrix

The sample covariance matrix is given as

$$\widehat{\mathbf{\Sigma}} = \begin{pmatrix} \widehat{\mathbf{\Sigma}}_{11} & \widehat{\mathbf{\Sigma}}_{12} \\ \widehat{\mathbf{\Sigma}}_{12}^T & \widehat{\mathbf{\Sigma}}_{22} \end{pmatrix} \tag{3.19}$$

where

$$\widehat{\mathbf{\Sigma}}_{11} = \widehat{\mathbf{P}}_1 - \hat{\mathbf{p}}_1\hat{\mathbf{p}}_1^T$$

$$\widehat{\mathbf{\Sigma}}_{22} = \widehat{\mathbf{P}}_2 - \hat{\mathbf{p}}_2\hat{\mathbf{p}}_2^T$$

$$\widehat{\mathbf{\Sigma}}_{12} = \widehat{\mathbf{P}}_{12} - \hat{\mathbf{p}}_1\hat{\mathbf{p}}_2^T$$

Here $\widehat{\mathbf{P}}_1 = \text{diag}(\hat{\mathbf{p}}_1)$ and $\widehat{\mathbf{P}}_2 = \text{diag}(\hat{\mathbf{p}}_2)$, and $\hat{\mathbf{p}}_1$ and $\hat{\mathbf{p}}_2$ specify the empirical probability mass functions for $\mathbf{X}_1$, and $\mathbf{X}_2$, respectively. Further, $\widehat{\mathbf{P}}_{12}$ specifies the empirical joint PMF for $\mathbf{X}_1$ and $\mathbf{X}_2$, given as

$$\widehat{\mathbf{P}}_{12}(i,j) = \hat{f}(\mathbf{e}_{1i}, \mathbf{e}_{2j}) = \frac{1}{n}\sum_{k=1}^n I_{ij}(\mathbf{x}_k) = \frac{n_{ij}}{n} = \hat{p}_{ij} \tag{3.20}$$

where I_{ij} is the indicator variable

$$I_{ij}(\mathbf{x}_k) = \begin{cases} 1 & \text{if } \mathbf{x}_{k1} = \mathbf{e}_{1i} \text{ and } \mathbf{x}_{k2} = \mathbf{e}_{2j} \\ 0 & \text{otherwise} \end{cases}$$

Taking the sum of $I_{ij}(\mathbf{x}_k)$ over all the n points in the sample yields the number of occurrences, n_{ij}, of the symbol pair (a_{1i}, a_{2j}) in the sample. One issue with the cross-attribute covariance matrix $\widehat{\mathbf{\Sigma}}_{12}$ is the need to estimate a quadratic number of parameters. That is, we need to obtain reliable counts n_{ij} to estimate the parameters p_{ij}, for a total of $O(m_1 \times m_2)$ parameters that have to be estimated, which can be a problem if the categorical attributes have many symbols. On the other hand, estimating $\widehat{\mathbf{\Sigma}}_{11}$ and $\widehat{\mathbf{\Sigma}}_{22}$ requires that we estimate m_1 and m_2 parameters, corresponding to p_i^1 and p_j^2, respectively. In total, computing $\mathbf{\Sigma}$ requires the estimation of $m_1 m_2 + m_1 + m_2$ parameters.

Example 3.8 (Bivariate Covariance Matrix). We continue with the bivariate categorical attributes X_1 and X_2 in Example 3.7. From Example 3.4, and from the

Table 3.4. Observed Counts (n_{ij}): sepal length and sepal width

		X_2		
		Short ($\mathbf{e}_{21}$)	Medium ($\mathbf{e}_{22}$)	Long ($\mathbf{e}_{23}$)
X_1	Very Short ($\mathbf{e}_{11}$)	7	33	5
	Short ($\mathbf{e}_{22}$)	24	18	8
	Long ($\mathbf{e}_{13}$)	13	30	0
	Very Long ($\mathbf{e}_{14}$)	3	7	2

occurrence counts for each of the values of sepal width in Table 3.3, we have

$$\hat{\mu}_1 = \hat{\mathbf{p}}_1 = \begin{pmatrix} 0.3 \\ 0.333 \\ 0.287 \\ 0.08 \end{pmatrix} \qquad \hat{\mu}_2 = \hat{\mathbf{p}}_2 = \frac{1}{150} \begin{pmatrix} 47 \\ 88 \\ 15 \end{pmatrix} = \begin{pmatrix} 0.313 \\ 0.587 \\ 0.1 \end{pmatrix}$$

Thus, the mean for $\mathbf{X} = \begin{pmatrix} \mathbf{X}_1 \\ \mathbf{X}_2 \end{pmatrix}$ is given as

$$\hat{\mu} = \begin{pmatrix} \hat{\mu}_1 \\ \hat{\mu}_2 \end{pmatrix} = \begin{pmatrix} \hat{\mathbf{p}}_1 \\ \hat{\mathbf{p}}_2 \end{pmatrix} = (0.3, 0.333, 0.287, 0.08 \mid 0.313, 0.587, 0.1)^T$$

From Example 3.5 we have

$$\widehat{\Sigma}_{11} = \begin{pmatrix} 0.21 & -0.1 & -0.086 & -0.024 \\ -0.1 & 0.222 & -0.096 & -0.027 \\ -0.086 & -0.096 & 0.204 & -0.023 \\ -0.024 & -0.027 & -0.023 & 0.074 \end{pmatrix}$$

In a similar manner we can obtain

$$\widehat{\Sigma}_{22} = \begin{pmatrix} 0.215 & -0.184 & -0.031 \\ -0.184 & 0.242 & -0.059 \\ -0.031 & -0.059 & 0.09 \end{pmatrix}$$

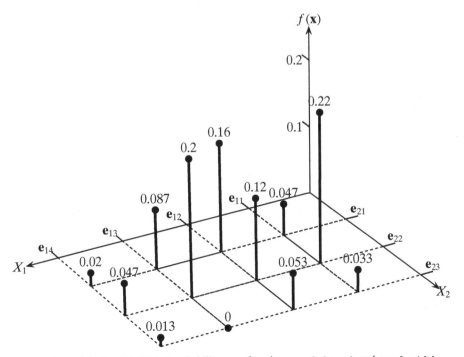

Figure 3.2. Empirical joint probability mass function: sepal length and sepal width.

Next, we use the observed counts in Table 3.4 to obtain the empirical joint PMF for $\mathbf{X}_1$ and $\mathbf{X}_2$ using Eq. (3.20), as plotted in Figure 3.2. From these probabilities we get

$$E[\mathbf{X}_1\mathbf{X}_2^T] = \widehat{\mathbf{P}}_{12} = \frac{1}{150}\begin{pmatrix} 7 & 33 & 5 \\ 24 & 18 & 8 \\ 13 & 30 & 0 \\ 3 & 7 & 2 \end{pmatrix} = \begin{pmatrix} 0.047 & 0.22 & 0.033 \\ 0.16 & 0.12 & 0.053 \\ 0.087 & 0.2 & 0 \\ 0.02 & 0.047 & 0.013 \end{pmatrix}$$

Further, we have

$$E[\mathbf{X}_1]E[\mathbf{X}_2]^T = \hat{\mu}_1\hat{\mu}_2^T = \hat{\mathbf{p}}_1\hat{\mathbf{p}}_2^T$$

$$= \begin{pmatrix} 0.3 \\ 0.333 \\ 0.287 \\ 0.08 \end{pmatrix}\begin{pmatrix} 0.313 & 0.587 & 0.1 \end{pmatrix}$$

$$= \begin{pmatrix} 0.094 & 0.176 & 0.03 \\ 0.104 & 0.196 & 0.033 \\ 0.09 & 0.168 & 0.029 \\ 0.025 & 0.047 & 0.008 \end{pmatrix}$$

We can now compute the across-attribute sample covariance matrix $\widehat{\mathbf{\Sigma}}_{12}$ for $\mathbf{X}_1$ and $\mathbf{X}_2$ using Eq. (3.18), as follows:

$$\widehat{\mathbf{\Sigma}}_{12} = \widehat{\mathbf{P}}_{12} - \hat{\mathbf{p}}_1\hat{\mathbf{p}}_2^T$$

$$= \begin{pmatrix} -0.047 & 0.044 & 0.003 \\ 0.056 & -0.076 & 0.02 \\ -0.003 & 0.032 & -0.029 \\ -0.005 & 0 & 0.005 \end{pmatrix}$$

One can observe that each row and column in $\widehat{\mathbf{\Sigma}}_{12}$ sums to zero. Putting it all together, from $\widehat{\mathbf{\Sigma}}_{11}$, $\widehat{\mathbf{\Sigma}}_{22}$ and $\widehat{\mathbf{\Sigma}}_{12}$ we obtain the sample covariance matrix as follows

$$\widehat{\mathbf{\Sigma}} = \begin{pmatrix} \widehat{\mathbf{\Sigma}}_{11} & \widehat{\mathbf{\Sigma}}_{12} \\ \widehat{\mathbf{\Sigma}}_{12}^T & \widehat{\mathbf{\Sigma}}_{22} \end{pmatrix}$$

$$= \left(\begin{array}{cccc|ccc} 0.21 & -0.1 & -0.086 & -0.024 & -0.047 & 0.044 & 0.003 \\ -0.1 & 0.222 & -0.096 & -0.027 & 0.056 & -0.076 & 0.02 \\ -0.086 & -0.096 & 0.204 & -0.023 & -0.003 & 0.032 & -0.029 \\ -0.024 & -0.027 & -0.023 & 0.074 & -0.005 & 0 & 0.005 \\ \hline -0.047 & 0.056 & -0.003 & -0.005 & 0.215 & -0.184 & -0.031 \\ 0.044 & -0.076 & 0.032 & 0 & -0.184 & 0.242 & -0.059 \\ 0.003 & 0.02 & -0.029 & 0.005 & -0.031 & -0.059 & 0.09 \end{array}\right)$$

In $\widehat{\mathbf{\Sigma}}$, each row and column also sums to zero.

3.2.1 Attribute Dependence: Contingency Analysis

Testing for the independence of the two categorical random variables X_1 and X_2 can be done via *contingency table analysis*. The main idea is to set up a hypothesis testing framework, where the null hypothesis H_0 is that $\mathbf{X}_1$ and $\mathbf{X}_2$ are independent, and the alternative hypothesis H_1 is that they are dependent. We then compute the value of the chi-square statistic χ^2 under the null hypothesis. Depending on the p-value, we either accept or reject the null hypothesis; in the latter case the attributes are considered to be dependent.

Contingency Table
A contingency table for $\mathbf{X}_1$ and $\mathbf{X}_2$ is the $m_1 \times m_2$ matrix of observed counts n_{ij} for all pairs of values $(\mathbf{e}_{1i}, \mathbf{e}_{2j})$ in the given sample of size n, defined as

$$\mathbf{N}_{12} = n \cdot \widehat{\mathbf{P}}_{12} = \begin{pmatrix} n_{11} & n_{12} & \cdots & n_{1m_2} \\ n_{21} & n_{22} & \cdots & n_{2m_2} \\ \vdots & \vdots & \ddots & \vdots \\ n_{m_1 1} & n_{m_1 2} & \cdots & n_{m_1 m_2} \end{pmatrix}$$

where $\widehat{\mathbf{P}}_{12}$ is the empirical joint PMF for $\mathbf{X}_1$ and $\mathbf{X}_2$, computed via Eq. (3.20). The contingency table is then augmented with row and column marginal counts, as follows:

$$\mathbf{N}_1 = n \cdot \hat{\mathbf{p}}_1 = \begin{pmatrix} n_1^1 \\ \vdots \\ n_{m_1}^1 \end{pmatrix} \qquad \mathbf{N}_2 = n \cdot \hat{\mathbf{p}}_2 = \begin{pmatrix} n_1^2 \\ \vdots \\ n_{m_2}^2 \end{pmatrix}$$

Note that the marginal row and column entries and the sample size satisfy the following constraints:

$$n_i^1 = \sum_{j=1}^{m_2} n_{ij} \qquad n_j^2 = \sum_{i=1}^{m_1} n_{ij} \qquad n = \sum_{i=1}^{m_1} n_i^1 = \sum_{j=1}^{m_2} n_j^2 = \sum_{i=1}^{m_1} \sum_{j=1}^{m_2} n_{ij}$$

It is worth noting that both $\mathbf{N}_1$ and $\mathbf{N}_2$ have a multinomial distribution with parameters $\mathbf{p}_1 = (p_1^1, \ldots, p_{m_1}^1)$ and $\mathbf{p}_2 = (p_1^2, \ldots, p_{m_2}^2)$, respectively. Further, $\mathbf{N}_{12}$ also has a multinomial distribution with parameters $\mathbf{P}_{12} = \{p_{ij}\}$, for $1 \leq i \leq m_1$ and $1 \leq j \leq m_2$.

Example 3.9 (Contingency Table). Table 3.4 shows the observed counts for the discretized sepal length (X_1) and sepal width (X_2) attributes. Augmenting the table with the row and column marginal counts and the sample size yields the final contingency table shown in Table 3.5.

χ^2 Statistic and Hypothesis Testing
Under the null hypothesis $\mathbf{X}_1$ and $\mathbf{X}_2$ are assumed to be independent, which means that their joint probability mass function is given as

$$\hat{p}_{ij} = \hat{p}_i^1 \cdot \hat{p}_j^2$$

Table 3.5. Contingency table: sepal length vs. sepal width

		Sepal width (X_2)			
		Short a_{21}	Medium a_{22}	Long a_{23}	Row Counts
Sepal length (X_1)	Very Short (a_{11})	7	33	5	$n_1^1 = 45$
	Short (a_{12})	24	18	8	$n_2^1 = 50$
	Long (a_{13})	13	30	0	$n_3^1 = 43$
	Very Long (a_{14})	3	7	2	$n_4^1 = 12$
	Column Counts	$n_1^2 = 47$	$n_2^2 = 88$	$n_3^2 = 15$	$n = 150$

Under this independence assumption, the expected frequency for each pair of values is given as

$$e_{ij} = n \cdot \hat{p}_{ij} = n \cdot \hat{p}_i^1 \cdot \hat{p}_j^2 = n \cdot \frac{n_i^1}{n} \cdot \frac{n_j^2}{n} = \frac{n_i^1 n_j^2}{n} \qquad (3.21)$$

However, from the sample we already have the observed frequency of each pair of values, n_{ij}. We would like to determine whether there is a significant difference in the observed and expected frequencies for each pair of values. If there is no significant difference, then the independence assumption is valid and we accept the null hypothesis that the attributes are independent. On the other hand, if there is a significant difference, then the null hypothesis should be rejected and we conclude that the attributes are dependent.

The χ^2 statistic quantifies the difference between observed and expected counts for each pair of values; it is defined as follows:

$$\chi^2 = \sum_{i=1}^{m_1} \sum_{j=1}^{m_2} \frac{(n_{ij} - e_{ij})^2}{e_{ij}} \qquad (3.22)$$

At this point, we need to determine the probability of obtaining the computed χ^2 value. In general, this can be rather difficult if we do not know the sampling distribution of a given statistic. Fortunately, for the χ^2 statistic it is known that its sampling distribution follows the *chi-squared* density function with q degrees of freedom:

$$f(x|q) = \frac{1}{2^{q/2}\Gamma(q/2)} x^{\frac{q}{2}-1} e^{-\frac{x}{2}} \qquad (3.23)$$

where the gamma function Γ is defined as

$$\Gamma(k > 0) = \int_0^\infty x^{k-1} e^{-x} dx \qquad (3.24)$$

The degrees of freedom, q, represent the number of independent parameters. In the contingency table there are $m_1 \times m_2$ observed counts n_{ij}. However, note that each row i and each column j must sum to n_i^1 and n_j^2, respectively. Further, the sum of the row and column marginals must also add to n; thus we have to remove $(m_1 + m_2)$ parameters from the number of independent parameters. However, doing this removes one of the parameters, say $n_{m_1 m_2}$, twice, so we have to add back one to the count. The total degrees of freedom is therefore

$$q = |dom(X_1)| \times |dom(X_2)| - (|dom(X_1)| + |dom(X_2)|) + 1$$
$$= m_1 m_2 - m_1 - m_2 + 1$$
$$= (m_1 - 1)(m_2 - 1)$$

p-value

The *p-value* of a statistic is defined as the probability of obtaining a value at least as extreme as the observed value under the null hypothesis. For the χ^2 statistic computed above, its p-value is defined as follows

$$\text{p-value}(\chi^2) = P(x \geq \chi^2) = 1 - F_q(\chi^2) \tag{3.25}$$

where F_q is the cumulative χ^2 probability distribution with q degrees of freedom.

The p-value gives a measure of how surprising is the observed value of the statistic. If the observed value lies in a low-probability region, then the value is more surprising. In general, the lower the p-value, the more surprising the observed value, and the more the grounds for rejecting the null hypothesis. The null hypothesis is rejected if the p-value is below some *significance level*, α. For example, if $\alpha = 0.01$, then we reject the null hypothesis if p-value$(\chi^2) \leq \alpha$. The significance level α corresponds to the least level of surprise we need to reject the null hypothesis. Note that the value $1 - \alpha$ is also called the *confidence level*. So equivalently, we say that we reject the null hypothesis at the $100(1 - \alpha)\%$ confidence level if p-value$(\chi^2) \leq \alpha$.

For a given significance level α (or equivalently, confidence level $1 - \alpha$), define the corresponding *critical value*, v_α, of the test statistic as follows:

$$P(x \geq v_\alpha) = 1 - F_q(v_\alpha) = \alpha, \text{ or equivalently } F_q(v_\alpha) = 1 - \alpha$$

For the given significance value α, we can find the critical value from the quantile function F_q^{-1}:

$$v_\alpha = F_q^{-1}(1 - \alpha)$$

An alternative test for rejection of the null hypothesis is to check if $\chi^2 \geq v_\alpha$, as in that case $P(x \geq \chi^2) \leq P(x \geq v_\alpha)$, and therefore, the p-value of the observed χ^2 value is bounded above by α, that is, p-value$(\chi^2) \leq $ p-value$(v_\alpha) = \alpha$.

Example 3.10. Consider the contingency table for sepal length and sepal width in Table 3.5. We compute the expected counts using Eq. (3.21); these counts are shown in Table 3.6. For example, we have

$$e_{11} = \frac{n_1^1 n_1^2}{n} = \frac{45 \cdot 47}{150} = \frac{2115}{150} = 14.1$$

Table 3.6. Expected counts

		X_2		
		Short (a_{21})	Medium (a_{22})	Long (a_{23})
X_1	Very Short (a_{11})	14.1	26.4	4.5
	Short (a_{12})	15.67	29.33	5.0
	Long (a_{13})	13.47	25.23	4.3
	Very Long (a_{14})	3.76	7.04	1.2

Next we use Eq. (3.22) to compute the value of the χ^2 statistic, which is given as $\chi^2 = 21.8$. Further, the number of degrees of freedom is given as

$$q = (m_1 - 1) \cdot (m_2 - 1) = 3 \cdot 2 = 6$$

The plot of the chi-squared density function with 6 degrees of freedom is shown in Figure 3.3. From the cumulative chi-squared distribution with $q = 6$ degrees of freedom, we obtain

$$\text{p-value}(21.8) = 1 - F_6(21.8) = 1 - 0.9987 = 0.0013$$

At a significance level of $\alpha = 0.01$, we would certainly be justified in rejecting the null hypothesis because the large value of the χ^2 statistic is indeed surprising. Further, at the $\alpha = 0.01$ significance level, the critical value of the statistic is

$$v_\alpha = F_6^{-1}(1 - \alpha) = F_6^{-1}(0.99) = 16.81$$

This critical value is also shown in Figure 3.3, and we can clearly see that the observed value of 21.8 is in the rejection region, as $21.8 > v_\alpha = 16.81$. In effect, we reject the null hypothesis that sepal length and sepal width are independent, and accept the alternative hypothesis that they are dependent.

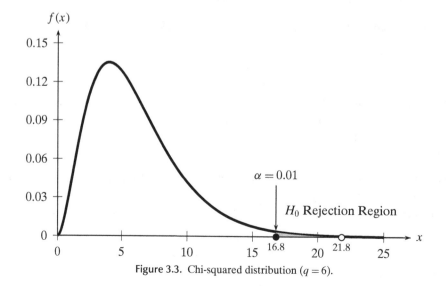

Figure 3.3. Chi-squared distribution ($q = 6$).

3.3 MULTIVARIATE ANALYSIS

Assume that the dataset comprises d categorical attributes X_j $(1 \leq j \leq d)$ with $dom(X_j) = \{a_{j1}, a_{j2}, \ldots, a_{jm_j}\}$. We are given n categorical points of the form $\mathbf{x}_i = (x_{i1}, x_{i2}, \ldots, x_{id})^T$ with $x_{ij} \in dom(X_j)$. The dataset is thus an $n \times d$ symbolic matrix

$$
\mathbf{D} = \begin{pmatrix}
X_1 & X_2 & \cdots & X_d \\
x_{11} & x_{12} & \cdots & x_{1d} \\
x_{21} & x_{22} & \cdots & x_{2d} \\
\vdots & \vdots & \ddots & \vdots \\
x_{n1} & x_{n2} & \cdots & x_{nd}
\end{pmatrix}
$$

Each attribute X_i is modeled as an m_i-dimensional multivariate Bernoulli variable $\mathbf{X}_i$, and their joint distribution is modeled as a $d' = \sum_{j=1}^{d} m_j$ dimensional vector random variable

$$
\mathbf{X} = \begin{pmatrix} \mathbf{X}_1 \\ \vdots \\ \mathbf{X}_d \end{pmatrix}
$$

Each categorical data point $\mathbf{v} = (v_1, v_2, \ldots, v_d)^T$ is therefore represented as a d'-dimensional binary vector

$$
\mathbf{X}(\mathbf{v}) = \begin{pmatrix} \mathbf{X}_1(v_1) \\ \vdots \\ \mathbf{X}_d(v_d) \end{pmatrix} = \begin{pmatrix} \mathbf{e}_{1k_1} \\ \vdots \\ \mathbf{e}_{dk_d} \end{pmatrix}
$$

provided $v_i = a_{ik_i}$, the k_ith symbol of X_i. Here $\mathbf{e}_{ik_i}$ is the k_ith standard basis vector in $\mathbb{R}^{m_i}$.

Mean
Generalizing from the bivariate case, the mean and sample mean for $\mathbf{X}$ are given as

$$
\boldsymbol{\mu} = E[\mathbf{X}] = \begin{pmatrix} \boldsymbol{\mu}_1 \\ \vdots \\ \boldsymbol{\mu}_d \end{pmatrix} = \begin{pmatrix} \mathbf{p}_1 \\ \vdots \\ \mathbf{p}_d \end{pmatrix} \qquad \hat{\boldsymbol{\mu}} = \begin{pmatrix} \hat{\boldsymbol{\mu}}_1 \\ \vdots \\ \hat{\boldsymbol{\mu}}_d \end{pmatrix} = \begin{pmatrix} \hat{\mathbf{p}}_1 \\ \vdots \\ \hat{\mathbf{p}}_d \end{pmatrix}
$$

where $\mathbf{p}_i = (p_1^i, \ldots, p_{m_i}^i)^T$ is the PMF for $\mathbf{X}_i$, and $\hat{\mathbf{p}}_i = (\hat{p}_1^i, \ldots, \hat{p}_{m_i}^i)^T$ is the empirical PMF for $\mathbf{X}_i$.

Covariance Matrix
The covariance matrix for $\mathbf{X}$, and its estimate from the sample, are given as the $d' \times d'$ matrices:

$$
\boldsymbol{\Sigma} = \begin{pmatrix}
\boldsymbol{\Sigma}_{11} & \boldsymbol{\Sigma}_{12} & \cdots & \boldsymbol{\Sigma}_{1d} \\
\boldsymbol{\Sigma}_{12}^T & \boldsymbol{\Sigma}_{22} & \cdots & \boldsymbol{\Sigma}_{2d} \\
\cdots & \cdots & \ddots & \cdots \\
\boldsymbol{\Sigma}_{1d}^T & \boldsymbol{\Sigma}_{2d}^T & \cdots & \boldsymbol{\Sigma}_{dd}
\end{pmatrix}
\qquad
\widehat{\boldsymbol{\Sigma}} = \begin{pmatrix}
\widehat{\boldsymbol{\Sigma}}_{11} & \widehat{\boldsymbol{\Sigma}}_{12} & \cdots & \widehat{\boldsymbol{\Sigma}}_{1d} \\
\widehat{\boldsymbol{\Sigma}}_{12}^T & \widehat{\boldsymbol{\Sigma}}_{22} & \cdots & \widehat{\boldsymbol{\Sigma}}_{2d} \\
\cdots & \cdots & \ddots & \cdots \\
\widehat{\boldsymbol{\Sigma}}_{1d}^T & \widehat{\boldsymbol{\Sigma}}_{2d}^T & \cdots & \widehat{\boldsymbol{\Sigma}}_{dd}
\end{pmatrix}
$$

where $d' = \sum_{i=1}^{d} m_i$, and $\boldsymbol{\Sigma}_{ij}$ (and $\widehat{\boldsymbol{\Sigma}}_{ij}$) is the $m_i \times m_j$ covariance matrix (and its estimate) for attributes $\mathbf{X}_i$ and $\mathbf{X}_j$:

$$\boldsymbol{\Sigma}_{ij} = \mathbf{P}_{ij} - \mathbf{p}_i \mathbf{p}_j^T \qquad\qquad \widehat{\boldsymbol{\Sigma}}_{ij} = \widehat{\mathbf{P}}_{ij} - \hat{\mathbf{p}}_i \hat{\mathbf{p}}_j^T \qquad (3.26)$$

Here $\mathbf{P}_{ij}$ is the joint PMF and $\widehat{\mathbf{P}}_{ij}$ is the empirical joint PMF for $\mathbf{X}_i$ and $\mathbf{X}_j$, which can be computed using Eq. (3.20).

Example 3.11 (Multivariate Analysis). Let us consider the 3-dimensional subset of the Iris dataset, with the discretized attributes sepal length (X_1) and sepal width (X_2), and the categorical attribute class (X_3). The domains for X_1 and X_2 are given in Table 3.1 and Table 3.3, respectively, and $dom(X_3) =$ {iris-versicolor, iris-setosa, iris-virginica}. Each value of X_3 occurs 50 times.

The categorical point $\mathbf{x} =$ (Short, Medium, iris-versicolor) is modeled as the vector

$$\mathbf{X}(\mathbf{x}) = \begin{pmatrix} \mathbf{e}_{12} \\ \mathbf{e}_{22} \\ \mathbf{e}_{31} \end{pmatrix} = (0,1,0,0 \mid 0,1,0 \mid 1,0,0)^T \in \mathbb{R}^{10}$$

From Example 3.8 and the fact that each value in $dom(X_3)$ occurs 50 times in a sample of $n = 150$, the sample mean is given as

$$\hat{\boldsymbol{\mu}} = \begin{pmatrix} \hat{\boldsymbol{\mu}}_1 \\ \hat{\boldsymbol{\mu}}_2 \\ \hat{\boldsymbol{\mu}}_3 \end{pmatrix} = \begin{pmatrix} \hat{\mathbf{p}}_1 \\ \hat{\mathbf{p}}_2 \\ \hat{\mathbf{p}}_3 \end{pmatrix} = (0.3, 0.333, 0.287, 0.08 \mid 0.313, 0.587, 0.1 \mid 0.33, 0.33, 0.33)^T$$

Using $\hat{\mathbf{p}}_3 = (0.33, 0.33, 0.33)^T$ we can compute the sample covariance matrix for X_3 using Eq. (3.15):

$$\widehat{\boldsymbol{\Sigma}}_{33} = \begin{pmatrix} 0.222 & -0.111 & -0.111 \\ -0.111 & 0.222 & -0.111 \\ -0.111 & -0.111 & 0.222 \end{pmatrix}$$

Using Eq. (3.26) we obtain

$$\widehat{\boldsymbol{\Sigma}}_{13} = \begin{pmatrix} -0.067 & 0.16 & -0.093 \\ 0.082 & -0.038 & -0.044 \\ 0.011 & -0.096 & 0.084 \\ -0.027 & -0.027 & 0.053 \end{pmatrix}$$

$$\widehat{\boldsymbol{\Sigma}}_{23} = \begin{pmatrix} 0.076 & -0.098 & 0.022 \\ -0.042 & 0.044 & -0.002 \\ -0.033 & 0.053 & -0.02 \end{pmatrix}$$

Combined with $\widehat{\boldsymbol{\Sigma}}_{11}$, $\widehat{\boldsymbol{\Sigma}}_{22}$ and $\widehat{\boldsymbol{\Sigma}}_{12}$ from Example 3.8, the final sample covariance matrix is the 10×10 symmetric matrix given as

$$\widehat{\boldsymbol{\Sigma}} = \begin{pmatrix} \widehat{\boldsymbol{\Sigma}}_{11} & \widehat{\boldsymbol{\Sigma}}_{12} & \widehat{\boldsymbol{\Sigma}}_{13} \\ \widehat{\boldsymbol{\Sigma}}_{12}^T & \widehat{\boldsymbol{\Sigma}}_{22} & \widehat{\boldsymbol{\Sigma}}_{23} \\ \widehat{\boldsymbol{\Sigma}}_{13}^T & \widehat{\boldsymbol{\Sigma}}_{23}^T & \widehat{\boldsymbol{\Sigma}}_{33} \end{pmatrix}$$

3.3.1 **Multiway Contingency Analysis**

For multiway dependence analysis, we have to first determine the empirical joint probability mass function for $\mathbf{X}$:

$$\hat{f}(\mathbf{e}_{1i_1}, \mathbf{e}_{2i_2}, \ldots, \mathbf{e}_{di_d}) = \frac{1}{n} \sum_{k=1}^{n} I_{i_1 i_2 \ldots i_d}(\mathbf{x}_k) = \frac{n_{i_1 i_2 \ldots i_d}}{n} = \hat{p}_{i_1 i_2 \ldots i_d}$$

where $I_{i_1 i_2 \ldots i_d}$ is the indicator variable

$$I_{i_1 i_2 \ldots i_d}(\mathbf{x}_k) = \begin{cases} 1 & \text{if } x_{k1} = \mathbf{e}_{1i_1}, x_{k2} = \mathbf{e}_{2i_2}, \ldots, x_{kd} = \mathbf{e}_{di_d} \\ 0 & \text{otherwise} \end{cases}$$

The sum of $I_{i_1 i_2 \ldots i_d}$ over all the n points in the sample yields the number of occurrences, $n_{i_1 i_2 \ldots i_d}$, of the symbolic vector $(a_{1i_1}, a_{2i_2}, \ldots, a_{di_d})$. Dividing the occurrences by the sample size results in the probability of observing those symbols. Using the notation $\mathbf{i} = (i_1, i_2, \ldots, i_d)$ to denote the index tuple, we can write the joint empirical PMF as the d-dimensional matrix $\widehat{\mathbf{P}}$ of size $m_1 \times m_2 \times \cdots \times m_d = \prod_{i=1}^{d} m_i$, given as

$$\widehat{\mathbf{P}}(\mathbf{i}) = \{\hat{p}_\mathbf{i}\} \text{ for all index tuples } \mathbf{i}, \text{ with } 1 \leq i_1 \leq m_1, \ldots, 1 \leq i_d \leq m_d$$

where $\hat{p}_\mathbf{i} = \hat{p}_{i_1 i_2 \ldots i_d}$. The d-dimensional contingency table is then given as

$$\mathbf{N} = n \times \widehat{\mathbf{P}} = \{n_\mathbf{i}\} \text{ for all index tuples } \mathbf{i}, \text{ with } 1 \leq i_1 \leq m_1, \ldots, 1 \leq i_d \leq m_d$$

where $n_\mathbf{i} = n_{i_1 i_2 \ldots i_d}$. The contingency table is augmented with the marginal count vectors $\mathbf{N}_i$ for all d attributes $\mathbf{X}_i$:

$$\mathbf{N}_i = n\hat{\mathbf{p}}_i = \begin{pmatrix} n_1^i \\ \vdots \\ n_{m_i}^i \end{pmatrix}$$

where $\hat{\mathbf{p}}_i$ is the empirical PMF for $\mathbf{X}_i$.

χ^2-**Test**

We can test for a d-way dependence between the d categorical attributes using the null hypothesis H_0 that they are d-way independent. The alternative hypothesis H_1 is that they are not d-way independent, that is, they are dependent in some way. Note that d-dimensional contingency analysis indicates whether all d attributes taken together are independent or not. In general we may have to conduct k-way contingency analysis to test if any subset of $k \leq d$ attributes are independent or not.

Under the null hypothesis, the expected number of occurrences of the symbol tuple $(a_{1i_1}, a_{2i_2}, \ldots, a_{di_d})$ is given as

$$e_\mathbf{i} = n \cdot \hat{p}_\mathbf{i} = n \cdot \prod_{j=1}^{d} \hat{p}_{i_j}^j = \frac{n_{i_1}^1 n_{i_2}^2 \ldots n_{i_d}^d}{n^{d-1}} \tag{3.27}$$

The chi-squared statistic measures the difference between the observed counts $n_{\mathbf{i}}$ and the expected counts $e_{\mathbf{i}}$:

$$\boxed{\chi^2 = \sum_{\mathbf{i}} \frac{(n_{\mathbf{i}} - e_{\mathbf{i}})^2}{e_{\mathbf{i}}}} = \sum_{i_1=1}^{m_1}\sum_{i_2=1}^{m_2}\cdots\sum_{i_d=1}^{m_d} \frac{(n_{i_1,i_2,\ldots,i_d} - e_{i_1,i_2,\ldots,i_d})^2}{e_{i_1,i_2,\ldots,i_d}} \qquad (3.28)$$

The χ^2 statistic follows a chi-squared density function with q degrees of freedom. For the d-way contingency table we can compute q by noting that there are ostensibly $\prod_{i=1}^{d} |dom(X_i)|$ independent parameters (the counts). However, we have to remove $\sum_{i=1}^{d} |dom(X_i)|$ degrees of freedom because the marginal count vector along each dimension $\mathbf{X}_i$ must equal $\mathbf{N}_i$. However, doing so removes one of the parameters d times, so we need to add back $d - 1$ to the free parameters count. The total number of degrees of freedom is given as

$$q = \prod_{i=1}^{d} |dom(X_i)| - \sum_{i=1}^{d} |dom(X_i)| + (d-1)$$

$$= \left(\prod_{i=1}^{d} m_i\right) - \left(\sum_{i=1}^{d} m_i\right) + d - 1 \qquad (3.29)$$

To reject the null hypothesis, we have to check whether the p-value of the observed χ^2 value is smaller than the desired significance level α (say $\alpha = 0.01$) using the chi-squared density with q degrees of freedom [Eq. (3.23)].

Example 3.12. Consider the 3-way contingency table in Figure 3.4. It shows the observed counts for each tuple of symbols (a_{1i}, a_{2j}, a_{3k}) for the three attributes sepal length (X_1), sepal width (X_2), and class (X_3). From the marginal counts for X_1 and X_2 in Table 3.5, and the fact that all three values of X_3 occur 50 times, we can compute the expected counts [Eq. (3.27)] for each cell. For instance,

$$e_{(4,1,1)} = \frac{n_4^1 \cdot n_1^2 \cdot n_1^3}{150^2} = \frac{45 \cdot 47 \cdot 50}{150 \cdot 150} = 4.7$$

The expected counts are the same for all three values of X_3 and are given in Table 3.7.

The value of the χ^2 statistic [Eq. (3.28)] is given as

$$\chi^2 = 231.06$$

Using Eq. (3.29), the number of degrees of freedom is given as

$$q = 4 \cdot 3 \cdot 3 - (4 + 3 + 3) + 2 = 36 - 10 + 2 = 28$$

In Figure 3.4 the counts in bold are the dependent parameters. All other counts are independent. In fact, any eight distinct cells could have been chosen as the dependent parameters.

For a significance level of $\alpha = 0.01$, the critical value of the chi-square distribution is $v_\alpha = 48.28$. The observed value of $\chi^2 = 231.06$ is much greater than v_α, and it is thus extremely unlikely to happen under the null hypothesis; its p-value is

$$\text{p-value}(231.06) = 7.91 \times 10^{-34}$$

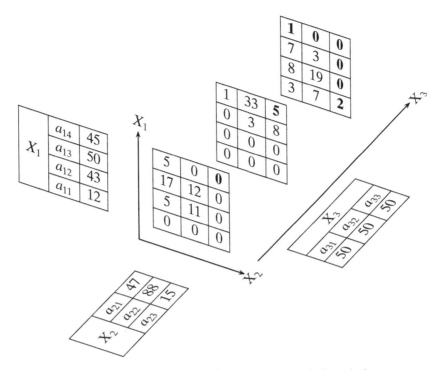

Figure 3.4. 3-Way contingency table (with marginal counts along each dimension).

Table 3.7. 3-Way expected counts

		$X_3(a_{31}/a_{32}/a_{33})$		
		X_2		
		a_{21}	a_{22}	a_{23}
X_1	a_{11}	1.25	2.35	0.40
	a_{12}	4.49	8.41	1.43
	a_{13}	5.22	9.78	1.67
	a_{14}	4.70	8.80	1.50

We conclude that the three attributes are not 3-way independent, but rather there is some dependence between them. However, this example also highlights one of the pitfalls of multiway contingency analysis. We can observe in Figure 3.4 that many of the observed counts are zero. This is due to the fact that the sample size is small, and we cannot reliably estimate all the multiway counts. Consequently, the dependence test may not be reliable as well.

3.4 DISTANCE AND ANGLE

With the modeling of categorical attributes as multivariate Bernoulli variables, it is possible to compute the distance or the angle between any two points $\mathbf{x}_i$ and $\mathbf{x}_j$:

$$\mathbf{x}_i = \begin{pmatrix} \mathbf{e}_{1i_1} \\ \vdots \\ \mathbf{e}_{di_d} \end{pmatrix} \qquad\qquad \mathbf{x}_j = \begin{pmatrix} \mathbf{e}_{1j_1} \\ \vdots \\ \mathbf{e}_{dj_d} \end{pmatrix}$$

The different measures of distance and similarity rely on the number of matching and mismatching values (or symbols) across the d attributes $\mathbf{X}_k$. For instance, we can compute the number of matching values s via the dot product:

$$s = \mathbf{x}_i^T \mathbf{x}_j = \sum_{k=1}^{d} (\mathbf{e}_{ki_k})^T \mathbf{e}_{kj_k}$$

On the other hand, the number of mismatches is simply $d - s$. Also useful is the norm of each point:

$$\|\mathbf{x}_i\|^2 = \mathbf{x}_i^T \mathbf{x}_i = d$$

Euclidean Distance

The Euclidean distance between $\mathbf{x}_i$ and $\mathbf{x}_j$ is given as

$$\|\mathbf{x}_i - \mathbf{x}_j\| = \sqrt{\mathbf{x}_i^T \mathbf{x}_i - 2\mathbf{x}_i \mathbf{x}_j + \mathbf{x}_j^T \mathbf{x}_j} = \sqrt{2(d - s)}$$

Thus, the maximum Euclidean distance between any two points is $\sqrt{2d}$, which happens when there are no common symbols between them, that is, when $s = 0$.

Hamming Distance

The *Hamming distance* between $\mathbf{x}_i$ and $\mathbf{x}_j$ is defined as the number of mismatched values:

$$\delta_H(\mathbf{x}_i, \mathbf{x}_j) = d - s = \frac{1}{2}\|\mathbf{x}_i - \mathbf{x}_j\|^2$$

Hamming distance is thus equivalent to half the squared Euclidean distance.

Cosine Similarity

The cosine of the angle between $\mathbf{x}_i$ and $\mathbf{x}_j$ is given as

$$\cos\theta = \frac{\mathbf{x}_i^T \mathbf{x}_j}{\|\mathbf{x}_i\| \cdot \|\mathbf{x}_j\|} = \frac{s}{d}$$

Jaccard Coefficient

The *Jaccard Coefficient* is a commonly used similarity measure between two categorical points. It is defined as the ratio of the number of matching values to the number of distinct values that appear in both $\mathbf{x}_i$ and $\mathbf{x}_j$, across the d attributes:

$$J(\mathbf{x}_i, \mathbf{x}_j) = \frac{s}{2(d - s) + s} = \frac{s}{2d - s}$$

where we utilize the observation that when the two points do not match for dimension k, they contribute 2 to the distinct symbol count; otherwise, if they match, the number of distinct symbols increases by 1. Over the $d - s$ mismatches and s matches, the number of distinct symbols is $2(d - s) + s$.

Example 3.13. Consider the 3-dimensional categorical data from Example 3.11. The symbolic point (Short, Medium, iris-versicolor) is modeled as the vector

$$\mathbf{x}_1 = \begin{pmatrix} \mathbf{e}_{12} \\ \mathbf{e}_{22} \\ \mathbf{e}_{31} \end{pmatrix} = (0,1,0,0 \mid 0,1,0 \mid 1,0,0)^T \in \mathbb{R}^{10}$$

and the symbolic point (VeryShort, Medium, iris-setosa) is modeled as

$$\mathbf{x}_2 = \begin{pmatrix} \mathbf{e}_{11} \\ \mathbf{e}_{22} \\ \mathbf{e}_{32} \end{pmatrix} = (1,0,0,0 \mid 0,1,0 \mid 0,1,0)^T \in \mathbb{R}^{10}$$

The number of matching symbols is given as

$$s = \mathbf{x}_1^T \mathbf{x}_2 = (\mathbf{e}_{12})^T \mathbf{e}_{11} + (\mathbf{e}_{22})^T \mathbf{e}_{22} + (\mathbf{e}_{31})^T \mathbf{e}_{32}$$

$$= \begin{pmatrix} 0 & 1 & 0 & 0 \end{pmatrix} \begin{pmatrix} 1 \\ 0 \\ 0 \\ 0 \end{pmatrix} + \begin{pmatrix} 0 & 1 & 0 \end{pmatrix} \begin{pmatrix} 0 \\ 1 \\ 0 \end{pmatrix} + \begin{pmatrix} 1 & 0 & 0 \end{pmatrix} \begin{pmatrix} 0 \\ 1 \\ 0 \end{pmatrix}$$

$$= 0 + 1 + 0 = 1$$

The Euclidean and Hamming distances are given as

$$\|\mathbf{x}_1 - \mathbf{x}_2\| = \sqrt{2(d - s)} = \sqrt{2 \cdot 2} = \sqrt{4} = 2$$
$$\delta_H(\mathbf{x}_1, \mathbf{x}_2) = d - s = 3 - 1 = 2$$

The cosine and Jaccard similarity are given as

$$\cos\theta = \frac{s}{d} = \frac{1}{3} = 0.333$$

$$J(\mathbf{x}_1, \mathbf{x}_2) = \frac{s}{2d - s} = \frac{1}{5} = 0.2$$

3.5 DISCRETIZATION

Discretization, also called *binning*, converts numeric attributes into categorical ones. It is usually applied for data mining methods that cannot handle numeric attributes. It can also help in reducing the number of values for an attribute, especially if there is noise in the numeric measurements; discretization allows one to ignore small and irrelevant differences in the values.

Formally, given a numeric attribute X, and a random sample $\{x_i\}_{i=1}^n$ of size n drawn from X, the discretization task is to divide the value range of X into k consecutive intervals, also called *bins*, by finding $k-1$ boundary values $v_1, v_2, \ldots, v_{k-1}$ that yield the k intervals:

$$[x_{min}, v_1], \ (v_1, v_2], \ \ldots, \ (v_{k-1}, x_{max}]$$

where the extremes of the range of X are given as

$$x_{min} = \min_i\{x_i\} \qquad\qquad x_{max} = \max_i\{x_i\}$$

The resulting k intervals or bins, which span the entire range of X, are usually mapped to symbolic values that comprise the domain for the new categorical attribute X.

Equal-Width Intervals

The simplest binning approach is to partition the range of X into k *equal-width* intervals. The interval width is simply the range of X divided by k:

$$w = \frac{x_{max} - x_{min}}{k}$$

Thus, the ith interval boundary is given as

$$v_i = x_{min} + iw, \text{ for } i = 1, \ldots, k-1$$

Equal-Frequency Intervals

In *equal-frequency* binning we divide the range of X into intervals that contain (approximately) equal number of points; equal frequency may not be possible due to repeated values. The intervals can be computed from the empirical quantile or inverse cumulative distribution function $\hat{F}^{-1}(q)$ for X [Eq. (2.2)]. Recall that $\hat{F}^{-1}(q) = \min\{x \mid P(X \le x) \ge q\}$, for $q \in [0, 1]$. In particular, we require that each interval contain $1/k$ of the probability mass; therefore, the interval boundaries are given as follows:

$$v_i = \hat{F}^{-1}(i/k) \text{ for } i = 1, \ldots, k-1$$

Example 3.14. Consider the `sepal length` attribute in the Iris dataset. Its minimum and maximum values are

$$x_{min} = 4.3 \qquad\qquad x_{max} = 7.9$$

We discretize it into $k = 4$ bins using equal-width binning. The width of an interval is given as

$$w = \frac{7.9 - 4.3}{4} = \frac{3.6}{4} = 0.9$$

and therefore the interval boundaries are

$$v_1 = 4.3 + 0.9 = 5.2 \qquad v_2 = 4.3 + 2 \cdot 0.9 = 6.1 \qquad v_3 = 4.3 + 3 \cdot 0.9 = 7.0$$

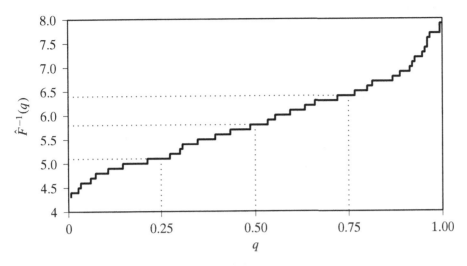

Figure 3.5. Empirical inverse CDF: `sepal length`.

Table 3.8. Equal-frequency discretization: `sepal length`

Bin	Width	Count
[4.3, 5.1]	0.8	$n_1 = 41$
(5.1, 5.8]	0.7	$n_2 = 39$
(5.8, 6.4]	0.6	$n_3 = 35$
(6.4, 7.9]	1.5	$n_4 = 35$

The four resulting bins for `sepal length` are shown in Table 3.1, which also shows the number of points n_i in each bin, which are not balanced among the bins.

For equal-frequency discretization, consider the empirical inverse cumulative distribution function (CDF) for `sepal length` shown in Figure 3.5. With $k = 4$ bins, the bin boundaries are the quartile values (which are shown as dashed lines):

$$v_1 = \hat{F}^{-1}(0.25) = 5.1 \qquad v_2 = \hat{F}^{-1}(0.50) = 5.8 \qquad v_3 = \hat{F}^{-1}(0.75) = 6.4$$

The resulting intervals are shown in Table 3.8. We can see that although the interval widths vary, they contain a more balanced number of points. We do not get identical counts for all the bins because many values are repeated; for instance, there are nine points with value 5.1 and there are seven points with value 5.8.

3.6 FURTHER READING

For a comprehensive introduction to categorical data analysis see Agresti (2012). Some aspects also appear in Wasserman (2004). For an entropy-based supervised discretization method that takes the class attribute into account see Fayyad and Irani (1993).

Agresti, A. (2012). *Categorical Data Analysis*. 3rd ed. Hoboken, NJ: John Wiley & Sons.

Fayyad, U. M. and Irani, K. B. (1993). Multi-interval discretization of continuous-valued attributes for classification learning. *Proceedings of the 13th International Joint Conference on Artificial Intelligence*. Morgan-Kaufmann, pp. 1022–1027.

Wasserman, L. (2004). *All of Statistics: A Concise Course in Statistical Inference*. New York: Springer Science + Business Media.

3.7 EXERCISES

Q1. Show that for categorical points, the cosine similarity between any two vectors in lies in the range $\cos\theta \in [0,1]$, and consequently $\theta \in [0°, 90°]$.

Q2. Prove that $E[(\mathbf{X}_1 - \boldsymbol{\mu}_1)(\mathbf{X}_2 - \boldsymbol{\mu}_2)^T] = E[\mathbf{X}_1\mathbf{X}_2^T] - E[\mathbf{X}_1]E[\mathbf{X}_2]^T$.

Table 3.9. Contingency table for Q3

	$Z = f$		$Z = g$	
	$Y = d$	$Y = e$	$Y = d$	$Y = e$
$X = a$	5	10	10	5
$X = b$	15	5	5	20
$X = c$	20	10	25	10

Q3. Consider the 3-way contingency table for attributes X, Y, Z shown in Table 3.9. Compute the χ^2 metric for the correlation between Y and Z. Are they dependent or independent at the 5% significance level? See Table 3.10 for the critical values of the χ^2 distribution.

Table 3.10. Critical values of the χ^2 distribution for different degrees of freedom (q) and significance levels (α): For example, for $q = 5$, the critical value at significance level $\alpha = 0.1$ is $v_\alpha = 9.236$.

$q \backslash \alpha$	0.995	0.99	0.975	0.95	0.90	0.10	0.05	0.025	0.01	0.005
1	—	—	0.001	0.004	0.016	2.706	3.841	5.024	6.635	7.879
2	0.010	0.020	0.051	0.103	0.211	4.605	5.991	7.378	9.210	10.597
3	0.072	0.115	0.216	0.352	0.584	6.251	7.815	9.348	11.345	12.838
4	0.207	0.297	0.484	0.711	1.064	7.779	9.488	11.143	13.277	14.860
5	0.412	0.554	0.831	1.145	1.610	9.236	11.070	12.833	15.086	16.750
6	0.676	0.872	1.237	1.635	2.204	10.645	12.592	14.449	16.812	18.548

Q4. Consider the "mixed" data given in Table 3.11. Here X_1 is a numeric attribute and X_2 is a categorical one. Assume that the domain of X_2 is given as $dom(X_2) = \{a, b\}$. Answer the following questions.

Table 3.11. Dataset for Q4 and Q5

X_1	X_2
0.3	a
−0.3	b
0.44	a
−0.60	a
0.40	a
1.20	b
−0.12	a
−1.60	b
1.60	b
−1.32	a

(a) What is the mean vector for this dataset?

(b) What is the covariance matrix?

Q5. In Table 3.11, assuming that X_1 is discretized into three bins, as follows:

$$c_1 = (-2, -0.5]$$
$$c_2 = (-0.5, 0.5]$$
$$c_3 = (0.5, 2]$$

Answer the following questions:

(a) Construct the contingency table between the discretized X_1 and X_2 attributes. Include the marginal counts.

(b) Compute the χ^2 statistic between them.

(c) Determine whether they are dependent or not at the 5% significance level. Use the χ^2 critical values from Table 3.10.

CHAPTER 4   Graph Data

The traditional paradigm in data analysis typically assumes that each data instance is independent of another. However, often data instances may be connected or linked to other instances via various types of relationships. The instances themselves may be described by various attributes. What emerges is a network or graph of instances (or nodes), connected by links (or edges). Both the nodes and edges in the graph may have several attributes that may be numerical or categorical, or even more complex (e.g., time series data). Increasingly, today's massive data is in the form of such graphs or networks. Examples include the World Wide Web (with its Web pages and hyperlinks), social networks (wikis, blogs, tweets, and other social media data), semantic networks (ontologies), biological networks (protein interactions, gene regulation networks, metabolic pathways), citation networks for scientific literature, and so on. In this chapter we look at the analysis of the link structure in graphs that arise from these kinds of networks. We will study basic topological properties as well as models that give rise to such graphs.

4.1 GRAPH CONCEPTS

Graphs

Formally, a *graph* $G = (V, E)$ is a mathematical structure consisting of a finite nonempty set V of *vertices* or *nodes*, and a set $E \subseteq V \times V$ of *edges* consisting of *unordered* pairs of vertices. An edge from a node to itself, (v_i, v_i), is called a *loop*. An undirected graph without loops is called a *simple graph*. Unless mentioned explicitly, we will consider a graph to be simple. An edge $e = (v_i, v_j)$ between v_i and v_j is said to be *incident with* nodes v_i and v_j; in this case we also say that v_i and v_j are *adjacent* to one another, and that they are *neighbors*. The number of nodes in the graph G, given as $|V| = n$, is called the *order* of the graph, and the number of edges in the graph, given as $|E| = m$, is called the *size* of G.

A *directed graph* or *digraph* has an edge set E consisting of *ordered* pairs of vertices. A directed edge (v_i, v_j) is also called an *arc*, and is said to be *from v_i to v_j*. We also say that v_i is the *tail* and v_j the *head* of the arc.

A *weighted graph* consists of a graph together with a weight w_{ij} for each edge $(v_i, v_j) \in E$. Every graph can be considered to be a weighted graph in which the edges have weight one.

Subgraphs

A graph $H = (V_H, E_H)$ is called a *subgraph* of $G = (V, E)$ if $V_H \subseteq V$ and $E_H \subseteq E$. We also say that G is a *supergraph* of H. Given a subset of the vertices $V' \subseteq V$, the *induced subgraph* $G' = (V', E')$ consists exactly of all the edges present in G between vertices in V'. More formally, for all $v_i, v_j \in V'$, $(v_i, v_j) \in E' \iff (v_i, v_j) \in E$. In other words, two nodes are adjacent in G' if and only if they are adjacent in G. A (sub)graph is called *complete* (or a *clique*) if there exists an edge between all pairs of nodes.

Degree

The *degree* of a node $v_i \in V$ is the number of edges incident with it, and is denoted as $d(v_i)$ or just d_i. The *degree sequence* of a graph is the list of the degrees of the nodes sorted in non-increasing order.

Let N_k denote the number of vertices with degree k. The *degree frequency distribution* of a graph is given as

$$(N_0, N_1, \ldots, N_t)$$

where t is the maximum degree for a node in G. Let X be a random variable denoting the degree of a node. The *degree distribution* of a graph gives the probability mass function f for X, given as

$$\left(f(0), f(1), \ldots, f(t) \right)$$

where $f(k) = P(X = k) = \frac{N_k}{n}$ is the probability of a node with degree k, given as the number of nodes N_k with degree k, divided by the total number of nodes n. In graph analysis, we typically make the assumption that the input graph represents a population, and therefore we write f instead of $\hat{f}$ for the probability distributions.

For directed graphs, the *indegree* of node v_i, denoted as $id(v_i)$, is the number of edges with v_i as head, that is, the number of incoming edges at v_i. The *outdegree* of v_i, denoted $od(v_i)$, is the number of edges with v_i as the tail, that is, the number of outgoing edges from v_i.

Path and Distance

A *walk* in a graph G between nodes x and y is an ordered sequence of vertices, starting at x and ending at y,

$$x = v_0, \; v_1, \; \ldots, \; v_{t-1}, \; v_t = y$$

such that there is an edge between every pair of consecutive vertices, that is, $(v_{i-1}, v_i) \in E$ for all $i = 1, 2, \ldots, t$. The length of the walk, t, is measured in terms of *hops* – the number of edges along the walk. In a walk, there is no restriction on the number of times a given vertex may appear in the sequence; thus both the vertices and edges may be repeated. A walk starting and ending at the same vertex (i.e., with $y = x$) is called *closed*. A *trail* is a walk with distinct edges, and a *path* is a walk with *distinct* vertices (with the exception of the start and end vertices). A closed path with length

$t \geq 3$ is called a *cycle*, that is, a cycle begins and ends at the same vertex and has distinct nodes.

A path of minimum length between nodes x and y is called a *shortest path*, and the length of the shortest path is called the *distance* between x and y, denoted as $d(x, y)$. If no path exists between the two nodes, the distance is assumed to be $d(x, y) = \infty$.

Connectedness

Two nodes v_i and v_j are said to be *connected* if there exists a path between them. A graph is *connected* if there is a path between all pairs of vertices. A *connected component*, or just *component*, of a graph is a maximal connected subgraph. If a graph has only one component it is connected; otherwise it is *disconnected*, as by definition there cannot be a path between two different components.

For a directed graph, we say that it is *strongly connected* if there is a (directed) path between all ordered pairs of vertices. We say that it is *weakly connected* if there exists a path between node pairs only by considering edges as undirected.

Example 4.1. Figure 4.1(a) shows a graph with $|V| = 8$ vertices and $|E| = 11$ edges. Because $(v_1, v_5) \in E$, we say that v_1 and v_5 are adjacent. The degree of v_1 is $d(v_1) = d_1 = 4$. The degree sequence of the graph is

$$(4, 4, 4, 3, 2, 2, 2, 1)$$

and therefore its degree frequency distribution is given as

$$(N_0, N_1, N_2, N_3, N_4) = (0, 1, 3, 1, 3)$$

We have $N_0 = 0$ because there are no isolated vertices, and $N_4 = 3$ because there are three nodes, v_1, v_4 and v_5, that have degree $k = 4$; the other numbers are obtained in a similar fashion. The degree distribution is given as

$$\left(f(0), f(1), f(2), f(3), f(4) \right) = (0, 0.125, 0.375, 0.125, 0.375)$$

The vertex sequence $(v_3, v_1, v_2, v_5, v_1, v_2, v_6)$ is a walk of length 6 between v_3 and v_6. We can see that vertices v_1 and v_2 have been visited more than once. In

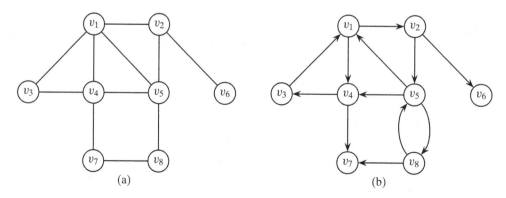

Figure 4.1. (a) A graph (undirected). (b) A directed graph.

contrast, the vertex sequence $(v_3, v_4, v_7, v_8, v_5, v_2, v_6)$ is a path of length 6 between v_3 and v_6. However, this is not the shortest path between them, which happens to be (v_3, v_1, v_2, v_6) with length 3. Thus, the distance between them is given as $d(v_3, v_6) = 3$.

Figure 4.1(b) shows a directed graph with 8 vertices and 12 edges. We can see that edge (v_5, v_8) is distinct from edge (v_8, v_5). The indegree of v_7 is $id(v_7) = 2$, whereas its outdegree is $od(v_7) = 0$. Thus, there is no (directed) path from v_7 to any other vertex.

Adjacency Matrix

A graph $G = (V, E)$, with $|V| = n$ vertices, can be conveniently represented in the form of an $n \times n$, symmetric binary *adjacency matrix*, $\mathbf{A}$, defined as

$$\mathbf{A}(i, j) = \begin{cases} 1 & \text{if } v_i \text{ is adjacent to } v_j \\ 0 & \text{otherwise} \end{cases} \tag{4.1}$$

If the graph is directed, then the adjacency matrix $\mathbf{A}$ is not symmetric, as $(v_i, v_j) \in E$ obviously does not imply that $(v_j, v_i) \in E$.

If the graph is weighted, then we obtain an $n \times n$ *weighted adjacency matrix*, $\mathbf{A}$, defined as

$$\mathbf{A}(i, j) = \begin{cases} w_{ij} & \text{if } v_i \text{ is adjacent to } v_j \\ 0 & \text{otherwise} \end{cases} \tag{4.2}$$

where w_{ij} is the weight on edge $(v_i, v_j) \in E$. A weighted adjacency matrix can always be converted into a binary one, if desired, by using some threshold τ on the edge weights

$$\mathbf{A}(i, j) = \begin{cases} 1 & \text{if } w_{ij} \geq \tau \\ 0 & \text{otherwise} \end{cases} \tag{4.3}$$

Graphs from Data Matrix

Many datasets that are not in the form of a graph can nevertheless be converted into one. Let $\mathbf{D}$ be a dataset consisting of n points $\mathbf{x}_i \in \mathbb{R}^d$ in a d-dimensional space. We can define a weighted graph $G = (V, E)$, where there exists a node for each point in $\mathbf{D}$, and there exists an edge between each pair of points, with weight

$$w_{ij} = sim(\mathbf{x}_i, \mathbf{x}_j)$$

where $sim(\mathbf{x}_i, \mathbf{x}_j)$ denotes the similarity between points $\mathbf{x}_i$ and $\mathbf{x}_j$. For instance, similarity can be defined as being inversely related to the Euclidean distance between the points via the transformation

$$w_{ij} = sim(\mathbf{x}_i, \mathbf{x}_j) = \exp\left\{ -\frac{\|\mathbf{x}_i - \mathbf{x}_j\|^2}{2\sigma^2} \right\} \tag{4.4}$$

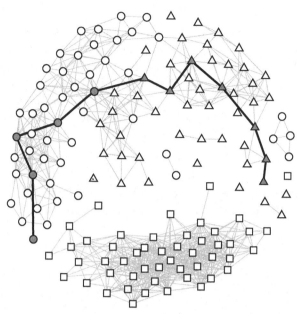

Figure 4.2. Iris similarity graph.

where σ is the spread parameter (equivalent to the standard deviation in the normal
density function). This transformation restricts the similarity function $sim()$ to lie in the
range $[0, 1]$. One can then choose an appropriate threshold τ and convert the weighted
adjacency matrix into a binary one via Eq. (4.3).

Example 4.2. Figure 4.2 shows the similarity graph for the Iris dataset (see
Table 1.1). The pairwise similarity between distinct pairs of points was computed
using Eq. (4.4), with $\sigma = 1/\sqrt{2}$ (we do not allow loops, to keep the graph simple).
The mean similarity between points was 0.197, with a standard deviation of 0.290.

A binary adjacency matrix was obtained via Eq. (4.3) using a threshold of $\tau =$
0.777, which results in an edge between points having similarity higher than two
standard deviations from the mean. The resulting Iris graph has 150 nodes and 753
edges.

The nodes in the Iris graph in Figure 4.2 have also been categorized according
to their class. The circles correspond to class `iris-versicolor`, the triangles
to `iris-virginica`, and the squares to `iris-setosa`. The graph has two big
components, one of which is exclusively composed of nodes labeled as `iris-setosa`.

4.2 TOPOLOGICAL ATTRIBUTES

In this section we study some of the purely topological, that is, edge-based or structural,
attributes of graphs. These attributes are *local* if they apply to only a single node (or
an edge), and *global* if they refer to the entire graph.

Degree

We have already defined the degree of a node v_i as the number of its neighbors. A more general definition that holds even when the graph is weighted is as follows:

$$d_i = \sum_j \mathbf{A}(i, j) \tag{4.5}$$

The degree is clearly a local attribute of each node. One of the simplest global attribute is the *average degree*:

$$\mu_d = \frac{\sum_i d_i}{n} \tag{4.6}$$

The preceding definitions can easily be generalized for (weighted) directed graphs. For example, we can obtain the indegree and outdegree by taking the summation over the incoming and outgoing edges, as follows:

$$id(v_i) = \sum_j \mathbf{A}(j, i)$$

$$od(v_i) = \sum_j \mathbf{A}(i, j)$$

The average indegree and average outdegree can be obtained likewise.

Average Path Length

The *average path length*, also called the *characteristic path length*, of a connected graph is given as

$$\mu_L = \frac{\sum_i \sum_{j>i} d(v_i, v_j)}{\binom{n}{2}} = \frac{2}{n(n-1)} \sum_i \sum_{j>i} d(v_i, v_j) \tag{4.7}$$

where n is the number of nodes in the graph, and $d(v_i, v_j)$ is the distance between v_i and v_j. For a directed graph, the average is over all ordered pairs of vertices:

$$\mu_L = \frac{1}{n(n-1)} \sum_i \sum_j d(v_i, v_j) \tag{4.8}$$

For a disconnected graph the average is taken over only the connected pairs of vertices.

Eccentricity

The *eccentricity* of a node v_i is the maximum distance from v_i to any other node in the graph:

$$e(v_i) = \max_j \{d(v_i, v_j)\} \tag{4.9}$$

If the graph is disconnected the eccentricity is computed only over pairs of vertices with finite distance, that is, only for vertices connected by a path.

Radius and Diameter

The *radius* of a connected graph, denoted $r(G)$, is the minimum eccentricity of any node in the graph:

$$r(G) = \min_i \{e(v_i)\} = \min_i \left\{ \max_j \{d(v_i, v_j)\} \right\} \tag{4.10}$$

The *diameter*, denoted $d(G)$, is the maximum eccentricity of any vertex in the graph:

$$d(G) = \max_i \{e(v_i)\} = \max_{i,j} \{d(v_i, v_j)\} \tag{4.11}$$

For a disconnected graph, the diameter is the maximum eccentricity over all the connected components of the graph.

The diameter of a graph G is sensitive to outliers. A more robust notion is *effective diameter*, defined as the minimum number of hops for which a large fraction, typically 90%, of all connected pairs of nodes can reach each other. More formally, let $H(k)$ denote the number of pairs of nodes that can reach each other in k hops or less. The effective diameter is defined as the smallest value of k such that $H(k) \geq 0.9 \times H(d(G))$.

Example 4.3. For the graph in Figure 4.1(a), the eccentricity of node v_4 is $e(v_4) = 3$ because the node farthest from it is v_6 and $d(v_4, v_6) = 3$. The radius of the graph is $r(G) = 2$; both v_1 and v_5 have the least eccentricity value of 2. The diameter of the graph is $d(G) = 4$, as the largest distance over all the pairs is $d(v_6, v_7) = 4$.

The diameter of the Iris graph is $d(G) = 11$, which corresponds to the bold path connecting the gray nodes in Figure 4.2. The degree distribution for the Iris graph is shown in Figure 4.3. The numbers at the top of each bar indicate the frequency.

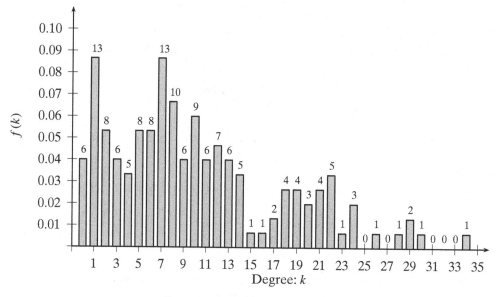

Figure 4.3. Iris graph: degree distribution.

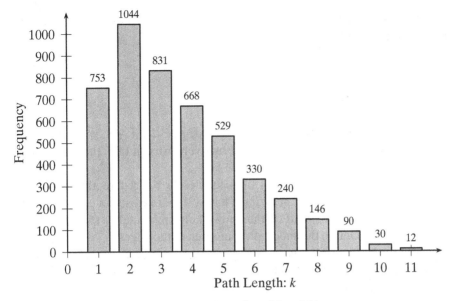

Figure 4.4. Iris graph: path length histogram.

For example, there are exactly 13 nodes with degree 7, which corresponds to the probability $f(7) = \frac{13}{150} = 0.0867$.

The path length histogram for the Iris graph is shown in Figure 4.4. For instance, 1044 node pairs have a distance of 2 hops between them. With $n = 150$ nodes, there are $\binom{n}{2} = 11,175$ pairs. Out of these 6502 pairs are unconnected, and there are a total of 4673 reachable pairs. Out of these $\frac{4175}{4673} = 0.89$ fraction are reachable in 6 hops, and $\frac{4415}{4673} = 0.94$ fraction are reachable in 7 hops. Thus, we can determine that the effective diameter is 7. The average path length is 3.58.

Clustering Coefficient

The *clustering coefficient* of a node v_i is a measure of the density of edges in the neighborhood of v_i. Let $G_i = (V_i, E_i)$ be the subgraph induced by the neighbors of vertex v_i. Note that $v_i \notin V_i$, as we assume that G is simple. Let $|V_i| = n_i$ be the number of neighbors of v_i, and $|E_i| = m_i$ be the number of edges among the neighbors of v_i. The clustering coefficient of v_i is defined as

$$C(v_i) = \frac{\text{no. of edges in } G_i}{\text{maximum number of edges in } G_i} = \frac{m_i}{\binom{n_i}{2}} = \frac{2 \cdot m_i}{n_i(n_i - 1)} \tag{4.12}$$

The clustering coefficient gives an indication about the "cliquishness" of a node's neighborhood, because the denominator corresponds to the case when G_i is a complete subgraph.

The *clustering coefficient* of a graph G is simply the average clustering coefficient over all the nodes, given as

$$C(G) = \frac{1}{n} \sum_i C(v_i) \qquad (4.13)$$

Because $C(v_i)$ is well defined only for nodes with degree $d(v_i) \geq 2$, we can define $C(v_i) = 0$ for nodes with degree less than 2. Alternatively, we can take the summation only over nodes with $d(v_i) \geq 2$.

The clustering coefficient $C(v_i)$ of a node is closely related to the notion of transitive relationships in a graph or network. That is, if there exists an edge between v_i and v_j, and another between v_i and v_k, then how likely are v_j and v_k to be linked or connected to each other. Define the subgraph composed of the edges (v_i, v_j) and (v_i, v_k) to be a *connected triple* centered at v_i. A connected triple centered at v_i that includes (v_j, v_k) is called a *triangle* (a complete subgraph of size 3). The clustering coefficient of node v_i can be expressed as

$$C(v_i) = \frac{\text{no. of triangles including } v_i}{\text{no. of connected triples centered at } v_i}$$

Note that the number of connected triples centered at v_i is simply $\binom{d_i}{2} = \frac{n_i(n_i-1)}{2}$, where $d_i = n_i$ is the number of neighbors of v_i.

Generalizing the aforementioned notion to the entire graph yields the *transitivity* of the graph, defined as

$$T(G) = \frac{3 \times \text{no. of triangles in } G}{\text{no. of connected triples in } G}$$

The factor 3 in the numerator is due to the fact that each triangle contributes to three connected triples centered at each of its three vertices. Informally, transitivity measures the degree to which a friend of your friend is also your friend, say, in a social network.

Efficiency

The *efficiency* for a pair of nodes v_i and v_j is defined as $\frac{1}{d(v_i,v_j)}$. If v_i and v_j are not connected, then $d(v_i, v_j) = \infty$ and the efficiency is $1/\infty = 0$. As such, the smaller the distance between the nodes, the more "efficient" the communication between them. The *efficiency* of a graph G is the average efficiency over all pairs of nodes, whether connected or not, given as

$$\frac{2}{n(n-1)} \sum_i \sum_{j>i} \frac{1}{d(v_i, v_j)}$$

The maximum efficiency value is 1, which holds for a complete graph.

The *local efficiency* for a node v_i is defined as the efficiency of the subgraph G_i induced by the neighbors of v_i. Because $v_i \notin G_i$, the local efficiency is an indication of the local fault tolerance, that is, how efficient is the communication between neighbors of v_i when v_i is removed or deleted from the graph.

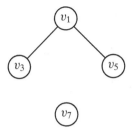

Figure 4.5. Subgraph G_4 induced by node v_4.

Example 4.4. For the graph in Figure 4.1(a), consider node v_4. Its neighborhood graph is shown in Figure 4.5. The clustering coefficient of node v_4 is given as

$$C(v_4) = \frac{2}{\binom{4}{2}} = \frac{2}{6} = 0.33$$

The clustering coefficient for the entire graph (over all nodes) is given as

$$C(G) = \frac{1}{8}\left(\frac{1}{2}+\frac{1}{3}+1+\frac{1}{3}+\frac{1}{3}+0+0+0\right) = \frac{2.5}{8} = 0.3125$$

The local efficiency of v_4 is given as

$$\frac{2}{4\cdot3}\left(\frac{1}{d(v_1,v_3)}+\frac{1}{d(v_1,v_5)}+\frac{1}{d(v_1,v_7)}+\frac{1}{d(v_3,v_5)}+\frac{1}{d(v_3,v_7)}+\frac{1}{d(v_5,v_7)}\right)$$
$$= \frac{1}{6}(1+1+0+0.5+0+0) = \frac{2.5}{6} = 0.417$$

4.3 CENTRALITY ANALYSIS

The notion of *centrality* is used to rank the vertices of a graph in terms of how "central" or important they are. A centrality can be formally defined as a function $c: V \to \mathbb{R}$, that induces a total order on V. We say that v_i is at least as central as v_j if $c(v_i) \geq c(v_j)$.

4.3.1 Basic Centralities

Degree Centrality
The simplest notion of centrality is the degree d_i of a vertex v_i – the higher the degree, the more important or central the vertex. For directed graphs, one may further consider the indegree centrality and outdegree centrality of a vertex.

Eccentricity Centrality
According to this notion, the less eccentric a node is, the more central it is. Eccentricity centrality is thus defined as follows:

$$c(v_i) = \frac{1}{e(v_i)} = \frac{1}{\max_j\{d(v_i,v_j)\}} \tag{4.14}$$

A node v_i that has the least eccentricity, that is, for which the eccentricity equals the graph radius, $e(v_i) = r(G)$, is called a *center node*, whereas a node that has the highest eccentricity, that is, for which eccentricity equals the graph diameter, $e(v_i) = d(G)$, is called a *periphery node*.

Eccentricity centrality is related to the problem of *facility location*, that is, choosing the optimum location for a resource or facility. The central node minimizes the maximum distance to any node in the network, and thus the most central node would be an ideal location for, say, a hospital, because it is desirable to minimize the maximum distance someone has to travel to get to the hospital quickly.

Closeness Centrality

Whereas eccentricity centrality uses the maximum of the distances from a given node, closeness centrality uses the sum of all the distances to rank how central a node is

$$c(v_i) = \frac{1}{\sum_j d(v_i, v_j)} \tag{4.15}$$

A node v_i with the smallest total distance, $\sum_j d(v_i, v_j)$, is called the *median node*.

Closeness centrality optimizes a different objective function for the facility location problem. It tries to minimize the total distance over all the other nodes, and thus a median node, which has the highest closeness centrality, is the optimal one to, say, locate a facility such as a new coffee shop or a mall, as in this case it is not as important to minimize the distance for the farthest node.

Betweenness Centrality

For a given vertex v_i the betweenness centrality measures how many shortest paths between all pairs of vertices include v_i. This gives an indication as to the central "monitoring" role played by v_i for various pairs of nodes. Let η_{jk} denote the number of shortest paths between vertices v_j and v_k, and let $\eta_{jk}(v_i)$ denote the number of such paths that include or contain v_i. Then the fraction of paths through v_i is denoted as

$$\gamma_{jk}(v_i) = \frac{\eta_{jk}(v_i)}{\eta_{jk}}$$

If the two vertices v_j and v_k are not connected, we assume $\gamma_{jk}(v_i) = 0$.

The betweenness centrality for a node v_i is defined as

$$c(v_i) = \sum_{\substack{j \neq i \\ k \neq i \\ k > j}} \sum \gamma_{jk}(v_i) = \sum_{\substack{j \neq i \\ k \neq i \\ k > j}} \sum \frac{\eta_{jk}(v_i)}{\eta_{jk}} \tag{4.16}$$

Example 4.5. Consider Figure 4.1(a). The values for the different node centrality measures are given in Table 4.1. According to degree centrality, nodes v_1, v_4, and v_5 are the most central. The eccentricity centrality is the highest for the center nodes in the graph, which are v_1 and v_5. It is the least for the periphery nodes, of which there are two, v_6 and, v_7.

Table 4.1. Centrality values

Centrality	v_1	v_2	v_3	v_4	v_5	v_6	v_7	v_8
Degree	4	3	2	4	4	1	2	2
Eccentricity $e(v_i)$	0.5 2	0.33 3	0.33 3	0.33 3	0.5 2	0.25 4	0.25 4	0.33 3
Closeness $\sum_j d(v_i, v_j)$	0.100 10	0.083 12	0.071 14	0.091 11	0.100 10	0.056 18	0.067 15	0.071 14
Betweenness	4.5	6	0	5	6.5	0	0.83	1.17

Nodes v_1 and v_5 have the highest closeness centrality value. In terms of betweenness, vertex v_5 is the most central, with a value of 6.5. We can compute this value by considering only those pairs of nodes v_j and v_k that have at least one shortest path passing through v_5, as only these node pairs have $\gamma_{jk}(v_5) > 0$ in Eq. (4.16). We have

$$c(v_5) = \gamma_{18}(v_5) + \gamma_{24}(v_5) + \gamma_{27}(v_5) + \gamma_{28}(v_5) + \gamma_{38}(v_5) + \gamma_{46}(v_5) + \gamma_{48}(v_5) + \gamma_{67}(v_5) + \gamma_{68}(v_5)$$

$$= 1 + \frac{1}{2} + \frac{2}{3} + 1 + \frac{2}{3} + \frac{1}{2} + \frac{1}{2} + \frac{2}{3} + 1 = 6.5$$

4.3.2 Web Centralities

We now consider directed graphs, especially in the context of the Web. For example, hypertext documents have directed links pointing from one document to another; citation networks of scientific articles have directed edges from a paper to the cited papers, and so on. We consider notions of centrality that are particularly suited to such Web-scale graphs.

Prestige

We first look at the notion of *prestige*, or the *eigenvector centrality*, of a node in a directed graph. As a centrality, prestige is supposed to be a measure of the importance or rank of a node. Intuitively the more the links that point to a given node, the higher its prestige. However, prestige does not depend simply on the indegree; it also (recursively) depends on the prestige of the nodes that point to it.

Let $G = (V, E)$ be a directed graph, with $|V| = n$. The adjacency matrix of G is an $n \times n$ asymmetric matrix $\mathbf{A}$ given as

$$\mathbf{A}(u, v) = \begin{cases} 1 & \text{if } (u, v) \in E \\ 0 & \text{if } (u, v) \notin E \end{cases}$$

Let $p(u)$ be a positive real number, called the *prestige* score for node u. Using the intuition that the prestige of a node depends on the prestige of other nodes pointing to

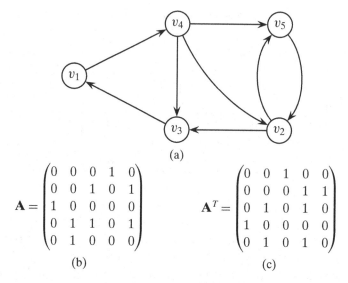

$$\mathbf{A} = \begin{pmatrix} 0 & 0 & 0 & 1 & 0 \\ 0 & 0 & 1 & 0 & 1 \\ 1 & 0 & 0 & 0 & 0 \\ 0 & 1 & 1 & 0 & 1 \\ 0 & 1 & 0 & 0 & 0 \end{pmatrix} \qquad \mathbf{A}^T = \begin{pmatrix} 0 & 0 & 1 & 0 & 0 \\ 0 & 0 & 0 & 1 & 1 \\ 0 & 1 & 0 & 1 & 0 \\ 1 & 0 & 0 & 0 & 0 \\ 0 & 1 & 0 & 1 & 0 \end{pmatrix}$$

(b) (c)

Figure 4.6. Example graph (a), adjacency matrix (b), and its transpose (c).

it, we can obtain the prestige score of a given node v as follows:

$$p(v) = \sum_u \mathbf{A}(u, v) \cdot p(u) = \sum_u \mathbf{A}^T(v, u) \cdot p(u)$$

For example, in Figure 4.6, the prestige of v_5 depends on the prestige of v_2 and v_4.

Across all the nodes, we can recursively express the prestige scores as

$$\mathbf{p}' = \mathbf{A}^T \mathbf{p} \tag{4.17}$$

where $\mathbf{p}$ is an n-dimensional column vector corresponding to the prestige scores for each vertex.

Starting from an initial prestige vector we can use Eq. (4.17) to obtain an updated prestige vector in an iterative manner. In other words, if $\mathbf{p}_{k-1}$ is the prestige vector across all the nodes at iteration $k - 1$, then the updated prestige vector at iteration k is given as

$$\begin{aligned} \mathbf{p}_k &= \mathbf{A}^T \mathbf{p}_{k-1} \\ &= \mathbf{A}^T (\mathbf{A}^T \mathbf{p}_{k-2}) = \left(\mathbf{A}^T\right)^2 \mathbf{p}_{k-2} \\ &= \left(\mathbf{A}^T\right)^2 (\mathbf{A}^T \mathbf{p}_{k-3}) = \left(\mathbf{A}^T\right)^3 \mathbf{p}_{k-3} \\ &= \vdots \\ &= \left(\mathbf{A}^T\right)^k \mathbf{p}_0 \end{aligned}$$

where $\mathbf{p}_0$ is the initial prestige vector. It is well known that the vector $\mathbf{p}_k$ converges to the dominant eigenvector of $\mathbf{A}^T$ with increasing k.

The dominant eigenvector of $\mathbf{A}^T$ and the corresponding eigenvalue can be computed using the *power iteration* approach whose pseudo-code is shown in

Algorithm 4.1. The method starts with the vector $\mathbf{p}_0$, which can be initialized to the vector $(1, 1, \ldots, 1)^T \in \mathbb{R}^n$. In each iteration, we multiply on the left by $\mathbf{A}^T$, and scale the intermediate $\mathbf{p}_k$ vector by dividing it by the maximum entry $\mathbf{p}_k[i]$ in $\mathbf{p}_k$ to prevent numeric overflow. The ratio of the maximum entry in iteration k to that in $k-1$, given as $\lambda = \frac{\mathbf{p}_k[i]}{\mathbf{p}_{k-1}[i]}$, yields an estimate for the eigenvalue. The iterations continue until the difference between successive eigenvector estimates falls below some threshold $\epsilon > 0$.

Algorithm 4.1: Power Iteration Method: Dominant Eigenvector

POWERITERATION ($\mathbf{A}, \epsilon$):

1   $k \leftarrow 0$ // iteration

2   $\mathbf{p}_0 \leftarrow \mathbf{1} \in \mathbb{R}^n$ // initial vector

3   **repeat**

4      $k \leftarrow k+1$

5      $\mathbf{p}_k \leftarrow \mathbf{A}^T \mathbf{p}_{k-1}$ // eigenvector estimate

6      $i \leftarrow \text{argmax}_j\{\mathbf{p}_k[j]\}$ // maximum value index

7      $\lambda \leftarrow \mathbf{p}_k[i]/\mathbf{p}_{k-1}[i]$ // eigenvalue estimate

8      $\mathbf{p}_k \leftarrow \frac{1}{\mathbf{p}_k[i]}\mathbf{p}_k$ // scale vector

9   **until** $\|\mathbf{p}_k - \mathbf{p}_{k-1}\| \le \epsilon$

10   $\mathbf{p} \leftarrow \frac{1}{\|\mathbf{p}_k\|}\mathbf{p}_k$ // normalize eigenvector

11   **return** $\mathbf{p}, \lambda$

Example 4.6. Consider the example shown in Figure 4.6. Starting with an initial prestige vector $\mathbf{p}_0 = (1, 1, 1, 1, 1)^T$, in Table 4.2 we show several iterations of the power method for computing the dominant eigenvector of $\mathbf{A}^T$. In each iteration we obtain $\mathbf{p}_k = \mathbf{A}^T \mathbf{p}_{k-1}$. For example,

$$\mathbf{p}_1 = \mathbf{A}^T \mathbf{p}_0 = \begin{pmatrix} 0 & 0 & 1 & 0 & 0 \\ 0 & 0 & 0 & 1 & 1 \\ 0 & 1 & 0 & 1 & 0 \\ 1 & 0 & 0 & 0 & 0 \\ 0 & 1 & 0 & 1 & 0 \end{pmatrix} \begin{pmatrix} 1 \\ 1 \\ 1 \\ 1 \\ 1 \end{pmatrix} = \begin{pmatrix} 1 \\ 2 \\ 2 \\ 1 \\ 2 \end{pmatrix}$$

Before the next iteration, we scale $\mathbf{p}_1$ by dividing each entry by the maximum value in the vector, which is 2 in this case, to obtain

$$\mathbf{p}_1 = \frac{1}{2} \begin{pmatrix} 1 \\ 2 \\ 2 \\ 1 \\ 2 \end{pmatrix} = \begin{pmatrix} 0.5 \\ 1 \\ 1 \\ 0.5 \\ 1 \end{pmatrix}$$

As k becomes large, we get

$$\mathbf{p}_k = \mathbf{A}^T \mathbf{p}_{k-1} \simeq \lambda \mathbf{p}_{k-1}$$

Table 4.2. Power method via scaling

$\mathbf{p}_0$	$\mathbf{p}_1$		$\mathbf{p}_2$		$\mathbf{p}_3$	
$\begin{pmatrix}1\\1\\1\\1\\1\end{pmatrix}$	$\begin{pmatrix}1\\2\\2\\1\\2\end{pmatrix} \rightarrow$	$\begin{pmatrix}0.5\\1\\1\\0.5\\1\end{pmatrix}$	$\begin{pmatrix}1\\1.5\\1.5\\0.5\\1.5\end{pmatrix} \rightarrow$	$\begin{pmatrix}0.67\\1\\1\\0.33\\1\end{pmatrix}$	$\begin{pmatrix}1\\1.33\\1.33\\0.67\\1.33\end{pmatrix} \rightarrow$	$\begin{pmatrix}0.75\\1\\1\\0.5\\1\end{pmatrix}$
λ	2		1.5		1.33	

$\mathbf{p}_4$		$\mathbf{p}_5$		$\mathbf{p}_6$		$\mathbf{p}_7$	
$\begin{pmatrix}1\\1.5\\1.5\\0.75\\1.5\end{pmatrix} \rightarrow$	$\begin{pmatrix}0.67\\1\\1\\0.5\\1\end{pmatrix}$	$\begin{pmatrix}1\\1.5\\1.5\\0.67\\1.5\end{pmatrix} \rightarrow$	$\begin{pmatrix}0.67\\1\\1\\0.44\\1\end{pmatrix}$	$\begin{pmatrix}1\\1.44\\1.44\\0.67\\1.44\end{pmatrix} \rightarrow$	$\begin{pmatrix}0.69\\1\\1\\0.46\\1\end{pmatrix}$	$\begin{pmatrix}1\\1.46\\1.46\\0.69\\1.46\end{pmatrix} \rightarrow$	$\begin{pmatrix}0.68\\1\\1\\0.47\\1\end{pmatrix}$
1.5		1.5		1.444		1.462	

which implies that the ratio of the maximum element of $\mathbf{p}_k$ to that of $\mathbf{p}_{k-1}$ should approach λ. The table shows this ratio for successive iterations. We can see in Figure 4.7 that within 10 iterations the ratio converges to $\lambda = 1.466$. The scaled dominant eigenvector converges to

$$\mathbf{p}_k = \begin{pmatrix} 1 \\ 1.466 \\ 1.466 \\ 0.682 \\ 1.466 \end{pmatrix}$$

After normalizing it to be a unit vector, the dominant eigenvector is given as

$$\mathbf{p} = \begin{pmatrix} 0.356 \\ 0.521 \\ 0.521 \\ 0.243 \\ 0.521 \end{pmatrix}$$

Thus, in terms of prestige, v_2, v_3, and v_5 have the highest values, as all of them have indegree 2 and are pointed to by nodes with the same incoming values of prestige. On the other hand, although v_1 and v_4 have the same indegree, v_1 is ranked higher, because v_3 contributes its prestige to v_1, but v_4 gets its prestige only from v_1.

PageRank

PageRank is a method for computing the prestige or centrality of nodes in the context of Web search. The Web graph consists of pages (the nodes) connected by hyperlinks

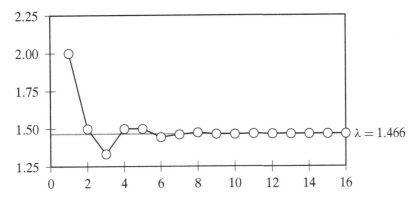

Figure 4.7. Convergence of the ratio to dominant eigenvalue.

(the edges). The method uses the so-called *random surfing* assumption that a person surfing the Web randomly chooses one of the outgoing links from the current page, or with some very small probability randomly jumps to any of the other pages in the Web graph. The PageRank of a Web page is defined to be the probability of a random web surfer landing at that page. Like prestige, the PageRank of a node v recursively depends on the PageRank of other nodes that point to it.

Normalized Prestige   We assume for the moment that each node u has outdegree at least 1. We discuss later how to handle the case when a node has no outgoing edges. Let $od(u) = \sum_v \mathbf{A}(u, v)$ denote the outdegree of node u. Because a random surfer can choose among any of its outgoing links, if there is a link from u to v, then the probability of visiting v from u is $\frac{1}{od(u)}$.

Starting from an initial probability or PageRank $p_0(u)$ for each node, such that

$$\sum_u p_0(u) = 1$$

we can compute an updated PageRank vector for v as follows:

$$p(v) = \sum_u \frac{\mathbf{A}(u, v)}{od(u)} \cdot p(u) = \sum_u \mathbf{N}(u, v) \cdot p(u) = \sum_u \mathbf{N}^T(v, u) \cdot p(u) \tag{4.18}$$

where $\mathbf{N}$ is the normalized adjacency matrix of the graph, given as

$$\mathbf{N}(u, v) = \begin{cases} \frac{1}{od(u)} & \text{if } (u, v) \in E \\ 0 & \text{if } (u, v) \notin E \end{cases}$$

Across all nodes, we can express the PageRank vector as follows:

$$\mathbf{p}' = \mathbf{N}^T\mathbf{p} \tag{4.19}$$

So far, the PageRank vector is essentially a normalized prestige vector.

Random Jumps   In the random surfing approach, there is a small probability of jumping from one node to any of the other nodes in the graph, even if they do not have a link between them. In essence, one can think of the Web graph as a (virtual) fully connected directed graph, with an adjacency matrix given as

$$\mathbf{A}_r = \mathbf{1}_{n \times n} = \begin{pmatrix} 1 & 1 & \cdots & 1 \\ 1 & 1 & \cdots & 1 \\ \vdots & \vdots & \ddots & \vdots \\ 1 & 1 & \cdots & 1 \end{pmatrix}$$

Here $\mathbf{1}_{n \times n}$ is the $n \times n$ matrix of all ones. For the random surfer matrix, the outdegree of each node is $od(u) = n$, and the probability of jumping from u to any node v is simply $\frac{1}{od(u)} = \frac{1}{n}$. Thus, if one allows only random jumps from one node to another, the PageRank can be computed analogously to Eq. (4.18):

$$p(v) = \sum_u \frac{\mathbf{A}_r(u, v)}{od(u)} \cdot p(u) = \sum_u \mathbf{N}_r(u, v) \cdot p(u) = \sum_u \mathbf{N}_r^T(v, u) \cdot p(u)$$

where $\mathbf{N}_r$ is the normalized adjacency matrix of the fully connected Web graph, given as

$$\mathbf{N}_r = \begin{pmatrix} \frac{1}{n} & \frac{1}{n} & \cdots & \frac{1}{n} \\ \frac{1}{n} & \frac{1}{n} & \cdots & \frac{1}{n} \\ \vdots & \vdots & \ddots & \vdots \\ \frac{1}{n} & \frac{1}{n} & \cdots & \frac{1}{n} \end{pmatrix} = \frac{1}{n}\mathbf{A}_r = \frac{1}{n}\mathbf{1}_{n \times n}$$

Across all the nodes the random jump PageRank vector can be represented as

$$\mathbf{p}' = \mathbf{N}_r^T \mathbf{p}$$

PageRank The full PageRank is computed by assuming that with some small probability, α, a random Web surfer jumps from the current node u to any other random node v, and with probability $1 - \alpha$ the user follows an existing link from u to v. In other words, we combine the normalized prestige vector, and the random jump vector, to obtain the final PageRank vector, as follows:

$$\mathbf{p}' = (1-\alpha)\mathbf{N}^T\mathbf{p} + \alpha\mathbf{N}_r^T\mathbf{p} = \left((1-\alpha)\mathbf{N}^T + \alpha\mathbf{N}_r^T\right)\mathbf{p} = \mathbf{M}^T\mathbf{p} \qquad (4.20)$$

where $\mathbf{M} = (1 - \alpha)\mathbf{N} + \alpha\mathbf{N}_r$ is the combined normalized adjacency matrix. The PageRank vector can be computed in an iterative manner, starting with an initial PageRank assignment $\mathbf{p}_0$, and updating it in each iteration using Eq. (4.20). One minor problem arises if a node u does not have any outgoing edges, that is, when $od(u) = 0$. Such a node acts like a sink for the normalized prestige score. Because there is no outgoing edge from u, the only choice u has is to simply jump to another random node. Thus, we need to make sure that if $od(u) = 0$ then for the row corresponding to u in $\mathbf{M}$, denoted as $\mathbf{M}_u$, we set $\alpha = 1$, that is,

$$\mathbf{M}_u = \begin{cases} \mathbf{M}_u & \text{if } od(u) > 0 \\ \frac{1}{n}\mathbf{1}_n^T & \text{if } od(u) = 0 \end{cases}$$

where $\mathbf{1}_n$ is the n-dimensional vector of all ones. We can use the power iteration method in Algorithm 4.1 to compute the dominant eigenvector of $\mathbf{M}^T$.

Example 4.7. Consider the graph in Figure 4.6. The normalized adjacency matrix is given as

$$\mathbf{N} = \begin{pmatrix} 0 & 0 & 0 & 1 & 0 \\ 0 & 0 & 0.5 & 0 & 0.5 \\ 1 & 0 & 0 & 0 & 0 \\ 0 & 0.33 & 0.33 & 0 & 0.33 \\ 0 & 1 & 0 & 0 & 0 \end{pmatrix}$$

Because there are $n = 5$ nodes in the graph, the normalized random jump adjacency matrix is given as

$$\mathbf{N}_r = \begin{pmatrix} 0.2 & 0.2 & 0.2 & 0.2 & 0.2 \\ 0.2 & 0.2 & 0.2 & 0.2 & 0.2 \\ 0.2 & 0.2 & 0.2 & 0.2 & 0.2 \\ 0.2 & 0.2 & 0.2 & 0.2 & 0.2 \\ 0.2 & 0.2 & 0.2 & 0.2 & 0.2 \end{pmatrix}$$

Assuming that $\alpha = 0.1$, the combined normalized adjacency matrix is given as

$$\mathbf{M} = 0.9\mathbf{N} + 0.1\mathbf{N}_r = \begin{pmatrix} 0.02 & 0.02 & 0.02 & 0.92 & 0.02 \\ 0.02 & 0.02 & 0.47 & 0.02 & 0.47 \\ 0.92 & 0.02 & 0.02 & 0.02 & 0.02 \\ 0.02 & 0.32 & 0.32 & 0.02 & 0.32 \\ 0.02 & 0.92 & 0.02 & 0.02 & 0.02 \end{pmatrix}$$

Computing the dominant eigenvector and eigenvalue of $\mathbf{M}^T$ we obtain $\lambda = 1$ and

$$\mathbf{p} = \begin{pmatrix} 0.419 \\ 0.546 \\ 0.417 \\ 0.422 \\ 0.417 \end{pmatrix}$$

Node v_2 has the highest PageRank value.

Hub and Authority Scores

Note that the PageRank of a node is independent of any query that a user may pose, as it is a global value for a Web page. However, for a specific user query, a page with a high global PageRank may not be that relevant. One would like to have a query-specific notion of the PageRank or prestige of a page. The Hyperlink Induced Topic Search (HITS) method is designed to do this. In fact, it computes two values to judge the importance of a page. The *authority score* of a page is analogous to PageRank or prestige, and it depends on how many "good" pages point to it. On the other hand, the *hub score* of a page is based on how many "good" pages it points to. In other words, a page with high authority has many hub pages pointing to it, and a page with high hub score points to many pages that have high authority.

Given a user query the HITS method first uses standard search engines to retrieve the set of relevant pages. It then expands this set to include any pages that point to some page in the set, or any pages that are pointed to by some page in the set. Any pages originating from the same host are eliminated. HITS is applied only on this expanded query specific graph G.

We denote by $a(u)$ the authority score and by $h(u)$ the hub score of node u. The authority score depends on the hub score and vice versa in the following manner:

$$a(v) = \sum_u \mathbf{A}^T(v, u) \cdot h(u)$$

$$h(v) = \sum_u \mathbf{A}(v, u) \cdot a(u)$$

In matrix notation, we obtain

$$\boxed{\mathbf{a}' = \mathbf{A}^T \mathbf{h}} \tag{4.21}$$

$$\boxed{\mathbf{h}' = \mathbf{A}\mathbf{a}} \tag{4.22}$$

In fact, we can rewrite the above recursively as follows:

$$\mathbf{a}_k = \mathbf{A}^T \mathbf{h}_{k-1} = \mathbf{A}^T(\mathbf{A}\mathbf{a}_{k-1}) = (\mathbf{A}^T\mathbf{A})\mathbf{a}_{k-1}$$

$$\mathbf{h}_k = \mathbf{A}\mathbf{a}_{k-1} = \mathbf{A}(\mathbf{A}^T\mathbf{h}_{k-1}) = (\mathbf{A}\mathbf{A}^T)\mathbf{h}_{k-1}$$

In other words, as $k \to \infty$, the authority score converges to the dominant eigenvector of $\mathbf{A}^T\mathbf{A}$, whereas the hub score converges to the dominant eigenvector of $\mathbf{A}\mathbf{A}^T$. The power iteration method can be used to compute the eigenvector in both cases. Starting with an initial authority vector $\mathbf{a} = \mathbf{1}_n$, the vector of all ones, we can compute the vector $\mathbf{h} = \mathbf{A}\mathbf{a}$. To prevent numeric overflows, we scale the vector by dividing by the maximum element. Next, we can compute $\mathbf{a} = \mathbf{A}^T\mathbf{h}$, and scale it too, which completes one iteration. This process is repeated until both $\mathbf{a}$ and $\mathbf{h}$ converge.

Example 4.8. For the graph in Figure 4.6, we can iteratively compute the authority and hub score vectors, by starting with $\mathbf{a} = (1, 1, 1, 1, 1)^T$. In the first iteration, we have

$$\mathbf{h} = \mathbf{A}\mathbf{a} = \begin{pmatrix} 0 & 0 & 0 & 1 & 0 \\ 0 & 0 & 1 & 0 & 1 \\ 1 & 0 & 0 & 0 & 0 \\ 0 & 1 & 1 & 0 & 1 \\ 0 & 1 & 0 & 0 & 0 \end{pmatrix} \begin{pmatrix} 1 \\ 1 \\ 1 \\ 1 \\ 1 \end{pmatrix} = \begin{pmatrix} 1 \\ 2 \\ 1 \\ 3 \\ 1 \end{pmatrix}$$

After scaling by dividing by the maximum value 3, we get

$$\mathbf{h}' = \begin{pmatrix} 0.33 \\ 0.67 \\ 0.33 \\ 1 \\ 0.33 \end{pmatrix}$$

Next we update **a** as follows:

$$\mathbf{a} = \mathbf{A}^T \mathbf{h}' = \begin{pmatrix} 0 & 0 & 1 & 0 & 0 \\ 0 & 0 & 0 & 1 & 1 \\ 0 & 1 & 0 & 1 & 0 \\ 1 & 0 & 0 & 0 & 0 \\ 0 & 1 & 0 & 1 & 0 \end{pmatrix} \begin{pmatrix} 0.33 \\ 0.67 \\ 0.33 \\ 1 \\ 0.33 \end{pmatrix} = \begin{pmatrix} 0.33 \\ 1.33 \\ 1.67 \\ 0.33 \\ 1.67 \end{pmatrix}$$

After scaling by dividing by the maximum value 1.67, we get

$$\mathbf{a}' = \begin{pmatrix} 0.2 \\ 0.8 \\ 1 \\ 0.2 \\ 1 \end{pmatrix}$$

This sets the stage for the next iteration. The process continues until **a** and **h** converge to the dominant eigenvectors of $\mathbf{A}^T \mathbf{A}$ and $\mathbf{A} \mathbf{A}^T$, respectively, given as

$$\mathbf{a} = \begin{pmatrix} 0 \\ 0.46 \\ 0.63 \\ 0 \\ 0.63 \end{pmatrix} \qquad \mathbf{h} = \begin{pmatrix} 0 \\ 0.58 \\ 0 \\ 0.79 \\ 0.21 \end{pmatrix}$$

From these scores, we conclude that v_4 has the highest hub score because it points to three nodes – v_2, v_3, and v_5 – with good authority. On the other hand, both v_3 and v_5 have high authority scores, as the two nodes v_4 and v_2 with the highest hub scores point to them.

4.4 GRAPH MODELS

Surprisingly, many real-world networks exhibit certain common characteristics, even though the underlying data can come from vastly different domains, such as social networks, biological networks, telecommunication networks, and so on. A natural question is to understand the underlying processes that might give rise to such real-world networks. We consider several network measures that will allow us to compare and contrast different graph models. Real-world networks are usually *large* and *sparse*. By large we mean that the order or the number of nodes n is very large, and by sparse we mean that the graph size or number of edges $m = O(n)$. The models we study below make a similar assumption that the graphs are large and sparse.

Small-world Property
It has been observed that many real-world graphs exhibit the so-called *small-world* property that there is a short path between any pair of nodes. We say that a graph G

exhibits small-world behavior if the average path length μ_L scales logarithmically with the number of nodes in the graph, that is, if

$$\mu_L \propto \log n \tag{4.23}$$

where n is the number of nodes in the graph. A graph is said to have *ultra-small-world* property if the average path length is much smaller than $\log n$, that is, if $\mu_L \ll \log n$.

Scale-free Property

In many real-world graphs it has been observed that the empirical degree distribution $f(k)$ exhibits a *scale-free* behavior captured by a power-law relationship with k, that is, the probability that a node has degree k satisfies the condition

$$f(k) \propto k^{-\gamma} \tag{4.24}$$

Intuitively, a power law indicates that the vast majority of nodes have very small degrees, whereas there are a few "hub" nodes that have high degrees, that is, they connect to or interact with lots of nodes. A power-law relationship leads to a scale-free or scale invariant behavior because scaling the argument by some constant c does not change the proportionality. To see this, let us rewrite Eq. (4.24) as an equality by introducing a proportionality constant α that does not depend on k, that is,

$$f(k) = \alpha k^{-\gamma} \tag{4.25}$$

Then we have

$$f(ck) = \alpha(ck)^{-\gamma} = (\alpha c^{-\gamma})k^{-\gamma} \propto k^{-\gamma}$$

Also, taking the logarithm on both sides of Eq. (4.25) gives

$$\log f(k) = \log(\alpha k^{-\gamma})$$
$$\text{or } \log f(k) = -\gamma \log k + \log \alpha$$

which is the equation of a straight line in the log-log plot of k versus $f(k)$, with $-\gamma$ giving the slope of the line. Thus, the usual approach to check whether a graph has scale-free behavior is to perform a least-square fit of the points $(\log k, \log f(k))$ to a line, as illustrated in Figure 4.8(a).

In practice, one of the problems with estimating the degree distribution for a graph is the high level of noise for the higher degrees, where frequency counts are the lowest. One approach to address the problem is to use the cumulative degree distribution $F(k)$, which tends to smooth out the noise. In particular, we use $F^c(k) = 1 - F(k)$, which gives the probability that a randomly chosen node has degree greater than k. If $f(k) \propto k^{-\gamma}$,

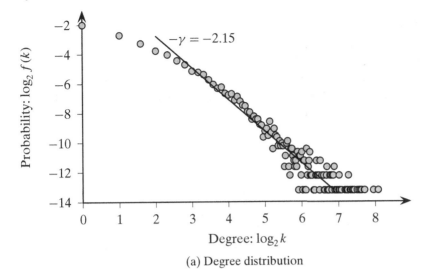

(a) Degree distribution

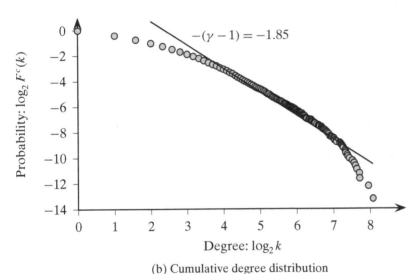

(b) Cumulative degree distribution

Figure 4.8. Degree distribution and its cumulative distribution.

and assuming that $\gamma > 1$, we have

$$F^c(k) = 1 - F(k) = 1 - \sum_0^k f(x) = \sum_k^\infty f(x) = \sum_k^\infty x^{-\gamma}$$

$$\simeq \int_k^\infty x^{-\gamma} dx = \frac{x^{-\gamma+1}}{-\gamma+1}\bigg|_k^\infty = \frac{1}{(\gamma-1)} \cdot k^{-(\gamma-1)}$$

$$\propto k^{-(\gamma-1)}$$

In other words, the log-log plot of $F^c(k)$ versus k will also be a power law with slope $-(\gamma-1)$ as opposed to $-\gamma$. Owing to the smoothing effect, plotting $\log k$ versus $\log F^c(k)$ and observing the slope gives a better estimate of the power law, as illustrated in Figure 4.8(b).

Clustering Effect

Real-world graphs often also exhibit a *clustering effect*, that is, two nodes are more likely to be connected if they share a common neighbor. The clustering effect is captured by a high clustering coefficient for the graph G. Let $C(k)$ denote the average clustering coefficient for all nodes with degree k; then the clustering effect also manifests itself as a power-law relationship between $C(k)$ and k:

$$C(k) \propto k^{-\gamma} \tag{4.26}$$

In other words, a log-log plot of k versus $C(k)$ exhibits a straight line behavior with negative slope $-\gamma$. Intuitively, the power-law behavior indicates hierarchical clustering of the nodes. That is, nodes that are sparsely connected (i.e., have smaller degrees) are part of highly clustered areas (i.e., have higher average clustering coefficients). Further, only a few hub nodes (with high degrees) connect these clustered areas (the hub nodes have smaller clustering coefficients).

Example 4.9. Figure 4.8(a) plots the degree distribution for a graph of human protein interactions, where each node is a protein and each edge indicates if the two incident proteins interact experimentally. The graph has $n = 9521$ nodes and $m = 37,060$ edges. A linear relationship between $\log k$ and $\log f(k)$ is clearly visible, although very small and very large degree values do not fit the linear trend. The best fit line after ignoring the extremal degrees yields a value of $\gamma = 2.15$. The plot of $\log k$ versus $\log F^c(k)$ makes the linear fit quite prominent. The slope obtained here is $-(\gamma - 1) = 1.85$, that is, $\gamma = 2.85$. We can conclude that the graph exhibits scale-free behavior (except at the degree extremes), with γ somewhere between 2 and 3, as is typical of many real-world graphs.

The diameter of the graph is $d(G) = 14$, which is very close to $\log_2 n = \log_2(9521) = 13.22$. The network is thus small-world.

Figure 4.9 plots the average clustering coefficient as a function of degree. The log-log plot has a very weak linear trend, as observed from the line of best fit that gives a slope of $-\gamma = -0.55$. We can conclude that the graph exhibits weak hierarchical clustering behavior.

4.4.1 Erdös–Rényi Random Graph Model

The Erdös–Rényi (ER) model generates a random graph such that any of the possible graphs with a fixed number of nodes and edges has equal probability of being chosen.

The ER model has two parameters: the number of nodes n and the number of edges m. Let M denote the maximum number of edges possible among the n nodes, that is,

$$M = \binom{n}{2} = \frac{n(n-1)}{2}$$

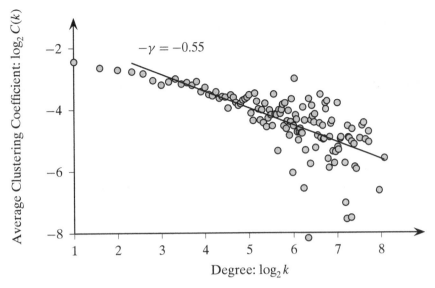

Figure 4.9. Average clustering coefficient distribution.

The ER model specifies a collection of graphs $\mathcal{G}(n, m)$ with n nodes and m edges, such that each graph $G \in \mathcal{G}$ has equal probability of being selected:

$$P(G) = \frac{1}{\binom{M}{m}} = \binom{M}{m}^{-1}$$

where $\binom{M}{m}$ is the number of possible graphs with m edges (with n nodes) corresponding to the ways of choosing the m edges out of a total of M possible edges.

Let $V = \{v_1, v_2, \ldots, v_n\}$ denote the set of n nodes. The ER method chooses a random graph $G = (V, E) \in \mathcal{G}$ via a generative process. At each step, it randomly selects two distinct vertices $v_i, v_j \in V$, and adds an edge (v_i, v_j) to E, provided the edge is not already in the graph G. The process is repeated until exactly m edges have been added to the graph.

Let X be a random variable denoting the degree of a node for $G \in \mathcal{G}$. Let p denote the probability of an edge in G, which can be computed as

$$p = \frac{m}{M} = \frac{m}{\binom{n}{2}} = \frac{2m}{n(n-1)}$$

Average Degree

For any given node in G its degree can be at most $n - 1$ (because we do not allow loops). Because p is the probability of an edge for any node, the random variable X, corresponding to the degree of a node, follows a binomial distribution with probability of success p, given as

$$f(k) = P(X = k) = \binom{n-1}{k} p^k (1 - p)^{n-1-k} \tag{4.27}$$

The average degree μ_d is then given as the expected value of X:

$$\mu_d = E[X] = (n-1)p$$

We can also compute the variance of the degrees among the nodes by computing the variance of X:

$$\sigma_d^2 = \text{var}(X) = (n-1)p(1-p)$$

Degree Distribution

To obtain the degree distribution for large and sparse random graphs, we need to derive an expression for $f(k) = P(X = k)$ as $n \to \infty$. Assuming that $m = O(n)$, we can write $p = \frac{m}{n(n-1)/2} = \frac{O(n)}{n(n-1)/2} = \frac{1}{O(n)} \to 0$. In other words, we are interested in the asymptotic behavior of the graphs as $n \to \infty$ and $p \to 0$.

Under these two trends, notice that the expected value and variance of X can be rewritten as

$$E[X] = (n-1)p \simeq np \text{ as } n \to \infty$$

$$\text{var}(X) = (n-1)p(1-p) \simeq np \text{ as } n \to \infty \text{ and } p \to 0$$

In other words, for large and sparse random graphs the expectation and variance of X are the same:

$$E[X] = \text{var}(X) = np$$

and the binomial distribution can be approximated by a Poisson distribution with parameter λ, given as

$$f(k) = \frac{\lambda^k e^{-\lambda}}{k!} \tag{4.28}$$

where $\lambda = np$ represents both the expected value and variance of the distribution. Using Stirling's approximation of the factorial $k! \simeq k^k e^{-k}\sqrt{2\pi k}$ we obtain

$$f(k) = \frac{\lambda^k e^{-\lambda}}{k!} \simeq \frac{\lambda^k e^{-\lambda}}{k^k e^{-k}\sqrt{2\pi k}} = \frac{e^{-\lambda}}{\sqrt{2\pi}} \frac{(\lambda e)^k}{\sqrt{k} k^k}$$

In other words, we have

$$f(k) \propto \alpha^k k^{-\frac{1}{2}} k^{-k}$$

for $\alpha = \lambda e = npe$. We conclude that large and sparse random graphs follow a Poisson degree distribution, which does not exhibit a power-law relationship. Thus, in one crucial respect, the ER random graph model is not adequate to describe real-world scale-free graphs.

Clustering Coefficient

Let us consider a node v_i in G with degree k. The clustering coefficient of v_i is given as

$$C(v_i) = \frac{2m_i}{k(k-1)}$$

where $k = n_i$ also denotes the number of nodes and m_i denotes the number of edges in the subgraph induced by neighbors of v_i. However, because p is the probability of an edge, the expected number of edges m_i among the neighbors of v_i is simply

$$m_i = \frac{pk(k-1)}{2}$$

Thus, we obtain

$$C(v_i) = \frac{2m_i}{k(k-1)} = p$$

In other words, the expected clustering coefficient across all nodes of all degrees is uniform, and thus the overall clustering coefficient is also uniform:

$$C(G) = \frac{1}{n} \sum_i C(v_i) = p \qquad (4.29)$$

Furthermore, for sparse graphs we have $p \to 0$, which in turn implies that $C(G) = C(v_i) \to 0$. Thus, large random graphs have no clustering effect whatsoever, which is contrary to many real-world networks.

Diameter

We saw earlier that the expected degree of a node is $\mu_d = \lambda$, which means that within one hop from a given node, we can reach λ other nodes. Because each of the neighbors of the initial node also has average degree λ, we can approximate the number of nodes that are two hops away as λ^2. In general, at a coarse level of approximation (i.e., ignoring shared neighbors), we can estimate the number of nodes at a distance of k hops away from a starting node v_i as λ^k. However, because there are a total of n distinct vertices in the graph, we have

$$\sum_{k=1}^{t} \lambda^k = n$$

where t denotes the maximum number of hops from v_i. We have

$$\sum_{k=1}^{t} \lambda^k = \frac{\lambda^{t+1} - 1}{\lambda - 1} \simeq \lambda^t$$

Plugging into the expression above, we have

$$\lambda^t \simeq n \quad \text{or}$$

$$t \log \lambda \simeq \log n \quad \text{which implies}$$

$$t \simeq \frac{\log n}{\log \lambda} \propto \log n$$

Because the path length from a node to the farthest node is bounded by t, it follows that the diameter of the graph is also bounded by that value, that is,

$$d(G) \propto \log n \qquad (4.30)$$

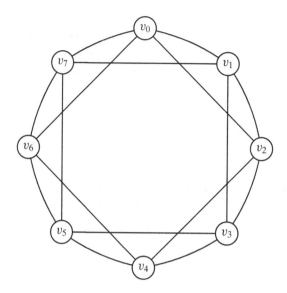

Figure 4.10. Watts–Strogatz regular graph: $n = 8, k = 2$.

assuming that the expected degree λ is fixed. We can thus conclude that random graphs satisfy at least one property of real-world graphs, namely that they exhibit small-world behavior.

4.4.2 Watts–Strogatz Small-world Graph Model

The random graph model fails to exhibit a high clustering coefficient, but it is small-world. The Watts–Strogatz (WS) model tries to explicitly model high local clustering by starting with a regular network in which each node is connected to its k neighbors on the right and left, assuming that the initial n vertices are arranged in a large circular backbone. Such a network will have a high clustering coefficient, but will not be small-world. Surprisingly, adding a small amount of randomness in the regular network by randomly *rewiring* some of the edges or by adding a small fraction of random edges leads to the emergence of the small-world phenomena.

The WS model starts with n nodes arranged in a circular layout, with each node connected to its immediate left and right neighbors. The edges in the initial layout are called *backbone* edges. Each node has edges to an additional $k - 1$ neighbors to the left and right. Thus, the WS model starts with a *regular* graph of degree $2k$, where each node is connected to its k neighbors on the right and k neighbors on the left, as illustrated in Figure 4.10.

Clustering Coefficient and Diameter of Regular Graph

Consider the subgraph G_v induced by the $2k$ neighbors of a node v. The clustering coefficient of v is given as

$$C(v) = \frac{m_v}{M_v} \tag{4.31}$$

where m_v is the actual number of edges, and M_v is the maximum possible number of edges, among the neighbors of v.

To compute m_v, consider some node r_i that is at a distance of i hops (with $1 \le i \le k$) from v to the right, considering only the backbone edges. The node r_i has edges to $k - i$ of its immediate right neighbors (restricted to the right neighbors of v), and to $k - 1$ of its left neighbors (all k left neighbors, excluding v). Owing to the symmetry about v, a node l_i that is at a distance of i backbone hops from v to the left has the same number of edges. Thus, the degree of any node in G_v that is i backbone hops away from v is given as

$$d_i = (k - i) + (k - 1) = 2k - i - 1$$

Because each edge contributes to the degree of its two incident nodes, summing the degrees of all neighbors of v, we obtain

$$2m_v = 2 \left(\sum_{i=1}^{k} 2k - i - 1 \right)$$

$$m_v = 2k^2 - \frac{k(k+1)}{2} - k$$

$$m_v = \frac{3}{2} k (k - 1) \tag{4.32}$$

On the other hand, the number of possible edges among the $2k$ neighbors of v is given as

$$M_v = \binom{2k}{2} = \frac{2k(2k-1)}{2} = k(2k - 1)$$

Plugging the expressions for m_v and M_v into Eq. (4.31), the clustering coefficient of a node v is given as

$$C(v) = \frac{m_v}{M_v} = \frac{3k - 3}{4k - 2} \tag{4.33}$$

As k increases, the clustering coefficient approaches $\frac{3}{4}$ because $C(G) = C(v) \to \frac{3}{4}$ as $k \to \infty$.

The WS regular graph thus has a high clustering coefficient. However, it does not satisfy the small-world property. To see this, note that along the backbone, the farthest node from v has a distance of at most $\frac{n}{2}$ hops. Further, because each node is connected to k neighbors on either side, one can reach the farthest node in at most $\frac{n/2}{k}$ hops. More precisely, the diameter of a regular WS graph is given as

$$d(G) = \begin{cases} \left\lceil \frac{n}{2k} \right\rceil & \text{if } n \text{ is even} \\ \left\lceil \frac{n-1}{2k} \right\rceil & \text{if } n \text{ is odd} \end{cases} \tag{4.34}$$

The regular graph has a diameter that scales linearly in the number of nodes, and thus it is not small-world.

Random Perturbation of Regular Graph

Edge Rewiring Starting with the regular graph of degree $2k$, the WS model perturbs the regular structure by adding some randomness to the network. One approach is to

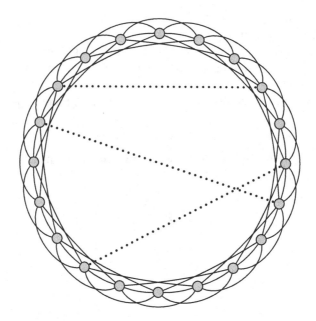

Figure 4.11. Watts–Strogatz graph ($n = 20$, $k = 3$): shortcut edges are shown dotted.

randomly rewire edges with probability r. That is, for each edge (u, v) in the graph, with probability r, replace v with another randomly chosen node avoiding loops and duplicate edges. Because the WS regular graph has $m = kn$ total edges, after rewiring, rm of the edges are random, and $(1 - r)m$ are regular.

Edge Shortcuts An alternative approach is that instead of rewiring edges, we add a few *shortcut* edges between random pairs of nodes, as shown in Figure 4.11. The total number of random shortcut edges added to the network is given as $mr = knr$, so that r can be considered as the probability, per edge, of adding a shortcut edge. The total number of edges in the graph is then simply $m + mr = (1 + r)m = (1 + r)kn$. Because $r \in [0, 1]$, the number of edges then lies in the range $[kn, 2kn]$.

In either approach, if the probability r of rewiring or adding shortcut edges is $r = 0$, then we are left with the original regular graph, with high clustering coefficient, but with no small-world property. On the other hand, if the rewiring or shortcut probability $r = 1$, the regular structure is disrupted, and the graph approaches a random graph, with little to no clustering effect, but with small-world property. Surprisingly, introducing only a small amount of randomness leads to a significant change in the regular network. As one can see in Figure 4.11, the presence of a few long-range shortcuts reduces the diameter of the network significantly. That is, even for a low value of r, the WS model retains most of the regular local clustering structure, but at the same time becomes small-world.

Properties of Watts–Strogatz Graphs
Degree Distribution Let us consider the shortcut approach, which is easier to analyze. In this approach, each vertex has degree at least $2k$. In addition there are the shortcut edges, which follow a binomial distribution. Each node can have $n' = n - 2k - 1$

additional shortcut edges, so we take n' as the number of independent trials to add edges. Because a node has degree $2k$, with shortcut edge probability of r, we expect roughly $2kr$ shortcuts from that node, but the node can connect to at most $n - 2k - 1$ other nodes. Thus, we can take the probability of success as

$$p = \frac{2kr}{n - 2k - 1} = \frac{2kr}{n'} \tag{4.35}$$

Let X denote the random variable denoting the number of shortcuts for each node. Then the probability of a node with j shortcut edges is given as

$$f(j) = P(X = j) = \binom{n'}{j} p^j (1 - p)^{n' - j}$$

with $E[X] = n'p = 2kr$. The expected degree of each node in the network is therefore

$$2k + E[X] = 2k + 2kr = 2k(1 + r)$$

It is clear that the degree distribution of the WS graph does not adhere to a power law. Thus, such networks are not scale-free.

Clustering Coefficient   After the shortcut edges have been added, each node v has expected degree $2k(1 + r)$, that is, it is on average connected to $2kr$ new neighbors, in addition to the $2k$ original ones. The number of possible edges among v's neighbors is given as

$$M_v = \frac{2k(1 + r)(2k(1 + r) - 1)}{2} = (1 + r)k(4kr + 2k - 1)$$

Because the regular WS graph remains intact even after adding shortcuts, the neighbors of v retain all $\frac{3k(k-1)}{2}$ initial edges, as given in Eq. (4.32). In addition, some of the shortcut edges may link pairs of nodes among v's neighbors. Let Y be the random variable that denotes the number of shortcut edges present among the $2k(1 + r)$ neighbors of v; then Y follows a binomial distribution with probability of success p, as given in Eq. (4.35). Thus, the expected number of shortcut edges is given as

$$E[Y] = pM_v$$

Let m_v be the random variable corresponding to the actual number of edges present among v's neighbors, whether regular or shortcut edges. The expected number of edges among the neighbors of v is then given as

$$E[m_v] = E\left[\frac{3k(k - 1)}{2} + Y\right] = \frac{3k(k - 1)}{2} + pM_v$$

Because the binomial distribution is essentially concentrated around the mean, we can now approximate the clustering coefficient by using the expected number of edges, as follows:

$$C(v) \simeq \frac{E[m_v]}{M_v} = \frac{\frac{3k(k-1)}{2} + pM_v}{M_v} = \frac{3k(k - 1)}{2M_v} + p$$

$$= \frac{3(k - 1)}{(1 + r)(4kr + 2(2k - 1))} + \frac{2kr}{n - 2k - 1}$$

using the value of p given in Eq. (4.35). For large graphs we have $n \to \infty$, so we can drop the second term above, to obtain

$$C(v) \simeq \frac{3(k-1)}{(1+r)(4kr+2(2k-1))} = \frac{3k-3}{4k-2+2r(2kr+4k-1)} \quad (4.36)$$

As $r \to 0$, the above expression becomes equivalent to Eq. (4.31). Thus, for small values of r the clustering coefficient remains high.

Diameter Deriving an analytical expression for the diameter of the WS model with random edge shortcuts is not easy. Instead we resort to an empirical study of the behavior of WS graphs when a small number of random shortcuts are added. In Example 4.10 we find that small values of shortcut edge probability r are enough to reduce the diameter from $O(n)$ to $O(\log n)$. The WS model thus leads to graphs that are small-world and that also exhibit the clustering effect. However, the WS graphs do not display a scale-free degree distribution.

Example 4.10. Figure 4.12 shows a simulation of the WS model, for a graph with $n = 1000$ vertices and $k = 3$. The x-axis shows different values of the probability r of adding random shortcut edges. The diameter values are shown as circles using the left y-axis, whereas the clustering values are shown as triangles using the right y-axis. These values are the averages over 10 runs of the WS model. The solid line gives the clustering coefficient from the analytical formula in Eq. (4.36), which is in perfect agreement with the simulation values.

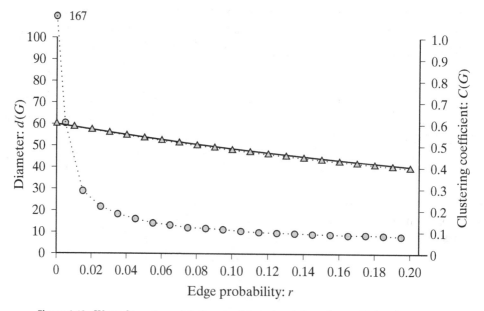

Figure 4.12. Watts–Strogatz model: diameter (circles) and clustering coefficient (triangles).

The initial regular graph has diameter

$$d(G) = \left\lceil \frac{n}{2k} \right\rceil = \left\lceil \frac{1000}{6} \right\rceil = 167$$

and its clustering coefficient is given as

$$C(G) = \frac{3(k-1)}{2(2k-1)} = \frac{6}{10} = 0.6$$

We can observe that the diameter quickly reduces, even with very small edge addition probability. For $r = 0.005$, the diameter is 61. For $r = 0.1$, the diameter shrinks to 11, which is on the same scale as $O(\log_2 n)$ because $\log_2 1000 \simeq 10$. On the other hand, we can observe that clustering coefficient remains high. For $r = 0.1$, the clustering coefficient is 0.48. Thus, the simulation study confirms that the addition of even a small number of random shortcut edges reduces the diameter of the WS regular graph from $O(n)$ (large-world) to $O(\log n)$ (small-world). At the same time the graph retains its local clustering property.

4.4.3 Barabási–Albert Scale-free Model

The Barabási–Albert (BA) model tries to capture the scale-free degree distributions of real-world graphs via a generative process that adds new nodes and edges at each time step. Further, the edge growth is based on the concept of *preferential attachment*; that is, edges from the new vertex are more likely to link to nodes with higher degrees. For this reason the model is also known as the *rich get richer* approach. The BA model mimics a dynamically growing graph by adding new vertices and edges at each time-step $t = 1, 2, \ldots$. Let G_t denote the graph at time t, and let n_t denote the number of nodes, and m_t the number of edges in G_t.

Initialization
The BA model starts at time-step $t = 0$, with an initial graph G_0 with n_0 nodes and m_0 edges. Each node in G_0 should have degree at least 1; otherwise it will never be chosen for preferential attachment. We will assume that each node has initial degree 2, being connected to its left and right neighbors in a circular layout. Thus $m_0 = n_0$.

Growth and Preferential Attachment
The BA model derives a new graph G_{t+1} from G_t by adding exactly one new node u and adding $q \le n_0$ new edges from u to q distinct nodes $v_j \in G_t$, where node v_j is chosen with probability $\pi_t(v_j)$ proportional to its degree in G_t, given as

$$\pi_t(v_j) = \frac{d_j}{\sum_{v_i \in G_t} d_i} \tag{4.37}$$

Because only one new vertex is added at each step, the number of nodes in G_t is given as

$$n_t = n_0 + t$$

Further, because exactly q new edges are added at each time-step, the number of edges in G_t is given as

$$m_t = m_0 + qt$$

Because the sum of the degrees is two times the number of edges in the graph, we have

$$\sum_{v_i \in G_t} d(v_i) = 2m_t = 2(m_0 + qt)$$

We can thus rewrite Eq. (4.37) as

$$\pi_t(v_j) = \frac{d_j}{2(m_0 + qt)} \tag{4.38}$$

As the network grows, owing to preferential attachment, one intuitively expects high degree hubs to emerge.

Example 4.11. Figure 4.13 shows a graph generated according to the BA model, with parameters $n_0 = 3, q = 2$, and $t = 12$. Initially, at time $t = 0$, the graph has $n_0 = 3$ vertices, namely $\{v_0, v_1, v_2\}$ (shown in gray), connected by $m_0 = 3$ edges (shown in bold). At each time step $t = 1, \ldots, 12$, vertex v_{t+2} is added to the growing network and is connected to $q = 2$ vertices chosen with a probability proportional to their degree.

For example, at $t = 1$, vertex v_3 is added, with edges to v_1 and v_2, chosen according to the distribution

$$\pi_0(v_i) = 1/3 \text{ for } i = 0, 1, 2$$

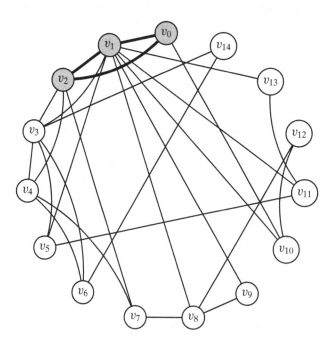

Figure 4.13. Barabási–Albert graph ($n_0 = 3, q = 2, t = 12$).

At $t = 2$, v_4 is added. Using Eq. (4.38), nodes v_2 and v_3 are preferentially chosen according to the probability distribution

$$\pi_1(v_0) = \pi_1(v_3) = \frac{2}{10} = 0.2$$

$$\pi_1(v_1) = \pi_1(v_2) = \frac{3}{10} = 0.3$$

The final graph after $t = 12$ time-steps shows the emergence of some hub nodes, such as v_1 (with degree 9) and v_3 (with degree 6).

Degree Distribution
We now study two different approaches to estimate the degree distribution for the BA model, namely the discrete approach, and the continuous approach.

Discrete Approach   The discrete approach is also called the *master-equation* method. Let X_t be a random variable denoting the degree of a node in G_t, and let $f_t(k)$ denote the probability mass function for X_t. That is, $f_t(k)$ is the degree distribution for the graph G_t at time-step t. Simply put, $f_t(k)$ is the fraction of nodes with degree k at time t. Let n_t denote the number of nodes and m_t the number of edges in G_t. Further, let $n_t(k)$ denote the number of nodes with degree k in G_t. Then we have

$$f_t(k) = \frac{n_t(k)}{n_t}$$

Because we are interested in large real-world graphs, as $t \to \infty$, the number of nodes and edges in G_t can be approximated as

$$n_t = n_0 + t \simeq t$$
$$m_t = m_0 + qt \simeq qt \tag{4.39}$$

Based on Eq. (4.37), at time-step $t + 1$, the probability $\pi_t(k)$ that some node with degree k in G_t is chosen for preferential attachment can be written as

$$\pi_t(k) = \frac{k \cdot n_t(k)}{\sum_i i \cdot n_t(i)}$$

Dividing the numerator and denominator by n_t, we have

$$\pi_t(k) = \frac{k \cdot \frac{n_t(k)}{n_t}}{\sum_i i \cdot \frac{n_t(i)}{n_t}} = \frac{k \cdot f_t(k)}{\sum_i i \cdot f_t(i)} \tag{4.40}$$

Note that the denominator is simply the expected value of X_t, that is, the mean degree in G_t, because

$$E[X_t] = \mu_d(G_t) = \sum_i i \cdot f_t(i) \tag{4.41}$$

Note also that in any graph the average degree is given as

$$\mu_d(G_t) = \frac{\sum_i d_i}{n_t} = \frac{2m_t}{n_t} \simeq \frac{2qt}{t} = 2q \tag{4.42}$$

where we used Eq. (4.39), that is, $m_t = qt$. Equating Eqs. (4.41) and (4.42), we can rewrite the preferential attachment probability [Eq. (4.40)] for a node of degree k as

$$\pi_t(k) = \frac{k \cdot f_t(k)}{2q} \tag{4.43}$$

We now consider the change in the number of nodes with degree k, when a new vertex u joins the growing network at time-step $t+1$. The net change in the number of nodes with degree k is given as the number of nodes with degree k at time $t+1$ minus the number of nodes with degree k at time t, given as

$$(n_t + 1) \cdot f_{t+1}(k) - n_t \cdot f_t(k)$$

Using the approximation that $n_t \simeq t$ from Eq. (4.39), the net change in degree k nodes is

$$(n_t + 1) \cdot f_{t+1}(k) - n_t \cdot f_t(k) = (t+1) \cdot f_{t+1}(k) - t \cdot f_t(k) \tag{4.44}$$

The number of nodes with degree k increases whenever u connects to a vertex v_i of degree $k-1$ in G_t, as in this case v_i will have degree k in G_{t+1}. Over the q edges added at time $t+1$, the number of nodes with degree $k-1$ in G_t that are chosen to connect to u is given as

$$q\pi_t(k-1) = \frac{q \cdot (k-1) \cdot f_t(k-1)}{2q} = \frac{1}{2} \cdot (k-1) \cdot f_t(k-1) \tag{4.45}$$

where we use Eq. (4.43) for $\pi_t(k-1)$. Note that Eq. (4.45) holds only when $k > q$. This is because v_i must have degree at least q, as each node that is added at time $t \geq 1$ has initial degree q. Therefore, if $d_i = k-1$, then $k-1 \geq q$ implies that $k > q$ (we can also ensure that the initial n_0 nodes have degree q by starting with clique of size $n_0 = q+1$).

At the same time, the number of nodes with degree k decreases whenever u connects to a vertex v_i with degree k in G_t, as in this case v_i will have a degree $k+1$ in G_{t+1}. Using Eq. (4.43), over the q edges added at time $t+1$, the number of nodes with degree k in G_t that are chosen to connect to u is given as

$$q \cdot \pi_t(k) = \frac{q \cdot k \cdot f_t(k)}{2q} = \frac{1}{2} \cdot k \cdot f_t(k) \tag{4.46}$$

Based on the preceding discussion, when $k > q$, the net change in the number of nodes with degree k is given as the difference between Eqs. (4.45) and (4.46) in G_t:

$$q \cdot \pi_t(k-1) - q \cdot \pi_t(k) = \frac{1}{2} \cdot (k-1) \cdot f_t(k-1) - \frac{1}{2}k \cdot f_t(k) \tag{4.47}$$

Equating Eqs. (4.44) and (4.47) we obtain the master equation for $k > q$:

$$(t+1) \cdot f_{t+1}(k) - t \cdot f_t(k) = \frac{1}{2} \cdot (k-1) \cdot f_t(k-1) - \frac{1}{2} \cdot k \cdot f_t(k) \tag{4.48}$$

On the other hand, when $k = q$, assuming that there are no nodes in the graph with degree less than q, then only the newly added node contributes to an increase in the number of nodes with degree $k = q$ by one. However, if u connects to an existing node v_i with degree k, then there will be a decrease in the number of degree k nodes because in this case v_i will have degree $k + 1$ in G_{t+1}. The net change in the number of nodes with degree k is therefore given as

$$1 - q \cdot \pi_t(k) = 1 - \frac{1}{2} \cdot k \cdot f_t(k) \tag{4.49}$$

Equating Eqs. (4.44) and (4.49) we obtain the master equation for the boundary condition $k = q$:

$$(t+1) \cdot f_{t+1}(k) - t \cdot f_t(k) = 1 - \frac{1}{2} \cdot k \cdot f_t(k) \tag{4.50}$$

Our goal is now to obtain the stationary or time-invariant solutions for the master equations. In other words, we study the solution when

$$f_{t+1}(k) = f_t(k) = f(k) \tag{4.51}$$

The stationary solution gives the degree distribution that is independent of time.

Let us first derive the stationary solution for $k = q$. Substituting Eq. (4.51) into Eq. (4.50) and setting $k = q$, we obtain

$$(t+1) \cdot f(q) - t \cdot f(q) = 1 - \frac{1}{2} \cdot q \cdot f(q)$$

$$2f(q) = 2 - q \cdot f(q), \text{ which implies that}$$

$$f(q) = \frac{2}{q+2} \tag{4.52}$$

The stationary solution for $k > q$ gives us a recursion for $f(k)$ in terms of $f(k-1)$:

$$(t+1) \cdot f(k) - t \cdot f(k) = \frac{1}{2} \cdot (k-1) \cdot f(k-1) - \frac{1}{2} \cdot k \cdot f(k)$$

$$2f(k) = (k-1) \cdot f(k-1) - k \cdot f(k), \text{ which implies that}$$

$$f(k) = \left(\frac{k-1}{k+2}\right) \cdot f(k-1) \tag{4.53}$$

Expanding (4.53) until the boundary condition $k = q$ yields

$$f(k) = \frac{(k-1)}{(k+2)} \cdot f(k-1)$$

$$= \frac{(k-1)(k-2)}{(k+2)(k+1)} \cdot f(k-2)$$

$$\vdots$$

$$= \frac{(k-1)(k-2)(k-3)(k-4)\cdots(q+3)(q+2)(q+1)(q)}{(k+2)(k+1)(k)(k-1)\cdots(q+6)(q+5)(q+4)(q+3)} \cdot f(q)$$

$$= \frac{(q+2)(q+1)q}{(k+2)(k+1)k} \cdot f(q)$$

Plugging in the stationary solution for $f(q)$ from Eq. (4.52) gives the general solution

$$f(k) = \frac{(q+2)(q+1)q}{(k+2)(k+1)k} \cdot \frac{2}{(q+2)} = \frac{2q(q+1)}{k(k+1)(k+2)}$$

For constant q and large k, it is easy to see that the degree distribution scales as

$$f(k) \propto k^{-3} \tag{4.54}$$

In other words, the BA model yields a power-law degree distribution with $\gamma = 3$, especially for large degrees.

Continuous Approach   The continuous approach is also called the *mean-field* method. In the BA model, the vertices that are added early on tend to have a higher degree, because they have more chances to acquire connections from the vertices that are added to the network at a later time. The time dependence of the degree of a vertex can be approximated as a continuous random variable. Let $k_i = d_t(i)$ denote the degree of vertex v_i at time t. At time t, the probability that the newly added node u links to v_i is given as $\pi_t(i)$. Further, the change in v_i's degree per time-step is given as $q \cdot \pi_t(i)$. Using the approximation that $n_t \simeq t$ and $m_t \simeq qt$ from Eq. (4.39), the rate of change of k_i with time can be written as

$$\frac{dk_i}{dt} = q \cdot \pi_t(i) = q \cdot \frac{k_i}{2qt} = \frac{k_i}{2t}$$

Rearranging the terms in the preceding equation $\frac{dk_i}{dt} = \frac{k_i}{2t}$ and integrating on both sides, we have

$$\int \frac{1}{k_i} dk_i = \int \frac{1}{2t} dt$$

$$\ln k_i = \frac{1}{2} \ln t + C$$

$$e^{\ln k_i} = e^{\ln t^{1/2}} \cdot e^C, \text{ which implies}$$

$$k_i = \alpha \cdot t^{1/2} \tag{4.55}$$

where C is the constant of integration, and thus $\alpha = e^C$ is also a constant.

Let t_i denote the time when node i was added to the network. Because the initial degree for any node is q, we obtain the boundary condition that $k_i = q$ at time $t = t_i$. Plugging these into Eq. (4.55), we get

$$k_i = \alpha \cdot t_i^{1/2} = q, \text{ which implies that}$$

$$\alpha = \frac{q}{\sqrt{t_i}} \tag{4.56}$$

Substituting Eq. (4.56) into Eq. (4.55) leads to the particular solution

$$k_i = \alpha \cdot \sqrt{t} = q \cdot \sqrt{t/t_i} \tag{4.57}$$

Intuitively, this solution confirms the rich-gets-richer phenomenon. It suggests that if a node v_i is added early to the network (i.e., t_i is small), then as time progresses (i.e., t gets larger), the degree of v_i keeps on increasing (as a square root of the time t).

Let us now consider the probability that the degree of v_i at time t is less than some value k, i.e., $P(k_i < k)$. Note that if $k_i < k$, then by Eq. (4.57), we have

$$k_i < k$$

$$q \cdot \sqrt{\frac{t}{t_i}} < k$$

$$\frac{t}{t_i} < \frac{k^2}{q^2}, \text{ which implies that}$$

$$t_i > \frac{q^2 t}{k^2}$$

Thus, we can write

$$P(k_i < k) = P\left(t_i > \frac{q^2 t}{k^2}\right) = 1 - P\left(t_i \le \frac{q^2 t}{k^2}\right)$$

In other words, the probability that node v_i has degree less than k is the same as the probability that the time t_i at which v_i enters the graph is greater than $\frac{q^2}{k^2}t$, which in turn can be expressed as 1 minus the probability that t_i is less than or equal to $\frac{q^2}{k^2}t$.

Note that vertices are added to the graph at a uniform rate of one vertex per time-step, that is, $\frac{1}{n_t} \simeq \frac{1}{t}$. Thus, the probability that t_i is less than or equal to $\frac{q^2}{k^2}t$ is given as

$$P(k_i < k) = 1 - P\left(t_i \le \frac{q^2 t}{k^2}\right)$$

$$= 1 - \frac{q^2 t}{k^2} \cdot \frac{1}{t}$$

$$= 1 - \frac{q^2}{k^2}$$

Because v_i is any generic node in the graph, $P(k_i < k)$ can be considered to be the cumulative degree distribution $F_t(k)$ at time t. We can obtain the degree distribution $f_t(k)$ by taking the derivative of $F_t(k)$ with respect to k to obtain

$$f_t(k) = \frac{d}{dk} F_t(k) = \frac{d}{dk} P(k_i < k)$$

$$= \frac{d}{dk}\left(1 - \frac{q^2}{k^2}\right)$$

$$= 0 - \left(\frac{k^2 \cdot 0 - q^2 \cdot 2k}{k^4}\right)$$

$$= \frac{2q^2}{k^3}$$

$$\propto k^{-3} \tag{4.58}$$

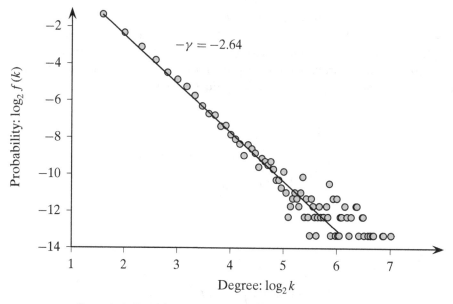

Figure 4.14. Barabási–Albert model ($n_0 = 3, t = 997, q = 3$): degree distribution.

In Eq. (4.58) we made use of the quotient rule for computing the derivative of the quotient $f(k) = \frac{g(k)}{h(k)}$, given as

$$\frac{df(k)}{dk} = \frac{h(k) \cdot \frac{dg(k)}{dk} - g(k) \cdot \frac{dh(k)}{dk}}{h(k)^2}$$

Here $g(k) = q^2$ and $h(k) = k^2$, and $\frac{dg(k)}{dk} = 0$ and $\frac{dh(k)}{dk} = 2k$.

Note that the degree distribution from the continuous approach, given in Eq. (4.58), is very close to that obtained from the discrete approach given in Eq. (4.54). Both solutions confirm that the degree distribution is proportional to k^{-3}, which gives the power-law behavior with $\gamma = 3$.

Clustering Coefficient and Diameter
Closed form solutions for the clustering coefficient and diameter for the BA model are difficult to derive. It has been shown that the diameter of BA graphs scales as

$$d(G_t) = O\left(\frac{\log n_t}{\log \log n_t}\right)$$

suggesting that they exhibit *ultra-small-world* behavior, when $q > 1$. Further, the expected clustering coefficient of the BA graphs scales as

$$E[C(G_t)] = O\left(\frac{(\log n_t)^2}{n_t}\right)$$

which is only slightly better than the clustering coefficient for random graphs, which scale as $O(n_t^{-1})$. In Example 4.12, we empirically study the clustering coefficient and diameter for random instances of the BA model with a given set of parameters.

Example 4.12. Figure 4.14 plots the empirical degree distribution obtained as the average of 10 different BA graphs generated with the parameters $n_0 = 3$, $q = 3$, and for $t = 997$ time-steps, so that the final graph has $n = 1000$ vertices. The slope of the line in the log-log scale confirms the existence of a power law, with the slope given as $-\gamma = -2.64$.

The average clustering coefficient over the 10 graphs was $C(G) = 0.019$, which is not very high, indicating that the BA model does not capture the clustering effect. On the other hand, the average diameter was $d(G) = 6$, indicating that ultra-small-world behavior.

4.5 FURTHER READING

The theory of random graphs was founded in Erdős and Rényi (1959); for a detailed treatment of the topic see Bollobás (2001). Alternative graph models for real-world networks were proposed in Watts and Strogatz (1998) and Barabási and Albert (1999). One of the first comprehensive books on graph data analysis was Wasserman and Faust (1994). More recent books on network science Lewis (2009) and Newman (2010). For PageRank see Brin and Page (1998), and for the hubs and authorities approach see Kleinberg (1999). For an up-to-date treatment of the patterns, laws, and models (including the RMat generator) for real-world networks, see Chakrabarti and Faloutsos (2012).

Barabási, A.-L. and Albert, R. (1999). Emergence of scaling in random networks. *Science*, 286 (5439), 509–512.

Bollobás, B. (2001). *Random Graphs*. 2nd ed. Vol. 73. New York: Cambridge University Press.

Brin, S. and Page, L. (1998). The anatomy of a large-scale hypertextual Web search engine. *Computer networks and ISDN systems*, 30 (1), 107–117.

Chakrabarti, D. and Faloutsos, C. (2012). Graph Mining: Laws, Tools, and Case Studies. *Synthesis Lectures on Data Mining and Knowledge Discovery*, 7 (1), 1–207.

Erdős, P. and Rényi, A. (1959). On random graphs. *Publicationes Mathematicae Debrecen*, 6, 290–297.

Kleinberg, J. M. (1999). Authoritative sources in a hyperlinked environment. *Journal of the ACM*, 46 (5), 604–632.

Lewis, T. G. (2009). *Network Science: Theory and Applications*. Hoboken, NJ: John Wiley & Sons.

Newman, M. (2010). *Networks: An Introduction*. Oxford: Oxford University Press.

Wasserman, S. and Faust, K. (1994). *Social Network Analysis: Methods and Applications*. Structural Analysis in the Social Sciences. New York: Cambridge University Press.

Watts, D. J. and Strogatz, S. H. (1998). Collective dynamics of 'small-world' networks. *Nature*, 393 (6684), 440–442.

4.6 EXERCISES

Q1. Given the graph in Figure 4.15, find the fixed-point of the prestige vector.

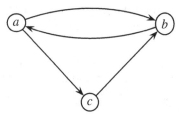

Figure 4.15. Graph for Q1

Q2. Given the graph in Figure 4.16, find the fixed-point of the authority and hub vectors.

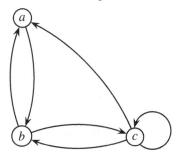

Figure 4.16. Graph for Q2.

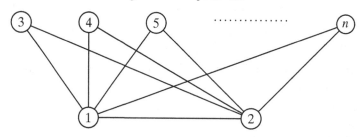

Figure 4.17. Graph for Q3.

Q3. Consider the double star graph given in Figure 4.17 with n nodes, where only nodes 1 and 2 are connected to all other vertices, and there are no other links. Answer the following questions (treating n as a variable).
  (a) What is the degree distribution for this graph?
  (b) What is the mean degree?
  (c) What is the clustering coefficient for vertex 1 and vertex 3?
  (d) What is the clustering coefficient $C(G)$ for the entire graph? What happens to the clustering coefficient as $n \to \infty$?
  (e) What is the transitivity $T(G)$ for the graph? What happens to $T(G)$ and $n \to \infty$?
  (f) What is the average path length for the graph?
  (g) What is the betweenness value for node 1?
  (h) What is the degree variance for the graph?

Q4. Consider the graph in Figure 4.18. Compute the hub and authority score vectors. Which nodes are the hubs and which are the authorities?

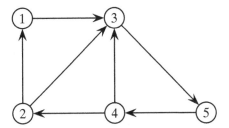

Figure 4.18. Graph for Q4.

Q5. Prove that in the BA model at time-step $t + 1$, the probability $\pi_t(k)$ that some node with degree k in G_t is chosen for preferential attachment is given as

$$\pi_t(k) = \frac{k \cdot n_t(k)}{\sum_i i \cdot n_t(i)}$$

CHAPTER 5

Kernel Methods

Before we can mine data, it is important to first find a suitable data representation that facilitates data analysis. For example, for complex data such as text, sequences, images, and so on, we must typically extract or construct a set of attributes or features, so that we can represent the data instances as multivariate vectors. That is, given a data instance $\mathbf{x}$ (e.g., a sequence), we need to find a mapping ϕ, so that $\phi(\mathbf{x})$ is the vector representation of $\mathbf{x}$. Even when the input data is a numeric data matrix, if we wish to discover nonlinear relationships among the attributes, then a nonlinear mapping ϕ may be used, so that $\phi(\mathbf{x})$ represents a vector in the corresponding high-dimensional space comprising nonlinear attributes. We use the term *input space* to refer to the data space for the input data $\mathbf{x}$ and *feature space* to refer to the space of mapped vectors $\phi(\mathbf{x})$. Thus, given a set of data objects or instances $\mathbf{x}_i$, and given a mapping function ϕ, we can transform them into feature vectors $\phi(\mathbf{x}_i)$, which then allows us to analyze complex data instances via numeric analysis methods.

Example 5.1 (Sequence-based Features). Consider a dataset of DNA sequences over the alphabet $\Sigma = \{A, C, G, T\}$. One simple feature space is to represent each sequence in terms of the probability distribution over symbols in Σ. That is, given a sequence $\mathbf{x}$ with length $|\mathbf{x}| = m$, the mapping into feature space is given as

$$\phi(\mathbf{x}) = \{P(A), P(C), P(G), P(T)\}$$

where $P(s) = \frac{n_s}{m}$ is the probability of observing symbol $s \in \Sigma$, and n_s is the number of times s appears in sequence $\mathbf{x}$. Here the input space is the set of sequences Σ^*, and the feature space is $\mathbb{R}^4$. For example, if $\mathbf{x} = ACAGCAGTA$, with $m = |\mathbf{x}| = 9$, since A occurs four times, C and G occur twice, and T occurs once, we have

$$\phi(\mathbf{x}) = (4/9, 2/9, 2/9, 1/9) = (0.44, 0.22, 0.22, 0.11)$$

Likewise, for another sequence $\mathbf{y} = AGCAAGCGAG$, we have

$$\phi(\mathbf{y}) = (4/10, 2/10, 4/10, 0) = (0.4, 0.2, 0.4, 0)$$

The mapping ϕ now allows one to compute statistics over the data sample to make inferences about the population. For example, we may compute the mean symbol composition. We can also define the distance between any two sequences, for example,

$$\|\phi(\mathbf{x}) - \phi(\mathbf{y})\| = \sqrt{(0.44 - 0.4)^2 + (0.22 - 0.2)^2 + (0.22 - 0.4)^2 + (0.11 - 0)^2} = 0.22$$

We can compute larger feature spaces by considering, for example, the probability distribution over all substrings or words of size up to k over the alphabet Σ, and so on.

Example 5.2 (Nonlinear Features). As an example of a nonlinear mapping consider the mapping ϕ that takes as input a vector $\mathbf{x} = (x_1, x_2)^T \in \mathbb{R}^2$ and maps it to a "quadratic" feature space via the nonlinear mapping

$$\phi(\mathbf{x}) = (x_1^2, x_2^2, \sqrt{2}x_1x_2)^T \in \mathbb{R}^3$$

For example, the point $\mathbf{x} = (5.9, 3)^T$ is mapped to the vector

$$\phi(\mathbf{x}) = (5.9^2, 3^2, \sqrt{2} \cdot 5.9 \cdot 3)^T = (34.81, 9, 25.03)^T$$

The main benefit of this transformation is that we may apply well-known linear analysis methods in the feature space. However, because the features are nonlinear combinations of the original attributes, this allows us to mine nonlinear patterns and relationships.

Whereas mapping into feature space allows one to analyze the data via algebraic and probabilistic modeling, the resulting feature space is usually very high-dimensional; it may even be infinite dimensional. Thus, transforming all the input points into feature space can be very expensive, or even impossible. Because the dimensionality is high, we also run into the curse of dimensionality highlighted later in Chapter 6.

Kernel methods avoid explicitly transforming each point $\mathbf{x}$ in the input space into the mapped point $\phi(\mathbf{x})$ in the feature space. Instead, the input objects are represented via their $n \times n$ pairwise similarity values. The similarity function, called a *kernel*, is chosen so that it represents a dot product in some high-dimensional feature space, yet it can be computed without directly constructing $\phi(\mathbf{x})$. Let $\mathcal{I}$ denote the input space, which can comprise any arbitrary set of objects, and let $\mathbf{D} \subset \mathcal{I}$ be a dataset comprising n objects $\mathbf{x}_i$ $(i = 1, 2, \cdots, n)$ in the input space. We can represent the pairwise similarity values between points in $\mathbf{D}$ via the $n \times n$ *kernel matrix*, defined as

$$\mathbf{K} = \begin{pmatrix} K(\mathbf{x}_1, \mathbf{x}_1) & K(\mathbf{x}_1, \mathbf{x}_2) & \cdots & K(\mathbf{x}_1, \mathbf{x}_n) \\ K(\mathbf{x}_2, \mathbf{x}_1) & K(\mathbf{x}_2, \mathbf{x}_2) & \cdots & K(\mathbf{x}_2, \mathbf{x}_n) \\ \vdots & \vdots & \ddots & \vdots \\ K(\mathbf{x}_n, \mathbf{x}_1) & K(\mathbf{x}_n, \mathbf{x}_2) & \cdots & K(\mathbf{x}_n, \mathbf{x}_n) \end{pmatrix}$$

where $K: \mathcal{I} \times \mathcal{I} \to \mathbb{R}$ is a *kernel function* on any two points in input space. However, we require that K corresponds to a dot product in some feature space. That is, for any

$\mathbf{x}_i, \mathbf{x}_j \in \mathcal{I}$, the kernel function should satisfy the condition

$$\boxed{K(\mathbf{x}_i, \mathbf{x}_j) = \phi(\mathbf{x}_i)^T \phi(\mathbf{x}_j)} \tag{5.1}$$

where $\phi : \mathcal{I} \to \mathcal{F}$ is a mapping from the input space $\mathcal{I}$ to the feature space $\mathcal{F}$. Intuitively, this means that we should be able to compute the value of the dot product using the original input representation $\mathbf{x}$, without having recourse to the mapping $\phi(\mathbf{x})$. Obviously, not just any arbitrary function can be used as a kernel; a valid kernel function must satisfy certain conditions so that Eq. (5.1) remains valid, as discussed in Section 5.1.

It is important to remark that the transpose operator for the dot product applies only when $\mathcal{F}$ is a vector space. When $\mathcal{F}$ is an abstract vector space with an inner product, the kernel is written as $K(\mathbf{x}_i, \mathbf{x}_j) = \langle \phi(\mathbf{x}_i), \phi(\mathbf{x}_j) \rangle$. However, for convenience we use the transpose operator throughout this chapter; when $\mathcal{F}$ is an inner product space it should be understood that

$$\phi(\mathbf{x}_i)^T \phi(\mathbf{x}_j) \equiv \langle \phi(\mathbf{x}_i), \phi(\mathbf{x}_j) \rangle$$

Example 5.3 (Linear and Quadratic Kernels). Consider the identity mapping, $\phi(\mathbf{x}) \to \mathbf{x}$. This naturally leads to the *linear kernel*, which is simply the dot product between two input vectors, and thus satisfies Eq. (5.1):

$$\phi(\mathbf{x})^T \phi(\mathbf{y}) = \mathbf{x}^T \mathbf{y} = K(\mathbf{x}, \mathbf{y})$$

For example, consider the first five points from the two-dimensional Iris dataset shown in Figure 5.1(a):

$$\mathbf{x}_1 = \begin{pmatrix} 5.9 \\ 3 \end{pmatrix} \qquad \mathbf{x}_2 = \begin{pmatrix} 6.9 \\ 3.1 \end{pmatrix} \qquad \mathbf{x}_3 = \begin{pmatrix} 6.6 \\ 2.9 \end{pmatrix} \qquad \mathbf{x}_4 = \begin{pmatrix} 4.6 \\ 3.2 \end{pmatrix} \qquad \mathbf{x}_5 = \begin{pmatrix} 6 \\ 2.2 \end{pmatrix}$$

The kernel matrix for the linear kernel is shown in Figure 5.1(b). For example,

$$K(\mathbf{x}_1, \mathbf{x}_2) = \mathbf{x}_1^T \mathbf{x}_2 = 5.9 \times 6.9 + 3 \times 3.1 = 40.71 + 9.3 = 50.01$$

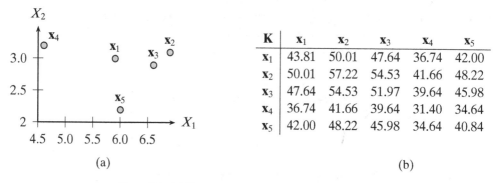

K	$\mathbf{x}_1$	$\mathbf{x}_2$	$\mathbf{x}_3$	$\mathbf{x}_4$	$\mathbf{x}_5$
$\mathbf{x}_1$	43.81	50.01	47.64	36.74	42.00
$\mathbf{x}_2$	50.01	57.22	54.53	41.66	48.22
$\mathbf{x}_3$	47.64	54.53	51.97	39.64	45.98
$\mathbf{x}_4$	36.74	41.66	39.64	31.40	34.64
$\mathbf{x}_5$	42.00	48.22	45.98	34.64	40.84

(a)   (b)

Figure 5.1. (a) Example points. (b) Linear kernel matrix.

Consider the quadratic mapping $\phi : \mathbb{R}^2 \to \mathbb{R}^3$ from Example 5.2, that maps $\mathbf{x} = (x_1, x_2)^T$ as follows:

$$\phi(\mathbf{x}) = (x_1^2, x_2^2, \sqrt{2}x_1x_2)^T$$

The dot product between the mapping for two input points $\mathbf{x}, \mathbf{y} \in \mathbb{R}^2$ is given as

$$\phi(\mathbf{x})^T\phi(\mathbf{y}) = x_1^2y_1^2 + x_2^2y_2^2 + 2x_1y_1x_2y_2$$

We can rearrange the preceding to obtain the (homogeneous) *quadratic kernel* function as follows:

$$\begin{aligned} \phi(\mathbf{x})^T\phi(\mathbf{y}) &= x_1^2y_1^2 + x_2^2y_2^2 + 2x_1y_1x_2y_2 \\ &= (x_1y_1 + x_2y_2)^2 \\ &= (\mathbf{x}^T\mathbf{y})^2 \\ &= K(\mathbf{x}, \mathbf{y}) \end{aligned}$$

We can thus see that the dot product in feature space can be computed by evaluating the kernel in input space, without explicitly mapping the points into feature space. For example, we have

$$\phi(\mathbf{x}_1) = (5.9^2, 3^2, \sqrt{2} \cdot 5.9 \cdot 3)^T = (34.81, 9, 25.03)^T$$

$$\phi(\mathbf{x}_2) = (6.9^2, 3.1^2, \sqrt{2} \cdot 6.9 \cdot 3.1)^T = (47.61, 9.61, 30.25)^T$$

$$\phi(\mathbf{x}_1)^T\phi(\mathbf{x}_2) = 34.81 \times 47.61 + 9 \times 9.61 + 25.03 \times 30.25 = 2501$$

We can verify that the homogeneous quadratic kernel gives the same value

$$K(\mathbf{x}_1, \mathbf{x}_2) = (\mathbf{x}_1^T\mathbf{x}_2)^2 = (50.01)^2 = 2501$$

We shall see that many data mining methods can be *kernelized*, that is, instead of mapping the input points into feature space, the data can be represented via the $n \times n$ kernel matrix $\mathbf{K}$, and all relevant analysis can be performed over $\mathbf{K}$. This is usually done via the so-called *kernel trick*, that is, show that the analysis task requires only dot products $\phi(\mathbf{x}_i)^T\phi(\mathbf{x}_j)$ in feature space, which can be replaced by the corresponding kernel $K(\mathbf{x}_i, \mathbf{x}_j) = \phi(\mathbf{x}_i)^T\phi(\mathbf{x}_j)$ that can be computed efficiently in input space. Once the kernel matrix has been computed, we no longer even need the input points $\mathbf{x}_i$, as all operations involving only dot products in the feature space can be performed over the $n \times n$ kernel matrix $\mathbf{K}$. An immediate consequence is that when the input data is the typical $n \times d$ numeric matrix $\mathbf{D}$ and we employ the linear kernel, the results obtained by analyzing $\mathbf{K}$ are equivalent to those obtained by analyzing $\mathbf{D}$ (as long as only dot products are involved in the analysis). Of course, kernel methods allow much more flexibility, as we can just as easily perform non-linear analysis by employing nonlinear kernels, or we may analyze (non-numeric) complex objects without explicitly constructing the mapping $\phi(\mathbf{x})$.

Example 5.4. Consider the five points from Example 5.3 along with the linear kernel matrix shown in Figure 5.1. The mean of the five points in feature space is simply the mean in input space, as ϕ is the identity function for the linear kernel:

$$\boldsymbol{\mu}_\phi = \frac{1}{5} \sum_{i=1}^{5} \phi(\mathbf{x}_i) = \frac{1}{5} \sum_{i=1}^{5} \mathbf{x}_i = (6.00, 2.88)^T$$

Now consider the squared magnitude of the mean in feature space:

$$\|\boldsymbol{\mu}_\phi\|^2 = \boldsymbol{\mu}_\phi^T \boldsymbol{\mu}_\phi = (6.0^2 + 2.88^2) = 44.29$$

Because this involves only a dot product in feature space, the squared magnitude can be computed directly from $\mathbf{K}$. As we shall see later [see Eq. (5.13)] the squared norm of the mean vector in feature space is equivalent to the average value of the kernel matrix $\mathbf{K}$. For the kernel matrix in Figure 5.1(b) we have

$$\frac{1}{5^2} \sum_{i=1}^{5} \sum_{j=1}^{5} K(\mathbf{x}_i, \mathbf{x}_j) = \frac{1107.36}{25} = 44.29$$

which matches the $\|\boldsymbol{\mu}_\phi\|^2$ value computed earlier. This example illustrates that operations involving dot products in feature space can be cast as operations over the kernel matrix $\mathbf{K}$.

Kernel methods offer a radically different view of the data. Instead of thinking of the data as vectors in input or feature space, we consider only the kernel values between pairs of points. The kernel matrix can also be considered as a weighted adjacency matrix for the complete graph over the n input points, and consequently there is a strong connection between kernels and graph analysis, in particular algebraic graph theory.

5.1 KERNEL MATRIX

Let $\mathcal{I}$ denote the input space, which can be any arbitrary set of data objects, and let $\mathbf{D} \subset \mathcal{I}$ denote a subset of n objects $\mathbf{x}_i$ in the input space. Let $\phi: \mathcal{I} \to \mathcal{F}$ be a mapping from the input space into the feature space $\mathcal{F}$, which is endowed with a dot product and norm. Let $K: \mathcal{I} \times \mathcal{I} \to \mathbb{R}$ be a function that maps pairs of input objects to their dot product value in feature space, that is, $K(\mathbf{x}_i, \mathbf{x}_j) = \phi(\mathbf{x}_i)^T \phi(\mathbf{x}_j)$, and let $\mathbf{K}$ be the $n \times n$ kernel matrix corresponding to the subset $\mathbf{D}$.

The function K is called a **positive semidefinite kernel** if and only if it is symmetric:

$$K(\mathbf{x}_i, \mathbf{x}_j) = K(\mathbf{x}_j, \mathbf{x}_i)$$

and the corresponding kernel matrix $\mathbf{K}$ for any subset $\mathbf{D} \subset \mathcal{I}$ is positive semidefinite, that is,

$$\mathbf{a}^T \mathbf{K} \mathbf{a} \geq 0, \text{ for all vectors } \mathbf{a} \in \mathbb{R}^n$$

which implies that

$$\sum_{i=1}^{n}\sum_{j=1}^{n}a_{i}a_{j}K(\mathbf{x}_{i},\mathbf{x}_{j}) \geq 0, \text{ for all } a_{i} \in \mathbb{R}, i \in [1,n] \tag{5.2}$$

We first verify that if $K(\mathbf{x}_i, \mathbf{x}_j)$ represents the dot product $\phi(\mathbf{x}_i)^T \phi(\mathbf{x}_j)$ in some feature space, then K is a positive semidefinite kernel. Consider any dataset $\mathbf{D}$, and let $\mathbf{K} = \{K(\mathbf{x}_i, \mathbf{x}_j)\}$ be the corresponding kernel matrix. First, K is symmetric since the dot product is symmetric, which also implies that $\mathbf{K}$ is symmetric. Second, $\mathbf{K}$ is positive semidefinite because

$$\mathbf{a}^{T}\mathbf{K}\mathbf{a} = \sum_{i=1}^{n}\sum_{j=1}^{n}a_{i}a_{j}K(\mathbf{x}_{i},\mathbf{x}_{j})$$

$$= \sum_{i=1}^{n}\sum_{j=1}^{n}a_{i}a_{j}\phi(\mathbf{x}_{i})^{T}\phi(\mathbf{x}_{j})$$

$$= \left(\sum_{i=1}^{n}a_{i}\phi(\mathbf{x}_{i})\right)^{T}\left(\sum_{j=1}^{n}a_{j}\phi(\mathbf{x}_{j})\right)$$

$$= \|\sum_{i=1}^{n}a_{i}\phi(\mathbf{x}_{i})\|^{2} \geq 0$$

Thus, K is a positive semidefinite kernel.

We now show that if we are given a positive semidefinite kernel $K: \mathcal{I} \times \mathcal{I} \to \mathbb{R}$, then it corresponds to a dot product in some feature space $\mathcal{F}$.

5.1.1 Reproducing Kernel Map

For the reproducing kernel map ϕ, we map each point $\mathbf{x} \in \mathcal{I}$ into a function in a *functional space* $\{f : \mathcal{I} \to \mathbb{R}\}$ comprising functions that map points in $\mathcal{I}$ into $\mathbb{R}$. Algebraically this space of functions is an abstract vector space where each point happens to be a function. In particular, any $\mathbf{x} \in \mathcal{I}$ in the input space is mapped to the following function:

$$\phi(\mathbf{x}) = K(\mathbf{x}, \cdot)$$

where the $\cdot$ stands for any argument in $\mathcal{I}$. That is, each object $\mathbf{x}$ in the input space gets mapped to a *feature point* $\phi(\mathbf{x})$, which is in fact a function $K(\mathbf{x}, \cdot)$ that represents its similarity to all other points in the input space $\mathcal{I}$.

Let $\mathcal{F}$ be the set of all functions or points that can be obtained as a linear combination of any subset of feature points, defined as

$$\mathcal{F} = span\{K(\mathbf{x}, \cdot) | \mathbf{x} \in \mathcal{I}\}$$

$$= \left\{\mathbf{f} = f(\cdot) = \sum_{i=1}^{m}\alpha_{i}\,K(\mathbf{x}_{i}, \cdot)\ \Big|\ m \in \mathbb{N}, \alpha_{i} \in \mathbb{R}, \{\mathbf{x}_{1}, \dots, \mathbf{x}_{m}\} \subseteq \mathcal{I}\right\}$$

We use the dual notation $\mathbf{f}$ and $f(\cdot)$ interchangeably to emphasize the fact that each point $\mathbf{f}$ in the feature space is in fact a function $f(\cdot)$. Note that by definition the feature point $\phi(\mathbf{x}) = K(\mathbf{x}, \cdot)$ belongs to $\mathcal{F}$.

Let $\mathbf{f}, \mathbf{g} \in \mathcal{F}$ be any two points in feature space:

$$\mathbf{f} = f(\cdot) = \sum_{i=1}^{m_a} \alpha_i\, K(\mathbf{x}_i, \cdot) \qquad\qquad \mathbf{g} = g(\cdot) = \sum_{j=1}^{m_b} \beta_j\, K(\mathbf{x}_j, \cdot)$$

Define the dot product between two points as

$$\mathbf{f}^T\mathbf{g} = f(\cdot)^T g(\cdot) = \sum_{i=1}^{m_a}\sum_{j=1}^{m_b} \alpha_i \beta_j K(\mathbf{x}_i, \mathbf{x}_j) \tag{5.3}$$

We emphasize that the notation $\mathbf{f}^T\mathbf{g}$ is only a convenience; it denotes the inner product $\langle \mathbf{f}, \mathbf{g}\rangle$ because $\mathcal{F}$ is an abstract vector space, with an inner product as defined above.

We can verify that the dot product is *bilinear*, that is, linear in both arguments, because

$$\mathbf{f}^T\mathbf{g} = \sum_{i=1}^{m_a}\sum_{j=1}^{m_b} \alpha_i\, \beta_j\, K(\mathbf{x}_i, \mathbf{x}_j) = \sum_{i=1}^{m_a} \alpha_i\, g(\mathbf{x}_i) = \sum_{j=1}^{m_b} \beta_j\, f(\mathbf{x}_j)$$

The fact that K is positive semidefinite implies that

$$\|\mathbf{f}\|^2 = \mathbf{f}^T\mathbf{f} = \sum_{i=1}^{m_a}\sum_{j=1}^{m_a} \alpha_i \alpha_j K(\mathbf{x}_i, \mathbf{x}_j) \geq 0$$

Thus, the space $\mathcal{F}$ is a *pre-Hilbert space*, defined as a normed inner product space, because it is endowed with a symmetric bilinear dot product and a norm. By adding the limit points of all Cauchy sequences that are convergent, $\mathcal{F}$ can be turned into a *Hilbert space*, defined as a normed inner product space that is complete. However, showing this is beyond the scope of this chapter.

The space $\mathcal{F}$ has the so-called *reproducing property*, that is, we can evaluate a function $f(\cdot) = \mathbf{f}$ at a point $\mathbf{x} \in \mathcal{I}$ by taking the dot product of $\mathbf{f}$ with $\phi(\mathbf{x})$, that is,

$$\mathbf{f}^T\phi(\mathbf{x}) = f(\cdot)^T K(\mathbf{x}, \cdot) = \sum_{i=1}^{m_a} \alpha_i\, K(\mathbf{x}_i, \mathbf{x}) = f(\mathbf{x})$$

For this reason, the space $\mathcal{F}$ is also called a *reproducing kernel Hilbert space*.

All we have to do now is to show that $K(\mathbf{x}_i, \mathbf{x}_j)$ corresponds to a dot product in the feature space $\mathcal{F}$. This is indeed the case, because using Eq. (5.3) for any two feature points $\phi(\mathbf{x}_i), \phi(\mathbf{x}_j) \in \mathcal{F}$ their dot product is given as

$$\phi(\mathbf{x}_i)^T\phi(\mathbf{x}_j) = K(\mathbf{x}_i, \cdot)^T K(\mathbf{x}_j, \cdot) = K(\mathbf{x}_i, \mathbf{x}_j)$$

The reproducing kernel map shows that any positive semidefinite kernel corresponds to a dot product in some feature space. This means we can apply well known algebraic and geometric methods to understand and analyze the data in these spaces.

Empirical Kernel Map

The reproducing kernel map ϕ maps the input space into a potentially infinite dimensional feature space. However, given a dataset $\mathbf{D}$ with n points $\mathbf{x}_i$ ($i = 1, 2, \cdots, n$), we can obtain a finite dimensional mapping by evaluating the kernel only on points in $\mathbf{D}$. That is, define the map ϕ as follows:

$$\phi(\mathbf{x}) = \left(K(\mathbf{x}_1, \mathbf{x}), K(\mathbf{x}_2, \mathbf{x}), \ldots, K(\mathbf{x}_n, \mathbf{x}) \right)^T \in \mathbb{R}^n$$

which maps each point $\mathbf{x} \in \mathcal{I}$ to the n-dimensional vector comprising the kernel values of $\mathbf{x}$ with each of the objects $\mathbf{x}_i \in \mathbf{D}$. We can define the dot product in feature space as

$$\phi(\mathbf{x}_i)^T \phi(\mathbf{x}_j) = \sum_{k=1}^{n} K(\mathbf{x}_k, \mathbf{x}_i) K(\mathbf{x}_k, \mathbf{x}_j) = \mathbf{K}_i^T \mathbf{K}_j \tag{5.4}$$

where $\mathbf{K}_i$ denotes the ith column of $\mathbf{K}$, which is also the same as the ith row of $\mathbf{K}$ (considered as a column vector), as $\mathbf{K}$ is symmetric. However, for ϕ to be a valid map, we require that $\phi(\mathbf{x}_i)^T \phi(\mathbf{x}_j) = K(\mathbf{x}_i, \mathbf{x}_j)$, which is clearly not satisfied by Eq. (5.4). One solution is to replace $\mathbf{K}_i^T \mathbf{K}_j$ in Eq. (5.4) with $\mathbf{K}_i^T \mathbf{A} \mathbf{K}_j$ for some positive semidefinite matrix $\mathbf{A}$ such that

$$\mathbf{K}_i^T \mathbf{A} \mathbf{K}_j = \mathbf{K}(\mathbf{x}_i, \mathbf{x}_j)$$

If we can find such an $\mathbf{A}$, it would imply that over all pairs of mapped points we have

$$\left\{ \mathbf{K}_i^T \mathbf{A} \mathbf{K}_j \right\}_{i,j=1}^{n} = \left\{ K(\mathbf{x}_i, \mathbf{x}_j) \right\}_{i,j=1}^{n}$$

which can be written compactly as

$$\mathbf{K} \mathbf{A} \mathbf{K} = \mathbf{K}$$

This immediately suggests that we take $\mathbf{A} = \mathbf{K}^{-1}$, the (pseudo) inverse of the kernel matrix $\mathbf{K}$. The modified map ϕ, called the *empirical kernel map*, is then defined as

$$\phi(\mathbf{x}) = \mathbf{K}^{-1/2} \cdot \left(K(\mathbf{x}_1, \mathbf{x}), K(\mathbf{x}_2, \mathbf{x}), \ldots, K(\mathbf{x}_n, \mathbf{x}) \right)^T \in \mathbb{R}^n$$

so that the dot product yields

$$\begin{aligned}
\phi(\mathbf{x}_i)^T \phi(\mathbf{x}_j) &= \left(\mathbf{K}^{-1/2} \, \mathbf{K}_i \right)^T \left(\mathbf{K}^{-1/2} \, \mathbf{K}_j \right) \\
&= \mathbf{K}_i^T \left(\mathbf{K}^{-1/2} \mathbf{K}^{-1/2} \right) \mathbf{K}_j \\
&= \mathbf{K}_i^T \, \mathbf{K}^{-1} \, \mathbf{K}_j
\end{aligned}$$

Over all pairs of mapped points, we have

$$\left\{ \mathbf{K}_i^T \mathbf{K}^{-1} \, \mathbf{K}_j \right\}_{i,j=1}^{n} = \mathbf{K} \, \mathbf{K}^{-1} \, \mathbf{K} = \mathbf{K}$$

as desired. However, it is important to note that this empirical feature representation is valid only for the n points in $\mathbf{D}$. If points are added to or removed from $\mathbf{D}$, the kernel map will have to be updated for all points.

5.1.2 Mercer Kernel Map

In general different feature spaces can be constructed for the same kernel K. We now describe how to construct the Mercer map.

Data-specific Kernel Map

The Mercer kernel map is best understood starting from the kernel matrix for the dataset $\mathbf{D}$ in input space. Because $\mathbf{K}$ is a symmetric positive semidefinite matrix, it has real and non-negative eigenvalues, and it can be decomposed as follows:

$$\mathbf{K} = \mathbf{U}\mathbf{\Lambda}\mathbf{U}^T$$

where $\mathbf{U}$ is the orthonormal matrix of eigenvectors $\mathbf{u}_i = (u_{i1}, u_{i2}, \ldots, u_{in})^T \in \mathbb{R}^n$ (for $i = 1, \ldots, n$), and $\mathbf{\Lambda}$ is the diagonal matrix of eigenvalues, with both arranged in non-increasing order of the eigenvalues $\lambda_1 \geq \lambda_2 \geq \ldots \geq \lambda_n \geq 0$:

$$\mathbf{U} = \begin{pmatrix} | & | & & | \\ \mathbf{u}_1 & \mathbf{u}_2 & \cdots & \mathbf{u}_n \\ | & | & & | \end{pmatrix} \qquad \mathbf{\Lambda} = \begin{pmatrix} \lambda_1 & 0 & \cdots & 0 \\ 0 & \lambda_2 & \cdots & 0 \\ \vdots & \vdots & \ddots & \vdots \\ 0 & 0 & \cdots & \lambda_n \end{pmatrix}$$

The kernel matrix $\mathbf{K}$ can therefore be rewritten as the spectral sum

$$\mathbf{K} = \lambda_1 \mathbf{u}_1 \mathbf{u}_1^T + \lambda_2 \mathbf{u}_2 \mathbf{u}_2^T + \cdots + \lambda_n \mathbf{u}_n \mathbf{u}_n^T$$

In particular the kernel function between $\mathbf{x}_i$ and $\mathbf{x}_j$ is given as

$$\mathbf{K}(\mathbf{x}_i, \mathbf{x}_j) = \lambda_1 \, u_{1i} \, u_{1j} + \lambda_2 \, u_{2i} \, u_{2j} \cdots + \lambda_n \, u_{ni} \, u_{nj}$$

$$= \sum_{k=1}^{n} \lambda_k \, u_{ki} \, u_{kj} \tag{5.5}$$

where u_{ki} denotes the ith component of eigenvector $\mathbf{u}_k$. It follows that if we define the Mercer map ϕ as follows:

$$\phi(\mathbf{x}_i) = \left(\sqrt{\lambda_1} \, u_{1i}, \sqrt{\lambda_2} \, u_{2i}, \ldots, \sqrt{\lambda_n} \, u_{ni} \right)^T \tag{5.6}$$

then $\mathbf{K}(\mathbf{x}_i, \mathbf{x}_j)$ is a dot product in feature space between the mapped points $\phi(\mathbf{x}_i)$ and $\phi(\mathbf{x}_j)$ because

$$\phi(\mathbf{x}_i)^T \phi(\mathbf{x}_j) = \left(\sqrt{\lambda_1} \, u_{1i}, \ldots, \sqrt{\lambda_n} \, u_{ni} \right) \left(\sqrt{\lambda_1} \, u_{1j}, \ldots, \sqrt{\lambda_n} \, u_{nj} \right)^T$$

$$= \lambda_1 \, u_{1i} \, u_{1j} + \cdots + \lambda_n \, u_{ni} \, u_{nj} = K(\mathbf{x}_i, \mathbf{x}_j)$$

Noting that $\mathbf{U}_i = (u_{1i}, u_{2i}, \ldots, u_{ni})^T$ is the ith row of $\mathbf{U}$, we can rewrite the Mercer map ϕ as

$$\phi(\mathbf{x}_i) = \sqrt{\mathbf{\Lambda}} \mathbf{U}_i \tag{5.7}$$

Thus, the kernel value is simply the dot product between scaled rows of $\mathbf{U}$:

$$\phi(\mathbf{x}_i)^T \phi(\mathbf{x}_j) = \left(\sqrt{\mathbf{\Lambda}} \mathbf{U}_i \right)^T \left(\sqrt{\mathbf{\Lambda}} \mathbf{U}_j \right) = \mathbf{U}_i^T \mathbf{\Lambda} \mathbf{U}_j$$

The Mercer map, defined equivalently in Eqs. (5.6) and (5.7), is obviously restricted to the input dataset $\mathbf{D}$, just like the empirical kernel map, and is therefore called the *data-specific Mercer kernel map*. It defines a data-specific feature space of dimensionality at most n, comprising the eigenvectors of $\mathbf{K}$.

Example 5.5. Let the input dataset comprise the five points shown in Figure 5.1(a), and let the corresponding kernel matrix be as shown in Figure 5.1(b). Computing the eigen-decomposition of $\mathbf{K}$, we obtain $\lambda_1 = 223.95$, $\lambda_2 = 1.29$, and $\lambda_3 = \lambda_4 = \lambda_5 = 0$. The effective dimensionality of the feature space is 2, comprising the eigenvectors $\mathbf{u}_1$ and $\mathbf{u}_2$. Thus, the matrix $\mathbf{U}$ is given as follows:

$$\mathbf{U} = \begin{pmatrix} & \mathbf{u}_1 & \mathbf{u}_2 \\ \hline \mathbf{U}_1 & -0.442 & 0.163 \\ \mathbf{U}_2 & -0.505 & -0.134 \\ \mathbf{U}_3 & -0.482 & -0.181 \\ \mathbf{U}_4 & -0.369 & 0.813 \\ \mathbf{U}_5 & -0.425 & -0.512 \end{pmatrix}$$

and we have

$$\Lambda = \begin{pmatrix} 223.95 & 0 \\ 0 & 1.29 \end{pmatrix} \quad \sqrt{\Lambda} = \begin{pmatrix} \sqrt{223.95} & 0 \\ 0 & \sqrt{1.29} \end{pmatrix} = \begin{pmatrix} 14.965 & 0 \\ 0 & 1.135 \end{pmatrix}$$

The kernel map is specified via Eq. (5.7). For example, for $\mathbf{x}_1 = (5.9, 3)^T$ and $\mathbf{x}_2 = (6.9, 3.1)^T$ we have

$$\phi(\mathbf{x}_1) = \sqrt{\Lambda}\mathbf{U}_1 = \begin{pmatrix} 14.965 & 0 \\ 0 & 1.135 \end{pmatrix} \begin{pmatrix} -0.442 \\ 0.163 \end{pmatrix} = \begin{pmatrix} -6.616 \\ 0.185 \end{pmatrix}$$

$$\phi(\mathbf{x}_2) = \sqrt{\Lambda}\mathbf{U}_2 = \begin{pmatrix} 14.965 & 0 \\ 0 & 1.135 \end{pmatrix} \begin{pmatrix} -0.505 \\ -0.134 \end{pmatrix} = \begin{pmatrix} -7.563 \\ -0.153 \end{pmatrix}$$

Their dot product is given as

$$\phi(\mathbf{x}_1)^T\phi(\mathbf{x}_2) = 6.616 \times 7.563 - 0.185 \times 0.153$$

$$= 50.038 - 0.028 = 50.01$$

which matches the kernel value $K(\mathbf{x}_1, \mathbf{x}_2)$ in Figure 5.1(b).

Mercer Kernel Map

For compact continuous spaces, analogous to the discrete case in Eq. (5.5), the kernel value between any two points can be written as the infinite spectral decomposition

$$K(\mathbf{x}_i, \mathbf{x}_j) = \sum_{k=1}^{\infty} \lambda_k \, \mathbf{u}_k(\mathbf{x}_i) \, \mathbf{u}_k(\mathbf{x}_j)$$

where $\{\lambda_1, \lambda_2, \ldots\}$ is the infinite set of eigenvalues, and $\{\mathbf{u}_1(\cdot), \mathbf{u}_2(\cdot), \ldots\}$ is the corresponding set of orthogonal and normalized *eigenfunctions*, that is, each function $\mathbf{u}_i(\cdot)$ is a solution to the integral equation

$$\int K(\mathbf{x}, \mathbf{y}) \, \mathbf{u}_i(\mathbf{y}) \, d\mathbf{y} = \lambda_i \mathbf{u}_i(\mathbf{x})$$

and K is a continuous positive semidefinite kernel, that is, for all functions $a(\cdot)$ with a finite square integral (i.e., $\int a(\mathbf{x})^2 \, d\mathbf{x} < \infty$) K satisfies the condition

$$\int \int K(\mathbf{x}_1, \mathbf{x}_2) \, a(\mathbf{x}_1) \, a(\mathbf{x}_2) \, d\mathbf{x}_1 \, d\mathbf{x}_2 \geq 0$$

We can see that this positive semidefinite kernel for compact continuous spaces is analogous to the the discrete kernel in Eq. (5.2). Further, similarly to the data-specific Mercer map [Eq. (5.6)], the general Mercer kernel map is given as

$$\phi(\mathbf{x}_i) = \left(\sqrt{\lambda_1} \, \mathbf{u}_1(\mathbf{x}_i), \sqrt{\lambda_2} \, \mathbf{u}_2(\mathbf{x}_i), \dots \right)^T$$

with the kernel value being equivalent to the dot product between two mapped points:

$$K(\mathbf{x}_i, \mathbf{x}_j) = \phi(\mathbf{x}_i)^T \phi(\mathbf{x}_j)$$

5.2 VECTOR KERNELS

We now consider two of the most commonly used vector kernels in practice. Kernels that map an (input) vector space into another (feature) vector space are called *vector kernels*. For multivariate input data, the input vector space will be the d-dimensional real space $\mathbb{R}^d$. Let $\mathbf{D}$ comprise n input points $\mathbf{x}_i \in \mathbb{R}^d$. Commonly used (nonlinear) kernel functions over vector data include the polynomial and Gaussian kernels, as described next.

Polynomial Kernel

Polynomial kernels are of two types: homogeneous or inhomogeneous. Let $\mathbf{x}, \mathbf{y} \in \mathbb{R}^d$. The *homogeneous polynomial kernel* is defined as

$$K_q(\mathbf{x}, \mathbf{y}) = \phi(\mathbf{x})^T \phi(\mathbf{y}) = (\mathbf{x}^T \mathbf{y})^q \tag{5.8}$$

where q is the degree of the polynomial. This kernel corresponds to a feature space spanned by all products of exactly q attributes.

The most typical cases are the *linear* (with $q = 1$) and *quadratic* (with $q = 2$) kernels, given as

$$K_1(\mathbf{x}, \mathbf{y}) = \mathbf{x}^T \mathbf{y}$$
$$K_2(\mathbf{x}, \mathbf{y}) = (\mathbf{x}^T \mathbf{y})^2$$

The *inhomogeneous polynomial kernel* is defined as

$$K_q(\mathbf{x}, \mathbf{y}) = \phi(\mathbf{x})^T \phi(\mathbf{y}) = (c + \mathbf{x}^T \mathbf{y})^q \tag{5.9}$$

where q is the degree of the polynomial, and $c \geq 0$ is some constant. When $c = 0$ we obtain the homogeneous kernel. When $c > 0$, this kernel corresponds to the feature space spanned by all products of at most q attributes. This can be seen from the binomial expansion

$$K_q(\mathbf{x}, \mathbf{y}) = (c + \mathbf{x}^T \mathbf{y})^q = \sum_{k=0}^{q} \binom{q}{k} c^{q-k} (\mathbf{x}^T \mathbf{y})^k$$

For example, for the typical value of $c = 1$, the inhomogeneous kernel is a weighted sum of the homogeneous polynomial kernels for all powers up to q, that is,

$$(1 + \mathbf{x}^T \mathbf{y})^q = 1 + q \mathbf{x}^T \mathbf{y} + \binom{q}{2} (\mathbf{x}^T \mathbf{y})^2 + \cdots + q (\mathbf{x}^T \mathbf{y})^{q-1} + (\mathbf{x}^T \mathbf{y})^q$$

Example 5.6. Consider the points $\mathbf{x}_1$ and $\mathbf{x}_2$ in Figure 5.1.

$$\mathbf{x}_1 = \begin{pmatrix} 5.9 \\ 3 \end{pmatrix} \qquad\qquad \mathbf{x}_2 = \begin{pmatrix} 6.9 \\ 3.1 \end{pmatrix}$$

The homogeneous quadratic kernel is given as

$$K(\mathbf{x}_1, \mathbf{x}_2) = (\mathbf{x}_1^T \mathbf{x}_2)^2 = 50.01^2 = 2501$$

The inhomogeneous quadratic kernel is given as

$$K(\mathbf{x}_1, \mathbf{x}_2) = (1 + \mathbf{x}_1^T \mathbf{x}_2)^2 = (1 + 50.01)^2 = 51.01^2 = 2602.02$$

For the polynomial kernel it is possible to construct a mapping ϕ from the input to the feature space. Let $n_0, n_1, \ldots, n_d$ denote non-negative integers, such that $\sum_{i=0}^{d} n_i = q$. Further, let $\mathbf{n} = (n_0, n_1, \ldots, n_d)$, and let $|\mathbf{n}| = \sum_{i=0}^{d} n_i = q$. Also, let $\binom{q}{\mathbf{n}}$ denote the multinomial coefficient

$$\binom{q}{\mathbf{n}} = \binom{q}{n_0, n_1, \ldots, n_d} = \frac{q!}{n_0! n_1! \ldots n_d!}$$

The multinomial expansion of the inhomogeneous kernel is then given as

$$K_q(\mathbf{x}, \mathbf{y}) = (c + \mathbf{x}^T \mathbf{y})^q = \left(c + \sum_{k=1}^{d} x_k y_k \right)^q = (c + x_1 y_1 + \cdots + x_d y_d)^q$$

$$= \sum_{|\mathbf{n}|=q} \binom{q}{\mathbf{n}} c^{n_0} (x_1 y_1)^{n_1} (x_2 y_2)^{n_2} \ldots (x_d y_d)^{n_d}$$

$$= \sum_{|\mathbf{n}|=q} \binom{q}{\mathbf{n}} c^{n_0} \left(x_1^{n_1} x_2^{n_2} \ldots x_d^{n_d} \right) \left(y_1^{n_1} y_2^{n_2} \ldots y_d^{n_d} \right)$$

$$= \sum_{|\mathbf{n}|=q} \left(\sqrt{a_{\mathbf{n}}} \prod_{k=1}^{d} x_k^{n_k} \right) \left(\sqrt{a_{\mathbf{n}}} \prod_{k=1}^{d} y_k^{n_k} \right)$$

$$= \phi(\mathbf{x})^T \phi(\mathbf{y})$$

where $a_{\mathbf{n}} = \binom{q}{\mathbf{n}} c^{n_0}$, and the summation is over all $\mathbf{n} = (n_0, n_1, \ldots, n_d)$ such that $|\mathbf{n}| = n_0 + n_1 + \cdots + n_d = q$. Using the notation $\mathbf{x}^{\mathbf{n}} = \prod_{k=1}^{d} x_k^{n_k}$, the mapping $\phi : \mathbb{R}^d \to \mathbb{R}^m$ is given as the vector

$$\phi(\mathbf{x}) = (\ldots, a_{\mathbf{n}} \mathbf{x}^{\mathbf{n}}, \ldots)^T = \left(\ldots, \sqrt{\binom{q}{\mathbf{n}}} c^{n_0} \prod_{k=1}^{d} x_k^{n_k}, \ldots \right)^T$$

where the variable $\mathbf{n} = (n_0, \ldots, n_d)$ ranges over all the possible assignments, such that $|\mathbf{n}| = q$. It can be shown that the dimensionality of the feature space is given as

$$m = \binom{d+q}{q}$$

Example 5.7 (Quadratic Polynomial Kernel). Let $\mathbf{x}, \mathbf{y} \in \mathbb{R}^2$ and let $c = 1$. The inhomogeneous quadratic polynomial kernel is given as

$$K(\mathbf{x}, \mathbf{y}) = (1 + \mathbf{x}^T \mathbf{y})^2 = (1 + x_1 y_1 + x_2 y_2)^2$$

The set of all assignments $\mathbf{n} = (n_0, n_1, n_2)$, such that $|\mathbf{n}| = q = 2$, and the corresponding terms in the multinomial expansion are shown below.

Assignments $\mathbf{n} = (n_0, n_1, n_2)$	Coefficient $a_{\mathbf{n}} = \binom{q}{\mathbf{n}} c^{n_0}$	Variables $\mathbf{x}^{\mathbf{n}} \mathbf{y}^{\mathbf{n}} = \prod_{k=1}^{d} (x_i y_i)^{n_i}$
$(1, 1, 0)$	2	$x_1 y_1$
$(1, 0, 1)$	2	$x_2 y_2$
$(0, 1, 1)$	2	$x_1 y_1 x_2 y_2$
$(2, 0, 0)$	1	1
$(0, 2, 0)$	1	$(x_1 y_1)^2$
$(0, 0, 2)$	1	$(x_2 y_2)^2$

Thus, the kernel can be written as

$$K(\mathbf{x}, \mathbf{y}) = 1 + 2x_1 y_1 + 2x_2 y_2 + 2x_1 y_1 x_2 y_2 + x_1^2 y_1^2 + x_2^2 y_2^2$$

$$= \left(1, \sqrt{2} x_1, \sqrt{2} x_2, \sqrt{2} x_1 x_2, x_1^2, x_2^2 \right) \left(1, \sqrt{2} y_1, \sqrt{2} y_2, \sqrt{2} y_1 y_2, y_1^2, y_2^2 \right)^T$$

$$= \phi(\mathbf{x})^T \phi(\mathbf{y})$$

When the input space is $\mathbb{R}^2$, the dimensionality of the feature space is given as

$$m = \binom{d+q}{q} = \binom{2+2}{2} = \binom{4}{2} = 6$$

In this case the inhomogeneous quadratic kernel with $c = 1$ corresponds to the mapping $\phi : \mathbb{R}^2 \to \mathbb{R}^6$, given as

$$\phi(\mathbf{x}) = \left(1, \sqrt{2} x_1, \sqrt{2} x_2, \sqrt{2} x_1 x_2, x_1^2, x_2^2 \right)^T$$

For example, for $\mathbf{x}_1 = (5.9, 3)^T$ and $\mathbf{x}_2 = (6.9, 3.1)^T$, we have

$$\phi(\mathbf{x}_1) = \left(1, \sqrt{2} \cdot 5.9, \sqrt{2} \cdot 3, \sqrt{2} \cdot 5.9 \cdot 3, 5.9^2, 3^2\right)^T$$

$$= (1, 8.34, 4.24, 25.03, 34.81, 9)^T$$

$$\phi(\mathbf{x}_2) = \left(1, \sqrt{2} \cdot 6.9, \sqrt{2} \cdot 3.1, \sqrt{2} \cdot 6.9 \cdot 3.1, 6.9^2, 3.1^2\right)^T$$

$$= (1, 9.76, 4.38, 30.25, 47.61, 9.61)^T$$

Thus, the inhomogeneous kernel value is

$$\phi(\mathbf{x}_1)^T \phi(\mathbf{x}_2) = 1 + 81.40 + 18.57 + 757.16 + 1657.30 + 86.49 = 2601.92$$

On the other hand, when the input space is $\mathbb{R}^2$, the homogeneous quadratic kernel corresponds to the mapping $\phi : \mathbb{R}^2 \to \mathbb{R}^3$, defined as

$$\phi(\mathbf{x}) = \left(\sqrt{2} x_1 x_2, x_1^2, x_2^2\right)^T$$

because only the degree 2 terms are considered. For example, for $\mathbf{x}_1$ and $\mathbf{x}_2$, we have

$$\phi(\mathbf{x}_1) = \left(\sqrt{2} \cdot 5.9 \cdot 3, 5.9^2, 3^2\right)^T = (25.03, 34.81, 9)^T$$

$$\phi(\mathbf{x}_2) = \left(\sqrt{2} \cdot 6.9 \cdot 3.1, 6.9^2, 3.1^2\right)^T = (30.25, 47.61, 9.61)^T$$

and thus

$$K(\mathbf{x}_1, \mathbf{x}_2) = \phi(\mathbf{x}_1)^T \phi(\mathbf{x}_2) = 757.16 + 1657.3 + 86.49 = 2500.95$$

These values essentially match those shown in Example 5.6 up to four significant digits.

Gaussian Kernel

The Gaussian kernel, also called the Gaussian radial basis function (RBF) kernel, is defined as

$$K(\mathbf{x}, \mathbf{y}) = \exp\left\{-\frac{\|\mathbf{x} - \mathbf{y}\|^2}{2\sigma^2}\right\} \tag{5.10}$$

where $\sigma > 0$ is the spread parameter that plays the same role as the standard deviation in a normal density function. Note that $K(\mathbf{x}, \mathbf{x}) = 1$, and further that the kernel value is inversely related to the distance between the two points $\mathbf{x}$ and $\mathbf{y}$.

Example 5.8. Consider again the points $\mathbf{x}_1$ and $\mathbf{x}_2$ in Figure 5.1:

$$\mathbf{x}_1 = \begin{pmatrix} 5.9 \\ 3 \end{pmatrix} \qquad \mathbf{x}_2 = \begin{pmatrix} 6.9 \\ 3.1 \end{pmatrix}$$

The squared distance between them is given as

$$\|\mathbf{x}_1 - \mathbf{x}_2\|^2 = \|(-1, -0.1)^T\|^2 = 1^2 + 0.1^2 = 1.01$$

With $\sigma = 1$, the Gaussian kernel is

$$K(\mathbf{x}_1, \mathbf{x}_2) = \exp\left\{-\frac{1.01}{2}\right\} = \exp\{-0.51\} = 0.6$$

It is interesting to note that a feature space for the Gaussian kernel has infinite dimensionality. To see this, note that the exponential function can be written as the infinite expansion

$$\exp\{a\} = \sum_{n=0}^{\infty} \frac{a^n}{n!} = 1 + a + \frac{1}{2!}a^2 + \frac{1}{3!}a^3 + \cdots$$

Further, using $\gamma = \frac{1}{2\sigma^2}$, and noting that $\|\mathbf{x} - \mathbf{y}\|^2 = \|\mathbf{x}\|^2 + \|\mathbf{y}\|^2 - 2\mathbf{x}^T\mathbf{y}$, we can rewrite the Gaussian kernel as follows:

$$K(\mathbf{x}, \mathbf{y}) = \exp\left\{-\gamma\|\mathbf{x} - \mathbf{y}\|^2\right\}$$
$$= \exp\left\{-\gamma\|\mathbf{x}\|^2\right\} \cdot \exp\left\{-\gamma\|\mathbf{y}\|^2\right\} \cdot \exp\left\{2\gamma\mathbf{x}^T\mathbf{y}\right\}$$

In particular, the last term is given as the infinite expansion

$$\exp\left\{2\gamma\mathbf{x}^T\mathbf{y}\right\} = \sum_{q=0}^{\infty} \frac{(2\gamma)^q}{q!}\left(\mathbf{x}^T\mathbf{y}\right)^q = 1 + (2\gamma)\mathbf{x}^T\mathbf{y} + \frac{(2\gamma)^2}{2!}\left(\mathbf{x}^T\mathbf{y}\right)^2 + \cdots$$

Using the multinomial expansion of $(\mathbf{x}^T\mathbf{y})^q$, we can write the Gaussian kernel as

$$K(\mathbf{x}, \mathbf{y}) = \exp\left\{-\gamma\|\mathbf{x}\|^2\right\}\exp\left\{-\gamma\|\mathbf{y}\|^2\right\}\sum_{q=0}^{\infty}\frac{(2\gamma)^q}{q!}\left(\sum_{|\mathbf{n}|=q}\binom{q}{\mathbf{n}}\prod_{k=1}^{d}(x_k y_k)^{n_k}\right)$$

$$= \sum_{q=0}^{\infty}\sum_{|\mathbf{n}|=q}\left(\sqrt{a_{q,\mathbf{n}}}\exp\left\{-\gamma\|\mathbf{x}\|^2\right\}\prod_{k=1}^{d}x_k^{n_k}\right)\left(\sqrt{a_{q,\mathbf{n}}}\exp\left\{-\gamma\|\mathbf{y}\|^2\right\}\prod_{k=1}^{d}y_k^{n_k}\right)$$

$$= \phi(\mathbf{x})^T\phi(\mathbf{y})$$

where $a_{q,\mathbf{n}} = \frac{(2\gamma)^q}{q!}\binom{q}{\mathbf{n}}$, and $\mathbf{n} = (n_1, n_2, \ldots, n_d)$, with $|\mathbf{n}| = n_1 + n_2 + \cdots + n_d = q$. The mapping into feature space corresponds to the function $\phi : \mathbb{R}^d \to \mathbb{R}^{\infty}$

$$\phi(\mathbf{x}) = \left(\ldots, \sqrt{\frac{(2\gamma)^q}{q!}\binom{q}{\mathbf{n}}}\exp\left\{-\gamma\|\mathbf{x}\|^2\right\}\prod_{k=1}^{d}x_k^{n_k}, \ldots\right)^T$$

with the dimensions ranging over all degrees $q = 0, \ldots, \infty$, and with the variable $\mathbf{n} = (n_1, \ldots, n_d)$ ranging over all possible assignments such that $|\mathbf{n}| = q$ for each value of q. Because ϕ maps the input space into an infinite dimensional feature space, we obviously cannot explicitly transform $\mathbf{x}$ into $\phi(\mathbf{x})$, yet computing the Gaussian kernel $K(\mathbf{x}, \mathbf{y})$ is straightforward.

5.3 BASIC KERNEL OPERATIONS IN FEATURE SPACE

Let us look at some of the basic data analysis tasks that can be performed solely via kernels, without instantiating $\phi(\mathbf{x})$.

Norm of a Point

We can compute the norm of a point $\phi(\mathbf{x})$ in feature space as follows:

$$\|\phi(\mathbf{x})\|^2 = \phi(\mathbf{x})^T \phi(\mathbf{x}) = K(\mathbf{x}, \mathbf{x}) \qquad (5.11)$$

which implies that $\|\phi(\mathbf{x})\| = \sqrt{K(\mathbf{x}, \mathbf{x})}$.

Distance between Points

The squared distance between two points $\phi(\mathbf{x}_i)$ and $\phi(\mathbf{x}_j)$ can be computed as

$$
\begin{aligned}
\|\phi(\mathbf{x}_i) - \phi(\mathbf{x}_j)\|^2 &= \|\phi(\mathbf{x}_i)\|^2 + \|\phi(\mathbf{x}_j)\|^2 - 2\phi(\mathbf{x}_i)^T\phi(\mathbf{x}_j) \qquad (5.12) \\
&= K(\mathbf{x}_i, \mathbf{x}_i) + K(\mathbf{x}_j, \mathbf{x}_j) - 2K(\mathbf{x}_i, \mathbf{x}_j)
\end{aligned}
$$

which implies that the distance is

$$\|\phi(\mathbf{x}_i) - \phi(\mathbf{x}_j)\| = \sqrt{K(\mathbf{x}_i, \mathbf{x}_i) + K(\mathbf{x}_j, \mathbf{x}_j) - 2K(\mathbf{x}_i, \mathbf{x}_j)}$$

Rearranging Eq. (5.12), we can see that the kernel value can be considered as a measure of the similarity between two points, as

$$\frac{1}{2}\left(\|\phi(\mathbf{x}_i)\|^2 + \|\phi(\mathbf{x}_j)\|^2 - \|\phi(\mathbf{x}_i) - \phi(\mathbf{x}_j)\|^2\right) = K(\mathbf{x}_i, \mathbf{x}_j) = \phi(\mathbf{x}_i)^T\phi(\mathbf{x}_j)$$

Thus, the more the distance $\|\phi(\mathbf{x}_i) - \phi(\mathbf{x}_j)\|$ between the two points in feature space, the less the kernel value, that is, the less the similarity.

Example 5.9. Consider the two points $\mathbf{x}_1$ and $\mathbf{x}_2$ in Figure 5.1:

$$\mathbf{x}_1 = \begin{pmatrix} 5.9 \\ 3 \end{pmatrix} \qquad\qquad \mathbf{x}_2 = \begin{pmatrix} 6.9 \\ 3.1 \end{pmatrix}$$

Assuming the homogeneous quadratic kernel, the norm of $\phi(\mathbf{x}_1)$ can be computed as

$$\|\phi(\mathbf{x}_1)\|^2 = K(\mathbf{x}_1, \mathbf{x}_1) = (\mathbf{x}_1^T\mathbf{x}_1)^2 = 43.81^2 = 1919.32$$

which implies that the norm of the transformed point is $\|\phi(\mathbf{x}_1)\| = \sqrt{43.81^2} = 43.81$.

The distance between $\phi(\mathbf{x}_1)$ and $\phi(\mathbf{x}_2)$ in feature space is given as

$$
\begin{aligned}
\|\phi(\mathbf{x}_1) - \phi(\mathbf{x}_2)\| &= \sqrt{K(\mathbf{x}_1, \mathbf{x}_1) + K(\mathbf{x}_2, \mathbf{x}_2) - 2K(\mathbf{x}_1, \mathbf{x}_2)} \\
&= \sqrt{1919.32 + 3274.13 - 2 \cdot 2501} = \sqrt{191.45} = 13.84
\end{aligned}
$$

Mean in Feature Space

The mean of the points in feature space is given as

$$\boldsymbol{\mu}_\phi = \frac{1}{n} \sum_{i=1}^{n} \phi(\mathbf{x}_i)$$

Because we do not, in general, have access to $\phi(\mathbf{x}_i)$, we cannot explicitly compute the mean point in feature space.

Nevertheless, we can compute the squared norm of the mean as follows:

$$\|\boldsymbol{\mu}_\phi\|^2 = \boldsymbol{\mu}_\phi^T \boldsymbol{\mu}_\phi = \left(\frac{1}{n} \sum_{i=1}^{n} \phi(\mathbf{x}_i)\right)^T \left(\frac{1}{n} \sum_{j=1}^{n} \phi(\mathbf{x}_j)\right) = \frac{1}{n^2} \sum_{i=1}^{n} \sum_{j=1}^{n} \phi(\mathbf{x}_i)^T \phi(\mathbf{x}_j)$$

which implies that

$$\|\boldsymbol{\mu}_\phi\|^2 = \frac{1}{n^2} \sum_{i=1}^{n} \sum_{j=1}^{n} K(\mathbf{x}_i, \mathbf{x}_j) \tag{5.13}$$

The above derivation implies that the squared norm of the mean in feature space is simply the average of the values in the kernel matrix $\mathbf{K}$.

Example 5.10. Consider the five points from Example 5.3, also shown in Figure 5.1. Example 5.4 showed the norm of the mean for the linear kernel. Let us consider the Gaussian kernel with $\sigma = 1$. The Gaussian kernel matrix is given as

$$\mathbf{K} = \begin{pmatrix} 1.00 & 0.60 & 0.78 & 0.42 & 0.72 \\ 0.60 & 1.00 & 0.94 & 0.07 & 0.44 \\ 0.78 & 0.94 & 1.00 & 0.13 & 0.65 \\ 0.42 & 0.07 & 0.13 & 1.00 & 0.23 \\ 0.72 & 0.44 & 0.65 & 0.23 & 1.00 \end{pmatrix}$$

The squared norm of the mean in feature space is therefore

$$\|\boldsymbol{\mu}_\phi\|^2 = \frac{1}{25} \sum_{i=1}^{5} \sum_{j=1}^{5} K(\mathbf{x}_i, \mathbf{x}_j) = \frac{14.98}{25} = 0.599$$

which implies that $\|\boldsymbol{\mu}_\phi\| = \sqrt{0.599} = 0.774$.

Total Variance in Feature Space

Let us first derive a formula for the squared distance of a point $\phi(\mathbf{x}_i)$ to the mean $\boldsymbol{\mu}_\phi$ in feature space:

$$\|\phi(\mathbf{x}_i) - \boldsymbol{\mu}_\phi\|^2 = \|\phi(\mathbf{x}_i)\|^2 - 2\phi(\mathbf{x}_i)^T \boldsymbol{\mu}_\phi + \|\boldsymbol{\mu}_\phi\|^2$$

$$= K(\mathbf{x}_i, \mathbf{x}_i) - \frac{2}{n} \sum_{j=1}^{n} K(\mathbf{x}_i, \mathbf{x}_j) + \frac{1}{n^2} \sum_{a=1}^{n} \sum_{b=1}^{n} K(\mathbf{x}_a, \mathbf{x}_b) \tag{5.14}$$

The total variance [Eq. (1.8)] in feature space is obtained by taking the average squared deviation of points from the mean in feature space:

$$\sigma_\phi^2 = \frac{1}{n}\sum_{i=1}^{n}\|\phi(\mathbf{x}_i) - \boldsymbol{\mu}_\phi\|^2$$

$$= \frac{1}{n}\sum_{i=1}^{n}\left(K(\mathbf{x}_i, \mathbf{x}_i) - \frac{2}{n}\sum_{j=1}^{n}K(\mathbf{x}_i, \mathbf{x}_j) + \frac{1}{n^2}\sum_{a=1}^{n}\sum_{b=1}^{n}K(\mathbf{x}_a, \mathbf{x}_b)\right)$$

$$= \frac{1}{n}\sum_{i=1}^{n}K(\mathbf{x}_i, \mathbf{x}_i) - \frac{2}{n^2}\sum_{i=1}^{n}\sum_{j=1}^{n}K(\mathbf{x}_i, \mathbf{x}_j) + \frac{n}{n^3}\sum_{a=1}^{n}\sum_{b=1}^{n}K(\mathbf{x}_a, \mathbf{x}_b)$$

That is

$$\sigma_\phi^2 = \frac{1}{n}\sum_{i=1}^{n}K(\mathbf{x}_i, \mathbf{x}_i) - \frac{1}{n^2}\sum_{i=1}^{n}\sum_{j=1}^{n}K(\mathbf{x}_i, \mathbf{x}_j) \qquad (5.15)$$

In other words, the total variance in feature space is given as the difference between the average of the diagonal entries and the average of the entire kernel matrix $\mathbf{K}$. Also notice that by Eq. (5.13) the second term is simply $\|\boldsymbol{\mu}_\phi\|^2$.

Example 5.11. Continuing Example 5.10, the total variance in feature space for the five points, for the Gaussian kernel, is given as

$$\sigma_\phi^2 = \left(\frac{1}{n}\sum_{i=1}^{n}K(\mathbf{x}_i, \mathbf{x}_i)\right) - \|\boldsymbol{\mu}_\phi\|^2 = \frac{1}{5}\times 5 - 0.599 = 0.401$$

The distance between $\phi(\mathbf{x}_1)$ and the mean $\boldsymbol{\mu}_\phi$ in feature space is given as

$$\|\phi(\mathbf{x}_1) - \boldsymbol{\mu}_\phi\|^2 = K(\mathbf{x}_1, \mathbf{x}_1) - \frac{2}{5}\sum_{j=1}^{5}K(\mathbf{x}_1, \mathbf{x}_j) + \|\boldsymbol{\mu}_\phi\|^2$$

$$= 1 - \frac{2}{5}(1 + 0.6 + 0.78 + 0.42 + 0.72) + 0.599$$

$$= 1 - 1.410 + 0.599 = 0.189$$

Centering in Feature Space

We can center each point in feature space by subtracting the mean from it, as follows:

$$\bar{\phi}(\mathbf{x}_i) = \phi(\mathbf{x}_i) - \boldsymbol{\mu}_\phi$$

Because we do not have explicit representation of $\phi(\mathbf{x}_i)$ or $\boldsymbol{\mu}_\phi$, we cannot explicitly center the points. However, we can still compute the *centered kernel matrix*, that is, the kernel matrix over centered points.

The centered kernel matrix is given as

$$\overline{\mathbf{K}} = \left\{ \overline{K}(\mathbf{x}_i, \mathbf{x}_j) \right\}_{i,j=1}^{n}$$

where each cell corresponds to the kernel between centered points, that is

$$\begin{aligned}
\overline{K}(\mathbf{x}_i, \mathbf{x}_j) &= \overline{\phi}(\mathbf{x}_i)^T \overline{\phi}(\mathbf{x}_j) \\
&= (\phi(\mathbf{x}_i) - \boldsymbol{\mu}_\phi)^T (\phi(\mathbf{x}_j) - \boldsymbol{\mu}_\phi) \\
&= \phi(\mathbf{x}_i)^T \phi(\mathbf{x}_j) - \phi(\mathbf{x}_i)^T \boldsymbol{\mu}_\phi - \phi(\mathbf{x}_j)^T \boldsymbol{\mu}_\phi + \boldsymbol{\mu}_\phi^T \boldsymbol{\mu}_\phi \\
&= K(\mathbf{x}_i, \mathbf{x}_j) - \frac{1}{n} \sum_{k=1}^{n} \phi(\mathbf{x}_i)^T \phi(\mathbf{x}_k) - \frac{1}{n} \sum_{k=1}^{n} \phi(\mathbf{x}_j)^T \phi(\mathbf{x}_k) + \|\boldsymbol{\mu}_\phi\|^2 \\
&= K(\mathbf{x}_i, \mathbf{x}_j) - \frac{1}{n} \sum_{k=1}^{n} K(\mathbf{x}_i, \mathbf{x}_k) - \frac{1}{n} \sum_{k=1}^{n} K(\mathbf{x}_j, \mathbf{x}_k) + \frac{1}{n^2} \sum_{a=1}^{n} \sum_{b=1}^{n} K(\mathbf{x}_a, \mathbf{x}_b)
\end{aligned}$$

In other words, we can compute the centered kernel matrix using only the kernel function. Over all the pairs of points, the centered kernel matrix can be written compactly as follows:

$$\overline{\mathbf{K}} = \mathbf{K} - \frac{1}{n} \mathbf{1}_{n \times n} \mathbf{K} - \frac{1}{n} \mathbf{K} \mathbf{1}_{n \times n} + \frac{1}{n^2} \mathbf{1}_{n \times n} \mathbf{K} \mathbf{1}_{n \times n} = \left(\mathbf{I} - \frac{1}{n} \mathbf{1}_{n \times n} \right) \mathbf{K} \left(\mathbf{I} - \frac{1}{n} \mathbf{1}_{n \times n} \right) \qquad (5.16)$$

where $\mathbf{1}_{n \times n}$ is the $n \times n$ singular matrix, all of whose entries equal 1.

Example 5.12. Consider the first five points from the 2-dimensional Iris dataset shown in Figure 5.1(a):

$$\mathbf{x}_1 = \begin{pmatrix} 5.9 \\ 3 \end{pmatrix} \qquad \mathbf{x}_2 = \begin{pmatrix} 6.9 \\ 3.1 \end{pmatrix} \qquad \mathbf{x}_3 = \begin{pmatrix} 6.6 \\ 2.9 \end{pmatrix} \qquad \mathbf{x}_4 = \begin{pmatrix} 4.6 \\ 3.2 \end{pmatrix} \qquad \mathbf{x}_5 = \begin{pmatrix} 6 \\ 2.2 \end{pmatrix}$$

Consider the linear kernel matrix shown in Figure 5.1(b). We can center it by first computing

$$\mathbf{I} - \frac{1}{5} \mathbf{1}_{5 \times 5} = \begin{pmatrix} 0.8 & -0.2 & -0.2 & -0.2 & -0.2 \\ -0.2 & 0.8 & -0.2 & -0.2 & -0.2 \\ -0.2 & -0.2 & 0.8 & -0.2 & -0.2 \\ -0.2 & -0.2 & -0.2 & 0.8 & -0.2 \\ -0.2 & -0.2 & -0.2 & -0.2 & 0.8 \end{pmatrix}$$

The centered kernel matrix [Eq. (5.16)] is given as

$$\bar{\mathbf{K}} = \left(\mathbf{I} - \frac{1}{5}\mathbf{1}_{5\times5}\right) \cdot \begin{pmatrix} 43.81 & 50.01 & 47.64 & 36.74 & 42.00 \\ 50.01 & 57.22 & 54.53 & 41.66 & 48.22 \\ 47.64 & 54.53 & 51.97 & 39.64 & 45.98 \\ 36.74 & 41.66 & 39.64 & 31.40 & 34.64 \\ 42.00 & 48.22 & 45.98 & 34.64 & 40.84 \end{pmatrix} \cdot \left(\mathbf{I} - \frac{1}{5}\mathbf{1}_{5\times5}\right)$$

$$= \begin{pmatrix} 0.02 & -0.06 & -0.06 & 0.18 & -0.08 \\ -0.06 & 0.86 & 0.54 & -1.19 & -0.15 \\ -0.06 & 0.54 & 0.36 & -0.83 & -0.01 \\ 0.18 & -1.19 & -0.83 & 2.06 & -0.22 \\ -0.08 & -0.15 & -0.01 & -0.22 & 0.46 \end{pmatrix}$$

To verify that $\bar{\mathbf{K}}$ is the same as the kernel matrix for the centered points, let us first center the points by subtracting the mean $\boldsymbol{\mu} = (6.0, 2.88)^T$. The centered points in feature space are given as

$$\bar{\mathbf{x}}_1 = \begin{pmatrix} -0.1 \\ 0.12 \end{pmatrix} \quad \bar{\mathbf{x}}_2 = \begin{pmatrix} 0.9 \\ 0.22 \end{pmatrix} \quad \bar{\mathbf{x}}_3 = \begin{pmatrix} 0.6 \\ 0.02 \end{pmatrix} \quad \bar{\mathbf{x}}_4 = \begin{pmatrix} -1.4 \\ 0.32 \end{pmatrix} \quad \bar{\mathbf{x}}_5 = \begin{pmatrix} 0.0 \\ -0.68 \end{pmatrix}$$

For example, the kernel between $\phi(\bar{\mathbf{x}}_1)$ and $\phi(\bar{\mathbf{x}}_2)$ is

$$\phi(\bar{\mathbf{x}}_1)^T \phi(\bar{\mathbf{x}}_2) = \bar{\mathbf{x}}_1^T \bar{\mathbf{x}}_2 = -0.09 + 0.03 = -0.06$$

which matches $\bar{\mathbf{K}}(\mathbf{x}_1, \mathbf{x}_2)$, as expected. The other entries can be verified in a similar manner. Thus, the kernel matrix obtained by centering the data and then computing the kernel is the same as that obtained via Eq. (5.16).

Normalizing in Feature Space

A common form of normalization is to ensure that points in feature space have unit length by replacing $\phi(\mathbf{x}_i)$ with the corresponding unit vector $\phi_n(\mathbf{x}_i) = \frac{\phi(\mathbf{x}_i)}{\|\phi(\mathbf{x}_i)\|}$. The dot product in feature space then corresponds to the cosine of the angle between the two mapped points, because

$$\phi_n(\mathbf{x}_i)^T \phi_n(\mathbf{x}_j) = \frac{\phi(\mathbf{x}_i)^T \phi(\mathbf{x}_j)}{\|\phi(\mathbf{x}_i)\| \cdot \|\phi(\mathbf{x}_j)\|} = \cos\theta$$

If the mapped points are both centered and normalized, then a dot product corresponds to the correlation between the two points in feature space.

The normalized kernel matrix, $\mathbf{K}_n$, can be computed using only the kernel function K, as

$$\mathbf{K}_n(\mathbf{x}_i, \mathbf{x}_j) = \frac{\phi(\mathbf{x}_i)^T \phi(\mathbf{x}_j)}{\|\phi(\mathbf{x}_i)\| \cdot \|\phi(\mathbf{x}_j)\|} = \frac{K(\mathbf{x}_i, \mathbf{x}_j)}{\sqrt{K(\mathbf{x}_i, \mathbf{x}_i) \cdot K(\mathbf{x}_j, \mathbf{x}_j)}} \tag{5.17}$$

$\mathbf{K}_n$ has all diagonal elements as 1.

Let $\mathbf{W}$ denote the diagonal matrix comprising the diagonal elements of $\mathbf{K}$:

$$\mathbf{W} = \mathrm{diag}(\mathbf{K}) = \begin{pmatrix} K(\mathbf{x}_1, \mathbf{x}_1) & 0 & \cdots & 0 \\ 0 & K(\mathbf{x}_2, \mathbf{x}_2) & \cdots & 0 \\ \vdots & \vdots & \ddots & \vdots \\ 0 & 0 & \cdots & K(\mathbf{x}_n, \mathbf{x}_n) \end{pmatrix}$$

The normalized kernel matrix can then be expressed compactly as

$$\mathbf{K}_n = \mathbf{W}^{-1/2} \cdot \mathbf{K} \cdot \mathbf{W}^{-1/2}$$

where $\mathbf{W}^{-1/2}$ is the diagonal matrix, defined as $\mathbf{W}^{-1/2}(\mathbf{x}_i, \mathbf{x}_i) = \frac{1}{\sqrt{K(\mathbf{x}_i, \mathbf{x}_i)}}$, with all other elements being zero.

Example 5.13. Consider the five points and the linear kernel matrix shown in Figure 5.1. We have

$$\mathbf{W} = \begin{pmatrix} 43.81 & 0 & 0 & 0 & 0 \\ 0 & 57.22 & 0 & 0 & 0 \\ 0 & 0 & 51.97 & 0 & 0 \\ 0 & 0 & 0 & 31.40 & 0 \\ 0 & 0 & 0 & 0 & 40.84 \end{pmatrix}$$

The normalized kernel is given as

$$\mathbf{K}_n = \mathbf{W}^{-1/2} \cdot \mathbf{K} \cdot \mathbf{W}^{-1/2} = \begin{pmatrix} 1.0000 & 0.9988 & 0.9984 & 0.9906 & 0.9929 \\ 0.9988 & 1.0000 & 0.9999 & 0.9828 & 0.9975 \\ 0.9984 & 0.9999 & 1.0000 & 0.9812 & 0.9980 \\ 0.9906 & 0.9828 & 0.9812 & 1.0000 & 0.9673 \\ 0.9929 & 0.9975 & 0.9980 & 0.9673 & 1.0000 \end{pmatrix}$$

The same kernel is obtained if we first normalize the feature vectors to have unit length and then take the dot products. For example, with the linear kernel, the normalized point $\phi_n(\mathbf{x}_1)$ is given as

$$\phi_n(\mathbf{x}_1) = \frac{\phi(\mathbf{x}_1)}{\|\phi(\mathbf{x}_1)\|} = \frac{\mathbf{x}_1}{\|\mathbf{x}_1\|} = \frac{1}{\sqrt{43.81}} \begin{pmatrix} 5.9 \\ 3 \end{pmatrix} = \begin{pmatrix} 0.8914 \\ 0.4532 \end{pmatrix}$$

Likewise, we have $\phi_n(\mathbf{x}_2) = \frac{1}{\sqrt{57.22}} \begin{pmatrix} 6.9 \\ 3.1 \end{pmatrix} = \begin{pmatrix} 0.9122 \\ 0.4098 \end{pmatrix}$. Their dot product is

$$\phi_n(\mathbf{x}_1)^T \phi_n(\mathbf{x}_2) = 0.8914 \cdot 0.9122 + 0.4532 \cdot 0.4098 = 0.9988$$

which matches $\mathbf{K}_n(\mathbf{x}_1, \mathbf{x}_2)$.

If we start with the centered kernel matrix $\bar{\mathbf{K}}$ from Example 5.12, and then normalize it, we obtain the normalized and centered kernel matrix $\bar{\mathbf{K}}_n$:

$$\bar{\mathbf{K}}_n = \begin{pmatrix} 1.00 & -0.44 & -0.61 & 0.80 & -0.77 \\ -0.44 & 1.00 & 0.98 & -0.89 & -0.24 \\ -0.61 & 0.98 & 1.00 & -0.97 & -0.03 \\ 0.80 & -0.89 & -0.97 & 1.00 & -0.22 \\ -0.77 & -0.24 & -0.03 & -0.22 & 1.00 \end{pmatrix}$$

As noted earlier, the kernel value $\bar{\mathbf{K}}_n(\mathbf{x}_i, \mathbf{x}_j)$ denotes the correlation between $\mathbf{x}_i$ and $\mathbf{x}_j$ in feature space, that is, it is cosine of the angle between the centered points $\phi(\mathbf{x}_i)$ and $\phi(\mathbf{x}_j)$.

5.4 KERNELS FOR COMPLEX OBJECTS

We conclude this chapter with some examples of kernels defined for complex data such as strings and graphs. The use of kernels for dimensionality reduction is described in Section 7.3, for clustering in Section 13.2 and Chapter 16, for discriminant analysis in Section 20.2, for classification in Sections 21.4 and 21.5, and for regression in Section 23.5.

5.4.1 Spectrum Kernel for Strings

Consider text or sequence data defined over an alphabet Σ. The l-spectrum feature map is the mapping $\phi : \Sigma^* \to \mathbb{R}^{|\Sigma|^l}$ from the set of substrings over Σ to the $|\Sigma|^l$-dimensional space representing the number of occurrences of all possible substrings of length l, defined as

$$\phi(\mathbf{x}) = \left(\cdots, \#(\alpha), \cdots \right)^T_{\alpha \in \Sigma^l}$$

where $\#(\alpha)$ is the number of occurrences of the l-length string α in $\mathbf{x}$.

The (full) spectrum map is an extension of the l-spectrum map, obtained by considering all lengths from $l = 0$ to $l = \infty$, leading to an infinite dimensional feature map $\phi : \Sigma^* \to \mathbb{R}^\infty$:

$$\phi(\mathbf{x}) = \left(\cdots, \#(\alpha), \cdots \right)^T_{\alpha \in \Sigma^*}$$

where $\#(\alpha)$ is the number of occurrences of the string α in $\mathbf{x}$.

The (l-)spectrum kernel between two strings $\mathbf{x}_i, \mathbf{x}_j$ is simply the dot product between their (l-)spectrum maps:

$$K(\mathbf{x}_i, \mathbf{x}_j) = \phi(\mathbf{x}_i)^T \phi(\mathbf{x}_j)$$

A naive computation of the l-spectrum kernel takes $O(|\Sigma|^l)$ time. However, for a given string $\mathbf{x}$ of length n, the vast majority of the l-length strings have an occurrence count of zero, which can be ignored. The l-spectrum map can be effectively computed in $O(n)$ time for a string of length n (assuming $n \gg l$) because there can be at most $n - l + 1$ substrings of length l, and the l-spectrum kernel can thus be computed in $O(n + m)$ time for any two strings of length n and m, respectively.

The feature map for the (full) spectrum kernel is infinite dimensional, but once again, for a given string $\mathbf{x}$ of length n, the vast majority of the strings will have an occurrence count of zero. A straightforward implementation of the spectrum map for a string $\mathbf{x}$ of length n can be computed in $O(n^2)$ time because $\mathbf{x}$ can have at most $\sum_{l=1}^{n} n - l + 1 = n(n+1)/2$ distinct nonempty substrings. The spectrum kernel can then be computed in $O(n^2 + m^2)$ time for any two strings of length n and m, respectively. However, a much more efficient computation is enabled via suffix trees (see Chapter 10), with a total time of $O(n + m)$.

Example 5.14. Consider sequences over the DNA alphabet $\Sigma = \{A, C, G, T\}$. Let $\mathbf{x}_1 = ACAGCAGTA$, and let $\mathbf{x}_2 = AGCAAGCGAG$. For $l = 3$, the feature space has dimensionality $|\Sigma|^l = 4^3 = 64$. Nevertheless, we do not have to map the input points into the full feature space; we can compute the reduced 3-spectrum mapping by counting the number of occurrences for only the length 3 substrings that occur in each input sequence, as follows:

$$\phi(\mathbf{x}_1) = (ACA:1, AGC:1, AGT:1, CAG:2, GCA:1, GTA:1)$$

$$\phi(\mathbf{x}_2) = (AAG:1, AGC:2, CAA:1, CGA:1, GAG:1, GCA:1, GCG:1)$$

where the notation $\alpha : \#(\alpha)$ denotes that substring α has $\#(\alpha)$ occurrences in $\mathbf{x}_i$. We can then compute the dot product by considering only the common substrings, as follows:

$$K(\mathbf{x}_1, \mathbf{x}_2) = 1 \times 2 + 1 \times 1 = 2 + 1 = 3$$

The first term in the dot product is due to the substring AGC, and the second is due to GCA, which are the only common length 3 substrings between $\mathbf{x}_1$ and $\mathbf{x}_2$.

The full spectrum can be computed by considering the occurrences of all common substrings over all possible lengths. For $\mathbf{x}_1$ and $\mathbf{x}_2$, the common substrings and their occurrence counts are given as

α	A	C	G	AG	CA	AGC	GCA	$AGCA$
$\#(\alpha)$ in $\mathbf{x}_1$	4	2	2	2	2	1	1	1
$\#(\alpha)$ in $\mathbf{x}_2$	4	2	4	3	1	2	1	1

Thus, the full spectrum kernel value is given as

$$K(\mathbf{x}_1, \mathbf{x}_2) = 16 + 4 + 8 + 6 + 2 + 2 + 1 + 1 = 40$$

5.4.2 Diffusion Kernels on Graph Nodes

Let $\mathbf{S}$ be some symmetric similarity matrix between nodes of a graph $G = (V, E)$. For instance, $\mathbf{S}$ can be the (weighted) adjacency matrix $\mathbf{A}$ [Eq. (4.2)] or the Laplacian matrix $\mathbf{L} = \mathbf{A} - \mathbf{\Delta}$ (or its negation), where $\mathbf{\Delta}$ is the degree matrix for an undirected graph G, defined as $\mathbf{\Delta}(i,i) = d_i$ and $\mathbf{\Delta}(i,j) = 0$ for all $i \neq j$, and d_i is the degree of node i.

Consider the similarity between any two nodes obtained by summing the product of the similarities over walks of length 2:

$$S^{(2)}(\mathbf{x}_i, \mathbf{x}_j) = \sum_{a=1}^{n} S(\mathbf{x}_i, \mathbf{x}_a) S(\mathbf{x}_a, \mathbf{x}_j) = \mathbf{S}_i^T \mathbf{S}_j$$

where

$$\mathbf{S}_i = \Big(S(\mathbf{x}_i, \mathbf{x}_1), S(\mathbf{x}_i, \mathbf{x}_2), \ldots, S(\mathbf{x}_i, \mathbf{x}_n) \Big)^T$$

denotes the (column) vector representing the ith row of $\mathbf{S}$ (and because $\mathbf{S}$ is symmetric, it also denotes the ith column of $\mathbf{S}$). Over all pairs of nodes the similarity matrix over walks of length 2, denoted $\mathbf{S}^{(2)}$, is thus given as the square of the base similarity matrix $\mathbf{S}$:

$$\mathbf{S}^{(2)} = \mathbf{S} \times \mathbf{S} = \mathbf{S}^2$$

In general, if we sum up the product of the base similarities over all l-length walks between two nodes, we obtain the l-length similarity matrix $\mathbf{S}^{(l)}$, which is simply the lth power of $\mathbf{S}$, that is,

$$\mathbf{S}^{(l)} = \mathbf{S}^l$$

Power Kernels

Even walk lengths lead to positive semidefinite kernels, but odd walk lengths are not guaranteed to do so, unless the base matrix $\mathbf{S}$ is itself a positive semidefinite matrix. In particular, $\mathbf{K} = \mathbf{S}^2$ is a valid kernel. To see this, assume that the ith row of $\mathbf{S}$ denotes the feature map for $\mathbf{x}_i$, that is, $\phi(\mathbf{x}_i) = \mathbf{S}_i$. The kernel value between any two points is then a dot product in feature space:

$$K(\mathbf{x}_i, \mathbf{x}_j) = S^{(2)}(\mathbf{x}_i, \mathbf{x}_j) = \mathbf{S}_i^T \mathbf{S}_j = \phi(\mathbf{x}_i)^T \phi(\mathbf{x}_j)$$

For a general walk length l, let $\mathbf{K} = \mathbf{S}^l$. Consider the eigen-decomposition of $\mathbf{S}$:

$$\mathbf{S} = \mathbf{U} \mathbf{\Lambda} \mathbf{U}^T = \sum_{i=1}^{n} \mathbf{u}_i \lambda_i \mathbf{u}_i^T$$

where $\mathbf{U}$ is the orthogonal matrix of eigenvectors and $\mathbf{\Lambda}$ is the diagonal matrix of eigenvalues of $\mathbf{S}$:

$$\mathbf{U} = \begin{pmatrix} | & | & & | \\ \mathbf{u}_1 & \mathbf{u}_2 & \cdots & \mathbf{u}_n \\ | & | & & | \end{pmatrix} \qquad \mathbf{\Lambda} = \begin{pmatrix} \lambda_1 & 0 & \cdots & 0 \\ 0 & \lambda_2 & \cdots & 0 \\ \vdots & \vdots & \ddots & 0 \\ 0 & 0 & \cdots & \lambda_n \end{pmatrix}$$

The eigen-decomposition of $\mathbf{K}$ can be obtained as follows:

$$\mathbf{K} = \mathbf{S}^l = \left(\mathbf{U} \mathbf{\Lambda} \mathbf{U}^T \right)^l = \mathbf{U} \left(\mathbf{\Lambda}^l \right) \mathbf{U}^T$$

where we used the fact that eigenvectors of $\mathbf{S}$ and $\mathbf{S}^l$ are identical, and further that eigenvalues of $\mathbf{S}^l$ are given as $(\lambda_i)^l$ (for all $i = 1, \ldots, n$), where λ_i is an eigenvalue of $\mathbf{S}$. For $\mathbf{K} = \mathbf{S}^l$ to be a positive semidefinite matrix, all its eigenvalues must be non-negative, which is guaranteed for all even walk lengths. Because $(\lambda_i)^l$ will be negative if l is odd and λ_i is negative, odd walk lengths lead to a positive semidefinite kernel only if $\mathbf{S}$ is positive semidefinite.

Exponential Diffusion Kernel

Instead of fixing the walk length *a priori*, we can obtain a new kernel between nodes of a graph by considering walks of all possible lengths, but by damping the contribution of longer walks, which leads to the *exponential diffusion kernel*, defined as

$$\mathbf{K} = \sum_{l=0}^{\infty} \frac{1}{l!} \beta^l \mathbf{S}^l = \mathbf{I} + \beta \mathbf{S} + \frac{1}{2!}\beta^2 \mathbf{S}^2 + \frac{1}{3!}\beta^3 \mathbf{S}^3 + \cdots = \exp\{\beta \mathbf{S}\} \tag{5.18}$$

where β is a damping factor, and $\exp\{\beta \mathbf{S}\}$ is the matrix exponential. The series on the right hand side above converges for all $\beta \geq 0$.

Substituting $\mathbf{S} = \mathbf{U} \boldsymbol{\Lambda} \mathbf{U}^T = \sum_{i=1}^{n} \lambda_i \mathbf{u}_i \mathbf{u}_i^T$ in Eq. (5.18), and utilizing the fact that $\mathbf{U} \mathbf{U}^T = \sum_{i=1}^{n} \mathbf{u}_i \mathbf{u}_i^T = \mathbf{I}$, we have

$$\mathbf{K} = \mathbf{I} + \beta \mathbf{S} + \frac{1}{2!}\beta^2 \mathbf{S}^2 + \cdots$$

$$= \left(\sum_{i=1}^{n} \mathbf{u}_i \mathbf{u}_i^T \right) + \left(\sum_{i=1}^{n} \mathbf{u}_i \beta \lambda_i \mathbf{u}_i^T \right) + \left(\sum_{i=1}^{n} \mathbf{u}_i \frac{1}{2!} \beta^2 \lambda_i^2 \mathbf{u}_i^T \right) + \cdots$$

$$= \sum_{i=1}^{n} \mathbf{u}_i \left(1 + \beta \lambda_i + \frac{1}{2!} \beta^2 \lambda_i^2 + \cdots \right) \mathbf{u}_i^T$$

$$= \sum_{i=1}^{n} \mathbf{u}_i \exp\{\beta \lambda_i\} \mathbf{u}_i^T$$

$$= \mathbf{U} \begin{pmatrix} \exp\{\beta \lambda_1\} & 0 & \cdots & 0 \\ 0 & \exp\{\beta \lambda_2\} & \cdots & 0 \\ \vdots & \vdots & \ddots & 0 \\ 0 & 0 & \cdots & \exp\{\beta \lambda_n\} \end{pmatrix} \mathbf{U}^T \tag{5.19}$$

Thus, the eigenvectors of $\mathbf{K}$ are the same as those for $\mathbf{S}$, whereas its eigenvalues are given as $\exp\{\beta \lambda_i\}$, where λ_i is an eigenvalue of $\mathbf{S}$. Further, $\mathbf{K}$ is symmetric because $\mathbf{S}$ is symmetric, and its eigenvalues are real and non-negative because the exponential of a real number is non-negative. $\mathbf{K}$ is thus a positive semidefinite kernel matrix. The complexity of computing the diffusion kernel is $O(n^3)$ corresponding to the complexity of computing the eigen-decomposition.

Von Neumann Diffusion Kernel

A related kernel based on powers of $\mathbf{S}$ is the *von Neumann diffusion kernel*, defined as

$$\mathbf{K} = \sum_{l=0}^{\infty} \beta^l \mathbf{S}^l \tag{5.20}$$

where $\beta \geq 0$. Expanding Eq. (5.20), we have

$$\begin{aligned}
\mathbf{K} &= \mathbf{I} + \beta \mathbf{S} + \beta^2 \mathbf{S}^2 + \beta^3 \mathbf{S}^3 + \cdots \\
&= \mathbf{I} + \beta \mathbf{S}(\mathbf{I} + \beta \mathbf{S} + \beta^2 \mathbf{S}^2 + \cdots) \\
&= \mathbf{I} + \beta \mathbf{S} \mathbf{K}
\end{aligned}$$

Rearranging the terms in the preceding equation, we obtain a closed form expression for the von Neumann kernel:

$$\begin{aligned}
\mathbf{K} - \beta \mathbf{S} \mathbf{K} &= \mathbf{I} \\
(\mathbf{I} - \beta \mathbf{S})\mathbf{K} &= \mathbf{I} \\
\mathbf{K} &= (\mathbf{I} - \beta \mathbf{S})^{-1} \tag{5.21}
\end{aligned}$$

Plugging in the eigen-decomposition $\mathbf{S} = \mathbf{U} \boldsymbol{\Lambda} \mathbf{U}^T$, and rewriting $\mathbf{I} = \mathbf{U}\mathbf{U}^T$, we have

$$\begin{aligned}
\mathbf{K} &= \left(\mathbf{U}\mathbf{U}^T - \mathbf{U}(\beta \boldsymbol{\Lambda})\mathbf{U}^T \right)^{-1} \\
&= \left(\mathbf{U}(\mathbf{I} - \beta \boldsymbol{\Lambda})\mathbf{U}^T \right)^{-1} \\
&= \mathbf{U}(\mathbf{I} - \beta \boldsymbol{\Lambda})^{-1}\mathbf{U}^T
\end{aligned}$$

where $(\mathbf{I} - \beta \boldsymbol{\Lambda})^{-1}$ is the diagonal matrix whose ith diagonal entry is $(1 - \beta \lambda_i)^{-1}$. The eigenvectors of $\mathbf{K}$ and $\mathbf{S}$ are identical, but the eigenvalues of $\mathbf{K}$ are given as $1/(1 - \beta \lambda_i)$. For $\mathbf{K}$ to be a positive semidefinite kernel, all its eigenvalues should be non-negative, which in turn implies that

$$\begin{aligned}
(1 - \beta \lambda_i)^{-1} &\geq 0 \\
1 - \beta \lambda_i &\geq 0 \\
\beta &\leq 1/\lambda_i
\end{aligned}$$

Further, the inverse matrix $(\mathbf{I} - \beta \boldsymbol{\Lambda})^{-1}$ exists only if

$$\det(\mathbf{I} - \beta \boldsymbol{\Lambda}) = \prod_{i=1}^{n}(1 - \beta \lambda_i) \neq 0$$

which implies that $\beta \neq 1/\lambda_i$ for all i. Thus, for $\mathbf{K}$ to be a valid kernel, we require that $\beta < 1/\lambda_i$ for all $i = 1, \ldots, n$. The von Neumann kernel is therefore guaranteed to be positive semidefinite if $|\beta| < 1/\rho(\mathbf{S})$, where $\rho(\mathbf{S}) = \max_i\{|\lambda_i|\}$ is called the *spectral radius* of $\mathbf{S}$, defined as the largest eigenvalue of $\mathbf{S}$ in absolute value.

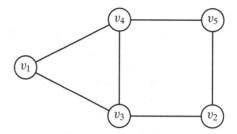

Figure 5.2. Graph diffusion kernel.

Example 5.15. Consider the graph in Figure 5.2. Its adjacency and degree matrices are given as

$$\mathbf{A} = \begin{pmatrix} 0 & 0 & 1 & 1 & 0 \\ 0 & 0 & 1 & 0 & 1 \\ 1 & 1 & 0 & 1 & 0 \\ 1 & 0 & 1 & 0 & 1 \\ 0 & 1 & 0 & 1 & 0 \end{pmatrix} \qquad \mathbf{\Delta} = \begin{pmatrix} 2 & 0 & 0 & 0 & 0 \\ 0 & 2 & 0 & 0 & 0 \\ 0 & 0 & 3 & 0 & 0 \\ 0 & 0 & 0 & 3 & 0 \\ 0 & 0 & 0 & 0 & 2 \end{pmatrix}$$

The negated Laplacian matrix for the graph is therefore

$$\mathbf{S} = -\mathbf{L} = \mathbf{A} - \mathbf{\Delta} = \begin{pmatrix} -2 & 0 & 1 & 1 & 0 \\ 0 & -2 & 1 & 0 & 1 \\ 1 & 1 & -3 & 1 & 0 \\ 1 & 0 & 1 & -3 & 1 \\ 0 & 1 & 0 & 1 & -2 \end{pmatrix}$$

The eigenvalues of $\mathbf{S}$ are as follows:

$$\lambda_1 = 0 \qquad \lambda_2 = -1.38 \qquad \lambda_3 = -2.38 \qquad \lambda_4 = -3.62 \qquad \lambda_5 = -4.62$$

and the eigenvectors of $\mathbf{S}$ are

$$\mathbf{U} = \begin{pmatrix} \mathbf{u}_1 & \mathbf{u}_2 & \mathbf{u}_3 & \mathbf{u}_4 & \mathbf{u}_5 \\ \hline 0.45 & -0.63 & 0.00 & 0.63 & 0.00 \\ 0.45 & 0.51 & -0.60 & 0.20 & -0.37 \\ 0.45 & -0.20 & -0.37 & -0.51 & 0.60 \\ 0.45 & -0.20 & 0.37 & -0.51 & -0.60 \\ 0.45 & 0.51 & 0.60 & 0.20 & 0.37 \end{pmatrix}$$

Assuming $\beta = 0.2$, the exponential diffusion kernel matrix is given as

$$\mathbf{K} = \exp\{0.2\mathbf{S}\} = \mathbf{U} \begin{pmatrix} \exp\{0.2\lambda_1\} & 0 & \cdots & 0 \\ 0 & \exp\{0.2\lambda_2\} & \cdots & 0 \\ \vdots & \vdots & \ddots & 0 \\ 0 & 0 & \cdots & \exp\{0.2\lambda_n\} \end{pmatrix} \mathbf{U}^T$$

$$= \begin{pmatrix} 0.70 & 0.01 & 0.14 & 0.14 & 0.01 \\ 0.01 & 0.70 & 0.13 & 0.03 & 0.14 \\ 0.14 & 0.13 & 0.59 & 0.13 & 0.03 \\ 0.14 & 0.03 & 0.13 & 0.59 & 0.13 \\ 0.01 & 0.14 & 0.03 & 0.13 & 0.70 \end{pmatrix}$$

For the von Neumann diffusion kernel, we have

$$(\mathbf{I} - 0.2\mathbf{\Lambda})^{-1} = \begin{pmatrix} 1 & 0.00 & 0.00 & 0.00 & 0.00 \\ 0 & 0.78 & 0.00 & 0.00 & 0.00 \\ 0 & 0.00 & 0.68 & 0.00 & 0.00 \\ 0 & 0.00 & 0.00 & 0.58 & 0.00 \\ 0 & 0.00 & 0.00 & 0.00 & 0.52 \end{pmatrix}$$

For instance, because $\lambda_2 = -1.38$, we have $1 - \beta\lambda_2 = 1 + 0.2 \times 1.38 = 1.28$, and therefore the second diagonal entry is $(1 - \beta\lambda_2)^{-1} = 1/1.28 = 0.78$. The von Neumann kernel is given as

$$\mathbf{K} = \mathbf{U}(\mathbf{I} - 0.2\mathbf{\Lambda})^{-1}\mathbf{U}^T = \begin{pmatrix} 0.75 & 0.02 & 0.11 & 0.11 & 0.02 \\ 0.02 & 0.74 & 0.10 & 0.03 & 0.11 \\ 0.11 & 0.10 & 0.66 & 0.10 & 0.03 \\ 0.11 & 0.03 & 0.10 & 0.66 & 0.10 \\ 0.02 & 0.11 & 0.03 & 0.10 & 0.74 \end{pmatrix}$$

5.5 FURTHER READING

Kernel methods have been extensively studied in machine learning and data mining. For an in-depth introduction and more advanced topics see Schölkopf and Smola (2002) and Shawe-Taylor and Cristianini (2004). For applications of kernel methods in bioinformatics see Schölkopf, Tsuda, and Vert (2004).

Schölkopf, B. and Smola, A. J. (2002). *Learning with Kernels: Support Vector Machines, Regularization, Optimization, and Beyond*. Cambridge, MA: MIT Press.
Schölkopf, B., Tsuda, K., and Vert, J.-P. (2004). *Kernel Methods in Computational Biology*. Cambridge, MA: MIT press.
Shawe-Taylor, J. and Cristianini, N. (2004). *Kernel Methods for Pattern Analysis*. New York: Cambridge University Press.

5.6 EXERCISES

Q1. Prove that the dimensionality of the feature space for the inhomogeneous polynomial kernel of degree q is $m = \binom{d+q}{q}$.

Q2. Consider the data shown in Table 5.1. Assume the following kernel function: $K(\mathbf{x}_i, \mathbf{x}_j) = \|\mathbf{x}_i - \mathbf{x}_j\|^2$. Compute the kernel matrix $\mathbf{K}$.

Table 5.1. Dataset for Q2

	X_1	X_2
$\mathbf{x}_1^T$	4	2.9
$\mathbf{x}_2^T$	2.5	1
$\mathbf{x}_3^T$	3.5	4
$\mathbf{x}_4^T$	2	2.1

Q3. Show that eigenvectors of $\mathbf{S}$ and $\mathbf{S}^l$ are identical, and further that eigenvalues of $\mathbf{S}^l$ are given as $(\lambda_i)^l$ (for all $i = 1, \ldots, n$), where λ_i is an eigenvalue of $\mathbf{S}$, and $\mathbf{S}$ is some $n \times n$ symmetric similarity matrix.

Q4. The von Neumann diffusion kernel is a valid positive semidefinite kernel if $|\beta| < \frac{1}{\rho(\mathbf{S})}$, where $\rho(\mathbf{S})$ is the spectral radius of $\mathbf{S}$. Can you derive better bounds for cases when $\beta > 0$ and when $\beta < 0$?

Q5. Given the three points $\mathbf{x}_1 = (2.5, 1)^T$, $\mathbf{x}_2 = (3.5, 4)^T$, and $\mathbf{x}_3 = (2, 2.1)^T$.
   (a) Compute the kernel matrix for the Gaussian kernel assuming that $\sigma^2 = 5$.
   (b) Compute the distance of the point $\phi(\mathbf{x}_1)$ from the mean in feature space.
   (c) Compute the dominant eigenvector and eigenvalue for the kernel matrix from (a).

CHAPTER 6

High-dimensional Data

In data mining typically the data is very high dimensional, as the number of attributes can easily be in the hundreds or thousands. Understanding the nature of high-dimensional space, or *hyperspace*, is very important, especially because hyperspace does not behave like the more familiar geometry in two or three dimensions.

6.1 HIGH-DIMENSIONAL OBJECTS

Consider the $n \times d$ data matrix

$$
\mathbf{D} = \begin{pmatrix}
 & X_1 & X_2 & \cdots & X_d \\
\hline
\mathbf{x}_1 & x_{11} & x_{12} & \cdots & x_{1d} \\
\mathbf{x}_2 & x_{21} & x_{22} & \cdots & x_{2d} \\
\vdots & \vdots & \vdots & \ddots & \vdots \\
\mathbf{x}_n & x_{n1} & x_{n2} & \cdots & x_{nd}
\end{pmatrix}
$$

where each point $\mathbf{x}_i \in \mathbb{R}^d$ and each attribute $X_j \in \mathbb{R}^n$.

Hypercube

Let the minimum and maximum values for each attribute X_j be given as

$$
\min(X_j) = \min_i \{x_{ij}\} \qquad\qquad \max(X_j) = \max_i \{x_{ij}\}
$$

The data hyperspace can be considered as a d-dimensional *hyper-rectangle*, defined as

$$
R_d = \prod_{j=1}^{d} \left[\min(X_j), \max(X_j) \right]
$$

$$
= \left\{ \mathbf{x} = (x_1, x_2, \ldots, x_d)^T \mid x_j \in [\min(X_j), \max(X_j)], \text{ for } j = 1, \ldots, d \right\}
$$

Assume the data is centered to have mean $\mu = 0$. Let m denote the largest absolute value in $\mathbf{D}$, given as

$$m = \max_{j=1}^{d} \max_{i=1}^{n} \left\{ |x_{ij}| \right\}$$

The data hyperspace can be represented as a *hypercube*, centered at $\mathbf{0}$, with all sides of length $l = 2m$, given as

$$H_d(l) = \left\{ \mathbf{x} = (x_1, x_2, \ldots, x_d)^T \mid \forall i, \; x_i \in [-l/2, l/2] \right\}$$

The hypercube in one dimension, $H_1(l)$, represents an interval, which in two dimensions, $H_2(l)$, represents a square, and which in three dimensions, $H_3(l)$, represents a cube, and so on. The *unit hypercube* has all sides of length $l = 1$, and is denoted as $H_d(1)$.

Hypersphere

Assume that the data has been centered, so that $\mu = 0$. Let r denote the largest magnitude among all points:

$$r = \max_i \left\{ \|\mathbf{x}_i\| \right\}$$

The data hyperspace can also be represented as a d-dimensional *hyperball* centered at $\mathbf{0}$ with radius r, defined as

$$B_d(r) = \left\{ \mathbf{x} \mid \|\mathbf{x}\| \leq r \right\} \tag{6.1}$$

$$\text{or } B_d(r) = \left\{ \mathbf{x} = (x_1, x_2, \ldots, x_d)^T \mid \sum_{j=1}^{d} x_j^2 \leq r^2 \right\} \tag{6.2}$$

The surface of the hyperball is called a *hypersphere*, and it consists of all the points exactly at distance r from the center of the hyperball, defined as

$$S_d(r) = \left\{ \mathbf{x} \mid \|\mathbf{x}\| = r \right\} \tag{6.3}$$

$$\text{or } S_d(r) = \left\{ \mathbf{x} = (x_1, x_2, \ldots, x_d)^T \mid \sum_{j=1}^{d} (x_j)^2 = r^2 \right\} \tag{6.4}$$

Because the hyperball consists of all the surface and interior points, it is also called a *closed hypersphere*.

Example 6.1. Consider the 2-dimensional, centered, Iris dataset, plotted in Figure 6.1. The largest absolute value along any dimension is $m = 2.06$, and the point with the largest magnitude is $(2.06, 0.75)$, with $r = 2.19$. In two dimensions, the hypercube representing the data space is a square with sides of length $l = 2m = 4.12$. The hypersphere marking the extent of the space is a circle (shown dashed) with radius $r = 2.19$.

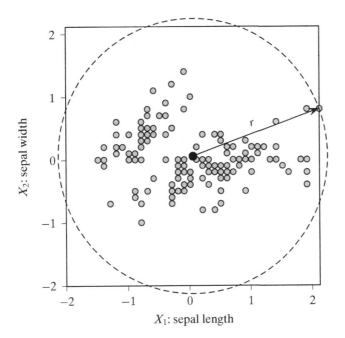

Figure 6.1. Iris data hyperspace: hypercube (solid; with $l = 4.12$) and hypersphere (dashed; with $r = 2.19$).

Hyperplanes

A hyperplane in d dimensions is given as the set of all points $\mathbf{x} \in \mathbb{R}^d$ that satisfy the equation $h(\mathbf{x}) = 0$, where $h(\mathbf{x})$ is the *hyperplane function*, defined as follows:

$$h(\mathbf{x}) = \mathbf{w}^T\mathbf{x} + b = w_1 x_1 + w_2 x_2 + \cdots + w_d x_d + b$$

Here, $\mathbf{w}$ is a d dimensional *weight vector* and b is a scalar, called the *bias*. For points that comprise the hyperplane, we have

$$h(\mathbf{x}) = \mathbf{w}^T\mathbf{x} + b = 0 \tag{6.5}$$

The hyperplane is thus defined as the set of all points such that $\mathbf{w}^T\mathbf{x} = -b$.

To see the role played by b, assuming that $w_1 \neq 0$, and setting $x_i = 0$ for all $i > 1$, we can obtain the offset where the hyperplane intersects the first axis, since by Eq. (6.5), we have

$$w_1 x_1 = -b \quad \text{or} \quad x_1 = -\frac{b}{w_1}$$

In other words, the point $(-\frac{b}{w_1}, 0, \ldots, 0)$ lies on the hyperplane. In a similar manner, we can obtain the offset where the hyperplane intersects each of the axes, which is given as $-\frac{b}{w_i}$ (provided $w_i \neq 0$).

Let $\mathbf{x}_1$ and $\mathbf{x}_2$ be two arbitrary points that lie on the hyperplane. From Eq. (6.5) we have

$$h(\mathbf{x}_1) = \mathbf{w}^T\mathbf{x}_1 + b = 0$$

$$h(\mathbf{x}_2) = \mathbf{w}^T\mathbf{x}_2 + b = 0$$

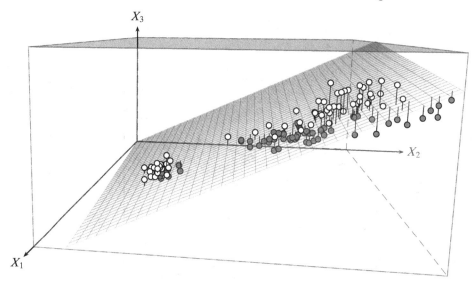

Figure 6.2. 3-dimensional Iris data hyperspace with a 2-dimensional hyperplane. Points in white are above the plane, whereas points in gray are below the plane.

Subtracting one from the other we obtain

$$\mathbf{w}^T(\mathbf{x}_1 - \mathbf{x}_2) = 0$$

This means that the weight vector $\mathbf{w}$ is orthogonal to the hyperplane because it is orthogonal to any arbitrary vector $(\mathbf{x}_1 - \mathbf{x}_2)$ on the hyperplane. In other words, the weight vector $\mathbf{w}$ specifies the direction that is normal to the hyperplane, which fixes the orientation of the hyperplane, whereas the bias b fixes the offset of the hyperplane in the d-dimensional space.

It is important to note that a hyperplane in d-dimensions has dimension $d-1$. For example, in $d=2$ dimensions, the hyperplane is a line, which has dimension 1; in $d=3$ dimensions the hyperplane is a plane, which has dimension 2, and so on. A hyperplane splits the original d-dimensional space into two *half-spaces*. Points on one side satisfy the equation $h(\mathbf{x}) > 0$, point on the other side satisfy the equation $h(\mathbf{x}) < 0$, and finally, points on the hyperplane satisfy the condition $h(\mathbf{x}) = 0$.

Example 6.2. Consider the 3-dimensional Iris dataset spanned by the attributes sepal length (X_1), petal length (X_2), and petal width (X_3). Figure 6.2 shows the scatterplot of the points, and also plots the hyperplane:

$$h(\mathbf{x}) = -0.082 \cdot x_1 + 0.45 \cdot x_2 - x_3 - 0.014 = 0$$

with the weight vector $\mathbf{w} = (w_1, w_2, w_3)^T = (-0.082, 0.45, -1)^T$ and bias $b = -0.014$. The hyperplane splits the space into two half-spaces, comprising the points above the plane (in white) and those below the plane (in gray).

6.2 HIGH-DIMENSIONAL VOLUMES

Hypercube

The volume of a hypercube with edge length l is given as

$$\text{vol}(H_d(l)) = l^d \tag{6.6}$$

Hypersphere

The volume of a hyperball and its corresponding hypersphere is identical because the volume measures the total content of the object, including all internal space. Consider the well known equations for the volume of a hypersphere in lower dimensions

$$\text{vol}(S_1(r)) = 2r \tag{6.7}$$

$$\text{vol}(S_2(r)) = \pi r^2 \tag{6.8}$$

$$\text{vol}(S_3(r)) = \frac{4}{3}\pi r^3 \tag{6.9}$$

As per the derivation in Appendix 6.7, the general equation for the volume of a d-dimensional hypersphere is given as

$$\text{vol}(S_d(r)) = K_d \cdot r^d = \left(\frac{\pi^{\frac{d}{2}}}{\Gamma\left(\frac{d}{2}+1\right)}\right) r^d \tag{6.10}$$

where

$$K_d = \frac{\pi^{d/2}}{\Gamma(\frac{d}{2}+1)} \tag{6.11}$$

is a scalar that depends on the dimensionality d, and Γ is the gamma function [Eq. (3.24)], defined as (for $\alpha > 0$)

$$\Gamma(\alpha) = \int_0^\infty x^{\alpha-1}e^{-x}dx \tag{6.12}$$

By direct integration of Eq. (6.12), we have

$$\Gamma(1) = 1 \quad \text{and} \quad \Gamma\left(\frac{1}{2}\right) = \sqrt{\pi} \tag{6.13}$$

The gamma function also has the following property for any $\alpha > 1$:

$$\Gamma(\alpha) = (\alpha - 1)\Gamma(\alpha - 1) \tag{6.14}$$

For any integer $n \geq 1$, we immediately have

$$\Gamma(n) = (n-1)! \tag{6.15}$$

Turning our attention back to Eq. (6.10), when d is even, then $\frac{d}{2}+1$ is an integer, and by Eq. (6.15) we have

$$\Gamma\left(\frac{d}{2}+1\right)=\left(\frac{d}{2}\right)!$$

and when d is odd, then by Eqs. (6.14) and (6.13), we have

$$\Gamma\left(\frac{d}{2}+1\right)=\left(\frac{d}{2}\right)\left(\frac{d-2}{2}\right)\left(\frac{d-4}{2}\right)\cdots\left(\frac{d-(d-1)}{2}\right)\Gamma\left(\frac{1}{2}\right)=\left(\frac{d!!}{2^{(d+1)/2}}\right)\sqrt{\pi}$$

where $d!!$ denotes the double factorial (or multifactorial), given as

$$d!!=\begin{cases}1 & \text{if } d=0 \text{ or } d=1 \\ d\cdot(d-2)!! & \text{if } d\geq 2\end{cases}$$

Putting it all together we have

$$\Gamma\left(\frac{d}{2}+1\right)=\begin{cases}\left(\frac{d}{2}\right)! & \text{if } d \text{ is even} \\ \sqrt{\pi}\left(\frac{d!!}{2^{(d+1)/2}}\right) & \text{if } d \text{ is odd}\end{cases} \tag{6.16}$$

Plugging in values of $\Gamma(d/2+1)$ in Eq. (6.10) gives us the equations for the volume of the hypersphere in different dimensions.

Example 6.3. By Eq. (6.16), we have for $d=1$, $d=2$ and $d=3$:

$$\Gamma(1/2+1)=\frac{1}{2}\sqrt{\pi}$$

$$\Gamma(2/2+1)=1!=1$$

$$\Gamma(3/2+1)=\frac{3}{4}\sqrt{\pi}$$

Thus, we can verify that the volume of a hypersphere in one, two, and three dimensions is given as

$$\text{vol}(S_1(r))=\frac{\sqrt{\pi}}{\frac{1}{2}\sqrt{\pi}}r=2r$$

$$\text{vol}(S_2(r))=\frac{\pi}{1}r^2=\pi r^2$$

$$\text{vol}(S_3(r))=\frac{\pi^{3/2}}{\frac{3}{4}\sqrt{\pi}}r^3=\frac{4}{3}\pi r^3$$

which match the expressions in Eqs. (6.7), (6.8), and (6.9), respectively.

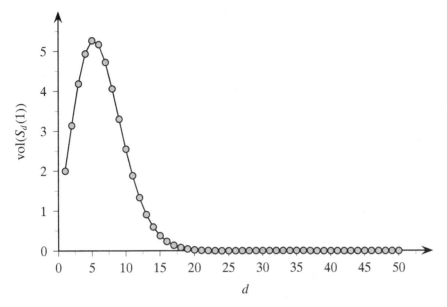

Figure 6.3. Volume of a unit hypersphere.

Surface Area The *surface area* of the hypersphere can be obtained by differentiating its volume with respect to r, given as

$$\text{area}(S_d(r)) = \frac{d}{dr}\,\text{vol}(S_d(r)) = \left(\frac{\pi^{\frac{d}{2}}}{\Gamma\left(\frac{d}{2}+1\right)}\right) d\,r^{d-1} = \left(\frac{2\pi^{\frac{d}{2}}}{\Gamma\left(\frac{d}{2}\right)}\right) r^{d-1}$$

We can quickly verify that for two dimensions the surface area of a circle is given as $2\pi r$, and for three dimensions the surface area of sphere is given as $4\pi r^2$.

Asymptotic Volume An interesting observation about the hypersphere volume is that as dimensionality increases, the volume first increases up to a point, and then starts to decrease, and ultimately vanishes. In particular, for the unit hypersphere with $r = 1$,

$$\lim_{d\to\infty} \text{vol}(S_d(1)) = \lim_{d\to\infty} \frac{\pi^{\frac{d}{2}}}{\Gamma(\frac{d}{2}+1)} \to 0 \tag{6.17}$$

Example 6.4. Figure 6.3 plots the volume of the unit hypersphere in Eq. (6.10) with increasing dimensionality. We see that initially the volume increases, and achieves the highest volume for $d = 5$ with $\text{vol}(S_5(1)) = 5.263$. Thereafter, the volume drops rapidly and essentially becomes zero by $d = 30$.

6.3 HYPERSPHERE INSCRIBED WITHIN HYPERCUBE

We next look at the space enclosed within the largest hypersphere that can be accommodated within a hypercube (which represents the dataspace). Consider a hypersphere of radius r inscribed in a hypercube with sides of length $2r$. When we take the ratio of the volume of the hypersphere of radius r to the hypercube with side length $l = 2r$, we observe the following trends.

In two dimensions, we have

$$\frac{\text{vol}(S_2(r))}{\text{vol}(H_2(2r))} = \frac{\pi r^2}{4r^2} = \frac{\pi}{4} = 78.5\%$$

Thus, an inscribed circle occupies $\frac{\pi}{4}$ of the volume of its enclosing square, as illustrated in Figure 6.4(a).

In three dimensions, the ratio is given as

$$\frac{\text{vol}(S_3(r))}{\text{vol}(H_3(2r))} = \frac{\frac{4}{3}\pi r^3}{8r^3} = \frac{\pi}{6} = 52.4\%$$

An inscribed sphere takes up only $\frac{\pi}{6}$ of the volume of its enclosing cube, as shown in Figure 6.4(b), which is quite a sharp decrease over the 2-dimensional case.

For the general case, as the dimensionality d increases asymptotically, we get

$$\lim_{d \to \infty} \frac{\text{vol}(S_d(r))}{\text{vol}(H_d(2r))} = \lim_{d \to \infty} \frac{\pi^{d/2}}{2^d \Gamma(\frac{d}{2} + 1)} \to 0 \tag{6.18}$$

This means that as the dimensionality increases, most of the volume of the hypercube is in the "corners," whereas the center is essentially empty. The mental picture that emerges is that high-dimensional space looks like a rolled-up porcupine, as illustrated in Figure 6.5.

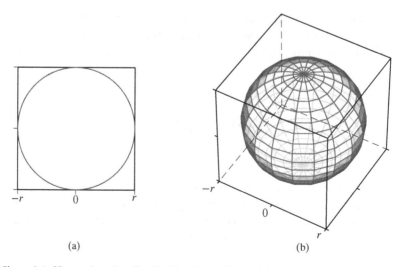

(a)   (b)

Figure 6.4. Hypersphere inscribed inside a hypercube: in (a) two and (b) three dimensions.

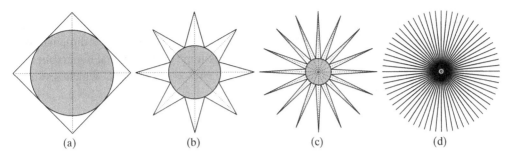

Figure 6.5. Conceptual view of high-dimensional space: (a) two, (b) three, (c) four, and (d) higher dimensions. In d dimensions there are 2^d "corners" and 2^{d-1} diagonals. The radius of the inscribed circle accurately reflects the difference between the volume of the hypercube and the inscribed hypersphere in d dimensions.

6.4 VOLUME OF THIN HYPERSPHERE SHELL

Let us now consider the volume of a thin hypersphere shell of width ϵ bounded by an outer hypersphere of radius r, and an inner hypersphere of radius $r - \epsilon$. The volume of the thin shell is given as the difference between the volumes of the two bounding hyperspheres, as illustrated in Figure 6.6.

Let $S_d(r, \epsilon)$ denote the thin hypershell of width ϵ. Its volume is given as

$$\text{vol}(S_d(r, \epsilon)) = \text{vol}(S_d(r)) - \text{vol}(S_d(r - \epsilon)) = K_d r^d - K_d (r - \epsilon)^d.$$

Let us consider the ratio of the volume of the thin shell to the volume of the outer sphere:

$$\frac{\text{vol}(S_d(r, \epsilon))}{\text{vol}(S_d(r))} = \frac{K_d r^d - K_d (r - \epsilon)^d}{K_d r^d} = 1 - \left(1 - \frac{\epsilon}{r}\right)^d.$$

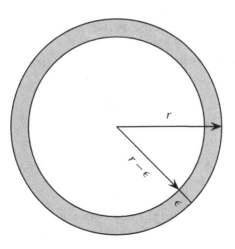

Figure 6.6. Volume of a thin shell (for $\epsilon > 0$).

Example 6.5. For example, for a circle in two dimensions, with $r = 1$ and $\epsilon = 0.01$ the volume of the thin shell is $1 - (0.99)^2 = 0.0199 \simeq 2\%$. As expected, in two-dimensions, the thin shell encloses only a small fraction of the volume of the original hypersphere. For three dimensions this fraction becomes $1 - (0.99)^3 = 0.0297 \simeq 3\%$, which is still a relatively small fraction.

Asymptotic Volume

As d increases, in the limit we obtain

$$\lim_{d \to \infty} \frac{\text{vol}(S_d(r, \epsilon))}{\text{vol}(S_d(r))} = \lim_{d \to \infty} 1 - \left(1 - \frac{\epsilon}{r}\right)^d \to 1 \tag{6.19}$$

That is, almost all of the volume of the hypersphere is contained in the thin shell as $d \to \infty$. This means that in high-dimensional spaces, unlike in lower dimensions, most of the volume is concentrated around the surface (within ϵ) of the hypersphere, and the center is essentially void. In other words, if the data is distributed uniformly in the d-dimensional space, then all of the points essentially lie on the boundary of the space (which is a $d - 1$ dimensional object). Combined with the fact that most of the hypercube volume is in the corners, we can observe that in high dimensions, data tends to get scattered on the boundary and corners of the space.

6.5 DIAGONALS IN HYPERSPACE

Another counterintuitive behavior of high-dimensional space deals with the diagonals. Let us assume that we have a d-dimensional hypercube, with origin $\mathbf{0}_d = (0_1, 0_2, \ldots, 0_d)^T$, and bounded in each dimension in the range $[-1, 1]$. Then each "corner" of the hyperspace is a d-dimensional vector of the form $(\pm 1_1, \pm 1_2, \ldots, \pm 1_d)^T$. Let $\mathbf{e}_i = (0_1, \ldots, 1_i, \ldots, 0_d)^T$ denote the d-dimensional canonical unit vector in dimension i, that is, the ith standard basis vector, and let $\mathbf{1}$ denote the d-dimensional ones vector $(1_1, 1_2, \ldots, 1_d)^T$.

Consider the angle θ_d between the ones vector $\mathbf{1}$ and the first standard basis vector $\mathbf{e}_1$, in d dimensions:

$$\cos \theta_d = \frac{\mathbf{e}_1^T \mathbf{1}}{\|\mathbf{e}_1\| \, \|\mathbf{1}\|} = \frac{\mathbf{e}_1^T \mathbf{1}}{\sqrt{\mathbf{e}_1^T \mathbf{e}_1} \sqrt{\mathbf{1}^T \mathbf{1}}} = \frac{1}{\sqrt{1}\sqrt{d}} = \frac{1}{\sqrt{d}}$$

As its name implies, the ones vector $\mathbf{1}$ makes the same angle, namely $\frac{1}{\sqrt{d}}$, with each of the standard basis vectors $\mathbf{e}_i$, for $i = 1, 2, \cdots, d$.

Example 6.6. Figure 6.7 illustrates the angle between the ones vector $\mathbf{1}$ and $\mathbf{e}_1$, for $d = 2$ and $d = 3$. In two dimensions, we have $\cos \theta_2 = \frac{1}{\sqrt{2}}$ whereas in three dimensions, we have $\cos \theta_3 = \frac{1}{\sqrt{3}}$.

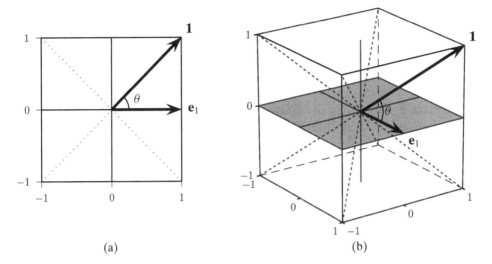

Figure 6.7. Angle between the ones vector **1** and $\mathbf{e}_1$: in (a) two and (b) three dimensions.

Asymptotic Angle

As d increases, the angle between the d-dimensional ones vector **1** and the first axis vector $\mathbf{e}_1$ is given as

$$\lim_{d \to \infty} \cos \theta_d = \lim_{d \to \infty} \frac{1}{\sqrt{d}} \to 0$$

which implies that

$$\lim_{d \to \infty} \theta_d \to \frac{\pi}{2} = 90° \tag{6.20}$$

This analysis holds for the angle between the ones vector $\mathbf{1}_d$ and any of the d principal axis vectors $\mathbf{e}_i$ (i.e., for all $i \in [1, d]$). In fact, the same result holds for any diagonal vector and any principal axis vector (in both directions). This implies that in high dimensions all of the diagonal vectors are perpendicular (or orthogonal) to all the coordinates axes! Because there are 2^d corners in a d-dimensional hyperspace, there are 2^d diagonal vectors from the origin to each of the corners. Because the diagonal vectors in opposite directions define a new axis, we obtain 2^{d-1} new axes, each of which is essentially orthogonal to all of the d principal coordinate axes! Thus, in effect, high-dimensional space has an exponential number of orthogonal "axes." A consequence of this strange property of high-dimensional space is that if there is a point or a group of points, say a cluster of interest, near a diagonal, these points will get projected into the origin and will not be visible in lower dimensional projections.

6.6 DENSITY OF THE MULTIVARIATE NORMAL

Let us consider how, for the standard multivariate normal distribution, the density of points around the mean changes in d dimensions. In particular, consider the probability of a point being within a fraction $\alpha > 0$, of the peak density at the mean.

For a multivariate normal distribution [Eq. (2.42)], with $\mu = \mathbf{0}_d$ (the d-dimensional zero vector), and $\Sigma = \mathbf{I}_d$ (the $d \times d$ identity matrix), we have

$$f(\mathbf{x}) = \frac{1}{(\sqrt{2\pi})^d} \exp\left\{-\frac{\mathbf{x}^T\mathbf{x}}{2}\right\} \qquad (6.21)$$

At the mean $\mu = \mathbf{0}_d$, the peak density is $f(\mathbf{0}_d) = \frac{1}{(\sqrt{2\pi})^d}$. Thus, the set of points $\mathbf{x}$ with density at least α fraction of the density at the mean, with $0 < \alpha < 1$, is given as

$$\frac{f(\mathbf{x})}{f(\mathbf{0})} \geq \alpha$$

which implies that

$$\exp\left\{-\frac{\mathbf{x}^T\mathbf{x}}{2}\right\} \geq \alpha$$

$$\text{or } \mathbf{x}^T\mathbf{x} \leq -2\ln(\alpha)$$

$$\text{and thus } \sum_{i=1}^{d}(x_i)^2 \leq -2\ln(\alpha) \qquad (6.22)$$

It is known that if the random variables X_1, X_2, ..., X_k are independent and identically distributed, and if each variable has a standard normal distribution, then their squared sum $X^2 + X_2^2 + \cdots + X_k^2$ follows a χ^2 distribution with k degrees of freedom, denoted as χ_k^2. Because the projection of the standard multivariate normal onto any attribute X_j is a standard univariate normal, we conclude that $\mathbf{x}^T\mathbf{x} = \sum_{i=1}^{d}(x_i)^2$ has a χ^2 distribution with d degrees of freedom. The probability that a point $\mathbf{x}$ is within α times the density at the mean can be computed from the χ_d^2 density function using Eq. (6.22), as follows:

$$P\left(\frac{f(\mathbf{x})}{f(\mathbf{0})} \geq \alpha\right) = P(\mathbf{x}^T\mathbf{x} \leq -2\ln(\alpha)) = \int_0^{-2\ln(\alpha)} f_{\chi_d^2}(\mathbf{x}^T\mathbf{x}) = F_{\chi_d^2}(-2\ln(\alpha)) \qquad (6.23)$$

where $f_{\chi_q^2}(x)$ is the chi-squared probability density function [Eq. (3.23)] with q degrees of freedom:

$$f_{\chi_q^2}(x) = \frac{1}{2^{q/2}\Gamma(q/2)} x^{\frac{q}{2}-1} e^{-\frac{x}{2}}$$

and $F_{\chi_q^2}(x)$ is its cumulative distribution function.

As dimensionality increases, this probability decreases sharply, and eventually tends to zero, that is,

$$\lim_{d\to\infty} P\left(\mathbf{x}^T\mathbf{x} \leq -2\ln(\alpha)\right) \to 0 \qquad (6.24)$$

Thus, in higher dimensions the probability density around the mean decreases very rapidly as one moves away from the mean. In essence the entire probability mass migrates to the tail regions.

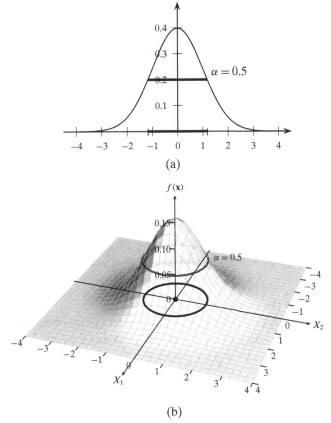

Figure 6.8. Density contour for α fraction of the density at the mean: in (a) one and (b) two dimensions.

Example 6.7. Consider the probability of a point being within 50% of the density at the mean, that is, $\alpha = 0.5$. From Eq. (6.23) we have

$$P\left(\mathbf{x}^T\mathbf{x} \leq -2\ln(0.5)\right) = F_{\chi_d^2}(1.386)$$

We can compute the probability of a point being within 50% of the peak density by evaluating the cumulative χ^2 distribution for different degrees of freedom (the number of dimensions). For $d = 1$, we find that the probability is $F_{\chi_1^2}(1.386) = 76.1\%$. For $d = 2$ the probability decreases to $F_{\chi_2^2}(1.386) = 50\%$, and for $d = 3$ it reduces to 29.12%. Looking at Figure 6.8, we can see that only about 24% of the density is in the tail regions for one dimension, but for two dimensions more than 50% of the density is in the tail regions. Figure 6.9 plots the χ_d^2 distribution and shows the probability $P\left(\mathbf{x}^T\mathbf{x} \leq 1.386\right)$ for two and three dimensions. This probability decreases rapidly with dimensionality; by $d = 10$, it decreases to 0.075%, that is, 99.925% of the points lie in the extreme or tail regions.

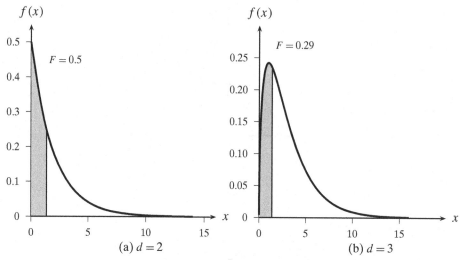

Figure 6.9. Probability $P(\mathbf{x}^T\mathbf{x} \le -2\ln(\alpha))$, with $\alpha = 0.5$.

Distance of Points from the Mean

Let us consider the average distance of a point $\mathbf{x}$ from the center of the standard multivariate normal. Let r^2 denote the square of the distance of a point $\mathbf{x}$ to the center $\boldsymbol{\mu} = \mathbf{0}$, given as

$$r^2 = \|\mathbf{x} - \mathbf{0}\|^2 = \mathbf{x}^T\mathbf{x} = \sum_{i=1}^{d} x_i^2$$

$\mathbf{x}^T\mathbf{x}$ follows a χ^2 distribution with d degrees of freedom, which has mean d and variance $2d$. It follows that the mean and variance of the random variable r^2 is

$$\mu_{r^2} = d \qquad\qquad\qquad \sigma_{r^2}^2 = 2d$$

By the central limit theorem, as $d \to \infty$, r^2 is approximately normal with mean d and variance $2d$, which implies that r^2 is concentrated about its mean value of d. As a consequence, the distance r of a point $\mathbf{x}$ to the center of the standard multivariate normal is likewise approximately concentrated around its mean $\sqrt{d}$.

Next, to estimate the spread of the distance r around its mean value, we need to derive the standard deviation of r from that of r^2. Assuming that σ_r is much smaller compared to r, then using the fact that $\frac{d\log r}{dr} = \frac{1}{r}$, after rearranging the terms, we have

$$\frac{dr}{r} = d\log r = \frac{1}{2}d\log r^2$$

Using the fact that $\frac{d\log r^2}{dr^2} = \frac{1}{r^2}$, and rearranging the terms, we obtain

$$\frac{dr}{r} = \frac{1}{2}\frac{dr^2}{r^2}$$

which implies that $dr = \frac{1}{2r}dr^2$. Setting the change in r^2 equal to the standard deviation of r^2, we have $dr^2 = \sigma_{r^2} = \sqrt{2d}$, and setting the mean radius $r = \sqrt{d}$, we have

$$\sigma_r = dr = \frac{1}{2\sqrt{d}}\sqrt{2d} = \frac{1}{\sqrt{2}}$$

We conclude that for large d, the radius r (or the distance of a point $\mathbf{x}$ from the origin $\mathbf{0}$) follows a normal distribution with mean $\sqrt{d}$ and standard deviation $1/\sqrt{2}$. Nevertheless, the density at the mean distance $r = \sqrt{d}$, is exponentially smaller than that at the peak density because

$$\frac{f(\mathbf{x})}{f(\mathbf{0})} = \exp\{-\mathbf{x}^T\mathbf{x}/2\} = \exp\{-d/2\}$$

Combined with the fact that the probability mass migrates away from the mean in high dimensions, we have another interesting observation, namely that, whereas the density of the standard multivariate normal is maximized at the center $\mathbf{0}$, most of the probability mass (the points) is concentrated in a small band around the mean distance of $\sqrt{d}$ from the center.

6.7 APPENDIX: DERIVATION OF HYPERSPHERE VOLUME

The volume of the hypersphere can be derived via integration using spherical polar coordinates. We consider the derivation in two and three dimensions, and then for a general d.

Volume in Two Dimensions

As illustrated in Figure 6.10, in $d = 2$ dimensions, the point $\mathbf{x} = (x_1, x_2) \in \mathbb{R}^2$ can be expressed in polar coordinates as follows:

$$x_1 = r \cos\theta_1 = rc_1$$
$$x_2 = r \sin\theta_1 = rs_1$$

where $r = \|\mathbf{x}\|$, and we use the notation $\cos\theta_1 = c_1$ and $\sin\theta_1 = s_1$ for convenience.

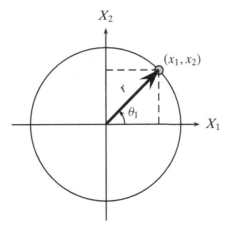

Figure 6.10. Polar coordinates in two dimensions.

The *Jacobian matrix* for this transformation is given as

$$J(\theta_1) = \begin{pmatrix} \frac{\partial x_1}{\partial r} & \frac{\partial x_1}{\partial \theta_1} \\ \frac{\partial x_2}{\partial r} & \frac{\partial x_2}{\partial \theta_1} \end{pmatrix} = \begin{pmatrix} c_1 & -rs_1 \\ s_1 & rc_1 \end{pmatrix}$$

The determinant of the Jacobian matrix is called the *Jacobian*. For $J(\theta_1)$, the Jacobian is given as

$$\det(J(\theta_1)) = rc_1^2 + rs_1^2 = r(c_1^2 + s_1^2) = r \tag{6.25}$$

Using the Jacobian in Eq. (6.25), the volume of the hypersphere in two dimensions can be obtained by integration over r and θ_1 (with $r > 0$, and $0 \le \theta_1 \le 2\pi$)

$$\mathrm{vol}(S_2(r)) = \int_r \int_{\theta_1} \left| \det(J(\theta_1)) \right| dr\, d\theta_1$$

$$= \int_0^r \int_0^{2\pi} r\, dr\, d\theta_1 = \int_0^r r\, dr \int_0^{2\pi} d\theta_1$$

$$= \frac{r^2}{2} \Big|_0^r \cdot \theta_1 \Big|_0^{2\pi} = \pi r^2$$

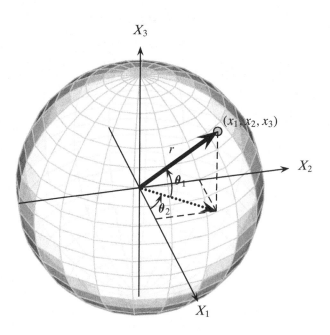

Figure 6.11. Polar coordinates in three dimensions.

Volume in Three Dimensions

As illustrated in Figure 6.11, in $d = 3$ dimensions, the point $\mathbf{x} = (x_1, x_2, x_3) \in \mathbb{R}^3$ can be expressed in polar coordinates as follows:

$$x_1 = r \cos\theta_1 \cos\theta_2 = r c_1 c_2$$

$$x_2 = r \cos\theta_1 \sin\theta_2 = r c_1 s_2$$

$$x_3 = r \sin\theta_1 = r s_1$$

where $r = \|\mathbf{x}\|$, and we used the fact that the dotted vector that lies in the X_1–X_2 plane in Figure 6.11 has magnitude $r \cos\theta_1$.

The Jacobian matrix is given as

$$J(\theta_1, \theta_2) = \begin{pmatrix} \frac{\partial x_1}{\partial r} & \frac{\partial x_1}{\partial \theta_1} & \frac{\partial x_1}{\partial \theta_2} \\ \frac{\partial x_2}{\partial r} & \frac{\partial x_2}{\partial \theta_1} & \frac{\partial x_2}{\partial \theta_2} \\ \frac{\partial x_3}{\partial r} & \frac{\partial x_3}{\partial \theta_1} & \frac{\partial x_3}{\partial \theta_2} \end{pmatrix} = \begin{pmatrix} c_1 c_2 & -r s_1 c_2 & -r c_1 s_2 \\ c_1 s_2 & -r s_1 s_2 & r c_1 c_2 \\ s_1 & r c_1 & 0 \end{pmatrix}$$

The Jacobian is then given as

$$\det(J(\theta_1, \theta_2)) = s_1(-r s_1)(c_1) \det(J(\theta_2)) - r c_1 c_1 c_1 \det(J(\theta_2))$$
$$= -r^2 c_1 (s_1^2 + c_2^2) = -r^2 c_1 \tag{6.26}$$

In computing this determinant we made use of the fact that if a column of a matrix $\mathbf{A}$ is multiplied by a scalar s, then the resulting determinant is $s \det(\mathbf{A})$. We also relied on the fact that the $(3, 1)$-*minor* of $J(\theta_1, \theta_2)$, obtained by deleting row 3 and column 1 is actually $J(\theta_2)$ with the first column multiplied by $-r s_1$ and the second column multiplied by c_1. Likewise, the $(3, 2)$-*minor* of $J(\theta_1, \theta_2)$ is $J(\theta_2)$ with both the columns multiplied by c_1.

The volume of the hypersphere for $d = 3$ is obtained via a triple integral with $r > 0$, $-\pi/2 \le \theta_1 \le \pi/2$, and $0 \le \theta_2 \le 2\pi$

$$\text{vol}(S_3(r)) = \int_r \int_{\theta_1} \int_{\theta_2} \left| \det(J(\theta_1, \theta_2)) \right| dr \, d\theta_1 \, d\theta_2$$

$$= \int_0^r \int_{-\pi/2}^{\pi/2} \int_0^{2\pi} r^2 \cos\theta_1 \, dr \, d\theta_1 \, d\theta_2 = \int_0^r r^2 \, dr \int_{-\pi/2}^{\pi/2} \cos\theta_1 d\theta_1 \int_0^{2\pi} d\theta_2$$

$$= \frac{r^3}{3}\Big|_0^r \cdot \sin\theta_1 \Big|_{-\pi/2}^{\pi/2} \cdot \theta_2 \Big|_0^{2\pi} = \frac{r^3}{3} \cdot 2 \cdot 2\pi = \frac{4}{3}\pi r^3 \tag{6.27}$$

Volume in d Dimensions

Before deriving a general expression for the hypersphere volume in d dimensions, let us consider the Jacobian in four dimensions. Generalizing the polar coordinates from three dimensions in Figure 6.11 to four dimensions, we obtain

$$x_1 = r\cos\theta_1\cos\theta_2\cos\theta_3 = rc_1c_2c_3$$
$$x_2 = r\cos\theta_1\cos\theta_2\sin\theta_3 = rc_1c_2s_3$$
$$x_3 = r\cos\theta_1\sin\theta_2 = rc_1s_2$$
$$x_4 = r\sin\theta_1 = rs_1$$

The Jacobian matrix is given as

$$J(\theta_1,\theta_2,\theta_3) = \begin{pmatrix} \frac{\partial x_1}{\partial r} & \frac{\partial x_1}{\partial\theta_1} & \frac{\partial x_1}{\partial\theta_2} & \frac{\partial x_1}{\partial\theta_3} \\ \frac{\partial x_2}{\partial r} & \frac{\partial x_2}{\partial\theta_1} & \frac{\partial x_2}{\partial\theta_2} & \frac{\partial x_2}{\partial\theta_3} \\ \frac{\partial x_3}{\partial r} & \frac{\partial x_3}{\partial\theta_1} & \frac{\partial x_3}{\partial\theta_2} & \frac{\partial x_3}{\partial\theta_3} \\ \frac{\partial x_4}{\partial r} & \frac{\partial x_4}{\partial\theta_1} & \frac{\partial x_4}{\partial\theta_2} & \frac{\partial x_4}{\partial\theta_3} \end{pmatrix} = \begin{pmatrix} c_1c_2c_3 & -rs_1c_2c_3 & -rc_1s_2c_3 & -rc_1c_2s_3 \\ c_1c_2s_3 & -rs_1c_2s_3 & -rc_1s_2s_3 & rc_1c_2c_3 \\ c_1s_2 & -rs_1s_2 & rc_1c_2 & 0 \\ s_1 & rc_1 & 0 & 0 \end{pmatrix}$$

Utilizing the Jacobian in three dimensions [Eq. (6.26)], the Jacobian in four dimensions is given as

$$\det(J(\theta_1,\theta_2,\theta_3)) = s_1(-rs_1)(c_1)(c_1)\det(J(\theta_2,\theta_3)) - rc_1(c_1)(c_1)(c_1)\det(J(\theta_2,\theta_3))$$
$$= r^3s_1^2c_1^2c_2 + r^3c_1^4c_2 = r^3c_1^2c_2(s_1^2 + c_1^2) = r^3c_1^2c_2$$

Jacobian in d Dimensions   By induction, we can obtain the d-dimensional Jacobian as follows:

$$\det(J(\theta_1,\theta_2,\ldots,\theta_{d-1})) = (-1)^d r^{d-1} c_1^{d-2} c_2^{d-3} \ldots c_{d-2}$$

The volume of the hypersphere is given by the d-dimensional integral with $r > 0$, $-\pi/2 \le \theta_i \le \pi/2$ for all $i = 1,\ldots,d-2$, and $0 \le \theta_{d-1} \le 2\pi$:

$$\text{vol}(S_d(r)) = \int_r \int_{\theta_1} \int_{\theta_2} \cdots \int_{\theta_{d-1}} \left| \det(J(\theta_1,\theta_2,\ldots,\theta_{d-1})) \right| dr\, d\theta_1\, d\theta_2 \ldots d\theta_{d-1}$$

$$= \int_0^r r^{d-1} dr \int_{-\pi/2}^{\pi/2} c_1^{d-2} d\theta_1 \cdots \int_{-\pi/2}^{\pi/2} c_{d-2} d\theta_{d-2} \int_0^{2\pi} d\theta_{d-1} \tag{6.28}$$

Consider one of the intermediate integrals:

$$\int_{-\pi/2}^{\pi/2} (\cos\theta)^k d\theta = 2\int_0^{\pi/2} \cos^k\theta\, d\theta \tag{6.29}$$

Let us substitute $u = \cos^2\theta$, then we have $\theta = \cos^{-1}(u^{1/2})$, and the Jacobian is

$$J = \frac{\partial\theta}{\partial u} = -\frac{1}{2}u^{-1/2}(1-u)^{-1/2} \tag{6.30}$$

Substituting Eq. (6.30) in Eq. (6.29), we get the new integral:

$$2 \int_0^{\pi/2} \cos^k \theta d\theta = \int_0^1 u^{(k-1)/2}(1-u)^{-1/2}du$$

$$= B\left(\frac{k+1}{2}, \frac{1}{2}\right) = \frac{\Gamma\left(\frac{k+1}{2}\right)\Gamma\left(\frac{1}{2}\right)}{\Gamma\left(\frac{k}{2}+1\right)} \tag{6.31}$$

where $B(\alpha, \beta)$ is the *beta function*, given as

$$B(\alpha, \beta) = \int_0^1 u^{\alpha-1}(1-u)^{\beta-1}du$$

and it can be expressed in terms of the gamma function [Eq. (6.12)] via the identity

$$B(\alpha, \beta) = \frac{\Gamma(\alpha)\Gamma(\beta)}{\Gamma(\alpha+\beta)}$$

Using the fact that $\Gamma(1/2) = \sqrt{\pi}$, and $\Gamma(1) = 1$, plugging Eq. (6.31) into Eq. (6.28), we get

$$\text{vol}(S_d(r)) = \frac{r^d}{d} \frac{\Gamma\left(\frac{d-1}{2}\right)\Gamma\left(\frac{1}{2}\right)}{\Gamma\left(\frac{d}{2}\right)} \frac{\Gamma\left(\frac{d-2}{2}\right)\Gamma\left(\frac{1}{2}\right)}{\Gamma\left(\frac{d-1}{2}\right)} \cdots \frac{\Gamma(1)\Gamma\left(\frac{1}{2}\right)}{\Gamma\left(\frac{3}{2}\right)} 2\pi$$

$$= \frac{\pi \Gamma\left(\frac{1}{2}\right)^{d/2-1} r^d}{\frac{d}{2}\Gamma\left(\frac{d}{2}\right)}$$

$$= \left(\frac{\pi^{d/2}}{\Gamma\left(\frac{d}{2}+1\right)}\right) r^d$$

which matches the expression in Eq. (6.10).

6.8 FURTHER READING

For an introduction to the geometry of d-dimensional spaces see Kendall (1961) and also Scott (1992, Section 1.5). The derivation of the mean distance for the multivariate normal is from MacKay (2003, p. 130).

Kendall, M. G. (1961). *A Course in the Geometry of n Dimensions*. New York: Hafner.
MacKay, D. J. (2003). *Information Theory, Inference and Learning Algorithms*. New York: Cambridge University Press.
Scott, D. W. (1992). *Multivariate Density Estimation: Theory, Practice, and Visualization*. New York: John Wiley & Sons.

6.9 EXERCISES

Q1. Given the gamma function in Eq. (6.12), show the following:

(a) $\Gamma(1) = 1$

(b) $\Gamma\left(\frac{1}{2}\right) = \sqrt{\pi}$

(c) $\Gamma(\alpha) = (\alpha - 1)\Gamma(\alpha - 1)$

Q2. Show that the asymptotic volume of the hypersphere $S_d(r)$ for any value of radius r eventually tends to zero as d increases.

Q3. The ball with center $\mathbf{c} \in \mathbb{R}^d$ and radius r is defined as

$$B_d(\mathbf{c}, r) = \left\{\mathbf{x} \in \mathbb{R}^d \mid \delta(\mathbf{x}, \mathbf{c}) \leq r\right\}$$

where $\delta(\mathbf{x}, \mathbf{c})$ is the distance between $\mathbf{x}$ and $\mathbf{c}$, which can be specified using the L_p-norm:

$$L_p(\mathbf{x}, \mathbf{c}) = \left(\sum_{i=1}^{d} |x_i - c_i|^p\right)^{\frac{1}{p}}$$

where $p \neq 0$ is any real number. The distance can also be specified using the L_∞-norm:

$$L_\infty(\mathbf{x}, \mathbf{c}) = \max_i\left\{|x_i - c_i|\right\}$$

Answer the following questions:

(a) For $d = 2$, sketch the shape of the hyperball inscribed inside the unit square, using the L_p-distance with $p = 0.5$ and with center $\mathbf{c} = (0.5, 0.5)^T$.

(b) With $d = 2$ and $\mathbf{c} = (0.5, 0.5)^T$, using the L_∞-norm, sketch the shape of the ball of radius $r = 0.25$ inside a unit square.

(c) Compute the formula for the maximum distance between any two points in the unit hypercube in d dimensions, when using the L_p-norm. What is the maximum distance for $p = 0.5$ when $d = 2$? What is the maximum distance for the L_∞-norm?

Q4. Consider the corner hypercubes of length $\epsilon \leq 1$ inside a unit hypercube. The 2-dimensional case is shown in Figure 6.12. Answer the following questions:

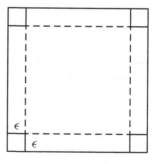

Figure 6.12. For Q4.

(a) Let $\epsilon = 0.1$. What is the fraction of the total volume occupied by the corner cubes in two dimensions?

(b) Derive an expression for the volume occupied by all of the corner hypercubes of length $\epsilon < 1$ as a function of the dimension d. What happens to the fraction of the volume in the corners as $d \to \infty$?

(c) What is the fraction of volume occupied by the thin hypercube shell of width $\epsilon < 1$ as a fraction of the total volume of the outer (unit) hypercube, as $d \to \infty$? For example, in two dimensions the thin shell is the space between the outer square (solid) and inner square (dashed).

Q5. Prove Eq. (6.24), that is, $\lim_{d \to \infty} P\left(\mathbf{x}^T \mathbf{x} \le -2\ln(\alpha)\right) \to 0$, for any $\alpha \in (0, 1)$ and $\mathbf{x} \in \mathbb{R}^d$.

Q6. Consider the conceptual view of high-dimensional space shown in Figure 6.5. Derive an expression for the radius of the inscribed circle, so that the area in the spokes accurately reflects the difference between the volume of the hypercube and the inscribed hypersphere in d dimensions. For instance, if the length of a half-diagonal is fixed at 1, then the radius of the inscribed circle is $\frac{1}{\sqrt{2}}$ in Figure 6.5(a).

Q7. Consider the unit hypersphere (with radius $r = 1$). Inside the hypersphere inscribe a hypercube (i.e., the largest hypercube you can fit inside the hypersphere). An example in two dimensions is shown in Figure 6.13. Answer the following questions:

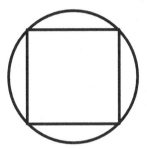

Figure 6.13. For Q7.

(a) Derive an expression for the volume of the inscribed hypercube for any given dimensionality d. Derive the expression for one, two, and three dimensions, and then generalize to higher dimensions.

(b) What happens to the ratio of the volume of the inscribed hypercube to the volume of the enclosing hypersphere as $d \to \infty$? Again, give the ratio in one, two and three dimensions, and then generalize.

Q8. Assume that a unit hypercube is given as $[0, 1]^d$, that is, the range is $[0, 1]$ in each dimension. The main diagonal in the hypercube is defined as the vector from $(\mathbf{0}, 0) = (\overbrace{0, \ldots, 0}^{d-1}, 0)$ to $(\mathbf{1}, 1) = (\overbrace{1, \ldots, 1}^{d-1}, 1)$. For example, when $d = 2$, the main diagonal goes from $(0, 0)$ to $(1, 1)$. On the other hand, the main anti-diagonal is defined as the vector from $(\mathbf{1}, 0) = (\overbrace{1, \ldots, 1}^{d-1}, 0)$ to $(\mathbf{0}, 1) = (\overbrace{0, \ldots, 0}^{d-1}, 1)$ For example, for $d = 2$, the anti-diagonal is from $(1, 0)$ to $(0, 1)$.

(a) Sketch the diagonal and anti-diagonal in $d = 3$ dimensions, and compute the angle between them.

(b) What happens to the angle between the main diagonal and anti-diagonal as $d \to \infty$. First compute a general expression for the d dimensions, and then take the limit as $d \to \infty$.

Q9. Draw a sketch of a hypersphere in four dimensions.

CHAPTER 7

Dimensionality Reduction

We saw in Chapter 6 that high-dimensional data has some peculiar characteristics, some of which are counterintuitive. For example, in high dimensions the center of the space is devoid of points, with most of the points being scattered along the surface of the space or in the corners. There is also an apparent proliferation of orthogonal axes. As a consequence high-dimensional data can cause problems for data mining and analysis, although in some cases high-dimensionality can help, for example, for nonlinear classification. Nevertheless, it is important to check whether the dimensionality can be reduced while preserving the essential properties of the full data matrix. This can aid data visualization as well as data mining. In this chapter we study methods that allow us to obtain optimal lower-dimensional projections of the data.

7.1 BACKGROUND

Let the data $\mathbf{D}$ consist of n points over d attributes, that is, it is an $n \times d$ matrix, given as

$$
\mathbf{D} = \begin{pmatrix}
 & X_1 & X_2 & \cdots & X_d \\
\hline
\mathbf{x}_1^T & x_{11} & x_{12} & \cdots & x_{1d} \\
\mathbf{x}_2^T & x_{21} & x_{22} & \cdots & x_{2d} \\
\vdots & \vdots & \vdots & \ddots & \vdots \\
\mathbf{x}_n^T & x_{n1} & x_{n2} & \cdots & x_{nd}
\end{pmatrix}
$$

Each point $\mathbf{x}_i = (x_{i1}, x_{i2}, \ldots, x_{id})^T$ is a vector in the ambient d-dimensional vector space spanned by the d standard basis vectors $\mathbf{e}_1, \mathbf{e}_2, \ldots, \mathbf{e}_d$, where $\mathbf{e}_i$ corresponds to the ith attribute X_i. Recall that the standard basis is an orthonormal basis for the data space, that is, the basis vectors are pairwise orthogonal, $\mathbf{e}_i^T \mathbf{e}_j = 0$, and have unit length $\|\mathbf{e}_i\| = 1$.

As such, given any other set of d orthonormal vectors $\mathbf{u}_1, \mathbf{u}_2, \ldots, \mathbf{u}_d$, with $\mathbf{u}_i^T \mathbf{u}_j = 0$ and $\|\mathbf{u}_i\| = 1$ (or $\mathbf{u}_i^T \mathbf{u}_i = 1$), we can re-express each point $\mathbf{x}$ as the linear combination

$$
\mathbf{x} = a_1 \mathbf{u}_1 + a_2 \mathbf{u}_2 + \cdots + a_d \mathbf{u}_d \tag{7.1}
$$

where the vector $\mathbf{a} = (a_1, a_2, \ldots, a_d)^T$ represents the coordinates of $\mathbf{x}$ in the new basis. The above linear combination can also be expressed as a matrix multiplication:

$$\boxed{\mathbf{x} = \mathbf{U}\mathbf{a}} \tag{7.2}$$

where $\mathbf{U}$ is the $d \times d$ matrix, whose ith column comprises the ith basis vector $\mathbf{u}_i$:

$$\mathbf{U} = \begin{pmatrix} | & | & & | \\ \mathbf{u}_1 & \mathbf{u}_2 & \cdots & \mathbf{u}_d \\ | & | & & | \end{pmatrix}$$

The matrix $\mathbf{U}$ is an *orthogonal* matrix, whose columns, the basis vectors, are *orthonormal*, that is, they are pairwise orthogonal and have unit length

$$\mathbf{u}_i^T \mathbf{u}_j = \begin{cases} 1 & \text{if } i = j \\ 0 & \text{if } i \neq j \end{cases}$$

Because $\mathbf{U}$ is orthogonal, this means that its inverse equals its transpose:

$$\mathbf{U}^{-1} = \mathbf{U}^T$$

which implies that $\mathbf{U}^T\mathbf{U} = \mathbf{I}$, where $\mathbf{I}$ is the $d \times d$ identity matrix.

Multiplying Eq. (7.2) on both sides by $\mathbf{U}^T$ yields the expression for computing the coordinates of $\mathbf{x}$ in the new basis

$$\mathbf{U}^T\mathbf{x} = \mathbf{U}^T\mathbf{U}\mathbf{a}$$

$$\boxed{\mathbf{a} = \mathbf{U}^T\mathbf{x}} \tag{7.3}$$

Example 7.1. Figure 7.1(a) shows the centered Iris dataset, with $n = 150$ points, in the $d = 3$ dimensional space comprising the sepal length (X_1), sepal width (X_2), and petal length (X_3) attributes. The space is spanned by the standard basis vectors

$$\mathbf{e}_1 = \begin{pmatrix} 1 \\ 0 \\ 0 \end{pmatrix} \qquad \mathbf{e}_2 = \begin{pmatrix} 0 \\ 1 \\ 0 \end{pmatrix} \qquad \mathbf{e}_3 = \begin{pmatrix} 0 \\ 0 \\ 1 \end{pmatrix}$$

Figure 7.1(b) shows the same points in the space spanned by the new basis vectors

$$\mathbf{u}_1 = \begin{pmatrix} -0.390 \\ 0.089 \\ -0.916 \end{pmatrix} \qquad \mathbf{u}_2 = \begin{pmatrix} -0.639 \\ -0.742 \\ 0.200 \end{pmatrix} \qquad \mathbf{u}_3 = \begin{pmatrix} -0.663 \\ 0.664 \\ 0.346 \end{pmatrix}$$

For example, the new coordinates of the centered point $\mathbf{x} = (-0.343, -0.754, 0.241)^T$ can be computed as

$$\mathbf{a} = \mathbf{U}^T\mathbf{x} = \begin{pmatrix} -0.390 & 0.089 & -0.916 \\ -0.639 & -0.742 & 0.200 \\ -0.663 & 0.664 & 0.346 \end{pmatrix} \begin{pmatrix} -0.343 \\ -0.754 \\ 0.241 \end{pmatrix} = \begin{pmatrix} -0.154 \\ 0.828 \\ -0.190 \end{pmatrix}$$

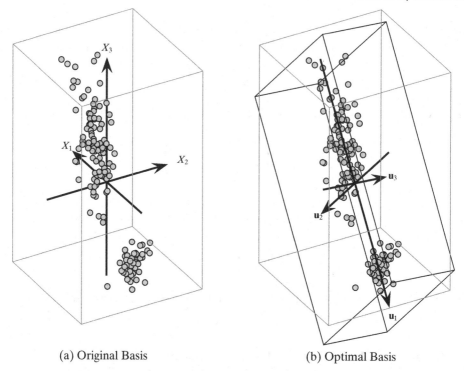

(a) Original Basis   (b) Optimal Basis

Figure 7.1. Iris data: optimal basis in three dimensions.

One can verify that **x** can be written as the linear combination

$$\mathbf{x} = -0.154\mathbf{u}_1 + 0.828\mathbf{u}_2 - 0.190\mathbf{u}_3$$

Because there are potentially infinite choices for the set of orthonormal basis vectors, one natural question is whether there exists an *optimal* basis, for a suitable notion of optimality. Further, it is often the case that the input dimensionality d is very large, which can cause various problems owing to the curse of dimensionality (see Chapter 6). It is natural to ask whether we can find a reduced dimensionality subspace that still preserves the essential characteristics of the data. That is, we are interested in finding the optimal r-dimensional representation of **D**, with $r \ll d$. In other words, given a point **x**, and assuming that the basis vectors have been sorted in decreasing order of importance, we can truncate its linear expansion [Eq. (7.1)] to just r terms, to obtain

$$\mathbf{x}' = a_1\mathbf{u}_1 + a_2\mathbf{u}_2 + \cdots + a_r\mathbf{u}_r = \sum_{i=1}^{r} a_i\mathbf{u}_i \qquad (7.4)$$

Here **x**′ is the projection of **x** onto the first r basis vectors, which can be written in matrix notation as follows:

$$\mathbf{x}' = \begin{pmatrix} | & | & & | \\ \mathbf{u}_1 & \mathbf{u}_2 & \cdots & \mathbf{u}_r \\ | & | & & | \end{pmatrix} \begin{pmatrix} a_1 \\ a_2 \\ \vdots \\ a_r \end{pmatrix} = \mathbf{U}_r \mathbf{a}_r \qquad (7.5)$$

where $\mathbf{U}_r$ is the matrix comprising the first r basis vectors, and $\mathbf{a}_r$ is a vector comprising the first r coordinates. Further, because $\mathbf{a} = \mathbf{U}^T\mathbf{x}$ from Eq. (7.3), restricting it to the first r terms, we get

$$\mathbf{a}_r = \mathbf{U}_r^T\mathbf{x} \tag{7.6}$$

Plugging this into Eq. (7.5), the projection of $\mathbf{x}$ onto the first r basis vectors can be compactly written as

$$\boxed{\mathbf{x}' = \mathbf{U}_r\mathbf{U}_r^T\mathbf{x} = \mathbf{P}_r\mathbf{x}} \tag{7.7}$$

where $\mathbf{P}_r = \mathbf{U}_r\mathbf{U}_r^T$ is the *orthogonal projection matrix* for the subspace spanned by the first r basis vectors. That is, $\mathbf{P}_r$ is symmetric and $\mathbf{P}_r^2 = \mathbf{P}_r$. This is easy to verify because $\mathbf{P}_r^T = (\mathbf{U}_r\mathbf{U}_r^T)^T = \mathbf{U}_r\mathbf{U}_r^T = \mathbf{P}_r$, and $\mathbf{P}_r^2 = (\mathbf{U}_r\mathbf{U}_r^T)(\mathbf{U}_r\mathbf{U}_r^T) = \mathbf{U}_r\mathbf{U}_r^T = \mathbf{P}_r$, where we use the observation that $\mathbf{U}_r^T\mathbf{U}_r = \mathbf{I}_{r\times r}$, the $r \times r$ identity matrix. The projection matrix $\mathbf{P}_r$ can also be written as the decomposition

$$\mathbf{P}_r = \mathbf{U}_r\mathbf{U}_r^T = \sum_{i=1}^{r}\mathbf{u}_i\mathbf{u}_i^T \tag{7.8}$$

From Eqs. (7.1) and (7.4), the projection of $\mathbf{x}$ onto the remaining dimensions comprises the *error vector*

$$\boxed{\boldsymbol{\epsilon} = \sum_{i=r+1}^{d} a_i\mathbf{u}_i = \mathbf{x} - \mathbf{x}'} \tag{7.9}$$

It is worth noting that that $\mathbf{x}'$ and $\boldsymbol{\epsilon}$ are orthogonal vectors:

$$\mathbf{x}'^T\boldsymbol{\epsilon} = \sum_{i=1}^{r}\sum_{j=r+1}^{d} a_i a_j\mathbf{u}_i^T\mathbf{u}_j = 0$$

This is a consequence of the basis being orthonormal. In fact, we can make an even stronger statement. The subspace spanned by the first r basis vectors

$$S_r = span\,(\mathbf{u}_1, \dots, \mathbf{u}_r)$$

and the subspace spanned by the remaining basis vectors

$$S_{d-r} = span\,(\mathbf{u}_{r+1}, \dots, \mathbf{u}_d)$$

are *orthogonal subspaces*, that is, all pairs of vectors $\mathbf{x} \in S_r$ and $\mathbf{y} \in S_{d-r}$ must be orthogonal. The subspace S_{d-r} is also called the *orthogonal complement* of S_r.

Example 7.2. Continuing Example 7.1, approximating the centered point $\mathbf{x} = (-0.343, -0.754, 0.241)^T$ by using only the first basis vector $\mathbf{u}_1 = (-0.390, 0.089, -0.916)^T$, we have

$$\mathbf{x}' = a_1\mathbf{u}_1 = -0.154\mathbf{u}_1 = \begin{pmatrix} 0.060 \\ -0.014 \\ 0.141 \end{pmatrix}$$

The projection of $\mathbf{x}$ on $\mathbf{u}_1$ could have been obtained directly from the projection matrix

$$\mathbf{P}_1 = \mathbf{u}_1 \mathbf{u}_1^T = \begin{pmatrix} -0.390 \\ 0.089 \\ -0.916 \end{pmatrix} \begin{pmatrix} -0.390 & 0.089 & -0.916 \end{pmatrix}$$

$$= \begin{pmatrix} 0.152 & -0.035 & 0.357 \\ -0.035 & 0.008 & -0.082 \\ 0.357 & -0.082 & 0.839 \end{pmatrix}$$

That is

$$\mathbf{x}' = \mathbf{P}_1 \mathbf{x} = \begin{pmatrix} 0.060 \\ -0.014 \\ 0.141 \end{pmatrix}$$

The error vector is given as

$$\boldsymbol{\epsilon} = a_2 \mathbf{u}_2 + a_3 \mathbf{u}_3 = \mathbf{x} - \mathbf{x}' = \begin{pmatrix} -0.40 \\ -0.74 \\ 0.10 \end{pmatrix}$$

One can verify that $\mathbf{x}'$ and $\boldsymbol{\epsilon}$ are orthogonal, i.e.,

$$\mathbf{x}'^T \boldsymbol{\epsilon} = \begin{pmatrix} 0.060 & -0.014 & 0.141 \end{pmatrix} \begin{pmatrix} -0.40 \\ -0.74 \\ 0.10 \end{pmatrix} = 0$$

The goal of dimensionality reduction is to seek an r-dimensional basis that gives the best possible approximation $\mathbf{x}'_i$ over all the points $\mathbf{x}_i \in \mathbf{D}$. Alternatively, we may seek to minimize the error $\boldsymbol{\epsilon}_i = \mathbf{x}_i - \mathbf{x}'_i$ over all the points.

7.2 PRINCIPAL COMPONENT ANALYSIS

Principal Component Analysis (PCA) is a technique that seeks a r-dimensional basis that best captures the variance in the data. The direction with the largest projected variance is called the first principal component. The orthogonal direction that captures the second largest projected variance is called the second principal component, and so on. As we shall see, the direction that maximizes the variance is also the one that minimizes the mean squared error.

7.2.1 Best Line Approximation

We will start with $r = 1$, that is, the one-dimensional subspace or line $\mathbf{u}$ that best approximates $\mathbf{D}$ in terms of the variance of the projected points. This will lead to the general PCA technique for the best $1 \le r \le d$ dimensional basis for $\mathbf{D}$.

Without loss of generality, we assume that $\mathbf{u}$ has magnitude $\|\mathbf{u}\|^2 = \mathbf{u}^T \mathbf{u} = 1$; otherwise it is possible to keep on increasing the projected variance by simply increasing the magnitude of $\mathbf{u}$. We also assume that the data matrix $\mathbf{D}$ has been centered by subtracting the mean μ. That is

$$\overline{\mathbf{D}} = \mathbf{D} - \mathbf{1} \cdot \mu^T$$

where $\overline{\mathbf{D}}$ is the centered data matrix, which has mean $\overline{\mu} = \mathbf{0}$.

The projection of the centered point $\overline{\mathbf{x}}_i \in \overline{\mathbf{D}}$ on the vector $\mathbf{u}$ (see Eq. (1.11)) is given as

$$\mathbf{x}_i' = \left(\frac{\mathbf{u}^T \overline{\mathbf{x}}_i}{\mathbf{u}^T \mathbf{u}} \right) \mathbf{u} = (\mathbf{u}^T \overline{\mathbf{x}}_i)\mathbf{u} = a_i \mathbf{u}$$

where

$$\boxed{a_i = \mathbf{u}^T \overline{\mathbf{x}}_i} \tag{7.10}$$

is the offset or scalar projection (Eq. (1.12)) of $\mathbf{x}_i$ on $\mathbf{u}$. We also call a_i a *projected point*. Note that the scalar projection of the mean $\overline{\mu}$ is 0. Therefore, the mean of the projected points a_i is also zero, since

$$\mu_a = \frac{1}{n} \sum_{i=1}^{n} a_i = \frac{1}{n} \sum_{i=1}^{n} \mathbf{u}^T (\overline{\mathbf{x}}_i) = \mathbf{u}^T \overline{\mu} = 0$$

We have to choose the direction $\mathbf{u}$ such that the variance of the projected points is maximized. The projected variance along $\mathbf{u}$ is given as

$$\sigma_{\mathbf{u}}^2 = \frac{1}{n} \sum_{i=1}^{n} (a_i - \mu_a)^2 = \frac{1}{n} \sum_{i=1}^{n} (\mathbf{u}^T \overline{\mathbf{x}}_i)^2 = \frac{1}{n} \sum_{i=1}^{n} \mathbf{u}^T \left(\overline{\mathbf{x}}_i \overline{\mathbf{x}}_i^T \right) \mathbf{u} = \mathbf{u}^T \left(\frac{1}{n} \sum_{i=1}^{n} \overline{\mathbf{x}}_i \overline{\mathbf{x}}_i^T \right) \mathbf{u}$$

Thus, we get

$$\boxed{\sigma_{\mathbf{u}}^2 = \mathbf{u}^T \Sigma \mathbf{u}} \tag{7.11}$$

where Σ is the sample covariance matrix for the centered data $\overline{\mathbf{D}}$[1].

To maximize the projected variance, we have to solve a constrained optimization problem, namely to maximize $\sigma_{\mathbf{u}}^2$ subject to the constraint that $\mathbf{u}^T \mathbf{u} = 1$. This can be solved by introducing a Lagrangian multiplier α for the constraint, to obtain the unconstrained maximization problem

$$\max_{\mathbf{u}} J(\mathbf{u}) = \mathbf{u}^T \Sigma \mathbf{u} - \alpha(\mathbf{u}^T \mathbf{u} - 1) \tag{7.12}$$

---

[1] The sample covariance matrix should be denoted as $\widehat{\Sigma}$, but we omit the "hat" to avoid clutter.

Setting the derivative of $J(\mathbf{u})$ with respect to $\mathbf{u}$ to the zero vector, we obtain

$$\frac{\partial}{\partial \mathbf{u}} J(\mathbf{u}) = \mathbf{0}$$

$$\frac{\partial}{\partial \mathbf{u}} \left(\mathbf{u}^T \mathbf{\Sigma} \mathbf{u} - \alpha (\mathbf{u}^T \mathbf{u} - 1) \right) = \mathbf{0}$$

$$2\mathbf{\Sigma} \mathbf{u} - 2\alpha \mathbf{u} = \mathbf{0}$$

$$\boxed{\mathbf{\Sigma} \mathbf{u} = \alpha \mathbf{u}} \tag{7.13}$$

This implies that α is an eigenvalue of the covariance matrix $\mathbf{\Sigma}$, with the associated eigenvector $\mathbf{u}$. Further, taking the dot product with $\mathbf{u}$ on both sides of Eq. (7.13) yields

$$\mathbf{u}^T \mathbf{\Sigma} \mathbf{u} = \mathbf{u}^T \alpha \mathbf{u} = \alpha \mathbf{u}^T \mathbf{u} = \alpha \tag{7.14}$$

To maximize the projected variance $\sigma_{\mathbf{u}}^2$, we should thus choose the largest eigenvalue of $\mathbf{\Sigma}$. In other words, the dominant eigenvector $\mathbf{u}_1$ specifies the direction of most variance, also called the *first principal component*, that is, $\mathbf{u} = \mathbf{u}_1$. Further, the largest eigenvalue λ_1 specifies the projected variance, that is, $\sigma_{\mathbf{u}}^2 = \alpha = \lambda_1$.

Minimum Squared Error Approach

We now show that the direction that maximizes the projected variance is also the one that minimizes the average squared error. As before, assume that the dataset $\mathbf{D}$ has been centered by subtracting the mean from each point. For a point $\bar{\mathbf{x}}_i \in \bar{\mathbf{D}}$, let $\mathbf{x}_i'$ denote its projection on $\mathbf{u}$, and let $\boldsymbol{\epsilon}_i = \bar{\mathbf{x}}_i - \mathbf{x}_i'$ denote the error vector. The mean squared error (*MSE*) optimization condition is defined as

$$MSE(\mathbf{u}) = \frac{1}{n} \sum_{i=1}^{n} \|\boldsymbol{\epsilon}_i\|^2 = \frac{1}{n} \sum_{i=1}^{n} \|\bar{\mathbf{x}}_i - \mathbf{x}_i'\|^2 = \frac{1}{n} \sum_{i=1}^{n} (\bar{\mathbf{x}}_i - \mathbf{x}_i')^T (\bar{\mathbf{x}}_i - \mathbf{x}_i')$$

$$= \frac{1}{n} \sum_{i=1}^{n} \left(\|\bar{\mathbf{x}}_i\|^2 - 2\bar{\mathbf{x}}_i^T \mathbf{x}_i' + (\mathbf{x}_i')^T \mathbf{x}_i' \right) \tag{7.15}$$

$$= \frac{1}{n} \sum_{i=1}^{n} \left(\|\bar{\mathbf{x}}_i\|^2 - 2\bar{\mathbf{x}}_i^T (\mathbf{u}^T \bar{\mathbf{x}}_i) \mathbf{u} + \left((\mathbf{u}^T \bar{\mathbf{x}}_i) \mathbf{u} \right)^T (\mathbf{u}^T \bar{\mathbf{x}}_i) \mathbf{u} \right), \text{ since } \mathbf{x}_i' = (\mathbf{u}^T \bar{\mathbf{x}}_i) \mathbf{u}$$

$$= \frac{1}{n} \sum_{i=1}^{n} \left(\|\bar{\mathbf{x}}_i\|^2 - 2(\mathbf{u}^T \bar{\mathbf{x}}_i)(\bar{\mathbf{x}}_i^T \mathbf{u}) + (\mathbf{u}^T \bar{\mathbf{x}}_i)(\bar{\mathbf{x}}_i^T \mathbf{u}) \mathbf{u}^T \mathbf{u} \right)$$

$$= \frac{1}{n} \sum_{i=1}^{n} \left(\|\bar{\mathbf{x}}_i\|^2 - (\mathbf{u}^T \bar{\mathbf{x}}_i)(\bar{\mathbf{x}}_i^T \mathbf{u}) \right)$$

$$= \frac{1}{n} \sum_{i=1}^{n} \|\bar{\mathbf{x}}_i\|^2 - \frac{1}{n} \sum_{i=1}^{n} \mathbf{u}^T (\bar{\mathbf{x}}_i \bar{\mathbf{x}}_i^T) \mathbf{u}$$

$$= \frac{1}{n} \sum_{i=1}^{n} \|\bar{\mathbf{x}}_i\|^2 - \mathbf{u}^T \left(\frac{1}{n} \sum_{i=1}^{n} \bar{\mathbf{x}}_i \bar{\mathbf{x}}_i^T \right) \mathbf{u}$$

which implies

$$MSE = \sum_{i=1}^{n} \frac{\|\bar{\mathbf{x}}_i\|^2}{n} - \mathbf{u}^T \mathbf{\Sigma} \mathbf{u} \tag{7.16}$$

Note that by Eq. (1.8) the total variance of the centered data (i.e., with $\bar{\mu} = \mathbf{0}$) is given as

$$\mathrm{var}(\bar{\mathbf{D}}) = \frac{1}{n} \sum_{i=1}^{n} \|\bar{\mathbf{x}}_i - \mathbf{0}\|^2 = \frac{1}{n} \sum_{i=1}^{n} \|\bar{\mathbf{x}}_i\|^2 = \frac{1}{n} \sum_{i=1}^{n} \|\mathbf{x}_i - \mu\|^2 = \mathrm{var}(\mathbf{D})$$

Further, by Eq. (2.35), we have

$$\mathrm{var}(\mathbf{D}) = tr(\mathbf{\Sigma}) = \sum_{i=1}^{d} \sigma_i^2 \tag{7.17}$$

Thus, we may rewrite Eq. (7.16) as

$$MSE(\mathbf{u}) = \mathrm{var}(\mathbf{D}) - \mathbf{u}^T \mathbf{\Sigma} \mathbf{u} = \sum_{i=1}^{d} \sigma_i^2 - \mathbf{u}^T \mathbf{\Sigma} \mathbf{u} \tag{7.18}$$

Because the first term, $\mathrm{var}(\mathbf{D})$, is a constant for a given dataset $\mathbf{D}$, the vector $\mathbf{u}$ that minimizes $MSE(\mathbf{u})$ is thus the same one that maximizes the second term, the projected variance $\mathbf{u}^T \mathbf{\Sigma} \mathbf{u}$. Because we know that $\mathbf{u}_1$, the dominant eigenvector of $\mathbf{\Sigma}$, maximizes the projected variance, we have

$$MSE(\mathbf{u}_1) = \mathrm{var}(\mathbf{D}) - \mathbf{u}_1^T \mathbf{\Sigma} \mathbf{u}_1 = \mathrm{var}(\mathbf{D}) - \mathbf{u}_1^T \lambda_1 \mathbf{u}_1 = \mathrm{var}(\mathbf{D}) - \lambda_1 \tag{7.19}$$

Thus, the principal component $\mathbf{u}_1$, which is the direction that maximizes the projected variance, is also the direction that minimizes the mean squared error.

Example 7.3. Figure 7.2 shows the first principal component, that is, the best one-dimensional approximation, for the three dimensional Iris dataset shown in Figure 7.1(a). The covariance matrix for this dataset is given as

$$\mathbf{\Sigma} = \begin{pmatrix} 0.681 & -0.039 & 1.265 \\ -0.039 & 0.187 & -0.320 \\ 1.265 & -0.320 & 3.092 \end{pmatrix}$$

The variance values σ_i^2 for each of the original dimensions are given along the main diagonal of $\mathbf{\Sigma}$. For example, $\sigma_1^2 = 0.681$, $\sigma_2^2 = 0.187$, and $\sigma_3^2 = 3.092$. The largest eigenvalue of $\mathbf{\Sigma}$ is $\lambda_1 = 3.662$, and the corresponding dominant eigenvector is $\mathbf{u}_1 = (-0.390, 0.089, -0.916)^T$. The unit vector $\mathbf{u}_1$ thus maximizes the projected variance, which is given as $J(\mathbf{u}_1) = \alpha = \lambda_1 = 3.662$. Figure 7.2 plots the principal component $\mathbf{u}_1$. It also shows the error vectors ϵ_i, as thin gray line segments.

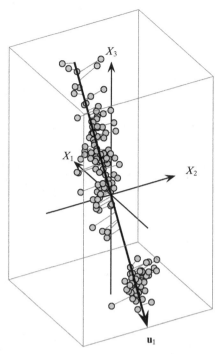

Figure 7.2. Best one-dimensional or line approximation.

The total variance of the data is given as

$$\text{var}(\mathbf{D}) = \frac{1}{n}\sum_{i=1}^{n}\|\bar{\mathbf{x}}\|^2 = \frac{1}{150}\cdot 594.04 = 3.96$$

We can also directly obtain the total variance as the trace of the covariance matrix:

$$\text{var}(\mathbf{D}) = tr(\mathbf{\Sigma}) = \sigma_1^2 + \sigma_2^2 + \sigma_3^2 = 0.681 + 0.187 + 3.092 = 3.96$$

Thus, using Eq. (7.19), the minimum value of the mean squared error is given as

$$MSE(\mathbf{u}_1) = \text{var}(\mathbf{D}) - \lambda_1 = 3.96 - 3.662 = 0.298$$

7.2.2 Best 2-dimensional Approximation

We are now interested in the best two-dimensional approximation to $\mathbf{D}$. As before, we center the data to obtain $\overline{\mathbf{D}}$, so that $\bar{\mu} = \mathbf{0}$. We already computed the direction with the most variance, namely $\mathbf{u}_1$, which is the eigenvector corresponding to the largest eigenvalue λ_1 of $\mathbf{\Sigma}$. We now want to find another direction $\mathbf{v}$, which also maximizes the projected variance, but is orthogonal to $\mathbf{u}_1$. According to Eq. (7.11) the projected variance along $\mathbf{v}$ is given as

$$\sigma_{\mathbf{v}}^2 = \mathbf{v}^T \mathbf{\Sigma} \mathbf{v}$$

We further require that $\mathbf{v}$ be a unit vector orthogonal to $\mathbf{u}_1$, that is,

$$\mathbf{v}^T \mathbf{u}_1 = 0$$
$$\mathbf{v}^T \mathbf{v} = 1$$

The optimization condition then becomes

$$\max_{\mathbf{v}} J(\mathbf{v}) = \mathbf{v}^T \boldsymbol{\Sigma} \mathbf{v} - \alpha(\mathbf{v}^T \mathbf{v} - 1) - \beta(\mathbf{v}^T \mathbf{u}_1 - 0) \qquad (7.20)$$

Taking the derivative of $J(\mathbf{v})$ with respect to $\mathbf{v}$, and setting it to the zero vector, gives

$$2\boldsymbol{\Sigma} \mathbf{v} - 2\alpha \mathbf{v} - \beta \mathbf{u}_1 = \mathbf{0} \qquad (7.21)$$

If we multiply on the left by $\mathbf{u}_1^T$ we get

$$2\mathbf{u}_1^T \boldsymbol{\Sigma} \mathbf{v} - 2\alpha \mathbf{u}_1^T \mathbf{v} - \beta \mathbf{u}_1^T \mathbf{u}_1 = 0$$
$$2\mathbf{v}^T \boldsymbol{\Sigma} \mathbf{u}_1 - \beta = 0, \text{ which implies that}$$
$$\beta = 2\mathbf{v}^T \lambda_1 \mathbf{u}_1 = 2\lambda_1 \mathbf{v}^T \mathbf{u}_1 = 0$$

In the derivation above we used the fact that $\mathbf{u}_1^T \boldsymbol{\Sigma} \mathbf{v} = \mathbf{v}^T \boldsymbol{\Sigma} \mathbf{u}_1$, and that $\mathbf{v}$ is orthogonal to $\mathbf{u}_1$. Plugging $\beta = 0$ into Eq. (7.21) gives us

$$2\boldsymbol{\Sigma} \mathbf{v} - 2\alpha \mathbf{v} = \mathbf{0}$$
$$\boldsymbol{\Sigma} \mathbf{v} = \alpha \mathbf{v}$$

This means that $\mathbf{v}$ is another eigenvector of $\boldsymbol{\Sigma}$. Also, as in Eq. (7.14), we have $\sigma_{\mathbf{v}}^2 = \alpha$. To maximize the variance along $\mathbf{v}$, we should choose $\alpha = \lambda_2$, the second largest eigenvalue of $\boldsymbol{\Sigma}$, with the *second principal component* being given by the corresponding eigenvector, that is, $\mathbf{v} = \mathbf{u}_2$.

Total Projected Variance
Let $\mathbf{U}_2$ be the matrix whose columns correspond to the two principal components, given as

$$\mathbf{U}_2 = \begin{pmatrix} | & | \\ \mathbf{u}_1 & \mathbf{u}_2 \\ | & | \end{pmatrix}$$

Given the point $\bar{\mathbf{x}}_i \in \overline{\mathbf{D}}$ its coordinates in the two-dimensional subspace spanned by $\mathbf{u}_1$ and $\mathbf{u}_2$ can be computed via Eq. (7.6), as follows:

$$\mathbf{a}_i = \mathbf{U}_2^T \bar{\mathbf{x}}_i$$

Assume that each point $\bar{\mathbf{x}}_i \in \mathbb{R}^d$ in $\overline{\mathbf{D}}$ has been projected to obtain its coordinates $\mathbf{a}_i \in \mathbb{R}^2$, yielding the new dataset $\mathbf{A}$. Further, because $\overline{\mathbf{D}}$ is centered, with $\bar{\mu} = \mathbf{0}$, the coordinates of the projected mean are also zero because $\mathbf{U}_2^T \bar{\mu} = \mathbf{U}_2^T \mathbf{0} = \mathbf{0}$. The total variance for $\mathbf{A}$ is given as

$$\text{var}(\mathbf{A}) = \frac{1}{n}\sum_{i=1}^{n}\|\mathbf{a}_i - \mathbf{0}\|^2 = \frac{1}{n}\sum_{i=1}^{n}\left(\mathbf{U}_2^T\bar{\mathbf{x}}_i\right)^T\left(\mathbf{U}_2^T\bar{\mathbf{x}}_i\right) = \frac{1}{n}\sum_{i=1}^{n}\bar{\mathbf{x}}_i^T\left(\mathbf{U}_2\mathbf{U}_2^T\right)\bar{\mathbf{x}}_i$$

$$= \frac{1}{n}\sum_{i=1}^{n}\bar{\mathbf{x}}_i^T\mathbf{P}_2\bar{\mathbf{x}}_i \tag{7.22}$$

where $\mathbf{P}_2$ is the orthogonal projection matrix [Eq. (7.8)] given as

$$\mathbf{P}_2 = \mathbf{U}_2\mathbf{U}_2^T = \mathbf{u}_1\mathbf{u}_1^T + \mathbf{u}_2\mathbf{u}_2^T$$

Substituting this into Eq. (7.22), the projected total variance is given as

$$\text{var}(\mathbf{A}) = \frac{1}{n}\sum_{i=1}^{n}\bar{\mathbf{x}}_i^T\mathbf{P}_2\bar{\mathbf{x}}_i \tag{7.23}$$

$$= \frac{1}{n}\sum_{i=1}^{n}\bar{\mathbf{x}}_i^T\left(\mathbf{u}_1\mathbf{u}_1^T + \mathbf{u}_2\mathbf{u}_2^T\right)\bar{\mathbf{x}}_i = \frac{1}{n}\sum_{i=1}^{n}(\mathbf{u}_1^T\bar{\mathbf{x}}_i)(\bar{\mathbf{x}}_i^T\mathbf{u}_1) + \frac{1}{n}\sum_{i=1}^{n}(\mathbf{u}_2^T\bar{\mathbf{x}}_i)(\bar{\mathbf{x}}_i^T\mathbf{u}_2)$$

$$= \mathbf{u}_1^T\Sigma\mathbf{u}_1 + \mathbf{u}_2^T\Sigma\mathbf{u}_2 \tag{7.24}$$

Because $\mathbf{u}_1$ and $\mathbf{u}_2$ are eigenvectors of Σ, we have $\Sigma\mathbf{u}_1 = \lambda_1\mathbf{u}_1$ and $\Sigma\mathbf{u}_2 = \lambda_2\mathbf{u}_2$, so that

$$\text{var}(\mathbf{A}) = \mathbf{u}_1^T\Sigma\mathbf{u}_1 + \mathbf{u}_2^T\Sigma\mathbf{u}_2 = \mathbf{u}_1^T\lambda_1\mathbf{u}_1 + \mathbf{u}_2^T\lambda_2\mathbf{u}_2 = \lambda_1 + \lambda_2 \tag{7.25}$$

Thus, the sum of the eigenvalues is the total variance of the projected points, and the first two principal components maximize this variance.

Mean Squared Error

We now show that the first two principal components also minimize the mean square error objective. The mean square error objective is given as

$$MSE = \frac{1}{n}\sum_{i=1}^{n}\|\bar{\mathbf{x}}_i - \mathbf{x}_i'\|^2$$

$$= \frac{1}{n}\sum_{i=1}^{n}\left(\|\bar{\mathbf{x}}_i\|^2 - 2\bar{\mathbf{x}}_i^T\mathbf{x}_i' + (\mathbf{x}_i')^T\mathbf{x}_i'\right), \text{ using Eq. (7.15)}$$

$$= \text{var}(\mathbf{D}) + \frac{1}{n}\sum_{i=1}^{n}\left(-2\bar{\mathbf{x}}_i^T\mathbf{P}_2\bar{\mathbf{x}}_i + (\mathbf{P}_2\bar{\mathbf{x}}_i)^T\mathbf{P}_2\bar{\mathbf{x}}_i\right), \text{ using Eq. (7.7) that } \mathbf{x}_i' = \mathbf{P}_2\bar{\mathbf{x}}_i$$

$$= \text{var}(\mathbf{D}) - \frac{1}{n}\sum_{i=1}^{n}\left(\bar{\mathbf{x}}_i^T\mathbf{P}_2\bar{\mathbf{x}}_i\right)$$

$$= \text{var}(\mathbf{D}) - \text{var}(\mathbf{A}), \text{ using Eq. (7.23)} \tag{7.26}$$

Thus, the MSE objective is minimized precisely when the total projected variance var($\mathbf{A}$) is maximized. From Eq. (7.25), we have

$$MSE = \text{var}(\mathbf{D}) - \lambda_1 - \lambda_2$$

Example 7.4. For the Iris dataset from Example 7.1, the two largest eigenvalues are $\lambda_1 = 3.662$, and $\lambda_2 = 0.239$, with the corresponding eigenvectors:

$$\mathbf{u}_1 = \begin{pmatrix} -0.390 \\ 0.089 \\ -0.916 \end{pmatrix} \qquad \mathbf{u}_2 = \begin{pmatrix} -0.639 \\ -0.742 \\ 0.200 \end{pmatrix}$$

The projection matrix is given as

$$\mathbf{P}_2 = \mathbf{U}_2\mathbf{U}_2^T = \begin{pmatrix} | & | \\ \mathbf{u}_1 & \mathbf{u}_2 \\ | & | \end{pmatrix} \begin{pmatrix} - & \mathbf{u}_1^T & - \\ - & \mathbf{u}_2^T & - \end{pmatrix} = \mathbf{u}_1\mathbf{u}_1^T + \mathbf{u}_2\mathbf{u}_2^T$$

$$= \begin{pmatrix} 0.152 & -0.035 & 0.357 \\ -0.035 & 0.008 & -0.082 \\ 0.357 & -0.082 & 0.839 \end{pmatrix} + \begin{pmatrix} 0.408 & 0.474 & -0.128 \\ 0.474 & 0.551 & -0.148 \\ -0.128 & -0.148 & 0.04 \end{pmatrix}$$

$$= \begin{pmatrix} 0.560 & 0.439 & 0.229 \\ 0.439 & 0.558 & -0.230 \\ 0.229 & -0.230 & 0.879 \end{pmatrix}$$

Thus, each centered point $\bar{\mathbf{x}}_i$ can be approximated by its projection onto the first two principal components $\mathbf{x}_i' = \mathbf{P}_2\bar{\mathbf{x}}_i$. Figure 7.3(a) plots this optimal 2-dimensional subspace spanned by $\mathbf{u}_1$ and $\mathbf{u}_2$. The error vector $\boldsymbol{\epsilon}_i$ for each point is shown as a thin line segment. The gray points are behind the 2-dimensional subspace, whereas the white points are in front of it. The total variance captured by the subspace is given as

$$\lambda_1 + \lambda_2 = 3.662 + 0.239 = 3.901$$

The mean squared error is given as

$$MSE = \text{var}(\mathbf{D}) - \lambda_1 - \lambda_2 = 3.96 - 3.662 - 0.239 = 0.059$$

Figure 7.3(b) plots a nonoptimal 2-dimensional subspace. As one can see the optimal subspace maximizes the variance, and minimizes the squared error, whereas the nonoptimal subspace captures less variance, and has a high mean squared error value, which can be pictorially seen from the lengths of the error vectors (line segments). In fact, this is the worst possible 2-dimensional subspace; its MSE is 3.662.

7.2.3 Best r-dimensional Approximation

We are now interested in the best r-dimensional approximation to $\mathbf{D}$, where $2 < r \leq d$. Assume that we have already computed the first $j - 1$ principal components or eigenvectors, $\mathbf{u}_1, \mathbf{u}_2, \ldots, \mathbf{u}_{j-1}$, corresponding to the $j - 1$ largest eigenvalues of $\mathbf{\Sigma}$, for $1 \leq j \leq r$. To compute the jth new basis vector $\mathbf{v}$, we have to ensure that it is normalized to unit length, that is, $\mathbf{v}^T\mathbf{v} = 1$, and is orthogonal to all previous components

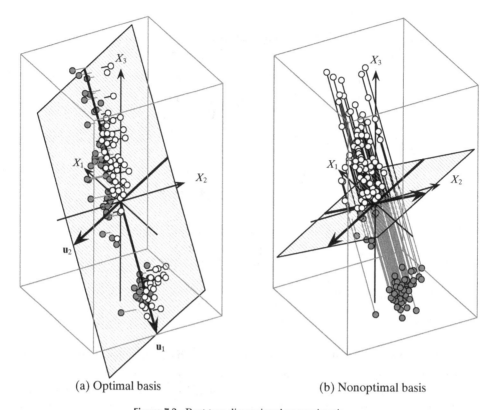

(a) Optimal basis   (b) Nonoptimal basis

Figure 7.3. Best two-dimensional approximation.

$\mathbf{u}_i$, i.e., $\mathbf{u}_i^T \mathbf{v} = 0$, for $1 \le i < j$. As before, the projected variance along $\mathbf{v}$ is given as

$$\sigma_\mathbf{v}^2 = \mathbf{v}^T \Sigma \mathbf{v}$$

Combined with the constraints on $\mathbf{v}$, this leads to the following maximization problem with Lagrange multipliers:

$$\max_{\mathbf{v}} J(\mathbf{v}) = \mathbf{v}^T \Sigma \mathbf{v} - \alpha (\mathbf{v}^T \mathbf{v} - 1) - \sum_{i=1}^{j-1} \beta_i (\mathbf{u}_i^T \mathbf{v} - 0)$$

Taking the derivative of $J(\mathbf{v})$ with respect to $\mathbf{v}$ and setting it to the zero vector gives

$$2 \Sigma \mathbf{v} - 2\alpha \mathbf{v} - \sum_{i=1}^{j-1} \beta_i \mathbf{u}_i = \mathbf{0} \qquad (7.27)$$

If we multiply on the left by $\mathbf{u}_k^T$, for $1 \le k < j$, we get

$$2 \mathbf{u}_k^T \Sigma \mathbf{v} - 2\alpha \mathbf{u}_k^T \mathbf{v} - \beta_k \mathbf{u}_k^T \mathbf{u}_k - \sum_{\substack{i=1 \\ i \ne k}}^{j-1} \beta_i \mathbf{u}_k^T \mathbf{u}_i = 0$$

$$2 \mathbf{v}^T \Sigma \mathbf{u}_k - \beta_k = 0$$

$$\beta_k = 2 \mathbf{v}^T \lambda_k \mathbf{u}_k = 2 \lambda_k \mathbf{v}^T \mathbf{u}_k = 0$$

where we used the fact that $\boldsymbol{\Sigma}\mathbf{u}_k = \lambda_k\mathbf{u}_k$, as $\mathbf{u}_k$ is the eigenvector corresponding to the kth largest eigenvalue λ_k of $\boldsymbol{\Sigma}$. Thus, we find that $\beta_i = 0$ for all $i < j$ in Eq. (7.27), which implies that

$$\boldsymbol{\Sigma}\mathbf{v} = \alpha\mathbf{v}$$

To maximize the variance along $\mathbf{v}$, we set $\alpha = \lambda_j$, the jth largest eigenvalue of $\boldsymbol{\Sigma}$, with $\mathbf{v} = \mathbf{u}_j$ giving the jth principal component.

In summary, to find the best r-dimensional approximation to $\mathbf{D}$, we compute the eigenvalues of $\boldsymbol{\Sigma}$. Because $\boldsymbol{\Sigma}$ is positive semidefinite, its eigenvalues must all be non-negative, and we can thus sort them in decreasing order as follows:

$$\lambda_1 \geq \lambda_2 \geq \cdots \lambda_r \geq \lambda_{r+1} \cdots \geq \lambda_d \geq 0$$

We then select the r largest eigenvalues, and their corresponding eigenvectors to form the best r-dimensional approximation.

Total Projected Variance
Let $\mathbf{U}_r$ be the r-dimensional basis vector matrix

$$\mathbf{U}_r = \begin{pmatrix} | & | & & | \\ \mathbf{u}_1 & \mathbf{u}_2 & \cdots & \mathbf{u}_r \\ | & | & & | \end{pmatrix}$$

with the projection matrix given as

$$\mathbf{P}_r = \mathbf{U}_r\mathbf{U}_r^T = \sum_{i=1}^{r}\mathbf{u}_i\mathbf{u}_i^T$$

Let $\mathbf{A}$ denote the dataset formed by the coordinates of the projected points in the r-dimensional subspace, that is, $\mathbf{a}_i = \mathbf{U}_r^T\bar{\mathbf{x}}_i$, and let $\mathbf{x}_i' = \mathbf{P}_r\bar{\mathbf{x}}_i$ denote the projected point in the original d-dimensional space. Following the derivation for Eqs. (7.22), (7.24), and (7.25), the projected variance is given as

$$\text{var}(\mathbf{A}) = \frac{1}{n}\sum_{i=1}^{n}\bar{\mathbf{x}}_i^T\mathbf{P}_r\bar{\mathbf{x}}_i = \sum_{i=1}^{r}\mathbf{u}_i^T\boldsymbol{\Sigma}\mathbf{u}_i = \sum_{i=1}^{r}\lambda_i$$

Thus, the total projected variance is simply the sum of the r largest eigenvalues of $\boldsymbol{\Sigma}$.

Mean Squared Error
Based on the derivation for Eq. (7.26), the mean squared error objective in r dimensions can be written as

$$MSE = \frac{1}{n}\sum_{i=1}^{n}\|\bar{\mathbf{x}}_i - \mathbf{x}_i'\|^2 = \text{var}(\mathbf{D}) - \text{var}(\mathbf{A})$$

$$= \text{var}(\mathbf{D}) - \sum_{i=1}^{r}\mathbf{u}_i^T\boldsymbol{\Sigma}\mathbf{u}_i = \text{var}(\mathbf{D}) - \sum_{i=1}^{r}\lambda_i$$

The first r-principal components maximize the projected variance $\text{var}(\mathbf{A})$, and thus they also minimize the MSE.

Total Variance

Note that the total variance of $\mathbf{D}$ is invariant to a change in basis vectors. Therefore, we have the following identity:

$$\text{var}(\mathbf{D}) = \sum_{i=1}^{d} \sigma_i^2 = \sum_{i=1}^{d} \lambda_i \tag{7.28}$$

Choosing the Dimensionality

Often we may not know how many dimensions, r, to use for a good approximation. One criteria for choosing r is to compute the fraction of the total variance captured by the first r principal components, computed as

$$f(r) = \frac{\lambda_1 + \lambda_2 + \cdots + \lambda_r}{\lambda_1 + \lambda_2 + \cdots + \lambda_d} = \frac{\sum_{i=1}^{r} \lambda_i}{\sum_{i=1}^{d} \lambda_i} = \frac{\sum_{i=1}^{r} \lambda_i}{\text{var}(\mathbf{D})} \tag{7.29}$$

Given a certain desired variance threshold, say α, starting from the first principal component, we keep on adding additional components, and stop at the smallest value r, for which $f(r) \geq \alpha$, given as

$$r = \min\{r' \mid f(r') \geq \alpha\} \tag{7.30}$$

In other words, we select the fewest number of dimensions such that the subspace spanned by those r dimensions captures at least α fraction of the total variance. In practice, α is usually set to 0.9 or higher, so that the reduced dataset captures at least 90% of the total variance.

Algorithm 7.1 gives the pseudo-code for the principal component analysis algorithm. Given the input data $\mathbf{D} \in \mathbb{R}^{n \times d}$, it first centers it by subtracting the mean from each point. Next, it computes the eigenvectors and eigenvalues of the covariance matrix Σ. Given the desired variance threshold α, it selects the smallest set of dimensions r that capture at least α fraction of the total variance. Finally, it computes the coordinates of each point in the new r-dimensional principal component subspace, to yield the new data matrix $\mathbf{A} \in \mathbb{R}^{n \times r}$.

Example 7.5. Given the 3-dimensional Iris dataset in Figure 7.1(a), its covariance matrix is

$$\Sigma = \begin{pmatrix} 0.681 & -0.039 & 1.265 \\ -0.039 & 0.187 & -0.320 \\ 1.265 & -0.32 & 3.092 \end{pmatrix}$$

The eigenvalues and eigenvectors of Σ are given as

$$\lambda_1 = 3.662 \qquad\qquad \lambda_2 = 0.239 \qquad\qquad \lambda_3 = 0.059$$

$$\mathbf{u}_1 = \begin{pmatrix} -0.390 \\ 0.089 \\ -0.916 \end{pmatrix} \qquad \mathbf{u}_2 = \begin{pmatrix} -0.639 \\ -0.742 \\ 0.200 \end{pmatrix} \qquad \mathbf{u}_3 = \begin{pmatrix} -0.663 \\ 0.664 \\ 0.346 \end{pmatrix}$$

Algorithm 7.1: Principal Component Analysis

PCA ($\mathbf{D}, \alpha$):

1 $\mu = \frac{1}{n} \sum_{i=1}^{n} \mathbf{x}_i$ // compute mean

2 $\overline{\mathbf{D}} = \mathbf{D} - \mathbf{1} \cdot \mu^T$ // center the data

3 $\Sigma = \frac{1}{n} \left(\overline{\mathbf{D}}^T \overline{\mathbf{D}} \right)$ // compute covariance matrix

4 $(\lambda_1, \lambda_2, \ldots, \lambda_d) = \text{eigenvalues}(\Sigma)$ // compute eigenvalues

5 $\mathbf{U} = \begin{pmatrix} \mathbf{u}_1 & \mathbf{u}_2 & \cdots & \mathbf{u}_d \end{pmatrix} = \text{eigenvectors}(\Sigma)$ // compute eigenvectors

6 $f(r) = \frac{\sum_{i=1}^{r} \lambda_i}{\sum_{i=1}^{d} \lambda_i}$, for all $r = 1, 2, \ldots, d$ // fraction of total variance

7 Choose smallest r so that $f(r) \geq \alpha$ // choose dimensionality

8 $\mathbf{U}_r = \begin{pmatrix} \mathbf{u}_1 & \mathbf{u}_2 & \cdots & \mathbf{u}_r \end{pmatrix}$ // reduced basis

9 $\mathbf{A} = \{ \mathbf{a}_i \mid \mathbf{a}_i = \mathbf{U}_r^T \overline{\mathbf{x}}_i, \text{for } i = 1, \ldots, n \}$ // reduced dimensionality data

---

The total variance is therefore $\lambda_1 + \lambda_2 + \lambda_3 = 3.662 + 0.239 + 0.059 = 3.96$. The optimal 3-dimensional basis is shown in Figure 7.1(b).

To find a lower dimensional approximation, let $\alpha = 0.95$. The fraction of total variance for different values of r is given as

r	1	2	3
$f(r)$	0.925	0.985	1.0

For example, for $r = 1$, the fraction of total variance is given as $f(1) = \frac{3.662}{3.96} = 0.925$. Thus, we need at least $r = 2$ dimensions to capture 95% of the total variance. This optimal 2-dimensional subspace is shown as the shaded plane in Figure 7.3(a). The reduced dimensionality dataset $\mathbf{A}$ is shown in Figure 7.4. It consists of the point coordinates $\mathbf{a}_i = \mathbf{U}_2^T \overline{\mathbf{x}}_i$ in the new 2-dimensional principal components basis comprising $\mathbf{u}_1$ and $\mathbf{u}_2$.

7.2.4 Geometry of PCA

Geometrically, when $r = d$, PCA corresponds to a orthogonal change of basis, so that the total variance is captured by the sum of the variances along each of the principal directions $\mathbf{u}_1, \mathbf{u}_2, \ldots, \mathbf{u}_d$, and further, all covariances are zero. This can be seen by looking at the collective action of the full set of principal components, which can be arranged in the $d \times d$ orthogonal matrix

$$\mathbf{U} = \begin{pmatrix} | & | & & | \\ \mathbf{u}_1 & \mathbf{u}_2 & \cdots & \mathbf{u}_d \\ | & | & & | \end{pmatrix}$$

with $\mathbf{U}^{-1} = \mathbf{U}^T$.

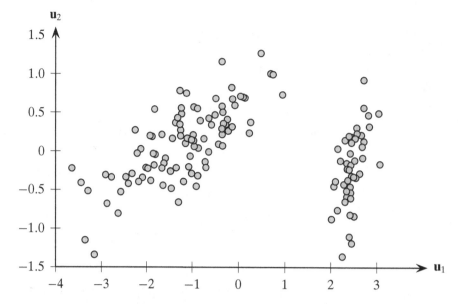

Figure 7.4. Reduced dimensionality dataset: Iris principal components.

Each principal component $\mathbf{u}_i$ corresponds to an eigenvector of the covariance matrix $\mathbf{\Sigma}$, that is,

$$\mathbf{\Sigma}\mathbf{u}_i = \lambda_i \mathbf{u}_i \text{ for all } 1 \le i \le d$$

which can be written compactly in matrix notation as follows:

$$\mathbf{\Sigma} \begin{pmatrix} | & | & & | \\ \mathbf{u}_1 & \mathbf{u}_2 & \cdots & \mathbf{u}_d \\ | & | & & | \end{pmatrix} = \begin{pmatrix} | & | & & | \\ \lambda_1\mathbf{u}_1 & \lambda_2\mathbf{u}_2 & \cdots & \lambda_d\mathbf{u}_d \\ | & | & & | \end{pmatrix}$$

$$\mathbf{\Sigma}\mathbf{U} = \mathbf{U} \begin{pmatrix} \lambda_1 & 0 & \cdots & 0 \\ 0 & \lambda_2 & \cdots & 0 \\ \vdots & \vdots & \ddots & \vdots \\ 0 & 0 & \cdots & \lambda_d \end{pmatrix}$$

$$\mathbf{\Sigma}\mathbf{U} = \mathbf{U}\mathbf{\Lambda} \tag{7.31}$$

If we multiply Eq. (7.31) on the left by $\mathbf{U}^{-1} = \mathbf{U}^T$ we obtain

$$\mathbf{U}^T\mathbf{\Sigma}\mathbf{U} = \mathbf{U}^T\mathbf{U}\mathbf{\Lambda} = \mathbf{\Lambda} = \begin{pmatrix} \lambda_1 & 0 & \cdots & 0 \\ 0 & \lambda_2 & \cdots & 0 \\ \vdots & \vdots & \ddots & \vdots \\ 0 & 0 & \cdots & \lambda_d \end{pmatrix}$$

This means that if we change the basis to $\mathbf{U}$, we change the covariance matrix $\mathbf{\Sigma}$ to a similar matrix $\mathbf{\Lambda}$, which in fact is the covariance matrix in the new basis. The fact that $\mathbf{\Lambda}$ is diagonal confirms that after the change of basis, all of the covariances vanish, and we are left with only the variances along each of the principal components, with the variance along each new direction $\mathbf{u}_i$ being given by the corresponding eigenvalue λ_i.

It is worth noting that in the new basis, the equation

$$\mathbf{x}^T \boldsymbol{\Sigma}^{-1} \mathbf{x} = 1 \tag{7.32}$$

defines a d-dimensional ellipsoid (or hyper-ellipse). The eigenvectors $\mathbf{u}_i$ of $\boldsymbol{\Sigma}$, that is, the principal components, are the directions for the principal axes of the ellipsoid. The square roots of the eigenvalues, that is, $\sqrt{\lambda_i}$, give the lengths of the semi-axes.

Multiplying Eq. (7.31) on the right by $\mathbf{U}^{-1} = \mathbf{U}^T$, we have

$$\boxed{\boldsymbol{\Sigma} = \mathbf{U} \boldsymbol{\Lambda} \mathbf{U}^T} \tag{7.33}$$

This equation is also called the *eigen-decomposition* of $\boldsymbol{\Sigma}$, since

$$\boxed{\boldsymbol{\Sigma} = \mathbf{U} \boldsymbol{\Lambda} \mathbf{U}^T = \lambda_1 \mathbf{u}_1 \mathbf{u}_1^T + \lambda_2 \mathbf{u}_2 \mathbf{u}_2^T + \ldots + \lambda_d \mathbf{u}_d \mathbf{u}_d^T = \sum_{i=1}^{d} \lambda_i \mathbf{u}_i \mathbf{u}_i^T} \tag{7.34}$$

In other words, the covariance matrix $\boldsymbol{\Sigma}$ can be expressed as the sum of rank one matrices derived from the eigenvectors, weighted by the eigenvalues, in decreasing order of importance.

Furthermore, assuming that $\boldsymbol{\Sigma}$ is invertible or nonsingular, we have

$$\boldsymbol{\Sigma}^{-1} = (\mathbf{U} \boldsymbol{\Lambda} \mathbf{U}^T)^{-1} = (\mathbf{U}^{-1})^T \boldsymbol{\Lambda}^{-1} \mathbf{U}^{-1} = \mathbf{U} \boldsymbol{\Lambda}^{-1} \mathbf{U}^T$$

where

$$\boldsymbol{\Lambda}^{-1} = \begin{pmatrix} \frac{1}{\lambda_1} & 0 & \cdots & 0 \\ 0 & \frac{1}{\lambda_2} & \cdots & 0 \\ \vdots & \vdots & \ddots & \vdots \\ 0 & 0 & \cdots & \frac{1}{\lambda_d} \end{pmatrix}$$

Substituting $\boldsymbol{\Sigma}^{-1}$ in Eq. (7.32), and using the fact that $\mathbf{x} = \mathbf{U}\mathbf{a}$ from Eq. (7.2), where $\mathbf{a} = (a_1, a_2, \ldots, a_d)^T$ represents the coordinates of $\mathbf{x}$ in the new basis, we get

$$\mathbf{x}^T \boldsymbol{\Sigma}^{-1} \mathbf{x} = 1$$

$$(\mathbf{a}^T \mathbf{U}^T) \mathbf{U} \boldsymbol{\Lambda}^{-1} \mathbf{U}^T (\mathbf{U}\mathbf{a}) = 1$$

$$\mathbf{a}^T \boldsymbol{\Lambda}^{-1} \mathbf{a} = 1$$

$$\sum_{i=1}^{d} \frac{a_i^2}{\lambda_i} = 1$$

which is precisely the equation for an ellipse centered at $\mathbf{0}$, with semi-axes lengths $\sqrt{\lambda_i}$. Thus $\mathbf{x}^T \boldsymbol{\Sigma}^{-1} \mathbf{x} = 1$, or equivalently $\mathbf{a}^T \boldsymbol{\Lambda}^{-1} \mathbf{a} = 1$ in the new principal components basis, defines an ellipsoid in d-dimensions, where the semi-axes lengths equal the standard deviations (squared root of the variance, $\sqrt{\lambda_i}$) along each axis. Likewise, the equation $\mathbf{x}^T \boldsymbol{\Sigma}^{-1} \mathbf{x} = s$, or equivalently $\mathbf{a}^T \boldsymbol{\Lambda}^{-1} \mathbf{a} = s$, for different values of the scalar s, represents concentric ellipsoids.

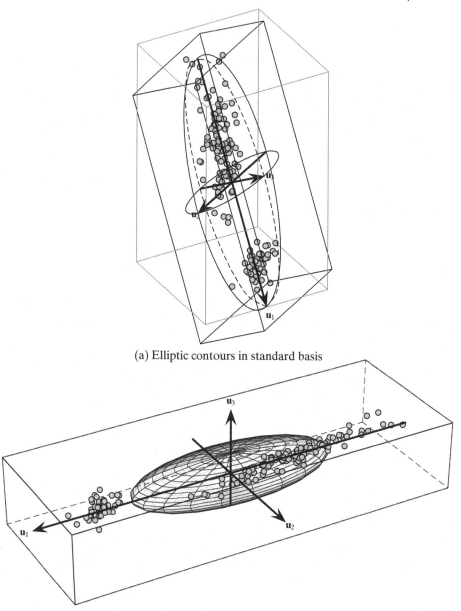

(a) Elliptic contours in standard basis

(b) Axis parallel ellipsoid in principal components basis

Figure 7.5. Iris data: standard and principal components basis in three dimensions.

Example 7.6. Figure 7.5(b) shows the ellipsoid $\mathbf{x}^T \mathbf{\Sigma}^{-1} \mathbf{x} = \mathbf{a}^T \mathbf{\Lambda}^{-1} \mathbf{a} = 1$ in the new principal components basis. Each semi-axis length corresponds to the standard deviation $\sqrt{\lambda_i}$ along that axis. Because all pairwise covariances are zero in the principal components basis, the ellipsoid is axis-parallel, that is, each of its axes coincides with a basis vector.

On the other hand, in the original standard d-dimensional basis for $\mathbf{D}$, the ellipsoid will not be axis-parallel, as shown by the contours of the ellipsoid in Figure 7.5(a). Here the semi-axis lengths correspond to half the value range in each direction; the length was chosen so that the ellipsoid encompasses most of the points.

7.3 KERNEL PRINCIPAL COMPONENT ANALYSIS

Principal component analysis can be extended to find nonlinear "directions" in the data using kernel methods. Kernel PCA finds the directions of most variance in the feature space instead of the input space. That is, instead of trying to find linear combinations of the input dimensions, kernel PCA finds linear combinations in the high-dimensional feature space obtained as some nonlinear transformation of the input dimensions. Thus, the linear principal components in the feature space correspond to nonlinear directions in the input space. As we shall see, using the *kernel trick*, all operations can be carried out in terms of the kernel function in input space, without having to transform the data into feature space.

Example 7.7. Consider the nonlinear Iris dataset shown in Figure 7.6, obtained via a nonlinear transformation applied on the centered Iris data. In particular, the sepal length (A_1) and sepal width attributes (A_2) were transformed as follows:

$$X_1 = 0.2A_1^2 + A_2^2 + 0.1A_1A_2$$
$$X_2 = A_2$$

The points show a clear quadratic (nonlinear) relationship between the two variables. Linear PCA yields the following two directions of most variance:

$$\lambda_1 = 0.197 \qquad \lambda_2 = 0.087$$

$$\mathbf{u}_1 = \begin{pmatrix} 0.301 \\ 0.953 \end{pmatrix} \qquad \mathbf{u}_2 = \begin{pmatrix} -0.953 \\ 0.301 \end{pmatrix}$$

These two principal components are illustrated in Figure 7.6. Also shown in the figure are lines of constant projections onto the principal components, that is, the set of all points in the input space that have the same coordinates when projected onto $\mathbf{u}_1$ and $\mathbf{u}_2$, respectively. For instance, the lines of constant projections in Figure 7.6(a) correspond to the solutions of $\mathbf{u}_1^T\mathbf{x} = s$ for different values of the coordinate s. Figure 7.7 shows the coordinates of each point in the principal components space comprising $\mathbf{u}_1$ and $\mathbf{u}_2$. It is clear from the figures that $\mathbf{u}_1$ and $\mathbf{u}_2$ do not fully capture the nonlinear relationship between X_1 and X_2. We shall see later in this section that kernel PCA is able to capture this dependence better.

Let ϕ correspond to a mapping from the input space to the feature space. Each point in feature space is given as the image $\phi(\mathbf{x}_i)$ of the point $\mathbf{x}_i$ in input space. In

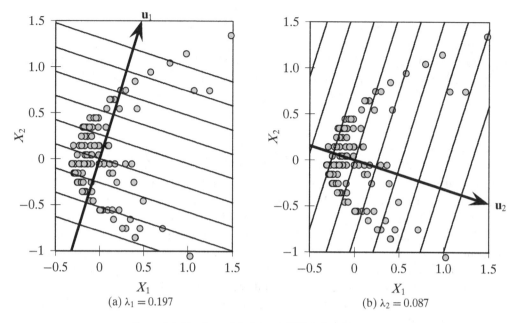

Figure 7.6. Nonlinear Iris dataset: PCA in input space.

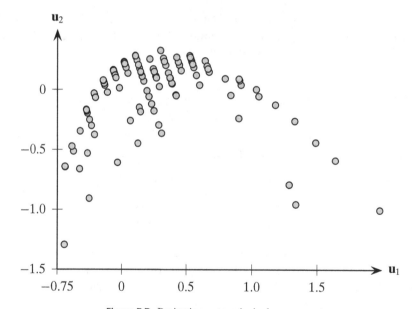

Figure 7.7. Projection onto principal components.

the input space, the first principal component captures the direction with the most projected variance; it is the eigenvector corresponding to the largest eigenvalue of the covariance matrix. Likewise, in feature space, we can find the first kernel principal component $\mathbf{u}_1$ (with $\mathbf{u}_1^T\mathbf{u}_1 = 1$), by solving for the eigenvector corresponding to the largest eigenvalue of the covariance matrix in feature space:

$$\boldsymbol{\Sigma}_\phi\mathbf{u}_1 = \lambda_1\mathbf{u}_1 \qquad (7.35)$$

where $\mathbf{\Sigma}_\phi$, the covariance matrix in feature space, is given as

$$\mathbf{\Sigma}_\phi = \frac{1}{n}\sum_{i=1}^n \left(\phi(\mathbf{x}_i) - \boldsymbol{\mu}_\phi\right)\left(\phi(\mathbf{x}_i) - \boldsymbol{\mu}_\phi\right)^T = \frac{1}{n}\sum_{i=1}^n \bar{\phi}(\mathbf{x}_i)\bar{\phi}(\mathbf{x}_i)^T \qquad (7.36)$$

where $\boldsymbol{\mu}_\phi$ is the mean in feature space, and $\bar{\phi}(\mathbf{x}_i) = \phi(\mathbf{x}_i) - \boldsymbol{\mu}_\phi$, is the centered point in feature space.

Plugging in the expansion of $\mathbf{\Sigma}_\phi$ from Eq. (7.36) into Eq. (7.35), we get

$$\left(\frac{1}{n}\sum_{i=1}^n \bar{\phi}(\mathbf{x}_i)\bar{\phi}(\mathbf{x}_i)^T\right)\mathbf{u}_1 = \lambda_1 \mathbf{u}_1 \qquad (7.37)$$

$$\frac{1}{n}\sum_{i=1}^n \bar{\phi}(\mathbf{x}_i)\left(\bar{\phi}(\mathbf{x}_i)^T\mathbf{u}_1\right) = \lambda_1\mathbf{u}_1$$

$$\sum_{i=1}^n \left(\frac{\bar{\phi}(\mathbf{x}_i)^T\mathbf{u}_1}{n\,\lambda_1}\right)\bar{\phi}(\mathbf{x}_i) = \mathbf{u}_1$$

$$\sum_{i=1}^n c_i\,\bar{\phi}(\mathbf{x}_i) = \mathbf{u}_1 \qquad (7.38)$$

where $c_i = \frac{\bar{\phi}(\mathbf{x}_i)^T\mathbf{u}_1}{n\lambda_1}$ is a scalar value. From Eq. (7.38) we see that the best direction in the feature space, $\mathbf{u}_1$, is just a linear combination of the transformed points, where the scalars c_i show the importance of each point toward the direction of most variance.

We can now substitute Eq. (7.38) back into Eq. (7.37) to get

$$\left(\frac{1}{n}\sum_{i=1}^n \bar{\phi}(\mathbf{x}_i)\bar{\phi}(\mathbf{x}_i)^T\right)\left(\sum_{j=1}^n c_j\,\bar{\phi}(\mathbf{x}_j)\right) = \lambda_1\sum_{i=1}^n c_i\,\bar{\phi}(\mathbf{x}_i)$$

$$\frac{1}{n}\sum_{i=1}^n\sum_{j=1}^n c_j\,\bar{\phi}(\mathbf{x}_i)\bar{\phi}(\mathbf{x}_i)^T\bar{\phi}(\mathbf{x}_j) = \lambda_1\sum_{i=1}^n c_i\,\bar{\phi}(\mathbf{x}_i)$$

$$\sum_{i=1}^n\left(\bar{\phi}(\mathbf{x}_i)\sum_{j=1}^n c_j\,\bar{\phi}(\mathbf{x}_i)^T\bar{\phi}(\mathbf{x}_j)\right) = n\lambda_1\sum_{i=1}^n c_i\,\bar{\phi}(\mathbf{x}_i)$$

In the preceding equation, we can replace the dot product in feature space, namely $\bar{\phi}(\mathbf{x}_i)^T\bar{\phi}(\mathbf{x}_j)$, by the corresponding kernel function in input space, namely $\bar{K}(\mathbf{x}_i, \mathbf{x}_j)$, which yields

$$\sum_{i=1}^n\left(\bar{\phi}(\mathbf{x}_i)\sum_{j=1}^n c_j\,\bar{K}(\mathbf{x}_i, \mathbf{x}_j)\right) = n\lambda_1\sum_{i=1}^n c_i\,\bar{\phi}(\mathbf{x}_i) \qquad (7.39)$$

Note that we assume that the points in feature space are centered, that is, we assume that the kernel matrix $\mathbf{K}$ has already been centered using Eq. (5.16):

$$\bar{\mathbf{K}} = \left(\mathbf{I} - \frac{1}{n}\mathbf{1}_{n\times n}\right)\mathbf{K}\left(\mathbf{I} - \frac{1}{n}\mathbf{1}_{n\times n}\right)$$

where $\mathbf{I}$ is the $n \times n$ identity matrix, and $\mathbf{1}_{n \times n}$ is the $n \times n$ matrix all of whose elements are 1.

We have so far managed to replace one of the dot products with the kernel function. To make sure that all computations in feature space are only in terms of dot products, we can take any point, say $\bar{\phi}(\mathbf{x}_k)$ and multiply Eq. (7.39) by $\bar{\phi}(\mathbf{x}_k)^T$ on both sides to obtain

$$\sum_{i=1}^{n} \left(\bar{\phi}(\mathbf{x}_k)^T \bar{\phi}(\mathbf{x}_i) \sum_{j=1}^{n} c_j \bar{K}(\mathbf{x}_i, \mathbf{x}_j) \right) = n\lambda_1 \sum_{i=1}^{n} c_i \bar{\phi}(\mathbf{x}_k)^T \bar{\phi}(\mathbf{x}_i)$$

$$\sum_{i=1}^{n} \left(\bar{K}(\mathbf{x}_k, \mathbf{x}_i) \sum_{j=1}^{n} c_j \bar{K}(\mathbf{x}_i, \mathbf{x}_j) \right) = n\lambda_1 \sum_{i=1}^{n} c_i \bar{K}(\mathbf{x}_k, \mathbf{x}_i) \tag{7.40}$$

Further, let $\bar{\mathbf{K}}_i$ denote row i of the centered kernel matrix, written as the column vector

$$\bar{\mathbf{K}}_i = \left(\bar{K}(\mathbf{x}_i, \mathbf{x}_1) \ \bar{K}(\mathbf{x}_i, \mathbf{x}_2) \ \cdots \ \bar{K}(\mathbf{x}_i, \mathbf{x}_n) \right)^T$$

Let $\mathbf{c}$ denote the column vector of weights

$$\mathbf{c} = (c_1 \ c_2 \ \cdots \ c_n)^T$$

We can plug $\bar{\mathbf{K}}_i$ and $\mathbf{c}$ into Eq. (7.40), and rewrite it as

$$\sum_{i=1}^{n} \bar{K}(\mathbf{x}_k, \mathbf{x}_i) \bar{\mathbf{K}}_i^T \mathbf{c} = n\lambda_1 \bar{\mathbf{K}}_k^T \mathbf{c}$$

In fact, because we can choose any of the n points, $\bar{\phi}(\mathbf{x}_k)$, in the feature space, to obtain Eq. (7.40), we have a set of n equations:

$$\sum_{i=1}^{n} \bar{K}(\mathbf{x}_1, \mathbf{x}_i) \bar{\mathbf{K}}_i^T \mathbf{c} = n\lambda_1 \bar{\mathbf{K}}_1^T \mathbf{c}$$

$$\sum_{i=1}^{n} \bar{K}(\mathbf{x}_2, \mathbf{x}_i) \bar{\mathbf{K}}_i^T \mathbf{c} = n\lambda_1 \bar{\mathbf{K}}_2^T \mathbf{c}$$

$$\vdots \qquad = \qquad \vdots$$

$$\sum_{i=1}^{n} \bar{K}(\mathbf{x}_n, \mathbf{x}_i) \bar{\mathbf{K}}_i^T \mathbf{c} = n\lambda_1 \bar{\mathbf{K}}_n^T \mathbf{c}$$

We can compactly represent all of these n equations as follows:

$$\bar{\mathbf{K}}^2 \mathbf{c} = n\lambda_1 \bar{\mathbf{K}} \mathbf{c}$$

where $\bar{\mathbf{K}}$ is the centered kernel matrix.

All non-zero eigenvalues and the corresponding eigenvectors of $\bar{\mathbf{K}}$ are solutions to the above equation. In particular, if η_1 is the largest eigenvalue of $\bar{\mathbf{K}}$ corresponding to the dominant eigenvector $\mathbf{c}$, we can verify that

$$\bar{\mathbf{K}}(\bar{\mathbf{K}}\mathbf{c}) = n\lambda_1\bar{\mathbf{K}}\mathbf{c}$$

$$\bar{\mathbf{K}}(\eta_1 \cdot \mathbf{c}) = n\lambda_1\eta_1\mathbf{c}$$

$$\bar{\mathbf{K}}\mathbf{c} = n\lambda_1\mathbf{c}$$

which implies

$$\boxed{\bar{\mathbf{K}}\mathbf{c} = \eta_1\mathbf{c}} \tag{7.41}$$

where $\eta_1 = n \cdot \lambda_1$. Thus, the weight vector $\mathbf{c}$ is the eigenvector corresponding to the largest eigenvalue η_1 of the kernel matrix $\bar{\mathbf{K}}$.

Once $\mathbf{c}$ is found, we can plug it back into Eq. (7.38) to obtain the first kernel principal component $\mathbf{u}_1$. The only constraint we impose is that $\mathbf{u}_1$ should be normalized to be a unit vector, as follows:

$$\mathbf{u}_1^T\mathbf{u}_1 = 1$$

$$\sum_{i=1}^{n}\sum_{j=1}^{n} c_i \, c_j \, \bar{\phi}(\mathbf{x}_i)^T \bar{\phi}(\mathbf{x}_j) = 1$$

$$\mathbf{c}^T\bar{\mathbf{K}}\mathbf{c} = 1$$

Noting that $\bar{\mathbf{K}}\mathbf{c} = \eta_1\mathbf{c}$ from Eq. (7.41), we get

$$\mathbf{c}^T(\eta_1\mathbf{c}) = 1$$

$$\eta_1\mathbf{c}^T\mathbf{c} = 1$$

$$\|\mathbf{c}\|^2 = \frac{1}{\eta_1}$$

However, because $\mathbf{c}$ is an eigenvector of $\bar{\mathbf{K}}$ it will have unit norm. Thus, to ensure that $\mathbf{u}_1$ is a unit vector, we have to scale the weight vector $\mathbf{c}$ so that its norm is $\|\mathbf{c}\| = \sqrt{\frac{1}{\eta_1}}$, which can be achieved by multiplying $\mathbf{c}$ by $\sqrt{\frac{1}{\eta_1}}$.

In general, because we do not map the input points into the feature space via ϕ, it is not possible to directly compute the principal direction, as it is specified in terms of $\bar{\phi}(\mathbf{x}_i)$, as seen in Eq. (7.38). However, what matters is that we can project any point $\bar{\phi}(\mathbf{x})$ onto the principal direction $\mathbf{u}_1$, as follows:

$$\mathbf{u}_1^T\bar{\phi}(\mathbf{x}) = \sum_{i=1}^{n}c_i\,\bar{\phi}(\mathbf{x}_i)^T\bar{\phi}(\mathbf{x}) = \sum_{i=1}^{n}c_i\,\bar{K}(\mathbf{x}_i,\mathbf{x})$$

which requires only kernel operations. When $\mathbf{x} = \mathbf{x}_i$ is one of the input points, the scalar projection of $\bar{\phi}(\mathbf{x}_i)$ onto the principal component $\mathbf{u}_1$ can be written as the dot product

$$a_{i1} = \mathbf{u}_1^T\bar{\phi}(\mathbf{x}_i) = \bar{\mathbf{K}}_i^T\mathbf{c} \tag{7.42}$$

where $\bar{\mathbf{K}}_i$ is the column vector corresponding to the ith row in the centered kernel matrix. Thus, we have shown that all computations, either for the solution of the

---

Algorithm 7.2: Kernel Principal Component Analysis

$\text{KERNELPCA } (\mathbf{D}, K, \alpha)\text{:}$

1 $\mathbf{K} = \left\{ K(\mathbf{x}_i, \mathbf{x}_j) \right\}_{i,j=1,\ldots,n}$ // compute $n \times n$ kernel matrix

2 $\overline{\mathbf{K}} = (\mathbf{I} - \frac{1}{n}\mathbf{1}_{n \times n})\mathbf{K}(\mathbf{I} - \frac{1}{n}\mathbf{1}_{n \times n})$ // center the kernel matrix

3 $(\eta_1, \eta_2, \ldots, \eta_n) = \text{eigenvalues}(\overline{\mathbf{K}})$ // compute eigenvalues

4 $\begin{pmatrix} \mathbf{c}_1 & \mathbf{c}_2 & \cdots & \mathbf{c}_n \end{pmatrix} = \text{eigenvectors}(\overline{\mathbf{K}})$ // compute eigenvectors

5 $\lambda_i = \frac{\eta_i}{n}$ for all $i = 1, \ldots, n$ // compute variance for each component

6 $\mathbf{c}_i = \sqrt{\frac{1}{\eta_i}} \cdot \mathbf{c}_i$ for all $i = 1, \ldots, n$ // ensure that $\mathbf{u}_i^T \mathbf{u}_i = 1$

7 $f(r) = \frac{\sum_{i=1}^{r} \lambda_i}{\sum_{i=1}^{d} \lambda_i}$, for all $r = 1, 2, \ldots, d$ // fraction of total variance

8 Choose smallest r so that $f(r) \geq \alpha$ // choose dimensionality

9 $\mathbf{C}_r = \begin{pmatrix} \mathbf{c}_1 & \mathbf{c}_2 & \cdots & \mathbf{c}_r \end{pmatrix}$ // reduced basis

10 $\mathbf{A} = \{\mathbf{a}_i \mid \mathbf{a}_i = \mathbf{C}_r^T \overline{\mathbf{K}}_i, \text{for } i = 1, \ldots, n\}$ // reduced dimensionality data

---

principal component, or for the projection of points, can be carried out using only the kernel function.

We can obtain the additional principal components by solving for the other eigenvalues and eigenvectors of Eq. (7.41). In other words, if we sort the eigenvalues of $\overline{\mathbf{K}}$ in decreasing order $\eta_1 \geq \eta_2 \geq \cdots \geq \eta_n \geq 0$, we can obtain the jth principal component as the corresponding eigenvector $\mathbf{c}_j$, which has to be normalized so that the norm is $\|\mathbf{c}_j\| = \sqrt{\frac{1}{\eta_j}}$, provided $\eta_j > 0$. Also, because $\eta_j = n\lambda_j$, the variance along the jth principal component is given as $\lambda_j = \frac{\eta_j}{n}$. To obtain a reduced dimensional dataset, say with dimensionality $r \ll n$, we can compute the scalar projection of $\overline{\phi}(\mathbf{x}_i)$ for each point $\mathbf{x}_i$ onto the principal component $\mathbf{u}_j$, for $j = 1, 2, \cdots, r$, as follows:

$$a_{ij} = \mathbf{u}_j^T \overline{\phi}(\mathbf{x}_i) = \overline{\mathbf{K}}_i^T \mathbf{c}_j$$

The new r-dimensional point corresponding to $\mathbf{x}_i$ is

$$\mathbf{a}_i = (a_{i1}, a_{i2}, \ldots, a_{ir})^T$$

We can also obtain $\mathbf{a}_i \in \mathbb{R}^r$ as follows:

$$\boxed{\mathbf{a}_i = \mathbf{C}_r^T \overline{\mathbf{K}}_i} \tag{7.43}$$

where $\mathbf{C}_r$ is the weight matrix whose columns comprise the top r eigenvectors, $\mathbf{c}_1, \mathbf{c}_2, \cdots, \mathbf{c}_r$. Algorithm 7.2 gives the pseudo-code for the kernel PCA method.

Example 7.8. Consider the nonlinear Iris data from Example 7.7 with $n = 150$ points. Let us use the homogeneous quadratic polynomial kernel in Eq. (5.8):

$$K(\mathbf{x}_i, \mathbf{x}_j) = \left(\mathbf{x}_i^T \mathbf{x}_j\right)^2$$

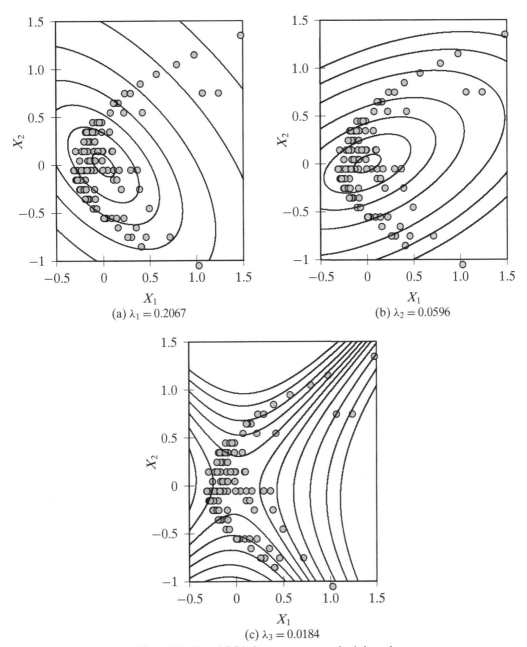

(a) $\lambda_1 = 0.2067$

(b) $\lambda_2 = 0.0596$

(c) $\lambda_3 = 0.0184$

Figure 7.8. Kernel PCA: homogeneous quadratic kernel.

The centered kernel matrix $\overline{\mathbf{K}}$ has three nonzero eigenvalues:

$$\eta_1 = 31.0 \qquad\qquad \eta_2 = 8.94 \qquad\qquad \eta_3 = 2.76$$

$$\lambda_1 = \frac{\eta_1}{150} = 0.2067 \qquad \lambda_2 = \frac{\eta_2}{150} = 0.0596 \qquad \lambda_3 = \frac{\eta_3}{150} = 0.0184$$

The corresponding eigenvectors $\mathbf{c}_1$, $\mathbf{c}_2$, and $\mathbf{c}_3$ are not shown because they lie in $\mathbb{R}^{150}$.

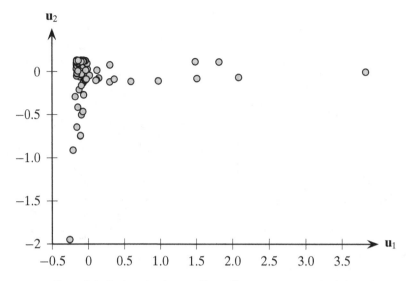

Figure 7.9. Projected point coordinates: homogeneous quadratic kernel.

Figure 7.8 shows the contour lines of constant projection onto the first three kernel principal components. These lines are obtained by solving the equations $\mathbf{u}_i^T \bar{\phi}(\mathbf{x}) = \sum_{j=1}^{n} c_{ij} \bar{K}(\mathbf{x}_j, \mathbf{x}) = s$ for different projection values s, for each of the eigenvectors $\mathbf{c}_i = (c_{i1}, c_{i2}, \ldots, c_{in})^T$ of the kernel matrix. For instance, for the first principal component this corresponds to the solutions $\mathbf{x} = (x_1, x_2)^T$, shown as contour lines, of the following equation:

$$1.0426 x_1^2 + 0.995 x_2^2 + 0.914 x_1 x_2 = s$$

for each chosen value of s. The principal components are also not shown in the figure, as it is typically not possible or feasible to map the points into feature space, and thus one cannot derive an explicit expression for $\mathbf{u}_i$. However, because the projection onto the principal components can be carried out via kernel operations via Eq. (7.42), Figure 7.9 shows the points $\mathbf{a}_i$ projected onto the first two kernel principal components, which capture $\frac{\lambda_1 + \lambda_2}{\lambda_1 + \lambda_2 + \lambda_3} = \frac{0.2663}{0.2847} = 93.5\%$ of the total variance.

Incidentally, the use of a linear kernel $K(\mathbf{x}_i, \mathbf{x}_j) = \mathbf{x}_i^T \mathbf{x}_j$ yields exactly the same principal components as shown in Figure 7.7.

7.4 SINGULAR VALUE DECOMPOSITION

Principal components analysis is a special case of a more general matrix decomposition method called *Singular Value Decomposition (SVD)*. We saw in Eq. (7.33) that PCA yields the following decomposition of the covariance matrix:

$$\mathbf{\Sigma} = \mathbf{U}\mathbf{\Lambda}\mathbf{U}^T \tag{7.44}$$

where the covariance matrix has been factorized into the orthogonal matrix $\mathbf{U}$ containing its eigenvectors, and a diagonal matrix $\mathbf{\Lambda}$ containing its eigenvalues (sorted in decreasing order). SVD generalizes the above factorization for any matrix. In particular for an $n \times d$ data matrix $\mathbf{D}$ with n points and d columns, SVD factorizes $\mathbf{D}$ as follows:

$$\mathbf{D} = \mathbf{L}\mathbf{\Delta}\mathbf{R}^T \tag{7.45}$$

where $\mathbf{L}$ is a orthogonal $n \times n$ matrix, $\mathbf{R}$ is an orthogonal $d \times d$ matrix, and $\mathbf{\Delta}$ is an $n \times d$ "diagonal" matrix. The columns of $\mathbf{L}$ are called the *left singular vectors*, and the columns of $\mathbf{R}$ (or rows of $\mathbf{R}^T$) are called the *right singular vectors*. The matrix $\mathbf{\Delta}$ is defined as

$$\mathbf{\Delta}(i, j) = \begin{cases} \delta_i & \text{If } i = j \\ 0 & \text{If } i \neq j \end{cases}$$

where $i = 1, \ldots, n$ and $j = 1, \ldots, d$. The entries $\mathbf{\Delta}(i, i) = \delta_i$ along the main diagonal of $\mathbf{\Delta}$ are called the *singular values* of $\mathbf{D}$, and they are all non-negative. If the rank of $\mathbf{D}$ is $r \leq \min(n, d)$, then there will be only r nonzero singular values, which we assume are ordered as follows:

$$\delta_1 \geq \delta_2 \geq \cdots \geq \delta_r > 0$$

One can discard those left and right singular vectors that correspond to zero singular values, to obtain the *reduced SVD* as

$$\mathbf{D} = \mathbf{L}_r \mathbf{\Delta}_r \mathbf{R}_r^T \tag{7.46}$$

where $\mathbf{L}_r$ is the $n \times r$ matrix of the left singular vectors, $\mathbf{R}_r$ is the $d \times r$ matrix of the right singular vectors, and $\mathbf{\Delta}_r$ is the $r \times r$ diagonal matrix containing the positive singular vectors. The reduced SVD leads directly to the *spectral decomposition* of $\mathbf{D}$, given as

$$\begin{aligned}
\mathbf{D} &= \mathbf{L}_r \mathbf{\Delta}_r \mathbf{R}_r^T \\
&= \begin{pmatrix} | & | & & | \\ l_1 & l_2 & \cdots & l_r \\ | & | & & | \end{pmatrix} \begin{pmatrix} \delta_1 & 0 & \cdots & 0 \\ 0 & \delta_2 & \cdots & 0 \\ \vdots & \vdots & \ddots & \vdots \\ 0 & 0 & \cdots & \delta_r \end{pmatrix} \begin{pmatrix} - & \mathbf{r}_1^T & - \\ - & \mathbf{r}_2^T & - \\ - & \vdots & - \\ - & \mathbf{r}_r^T & - \end{pmatrix} \\
&= \delta_1 l_1 \mathbf{r}_1^T + \delta_2 l_2 \mathbf{r}_2^T + \cdots + \delta_r l_r \mathbf{r}_r^T
\end{aligned}$$

That is,

$$\mathbf{D} = \sum_{i=1}^{r} \delta_i l_i \mathbf{r}_i^T \tag{7.47}$$

The spectral decomposition represents $\mathbf{D}$ as a sum of rank one matrices of the form $\delta_i l_i \mathbf{r}_i^T$. By selecting the q largest singular values $\delta_1, \delta_2, \ldots, \delta_q$ and the corresponding left and right singular vectors, we obtain the best rank q approximation to the original matrix $\mathbf{D}$. That is, if $\mathbf{D}_q$ is the matrix defined as

$$\mathbf{D}_q = \sum_{i=1}^{q} \delta_i l_i \mathbf{r}_i^T$$

then it can be shown that $\mathbf{D}_q$ is the rank q matrix that minimizes the expression

$$\|\mathbf{D} - \mathbf{D}_q\|_F$$

where $\|\mathbf{A}\|_F$ is called the *Frobenius Norm* of the $n \times d$ matrix $\mathbf{A}$, defined as

$$\|\mathbf{A}\|_F = \sqrt{\sum_{i=1}^{n} \sum_{j=1}^{d} \mathbf{A}(i, j)^2}$$

7.4.1 Geometry of SVD

In general, any $n \times d$ matrix $\mathbf{D}$ represents a *linear transformation*, $\mathbf{D} \colon \mathbb{R}^d \to \mathbb{R}^n$, from the space of d-dimensional vectors to the space of n-dimensional vectors because for any $\mathbf{x} \in \mathbb{R}^d$ there exists $\mathbf{y} \in \mathbb{R}^n$ such that

$$\mathbf{D}\mathbf{x} = \mathbf{y}$$

The set of all vectors $\mathbf{y} \in \mathbb{R}^n$ such that $\mathbf{D}\mathbf{x} = \mathbf{y}$ over all possible $\mathbf{x} \in \mathbb{R}^d$ is called the *column space* of $\mathbf{D}$, and the set of all vectors $\mathbf{x} \in \mathbb{R}^d$, such that $\mathbf{D}^T\mathbf{y} = \mathbf{x}$ over all $\mathbf{y} \in \mathbb{R}^n$, is called the *row space* of $\mathbf{D}$, which is equivalent to the column space of $\mathbf{D}^T$. In other words, the column space of $\mathbf{D}$ is the set of all vectors that can be obtained as linear combinations of columns of $\mathbf{D}$, and the row space of $\mathbf{D}$ is the set of all vectors that can be obtained as linear combinations of the rows of $\mathbf{D}$ (or columns of $\mathbf{D}^T$). Also note that the set of all vectors $\mathbf{x} \in \mathbb{R}^d$, such that $\mathbf{D}\mathbf{x} = \mathbf{0}$ is called the *null space* of $\mathbf{D}$, and finally, the set of all vectors $\mathbf{y} \in \mathbb{R}^n$, such that $\mathbf{D}^T\mathbf{y} = \mathbf{0}$ is called the *left null space* of $\mathbf{D}$.

One of the main properties of SVD is that it gives a basis for each of the four fundamental spaces associated with the matrix $\mathbf{D}$. If $\mathbf{D}$ has rank r, it means that it has only r independent columns, and also only r independent rows. Thus, the r left singular vectors $l_1, l_2, \ldots, l_r$ corresponding to the r nonzero singular values of $\mathbf{D}$ in Eq. (7.45) represent a basis for the column space of $\mathbf{D}$. The remaining $n - r$ left singular vectors $l_{r+1}, \ldots, l_n$ represent a basis for the left null space of $\mathbf{D}$. For the row space, the r right singular vectors $\mathbf{r}_1, \mathbf{r}_2, \ldots, \mathbf{r}_r$ corresponding to the r non-zero singular values, represent a basis for the row space of $\mathbf{D}$, and the remaining $d - r$ right singular vectors $\mathbf{r}_j$ ($j = r+1, \ldots, d$), represent a basis for the null space of $\mathbf{D}$.

Consider the reduced SVD expression in Eq. (7.46). Right multiplying both sides of the equation by $\mathbf{R}_r$ and noting that $\mathbf{R}_r^T\mathbf{R}_r = \mathbf{I}_r$, where $\mathbf{I}_r$ is the $r \times r$ identity matrix, we have

$$\mathbf{D}\mathbf{R}_r = \mathbf{L}_r\mathbf{\Delta}_r\mathbf{R}_r^T\mathbf{R}_r$$

$$\mathbf{D}\mathbf{R}_r = \mathbf{L}_r\mathbf{\Delta}_r$$

$$\mathbf{D}\mathbf{R}_r = \mathbf{L}_r\begin{pmatrix} \delta_1 & 0 & \cdots & 0 \\ 0 & \delta_2 & \cdots & 0 \\ \vdots & \vdots & \ddots & \vdots \\ 0 & 0 & \cdots & \delta_r \end{pmatrix}$$

$$\mathbf{D}\begin{pmatrix} | & | & & | \\ \mathbf{r}_1 & \mathbf{r}_2 & \cdots & \mathbf{r}_r \\ | & | & & | \end{pmatrix} = \begin{pmatrix} | & | & & | \\ \delta_1\mathbf{l}_1 & \delta_2\mathbf{l}_2 & \cdots & \delta_r\mathbf{l}_r \\ | & | & & | \end{pmatrix}$$

From the above, we conclude that

$$\mathbf{D}\mathbf{r}_i = \delta_i\mathbf{l}_i \quad \text{for all } i = 1,\dots,r$$

In other words, SVD is a special factorization of the matrix $\mathbf{D}$, such that any basis vector $\mathbf{r}_i$ for the row space is mapped to the corresponding basis vector $\mathbf{l}_i$ in the column space, scaled by the singular value δ_i. As such, we can think of the SVD as a mapping from an orthonormal basis $(\mathbf{r}_1, \mathbf{r}_2, \dots, \mathbf{r}_r)$ in $\mathbb{R}^d$ (the row space) to an orthonormal basis $(\mathbf{l}_1, \mathbf{l}_2, \dots, \mathbf{l}_r)$ in $\mathbb{R}^n$ (the column space), with the corresponding axes scaled according to the singular values $\delta_1, \delta_2, \dots, \delta_r$.

7.4.2 Connection between SVD and PCA

Assume that the matrix $\mathbf{D}$ has been centered, and assume that the centered matrix $\overline{\mathbf{D}}$ has been factorized via SVD [Eq. (7.45)] as $\overline{\mathbf{D}} = \mathbf{L}\mathbf{\Delta}\mathbf{R}^T$. Consider the *scatter matrix* for $\overline{\mathbf{D}}$, given as $\overline{\mathbf{D}}^T\overline{\mathbf{D}}$. We have

$$\begin{aligned} \overline{\mathbf{D}}^T\overline{\mathbf{D}} &= \left(\mathbf{L}\mathbf{\Delta}\mathbf{R}^T\right)^T\left(\mathbf{L}\mathbf{\Delta}\mathbf{R}^T\right) \\ &= \mathbf{R}\mathbf{\Delta}^T\mathbf{L}^T\mathbf{L}\mathbf{\Delta}\mathbf{R}^T \\ &= \mathbf{R}(\mathbf{\Delta}^T\mathbf{\Delta})\mathbf{R}^T \\ &= \mathbf{R}\mathbf{\Delta}_d^2\mathbf{R}^T \end{aligned} \tag{7.48}$$

where $\mathbf{\Delta}_d^2$ is the $d \times d$ diagonal matrix defined as $\mathbf{\Delta}_d^2(i,i) = \delta_i^2$, for $i = 1,\dots,d$. We conclude that each $\mathbf{r}_i$ is an eigenvector of $\overline{\mathbf{D}}^T\overline{\mathbf{D}}$, with the corresponding eigenvalue δ_i^2. Only $r \leq \min(d,n)$ of these eigenvalues are positive, whereas the rest are all zeros.

Because the covariance matrix of $\overline{\mathbf{D}}$ is given as $\mathbf{\Sigma} = \frac{1}{n}\overline{\mathbf{D}}^T\overline{\mathbf{D}}$, and because it can be decomposed as $\mathbf{\Sigma} = \mathbf{U}\mathbf{\Lambda}\mathbf{U}^T$ via PCA [Eq. (7.44)], we have

$$\begin{aligned} \overline{\mathbf{D}}^T\overline{\mathbf{D}} &= n\mathbf{\Sigma} \\ &= n\mathbf{U}\mathbf{\Lambda}\mathbf{U}^T \\ &= \mathbf{U}(n\mathbf{\Lambda})\mathbf{U}^T \end{aligned} \tag{7.49}$$

Equating Eq. (7.48) and Eq. (7.49), we conclude that the right singular vectors $\mathbf{R}$ are the same as the eigenvectors of Σ. Further, the corresponding singular values of $\overline{\mathbf{D}}$ are related to the eigenvalues of Σ by the expression

$$n\lambda_i = \delta_i^2$$

$$\text{or, } \lambda_i = \frac{\delta_i^2}{n}, \text{ for } i = 1, \ldots, d \tag{7.50}$$

Let us now consider the matrix $\overline{\mathbf{D}}\overline{\mathbf{D}}^T$. We have

$$\begin{aligned}
\overline{\mathbf{D}}\overline{\mathbf{D}}^T &= (\mathbf{L}\mathbf{\Delta}\mathbf{R}^T)(\mathbf{L}\mathbf{\Delta}\mathbf{R}^T)^T \\
&= \mathbf{L}\mathbf{\Delta}\mathbf{R}^T\mathbf{R}\mathbf{\Delta}^T\mathbf{L}^T \\
&= \mathbf{L}(\mathbf{\Delta}\mathbf{\Delta}^T)\mathbf{L}^T \\
&= \mathbf{L}\mathbf{\Delta}_n^2\mathbf{L}^T
\end{aligned}$$

where $\mathbf{\Delta}_n^2$ is the $n \times n$ diagonal matrix given as $\mathbf{\Delta}_n^2(i,i) = \delta_i^2$, for $i = 1, \ldots, n$. Only r of these singular values are positive, whereas the rest are all zeros. Thus, the left singular vectors in $\mathbf{L}$ are the eigenvectors of the $n \times n$ matrix $\overline{\mathbf{D}}\overline{\mathbf{D}}^T$, and the corresponding eigenvalues are given as δ_i^2.

Example 7.9. Let us consider the $n \times d$ centered Iris data matrix $\mathbf{D}$ from Example 7.1, with $n = 150$ and $d = 3$. In Example 7.5 we computed the eigenvectors and eigenvalues of the covariance matrix Σ as follows:

$$\lambda_1 = 3.662 \qquad\qquad \lambda_2 = 0.239 \qquad\qquad \lambda_3 = 0.059$$

$$\mathbf{u}_1 = \begin{pmatrix} -0.390 \\ 0.089 \\ -0.916 \end{pmatrix} \qquad \mathbf{u}_2 = \begin{pmatrix} -0.639 \\ -0.742 \\ 0.200 \end{pmatrix} \qquad \mathbf{u}_3 = \begin{pmatrix} -0.663 \\ 0.664 \\ 0.346 \end{pmatrix}$$

Computing the SVD of $\overline{\mathbf{D}}$ yields the following nonzero singular values and the corresponding right singular vectors

$$\delta_1 = 23.437 \qquad\qquad \delta_2 = 5.992 \qquad\qquad \delta_3 = 2.974$$

$$\mathbf{r}_1 = \begin{pmatrix} -0.390 \\ 0.089 \\ -0.916 \end{pmatrix} \qquad \mathbf{r}_2 = \begin{pmatrix} 0.639 \\ 0.742 \\ -0.200 \end{pmatrix} \qquad \mathbf{r}_3 = \begin{pmatrix} -0.663 \\ 0.664 \\ 0.346 \end{pmatrix}$$

We do not show the left singular vectors l_1, l_2, l_3 because they lie in $\mathbb{R}^{150}$. Using Eq. (7.50) one can verify that $\lambda_i = \frac{\delta_i^2}{n}$. For example,

$$\lambda_1 = \frac{\delta_1^2}{n} = \frac{23.437^2}{150} = \frac{549.29}{150} = 3.662$$

Notice also that the right singular vectors are equivalent to the principal components or eigenvectors of Σ, up to isomorphism. That is, they may potentially be reversed in direction. For the Iris dataset, we have $\mathbf{r}_1 = \mathbf{u}_1$, $\mathbf{r}_2 = -\mathbf{u}_2$, and $\mathbf{r}_3 = \mathbf{u}_3$. Here the second right singular vector is reversed in sign when compared to the second principal component.

7.5 FURTHER READING

Principal component analysis was pioneered in Pearson (1901). For a comprehensive description of PCA see Jolliffe (2002). Kernel PCA was first introduced in Schölkopf, Smola, and Müller (1998). For further exploration of non-linear dimensionality reduction methods see Lee and Verleysen (2007). The requisite linear algebra background can be found in Strang (2006).

Jolliffe, I. (2002). *Principal Component Analysis*. 2nd ed. Springer Series in Statistics. New York: Springer Science + Business Media.

Lee, J. A. and Verleysen, M. (2007). *Nonlinear Dimensionality Reduction*. New York: Springer Science + Business Media.

Pearson, K. (1901). On lines and planes of closest fit to systems of points in space. *The London, Edinburgh, and Dublin Philosophical Magazine and Journal of Science*, 2 (11), 559–572.

Schölkopf, B., Smola, A. J., and Müller, K.-R. (1998). Nonlinear component analysis as a kernel eigenvalue problem. *Neural Computation*, 10 (5), 1299–1319.

Strang, G. (2006). *Linear Algebra and Its Applications*. 4th ed. Independence, KY: Thomson Brooks/Cole, Cengage learning.

7.6 EXERCISES

Q1. Consider the following data matrix **D**:

X_1	X_2
8	−20
0	−1
10	−19
10	−20
2	0

(a) Compute the mean μ and covariance matrix Σ for **D**.

(b) Compute the eigenvalues of Σ.

(c) What is the "intrinsic" dimensionality of this dataset (discounting some small amount of variance)?

(d) Compute the first principal component.

(e) If the μ and Σ from above characterize the normal distribution from which the points were generated, sketch the orientation/extent of the 2-dimensional normal density function.

Q2. Given the covariance matrix $\boldsymbol{\Sigma} = \begin{pmatrix} 5 & 4 \\ 4 & 5 \end{pmatrix}$, answer the following questions:

  (a) Compute the eigenvalues of $\boldsymbol{\Sigma}$ by solving the equation $\det(\boldsymbol{\Sigma} - \lambda \mathbf{I}) = 0$.

  (b) Find the corresponding eigenvectors by solving the equation $\boldsymbol{\Sigma}\mathbf{u}_i = \lambda_i \mathbf{u}_i$.

Q3. Compute the singular values and the left and right singular vectors of the following matrix:

$$\mathbf{A} = \begin{pmatrix} 1 & 1 & 0 \\ 0 & 0 & 1 \end{pmatrix}$$

Q4. Consider the data in Table 7.1. Using the linear kernel, answer the following questions:

  (a) Compute the kernel matrix $\mathbf{K}$ and the centered kernel matrix $\overline{\mathbf{K}}$.

  (b) Find the first kernel principal component.

Table 7.1. Dataset for Q4

	X_1	X_2
$\mathbf{x}_1^T$	4	2.9
$\mathbf{x}_2^T$	2.5	1
$\mathbf{x}_3^T$	3.5	4
$\mathbf{x}_4^T$	2	2.1

Q5. Given the two points $\mathbf{x}_1 = (1, 2)^T$, and $\mathbf{x}_2 = (2, 1)^T$, use the kernel function

$$K(\mathbf{x}_i, \mathbf{x}_j) = (\mathbf{x}_i^T \mathbf{x}_j)^2$$

to find the kernel principal component, by solving the equation $\overline{\mathbf{K}}\mathbf{c} = \eta_1 \mathbf{c}$.

Q6. Show that the following relationship holds for the total variance of a dataset $\mathbf{D}$:

$$\mathrm{var}(\mathbf{D}) = tr(\boldsymbol{\Sigma}) = tr(\boldsymbol{\Lambda})$$

where $\boldsymbol{\Sigma}$ is the sample covariance matrix for $\mathbf{D}$, and $\boldsymbol{\Lambda}$ is the diagonal matrix of the eigenvalues of $\boldsymbol{\Sigma}$ in decreasing order.

Q7. Prove that if $\lambda_i \neq \lambda_j$ are two distinct eigenvalues of $\boldsymbol{\Sigma}$, then the corresponding eigenvectors $\mathbf{u}_i$ and $\mathbf{u}_j$ are orthogonal.

Q8. Let $\mathbf{U}$ be the matrix of eigenvectors of $\boldsymbol{\Sigma}$. Show that its left and right inverse is $\mathbf{U}^T$.

Q9. Let $\eta_i > 0$ be a non-zero eigenvalue of $\mathbf{K}$. Show that $\mathbf{c}_i$ is an eigenvector of $\mathbf{K}$ corresponding to η_i if and only if $\mathbf{K}^2 \mathbf{c}_i = \eta_i \mathbf{K} \mathbf{c}_i$.

Q10. Let $\mathbf{u}_i = \sum_{j=1}^{n} c_{ij} \phi(\mathbf{x}_j)$ denote the ith kernel principal component (PC), where $\mathbf{c}_i = (c_{i1}, c_{i2}, \ldots, c_{in})^T$ is the ith eigenvector of the kernel matrix $\mathbf{K}$ (with corresponding eigenvalue η_i). Show that $\mathbf{u}_i$ and $\mathbf{u}_j$ are orthogonal for any two different kernel PCs.

PART TWO

FREQUENT PATTERN MINING

Frequent pattern mining refers to the task of extracting informative and useful patterns in massive and complex datasets. Patterns comprise sets of co-occurring attribute values, called *itemsets*, or more complex patterns, such as sequences, which consider explicit precedence relationships (either positional or temporal), and graphs, which consider arbitrary relationships between entities. The key goal is to discover hidden relationships in the data to better understand the interactions among the data points and attributes.

This part begins by presenting efficient algorithms for frequent itemset mining in Chapter 8. The key methods include the level-wise Apriori algorithm, the "vertical" intersection based Eclat algorithm, and the frequent pattern tree and projection based FPGrowth method. Typically the mining process results in too many frequent patterns that can be hard to interpret. In Chapter 9, we consider approaches to summarize the mined patterns; these include maximal (GenMax algorithm), closed (Charm algorithm), and non-derivable itemsets.

We describe effective methods for frequent sequence mining in Chapter 10, which include the level-wise GSP method, the vertical SPADE algorithm, and the projection-based PrefixSpan approach. We also describe how consecutive subsequences, also called substrings, can be mined much more efficiently via Ukkonen's linear time and space suffix tree method.

Moving beyond sequences to arbitrary graphs, we describe the popular and efficient gSpan algorithm for frequent subgraph mining in Chapter 11. Graph mining involves two key steps, namely graph isomorphism checks to eliminate duplicate patterns during pattern enumeration and subgraph isomorphism checks during frequency computation. These operations can be performed in polynomial time for sets and sequences, but for graphs it is known that subgraph isomorphism is NP-hard, and thus there is no polynomial time method possible, unless $P = NP$. The gSpan method proposes a new canonical code and a systematic approach to subgraph extension, which allow it to efficiently detect duplicates and to perform several subgraph isomorphism checks much more efficiently than performing them individually.

Given that pattern mining methods generate many output results, it is very important to assess the mined patterns. We discuss strategies for assessing both the frequent patterns and rules that can be mined from them in Chapter 12, emphasizing methods for significance testing.

CHAPTER 8

Itemset Mining

In many applications one is interested in how often two or more objects of interest co-occur. For example, consider a popular website, which logs all incoming traffic to its site in the form of weblogs. Weblogs typically record the source and destination pages requested by some user, as well as the time, return code whether the request was successful or not, and so on. Given such weblogs, one might be interested in finding if there are sets of web pages that many users tend to browse whenever they visit the website. Such "frequent" sets of web pages give clues to user browsing behavior and can be used for improving the browsing experience.

The quest to mine frequent patterns appears in many other domains. The prototypical application is *market basket analysis*, that is, to mine the sets of items that are frequently bought together at a supermarket by analyzing the customer shopping carts (the so-called "market baskets"). Once we mine the frequent sets, they allow us to extract *association rules* among the item sets, where we make some statement about how likely are two sets of items to co-occur or to conditionally occur. For example, in the weblog scenario frequent sets allow us to extract rules like, "Users who visit the sets of pages main, laptops and rebates also visit the pages shopping-cart and checkout", indicating, perhaps, that the special rebate offer is resulting in more laptop sales. In the case of market baskets, we can find rules such as "Customers who buy milk and cereal also tend to buy bananas," which may prompt a grocery store to co-locate bananas in the cereal aisle. We begin this chapter with algorithms to mine frequent itemsets, and then show how they can be used to extract association rules.

8.1 FREQUENT ITEMSETS AND ASSOCIATION RULES

Itemsets and Tidsets

Let $\mathcal{I} = \{x_1, x_2, \ldots, x_m\}$ be a set of elements called *items*. A set $X \subseteq \mathcal{I}$ is called an *itemset*. The set of items $\mathcal{I}$ may denote, for example, the collection of all products sold at a supermarket, the set of all web pages at a website, and so on. An itemset of cardinality (or size) k is called a k-itemset. Further, we denote by $\mathcal{I}^{(k)}$ the set of all k-itemsets, that is, subsets of $\mathcal{I}$ with size k. Let $\mathcal{T} = \{t_1, t_2, \ldots, t_n\}$ be another set of elements called transaction identifiers or *tids*. A set $T \subseteq \mathcal{T}$ is called a *tidset*. We assume that itemsets and tidsets are kept sorted in lexicographic order.

A *transaction* is a tuple of the form $\langle t, X \rangle$, where $t \in \mathcal{T}$ is a unique transaction identifier, and X is an itemset. The set of transactions $\mathcal{T}$ may denote the set of all customers at a supermarket, the set of all the visitors to a website, and so on. For convenience, we refer to a transaction $\langle t, X \rangle$ by its identifier t.

Database Representation

A binary database $\mathbf{D}$ is a binary relation on the set of tids and items, that is, $\mathbf{D} \subseteq \mathcal{T} \times \mathcal{I}$. We say that tid $t \in \mathcal{T}$ *contains* item $x \in \mathcal{I}$ iff $(t, x) \in \mathbf{D}$. In other words, $(t, x) \in \mathbf{D}$ iff $x \in X$ in the tuple $\langle t, X \rangle$. We say that tid t *contains* itemset $X = \{x_1, x_2, \ldots, x_k\}$ iff $(t, x_i) \in \mathbf{D}$ for all $i = 1, 2, \ldots, k$.

Example 8.1. Figure 8.1(a) shows an example binary database. Here $\mathcal{I} = \{A, B, C, D, E\}$, and $\mathcal{T} = \{1, 2, 3, 4, 5, 6\}$. In the binary database, the cell in row t and column x is 1 iff $(t, x) \in \mathbf{D}$, and 0 otherwise. We can see that transaction 1 contains item B, and it also contains the itemset BE, and so on.

For a set X, we denote by 2^X the powerset of X, that is, the set of all subsets of X. Let $\mathbf{i}: 2^{\mathcal{T}} \to 2^{\mathcal{I}}$ be a function, defined as follows:

$$\mathbf{i}(T) = \{x \mid \forall t \in T, t \text{ contains } x\} \tag{8.1}$$

where $T \subseteq \mathcal{T}$, and $\mathbf{i}(T)$ is the set of items that are common to *all* the transactions in the tidset T. In particular, $\mathbf{i}(t)$ is the set of items contained in tid $t \in \mathcal{T}$. Note that in this chapter we drop the set notation for convenience (e.g., we write $\mathbf{i}(t)$ instead of $\mathbf{i}(\{t\})$). It is sometimes convenient to consider the binary database $\mathbf{D}$, as a *transaction database* consisting of tuples of the form $\langle t, \mathbf{i}(t) \rangle$, with $t \in \mathcal{T}$. The transaction or itemset database can be considered as a horizontal representation of the binary database, where we omit items that are not contained in a given tid.

Let $\mathbf{t}: 2^{\mathcal{I}} \to 2^{\mathcal{T}}$ be a function, defined as follows:

$$\mathbf{t}(X) = \{t \mid t \in \mathcal{T} \text{ and } t \text{ contains } X\} \tag{8.2}$$

where $X \subseteq \mathcal{I}$, and $\mathbf{t}(X)$ is the set of tids that contain *all* the items in the itemset X. In particular, $\mathbf{t}(x)$ is the set of tids that contain the single item $x \in \mathcal{I}$. It is also sometimes convenient to think of the binary database $\mathbf{D}$, as a tidset database containing a collection of tuples of the form $\langle x, \mathbf{t}(x) \rangle$, with $x \in \mathcal{I}$. The tidset database is a vertical representation of the binary database, where we omit tids that do not contain a given item.

Example 8.2. Figure 8.1(b) shows the corresponding transaction database for the binary database in Figure 8.1(a). For instance, the first transaction is $\langle 1, \{A, B, D, E\} \rangle$, where we omit item C since $(1, C) \notin \mathbf{D}$. Henceforth, for convenience, we drop the set notation for itemsets and tidsets if there is no confusion. Thus, we write $\langle 1, \{A, B, D, E\} \rangle$ as $\langle 1, ABDE \rangle$.

D	*A*	*B*	*C*	*D*	*E*
1	1	1	0	1	1
2	0	1	1	0	1
3	1	1	0	1	1
4	1	1	1	0	1
5	1	1	1	1	1
6	0	1	1	1	0

t	i(*t*)
1	*ABDE*
2	*BCE*
3	*ABDE*
4	*ABCE*
5	*ABCDE*
6	*BCD*

x	*A*	*B*	*C*	*D*	*E*
	1	1	2	1	1
	3	2	4	3	2
t(*x*)	4	3	5	5	3
	5	4	6	6	4
		5			5
		6			

(a) Binary database   (b) Transaction database   (c) Vertical database

Figure 8.1. An example database.

Figure 8.1(c) shows the corresponding vertical database for the binary database in Figure 8.1(a). For instance, the tuple corresponding to item A, shown in the first column, is $\langle A, \{1,3,4,5\}\rangle$, which we write as $\langle A, 1345\rangle$ for convenience; we omit tids 2 and 6 because $(2, A) \notin \mathbf{D}$ and $(6, A) \notin \mathbf{D}$.

Support and Frequent Itemsets

The *support* of an itemset X in a dataset $\mathbf{D}$, denoted $sup(X, \mathbf{D})$, is the number of transactions in $\mathbf{D}$ that contain X:

$$sup(X, \mathbf{D}) = \left|\{t \mid \langle t, \mathbf{i}(t)\rangle \in \mathbf{D} \text{ and } X \subseteq \mathbf{i}(t)\}\right| = |\mathbf{t}(X)| \tag{8.3}$$

The *relative support* of X is the fraction of transactions that contain X:

$$rsup(X, \mathbf{D}) = \frac{sup(X, \mathbf{D})}{|\mathbf{D}|} \tag{8.4}$$

It is an estimate of the *joint probability* of the items comprising X.

An itemset X is said to be *frequent* in $\mathbf{D}$ if $sup(X, \mathbf{D}) \geq minsup$, where *minsup* is a user defined *minimum support threshold*. When there is no confusion about the database $\mathbf{D}$, we write support as $sup(X)$, and relative support as $rsup(X)$. If *minsup* is specified as a fraction, then we assume that relative support is implied. We use the set $\mathcal{F}$ to denote the set of all frequent itemsets, and $\mathcal{F}^{(k)}$ to denote the set of frequent k-itemsets.

Example 8.3. Given the example dataset in Figure 8.1, let *minsup* = 3 (in relative support terms we mean *minsup* = 0.5). Table 8.1 shows all the 19 frequent itemsets in the database, grouped by their support value. For example, the itemset *BCE* is contained in tids 2, 4, and 5, so $\mathbf{t}(BCE) = 245$ and $sup(BCE) = |\mathbf{t}(BCE)| = 3$. Thus, *BCE* is a frequent itemset. The 19 frequent itemsets shown in the table comprise the set $\mathcal{F}$. The sets of all frequent k-itemsets are

$$\mathcal{F}^{(1)} = \{A, B, C, D, E\}$$
$$\mathcal{F}^{(2)} = \{AB, AD, AE, BC, BD, BE, CE, DE\}$$
$$\mathcal{F}^{(3)} = \{ABD, ABE, ADE, BCE, BDE\}$$
$$\mathcal{F}^{(4)} = \{ABDE\}$$

Table 8.1. Frequent itemsets with $minsup = 3$

sup	itemsets
6	B
5	E, BE
4	$A, C, D, AB, AE, BC, BD, ABE$
3	$AD, CE, DE, ABD, ADE, BCE, BDE, ABDE$

Association Rules

An *association rule* is an expression $X \xrightarrow{s,c} Y$, where X and Y are itemsets and they are disjoint, that is, $X, Y \subseteq \mathcal{I}$, and $X \cap Y = \emptyset$. Let the itemset $X \cup Y$ be denoted as XY. The *support* of the rule is the number of transactions in which both X and Y co-occur as subsets:

$$s = sup(X \longrightarrow Y) = |\mathbf{t}(XY)| = sup(XY)$$

The *relative support* of the rule is defined as the fraction of transactions where X and Y co-occur, and it provides an estimate of the joint probability of X and Y:

$$rsup(X \longrightarrow Y) = \frac{sup(XY)}{|\mathbf{D}|} = P(X \wedge Y)$$

The *confidence* of a rule is the conditional probability that a transaction contains Y given that it contains X:

$$c = conf(X \longrightarrow Y) = P(Y|X) = \frac{P(X \wedge Y)}{P(X)} = \frac{sup(XY)}{sup(X)}$$

A rule is *frequent* if the itemset XY is frequent, that is, $sup(XY) \geq minsup$ and a rule is *strong* if $conf \geq minconf$, where *minconf* is a user-specified minimum confidence threshold.

Example 8.4. Consider the association rule $BC \longrightarrow E$. Using the itemset support values shown in Table 8.1, the support and confidence of the rule are as follows:

$$s = sup(BC \longrightarrow E) = sup(BCE) = 3$$

$$c = conf(BC \longrightarrow E) = \frac{sup(BCE)}{sup(BC)} = 3/4 = 0.75$$

Itemset and Rule Mining

From the definition of rule support and confidence, we can observe that to generate frequent and high confidence association rules, we need to first enumerate all the frequent itemsets along with their support values. Formally, given a binary database $\mathbf{D}$ and a user defined minimum support threshold *minsup*, the task of frequent itemset mining is to enumerate all itemsets that are frequent, i.e., those that have support at least *minsup*. Next, given the set of frequent itemsets $\mathcal{F}$ and a minimum confidence value *minconf*, the association rule mining task is to find all frequent and strong rules.

8.2 ITEMSET MINING ALGORITHMS

We begin by describing a naive or brute-force algorithm that enumerates all the possible itemsets $X \subseteq \mathcal{I}$, and for each such subset determines its support in the input dataset $\mathbf{D}$. The method comprises two main steps: (1) candidate generation and (2) support computation.

Candidate Generation

This step generates all the subsets of $\mathcal{I}$, which are called *candidates*, as each itemset is potentially a candidate frequent pattern. The candidate itemset search space is clearly exponential because there are $2^{|\mathcal{I}|}$ potentially frequent itemsets. It is also instructive to note the structure of the itemset search space; the set of all itemsets forms a lattice structure where any two itemsets X and Y are connected by a link iff X is an *immediate subset* of Y, that is, $X \subseteq Y$ and $|X| = |Y| - 1$. In terms of a practical search strategy, the itemsets in the lattice can be enumerated using either a breadth-first (BFS) or depth-first (DFS) search on the *prefix tree*, where two itemsets X, Y are connected by a link iff X is an immediate subset and prefix of Y. This allows one to enumerate itemsets starting with an empty set, and adding one more item at a time.

Support Computation

This step computes the support of each candidate pattern X and determines if it is frequent. For each transaction $\langle t, \mathbf{i}(t) \rangle$ in the database, we determine if X is a subset of $\mathbf{i}(t)$. If so, we increment the support of X.

The pseudo-code for the brute-force method is shown in Algorithm 8.1. It enumerates each itemset $X \subseteq \mathcal{I}$, and then computes its support by checking if $X \subseteq \mathbf{i}(t)$ for each $t \in \mathcal{T}$.

Algorithm 8.1: Algorithm BRUTEFORCE

BRUTEFORCE (D, $\mathcal{I}$, *minsup*):

1   $\mathcal{F} \leftarrow \emptyset$ // set of frequent itemsets
2   **foreach** $X \subseteq \mathcal{I}$ **do**
3     $sup(X) \leftarrow$ COMPUTESUPPORT $(X, \mathbf{D})$
4   **if** $sup(X) \geq minsup$ **then**
5       $\mathcal{F} \leftarrow \mathcal{F} \cup \{(X, sup(X))\}$

6   **return** $\mathcal{F}$

COMPUTESUPPORT $(X, \mathbf{D})$:

7   $sup(X) \leftarrow 0$
8   **foreach** $\langle t, \mathbf{i}(t) \rangle \in \mathbf{D}$ **do**
9   **if** $X \subseteq \mathbf{i}(t)$ **then**
10      $sup(X) \leftarrow sup(X) + 1$

11   **return** $sup(X)$

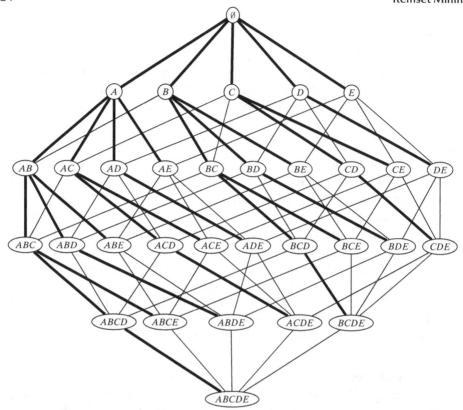

Figure 8.2. Itemset lattice and prefix-based search tree (in bold).

Example 8.5. Figure 8.2 shows the itemset lattice for the set of items $\mathcal{I} = \{A, B, C, D, E\}$. There are $2^{|\mathcal{I}|} = 2^5 = 32$ possible itemsets including the empty set. The corresponding prefix search tree is also shown (in bold). The brute-force method explores the entire itemset search space, regardless of the *minsup* threshold employed. If *minsup* = 3, then the brute-force method would output the set of frequent itemsets shown in Table 8.1.

Computational Complexity

Support computation takes time $O(|\mathcal{I}| \cdot |\mathbf{D}|)$ in the worst case, and because there are $O(2^{|\mathcal{I}|})$ possible candidates, the computational complexity of the brute-force method is $O(|\mathcal{I}| \cdot |\mathbf{D}| \cdot 2^{|\mathcal{I}|})$. Because the database $\mathbf{D}$ can be very large, it is also important to measure the input/output (I/O) complexity. Because we make one complete database scan to compute the support of each candidate, the I/O complexity of BRUTEFORCE is $O(2^{|\mathcal{I}|})$ database scans. Thus, the brute force approach is computationally infeasible for even small itemset spaces, whereas in practice $\mathcal{I}$ can be very large (e.g., a supermarket carries thousands of items). The approach is impractical from an I/O perspective as well.

We shall see next how to systematically improve on the brute force approach, by improving both the candidate generation and support counting steps.

8.2.1 Level-wise Approach: Apriori Algorithm

The brute force approach enumerates all possible itemsets in its quest to determine the frequent ones. This results in a lot of wasteful computation because many of the candidates may not be frequent. Let $X, Y \subseteq \mathcal{I}$ be any two itemsets. Note that if $X \subseteq Y$, then $sup(X) \geq sup(Y)$, which leads to the following two observations: (1) if X is frequent, then any subset $Y \subseteq X$ is also frequent, and (2) if X is not frequent, then any superset $Y \supseteq X$ cannot be frequent. The *Apriori algorithm* utilizes these two properties to significantly improve the brute-force approach. It employs a level-wise or breadth-first exploration of the itemset search space, and prunes all supersets of any infrequent candidate, as no superset of an infrequent itemset can be frequent. It also avoids generating any candidate that has an infrequent subset. In addition to improving the candidate generation step via itemset pruning, the Apriori method also significantly improves the I/O complexity. Instead of counting the support for a single itemset, it explores the prefix tree in a breadth-first manner, and computes the support of all the valid candidates of size k that comprise level k in the prefix tree.

Example 8.6. Consider the example dataset in Figure 8.1; let *minsup* = 3. Figure 8.3 shows the itemset search space for the Apriori method, organized as a prefix tree where two itemsets are connected if one is a prefix and immediate subset of the

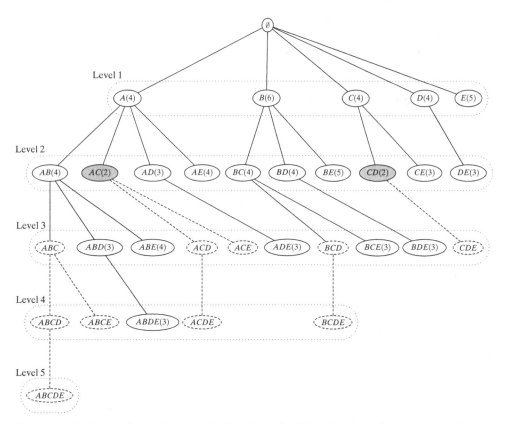

Figure 8.3. Apriori: prefix search tree and effect of pruning. Shaded nodes indicate infrequent itemsets; dashed nodes and lines indicate all of the pruned nodes and branches; solid lines indicate frequent itemsets.

Algorithm 8.2: Algorithm APRIORI

APRIORI ($\mathbf{D}, \mathcal{I}, minsup$):

1 $\mathcal{F} \leftarrow \emptyset$
2 $\mathcal{C}^{(1)} \leftarrow \{\emptyset\}$ // Initial prefix tree with single items
3 **foreach** $i \in \mathcal{I}$ **do** Add i as child of $\emptyset$ in $\mathcal{C}^{(1)}$ with $sup(i) \leftarrow 0$
4 $k \leftarrow 1$ // k denotes the level
5 **while** $\mathcal{C}^{(k)} \neq \emptyset$ **do**
6 $\quad$ COMPUTESUPPORT ($\mathcal{C}^{(k)}, \mathbf{D}$)
7 $\quad$ **foreach** *leaf* $X \in \mathcal{C}^{(k)}$ **do**
8 $\quad\quad$ **if** $sup(X) \geq minsup$ **then** $\mathcal{F} \leftarrow \mathcal{F} \cup \{(X, sup(X))\}$
9 $\quad\quad$ **else** remove X from $\mathcal{C}^{(k)}$
10 $\quad$ $\mathcal{C}^{(k+1)} \leftarrow$ EXTENDPREFIXTREE ($\mathcal{C}^{(k)}$)
11 $\quad$ $k \leftarrow k + 1$
12 **return** $\mathcal{F}^{(k)}$

COMPUTESUPPORT ($\mathcal{C}^{(k)}, \mathbf{D}$):

13 **foreach** $\langle t, \mathbf{i}(t) \rangle \in \mathbf{D}$ **do**
14 $\quad$ **foreach** k-*subset* $X \subseteq \mathbf{i}(t)$ **do**
15 $\quad\quad$ **if** $X \in \mathcal{C}^{(k)}$ **then** $sup(X) \leftarrow sup(X) + 1$

EXTENDPREFIXTREE ($\mathcal{C}^{(k)}$):

16 **foreach** *leaf* $X_a \in \mathcal{C}^{(k)}$ **do**
17 $\quad$ **foreach** *leaf* $X_b \in$ SIBLING(X_a), *such that* $b > a$ **do**
18 $\quad\quad$ $X_{ab} \leftarrow X_a \cup X_b$
$\quad\quad$ // prune candidate if there are any infrequent subsets
19 $\quad\quad$ **if** $X_j \in \mathcal{C}^{(k)}$, *for all* $X_j \subset X_{ab}$, *such that* $|X_j| = |X_{ab}| - 1$ **then**
20 $\quad\quad\quad$ Add X_{ab} as child of X_a with $sup(X_{ab}) \leftarrow 0$
21 $\quad$ **if** *no extensions from* X_a **then**
22 $\quad\quad$ remove X_a, and all ancestors of X_a with no extensions, from $\mathcal{C}^{(k)}$
23 **return** $\mathcal{C}^{(k)}$

---

other. Each node shows an itemset along with its support, thus $AC(2)$ indicates that $sup(AC) = 2$. Apriori enumerates the candidate patterns in a level-wise manner, as shown in the figure, which also demonstrates the power of pruning the search space via the two Apriori properties. For example, once we determine that AC is infrequent, we can prune any itemset that has AC as a prefix, that is, the entire subtree under AC can be pruned. Likewise for CD. Also, the extension BCD from BC can be pruned, since it has an infrequent subset, namely CD.

Algorithm 8.2 shows the pseudo-code for the Apriori method. Let $\mathcal{C}^{(k)}$ denote the prefix tree comprising all the candidate k-itemsets. The method begins by inserting the single items into an initially empty prefix tree to populate $\mathcal{C}^{(1)}$. The while loop (lines

5–11) first computes the support for the current set of candidates at level k via the COMPUTESUPPORT procedure that generates k-subsets of each transaction in the database **D**, and for each such subset it increments the support of the corresponding candidate in $\mathcal{C}^{(k)}$ if it exists. This way, the database is scanned only once per level, and the supports for all candidate k-itemsets are incremented during that scan. Next, we remove any infrequent candidate (line 9). The leaves of the prefix tree that survive comprise the set of frequent k-itemsets $\mathcal{F}^{(k)}$, which are used to generate the candidate $(k + 1)$-itemsets for the next level (line 10). The EXTENDPREFIXTREE procedure employs prefix-based extension for candidate generation. Given two frequent k-itemsets X_a and X_b with a common $k - 1$ length prefix, that is, given two sibling leaf nodes with a common parent, we generate the $(k + 1)$-length candidate $X_{ab} = X_a \cup X_b$. This candidate is retained only if it has no infrequent subset. Finally, if a k-itemset X_a has no extension, it is pruned from the prefix tree, and we recursively prune any of its ancestors with no k-itemset extension, so that in $\mathcal{C}^{(k)}$ all leaves are at level k. If new candidates were added, the whole process is repeated for the next level. This process continues until no new candidates are added.

Example 8.7. Figure 8.4 illustrates the Apriori algorithm on the example dataset from Figure 8.1 using $minsup = 3$. All the candidates $\mathcal{C}^{(1)}$ are frequent (see Figure 8.4(a)). During extension all the pairwise combinations will be considered, since they all share the empty prefix $\emptyset$ as their parent. These comprise the new prefix tree $\mathcal{C}^{(2)}$ in Figure 8.4(b); because E has no prefix-based extensions, it is removed from the tree. After support computation $AC(2)$ and $CD(2)$ are eliminated (shown in gray) since they are infrequent. The next level prefix tree is shown in Figure 8.4(c). The candidate BCD is pruned due to the presence of the infrequent subset CD. All of the candidates at level 3 are frequent. Finally, $\mathcal{C}^{(4)}$ (shown in Figure 8.4(d)) has only one candidate $X_{ab} = ABDE$, which is generated from $X_a = ABD$ and $X_b = ABE$ because this is the only pair of siblings. The mining process stops after this step, since no more extensions are possible.

The worst-case computational complexity of the Apriori algorithm is still $O(|\mathcal{I}| \cdot |\mathbf{D}| \cdot 2^{|\mathcal{I}|})$, as all itemsets may be frequent. In practice, due to the pruning of the search space the cost is much lower. However, in terms of I/O cost Apriori requires $O(|\mathcal{I}|)$ database scans, as opposed to the $O(2^{|\mathcal{I}|})$ scans in the brute-force method. In practice, it requires only l database scans, where l is the length of the longest frequent itemset.

8.2.2 Tidset Intersection Approach: Eclat Algorithm

The support counting step can be improved significantly if we can index the database in such a way that it allows fast frequency computations. Notice that in the level-wise approach, to count the support, we have to generate subsets of each transaction and check whether they exist in the prefix tree. This can be expensive because we may end up generating many subsets that do not exist in the prefix tree.

The Eclat algorithm leverages the tidsets directly for support computation. The basic idea is that the support of a candidate itemset can be computed by intersecting the tidsets of suitably chosen subsets. In general, given $\mathbf{t}(X)$ and $\mathbf{t}(Y)$ for any two frequent

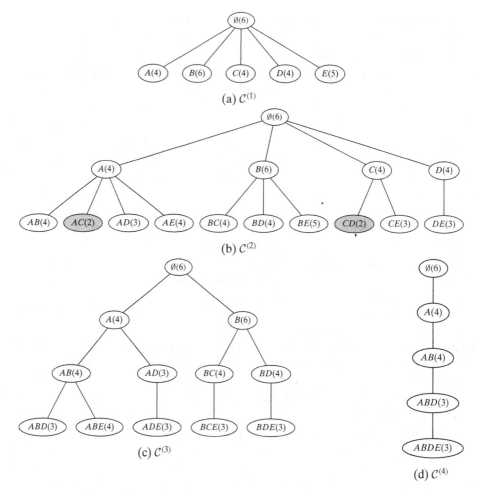

Figure 8.4. Itemset mining: Apriori algorithm. The prefix search trees $C^{(k)}$ at each level are shown. Leaves (unshaded) comprise the set of frequent k-itemsets $\mathcal{F}^{(k)}$.

itemsets X and Y, we have

$$\mathbf{t}(XY) = \mathbf{t}(X) \cap \mathbf{t}(Y)$$

The support of candidate XY is simply the cardinality of $\mathbf{t}(XY)$, that is, $sup(XY) = |\mathbf{t}(XY)|$. Eclat intersects the tidsets only if the frequent itemsets share a common prefix, and it traverses the prefix search tree in a DFS-like manner, processing a group of itemsets that have the same prefix, also called a *prefix equivalence class*.

Example 8.8. For example, if we know that the tidsets for item A and C are $\mathbf{t}(A) = 1345$ and $\mathbf{t}(C) = 2456$, respectively, then we can determine the support of AC by intersecting the two tidsets, to obtain $\mathbf{t}(AC) = \mathbf{t}(A) \cap \mathbf{t}(C) = 1345 \cap 2456 = 45$. In this case, we have $sup(AC) = |45| = 2$. An example of a prefix equivalence class is the set $P_A = \{AB, AC, AD, AE\}$, as all the elements of P_A share A as the prefix.

The pseudo-code for Eclat is given in Algorithm 8.3. It employs a vertical representation of the binary database **D**. Thus, the input is the set of tuples $\langle i, \mathbf{t}(i) \rangle$ for all frequent items $i \in \mathcal{I}$, which comprise an equivalence class P (they all share the empty prefix); it is assumed that P contains only frequent itemsets. In general, given a prefix equivalence class P, for each frequent itemset $X_a \in P$, we try to intersect its tidset with the tidsets of all other itemsets $X_b \in P$. The candidate pattern is $X_{ab} = X_a \cup X_b$, and we check the cardinality of the intersection $\mathbf{t}(X_a) \cap \mathbf{t}(X_b)$ to determine whether it is frequent. If so, X_{ab} is added to the new equivalence class P_a that contains all itemsets that share X_a as a prefix. A recursive call to Eclat then finds all extensions of the X_a branch in the search tree. This process continues until no extensions are possible over all branches.

Example 8.9. Figure 8.5 illustrates the Eclat algorithm. Here $minsup = 3$, and the initial prefix equivalence class is

$$P_\emptyset = \big\{ \langle A, 1345 \rangle, \langle B, 123456 \rangle, \langle C, 2456 \rangle, \langle D, 1356 \rangle, \langle E, 12345 \rangle \big\}$$

Eclat intersects $\mathbf{t}(A)$ with each of $\mathbf{t}(B)$, $\mathbf{t}(C)$, $\mathbf{t}(D)$, and $\mathbf{t}(E)$ to obtain the tidsets for AB, AC, AD and AE, respectively. Out of these AC is infrequent and is pruned (marked gray). The frequent itemsets and their tidsets comprise the new prefix equivalence class

$$P_A = \big\{ \langle AB, 1345 \rangle, \langle AD, 135 \rangle, \langle AE, 1345 \rangle \big\}$$

which is recursively processed. On return, Eclat intersects $\mathbf{t}(B)$ with $\mathbf{t}(C)$, $\mathbf{t}(D)$, and $\mathbf{t}(E)$ to obtain the equivalence class

$$P_B = \big\{ \langle BC, 2456 \rangle, \langle BD, 1356 \rangle, \langle BE, 12345 \rangle \big\}$$

Other branches are processed in a similar manner; the entire search space that Eclat explores is shown in Figure 8.5. The gray nodes indicate infrequent itemsets, whereas the rest constitute the set of frequent itemsets.

Algorithm 8.3: Algorithm ECLAT

    // Initial Call: $\mathcal{F} \leftarrow \emptyset, P \leftarrow \big\{ \langle i, \mathbf{t}(i) \rangle \mid i \in \mathcal{I}, |\mathbf{t}(i)| \geq minsup \big\}$

    ECLAT $(P, minsup, \mathcal{F})$:

1 **foreach** $\langle X_a, \mathbf{t}(X_a) \rangle \in P$ **do**

2     $\mathcal{F} \leftarrow \mathcal{F} \cup \big\{ (X_a, sup(X_a)) \big\}$

3     $P_a \leftarrow \emptyset$

4   **foreach** $\langle X_b, \mathbf{t}(X_b) \rangle \in P$, *with* $X_b > X_a$ **do**

5         $X_{ab} = X_a \cup X_b$

6         $\mathbf{t}(X_{ab}) = \mathbf{t}(X_a) \cap \mathbf{t}(X_b)$

7   **if** $sup(X_{ab}) \geq minsup$ **then**

8             $P_a \leftarrow P_a \cup \big\{ \langle X_{ab}, \mathbf{t}(X_{ab}) \rangle \big\}$

9   **if** $P_a \neq \emptyset$ **then** ECLAT $(P_a, minsup, \mathcal{F})$

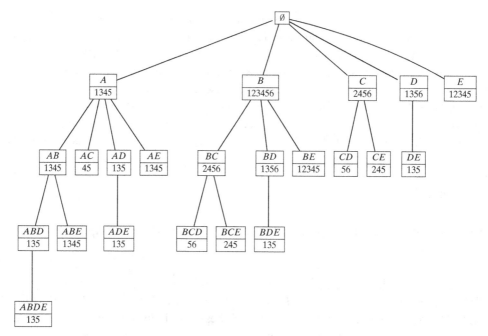

Figure 8.5. Eclat algorithm: tidlist intersections (gray boxes indicate infrequent itemsets).

The computational complexity of Eclat is $O(|\mathbf{D}| \cdot 2^{|\mathcal{I}|})$ in the worst case, since there can be $2^{|\mathcal{I}|}$ frequent itemsets, and an intersection of two tidsets takes at most $O(|\mathbf{D}|)$ time. The I/O complexity of Eclat is harder to characterize, as it depends on the size of the intermediate tidsets. With t as the average tidset size, the initial database size is $O(t \cdot |\mathcal{I}|)$, and the total size of all the intermediate tidsets is $O(t \cdot 2^{|\mathcal{I}|})$. Thus, Eclat requires $\frac{t \cdot 2^{|\mathcal{I}|}}{t \cdot |\mathcal{I}|} = O(2^{|\mathcal{I}|} / |\mathcal{I}|)$ database scans in the worst case.

Diffsets: Difference of Tidsets

The Eclat algorithm can be significantly improved if we can shrink the size of the intermediate tidsets. This can be achieved by keeping track of the differences in the tidsets as opposed to the full tidsets. Formally, let $X_k = \{x_1, x_2, \ldots, x_{k-1}, x_k\}$ be a k-itemset. Define the *diffset* of X_k as the set of tids that contain the prefix $X_{k-1} = \{x_1, \ldots, x_{k-1}\}$ but do not contain the item x_k, given as

$$\mathbf{d}(X_k) = \mathbf{t}(X_{k-1}) \setminus \mathbf{t}(X_k)$$

Consider two k-itemsets $X_a = \{x_1, \ldots, x_{k-1}, x_a\}$ and $X_b = \{x_1, \ldots, x_{k-1}, x_b\}$ that share the common $(k-1)$-itemset $X = \{x_1, x_2, \ldots, x_{k-1}\}$ as a prefix. The diffsets of X_a and X_b are given as

$$\mathbf{d}(X_a) = \mathbf{t}(X) \setminus \mathbf{t}(X_a) \qquad\qquad \mathbf{d}(X_b) = \mathbf{t}(X) \setminus \mathbf{t}(X_b)$$

Since $\mathbf{t}(X_a) \subseteq \mathbf{t}(X)$ and $\mathbf{t}(X_b) \subseteq \mathbf{t}(X)$, we get

$$\mathbf{t}(X_a) = \mathbf{t}(X) \setminus \mathbf{d}(X_a) \qquad\qquad \mathbf{t}(X_b) = \mathbf{t}(X) \setminus \mathbf{d}(X_b)$$

Finally, note that for any sets X and Y,

$$\mathbf{t}(X) \setminus \mathbf{t}(Y) = \mathbf{t}(X) \cap \overline{\mathbf{t}(Y)}$$

Now, consider the diffset of $X_{ab} = X_a \cup X_b = \{x_1, \ldots, x_{k-1}, x_a, x_b\}$, we have

$$\mathbf{d}(X_{ab}) = \mathbf{t}(X_a) \setminus \mathbf{t}(X_{ab}) \tag{8.5}$$

$$= \mathbf{t}(X_a) \setminus \mathbf{t}(X_b)$$

$$= \big(\mathbf{t}(X) \setminus \mathbf{d}(X_a)\big) \setminus \big(\mathbf{t}(X) \setminus \mathbf{d}(X_b)\big)$$

$$= \big(\mathbf{t}(X) \cap \overline{\mathbf{d}(X_a)}\big) \cap \overline{\big(\mathbf{t}(X) \cap \overline{\mathbf{d}(X_b)}\big)}$$

$$= \big(\mathbf{t}(X) \cap \overline{\mathbf{d}(X_a)}\big) \cap \big(\mathbf{d}(X_b) \cup \overline{\mathbf{t}(X)}\big)$$

$$= \mathbf{t}(X) \cap \mathbf{d}(X_b) \cap \overline{\mathbf{d}(X_a)}$$

$$= \mathbf{d}(X_b) \setminus \mathbf{d}(X_a)$$

Thus, the diffset of X_{ab} can be obtained from the diffsets of its subsets X_a and X_b, which means that we can replace all intersection operations in Eclat with diffset operations. Using diffsets the support of a candidate itemset can be obtained by subtracting the diffset size from the support of the prefix itemset:

$$sup(X_{ab}) = sup(X_a) - |\mathbf{d}(X_{ab})| \tag{8.6}$$

which follows directly from Eq. (8.5).

The variant of Eclat that uses the diffset optimization is called dEclat, whose pseudo-code is shown in Algorithm 8.4. The input comprises all the frequent single items $i \in \mathcal{I}$ along with their diffsets, which are computed as

$$\mathbf{d}(i) = \mathbf{t}(\emptyset) \setminus \mathbf{t}(i) = \mathcal{T} \setminus \mathbf{t}(i)$$

Given an equivalence class P, for each pair of distinct itemsets X_a and X_b we generate the candidate pattern $X_{ab} = X_a \cup X_b$ and check whether it is frequent via the use of diffsets (lines 6–7). Recursive calls are made to find further extensions. It is important to note that the switch from tidsets to diffsets can be made during any recursive call to

---

Algorithm 8.4: Algorithm DECLAT

// Initial Call: $\mathcal{F} \leftarrow \emptyset$,
$\quad P \leftarrow \big\{\langle i, \mathbf{d}(i), sup(i)\rangle \mid i \in \mathcal{I}, \mathbf{d}(i) = \mathcal{T} \setminus \mathbf{t}(i), sup(i) \geq minsup\big\}$
DECLAT (P, $minsup$, $\mathcal{F}$):

1   **foreach** $\langle X_a, \mathbf{d}(X_a), sup(X_a)\rangle \in P$ **do**
2      $\mathcal{F} \leftarrow \mathcal{F} \cup \big\{(X_a, sup(X_a))\big\}$
3      $P_a \leftarrow \emptyset$
4   **foreach** $\langle X_b, \mathbf{d}(X_b), sup(X_b)\rangle \in P$, *with* $X_b > X_a$ **do**
5        $X_{ab} = X_a \cup X_b$
6        $\mathbf{d}(X_{ab}) = \mathbf{d}(X_b) \setminus \mathbf{d}(X_a)$
7        $sup(X_{ab}) = sup(X_a) - |\mathbf{d}(X_{ab})|$
8   **if** $sup(X_{ab}) \geq minsup$ **then**
9          $P_a \leftarrow P_a \cup \big\{\langle X_{ab}, \mathbf{d}(X_{ab}), sup(X_{ab})\rangle\big\}$

10   **if** $P_a \neq \emptyset$ **then** DECLAT (P_a, $minsup$, $\mathcal{F}$)

the method. In particular, if the initial tidsets have small cardinality, then the initial call should use tidset intersections, with a switch to diffsets starting with 2-itemsets. Such optimizations are not described in the pseudo-code for clarity.

Example 8.10. Figure 8.6 illustrates the dEclat algorithm. Here *minsup* = 3, and the initial prefix equivalence class comprises all frequent items and their diffsets, computed as follows:

$$\mathbf{d}(A) = \mathcal{T} \setminus 1345 = 26$$

$$\mathbf{d}(B) = \mathcal{T} \setminus 123456 = \emptyset$$

$$\mathbf{d}(C) = \mathcal{T} \setminus 2456 = 13$$

$$\mathbf{d}(D) = \mathcal{T} \setminus 1356 = 24$$

$$\mathbf{d}(E) = \mathcal{T} \setminus 12345 = 6$$

where $\mathcal{T} = 123456$. To process candidates with A as a prefix, dEclat computes the diffsets for AB, AC, AD and AE. For instance, the diffsets of AB and AC are given as

$$\mathbf{d}(AB) = \mathbf{d}(B) \setminus \mathbf{d}(A) = \emptyset \setminus \{2, 6\} = \emptyset$$

$$\mathbf{d}(AC) = \mathbf{d}(C) \setminus \mathbf{d}(A) = \{1, 3\} \setminus \{2, 6\} = 13$$

and their support values are

$$sup(AB) = sup(A) - |\mathbf{d}(AB)| = 4 - 0 = 4$$

$$sup(AC) = sup(A) - |\mathbf{d}(AC)| = 4 - 2 = 2$$

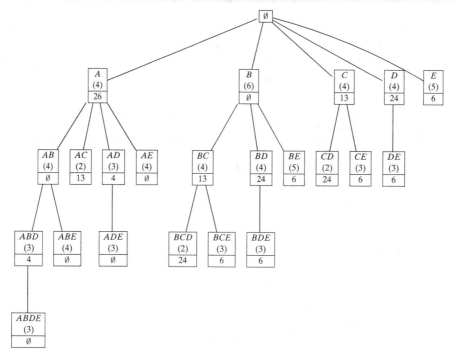

Figure 8.6. dEclat algorithm: diffsets (gray boxes indicate infrequent itemsets).

Whereas AB is frequent, we can prune AC because it is not frequent. The frequent itemsets and their diffsets and support values comprise the new prefix equivalence class:

$$P_A = \left\{ \langle AB, \emptyset, 4 \rangle, \langle AD, 4, 3 \rangle, \langle AE, \emptyset, 4 \rangle \right\}$$

which is recursively processed. Other branches are processed in a similar manner. The entire search space for dEclat is shown in Figure 8.6. The support of an itemset is shown within brackets. For example, A has support 4 and diffset $\mathbf{d}(A) = 26$.

8.2.3 Frequent Pattern Tree Approach: FPGrowth Algorithm

The FPGrowth method indexes the database for fast support computation via the use of an augmented prefix tree called the *frequent pattern tree* (FP-tree). Each node in the tree is labeled with a single item, and each child node represents a different item. Each node also stores the support information for the itemset comprising the items on the path from the root to that node. The FP-tree is constructed as follows. Initially the tree contains as root the null item $\emptyset$. Next, for each tuple $\langle t, X \rangle \in \mathbf{D}$, where $X = \mathbf{i}(t)$, we insert the itemset X into the FP-tree, incrementing the count of all nodes along the path that represents X. If X shares a prefix with some previously inserted transaction, then X will follow the same path until the common prefix. For the remaining items in X, new nodes are created under the common prefix, with counts initialized to 1. The FP-tree is complete when all transactions have been inserted.

The FP-tree can be considered as a prefix compressed representation of $\mathbf{D}$. Because we want the tree to be as compact as possible, we want the most frequent items to be at the top of the tree. FPGrowth therefore reorders the items in decreasing order of support, that is, from the initial database, it first computes the support of all single items $i \in \mathcal{I}$. Next, it discards the infrequent items, and sorts the frequent items by decreasing support. Finally, each tuple $\langle t, X \rangle \in \mathbf{D}$ is inserted into the FP-tree after reordering X by decreasing item support.

Example 8.11. Consider the example database in Figure 8.1. We add each transaction one by one into the FP-tree, and keep track of the count at each node. For our example database the sorted item order is $\{B(6), E(5), A(4), C(4), D(4)\}$. Next, each transaction is reordered in this same order; for example, $\langle 1, ABDE \rangle$ becomes $\langle 1, BEAD \rangle$. Figure 8.7 illustrates step-by-step FP-tree construction as each sorted transaction is added to it. The final FP-tree for the database is shown in Figure 8.7(f).

Once the FP-tree has been constructed, it serves as an index in lieu of the original database. All frequent itemsets can be mined from the tree directly via the FPGROWTH method, whose pseudo-code is shown in Algorithm 8.5. The method accepts as input a FP-tree R constructed from the input database $\mathbf{D}$, and the current itemset prefix P, which is initially empty.

Given a FP-tree R, projected FP-trees are built for each frequent item i in R in increasing order of support. To project R on item i, we find all the occurrences of i in the tree, and for each occurrence, we determine the corresponding path from the root to i (line 13). The count of item i on a given path is recorded in $cnt(i)$ (line 14), and

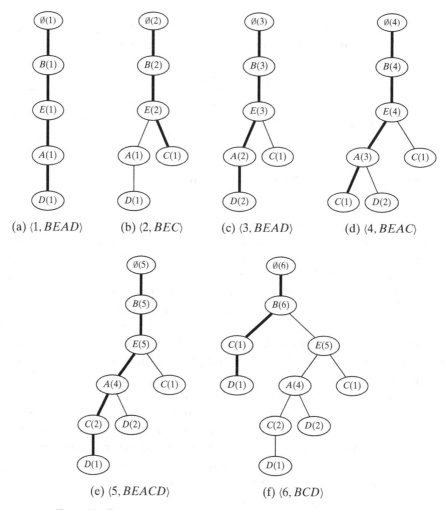

(a) ⟨1, *BEAD*⟩   (b) ⟨2, *BEC*⟩   (c) ⟨3, *BEAD*⟩   (d) ⟨4, *BEAC*⟩

(e) ⟨5, *BEACD*⟩   (f) ⟨6, *BCD*⟩

Figure 8.7. Frequent pattern tree: bold edges indicate current transaction.

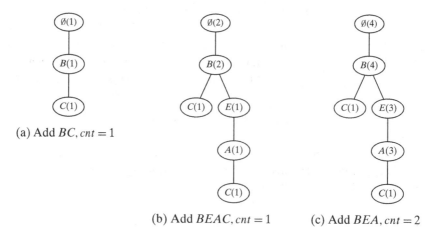

(a) Add *BC*, *cnt* = 1

(b) Add *BEAC*, *cnt* = 1   (c) Add *BEA*, *cnt* = 2

Figure 8.8. Projected frequent pattern tree for *D*.

Algorithm 8.5: Algorithm FPGROWTH

// Initial Call: $R \leftarrow$ FP-tree($\mathbf{D}$), $P \leftarrow \emptyset$, $\mathcal{F} \leftarrow \emptyset$

FPGROWTH ($R, P, \mathcal{F}, minsup$):

1 Remove infrequent items from R
2 **if** ISPATH(R) **then** // insert subsets of R into $\mathcal{F}$
3   **foreach** $Y \subseteq R$ **do**
4    $X \leftarrow P \cup Y$
5    $sup(X) \leftarrow \min_{x \in Y}\{cnt(x)\}$
6    $\mathcal{F} \leftarrow \mathcal{F} \cup \{(X, sup(X))\}$
7 **else**   // process projected FP-trees for each frequent item i
8   **foreach** $i \in R$ *in increasing order of* $sup(i)$ **do**
9    $X \leftarrow P \cup \{i\}$
10   $sup(X) \leftarrow sup(i)$ // sum of $cnt(i)$ for all nodes labeled i
11   $\mathcal{F} \leftarrow \mathcal{F} \cup \{(X, sup(X))\}$
12   $R_X \leftarrow \emptyset$ // projected FP-tree for X
13   **foreach** $path \in$ PATHFROMROOT(i) **do**
14    $cnt(i) \leftarrow$ count of i in $path$
15   Insert $path$, excluding i, into FP-tree R_X with count $cnt(i)$
16   **if** $R_X \neq \emptyset$ **then** FPGROWTH ($R_X, X, \mathcal{F}, minsup$)

---

the path is inserted into the new projected tree R_X, where X is the itemset obtained by extending the prefix P with the item i. While inserting the path, the count of each node in R_X along the given path is incremented by the path count $cnt(i)$. We omit the item i from the path, as it is now part of the prefix. The resulting FP-tree is a projection of the itemset X that comprises the current prefix extended with item i (line 9). We then call FPGROWTH recursively with projected FP-tree R_X and the new prefix itemset X as the parameters (line 16). The base case for the recursion happens when the input FP-tree R is a single path. FP-trees that are paths are handled by enumerating all itemsets that are subsets of the path, with the support of each such itemset being given by the least frequent item in it (lines 2–6).

Example 8.12. We illustrate the FPGrowth method on the FP-tree R built in Example 8.11, as shown in Figure 8.7(f). Let $minsup = 3$. The initial prefix is $P = \emptyset$, and the set of frequent items i in R are $B(6)$, $E(5)$, $A(4)$, $C(4)$, and $D(4)$. FPGrowth creates a projected FP-tree for each item, but in increasing order of support.

The projected FP-tree for item D is shown in Figure 8.8(c). Given the initial FP-tree R shown in Figure 8.7(f), there are three paths from the root to a node labeled D, namely

$$BCD, \quad cnt(D) = 1$$
$$BEACD, \quad cnt(D) = 1$$
$$BEAD, \quad cnt(D) = 2$$

These three paths, excluding the last item $i = D$, are inserted into the new FP-tree R_D with the counts incremented by the corresponding $cnt(D)$ values, that is, we insert into R_D, the paths BC with count of 1, $BEAC$ with count of 1, and finally BEA with count of 2, as shown in Figure 8.8(a)–Figure 8.8(c). The projected FP-tree for D is shown in Figure 8.8(c), which is processed recursively.

When we process R_D, we have the prefix itemset $P = D$, and after removing the infrequent item C (which has support 2), we find that the resulting FP-tree is a single path $B(4)$–$E(3)$–$A(3)$. Thus, we enumerate all subsets of this path and prefix them with D, to obtain the frequent itemsets $DB(4)$, $DE(3)$, $DA(3)$, $DBE(3)$, $DBA(3)$, $DEA(3)$, and $DBEA(3)$. At this point the call from D returns.

In a similar manner, we process the remaining items at the top level. The projected trees for C, A, and E are all single-path trees, allowing us to generate the frequent itemsets $\{CB(4), CE(3), CBE(3)\}$, $\{AE(4), AB(4), AEB(4)\}$, and $\{EB(5)\}$, respectively. This process is illustrated in Figure 8.9.

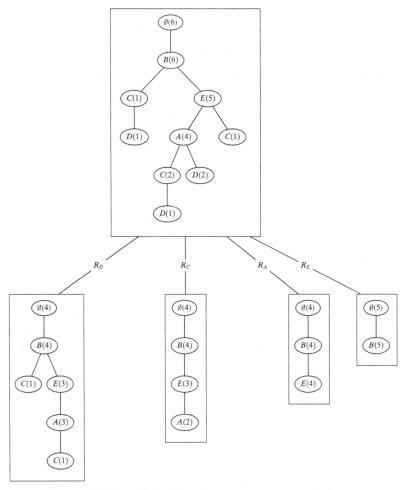

Figure 8.9. FPGrowth algorithm: frequent pattern tree projection.

8.3 GENERATING ASSOCIATION RULES

Given a collection of frequent itemsets $\mathcal{F}$, to generate association rules we iterate over all itemsets $Z \in \mathcal{F}$, and calculate the confidence of various rules that can be derived from the itemset. Formally, given a frequent itemset $Z \in \mathcal{F}$, we look at all proper subsets $X \subset Z$ to compute rules of the form

$$X \xrightarrow{s,c} Y, \text{ where } Y = Z \setminus X$$

where $Z \setminus X = Z - X$. The rule must be frequent because

$$s = sup(XY) = sup(Z) \geq minsup$$

Thus, we have to only check whether the rule confidence satisfies the *minconf* threshold. We compute the confidence as follows:

$$c = \frac{sup(X \cup Y)}{sup(X)} = \frac{sup(Z)}{sup(X)} \tag{8.7}$$

If $c \geq minconf$, then the rule is a strong rule. On the other hand, if $conf(X \longrightarrow Y) < c$, then $conf(W \longrightarrow Z \setminus W) < c$ for all subsets $W \subset X$, as $sup(W) \geq sup(X)$. We can thus avoid checking subsets of X.

Algorithm 8.6 shows the pseudo-code for the association rule mining algorithm. For each frequent itemset $Z \in \mathcal{F}$, with size at least 2, we initialize the set of antecedents $\mathcal{A}$ with all the nonempty subsets of Z (line 2). For each $X \in \mathcal{A}$ we check whether the confidence of the rule $X \longrightarrow Z \setminus X$ is at least *minconf* (line 7). If so, we output the rule. Otherwise, we remove all subsets $W \subset X$ from the set of possible antecedents (line 10).

Example 8.13. Consider the frequent itemset $ABDE(3)$ from Table 8.1, whose support is shown within the brackets. Assume that *minconf* = 0.9. To generate strong

---

Algorithm 8.6: Algorithm ASSOCIATIONRULES

    ASSOCIATIONRULES ($\mathcal{F}$, *minconf*):

1 **foreach** $Z \in \mathcal{F}$, *such that* $|Z| \geq 2$ **do**

2     $\mathcal{A} \leftarrow \{X \mid X \subset Z, X \neq \emptyset\}$

3   **while** $\mathcal{A} \neq \emptyset$ **do**

4         $X \leftarrow$ maximal element in $\mathcal{A}$

5         $\mathcal{A} \leftarrow \mathcal{A} \setminus X$// remove X from $\mathcal{A}$

6         $c \leftarrow sup(Z)/sup(X)$

7   **if** $c \geq minconf$ **then**

8   print $X \longrightarrow Y, sup(Z), c$

9   **else**

10           $\mathcal{A} \leftarrow \mathcal{A} \setminus \{W \mid W \subset X\}$ // remove subsets of X from $\mathcal{A}$

association rules we initialize the set of antecedents to

$$\mathcal{A} = \{ABD(3), ABE(4), ADE(3), BDE(3), AB(4), AD(3), AE(4),$$

$$BD(4), BE(5), DE(3), A(4), B(6), D(4), E(5)\}$$

The first subset is $X = ABD$, and the confidence of $ABD \longrightarrow E$ is $3/3 = 1.0$, so we output it. The next subset is $X = ABE$, but the corresponding rule $ABE \longrightarrow D$ is not strong since $conf(ABE \longrightarrow D) = 3/4 = 0.75$. We can thus remove from $\mathcal{A}$ all subsets of ABE; the updated set of antecedents is therefore

$$\mathcal{A} = \{ADE(3), BDE(3), AD(3), BD(4), DE(3), D(4)\}$$

Next, we select $X = ADE$, which yields a strong rule, and so do $X = BDE$ and $X = AD$. However, when we process $X = BD$, we find that $conf(BD \longrightarrow AE) = 3/4 = 0.75$, and thus we can prune all subsets of BD from $\mathcal{A}$, to yield

$$\mathcal{A} = \{DE(3)\}$$

The last rule to be tried is $DE \longrightarrow AB$ which is also strong. The final set of strong rules that are output are as follows:

$$ABD \longrightarrow E, conf = 1.0$$

$$ADE \longrightarrow B, conf = 1.0$$

$$BDE \longrightarrow A, conf = 1.0$$

$$AD \longrightarrow BE, conf = 1.0$$

$$DE \longrightarrow AB, conf = 1.0$$

8.4 FURTHER READING

The association rule mining problem was introduced in Agrawal, Imieliński, and Swami (1993). The Apriori method was proposed in Agrawal and Srikant (1994), and a similar approach was outlined independently in Mannila, Toivonen, and Verkamo (1994). The tidlist intersection based Eclat method is described in Zaki et al. (1997), and the dEclat approach that uses diffset appears in Zaki and Gouda (2003). Finally, the FPGrowth algorithm is described in Han, Pei, and Yin (2000). For an experimental comparison between several of the frequent itemset mining algorithms see Goethals and Zaki (2004). There is a very close connection between itemset mining and association rules, and formal concept analysis; see Ganter, Wille, and Franzke, 1997. For example, association rules can be considered to be *partial implications* with frequency constraints; see Luxenburger (1991).

Agrawal, R., Imieliński, T., and Swami, A. (1993). Mining association rules between sets of items in large databases. *Proceedings of the ACM SIGMOD International Conference on Management of Data*. ACM, pp. 207–216.

Agrawal, R. and Srikant, R. (1994). Fast algorithms for mining association rules. *Proceedings of the 20th International Conference on Very Large Data Bases*, pp. 487–499.

Ganter, B., Wille, R., and Franzke, C. (1997). *Formal Concept Analysis: Mathematical Foundations*. New York: Springer-Verlag.

Goethals, B. and Zaki, M. J. (2004). Advances in frequent itemset mining implementations: Report on FIMI'03. *ACM SIGKDD Explorations Newsletter*, 6 (1), 109–117.

Han, J., Pei, J., and Yin, Y. (2000). Mining frequent patterns without candidate generation. *Proceedings of the ACM SIGMOD International Conference on Management of Data*. ACM, pp. 1–12.

Luxenburger, M. (1991). Implications partielles dans un contexte. *Mathématiques et Sciences Humaines*, 113, 35–55.

Mannila, H., Toivonen, H., and Verkamo, I. A. (1994). Efficient algorithms for discovering association rules. *AAAI Workshop on Knowledge Discovery in Databases*. AAAI Press, pp. 181–192.

Zaki, M. J. and Gouda, K. (2003). Fast vertical mining using diffsets. *Proceedings of the 9th ACM SIGKDD International Conference on Knowledge Discovery and Data Mining*. ACM, pp. 326–335.

Zaki, M. J., Parthasarathy, S., Ogihara, M., and Li, W. (1997). New algorithms for fast discovery of association rules. *Proceedings of the 3rd International Conference on Knowledge Discovery and Data Mining*, pp. 283–286.

8.5 EXERCISES

Q1. Given the database in Table 8.2.

   (a) Using *minsup* = 3/8, show how the Apriori algorithm enumerates all frequent patterns from this dataset.

   (b) With *minsup* = 2/8, show how FPGrowth enumerates the frequent itemsets.

Table 8.2. Transaction database for Q1

tid	itemset
t_1	$ABCD$
t_2	$ACDF$
t_3	$ACDEG$
t_4	$ABDF$
t_5	BCG
t_6	DFG
t_7	ABG
t_8	$CDFG$

Q2. Consider the vertical database shown in Table 8.3. Assuming that $minsup = 3$, enumerate all the frequent itemsets using the Eclat method.

Table 8.3. Dataset for Q2

A	B	C	D	E
1	2	1	1	2
3	3	2	6	3
5	4	3		4
6	5	5		5
	6	6		

Q3. Given two k-itemsets $X_a = \{x_1, \ldots, x_{k-1}, x_a\}$ and $X_b = \{x_1, \ldots, x_{k-1}, x_b\}$ that share the common $(k-1)$-itemset $X = \{x_1, x_2, \ldots, x_{k-1}\}$ as a prefix, prove that

$$sup(X_{ab}) = sup(X_a) - |\mathbf{d}(X_{ab})|$$

where $X_{ab} = X_a \cup X_b$, and $\mathbf{d}(X_{ab})$ is the diffset of X_{ab}.

Q4. Given the database in Table 8.4. Show all rules that one can generate from the set ABE.

Table 8.4. Dataset for Q4

tid	itemset
t_1	ACD
t_2	BCE
t_3	$ABCE$
t_4	BDE
t_5	$ABCE$
t_6	$ABCD$

Q5. Consider the *partition* algorithm for itemset mining. It divides the database into k partitions, not necessarily equal, such that $\mathbf{D} = \cup_{i=1}^{k} \mathbf{D}_i$, where $\mathbf{D}_i$ is partition i, and for any $i \neq j$, we have $\mathbf{D}_i \cap \mathbf{D}_j = \emptyset$. Also let $n_i = |\mathbf{D}_i|$ denote the number of transactions in partition $\mathbf{D}_i$. The algorithm first mines only locally frequent itemsets, that is, itemsets whose relative support is above the *minsup* threshold specified as a fraction. In the second step, it takes the union of all locally frequent itemsets, and computes their support in the entire database $\mathbf{D}$ to determine which of them are globally frequent. Prove that if a pattern is globally frequent in the database, then it must be locally frequent in at least one partition.

Q6. Consider Figure 8.10. It shows a simple taxonomy on some food items. Each leaf is a simple item and an internal node represents a higher-level category or item. Each item (single or high-level) has a unique integer label noted under it. Consider the database composed of the simple items shown in Table 8.5 Answer the following questions:

(a) What is the size of the itemset search space if one restricts oneself to only itemsets composed of simple items?

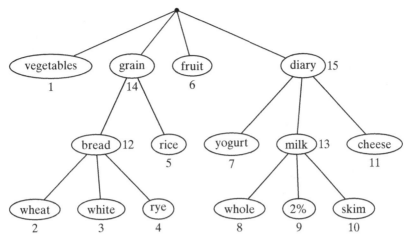

Figure 8.10. Item taxonomy for Q6.

Table 8.5. Dataset for Q6

tid	itemset
1	2 3 6 7
2	1 3 4 8 11
3	3 9 11
4	1 5 6 7
5	1 3 8 10 11
6	3 5 7 9 11
7	4 6 8 10 11
8	1 3 5 8 11

(b) Let $X = \{x_1, x_2, \ldots, x_k\}$ be a frequent itemset. Let us replace some $x_i \in X$ with its parent in the taxonomy (provided it exists) to obtain X', then the support of the new itemset X' is:

   i. more than support of X

  ii. less than support of X

 iii. not equal to support of X

  iv. more than or equal to support of X

   v. less than or equal to support of X

(c) Use *minsup* = 7/8. Find all frequent itemsets composed only of high-level items in the taxonomy. Keep in mind that if a simple item appears in a transaction, then its high-level ancestors are all assumed to occur in the transaction as well.

Q7. Let **D** be a database with n transactions. Consider a sampling approach for mining frequent itemsets, where we extract a random sample $\mathbf{S} \subset \mathbf{D}$, with say m transactions, and we mine all the frequent itemsets in the sample, denoted as $\mathcal{F}_S$. Next, we make one complete scan of **D**, and for each $X \in \mathcal{F}_S$, we find its actual support in the whole database. Some of the itemsets in the sample may not be truly frequent in the database; these are the false positives. Also, some of the true frequent itemsets in the original database may never be present in the sample at all; these are the false negatives.

Prove that if X is a false negative, then this case can be detected by counting the support in $\mathbf{D}$ for every itemset belonging to the *negative border* of $\mathcal{F}_S$, denoted $Bd^-(\mathcal{F}_S)$, which is defined as the set of minimal infrequent itemsets in sample $\mathbf{S}$. Formally,

$$Bd^-(\mathcal{F}_S) = \inf\{Y \mid sup(Y) < minsup \text{ and } \forall Z \subset Y, sup(Z) \geq minsup\}$$

where inf returns the minimal elements of the set.

Q8. Assume that we want to mine frequent patterns from relational tables. For example consider Table 8.6, with three attributes A, B, and C, and six records. Each attribute has a domain from which it draws its values, for example, the domain of A is $dom(A) = \{a_1, a_2, a_3\}$. Note that no record can have more than one value of a given attribute.

Table 8.6. Data for Q8

tid	A	B	C
1	a_1	b_1	c_1
2	a_2	b_3	c_2
3	a_2	b_3	c_3
4	a_2	b_1	c_1
5	a_2	b_3	c_3
6	a_3	b_3	c_3

We define a *relational pattern* P over some k attributes $X_1, X_2, \ldots, X_k$ to be a subset of the Cartesian product of the domains of the attributes, i.e., $P \subseteq dom(X_1) \times dom(X_2) \times \cdots \times dom(X_k)$. That is, $P = P_1 \times P_2 \times \cdots \times P_k$, where each $P_i \subseteq dom(X_i)$. For example, $\{a_1, a_2\} \times \{c_1\}$ is a possible pattern over attributes A and C, whereas $\{a_1\} \times \{b_1\} \times \{c_1\}$ is another pattern over attributes A, B and C.

The support of relational pattern $P = P_1 \times P_2 \times \cdots \times P_k$ in dataset $\mathbf{D}$ is defined as the number of records in the dataset that belong to it; it is given as

$$sup(P) = \left|\{r = (r_1, r_2, \ldots, r_n) \in \mathbf{D} : r_i \in P_i \text{ for all } P_i \text{ in } P\}\right|$$

For example, $sup(\{a_1, a_2\} \times \{c_1\}) = 2$, as both records 1 and 4 contribute to its support. Note, however that the pattern $\{a_1\} \times \{c_1\}$ has a support of 1, since only record 1 belongs to it. Thus, relational patterns **do not** satisfy the Apriori property that we used for frequent itemsets, that is, subsets of a frequent relational pattern can be infrequent.

We call a relational pattern $P = P_1 \times P_2 \times \cdots \times P_k$ over attributes $X_1, \ldots, X_k$ as *valid* iff for all $u \in P_i$ and all $v \in P_j$, the pair of values $(X_i = u, X_j = v)$ occurs together in some record. For example, $\{a_1, a_2\} \times \{c_1\}$ is a valid pattern since both $(A = a_1, C = c_1)$ and $(A = a_2, C = c_1)$ occur in some records (namely, records 1 and 4, respectively), whereas $\{a_1, a_2\} \times \{c_2\}$ is not a valid pattern, since there is no record that has the values $(A = a_1, C = c_2)$. Thus, for a pattern to be valid every pair of values in P from distinct attributes must belong to some record.

Given that $minsup = 2$, find all frequent, valid, relational patterns in the dataset in Table 8.6.

Q9. Given the following multiset dataset:

tid	multiset
1	*ABCA*
2	*ABABA*
3	*CABBA*

Using $minsup = 2$, answer the following:

(a) Find all frequent multisets. Recall that a multiset is still a set (i.e., order is not important), but it allows multiple occurrences of an item.

(b) Find all minimal infrequent multisets, that is, those multisets that have no infrequent sub-multisets.

CHAPTER 9

Summarizing Itemsets

The search space for frequent itemsets is usually very large and it grows exponentially with the number of items. In particular, a low minimum support value may result in an intractable number of frequent itemsets. An alternative approach, studied in this chapter, is to determine condensed representations of the frequent itemsets that summarize their essential characteristics. The use of condensed representations can not only reduce the computational and storage demands, but it can also make it easier to analyze the mined patterns. In this chapter we discuss three of these representations: closed, maximal, and nonderivable itemsets.

9.1 MAXIMAL AND CLOSED FREQUENT ITEMSETS

Given a binary database $\mathbf{D} \subseteq \mathcal{T} \times \mathcal{I}$, over the tids $\mathcal{T}$ and items $\mathcal{I}$, let $\mathcal{F}$ denote the set of all frequent itemsets, that is,

$$\mathcal{F} = \{X \mid X \subseteq \mathcal{I} \text{ and } sup(X) \geq minsup\} \tag{9.1}$$

Maximal Frequent Itemsets

A frequent itemset $X \in \mathcal{F}$ is called *maximal* if it has no frequent supersets. Let $\mathcal{M}$ be the set of all maximal frequent itemsets, given as

$$\mathcal{M} = \{X \mid X \in \mathcal{F} \text{ and } \nexists Y \supset X, \text{ such that } Y \in \mathcal{F}\} \tag{9.2}$$

The set $\mathcal{M}$ is a condensed representation of the set of all frequent itemset $\mathcal{F}$, because we can determine whether any itemset X is frequent or not using $\mathcal{M}$. If there exists a maximal itemset Z such that $X \subseteq Z$, then X must be frequent; otherwise X cannot be frequent. On the other hand, we cannot determine $sup(X)$ using $\mathcal{M}$ alone, although we can lower-bound it, that is, $sup(X) \geq sup(Z)$ if $X \subseteq Z \in \mathcal{M}$.

Example 9.1. Consider the dataset given in Figure 9.1(a). Using any of the algorithms discussed in Chapter 8 and *minsup* $= 3$, we obtain the frequent itemsets shown

Tid	Itemset
1	$ABDE$
2	BCE
3	$ABDE$
4	$ABCE$
5	$ABCDE$
6	BCD

(a) Transaction database

sup	Itemsets
6	B
5	E, BE
4	$A, C, D, AB, AE, BC, BD, ABE$
3	$AD, CE, DE, ABD, ADE, BCE, BDE, ABDE$

(b) Frequent itemsets ($minsup = 3$)

Figure 9.1. An example database.

in Figure 9.1(b). Notice that there are 19 frequent itemsets out of the $2^5 - 1 = 31$ possible nonempty itemsets. Out of these, there are only two maximal itemsets, $ABDE$ and BCE. Any other frequent itemset must be a subset of one of the maximal itemsets. For example, we can determine that ABE is frequent, since $ABE \subset ABDE$, and we can establish that $sup(ABE) \geq sup(ABDE) = 3$.

Closed Frequent Itemsets

Recall that the function $\mathbf{t}: 2^{\mathcal{I}} \to 2^{\mathcal{T}}$ [Eq. (8.2)] maps itemsets to tidsets, and the function $\mathbf{i}: 2^{\mathcal{T}} \to 2^{\mathcal{I}}$ [Eq. (8.1)] maps tidsets to itemsets. That is, given $T \subseteq \mathcal{T}$, and $X \subseteq \mathcal{I}$, we have

$$\mathbf{t}(X) = \{t \in \mathcal{T} \mid t \text{ contains } X\}$$

$$\mathbf{i}(T) = \{x \in \mathcal{I} \mid \forall t \in T, t \text{ contains } x\}$$

Define by $\mathbf{c}: 2^{\mathcal{I}} \to 2^{\mathcal{I}}$ the *closure operator*, given as

$$\mathbf{c}(X) = \mathbf{i} \circ \mathbf{t}(X) = \mathbf{i}(\mathbf{t}(X))$$

The closure operator $\mathbf{c}$ maps itemsets to itemsets, and it satisfies the following three properties:

- *Extensive*: $X \subseteq \mathbf{c}(X)$
- *Monotonic*: If $X_i \subseteq X_j$, then $\mathbf{c}(X_i) \subseteq \mathbf{c}(X_j)$
- *Idempotent*: $\mathbf{c}(\mathbf{c}(X)) = \mathbf{c}(X)$

An itemset X is called *closed* if $\mathbf{c}(X) = X$, that is, if X is a fixed point of the closure operator $\mathbf{c}$. On the other hand, if $X \neq \mathbf{c}(X)$, then X is not closed, but the set $\mathbf{c}(X)$ is called its closure. From the properties of the closure operator, both X and $\mathbf{c}(X)$ have the same tidset. It follows that a frequent set $X \in \mathcal{F}$ is closed if it has no frequent superset *with the same frequency* because by definition, it is the largest itemset common to all the tids in the tidset $\mathbf{t}(X)$. The set of all closed frequent itemsets is thus defined as

$$\mathcal{C} = \big\{ X \mid X \in \mathcal{F} \text{ and } \nexists Y \supset X \text{ such that } sup(X) = sup(Y) \big\} \qquad (9.3)$$

Put differently, X is closed if all supersets of X have strictly less support, that is, $sup(X) > sup(Y)$, for all $Y \supset X$.

The set of all closed frequent itemsets $\mathcal{C}$ is a condensed representation, as we can determine whether an itemset X is frequent, as well as the exact support of X using $\mathcal{C}$ alone. The itemset X is frequent if there exists a closed frequent itemset $Z \in \mathcal{C}$ such that $X \subseteq Z$. Further, the support of X is given as

$$sup(X) = \max\big\{ sup(Z) \mid Z \in \mathcal{C}, X \subseteq Z \big\}$$

The following relationship holds between the set of all, closed, and maximal frequent itemsets:

$$\mathcal{M} \subseteq \mathcal{C} \subseteq \mathcal{F} \qquad (9.4)$$

Minimal Generators

A frequent itemset X is a *minimal generator* if it has no subsets with the same support:

$$\mathcal{G} = \big\{ X \mid X \in \mathcal{F} \text{ and } \nexists Y \subset X, \text{ such that } sup(X) = sup(Y) \big\} \qquad (9.5)$$

In other words, all subsets of X have strictly higher support, that is, $sup(X) < sup(Y)$, for all $Y \subset X$. The concept of minimum generator is closely related to the notion of closed itemsets. Given an equivalence class of itemsets that have the same tidset, a closed itemset is the unique maximum element of the class, whereas the minimal generators are the minimal elements of the class.

Example 9.2. Consider the example dataset in Figure 9.1(a). The frequent closed (as well as maximal) itemsets using *minsup* $= 3$ are shown in Figure 9.2. We can see, for instance, that the itemsets AD, DE, ABD, ADE, BDE, and $ABDE$, occur in the same three transactions, namely 135, and thus constitute an equivalence class. The largest itemset among these, namely $ABDE$, is the closed itemset. Using the closure operator yields the same result; we have $\mathbf{c}(AD) = \mathbf{i}(\mathbf{t}(AD)) = \mathbf{i}(135) = ABDE$, which indicates that the closure of AD is $ABDE$. To verify that $ABDE$ is closed note that $\mathbf{c}(ABDE) = \mathbf{i}(\mathbf{t}(ABDE)) = \mathbf{i}(135) = ABDE$. The minimal elements of the equivalence class, namely AD and DE, are the minimal generators. No subset of these itemsets shares the same tidset.

The set of all closed frequent itemsets, and the corresponding set of minimal generators, is as follows:

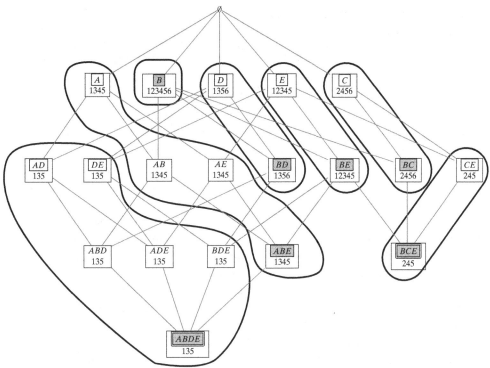

Figure 9.2. Frequent, closed, minimal generators, and maximal frequent itemsets. Itemsets that are boxed and shaded are closed, whereas those within boxes (but unshaded) are the minimal generators; maximal itemsets are shown boxed with double lines.

Tidset	C	G
1345	ABE	A
123456	B	B
1356	BD	D
12345	BE	E
2456	BC	C
135	$ABDE$	AD, DE
245	BCE	CE

Out of the closed itemsets, the maximal ones are $ABDE$ and BCE. Consider itemset AB. Using C we can determine that

$$sup(AB) = \max\{sup(ABE), sup(ABDE)\} = \max\{4, 3\} = 4$$

9.2 MINING MAXIMAL FREQUENT ITEMSETS: GENMAX ALGORITHM

Mining maximal itemsets requires additional steps beyond simply determining the frequent itemsets. Assuming that the set of maximal frequent itemsets is initially empty, that is, $\mathcal{M} = \emptyset$, each time we generate a new frequent itemset X, we have to perform the following maximality checks

- **Subset Check:** $\nexists Y \in \mathcal{M}$, such that $X \subset Y$. If such a Y exists, then clearly X is not maximal. Otherwise, we add X to $\mathcal{M}$, as a potentially maximal itemset.
- **Superset Check:** $\nexists Y \in \mathcal{M}$, such that $Y \subset X$. If such a Y exists, then Y cannot be maximal, and we have to remove it from $\mathcal{M}$.

These two maximality checks take $O(|\mathcal{M}|)$ time, which can get expensive, especially as $\mathcal{M}$ grows; thus for efficiency reasons it is crucial to minimize the number of times these checks are performed. As such, any of the frequent itemset mining algorithms from Chapter 8 can be extended to mine maximal frequent itemsets by adding the maximality checking steps. Here we consider the GenMax method, which is based on the tidset intersection approach of Eclat (see Section 8.2.2). We shall see that it never inserts a nonmaximal itemset into $\mathcal{M}$. It thus eliminates the superset checks and requires only subset checks to determine maximality.

Algorithm 9.1 shows the pseudo-code for GenMax. The initial call takes as input the set of frequent items along with their tidsets, $\langle i, \mathbf{t}(i) \rangle$, and the initially empty set of maximal itemsets, $\mathcal{M}$. Given a set of itemset–tidset pairs, called IT-pairs, of the form $\langle X, \mathbf{t}(X) \rangle$, the recursive GenMax method works as follows. In lines 1–3, we check if the entire current branch can be pruned by checking if the union of all the itemsets, $Y = \bigcup X_i$, is already subsumed by (or contained in) some maximal pattern $Z \in \mathcal{M}$. If so, no maximal itemset can be generated from the current branch, and it is pruned. On the other hand, if the branch is not pruned, we intersect each IT-pair $\langle X_i, \mathbf{t}(X_i) \rangle$ with all the other IT-pairs $\langle X_j, \mathbf{t}(X_j) \rangle$, with $j > i$, to generate new candidates X_{ij}, which are added to the IT-pair set P_i (lines 6–9). If P_i is not empty, a recursive call to GENMAX is made to find other potentially frequent extensions of X_i. On the other hand, if P_i is empty, it means that X_i cannot be extended, and it is potentially maximal. In this case, we add

---

Algorithm 9.1: Algorithm GENMAX

// Initial Call: $\mathcal{M} \leftarrow \emptyset$, $P \leftarrow \{ \langle i, \mathbf{t}(i) \rangle \mid i \in \mathcal{I}, sup(i) \geq minsup \}$

GENMAX ($P, minsup, \mathcal{M}$):

1   $Y \leftarrow \bigcup X_i$

2   **if** $\exists Z \in \mathcal{M}$, *such that* $Y \subseteq Z$ **then**

3     $\lfloor$ **return** // prune entire branch

4   **foreach** $\langle X_i, \mathbf{t}(X_i) \rangle \in P$ **do**

5     $P_i \leftarrow \emptyset$

6   **foreach** $\langle X_j, \mathbf{t}(X_j) \rangle \in P$, *with* $j > i$ **do**

7       $X_{ij} \leftarrow X_i \cup X_j$

8       $\mathbf{t}(X_{ij}) = \mathbf{t}(X_i) \cap \mathbf{t}(X_j)$

9   **if** $sup(X_{ij}) \geq minsup$ **then** $P_i \leftarrow P_i \cup \{ \langle X_{ij}, \mathbf{t}(X_{ij}) \rangle \}$

10   **if** $P_i \neq \emptyset$ **then** GENMAX ($P_i, minsup, \mathcal{M}$)

11   **else if** $\nexists Z \in \mathcal{M}, X_i \subseteq Z$ **then**

12     $\lfloor$ $\mathcal{M} = \mathcal{M} \cup X_i$ // add X_i to maximal set

X_i to the set $\mathcal{M}$, provided that X_i is not contained in any previously added maximal set $Z \in \mathcal{M}$ (line 12). Note also that, because of this check for maximality before inserting any itemset into $\mathcal{M}$, we never have to remove any itemsets from it. In other words, all itemsets in $\mathcal{M}$ are guaranteed to be maximal. On termination of GenMax, the set $\mathcal{M}$ contains the final set of all maximal frequent itemsets. The GenMax approach also includes a number of other optimizations to reduce the maximality checks and to improve the support computations. Further, GenMax utilizes diffsets (differences of tidsets) for fast support computation, which were described in Section 8.2.2. We omit these optimizations here for clarity.

Example 9.3. Figure 9.3 shows the execution of GenMax on the example database from Figure 9.1(a) using *minsup* = 3. Initially the set of maximal itemsets is empty. The root of the tree represents the initial call with all IT-pairs consisting of frequent single items and their tidsets. We first intersect $\mathbf{t}(A)$ with the tidsets of the other items. The set of frequent extensions from A are

$$P_A = \left\{ \langle AB, 1345 \rangle, \langle AD, 135 \rangle, \langle AE, 1345 \rangle \right\}$$

Choosing $X_i = AB$, leads to the next set of extensions, namely

$$P_{AB} = \left\{ \langle ABD, 135 \rangle, \langle ABE, 1345 \rangle \right\}$$

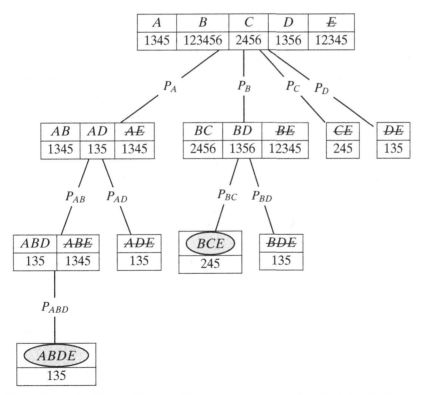

Figure 9.3. Mining maximal frequent itemsets. Maximal itemsets are shown as shaded ovals, whereas pruned branches are shown with the strike-through. Infrequent itemsets are not shown.

Finally, we reach the left-most leaf corresponding to $P_{ABD} = \{\langle ABDE, 135 \rangle\}$. At this point, we add $ABDE$ to the set of maximal frequent itemsets because it has no other extensions, so that $\mathcal{M} = \{ABDE\}$.

The search then backtracks one level, and we try to process ABE, which is also a candidate to be maximal. However, it is contained in $ABDE$, so it is pruned. Likewise, when we try to process $P_{AD} = \{\langle ADE, 135 \rangle\}$ it will get pruned because it is also subsumed by $ABDE$, and similarly for AE. At this stage, all maximal itemsets starting with A have been found, and we next proceed with the B branch. The left-most B branch, namely BCE, cannot be extended further. Because BCE is not a subset of any maximal itemset in $\mathcal{M}$, we insert it as a maximal itemset, so that $\mathcal{M} = \{ABDE, BCE\}$. Subsequently, all remaining branches are subsumed by one of these two maximal itemsets, and are thus pruned.

9.3 MINING CLOSED FREQUENT ITEMSETS: CHARM ALGORITHM

Mining closed frequent itemsets requires that we perform closure checks, that is, whether $X = \mathbf{c}(X)$. Direct closure checking can be very expensive, as we would have to verify that X is the largest itemset common to all the tids in $\mathbf{t}(X)$, that is, $X = \bigcap_{t \in \mathbf{t}(X)} \mathbf{i}(t)$. Instead, we will describe a vertical tidset intersection based method called CHARM that performs more efficient closure checking. Given a collection of IT-pairs $\{\langle X_i, \mathbf{t}(X_i) \rangle\}$, the following three properties hold:

Property (1) If $\mathbf{t}(X_i) = \mathbf{t}(X_j)$, then $\mathbf{c}(X_i) = \mathbf{c}(X_j) = \mathbf{c}(X_i \cup X_j)$, which implies that we can replace every occurrence of X_i with $X_i \cup X_j$ and prune the branch under X_j because its closure is identical to the closure of $X_i \cup X_j$.

Property (2) If $\mathbf{t}(X_i) \subset \mathbf{t}(X_j)$, then $\mathbf{c}(X_i) \neq \mathbf{c}(X_j)$ but $\mathbf{c}(X_i) = \mathbf{c}(X_i \cup X_j)$, which means that we can replace every occurrence of X_i with $X_i \cup X_j$, but we cannot prune X_j because it generates a different closure. Note that if $\mathbf{t}(X_i) \supset \mathbf{t}(X_j)$ then we simply interchange the role of X_i and X_j.

Property (3) If $\mathbf{t}(X_i) \neq \mathbf{t}(X_j)$, then $\mathbf{c}(X_i) \neq \mathbf{c}(X_j) \neq \mathbf{c}(X_i \cup X_j)$. In this case we cannot remove either X_i or X_j, as each of them generates a different closure.

Algorithm 9.2 presents the pseudo-code for Charm, which is also based on the Eclat algorithm described in Section 8.2.2. It takes as input the set of all frequent single items along with their tidsets. Also, initially the set of all closed itemsets, $\mathcal{C}$, is empty. Given any IT-pair set $P = \{\langle X_i, \mathbf{t}(X_i) \rangle\}$, the method first sorts them in increasing order of support. For each itemset X_i we try to extend it with all other items X_j in the sorted order, and we apply the above three properties to prune branches where possible. First we make sure that $X_{ij} = X_i \cup X_j$ is frequent, by checking the cardinality of $\mathbf{t}(X_{ij})$. If yes, then we check properties 1 and 2 (lines 8 and 12). Note that whenever we replace X_i with $X_{ij} = X_i \cup X_j$, we make sure to do so in the current set P, as well as the new set P_i. Only when property 3 holds do we add the new extension X_{ij} to the set P_i (line 14).

Algorithm 9.2: Algorithm CHARM

// Initial Call: $\mathcal{C} \leftarrow \emptyset$, $P \leftarrow \{\langle i, \mathbf{t}(i)\rangle : i \in \mathcal{I}, sup(i) \geq minsup\}$

CHARM ($P, minsup, \mathcal{C}$):

1 Sort P in increasing order of support (i.e., by increasing $|\mathbf{t}(X_i)|$)
2 **foreach** $\langle X_i, \mathbf{t}(X_i)\rangle \in P$ **do**
3 $\quad$ $P_i \leftarrow \emptyset$
4 $\quad$ **foreach** $\langle X_j, \mathbf{t}(X_j)\rangle \in P$, *with* $j > i$ **do**
5 $\quad\quad$ $X_{ij} = X_i \cup X_j$
6 $\quad\quad$ $\mathbf{t}(X_{ij}) = \mathbf{t}(X_i) \cap \mathbf{t}(X_j)$
7 $\quad\quad$ **if** $sup(X_{ij}) \geq minsup$ **then**
8 $\quad\quad\quad$ **if** $\mathbf{t}(X_i) = \mathbf{t}(X_j)$ **then** // Property 1
9 $\quad\quad\quad\quad$ Replace X_i with X_{ij} in P and P_i
10 $\quad\quad\quad\quad$ Remove $\langle X_j, \mathbf{t}(X_j)\rangle$ from P
11 $\quad\quad\quad$ **else**
12 $\quad\quad\quad\quad$ **if** $\mathbf{t}(X_i) \subset \mathbf{t}(X_j)$ **then** // Property 2
13 $\quad\quad\quad\quad\quad$ Replace X_i with X_{ij} in P and P_i
14 $\quad\quad\quad\quad$ **else** // Property 3
15 $\quad\quad\quad\quad\quad$ $P_i \leftarrow P_i \cup \{\langle X_{ij}, \mathbf{t}(X_{ij})\rangle\}$

16 $\quad$ **if** $P_i \neq \emptyset$ **then** CHARM ($P_i, minsup, \mathcal{C}$)
17 $\quad$ **if** $\nexists Z \in \mathcal{C}$, *such that* $X_i \subseteq Z$ *and* $\mathbf{t}(X_i) = \mathbf{t}(Z)$ **then**
18 $\quad\quad$ $\mathcal{C} = \mathcal{C} \cup X_i$ // Add X_i to closed set

---

If the set P_i is not empty, then we make a recursive call to Charm. Finally, if X_i is not a subset of any closed set Z with the same support, we can safely add it to the set of closed itemsets, $\mathcal{C}$ (line 18). For fast support computation, Charm uses the diffset optimization described in Section 8.2.2; we omit it here for clarity.

Example 9.4. We illustrate the Charm algorithm for mining frequent closed itemsets from the example database in Figure 9.1(a), using $minsup = 3$. Figure 9.4 shows the sequence of steps. The initial set of IT-pairs, after support based sorting, is shown at the root of the search tree. The sorted order is A, C, D, E, and B. We first process extensions from A, as shown in Figure 9.4(a). Because AC is not frequent, it is pruned. AD is frequent and because $\mathbf{t}(A) \neq \mathbf{t}(D)$, we add $\langle AD, 135\rangle$ to the set P_A (property 3). When we combine A with E, property 2 applies, and we simply replace all occurrences of A in both P and P_A with AE, which is illustrated with the strike-through. Likewise, because $\mathbf{t}(A) \subset \mathbf{t}(B)$ all current occurrences of A, actually AE, in both P and P_A are replaced by AEB. The set P_A thus contains only one itemset $\{\langle ADEB, 135\rangle\}$. When CHARM is invoked with P_A as the IT-pair, it jumps straight to line 18, and adds $ADEB$ to the set of closed itemsets $\mathcal{C}$. When the call returns, we check whether AEB can be added as a closed itemset. AEB is a subset of $ADEB$, but it does not have the same support, thus AEB is also added to $\mathcal{C}$. At this point all closed itemsets containing A have been found.

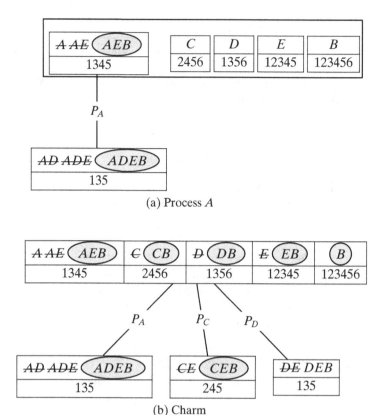

Figure 9.4. Mining closed frequent itemsets. Closed itemsets are shown as shaded ovals. Strike-through represents itemsets X_i replaced by $X_i \cup X_j$ during execution of the algorithm. Infrequent itemsets are not shown.

The Charm algorithm proceeds with the remaining branches as shown in Figure 9.4(b). For instance, C is processed next. CD is infrequent and thus pruned. CE is frequent and it is added to P_C as a new extension (via property 3). Because $\mathbf{t}(C) \subset \mathbf{t}(B)$, all occurrences of C are replaced by CB, and $P_C = \{\langle CEB, 245\rangle\}$. CEB and CB are both found to be closed. The computation proceeds in this manner until all closed frequent itemsets are enumerated. Note that when we get to DEB and perform the closure check, we find that it is a subset of $ADEB$ and also has the same support; thus DEB is not closed.

9.4 NONDERIVABLE ITEMSETS

An itemset is called *nonderivable* if its support cannot be deduced from the supports of its subsets. The set of all frequent nonderivable itemsets is a summary or condensed representation of the set of all frequent itemsets. Further, it is lossless with respect to support, that is, the exact support of all other frequent itemsets can be deduced from it.

Generalized Itemsets

Let $\mathcal{T}$ be a set of tids, let $\mathcal{I}$ be a set of items, and let X be a k-itemset, that is, $X = \{x_1, x_2, \ldots, x_k\}$. Consider the tidsets $\mathbf{t}(x_i)$ for each item $x_i \in X$. These k tidsets induce a partitioning of the set of all tids into 2^k regions, some of which may be empty, where each partition contains the tids for some subset of items $Y \subseteq X$, but for none of the remaining items $Z = X \setminus Y$. Each such region is therefore the tidset of a *generalized itemset* comprising items in X or their negations. As such a generalized itemset can be represented as $Y\overline{Z}$, where Y consists of regular items and Z consists of negated items. We define the support of a generalized itemset $Y\overline{Z}$ as the number of transactions that contain all items in Y but no item in Z:

$$sup(Y\overline{Z}) = \left| \{t \in \mathcal{T} \mid Y \subseteq \mathbf{i}(t) \text{ and } Z \cap \mathbf{i}(t) = \emptyset \} \right| \qquad (9.6)$$

Example 9.5. Consider the example dataset in Figure 9.1(a). Let $X = ACD$. We have $\mathbf{t}(A) = 1345$, $\mathbf{t}(C) = 2456$, and $\mathbf{t}(D) = 1356$. These three tidsets induce a partitioning on the space of all tids, as illustrated in the Venn diagram shown in Figure 9.5. For example, the region labeled $\mathbf{t}(AC\overline{D}) = 4$ represents those tids that contain A and C but not D. Thus, the support of the generalized itemset $AC\overline{D}$ is 1. The tids that belong to all the eight regions are shown. Some regions are empty, which means that the support of the corresponding generalized itemset is 0.

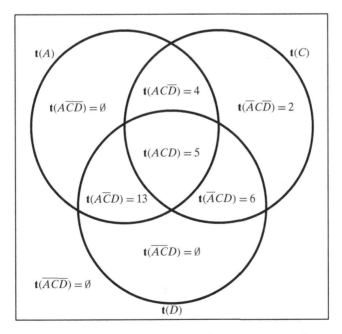

Figure 9.5. Tidset partitioning induced by $\mathbf{t}(A)$, $\mathbf{t}(C)$, and $\mathbf{t}(D)$.

Inclusion–Exclusion Principle

Let $Y\overline{Z}$ be a generalized itemset, and let $X = Y \cup Z = YZ$. The inclusion–exclusion principle allows one to directly compute the support of $Y\overline{Z}$ as a combination of the supports for all itemsets W, such that $Y \subseteq W \subseteq X$:

$$sup(Y\overline{Z}) = \sum_{Y \subseteq W \subseteq X} -1^{|W \setminus Y|} \cdot sup(W) \qquad (9.7)$$

Example 9.6. Let us compute the support of the generalized itemset $\overline{A}C\overline{D} = C\overline{AD}$, where $Y = C$, $Z = AD$ and $X = YZ = ACD$. In the Venn diagram shown in Figure 9.5, we start with all the tids in $\mathbf{t}(C)$, and remove the tids contained in $\mathbf{t}(AC)$ and $\mathbf{t}(CD)$. However, we realize that in terms of support this removes $sup(ACD)$ twice, so we need to add it back. In other words, the support of $C\overline{AD}$ is given as

$$sup(C\overline{AD}) = sup(C) - sup(AC) - sup(CD) + sup(ACD)$$

$$= 4 - 2 - 2 + 1 = 1$$

But, this is precisely what the inclusion–exclusion formula gives:

$$
\begin{aligned}
sup(C\overline{AD}) = \ &(-1)^0 \, sup(C) + &&W = C, |W \setminus Y| = 0 \\
&(-1)^1 \, sup(AC) + &&W = AC, |W \setminus Y| = 1 \\
&(-1)^1 \, sup(CD) + &&W = CD, |W \setminus Y| = 1 \\
&(-1)^2 \, sup(ACD) &&W = ACD, |W \setminus Y| = 2 \\
= \ &sup(C) - sup(AC) - sup(CD) + sup(ACD)
\end{aligned}
$$

We can see that the support of $C\overline{AD}$ is a combination of the support values over all itemsets W such that $C \subseteq W \subseteq ACD$.

Support Bounds for an Itemset

Notice that the inclusion–exclusion formula in Eq. (9.7) for the support of $Y\overline{Z}$ has terms for all subsets between Y and $X = YZ$. Put differently, for a given k-itemset X, there are 2^k generalized itemsets of the form $Y\overline{Z}$, with $Y \subseteq X$ and $Z = X \setminus Y$, and each such generalized itemset has a term for $sup(X)$ in the inclusion–exclusion equation; this happens when $W = X$. Because the support of any (generalized) itemset must be non-negative, we can derive a bound on the support of X from each of the 2^k generalized itemsets by setting $sup(Y\overline{Z}) \geq 0$. However, note that whenever $|X \setminus Y|$ is even, the coefficient of $sup(X)$ is $+1$, but when $|X \setminus Y|$ is odd, the coefficient of $sup(X)$ is -1 in Eq. (9.7). Thus, from the 2^k possible subsets $Y \subseteq X$, we derive 2^{k-1} lower bounds and 2^{k-1} upper bounds for $sup(X)$, obtained after setting $sup(Y\overline{Z}) \geq 0$, and rearranging the terms in the inclusion–exclusion formula, so that $sup(X)$ is on the left hand side and the the remaining terms are on the right hand side

> **Upper Bounds** ($|X \setminus Y|$ is odd): $sup(X) \leq \displaystyle\sum_{Y \subseteq W \subset X} -1^{(|X \setminus W|+1)} sup(W)$ (9.8)
>
> **Lower Bounds** ($|X \setminus Y|$ is even): $sup(X) \geq \displaystyle\sum_{Y \subseteq W \subset X} -1^{(|X \setminus W|+1)} sup(W)$ (9.9)

Example 9.7. Consider Figure 9.5, which shows the partitioning induced by the tidsets of A, C, and D. We wish to determine the support bounds for $X = ACD$ using each of the generalized itemsets $Y\overline{Z}$ where $Y \subseteq X$. For example, if $Y = C$, then the inclusion-exclusion principle [Eq. (9.7)] gives us

$$sup(\overline{CAD}) = sup(C) - sup(AC) - sup(CD) + sup(ACD)$$

Setting $sup(\overline{CAD}) \geq 0$, and rearranging the terms, we obtain

$$sup(ACD) \geq -sup(C) + sup(AC) + sup(CD)$$

which is precisely the expression from the lower-bound formula in Eq. (9.9) because $|X \setminus Y| = |ACD - C| = |AD| = 2$ is even.

As another example, let $Y = \emptyset$. Setting $sup(\overline{ACD}) \geq 0$, we have

$$sup(\overline{ACD}) = sup(\emptyset) - sup(A) - sup(C) - sup(D) +$$
$$sup(AC) + sup(AD) + sup(CD) - sup(ACD) \geq 0$$
$$\implies sup(ACD) \leq sup(\emptyset) - sup(A) - sup(C) - sup(D) +$$
$$sup(AC) + sup(AD) + sup(CD)$$

Notice that this rule gives an upper bound on the support of ACD, which also follows from Eq. (9.8) because $|X \setminus Y| = 3$ is odd.

In fact, from each of the regions in Figure 9.5, we get one bound, and out of the eight possible regions, exactly four give upper bounds and the other four give lower bounds for the support of ACD:

$$
\begin{aligned}
sup(ACD) \quad &\geq 0 && \text{when } Y = ACD \\
&\leq sup(AC) && \text{when } Y = AC \\
&\leq sup(AD) && \text{when } Y = AD \\
&\leq sup(CD) && \text{when } Y = CD \\
&\geq sup(AC) + sup(AD) - sup(A) && \text{when } Y = A \\
&\geq sup(AC) + sup(CD) - sup(C) && \text{when } Y = C \\
&\geq sup(AD) + sup(CD) - sup(D) && \text{when } Y = D \\
&\leq sup(AC) + sup(AD) + sup(CD) - && \\
&\quad sup(A) - sup(C) - sup(D) + sup(\emptyset) && \text{when } Y = \emptyset
\end{aligned}
$$

This derivation of the bounds is schematically summarized in Figure 9.6. For instance, at level 2 the inequality is $\geq$, which implies that if Y is any itemset at this level, we will obtain a lower bound. The signs at different levels indicate the coefficient of the

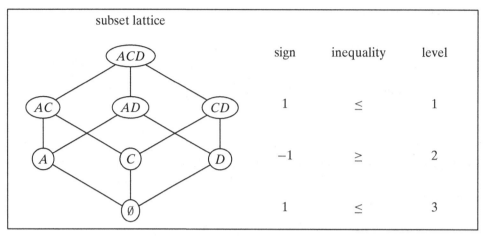

Figure 9.6. Support bounds from subsets.

corresponding itemset in the upper or lower bound computations via Eq. (9.8) and Eq. (9.9). Finally, the subset lattice shows which intermediate terms W have to be considered in the summation. For instance, if $Y = A$, then the intermediate terms are $W \in \{AC, AD, A\}$, with the corresponding signs $\{+1, +1, -1\}$, so that we obtain the lower bound rule:

$$sup(ACD) \geq sup(AC) + sup(AD) - sup(A)$$

Nonderivable Itemsets

Given an itemset X, and $Y \subseteq X$, let $IE(Y)$ denote the summation

$$IE(Y) = \sum_{Y \subseteq W \subset X} -1^{(|X \setminus W| + 1)} \cdot sup(W)$$

Then, the sets of all upper and lower bounds for $sup(X)$ are given as

$$UB(X) = \Big\{ IE(Y) \,\Big|\, Y \subseteq X, \, |X \setminus Y| \text{ is odd} \Big\} \tag{9.10}$$

$$LB(X) = \Big\{ IE(Y) \,\Big|\, Y \subseteq X, \, |X \setminus Y| \text{ is even} \Big\} \tag{9.11}$$

An itemset X is called *nonderivable* if $\max\{LB(X)\} \neq \min\{UB(X)\}$, which implies that the support of X cannot be derived from the support values of its subsets; we know only the range of possible values, that is,

$$sup(X) \in \Big[\max\{LB(X)\}, \min\{UB(X)\} \Big]$$

On the other hand, X is derivable if $sup(X) = \max\{LB(X)\} = \min\{UB(X)\}$ because in this case $sup(X)$ can be derived exactly using the supports of its subsets. Thus, the set of all frequent nonderivable itemsets is given as

$$\mathcal{N} = \left\{ X \in \mathcal{F} \mid \max\{LB(X)\} \neq \min\{UB(X)\} \right\}$$

where $\mathcal{F}$ is the set of all frequent itemsets.

Example 9.8. Consider the set of upper bound and lower bound formulas for $sup(ACD)$ outlined in Example 9.7. Using the tidset information in Figure 9.5, the support lower bounds are

$$sup(ACD) \geq 0$$
$$\geq sup(AC) + sup(AD) - sup(A) = 2 + 3 - 4 = 1$$
$$\geq sup(AC) + sup(CD) - sup(C) = 2 + 2 - 4 = 0$$
$$\geq sup(AD) + sup(CD) - sup(D) = 3 + 2 - 4 = 0$$

and the upper bounds are

$$sup(ACD) \leq sup(AC) = 2$$
$$\leq sup(AD) = 3$$
$$\leq sup(CD) = 2$$
$$\leq sup(AC) + sup(AD) + sup(CD) - sup(A) - sup(C) -$$
$$sup(D) + sup(\emptyset) = 2 + 3 + 2 - 4 - 4 - 4 + 6 = 1$$

Thus, we have

$$LB(ACD) = \{0, 1\} \qquad\qquad \max\{LB(ACD)\} = 1$$
$$UB(ACD) = \{1, 2, 3\} \qquad\qquad \min\{UB(ACD)\} = 1$$

Because $\max\{LB(ACD)\} = \min\{UB(ACD)\}$ we conclude that ACD is derivable.

Note that is it not essential to derive all the upper and lower bounds before one can conclude whether an itemset is derivable. For example, let $X = ABDE$. Considering its immediate subsets, we can obtain the following upper bound values:

$$sup(ABDE) \leq sup(ABD) = 3$$
$$\leq sup(ABE) = 4$$
$$\leq sup(ADE) = 3$$
$$\leq sup(BDE) = 3$$

From these upper bounds, we know for sure that $sup(ABDE) \leq 3$. Now, let us consider the lower bound derived from $Y = AB$:

$$sup(ABDE) \geq sup(ABD) + sup(ABE) - sup(AB) = 3 + 4 - 4 = 3$$

At this point we know that $sup(ABDE) \geq 3$, so without processing any further bounds, we can conclude that $sup(ABDE) \in [3, 3]$, which means that $ABDE$ is derivable.

For the example database in Figure 9.1(a), the set of all frequent nonderivable itemsets, along with their support bounds, is

$$\mathcal{N} = \{A[0,6], B[0,6], C[0,6], D[0,6], E[0,6],$$
$$AD[2,4], AE[3,4], CE[3,4], DE[3,4]\}$$

Notice that single items are always nonderivable by definition.

9.5 FURTHER READING

The concept of closed itemsets is based on the elegant lattice theoretic framework of formal concept analysis in Ganter, Wille, and Franzke (1997).The Charm algorithm for mining frequent closed itemsets appears in Zaki and Hsiao (2005), and the GenMax method for mining maximal frequent itemsets is described in Gouda and Zaki (2005). For an Apriori style algorithm for maximal patterns, called MaxMiner, that uses very effective support lower bound based itemset pruning see Bayardo Jr (1998). The notion of minimal generators was proposed in Bastide et al. (2000); they refer to them as *key patterns*. Nonderivable itemset mining task was introduced in Calders and Goethals (2007).

Bastide, Y., Taouil, R., Pasquier, N., Stumme, G., and Lakhal, L. (2000). Mining frequent patterns with counting inference. *ACM SIGKDD Explorations Newsletter*, 2 (2), 66–75.

Bayardo Jr, R. J. (1998). Efficiently mining long patterns from databases. *Proceedings of the ACM SIGMOD International Conference on Management of Data*. ACM, pp. 85–93.

Calders, T. and Goethals, B. (2007). Non-derivable itemset mining. *Data Mining and Knowledge Discovery*, 14 (1), 171–206.

Ganter, B., Wille, R., and Franzke, C. (1997). *Formal Concept Analysis: Mathematical Foundations*. New York: Springer-Verlag.

Gouda, K. and Zaki, M. J. (2005). Genmax: An efficient algorithm for mining maximal frequent itemsets. *Data Mining and Knowledge Discovery*, 11 (3), 223–242.

Zaki, M. J. and Hsiao, C.-J. (2005). Efficient algorithms for mining closed itemsets and their lattice structure. *IEEE Transactions on Knowledge and Data Engineering*, 17 (4), 462–478.

9.6 EXERCISES

Q1. True or False:
   (a) Maximal frequent itemsets are sufficient to determine all frequent itemsets with their supports.
   (b) An itemset and its closure share the same set of transactions.

(c) The set of all maximal frequent sets is a subset of the set of all closed frequent itemsets.

(d) The set of all maximal frequent sets is the set of longest possible frequent itemsets.

Table 9.1. Dataset for Q2

Tid	Itemset
t_1	ACD
t_2	BCE
t_3	$ABCE$
t_4	BDE
t_5	$ABCE$
t_6	$ABCD$

Q2. Given the database in Table 9.1

(a) Show the application of the closure operator on AE, that is, compute $\mathbf{c}(AE)$. Is AE closed?

(b) Find all frequent, closed, and maximal itemsets using $minsup = 2/6$.

Table 9.2. Dataset for Q3

Tid	Itemset
1	ACD
2	BCD
3	AC
4	ABD
5	$ABCD$
6	BCD

Q3. Given the database in Table 9.2, find all minimal generators using $minsup = 1$.

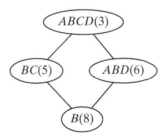

Figure 9.7. Closed itemset lattice for Q4.

Q4. Consider the frequent closed itemset lattice shown in Figure 9.7. Assume that the item space is $\mathcal{I} = \{A, B, C, D, E\}$. Answer the following questions:

(a) What is the frequency of CD?

(b) Find all frequent itemsets and their frequency, for itemsets in the subset interval $[B, ABD]$.

(c) Is ADE frequent? If yes, show its support. If not, why?

Q5. Let $\mathcal{C}$ be the set of all closed frequent itemsets and $\mathcal{M}$ the set of all maximal frequent itemsets for some database. Prove that $\mathcal{M} \subseteq \mathcal{C}$.

Q6. Prove that the closure operator $\mathbf{c} = \mathbf{i} \circ \mathbf{t}$ satisfies the following properties (X and Y are some itemsets):

    (a) Extensive: $X \subseteq \mathbf{c}(X)$

    (b) Monotonic: If $X \subseteq Y$ then $\mathbf{c}(X) \subseteq \mathbf{c}(Y)$

    (c) Idempotent: $\mathbf{c}(X) = \mathbf{c}(\mathbf{c}(X))$

Table 9.3. Dataset for Q7

Tid	Itemset
1	ACD
2	BCD
3	ACD
4	ABD
5	$ABCD$
6	BC

Q7. Let δ be an integer. An itemset X is called a δ-*free* itemset iff for all subsets $Y \subset X$, we have $sup(Y) - sup(X) > \delta$. For any itemset X, we define the δ-*closure* of X as follows:

$$\delta\text{-closure}(X) = \{Y \mid X \subset Y, sup(X) - sup(Y) \leq \delta, \text{ and } Y \text{ is maximal}\}$$

Consider the database shown in Table 9.3. Answer the following questions:

    (a) Given $\delta = 1$, compute all the δ-free itemsets.

    (b) For each of the δ-free itemsets, compute its δ-closure for $\delta = 1$.

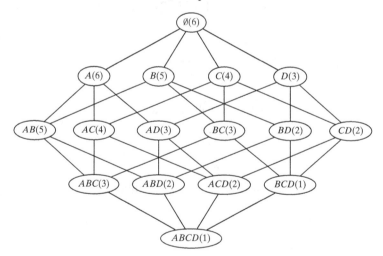

Figure 9.8. Frequent itemset lattice for Q8.

Q8. Given the lattice of frequent itemsets (along with their supports) shown in Figure 9.8, answer the following questions:

    (a) List all the closed itemsets.

    (b) Is BCD derivable? What about $ABCD$? What are the bounds on their supports.

Q9. Prove that if an itemset X is derivable, then so is any superset $Y \supset X$. Using this observation describe an algorithm to mine all nonderivable itemsets.

Q10. Prove that if X is a minimal generator, then all subsets $Y \subset X$ are also minimal generators (with different support than X).

CHAPTER 10

Sequence Mining

Many real-world applications such as bioinformatics, Web mining, and text mining have to deal with sequential and temporal data. Sequence mining helps discover patterns across time or positions in a given dataset. In this chapter we consider methods to mine frequent sequences, which allow gaps between elements, as well as methods to mine frequent substrings, which do not allow gaps between consecutive elements.

10.1 FREQUENT SEQUENCES

Let Σ denote an *alphabet*, defined as a finite set of characters or symbols, and let $|\Sigma|$ denote its cardinality. A *sequence* or a *string* is defined as an ordered list of symbols, and is written as $\mathbf{s} = s_1 s_2 \ldots s_k$, where $s_i \in \Sigma$ is a symbol at position i, also denoted as $\mathbf{s}[i]$. Here $|\mathbf{s}| = k$ denotes the *length* of the sequence. A sequence with length k is also called a *k-sequence*. We use the notation $\mathbf{s}[i:j] = s_i s_{i+1} \cdots s_{j-1} s_j$ to denote the *substring* or sequence of consecutive symbols in positions i through j, where $j > i$. Define the *prefix* of a sequence $\mathbf{s}$ as any substring of the form $\mathbf{s}[1:i] = s_1 s_2 \ldots s_i$, with $0 \le i \le n$. Also, define the *suffix* of $\mathbf{s}$ as any substring of the form $\mathbf{s}[i:n] = s_i s_{i+1} \ldots s_n$, with $1 \le i \le n+1$. Note that $\mathbf{s}[1:0]$ is the empty prefix, and $\mathbf{s}[n+1:n]$ is the empty suffix. Let $\Sigma^\star$ be the set of all possible sequences that can be constructed using the symbols in Σ, including the empty sequence $\emptyset$ (which has length zero).

Let $\mathbf{s} = s_1 s_2 \ldots s_n$ and $\mathbf{r} = r_1 r_2 \ldots r_m$ be two sequences over Σ. We say that $\mathbf{r}$ is a *subsequence* of $\mathbf{s}$ denoted $\mathbf{r} \subseteq \mathbf{s}$, if there exists a one-to-one mapping $\phi : [1, m] \to [1, n]$, such that $\mathbf{r}[i] = \mathbf{s}[\phi(i)]$ and for any two positions i, j in $\mathbf{r}$, $i < j \implies \phi(i) < \phi(j)$. In other words, each position in $\mathbf{r}$ is mapped to a different position in $\mathbf{s}$, and the order of symbols is preserved, even though there may be intervening gaps between consecutive elements of $\mathbf{r}$ in the mapping. If $\mathbf{r} \subseteq \mathbf{s}$, we also say that $\mathbf{s}$ *contains* $\mathbf{r}$. The sequence $\mathbf{r}$ is called a *consecutive subsequence* or substring of $\mathbf{s}$ provided $r_1 r_2 \ldots r_m = s_j s_{j+1} \ldots s_{j+m-1}$, i.e., $\mathbf{r}[1:m] = \mathbf{s}[j:j+m-1]$, with $1 \le j \le n-m+1$. For substrings we do not allow any gaps between the elements of $\mathbf{r}$ in the mapping.

Example 10.1. Let $\Sigma = \{A, C, G, T\}$, and let $\mathbf{s} = ACTGAACG$. Then $\mathbf{r}_1 = CGAAG$ is a subsequence of $\mathbf{s}$, and $\mathbf{r}_2 = CTGA$ is a substring of $\mathbf{s}$. The sequence $\mathbf{r}_3 = ACT$ is a prefix of $\mathbf{s}$, and so is $\mathbf{r}_4 = ACTGA$, whereas $\mathbf{r}_5 = GAACG$ is one of the suffixes of $\mathbf{s}$.

Given a database $\mathbf{D} = \{\mathbf{s}_1, \mathbf{s}_2, \ldots, \mathbf{s}_N\}$ of N sequences, and given some sequence $\mathbf{r}$, the *support* of $\mathbf{r}$ in the database $\mathbf{D}$ is defined as the total number of sequences in $\mathbf{D}$ that contain $\mathbf{r}$

$$sup(\mathbf{r}) = \left| \left\{ \mathbf{s}_i \in \mathbf{D} | \mathbf{r} \subseteq \mathbf{s}_i \right\} \right| \tag{10.1}$$

The *relative support* of $\mathbf{r}$ is the fraction of sequences that contain $\mathbf{r}$

$$rsup(\mathbf{r}) = sup(\mathbf{r})/N$$

Given a user-specified *minsup* threshold, we say that a sequence $\mathbf{r}$ is *frequent* in database $\mathbf{D}$ if $sup(\mathbf{r}) \geq minsup$. A frequent sequence is *maximal* if it is not a subsequence of any other frequent sequence, and a frequent sequence is *closed* if it is not a subsequence of any other frequent sequence with the same support.

10.2 MINING FREQUENT SEQUENCES

For sequence mining the order of the symbols matters, and thus we have to consider all possible *permutations* of the symbols as the possible frequent candidates. Contrast this with itemset mining, where we had only to consider *combinations* of the items. The sequence search space can be organized in a prefix search tree. The root of the tree, at level 0, contains the empty sequence, with each symbol $x \in \Sigma$ as one of its children. As such, a node labeled with the sequence $\mathbf{s} = s_1 s_2 \ldots s_k$ at level k has children of the form $\mathbf{s}' = s_1 s_2 \ldots s_k s_{k+1}$ at level $k+1$. In other words, $\mathbf{s}$ is a prefix of each child $\mathbf{s}'$, which is also called an *extension* of $\mathbf{s}$.

Example 10.2. Let $\Sigma = \{A, C, G, T\}$ and let the sequence database $\mathbf{D}$ consist of the three sequences shown in Table 10.1. The sequence search space organized as a prefix search tree is illustrated in Figure 10.1. The support of each sequence is shown within brackets. For example, the node labeled A has three extensions AA, AG, and AT, out of which AT is infrequent if $minsup = 3$.

The subsequence search space is conceptually infinite because it comprises all sequences in Σ^*, that is, all sequences of length zero or more that can be created using symbols in Σ. In practice, the database $\mathbf{D}$ consists of bounded length sequences. Let l denote the length of the longest sequence in the database, then, in the worst case, we will have to consider all candidate sequences of length up to l, which gives the following

Table 10.1. Example sequence database

Id	Sequence
$\mathbf{s}_1$	$CAGAAGT$
$\mathbf{s}_2$	$TGACAG$
$\mathbf{s}_3$	$GAAGT$

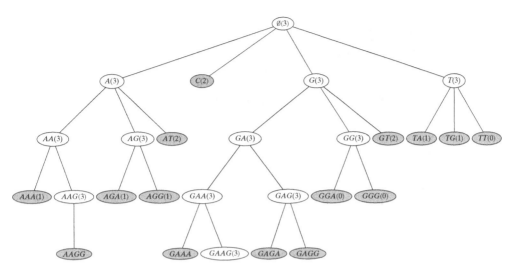

Figure 10.1. Sequence search space: shaded ovals represent candidates that are infrequent; those without support in brackets can be pruned based on an infrequent subsequence. Unshaded ovals represent frequent sequences.

bound on the size of the search space:

$$|\Sigma|^1 + |\Sigma|^2 + \cdots + |\Sigma|^l = O(|\Sigma|^l) \qquad (10.2)$$

since at level k there are $|\Sigma|^k$ possible subsequences of length k.

10.2.1 Level-wise Mining: GSP

We can devise an effective sequence mining algorithm that searches the sequence prefix tree using a level-wise or breadth-first search. Given the set of frequent sequences at level k, we generate all possible sequence extensions or *candidates* at level $k+1$. We next compute the support of each candidate and prune those that are not frequent. The search stops when no more frequent extensions are possible.

The pseudo-code for the level-wise, generalized sequential pattern (GSP) mining method is shown in Algorithm 10.1. It uses the antimonotonic property of support to prune candidate patterns, that is, no supersequence of an infrequent sequence can be frequent, and all subsequences of a frequent sequence must be frequent. The prefix search tree at level k is denoted $\mathcal{C}^{(k)}$. Initially $\mathcal{C}^{(1)}$ comprises all the symbols in Σ. Given the current set of candidate k-sequences $\mathcal{C}^{(k)}$, the method first computes their support (line 6). For each database sequence $\mathbf{s}_i \in \mathbf{D}$, we check whether a candidate sequence $\mathbf{r} \in \mathcal{C}^{(k)}$ is a subsequence of $\mathbf{s}_i$. If so, we increment the support of $\mathbf{r}$. Once the frequent sequences at level k have been found, we generate the candidates for level $k+1$ (line 10). For the extension, each leaf $\mathbf{r}_a$ is extended with the last symbol of any other leaf $\mathbf{r}_b$ that shares the same prefix (i.e., has the same parent), to obtain the new candidate $(k+1)$-sequence $\mathbf{r}_{ab} = \mathbf{r}_a + \mathbf{r}_b[k]$ (line 18). If the new candidate $\mathbf{r}_{ab}$ contains any infrequent k-sequence, we prune it.

The computational complexity of GSP is $O(|\Sigma|^l)$ as per Eq. (10.2), where l is the length of the longest frequent sequence. The I/O complexity is $O(l \cdot \mathbf{D})$ because we compute the support of an entire level in one scan of the database.

Algorithm 10.1: Algorithm GSP

GSP (D, Σ, *minsup*):

1 $\mathcal{F} \leftarrow \emptyset$
2 $\mathcal{C}^{(1)} \leftarrow \{\emptyset\}$ // Initial prefix tree with single symbols
3 **foreach** $s \in \Sigma$ **do** Add s as child of $\emptyset$ in $\mathcal{C}^{(1)}$ with $sup(s) \leftarrow 0$
4 $k \leftarrow 1$ // k denotes the level
5 **while** $\mathcal{C}^{(k)} \neq \emptyset$ **do**
6   COMPUTESUPPORT ($\mathcal{C}^{(k)}$, **D**)
7   **foreach** *leaf* **s** $\in \mathcal{C}^{(k)}$ **do**
8   **if** $sup(\mathbf{r}) \geq minsup$ **then** $\mathcal{F} \leftarrow \mathcal{F} \cup \{(\mathbf{r}, sup(\mathbf{r}))\}$
9   **else** remove **s** from $\mathcal{C}^{(k)}$
10     $\mathcal{C}^{(k+1)} \leftarrow$ EXTENDPREFIXTREE ($\mathcal{C}^{(k)}$)
11     $k \leftarrow k+1$
12 **return** $\mathcal{F}^{(k)}$

COMPUTESUPPORT ($\mathcal{C}^{(k)}$, D):

13 **foreach** $\mathbf{s}_i \in \mathbf{D}$ **do**
14   **foreach** $\mathbf{r} \in \mathcal{C}^{(k)}$ **do**
15   **if** $\mathbf{r} \subseteq \mathbf{s}_i$ **then** $sup(\mathbf{r}) \leftarrow sup(\mathbf{r}) + 1$

EXTENDPREFIXTREE ($\mathcal{C}^{(k)}$):

16 **foreach** *leaf* $\mathbf{r}_a \in \mathcal{C}^{(k)}$ **do**
17   **foreach** *leaf* $\mathbf{r}_b \in$ CHILDREN(PARENT($\mathbf{r}_a$)) **do**
18        $\mathbf{r}_{ab} \leftarrow \mathbf{r}_a + \mathbf{r}_b[k]$ // extend $\mathbf{r}_a$ with last item of $\mathbf{r}_b$
       // prune if there are any infrequent subsequences
19   **if** $\mathbf{r}_c \in \mathcal{C}^{(k)}$, *for all* $\mathbf{r}_c \subset \mathbf{r}_{ab}$, *such that* $|\mathbf{r}_c| = |\mathbf{r}_{ab}| - 1$ **then**
20   Add $\mathbf{r}_{ab}$ as child of $\mathbf{r}_a$ with $sup(\mathbf{r}_{ab}) \leftarrow 0$
21   **if** *no extensions from* $\mathbf{r}_a$ **then**
22   remove $\mathbf{r}_a$, and all ancestors of $\mathbf{r}_a$ with no extensions, from $\mathcal{C}^{(k)}$
23 **return** $\mathcal{C}^{(k)}$

Example 10.3. For example, let us mine the database shown in Table 10.1 using *minsup* = 3. That is, we want to find only those subsequences that occur in all three database sequences. Figure 10.1 shows that we begin by extending the empty sequence $\emptyset$ at level 0, to obtain the candidates A, C, G, and T at level 1. Out of these C can be pruned because it is not frequent. Next we generate all possible candidates at level 2. Notice that using A as the prefix we generate all possible extensions AA, AG, and AT. A similar process is repeated for the other two symbols G and T. Some candidate extensions can be pruned without counting. For example, the extension $GAAA$ obtained from GAA can be pruned because it has an infrequent subsequence AAA. The figure shows all the frequent sequences (unshaded), out of which $GAAG(3)$ and $T(3)$ are the maximal ones.

10.2.2 Vertical Sequence Mining: Spade

The Spade algorithm uses a vertical database representation for sequence mining. The idea is to record for each symbol the sequence identifiers and the positions where it occurs. For each symbol $s \in \Sigma$, we keep a set of tuples of the form $\langle i, pos(s) \rangle$, where $pos(s)$ is the set of positions in the database sequence $\mathbf{s}_i \in \mathbf{D}$ where symbol s appears. Let $\mathcal{L}(s)$ denote the set of such sequence-position tuples for symbol s, which we refer to as the *poslist*. The set of poslists for each symbol $s \in \Sigma$ thus constitutes a vertical representation of the input database. In general, given k-sequence $\mathbf{r}$, its poslist $\mathcal{L}(\mathbf{r})$ maintains the list of positions for the occurrences of the last symbol $\mathbf{r}[k]$ in each database sequence $\mathbf{s}_i$, provided $\mathbf{r} \subseteq \mathbf{s}_i$. The support of sequence $\mathbf{r}$ is simply the number of distinct sequences in which $\mathbf{r}$ occurs, that is, $sup(\mathbf{r}) = |\mathcal{L}(\mathbf{r})|$.

Example 10.4. In Table 10.1, the symbol A occurs in $\mathbf{s}_1$ at positions 2, 4, and 5. Thus, we add the tuple $\langle 1, \{2, 4, 5\} \rangle$ to $\mathcal{L}(A)$. Because A also occurs at positions 3 and 5 in sequence $\mathbf{s}_2$, and at positions 2 and 3 in $\mathbf{s}_3$, the complete poslist for A is $\{\langle 1, \{2, 4, 5\} \rangle, \langle 2, \{3, 5\} \rangle, \langle 1, \{2, 3\} \rangle\}$. We have $sup(A) = 3$, as its poslist contains three tuples. Figure 10.2 shows the poslist for each symbol, as well as other sequences.

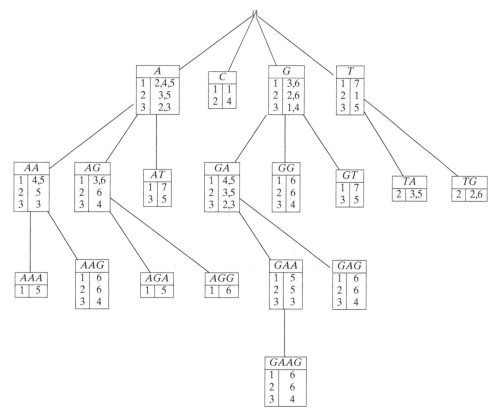

Figure 10.2. Sequence mining via Spade: infrequent sequences with at least one occurrence are shown shaded; those with zero support are not shown.

Algorithm 10.2: Algorithm SPADE

```
// Initial Call: F ← ∅, k ← 0,
    P ← {⟨s, L(s)⟩ | s ∈ Σ, sup(s) ≥ minsup}
```
SPADE ($P, minsup, F, k$):

1 **foreach** $\mathbf{r}_a \in P$ **do**
2     $F \leftarrow F \cup \{(\mathbf{r}_a, sup(\mathbf{r}_a))\}$
3     $P_a \leftarrow \emptyset$
4   **foreach** $\mathbf{r}_b \in P$ **do**
5        $\mathbf{r}_{ab} = \mathbf{r}_a + \mathbf{r}_b[k]$
6        $L(\mathbf{r}_{ab}) = L(\mathbf{r}_a) \cap L(\mathbf{r}_b)$
7   **if** $sup(\mathbf{r}_{ab}) \geq minsup$ **then**
8           $P_a \leftarrow P_a \cup \{\langle \mathbf{r}_{ab}, L(\mathbf{r}_{ab})\rangle\}$
9   **if** $P_a \neq \emptyset$ **then** SPADE ($P_a, minsup, F, k+1$)

For example, for sequence GT, we find that it is a subsequence of $\mathbf{s}_1$ and $\mathbf{s}_3$. Even though there are two occurrences of GT in $\mathbf{s}_1$, the last symbol T occurs at position 7 in both occurrences, thus the poslist for GT has the tuple $\langle 1, 7 \rangle$. The full poslist for GT is $L(GT) = \{\langle 1, 7 \rangle, \langle 3, 5 \rangle\}$. The support of GT is $sup(GT) = |L(GT)| = 2$.

Support computation in Spade is done via *sequential join* operations. Given the poslists for any two k-sequences $\mathbf{r}_a$ and $\mathbf{r}_b$ that share the same $(k-1)$ length prefix, the idea is to perform sequential joins on the poslists to compute the support for the new $(k+1)$ length candidate sequence $\mathbf{r}_{ab} = \mathbf{r}_a + \mathbf{r}_b[k]$. Given a tuple $\langle i, pos(\mathbf{r}_b[k])\rangle \in L(\mathbf{r}_b)$, we first check if there exists a tuple $\langle i, pos(\mathbf{r}_a[k])\rangle \in L(\mathbf{r}_a)$, that is, both sequences must occur in the same database sequence $\mathbf{s}_i$. Next, for each position $p \in pos(\mathbf{r}_b[k])$, we check whether there exists a position $q \in pos(\mathbf{r}_a[k])$ such that $q < p$. If yes, this means that the symbol $\mathbf{r}_b[k]$ occurs after the last position of $\mathbf{r}_a$ and thus we retain p as a valid occurrence of $\mathbf{r}_{ab}$. The poslist $L(\mathbf{r}_{ab})$ comprises all such valid occurrences. Notice how we keep track of positions only for the last symbol in the candidate sequence. This is because we extend sequences from a common prefix, so there is no need to keep track of all the occurrences of the symbols in the prefix. We denote the sequential join as $L(\mathbf{r}_{ab}) = L(\mathbf{r}_a) \cap L(\mathbf{r}_b)$.

The main advantage of the vertical approach is that it enables different search strategies over the sequence search space, including breadth or depth-first search. Algorithm 10.2 shows the pseudo-code for Spade. Given a set of sequences P that share the same prefix, along with their poslists, the method creates a new prefix equivalence class P_a for each sequence $\mathbf{r}_a \in P$ by performing sequential joins with every sequence $\mathbf{r}_b \in P$, including self-joins. After removing the infrequent extensions, the new equivalence class P_a is then processed recursively.

Example 10.5. Consider the poslists for A and G shown in Figure 10.2. To obtain $\mathcal{L}(AG)$, we perform a sequential join over the poslists $\mathcal{L}(A)$ and $\mathcal{L}(G)$. For the tuples $\langle 1, \{2, 4, 5\}\rangle \in \mathcal{L}(A)$ and $\langle 1, \{3, 6\}\rangle \in \mathcal{L}(G)$, both positions 3 and 6 for G, occur after some occurrence of A, for example, at position 2. Thus, we add the tuple $\langle 1, \{3, 6\}\rangle$ to $\mathcal{L}(AG)$. The complete poslist for AG is $\mathcal{L}(AG) = \{\langle 1, \{3, 6\}\rangle, \langle 2, 6\rangle, \langle 3, 4\rangle\}$.

Figure 10.2 illustrates the complete working of the Spade algorithm, along with all the candidates and their poslists.

10.2.3 Projection-Based Sequence Mining: PrefixSpan

Let $\mathbf{D}$ denote a database, and let $s \in \Sigma$ be any symbol. The *projected database* with respect to s, denoted $\mathbf{D}_s$, is obtained by finding the the first occurrence of s in $\mathbf{s}_i$, say at position p. Next, we retain in $\mathbf{D}_s$ only the suffix of $\mathbf{s}_i$ starting at position $p+1$. Further, any infrequent symbols are removed from the suffix. This is done for each sequence $\mathbf{s}_i \in \mathbf{D}$.

Example 10.6. Consider the three database sequences in Table 10.1. Given that the symbol G first occurs at position 3 in $\mathbf{s}_1 = CAGAAGT$, the projection of $\mathbf{s}_1$ with respect to G is the suffix $AAGT$. The projected database for G, denoted $\mathbf{D}_G$ is therefore given as: $\{\mathbf{s}_1 : AAGT, \mathbf{s}_2 : AAG, \mathbf{s}_3 : AAGT\}$.

The main idea in PrefixSpan is to compute the support for only the individual symbols in the projected database $\mathbf{D}_s$, and then to perform recursive projections on the frequent symbols in a depth-first manner. The PrefixSpan method is outlined in Algorithm 10.3. Here $\mathbf{r}$ is a frequent subsequence, and $\mathbf{D}_\mathbf{r}$ is the projected dataset for $\mathbf{r}$. Initially $\mathbf{r}$ is empty and $\mathbf{D}_\mathbf{r}$ is the entire input dataset $\mathbf{D}$. Given a database of (projected) sequences $\mathbf{D}_\mathbf{r}$, PrefixSpan first finds all the frequent symbols in the projected dataset. For each such symbol s, we extend $\mathbf{r}$ by appending s to obtain the new frequent

---

Algorithm 10.3: Algorithm PREFIXSPAN

```
    // Initial Call: Dr ← D, r ← ∅, F ← ∅
    PREFIXSPAN (Dr, r, minsup, F):
1   foreach s ∈ Σ such that sup(s, Dr) ≥ minsup do
2       rs = r + s // extend r by symbol s
3       F ← F ∪ {(rs, sup(s, Dr))}
4       Ds ← ∅ // create projected data for symbol s
5       foreach si ∈ Dr do
6           s′i ← projection of si w.r.t symbol s
7           Remove any infrequent symbols from s′i
8           Add s′i to Ds if s′i ≠ ∅
9       if Ds ≠ ∅ then PREFIXSPAN (Ds, rs, minsup, F)
```

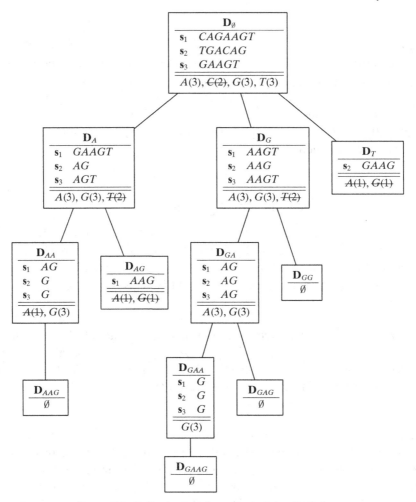

Figure 10.3. Projection-based sequence mining: PrefixSpan.

subsequence $\mathbf{r}_s$. Next, we create the projected dataset $\mathbf{D}_s$ by projecting $\mathbf{D_r}$ on symbol s. A recursive call to PrefixSpan is then made with $\mathbf{r}_s$ and $\mathbf{D}_s$.

Example 10.7. Figure 10.3 shows the projection-based PrefixSpan mining approach for the example dataset in Table 10.1 using *minsup* = 3. Initially we start with the whole database $\mathbf{D}$, which can also be denoted as $\mathbf{D}_\emptyset$. We compute the support of each symbol, and find that C is not frequent (shown crossed out). Among the frequent symbols, we first create a new projected dataset $\mathbf{D}_A$. For $\mathbf{s}_1$, we find that the first A occurs at position 2, so we retain only the suffix $GAAGT$. In $\mathbf{s}_2$, the first A occurs at position 3, so the suffix is CAG. After removing C (because it is infrequent), we are left with only AG as the projection of $\mathbf{s}_2$ on A. In a similar manner we obtain the projection for $\mathbf{s}_3$ as AGT. The left child of the root shows the final projected dataset $\mathbf{D}_A$. Now the mining proceeds recursively. Given $\mathbf{D}_A$, we count the symbol supports in $\mathbf{D}_A$, finding that only A and G are frequent, which will lead to the projection $\mathbf{D}_{AA}$ and then $\mathbf{D}_{AG}$, and so on. The complete projection-based approach is illustrated in Figure 10.3.

10.3 SUBSTRING MINING VIA SUFFIX TREES

We now look at efficient methods for mining frequent substrings. Let $\mathbf{s}$ be a sequence having length n, then there are at most $O(n^2)$ possible distinct substrings contained in $\mathbf{s}$. To see this consider substrings of length w, of which there are $n - w + 1$ possible ones in $\mathbf{s}$. Adding over all substring lengths we get

$$\sum_{w=1}^{n}(n - w + 1) = n + (n - 1) + \cdots + 2 + 1 = O(n^2)$$

This is a much smaller search space compared to subsequences, and consequently we can design more efficient algorithms for solving the frequent substring mining task. In fact, we can mine all the frequent substrings in worst case $O(Nn^2)$ time for a dataset $\mathbf{D} = \{\mathbf{s}_1, \mathbf{s}_2, \ldots, \mathbf{s}_N\}$ with N sequences.

10.3.1 Suffix Tree

Let Σ denote the alphabet, and let $\$ \notin \Sigma$ be a *terminal* character used to mark the end of a string. Given a sequence $\mathbf{s}$, we append the terminal character so that $\mathbf{s} = s_1 s_2 \ldots s_n s_{n+1}$, where $s_{n+1} = \$$, and the jth suffix of $\mathbf{s}$ is given as $\mathbf{s}[j : n + 1] = s_j s_{j+1} \ldots s_{n+1}$. The *suffix tree* of the sequences in the database $\mathbf{D}$, denoted $\mathcal{T}$, stores all the suffixes for each $\mathbf{s}_i \in \mathbf{D}$ in a tree structure, where suffixes that share a common prefix lie on the same path from the root of the tree. The substring obtained by concatenating all the symbols from the root node to a node v is called the *node label* of v, and is denoted as $L(v)$. The substring that appears on an edge (v_a, v_b) is called an *edge label*, and is denoted as $L(v_a, v_b)$. A suffix tree has two kinds of nodes: internal and leaf nodes. An internal node in the suffix tree (except for the root) has at least two children, where each edge label to a child begins with a different symbol. Because the terminal character is unique, there are as many leaves in the suffix tree as there are unique suffixes over all the sequences. Each leaf node corresponds to a suffix shared by one or more sequences in $\mathbf{D}$.

It is straightforward to obtain a quadratic time and space suffix tree construction algorithm. Initially, the suffix tree $\mathcal{T}$ is empty. Next, for each sequence $\mathbf{s}_i \in \mathbf{D}$, with $|\mathbf{s}_i| = n_i$, we generate all its suffixes $\mathbf{s}_i[j : n_i + 1]$, with $1 \le j \le n_i$, and insert each of them into the tree by following the path from the root until we either reach a leaf or there is a mismatch in one of the symbols along an edge. If we reach a leaf, we insert the pair (i, j) into the leaf, noting that this is the jth suffix of sequence $\mathbf{s}_i$. If there is a mismatch in one of the symbols, say at position $p \ge j$, we add an internal vertex just before the mismatch, and create a new leaf node containing (i, j) with edge label $\mathbf{s}_i[p : n_i + 1]$.

Example 10.8. Consider the database in Table 10.1 with three sequences. In particular, let us focus on $\mathbf{s}_1 = CAGAAGT$. Figure 10.4 shows what the suffix tree $\mathcal{T}$ looks like after inserting the jth suffix of $\mathbf{s}_1$ into $\mathcal{T}$. The first suffix is the entire sequence $\mathbf{s}_1$ appended with the terminal symbol; thus the suffix tree contains a single leaf containing $(1, 1)$ under the root (Figure 10.4(a)). The second suffix is $AGAAGT\$$, and Figure 10.4(b) shows the resulting suffix tree, which now has two leaves. The third suffix $GAAGT\$$ begins with G, which has not yet been observed,

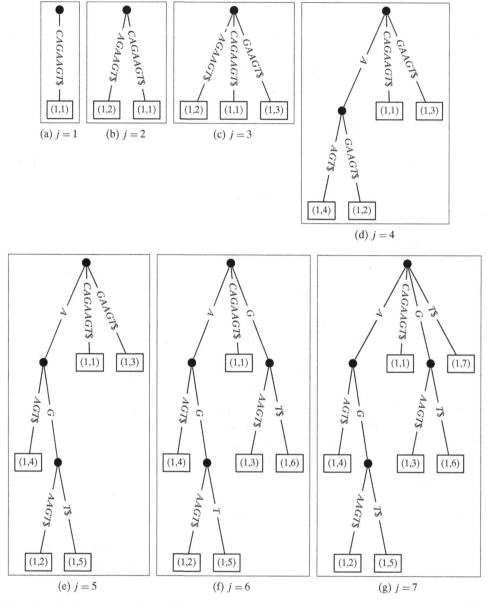

Figure 10.4. Suffix tree construction: (a)–(g) show the successive changes to the tree, after we add the jth suffix of $\mathbf{s}_1 = CAGAAGT\$$ for $j = 1, \ldots, 7$.

so it creates a new leaf in $\mathcal{T}$ under the root. The fourth suffix $AAGT\$$ shares the prefix A with the second suffix, so it follows the path beginning with A from the root. However, because there is a mismatch at position 2, we create an internal node right before it and insert the leaf $(1,4)$, as shown in Figure 10.4(d). The suffix tree obtained after inserting all of the suffixes of $\mathbf{s}_1$ is shown in Figure 10.4(g), and the complete suffix tree for all three sequences is shown in Figure 10.5.

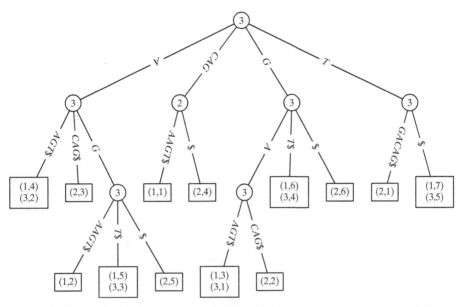

Figure 10.5. Suffix tree for all three sequences in Table 10.1. Internal nodes store support information. Leaves also record the support (not shown).

In terms of the time and space complexity, the algorithm sketched above requires $O(Nn^2)$ time and space, where N is the number of sequences in **D**, and n is the longest sequence length. The time complexity follows from the fact that the method always inserts a new suffix starting from the root of the suffix tree. This means that in the worst case it compares $O(n)$ symbols per suffix insertion, giving the worst case bound of $O(n^2)$ over all n suffixes. The space complexity comes from the fact that each suffix is explicitly represented in the tree, taking $n + (n-1) + \cdots + 1 = O(n^2)$ space. Over all the N sequences in the database, we obtain $O(Nn^2)$ as the worst case time and space bounds.

Frequent Substrings

Once the suffix tree is built, we can compute all the frequent substrings by checking how many different sequences appear in a leaf node or under an internal node. The node labels for the nodes with support at least *minsup* yield the set of frequent substrings; all the prefixes of such node labels are also frequent. The suffix tree can also support ad hoc queries for finding all the occurrences in the database for any query substring **q**. For each symbol in **q**, we follow the path from the root until all symbols in **q** have been seen, or until there is a mismatch at any position. If **q** is found, then the set of leaves under that path is the list of occurrences of the query **q**. On the other hand, if there is mismatch that means the query does not occur in the database. In terms of the query time complexity, because we have to match each character in **q**, we immediately get $O(|\mathbf{q}|)$ as the time bound (assuming that $|\Sigma|$ is a constant), which is *independent* of the size of the database. Listing all the matches takes additional time, for a total time complexity of $O(|\mathbf{q}| + k)$, if there are k matches.

Example 10.9. Consider the suffix tree shown in Figure 10.5, which stores all the suffixes for the sequence database in Table 10.1. To facilitate frequent substring enumeration, we store the support for each internal as well as leaf node, that is, we store the number of distinct sequence ids that occur at or under each node. For example, the leftmost child of the root node on the path labeled A has support 3 because there are three distinct sequences under that subtree. If $minsup = 3$, then the frequent substrings are A, AG, G, GA, and T. Out of these, the maximal ones are AG, GA, and T. If $minsup = 2$, then the maximal frequent substrings are $GAAGT$ and CAG.

For ad hoc querying consider $\mathbf{q} = GAA$. Searching for symbols in $\mathbf{q}$ starting from the root leads to the leaf node containing the occurrences $(1, 3)$ and $(3, 1)$, which means that GAA appears at position 3 in $\mathbf{s}_1$ and at position 1 in $\mathbf{s}_3$. On the other hand if $\mathbf{q} = CAA$, then the search terminates with a mismatch at position 3 after following the branch labeled CAG from the root. This means that $\mathbf{q}$ does not occur in the database.

10.3.2 Ukkonen's Linear Time Algorithm

We now present a linear time and space algorithm for constructing suffix trees. We first consider how to build the suffix tree for a single sequence $\mathbf{s} = s_1 s_2 \ldots s_n s_{n+1}$, with $s_{n+1} = \$$. The suffix tree for the entire dataset of N sequences can be obtained by inserting each sequence one by one.

Achieving Linear Space

Let us see how to reduce the space requirements of a suffix tree. If an algorithm stores all the symbols on each edge label, then the space complexity is $O(n^2)$, and we cannot achieve linear time construction either. The trick is to not explicitly store all the edge labels, but rather to use an *edge-compression* technique, where we store only the starting and ending positions of the edge label in the input string $\mathbf{s}$. That is, if an edge label is given as $\mathbf{s}[i : j]$, then we represent is as the interval $[i, j]$.

Example 10.10. Consider the suffix tree for $\mathbf{s}_1 = CAGAAGT\$$ shown in Figure 10.4(g). The edge label $CAGAAGT\$$ for the suffix $(1, 1)$ can be represented via the interval $[1, 8]$ because the edge label denotes the substring $\mathbf{s}_1[1 : 8]$. Likewise, the edge label $AAGT\$$ leading to suffix $(1, 2)$ can be compressed as $[4, 8]$ because $AAGT\$ = \mathbf{s}_1[4 : 8]$. The complete suffix tree for $\mathbf{s}_1$ with compressed edge labels is shown in Figure 10.6.

In terms of space complexity, note that when we add a new suffix to the tree $\mathcal{T}$, it can create at most one new internal node. As there are n suffixes, there are n leaves in $\mathcal{T}$ and at most n internal nodes. With at most $2n$ nodes, the tree has at most $2n - 1$ edges, and thus the total space required to store an interval for each edge is $2(2n - 1) = 4n - 2 = O(n)$.

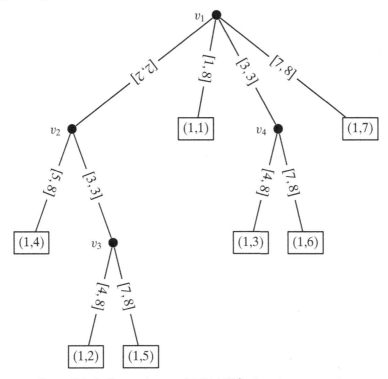

Figure 10.6. Suffix tree for $s_1 = CAGAAGT\$$ using edge-compression.

Achieving Linear Time

Ukkonen's method is an *online* algorithm, that is, given a string $\mathbf{s} = s_1 s_2 \ldots s_n\$$ it constructs the full suffix tree in phases. Phase i builds the tree up to the ith symbol in $\mathbf{s}$, that is, it updates the suffix tree from the previous phase by adding the next symbol s_i. Let $\mathcal{T}_i$ denote the suffix tree up to the ith prefix $\mathbf{s}[1:i]$, with $1 \leq i \leq n$. Ukkonen's algorithm constructs $\mathcal{T}_i$ from $\mathcal{T}_{i-1}$, by making sure that all suffixes including the *current* character s_i are in the new intermediate tree $\mathcal{T}_i$. In other words, in the ith phase, it inserts all the suffixes $\mathbf{s}[j:i]$ from $j = 1$ to $j = i$ into the tree $\mathcal{T}_i$. Each such insertion is called the jth *extension* of the ith *phase*. Once we process the terminal character at position $n + 1$ we obtain the final suffix tree $\mathcal{T}$ for $\mathbf{s}$.

Algorithm 10.4 shows the code for a naive implementation of Ukkonen's approach. This method has cubic time complexity because to obtain $\mathcal{T}_i$ from $\mathcal{T}_{i-1}$ takes $O(i^2)$ time, with the last phase requiring $O(n^2)$ time. With n phases, the total time is $O(n^3)$. Our goal is to show that this time can be reduced to just $O(n)$ via the optimizations described in the following paragraghs.

Implicit Suffixes   This optimization states that, in phase i, if the jth extension $\mathbf{s}[j:i]$ is found in the tree, then any subsequent extensions will also be found, and consequently there is no need to process further extensions in phase i. Thus, the suffix tree $\mathcal{T}_i$ at the end of phase i has *implicit suffixes* corresponding to extensions $j + 1$ through i. It is important to note that all suffixes will become explicit the first time we encounter a new substring that does not already exist in the tree. This will surely happen in phase $n + 1$ when we process the terminal character \$, as it cannot occur anywhere else in $\mathbf{s}$ (after all, $\$ \notin \Sigma$).

Algorithm 10.4: Algorithm NAIVEUKKONEN

NAIVEUKKONEN (s):

1 $n \leftarrow |\mathbf{s}|$
2 $\mathbf{s}[n+1] \leftarrow \$$ // append terminal character
3 $\mathcal{T} \leftarrow \emptyset$ // add empty string as root
4 **foreach** $i = 1, \dots, n+1$ **do** // phase i - construct $\mathcal{T}_i$
5   **foreach** $j = 1, \dots, i$ **do** // extension j for phase i
      // Insert $\mathbf{s}[j:i]$ into the suffix tree
6   Find end of the path with label $\mathbf{s}[j:i-1]$ in $\mathcal{T}$
7   Insert s_i at end of path;

8 **return** $\mathcal{T}$

Implicit Extensions Let the current phase be i, and let $l \le i - 1$ be the last explicit suffix in the previous tree $\mathcal{T}_{i-1}$. All explicit suffixes in $\mathcal{T}_{i-1}$ have edge labels of the form $[x, i-1]$ leading to the corresponding leaf nodes, where the starting position x is node specific, but the ending position must be $i - 1$ because s_{i-1} was added to the end of these paths in phase $i - 1$. In the current phase i, we would have to extend these paths by adding s_i at the end. However, instead of explicitly incrementing all the ending positions, we can replace the ending position by a pointer e which keeps track of the current phase being processed. If we replace $[x, i-1]$ with $[x, e]$, then in phase i, if we set $e = i$, then immediately all the l existing suffixes get *implicitly* extended to $[x, i]$. Thus, in one operation of incrementing e we have, in effect, taken care of extensions 1 through l for phase i.

Example 10.11. Let $\mathbf{s}_1 = CAGAAGT\$$. Assume that we have already performed the first six phases, which result in the tree $\mathcal{T}_6$ shown in Figure 10.7(a). The last explicit suffix in $\mathcal{T}_6$ is $l = 4$. In phase $i = 7$ we have to execute the following extensions:

$$\begin{array}{ll}
CAGAAGT & \text{extension 1} \\
AGAAGT & \text{extension 2} \\
GAAGT & \text{extension 3} \\
AAGT & \text{extension 4} \\
AGT & \text{extension 5} \\
GT & \text{extension 6} \\
T & \text{extension 7}
\end{array}$$

At the start of the seventh phase, we set $e = 7$, which yields implicit extensions for all suffixes explicitly in the tree, as shown in Figure 10.7(b). Notice how symbol $s_7 = T$ is now implicitly on each of the leaf edges, for example, the label $[5, e] = AG$ in $\mathcal{T}_6$ now becomes $[5, e] = AGT$ in $\mathcal{T}_7$. Thus, the first four extensions listed above are taken care of by simply incrementing e. To complete phase 7 we have to process the remaining extensions.

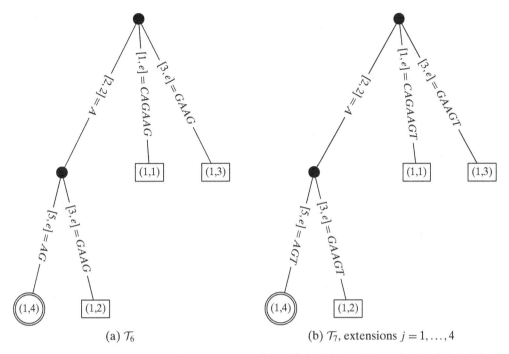

(a) $\mathcal{T}_6$ (b) $\mathcal{T}_7$, extensions $j = 1, \ldots, 4$

Figure 10.7. Implicit extensions in phase $i = 7$. Last explicit suffix in $\mathcal{T}_6$ is $l = 4$ (shown double-circled). Edge labels shown for convenience; only the intervals are stored.

Skip/Count Trick For the jth extension of phase i, we have to search for the substring $\mathbf{s}[j : i-1]$ so that we can add s_i at the end. However, note that this string must exist in $\mathcal{T}_{i-1}$ because we have already processed symbol s_{i-1} in the previous phase. Thus, instead of searching for each character in $\mathbf{s}[j : i-1]$ starting from the root, we first *count* the number of symbols on the edge beginning with character s_j; let this length be m. If m is longer than the length of the substring (i.e., if $m > i - j$), then the substring must end on this edge, so we simply jump to position $i - j$ and insert s_i. On the other hand, if $m \le i - j$, then we can *skip* directly to the child node, say v_c, and search for the remaining string $\mathbf{s}[j + m : i-1]$ from v_c using the same skip/count technique. With this optimization, the cost of an extension becomes proportional to the number of nodes on the path, as opposed to the number of characters in $\mathbf{s}[j : i-1]$.

Suffix Links We saw that with the skip/count optimization we can search for the substring $\mathbf{s}[j : i-1]$ by following nodes from parent to child. However, we still have to start from the root node each time. We can avoid searching from the root via the use of *suffix links*. For each internal node v_a we maintain a link to the internal node v_b, where $L(v_b)$ is the immediate suffix of $L(v_a)$. In extension $j-1$, let v_p denote the internal node under which we find $\mathbf{s}[j-1 : i]$, and let m be the length of the node label of v_p. To insert the jth extension $\mathbf{s}[j : i]$, we follow the suffix link from v_p to another node, say v_s, and search for the remaining substring $\mathbf{s}[j + m - 1 : i-1]$ from v_s. The use of suffix links allows us to jump internally within the tree for different extensions, as opposed to searching from the root each time. As a final observation, if extension j

---

Algorithm 10.5: Algorithm UKKONEN

UKKONEN (s):

1 $n \leftarrow |\mathbf{s}|$
2 $\mathbf{s}[n+1] \leftarrow \$$ // append terminal character
3 $\mathcal{T} \leftarrow \emptyset$ // add empty string as root
4 $l \leftarrow 0$ // last explicit suffix
5 **foreach** $i = 1, \ldots, n+1$ **do** // phase i - construct $\mathcal{T}_i$
6    $e \leftarrow i$ // implicit extensions
7   **foreach** $j = l+1, \ldots, i$ **do** // extension j for phase i
      // Insert $\mathbf{s}[j:i]$ into the suffix tree
8   Find end of $\mathbf{s}[j:i-1]$ in $\mathcal{T}$ via skip/count and suffix links
9   **if** $s_i \in \mathcal{T}$ **then** // implicit suffixes
10   **break**
11   **else**
12   Insert s_i at end of path
13   Set last explicit suffix l if needed

14 **return** $\mathcal{T}$

---

creates a new internal node, then its suffix link will point to the new internal node that will be created during extension $j+1$.

The pseudo-code for the optimized Ukkonen's algorithm is shown in Algorithm 10.5. It is important to note that it achieves linear time and space only with all of the optimizations in conjunction, namely implicit extensions (line 6), implicit suffixes (line 9), and skip/count and suffix links for inserting extensions in $\mathcal{T}$ (line 8).

Example 10.12. Let us look at the execution of Ukkonen's algorithm on the sequence $\mathbf{s}_1 = CAGAAGT\$$, as shown in Figure 10.8. In phase 1, we process character $s_1 = C$ and insert the suffix $(1, 1)$ into the tree with edge label $[1, e]$ (see Figure 10.8(a)). In phases 2 and 3, new suffixes $(1, 2)$ and $(1, 3)$ are added (see Figures 10.8(b)–10.8(c)). For phase 4, when we want to process $s_4 = A$, we note that all suffixes up to $l = 3$ are already explicit. Setting $e = 4$ implicitly extends all of them, so we have only to make sure that the last extension $(j = 4)$ consisting of the single character A is in the tree. Searching from the root, we find A in the tree implicitly, and we thus proceed to the next phase. In the next phase, we set $e = 5$, and the suffix $(1, 4)$ becomes explicit when we try to add the extension AA, which is not in the tree. For $e = 6$, we find the extension AG already in the tree and we skip ahead to the next phase. At this point the last explicit suffix is still $(1, 4)$. For $e = 7$, T is a previously unseen symbol, and so all suffixes will become explicit, as shown in Figure 10.8(g).

It is instructive to see the extensions in the last phase $(i = 7)$. As described in Example 10.11, the first four extensions will be done implicitly. Figure 10.9(a) shows the suffix tree after these four extensions. For extension 5, we begin at the last explicit

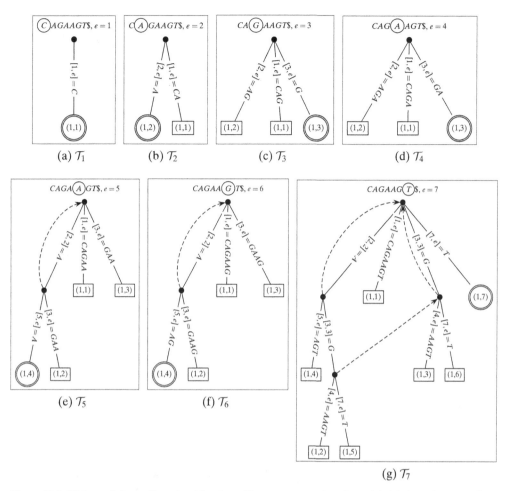

Figure 10.8. Ukkonen's linear time algorithm for suffix tree construction. Steps (a)–(g) show the successive changes to the tree after the ith phase. The suffix links are shown with dashed lines. The double-circled leaf denotes the last explicit suffix in the tree. The last step is not shown because when $e = 8$, the terminal character $ will not alter the tree. All the edge labels are shown for ease of understanding, although the actual suffix tree keeps only the intervals for each edge.

leaf, follow its parent's suffix link, and begin searching for the remaining characters from that point. In our example, the suffix link points to the root, so we search for $s[5:7] = AGT$ from the root. We skip to node v_A, and look for the remaining string GT, which has a mismatch inside the edge $[3, e]$. We thus create a new internal node after G, and insert the explicit suffix $(1, 5)$, as shown in Figure 10.9(b). The next extension $s[6:7] = GT$ begins at the newly created leaf node $(1, 5)$. Following the closest suffix link leads back to the root, and a search for GT gets a mismatch on the edge out of the root to leaf $(1, 3)$. We then create a new internal node v_G at that point, add a suffix link from the previous internal node v_{AG} to v_G, and add a new explicit leaf $(1, 6)$, as shown in Figure 10.9(c). The last extension, namely $j = 7$, corresponding to

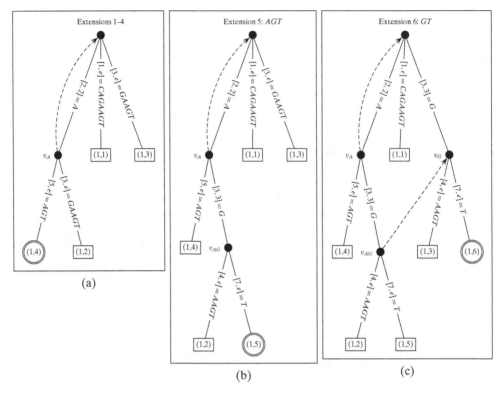

Figure 10.9. Extensions in phase $i = 7$. Initially the last explicit suffix is $l = 4$ and is shown double-circled. All the edge labels are shown for convenience; the actual suffix tree keeps only the intervals for each edge.

$\mathbf{s}[7:7] = T$, results in making all the suffixes explicit because the symbol T has been seen for the first time. The resulting tree is shown in Figure 10.8(g).

Once $\mathbf{s}_1$ has been processed, we can then insert the remaining sequences in the database $\mathbf{D}$ into the existing suffix tree. The final suffix tree for all three sequences is shown in Figure 10.5, with additional suffix links (not shown) from all the internal nodes.

Ukkonen's algorithm has time complexity of $O(n)$ for a sequence of length n because it does only a constant amount of work (amortized) to make each suffix explicit. Note that, for each phase, a certain number of extensions are done implicitly just by incrementing e. Out of the i extensions from $j = 1$ to $j = i$, let us say that l are done implicitly. For the remaining extensions, we stop the first time some suffix is implicitly in the tree; let that extension be k. Thus, phase i needs to add explicit suffixes only for suffixes $l + 1$ through $k - 1$. For creating each explicit suffix, we perform a constant number of operations, which include following the closest suffix link, skip/counting to look for the first mismatch, and inserting if needed a new suffix leaf node. Because each leaf becomes explicit only once, and the number of skip/count steps are bounded by $O(n)$ over the whole tree, we get a worst-case $O(n)$

time algorithm. The total time over the entire database of N sequences is thus $O(Nn)$, if n is the longest sequence length.

10.4 FURTHER READING

The level-wise GSP method for mining sequential patterns was proposed in Srikant and Agrawal (1996). Spade is described in Zaki (2001), and the PrefixSpan algorithm in Pei et al. (2004). Ukkonen's linear time suffix tree construction method appears in Ukkonen (1995). For an excellent introduction to suffix trees and their numerous applications see Gusfield (1997); the suffix tree description in this chapter has been heavily influenced by it.

Gusfield, D. (1997). *Algorithms on Strings, Trees and Sequences: Computer Science and Computational Biology*. New York: Cambridge University Press.

Pei, J., Han, J., Mortazavi-Asl, B., Wang, J., Pinto, H., Chen, Q., Dayal, U., and Hsu, M.-C. (2004). Mining sequential patterns by pattern-growth: The Prefixspan approach. *IEEE Transactions on Knowledge and Data Engineering*, 16 (11), 1424–1440.

Srikant, R. and Agrawal, R. (Mar. 1996). Mining sequential patterns: Generalizations and performance improvements. *Proceedings of the 5th International Conference on Extending Database Technology*. New York: Springer-Verlag, pp. 1–17.

Ukkonen, E. (1995). On-line construction of suffix trees. *Algorithmica*, 14 (3), 249–260.

Zaki, M. J. (2001). SPADE: An efficient algorithm for mining frequent sequences. *Machine Learning*, 42 (1-2), 31–60.

10.5 EXERCISES

Q1. Consider the database shown in Table 10.2. Answer the following questions:
   (a) Let *minsup* $= 4$. Find all frequent sequences.
   (b) Given that the alphabet is $\Sigma = \{A, C, G, T\}$. How many possible sequences of length k can there be?

Table 10.2. Sequence database for Q1

Id	Sequence
s_1	*AATACAAGAAC*
s_2	*GTATGGTGAT*
s_3	*AACATGGCCAA*
s_4	*AAGCGTGGTCAA*

Q2. Given the DNA sequence database in Table 10.3, answer the following questions using *minsup* $= 4$
   (a) Find the maximal frequent sequences.
   (b) Find all the closed frequent sequences.
   (c) Find the maximal frequent substrings.

(d) Show how Spade would work on this dataset.

(e) Show the steps of the PrefixSpan algorithm.

Table 10.3. Sequence database for Q2

Id	Sequence
s_1	$ACGTCACG$
s_2	$TCGA$
s_3	$GACTGCA$
s_4	$CAGTC$
s_5	$AGCT$
s_6	$TGCAGCTC$
s_7	$AGTCAG$

Q3. Given $\mathbf{s} = AABBACBBAA$, and $\Sigma = \{A, B, C\}$. Define support as the number of occurrence of a subsequence in $\mathbf{s}$. Using $minsup = 2$, answer the following questions:

(a) Show how the vertical Spade method can be extended to mine all frequent substrings (consecutive subsequences) in $\mathbf{s}$.

(b) Construct the suffix tree for $\mathbf{s}$ using Ukkonen's method. Show all intermediate steps, including all suffix links.

(c) Using the suffix tree from the previous step, find all the occurrences of the query $\mathbf{q} = ABBA$ allowing for at most two mismatches.

(d) Show the suffix tree when we add another character A just before the $. That is, you must undo the effect of adding the $, add the new symbol A, and then add $ back again.

(e) Describe an algorithm to extract all the maximal frequent substrings from a suffix tree. Show all maximal frequent substrings in $\mathbf{s}$.

Q4. Consider a bitvector based approach for mining frequent subsequences. For instance, in Table 10.2, for s_1, the symbol C occurs at positions 5 and 11. Thus, the bitvector for C in s_1 is given as 00001000001. Because C does not appear in s_2 its bitvector can be omitted for s_2. The complete set of bitvectors for symbol C is

$$(s_1, 00001000001)$$

$$(s_3, 00100001100)$$

$$(s_4, 000100000100)$$

Given the set of bitvectors for each symbol show how we can mine all frequent subsequences by using bit operations on the bitvectors. Show the frequent subsequences and their bitvectors using $minsup = 4$.

Q5. Consider the database shown in Table 10.4. Each sequence comprises itemset events that happen at the same time. For example, sequence s_1 can be considered to be a sequence of itemsets $(AB)_{10}(B)_{20}(AB)_{30}(AC)_{40}$, where symbols within brackets are considered to co-occur at the same time, which is given in the subscripts. Describe an algorithm that can mine all the frequent subsequences over itemset events. The

Table 10.4. Sequences for Q5

Id	Time	Items
s_1	10	A, B
	20	B
	30	A, B
	40	A, C
s_2	20	A, C
	30	A, B, C
	50	B
s_3	10	A
	30	B
	40	A
	50	C
	60	B
s_4	30	A, B
	40	A
	50	B
	60	C

itemsets can be of any length as long as they are frequent. Find all frequent itemset sequences with $minsup = 3$.

Q6. The suffix tree shown in Figure 10.5 contains all suffixes for the three sequences s_1, s_2, s_3 in Table 10.1. Note that a pair (i, j) in a leaf denotes the jth suffix of sequence s_i.

(a) Add a new sequence $s_4 = GAAGCAGAA$ to the existing suffix tree, using the Ukkonen algorithm. Show the last character position (e), along with the suffixes (l) as they become explicit in the tree for s_4. Show the final suffix tree after all suffixes of s_4 have become explicit.

(b) Find all closed frequent substrings with $minsup = 2$ using the final suffix tree.

Q7. Given the following three sequences:

$$s_1 : GAAGT$$

$$s_2 : CAGAT$$

$$s_3 : ACGT$$

Find all the frequent subsequences with $minsup = 2$, but allowing at most a gap of 1 position between successive sequence elements.

CHAPTER 11

Graph Pattern Mining

Graph data is becoming increasingly more ubiquitous in today's networked world. Examples include social networks as well as cell phone networks and blogs. The Internet is another example of graph data, as is the hyperlinked structure of the World Wide Web (WWW). Bioinformatics, especially systems biology, deals with understanding interaction networks between various types of biomolecules, such as protein–protein interactions, metabolic networks, gene networks, and so on. Another prominent source of graph data is the Semantic Web, and linked open data, with graphs represented using the Resource Description Framework (RDF) data model.

The goal of graph mining is to extract interesting subgraphs from a single large graph (e.g., a social network), or from a database of many graphs. In different applications we may be interested in different kinds of subgraph patterns, such as subtrees, complete graphs or cliques, bipartite cliques, dense subgraphs, and so on. These may represent, for example, communities in a social network, hub and authority pages on the WWW, cluster of proteins involved in similar biochemical functions, and so on. In this chapter we outline methods to mine all the frequent subgraphs that appear in a database of graphs.

11.1 ISOMORPHISM AND SUPPORT

A graph is a pair $G = (V, E)$ where V is a set of vertices, and $E \subseteq V \times V$ is a set of edges. We assume that edges are unordered, so that the graph is undirected. If (u, v) is an edge, we say that u and v are *adjacent* and that v is a *neighbor* of u, and vice versa. The set of all neighbors of u in G is given as $N(u) = \{v \in V \mid (u, v) \in E\}$. A *labeled graph* has labels associated with its vertices as well as edges. We use $L(u)$ to denote the label of the vertex u, and $L(u, v)$ to denote the label of the edge (u, v), with the set of vertex labels denoted as Σ_V and the set of edge labels as Σ_E. Given an edge $(u, v) \in G$, the tuple $\langle u, v, L(u), L(v), L(u, v) \rangle$ that augments the edge with the node and edge labels is called an *extended edge*.

Example 11.1. Figure 11.1(a) shows an example of an unlabeled graph, whereas Figure 11.1(b) shows the same graph, with labels on the vertices, taken from the

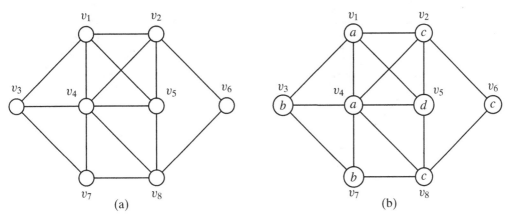

Figure 11.1. An unlabeled (a) and labeled (b) graph with eight vertices.

vertex label set $\Sigma_V = \{a, b, c, d\}$. In this example, edges are all assumed to be unlabeled, and are therefore edge labels are not shown. Considering Figure 11.1(b), the label of vertex v_4 is $L(v_4) = a$, and its neighbors are $N(v_4) = \{v_1, v_2, v_3, v_5, v_7, v_8\}$. The edge (v_4, v_1) leads to the extended edge $\langle v_4, v_1, a, a \rangle$, where we omit the edge label $L(v_4, v_1)$ because it is empty.

Subgraphs
A graph $G' = (V', E')$ is said to be a *subgraph* of G if $V' \subseteq V$ and $E' \subseteq E$. Note that this definition allows for disconnected subgraphs. However, typically data mining applications call for *connected subgraphs*, defined as a subgraph G' such that $V' \subseteq V$, $E' \subseteq E$, and for any two nodes $u, v \in V'$, there exists a *path* from u to v in G'.

Example 11.2. The graph defined by the bold edges in Figure 11.2(a) is a subgraph of the larger graph; it has vertex set $V' = \{v_1, v_2, v_4, v_5, v_6, v_8\}$. However, it is a disconnected subgraph. Figure 11.2(b) shows an example of a connected subgraph on the same vertex set V'.

Graph and Subgraph Isomorphism
A graph $G' = (V', E')$ is said to be *isomorphic* to another graph $G = (V, E)$ if there exists a bijective function $\phi : V' \to V$, i.e., both injective (into) and surjective (onto), such that

1. $(u, v) \in E' \iff (\phi(u), \phi(v)) \in E$

2. $\forall u \in V'$, $L(u) = L(\phi(u))$

3. $\forall (u, v) \in E'$, $L(u, v) = L(\phi(u), \phi(v))$

In other words, the *isomorphism* ϕ preserves the edge adjacencies as well as the vertex and edge labels. Put differently, the extended tuple $\langle u, v, L(u), L(v), L(u, v) \rangle \in G'$ if and only if $\langle \phi(u), \phi(v), L(\phi(u)), L(\phi(v)), L(\phi(u), \phi(v)) \rangle \in G$.

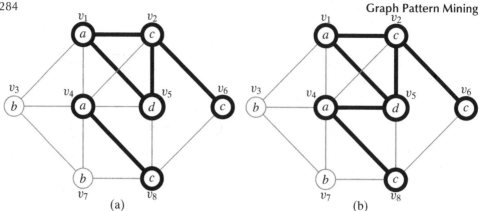

Figure 11.2. A subgraph (a) and connected subgraph (b).

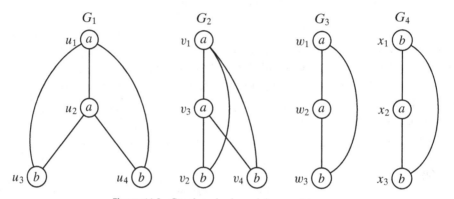

Figure 11.3. Graph and subgraph isomorphism.

If the function ϕ is only injective but not surjective, we say that the mapping ϕ is a *subgraph isomorphism* from G' to G. In this case, we say that G' is isomorphic to a subgraph of G, that is, G' is *subgraph isomorphic* to G, denoted $G' \subseteq G$; we also say that G *contains* G'.

Example 11.3. In Figure 11.3, $G_1 = (V_1, E_1)$ and $G_2 = (V_2, E_2)$ are isomorphic graphs. There are several possible isomorphisms between G_1 and G_2. An example of an isomorphism $\phi : V_2 \to V_1$ is

$$\phi(v_1) = u_1 \qquad \phi(v_2) = u_3 \qquad \phi(v_3) = u_2 \qquad \phi(v_4) = u_4$$

The inverse mapping ϕ^{-1} specifies the isomorphism from G_1 to G_2. For example, $\phi^{-1}(u_1) = v_1$, $\phi^{-1}(u_2) = v_3$, and so on. The set of all possible isomorphisms from G_2 to G_1 are as follows:

	v_1	v_2	v_3	v_4
ϕ_1	u_1	u_3	u_2	u_4
ϕ_2	u_1	u_4	u_2	u_3
ϕ_3	u_2	u_3	u_1	u_4
ϕ_4	u_2	u_4	u_1	u_3

The graph G_3 is subgraph isomorphic to both G_1 and G_2. The set of all possible subgraph isomorphisms from G_3 to G_1 are as follows:

	w_1	w_2	w_3
ϕ_1	u_1	u_2	u_3
ϕ_2	u_1	u_2	u_4
ϕ_3	u_2	u_1	u_3
ϕ_4	u_2	u_1	u_4

The graph G_4 is not subgraph isomorphic to either G_1 or G_2, and it is also not isomorphic to G_3 because the extended edge $\langle x_1, x_3, b, b \rangle$ has no possible mappings in G_1, G_2 or G_3.

Subgraph Support

Given a database of graphs, $\mathbf{D} = \{G_1, G_2, \ldots, G_n\}$, and given some graph G, the support of G in $\mathbf{D}$ is defined as follows:

$$sup(G) = \left| \{ G_i \in \mathbf{D} \mid G \subseteq G_i \} \right| \qquad (11.1)$$

The support is simply the number of graphs in the database that contain G. Given a *minsup* threshold, the goal of graph mining is to mine all frequent connected subgraphs with $sup(G) \geq minsup$.

To mine all the frequent subgraphs, one has to search over the space of all possible graph patterns, which is exponential in size. If we consider subgraphs with m vertices, then there are $\binom{m}{2} = O(m^2)$ possible edges. The number of possible subgraphs with m nodes is then $O(2^{m^2})$ because we may decide either to include or exclude each of the edges. Many of these subgraphs will not be connected, but $O(2^{m^2})$ is a convenient upper bound. When we add labels to the vertices and edges, the number of labeled graphs will be even more. Assume that $|\Sigma_V| = |\Sigma_E| = s$, then there are s^m possible ways to label the vertices and there are s^{m^2} ways to label the edges. Thus, the number of possible labeled subgraphs with m vertices is $2^{m^2} s^m s^{m^2} = O\big((2s)^{m^2}\big)$. This is the worst case bound, as many of these subgraphs will be isomorphic to each other, with the number of distinct subgraphs being much less. Nevertheless, the search space is still enormous because we typically have to search for all subgraphs ranging from a single vertex to some maximum number of vertices given by the largest frequent subgraph.

There are two main challenges in frequent subgraph mining. The first is to systematically generate candidate subgraphs. We use *edge-growth* as the basic mechanism for extending the candidates. The mining process proceeds in a breadth-first (level-wise) or a depth-first manner, starting with an empty subgraph (i.e., with no edge), and adding a new edge each time. Such an edge may either connect two existing vertices in the graph or it may introduce a new vertex as one end of a new edge. The key is to perform nonredundant subgraph enumeration, such that we do not generate the same graph candidate more than once. This means that we have to perform graph isomorphism checking to make sure that duplicate graphs are removed. The second challenge is to count the support of a graph in the database. This involves subgraph isomorphism checking, as we have to find the set of graphs that contain a given candidate.

11.2 CANDIDATE GENERATION

An effective strategy to enumerate subgraph patterns is the so-called *rightmost path extension*. Given a graph G, we perform a depth-first search (DFS) over its vertices, and create a DFS spanning tree, that is, one that covers or spans all the vertices. Edges that are included in the DFS tree are called *forward* edges, and all other edges are called *backward* edges. Backward edges create cycles in the graph. Once we have a DFS tree, define the *rightmost* path as the path from the root to the rightmost leaf, that is, to the leaf with the highest index in the DFS order.

Example 11.4. Consider the graph shown in Figure 11.4(a). One of the possible DFS spanning trees is shown in Figure 11.4(b) (illustrated via bold edges), obtained by starting at v_1 and then choosing the vertex with the smallest index at each step. Figure 11.5 shows the same graph (ignoring the dashed edges), rearranged to emphasize the DFS tree structure. For instance, the edges (v_1, v_2) and (v_2, v_3) are examples of forward edges, whereas (v_3, v_1), (v_4, v_1), and (v_6, v_1) are all backward edges. The bold edges (v_1, v_5), (v_5, v_7) and (v_7, v_8) comprise the rightmost path.

For generating new candidates from a given graph G, we extend it by adding a new edge to vertices only on the rightmost path. We can either extend G by adding backward edges from the *rightmost vertex* to some other vertex on the rightmost path (disallowing self-loops or multi-edges), or we can extend G by adding forward edges from any of the vertices on the rightmost path. A backward extension does not add a new vertex, whereas a forward extension adds a new vertex.

For systematic candidate generation we impose a total order on the extensions, as follows: First, we try all backward extensions from the rightmost vertex, and then we try forward extensions from vertices on the rightmost path. Among the backward edge extensions, if u_r is the rightmost vertex, the extension (u_r, v_i) is tried before (u_r, v_j) if $i < j$. In other words, backward extensions closer to the root are considered before those farther away from the root along the rightmost path. Among the forward edge

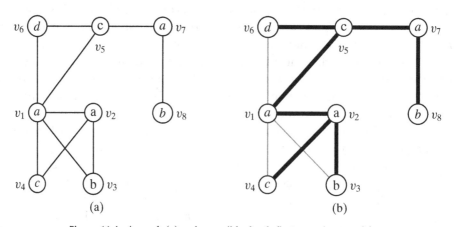

Figure 11.4. A graph (a) and a possible depth-first spanning tree (b).

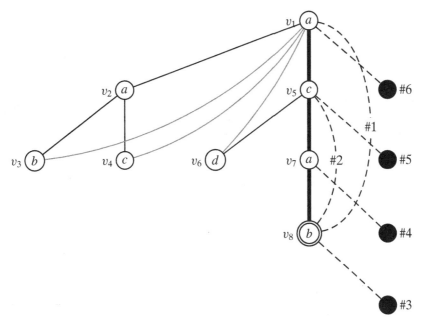

Figure 11.5. Rightmost path extensions. The bold path is the rightmost path in the DFS tree. The *rightmost vertex* is v_8, shown double circled. Solid black lines (thin and bold) indicate the *forward* edges, which are part of the DFS tree. The *backward* edges, which by definition are not part of the DFS tree, are shown in gray. The set of possible extensions on the rightmost path are shown with dashed lines. The precedence ordering of the extensions is also shown.

extensions, if v_x is the new vertex to be added, the extension (v_i, v_x) is tried before (v_j, v_x) if $i > j$. In other words, the vertices farther from the root (those at greater depth) are extended before those closer to the root. Also note that the new vertex will be numbered $x = r + 1$, as it will become the new rightmost vertex after the extension.

Example 11.5. Consider the order of extensions shown in Figure 11.5. Node v_8 is the rightmost vertex; thus we try backward extensions only from v_8. The first extension, denoted #1 in Figure 11.5, is the backward edge (v_8, v_1) connecting v_8 to the root, and the next extension is (v_8, v_5), denoted #2, which is also backward. No other backward extensions are possible without introducing multiple edges between the same pair of vertices. The forward extensions are tried in reverse order, starting from the rightmost vertex v_8 (extension denoted as #3) and ending at the root (extension denoted as #6). Thus, the forward extension (v_8, v_x), denoted #3, comes before the forward extension (v_7, v_x), denoted #4, and so on.

11.2.1 Canonical Code

When generating candidates using rightmost path extensions, it is possible that duplicate, that is, isomorphic, graphs are generated via different extensions. Among the isomorphic candidates, we need to keep only one for further extension, whereas the others can be pruned to avoid redundant computation. The main idea is that if we can somehow sort or rank the isomorphic graphs, we can pick the *canonical representative*, say the one with the least rank, and extend only that graph.

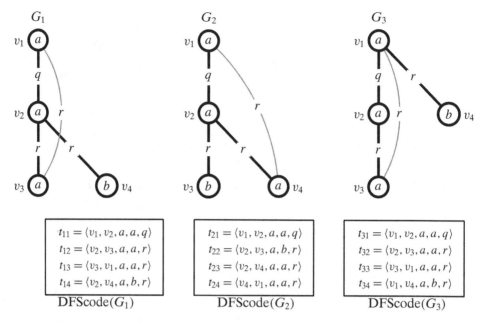

Figure 11.6. Canonical DFS code. G_1 is canonical, whereas G_2 and G_3 are noncanonical. Vertex label set $\Sigma_V = \{a, b\}$, and edge label set $\Sigma_E = \{q, r\}$. The vertices are numbered in DFS order.

Let G be a graph and let T_G be a DFS spanning tree for G. The DFS tree T_G defines an ordering of both the nodes and edges in G. The DFS node ordering is obtained by numbering the nodes consecutively in the order they are visited in the DFS walk. We assume henceforth that for a pattern graph G the nodes are numbered according to their position in the DFS ordering, so that $i < j$ implies that v_i comes before v_j in the DFS walk. The DFS edge ordering is obtained by following the edges between consecutive nodes in DFS order, with the condition that all the backward edges incident with vertex v_i are listed before any of the forward edges incident with it. The *DFS code* for a graph G, for a given DFS tree T_G, denoted DFScode(G), is defined as the sequence of extended edge tuples of the form $\langle v_i, v_j, L(v_i), L(v_j), L(v_i, v_j) \rangle$ listed in the DFS edge order.

Example 11.6. Figure 11.6 shows the DFS codes for three graphs, which are all isomorphic to each other. The graphs have node and edge labels drawn from the label sets $\Sigma_V = \{a, b\}$ and $\Sigma_E = \{q, r\}$. The edge labels are shown centered on the edges. The bold edges comprise the DFS tree for each graph. For G_1, the DFS node ordering is v_1, v_2, v_3, v_4, whereas the DFS edge ordering is $(v_1, v_2), (v_2, v_3), (v_3, v_1)$, and (v_2, v_4). Based on the DFS edge ordering, the first tuple in the DFS code for G_1 is therefore $\langle v_1, v_2, a, a, q \rangle$. The next tuple is $\langle v_2, v_3, a, a, r \rangle$ and so on. The DFS code for each graph is shown in the corresponding box below the graph.

Canonical DFS Code

A subgraph is *canonical* if it has the smallest DFS code among all possible isomorphic graphs, with the ordering between codes defined as follows. Let t_1 and t_2 be any two

DFS code tuples:

$$t_1 = \langle v_i, v_j, L(v_i), L(v_j), L(v_i, v_j) \rangle$$
$$t_2 = \langle v_x, v_y, L(v_x), L(v_y), L(v_x, v_y) \rangle$$

We say that t_1 is smaller than t_2, written $t_1 < t_2$, iff

    i) $(v_i, v_j) <_e (v_x, v_y)$, or

    ii) $(v_i, v_j) = (v_x, v_y)$ and   (11.2)

        $\langle L(v_i), L(v_j), L(v_i, v_j) \rangle <_l \langle L(v_x), L(v_y), L(v_x, v_y) \rangle$

where $<_e$ is an ordering on the edges and $<_l$ is an ordering on the vertex and edge labels. The *label order* $<_l$ is the standard lexicographic order on the vertex and edge labels. The *edge order* $<_e$ is derived from the rules for rightmost path extension, namely that all of a node's backward extensions must be considered before any forward edge from that node, and deep DFS trees are preferred over bushy DFS trees. Formally, Let $e_{ij} = (v_i, v_j)$ and $e_{xy} = (v_x, v_y)$ be any two edges. We say that $e_{ij} <_e e_{xy}$ iff

Condition (1) If e_{ij} and e_{xy} are both forward edges, then (a) $j < y$, or (b) $j = y$ and $i > x$. That is, (a) a forward extension to a node earlier in the DFS node order is smaller, or (b) if both the forward edges point to a node with the same DFS node order, then the forward extension from a node deeper in the tree is smaller.

Condition (2) If e_{ij} and e_{xy} are both backward edges, then (a) $i < x$, or (b) $i = x$ and $j < y$. That is, (a) a backward edge from a node earlier in the DFS node order is smaller, or (b) if both the backward edges originate from a node with the same DFS node order, then the backward edge to a node earlier in DFS node order (i.e., closer to the root along the rightmost path) is smaller.

Condition (3) If e_{ij} is a forward and e_{xy} is a backward edge, then $j \le x$. That is, a forward edge to a node earlier in the DFS node order is smaller than a backward edge from that node or any node that comes after it in DFS node order.

Condition (4) If e_{ij} is a backward and e_{xy} is a forward edge, then $i < y$. That is, a backward edge from a node earlier in DFS node order is smaller than a forward edge to any later node.

Given any two DFS codes, we can compare them tuple by tuple to check which is smaller. In particular, the *canonical DFS code* for a graph G is defined as follows:

$$C = \min_{G'} \left\{ \text{DFScode}(G') \mid G' \text{ is isomorphic to } G \right\}$$

Given a candidate subgraph G, we can first determine whether its DFS code is canonical or not. Only canonical graphs need to be retained for extension, whereas noncanonical candidates can be removed from further consideration.

Example 11.7. Consider the DFS codes for the three graphs shown in Figure 11.6. Comparing G_1 and G_2, we find that $t_{11} = t_{21}$, but $t_{12} < t_{22}$ because $\langle a, a, r \rangle <_l \langle a, b, r \rangle$. Comparing the codes for G_1 and G_3, we find that the first three tuples are equal for both the graphs, but $t_{14} < t_{34}$ because

$$(v_i, v_j) = (v_2, v_4) <_e (v_1, v_4) = (v_x, v_y)$$

due to condition (1) above. That is, both are forward edges, and we have $v_j = v_4 = v_y$ with $v_i = v_2 > v_1 = v_x$. In fact, it can be shown that the code for G_1 is the canonical DFS code for all graphs isomorphic to G_1. Thus, G_1 is the canonical candidate.

11.3 THE GSPAN ALGORITHM

We describe the gSpan algorithm to mine all frequent subgraphs from a database of graphs. Given a database $\mathbf{D} = \{G_1, G_2, \ldots, G_n\}$ comprising n graphs, and given a minimum support threshold *minsup*, the goal is to enumerate all (connected) subgraphs G that are frequent, that is, $sup(G) \geq minsup$. In gSpan, each graph is represented by its canonical DFS code, so that the task of enumerating frequent subgraphs is equivalent to the task of generating all canonical DFS codes for frequent subgraphs. Algorithm 11.1 shows the pseudo-code for gSpan.

gSpan enumerates patterns in a depth-first manner, starting with the empty code. Given a canonical and frequent code C, gSpan first determines the set of possible edge extensions along the rightmost path (line 1). The function RIGHTMOSTPATH-EXTENSIONS returns the set of edge extensions along with their support values, $\mathcal{E}$. Each extended edge t in $\mathcal{E}$ leads to a new candidate DFS code $C' = C \cup \{t\}$, with support $sup(C') = sup(t)$ (lines 3–4). For each new candidate code, gSpan checks whether it is frequent and canonical, and if so gSpan recursively extends C' (lines 5–6). The algorithm stops when there are no more frequent and canonical extensions possible.

Algorithm 11.1: Algorithm GSPAN

    // Initial Call: $C \leftarrow \emptyset$
    GSPAN $(C, \mathbf{D}, minsup)$:
1 $\mathcal{E} \leftarrow$ RIGHTMOSTPATH-EXTENSIONS$(C, \mathbf{D})$ // extensions and
      supports
2 **foreach** $(t, sup(t)) \in \mathcal{E}$ **do**
3 | $C' \leftarrow C \cup t$ // extend the code with extended edge tuple t
4 | $sup(C') \leftarrow sup(t)$ // record the support of new extension
     | // recursively call GSPAN if code is frequent and
     | canonical
5 | **if** $sup(C') \geq minsup$ **and** ISCANONICAL (C') **then**
6 | | GSPAN $(C', \mathbf{D}, minsup)$

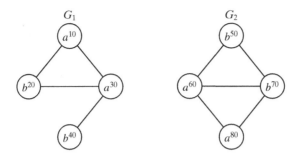

Figure 11.7. Example graph database.

Example 11.8. Consider the example graph database comprising G_1 and G_2 shown in Figure 11.7. Let $minsup = 2$, that is, assume that we are interested in mining subgraphs that appear in both the graphs in the database. For each graph the node labels and node numbers are both shown, for example, the node a^{10} in G_1 means that node 10 has label a.

Figure 11.8 shows the candidate patterns enumerated by gSpan. For each candidate the nodes are numbered in the DFS tree order. The solid boxes show frequent subgraphs, whereas the dotted boxes show the infrequent ones. The dashed boxes represent noncanonical codes. Subgraphs that do not occur even once are not shown. The figure also shows the DFS codes and their corresponding graphs.

The mining process begins with the empty DFS code C_0 corresponding to the empty subgraph. The set of possible 1-edge extensions comprises the new set of candidates. Among these, C_3 is pruned because it is not canonical (it is isomorphic to C_2), whereas C_4 is pruned because it is not frequent. The remaining two candidates, C_1 and C_2, are both frequent and canonical, and are thus considered for further extension. The depth-first search considers C_1 before C_2, with the rightmost path extensions of C_1 being C_5 and C_6. However, C_6 is not canonical; it is isomorphic to C_5, which has the canonical DFS code. Further extensions of C_5 are processed recursively. Once the recursion from C_1 completes, gSpan moves on to C_2, which will be recursively extended via rightmost edge extensions as illustrated by the subtree under C_2. After processing C_2, gSpan terminates because no other frequent and canonical extensions are found. In this example, C_{12} is a maximal frequent subgraph, that is, no supergraph of C_{12} is frequent.

This example also shows the importance of duplicate elimination via canonical checking. The groups of isomorphic subgraphs encountered during the execution of gSpan are as follows: $\{C_2, C_3\}$, $\{C_5, C_6, C_{17}\}$, $\{C_7, C_{19}\}$, $\{C_9, C_{25}\}$, $\{C_{20}, C_{21}, C_{22}, C_{24}\}$, and $\{C_{12}, C_{13}, C_{14}\}$. Within each group the first graph is canonical and thus the remaining codes are pruned.

For a complete description of gSpan we have to specify the algorithm for enumerating the rightmost path extensions and their support, so that infrequent patterns can be eliminated, and the procedure for checking whether a given DFS code is canonical, so that duplicate patterns can be pruned. These are detailed next.

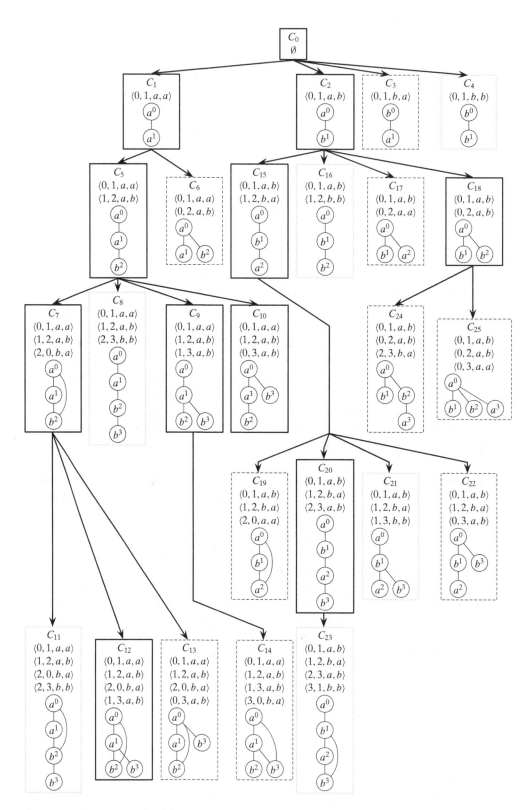

Figure 11.8. Frequent graph mining: *minsup* = 2. Solid boxes indicate the frequent subgraphs, dotted the infrequent, and dashed the noncanonical subgraphs.

Algorithm 11.2: Rightmost Path Extensions and Their Support

RIGHTMOSTPATH-EXTENSIONS $(C, \mathbf{D})$:

1 $R \leftarrow$ nodes on the rightmost path in C
2 $u_r \leftarrow$ rightmost child in C // dfs number
3 $\mathcal{E} \leftarrow \emptyset$ // set of extensions from C
4 **foreach** $G_i \in \mathbf{D}$, $i = 1, \ldots, n$ **do**
5 $\quad$ **if** $C = \emptyset$ **then**
$\quad\quad$ // add distinct label tuples in G_i as forward
$\quad\quad$ extensions
6 $\quad\quad$ **foreach** *distinct* $\langle L(x), L(y), L(x, y) \rangle \in G_i$ **do**
7 $\quad\quad\quad$ $f = \langle 0, 1, L(x), L(y), L(x, y) \rangle$
8 $\quad\quad\quad$ Add tuple f to $\mathcal{E}$ along with graph id i
9 $\quad$ **else**
10 $\quad\quad$ $\Phi_i = \text{SUBGRAPHISOMORPHISMS}(C, G_i)$
11 $\quad\quad$ **foreach** *isomorphism* $\phi \in \Phi_i$ **do**
$\quad\quad\quad$ // backward extensions from rightmost child
12 $\quad\quad\quad$ **foreach** $x \in N_{G_i}(\phi(u_r))$ *such that* $\exists v \leftarrow \phi^{-1}(x)$ **do**
13 $\quad\quad\quad\quad$ **if** $v \in R$ *and* $(u_r, v) \notin G(C)$ **then**
14 $\quad\quad\quad\quad\quad$ $b = \langle u_r, v, L(\phi(u_r)), L(\phi(v)), L(\phi(u_r), \phi(v)) \rangle$
15 $\quad\quad\quad\quad\quad$ Add tuple b to $\mathcal{E}$ along with graph id i

$\quad\quad\quad$ // forward extensions from nodes on rightmost path
16 $\quad\quad\quad$ **foreach** $u \in R$ **do**
17 $\quad\quad\quad\quad$ **foreach** $x \in N_{G_i}(\phi(u))$ *and* $\nexists \phi^{-1}(x)$ **do**
18 $\quad\quad\quad\quad\quad$ $f = \langle u, u_r + 1, L(\phi(u)), L(x), L(\phi(u), x) \rangle$
19 $\quad\quad\quad\quad\quad$ Add tuple f to $\mathcal{E}$ along with graph id i

// Compute the support of each extension
20 **foreach** *distinct extension* $s \in \mathcal{E}$ **do**
21 $\quad$ $sup(s) =$ number of distinct graph ids that support tuple s

22 **return** *set of pairs* $\langle s, sup(s) \rangle$ *for extensions* $s \in \mathcal{E}$, *in tuple sorted order*

11.3.1 Extension and Support Computation

The support computation task is to find the number of graphs in the database $\mathbf{D}$ that contain a candidate subgraph, which is very expensive because it involves subgraph isomorphism checks. gSpan combines the tasks of enumerating candidate extensions and support computation.

Assume that $\mathbf{D} = \{G_1, G_2, \ldots, G_n\}$ comprises n graphs. Let $C = \{t_1, t_2, \ldots, t_k\}$ denote a frequent canonical DFS code comprising k edges, and let $G(C)$ denote the graph corresponding to code C. The task is to compute the set of possible rightmost path extensions from C, along with their support values, which is accomplished via the pseudo-code in Algorithm 11.2.

Given code C, gSpan first records the nodes on the rightmost path (R), and the rightmost child (u_r). Next, gSpan considers each graph $G_i \in \mathbf{D}$. If $C = \emptyset$, then each distinct label tuple of the form $\langle L(x), L(y), L(x, y) \rangle$ for adjacent nodes x and y in G_i contributes a forward extension $\langle 0, 1, L(x), L(y), L(x, y) \rangle$ (lines 6-8). On the other hand, if C is not empty, then gSpan enumerates all possible subgraph isomorphisms Φ_i between the code C and graph G_i via the function SUBGRAPHISOMORPHISMS (line 10). Given subgraph isomorphism $\phi \in \Phi_i$, gSpan finds all possible forward and backward edge extensions, and stores them in the extension set $\mathcal{E}$.

Backward extensions (lines 12–15) are allowed only from the rightmost child u_r in C to some other node on the rightmost path R. The method considers each neighbor x of $\phi(u_r)$ in G_i and checks whether it is a mapping for some vertex $v = \phi^{-1}(x)$ along the rightmost path R in C. If the edge (u_r, v) does not already exist in C, it is a new extension, and the extended tuple $b = \langle u_r, v, L(u_r), L(v), L(u_r, v) \rangle$ is added to the set of extensions $\mathcal{E}$, along with the graph id i that contributed to that extension.

Forward extensions (lines 16–19) are allowed only from nodes on the rightmost path R to new nodes. For each node u in R, the algorithm finds a neighbor x in G_i that is not in a mapping from some node in C. For each such node x, the forward extension $f = \langle u, u_r + 1, L(\phi(u)), L(x), L(\phi(u), x) \rangle$ is added to $\mathcal{E}$, along with the graph id i. Because a forward extension adds a new vertex to the graph $G(C)$, the id of the new node in C must be $u_r + 1$, that is, one more than the highest numbered node in C, which by definition is the rightmost child u_r.

Once all the backward and forward extensions have been cataloged over all graphs G_i in the database $\mathbf{D}$, we compute their support by counting the number of distinct graph ids that contribute to each extension. Finally, the method returns the set of all extensions and their supports in sorted order (increasing) based on the tuple comparison operator in Eq. (11.2).

Example 11.9. Consider the canonical code C and the corresponding graph $G(C)$ shown in Figure 11.9(a). For this code all the vertices are on the rightmost path, that is, $R = \{0, 1, 2\}$, and the rightmost child is $u_r = 2$.

The sets of all possible isomorphisms from C to graphs G_1 and G_2 in the database (shown in Figure 11.7) are listed in Figure 11.9(b) as Φ_1 and Φ_2. For example, the first isomorphism $\phi_1 : G(C) \rightarrow G_1$ is defined as

$$\phi_1(0) = 10 \qquad\qquad \phi_1(1) = 30 \qquad\qquad \phi_1(2) = 20$$

The list of possible backward and forward extensions for each isomorphism is shown in Figure 11.9(c). For example, there are two possible edge extensions from the isomorphism ϕ_1. The first is a backward edge extension $\langle 2, 0, b, a \rangle$, as $(20, 10)$ is a valid backward edge in G_1. That is, the node $x = 10$ is a neighbor of $\phi(2) = 20$ in G_1, $\phi^{-1}(10) = 0 = v$ is on the rightmost path, and the edge $(2, 0)$ is not already in $G(C)$, which satisfy the backward extension steps in lines 12–15 in Algorithm 11.2. The second extension is a forward one $\langle 1, 3, a, b \rangle$, as $\langle 30, 40, a, b \rangle$ is a valid extended edge in G_1. That is, $x = 40$ is a neighbor of $\phi(1) = 30$ in G_1, and node 40 has not already been mapped by any node in $G(C)$, that is, $\phi_1^{-1}(40)$ does not exist. These conditions satisfy the forward extension steps in lines 16–19 in Algorithm 11.2.

C

| $t_1 : \langle 0, 1, a, a \rangle$ |
| $t_2 : \langle 1, 2, a, b \rangle$ |

$G(C)$

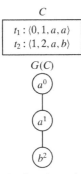

(a) Code C and graph $G(C)$

Φ	ϕ	0	1	2
	ϕ_1	10	30	20
Φ_1	ϕ_2	10	30	40
	ϕ_3	30	10	20
	ϕ_4	60	80	70
Φ_2	ϕ_5	80	60	50
	ϕ_6	80	60	70

(b) Subgraph isomorphisms

Id	ϕ	Extensions
	ϕ_1	$\{\langle 2, 0, b, a \rangle, \langle 1, 3, a, b \rangle\}$
G_1	ϕ_2	$\{\langle 1, 3, a, b \rangle, \langle 0, 3, a, b \rangle\}$
	ϕ_3	$\{\langle 2, 0, b, a \rangle, \langle 0, 3, a, b \rangle\}$
	ϕ_4	$\{\langle 2, 0, b, a \rangle, \langle 2, 3, b, b \rangle, \langle 0, 3, a, b \rangle\}$
G_2	ϕ_5	$\{\langle 2, 3, b, b \rangle, \langle 1, 3, a, b \rangle, \langle 0, 3, a, b \rangle\}$
	ϕ_6	$\{\langle 2, 0, b, a \rangle, \langle 2, 3, b, b \rangle, \langle 1, 3, a, b \rangle\}$

(c) Edge extensions

Extension	Support
$\langle 2, 0, b, a \rangle$	2
$\langle 2, 3, b, b \rangle$	1
$\langle 1, 3, a, b \rangle$	2
$\langle 0, 3, a, b \rangle$	2

(d) Extensions (sorted) and supports

Figure 11.9. Rightmost path extensions.

Given the set of all the edge extensions, and the graph ids that contribute to them, we obtain support for each extension by counting how many graphs contribute to it. The final set of extensions, in sorted order, along with their support values is shown in Figure 11.9(d). With *minsup* $= 2$, the only infrequent extension is $\langle 2, 3, b, b \rangle$.

Subgraph Isomorphisms

The key step in listing the edge extensions for a given code C is to enumerate all the possible isomorphisms from C to each graph $G_i \in \mathbf{D}$. The function SUBGRAPHI-SOMORPHISMS, shown in Algorithm 11.3, accepts a code C and a graph G, and returns the set of all isomorphisms between C and G. The set of isomorphisms Φ is initialized by mapping vertex 0 in C to each vertex x in G that shares the same label as 0, that is, if $L(x) = L(0)$ (line 1). The method considers each tuple t_i in C and extends the current set of partial isomorphisms. Let $t_i = \langle u, v, L(u), L(v), L(u, v) \rangle$. We have to check if each isomorphism $\phi \in \Phi$ can be extended in G using the information from t_i (lines 5–12). If t_i is a forward edge, then we seek a neighbor x of $\phi(u)$ in G such that x has not already been mapped by some vertex in C, that is, $\phi^{-1}(x)$ should not exist, and the node and edge labels should match, that is, $L(x) = L(v)$, and $L(\phi(u), x) = L(u, v)$. If so, ϕ can be extended with the mapping $\phi(v) \to x$. The new extended isomorphism, denoted ϕ', is added to the initially empty set of isomorphisms Φ'. If t_i is a backward edge, we have to check if $\phi(v)$ is a neighbor of $\phi(u)$ in G. If so, we add the current isomorphism ϕ to Φ'. Thus,

---

Algorithm 11.3: Enumerate Subgraph Isomorphisms

SUBGRAPHISOMORPHISMS $(C = \{t_1, t_2, \ldots, t_k\}, G)$:

1   $\Phi \leftarrow \{\phi(0) \rightarrow x \mid x \in G \text{ and } L(x) = L(0)\}$

2   **foreach** $t_i \in C, i = 1, \ldots, k$ **do**

3      $\langle u, v, L(u), L(v), L(u, v) \rangle \leftarrow t_i$ // expand extended edge t_i

4      $\Phi' \leftarrow \emptyset$ // partial isomorphisms including t_i

5   **foreach** *partial isomorphism* $\phi \in \Phi$ **do**

6   **if** $v > u$ **then**

            // forward edge

7   **foreach** $x \in N_G(\phi(u))$ **do**

8   **if** $\nexists \phi^{-1}(x)$ *and* $L(x) = L(v)$ *and* $L(\phi(u), x) = L(u, v)$ **then**

9                 $\phi' \leftarrow \phi \cup \{\phi(v) \rightarrow x\}$

10   Add ϕ' to Φ'

11   **else**

            // backward edge

12   **if** $\phi(v) \in N_G(\phi(u))$ **then** Add ϕ to Φ' // valid isomorphism

13      $\Phi \leftarrow \Phi'$ // update partial isomorphisms

14 **return** Φ

---

only those isomorphisms that can be extended in the forward case, or those that satisfy the backward edge, are retained for further checking. Once all the extended edges in C have been processed, the set Φ contains all the valid isomorphisms from C to G.

Example 11.10. Figure 11.10 illustrates the subgraph isomorphism enumeration algorithm from the code C to each of the graphs G_1 and G_2 in the database shown in Figure 11.7.

For G_1, the set of isomorphisms Φ is initialized by mapping the first node of C to all nodes labeled a in G_1 because $L(0) = a$. Thus, $\Phi = \{\phi_1(0) \rightarrow 10, \phi_2(0) \rightarrow 30\}$. We next consider each tuple in C, and see which isomorphisms can be extended. The first tuple $t_1 = \langle 0, 1, a, a \rangle$ is a forward edge, thus for ϕ_1, we consider neighbors x of 10 that are labeled a and not included in the isomorphism yet. The only other vertex that satisfies this condition is 30; thus the isomorphism is extended by mapping $\phi_1(1) \rightarrow$ 30. In a similar manner the second isomorphism ϕ_2 is extended by adding $\phi_2(1) \rightarrow 10$, as shown in Figure 11.10. For the second tuple $t_2 = \langle 1, 2, a, b \rangle$, the isomorphism ϕ_1 has two possible extensions, as 30 has two neighbors labeled b, namely 20 and 40. The extended mappings are denoted ϕ'_1 and ϕ''_1. For ϕ_2 there is only one extension.

The isomorphisms of C in G_2 can be found in a similar manner. The complete sets of isomorphisms in each database graph are shown in Figure 11.10.

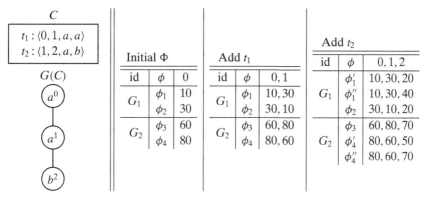

Figure 11.10. Subgraph isomorphisms.

11.3.2 Canonicality Checking

Given a DFS code $C = \{t_1, t_2, \ldots, t_k\}$ comprising k extended edge tuples and the corresponding graph $G(C)$, the task is to check whether the code C is canonical. This can be accomplished by trying to reconstruct the canonical code C^* for $G(C)$ in an iterative manner starting from the empty code and selecting the least rightmost path extension at each step, where the least edge extension is based on the extended tuple comparison operator in Eq. (11.2). If at any step the current (partial) canonical DFS code C^* is smaller than C, then we know that C cannot be canonical and can thus be pruned. On the other hand, if no smaller code is found after k extensions then C must be canonical. The pseudo-code for canonicality checking is given in Algorithm 11.4. The method can be considered as a restricted version of gSpan in that the graph $G(C)$ plays the role of a graph in the database, and C^* plays the role of a candidate extension. The key difference is that we consider only the smallest rightmost path edge extension among all the possible candidate extensions.

Algorithm 11.4: Canonicality Checking: Algorithm IsCANONICAL

ISCANONICAL $(C = \{t_1, t_2, \ldots, t_k\})$:

1 $\mathbf{D}_C \leftarrow \{G(C)\}$ // graph corresponding to code C

2 $C^* \leftarrow \emptyset$ // initialize canonical DFScode

3 **for** $i = 1 \cdots k$ **do**

4 $\quad \mathcal{E} = \text{RIGHTMOSTPATH-EXTENSIONS}(C^*, \mathbf{D}_C)$ // extensions of C^*

5 $\quad (s_i, sup(s_i)) \leftarrow \min\{\mathcal{E}\}$ // least rightmost edge extension of C^*

6 $\quad$ **if** $s_i < t_i$ **then**

7 $\quad\quad$ **return** *false* // C^* is smaller, thus C is not canonical

8 $\quad C^* \leftarrow C^* \cup s_i$

9 **return** *true* // no smaller code exists; C is canonical

---

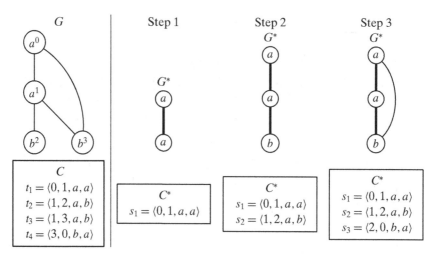

Figure 11.11. Canonicality checking.

Example 11.11. Consider the subgraph candidate C_{14} from Figure 11.8, which is replicated as graph G in Figure 11.11, along with its DFS code C. From an initial canonical code $C^* = \emptyset$, the smallest rightmost edge extension s_1 is added in Step 1. Because $s_1 = t_1$, we proceed to the next step, which finds the smallest edge extension s_2. Once again $s_2 = t_2$, so we proceed to the third step. The least possible edge extension for G^* is the extended edge s_3. However, we find that $s_3 < t_3$, which means that C cannot be canonical, and there is no need to try further edge extensions.

11.4 FURTHER READING

The gSpan algorithm was described in Yan and Han (2002), along with the notion of canonical DFS code. A different notion of canonical graphs using canonical adjacency matrices was described in Huan, Wang, and Prins (2003). Level-wise algorithms to mine frequent subgraphs appear in Kuramochi and Karypis (2001) and Inokuchi, Washio, and Motoda (2000). Markov chain Monte Carlo methods to sample a set of representative graph patterns were proposed in Al Hasan and Zaki (2009). For an efficient algorithm to mine frequent tree patterns see Zaki (2002).

Al Hasan, M. and Zaki, M. J. (2009). Output space sampling for graph patterns. *Proceedings of the VLDB Endowment*, 2 (1), 730–741.

Huan, J., Wang, W., and Prins, J. (2003). Efficient mining of frequent subgraphs in the presence of isomorphism. *Proceedings of the IEEE International Conference on Data Mining*. IEEE, pp. 549–552.

Inokuchi, A., Washio, T., and Motoda, H. (2000). An apriori-based algorithm for mining frequent substructures from graph data. *Proceedings of the European Conference on Principles of Data Mining and Knowledge Discovery*. Springer, pp. 13–23.

Kuramochi, M. and Karypis, G. (2001). Frequent subgraph discovery. *Proceedings of the IEEE International Conference on Data Mining.* IEEE, pp. 313–320.

Yan, X. and Han, J. (2002). gSpan: Graph-based substructure pattern mining. *Proceedings of the IEEE International Conference on Data Mining.* IEEE, pp. 721–724.

Zaki, M. J. (2002). Efficiently mining frequent trees in a forest. *Proceedings of the 8th ACM SIGKDD International Conference on Knowledge Discovery and Data Mining.* ACM, pp. 71–80.

11.5 EXERCISES

Q1. Find the canonical DFS code for the graph in Figure 11.12. Try to eliminate some codes without generating the complete search tree. For example, you can eliminate a code if you can show that it will have a larger code than some other code.

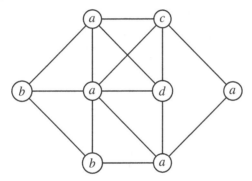

Figure 11.12. Graph for Q1.

Q2. Given the graph in Figure 11.13. Mine all the frequent subgraphs with *minsup* = 1. For each frequent subgraph, also show its canonical code.

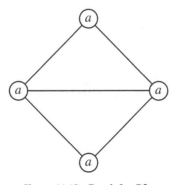

Figure 11.13. Graph for Q2.

Q3. Consider the graph shown in Figure 11.14. Show all its isomorphic graphs and their DFS codes, and find the canonical representative (you may omit isomorphic graphs that can definitely not have canonical codes).

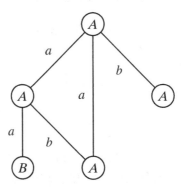

Figure 11.14. Graph for Q3.

Q4. Given the graphs in Figure 11.15, separate them into isomorphic groups.

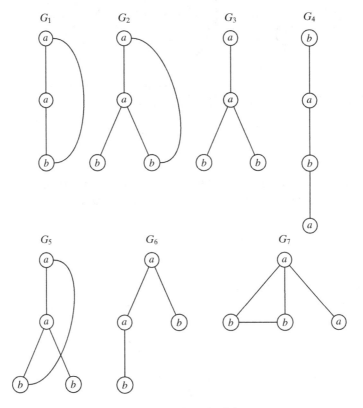

Figure 11.15. Data for Q4.

Q5. Given the graph in Figure 11.16. Find the *maximum* DFS code for the graph, subject to the constraint that all extensions (whether forward or backward) are done only from the right most path.

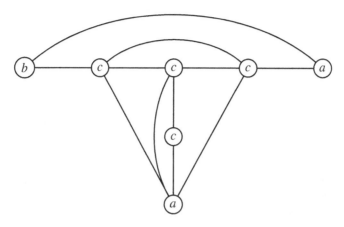

Figure 11.16. Graph for Q5.

Q6. For an edge labeled undirected graph $G = (V, E)$, define its labeled adjacency matrix **A** as follows:

$$\mathbf{A}(i, j) = \begin{cases} L(v_i) & \text{if } i = j \\ L(v_i, v_j) & \text{if } (v_i, v_j) \in E \\ 0 & \text{Otherwise} \end{cases}$$

where $L(v_i)$ is the label for vertex v_i and $L(v_i, v_j)$ is the label for edge (v_i, v_j). In other words, the labeled adjacency matrix has the node labels on the main diagonal, and it has the label of the edge (v_i, v_j) in cell $\mathbf{A}(i, j)$. Finally, a 0 in cell $\mathbf{A}(i, j)$ means that there is no edge between v_i and v_j.

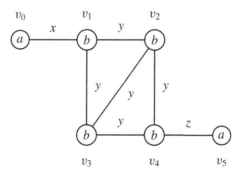

Figure 11.17. Graph for Q6.

Given a particular permutation of the vertices, a *matrix code* for the graph is obtained by concatenating the lower triangular submatrix of **A** row-by-row. For example, one possible matrix corresponding to the default vertex permutation $v_0 v_1 v_2 v_3 v_4 v_5$ for the graph in Figure 11.17 is given as

a					
x	b				
0	y	b			
0	y	y	b		
0	0	y	y	b	
0	0	0	0	z	a

The code for the matrix above is $axb0yb0yyb00yyb0000za$. Given the total ordering on the labels

$$0 < a < b < x < y < z$$

find the maximum matrix code for the graph in Figure 11.17. That is, among all possible vertex permutations and the corresponding matrix codes, you have to choose the lexicographically largest code.

CHAPTER 12

Pattern and Rule Assessment

In this chapter we discuss how to assess the significance of the mined frequent patterns, as well as the association rules derived from them. Ideally, the mined patterns and rules should satisfy desirable properties such as conciseness, novelty, utility, and so on. We outline several rule and pattern assessment measures that aim to quantify different properties of the mined results. Typically, the question of whether a pattern or rule is interesting is to a large extent a subjective one. However, we can certainly try to eliminate rules and patterns that are not statistically significant. Methods to test for the statistical significance and to obtain confidence bounds on the test statistic value are also considered in this chapter.

12.1 RULE AND PATTERN ASSESSMENT MEASURES

Let $\mathcal{I}$ be a set of items and $\mathcal{T}$ a set of tids, and let $\mathbf{D} \subseteq \mathcal{T} \times \mathcal{I}$ be a binary database. Recall that an *association rule* is an expression $X \longrightarrow Y$, where X and Y are itemsets, i.e., $X, Y \subseteq \mathcal{I}$, and $X \cap Y = \emptyset$. We call X the antecedent of the rule and Y the consequent.

The tidset for an itemset X is the set of all tids that contain X, given as

$$\mathbf{t}(X) = \left\{ t \in \mathcal{T} \mid X \text{ is contained in } t \right\}$$

The support of X is thus $sup(X) = |\mathbf{t}(X)|$. In the discussion that follows we use the short form XY to denote the union, $X \cup Y$, of the itemsets X and Y.

Given a frequent itemset $Z \in \mathcal{F}$, where $\mathcal{F}$ is the set of all frequent itemsets, we can derive different association rules by considering each proper subset of Z as the antecedent and the remaining items as the consequent, that is, for each $Z \in \mathcal{F}$, we can derive a set of rules of the form $X \longrightarrow Y$, where $X \subset Z$ and $Y = Z \setminus X$.

12.1.1 Rule Assessment Measures

Different rule interestingness measures try to quantify the dependence between the consequent and antecedent. Below we review some of the common rule assessment measures, starting with support and confidence.

Table 12.1. Example Dataset

Tid	Items
1	$ABDE$
2	BCE
3	$ABDE$
4	$ABCE$
5	$ABCDE$
6	BCD

Table 12.2. Frequent itemsets with $minsup = 3$ (relative minimum support 50%)

sup	rsup	Itemsets
3	0.5	$ABD, ABDE, AD, ADE, BCE, BDE, CE, DE$
4	0.67	$A, C, D, AB, ABE, AE, BC, BD$
5	0.83	E, BE
6	1.0	B

Support

The *support* of the rule is defined as the number of transactions that contain both X and Y, that is,

$$sup(X \longrightarrow Y) = sup(XY) = |\mathbf{t}(XY)| \qquad (12.1)$$

The *relative support* is the fraction of transactions that contain both X and Y, that is, the empirical joint probability of the items comprising the rule

$$rsup(X \longrightarrow Y) = P(XY) = rsup(XY) = \frac{sup(XY)}{|\mathbf{D}|} \qquad (12.2)$$

Typically we are interested in frequent rules, with $sup(X \longrightarrow Y) \geq minsup$, where *minsup* is a user-specified minimum support threshold. When minimum support is specified as a fraction then relative support is implied. Notice that (relative) support is a symmetric measure because $sup(X \longrightarrow Y) = sup(Y \longrightarrow X)$.

Example 12.1. We illustrate the rule assessment measures using the example binary dataset $\mathbf{D}$ in Table 12.1, shown in transactional form. It has six transactions over a set of five items $\mathcal{I} = \{A, B, C, D, E\}$. The set of all frequent itemsets with $minsup = 3$ is listed in Table 12.2. The table shows the support and relative support for each frequent itemset. The association rule $AB \longrightarrow DE$ derived from the itemset $ABDE$ has support $sup(AB \longrightarrow DE) = sup(ABDE) = 3$, and its relative support is $rsup(AB \longrightarrow DE) = sup(ABDE)/|\mathbf{D}| = 3/6 = 0.5$.

Table 12.3. Rule confidence

Rule			$conf$
A	$\longrightarrow$	E	1.00
E	$\longrightarrow$	A	0.80
B	$\longrightarrow$	E	0.83
E	$\longrightarrow$	B	1.00
E	$\longrightarrow$	BC	0.60
BC	$\longrightarrow$	E	0.75

Confidence

The *confidence* of a rule is the conditional probability that a transaction contains the consequent Y given that it contains the antecedent X:

$$conf(X \longrightarrow Y) = P(Y|X) = \frac{P(XY)}{P(X)} = \frac{rsup(XY)}{rsup(X)} = \frac{sup(XY)}{sup(X)} \tag{12.3}$$

Typically we are interested in high confidence rules, with $conf(X \longrightarrow Y) \geq minconf$, where *minconf* is a user-specified minimum confidence value. Confidence is not a symmetric measure because by definition it is conditional on the antecedent.

Example 12.2. Table 12.3 shows some example association rules along with their confidence generated from the example dataset in Table 12.1. For instance, the rule $A \longrightarrow E$ has confidence $sup(AE)/sup(A) = 4/4 = 1.0$. To see the asymmetry of confidence, observe that the rule $E \longrightarrow A$ has confidence $sup(AE)/sup(E) = 4/5 = 0.8$.

Care must be exercised in interpreting the goodness of a rule. For instance, the rule $E \longrightarrow BC$ has confidence $P(BC|E) = 0.60$, that is, given E we have a probability of 60% of finding BC. However, the unconditional probability of BC is $P(BC) = 4/6 = 0.67$, which means that E, in fact, has a deleterious effect on BC.

Lift

Lift is defined as the ratio of the observed joint probability of X and Y to the expected joint probability if they were statistically independent, that is,

$$lift(X \longrightarrow Y) = \frac{P(XY)}{P(X) \cdot P(Y)} = \frac{rsup(XY)}{rsup(X) \cdot rsup(Y)} = \frac{conf(X \longrightarrow Y)}{rsup(Y)} \tag{12.4}$$

One common use of lift is to measure the surprise of a rule. A lift value close to 1 means that the support of a rule is expected considering the supports of its components. We usually look for values that are much larger (i.e., above expectation) or smaller than 1 (i.e., below expectation).

Notice that lift is a symmetric measure, and it is always larger than or equal to the confidence because it is the confidence divided by the consequent's probability. Lift

Table 12.4. Rule lift

Rule			lift
AE	$\longrightarrow$	BC	0.75
CE	$\longrightarrow$	AB	1.00
BE	$\longrightarrow$	AC	1.20

is also not downward closed, that is, assuming that $X' \subset X$ and $Y' \subset Y$, it can happen that $lift(X' \longrightarrow Y')$ may be higher than $lift(X \longrightarrow Y)$. Lift can be susceptible to noise in small datasets, as rare or infrequent itemsets that occur only a few times can have very high lift values.

Example 12.3. Table 12.4 shows three rules and their lift values, derived from the itemset $ABCE$, which has support $sup(ABCE) = 2$ in our example database in Table 12.1.

The lift for the rule $AE \longrightarrow BC$ is given as

$$lift(AE \longrightarrow BC) = \frac{rsup(ABCE)}{rsup(AE) \cdot rsup(BC)} = \frac{2/6}{4/6 \times 4/6} = 6/8 = 0.75$$

Since the lift value is less than 1, the observed rule support is less than the expected support. On the other hand, the rule $BE \longrightarrow AC$ has lift

$$lift(BE \longrightarrow AC) = \frac{2/6}{2/6 \times 5/6} = 6/5 = 1.2$$

indicating that it occurs more than expected. Finally, the rule $CE \longrightarrow AB$ has lift equal to 1.0, which means that the observed support and the expected support match.

Example 12.4. It is interesting to compare confidence and lift. Consider the three rules shown in Table 12.5 as well as their relative support, confidence, and lift values. Comparing the first two rules, we can see that despite having lift greater than 1, they provide different information. Whereas $E \longrightarrow AC$ is a weak rule ($conf = 0.4$), $E \longrightarrow AB$ is not only stronger in terms of confidence, but it also has more support. Comparing the second and third rules, we can see that although $B \longrightarrow E$ has lift equal to 1.0, meaning that B and E are independent events, its confidence is higher and so is its support. This example underscores the point that whenever we analyze association rules, we should evaluate them using multiple interestingness measures.

Table 12.5. Comparing support, confidence, and lift

Rule			rsup	conf	lift
E	$\longrightarrow$	AC	0.33	0.40	1.20
E	$\longrightarrow$	AB	0.67	0.80	1.20
B	$\longrightarrow$	E	0.83	0.83	1.00

Table 12.6. Rule leverage

Rule			rsup	lift	leverage
ACD	$\longrightarrow$	E	0.17	1.20	0.03
AC	$\longrightarrow$	E	0.33	1.20	0.06
AB	$\longrightarrow$	D	0.50	1.12	0.06
A	$\longrightarrow$	E	0.67	1.20	0.11

Leverage

Leverage measures the difference between the observed and expected joint probability of XY assuming that X and Y are independent

$$leverage(X \longrightarrow Y) = P(XY) - P(X) \cdot P(Y) = rsup(XY) - rsup(X) \cdot rsup(Y) \qquad (12.5)$$

Leverage gives an "absolute" measure of how surprising a rule is and it should be used together with lift. Like lift it is symmetric.

Example 12.5. Consider the rules shown in Table 12.6, which are based on the example dataset in Table 12.1. The leverage of the rule $ACD \longrightarrow E$ is

$$leverage(ACD \longrightarrow E) = P(ACDE) - P(ACD) \cdot P(E) = 1/6 - 1/6 \times 5/6 = 0.03$$

Similarly, we can calculate the leverage for other rules. The first two rules have the same lift; however, the leverage of the first rule is half that of the second rule, mainly due to the higher support of ACE. Thus, considering lift in isolation may be misleading because rules with different support may have the same lift. On the other hand, the second and third rules have different lift but the same leverage. Finally, we emphasize the need to consider leverage together with other metrics by comparing the first, second, and fourth rules, which, despite having the same lift, have different leverage values. In fact, the fourth rule $A \longrightarrow E$ may be preferable over the first two because it is simpler and has higher leverage.

Jaccard

The Jaccard coefficient measures the similarity between two sets. When applied as a rule assessment measure it computes the similarity between the tidsets of X and Y:

$$jaccard(X \longrightarrow Y) = \frac{|\mathbf{t}(X) \cap \mathbf{t}(Y)|}{|\mathbf{t}(X) \cup \mathbf{t}(Y)|} = \frac{sup(XY)}{sup(X) + sup(Y) - sup(XY)}$$

$$= \frac{P(XY)}{P(X) + P(Y) - P(XY)} \qquad (12.6)$$

Jaccard is a symmetric measure.

Example 12.6. Consider the three rules and their Jaccard values shown in Table 12.7. For example, we have

$$jaccard(A \longrightarrow C) = \frac{sup(AC)}{sup(A) + sup(C) - sup(AC)} = \frac{2}{4 + 4 - 2} = 2/6 = 0.33$$

Table 12.7. Jaccard coefficient

Rule			$rsup$	$lift$	$jaccard$
A	$\longrightarrow$	C	0.33	0.75	0.33
A	$\longrightarrow$	E	0.67	1.20	0.80
A	$\longrightarrow$	B	0.67	1.00	0.67

Conviction

All of the rule assessment measures we considered above use only the joint probability of X and Y. Define $\neg X$ to be the event that X is not contained in a transaction, that is, $X \not\subseteq t \in \mathcal{T}$, and likewise for $\neg Y$. There are, in general, four possible events depending on the occurrence or non-occurrence of the itemsets X and Y as depicted in the contingency table shown in Table 12.9.

Conviction measures the expected error of the rule, that is, how often X occurs in a transaction where Y does not. It is thus a measure of the strength of a rule with respect to the complement of the consequent, defined as

$$conv(X \longrightarrow Y) = \frac{P(X) \cdot P(\neg Y)}{P(X \neg Y)} = \frac{1}{lift(X \longrightarrow \neg Y)} \tag{12.7}$$

If the joint probability of $X \neg Y$ is less than that expected under independence of X and $\neg Y$, then conviction is high, and vice versa. It is an asymmetric measure.

From Table 12.9 we observe that $P(X) = P(XY) + P(X \neg Y)$, which implies that $P(X \neg Y) = P(X) - P(XY)$. Further, $P(\neg Y) = 1 - P(Y)$. We thus have

$$conv(X \longrightarrow Y) = \frac{P(X) \cdot P(\neg Y)}{P(X) - P(XY)} = \frac{P(\neg Y)}{1 - P(XY)/P(X)} = \frac{1 - rsup(Y)}{1 - conf(X \longrightarrow Y)}$$

We conclude that conviction is infinite if confidence is one. If X and Y are independent, then conviction is 1.

Example 12.7. For the rule $A \longrightarrow DE$, we have

$$conv(A \longrightarrow DE) = \frac{1 - rsup(DE)}{1 - conf(A)} = 2.0$$

Table 12.8 shows this and some other rules, along with their conviction, support, confidence, and lift values.

Table 12.8. Rule conviction

Rule			$rsup$	$conf$	$lift$	$conv$
A	$\longrightarrow$	DE	0.50	0.75	1.50	2.00
DE	$\longrightarrow$	A	0.50	1.00	1.50	∞
E	$\longrightarrow$	C	0.50	0.60	0.90	0.83
C	$\longrightarrow$	E	0.50	0.75	0.90	0.68

Table 12.9. Contingency table for X and Y

	Y	$\neg Y$	
X	$sup(XY)$	$sup(X\neg Y)$	$sup(X)$
$\neg X$	$sup(\neg XY)$	$sup(\neg X\neg Y)$	$sup(\neg X)$
	$sup(Y)$	$sup(\neg Y)$	$|\mathbf{D}|$

Odds Ratio

The odds ratio utilizes all four entries from the contingency table shown in Table 12.9. Let us divide the dataset into two groups of transactions – those that contain X and those that do not contain X. Define the odds of Y in these two groups as follows:

$$odds(Y|X) = \frac{P(XY)/P(X)}{P(X\neg Y)/P(X)} = \frac{P(XY)}{P(X\neg Y)}$$

$$odds(Y|\neg X) = \frac{P(\neg XY)/P(\neg X)}{P(\neg X\neg Y)/P(\neg X)} = \frac{P(\neg XY)}{P(\neg X\neg Y)}$$

The odds ratio is then defined as the ratio of these two odds:

$$oddsratio(X \longrightarrow Y) = \frac{odds(Y|X)}{odds(Y|\neg X)} = \frac{P(XY) \cdot P(\neg X\neg Y)}{P(X\neg Y) \cdot P(\neg XY)}$$

$$= \boxed{\frac{sup(XY) \cdot sup(\neg X\neg Y)}{sup(X\neg Y) \cdot sup(\neg XY)}} \qquad (12.8)$$

The odds ratio is a symmetric measure, and if X and Y are independent, then it has value 1. Thus, values close to 1 may indicate that there is little dependence between X and Y. Odds ratios greater than 1 imply higher odds of Y occurring in the presence of X as opposed to its complement $\neg X$, whereas odds smaller than one imply higher odds of Y occurring with $\neg X$.

Example 12.8. Let us compare the odds ratio for two rules, $C \longrightarrow A$ and $D \longrightarrow A$, using the example data in Table 12.1. The contingency tables for A and C, and for A and D, are given below:

	C	$\neg C$
A	2	2
$\neg A$	2	0

	D	$\neg D$
A	3	1
$\neg A$	1	1

The odds ratio values for the two rules are given as

$$oddsratio(C \longrightarrow A) = \frac{sup(AC) \cdot sup(\neg A\neg C)}{sup(A\neg C) \cdot sup(\neg AC)} = \frac{2 \times 0}{2 \times 2} = 0$$

$$oddsratio(D \longrightarrow A) = \frac{sup(AD) \cdot sup(\neg A\neg D)}{sup(A\neg D) \cdot sup(\neg AD)} = \frac{3 \times 1}{1 \times 1} = 3$$

Thus, $D \longrightarrow A$ is a stronger rule than $C \longrightarrow A$, which is also indicated by looking at other measures like lift and confidence:

$$conf(C \longrightarrow A) = 2/4 = 0.5 \qquad\qquad conf(D \longrightarrow A) = 3/4 = 0.75$$

$$lift(C \longrightarrow A) = \frac{2/6}{4/6 \times 4/6} = 0.75 \qquad lift(D \longrightarrow A) = \frac{3/6}{4/6 \times 4/6} = 1.125$$

$C \longrightarrow A$ has less confidence and lift than $D \longrightarrow A$.

Example 12.9. We apply the different rule assessment measures on the Iris dataset, which has $n = 150$ examples, over one categorical attribute (class), and four numeric attributes (sepal length, sepal width, petal length, and petal width). To generate association rules we first discretize the numeric attributes as shown in Table 12.10. In particular, we want to determine representative class-specific rules that characterize each of the three Iris classes: iris setosa, iris virginica and iris versicolor, that is, we generate rules of the form $X \longrightarrow y$, where X is an itemset over the discretized numeric attributes, and y is a single item representing one of the Iris classes.

We start by generating all class-specific association rules using $minsup = 10$ and a minimum lift value of 0.1, which results in a total of 79 rules. Figure 12.1(a) plots the relative support and confidence of these 79 rules, with the three classes represented by different symbols. To look for the most surprising rules, we also plot in Figure 12.1(b) the lift and conviction value for the same 79 rules. For each class we select the most specific (i.e., with maximal antecedent) rule with the highest relative support and then confidence, and also those with the highest conviction and then lift. The selected rules are listed in Table 12.11 and Table 12.12, respectively. They

Table 12.10. Iris dataset discretization and labels employed

Attribute	Range or value	Label
Sepal length	4.30–5.55	sl_1
	5.55–6.15	sl_2
	6.15–7.90	sl_3
Sepal width	2.00–2.95	sw_1
	2.95–3.35	sw_2
	3.35–4.40	sw_3
Petal length	1.00–2.45	pl_1
	2.45–4.75	pl_2
	4.75–6.90	pl_3
Petal width	0.10–0.80	pw_1
	0.80–1.75	pw_2
	1.75–2.50	pw_3
Class	Iris-setosa	c_1
	Iris-versicolor	c_2
	Iris-virginica	c_3

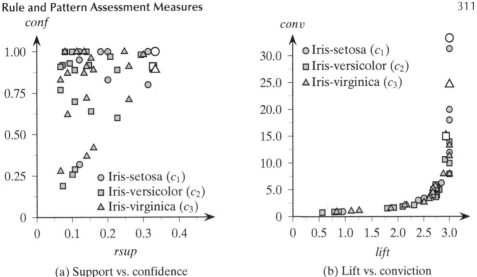

Figure 12.1. Iris: support vs. confidence, and conviction vs. lift for class-specific rules. The best rule for each class is shown in white.

Table 12.11. Iris: best class-specific rules according to support and confidence

Rule	rsup	conf	lift	conv
$\{pl_1, pw_1\} \longrightarrow c_1$	0.333	1.00	3.00	33.33
$pw_2 \longrightarrow c_2$	0.327	0.91	2.72	6.00
$pl_3 \longrightarrow c_3$	0.327	0.89	2.67	5.24

Table 12.12. Iris: best class-specific rules according to lift and conviction

Rule	rsup	conf	lift	conv
$\{pl_1, pw_1\} \longrightarrow c_1$	0.33	1.00	3.00	33.33
$\{pl_2, pw_2\} \longrightarrow c_2$	0.29	0.98	2.93	15.00
$\{sl_3, pl_3, pw_3\} \longrightarrow c_3$	0.25	1.00	3.00	24.67

are also highlighted in Figure 12.1 (as larger white symbols). Compared to the top rules for support and confidence, we observe that the best rule for c_1 is the same, but the rules for c_2 and c_3 are not the same, suggesting a trade-off between support and novelty among these rules.

12.1.2 Pattern Assessment Measures

We now turn our focus on measures for pattern assessment.

Support
The most basic measures are support and relative support, giving the number and fraction of transactions in **D** that contain the itemset X:

$$sup(X) = |\mathbf{t}(X)| \qquad\qquad rsup(X) = \frac{sup(X)}{|\mathbf{D}|}$$

Lift

The *lift* of a k-itemset $X = \{x_1, x_2, \ldots, x_k\}$ in dataset $\mathbf{D}$ is defined as

$$lift(X, \mathbf{D}) = \frac{P(X)}{\prod_{i=1}^{k} P(x_i)} = \frac{rsup(X)}{\prod_{i=1}^{k} rsup(x_i)} \tag{12.9}$$

that is, the ratio of the observed joint probability of items in X to the expected joint probability if all the items $x_i \in X$ were independent.

We may further generalize the notion of lift of an itemset X by considering all the different ways of partitioning it into nonempty and disjoint subsets. For instance, assume that the set $\{X_1, X_2, \ldots, X_q\}$ is a q-partition of X, i.e., a partitioning of X into q nonempty and disjoint itemsets X_i, such that $X_i \cap X_j = \emptyset$ and $\cup_i X_i = X$. Define the generalized lift of X over partitions of size q as follows:

$$lift_q(X) = \min_{X_1, \ldots, X_q} \left\{ \frac{P(X)}{\prod_{i=1}^{q} P(X_i)} \right\} \tag{12.10}$$

This is, the least value of lift over all q-partitions X. Viewed in this light, $lift(X) = lift_k(X)$, that is, lift is the value obtained from the unique k-partition of X.

Rule-based Measures

Given an itemset X, we can evaluate it using rule assessment measures by considering all possible rules that can be generated from X. Let Θ be some rule assessment measure. We generate all possible rules from X of the form $X_1 \longrightarrow X_2$ and $X_2 \longrightarrow X_1$, where the set $\{X_1, X_2\}$ is a 2-partition, or a bipartition, of X. We then compute the measure Θ for each such rule, and use summary statistics such as the mean, maximum, and minimum to characterize X. If Θ is a symmetric measure, then $\Theta(X_1 \longrightarrow X_2) = \Theta(X_2 \longrightarrow X_1)$, and we have to consider only half of the rules. For example, if Θ is rule lift, then we can define the average, maximum, and minimum lift values for X as follows:

$$AvgLift(X) = \underset{X_1, X_2}{avg} \left\{ lift(X_1 \longrightarrow X_2) \right\}$$

$$MaxLift(X) = \underset{X_1, X_2}{\max} \left\{ lift(X_1 \longrightarrow X_2) \right\}$$

$$MinLift(X) = \underset{X_1, X_2}{\min} \left\{ lift(X_1 \longrightarrow X_2) \right\}$$

We can also do the same for other rule measures such as leverage, confidence, and so on. In particular, when we use rule lift, then $MinLift(X)$ is identical to the generalized lift $lift_2(X)$ over all 2-partitions of X.

Example 12.10. Consider the itemset $X = \{pl_2, pw_2, c_2\}$, whose support in the discretized Iris dataset is shown in Table 12.13, along with the supports for all of its subsets. Note that the size of the database is $|\mathbf{D}| = n = 150$.

Table 12.13. Support values for $\{pl_2, pw_2, c_2\}$ and its subsets

Itemset	sup	rsup
$\{pl_2, pw_2, c_2\}$	44	0.293
$\{pl_2, pw_2\}$	45	0.300
$\{pl_2, c_2\}$	44	0.293
$\{pw_2, c_2\}$	49	0.327
$\{pl_2\}$	45	0.300
$\{pw_2\}$	54	0.360
$\{c_2\}$	50	0.333

Table 12.14. Rules generated from itemset $\{pl_2, pw_2, c_2\}$

Bipartition	Rule	lift	leverage	conf
$\big\{\{pl_2\}, \{pw_2, c_2\}\big\}$	$pl_2 \longrightarrow \{pw_2, c_2\}$	2.993	0.195	0.978
	$\{pw_2, c_2\} \longrightarrow pl_2$	2.993	0.195	0.898
$\big\{\{pw_2\}, \{pl_2, c_2\}\big\}$	$pw_2 \longrightarrow \{pl_2, c_2\}$	2.778	0.188	0.815
	$\{pl_2, c_2\} \longrightarrow pw_2$	2.778	0.188	1.000
$\big\{\{c_2\}, \{pl_2, pw_2\}\big\}$	$c_2 \longrightarrow \{pl_2, pw_2\}$	2.933	0.193	0.880
	$\{pl_2, pw_2\} \longrightarrow c_2$	2.933	0.193	0.978

Using Eq. (12.9), the lift of X is given as

$$lift(X) = \frac{rsup(X)}{rsup(pl_2) \cdot rsup(pw_2) \cdot rsup(c_2)} = \frac{0.293}{0.3 \cdot 0.36 \cdot 0.333} = 8.16$$

Table 12.14 shows all the possible rules that can be generated from X, along with the rule lift and leverage values. Note that because both of these measures are symmetric, we need to consider only the distinct bipartitions of which there are three, as shown in the table. The maximum, minimum, and average lift values are as follows:

$$MaxLift(X) = \max\{2.993, 2.778, 2.933\} = 2.998$$

$$MinLift(X) = \min\{2.993, 2.778, 2.933\} = 2.778$$

$$AvgLift(X) = \text{avg}\{2.993, 2.778, 2.933\} = 2.901$$

We may use other measures too. For example, the average leverage of X is given as

$$AvgLeverage(X) = \text{avg}\{0.195, 0.188, 0.193\} = 0.192$$

However, because confidence is not a symmetric measure, we have to consider all the six rules and their confidence values, as shown in Table 12.14. The average confidence for X is

$$AvgConf(X) = \text{avg}\{0.978, 0.898, 0.815, 1.0, 0.88, 0.978\} = 5.549/6 = 0.925$$

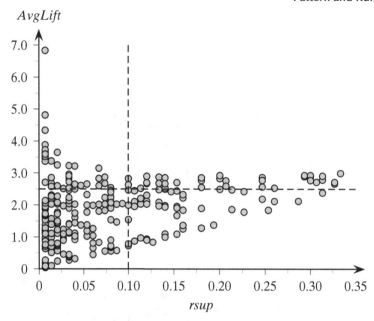

Figure 12.2. Iris: support and average lift of patterns assessed.

Example 12.11. Consider all frequent itemsets in the discretized Iris dataset from Example 12.9, using $minsup = 1$. We analyze the set of all possible rules that can be generated from these frequent itemsets. Figure 12.2 plots the relative support and average lift values for all the 306 frequent patterns with size at least 2 (since nontrivial rules can only be generated from itemsets of size 2 or more). We can see that with the exception of low support itemsets, the average lift value is bounded above by 3.0. From among these we may select those patterns with the highest support for further analysis. For instance, the itemset $X = \{pl_1, pw_1, c_1\}$ is a maximal itemset with support $rsup(X) = 0.33$, all of whose subsets also have support $rsup = 0.33$. Thus, all of the rules that can be derived from it have a lift of 3.0, and the minimum lift of X is 3.0.

12.1.3 Comparing Multiple Rules and Patterns

We now turn our attention to comparing different rules and patterns. In general, the number of frequent itemsets and association rules can be very large and many of them may not be very relevant. We highlight cases when certain patterns and rules can be pruned, as the information contained in them may be subsumed by other more relevant ones.

Comparing Itemsets
When comparing multiple itemsets we may choose to focus on the maximal itemsets that satisfy some property, or we may consider closed itemsets that capture all of the support information. We consider these and other measures in the following paragraphs.

Maximal Itemsets An frequent itemset X is *maximal* if all of its supersets are not frequent, that is, X is maximal iff

$$sup(X) \geq minsup, \text{ and for all } Y \supset X, sup(Y) < minsup$$

Table 12.15. Iris: maximal patterns according to average lift

Pattern	Avg. lift
$\{sl_1, sw_2, pl_1, pw_1, c_1\}$	2.90
$\{sl_1, sw_3, pl_1, pw_1, c_1\}$	2.86
$\{sl_2, sw_1, pl_2, pw_2, c_2\}$	2.83
$\{sl_3, sw_2, pl_3, pw_3, c_3\}$	2.88
$\{sw_1, pl_3, pw_3, c_3\}$	2.52

Given a collection of frequent itemsets, we may choose to retain only the maximal ones, especially among those that already satisfy some other constraints on pattern assessment measures like lift or leverage.

Example 12.12. Consider the discretized Iris dataset from Example 12.9. To gain insights into the maximal itemsets that pertain to each of the Iris classes, we focus our attention on the class-specific itemsets, that is, those itemsets X that contain a class as one of the items. From the itemsets plotted in Figure 12.2, using $minsup(X) \geq 15$ (which corresponds to a relative support of 10%) and retaining only those itemsets with an average lift value of at least 2.5, we retain 37 class-specific itemsets (in the top right quadrant). Among these, the maximal class-specific itemsets are shown in Table 12.15, which highlight the features that characterize each of the three classes. For instance, for class c_1 (Iris-setosa), the essential items are sl_1, pl_1, pw_1 and either sw_2 or sw_3. Looking at the range values in Table 12.10, we conclude that Iris-setosa class is characterized by sepal-length in the range $sl_1 = [4.30, 5.55]$, petal-length in the range $pl_1 = [1, 2.45]$, and so on. A similar interpretation can be carried out for the other two Iris classes.

Closed Itemsets and Minimal Generators An itemset X is *closed* if all of its supersets have strictly less support, that is,

$$sup(X) > sup(Y), \text{ for all } Y \supset X$$

An itemset X is a *minimal generator* if all its subsets have strictly higher support, that is,

$$sup(X) < sup(Y), \text{ for all } Y \subset X$$

If an itemset X is not a minimal generator, then it implies that it has some redundant items, that is, we can find some subset $Y \subset X$, which can be replaced with an even smaller subset $W \subset Y$ without changing the support of X, that is, there exists a $W \subset Y$, such that

$$sup(X) = sup(Y \cup (X \setminus Y)) = sup(W \cup (X \setminus Y))$$

One can show that all subsets of a minimal generator must themselves be minimal generators.

Table 12.16. Closed itemsets and minimal generators

sup	Closed Itemset	Minimal Generators
3	$ABDE$	AD, DE
3	BCE	CE
4	ABE	A
4	BC	C
4	BD	D
5	BE	E
6	B	B

Example 12.13. Consider the dataset in Table 12.1 and the set of frequent itemsets with $minsup = 3$ as shown in Table 12.2. There are only two maximal frequent itemsets, namely $ABDE$ and BCE, which capture essential information about whether another itemset is frequent or not: an itemset is frequent only if it is a subset of one of these two.

Table 12.16 shows the seven closed itemsets and the corresponding minimal generators. Both of these sets allow one to infer the exact support of any other frequent itemset. The support of an itemset X is the maximum support among all closed itemsets that contain it. Alternatively, the support of X is the minimum support among all minimal generators that are subsets of X. For example, the itemset AE is a subset of the closed sets ABE and $ABDE$, and it is a superset of the minimal generators A, and E; we can observe that

$$sup(AE) = \max\{sup(ABE), sup(ABDE)\} = 4$$

$$sup(AE) = \min\{sup(A), sup(E)\} = 4$$

Productive Itemsets An itemset X is *productive* if its relative support is higher than the expected relative support over all of its bipartitions, assuming they are independent. More formally, let $|X| \geq 2$, and let $\{X_1, X_2\}$ be a bipartition of X. We say that X is productive provided

$$\boxed{rsup(X) > rsup(X_1) \times rsup(X_2), \text{ for all bipartitions } \{X_1, X_2\} \text{ of } X} \qquad (12.11)$$

This immediately implies that X is productive if its minimum lift is greater than one, as

$$MinLift(X) = \min_{X_1, X_2}\left\{\frac{rsup(X)}{rsup(X_1) \cdot rsup(X_2)}\right\} > 1$$

In terms of leverage, X is productive if its minimum leverage is above zero because

$$MinLeverage(X) = \min_{X_1, X_2}\left\{rsup(X) - rsup(X_1) \times rsup(X_2)\right\} > 0$$

Example 12.14. Considering the frequent itemsets in Table 12.2, the set $ABDE$ is not productive because there exists a bipartition with lift value of 1. For instance, for its bipartition $\{B, ADE\}$ we have

$$lift(B \longrightarrow ADE) = \frac{rsup(ABDE)}{rsup(B) \cdot rsup(ADE)} = \frac{3/6}{6/6 \cdot 3/6} = 1$$

On the other hand, ADE is productive because it has three distinct bipartitions and all of them have lift above 1:

$$lift(A \longrightarrow DE) = \frac{rsup(ADE)}{rsup(A) \cdot rsup(DE)} = \frac{3/6}{4/6 \cdot 3/6} = 1.5$$

$$lift(D \longrightarrow AE) = \frac{rsup(ADE)}{rsup(D) \cdot rsup(AE)} = \frac{3/6}{4/6 \cdot 4/6} = 1.125$$

$$lift(E \longrightarrow AD) = \frac{rsup(ADE)}{rsup(E) \cdot rsup(AD)} = \frac{3/6}{5/6 \cdot 3/6} = 1.2$$

Comparing Rules

Given two rules $R : X \longrightarrow Y$ and $R' : W \longrightarrow Y$ that have the same consequent, we say that R is *more specific* than R', or equivalently, that R' is *more general* than R provided $W \subset X$.

Nonredundant Rules   We say that a rule $R : X \longrightarrow Y$ is *redundant* provided there exists a more general rule $R' : W \longrightarrow Y$ that has the same support, that is, $W \subset X$ and $sup(R) = sup(R')$. On the other hand, if $sup(R) < sup(R')$ over all its generalizations R', then R is *nonredundant*.

Improvement and Productive Rules   Define the *improvement* of a rule $X \longrightarrow Y$ as follows:

$$imp(X \longrightarrow Y) = conf(X \longrightarrow Y) - \max_{W \subset X} \left\{ conf(W \longrightarrow Y) \right\} \tag{12.12}$$

Improvement quantifies the minimum difference between the confidence of a rule and any of its generalizations. A rule $R : X \longrightarrow Y$ is *productive* if its improvement is greater than zero, which implies that for all more general rules $R' : W \longrightarrow Y$ we have $conf(R) > conf(R')$. On the other hand, if there exists a more general rule R' with $conf(R') \geq conf(R)$, then R is *unproductive*. If a rule is redundant, it is also unproductive because its improvement is zero.

The smaller the improvement of a rule $R : X \longrightarrow Y$, the more likely it is to be unproductive. We can generalize this notion to consider rules that have at least some minimum level of improvement, that is, we may require that $imp(X \longrightarrow Y) \geq t$, where t is a user-specified minimum improvement threshold.

Example 12.15. Consider the example dataset in Table 12.1, and the set of frequent itemsets in Table 12.2. Consider rule $R : BE \longrightarrow C$, which has support 3, and confidence $3/5 = 0.60$. It has two generalizations, namely

$$R_1' : E \longrightarrow C, \quad sup = 3, conf = 3/5 = 0.6$$
$$R_2' : B \longrightarrow C, \quad sup = 4, conf = 4/6 = 0.67$$

Thus, $BE \longrightarrow C$ is redundant w.r.t. $E \longrightarrow C$ because they have the same support, that is, $sup(BCE) = sup(BC)$. Further, $BE \longrightarrow C$ is also unproductive, since $imp(BE \longrightarrow C) = 0.6 - \max\{0.6, 0.67\} = -0.07$; it has a more general rule, namely R_2', with higher confidence.

12.2 SIGNIFICANCE TESTING AND CONFIDENCE INTERVALS

We now consider how to assess the statistical significance of patterns and rules, and how to derive confidence intervals for a given assessment measure.

12.2.1 Fisher Exact Test for Productive Rules

We begin by discussing the Fisher exact test for rule improvement. That is, we directly test whether the rule $R : X \longrightarrow Y$ is productive by comparing its confidence with that of each of its generalizations $R' : W \longrightarrow Y$, including the default or trivial rule $\emptyset \longrightarrow Y$.

Let $R : X \longrightarrow Y$ be an association rule. Consider its generalization $R' : W \longrightarrow Y$, where $W = X \setminus Z$ is the new antecedent formed by removing from X the subset $Z \subseteq X$. Given an input dataset **D**, conditional on the fact that W occurs, we can create a 2×2 contingency table between Z and the consequent Y as shown in Table 12.17. The different cell values are as follows:

$$a = sup(WZY) = sup(XY) \qquad b = sup(WZ\neg Y) = sup(X\neg Y)$$
$$c = sup(W\neg ZY) \qquad\qquad d = sup(W\neg Z\neg Y)$$

Here, a denotes the number of transactions that contain both X and Y, b denotes the number of transactions that contain X but not Y, c denotes the number of transactions that contain W and Y but not Z, and finally d denotes the number of transactions that contain W but neither Z nor Y. The marginal counts are given as

row marginals: $a+b = sup(WZ) = sup(X), \quad c+d = sup(W\neg Z)$

column marginals: $a+c = sup(WY), \quad b+d = sup(W\neg Y)$

where the row marginals give the occurrence frequency of W with and without Z, and the column marginals specify the occurrence counts of W with and without Y. Finally, we can observe that the sum of all the cells is simply $n = a+b+c+d = sup(W)$. Notice that when $Z = X$, we have $W = \emptyset$, and the contingency table defaults to the one shown in Table 12.9.

Given a contingency table conditional on W, we are interested in the odds ratio obtained by comparing the presence and absence of Z, that is,

$$oddsratio = \frac{a/(a+b)}{b/(a+b)} \Bigg/ \frac{c/(c+d)}{d/(c+d)} = \frac{ad}{bc} \qquad (12.13)$$

Table 12.17. Contingency table for Z and Y, conditional on $W = X \setminus Z$

W	Y	$\neg Y$	
Z	a	b	$a+b$
$\neg Z$	c	d	$c+d$
	$a+c$	$b+d$	$n = sup(W)$

Recall that the odds ratio measures the odds of X, that is, W and Z, occurring with Y versus the odds of its subset W, but not Z, occurring with Y. Under the null hypothesis H_0 that Z and Y are independent given W the odds ratio is 1. To see this, note that under the independence assumption the count in a cell of the contingency table is equal to the product of the corresponding row and column marginal counts divided by n, that is, under H_0:

$$a = (a+b)(a+c)/n \qquad\qquad b = (a+b)(b+d)/n$$

$$c = (c+d)(a+c)/n \qquad\qquad d = (c+d)(b+d)/n$$

Plugging these values in Eq. (12.13), we obtain

$$oddsratio = \frac{ad}{bc} = \frac{(a+b)(c+d)(b+d)(a+c)}{(a+c)(b+d)(a+b)(c+d)} = 1$$

The null hypothesis therefore corresponds to $H_0 : oddsratio = 1$, and the alternative hypothesis is $H_a : oddsratio > 1$. Under the null hypothesis, if we further assume that the row and column marginals are fixed, then a uniquely determines the other three values b, c, and d, and the probability mass function of observing the value a in the contingency table is given by the hypergeometric distribution. Recall that the hypergeometric distribution gives the probability of choosing s successes in t trails if we sample *without replacement* from a finite population of size T that has S successes in total, given as

$$P(s \mid t, S, T) = \binom{S}{s} \cdot \binom{T-S}{t-s} \Big/ \binom{T}{t}$$

In our context, we take the occurrence of Z as a success. The population size is $T = sup(W) = n$ because we assume that W always occurs, and the total number of successes is the support of Z given W, that is, $S = a+b$. In $t = a+c$ trials, the hypergeometric distribution gives the probability of $s = a$ successes:

$$P\left(a \mid (a+c), (a+b), n\right) = \frac{\binom{a+b}{a} \cdot \binom{n-(a+b)}{(a+c)-a}}{\binom{n}{a+c}} = \frac{\binom{a+b}{a} \cdot \binom{c+d}{c}}{\binom{n}{a+c}}$$

$$= \frac{(a+b)! \, (c+d)!}{a! \, b! \, c! \, d!} \Big/ \frac{n!}{(a+c)! \, (n-(a+c))!}$$

$$= \frac{(a+b)! \, (c+d)! \, (a+c)! \, (b+d)!}{n! \, a! \, b! \, c! \, d!} \qquad (12.14)$$

Our aim is to contrast the null hypothesis H_0 that $oddsratio = 1$ with the alternative hypothesis H_a that $oddsratio > 1$. Because a determines the rest of the cells

Table 12.18. Contingency table: increase a by i

W	Y	$\neg Y$	
Z	$a+i$	$b-i$	$a+b$
$\neg Z$	$c-i$	$d+i$	$c+d$
	$a+c$	$b+d$	$n = sup(W)$

under fixed row and column marginals, we can see from Eq. (12.13) that the larger the a the larger the odds ratio, and consequently the greater the evidence for H_a. We can obtain the p-value for a contingency table as extreme as that in Table 12.17 by summing Eq. (12.14) over all possible values a or larger:

$$\text{p-value}(a) = \sum_{i=0}^{\min(b,c)} P(a+i \mid (a+c),(a+b),n)$$

$$= \sum_{i=0}^{\min(b,c)} \frac{(a+b)!\,(c+d)!\,(a+c)!\,(b+d)!}{n!\,(a+i)!\,(b-i)!\,(c-i)!\,(d+i)!} \tag{12.15}$$

which follows from the fact that when we increase the count of a by i, then because the row and column marginals are fixed, b and c must decrease by i, and d must increase by i, as shown in Table 12.18. The lower the p-value the stronger the evidence that the odds ratio is greater than one, and thus, we may reject the null hypothesis H_0 if p-value $\leq \alpha$, where α is the significance level (e.g., $\alpha = 0.01$). This test is known as the *Fisher Exact Test*.

In summary, to check whether a rule $R : X \longrightarrow Y$ is productive, we must compute p-value$(a) = $ p-value$(sup(XY))$ of the contingency tables obtained from each of its generalizations $R' : W \longrightarrow Y$, where $W = X \setminus Z$, for $Z \subseteq X$. If p-value$(sup(XY)) > \alpha$ for any of these comparisons, then we can reject the rule $R : X \longrightarrow Y$ as nonproductive. On the other hand, if p-value$(sup(XY)) \leq \alpha$ for all the generalizations, then R is productive. However, note that if $|X| = k$, then there are $2^k - 1$ possible generalizations; to avoid this exponential complexity for large antecedents, we typically restrict our attention to only the immediate generalizations of the form $R' : X \setminus z \longrightarrow Y$, where $z \in X$ is one of the attribute values in the antecedent. However, we do include the trivial rule $\emptyset \longrightarrow Y$ because the conditional probability $P(Y|X) = conf(X \longrightarrow Y)$ should also be higher than the prior probability $P(Y) = conf(\emptyset \longrightarrow Y)$.

Example 12.16. Consider the rule $R : pw_2 \longrightarrow c_2$ obtained from the discretized Iris dataset. To test if it is productive, because there is only a single item in the antecedent, we compare it only with the default rule $\emptyset \longrightarrow c_2$. Using Table 12.17, the various cell values are

$$a = sup(pw_2, c_2) = 49 \qquad\qquad b = sup(pw_2, \neg c_2) = 5$$

$$c = sup(\neg pw_2, c_2) = 1 \qquad\qquad d = sup(\neg pw_2, \neg c_2) = 95$$

with the contingency table given as

	c_2	$\neg c_2$	
pw_2	49	5	54
$\neg pw_2$	1	95	96
	50	100	150

Thus the p-value is given as

$$\text{p-value} = \sum_{i=0}^{\min(b,c)} P(a+i \mid (a+c),(a+b),n)$$

$$= P(49 \mid 50,54,150) + P(50 \mid 50,54,150)$$

$$= \binom{54}{49}\cdot\binom{96}{95}\bigg/\binom{150}{50} + \binom{54}{50}\cdot\binom{96}{96}\bigg/\binom{150}{50}$$

$$= 1.51 \times 10^{-32} + 1.57 \times 10^{-35} = 1.51 \times 10^{-32}$$

Since the p-value is extremely small, we can safely reject the null hypothesis that the odds ratio is 1. Instead, there is a strong relationship between $X = pw_2$ and $Y = c_2$, and we conclude that $R : pw_2 \longrightarrow c_2$ is a productive rule.

Example 12.17. Consider another rule $\{sw_1, pw_2\} \longrightarrow c_2$, with $X = \{sw_1, pw_2\}$ and $Y = c_2$. Consider its three generalizations, and the corresponding contingency tables and p-values:

$R'_1 : pw_2 \longrightarrow c_2$
$Z = \{sw_1\}$
$W = X \setminus Z = \{pw_2\}$
p-value $= 0.84$

$W = pw_2$	c_2	$\neg c_2$	
sw_1	34	4	38
$\neg sw_1$	15	1	16
	49	5	54

$R'_2 : sw_1 \longrightarrow c_2$
$Z = \{pw_2\}$
$W = X \setminus Z = \{sw_1\}$
p-value $= 1.39 \times 10^{-11}$

$W = sw_1$	c_2	$\neg c_2$	
pw_2	34	4	38
$\neg pw_2$	0	19	19
	34	23	57

$R'_3 : \emptyset \longrightarrow c_2$
$Z = \{sw_1, pw_2\}$
$W = X \setminus Z = \emptyset$
p-value $= 3.55 \times 10^{-17}$

$W = \emptyset$	c_2	$\neg c_2$	
$\{sw_1, pw_2\}$	34	4	38
$\neg\{sw_1, pw_2\}$	16	96	112
	50	100	150

We can see that whereas the p-value with respect to R'_2 and R'_3 is small, for R'_1 we have p-value $= 0.84$, which is too high and thus we cannot reject the null hypothesis. We conclude that $R : \{sw_1, pw_2\} \longrightarrow c_2$ is not productive. In fact, its generalization R'_1 is the one that is productive, as shown in Example 12.16.

Multiple Hypothesis Testing

Given an input dataset **D**, there can be an exponentially large number of rules that need to be tested to check whether they are productive or not. We thus run into the multiple hypothesis testing problem, that is, just by the sheer number of hypothesis tests some unproductive rules will pass the p-value $\leq \alpha$ threshold by random chance. A strategy for overcoming this problem is to use the *Bonferroni correction* of the significance level that explicitly takes into account the number of experiments performed during the hypothesis testing process. Instead of using the given α threshold, we should use an adjusted threshold $\alpha' = \frac{\alpha}{\#r}$, where $\#r$ is the number of rules to be tested or its estimate. This correction ensures that the rule false discovery rate is bounded by α, where a false discovery is to claim that a rule is productive when it is not.

Example 12.18. Consider the discretized Iris dataset, using the discretization shown in Table 12.10. Let us focus only on class-specific rules, that is, rules of the form $X \rightarrow c_i$. Since each example can take on only one value at a time for a given attribute, the maximum antecedent length is four, and the maximum number of class-specific rules that can be generated from the Iris dataset is given as

$$\#r = c \times \left(\sum_{i=1}^{4} \binom{4}{i} b^i \right)$$

where c is the number of Iris classes, and b is the maximum number of bins for any other attribute. The summation is over the antecedent size i, that is, the number of attributes to be used in the antecedent. Finally, there are b^i possible combinations for the chosen set of i attributes. Because there are three Iris classes, and because each attribute has three bins, we have $c = 3$ and $b = 3$, and the number of possible rules is

$$\#r = 3 \times \left(\sum_{i=1}^{4} \binom{4}{i} 3^i \right) = 3(12 + 54 + 108 + 81) = 3 \cdot 255 = 765$$

Thus, if the input significance level is $\alpha = 0.01$, then the adjusted significance level using the Bonferroni correction is $\alpha' = \alpha/\#r = 0.01/765 = 1.31 \times 10^{-5}$. The rule $pw_2 \longrightarrow c_2$ in Example 12.16 has p-value $= 1.51 \times 10^{-32}$, and thus it remains productive even when we use α'.

12.2.2 Permutation Test for Significance

A *permutation* or *randomization* test determines the distribution of a given test statistic Θ by randomly modifying the observed data several times to obtain a random sample of datasets, which can in turn be used for significance testing. In the context of pattern assessment, given an input dataset $\mathbf{D}$, we first generate k randomly permuted datasets $\mathbf{D}_1, \mathbf{D}_2, \ldots, \mathbf{D}_k$. We can then perform different types of significance tests. For instance, given a pattern or rule we can check whether it is statistically significant by first computing the empirical probability mass function (EPMF) for the test statistic Θ by computing its value θ_i in the ith randomized dataset $\mathbf{D}_i$ for all $i \in [1, k]$. From these values we can generate the empirical cumulative distribution function

$$\hat{F}(x) = \hat{P}(\Theta \le x) = \frac{1}{k} \sum_{i=1}^{k} I(\theta_i \le x)$$

where I is an indicator variable that takes on the value 1 when its argument is true, and is 0 otherwise. Let θ be the value of the test statistic in the input dataset $\mathbf{D}$, then p-value(θ), that is, the probability of obtaining a value as high as θ by random chance can be computed as

$$\text{p-value}(\theta) = 1 - \hat{F}(\theta)$$

Given a significance level α, if p-value(θ) $> \alpha$, then we accept the null hypothesis that the pattern/rule is not statistically significant. On the other hand, if p-value(θ) $\le \alpha$, then we can reject the null hypothesis and conclude that the pattern is significant because a value as high as θ is highly improbable. The permutation test approach can also be used to assess an entire set of rules or patterns. For instance, we may test a collection of frequent itemsets by comparing the number of frequent itemsets in $\mathbf{D}$ with the distribution of the number of frequent itemsets empirically derived from the permuted datasets $\mathbf{D}_i$. We may also do this analysis as a function of *minsup*, and so on.

Swap Randomization
A key question in generating the permuted datasets $\mathbf{D}_i$ is which characteristics of the input dataset $\mathbf{D}$ we should preserve. The *swap randomization* approach maintains as invariant the column and row margins for a given dataset, that is, the permuted datasets preserve the support of each item (the column margin) as well as the number of items in each transaction (the row margin). Given a dataset $\mathbf{D}$, we randomly create k datasets that have the same row and column margins. We then mine frequent patterns in $\mathbf{D}$ and check whether the pattern statistics are different from those obtained using the randomized datasets. If the differences are not significant, we may conclude that the patterns arise solely from the row and column margins, and not from any interesting properties of the data.

Given a binary matrix $\mathbf{D} \subseteq \mathcal{T} \times \mathcal{I}$, the swap randomization method exchanges two nonzero cells of the matrix via a *swap* that leaves the row and column margins unchanged. To illustrate how swap works, consider any two transactions $t_a, t_b \in \mathcal{T}$ and any two items $i_a, i_b \in \mathcal{I}$ such that $(t_a, i_a), (t_b, i_b) \in \mathbf{D}$ and $(t_a, i_b), (t_b, i_a) \notin \mathbf{D}$, which corresponds to the 2×2 submatrix in $\mathbf{D}$, given as

$$\mathbf{D}(t_a, i_a; t_b, i_b) = \begin{pmatrix} 1 & 0 \\ 0 & 1 \end{pmatrix}$$

After a swap operation we obtain the new submatrix

$$\mathbf{D}(t_a, i_b; t_b, i_a) = \begin{pmatrix} 0 & 1 \\ 1 & 0 \end{pmatrix}$$

Algorithm 12.1: Generate Swap Randomized Dataset

SWAPRANDOMIZATION($t, \mathbf{D} \subseteq \mathcal{T} \times \mathcal{I}$):

1 **while** $t > 0$ **do**
2   Select pairs $(t_a, i_a), (t_b, i_b) \in \mathbf{D}$ randomly
3   **if** $(t_a, i_b) \notin \mathbf{D}$ *and* $(t_b, i_a) \notin \mathbf{D}$ **then**
4          $\mathbf{D} \leftarrow \mathbf{D} \setminus \{(t_a, i_a), (t_b, i_b)\} \cup \{(t_a, i_b), (t_b, i_a)\}$
5      $t \leftarrow t - 1$
6 **return** $\mathbf{D}$

---

where we exchange the elements in $\mathbf{D}$ so that $(t_a, i_b), (t_b, i_a) \in \mathbf{D}$, and $(t_a, i_a), (t_b, i_b) \notin \mathbf{D}$. We denote this operation as $Swap(t_a, i_a; t_b, i_b)$. Notice that a swap does not affect the row and column margins, and we can thus generate a permuted dataset with the same row and column sums as $\mathbf{D}$ through a sequence of swaps. Algorithm 12.1 shows the pseudo-code for generating a swap randomized dataset. The algorithm performs t swap trials by selecting two pairs $(t_a, i_a), (t_b, i_b) \in \mathbf{D}$ at random; a swap is successful only if both $(t_a, i_b), (t_b, i_a) \notin \mathbf{D}$.

Example 12.19. Consider the input binary dataset $\mathbf{D}$ shown in Table 12.19(a), whose row and column sums are also shown. Table 12.19(b) shows the resulting dataset after a single swap operation $Swap(1, D; 4, C)$, highlighted by the gray cells. When we apply another swap, namely $Swap(2, C; 4, A)$, we obtain the data in Table 12.19(c). We can observe that the marginal counts remain invariant.

From the input dataset $\mathbf{D}$ in Table 12.19(a) we generated $k = 100$ swap randomized datasets, each of which is obtained by performing 150 swaps (the product of all possible transaction pairs and item pairs, that is, $\binom{6}{2} \cdot \binom{5}{2} = 150$). Let the test statistic be the total number of frequent itemsets using $minsup = 3$. Mining $\mathbf{D}$ results in $|\mathcal{F}| = 19$ frequent itemsets. Likewise, mining each of the $k = 100$ permuted datasets results in the following empirical PMF for $|\mathcal{F}|$:

$$P(|\mathcal{F}| = 19) = 0.67 \qquad\qquad P(|\mathcal{F}| = 17) = 0.33$$

Because p-value(19) = 0.67, we may conclude that the set of frequent itemsets is essentially determined by the row and column marginals.

Focusing on a specific itemset, consider $ABDE$, which is one of the maximal frequent itemsets in $\mathbf{D}$, with $sup(ABDE) = 3$. The probability that $ABDE$ is frequent is $17/100 = 0.17$ because it is frequent in 17 of the 100 swapped datasets. As this probability is not very low, we may conclude that $ABDE$ is not a statistically significant pattern; it has a relatively high chance of being frequent in random datasets. Consider another itemset BCD that is not frequent in $\mathbf{D}$ because $sup(BCD) = 2$. The empirical PMF for the support of BCD is given as

$$P(sup = 2) = 0.54 \qquad P(sup = 3) = 0.44 \qquad P(sup = 4) = 0.02$$

In a majority of the datasets BCD is infrequent, and if $minsup = 4$, then p-value($sup = 4$) = 0.02 implies that BCD is highly unlikely to be a frequent pattern.

Table 12.19. Input data **D** and swap randomization

Tid	Items					Sum
	A	B	C	D	E	
1	1	1	0	1	1	4
2	0	1	1	0	1	3
3	1	1	0	1	1	4
4	1	1	1	0	1	4
5	1	1	1	1	1	5
6	0	1	1	1	0	3
Sum	4	6	4	4	5	

(a) Input binary data **D**

Tid	Items					Sum
	A	B	C	D	E	
1	1	1	1	0	1	4
2	0	1	1	0	1	3
3	1	1	0	1	1	4
4	1	1	0	1	1	4
5	1	1	1	1	1	5
6	0	1	1	1	0	3
Sum	4	6	4	4	5	

(b) $Swap(1, D; 4, C)$

Tid	Items					Sum
	A	B	C	D	E	
1	1	1	1	0	1	4
2	1	1	0	0	1	3
3	1	1	0	1	1	4
4	0	1	1	1	1	4
5	1	1	1	1	1	5
6	0	1	1	1	0	3
Sum	4	6	4	4	5	

(c) $Swap(2, C; 4, A)$

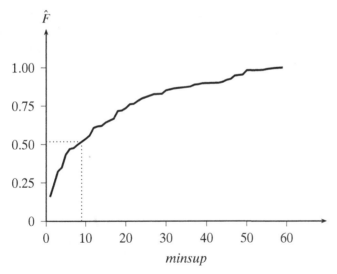

Figure 12.3. Cumulative distribution of the number of frequent itemsets as a function of minimum support.

Example 12.20. We apply the swap randomization approach to the discretized Iris dataset. Figure 12.3 shows the cumulative distribution of the number of frequent itemsets in **D** at various minimum support levels. We choose $minsup = 10$, for which we have $\hat{F}(10) = P(sup < 10) = 0.517$. Put differently, $P(sup \geq 10) = 1 - 0.517 = 0.483$, that is, 48.3% of the itemsets that occur at least once are frequent using $minsup = 10$.

Define the test statistic to be the *relative lift*, defined as the relative change in the lift value of itemset X when comparing the input dataset $\mathbf{D}$ and a randomized dataset $\mathbf{D}_i$, that is,

$$rlift(X, \mathbf{D}, \mathbf{D}_i) = \frac{lift(X, \mathbf{D}) - lift(X, \mathbf{D}_i)}{lift(X, \mathbf{D})}$$

For an m-itemset $X = \{x_1, \ldots, x_m\}$, by Eq. (12.9) note that

$$lift(X, \mathbf{D}) = rsup(X, \mathbf{D}) \bigg/ \prod_{j=1}^{m} rsup(x_j, \mathbf{D})$$

Because the swap randomization process leaves item supports (the column margins) intact, and does not change the number of transactions, we have $rsup(x_j, \mathbf{D}) = rsup(x_j, \mathbf{D}_i)$, and $|\mathbf{D}| = |\mathbf{D}_i|$. We can thus rewrite the relative lift statistic as

$$rlift(X, \mathbf{D}, \mathbf{D}_i) = \frac{sup(X, \mathbf{D}) - sup(X, \mathbf{D}_i)}{sup(X, \mathbf{D})} = 1 - \frac{sup(X, \mathbf{D}_i)}{sup(X, \mathbf{D})}$$

We generate $k = 100$ randomized datasets and compute the average relative lift for each of the 140 frequent itemsets of size two or more in the input dataset, as lift values are not defined for single items. Figure 12.4 shows the cumulative distribution for average relative lift, which ranges from -0.55 to 0.998. An average relative lift close to 1 means that the corresponding frequent pattern hardly ever occurs in any of the randomized datasets. On the other hand, a larger negative average relative lift value means that the support in randomized datasets is higher than in the input dataset. Finally, a value close to zero means that the support of the itemset is the same in both the original and randomized datasets; it is mainly a consequence of the marginal counts, and thus of little interest.

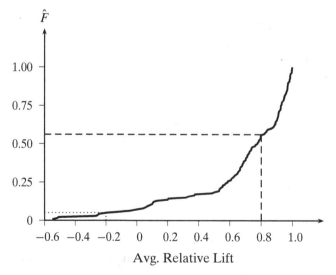

Figure 12.4. Cumulative distribution for average relative lift.

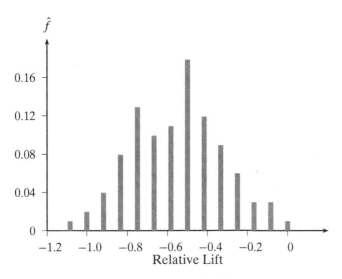

Figure 12.5. PMF for relative lift for $\{sl_1, pw_2\}$.

Figure 12.4 indicates that 44% of the frequent itemsets have average relative lift values above 0.8. These patterns are likely to be of interest. The pattern with the highest lift value of 0.998 is $\{sl_1, sw_3, pl_1, pw_1, c_1\}$. The itemset that has more or less the same support in the input and randomized datasets is $\{sl_2, c_3\}$; its average relative lift is -0.002. On the other hand, 5% of the frequent itemsets have average relative lift below -0.2. These are also of interest because they indicate more of a dis-association among the items, that is, the itemsets are more frequent by random chance. An example of such a pattern is $\{sl_1, pw_2\}$. Figure 12.5 shows the empirical probability mass function for its relative lift values across the 100 swap randomized datasets. Its average relative lift value is -0.55, and p-value$(-0.2) = 0.069$, which indicates that the itemset is likely to be disassociative.

12.2.3 Bootstrap Sampling for Confidence Interval

Typically the input transaction database $\mathbf{D}$ is just a sample from some population, and it is not enough to claim that a pattern X is frequent in $\mathbf{D}$ with support $sup(X)$. What can we say about the range of possible support values for X? Likewise, for a rule R with a given lift value in $\mathbf{D}$, what can we say about the range of lift values in different samples? In general, given a test assessment statistic Θ, bootstrap sampling allows one to infer the confidence interval for the possible values of Θ at a desired confidence level $1 - \alpha$, where $\alpha \in (0, 1)$ is the significance level. For example if $1 - \alpha = 0.95$, which corresponds to the 95% confidence level, the corresponding significance level is $\alpha = 0.05$.

The main idea is to generate k bootstrap samples from $\mathbf{D}$ using sampling *with replacement*, that is, assuming $|\mathbf{D}| = n$, each sample $\mathbf{D}_i$ is obtained by selecting at random n transactions from $\mathbf{D}$ with replacement. Given pattern X or rule $R : X \longrightarrow Y$, we can obtain the value of the test statistic in each of the bootstrap samples; let

θ_i denote the value in sample $\mathbf{D}_i$. From these values we can generate the empirical cumulative distribution function for the statistic

$$\hat{F}(x) = \hat{P}\left(\Theta \leq x\right) = \frac{1}{k}\sum_{i=1}^{k} I(\theta_i \leq x)$$

where I is an indicator variable that takes on the value 1 when its argument is true, and 0 otherwise. Given a desired confidence level $1 - \alpha$ (e.g., $1 - \alpha = 0.95$) we can compute the interval for the test statistic by discarding values from the tail ends of $\hat{F}$ on both sides that encompass $\alpha/2$ of the probability mass. Formally, let v_t denote the critical value of the test statistic, defined as

$$P(x \geq v_t) = 1 - \hat{F}(v_t) = t \text{ or equivalently } \hat{F}(v_t) = 1 - t$$

The critical value can be obtained from quantile function as $v_t = \hat{F}^{-1}(1 - t)$. We then have

$$P\left(\Theta \in [v_{1-\alpha/2}, v_{\alpha/2}]\right) = \hat{F}\left(v_{\alpha/2}\right) - \hat{F}\left(v_{1-\alpha/2}\right) = 1 - \tfrac{\alpha}{2} - (1 - (1 - \tfrac{\alpha}{2}))$$

$$= 1 - \tfrac{\alpha}{2} - \tfrac{\alpha}{2} = 1 - \alpha$$

In other words, the interval $[v_{1-\alpha/2}, v_{\alpha/2}]$ encompasses $1 - \alpha$ fraction of the probability mass, and therefore it is called the $100(1 - \alpha)\%$ confidence interval for the chosen test statistic Θ. The pseudo-code for bootstrap sampling for estimating the confidence interval is shown in Algorithm 12.2.

Algorithm 12.2: Bootstrap Resampling Method

BOOTSTRAP-CONFIDENCEINTERVAL($X, 1 - \alpha, k, \mathbf{D}$):

1 **for** $i \in [1, k]$ **do**
2 $\quad$ $\mathbf{D}_i \leftarrow$ sample of size n with replacement from $\mathbf{D}$
3 $\quad$ $\theta_i \leftarrow$ compute test statistic for X on $\mathbf{D}_i$
4 $\hat{F}(x) \leftarrow P\left(\Theta \leq x\right) = \frac{1}{k}\sum_{i=1}^{k} I(\theta_i \leq x)$
5 $v_{\alpha/2} \leftarrow \hat{F}^{-1}\left(1 - \tfrac{\alpha}{2}\right)$
6 $v_{1-\alpha/2} \leftarrow \hat{F}^{-1}\left(\tfrac{\alpha}{2}\right)$
7 **return** $[v_{1-\alpha/2}, v_{\alpha/2}]$

Example 12.21. Let the relative support *rsup* be the test statistic. Consider the itemset $X = \{sw_1, pl_3, pw_3, cl_3\}$, which has relative support $rsup(X, \mathbf{D}) = 0.113$ (or $sup(X, \mathbf{D}) = 17$) in the Iris dataset.

Using $k = 100$ bootstrap samples, we first compute the relative support of X in each of the samples ($rsup(X, \mathbf{D}_i)$). The empirical probability mass function for the relative support of X is shown in Figure 12.6 and the corresponding empirical cumulative distribution is shown in Figure 12.7. Let the confidence level be $1 - \alpha = 0.9$, which corresponds to a significance level of $\alpha = 0.1$. To obtain the confidence

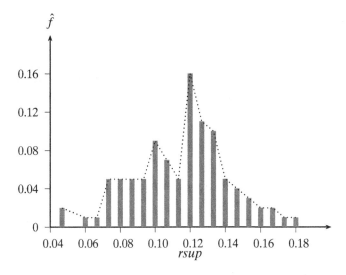

Figure 12.6. Empirical PMF for relative support.

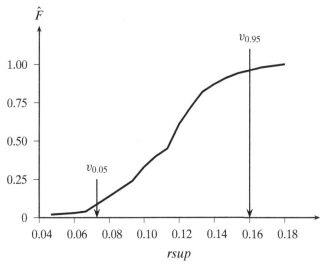

Figure 12.7. Empirical cumulative distribution for relative support.

interval we have to discard the values that account for $\alpha/2 = 0.05$ of the probability mass at both ends of the relative support values. The critical values at the left and right ends are as follows:

$$v_{1-\alpha/2} = v_{0.95} = 0.073$$

$$v_{\alpha/2} = v_{0.05} = 0.16$$

Thus, the 90% confidence interval for the relative support of X is $[0.073, 0.16]$, which corresponds to the interval $[11, 24]$ for its absolute support. Note that the relative support of X in the input dataset is 0.113, which has p-value$(0.113) = 0.45$, and the expected relative support value of X is $\mu_{rsup} = 0.115$.

12.3 FURTHER READING

Reviews of various measures for rule and pattern interestingness appear in Tan, Kumar, and Srivastava (2002) and Geng and Hamilton (2006) and Lallich, Teytaud, and Prudhomme (2007). Randomization and resampling methods for significance testing and confidence intervals are described in Megiddo and Srikant (1998) and Gionis et al. (2007). Statistical testing and validation approaches also appear in Webb (2006) and Lallich, Teytaud, and Prudhomme (2007).

Geng, L. and Hamilton, H. J. (2006). Interestingness measures for data mining: A survey. *ACM Computing Surveys*, 38 (3), 9.

Gionis, A., Mannila, H., Mielikäinen, T., and Tsaparas, P. (2007). Assessing data mining results via swap randomization. *ACM Transactions on Knowledge Discovery from Data*, 1 (3), 14.

Lallich, S., Teytaud, O., and Prudhomme, E. (2007). "Association rule interestingness: measure and statistical validation". In: *Quality Measures in Data Mining*. New York: Springer Science + Business Media, pp. 251–275.

Megiddo, N. and Srikant, R. (1998). Discovering predictive association rules. *Proceedings of the 4th International Conference on Knowledge Discovery in Databases and Data Mining*, pp. 274–278.

Tan, P.-N., Kumar, V., and Srivastava, J. (2002). Selecting the right interestingness measure for association patterns. *Proceedings of the 8th ACM SIGKDD International Conference on Knowledge Discovery and Data Mining*. ACM, pp. 32–41.

Webb, G. I. (2006). Discovering significant rules. *Proceedings of the 12th ACM SIGKDD International Conference on Knowledge Discovery and Data Mining*. ACM, pp. 434–443.

12.4 EXERCISES

Q1. Show that if X and Y are independent, then $conv(X \longrightarrow Y) = 1$.

Q2. Show that if X and Y are independent then $oddsratio(X \longrightarrow Y) = 1$.

Q3. Show that for a frequent itemset X, the value of the relative lift statistic defined in Example 12.20 lies in the range

$$\left[1 - |\mathbf{D}|/minsup,\ 1\right]$$

Q4. Let $\mathbf{D}$ be a binary database spanning one trillion (10^9) transactions. Because it is too time consuming to mine it directly, we use Monte Carlo sampling to find the bounds on the frequency of a given itemset X. We run 200 sampling trials $\mathbf{D}_i$ ($i = 1 \ldots 200$), with each sample of size 100, 000, and we obtain the support values for X in the various samples, as shown in Table 12.20. The table shows the number of samples where the support of the itemset was a given value. For instance, in 5 samples its support was 10,000. Answer the following questions:

Table 12.20. Data for Q4

Support	No. of samples
10,000	5
15,000	20
20,000	40
25,000	50
30,000	20
35,000	50
40,000	5
45,000	10

(a) Draw a histogram for the table, and calculate the mean and variance of the support across the different samples.

(b) Find the lower and upper bound on the support of X at the 95% confidence level. The support values given should be for the entire database **D**.

(c) Assume that $minsup = 0.25$, and let the observed support of X in a sample be $sup(X) = 32500$. Set up a hypothesis testing framework to check if the support of X is significantly higher than the $minsup$ value. What is the p-value?

Q5. Let A and B be two binary attributes. While mining association rules at 30% minimum support and 60% minimum confidence, the following rule was mined: $A \longrightarrow B$, with $sup = 0.4$, and $conf = 0.66$. Assume that there are a total of 10,000 customers, and that 4000 of them buy both A and B; 2000 buy A but not B, 3500 buy B but not A, and 500 buy neither A nor B.

Compute the dependence between A and B via the χ^2-statistic from the corresponding contingency table. Do you think the discovered association is truly a strong rule, that is, does A predict B strongly? Set up a hypothesis testing framework, writing down the null and alternate hypotheses, to answer the above question, at the 5% significance level. The critical values of the chi-squared statistic for the 5% significance level for various degrees of freedom (df) are shown below:

df	χ^2
1	3.84
2	5.99
3	7.82
4	9.49
5	11.07
6	12.59

PART THREE CLUSTERING

Clustering is the task of partitioning the data points into *natural groups* called clusters, such that points within a group are very similar, whereas points between different groups are as dissimilar as possible. Depending on the data and desired cluster characteristics, there are different types of clustering paradigms such as representative-based, hierarchical, density-based, graph-based, and spectral clustering. Clustering is an *unsupervised learning* approach since it does not require a separate training dataset to learn the model parameters.

This part starts with representative-based clustering methods (Chapter 13), which include the K-means and Expectation-Maximization (EM) algorithms. K-means is a greedy algorithm that minimizes the squared distance of points from their respective cluster means, and it performs hard clustering, that is, each point is assigned to only one cluster. We also show how kernel K-means can be used for nonlinear clusters. EM generalizes K-means by modeling the data as a mixture of normal distributions, and it finds the cluster parameters (the mean and covariance matrix) by maximizing the likelihood of the data. It is a soft clustering approach, that is, instead of making a hard assignment, it returns the probability that a point belongs to each cluster.

In Chapter 14, we consider various agglomerative hierarchical clustering methods, which start from each point in its own cluster, and successively merge (or agglomerate) pairs of clusters until the desired number of clusters have been found. We consider various cluster proximity measures that distinguish the different hierarchical methods. There are some datasets where the points from different clusters may in fact be closer in distance than points from the same cluster; this usually happens when the clusters are nonconvex in shape. Density-based clustering methods described in Chapter 15 use the density or connectedness properties to find such nonconvex clusters. The two main methods are DBSCAN and its generalization DENCLUE, which is based on kernel density estimation.

We consider graph clustering methods in Chapter 16, which are typically based on spectral analysis of graph data. Graph clustering can be considered as an optimization problem over a k-way cut in a graph; different objectives can be cast as spectral decomposition of different graph matrices, such as the (normalized) adjacency matrix, Laplacian matrix, and so on, derived from the original graph data or from the kernel matrix.

Finally, given the proliferation of different types of clustering methods, it is important to assess the mined clusters as to how good they are in capturing the natural groups in data. In Chapter 17, we describe various clustering validation and evaluation strategies, spanning external and internal measures to compare a clustering with the ground-truth if it is available, or to compare two clusterings. We also highlight methods for clustering stability, that is, the sensitivity of the clustering to data perturbation, and clustering tendency, that is, the clusterability of the data. We also consider methods to choose the parameter k, which is the user-specified value for the number of clusters to discover.

CHAPTER 13

Representative-based Clustering

Given a dataset $\mathbf{D}$ with n points $\mathbf{x}_i$ in a d-dimensional space, and given the number of desired clusters k, the goal of representative-based clustering is to partition the dataset into k groups or clusters, which is called a *clustering* and is denoted as $\mathcal{C} = \{C_1, C_2, \ldots, C_k\}$. Further, for each cluster C_i there exists a representative point that summarizes the cluster, a common choice being the mean (also called the *centroid*) $\boldsymbol{\mu}_i$ of all points in the cluster, that is,

$$\boldsymbol{\mu}_i = \frac{1}{n_i} \sum_{\mathbf{x}_j \in C_i} \mathbf{x}_j$$

where $n_i = |C_i|$ is the number of points in cluster C_i.

A brute-force or exhaustive algorithm for finding a good clustering is simply to generate all possible partitions of n points into k clusters, evaluate some optimization score for each of them, and retain the clustering that yields the best score. The *exact* number of ways of partitioning n points into k nonempty and disjoint parts is given by the *Stirling numbers of the second kind*, given as

$$S(n, k) = \frac{1}{k!} \sum_{t=0}^{k} (-1)^t \binom{k}{t} (k-t)^n$$

Informally, each point can be assigned to any one of the k clusters, so there are at most k^n possible clusterings. However, any permutation of the k clusters within a given clustering yields an equivalent clustering; therefore, there are $O(k^n/k!)$ clusterings of n points into k groups. It is clear that exhaustive enumeration and scoring of all possible clusterings is not practically feasible. In this chapter we describe two approaches for representative-based clustering, namely the K-means and expectation-maximization algorithms.

13.1 K-MEANS ALGORITHM

Given a clustering $\mathcal{C} = \{C_1, C_2, \ldots, C_k\}$ we need some scoring function that evaluates its quality or goodness. This *sum of squared errors* scoring function is defined as

$$SSE(\mathcal{C}) = \sum_{i=1}^{k} \sum_{\mathbf{x}_j \in C_i} \|\mathbf{x}_j - \boldsymbol{\mu}_i\|^2 \qquad (13.1)$$

The goal is to find the clustering that minimizes the SSE score:

$$\mathcal{C}^* = \arg\min_{\mathcal{C}} \{SSE(\mathcal{C})\}$$

K-means employs a greedy iterative approach to find a clustering that minimizes the SSE objective [Eq. (13.1)]. As such it can converge to a local optima instead of a globally optimal clustering.

K-means initializes the cluster means by randomly generating k points in the data space. This is typically done by generating a value uniformly at random within the range for each dimension. Each iteration of K-means consists of two steps: (1) cluster assignment, and (2) centroid update. Given the k cluster means, in the cluster assignment step, each point $\mathbf{x}_j \in \mathbf{D}$ is assigned to the closest mean, which induces a clustering, with each cluster C_i comprising points that are closer to $\boldsymbol{\mu}_i$ than any other cluster mean. That is, each point $\mathbf{x}_j$ is assigned to cluster C_{i^*}, where

$$i^* = \arg\min_{i=1}^{k} \left\{ \|\mathbf{x}_j - \boldsymbol{\mu}_i\|^2 \right\} \qquad (13.2)$$

Given a set of clusters $C_i, i = 1, \ldots, k$, in the centroid update step, new mean values are computed for each cluster from the points in C_i. The cluster assignment and centroid update steps are carried out iteratively until we reach a fixed point or local minima. Practically speaking, one can assume that K-means has converged if the centroids do not change from one iteration to the next. For instance, we can stop if $\sum_{i=1}^{k} \|\boldsymbol{\mu}_i^t - \boldsymbol{\mu}_i^{t-1}\|^2 \le \epsilon$, where $\epsilon > 0$ is the convergence threshold, t denotes the current iteration, and $\boldsymbol{\mu}_i^t$ denotes the mean for cluster C_i in iteration t.

The pseudo-code for K-means is given in Algorithm 13.1. Because the method starts with a random guess for the initial centroids, K-means is typically run several times, and the run with the lowest SSE value is chosen to report the final clustering. It is also worth noting that K-means generates convex-shaped clusters because the region in the data space corresponding to each cluster can be obtained as the intersection of half-spaces resulting from hyperplanes that bisect and are normal to the line segments that join pairs of cluster centroids.

In terms of the computational complexity of K-means, we can see that the cluster assignment step take $O(nkd)$ time because for each of the n points we have to compute its distance to each of the k clusters, which takes d operations in d dimensions. The centroid re-computation step takes $O(nd)$ time because we have to add at total of n d-dimensional points. Assuming that there are t iterations, the total time for K-means is given as $O(tnkd)$. In terms of the I/O cost it requires $O(t)$ full database scans, because we have to read the entire database in each iteration.

Example 13.1. Consider the one-dimensional data shown in Figure 13.1(a). Assume that we want to cluster the data into $k = 2$ groups. Let the initial centroids be $\mu_1 = 2$

Algorithm 13.1: K-means Algorithm

K-MEANS $(\mathbf{D}, k, \epsilon)$:

1   $t = 0$
2   Randomly initialize k centroids: $\boldsymbol{\mu}_1^t, \boldsymbol{\mu}_2^t, \ldots, \boldsymbol{\mu}_k^t \in \mathbb{R}^d$
3   **repeat**
4      $t \leftarrow t + 1$
5      $C_i \leftarrow \emptyset$ for all $i = 1, \cdots, k$
     `// Cluster Assignment Step`
6   **foreach** $\mathbf{x}_j \in \mathbf{D}$ **do**
7         $i^* \leftarrow \operatorname{argmin}_i \left\{ \| \mathbf{x}_j - \boldsymbol{\mu}_i^{t-1} \|^2 \right\}$
8         $C_{i^*} \leftarrow C_{i^*} \cup \{\mathbf{x}_j\}$ `// Assign` $\mathbf{x}_j$ `to closest centroid`
     `// Centroid Update Step`
9   **foreach** $i = 1, \cdots, k$ **do**
10        $\boldsymbol{\mu}_i^t \leftarrow \frac{1}{|C_i|} \sum_{\mathbf{x}_j \in C_i} \mathbf{x}_j$
11 **until** $\sum_{i=1}^{k} \| \boldsymbol{\mu}_i^t - \boldsymbol{\mu}_i^{t-1} \|^2 \leq \epsilon$

---

and $\mu_2 = 4$. In the first iteration, we first compute the clusters, assigning each point to the closest mean, to obtain

$$C_1 = \{2, 3\} \qquad\qquad C_2 = \{4, 10, 11, 12, 20, 25, 30\}$$

We next update the means as follows:

$$\mu_1 = \frac{2+3}{2} = \frac{5}{2} = 2.5$$

$$\mu_2 = \frac{4+10+11+12+20+25+30}{7} = \frac{112}{7} = 16$$

The new centroids and clusters after the first iteration are shown in Figure 13.1(b). For the second step, we repeat the cluster assignment and centroid update steps, as shown in Figure 13.1(c), to obtain the new clusters:

$$C_1 = \{2, 3, 4\} \qquad\qquad C_2 = \{10, 11, 12, 20, 25, 30\}$$

and the new means:

$$\mu_1 = \frac{2+3+4}{4} = \frac{9}{3} = 3$$

$$\mu_2 = \frac{10+11+12+20+25+30}{6} = \frac{108}{6} = 18$$

The complete process until convergence is illustrated in Figure 13.1. The final clusters are given as

$$C_1 = \{2, 3, 4, 10, 11, 12\} \qquad\qquad C_2 = \{20, 25, 30\}$$

with representatives $\mu_1 = 7$ and $\mu_2 = 25$.

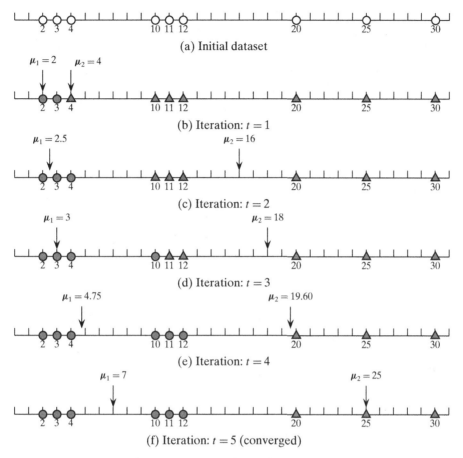

Figure 13.1. K-means in one dimension.

Example 13.2 (K-means in Two Dimensions). In Figure 13.2 we illustrate the K-means algorithm on the Iris dataset, using the first two principal components as the two dimensions. Iris has $n = 150$ points, and we want to find $k = 3$ clusters, corresponding to the three types of Irises. A random initialization of the cluster means yields

$$\mu_1 = (-0.98, -1.24)^T \qquad \mu_2 = (-2.96, 1.16)^T \qquad \mu_3 = (-1.69, -0.80)^T$$

as shown in Figure 13.2(a). With these initial clusters, K-means takes eight iterations to converge. Figure 13.2(b) shows the clusters and their means after one iteration:

$$\mu_1 = (1.56, -0.08)^T \qquad \mu_2 = (-2.86, 0.53)^T \qquad \mu_3 = (-1.50, -0.05)^T$$

Finally, Figure 13.2(c) shows the clusters on convergence. The final means are as follows:

$$\mu_1 = (2.64, 0.19)^T \qquad \mu_2 = (-2.35, 0.27)^T \qquad \mu_3 = (-0.66, -0.33)^T$$

Figure 13.2 shows the cluster means as black points, and shows the convex regions of data space that correspond to each of the three clusters. The dashed lines

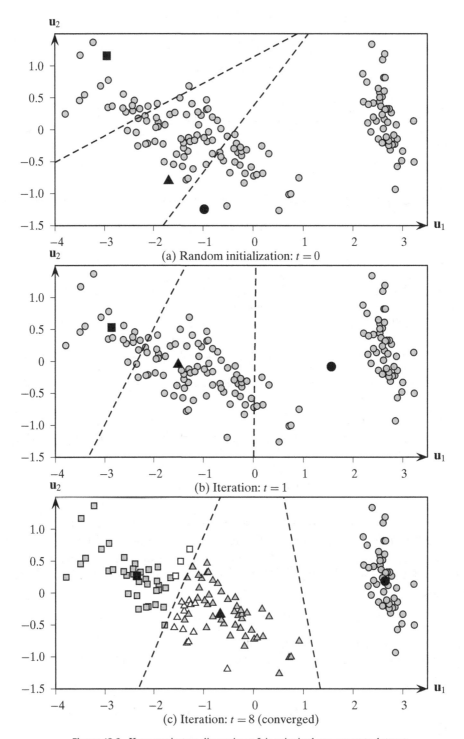

Figure 13.2. K-means in two dimensions: Iris principal components dataset.

(hyperplanes) are the perpendicular bisectors of the line segments joining two cluster centers. The resulting convex partition of the points comprises the clustering.

Figure 13.2(c) shows the final three clusters: C_1 as circles, C_2 as squares, and C_3 as triangles. White points indicate a wrong grouping when compared to the known Iris types. Thus, we can see that C_1 perfectly corresponds to iris-setosa, and the majority of the points in C_2 correspond to iris-virginica, and in C_3 to iris-versicolor. For example, three points (white squares) of type iris-versicolor are wrongly clustered in C_2, and 14 points from iris-virginica are wrongly clustered in C_3 (white triangles). Of course, because the Iris class label is not used in clustering, it is reasonable to expect that we will not obtain a perfect clustering.

13.2 KERNEL K-MEANS

In K-means, the separating boundary between clusters is linear. Kernel K-means allows one to extract nonlinear boundaries between clusters via the use of the kernel trick outlined in Chapter 5. This way the method can be used to detect nonconvex clusters.

In kernel K-means, the main idea is to conceptually map a data point $\mathbf{x}_i$ in input space to a point $\phi(\mathbf{x}_i)$ in some high-dimensional feature space, via an appropriate nonlinear mapping ϕ. However, the kernel trick allows us to carry out the clustering in feature space purely in terms of the kernel function $K(\mathbf{x}_i, \mathbf{x}_j)$, which can be computed in input space, but corresponds to a dot (or inner) product $\phi(\mathbf{x}_i)^T \phi(\mathbf{x}_j)$ in feature space.

Assume for the moment that all points $\mathbf{x}_i \in \mathbf{D}$ have been mapped to their corresponding images $\phi(\mathbf{x}_i)$ in feature space. Let $\mathbf{K} = \{K(\mathbf{x}_i, \mathbf{x}_j)\}_{i,j=1,\ldots,n}$ denote the $n \times n$ symmetric kernel matrix, where $K(\mathbf{x}_i, \mathbf{x}_j) = \phi(\mathbf{x}_i)^T \phi(\mathbf{x}_j)$. Let $\{C_1, \ldots, C_k\}$ specify the partitioning of the n points into k clusters, and let the corresponding cluster means in feature space be given as $\{\boldsymbol{\mu}_1^\phi, \ldots, \boldsymbol{\mu}_k^\phi\}$, where

$$\boldsymbol{\mu}_i^\phi = \frac{1}{n_i} \sum_{\mathbf{x}_j \in C_i} \phi(\mathbf{x}_j)$$

is the mean of cluster C_i in feature space, with $n_i = |C_i|$.

In feature space, the kernel K-means sum of squared errors objective can be written as

$$\min_{\mathcal{C}} SSE(\mathcal{C}) = \sum_{i=1}^{k} \sum_{\mathbf{x}_j \in C_i} \|\phi(\mathbf{x}_j) - \boldsymbol{\mu}_i^\phi\|^2$$

Expanding the kernel SSE objective in terms of the kernel function, we get

$$SSE(\mathcal{C}) = \sum_{i=1}^{k} \sum_{\mathbf{x}_j \in C_i} \|\phi(\mathbf{x}_j) - \boldsymbol{\mu}_i^\phi\|^2$$

$$= \sum_{i=1}^{k} \sum_{\mathbf{x}_j \in C_i} \|\phi(\mathbf{x}_j)\|^2 - 2\phi(\mathbf{x}_j)^T \boldsymbol{\mu}_i^\phi + \|\boldsymbol{\mu}_i^\phi\|^2$$

$$= \sum_{i=1}^{k} \left(\left(\sum_{\mathbf{x}_j \in C_i} \|\phi(\mathbf{x}_j)\|^2 \right) - 2n_i \left(\frac{1}{n_i} \sum_{\mathbf{x}_j \in C_i} \phi(\mathbf{x}_j) \right)^T \boldsymbol{\mu}_i^\phi + n_i \|\boldsymbol{\mu}_i^\phi\|^2 \right)$$

$$= \left(\sum_{i=1}^{k} \sum_{\mathbf{x}_j \in C_i} \phi(\mathbf{x}_j)^T \phi(\mathbf{x}_j) \right) - \left(\sum_{i=1}^{k} n_i \|\boldsymbol{\mu}_i^\phi\|^2 \right)$$

$$= \sum_{i=1}^{k} \sum_{\mathbf{x}_j \in C_i} K(\mathbf{x}_j, \mathbf{x}_j) - \sum_{i=1}^{k} \frac{1}{n_i} \sum_{\mathbf{x}_a \in C_i} \sum_{\mathbf{x}_b \in C_i} K(\mathbf{x}_a, \mathbf{x}_b)$$

$$= \sum_{j=1}^{n} K(\mathbf{x}_j, \mathbf{x}_j) - \sum_{i=1}^{k} \frac{1}{n_i} \sum_{\mathbf{x}_a \in C_i} \sum_{\mathbf{x}_b \in C_i} K(\mathbf{x}_a, \mathbf{x}_b) \qquad (13.3)$$

Thus, the kernel K-means SSE objective function can be expressed purely in terms of the kernel function. Like K-means, to minimize the SSE objective we adopt a greedy iterative approach. The basic idea is to assign each point to the closest mean in feature space, resulting in a new clustering, which in turn can be used obtain new estimates for the cluster means. However, the main difficulty is that we cannot explicitly compute the mean of each cluster in feature space. Fortunately, explicitly obtaining the cluster means is not required; all operations can be carried out in terms of the kernel function $K(\mathbf{x}_i, \mathbf{x}_j) = \phi(\mathbf{x}_i)^T \phi(\mathbf{x}_j)$.

Consider the distance of a point $\phi(\mathbf{x}_j)$ to the mean $\boldsymbol{\mu}_i^\phi$ in feature space, which can be computed as

$$\|\phi(\mathbf{x}_j) - \boldsymbol{\mu}_i^\phi\|^2 = \|\phi(\mathbf{x}_j)\|^2 - 2\phi(\mathbf{x}_j)^T \boldsymbol{\mu}_i^\phi + \|\boldsymbol{\mu}_i^\phi\|^2$$

$$= \phi(\mathbf{x}_j)^T \phi(\mathbf{x}_j) - \frac{2}{n_i} \sum_{\mathbf{x}_a \in C_i} \phi(\mathbf{x}_j)^T \phi(\mathbf{x}_a) + \frac{1}{n_i^2} \sum_{\mathbf{x}_a \in C_i} \sum_{\mathbf{x}_b \in C_i} \phi(\mathbf{x}_a)^T \phi(\mathbf{x}_b)$$

$$= K(\mathbf{x}_j, \mathbf{x}_j) - \frac{2}{n_i} \sum_{\mathbf{x}_a \in C_i} K(\mathbf{x}_a, \mathbf{x}_j) + \frac{1}{n_i^2} \sum_{\mathbf{x}_a \in C_i} \sum_{\mathbf{x}_b \in C_i} K(\mathbf{x}_a, \mathbf{x}_b) \qquad (13.4)$$

Thus, the distance of a point to a cluster mean in feature space can be computed using only kernel operations. In the cluster assignment step of kernel K-means, we assign a point to the closest cluster mean as follows:

$$C^*(\mathbf{x}_j) = \arg\min_{i} \left\{ \|\phi(\mathbf{x}_j) - \boldsymbol{\mu}_i^\phi\|^2 \right\}$$

$$= \arg\min_{i} \left\{ K(\mathbf{x}_j, \mathbf{x}_j) - \frac{2}{n_i} \sum_{\mathbf{x}_a \in C_i} K(\mathbf{x}_a, \mathbf{x}_j) + \frac{1}{n_i^2} \sum_{\mathbf{x}_a \in C_i} \sum_{\mathbf{x}_b \in C_i} K(\mathbf{x}_a, \mathbf{x}_b) \right\}$$

$$= \boxed{ \arg\min_{i} \left\{ \frac{1}{n_i^2} \sum_{\mathbf{x}_a \in C_i} \sum_{\mathbf{x}_b \in C_i} K(\mathbf{x}_a, \mathbf{x}_b) - \frac{2}{n_i} \sum_{\mathbf{x}_a \in C_i} K(\mathbf{x}_a, \mathbf{x}_j) \right\} } \qquad (13.5)$$

Algorithm 13.2: Kernel K-means Algorithm

KERNEL-KMEANS($\mathbf{K}, k, \epsilon$):

1 $t \leftarrow 0$
2 $\mathcal{C}^t \leftarrow \{C_1^t, \ldots, C_k^t\}$ // Randomly partition points into k clusters
3 **repeat**
4     $t \leftarrow t + 1$
5   **foreach** $C_i \in \mathcal{C}^{t-1}$ **do** // Compute squared norm of cluster means
6        $\text{sqnorm}_i \leftarrow \frac{1}{n_i^2} \sum_{\mathbf{x}_a \in C_i} \sum_{\mathbf{x}_b \in C_i} K(\mathbf{x}_a, \mathbf{x}_b)$
7   **foreach** $\mathbf{x}_j \in \mathbf{D}$ **do** // Average kernel value for $\mathbf{x}_j$ and C_i
8   **foreach** $C_i \in \mathcal{C}^{t-1}$ **do**
9           $\text{avg}_{ji} \leftarrow \frac{1}{n_i} \sum_{\mathbf{x}_a \in C_i} K(\mathbf{x}_a, \mathbf{x}_j)$

   // Find closest cluster for each point
10   **foreach** $\mathbf{x}_j \in \mathbf{D}$ **do**
11   **foreach** $C_i \in \mathcal{C}^{t-1}$ **do**
12          $d(\mathbf{x}_j, C_i) \leftarrow \text{sqnorm}_i - 2 \cdot \text{avg}_{ji}$
13       $i^* \leftarrow \arg\min_i \{d(\mathbf{x}_j, C_i)\}$
14       $C_{i^*}^t \leftarrow C_{i^*}^t \cup \{\mathbf{x}_j\}$ // Cluster reassignment
15    $\mathcal{C}^t \leftarrow \{C_1^t, \ldots, C_k^t\}$
16 **until** $1 - \frac{1}{n} \sum_{i=1}^k \left| C_i^t \cap C_i^{t-1} \right| \leq \epsilon$

---

where we drop the $K(\mathbf{x}_j, \mathbf{x}_j)$ term because it remains the same for all k clusters and does not impact the cluster assignment decision. Also note that the first term is simply the average pairwise kernel value for cluster C_i and is independent of the point $\mathbf{x}_j$. It is in fact the squared norm of the cluster mean in feature space. The second term is twice the average kernel value for points in C_i with respect to $\mathbf{x}_j$.

Algorithm 13.2 shows the pseudo-code for the kernel K-means method. It starts from an initial random partitioning of the points into k clusters. It then iteratively updates the cluster assignments by reassigning each point to the closest mean in feature space via Eq. (13.5). To facilitate the distance computation, it first computes the average kernel value, that is, the squared norm of the cluster mean, for each cluster (for loop in line 5). Next, it computes the average kernel value for each point $\mathbf{x}_j$ with points in cluster C_i (for loop in line 7). The main cluster assignment step uses these values to compute the distance of $\mathbf{x}_j$ from each of the clusters C_i and assigns $\mathbf{x}_j$ to the closest mean. This reassignment information is used to re-partition the points into a new set of clusters. That is, all points $\mathbf{x}_j$ that are closer to the mean for C_i make up the new cluster for the next iteration. This iterative process is repeated until convergence.

For convergence testing, we check if there is any change in the cluster assignments of the points. The number of points that do not change clusters is given as the sum $\sum_{i=1}^k |C_i^t \cap C_i^{t-1}|$, where t specifies the current iteration. The fraction of points

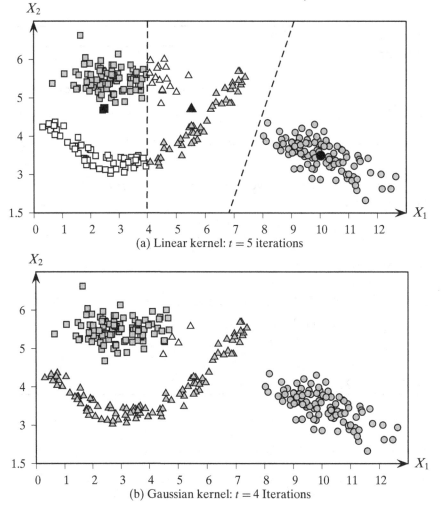

(a) Linear kernel: $t = 5$ iterations

(b) Gaussian kernel: $t = 4$ Iterations

Figure 13.3. Kernel K-means: linear versus Gaussian kernel.

reassigned to a different cluster in the current iteration is given as

$$\frac{n - \sum_{i=1}^{k} |C_i^t \cap C_i^{t-1}|}{n} = 1 - \frac{1}{n} \sum_{i=1}^{k} |C_i^t \cap C_i^{t-1}|$$

Kernel K-means stops when the fraction of points with new cluster assignments falls below some threshold $\epsilon \geq 0$. For example, one can iterate until no points change clusters.

Computational Complexity

Computing the average kernel value for each cluster C_i takes time $O(n^2)$ across all clusters. Computing the average kernel value of each point with respect to each of the k clusters also takes $O(n^2)$ time. Finally, computing the closest mean for each point and cluster reassignment takes $O(kn)$ time. The total computational complexity of kernel K-means is thus $O(tn^2)$, where t is the number of iterations until convergence. The I/O complexity is $O(t)$ scans of the kernel matrix **K**.

Example 13.3. Figure 13.3 shows an application of the kernel K-means approach on a synthetic dataset with three embedded clusters. Each cluster has 100 points, for a total of $n = 300$ points in the dataset.

Using the linear kernel $K(\mathbf{x}_i, \mathbf{x}_j) = \mathbf{x}_i^T \mathbf{x}_j$ is equivalent to the K-means algorithm because in this case Eq. (13.5) is the same as Eq. (13.2). Figure 13.3(a) shows the resulting clusters; points in C_1 are shown as squares, in C_2 as triangles, and in C_3 as circles. We can see that K-means is not able to separate the three clusters due to the presence of the parabolic shaped cluster. The white points are those that are wrongly clustered, comparing with the ground truth in terms of the generated cluster labels.

Using the Gaussian kernel $K(\mathbf{x}_i, \mathbf{x}_j) = \exp\left\{-\frac{\|\mathbf{x}_i - \mathbf{x}_j\|^2}{2\sigma^2}\right\}$ from Eq. (5.10), with $\sigma = 1.5$, results in a near-perfect clustering, as shown in Figure 13.3(b). Only four points (white triangles) are grouped incorrectly with cluster C_2, whereas they should belong to cluster C_1. We can see from this example that kernel K-means is able to handle nonlinear cluster boundaries. One caveat is that the value of the spread parameter σ has to be set by trial and error.

13.3 EXPECTATION-MAXIMIZATION CLUSTERING

The K-means approach is an example of a *hard assignment* clustering, where each point can belong to only one cluster. We now generalize the approach to consider *soft assignment* of points to clusters, so that each point has a probability of belonging to each cluster.

Let $\mathbf{D}$ consist of n points $\mathbf{x}_j$ in d-dimensional space $\mathbb{R}^d$. Let X_a denote the random variable corresponding to the ath attribute. We also use X_a to denote the ath column vector, corresponding to the n data samples from X_a. Let $\mathbf{X} = (X_1, X_2, \ldots, X_d)$ denote the vector random variable across the d-attributes, with $\mathbf{x}_j$ being a data sample from $\mathbf{X}$.

Gaussian Mixture Model

We assume that each cluster C_i is characterized by a multivariate normal distribution, that is,

$$f_i(\mathbf{x}) = f(\mathbf{x}|\boldsymbol{\mu}_i, \boldsymbol{\Sigma}_i) = \frac{1}{(2\pi)^{\frac{d}{2}} |\boldsymbol{\Sigma}_i|^{\frac{1}{2}}} \exp\left\{-\frac{(\mathbf{x} - \boldsymbol{\mu}_i)^T \boldsymbol{\Sigma}_i^{-1} (\mathbf{x} - \boldsymbol{\mu}_i)}{2}\right\} \tag{13.6}$$

where the cluster mean $\boldsymbol{\mu}_i \in \mathbb{R}^d$ and covariance matrix $\boldsymbol{\Sigma}_i \in \mathbb{R}^{d \times d}$ are both unknown parameters. $f_i(\mathbf{x})$ is the probability density at $\mathbf{x}$ attributable to cluster C_i. We assume that the probability density function of $\mathbf{X}$ is given as a *Gaussian mixture model* over all the k cluster normals, defined as

$$f(\mathbf{x}) = \sum_{i=1}^{k} f_i(\mathbf{x}) P(C_i) = \sum_{i=1}^{k} f(\mathbf{x}|\boldsymbol{\mu}_i, \boldsymbol{\Sigma}_i) P(C_i) \tag{13.7}$$

where the prior probabilities $P(C_i)$ are called the *mixture parameters*, which must satisfy the condition

$$\sum_{i=1}^{k} P(C_i) = 1$$

The Gaussian mixture model is thus characterized by the mean $\boldsymbol{\mu}_i$, the covariance matrix $\boldsymbol{\Sigma}_i$, and the mixture probability $P(C_i)$ for each of the k normal distributions. We write the set of all the model parameters compactly as

$$\boldsymbol{\theta} = \left\{ \boldsymbol{\mu}_1, \boldsymbol{\Sigma}_1, P(C_1) \ldots, \boldsymbol{\mu}_k, \boldsymbol{\Sigma}_k, P(C_k) \right\}$$

Maximum Likelihood Estimation

Given the dataset $\mathbf{D}$, we define the *likelihood* of $\boldsymbol{\theta}$ as the conditional probability of the data $\mathbf{D}$ given the model parameters $\boldsymbol{\theta}$, denoted as $P(\mathbf{D}|\boldsymbol{\theta})$. Because each of the n points $\mathbf{x}_j$ is considered to be a random sample from $\mathbf{X}$ (i.e., independent and identically distributed as $\mathbf{X}$), the likelihood of $\boldsymbol{\theta}$ is given as

$$P(\mathbf{D}|\boldsymbol{\theta}) = \prod_{j=1}^{n} f(\mathbf{x}_j)$$

The goal of maximum likelihood estimation (MLE) is to choose the parameters $\boldsymbol{\theta}$ that maximize the likelihood, that is,

$$\boldsymbol{\theta}^* = \arg\max_{\boldsymbol{\theta}} \{ P(\mathbf{D}|\boldsymbol{\theta}) \}$$

It is typical to maximize the log of the likelihood function because it turns the product over the points into a summation and the maximum value of the likelihood and log-likelihood coincide. That is, MLE maximizes

$$\boldsymbol{\theta}^* = \arg\max_{\boldsymbol{\theta}} \{ \ln P(\mathbf{D}|\boldsymbol{\theta}) \}$$

where the *log-likelihood* function is given as

$$\ln P(\mathbf{D}|\boldsymbol{\theta}) = \sum_{j=1}^{n} \ln f(\mathbf{x}_j) = \sum_{j=1}^{n} \ln \left(\sum_{i=1}^{k} f(\mathbf{x}_j|\boldsymbol{\mu}_i, \boldsymbol{\Sigma}_i) P(C_i) \right) \tag{13.8}$$

Directly maximizing the log-likelihood over $\boldsymbol{\theta}$ is hard. Instead, we can use the expectation-maximization (EM) approach for finding the maximum likelihood estimates for the parameters $\boldsymbol{\theta}$. EM is a two-step iterative approach that starts from an initial guess for the parameters $\boldsymbol{\theta}$. Given the current estimates for $\boldsymbol{\theta}$, in the *expectation step* EM computes the cluster posterior probabilities $P(C_i|\mathbf{x}_j)$ via the Bayes theorem:

$$P(C_i|\mathbf{x}_j) = \frac{P(C_i \text{ and } \mathbf{x}_j)}{P(\mathbf{x}_j)} = \frac{P(\mathbf{x}_j|C_i) P(C_i)}{\sum_{a=1}^{k} P(\mathbf{x}_j|C_a) P(C_a)}$$

Because each cluster is modeled as a multivariate normal distribution [Eq. (13.6)], the probability of $\mathbf{x}_j$ given cluster C_i can be obtained by considering a small interval $\epsilon > 0$ centered at $\mathbf{x}_j$, as follows:

$$P(\mathbf{x}_j|C_i) \simeq 2\epsilon \cdot f(\mathbf{x}_j|\boldsymbol{\mu}_i, \boldsymbol{\Sigma}_i) = 2\epsilon \cdot f_i(\mathbf{x}_j)$$

The posterior probability of C_i given $\mathbf{x}_j$ is thus given as

$$P(C_i|\mathbf{x}_j) = \frac{f_i(\mathbf{x}_j) \cdot P(C_i)}{\sum_{a=1}^{k} f_a(\mathbf{x}_j) \cdot P(C_a)} \tag{13.9}$$

and $P(C_i|\mathbf{x}_j)$ can be considered as the weight or contribution of the point $\mathbf{x}_j$ to cluster C_i. Next, in the *maximization step*, using the weights $P(C_i|\mathbf{x}_j)$ EM re-estimates $\boldsymbol{\theta}$, that is, it re-estimates the parameters $\boldsymbol{\mu}_i$, $\boldsymbol{\Sigma}_i$, and $P(C_i)$ for each cluster C_i. The re-estimated mean is given as the weighted average of all the points, the re-estimated covariance matrix is given as the weighted covariance over all pairs of dimensions, and the re-estimated prior probability for each cluster is given as the fraction of weights that contribute to that cluster. In Section 13.3.3 we formally derive the expressions for the MLE estimates for the cluster parameters, and in Section 13.3.4 we describe the generic EM approach in more detail. We begin with the application of the EM clustering algorithm for the one-dimensional and general d-dimensional cases.

13.3.1 EM in One Dimension

Consider a dataset $\mathbf{D}$ consisting of a single attribute X, where each point $x_j \in \mathbb{R}$ ($j = 1, \ldots, n$) is a random sample from X. For the mixture model [Eq. (13.7)], we use univariate normals for each cluster:

$$f_i(x) = f(x|\mu_i, \sigma_i^2) = \frac{1}{\sqrt{2\pi}\sigma_i} \exp\left\{-\frac{(x-\mu_i)^2}{2\sigma_i^2}\right\}$$

with the cluster parameters μ_i, σ_i^2, and $P(C_i)$. The EM approach consists of three steps: initialization, expectation step, and maximization step.

Initialization
For each cluster C_i, with $i = 1, 2, \ldots, k$, we can randomly initialize the cluster parameters μ_i, σ_i^2, and $P(C_i)$. The mean μ_i is selected uniformly at random from the range of possible values for X. It is typical to assume that the initial variance is given as $\sigma_i^2 = 1$. Finally, the cluster prior probabilities are initialized to $P(C_i) = \frac{1}{k}$, so that each cluster has an equal probability.

Expectation Step
Assume that for each of the k clusters, we have an estimate for the parameters, namely the mean μ_i, variance σ_i^2, and prior probability $P(C_i)$. Given these values the clusters posterior probabilities are computed using Eq. (13.9):

$$P(C_i|x_j) = \frac{f(x_j|\mu_i, \sigma_i^2) \cdot P(C_i)}{\sum_{a=1}^{k} f(x_j|\mu_a, \sigma_a^2) \cdot P(C_a)}$$

For convenience, we use the notation $w_{ij} = P(C_i|x_j)$, treating the posterior probability as the weight or contribution of the point x_j to cluster C_i. Further, let

$$\mathbf{w}_i = (w_{i1}, \ldots, w_{in})^T$$

denote the weight vector for cluster C_i across all the n points.

Maximization Step

Assuming that all the posterior probability values or weights $w_{ij} = P(C_i|x_j)$ are known, the maximization step, as the name implies, computes the maximum likelihood estimates of the cluster parameters by re-estimating μ_i, σ_i^2, and $P(C_i)$.

The re-estimated value for the cluster mean, μ_i, is computed as the weighted mean of all the points:

$$\mu_i = \frac{\sum_{j=1}^n w_{ij} \cdot x_j}{\sum_{j=1}^n w_{ij}}$$

In terms of the weight vector $\mathbf{w}_i$ and the attribute vector $X = (x_1, x_2, \ldots, x_n)^T$, we can rewrite the above as

$$\mu_i = \frac{\mathbf{w}_i^T X}{\mathbf{w}_i^T \mathbf{1}}$$

The re-estimated value of the cluster variance is computed as the weighted variance across all the points:

$$\sigma_i^2 = \frac{\sum_{j=1}^n w_{ij}(x_j - \mu_i)^2}{\sum_{j=1}^n w_{ij}}$$

Let $\bar{X}_i = X - \mu_i \mathbf{1} = (x_1 - \mu_i, x_2 - \mu_i, \ldots, x_n - \mu_i)^T = (\bar{x}_{i1}, \bar{x}_{i2}, \ldots, \bar{x}_{in})^T$ be the centered attribute vector for cluster C_i, and let $\bar{X}_i^s$ be the squared vector given as $\bar{X}_i^s = (\bar{x}_{i1}^2, \ldots, \bar{x}_{in}^2)^T$. The variance can be expressed compactly in terms of the dot product between the weight vector and the squared centered vector:

$$\sigma_i^2 = \frac{\mathbf{w}_i^T \bar{X}_i^s}{\mathbf{w}_i^T \mathbf{1}}$$

Finally, the prior probability of cluster C_i is re-estimated as the fraction of the total weight belonging to C_i, computed as

$$P(C_i) = \frac{\sum_{j=1}^n w_{ij}}{\sum_{a=1}^k \sum_{j=1}^n w_{aj}} = \frac{\sum_{j=1}^n w_{ij}}{\sum_{j=1}^n 1} = \frac{\sum_{j=1}^n w_{ij}}{n} \tag{13.10}$$

where we made use of the fact that

$$\sum_{i=1}^k w_{ij} = \sum_{i=1}^k P(C_i|x_j) = 1$$

In vector notation the prior probability can be written as

$$P(C_i) = \frac{\mathbf{w}_i^T \mathbf{1}}{n}$$

Iteration

Starting from an initial set of values for the cluster parameters μ_i, σ_i^2 and $P(C_i)$ for all $i = 1, \ldots, k$, the EM algorithm applies the expectation step to compute the weights $w_{ij} = P(C_i|x_j)$. These values are then used in the maximization step to compute the updated cluster parameters μ_i, σ_i^2 and $P(C_i)$. Both the expectation and maximization steps are iteratively applied until convergence, for example, until the means change very little from one iteration to the next.

Example 13.4 (EM in 1D). Figure 13.4 illustrates the EM algorithm on the one-dimensional dataset:

$x_1 = 1.0$	$x_2 = 1.3$	$x_3 = 2.2$	$x_4 = 2.6$	$x_5 = 2.8$
$x_6 = 5.0$	$x_7 = 7.3$	$x_8 = 7.4$	$x_9 = 7.5$	$x_{10} = 7.7$	$x_{11} = 7.9$

We assume that $k = 2$. The initial random means are shown in Figure 13.4(a), with the initial parameters given as

$$\mu_1 = 6.63 \qquad \sigma_1^2 = 1 \qquad P(C_2) = 0.5$$
$$\mu_2 = 7.57 \qquad \sigma_2^2 = 1 \qquad P(C_2) = 0.5$$

After repeated expectation and maximization steps, the EM method converges after five iterations. After $t = 1$ (see Figure 13.4(b)) we have

$$\mu_1 = 3.72 \qquad \sigma_1^2 = 6.13 \qquad P(C_1) = 0.71$$
$$\mu_2 = 7.4 \qquad \sigma_2^2 = 0.69 \qquad P(C_2) = 0.29$$

After the final iteration ($t = 5$), as shown in Figure 13.4(c), we have

$$\mu_1 = 2.48 \qquad \sigma_1^2 = 1.69 \qquad P(C_1) = 0.55$$
$$\mu_2 = 7.56 \qquad \sigma_2^2 = 0.05 \qquad P(C_2) = 0.45$$

One of the main advantages of the EM algorithm over K-means is that it returns the probability $P(C_i|\mathbf{x}_j)$ of each cluster C_i for each point $\mathbf{x}_j$. However, in this 1-dimensional example, these values are essentially binary; assigning each point to the cluster with the highest posterior probability, we obtain the hard clustering

$$C_1 = \{x_1, x_2, x_3, x_4, x_5, x_6\} \text{ (white points)}$$
$$C_2 = \{x_7, x_8, x_9, x_{10}, x_{11}\} \text{ (gray points)}$$

as illustrated in Figure 13.4(c).

13.3.2 EM in d Dimensions

We now consider the EM method in d dimensions, where each cluster is characterized by a multivariate normal distribution [Eq. (13.6)], with parameters μ_i, Σ_i, and $P(C_i)$. For each cluster C_i, we thus need to estimate the d-dimensional mean vector:

$$\mu_i = (\mu_{i1}, \mu_{i2}, \ldots, \mu_{id})^T$$

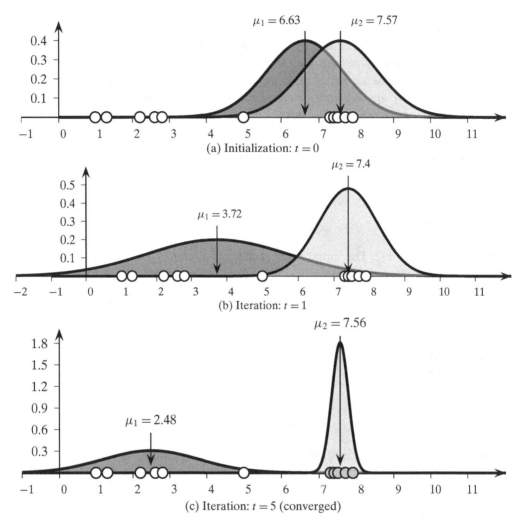

Figure 13.4. EM in one dimension.

and the $d \times d$ covariance matrix:

$$\boldsymbol{\Sigma}_i = \begin{pmatrix} (\sigma_1^i)^2 & \sigma_{12}^i & \cdots & \sigma_{1d}^i \\ \sigma_{21}^i & (\sigma_2^i)^2 & \cdots & \sigma_{2d}^i \\ \vdots & \vdots & \ddots & \\ \sigma_{d1}^i & \sigma_{d2}^i & \cdots & (\sigma_d^i)^2 \end{pmatrix}$$

Because the covariance matrix is symmetric, we have to estimate $\binom{d}{2} = \frac{d(d-1)}{2}$ pairwise covariances and d variances, for a total of $\frac{d(d+1)}{2}$ parameters for $\boldsymbol{\Sigma}_i$. This may be too many parameters for practical purposes because we may not have enough data to estimate all of them reliably. For example, if $d = 100$, then we have to estimate $100 \cdot 101/2 = 5050$ parameters! One simplification is to assume that all dimensions are independent, which leads to a diagonal covariance matrix:

$$\boldsymbol{\Sigma}_i = \begin{pmatrix} (\sigma_1^i)^2 & 0 & \cdots & 0 \\ 0 & (\sigma_2^i)^2 & \cdots & 0 \\ \vdots & \vdots & \ddots & \\ 0 & 0 & \cdots & (\sigma_d^i)^2 \end{pmatrix}$$

Under the independence assumption we have only d parameters to estimate for the diagonal covariance matrix.

Initialization

For each cluster C_i, with $i = 1, 2, \ldots, k$, we randomly initialize the mean $\boldsymbol{\mu}_i$ by selecting a value μ_{ia} for each dimension X_a uniformly at random from the range of X_a. The covariance matrix is initialized as the $d \times d$ identity matrix, $\boldsymbol{\Sigma}_i = \mathbf{I}$. Finally, the cluster prior probabilities are initialized to $P(C_i) = \frac{1}{k}$, so that each cluster has an equal probability.

Expectation Step

In the expectation step, we compute the posterior probability of cluster C_i given point $\mathbf{x}_j$ using Eq. (13.9), with $i = 1, \ldots, k$ and $j = 1, \ldots, n$. As before, we use the shorthand notation $w_{ij} = P(C_i|\mathbf{x}_j)$ to denote the fact that $P(C_i|\mathbf{x}_j)$ can be considered as the weight or contribution of point $\mathbf{x}_j$ to cluster C_i, and we use the notation $\mathbf{w}_i = (w_{i1}, w_{i2}, \ldots, w_{in})^T$ to denote the weight vector for cluster C_i, across all the n points.

Maximization Step

Given the weights w_{ij}, in the maximization step, we re-estimate $\boldsymbol{\Sigma}_i$, $\boldsymbol{\mu}_i$ and $P(C_i)$. The mean $\boldsymbol{\mu}_i$ for cluster C_i can be estimated as

$$\boldsymbol{\mu}_i = \frac{\sum_{j=1}^n w_{ij} \cdot \mathbf{x}_j}{\sum_{j=1}^n w_{ij}} \tag{13.11}$$

which can be expressed compactly in matrix form as

$$\boldsymbol{\mu}_i = \frac{\mathbf{D}^T \mathbf{w}_i}{\mathbf{w}_i^T \mathbf{1}}$$

Let $\overline{\mathbf{D}}_i = \mathbf{D} - \mathbf{1} \cdot \boldsymbol{\mu}_i^T$ be the centered data matrix for cluster C_i. Let $\overline{\mathbf{x}}_{ji} = \mathbf{x}_j - \boldsymbol{\mu}_i \in \mathbb{R}^d$ denote the jth centered point in $\overline{\mathbf{D}}_i$. We can express $\boldsymbol{\Sigma}_i$ compactly using the outer-product form

$$\boldsymbol{\Sigma}_i = \frac{\sum_{j=1}^n w_{ij} \overline{\mathbf{x}}_{ji} \overline{\mathbf{x}}_{ji}^T}{\mathbf{w}_i^T \mathbf{1}} \tag{13.12}$$

Considering the pairwise attribute view, the covariance between dimensions X_a and X_b is estimated as

$$\sigma_{ab}^i = \frac{\sum_{j=1}^n w_{ij}(x_{ja} - \mu_{ia})(x_{jb} - \mu_{ib})}{\sum_{j=1}^n w_{ij}}$$

where x_{ja} and μ_{ia} denote the values of the ath dimension for $\mathbf{x}_j$ and $\boldsymbol{\mu}_i$, respectively.

Finally, the prior probability $P(C_i)$ for each cluster is the same as in the one-dimensional case [Eq. (13.10)], given as

$$P(C_i) = \frac{\sum_{j=1}^{n} w_{ij}}{n} = \frac{\mathbf{w}_i^T \mathbf{1}}{n} \tag{13.13}$$

A formal derivation of these re-estimates for $\boldsymbol{\mu}_i$ [Eq. (13.11)], $\boldsymbol{\Sigma}_i$ [Eq. (13.12)], and $P(C_i)$ [Eq. (13.13)] is given in Section 13.3.3.

EM Clustering Algorithm

The pseudo-code for the multivariate EM clustering algorithm is given in Algorithm 13.3. After initialization of $\boldsymbol{\mu}_i$, $\boldsymbol{\Sigma}_i$, and $P(C_i)$ for all $i = 1, \ldots, k$, the expectation and maximization steps are repeated until convergence. For the convergence test, we check whether $\sum_i \|\boldsymbol{\mu}_i^t - \boldsymbol{\mu}_i^{t-1}\|^2 \leq \epsilon$, where $\epsilon > 0$ is the convergence threshold, and t denotes the iteration. In words, the iterative process continues until the change in the cluster means becomes very small.

Algorithm 13.3: Expectation-Maximization (EM) Algorithm

EXPECTATION-MAXIMIZATION ($\mathbf{D}, k, \epsilon$):

1 $t \leftarrow 0$
    // Initialization
2 Randomly initialize $\boldsymbol{\mu}_1^t, \ldots, \boldsymbol{\mu}_k^t$
3 $\boldsymbol{\Sigma}_i^t \leftarrow \mathbf{I}, \forall i = 1, \ldots, k$
4 $P^t(C_i) \leftarrow \frac{1}{k}, \forall i = 1, \ldots, k$
5 **repeat**
6    $t \leftarrow t + 1$
      // Expectation Step
7   **for** $i = 1, \ldots, k$ *and* $j = 1, \ldots, n$ **do**
8      $w_{ij} \leftarrow \frac{f(\mathbf{x}_j | \boldsymbol{\mu}_i, \boldsymbol{\Sigma}_i) \cdot P(C_i)}{\sum_{a=1}^{k} f(\mathbf{x}_j | \boldsymbol{\mu}_a, \boldsymbol{\Sigma}_a) \cdot P(C_a)}$ // posterior probability $P^t(C_i | \mathbf{x}_j)$
      // Maximization Step
9   **for** $i = 1, \ldots, k$ **do**
10    $\boldsymbol{\mu}_i^t \leftarrow \frac{\sum_{j=1}^{n} w_{ij} \cdot \mathbf{x}_j}{\sum_{j=1}^{n} w_{ij}}$ // re-estimate mean
11    $\boldsymbol{\Sigma}_i^t \leftarrow \frac{\sum_{j=1}^{n} w_{ij} (\mathbf{x}_j - \boldsymbol{\mu}_i)(\mathbf{x}_j - \boldsymbol{\mu}_i)^T}{\sum_{j=1}^{n} w_{ij}}$ // re-estimate covariance matrix
12    $P^t(C_i) \leftarrow \frac{\sum_{j=1}^{n} w_{ij}}{n}$ // re-estimate priors
13 **until** $\sum_{i=1}^{k} \|\boldsymbol{\mu}_i^t - \boldsymbol{\mu}_i^{t-1}\|^2 \leq \epsilon$

Example 13.5 (EM in 2D). Figure 13.5 illustrates the EM algorithm for the two-dimensional Iris dataset, where the two attributes are its first two principal components. The dataset consists of $n = 150$ points, and EM was run using $k = 3$, with full covariance matrix for each cluster. The initial cluster parameters are $\Sigma_i = \begin{pmatrix} 1 & 0 \\ 0 & 1 \end{pmatrix}$ and $P(C_i) = 1/3$, with the means chosen as

$$\mu_1 = (-3.59, 0.25)^T \qquad \mu_2 = (-1.09, -0.46)^T \qquad \mu_3 = (0.75, 1.07)^T$$

The cluster means (shown in black) and the joint probability density function are shown in Figure 13.5(a).

The EM algorithm took 36 iterations to converge (using $\epsilon = 0.001$). An intermediate stage of the clustering is shown in Figure 13.5(b), for $t = 1$. Finally at iteration $t = 36$, shown in Figure 13.5(c), the three clusters have been correctly identified, with the following parameters:

$$\mu_1 = (-2.02, 0.017)^T \qquad \mu_2 = (-0.51, -0.23)^T \qquad \mu_3 = (2.64, 0.19)^T$$

$$\Sigma_1 = \begin{pmatrix} 0.56 & -0.29 \\ -0.29 & 0.23 \end{pmatrix} \qquad \Sigma_2 = \begin{pmatrix} 0.36 & -0.22 \\ -0.22 & 0.19 \end{pmatrix} \qquad \Sigma_3 = \begin{pmatrix} 0.05 & -0.06 \\ -0.06 & 0.21 \end{pmatrix}$$

$$P(C_1) = 0.36 \qquad\qquad P(C_2) = 0.31 \qquad\qquad P(C_3) = 0.33$$

To see the effect of a full versus diagonal covariance matrix, we ran the EM algorithm on the Iris principal components dataset under the independence assumption, which took $t = 29$ iterations to converge. The final cluster parameters were

$$\mu_1 = (-2.1, 0.28)^T \qquad \mu_2 = (-0.67, -0.40)^T \qquad \mu_3 = (2.64, 0.19)^T$$

$$\Sigma_1 = \begin{pmatrix} 0.59 & 0 \\ 0 & 0.11 \end{pmatrix} \qquad \Sigma_2 = \begin{pmatrix} 0.49 & 0 \\ 0 & 0.11 \end{pmatrix} \qquad \Sigma_3 = \begin{pmatrix} 0.05 & 0 \\ 0 & 0.21 \end{pmatrix}$$

$$P(C_1) = 0.30 \qquad\qquad P(C_2) = 0.37 \qquad\qquad P(C_3) = 0.33$$

Figure 13.6(b) shows the clustering results. Also shown are the contours of the normal density function for each cluster (plotted so that the contours do not intersect). The results for the full covariance matrix are shown in Figure 13.6(a), which is a projection of Figure 13.5(c) onto the 2D plane. Points in C_1 are shown as squares, in C_2 as triangles, and in C_3 as circles.

One can observe that the diagonal assumption leads to axis parallel contours for the normal density, contrasted with the rotated contours for the full covariance matrix. The full matrix yields much better clustering, which can be observed by considering the number of points grouped with the wrong Iris type (the white points). For the full covariance matrix only three points are in the wrong group, whereas for the diagonal covariance matrix 25 points are in the wrong cluster, 15 from iris-virginica (white triangles) and 10 from iris-versicolor (white squares). The points corresponding to iris-setosa are correctly clustered as C_3 in both approaches.

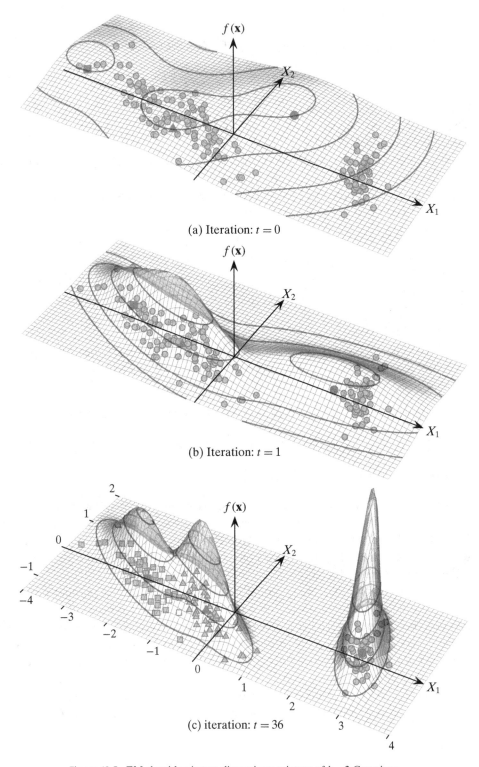

(a) Iteration: $t = 0$

(b) Iteration: $t = 1$

(c) iteration: $t = 36$

Figure 13.5. EM algorithm in two dimensions: mixture of $k = 3$ Gaussians.

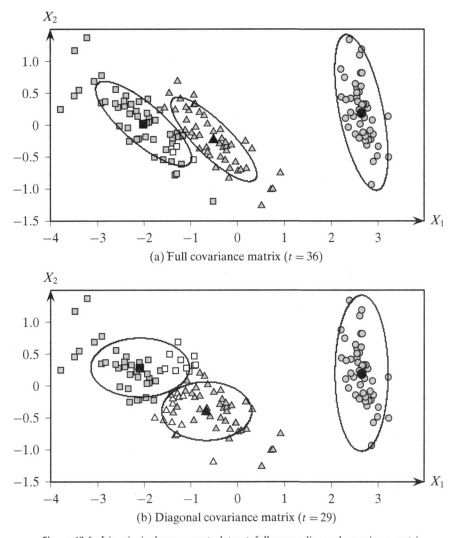

(a) Full covariance matrix ($t = 36$)

(b) Diagonal covariance matrix ($t = 29$)

Figure 13.6. Iris principal components dataset: full versus diagonal covariance matrix.

Computational Complexity

For the expectation step, to compute the cluster posterior probabilities, we need to invert Σ_i and compute its determinant $|\Sigma_i|$, which takes $O(d^3)$ time. Across the k clusters the time is $O(kd^3)$. For the expectation step, evaluating the density $f(\mathbf{x}_j | \boldsymbol{\mu}_i, \Sigma_i)$ takes $O(d^2)$ time, for a total time of $O(knd^2)$ over the n points and k clusters. For the maximization step, the time is dominated by the update for Σ_i, which takes $O(knd^2)$ time over all k clusters. The computational complexity of the EM method is thus $O(t(kd^3 + nkd^2))$, where t is the number of iterations. If we use a diagonal covariance matrix, then inverse and determinant of Σ_i can be computed in $O(d)$ time. Density computation per point takes $O(d)$ time, so that the time for the expectation step is $O(knd)$. The maximization step also takes $O(knd)$ time to re-estimate Σ_i. The total time for a diagonal covariance matrix is therefore $O(tnkd)$. The I/O complexity for the EM algorithm is $O(t)$ complete database scans because we read the entire set of points in each iteration.

K-means as Specialization of EM

Although we assumed a normal mixture model for the clusters, the EM approach can be applied with other models for the cluster density distribution $P(\mathbf{x}_j|C_i)$. For instance, K-means can be considered as a special case of the EM algorithm, obtained as follows:

$$P(\mathbf{x}_j|C_i) = \begin{cases} 1 & \text{if } C_i = \arg\min_{C_a}\left\{\|\mathbf{x}_j - \boldsymbol{\mu}_a\|^2\right\} \\ 0 & \text{otherwise} \end{cases}$$

Using Eq. (13.9), the posterior probability $P(C_i|\mathbf{x}_j)$ is given as

$$P(C_i|\mathbf{x}_j) = \frac{P(\mathbf{x}_j|C_i)P(C_i)}{\sum_{a=1}^{k} P(\mathbf{x}_j|C_a)P(C_a)}$$

One can see that if $P(\mathbf{x}_j|C_i) = 0$, then $P(C_i|\mathbf{x}_j) = 0$. Otherwise, if $P(\mathbf{x}_j|C_i) = 1$, then $P(\mathbf{x}_j|C_a) = 0$ for all $a \neq i$, and thus $P(C_i|\mathbf{x}_j) = \frac{1 \cdot P(C_i)}{1 \cdot P(C_i)} = 1$. Putting it all together, the posterior probability is given as

$$P(C_i|\mathbf{x}_j) = \begin{cases} 1 & \text{if } \mathbf{x}_j \in C_i, \text{i.e., if } C_i = \arg\min_{C_a}\left\{\|\mathbf{x}_j - \boldsymbol{\mu}_a\|^2\right\} \\ 0 & \text{otherwise} \end{cases} \tag{13.14}$$

It is clear that for K-means the cluster parameters are $\boldsymbol{\mu}_i$ and $P(C_i)$; we can ignore the covariance matrix.

13.3.3 Maximum Likelihood Estimation

In this section, we derive the maximum likelihood estimates for the cluster parameters $\boldsymbol{\mu}_i$, $\boldsymbol{\Sigma}_i$ and $P(C_i)$. We do this by taking the derivative of the log-likelihood function with respect to each of these parameters and setting the derivative to zero.

The partial derivative of the log-likelihood function [Eq. (13.8)] with respect to some parameter $\boldsymbol{\theta}_i$ for cluster C_i is given as

$$\frac{\partial}{\partial \boldsymbol{\theta}_i} \ln\Big(P(\mathbf{D}|\boldsymbol{\theta})\Big) = \frac{\partial}{\partial \boldsymbol{\theta}_i}\left(\sum_{j=1}^{n} \ln f(\mathbf{x}_j)\right)$$

$$= \sum_{j=1}^{n}\left(\frac{1}{f(\mathbf{x}_j)} \cdot \frac{\partial f(\mathbf{x}_j)}{\partial \boldsymbol{\theta}_i}\right)$$

$$= \sum_{j=1}^{n}\left(\frac{1}{f(\mathbf{x}_j)} \sum_{a=1}^{k} \frac{\partial}{\partial \boldsymbol{\theta}_i}\Big(f(\mathbf{x}_j|\boldsymbol{\mu}_a, \boldsymbol{\Sigma}_a)P(C_a)\Big)\right)$$

$$= \sum_{j=1}^{n}\left(\frac{1}{f(\mathbf{x}_j)} \cdot \frac{\partial}{\partial \boldsymbol{\theta}_i}\Big(f(\mathbf{x}_j|\boldsymbol{\mu}_i, \boldsymbol{\Sigma}_i)P(C_i)\Big)\right)$$

The last step follows from the fact that because $\boldsymbol{\theta}_i$ is a parameter for the ith cluster the mixture components for the other clusters are constants with respect to $\boldsymbol{\theta}_i$. Using the fact that $|\boldsymbol{\Sigma}_i| = \frac{1}{|\boldsymbol{\Sigma}_i^{-1}|}$ the multivariate normal density in Eq. (13.6) can be written as

$$f(\mathbf{x}_j|\boldsymbol{\mu}_i, \boldsymbol{\Sigma}_i) = (2\pi)^{-\frac{d}{2}} \, |\boldsymbol{\Sigma}_i^{-1}|^{\frac{1}{2}} \, \exp\big\{g(\boldsymbol{\mu}_i, \boldsymbol{\Sigma}_i)\big\} \tag{13.15}$$

where

$$g(\boldsymbol{\mu}_i, \boldsymbol{\Sigma}_i) = -\frac{1}{2}(\mathbf{x}_j - \boldsymbol{\mu}_i)^T \boldsymbol{\Sigma}_i^{-1}(\mathbf{x}_j - \boldsymbol{\mu}_i) \qquad (13.16)$$

Thus, the derivative of the log-likelihood function can be written as

$$\frac{\partial}{\partial \boldsymbol{\theta}_i} \ln\left(P(\mathbf{D}|\boldsymbol{\theta})\right) = \sum_{j=1}^{n} \left(\frac{1}{f(\mathbf{x}_j)} \cdot \frac{\partial}{\partial \boldsymbol{\theta}_i} \left((2\pi)^{-\frac{d}{2}} |\boldsymbol{\Sigma}_i^{-1}|^{\frac{1}{2}} \exp\{g(\boldsymbol{\mu}_i, \boldsymbol{\Sigma}_i)\} P(C_i) \right) \right) \qquad (13.17)$$

Below, we make use of the fact that

$$\frac{\partial}{\partial \boldsymbol{\theta}_i} \exp\{g(\boldsymbol{\mu}_i, \boldsymbol{\Sigma}_i)\} = \exp\{g(\boldsymbol{\mu}_i, \boldsymbol{\Sigma}_i)\} \cdot \frac{\partial}{\partial \boldsymbol{\theta}_i} g(\boldsymbol{\mu}_i, \boldsymbol{\Sigma}_i) \qquad (13.18)$$

Estimation of Mean

To derive the maximum likelihood estimate for the mean $\boldsymbol{\mu}_i$, we have to take the derivative of the log-likelihood with respect to $\boldsymbol{\theta}_i = \boldsymbol{\mu}_i$. As per Eq. (13.17), the only term involving $\boldsymbol{\mu}_i$ is $\exp\{g(\boldsymbol{\mu}_i, \boldsymbol{\Sigma}_i)\}$. Using the fact that

$$\frac{\partial}{\partial \boldsymbol{\mu}_i} g(\boldsymbol{\mu}_i, \boldsymbol{\Sigma}_i) = \boldsymbol{\Sigma}_i^{-1}(\mathbf{x}_j - \boldsymbol{\mu}_i) \qquad (13.19)$$

and making use of Eq. (13.18), the partial derivative of the log-likelihood [Eq. (13.17)] with respect to $\boldsymbol{\mu}_i$ is

$$\frac{\partial}{\partial \boldsymbol{\mu}_i} \ln(P(\mathbf{D}|\boldsymbol{\theta})) = \sum_{j=1}^{n} \left(\frac{1}{f(\mathbf{x}_j)} (2\pi)^{-\frac{d}{2}} |\boldsymbol{\Sigma}_i^{-1}|^{\frac{1}{2}} \exp\{g(\boldsymbol{\mu}_i, \boldsymbol{\Sigma}_i)\} P(C_i) \, \boldsymbol{\Sigma}_i^{-1}(\mathbf{x}_j - \boldsymbol{\mu}_i) \right)$$

$$= \sum_{j=1}^{n} \left(\frac{f(\mathbf{x}_j|\boldsymbol{\mu}_i, \boldsymbol{\Sigma}_i) P(C_i)}{f(\mathbf{x}_j)} \cdot \boldsymbol{\Sigma}_i^{-1}(\mathbf{x}_j - \boldsymbol{\mu}_i) \right)$$

$$= \sum_{j=1}^{n} w_{ij} \boldsymbol{\Sigma}_i^{-1}(\mathbf{x}_j - \boldsymbol{\mu}_i)$$

where we made use of Eqs. (13.15) and (13.9), and the fact that

$$w_{ij} = P(C_i|\mathbf{x}_j) = \frac{f(\mathbf{x}_j|\boldsymbol{\mu}_i, \boldsymbol{\Sigma}_i) P(C_i)}{f(\mathbf{x}_j)}$$

Setting the partial derivative of the log-likelihood to the zero vector, and multiplying both sides by $\boldsymbol{\Sigma}_i$, we get

$$\sum_{j=1}^{n} w_{ij}(\mathbf{x}_j - \boldsymbol{\mu}_i) = \mathbf{0}, \text{ which implies that}$$

$$\sum_{j=1}^{n} w_{ij}\mathbf{x}_j = \boldsymbol{\mu}_i \sum_{j=1}^{n} w_{ij}, \text{ and therefore}$$

$$\boldsymbol{\mu}_i = \frac{\sum_{j=1}^{n} w_{ij}\mathbf{x}_j}{\sum_{j=1}^{n} w_{ij}} \qquad (13.20)$$

which is precisely the re-estimation formula we used in Eq. (13.11).

Estimation of Covariance Matrix

To re-estimate the covariance matrix Σ_i, we take the partial derivative of Eq. (13.17) with respect to Σ_i^{-1} using the product rule for the differentiation of the term $|\Sigma_i^{-1}|^{\frac{1}{2}} \exp\{g(\mu_i, \Sigma_i)\}$.

Using the fact that for any square matrix $\mathbf{A}$, we have $\frac{\partial |\mathbf{A}|}{\partial \mathbf{A}} = |\mathbf{A}| \cdot (\mathbf{A}^{-1})^T$ the derivative of $|\Sigma_i^{-1}|^{\frac{1}{2}}$ with respect to Σ_i^{-1} is

$$\frac{\partial |\Sigma_i^{-1}|^{\frac{1}{2}}}{\partial \Sigma_i^{-1}} = \frac{1}{2} \cdot |\Sigma_i^{-1}|^{-\frac{1}{2}} \cdot |\Sigma_i^{-1}| \cdot \Sigma_i = \frac{1}{2} \cdot |\Sigma_i^{-1}|^{\frac{1}{2}} \cdot \Sigma_i \tag{13.21}$$

Next, using the fact that for the square matrix $\mathbf{A} \in \mathbb{R}^{d \times d}$ and vectors $\mathbf{a}, \mathbf{b} \in \mathbb{R}^d$, we have $\frac{\partial}{\partial \mathbf{A}} \mathbf{a}^T \mathbf{A} \mathbf{b} = \mathbf{a}\mathbf{b}^T$ the derivative of $\exp\{g(\mu_i, \Sigma_i)\}$ with respect to Σ_i^{-1} is obtained from Eq. (13.18) as follows:

$$\frac{\partial}{\partial \Sigma_i^{-1}} \exp\{g(\mu_i, \Sigma_i)\} = -\frac{1}{2} \exp\{g(\mu_i, \Sigma_i)\}(\mathbf{x}_j - \mu_i)(\mathbf{x}_j - \mu_i)^T \tag{13.22}$$

Using the product rule on Eqs. (13.21) and (13.22), we get

$$\frac{\partial}{\partial \Sigma_i^{-1}} |\Sigma_i^{-1}|^{\frac{1}{2}} \exp\{g(\mu_i, \Sigma_i)\}$$

$$= \frac{1}{2} |\Sigma_i^{-1}|^{\frac{1}{2}} \Sigma_i \exp\{g(\mu_i, \Sigma_i)\} - \frac{1}{2} |\Sigma_i^{-1}|^{\frac{1}{2}} \exp\{g(\mu_i, \Sigma_i)\}(\mathbf{x}_j - \mu_i)(\mathbf{x}_j - \mu_i)^T$$

$$= \frac{1}{2} \cdot |\Sigma_i^{-1}|^{\frac{1}{2}} \cdot \exp\{g(\mu_i, \Sigma_i)\}\left(\Sigma_i - (\mathbf{x}_j - \mu_i)(\mathbf{x}_j - \mu_i)^T\right) \tag{13.23}$$

Plugging Eq. (13.23) into Eq. (13.17) the derivative of the log-likelihood function with respect to Σ_i^{-1} is given as

$$\frac{\partial}{\partial \Sigma_i^{-1}} \ln(P(\mathbf{D}|\theta)) = \frac{1}{2} \sum_{j=1}^{n} \frac{(2\pi)^{-\frac{d}{2}} |\Sigma_i^{-1}|^{\frac{1}{2}} \exp\{g(\mu_i, \Sigma_i)\} P(C_i)}{f(\mathbf{x}_j)} \left(\Sigma_i - (\mathbf{x}_j - \mu_i)(\mathbf{x}_j - \mu_i)^T\right)$$

$$= \frac{1}{2} \sum_{j=1}^{n} \frac{f(\mathbf{x}_j|\mu_i, \Sigma_i) P(C_i)}{f(\mathbf{x}_j)} \cdot \left(\Sigma_i - (\mathbf{x}_j - \mu_i)(\mathbf{x}_j - \mu_i)^T\right)$$

$$= \frac{1}{2} \sum_{j=1}^{n} w_{ij} \left(\Sigma_i - (\mathbf{x}_j - \mu_i)(\mathbf{x}_j - \mu_i)^T\right)$$

Setting the derivative to the $d \times d$ zero matrix $\mathbf{0}_{d \times d}$, we can solve for Σ_i:

$$\sum_{j=1}^{n} w_{ij} \left(\Sigma_i - (\mathbf{x}_j - \mu_i)(\mathbf{x}_j - \mu_i)^T\right) = \mathbf{0}_{d \times d}, \text{ which implies that}$$

$$\Sigma_i = \frac{\sum_{j=1}^{n} w_{ij}(\mathbf{x}_j - \mu_i)(\mathbf{x}_j - \mu_i)^T}{\sum_{j=1}^{n} w_{ij}} \tag{13.24}$$

Thus, we can see that the maximum likelihood estimate for the covariance matrix is given as the weighted outer-product form in Eq. (13.12).

Estimating the Prior Probability: Mixture Parameters

To obtain a maximum likelihood estimate for the mixture parameters or the prior probabilities $P(C_i)$, we have to take the partial derivative of the log-likelihood [Eq. (13.17)] with respect to $P(C_i)$. However, we have to introduce a Lagrange multiplier α for the constraint that $\sum_{a=1}^{k} P(C_a) = 1$. We thus take the following derivative:

$$\frac{\partial}{\partial P(C_i)} \left(\ln(P(\mathbf{D}|\boldsymbol{\theta})) + \alpha \left(\sum_{a=1}^{k} P(C_a) - 1 \right) \right) \tag{13.25}$$

The partial derivative of the log-likelihood in Eq. (13.17) with respect to $P(C_i)$ gives

$$\frac{\partial}{\partial P(C_i)} \ln(P(\mathbf{D}|\boldsymbol{\theta})) = \sum_{j=1}^{n} \frac{f(\mathbf{x}_j|\boldsymbol{\mu}_i, \boldsymbol{\Sigma}_i)}{f(\mathbf{x}_j)}$$

The derivative in Eq. (13.25) thus evaluates to

$$\left(\sum_{j=1}^{n} \frac{f(\mathbf{x}_j|\boldsymbol{\mu}_i, \boldsymbol{\Sigma}_i)}{f(\mathbf{x}_j)} \right) + \alpha$$

Setting the derivative to zero, and multiplying on both sides by $P(C_i)$, we get

$$\sum_{j=1}^{n} \frac{f(\mathbf{x}_j|\boldsymbol{\mu}_i, \boldsymbol{\Sigma}_i) P(C_i)}{f(\mathbf{x}_j)} = -\alpha P(C_i)$$

$$\sum_{j=1}^{n} w_{ij} = -\alpha P(C_i) \tag{13.26}$$

Taking the summation of Eq. (13.26) over all clusters yields

$$\sum_{i=1}^{k} \sum_{j=1}^{n} w_{ij} = -\alpha \sum_{i=1}^{k} P(C_i)$$

$$\text{or } n = -\alpha \tag{13.27}$$

The last step follows from the fact that $\sum_{i=1}^{k} w_{ij} = 1$. Plugging Eq. (13.27) into Eq. (13.26), gives us the maximum likelihood estimate for $P(C_i)$ as follows:

$$P(C_i) = \frac{\sum_{j=1}^{n} w_{ij}}{n} \tag{13.28}$$

which matches the formula in Eq. (13.13).

We can see that all three parameters $\boldsymbol{\mu}_i$, $\boldsymbol{\Sigma}_i$, and $P(C_i)$ for cluster C_i depend on the weights w_{ij}, which correspond to the cluster posterior probabilities $P(C_i|\mathbf{x}_j)$. Equations (13.20), (13.24), and (13.28) thus do not represent a closed-form solution for maximizing the log-likelihood function. Instead, we use the iterative EM approach to compute the w_{ij} in the expectation step, and we then re-estimate $\boldsymbol{\mu}_i$, $\boldsymbol{\Sigma}_i$ and $P(C_i)$ in the maximization step. Next, we describe the EM framework in some more detail.

13.3.4 EM Approach

Maximizing the log-likelihood function [Eq. (13.8)] directly is hard because the mixture term appears inside the logarithm. The problem is that for any point $\mathbf{x}_j$ we do not know which normal, or mixture component, it comes from. Suppose that we knew this information, that is, suppose each point $\mathbf{x}_j$ had an associated value indicating the cluster that generated the point. As we shall see, it is much easier to maximize the log-likelihood given this information.

The categorical attribute corresponding to the cluster label can be modeled as a vector random variable $\mathbf{C} = (C_1, C_2, \ldots, C_k)$, where C_i is a Bernoulli random variable (see Section 3.1.2 for details on how to model a categorical variable). If a given point is generated from cluster C_i, then $C_i = 1$, otherwise $C_i = 0$. The parameter $P(C_i)$ gives the probability $P(C_i = 1)$. Because each point can be generated from only one cluster, if $C_a = 1$ for a given point, then $C_i = 0$ for all $i \neq a$. It follows that $\sum_{i=1}^{k} P(C_i) = 1$.

For each point $\mathbf{x}_j$, let its cluster vector be $\mathbf{c}_j = (c_{j1}, \ldots, c_{jk})^T$. Only one component of $\mathbf{c}_j$ has value 1. If $c_{ji} = 1$, it means that $C_i = 1$, that is, the cluster C_i generates the point $\mathbf{x}_j$. The probability mass function of $\mathbf{C}$ is given as

$$P(\mathbf{C} = \mathbf{c}_j) = \prod_{i=1}^{k} P(C_i)^{c_{ji}}$$

Given the cluster information $\mathbf{c}_j$ for each point $\mathbf{x}_j$, the conditional probability density function for $\mathbf{X}$ is given as

$$f(\mathbf{x}_j | \mathbf{c}_j) = \prod_{i=1}^{k} f(\mathbf{x}_j | \boldsymbol{\mu}_i, \boldsymbol{\Sigma}_i)^{c_{ji}}$$

Only one cluster can generate $\mathbf{x}_j$, say C_a, in which case $c_{ja} = 1$, and the above expression would simplify to $f(\mathbf{x}_j | \mathbf{c}_j) = f(\mathbf{x}_j | \boldsymbol{\mu}_a, \boldsymbol{\Sigma}_a)$.

The pair $(\mathbf{x}_j, \mathbf{c}_j)$ is a random sample drawn from the joint distribution of vector random variables $\mathbf{X} = (X_1, \ldots, X_d)$ and $\mathbf{C} = (C_1, \ldots, C_k)$, corresponding to the d data attributes and k cluster attributes. The joint density function of $\mathbf{X}$ and $\mathbf{C}$ is given as

$$f(\mathbf{x}_j \text{ and } \mathbf{c}_j) = f(\mathbf{x}_j | \mathbf{c}_j) P(\mathbf{c}_j) = \prod_{i=1}^{k} \left(f(\mathbf{x}_j | \boldsymbol{\mu}_i, \boldsymbol{\Sigma}_i) P(C_i) \right)^{c_{ji}}$$

The log-likelihood for the data given the cluster information is as follows:

$$\ln P(\mathbf{D} | \boldsymbol{\theta}) = \ln \prod_{j=1}^{n} f(\mathbf{x}_j \text{ and } \mathbf{c}_j | \boldsymbol{\theta})$$

$$= \sum_{j=1}^{n} \ln f(\mathbf{x}_j \text{ and } \mathbf{c}_j | \boldsymbol{\theta})$$

$$= \sum_{j=1}^{n} \ln \left(\prod_{i=1}^{k} \left(f(\mathbf{x}_j | \boldsymbol{\mu}_i, \boldsymbol{\Sigma}_i) P(C_i) \right)^{c_{ji}} \right)$$

$$= \sum_{j=1}^{n} \sum_{i=1}^{k} c_{ji} \left(\ln f(\mathbf{x}_j | \boldsymbol{\mu}_i, \boldsymbol{\Sigma}_i) + \ln P(C_i) \right) \tag{13.29}$$

Expectation Step

In the expectation step, we compute the expected value of the log-likelihood for the labeled data given in Eq. (13.29). The expectation is over the missing cluster information c_j treating μ_i, Σ_i, $P(C_i)$, and x_j as fixed. Owing to the linearity of expectation, the expected value of the log-likelihood is given as

$$E[\ln P(\mathbf{D}|\theta)] = \sum_{j=1}^{n}\sum_{i=1}^{k} E[c_{ji}]\Big(\ln f(\mathbf{x}_j|\mu_i, \Sigma_i) + \ln P(C_i)\Big)$$

The expected value $E[c_{ji}]$ can be computed as

$$E[c_{ji}] = 1 \cdot P(c_{ji} = 1|\mathbf{x}_j) + 0 \cdot P(c_{ji} = 0|\mathbf{x}_j) = P(c_{ji} = 1|\mathbf{x}_j) = P(C_i|\mathbf{x}_j)$$

$$= \frac{P(\mathbf{x}_j|C_i)P(C_i)}{P(\mathbf{x}_j)} = \frac{f(\mathbf{x}_j|\mu_i, \Sigma_i)P(C_i)}{f(\mathbf{x}_j)}$$

$$= w_{ij} \tag{13.30}$$

Thus, in the expectation step we use the values of $\theta = \{\mu_i, \Sigma_i, P(C_i)\}_{i=1}^{k}$ to estimate the posterior probabilities or weights w_{ij} for each point for each cluster. Using $E[c_{ji}] = w_{ij}$, the expected value of the log-likelihood function can be rewritten as

$$E[\ln P(\mathbf{D}|\theta)] = \sum_{j=1}^{n}\sum_{i=1}^{k} w_{ij}\Big(\ln f(\mathbf{x}_j|\mu_i, \Sigma_i) + \ln P(C_i)\Big) \tag{13.31}$$

Maximization Step

In the maximization step, we maximize the expected value of the log-likelihood [Eq. (13.31)]. Taking the derivative with respect to μ_i, Σ_i or $P(C_i)$ we can ignore the terms for all the other clusters.

The derivative of Eq. (13.31) with respect to μ_i is given as

$$\frac{\partial}{\partial \mu_i}\ln E[P(\mathbf{D}|\theta)] = \frac{\partial}{\partial \mu_i}\sum_{j=1}^{n} w_{ij}\ln f(\mathbf{x}_j|\mu_i, \Sigma_i)$$

$$= \sum_{j=1}^{n} w_{ij} \cdot \frac{1}{f(\mathbf{x}_j|\mu_i, \Sigma_i)}\frac{\partial}{\partial \mu_i}f(\mathbf{x}_j|\mu_i, \Sigma_i)$$

$$= \sum_{j=1}^{n} w_{ij} \cdot \frac{1}{f(\mathbf{x}_j|\mu_i, \Sigma_i)} \cdot f(\mathbf{x}_j|\mu_i, \Sigma_i)\,\Sigma_i^{-1}(\mathbf{x}_j - \mu_i)$$

$$= \sum_{j=1}^{n} w_{ij}\,\Sigma_i^{-1}(\mathbf{x}_j - \mu_i)$$

where we used the observation that

$$\frac{\partial}{\partial \mu_i}f(\mathbf{x}_j|\mu_i, \Sigma_i) = f(\mathbf{x}_j|\mu_i, \Sigma_i)\,\Sigma_i^{-1}(\mathbf{x}_j - \mu_i)$$

which follows from Eqs. (13.15), (13.18), and (13.19). Setting the derivative of the expected value of the log-likelihood to the zero vector, and multiplying on both sides by $\mathbf{\Sigma}_i$, we get

$$\boldsymbol{\mu}_i = \frac{\sum_{j=1}^n w_{ij}\mathbf{x}_j}{\sum_{j=1}^n w_{ij}}$$

matching the formula in Eq. (13.11).

Making use of Eqs. (13.23) and (13.15), we obtain the derivative of Eq. (13.31) with respect to $\mathbf{\Sigma}_i^{-1}$ as follows:

$$\frac{\partial}{\partial \mathbf{\Sigma}_i^{-1}} \ln E[P(\mathbf{D}|\boldsymbol{\theta})]$$

$$= \sum_{j=1}^n w_{ij} \cdot \frac{1}{f(\mathbf{x}_j|\boldsymbol{\mu}_i, \mathbf{\Sigma}_i)} \cdot \frac{1}{2} f(\mathbf{x}_j|\boldsymbol{\mu}_i, \mathbf{\Sigma}_i)\big(\mathbf{\Sigma}_i - (\mathbf{x}_j - \boldsymbol{\mu}_i)(\mathbf{x}_j - \boldsymbol{\mu}_i)^T\big)$$

$$= \frac{1}{2} \sum_{j=1}^n w_{ij} \cdot \big(\mathbf{\Sigma}_i - (\mathbf{x}_j - \boldsymbol{\mu}_i)(\mathbf{x}_j - \boldsymbol{\mu}_i)^T\big)$$

Setting the derivative to the $d \times d$ zero matrix and solving for $\mathbf{\Sigma}_i$ yields

$$\mathbf{\Sigma}_i = \frac{\sum_{j=1}^n w_{ij}(\mathbf{x}_j - \boldsymbol{\mu}_i)(\mathbf{x}_j - \boldsymbol{\mu}_i)^T}{\sum_{j=1}^n w_{ij}}$$

which is the same as that in Eq. (13.12).

Using the Lagrange multiplier α for the constraint $\sum_{i=1}^k P(C_i) = 1$, and noting that in the log-likelihood function [Eq. (13.31)], the term $\ln f(\mathbf{x}_j|\boldsymbol{\mu}_i, \mathbf{\Sigma}_i)$ is a constant with respect to $P(C_i)$, we obtain the following:

$$\frac{\partial}{\partial P(C_i)}\left(\ln E[P(\mathbf{D}|\boldsymbol{\theta})] + \alpha\left(\sum_{i=1}^k P(C_i) - 1\right)\right) = \frac{\partial}{\partial P(C_i)}\big(w_{ij}\ln P(C_i) + \alpha P(C_i)\big)$$

$$= \left(\sum_{j=1}^n w_{ij} \cdot \frac{1}{P(C_i)}\right) + \alpha$$

Setting the derivative to zero, we get

$$\sum_{j=1}^n w_{ij} = -\alpha \cdot P(C_i)$$

Using the same derivation as in Eq. (13.27) we obtain

$$P(C_i) = \frac{\sum_{j=1}^n w_{ij}}{n}$$

which is identical to the re-estimation formula in Eq. (13.13).

13.4 FURTHER READING

The K-means algorithm was proposed in several contexts during the 1950s and 1960s; among the first works to develop the method include MacQueen (1967); Lloyd (1982) and Hartigan (1975). Kernel k-means was first proposed in Schölkopf, Smola, and Müller (1996). The EM algorithm was proposed in Dempster, Laird, and Rubin (1977). A good review on EM method can be found in McLachlan and Krishnan (2008). For a scalable and incremental representative-based clustering method that can also generate hierarchical clusterings see Zhang, Ramakrishnan, and Livny (1996).

Dempster, A. P., Laird, N. M., and Rubin, D. B. (1977). Maximum likelihood from incomplete data via the EM algorithm. *Journal of the Royal Statistical Society, Series B*, 39 (1), 1–38.

Hartigan, J. A. (1975). *Clustering Algorithms*. New York: New York: John Wiley & Sons.

Lloyd, S. (1982). Least squares quantization in PCM. *IEEE Transactions on Information Theory*, 28 (2), 129–137.

MacQueen, J. (1967). Some methods for classification and analysis of multivariate observations. *Proceedings of the 5th Berkeley Symposium on Mathematical Statistics and Probability*. Vol. 1. 281-297. University of California Press, Berkeley, p. 14.

McLachlan, G. and Krishnan, T. (2008). *The EM Algorithm and Extensions, 2nd ed.* New Jersey: Hoboken, NJ: John Wiley & Sons.

Schölkopf, B., Smola, A., and Müller, K.-R. (1996). *Nonlinear component analysis as a kernel eigenvalue problem*. Technical Report No. 44. Tübingen, Germany: Max-Planck-Institut für biologische Kybernetik.

Zhang, T., Ramakrishnan, R., and Livny, M. (1996). BIRCH: An efficient data clustering method for very large databases. *ACM SIGMOD Record*. Vol. 25. 2. ACM, pp. 103–114.

13.5 EXERCISES

Q1. Given the following points: $2, 4, 10, 12, 3, 20, 30, 11, 25$. Assume $k = 3$, and that we randomly pick the initial means $\mu_1 = 2$, $\mu_2 = 4$ and $\mu_3 = 6$. Show the clusters obtained using K-means algorithm after one iteration, and show the new means for the next iteration.

Table 13.1. Dataset for Q2

x	$P(C_1|x)$	$P(C_2|x)$
2	0.9	0.1
3	0.8	0.1
7	0.3	0.7
9	0.1	0.9
2	0.9	0.1
1	0.8	0.2

Q2. Given the data points in Table 13.1, and their probability of belonging to two clusters. Assume that these points were produced by a mixture of two univariate normal distributions. Answer the following questions:

(a) Find the maximum likelihood estimate of the means μ_1 and μ_2.

(b) Assume that $\mu_1 = 2$, $\mu_2 = 7$, and $\sigma_1 = \sigma_2 = 1$. Find the probability that the point $x = 5$ belongs to cluster C_1 and to cluster C_2. You may assume that the prior probability of each cluster is equal (i.e., $P(C_1) = P(C_2) = 0.5$), and the prior probability $P(x = 5) = 0.029$.

Table 13.2. Dataset for Q3

	X_1	X_2
$\mathbf{x}_1^T$	0	2
$\mathbf{x}_2^T$	0	0
$\mathbf{x}_3^T$	1.5	0
$\mathbf{x}_4^T$	5	0
$\mathbf{x}_5^T$	5	2

Q3. Given the two-dimensional points in Table 13.2, assume that $k = 2$, and that initially the points are assigned to clusters as follows: $C_1 = \{\mathbf{x}_1, \mathbf{x}_2, \mathbf{x}_4\}$ and $C_2 = \{\mathbf{x}_3, \mathbf{x}_5\}$. Answer the following questions:

(a) Apply the K-means algorithm until convergence, that is, the clusters do not change, assuming (1) the usual Euclidean distance or the L_2-*norm* as the distance between points, defined as $\|\mathbf{x}_i - \mathbf{x}_j\|_2 = \left(\sum_{a=1}^{d}(x_{ia} - x_{ja})^2\right)^{1/2}$, and (2) the Manhattan distance or the L_1-*norm* defined as $\|\mathbf{x}_i - \mathbf{x}_j\|_1 = \sum_{a=1}^{d}|x_{ia} - x_{ja}|$.

(b) Apply the EM algorithm with $k = 2$ assuming that the dimensions are independent. Show one complete execution of the expectation and the maximization steps. Start with the assumption that $P(C_i|x_{ja}) = 0.5$ for $a = 1, 2$ and $j = 1, \ldots, 5$.

Q4. Given the categorical database in Table 13.3. Find $k = 2$ clusters in this data using the EM method. Assume that each attribute is independent, and that the domain of each attribute is $\{A, C, T\}$. Initially assume that the points are partitioned as follows: $C_1 = \{\mathbf{x}_1, \mathbf{x}_4\}$, and $C_2 = \{\mathbf{x}_2, \mathbf{x}_3\}$. Assume that $P(C_1) = P(C_2) = 0.5$.

Table 13.3. Dataset for Q4

	X_1	X_2
$\mathbf{x}_1^T$	A	T
$\mathbf{x}_2^T$	A	A
$\mathbf{x}_3^T$	C	C
$\mathbf{x}_4^T$	A	C

The probability of an attribute value given a cluster is given as

$$P(x_{ja}|C_i) = \frac{\text{No. of times the symbol } x_{ja} \text{ occurs in cluster } C_i}{\text{No. of objects in cluster } C_i}$$

for $a = 1, 2$. The probability of a point given a cluster is then given as

$$P(\mathbf{x}_j|C_i) = \prod_{a=1}^{2} P(x_{ja}|C_i)$$

Instead of computing the mean for each cluster, generate a partition of the objects by doing a hard assignment. That is, in the expectation step compute $P(C_i|\mathbf{x}_j)$, and in the maximization step assign the point $\mathbf{x}_j$ to the cluster with the largest $P(C_i|\mathbf{x}_j)$ value, which gives a new partitioning of the points. Show one full iteration of the EM algorithm and show the resulting clusters.

Table 13.4. Dataset for Q5

	X_1	X_2	X_3
$\mathbf{x}_1^T$	0.5	4.5	2.5
$\mathbf{x}_2^T$	2.2	1.5	0.1
$\mathbf{x}_3^T$	3.9	3.5	1.1
$\mathbf{x}_4^T$	2.1	1.9	4.9
$\mathbf{x}_5^T$	0.5	3.2	1.2
$\mathbf{x}_6^T$	0.8	4.3	2.6
$\mathbf{x}_7^T$	2.7	1.1	3.1
$\mathbf{x}_8^T$	2.5	3.5	2.8
$\mathbf{x}_9^T$	2.8	3.9	1.5
$\mathbf{x}_{10}^T$	0.1	4.1	2.9

Q5. Given the points in Table 13.4, assume that there are two clusters: C_1 and C_2, with $\mu_1 = (0.5, 4.5, 2.5)^T$ and $\mu_2 = (2.5, 2, 1.5)^T$. Initially assign each point to the closest mean, and compute the covariance matrices Σ_i and the prior probabilities $P(C_i)$ for $i = 1, 2$. Next, answer which cluster is more likely to have produced $\mathbf{x}_8$?

Q6. Consider the data in Table 13.5. Answer the following questions:

(a) Compute the kernel matrix $\mathbf{K}$ between the points assuming the following kernel:

$$K(\mathbf{x}_i, \mathbf{x}_j) = 1 + \mathbf{x}_i^T \mathbf{x}_j$$

(b) Assume initial cluster assignments of $C_1 = \{\mathbf{x}_1, \mathbf{x}_2\}$ and $C_2 = \{\mathbf{x}_3, \mathbf{x}_4\}$. Using kernel K-means, which cluster should $\mathbf{x}_1$ belong to in the next step?

Table 13.5. Data for Q6

	X_1	X_2	X_3
$\mathbf{x}_1^T$	0.4	0.9	0.6
$\mathbf{x}_2^T$	0.5	0.1	0.6
$\mathbf{x}_3^T$	0.6	0.3	0.6
$\mathbf{x}_4^T$	0.4	0.8	0.5

Q7. Prove the following equivalence for the multivariate normal density function:

$$\frac{\partial}{\partial \mu_i} f(\mathbf{x}_j|\mu_i, \Sigma_i) = f(\mathbf{x}_j|\mu_i, \Sigma_i) \, \Sigma_i^{-1} (\mathbf{x}_j - \mu_i)$$

CHAPTER 14

Hierarchical Clustering

Given n points in a d-dimensional space, the goal of hierarchical clustering is to create a sequence of nested partitions, which can be conveniently visualized via a tree or hierarchy of clusters, also called the cluster *dendrogram*. The clusters in the hierarchy range from the fine-grained to the coarse-grained – the lowest level of the tree (the leaves) consists of each point in its own cluster, whereas the highest level (the root) consists of all points in one cluster. Both of these may be considered to be *trivial* clusterings. At some intermediate level, we may find meaningful clusters. If the user supplies k, the desired number of clusters, we can choose the level at which there are k clusters.

There are two main algorithmic approaches to mine hierarchical clusters: agglomerative and divisive. Agglomerative strategies work in a bottom-up manner. That is, starting with each of the n points in a separate cluster, they repeatedly merge the most similar pair of clusters until all points are members of the same cluster. Divisive strategies do just the opposite, working in a top-down manner. Starting with all the points in the same cluster, they recursively split the clusters until all points are in separate clusters. In this chapter we focus on agglomerative strategies. We discuss some divisive strategies in Chapter 16, in the context of graph partitioning.

14.1 PRELIMINARIES

Given a dataset $\mathbf{D}$ comprising n points $\mathbf{x}_i \in \mathbb{R}^d$ ($i = 1, 2, \cdots, n$), a clustering $\mathcal{C} = \{C_1, \ldots, C_k\}$ is a partition of $\mathbf{D}$, that is, each cluster is a set of points $C_i \subseteq \mathbf{D}$, such that the clusters are pairwise disjoint $C_i \cap C_j = \emptyset$ (for all $i \neq j$), and $\cup_{i=1}^k C_i = \mathbf{D}$. A clustering $\mathcal{A} = \{A_1, \ldots, A_r\}$ is said to be nested in another clustering $\mathcal{B} = \{B_1, \ldots, B_s\}$ if and only if $r > s$, and for each cluster $A_i \in \mathcal{A}$, there exists a cluster $B_j \in \mathcal{B}$, such that $A_i \subseteq B_j$. Hierarchical clustering yields a sequence of n nested partitions $\mathcal{C}_1, \ldots, \mathcal{C}_n$, ranging from the trivial clustering $\mathcal{C}_1 = \{\{\mathbf{x}_1\}, \ldots, \{\mathbf{x}_n\}\}$ where each point is in a separate cluster, to the other trivial clustering $\mathcal{C}_n = \{\{\mathbf{x}_1, \ldots, \mathbf{x}_n\}\}$, where all points are in one cluster. In general, the clustering $\mathcal{C}_{t-1}$ is nested in the clustering $\mathcal{C}_t$. The cluster dendrogram is a rooted binary tree that captures this nesting structure, with edges between cluster $C_i \in \mathcal{C}_{t-1}$ and cluster $C_j \in \mathcal{C}_t$ if C_i is nested in C_j, that is, if $C_i \subset C_j$. In this way the dendrogram captures the entire sequence of nested clusterings.

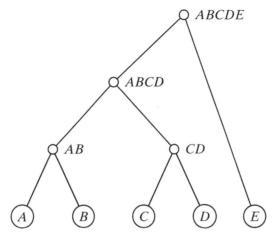

Figure 14.1. Hierarchical clustering dendrogram.

Example 14.1. Figure 14.1 shows an example of hierarchical clustering of five labeled points: A, B, C, D, and E. The dendrogram represents the following sequence of nested partitions:

Clustering	Clusters
C_1	$\{A\}, \{B\}, \{C\}, \{D\}, \{E\}$
C_2	$\{AB\}, \{C\}, \{D\}, \{E\}$
C_3	$\{AB\}, \{CD\}, \{E\}$
C_4	$\{ABCD\}, \{E\}$
C_5	$\{ABCDE\}$

with $C_{t-1} \subset C_t$ for $t = 2, \ldots, 5$. We assume that A and B are merged before C and D.

Number of Hierarchical Clusterings

The number of different nested or hierarchical clusterings corresponds to the number of different binary rooted trees or dendrograms with n leaves with distinct labels. Any tree with t nodes has $t - 1$ edges. Also, any rooted binary tree with m leaves has $m - 1$ internal nodes. Thus, a dendrogram with m leaf nodes has a total of $t = m + m - 1 = 2m - 1$ nodes, and consequently $t - 1 = 2m - 2$ edges. To count the number of different dendrogram topologies, let us consider how we can extend a dendrogram with m leaves by adding an extra leaf, to yield a dendrogram with $m + 1$ leaves. Note that we can add the extra leaf by splitting (i.e., branching from) any of the $2m - 2$ edges. Further, we can also add the new leaf as a child of a new root, giving $2m - 2 + 1 = 2m - 1$ new dendrograms with $m + 1$ leaves. The total number of different dendrograms with n leaves is thus obtained by the following product:

$$\prod_{m=1}^{n-1} (2m - 1) = 1 \times 3 \times 5 \times 7 \times \cdots \times (2n - 3) = (2n - 3)!! \tag{14.1}$$

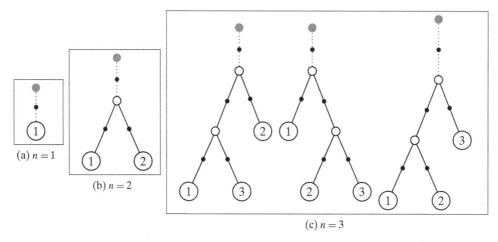

Figure 14.2. Number of hierarchical clusterings.

The index m in Eq. (14.1) goes up to $n - 1$ because the last term in the product denotes the number of dendrograms one obtains when we extend a dendrogram with $n - 1$ leaves by adding one more leaf, to yield dendrograms with n leaves.

The number of possible hierarchical clusterings is thus given as $(2n - 3)!!$, which grows extremely rapidly. It is obvious that a naive approach of enumerating all possible hierarchical clusterings is simply infeasible.

Example 14.2. Figure 14.2 shows the number of trees with one, two, and three leaves. The gray nodes are the virtual roots, and the black dots indicate locations where a new leaf can be added. There is only one tree possible with a single leaf, as shown in Figure 14.2(a). It can be extended in only one way to yield the unique tree with two leaves in Figure 14.2(b). However, this tree has three possible locations where the third leaf can be added. Each of these cases is shown in Figure 14.2(c). We can further see that each of the trees with $m = 3$ leaves has five locations where the fourth leaf can be added, and so on, which confirms the equation for the number of hierarchical clusterings in Eq. (14.1).

14.2 AGGLOMERATIVE HIERARCHICAL CLUSTERING

In agglomerative hierarchical clustering, we begin with each of the n points in a separate cluster. We repeatedly merge the two closest clusters until all points are members of the same cluster, as shown in the pseudo-code given in Algorithm 14.1. Formally, given a set of clusters $\mathcal{C} = \{C_1, C_2, .., C_m\}$, we find the *closest* pair of clusters C_i and C_j and merge them into a new cluster $C_{ij} = C_i \cup C_j$. Next, we update the set of clusters by removing C_i and C_j and adding C_{ij}, as follows $\mathcal{C} = (\mathcal{C} \setminus \{C_i, C_j\}) \cup \{C_{ij}\}$. We repeat the process until $\mathcal{C}$ contains only one cluster. Because the number of clusters decreases by one in each step, this process results in a sequence of n nested clusterings. If specified, we can stop the merging process when there are exactly k clusters remaining.

Algorithm 14.1: Agglomerative Hierarchical Clustering Algorithm

AGGLOMERATIVECLUSTERING($\mathbf{D}, k$):

1 $\mathcal{C} \leftarrow \{C_i = \{\mathbf{x}_i\} \mid \mathbf{x}_i \in \mathbf{D}\}$ // Each point in separate cluster
2 $\Delta \leftarrow \{\|\mathbf{x}_i - \mathbf{x}_j\| : \mathbf{x}_i, \mathbf{x}_j \in \mathbf{D}\}$ // Compute distance matrix
3 **repeat**
4   Find the closest pair of clusters $C_i, C_j \in \mathcal{C}$
5      $C_{ij} \leftarrow C_i \cup C_j$ // Merge the clusters
6      $\mathcal{C} \leftarrow \big(\mathcal{C} \setminus \{C_i, C_j\}\big) \cup \{C_{ij}\}$ // Update the clustering
7   Update distance matrix Δ to reflect new clustering
8 **until** $|\mathcal{C}| = k$

14.2.1 Distance between Clusters

The main step in the algorithm is to determine the closest pair of clusters. Several distance measures, such as single link, complete link, group average, and others discussed in the following paragraphs, can be used to compute the distance between any two clusters. The between-cluster distances are ultimately based on the distance between two points, which is typically computed using the Euclidean distance or L_2-norm, defined as

$$\|\mathbf{x} - \mathbf{y}\| = \left(\sum_{i=1}^{d}(x_i - y_i)^2\right)^{1/2}$$

However, one may use other distance metrics, or if available one may a user-specified distance matrix.

Single Link

Given two clusters C_i and C_j, the distance between them, denoted $\delta(C_i, C_j)$, is defined as the minimum distance between a point in C_i and a point in C_j

$$\delta(C_i, C_j) = \min\{\|\mathbf{x} - \mathbf{y}\| \mid \mathbf{x} \in C_i, \mathbf{y} \in C_j\} \tag{14.2}$$

The name *single link* comes from the observation that if we choose the minimum distance between points in the two clusters and connect those points, then (typically) only a single link would exist between those clusters because all other pairs of points would be farther away.

Complete Link

The distance between two clusters is defined as the maximum distance between a point in C_i and a point in C_j:

$$\delta(C_i, C_j) = \max\{\|\mathbf{x} - \mathbf{y}\| \mid \mathbf{x} \in C_i, \mathbf{y} \in C_j\} \tag{14.3}$$

The name *complete link* conveys the fact that if we connect all pairs of points from the two clusters with distance at most $\delta(C_i, C_j)$, then all possible pairs would be connected, that is, we get a complete linkage.

Group Average

The distance between two clusters is defined as the average pairwise distance between points in C_i and C_j:

$$\delta(C_i, C_j) = \frac{\sum_{\mathbf{x} \in C_i} \sum_{\mathbf{y} \in C_j} \|\mathbf{x} - \mathbf{y}\|}{n_i \cdot n_j} \tag{14.4}$$

where $n_i = |C_i|$ denotes the number of points in cluster C_i.

Mean Distance

The distance between two clusters is defined as the distance between the means or centroids of the two clusters:

$$\delta(C_i, C_j) = \|\boldsymbol{\mu}_i - \boldsymbol{\mu}_j\| \tag{14.5}$$

where $\boldsymbol{\mu}_i = \frac{1}{n_i} \sum_{\mathbf{x} \in C_i} \mathbf{x}$.

Minimum Variance: Ward's Method

The distance between two clusters is defined as the increase in the sum of squared errors (SSE) when the two clusters are merged. The SSE for a given cluster C_i is given as

$$SSE_i = \sum_{\mathbf{x} \in C_i} \|\mathbf{x} - \boldsymbol{\mu}_i\|^2$$

which can also be written as

$$\begin{aligned}
SSE_i &= \sum_{\mathbf{x} \in C_i} \|\mathbf{x} - \boldsymbol{\mu}_i\|^2 \\
&= \sum_{\mathbf{x} \in C_i} \mathbf{x}^T \mathbf{x} - 2 \sum_{\mathbf{x} \in C_i} \mathbf{x}^T \boldsymbol{\mu}_i + \sum_{\mathbf{x} \in C_i} \boldsymbol{\mu}_i^T \boldsymbol{\mu}_i \\
&= \left(\sum_{\mathbf{x} \in C_i} \mathbf{x}^T \mathbf{x} \right) - n_i \boldsymbol{\mu}_i^T \boldsymbol{\mu}_i
\end{aligned} \tag{14.6}$$

The SSE for a clustering $\mathcal{C} = \{C_1, \ldots, C_m\}$ is given as

$$SSE = \sum_{i=1}^{m} SSE_i = \sum_{i=1}^{m} \sum_{\mathbf{x} \in C_i} \|\mathbf{x} - \boldsymbol{\mu}_i\|^2$$

Ward's measure defines the distance between two clusters C_i and C_j as the net change in the SSE value when we merge C_i and C_j into C_{ij}, given as

$$\delta(C_i, C_j) = \Delta SSE_{ij} = SSE_{ij} - SSE_i - SSE_j \tag{14.7}$$

We can obtain a simpler expression for the Ward's measure by plugging Eq. (14.6) into Eq. (14.7), and noting that because $C_{ij} = C_i \cup C_j$ and $C_i \cap C_j = \emptyset$, we have $|C_{ij}| = n_{ij} = n_i + n_j$, and therefore

$$\delta(C_i, C_j) = \Delta SSE_{ij}$$

$$= \sum_{\mathbf{z} \in C_{ij}} \|\mathbf{z} - \boldsymbol{\mu}_{ij}\|^2 - \sum_{\mathbf{x} \in C_i} \|\mathbf{x} - \boldsymbol{\mu}_i\|^2 - \sum_{\mathbf{y} \in C_j} \|\mathbf{y} - \boldsymbol{\mu}_j\|^2$$

$$= \sum_{\mathbf{z} \in C_{ij}} \mathbf{z}^T\mathbf{z} - n_{ij}\boldsymbol{\mu}_{ij}^T\boldsymbol{\mu}_{ij} - \sum_{\mathbf{x} \in C_i} \mathbf{x}^T\mathbf{x} + n_i\boldsymbol{\mu}_i^T\boldsymbol{\mu}_i - \sum_{\mathbf{y} \in C_j} \mathbf{y}^T\mathbf{y} + n_j\boldsymbol{\mu}_j^T\boldsymbol{\mu}_j$$

$$= n_i\boldsymbol{\mu}_i^T\boldsymbol{\mu}_i + n_j\boldsymbol{\mu}_j^T\boldsymbol{\mu}_j - (n_i + n_j)\boldsymbol{\mu}_{ij}^T\boldsymbol{\mu}_{ij} \tag{14.8}$$

The last step follows from the fact that $\sum_{\mathbf{z} \in C_{ij}} \mathbf{z}^T\mathbf{z} = \sum_{\mathbf{x} \in C_i} \mathbf{x}^T\mathbf{x} + \sum_{\mathbf{y} \in C_j} \mathbf{y}^T\mathbf{y}$. Noting that

$$\boldsymbol{\mu}_{ij} = \frac{n_i\boldsymbol{\mu}_i + n_j\boldsymbol{\mu}_j}{n_i + n_j}$$

we obtain

$$\boldsymbol{\mu}_{ij}^T\boldsymbol{\mu}_{ij} = \frac{1}{(n_i + n_j)^2} \left(n_i^2\boldsymbol{\mu}_i^T\boldsymbol{\mu}_i + 2n_in_j\boldsymbol{\mu}_i^T\boldsymbol{\mu}_j + n_j^2\boldsymbol{\mu}_j^T\boldsymbol{\mu}_j \right)$$

Plugging the above into Eq. (14.8), we finally obtain

$$\delta(C_i, C_j) = \Delta SSE_{ij}$$

$$= n_i\boldsymbol{\mu}_i^T\boldsymbol{\mu}_i + n_j\boldsymbol{\mu}_j^T\boldsymbol{\mu}_j - \frac{1}{(n_i + n_j)} \left(n_i^2\boldsymbol{\mu}_i^T\boldsymbol{\mu}_i + 2n_in_j\boldsymbol{\mu}_i^T\boldsymbol{\mu}_j + n_j^2\boldsymbol{\mu}_j^T\boldsymbol{\mu}_j \right)$$

$$= \frac{n_i(n_i + n_j)\boldsymbol{\mu}_i^T\boldsymbol{\mu}_i + n_j(n_i + n_j)\boldsymbol{\mu}_j^T\boldsymbol{\mu}_j - n_i^2\boldsymbol{\mu}_i^T\boldsymbol{\mu}_i - 2n_in_j\boldsymbol{\mu}_i^T\boldsymbol{\mu}_j - n_j^2\boldsymbol{\mu}_j^T\boldsymbol{\mu}_j}{n_i + n_j}$$

$$= \frac{n_in_j \left(\boldsymbol{\mu}_i^T\boldsymbol{\mu}_i - 2\boldsymbol{\mu}_i^T\boldsymbol{\mu}_j + \boldsymbol{\mu}_j^T\boldsymbol{\mu}_j \right)}{n_i + n_j}$$

$$= \boxed{\left(\frac{n_in_j}{n_i + n_j} \right) \|\boldsymbol{\mu}_i - \boldsymbol{\mu}_j\|^2} \tag{14.9}$$

Ward's measure is therefore a weighted version of the square of the mean distance measure in Eq. (14.5). In essence, Ward's measure weighs the squared distance between the means by half of the harmonic mean of the cluster sizes, where the harmonic mean of two numbers n_1 and n_2 is given as $\frac{2}{\frac{1}{n_1} + \frac{1}{n_2}} = \frac{2n_1n_2}{n_1 + n_2}$.

Example 14.3 (Single Link). Consider the single link clustering shown in Figure 14.3 on a dataset of five points, whose pairwise distances are also shown on the bottom

δ	E
ABCD	③

δ	CD	E
AB	②	3
CD		3

δ	C	D	E
AB	3	2	3
C		①	3
D			5

δ	B	C	D	E
A	①	3	2	4
B		3	2	3
C			1	3
D				5

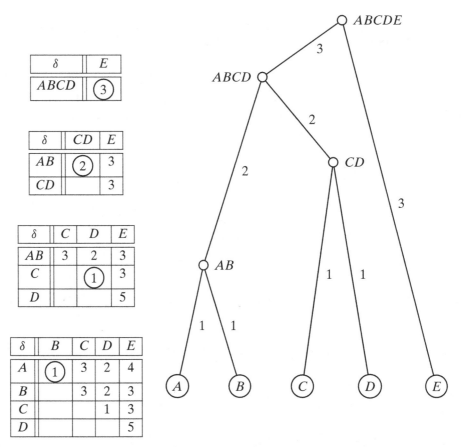

Figure 14.3. Single link agglomerative clustering.

left. Initially, all points are in their own cluster. The closest pair of points are (A, B) and (C, D), both with $\delta = 1$. We choose to first merge A and B, and derive a new distance matrix for the merged cluster. Essentially, we have to compute the distances of the new cluster AB to all other clusters. For example, $\delta(AB, E) = 3$ because $\delta(AB, E) = \min\{\delta(A, E), \delta(B, E)\} = \min\{4, 3\} = 3$. In the next step we merge C and D because they are the closest clusters, and we obtain a new distance matrix for the resulting set of clusters. After this, AB and CD are merged, and finally, E is merged with $ABCD$. In the distance matrices, we have shown (circled) the minimum distance used at each iteration that results in a merging of the two closest pairs of clusters.

14.2.2 Updating Distance Matrix

Whenever two clusters C_i and C_j are merged into C_{ij}, we need to update the distance matrix by recomputing the distances from the newly created cluster C_{ij} to all other clusters C_r ($r \neq i$ and $r \neq j$). The Lance–Williams formula provides a general equation to recompute the distances for all of the cluster proximity measures we considered

Table 14.1. Lance–Williams formula for cluster proximity

Measure	α_i	α_j	β	γ
Single link	$\frac{1}{2}$	$\frac{1}{2}$	0	$-\frac{1}{2}$
Complete link	$\frac{1}{2}$	$\frac{1}{2}$	0	$\frac{1}{2}$
Group average	$\frac{n_i}{n_i+n_j}$	$\frac{n_j}{n_i+n_j}$	0	0
Mean distance	$\frac{n_i}{n_i+n_j}$	$\frac{n_j}{n_i+n_j}$	$\frac{-n_i \cdot n_j}{(n_i+n_j)^2}$	0
Ward's measure	$\frac{n_i+n_r}{n_i+n_j+n_r}$	$\frac{n_j+n_r}{n_i+n_j+n_r}$	$\frac{-n_r}{n_i+n_j+n_r}$	0

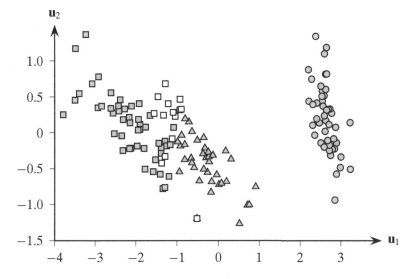

Figure 14.4. Iris dataset: complete link.

earlier; it is given as

$$\delta(C_{ij}, C_r) = \alpha_i \cdot \delta(C_i, C_r) + \alpha_j \cdot \delta(C_j, C_r) +$$
$$\beta \cdot \delta(C_i, C_j) + \gamma \cdot \left| \delta(C_i, C_r) - \delta(C_j, C_r) \right| \qquad (14.10)$$

The coefficients $\alpha_i, \alpha_j, \beta$, and γ differ from one measure to another. Let $n_i = |C_i|$ denote the cardinality of cluster C_i; then the coefficients for the different distance measures are as shown in Table 14.1.

Example 14.4. Consider the two-dimensional Iris principal components dataset shown in Figure 14.4, which also illustrates the results of hierarchical clustering using the complete-link method, with $k = 3$ clusters. Table 14.2 shows the contingency table comparing the clustering results with the ground-truth Iris types (which are not used in clustering). We can observe that 15 points are misclustered in total; these points are shown in white in Figure 14.4. Whereas `iris-setosa` is well separated, the other two Iris types are harder to separate.

Table 14.2. Contingency table: clusters versus Iris types

	iris-setosa	iris-virginica	iris-versicolor
C_1 (circle)	50	0	0
C_2 (triangle)	0	1	36
C_3 (square)	0	49	14

14.2.3 Computational Complexity

In agglomerative clustering, we need to compute the distance of each cluster to all other clusters, and at each step the number of clusters decreases by 1. Initially it takes $O(n^2)$ time to create the pairwise distance matrix, unless it is specified as an input to the algorithm.

At each merge step, the distances from the merged cluster to the other clusters have to be recomputed, whereas the distances between the other clusters remain the same. This means that in step t, we compute $O(n - t)$ distances. The other main operation is to find the closest pair in the distance matrix. For this we can keep the n^2 distances in a heap data structure, which allows us to find the minimum distance in $O(1)$ time; creating the heap takes $O(n^2)$ time. Deleting/updating distances from the heap takes $O(\log n)$ time for each operation, for a total time across all merge steps of $O(n^2 \log n)$. Thus, the computational complexity of hierarchical clustering is $O(n^2 \log n)$.

14.3 FURTHER READING

Hierarchical clustering has a long history, especially in taxonomy or classificatory systems, and phylogenetics; see, for example, Sokal and Sneath (1963). The generic Lance–Williams formula for distance updates appears in Lance and Williams (1967). Ward's measure is from Ward (1963). Efficient methods for single-link and complete-link measures with $O(n^2)$ complexity are given in Sibson (1973) and Defays (1977), respectively. For a good discussion of hierarchical clustering, and clustering in general, see Jain and Dubes (1988).

Defays, D. (1977). An efficient algorithm for a complete link method. *Computer Journal*, 20 (4), 364–366.

Jain, A. K. and Dubes, R. C. (1988). *Algorithms for Clustering Data*. Upper Saddle River, NJ: Prentice-Hall.

Lance, G. N. and Williams, W. T. (1967). A general theory of classificatory sorting strategies 1. Hierarchical systems. *The Computer Journal*, 9 (4), 373–380.

Sibson, R. (1973). SLINK: An optimally efficient algorithm for the single-link cluster method. *Computer Journal*, 16 (1), 30–34.

Sokal, R. R. and Sneath, P. H. (1963). *The Principles of Numerical Taxonomy*. San Francisco: W.H. Freeman.

Ward, J. H. (1963). Hierarchical grouping to optimize an objective function. *Journal of the American Statistical Association*, 58 (301), 236–244.

14.4 EXERCISES

Q1. Consider the 5-dimensional categorical data shown in Table 14.3.

Table 14.3. Data for Q1

Point	X_1	X_2	X_3	X_4	X_5
$\mathbf{x}_1^T$	1	0	1	1	0
$\mathbf{x}_2^T$	1	1	0	1	0
$\mathbf{x}_3^T$	0	0	1	1	0
$\mathbf{x}_4^T$	0	1	0	1	0
$\mathbf{x}_5^T$	1	0	1	0	1
$\mathbf{x}_6^T$	0	1	1	0	0

The similarity between categorical data points can be computed in terms of the number of matches and mismatches for the different attributes. Let n_{11} be the number of attributes on which two points $\mathbf{x}_i$ and $\mathbf{x}_j$ assume the value 1, and let n_{10} denote the number of attributes where $\mathbf{x}_i$ takes value 1, but $\mathbf{x}_j$ takes on the value of 0. Define n_{01} and n_{00} in a similar manner. The contingency table for measuring the similarity is then given as

		$\mathbf{x}_j$	
		1	0
$\mathbf{x}_i$	1	n_{11}	n_{10}
	0	n_{01}	n_{00}

Define the following similarity measures:
- Simple matching coefficient: $SMC(\mathbf{x}_i, \mathbf{x}_j) = \frac{n_{11}+n_{00}}{n_{11}+n_{10}+n_{01}+n_{00}}$
- Jaccard coefficient: $JC(\mathbf{x}_i, \mathbf{x}_j) = \frac{n_{11}}{n_{11}+n_{10}+n_{01}}$
- Rao's coefficient: $RC(\mathbf{x}_i, \mathbf{x}_j) = \frac{n_{11}}{n_{11}+n_{10}+n_{01}+n_{00}}$

Find the cluster dendrograms produced by the hierarchical clustering algorithm under the following scenarios:

(a) We use single link with RC.

(b) We use complete link with SMC.

(c) We use group average with JC.

Q2. Given the dataset in Figure 14.5, show the dendrogram resulting from the single-link hierarchical agglomerative clustering approach using the L_1-*norm* as the distance between points

$$\|\mathbf{x} - \mathbf{y}\|_1 = \sum_{d=1}^{2} |x_{id} - y_{id}|$$

Whenever there is a choice, merge the cluster that has the lexicographically smallest labeled point. Show the cluster merge order in the tree, stopping when you have $k = 4$ clusters. Show the full distance matrix at each step.

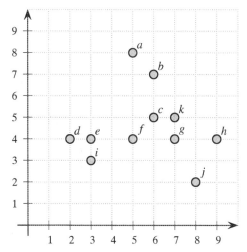

Figure 14.5. Dataset for Q2.

Table 14.4. Dataset for Q3

	A	B	C	D	E
A	0	1	3	2	4
B		0	3	2	3
C			0	1	3
D				0	5
E					0

Q3. Using the distance matrix from Table 14.4, use the average link method to generate hierarchical clusters. Show the merging distance thresholds.

Q4. Prove that in the Lance–Williams formula [Eq. (14.10)]
  (a) If $\alpha_i = \frac{n_i}{n_i+n_j}$, $\alpha_j = \frac{n_j}{n_i+n_j}$, $\beta = 0$ and $\gamma = 0$, then we obtain the group average measure.
  (b) If $\alpha_i = \frac{n_i+n_r}{n_i+n_j+n_r}$, $\alpha_j = \frac{n_j+n_r}{n_i+n_j+n_r}$, $\beta = \frac{-n_r}{n_i+n_j+n_r}$ and $\gamma = 0$, then we obtain Ward's measure.

Q5. If we treat each point as a vertex, and add edges between two nodes with distance less than some threshold value, then the single-link method corresponds to a well known graph algorithm. Describe this graph-based algorithm to hierarchically cluster the nodes via single-link measure, using successively higher distance thresholds.

CHAPTER 15

Density-based Clustering

The representative-based clustering methods like K-means and expectation-maximization are suitable for finding ellipsoid-shaped clusters, or at best convex clusters. However, for nonconvex clusters, such as those shown in Figure 15.1, these methods have trouble finding the true clusters, as two points from different clusters may be closer than two points in the same cluster. The density-based methods we consider in this chapter are able to mine such nonconvex clusters.

15.1 THE DBSCAN ALGORITHM

Density-based clustering uses the local density of points to determine the clusters, rather than using only the distance between points. We define a ball of radius ϵ around a point $\mathbf{x} \in \mathbb{R}^d$, called the ϵ-*neighborhood* of $\mathbf{x}$, as follows:

$$N_\epsilon(\mathbf{x}) = B_d(\mathbf{x}, \epsilon) = \{\mathbf{y} \mid \|\mathbf{x} - \mathbf{y}\| \leq \epsilon\} \tag{15.1}$$

Here $\|\mathbf{x} - \mathbf{y}\|$ is the Euclidean distance between points $\mathbf{x}$ and $\mathbf{y}$. However, other distance metrics can also be used.

For any point $\mathbf{x} \in \mathbf{D}$, we say that $\mathbf{x}$ is a *core point* if there are at least *minpts* points in its ϵ-neighborhood. In other words, $\mathbf{x}$ is a core point if $|N_\epsilon(\mathbf{x})| \geq minpts$, where *minpts* is a user-defined local density or frequency threshold. A *border point* is defined as a point that does not meet the *minpts* threshold, that is, it has $|N_\epsilon(\mathbf{x})| < minpts$, but it belongs to the ϵ-neighborhood of some core point $\mathbf{z}$, that is, $\mathbf{x} \in N_\epsilon(\mathbf{z})$. Finally, if a point is neither a core nor a border point, then it is called a *noise point* or an outlier.

Example 15.1. Figure 15.2(a) shows the ϵ-neighborhood of the point $\mathbf{x}$, using the Euclidean distance metric. Figure 15.2(b) shows the three different types of points, using $minpts = 6$. Here $\mathbf{x}$ is a core point because $|N_\epsilon(\mathbf{x})| = 6$, $\mathbf{y}$ is a border point because $|N_\epsilon(\mathbf{y})| < minpts$, but it belongs to the ϵ-neighborhood of the core point $\mathbf{x}$, i.e., $\mathbf{y} \in N_\epsilon(\mathbf{x})$. Finally, $\mathbf{z}$ is a noise point.

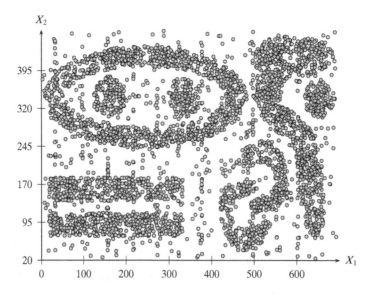

Figure 15.1. Density-based dataset.

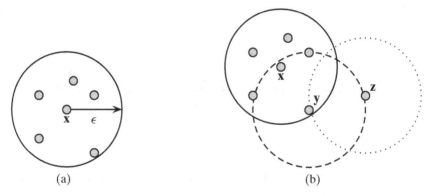

Figure 15.2. (a) Neighborhood of a point. (b) Core, border, and noise points.

We say that a point $\mathbf{x}$ is *directly density reachable* from another point $\mathbf{y}$ if $\mathbf{x} \in N_\epsilon(\mathbf{y})$ and $\mathbf{y}$ is a core point. We say that $\mathbf{x}$ is *density reachable* from $\mathbf{y}$ if there exists a chain of points, $\mathbf{x}_0, \mathbf{x}_1, \ldots, \mathbf{x}_l$, such that $\mathbf{x} = \mathbf{x}_0$ and $\mathbf{y} = \mathbf{x}_l$, and $\mathbf{x}_i$ is directly density reachable from $\mathbf{x}_{i-1}$ for all $i = 1, \ldots, l$. In other words, there is set of core points leading from $\mathbf{y}$ to $\mathbf{x}$. Note that density reachability is an asymmetric or directed relationship. Define any two points $\mathbf{x}$ and $\mathbf{y}$ to be *density connected* if there exists a core point $\mathbf{z}$, such that both $\mathbf{x}$ and $\mathbf{y}$ are density reachable from $\mathbf{z}$. A *density-based cluster* is defined as a maximal set of density connected points.

The pseudo-code for the DBSCAN density-based clustering method is shown in Algorithm 15.1. First, DBSCAN computes the ϵ-neighborhood $N_\epsilon(\mathbf{x}_i)$ for each point $\mathbf{x}_i$ in the dataset $\mathbf{D}$, and checks if it is a core point (lines 2–5). It also sets the cluster id $id(\mathbf{x}_i) = \emptyset$ for all points, indicating that they are not assigned to any cluster. Next,

---

Algorithm 15.1: Density-based Clustering Algorithm

$\textbf{DBSCAN} (\mathbf{D}, \epsilon, minpts)$:

1 $Core \leftarrow \emptyset$
2 **foreach** $\mathbf{x}_i \in \mathbf{D}$ **do** // Find the core points
3 $\quad$ Compute $N_\epsilon(\mathbf{x}_i)$
4 $\quad$ $id(\mathbf{x}_i) \leftarrow \emptyset$ // cluster id for $\mathbf{x}_i$
5 $\quad$ **if** $N_\epsilon(\mathbf{x}_i) \geq minpts$ **then** $Core \leftarrow Core \cup \{\mathbf{x}_i\}$

6 $k \leftarrow 0$ // cluster id
7 **foreach** $\mathbf{x}_i \in Core$, such that $id(\mathbf{x}_i) = \emptyset$ **do**
8 $\quad$ $k \leftarrow k+1$
9 $\quad$ $id(\mathbf{x}_i) \leftarrow k$ // assign $\mathbf{x}_i$ to cluster id k
10 $\quad$ DENSITYCONNECTED $(\mathbf{x}_i, k)$

11 $\mathcal{C} \leftarrow \{C_i\}_{i=1}^k$, where $C_i \leftarrow \{\mathbf{x} \in \mathbf{D} \mid id(\mathbf{x}) = i\}$
12 $Noise \leftarrow \{\mathbf{x} \in \mathbf{D} \mid id(\mathbf{x}) = \emptyset\}$
13 $Border \leftarrow \mathbf{D} \setminus \{Core \cup Noise\}$
14 **return** $\mathcal{C}, Core, Border, Noise$

$\textbf{DENSITYCONNECTED} (\mathbf{x}, k)$:

15 **foreach** $\mathbf{y} \in N_\epsilon(\mathbf{x})$ **do**
16 $\quad$ $id(\mathbf{y}) \leftarrow k$ // assign $\mathbf{y}$ to cluster id k
17 $\quad$ **if** $\mathbf{y} \in Core$ **then** DENSITYCONNECTED $(\mathbf{y}, k)$

---

starting from each unassigned core point, the method recursively finds all its density connected points, which are assigned to the same cluster (line 10). Some border point may be reachable from core points in more than one cluster; they may either be arbitrarily assigned to one of the clusters or to all of them (if overlapping clusters are allowed). Those points that do not belong to any cluster are treated as outliers or noise.

DBSCAN can also be considered as a search for the connected components in a graph where the vertices correspond to the core points in the dataset, and there exists an (undirected) edge between two vertices (core points) if the distance between them is less than ϵ, that is, each of them is in the ϵ-neighborhood of the other point. The connected components of this graph correspond to the core points of each cluster. Next, each core point incorporates into its cluster any border points in its neighborhood.

One limitation of DBSCAN is that it is sensitive to the choice of ϵ, in particular if clusters have different densities. If ϵ is too small, sparser clusters will be categorized as noise. If ϵ is too large, denser clusters may be merged together. In other words, if there are clusters with different local densities, then a single ϵ value may not suffice.

Example 15.2. Figure 15.3 shows the clusters discovered by DBSCAN on the density-based dataset in Figure 15.1. For the parameter values $\epsilon = 15$ and $minpts = 10$, found after parameter tuning, DBSCAN yields a near-perfect clustering

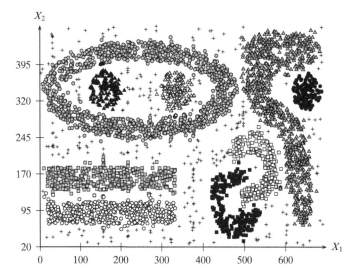

Figure 15.3. Density-based clusters.

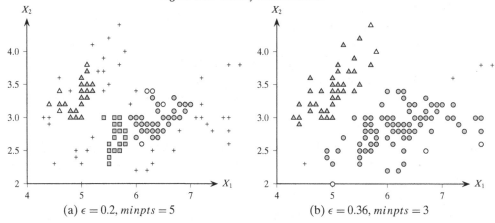

Figure 15.4. DBSCAN clustering: Iris dataset.

comprising all nine clusters. Cluster are shown using different symbols and shading; noise points are shown as plus symbols.

Example 15.3. Figure 15.4 shows the clusterings obtained via DBSCAN on the two-dimensional Iris dataset (over sepal length and sepal width attributes) for two different parameter settings. Figure 15.4(a) shows the clusters obtained with radius $\epsilon = 0.2$ and core threshold $minpts = 5$. The three clusters are plotted using different shaped points, namely circles, squares, and triangles. Shaded points are core points, whereas the border points for each cluster are showed unshaded (white). Noise points are shown as plus symbols. Figure 15.4(b) shows the clusters obtained with a larger value of radius $\epsilon = 0.36$, with $minpts = 3$. Two clusters are found, corresponding to the two dense regions of points.

For this dataset tuning the parameters is not that easy, and DBSCAN is not very effective in discovering the three Iris classes. For instance it identifies too many points (47 of them) as noise in Figure 15.4(a). However, DBSCAN is able to find the two main dense sets of points, distinguishing iris-setosa (in triangles) from the other types of Irises, in Figure 15.4(b). Increasing the radius more than $\epsilon = 0.36$ collapses all points into a single large cluster.

Computational Complexity

The main cost in DBSCAN is for computing the ϵ-neighborhood for each point. If the dimensionality is not too high this can be done efficiently using a spatial index structure in $O(n \log n)$ time. When dimensionality is high, it takes $O(n^2)$ to compute the neighborhood for each point. Once $N_\epsilon(\mathbf{x})$ has been computed the algorithm needs only a single pass over all the points to find the density connected clusters. Thus, the overall complexity of DBSCAN is $O(n^2)$ in the worst-case.

15.2 KERNEL DENSITY ESTIMATION

There is a close connection between density-based clustering and density estimation. The goal of density estimation is to determine the unknown probability density function by finding the dense regions of points, which can in turn be used for clustering. Kernel density estimation is a nonparametric technique that does not assume any fixed probability model of the clusters, as in the case of K-means or the mixture model assumed in the EM algorithm. Instead, it tries to directly infer the underlying probability density at each point in the dataset.

15.2.1 Univariate Density Estimation

Assume that X is a continuous random variable, and let $x_1, x_2, \ldots, x_n$ be a random sample drawn from the underlying probability density function $f(x)$, which is assumed to be unknown. We can directly estimate the cumulative distribution function from the data by counting how many points are less than or equal to x:

$$\hat{F}(x) = \frac{1}{n} \sum_{i=1}^{n} I(x_i \le x)$$

where I is an indicator function that has value 1 only when its argument is true, and 0 otherwise. We can estimate the density function by taking the derivative of $\hat{F}(x)$, by considering a window of small width h centered at x, that is,

$$\hat{f}(x) = \frac{\hat{F}\left(x + \frac{h}{2}\right) - \hat{F}\left(x - \frac{h}{2}\right)}{h} = \frac{k/n}{h} = \frac{k}{nh} \tag{15.2}$$

where k is the number of points that lie in the window of width h centered at x, that is, within the closed interval $[x - \frac{h}{2}, x + \frac{h}{2}]$. Thus, the density estimate is the ratio of the fraction of the points in the window (k/n) to the volume of the window (h). Here

h plays the role of "influence." That is, a large h estimates the probability density over a large window by considering many points, which has the effect of smoothing the estimate. On the other hand, if h is small, then only the points in close proximity to x are considered. In general we want a small value of h, but not too small, as in that case no points will fall in the window and we will not be able to get an accurate estimate of the probability density.

Kernel Estimator

Kernel density estimation relies on a *density kernel function K* that is non-negative, symmetric, and integrates to 1, that is, $K(x) \geq 0$, $K(-x) = K(x)$ for all values x, and $\int K(x)dx = 1$. Thus, K is essentially a probability density function. Note that K should not be confused with the positive semidefinite kernel mentioned in Chapter 5.

Discrete Kernel   The density estimate $\hat{f}(x)$ from Eq. (15.2) can also be rewritten in terms of the kernel function as follows:

$$\hat{f}(x) = \frac{1}{nh} \sum_{i=1}^{n} K\left(\frac{x - x_i}{h}\right) \tag{15.3}$$

where the **discrete kernel** function K computes the number of points in a window of width h, and is defined as

$$K(z) = \begin{cases} 1 & \text{If } |z| \leq \frac{1}{2} \\ 0 & \text{Otherwise} \end{cases} \tag{15.4}$$

We can see that if $|z| = |\frac{x-x_i}{h}| \leq \frac{1}{2}$, then the point x_i is within a window of width h centered at x, as

$$\left|\frac{x - x_i}{h}\right| \leq \frac{1}{2} \text{ implies that } -\frac{1}{2} \leq \frac{x_i - x}{h} \leq \frac{1}{2}, \text{ or}$$

$$-\frac{h}{2} \leq x_i - x \leq \frac{h}{2}, \text{ and finally}$$

$$x - \frac{h}{2} \leq x_i \leq x + \frac{h}{2}$$

Example 15.4. Figure 15.5 shows the kernel density estimates using the discrete kernel for different values of the influence parameter h, for the one-dimensional Iris dataset comprising the sepal length attribute. The x-axis plots the $n = 150$ data points. Because several points have the same value, they are shown stacked, where the stack height corresponds to the frequency of that value.

When h is small, as shown in Figure 15.5(a), the density function has many local maxima or modes. However, as we increase h from 0.25 to 2, the number of modes decreases, until h becomes large enough to yield a unimodal distribution, as shown in Figure 15.5(d). We can observe that the discrete kernel yields a non-smooth (or jagged) density function.

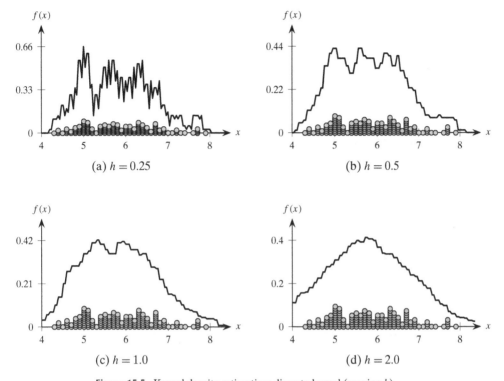

Figure 15.5. Kernel density estimation: discrete kernel (varying h).

Gaussian Kernel The width h is a parameter that denotes the spread or smoothness of the density estimate. If the spread is too large we get a more averaged value. If it is too small we do not have enough points in the window. Further, the kernel function in Eq. (15.4) has an abrupt influence. For points within the window ($|z| \leq \frac{1}{2}$) there is a net contribution of $\frac{1}{hn}$ to the probability estimate $\hat{f}(x)$. On the other hand, points outside the window ($|z| > \frac{1}{2}$) contribute 0.

Instead of the discrete kernel, we can define a more smooth transition of influence via a Gaussian kernel:

$$K(z) = \frac{1}{\sqrt{2\pi}} \exp\left\{-\frac{z^2}{2}\right\}$$

Thus, we have

$$K\left(\frac{x - x_i}{h}\right) = \frac{1}{\sqrt{2\pi}} \exp\left\{-\frac{(x - x_i)^2}{2h^2}\right\} \tag{15.5}$$

Here x, which is at the center of the window, plays the role of the mean, and h acts as the standard deviation.

Example 15.5. Figure 15.6 shows the univariate density function for the 1-dimensional Iris dataset (over `sepal length`) using the Gaussian kernel. Plots are

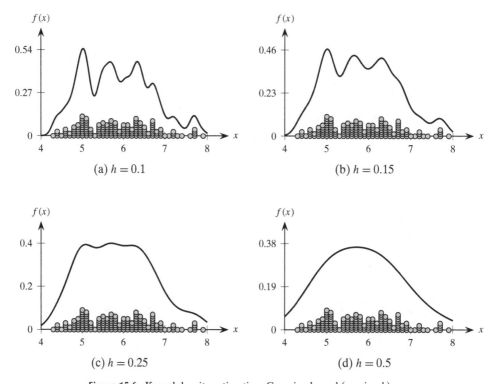

Figure 15.6. Kernel density estimation: Gaussian kernel (varying h).

shown for increasing values of the spread parameter h. The data points are shown stacked along the x-axis, with the heights corresponding to the value frequencies.

As h varies from 0.1 to 0.5, we can see the smoothing effect of increasing h on the density function. For instance, for $h = 0.1$ there are many local maxima, whereas for $h = 0.5$ there is only one density peak. Compared to the discrete kernel case shown in Figure 15.5, we can clearly see that the Gaussian kernel yields much smoother estimates, without discontinuities.

15.2.2 Multivariate Density Estimation

To estimate the probability density at a d-dimensional point $\mathbf{x} = (x_1, x_2, \ldots, x_d)^T$, we define the d-dimensional "window" as a hypercube in d dimensions, that is, a hypercube centered at $\mathbf{x}$ with edge length h. The volume of such a d-dimensional hypercube is given as

$$\text{vol}(H_d(h)) = h^d$$

The density is then estimated as the fraction of the point weight lying within the d-dimensional window centered at $\mathbf{x}$, divided by the volume of the hypercube:

$$\hat{f}(\mathbf{x}) = \frac{1}{nh^d} \sum_{i=1}^{n} K\left(\frac{\mathbf{x} - \mathbf{x}_i}{h}\right) \tag{15.6}$$

where the multivariate kernel function K satisfies the condition $\int K(\mathbf{z})d\mathbf{z} = 1$.

Discrete Kernel   For any d-dimensional vector $\mathbf{z} = (z_1, z_2, \ldots, z_d)^T$, the discrete kernel function in d-dimensions is given as

$$K(\mathbf{z}) = \begin{cases} 1 & \text{If } |z_j| \leq \frac{1}{2}, \text{ for all dimensions } j = 1, \ldots, d \\ 0 & \text{Otherwise} \end{cases} \tag{15.7}$$

For $\mathbf{z} = \frac{\mathbf{x} - \mathbf{x}_i}{h}$, we see that the kernel computes the number of points within the hypercube centered at $\mathbf{x}$ because $K(\frac{\mathbf{x} - \mathbf{x}_i}{h}) = 1$ if and only if $|\frac{x_j - x_{ij}}{h}| \leq \frac{1}{2}$ for all dimensions j. Each point within the hypercube thus contributes a weight of $\frac{1}{n}$ to the density estimate.

Gaussian Kernel   The d-dimensional Gaussian kernel is given as

$$K(\mathbf{z}) = \frac{1}{(2\pi)^{d/2}} \exp\left\{-\frac{\mathbf{z}^T \mathbf{z}}{2}\right\} \tag{15.8}$$

where we assume that the covariance matrix is the $d \times d$ identity matrix, that is, $\mathbf{\Sigma} = \mathbf{I}_d$. Plugging $\mathbf{z} = \frac{\mathbf{x} - \mathbf{x}_i}{h}$ in Eq. (15.8), we have

$$K\left(\frac{\mathbf{x} - \mathbf{x}_i}{h}\right) = \frac{1}{(2\pi)^{d/2}} \exp\left\{-\frac{(\mathbf{x} - \mathbf{x}_i)^T(\mathbf{x} - \mathbf{x}_i)}{2h^2}\right\} \tag{15.9}$$

Each point contributes a weight to the density estimate inversely proportional to its distance from $\mathbf{x}$ tempered by the width parameter h.

Example 15.6. Figure 15.7 shows the probability density function for the 2D Iris dataset comprising the sepal length and sepal width attributes, using the Gaussian kernel. As expected, for small values of h the density function has several local maxima, whereas for larger values the number of maxima reduce, and ultimately for a large enough value we obtain a unimodal distribution.

Example 15.7. Figure 15.8 shows the kernel density estimate for the density-based dataset in Figure 15.1, using a Gaussian kernel with $h = 20$. One can clearly discern that the density peaks closely correspond to regions with higher density of points.

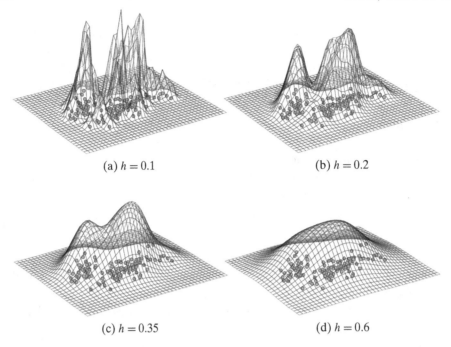

(a) $h = 0.1$ (b) $h = 0.2$

(c) $h = 0.35$ (d) $h = 0.6$

Figure 15.7. Density estimation: 2D Iris dataset (varying h).

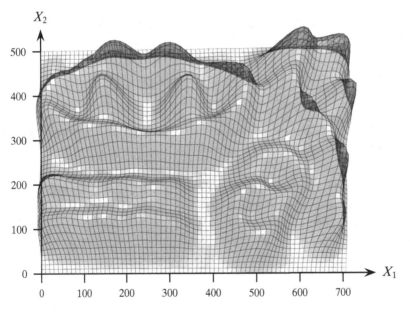

Figure 15.8. Density estimation: density-based dataset.

15.2.3 Nearest Neighbor Density Estimation

In the preceding density estimation formulation we implicitly fixed the volume by fixing the width h, and we used the kernel function to find out the number or weight of points that lie inside the fixed volume region. An alternative approach to density estimation is to fix k, the number of points required to estimate the density, and allow the volume of the enclosing region to vary to accommodate those k points. This approach is called the k nearest neighbors (KNN) approach to density estimation. Like kernel density estimation, KNN density estimation is also a nonparametric approach.

Given k, the number of neighbors, we estimate the density at $\mathbf{x}$ as follows:

$$\hat{f}(\mathbf{x}) = \frac{k}{n \operatorname{vol}(S_d(h_\mathbf{x}))}$$

where $h_\mathbf{x}$ is the distance from $\mathbf{x}$ to its kth nearest neighbor, and $\operatorname{vol}(S_d(h_\mathbf{x}))$ is the volume of the d-dimensional hypersphere $S_d(h_\mathbf{x})$ centered at $\mathbf{x}$, with radius $h_\mathbf{x}$ [Eq. (6.10)]. In other words, the width (or radius) $h_\mathbf{x}$ is now a variable, which depends on $\mathbf{x}$ and the chosen value k.

15.3 DENSITY-BASED CLUSTERING: DENCLUE

Having laid the foundations of kernel density estimation, we can develop a general formulation of density-based clustering. The basic approach is to find the peaks in the density landscape via gradient-based optimization, and find the regions with density above a given threshold.

Density Attractors and Gradient

A point $\mathbf{x}^*$ is called a *density attractor* if it is a local maxima of the probability density function f. A density attractor can be found via a gradient ascent approach starting at some point $\mathbf{x}$. The idea is to compute the density gradient, the direction of the largest increase in the density, and to move in the direction of the gradient in small steps, until we reach a local maxima.

The gradient at a point $\mathbf{x}$ can be computed as the multivariate derivative of the probability density estimate in Eq. (15.6), given as

$$\nabla \hat{f}(\mathbf{x}) = \frac{\partial}{\partial \mathbf{x}} \hat{f}(\mathbf{x}) = \frac{1}{nh^d} \sum_{i=1}^{n} \frac{\partial}{\partial \mathbf{x}} K\left(\frac{\mathbf{x} - \mathbf{x}_i}{h}\right) \tag{15.10}$$

For the Gaussian kernel [Eq. (15.8)], we have

$$\frac{\partial}{\partial \mathbf{x}} K(\mathbf{z}) = \left(\frac{1}{(2\pi)^{d/2}} \exp\left\{-\frac{\mathbf{z}^T \mathbf{z}}{2}\right\}\right) \cdot -\mathbf{z} \cdot \frac{\partial \mathbf{z}}{\partial \mathbf{x}}$$

$$= K(\mathbf{z}) \cdot -\mathbf{z} \cdot \frac{\partial \mathbf{z}}{\partial \mathbf{x}}$$

Setting $\mathbf{z} = \frac{\mathbf{x} - \mathbf{x}_i}{h}$ above, we get

$$\frac{\partial}{\partial \mathbf{x}} K\left(\frac{\mathbf{x} - \mathbf{x}_i}{h}\right) = K\left(\frac{\mathbf{x} - \mathbf{x}_i}{h}\right) \cdot \left(\frac{\mathbf{x}_i - \mathbf{x}}{h}\right) \cdot \left(\frac{1}{h}\right)$$

which follows from the fact that $\frac{\partial}{\partial \mathbf{x}}\left(\frac{\mathbf{x}-\mathbf{x}_i}{h}\right) = \frac{1}{h}$. Substituting the above in Eq. (15.10), the gradient at a point $\mathbf{x}$ is given as

$$\nabla \hat{f}(\mathbf{x}) = \frac{1}{nh^{d+2}} \sum_{i=1}^{n} K\left(\frac{\mathbf{x}-\mathbf{x}_i}{h}\right) \cdot (\mathbf{x}_i - \mathbf{x}) \tag{15.11}$$

This equation can be thought of as having two parts: a vector $(\mathbf{x}_i - \mathbf{x})$ and a scalar *influence* value $K(\frac{\mathbf{x}-\mathbf{x}_i}{h})$. For each point $\mathbf{x}_i$, we first compute the direction away from $\mathbf{x}$, that is, the vector $(\mathbf{x}_i - \mathbf{x})$. Next, we scale it using the Gaussian kernel value as the weight $K\left(\frac{\mathbf{x}-\mathbf{x}_i}{h}\right)$. Finally, the vector $\nabla \hat{f}(\mathbf{x})$ is the net influence at $\mathbf{x}$, as illustrated in Figure 15.9, that is, the weighted sum of the difference vectors.

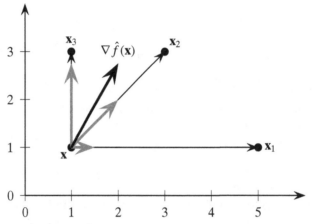

Figure 15.9. The gradient vector $\nabla \hat{f}(\mathbf{x})$ (shown in thick black) obtained as the sum of difference vectors $\mathbf{x}_i - \mathbf{x}$ (shown in gray).

We say that $\mathbf{x}^*$ is a *density attractor* for $\mathbf{x}$, or alternatively that $\mathbf{x}$ is *density attracted* to $\mathbf{x}^*$, if a hill climbing process started at $\mathbf{x}$ converges to $\mathbf{x}^*$. That is, there exists a sequence of points $\mathbf{x} = \mathbf{x}_0 \to \mathbf{x}_1 \to \ldots \to \mathbf{x}_m$, starting from $\mathbf{x}$ and ending at $\mathbf{x}_m$, such that $\|\mathbf{x}_m - \mathbf{x}^*\| \le \epsilon$, that is, $\mathbf{x}_m$ converges to the attractor $\mathbf{x}^*$.

The typical approach is to use the gradient-ascent method to compute $\mathbf{x}^*$, that is, starting from $\mathbf{x}$, we iteratively update it at each step t via the update rule:

$$\mathbf{x}_{t+1} = \mathbf{x}_t + \eta \cdot \nabla \hat{f}(\mathbf{x}_t)$$

where $\eta > 0$ is the step size. That is, each intermediate point is obtained after a small move in the direction of the gradient vector. However, the gradient-ascent approach can be slow to converge. Instead, one can directly optimize the move direction by setting the gradient [Eq. (15.11)] to the zero vector:

$$\nabla \hat{f}(\mathbf{x}) = \mathbf{0}$$

$$\frac{1}{nh^{d+2}} \sum_{i=1}^{n} K\left(\frac{\mathbf{x}-\mathbf{x}_i}{h}\right) \cdot (\mathbf{x}_i - \mathbf{x}) = \mathbf{0}$$

$$\mathbf{x} \cdot \sum_{i=1}^{n} K\left(\frac{\mathbf{x} - \mathbf{x}_i}{h}\right) = \sum_{i=1}^{n} K\left(\frac{\mathbf{x} - \mathbf{x}_i}{h}\right)\mathbf{x}_i$$

$$\mathbf{x} = \frac{\sum_{i=1}^{n} K\left(\frac{\mathbf{x} - \mathbf{x}_i}{h}\right)\mathbf{x}_i}{\sum_{i=1}^{n} K\left(\frac{\mathbf{x} - \mathbf{x}_i}{h}\right)}$$

The point $\mathbf{x}$ is involved on both the left- and right-hand sides above; however, it can be used to obtain the following iterative update rule:

$$\mathbf{x}_{t+1} = \frac{\sum_{i=1}^{n} K\left(\frac{\mathbf{x}_t - \mathbf{x}_i}{h}\right)\mathbf{x}_i}{\sum_{i=1}^{n} K\left(\frac{\mathbf{x}_t - \mathbf{x}_i}{h}\right)} \qquad (15.12)$$

where t denotes the current iteration and $\mathbf{x}_{t+1}$ is the updated value for the current vector $\mathbf{x}_t$. This direct update rule is essentially a weighted average of the influence (computed via the kernel function K) of each point $\mathbf{x}_i \in \mathbf{D}$ on the current point $\mathbf{x}_t$. The direct update rule results in much faster convergence of the hill-climbing process.

Center-defined Cluster

A cluster $C \subseteq \mathbf{D}$, is called a *center-defined cluster* if all the points $\mathbf{x} \in C$ are density attracted to a unique density attractor $\mathbf{x}^*$, such that $\hat{f}(\mathbf{x}^*) \geq \xi$, where ξ is a user-defined minimum density threshold. In other words,

$$\hat{f}(\mathbf{x}^*) = \frac{1}{nh^d} \sum_{i=1}^{n} K\left(\frac{\mathbf{x}^* - \mathbf{x}_i}{h}\right) \geq \xi$$

Density-based Cluster

An arbitrary-shaped cluster $C \subseteq \mathbf{D}$ is called a *density-based cluster* if there exists a set of density attractors $\mathbf{x}_1^*, \mathbf{x}_2^*, \ldots, \mathbf{x}_m^*$, such that

1. Each point $\mathbf{x} \in C$ is attracted to some attractor $\mathbf{x}_i^*$.

2. Each density attractor has density above ξ. That is, $\hat{f}(\mathbf{x}_i^*) \geq \xi$.

3. Any two density attractors $\mathbf{x}_i^*$ and $\mathbf{x}_j^*$ are *density reachable*, that is, there exists a path from $\mathbf{x}_i^*$ to $\mathbf{x}_j^*$, such that for all points $\mathbf{y}$ on the path, $\hat{f}(\mathbf{y}) \geq \xi$.

DENCLUE Algorithm

The pseudo-code for DENCLUE is shown in Algorithm 15.2. The first step is to compute the density attractor $\mathbf{x}^*$ for each point $\mathbf{x}$ in the dataset (line 3). If the density at $\mathbf{x}^*$ is above the minimum density threshold ξ, the attractor is added to the set of attractors $\mathcal{A}$. The data point $\mathbf{x}$ is also added to the set of points $R(\mathbf{x}^*)$ attracted to $\mathbf{x}^*$ (line 6). In the second step, DENCLUE finds all the maximal subsets of attractors $C \subseteq \mathcal{A}$, such that any pair of attractors in C is density-reachable from each other (line 7). These maximal subsets of mutually reachable attractors form the seed for each density-based cluster. Finally, for each attractor $\mathbf{x}^* \in C$, we add to the cluster all of the points $R(\mathbf{x}^*)$ that are attracted to $\mathbf{x}^*$, which results in the final set of clusters $\mathcal{C}$.

Algorithm 15.2: DENCLUE Algorithm

DENCLUE $(\mathbf{D}, h, \xi, \epsilon)$:

1 $\mathcal{A} \leftarrow \emptyset$
2 **foreach** $\mathbf{x} \in \mathbf{D}$ **do** // find density attractors
3 $\quad$ $\mathbf{x}^* \leftarrow$ FINDATTRACTOR$(\mathbf{x}, \mathbf{D}, h, \epsilon)$
4 $\quad$ **if** $\hat{f}(\mathbf{x}^*) \geq \xi$ **then**
5 $\quad\quad$ $\mathcal{A} \leftarrow \mathcal{A} \cup \{\mathbf{x}^*\}$
6 $\quad\quad$ $R(\mathbf{x}^*) \leftarrow R(\mathbf{x}^*) \cup \{\mathbf{x}\}$

7 $\mathcal{C} \leftarrow \{$maximal $C \subseteq \mathcal{A} \mid \forall \mathbf{x}_i^*, \mathbf{x}_j^* \in C, \mathbf{x}_i^*$ and $\mathbf{x}_j^*$ are density reachable$\}$
8 **foreach** $C \in \mathcal{C}$ **do** // density-based clusters
9 $\quad$ **foreach** $\mathbf{x}^* \in C$ **do** $C \leftarrow C \cup R(\mathbf{x}^*)$
10 **return** $\mathcal{C}$

FINDATTRACTOR $(\mathbf{x}, \mathbf{D}, h, \epsilon)$:

11 $t \leftarrow 0$
12 $\mathbf{x}_t \leftarrow \mathbf{x}$
13 **repeat**
14 $\quad$ $\mathbf{x}_{t+1} \leftarrow \dfrac{\sum_{i=1}^n K\left(\frac{\mathbf{x}_t - \mathbf{x}_i}{h}\right) \cdot \mathbf{x}_i}{\sum_{i=1}^n K\left(\frac{\mathbf{x}_t - \mathbf{x}_i}{h}\right)}$
15 $\quad$ $t \leftarrow t + 1$
16 **until** $\|\mathbf{x}_t - \mathbf{x}_{t-1}\| \leq \epsilon$
17 **return** $\mathbf{x}_t$

The FINDATTRACTOR method implements the hill-climbing process using the direct update rule [Eq. (15.12)], which results in fast convergence. To further speed up the influence computation, it is possible to compute the kernel values for only the nearest neighbors of $\mathbf{x}_t$. That is, we can index the points in the dataset $\mathbf{D}$ using a spatial index structure, so that we can quickly compute all the nearest neighbors of $\mathbf{x}_t$ within some radius r. For the Gaussian kernel, we can set $r = h \cdot z$, where h is the influence parameter that plays the role of standard deviation, and z specifies the number of standard deviations. Let $B_d(\mathbf{x}_t, r)$ denote the set of all points in $\mathbf{D}$ that lie within a d-dimensional ball of radius r centered at $\mathbf{x}_t$. The nearest neighbor based update rule can then be expressed as

$$\mathbf{x}_{t+1} = \frac{\sum_{\mathbf{x}_i \in B_d(\mathbf{x}_t, r)} K\left(\frac{\mathbf{x}_t - \mathbf{x}_i}{h}\right) \mathbf{x}_i}{\sum_{\mathbf{x}_i \in B_d(\mathbf{x}_t, r)} K\left(\frac{\mathbf{x}_t - \mathbf{x}_i}{h}\right)}$$

which can be used in line 14 in Algorithm 15.2. When the data dimensionality is not high, this can result in a significant speedup. However, the effectiveness deteriorates rapidly with increasing number of dimensions. This is due to two effects. The first is that finding $B_d(\mathbf{x}_t, r)$ reduces to a linear-scan of the data taking $O(n)$ time for each query. Second, due to the *curse of dimensionality* (see Chapter 6), nearly all points appear to be equally close to $\mathbf{x}_t$, thereby nullifying any benefits of computing the nearest neighbors.

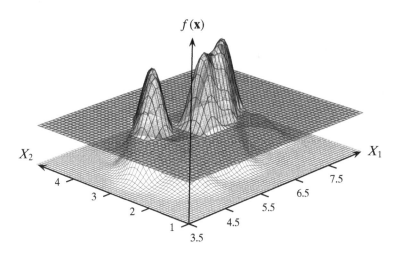

$f(\mathbf{x})$

X_2

X_1

4
3
2
1
3.5
4.5
5.5
6.5
7.5

Figure 15.10. DENCLUE: Iris 2D dataset.

Example 15.8. Figure 15.10 shows the DENCLUE clustering for the 2-dimensional Iris dataset comprising the sepal length and sepal width attributes. The results were obtained with $h = 0.2$ and $\xi = 0.08$, using a Gaussian kernel. The clustering is obtained by thresholding the probability density function in Figure 15.7(b) at $\xi = 0.08$. The two peaks correspond to the two final clusters. Whereas iris setosa is well separated, it is hard to separate the other two types of Irises.

Example 15.9. Figure 15.11 shows the clusters obtained by DENCLUE on the density-based dataset from Figure 15.1. Using the parameters $h = 10$ and $\xi = 9.5 \times 10^{-5}$, with a Gaussian kernel, we obtain eight clusters. The figure is obtained by slicing the density function at the density value ξ; only the regions above that value are plotted. All the clusters are correctly identified, with the exception of the two semicircular clusters on the lower right that appear merged into one cluster.

DENCLUE: Special Cases
It can be shown that DBSCAN is a special case of the general kernel density estimate based clustering approach, DENCLUE. If we let $h = \epsilon$ and $\xi = minpts$, then using a discrete kernel DENCLUE yields exactly the same clusters as DBSCAN. Each density attractor corresponds to a core point, and the set of connected core points define the attractors of a density-based cluster. It can also be shown that K-means is a special case of density-based clustering for appropriates value of h and ξ, with the density attractors corresponding to the cluster centroids. Further, it is worth noting that the density-based approach can produce hierarchical clusters, by varying the ξ threshold. For example, decreasing ξ can result in the merging of several clusters found at higher

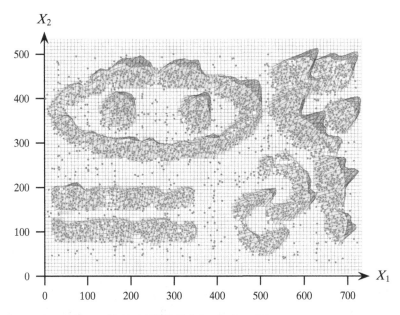

Figure 15.11. DENCLUE: density-based dataset.

thresholds values. At the same time it can also lead to new clusters if the peak density satisfies the lower ξ value.

Computational Complexity

The time for DENCLUE is dominated by the cost of the hill-climbing process. For each point $\mathbf{x} \in \mathbf{D}$, finding the density attractor takes $O(nt)$ time, where t is the maximum number of hill-climbing iterations. This is because each iteration takes $O(n)$ time for computing the sum of the influence function over all the points $\mathbf{x}_i \in \mathbf{D}$. The total cost to compute density attractors is therefore $O(n^2 t)$. We assume that for reasonable values of h and ξ, there are only a few density attractors, that is, $|\mathcal{A}| = m \ll n$. The cost of finding the maximal reachable subsets of attractors is $O(m^2)$, and the final clusters can be obtained in $O(n)$ time.

15.4 FURTHER READING

Kernel density estimation was developed independently in Rosenblatt (1956) and Parzen (1962). For an excellent description of density estimation techniques see Silverman (1986). The density-based DBSCAN algorithm was introduced in Ester et al. (1996). The DENCLUE method was proposed in Hinneburg and Keim (1998), with the faster direct update rule appearing in Hinneburg and Gabriel (2007). However, the direct update rule is essentially the *mean-shift* algorithm first proposed in Fukunaga and Hostetler (1975). See Cheng (1995) for convergence properties and generalizations of the mean-shift method.

Cheng, Y. (1995). Mean shift, mode seeking, and clustering. *IEEE Transactions on Pattern Analysis and Machine Intelligence*, 17 (8), 790–799.

Ester, M., Kriegel, H.-P., Sander, J., and Xu, X. (1996). A density-based algorithm for discovering clusters in large spatial databases with noise. *Proceedings of the 2nd ACM SIGKDD International Conference on Knowledge Discovery and Data Mining*. Palo Alto, CA: AAAI Press, pp. 226–231.

Fukunaga, K. and Hostetler, L. (1975). The estimation of the gradient of a density function, with applications in pattern recognition. *IEEE Transactions on Information Theory*, 21 (1), 32–40.

Hinneburg, A. and Gabriel, H.-H. (2007). Denclue 2.0: Fast clustering based on kernel density estimation. *Proceedings of the 7th International Symposium on Intelligent Data Analysis*. New York: Springer Science + Business Media, pp. 70–80.

Hinneburg, A. and Keim, D. A. (1998). An efficient approach to clustering in large multimedia databases with noise. *Proceedings of the 4th ACM SIGKDD International Conference on Knowledge Discovery and Data Mining*. Palo Alto, CA: AAAI Press, pp. 58–65.

Parzen, E. (1962). On estimation of a probability density function and mode. *The Annals of Mathematical Statistics*, 33 (3), 1065–1076.

Rosenblatt, M. (1956). Remarks on some nonparametric estimates of a density function. *The Annals of Mathematical Statistics*, 27 (3), 832–837.

Silverman, B. (1986). *Density Estimation for Statistics and Data Analysis*. Monographs on Statistics and Applied Probability. Boca Raton, FL: Chapman and Hall / CRC.

15.5 EXERCISES

Q1. Consider Figure 15.12 and answer the following questions, assuming that we use the Euclidean distance between points, and that $\epsilon = 2$ and $minpts = 3$

    (a) List all the core points.

    (b) Is a directly density reachable from d?

    (c) Is o density reachable from i? Show the intermediate points on the chain or the point where the chain breaks.

    (d) Is density reachable a symmetric relationship, that is, if x is density reachable from y, does it imply that y is density reachable from x? Why or why not?

    (e) Is l density connected to x? Show the intermediate points that make them density connected or violate the property, respectively.

    (f) Is density connected a symmetric relationship?

    (g) Show the density-based clusters and the noise points.

Q2. Consider the points in Figure 15.13. Define the following distance measures:

$$L_\infty(\mathbf{x}, \mathbf{y}) = \max_{i=1}^{d}\{|x_i - y_i|\}$$

$$L_{\frac{1}{2}}(\mathbf{x}, \mathbf{y}) = \left(\sum_{i=1}^{d} |x_i - y_i|^{\frac{1}{2}}\right)^2$$

$$L_{\min}(\mathbf{x}, \mathbf{y}) = \min_{i=1}^{d}\{|x_i - y_i|\}$$

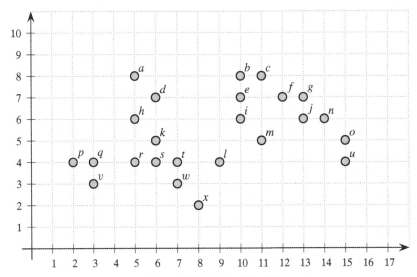

Figure 15.12. Dataset for Q1.

$$L_{pow}(\mathbf{x}, \mathbf{y}) = \left(\sum_{i=1}^{d} 2^{i-1}(x_i - y_i)^2 \right)^{1/2}$$

(a) Using $\epsilon = 2$, $minpts = 5$, and L_∞ distance, find all core, border, and noise points.

(b) Show the shape of the ball of radius $\epsilon = 4$ using the $L_{\frac{1}{2}}$ distance. Using $minpts = 3$ show all the clusters found by DBSCAN.

(c) Using $\epsilon = 1$, $minpts = 6$, and L_{min}, list all core, border, and noise points.

(d) Using $\epsilon = 4$, $minpts = 3$, and L_{pow}, show all clusters found by DBSCAN.

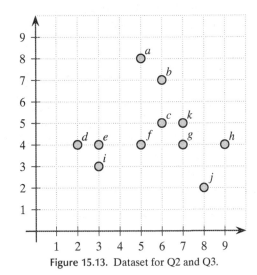

Figure 15.13. Dataset for Q2 and Q3.

Q3. Consider the points shown in Figure 15.13. Define the following two kernels:

$$K_1(\mathbf{z}) = \begin{cases} 1 & \text{If } L_\infty(\mathbf{z}, \mathbf{0}) \leq 1 \\ 0 & \text{Otherwise} \end{cases}$$

$$K_2(\mathbf{z}) = \begin{cases} 1 & \text{If } \sum_{j=1}^{d} |z_j| \leq 1 \\ 0 & \text{Otherwise} \end{cases}$$

Using each of the two kernels K_1 and K_2, answer the following questions assuming that $h = 2$:

(a) What is the probability density at e?

(b) List all the density attractors for this dataset.

(c) What is the gradient at e using the Gaussian kernel and using only the neighboring points d, i, and f?

Q4. The Hessian matrix is defined as the set of partial derivatives of the gradient vector with respect to $\mathbf{x}$. What is the Hessian matrix for the Gaussian kernel? Use the gradient in Eq. (15.11).

Q5. Let us compute the probability density at a point x using the k-nearest neighbor approach, given as

$$\hat{f}(x) = \frac{k}{nV_x}$$

where k is the number of nearest neighbors, n is the total number of points, and V_x is the volume of the region encompassing the k nearest neighbors of x. In other words, we fix k and allow the volume to vary based on those k nearest neighbors of x. Given the following points

$$2, 2.5, 3, 4, 4.5, 5, 6.1$$

Find the peak density in this dataset, assuming $k = 4$. Keep in mind that this may happen at a point other than those given above. Also, a point is its own nearest neighbor.

CHAPTER 16

Spectral and Graph Clustering

In this chapter we consider clustering over graph data, that is, given a graph, the goal is to cluster the nodes by using the edges and their weights, which represent the similarity between the incident nodes. Graph clustering is related to divisive hierarchical clustering, as many methods partition the set of nodes to obtain the final clusters using the pairwise similarity matrix between nodes. As we shall see, graph clustering also has a very strong connection to spectral decomposition of graph-based matrices. Finally, if the similarity matrix is positive semidefinite, it can be considered as a kernel matrix, and graph clustering is therefore also related to kernel-based clustering.

16.1 GRAPHS AND MATRICES

Given a dataset $\mathbf{D}$ comprising n points $\mathbf{x}_i \in \mathbb{R}^d$ ($i = 1, 2, \cdots, n$), let $\mathbf{A}$ denote the $n \times n$ symmetric *similarity matrix* between the points, given as

$$\mathbf{A} = \begin{pmatrix} a_{11} & a_{12} & \cdots & a_{1n} \\ a_{21} & a_{22} & \cdots & a_{2n} \\ \vdots & \vdots & \cdots & \vdots \\ a_{n1} & a_{n2} & \cdots & a_{nn} \end{pmatrix} \tag{16.1}$$

where $\mathbf{A}(i, j) = a_{ij}$ denotes the similarity or affinity between points $\mathbf{x}_i$ and $\mathbf{x}_j$. We require the similarity to be symmetric and non-negative, that is, $a_{ij} = a_{ji}$ and $a_{ij} \geq 0$, respectively. The matrix $\mathbf{A}$ may be considered to be a *weighted adjacency matrix* of the weighted (undirected) graph $G = (V, E)$, where each vertex is a point and each edge joins a pair of points, that is,

$$V = \{\mathbf{x}_i \mid i = 1, \ldots, n\}$$

$$E = \left\{ (\mathbf{x}_i, \mathbf{x}_j) \mid 1 \leq i, j \leq n \right\}$$

Further, the similarity matrix $\mathbf{A}$ gives the weight on each edge, that is, a_{ij} denotes the weight of the edge $(\mathbf{x}_i, \mathbf{x}_j)$. If all affinities are 0 or 1, then $\mathbf{A}$ represents the regular adjacency relationship between the vertices.

For a vertex $\mathbf{x}_i$, let d_i denote the *degree* of the vertex, defined as

$$d_i = \sum_{j=1}^{n} a_{ij}$$

We define the *degree matrix* $\mathbf{\Delta}$ of graph G as the $n \times n$ diagonal matrix:

$$\mathbf{\Delta} = \begin{pmatrix} d_1 & 0 & \cdots & 0 \\ 0 & d_2 & \cdots & 0 \\ \vdots & \vdots & \ddots & \vdots \\ 0 & 0 & \cdots & d_n \end{pmatrix} = \begin{pmatrix} \sum_{j=1}^{n} a_{1j} & 0 & \cdots & 0 \\ 0 & \sum_{j=1}^{n} a_{2j} & \cdots & 0 \\ \vdots & \vdots & \ddots & \vdots \\ 0 & 0 & \cdots & \sum_{j=1}^{n} a_{nj} \end{pmatrix} \tag{16.2}$$

$\mathbf{\Delta}$ can be compactly written as $\mathbf{\Delta}(i, i) = d_i$ for all $1 \leq i \leq n$.

Example 16.1. Figure 16.1 shows the similarity graph for the Iris dataset, obtained as follows. Each of the $n = 150$ points $\mathbf{x}_i \in \mathbb{R}^4$ in the Iris dataset is represented by a node in G. To create the edges, we first compute the pairwise similarity between the points using the Gaussian kernel [Eq. (5.10)]:

$$a_{ij} = \exp\left\{ -\frac{\|\mathbf{x}_i - \mathbf{x}_j\|^2}{2\sigma^2} \right\}$$

using $\sigma = 1$. Each edge $(\mathbf{x}_i, \mathbf{x}_j)$ has the weight a_{ij}. Next, for each node $\mathbf{x}_i$ we compute the top q nearest neighbors in terms of the similarity value, given as

$$N_q(\mathbf{x}_i) = \left\{ \mathbf{x}_j \in V : a_{ij} \leq a_{iq} \right\}$$

where a_{iq} represents the similarity value between $\mathbf{x}_i$ and its qth nearest neighbor. We used a value of $q = 16$, as in this case each node records at least 15 nearest neighbors (not including the node itself), which corresponds to 10% of the nodes. An edge is added between nodes $\mathbf{x}_i$ and $\mathbf{x}_j$ if and only if both nodes are *mutual nearest neighbors*, that is, if $\mathbf{x}_j \in N_q(\mathbf{x}_i)$ and $\mathbf{x}_i \in N_q(\mathbf{x}_j)$. Finally, if the resulting graph is disconnected, we add the top q most similar (i.e., highest weighted) edges between any two connected components.

The resulting Iris similarity graph is shown in Figure 16.1. It has $|V| = n = 150$ nodes and $|E| = m = 1730$ edges. Edges with similarity $a_{ij} \geq 0.9$ are shown in black, and the remaining edges are shown in gray. Although $a_{ii} = 1.0$ for all nodes, we do not show the self-edges or loops.

Normalized Adjacency Matrix

The normalized adjacency matrix is obtained by dividing each row of the adjacency matrix by the degree of the corresponding node. Given the weightedadjacency matrix

Figure 16.1. Iris similarity graph.

A for a graph G, its normalized adjacency matrix is defined as

$$\mathbf{M} = \mathbf{\Delta}^{-1}\mathbf{A} = \begin{pmatrix} \frac{a_{11}}{d_1} & \frac{a_{12}}{d_1} & \cdots & \frac{a_{1n}}{d_1} \\ \frac{a_{21}}{d_2} & \frac{a_{22}}{d_2} & \cdots & \frac{a_{2n}}{d_2} \\ \vdots & \vdots & \ddots & \vdots \\ \frac{a_{n1}}{d_n} & \frac{a_{n2}}{d_n} & \cdots & \frac{a_{nn}}{d_n} \end{pmatrix} \tag{16.3}$$

Because **A** is assumed to have non-negative elements, this implies that each element of **M**, namely m_{ij} is also non-negative, as $m_{ij} = \frac{a_{ij}}{d_i} \geq 0$. Consider the sum of the ith row in **M**; we have

$$\sum_{j=1}^{n} m_{ij} = \sum_{j=1}^{n} \frac{a_{ij}}{d_i} = \frac{d_i}{d_i} = 1 \tag{16.4}$$

Thus, each row in **M** sums to 1. This implies that 1 is an eigenvalue of **M**. In fact, $\lambda_1 = 1$ is the largest eigenvalue of **M**, and the other eigenvalues satisfy the property that $|\lambda_i| \leq 1$. Also, if G is connected then the eigenvector corresponding to λ_1 is $\mathbf{u}_1 = \frac{1}{\sqrt{n}}(1, 1, \dots, 1)^T = \frac{1}{\sqrt{n}}\mathbf{1}$. Because **M** is not symmetric, its eigenvectors are not necessarily orthogonal.

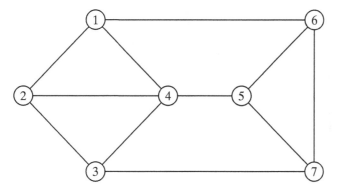

Figure 16.2. Example graph.

Example 16.2. Consider the graph in Figure 16.2. Its adjacency and degree matrices are given as

$$
\mathbf{A} = \begin{pmatrix}
0 & 1 & 0 & 1 & 0 & 1 & 0 \\
1 & 0 & 1 & 1 & 0 & 0 & 0 \\
0 & 1 & 0 & 1 & 0 & 0 & 1 \\
1 & 1 & 1 & 0 & 1 & 0 & 0 \\
0 & 0 & 0 & 1 & 0 & 1 & 1 \\
1 & 0 & 0 & 0 & 1 & 0 & 1 \\
0 & 0 & 1 & 0 & 1 & 1 & 0
\end{pmatrix}
\qquad
\mathbf{\Delta} = \begin{pmatrix}
3 & 0 & 0 & 0 & 0 & 0 & 0 \\
0 & 3 & 0 & 0 & 0 & 0 & 0 \\
0 & 0 & 3 & 0 & 0 & 0 & 0 \\
0 & 0 & 0 & 4 & 0 & 0 & 0 \\
0 & 0 & 0 & 0 & 3 & 0 & 0 \\
0 & 0 & 0 & 0 & 0 & 3 & 0 \\
0 & 0 & 0 & 0 & 0 & 0 & 3
\end{pmatrix}
$$

The normalized adjacency matrix is as follows:

$$
\mathbf{M} = \mathbf{\Delta}^{-1}\mathbf{A} = \begin{pmatrix}
0 & 0.33 & 0 & 0.33 & 0 & 0.33 & 0 \\
0.33 & 0 & 0.33 & 0.33 & 0 & 0 & 0 \\
0 & 0.33 & 0 & 0.33 & 0 & 0 & 0.33 \\
0.25 & 0.25 & 0.25 & 0 & 0.25 & 0 & 0 \\
0 & 0 & 0 & 0.33 & 0 & 0.33 & 0.33 \\
0.33 & 0 & 0 & 0 & 0.33 & 0 & 0.33 \\
0 & 0 & 0.33 & 0 & 0.33 & 0.33 & 0
\end{pmatrix}
$$

The eigenvalues of $\mathbf{M}$ sorted in decreasing order are as follows:

$$\lambda_1 = 1 \qquad\qquad \lambda_2 = 0.483 \qquad\qquad \lambda_3 = 0.206 \qquad\qquad \lambda_4 = -0.045$$

$$\lambda_5 = -0.405 \qquad\qquad \lambda_6 = -0.539 \qquad\qquad \lambda_7 = -0.7$$

The eigenvector corresponding to $\lambda_1 = 1$ is

$$\mathbf{u}_1 = \frac{1}{\sqrt{7}}(1,1,1,1,1,1,1)^T = (0.38, 0.38, 0.38, 0.38, 0.38, 0.38, 0.38)^T$$

Graph Laplacian Matrices

The *Laplacian matrix* of a graph is defined as

$$\mathbf{L} = \mathbf{\Delta} - \mathbf{A}$$

$$= \begin{pmatrix} \sum_{j=1}^{n} a_{1j} & 0 & \cdots & 0 \\ 0 & \sum_{j=1}^{n} a_{2j} & \cdots & 0 \\ \vdots & \vdots & \ddots & \vdots \\ 0 & 0 & \cdots & \sum_{j=1}^{n} a_{nj} \end{pmatrix} - \begin{pmatrix} a_{11} & a_{12} & \cdots & a_{1n} \\ a_{21} & a_{22} & \cdots & a_{2n} \\ \vdots & \vdots & \cdots & \vdots \\ a_{n1} & a_{n2} & \cdots & a_{nn} \end{pmatrix}$$

$$= \begin{pmatrix} \sum_{j \neq 1} a_{1j} & -a_{12} & \cdots & -a_{1n} \\ -a_{21} & \sum_{j \neq 2} a_{2j} & \cdots & -a_{2n} \\ \vdots & \vdots & \cdots & \vdots \\ -a_{n1} & -a_{n2} & \cdots & \sum_{j \neq n} a_{nj} \end{pmatrix} \qquad (16.5)$$

It is interesting to note that $\mathbf{L}$ is a symmetric, positive semidefinite matrix, as for any $\mathbf{c} \in \mathbb{R}^n$, we have

$$\mathbf{c}^T \mathbf{L} \mathbf{c} = \mathbf{c}^T (\mathbf{\Delta} - \mathbf{A}) \mathbf{c} = \mathbf{c}^T \mathbf{\Delta} \mathbf{c} - \mathbf{c}^T \mathbf{A} \mathbf{c}$$

$$= \sum_{i=1}^{n} d_i c_i^2 - \sum_{i=1}^{n} \sum_{j=1}^{n} c_i c_j a_{ij}$$

$$= \frac{1}{2} \left(\sum_{i=1}^{n} d_i c_i^2 - 2 \sum_{i=1}^{n} \sum_{j=1}^{n} c_i c_j a_{ij} + \sum_{j=1}^{n} d_j c_j^2 \right)$$

$$= \frac{1}{2} \left(\sum_{i=1}^{n} \sum_{j=1}^{n} a_{ij} c_i^2 - 2 \sum_{i=1}^{n} \sum_{j=1}^{n} c_i c_j a_{ij} + \sum_{i=j}^{n} \sum_{i=1}^{n} a_{ij} c_j^2 \right) \qquad (16.6)$$

$$= \frac{1}{2} \sum_{i=1}^{n} \sum_{j=1}^{n} a_{ij} (c_i - c_j)^2$$

$$\geq 0 \qquad \text{because } a_{ij} \geq 0 \text{ and } (c_i - c_j)^2 \geq 0$$

This means that $\mathbf{L}$ has n real, non-negative eigenvalues, which can be arranged in decreasing order as follows: $\lambda_1 \geq \lambda_2 \geq \cdots \geq \lambda_n \geq 0$. Because $\mathbf{L}$ is symmetric, its eigenvectors are orthonormal. Further, from Eq. (16.5) we can see that the first column (and the first row) is a linear combination of the remaining columns (rows). That is, if L_i denotes the ith column of $\mathbf{L}$, then we can observe that $L_1 + L_2 + L_3 + \cdots + L_n = \mathbf{0}$. This implies that the rank of $\mathbf{L}$ is at most $n-1$, and the smallest eigenvalue is $\lambda_n = 0$, with the corresponding eigenvector given as $\mathbf{u}_n = \frac{1}{\sqrt{n}}(1, 1, \ldots, 1)^T = \frac{1}{\sqrt{n}} \mathbf{1}$, provided the graph is connected. If the graph is disconnected, then the number of eigenvalues equal to zero specifies the number of connected components in the graph.

Example 16.3. Consider the graph in Figure 16.2, whose adjacency and degree matrices are shown in Example 16.2. The graph Laplacian is given as

$$\mathbf{L} = \mathbf{\Delta} - \mathbf{A} = \begin{pmatrix} 3 & -1 & 0 & -1 & 0 & -1 & 0 \\ -1 & 3 & -1 & -1 & 0 & 0 & 0 \\ 0 & -1 & 3 & -1 & 0 & 0 & -1 \\ -1 & -1 & -1 & 4 & -1 & 0 & 0 \\ 0 & 0 & 0 & -1 & 3 & -1 & -1 \\ -1 & 0 & 0 & 0 & -1 & 3 & -1 \\ 0 & 0 & -1 & 0 & -1 & -1 & 3 \end{pmatrix}$$

The eigenvalues of $\mathbf{L}$ are as follows:

$$\lambda_1 = 5.618 \qquad \lambda_2 = 4.618 \qquad \lambda_3 = 4.414 \qquad \lambda_4 = 3.382$$

$$\lambda_5 = 2.382 \qquad \lambda_6 = 1.586 \qquad \lambda_7 = 0$$

The eigenvector corresponding to $\lambda_7 = 0$ is

$$\mathbf{u}_7 = \frac{1}{\sqrt{7}}(1,1,1,1,1,1,1)^T = (0.38, 0.38, 0.38, 0.38, 0.38, 0.38, 0.38)^T$$

The *normalized symmetric Laplacian matrix* of a graph is defined as

$$\mathbf{L}^s = \mathbf{\Delta}^{-1/2} \mathbf{L} \mathbf{\Delta}^{-1/2} \tag{16.7}$$

$$= \mathbf{\Delta}^{-1/2}(\mathbf{\Delta} - \mathbf{A})\mathbf{\Delta}^{-1/2} = \mathbf{\Delta}^{-1/2}\mathbf{\Delta}\mathbf{\Delta}^{-1/2} - \mathbf{\Delta}^{-1/2}\mathbf{A}\mathbf{\Delta}^{-1/2}$$

$$= \mathbf{I} - \mathbf{\Delta}^{-1/2}\mathbf{A}\mathbf{\Delta}^{-1/2}$$

where $\mathbf{\Delta}^{1/2}$ is the diagonal matrix given as $\mathbf{\Delta}^{1/2}(i,i) = \sqrt{d_i}$, and $\mathbf{\Delta}^{-1/2}$ is the diagonal matrix given as $\mathbf{\Delta}^{-1/2}(i,i) = \frac{1}{\sqrt{d_i}}$ (assuming that $d_i \neq 0$), for $1 \leq i \leq n$. In other words, the normalized Laplacian is given as

$$\mathbf{L}^s = \mathbf{\Delta}^{-1/2} \mathbf{L} \mathbf{\Delta}^{-1/2}$$

$$= \begin{pmatrix} \frac{\sum_{j\neq 1} a_{1j}}{\sqrt{d_1 d_1}} & -\frac{a_{12}}{\sqrt{d_1 d_2}} & \cdots & -\frac{a_{1n}}{\sqrt{d_1 d_n}} \\ -\frac{a_{21}}{\sqrt{d_2 d_1}} & \frac{\sum_{j\neq 2} a_{2j}}{\sqrt{d_2 d_2}} & \cdots & -\frac{a_{2n}}{\sqrt{d_2 d_n}} \\ \vdots & \vdots & \ddots & \vdots \\ -\frac{a_{n1}}{\sqrt{d_n d_1}} & -\frac{a_{n2}}{\sqrt{d_n d_2}} & \cdots & \frac{\sum_{j\neq n} a_{nj}}{\sqrt{d_n d_n}} \end{pmatrix} \tag{16.8}$$

Like the derivation in Eq. (16.6), we can show that $\mathbf{L}^s$ is also positive semidefinite because for any $\mathbf{c} \in \mathbb{R}^d$, we get

$$\mathbf{c}^T \mathbf{L}^s \mathbf{c} = \frac{1}{2} \sum_{i=1}^{n} \sum_{j=1}^{n} a_{ij} \left(\frac{c_i}{\sqrt{d_i}} - \frac{c_j}{\sqrt{d_j}} \right)^2 \geq 0 \tag{16.9}$$

Further, if L_i^s denotes the ith column of $\mathbf{L}^s$, then from Eq. (16.8) we can see that

$$\sqrt{d_1}L_1^s + \sqrt{d_2}L_2^s + \sqrt{d_3}L_3^s + \cdots + \sqrt{d_n}L_n^s = \mathbf{0}$$

That is, the first column is a linear combination of the other columns, which means that $\mathbf{L}^s$ has rank at most $n - 1$, with the smallest eigenvalue $\lambda_n = 0$, and the corresponding eigenvector $\frac{1}{\sqrt{\sum_i d_i}}(\sqrt{d_1}, \sqrt{d_2}, \ldots, \sqrt{d_n})^T = \frac{1}{\sqrt{\sum_i d_i}}\mathbf{\Delta}^{1/2}\mathbf{1}$. Combined with the fact that $\mathbf{L}^s$ is positive semidefinite, we conclude that $\mathbf{L}^s$ has n (not necessarily distinct) real, positive eigenvalues $\lambda_1 \geq \lambda_2 \geq \cdots \geq \lambda_n = 0$.

Example 16.4. We continue with Example 16.3. For the graph in Figure 16.2, its normalized symmetric Laplacian is given as

$$\mathbf{L}^s = \begin{pmatrix} 1 & -0.33 & 0 & -0.29 & 0 & -0.33 & 0 \\ -0.33 & 1 & -0.33 & -0.29 & 0 & 0 & 0 \\ 0 & -0.33 & 1 & -0.29 & 0 & 0 & -0.33 \\ -0.29 & -0.29 & -0.29 & 1 & -0.29 & 0 & 0 \\ 0 & 0 & 0 & -0.29 & 1 & -0.33 & -0.33 \\ -0.33 & 0 & 0 & 0 & -0.33 & 1 & -0.33 \\ 0 & 0 & -0.33 & 0 & -0.33 & -0.33 & 1 \end{pmatrix}$$

The eigenvalues of $\mathbf{L}^s$ are as follows:

$$\lambda_1 = 1.7 \qquad \lambda_2 = 1.539 \qquad \lambda_3 = 1.405 \qquad \lambda_4 = 1.045$$

$$\lambda_5 = 0.794 \qquad \lambda_6 = 0.517 \qquad \lambda_7 = 0$$

The eigenvector corresponding to $\lambda_7 = 0$ is

$$\mathbf{u}_7 = \frac{1}{\sqrt{22}}(\sqrt{3}, \sqrt{3}, \sqrt{3}, \sqrt{4}, \sqrt{3}, \sqrt{3}, \sqrt{3})^T$$

$$= (0.37, 0.37, 0.37, 0.43, 0.37, 0.37, 0.37)^T$$

The *normalized asymmetric Laplacian* matrix is defined as

$$\begin{aligned} \mathbf{L}^a &= \mathbf{\Delta}^{-1}\mathbf{L} \\ &= \mathbf{\Delta}^{-1}(\mathbf{\Delta} - \mathbf{A}) = \mathbf{I} - \mathbf{\Delta}^{-1}\mathbf{A} \\ &= \begin{pmatrix} \frac{\sum_{j \neq 1} a_{1j}}{d_1} & -\frac{a_{12}}{d_1} & \cdots & -\frac{a_{1n}}{d_1} \\ -\frac{a_{21}}{d_2} & \frac{\sum_{j \neq 2} a_{2j}}{d_2} & \cdots & -\frac{a_{2n}}{d_2} \\ \vdots & \vdots & \ddots & \vdots \\ -\frac{a_{n1}}{d_n} & -\frac{a_{n2}}{d_n} & \cdots & \frac{\sum_{j \neq n} a_{nj}}{d_n} \end{pmatrix} \end{aligned} \qquad (16.10)$$

Consider the eigenvalue equation for the symmetric Laplacian $\mathbf{L}^s$:

$$\mathbf{L}^s\mathbf{u} = \lambda\mathbf{u}$$

Left multiplying by $\boldsymbol{\Delta}^{-1/2}$ on both sides, we get

$$\boldsymbol{\Delta}^{-1/2}\mathbf{L}^s\mathbf{u} = \lambda\boldsymbol{\Delta}^{-1/2}\mathbf{u}$$

$$\boldsymbol{\Delta}^{-1/2}\left(\boldsymbol{\Delta}^{-1/2}\mathbf{L}\boldsymbol{\Delta}^{-1/2}\right)\mathbf{u} = \lambda\boldsymbol{\Delta}^{-1/2}\mathbf{u}$$

$$\boldsymbol{\Delta}^{-1}\mathbf{L}\left(\boldsymbol{\Delta}^{-1/2}\mathbf{u}\right) = \lambda\left(\boldsymbol{\Delta}^{-1/2}\mathbf{u}\right)$$

$$\mathbf{L}^a\mathbf{v} = \lambda\mathbf{v}$$

where $\mathbf{v} = \boldsymbol{\Delta}^{-1/2}\mathbf{u}$ is an eigenvector of $\mathbf{L}^a$, and $\mathbf{u}$ is an eigenvector of $\mathbf{L}^s$. Further, $\mathbf{L}^a$ has the same set of eigenvalues as $\mathbf{L}^s$, which means that $\mathbf{L}^a$ is a positive semi-definite matrix with n real eigenvalues $\lambda_1 \geq \lambda_2 \geq \cdots \geq \lambda_n = 0$. From Eq. (16.10) we can see that if L_i^a denotes the ith column of $\mathbf{L}^a$, then $L_1^a + L_2^a + \cdots + L_n^a = 0$, which implies that $\mathbf{v}_n = \frac{1}{\sqrt{n}}\mathbf{1}$ is the eigenvector corresponding to the smallest eigenvalue $\lambda_n = 0$.

Example 16.5. For the graph in Figure 16.2, its normalized asymmetric Laplacian matrix is given as

$$\mathbf{L}^a = \boldsymbol{\Delta}^{-1}\mathbf{L} = \begin{pmatrix} 1 & -0.33 & 0 & -0.33 & 0 & -0.33 & 0 \\ -0.33 & 1 & -0.33 & -0.33 & 0 & 0 & 0 \\ 0 & -0.33 & 1 & -0.33 & 0 & 0 & -0.33 \\ -0.25 & -0.25 & -0.25 & 1 & -0.25 & 0 & 0 \\ 0 & 0 & 0 & -0.33 & 1 & -0.33 & -0.33 \\ -0.33 & 0 & 0 & 0 & -0.33 & 1 & -0.33 \\ 0 & 0 & -0.33 & 0 & -0.33 & -0.33 & 1 \end{pmatrix}$$

The eigenvalues of $\mathbf{L}^a$ are identical to those for $\mathbf{L}^s$, namely

$$\lambda_1 = 1.7 \qquad \lambda_2 = 1.539 \qquad \lambda_3 = 1.405 \qquad \lambda_4 = 1.045$$

$$\lambda_5 = 0.794 \qquad \lambda_6 = 0.517 \qquad \lambda_7 = 0$$

The eigenvector corresponding to $\lambda_7 = 0$ is

$$\mathbf{u}_7 = \frac{1}{\sqrt{7}}(1,1,1,1,1,1,1)^T = (0.38, 0.38, 0.38, 0.38, 0.38, 0.38, 0.38)^T$$

16.2 CLUSTERING AS GRAPH CUTS

A *k-way cut* in a graph is a partitioning or clustering of the vertex set, given as $\mathcal{C} = \{C_1, \ldots, C_k\}$, such that $C_i \neq \emptyset$ for all i, $C_i \cap C_j = \emptyset$ for all i, j, and $V = \bigcup_i C_i$. We require $\mathcal{C}$ to optimize some objective function that captures the intuition that nodes within a cluster should have high similarity, and nodes from different clusters should have low similarity.

Given a weighted graph G defined by its similarity matrix [Eq. (16.1)], let $S, T \subseteq V$ be any two subsets of the vertices. We denote by $W(S, T)$ the sum of the weights on all edges with one vertex in S and the other in T, given as

$$W(S, T) = \sum_{v_i \in S} \sum_{v_j \in T} a_{ij} \qquad (16.11)$$

Given $S \subseteq V$, we denote by $\overline{S}$ the complementary set of vertices, that is, $\overline{S} = V - S$. A *(vertex) cut* in a graph is defined as a partitioning of V into $S \subset V$ and $\overline{S}$. The *weight of the cut* or *cut weight* is defined as the sum of all the weights on edges between vertices in S and $\overline{S}$, given as $W(S, \overline{S})$.

Given a clustering $\mathcal{C} = \{C_1, \ldots, C_k\}$ comprising k clusters, the *size* of a cluster C_i is the number of nodes in the cluster, given as $|C_i|$. The *volume* of a cluster C_i is defined as the sum of all the weights on edges with one end in cluster C_i:

$$vol(C_i) = \sum_{v_j \in C_i} d_j = \sum_{v_j \in C_i} \sum_{v_r \in V} a_{jr} = W(C_i, V) \qquad (16.12)$$

Let $\mathbf{c}_i \in \{0, 1\}^n$ be the *cluster indicator vector* that records the cluster membership for cluster C_i, defined as

$$c_{ij} = \begin{cases} 1 & \text{if } v_j \in C_i \\ 0 & \text{if } v_j \notin C_i \end{cases}$$

Because a clustering creates pairwise disjoint clusters, we immediately have

$$\mathbf{c}_i^T \mathbf{c}_j = 0$$

Further, the cluster size can be written as

$$|C_i| = \mathbf{c}_i^T \mathbf{c}_i = \|\mathbf{c}_i\|^2 \qquad (16.13)$$

The following identities allow us to express the weight of a cut in terms of matrix operations. Let us derive an expression for the sum of the weights for all edges with one end in C_i. These edges include internal cluster edges (with both ends in C_i), as well as external cluster edges (with the other end in another cluster $C_{j \neq i}$).

$$vol(C_i) = W(C_i, V) \qquad = \sum_{v_r \in C_i} d_r = \sum_{v_r \in C_i} c_{ir} d_r c_{ir} = \sum_{r=1}^{n} \sum_{s=1}^{n} c_{ir} \mathbf{\Delta}_{rs} c_{is}$$

Therefore, the volume of the cluster can be written as:

$$vol(C_i) = \mathbf{c}_i^T \mathbf{\Delta} \mathbf{c}_i \qquad (16.14)$$

Consider the sum of weights of all internal edges:

$$W(C_i, C_i) = \sum_{v_r \in C_i} \sum_{v_s \in C_i} a_{rs} = \sum_{r=1}^{n} \sum_{s=1}^{n} c_{ir} a_{rs} c_{is}$$

We can therefore rewrite the sum of internal weights as

$$W(C_i, C_i) = \mathbf{c}_i^T \mathbf{A} \mathbf{c}_i \qquad (16.15)$$

We can get the sum of weights for all the external edges, or the cut weight by subtracting Eq. (16.15) from Eq. (16.14), as follows:

$$W(C_i, \overline{C_i}) = \sum_{v_r \in C_i} \sum_{v_s \in V - C_i} a_{rs} = W(C_i, V) - W(C_i, C_i)$$

$$= \mathbf{c}_i(\mathbf{\Delta} - \mathbf{A})\mathbf{c}_i = \mathbf{c}_i^T \mathbf{L} \mathbf{c}_i \qquad (16.16)$$

Example 16.6. Consider the graph in Figure 16.2. Assume that $C_1 = \{1, 2, 3, 4\}$ and $C_2 = \{5, 6, 7\}$ are two clusters. Their cluster indicator vectors are given as

$$\mathbf{c}_1 = (1, 1, 1, 1, 0, 0, 0)^T \qquad\qquad \mathbf{c}_2 = (0, 0, 0, 0, 1, 1, 1)^T$$

As required, we have $\mathbf{c}_1^T \mathbf{c}_2 = 0$, and $\mathbf{c}_1^T \mathbf{c}_1 = \|\mathbf{c}_1\|^2 = 4$ and $\mathbf{c}_2^T \mathbf{c}_2 = 3$ give the cluster sizes. Consider the cut weight between C_1 and C_2. Because there are three edges between the two clusters, we have $W(C_1, \overline{C_1}) = W(C_1, C_2) = 3$. Using the Laplacian matrix from Example 16.3, by Eq. (16.16) we have

$$W(C_1, \overline{C_1}) = \mathbf{c}_1^T \mathbf{L} \mathbf{c}_1$$

$$= (1, 1, 1, 1, 0, 0, 0) \begin{pmatrix} 3 & -1 & 0 & -1 & 0 & -1 & 0 \\ -1 & 3 & -1 & -1 & 0 & 0 & 0 \\ 0 & -1 & 3 & -1 & 0 & 0 & -1 \\ -1 & -1 & -1 & 4 & -1 & 0 & 0 \\ 0 & 0 & 0 & -1 & 3 & -1 & -1 \\ -1 & 0 & 0 & 0 & -1 & 3 & -1 \\ 0 & 0 & -1 & 0 & -1 & -1 & 3 \end{pmatrix} \begin{pmatrix} 1 \\ 1 \\ 1 \\ 1 \\ 0 \\ 0 \\ 0 \end{pmatrix}$$

$$= (1, 0, 1, 1, -1, -1, -1)(1, 1, 1, 1, 0, 0, 0)^T = 3$$

16.2.1 Clustering Objective Functions: Ratio and Normalized Cut

The clustering objective function can be formulated as an optimization problem over the k-way cut $\mathcal{C} = \{C_1, \ldots, C_k\}$. We consider two common minimization objectives, namely ratio and normalized cut. We consider maximization objectives in Section 16.2.3, after describing the spectral clustering algorithm.

Ratio Cut

The *ratio cut* objective is defined over a k-way cut as follows:

$$\min_{\mathcal{C}} J_{rc}(\mathcal{C}) = \sum_{i=1}^{k} \frac{W(C_i, \overline{C_i})}{|C_i|} = \sum_{i=1}^{k} \frac{\mathbf{c}_i^T \mathbf{L} \mathbf{c}_i}{\mathbf{c}_i^T \mathbf{c}_i} = \sum_{i=1}^{k} \frac{\mathbf{c}_i^T \mathbf{L} \mathbf{c}_i}{\|\mathbf{c}_i\|^2} \qquad (16.17)$$

where we make use of Eq. (16.16), that is, $W(C_i, \overline{C_i}) = \mathbf{c}_i^T \mathbf{L} \mathbf{c}_i$.

Ratio cut tries to minimize the sum of the similarities from a cluster C_i to other points not in the cluster $\overline{C_i}$, taking into account the size of each cluster. One can observe that the objective function has a lower value when the cut weight is minimized and when the cluster size is large.

Unfortunately, for binary cluster indicator vectors $\mathbf{c}_i$, the ratio cut objective is NP-hard. An obvious relaxation is to allow $\mathbf{c}_i$ to take on any real value. In this case, we can rewrite the objective as

$$\min_{\mathcal{C}} J_{rc}(\mathcal{C}) = \sum_{i=1}^{k} \frac{\mathbf{c}_i^T \mathbf{L} \mathbf{c}_i}{\|\mathbf{c}_i\|^2} = \sum_{i=1}^{k} \left(\frac{\mathbf{c}_i}{\|\mathbf{c}_i\|} \right)^T \mathbf{L} \left(\frac{\mathbf{c}_i}{\|\mathbf{c}_i\|} \right) = \sum_{i=1}^{k} \mathbf{u}_i^T \mathbf{L} \mathbf{u}_i \qquad (16.18)$$

where $\mathbf{u}_i = \frac{\mathbf{c}_i}{\|\mathbf{c}_i\|}$ is the unit vector in the direction of $\mathbf{c}_i \in \mathbb{R}^n$, that is, $\mathbf{c}_i$ is assumed to be an arbitrary real vector.

To minimize J_{rc} we take its derivative with respect to $\mathbf{u}_i$ and set it to the zero vector. To incorporate the constraint that $\mathbf{u}_i^T \mathbf{u}_i = 1$, we introduce the Lagrange multiplier λ_i for each cluster C_i. We have

$$\frac{\partial}{\partial \mathbf{u}_i} \left(\sum_{i=1}^{k} \mathbf{u}_i^T \mathbf{L} \mathbf{u}_i + \sum_{i=1}^{n} \lambda_i (1 - \mathbf{u}_i^T \mathbf{u}_i) \right) = \mathbf{0}, \text{ which implies that}$$

$$2\mathbf{L}\mathbf{u}_i - 2\lambda_i \mathbf{u}_i = \mathbf{0}, \text{ and thus}$$

$$\mathbf{L}\mathbf{u}_i = \lambda_i \mathbf{u}_i \qquad (16.19)$$

This implies that $\mathbf{u}_i$ is one of the eigenvectors of the Laplacian matrix $\mathbf{L}$, corresponding to the eigenvalue λ_i. Using Eq. (16.19), we can see that

$$\mathbf{u}_i^T \mathbf{L} \mathbf{u}_i = \mathbf{u}_i^T \lambda_i \mathbf{u}_i = \lambda_i$$

which in turn implies that to minimize the ratio cut objective [Eq. (16.18)], we should choose the k smallest eigenvalues, and the corresponding eigenvectors, so that

$$\min_{\mathcal{C}} J_{rc}(\mathcal{C}) = \mathbf{u}_n^T \mathbf{L} \mathbf{u}_n + \cdots + \mathbf{u}_{n-k+1}^T \mathbf{L} \mathbf{u}_{n-k+1}$$

$$= \lambda_n + \cdots + \lambda_{n-k+1} \qquad (16.20)$$

where we assume that the eigenvalues have been sorted so that $\lambda_1 \geq \lambda_2 \geq \cdots \geq \lambda_n$. Noting that the smallest eigenvalue of $\mathbf{L}$ is $\lambda_n = 0$, the k smallest eigenvalues are as follows: $0 = \lambda_n \leq \lambda_{n-1} \leq \lambda_{n-k+1}$. The corresponding eigenvectors $\mathbf{u}_n, \mathbf{u}_{n-1}, \ldots, \mathbf{u}_{n-k+1}$ represent the relaxed cluster indicator vectors. However, because $\mathbf{u}_n = \frac{1}{\sqrt{n}} \mathbf{1}$, it does not provide any guidance on how to separate the graph nodes if the graph is connected.

Normalized Cut

Normalized cut is similar to ratio cut, except that it divides the cut weight of each cluster by the volume of a cluster instead of its size. The objective function is given as

$$\min_{\mathcal{C}} J_{nc}(\mathcal{C}) = \sum_{i=1}^{k} \frac{W(C_i, \overline{C_i})}{vol(C_i)} = \sum_{i=1}^{k} \frac{\mathbf{c}_i^T \mathbf{L} \mathbf{c}_i}{\mathbf{c}_i^T \mathbf{\Delta} \mathbf{c}_i} \tag{16.21}$$

where we use Eqs. (16.16) and (16.14), that is, $W(C_i, \overline{C_i}) = \mathbf{c}_i^T \mathbf{L} \mathbf{c}_i$ and $vol(C_i) = \mathbf{c}_i^T \mathbf{\Delta} \mathbf{c}_i$, respectively. The J_{nc} objective function has lower values when the cut weight is low and when the cluster volume is high, as desired.

As in the case of ratio cut, we can obtain an optimal solution to the normalized cut objective if we relax the condition that $\mathbf{c}_i$ be a binary cluster indicator vector. Instead we assume $\mathbf{c}_i$ to be an arbitrary real vector. Using the observation that the diagonal degree matrix $\mathbf{\Delta}$ can be written as $\mathbf{\Delta} = \mathbf{\Delta}^{1/2} \mathbf{\Delta}^{1/2}$, and using the fact that $\mathbf{I} = \mathbf{\Delta}^{1/2} \mathbf{\Delta}^{-1/2}$ and $\mathbf{\Delta}^T = \mathbf{\Delta}$ (because $\mathbf{\Delta}$ is diagonal), we can rewrite the normalized cut objective in terms of the normalized symmetric Laplacian, as follows:

$$
\begin{aligned}
\min_{\mathcal{C}} J_{nc}(\mathcal{C}) &= \sum_{i=1}^{k} \frac{\mathbf{c}_i^T \mathbf{L} \mathbf{c}_i}{\mathbf{c}_i^T \mathbf{\Delta} \mathbf{c}_i} = \sum_{i=1}^{k} \frac{\mathbf{c}_i^T (\mathbf{\Delta}^{1/2} \mathbf{\Delta}^{-1/2}) \mathbf{L} (\mathbf{\Delta}^{-1/2} \mathbf{\Delta}^{1/2}) \mathbf{c}_i}{\mathbf{c}_i^T (\mathbf{\Delta}^{1/2} \mathbf{\Delta}^{1/2}) \mathbf{c}_i} \\
&= \sum_{i=1}^{k} \frac{(\mathbf{\Delta}^{1/2} \mathbf{c}_i)^T (\mathbf{\Delta}^{-1/2} \mathbf{L} \mathbf{\Delta}^{-1/2})(\mathbf{\Delta}^{1/2} \mathbf{c}_i)}{(\mathbf{\Delta}^{1/2} \mathbf{c}_i)^T (\mathbf{\Delta}^{1/2} \mathbf{c}_i)} \\
&= \sum_{i=1}^{k} \left(\frac{\mathbf{\Delta}^{1/2} \mathbf{c}_i}{\| \mathbf{\Delta}^{1/2} \mathbf{c}_i \|} \right)^T \mathbf{L}^s \left(\frac{\mathbf{\Delta}^{1/2} \mathbf{c}_i}{\| \mathbf{\Delta}^{1/2} \mathbf{c}_i \|} \right) = \sum_{i=1}^{k} \mathbf{u}_i^T \mathbf{L}^s \mathbf{u}_i
\end{aligned}
$$

where $\mathbf{u}_i = \frac{\mathbf{\Delta}^{1/2} \mathbf{c}_i}{\| \mathbf{\Delta}^{1/2} \mathbf{c}_i \|}$ is the unit vector in the direction of $\mathbf{\Delta}^{1/2} \mathbf{c}_i$. Following the same approach as in Eq. (16.19), we conclude that the normalized cut objective is optimized by selecting the k smallest eigenvalues of the normalized Laplacian matrix $\mathbf{L}^s$, namely $0 = \lambda_n \leq \cdots \leq \lambda_{n-k+1}$.

The normalized cut objective [Eq. (16.21)], can also be expressed in terms of the normalized asymmetric Laplacian, by differentiating Eq. (16.21) with respect to $\mathbf{c}_i$ and setting the result to the zero vector. Noting that all terms other than that for $\mathbf{c}_i$ are constant with respect to $\mathbf{c}_i$, we have:

$$\frac{\partial}{\partial \mathbf{c}_i} \left(\sum_{j=1}^{k} \frac{\mathbf{c}_j^T \mathbf{L} \mathbf{c}_j}{\mathbf{c}_j^T \mathbf{\Delta} \mathbf{c}_j} \right) = \frac{\partial}{\partial \mathbf{c}_i} \left(\frac{\mathbf{c}_i^T \mathbf{L} \mathbf{c}_i}{\mathbf{c}_i^T \mathbf{\Delta} \mathbf{c}_i} \right) = \mathbf{0}$$

$$\frac{\mathbf{L} \mathbf{c}_i (\mathbf{c}_i^T \mathbf{\Delta} \mathbf{c}_i) - \mathbf{\Delta} \mathbf{c}_i (\mathbf{c}_i^T \mathbf{L} \mathbf{c}_i)}{(\mathbf{c}_i^T \mathbf{\Delta} \mathbf{c}_i)^2} = \mathbf{0}$$

$$\mathbf{L} \mathbf{c}_i = \left(\frac{\mathbf{c}_i^T \mathbf{L} \mathbf{c}_i}{\mathbf{c}_i^T \mathbf{\Delta} \mathbf{c}_i} \right) \mathbf{\Delta} \mathbf{c}_i$$

$$\mathbf{\Delta}^{-1} \mathbf{L} \mathbf{c}_i = \lambda_i \mathbf{c}_i$$

$$\mathbf{L}^a \mathbf{c}_i = \lambda_i \mathbf{c}_i$$

where $\lambda_i = \frac{\mathbf{c}_i^T \mathbf{L} \mathbf{c}_i}{\mathbf{c}_i^T \Delta \mathbf{c}_i}$ is the eigenvalue corresponding to the ith eigenvector $\mathbf{c}_i$ of the asymmetric Laplacian matrix $\mathbf{L}^a$. To minimize the normalized cut objective we therefore choose the k smallest eigenvalues of $\mathbf{L}^a$, namely, $0 = \lambda_n \le \cdots \le \lambda_{n-k+1}$.

To derive the clustering, for $\mathbf{L}^a$, we can use the corresponding eigenvectors $\mathbf{u}_n, \ldots, \mathbf{u}_{n-k+1}$, with $\mathbf{c}_i = \mathbf{u}_i$ representing the real-valued cluster indicator vectors. However, note that for $\mathbf{L}^a$, we have $\mathbf{c}_n = \mathbf{u}_n = \frac{1}{\sqrt{n}}\mathbf{1}$. Further, for the normalized symmetric Laplacian $\mathbf{L}^s$, the real-valued cluster indicator vectors are given as $\mathbf{c}_i = \Delta^{-1/2}\mathbf{u}_i$, which again implies that $\mathbf{c}_n = \frac{1}{\sqrt{n}}\mathbf{1}$. This means that the eigenvector $\mathbf{u}_n$ corresponding to the smallest eigenvalue $\lambda_n = 0$ does not by itself contain any useful information for clustering if the graph is connected.

16.2.2 Spectral Clustering Algorithm

Algorithm 16.1 gives the pseudo-code for the spectral clustering approach. We assume that the underlying graph is connected. The method takes a dataset $\mathbf{D}$ as input and computes the similarity matrix $\mathbf{A}$. Alternatively, the matrix $\mathbf{A}$ may be directly input as well. Depending on the objective function, we choose the corresponding matrix $\mathbf{B}$. For instance, for normalized cut $\mathbf{B}$ is chosen to be either $\mathbf{L}^s$ or $\mathbf{L}^a$, whereas for ratio cut we choose $\mathbf{B} = \mathbf{L}$. Next, we compute the k smallest eigenvalues and eigenvectors of $\mathbf{B}$. However, the main problem we face is that the eigenvectors $\mathbf{u}_i$ are not binary, and thus it is not immediately clear how we can assign points to clusters. One solution to this problem is to treat the $n \times k$ matrix of eigenvectors as a new data matrix:

$$\mathbf{U} = \begin{pmatrix} | & | & & | \\ \mathbf{u}_n & \mathbf{u}_{n-1} & \cdots & \mathbf{u}_{n-k+1} \\ | & | & & | \end{pmatrix} = \begin{pmatrix} u_{n,1} & u_{n-1,1} & \cdots & u_{n-k+1,1} \\ u_{n2} & u_{n-1,2} & \cdots & u_{n-k+1,2} \\ | & | & \cdots & | \\ u_{n,n} & u_{n-1,n} & \cdots & u_{n-k+1,n} \end{pmatrix} \tag{16.22}$$

Next, we normalize each row of $\mathbf{U}$ to obtain the unit vector:

$$\mathbf{y}_i = \frac{1}{\sqrt{\sum_{j=1}^{k} u_{n-j+1,i}^2}} (u_{n,i}, \ u_{n-1,i}, \ \ldots, \ u_{n-k+1,i})^T \tag{16.23}$$

Algorithm 16.1: Spectral Clustering Algorithm

SPECTRAL CLUSTERING $(\mathbf{D}, k)$:

1 Compute the similarity matrix $\mathbf{A} \in \mathbb{R}^{n \times n}$
2 **if** *ratio cut* **then** $\mathbf{B} \leftarrow \mathbf{L}$
3 **else if** *normalized cut* **then** $\mathbf{B} \leftarrow \mathbf{L}^s$ or $\mathbf{L}^a$
4 Solve $\mathbf{B}\mathbf{u}_i = \lambda_i \mathbf{u}_i$ for $i = n, \ldots, n-k+1$, where $\lambda_n \le \lambda_{n-1} \le \cdots \le \lambda_{n-k+1}$
5 $\mathbf{U} \leftarrow \begin{pmatrix} \mathbf{u}_n & \mathbf{u}_{n-1} & \cdots & \mathbf{u}_{n-k+1} \end{pmatrix}$
6 $\mathbf{Y} \leftarrow$ normalize rows of $\mathbf{U}$ using Eq. (16.23)
7 $\mathcal{C} \leftarrow \{C_1, \ldots, C_k\}$ via K-means on $\mathbf{Y}$

---

which yields the new normalized data matrix $\mathbf{Y} \in \mathbb{R}^{n \times k}$ comprising n points in a reduced k dimensional space:

$$\mathbf{Y} = \begin{pmatrix} - & \mathbf{y}_1^T & - \\ - & \mathbf{y}_2^T & - \\ & \vdots & \\ - & \mathbf{y}_n^T & - \end{pmatrix}$$

We can now cluster the new points in $\mathbf{Y}$ into k clusters via the K-means algorithm or any other fast clustering method, as it is expected that the clusters are well-separated in the k-dimensional eigen-space. Note that for $\mathbf{L}$, $\mathbf{L}^s$, and $\mathbf{L}^a$, the cluster indicator vector corresponding to the smallest eigenvalue $\lambda_n = 0$ is a vector of all 1's, which does not provide any information about how to separate the nodes. The real information for clustering is contained in eigenvectors starting from the second smallest eigenvalue. However, if the graph is disconnected, then even the eigenvector corresponding to λ_n can contain information valuable for clustering. Thus, we retain all k eigenvectors in $\mathbf{U}$ in Eq. (16.22).

Strictly speaking, the normalization step [Eq. (16.23)] is recommended only for the normalized symmetric Laplacian $\mathbf{L}^s$. This is because the eigenvectors of $\mathbf{L}^s$ and the cluster indicator vectors are related as $\mathbf{\Delta}^{1/2}\mathbf{c}_i = \mathbf{u}_i$. The jth entry of $\mathbf{u}_i$, corresponding to vertex v_j, is given as

$$u_{ij} = \frac{\sqrt{d_j} c_{ij}}{\sqrt{\sum_{r=1}^n d_r c_{ir}^2}}$$

If vertex degrees vary a lot, vertices with small degrees would have very small values u_{ij}. This can cause problems for K-means for correctly clustering these vertices. The normalization step helps alleviate this problem for $\mathbf{L}^s$, though it can also help other objectives.

Computational Complexity

The computational complexity of the spectral clustering algorithm is $O(n^3)$, because computing the eigenvectors takes that much time. However, if the graph is sparse, the complexity to compute the eigenvectors is $O(mn)$ where m is the number of edges in the graph. In particular, if $m = O(n)$, then the complexity reduces to $O(n^2)$. Running the K-means method on $\mathbf{Y}$ takes $O(tnk^2)$ time, where t is the number of iterations K-means takes to converge.

Example 16.7. Consider the normalized cut approach applied to the graph in Figure 16.2. Assume that we want to find $k = 2$ clusters. For the normalized asymmetric Laplacian matrix from Example 16.5, we compute the eigenvectors, $\mathbf{v}_7$ and $\mathbf{v}_6$, corresponding to the two smallest eigenvalues, $\lambda_7 = 0$ and $\lambda_6 = 0.517$. The matrix composed of both the eigenvectors is given as

$$U = \begin{pmatrix} \mathbf{u}_1 & \mathbf{u}_2 \\ -0.378 & -0.226 \\ -0.378 & -0.499 \\ -0.378 & -0.226 \\ -0.378 & -0.272 \\ -0.378 & 0.425 \\ -0.378 & 0.444 \\ -0.378 & 0.444 \end{pmatrix}$$

We treat the ith component of $\mathbf{u}_1$ and $\mathbf{u}_2$ as the ith point $(u_{1i}, u_{2i}) \in \mathbb{R}^2$, and after normalizing all points to have unit length we obtain the new dataset:

$$Y = \begin{pmatrix} -0.859 & -0.513 \\ -0.604 & -0.797 \\ -0.859 & -0.513 \\ -0.812 & -0.584 \\ -0.664 & 0.747 \\ -0.648 & 0.761 \\ -0.648 & 0.761 \end{pmatrix}$$

For instance the first point is computed as

$$\mathbf{y}_1 = \frac{1}{\sqrt{(-0.378)^2 + (-0.226^2)}} (-0.378, -0.226)^T = (-0.859, -0.513)^T$$

Figure 16.3 plots the new dataset $\mathbf{Y}$. Clustering the points into $k = 2$ groups using K-means yields the two clusters $C_1 = \{1, 2, 3, 4\}$ and $C_2 = \{5, 6, 7\}$.

Example 16.8. We apply spectral clustering on the Iris graph in Figure 16.1 using the normalized cut objective with the asymmetric Laplacian matrix $\mathbf{L}^a$. Figure 16.4 shows the $k = 3$ clusters. Comparing them with the true Iris classes (not used in the clustering), we obtain the contingency table shown in Table 16.1, indicating the number of points clustered correctly (on the main diagonal) and incorrectly (off-diagonal). We can see that cluster C_1 corresponds mainly to iris-setosa, C_2 to iris-virginica, and C_3 to iris-versicolor. The latter two are more difficult to separate. In total there are 18 points that are misclustered when compared to the true Iris types.

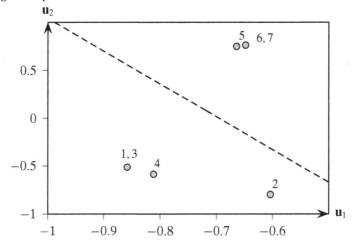

Figure 16.3. K-means on spectral dataset **Y**.

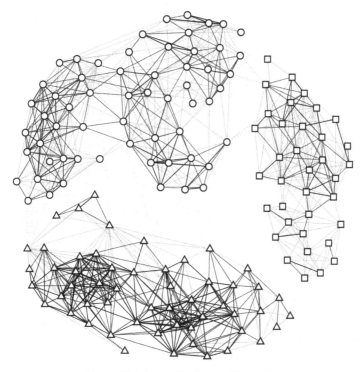

Figure 16.4. Normalized cut on Iris graph.

Table 16.1. Contingency table: clusters versus Iris types

	iris-setosa	iris-virginica	iris-versicolor
C_1 (triangle)	50	0	4
C_2 (square)	0	36	0
C_3 (circle)	0	14	46

16.2.3 Maximization Objectives: Average Cut and Modularity

We now discuss two clustering objective functions that can be formulated as maximization problems over the k-way cut $\mathcal{C} = \{C_1, \ldots, C_k\}$. These include average weight and modularity. We also explore their connections with normalized cut and kernel K-means.

Average Weight

The *average weight* objective is defined as

$$
\max_{\mathcal{C}} J_{aw}(\mathcal{C}) = \sum_{i=1}^{k} \frac{W(C_i, C_i)}{|C_i|} = \sum_{i=1}^{k} \frac{\mathbf{c}_i^T \mathbf{A} \mathbf{c}_i}{\mathbf{c}_i^T \mathbf{c}_i} \tag{16.24}
$$

where we used the equivalence $W(C_i, C_i) = \mathbf{c}_i^T \mathbf{A} \mathbf{c}_i$ established in Eq. (16.15). Instead of trying to minimize the weights on edges between clusters as in ratio cut, average weight tries to maximize the within cluster weights. The problem of maximizing J_{aw} for binary cluster indicator vectors is also NP-hard; we can obtain a solution by relaxing the constraint on $\mathbf{c}_i$, by assuming that it can take on any real values for its elements. This leads to the relaxed objective

$$
\max_{\mathcal{C}} J_{aw}(\mathcal{C}) = \sum_{i=1}^{k} \mathbf{u}_i^T \mathbf{A} \mathbf{u}_i \tag{16.25}
$$

where $\mathbf{u}_i = \frac{\mathbf{c}_i}{\|\mathbf{c}_i\|}$. Following the same approach as in Eq. (16.19), we can maximize the objective by selecting the k largest eigenvalues of $\mathbf{A}$, and the corresponding eigenvectors

$$
\max_{\mathcal{C}} J_{aw}(\mathcal{C}) = \mathbf{u}_1^T \mathbf{A} \mathbf{u}_1 + \cdots + \mathbf{u}_k^T \mathbf{A} \mathbf{u}_k
$$

$$
= \lambda_1 + \cdots + \lambda_k
$$

where $\lambda_1 \geq \lambda_2 \geq \cdots \geq \lambda_n$.

If we assume that $\mathbf{A}$ is the weighted adjacency matrix obtained from a symmetric and positive semidefinite kernel, that is, with $a_{ij} = K(\mathbf{x}_i, \mathbf{x}_j)$, then $\mathbf{A}$ will be positive semidefinite and will have non-negative real eigenvalues. In general, if we threshold $\mathbf{A}$ or if $\mathbf{A}$ is the unweighted adjacency matrix for an undirected graph, then even though $\mathbf{A}$ is symmetric, it may not be positive semidefinite. This means that in general $\mathbf{A}$ can have negative eigenvalues, though they are all real. Because J_{aw} is a maximization problem, this means that we must consider only the positive eigenvalues and the corresponding eigenvectors.

Example 16.9. For the graph in Figure 16.2, with the adjacency matrix shown in Example 16.3, its eigenvalues are as follows:

$$\lambda_1 = 3.18 \qquad \lambda_2 = 1.49 \qquad \lambda_3 = 0.62 \qquad \lambda_4 = -0.15$$

$$\lambda_5 = -1.27 \qquad \lambda_6 = -1.62 \qquad \lambda_7 = -2.25$$

We can see that the eigenvalues can be negative, as $\mathbf{A}$ is the adjacency graph and is not positive semidefinite.

Average Weight and Kernel K-means   The average weight objective leads to an interesting connection between kernel K-means and graph cuts. If the weighted adjacency matrix $\mathbf{A}$ represents the kernel value between a pair of points, so that $a_{ij} = K(\mathbf{x}_i, \mathbf{x}_j)$, then we may use the sum of squared errors objective [Eq. (13.3)] of kernel K-means for graph clustering. The SSE objective is given as

$$
\begin{aligned}
\min_{\mathcal{C}} J_{sse}(\mathcal{C}) &= \sum_{j=1}^{n} K(\mathbf{x}_j, \mathbf{x}_j) - \sum_{i=1}^{k} \frac{1}{|C_i|} \sum_{\mathbf{x}_r \in C_i} \sum_{\mathbf{x}_s \in C_i} K(\mathbf{x}_r, \mathbf{x}_s) \\
&= \sum_{j=1}^{n} a_{jj} - \sum_{i=1}^{k} \frac{1}{|C_i|} \sum_{v_r \in C_i} \sum_{v_s \in C_i} a_{rs} \\
&= \sum_{j=1}^{n} a_{jj} - \sum_{i=1}^{k} \frac{\mathbf{c}_i^T \mathbf{A} \mathbf{c}_i}{\mathbf{c}_i^T \mathbf{c}_i} \\
&= \sum_{j=1}^{n} a_{jj} - J_{aw}(\mathcal{C})
\end{aligned}
\tag{16.26}
$$

We can observe that because $\sum_{j=1}^{n} a_{jj}$ is independent of the clustering, minimizing the SSE objective is the same as maximizing the average weight objective. In particular, if a_{ij} represents the linear kernel $\mathbf{x}_i^T \mathbf{x}_j$ between the nodes, then maximizing the average weight objective [Eq. (16.24)] is equivalent to minimizing the regular K-means SSE objective [Eq. (13.1)]. Thus, spectral clustering using J_{aw} and kernel K-means represent two different approaches to solve the same problem. Kernel K-means tries to solve the NP-hard problem by using a greedy iterative approach to directly optimize the SSE objective, whereas the graph cut formulation tries to solve the same NP-hard problem by optimally solving a relaxed problem.

Modularity

Informally, modularity is defined as the difference between the observed and expected fraction of edges within a cluster. It measures the extent to which nodes of the same type (in our case, the same cluster) are linked to each other.

Unweighted Graphs   Let us assume for the moment that the graph G is unweighted, and that $\mathbf{A}$ is its binary adjacency matrix. The number of edges within a cluster C_i is given as

$$
\frac{1}{2} \sum_{v_r \in C_i} \sum_{v_s \in C_i} a_{rs}
$$

where we divide by $\frac{1}{2}$ because each edge is counted twice in the summation. Over all the clusters, the observed number of edges within the same cluster is given as

$$\frac{1}{2}\sum_{i=1}^{k}\sum_{v_r \in C_i}\sum_{v_s \in C_i} a_{rs} \tag{16.27}$$

Let us compute the expected number of edges between any two vertices v_r and v_s, assuming that edges are placed at random, and allowing multiple edges between the same pair of vertices. Let $|E| = m$ be the total number of edges in the graph. The probability that one end of an edge is v_r is given as $\frac{d_r}{2m}$, where d_r is the degree of v_r. The probability that one end is v_r and the other v_s is then given as

$$p_{rs} = \frac{d_r}{2m} \cdot \frac{d_s}{2m} = \frac{d_r d_s}{4m^2}$$

The number of edges between v_r and v_s follows a binomial distribution with success probability p_{rs} over $2m$ trials (because we are selecting the two ends of m edges). The expected number of edges between v_r and v_s is given as

$$2m \cdot p_{rs} = \frac{d_r d_s}{2m}$$

The expected number of edges within a cluster C_i is then

$$\frac{1}{2}\sum_{v_r \in C_i}\sum_{v_s \in C_i} \frac{d_r d_s}{2m}$$

and the expected number of edges within the same cluster, summed over all k clusters, is given as

$$\frac{1}{2}\sum_{i=1}^{k}\sum_{v_r \in C_i}\sum_{v_s \in C_i} \frac{d_r d_s}{2m} \tag{16.28}$$

where we divide by 2 because each edge is counted twice. The *modularity* of the clustering $\mathcal{C}$ is defined as the difference between the observed and expected fraction of edges within the same cluster, obtained by subtracting Eq. (16.28) from Eq. (16.27), and dividing by the number of edges:

$$Q = \frac{1}{2m}\sum_{i=1}^{k}\sum_{v_r \in C_i}\sum_{v_s \in C_i} \left(a_{rs} - \frac{d_r d_s}{2m} \right)$$

Because $2m = \sum_{i=1}^{n} d_i$, we can rewrite modularity as follows:

$$Q = \sum_{i=1}^{k}\sum_{v_r \in C_i}\sum_{v_s \in C_i} \left(\frac{a_{rs}}{\sum_{j=1}^{n} d_j} - \frac{d_r d_s}{\left(\sum_{j=1}^{n} d_j\right)^2} \right) \tag{16.29}$$

Weighted Graphs One advantage of the modularity formulation in Eq. (16.29) is that it directly generalizes to weighted graphs. Assume that $\mathbf{A}$ is the weighted adjacency matrix; we interpret the modularity of a clustering as the difference between the observed and expected fraction of weights on edges within the clusters.

From Eq. (16.15) we have

$$\sum_{v_r \in C_i} \sum_{v_s \in C_i} a_{rs} = W(C_i, C_i)$$

and from Eq. (16.14) we have

$$\sum_{v_r \in C_i} \sum_{v_s \in C_i} d_r d_s = \left(\sum_{v_r \in C_i} d_r \right) \left(\sum_{v_s \in C_i} d_s \right) = W(C_i, V)^2$$

Further, note that

$$\sum_{j=1}^{n} d_j = W(V, V)$$

Using the above equivalences, can write the modularity objective [Eq. (16.29)] in terms of the weight function W as follows:

$$\max_{\mathcal{C}} J_Q(\mathcal{C}) = \sum_{i=1}^{k} \left(\frac{W(C_i, C_i)}{W(V, V)} - \left(\frac{W(C_i, V)}{W(V, V)} \right)^2 \right) \tag{16.30}$$

We now express the modularity objective [Eq. (16.30)] in matrix terms. From Eq. (16.15), we have

$$W(C_i, C_i) = \mathbf{c}_i^T \mathbf{A} \mathbf{c}_i$$

Also note that

$$W(C_i, V) = \sum_{v_r \in C_i} d_r = \sum_{v_r \in C_i} d_r c_{ir} = \sum_{j=1}^{n} d_j c_{ij} = \mathbf{d}^T \mathbf{c}_i$$

where $\mathbf{d} = (d_1, d_2, \ldots, d_n)^T$ is the vector of vertex degrees. Further, we have

$$W(V, V) = \sum_{j=1}^{n} d_j = tr(\mathbf{\Delta})$$

where $tr(\mathbf{\Delta})$ is the trace of $\mathbf{\Delta}$, that is, sum of the diagonal entries of $\mathbf{\Delta}$.

The clustering objective based on modularity can then be written as

$$\max_{\mathcal{C}} J_Q(\mathcal{C}) = \sum_{i=1}^{k} \left(\frac{\mathbf{c}_i^T \mathbf{A} \mathbf{c}_i}{tr(\mathbf{\Delta})} - \frac{(\mathbf{d}^T \mathbf{c}_i)^2}{tr(\mathbf{\Delta})^2} \right)$$

$$= \sum_{i=1}^{k} \left(\mathbf{c}_i^T \left(\frac{\mathbf{A}}{tr(\mathbf{\Delta})} \right) \mathbf{c}_i - \mathbf{c}_i^T \left(\frac{\mathbf{d} \cdot \mathbf{d}^T}{tr(\mathbf{\Delta})^2} \right) \mathbf{c}_i \right)$$

$$= \sum_{i=1}^{k} \mathbf{c}_i^T \mathbf{Q} \mathbf{c}_i \tag{16.31}$$

where $\mathbf{Q}$ is the *modularity matrix*:

$$\mathbf{Q} = \frac{1}{tr(\mathbf{\Delta})}\left(\mathbf{A} - \frac{\mathbf{d}\cdot\mathbf{d}^T}{tr(\mathbf{\Delta})}\right)$$

Directly maximizing objective Eq. (16.31) for binary cluster vectors $\mathbf{c}_i$ is hard. We resort to the approximation that elements of $\mathbf{c}_i$ can take on real values. Further, we require that $\mathbf{c}_i^T\mathbf{c}_i = \|\mathbf{c}_i\|^2 = 1$ to ensure that J_Q does not increase without bound. Following the approach in Eq. (16.19), we conclude that $\mathbf{c}_i$ is an eigenvector of $\mathbf{Q}$. However, because this a maximization problem, instead of selecting the k smallest eigenvalues, we select the k largest eigenvalues and the corresponding eigenvectors to obtain

$$\max_{\mathcal{C}} J_Q(\mathcal{C}) = \mathbf{u}_1^T\mathbf{Q}\mathbf{u}_1 + \cdots + \mathbf{u}_k^T\mathbf{Q}\mathbf{u}_k$$

$$= \lambda_1 + \cdots + \lambda_k$$

where $\mathbf{u}_i$ is the eigenvector corresponding to λ_i, and the eigenvalues are sorted so that $\lambda_1 \geq \cdots \geq \lambda_n$. The relaxed cluster indicator vectors are given as $\mathbf{c}_i = \mathbf{u}_i$. Note that the modularity matrix $\mathbf{Q}$ is symmetric, but it is not positive semidefinite. This means that although it has real eigenvalues, they may be negative too. Also note that if Q_i denotes the ith column of $\mathbf{Q}$, then we have $Q_1 + Q_2 + \cdots + Q_n = \mathbf{0}$, which implies that 0 is an eigenvalue of $\mathbf{Q}$ with the corresponding eigenvector $\frac{1}{\sqrt{n}}\mathbf{1}$. Thus, for maximizing the modularity one should use only the positive eigenvalues.

Example 16.10. Consider the graph in Figure 16.2. The degree vector is $\mathbf{d} = (3,3,3,4,3,3,3)^T$, and the sum of degrees is $tr(\mathbf{\Delta}) = 22$. The modularity matrix is given as

$$\mathbf{Q} = \frac{1}{tr(\mathbf{\Delta})}\mathbf{A} - \frac{1}{tr(\mathbf{\Delta})^2}\mathbf{d}\cdot\mathbf{d}^T$$

$$= \frac{1}{22}\begin{pmatrix} 0 & 1 & 0 & 1 & 0 & 1 & 0 \\ 1 & 0 & 1 & 1 & 0 & 0 & 0 \\ 0 & 1 & 0 & 1 & 0 & 0 & 1 \\ 1 & 1 & 1 & 0 & 1 & 0 & 0 \\ 0 & 0 & 0 & 1 & 0 & 1 & 1 \\ 1 & 0 & 0 & 0 & 1 & 0 & 1 \\ 0 & 0 & 1 & 0 & 1 & 1 & 0 \end{pmatrix} - \frac{1}{484}\begin{pmatrix} 9 & 9 & 9 & 12 & 9 & 9 & 9 \\ 9 & 9 & 9 & 12 & 9 & 9 & 9 \\ 9 & 9 & 9 & 12 & 9 & 9 & 9 \\ 12 & 12 & 12 & 16 & 12 & 12 & 12 \\ 9 & 9 & 9 & 12 & 9 & 9 & 9 \\ 9 & 9 & 9 & 12 & 9 & 9 & 9 \\ 9 & 9 & 9 & 12 & 9 & 9 & 9 \end{pmatrix}$$

$$= \begin{pmatrix} -0.019 & 0.027 & -0.019 & 0.021 & -0.019 & 0.027 & -0.019 \\ 0.027 & -0.019 & 0.027 & 0.021 & -0.019 & -0.019 & -0.019 \\ -0.019 & 0.027 & -0.019 & 0.021 & -0.019 & -0.019 & 0.027 \\ 0.021 & 0.021 & 0.021 & -0.033 & 0.021 & -0.025 & -0.025 \\ -0.019 & -0.019 & -0.019 & 0.021 & -0.019 & 0.027 & 0.027 \\ 0.027 & -0.019 & -0.019 & -0.025 & 0.027 & -0.019 & 0.027 \\ -0.019 & -0.019 & 0.027 & -0.025 & 0.027 & 0.027 & -0.019 \end{pmatrix}$$

The eigenvalues of $\mathbf{Q}$ are as follows:

$$\lambda_1 = 0.0678 \qquad \lambda_2 = 0.0281 \qquad \lambda_3 = 0 \qquad\qquad \lambda_4 = -0.0068$$

$$\lambda_5 = -0.0579 \qquad \lambda_6 = -0.0736 \qquad \lambda_7 = -0.1024$$

The eigenvector corresponding to $\lambda_3 = 0$ is

$$\mathbf{u}_3 = \frac{1}{\sqrt{7}}(1,1,1,1,1,1,1)^T = (0.38, 0.38, 0.38, 0.38, 0.38, 0.38, 0.38)^T$$

Modularity as Average Weight Consider what happens to the modularity matrix $\mathbf{Q}$ if we use the normalized adjacency matrix $\mathbf{M} = \mathbf{\Delta}^{-1}\mathbf{A}$ in place of the standard adjacency matrix $\mathbf{A}$ in Eq. (16.31). In this case, we know by Eq. (16.4) that each row of $\mathbf{M}$ sums to 1, that is,

$$\sum_{j=1}^{n} m_{ij} = d_i = 1, \text{ for all } i = 1, \ldots, n$$

We thus have $tr(\mathbf{\Delta}) = \sum_{i=1}^{n} d_i = n$, and further $\mathbf{d} \cdot \mathbf{d}^T = \mathbf{1}_{n \times n}$, where $\mathbf{1}_{n \times n}$ is the $n \times n$ matrix of all 1's. The modularity matrix can then be written as

$$\mathbf{Q} = \frac{1}{n}\mathbf{M} - \frac{1}{n^2}\mathbf{1}_{n \times n}$$

For large graphs with many nodes, n is large and the second term practically vanishes, as $\frac{1}{n^2}$ will be very small. Thus, the modularity matrix can be reasonably approximated as

$$\mathbf{Q} \simeq \frac{1}{n}\mathbf{M} \tag{16.32}$$

Substituting the above in the modularity objective [Eq. (16.31)], we get

$$\max_{\mathcal{C}} J_Q(\mathcal{C}) = \sum_{i=1}^{k} \mathbf{c}_i^T \mathbf{Q} \mathbf{c}_i = \sum_{i=1}^{k} \mathbf{c}_i^T \mathbf{M} \mathbf{c}_i \tag{16.33}$$

where we dropped the $\frac{1}{n}$ factor because it is a constant for a given graph; it only scales the eigenvalues without effecting the eigenvectors.

In conclusion, if we use the normalized adjacency matrix, maximizing the modularity is equivalent to selecting the k largest eigenvalues and the corresponding eigenvectors of the normalized adjacency matrix $\mathbf{M}$. Note that in this case modularity is also equivalent to the average weight objective and kernel K-means as established in Eq. (16.26).

Normalized Modularity as Normalized Cut Define the *normalized modularity* objective as follows:

$$\max_{\mathcal{C}} J_{nQ}(\mathcal{C}) = \sum_{i=1}^{k} \frac{1}{W(C_i, V)} \left(\frac{W(C_i, C_i)}{W(V, V)} - \left(\frac{W(C_i, V)}{W(V, V)} \right)^2 \right) \tag{16.34}$$

We can observe that the main difference from the modularity objective [Eq. (16.30)] is that we divide by $vol(C_i) = W(C, V_i)$ for each cluster. Simplifying the above, we obtain

$$J_{nQ}(\mathcal{C}) = \frac{1}{W(V, V)} \sum_{i=1}^{k} \left(\frac{W(C_i, C_i)}{W(C_i, V)} - \frac{W(C_i, V)}{W(V, V)} \right)$$

$$= \frac{1}{W(V, V)} \left(\sum_{i=1}^{k} \left(\frac{W(C_i, C_i)}{W(C_i, V)} \right) - \sum_{i=1}^{k} \left(\frac{W(C_i, V)}{W(V, V)} \right) \right)$$

$$= \frac{1}{W(V, V)} \left(\sum_{i=1}^{k} \left(\frac{W(C_i, C_i)}{W(C_i, V)} \right) - 1 \right)$$

Now consider the expression $(k-1) - W(V, V) \cdot J_{nQ}(\mathcal{C})$, we have

$$(k-1) - W(V, V) J_{nQ}(\mathcal{C}) = (k-1) - \left(\sum_{i=1}^{k} \left(\frac{W(C_i, C_i)}{W(C_i, V)} \right) - 1 \right)$$

$$= k - \sum_{i=1}^{k} \frac{W(C_i, C_i)}{W(C_i, V)}$$

$$= \sum_{i=1}^{k} 1 - \frac{W(C_i, C_i)}{W(C_i, V)}$$

$$= \sum_{i=1}^{k} \frac{W(C_i, V) - W(C_i, C_i)}{W(C_i, V)}$$

$$= \sum_{i=1}^{k} \frac{W(C_i, \overline{C_i})}{W(C_i, V)}$$

$$= \sum_{i=1}^{k} \frac{W(C_i, \overline{C_i})}{vol(C_i)}$$

$$= J_{nc}(\mathcal{C})$$

In other words the normalized cut objective [Eq. (16.21)] is related to the normalized modularity objective [Eq. (16.34)] by the following equation:

$$J_{nc}(\mathcal{C}) = (k-1) - W(V, V) \cdot J_{nQ}(\mathcal{C})$$

Since $W(V, V)$ is a constant for a given graph, we observe that minimizing normalized cut is equivalent to maximizing normalized modularity.

Spectral Clustering Algorithm

Both average weight and modularity are maximization objectives; therefore we have to slightly modify Algorithm 16.1 for spectral clustering to use these objectives. The matrix $\mathbf{B}$ is chosen to be $\mathbf{A}$ if we are maximizing average weight or $\mathbf{Q}$ for the modularity objective. Next, instead of computing the k smallest eigenvalues we have to select the k largest eigenvalues and their corresponding eigenvectors. Because both $\mathbf{A}$ and $\mathbf{Q}$ can have negative eigenvalues, we must select only the positive eigenvalues. The rest of the algorithm remains the same.

16.3 MARKOV CLUSTERING

We now consider a graph clustering method based on simulating a random walk on a weighted graph. The basic intuition is that if node transitions reflect the weights on the edges, then transitions from one node to another within a cluster are much more likely than transitions between nodes from different clusters. This is because nodes within a cluster have higher similarities or weights, and nodes across clusters have lower similarities.

Given the weighted adjacency matrix $\mathbf{A}$ for a graph G, the normalized adjacency matrix [Eq. (16.3)] is given as $\mathbf{M} = \mathbf{\Delta}^{-1}\mathbf{A}$. The matrix $\mathbf{M}$ can be interpreted as the $n \times n$ *transition matrix* where the entry $m_{ij} = \frac{a_{ij}}{d_i}$ can be interpreted as the probability of transitioning or jumping from node i to node j in the graph G. This is because $\mathbf{M}$ is a *row stochastic* or *Markov* matrix, which satisfies the following conditions: (1) elements of the matrix are non-negative, that is, $m_{ij} \geq 0$, which follows from the fact that $\mathbf{A}$ is non-negative, and (2) rows of $\mathbf{M}$ are probability vectors, that is, row elements add to 1, because

$$\sum_{j=1}^{n} m_{ij} = \sum_{j=1}^{n} \frac{a_{ij}}{d_i} = 1$$

The matrix $\mathbf{M}$ is thus the transition matrix for a *Markov chain* or a Markov random walk on graph G. A Markov chain is a discrete-time stochastic process over a set of states, in our case the set of vertices V. The Markov chain makes a transition from one node to another at discrete timesteps $t = 1, 2, \ldots$, with the probability of making a transition from node i to node j given as m_{ij}. Let the random variable X_t denote the state at time t. The Markov property means that the probability distribution of X_t over the states at time t depends only on the probability distribution of X_{t-1}, that is,

$$P(X_t = i | X_0, X_1, \ldots, X_{t-1}) = P(X_t = i | X_{t-1})$$

Further, we assume that the Markov chain is *homogeneous*, that is, the transition probability

$$P(X_t = j | X_{t-1} = i) = m_{ij}$$

is independent of the time step t.

Given node i the transition matrix $\mathbf{M}$ specifies the probabilities of reaching any other node j in one time step. Starting from node i at $t = 0$, let us consider the probability of being at node j at $t = 2$, that is, after two steps. We denote by $m_{ij}(2)$ the probability of reaching j from i in two time steps. We can compute this as follows:

$$m_{ij}(2) = P(X_2 = j | X_0 = i) = \sum_{a=1}^{n} P(X_1 = a | X_0 = i) P(X_2 = j | X_1 = a)$$

$$= \sum_{a=1}^{n} m_{ia} m_{aj} = \mathbf{m}_i^T M_j \tag{16.35}$$

where $\mathbf{m}_i = (m_{i1}, m_{i2}, \ldots, m_{in})^T$ denotes the vector corresponding to the ith row of $\mathbf{M}$ and $M_j = (m_{1j}, m_{2j}, \ldots, m_{nj})^T$ denotes the vector corresponding to the jth column of $\mathbf{M}$.

Consider the product of $\mathbf{M}$ with itself:

$$\mathbf{M}^2 = \mathbf{M} \cdot \mathbf{M} = \begin{pmatrix} - \mathbf{m}_1^T - \\ - \mathbf{m}_2^T - \\ \vdots \\ - \mathbf{m}_n^T - \end{pmatrix} \begin{pmatrix} | & | & & | \\ M_1 & M_2 & \cdots & M_n \\ | & | & & | \end{pmatrix}$$

$$= \left\{ \mathbf{m}_i^T M_j \right\}_{i,j=1}^{n} = \left\{ m_{ij}(2) \right\}_{i,j=1}^{n} \tag{16.36}$$

Equations (16.35) and (16.36) imply that $\mathbf{M}^2$ is precisely the transition probability matrix for the Markov chain over two time-steps. Likewise, the three-step transition matrix is $\mathbf{M}^2 \cdot \mathbf{M} = \mathbf{M}^3$. In general, the transition probability matrix for t time steps is given as

$$\mathbf{M}^{t-1} \cdot \mathbf{M} = \mathbf{M}^t \tag{16.37}$$

A random walk on G thus corresponds to taking successive powers of the transition matrix $\mathbf{M}$. Let $\boldsymbol{\pi}_0$ specify the initial state probability vector at time $t = 0$, that is, $\pi_{0i} = P(X_0 = i)$ is the probability of starting at node i, for all $i = 1, \ldots, n$. Starting from $\boldsymbol{\pi}_0$, we can obtain the state probability vector for X_t, that is, the probability of being at node i at time-step t, as follows

$$\boldsymbol{\pi}_t^T = \boldsymbol{\pi}_{t-1}^T \mathbf{M}$$
$$= \left(\boldsymbol{\pi}_{t-2}^T \mathbf{M} \right) \cdot \mathbf{M} = \boldsymbol{\pi}_{t-2}^T \mathbf{M}^2$$
$$= \left(\boldsymbol{\pi}_{t-3}^T \mathbf{M}^2 \right) \cdot \mathbf{M} = \boldsymbol{\pi}_{t-3}^T \mathbf{M}^3$$
$$= \vdots$$
$$= \boldsymbol{\pi}_0^T \mathbf{M}^t$$

Equivalently, taking transpose on both sides, we get

$$\boldsymbol{\pi}_t = (M^t)^T \boldsymbol{\pi}_0 = (\mathbf{M}^T)^t \boldsymbol{\pi}_0$$

The state probability vector thus converges to the dominant eigenvector of $\mathbf{M}^T$, reflecting the steady-state probability of reaching any node in the graph, regardless of the starting node. Note that if the graph is directed, then the steady-state vector is equivalent to the normalized prestige vector [Eq. (4.19)].

Transition Probability Inflation

We now consider a variation of the random walk, where the probability of transitioning from node i to j is inflated by taking each element m_{ij} to the power $r \geq 1$. Given a transition matrix $\mathbf{M}$, define the inflation operator Υ as follows:

$$\Upsilon(\mathbf{M}, r) = \left\{ \frac{(m_{ij})^r}{\sum_{a=1}^{n}(m_{ia})^r} \right\}_{i,j=1}^{n} \tag{16.38}$$

The inflation operation results in a transformed or inflated transition probability matrix because the elements remain non-negative, and each row is normalized to sum to 1. The net effect of the inflation operator is to increase the higher probability transitions and decrease the lower probability transitions.

16.3.1 Markov Clustering Algorithm

The Markov clustering algorithm (MCL) is an iterative method that interleaves matrix expansion and inflation steps. Matrix expansion corresponds to taking successive powers of the transition matrix, leading to random walks of longer lengths. On the other hand, matrix inflation makes the higher probability transitions even more likely and reduces the lower probability transitions. Because nodes in the same cluster are expected to have higher weights, and consequently higher transition probabilities between them, the inflation operator makes it more likely to stay within the cluster. It thus limits the extent of the random walk.

The pseudo-code for MCL is given in Algorithm 16.2. The method works on the weighted adjacency matrix for a graph. Instead of relying on a user-specified value for k, the number of output clusters, MCL takes as input the inflation parameter $r \geq 1$. Higher values lead to more, smaller clusters, whereas smaller values lead to fewer, but larger clusters. However, the exact number of clusters cannot be pre-determined. Given the adjacency matrix $\mathbf{A}$, MCL first adds *loops* or self-edges to $\mathbf{A}$ if they do not exist. If $\mathbf{A}$ is a similarity matrix, then this is not required, as a node is most similar to itself, and thus $\mathbf{A}$ should have high values on the diagonals. For simple, undirected graphs, if $\mathbf{A}$ is the adjacency matrix, then adding self-edges associates return probabilities with each node.

The iterative MCL expansion and inflation process stops when the transition matrix converges, that is, when the difference between the transition matrix from two successive iterations falls below some threshold $\epsilon \geq 0$. The matrix difference is given in terms of the *Frobenius norm*:

$$\|\mathbf{M}_t - \mathbf{M}_{t-1}\|_F = \sqrt{\sum_{i=1}^{n}\sum_{j=1}^{n}\Big(\mathbf{M}_t(i, j) - \mathbf{M}_{t-1}(i, j)\Big)^2}$$

The MCL process stops when $\|\mathbf{M}_t - \mathbf{M}_{t-1}\|_F \leq \epsilon$.

MCL Graph

The final clusters are found by enumerating the weakly connected components in the directed graph induced by the converged transition matrix $\mathbf{M}_t$. The directed

---

Algorithm 16.2: Markov Clustering Algorithm (MCL)

MARKOV CLUSTERING ($\mathbf{A}, r, \epsilon$):

1 $t \leftarrow 0$
2 Add self-edges to $\mathbf{A}$ if they do not exist
3 $\mathbf{M}_t \leftarrow \Delta^{-1}\mathbf{A}$
4 **repeat**
5 $\quad$ $t \leftarrow t+1$
6 $\quad$ $\mathbf{M}_t \leftarrow \mathbf{M}_{t-1} \cdot \mathbf{M}_{t-1}$
7 $\quad$ $\mathbf{M}_t \leftarrow \Upsilon(\mathbf{M}_t, r)$
8 **until** $\|\mathbf{M}_t - \mathbf{M}_{t-1}\|_F \leq \epsilon$
9 $G_t \leftarrow$ directed graph induced by $\mathbf{M}_t$
10 $\mathcal{C} \leftarrow$ {weakly connected components in G_t}

---

graph induced by $\mathbf{M}_t$ is denoted as $G_t = (V_t, E_t)$. The vertex set is the same as the set of nodes in the original graph, that is, $V_t = V$, and the edge set is given as

$$E_t = \big\{(i,j) \mid \mathbf{M}_t(i,j) > 0\big\}$$

In other words, a directed edge (i,j) exists only if node i can transition to node j within t steps of the expansion and inflation process. A node j is called an *attractor* if $\mathbf{M}_t(j,j) > 0$, and we say that node i is attracted to attractor j if $\mathbf{M}_t(i,j) > 0$. The MCL process yields a set of attractor nodes, $V_a \subseteq V$, such that other nodes are attracted to at least one attractor in V_a. That is, for all nodes i there exists a node $j \in V_a$, such that $(i,j) \in E_t$. A strongly connectedcomponent in a directed graph is defined a maximal subgraph such that there exists a directed path between all pairs of vertices in the subgraph. To extract the clusters from G_t, MCL first finds the strongly connected components $S_1, S_2, \ldots, S_q$ over the set of attractors V_a. Next, for each strongly connected set of attractors S_j, MCL finds the weakly connected components consisting of all nodes $i \in V_t - V_a$ attracted to an attractor in S_j. If a node i is attracted to multiple strongly connected components, it is added to each such cluster, resulting in possibly overlapping clusters.

Example 16.11. We apply the MCL method to find $k = 2$ clusters for the graph shown in Figure 16.2. We add the self-loops to the graph to obtain the adjacency matrix:

$$\mathbf{A} = \begin{pmatrix} 1 & 1 & 0 & 1 & 0 & 1 & 0 \\ 1 & 1 & 1 & 1 & 0 & 0 & 0 \\ 0 & 1 & 1 & 1 & 0 & 0 & 1 \\ 1 & 1 & 1 & 1 & 1 & 0 & 0 \\ 0 & 0 & 0 & 1 & 1 & 1 & 1 \\ 1 & 0 & 0 & 0 & 1 & 1 & 1 \\ 0 & 0 & 1 & 0 & 1 & 1 & 1 \end{pmatrix}$$

The corresponding Markov matrix is given as

$$
\mathbf{M}_0 = \boldsymbol{\Delta}^{-1}\mathbf{A} = \begin{pmatrix}
0.25 & 0.25 & 0 & 0.25 & 0 & 0.25 & 0 \\
0.25 & 0.25 & 0.25 & 0.25 & 0 & 0 & 0 \\
0 & 0.25 & 0.25 & 0.25 & 0 & 0 & 0.25 \\
0.20 & 0.20 & 0.20 & 0.20 & 0.20 & 0 & 0 \\
0 & 0 & 0 & 0.25 & 0.25 & 0.25 & 0.25 \\
0.25 & 0 & 0 & 0 & 0.25 & 0.25 & 0.25 \\
0 & 0 & 0.25 & 0 & 0.25 & 0.25 & 0.25
\end{pmatrix}
$$

In the first iteration, we apply expansion and then inflation (with $r = 2.5$) to obtain

$$
\mathbf{M}_1 = \mathbf{M}_0 \cdot \mathbf{M}_0 = \begin{pmatrix}
0.237 & 0.175 & 0.113 & 0.175 & 0.113 & 0.125 & 0.062 \\
0.175 & 0.237 & 0.175 & 0.237 & 0.050 & 0.062 & 0.062 \\
0.113 & 0.175 & 0.237 & 0.175 & 0.113 & 0.062 & 0.125 \\
0.140 & 0.190 & 0.140 & 0.240 & 0.090 & 0.100 & 0.100 \\
0.113 & 0.050 & 0.113 & 0.113 & 0.237 & 0.188 & 0.188 \\
0.125 & 0.062 & 0.062 & 0.125 & 0.188 & 0.250 & 0.188 \\
0.062 & 0.062 & 0.125 & 0.125 & 0.188 & 0.188 & 0.250
\end{pmatrix}
$$

$$
\mathbf{M}_1 = \Upsilon(\mathbf{M}_1, 2.5) = \begin{pmatrix}
0.404 & 0.188 & 0.062 & 0.188 & 0.062 & 0.081 & 0.014 \\
0.154 & 0.331 & 0.154 & 0.331 & 0.007 & 0.012 & 0.012 \\
0.062 & 0.188 & 0.404 & 0.188 & 0.062 & 0.014 & 0.081 \\
0.109 & 0.234 & 0.109 & 0.419 & 0.036 & 0.047 & 0.047 \\
0.060 & 0.008 & 0.060 & 0.060 & 0.386 & 0.214 & 0.214 \\
0.074 & 0.013 & 0.013 & 0.074 & 0.204 & 0.418 & 0.204 \\
0.013 & 0.013 & 0.074 & 0.074 & 0.204 & 0.204 & 0.418
\end{pmatrix}
$$

MCL converges in 10 iterations (using $\epsilon = 0.001$), with the final transition matrix

$$
\mathbf{M} =
\begin{array}{c|ccccccc}
 & 1 & 2 & 3 & 4 & 5 & 6 & 7 \\
\hline
1 & 0 & 0 & 0 & 1 & 0 & 0 & 0 \\
2 & 0 & 0 & 0 & 1 & 0 & 0 & 0 \\
3 & 0 & 0 & 0 & 1 & 0 & 0 & 0 \\
4 & 0 & 0 & 0 & 1 & 0 & 0 & 0 \\
5 & 0 & 0 & 0 & 0 & 0 & 0.5 & 0.5 \\
6 & 0 & 0 & 0 & 0 & 0 & 0.5 & 0.5 \\
7 & 0 & 0 & 0 & 0 & 0 & 0.5 & 0.5
\end{array}
$$

Figure 16.5 shows the directed graph induced by the converged $\mathbf{M}$ matrix, where an edge (i, j) exists if and only if $\mathbf{M}(i, j) > 0$. The nonzero diagonal elements of $\mathbf{M}$ are the attractors (nodes with self-loops, shown in gray). We can observe that $\mathbf{M}(4, 4)$, $\mathbf{M}(6, 6)$, and $\mathbf{M}(7, 7)$ are all greater than zero, making nodes 4, 6, and 7 the three attractors. Because both 6 and 7 can reach each other, the equivalence classes of attractors are $\{4\}$ and $\{6, 7\}$. Nodes 1, 2, and 3 are attracted to 4, and node 5 is attracted to both 6 and 7. Thus, the two weakly connected components that make up the two clusters are $C_1 = \{1, 2, 3, 4\}$ and $C_2 = \{5, 6, 7\}$.

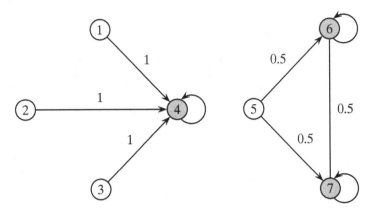

Figure 16.5. MCL attractors and clusters.

Example 16.12. Figure 16.6(a) shows the clusters obtained via the MCL algorithm on the Iris graph from Figure 16.1, using $r = 1.3$ in the inflation step. MCL yields three attractors (shown as gray nodes; self-loops omitted), which separate the graph into three clusters. The contingency table for the discovered clusters versus the true Iris types is given in Table 16.2. One point with class iris-versicolor is (wrongly) grouped with iris-setosa in C_1, but 14 points from iris-virginica are misclustered.

Notice that the only parameter for MCL is r, the exponent for the inflation step. The number of clusters is not explicitly specified, but higher values of r result in more clusters. The value of $r = 1.3$ was used above because it resulted in three clusters. Figure 16.6(b) shows the results for $r = 2$. MCL yields nine clusters, where one of the clusters (top-most) has two attractors.

Computational Complexity

The computational complexity of the MCL algorithm is $O(tn^3)$, where t is the number of iterations until convergence. This follows from the fact that whereas the inflation operation takes $O(n^2)$ time, the expansion operation requires matrix multiplication, which takes $O(n^3)$ time. However, the matrices become sparse very quickly, and it is possible to use sparse matrix multiplication to obtain $O(n^2)$ complexity for expansion in later iterations. On convergence, the weakly connected components in G_t can be found in $O(n + m)$ time, where m is the number of edges. Because G_t is very sparse, with $m = O(n)$, the final clustering step takes $O(n)$ time.

16.4 FURTHER READING

Spectral partitioning of graphs was first proposed in Donath and Hoffman (1973). Properties of the second smallest eigenvalue of the Laplacian matrix, also called *algebraic connectivity*, were studied in Fiedler (1973). A recursive bipartitioning

Table 16.2. Contingency table: MCL clusters versus Iris types

	iris-setosa	iris-virginica	iris-versicolor
C_1 (triangle)	50	0	1
C_2 (square)	0	36	0
C_3 (circle)	0	14	49

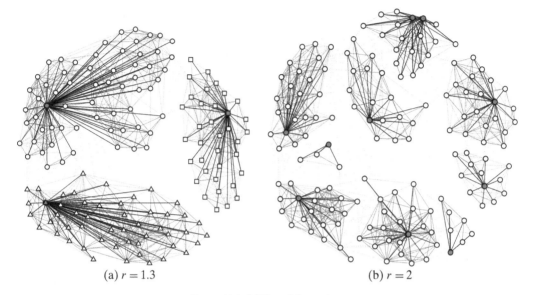

(a) $r = 1.3$ (b) $r = 2$

Figure 16.6. MCL on Iris graph.

approach to find k clusters using the normalized cut objective was given in Shi and Malik (2000). The direct k-way partitioning approach for normalized cut, using the normalized symmetric Laplacian matrix, was proposed in Ng, Jordan, and Weiss (2001). The connection between spectral clustering objective and kernel K-means was established in Dhillon, Guan, and Kulis (2007). The modularity objective was introduced in Newman (2003), where it was called *assortativity coefficient*. The spectral algorithm using the modularity matrix was first proposed in White and Smyth (2005). The relationship between modularity and normalized cut was shown in Yu and Ding (2010). For an excellent tutorial on spectral clustering techniques see Luxburg (2007). The Markov clustering algorithm was originally proposed in Dongen (2000). For an extensive review of graph clustering methods see Fortunato (2010).

Dhillon, I. S., Guan, Y., and Kulis, B. (2007). Weighted graph cuts without eigenvectors a multilevel approach. *IEEE Transactions on Pattern Analysis and Machine Intelligence*, 29 (11), 1944–1957.

Donath, W. E. and Hoffman, A. J. (1973). Lower bounds for the partitioning of graphs. *IBM Journal of Research and Development*, 17 (5), 420–425.

Dongen, S. M. van (2000). "Graph clustering by flow simulation". PhD thesis. The University of Utrecht, The Netherlands.

Fiedler, M. (1973). Algebraic connectivity of graphs. *Czechoslovak Mathematical Journal*, 23 (2), 298–305.

Fortunato, S. (2010). Community detection in graphs. *Physics Reports*, 486 (3), 75–174.

Luxburg, U. (2007). A tutorial on spectral clustering. *Statistics and Computing*, 17 (4), 395–416.

Newman, M. E. (2003). Mixing patterns in networks. *Physical Review E*, 67 (2), 026126.

Ng, A. Y., Jordan, M. I., and Weiss, Y. (2001). On spectral clustering: Analysis and an algorithm. *Advances in Neural Information Processing Systems 14*. Cambridge, MA: MIT Press, pp. 849–856.

Shi, J. and Malik, J. (2000). Normalized cuts and image segmentation. *IEEE Transactions on Pattern Analysis Machine Intelligence*, 22 (8), 888–905.

White, S. and Smyth, P. (2005). A spectral clustering approach to finding communities in graphs. *Proceedings of the 5th SIAM International Conference on Data Mining*. Philadelphia: SIAM, pp. 76–84.

Yu, L. and Ding, C. (2010). Network community discovery: solving modularity clustering via normalized cut. *Proceedings of the 8th Workshop on Mining and Learning with Graphs*. ACM, pp. 34–36.

16.5 EXERCISES

Q1. Show that if Q_i denotes the ith column of the modularity matrix $\mathbf{Q}$, then $\sum_{i=1}^{n} Q_i = \mathbf{0}$.

Q2. Prove that the normalized symmetric Laplacian matrix $\mathbf{L}^s$ [Eq. (16.8)] is positive semidefinite. Also prove that the normalized asymmetric Laplacian matrix $\mathbf{L}^a$ [Eq. (16.10)] behaves like a positive semidefinite matrix. Show that the smallest eigenvalue is $\lambda_n = 0$ for both.

Q3. Prove that the largest eigenvalue of the normalized adjacency matrix $\mathbf{M}$ [Eq. (16.3)] is 1, and further that all eigenvalues satisfy the condition that $|\lambda_i| \leq 1$.

Q4. Show that $\sum_{v_r \in C_i} c_{ir} d_r c_{ir} = \sum_{r=1}^{n} \sum_{s=1}^{n} c_{ir} \mathbf{\Delta}_{rs} c_{is}$, where $\mathbf{c}_i$ is the cluster indicator vector for cluster C_i and $\mathbf{\Delta}$ is the degree matrix for the graph.

Q5. For the normalized symmetric Laplacian $\mathbf{L}^s$, show that for the normalized cut objective the real-valued cluster indicator vector corresponding to the smallest eigenvalue $\lambda_n = 0$ is given as $\mathbf{c}_n = \frac{1}{\sqrt{\sum_{i=1}^{n} d_i}} \mathbf{\Delta}^{1/2} \mathbf{1}$.

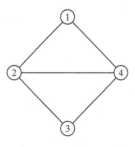

Figure 16.7. Graph for Q6.

Q6. Given the graph in Figure 16.7, answer the following questions:

   (a) Cluster the graph into two clusters using ratio cut and normalized cut.

   (b) Use the normalized adjacency matrix $\mathbf{M}$ for the graph and cluster it into two clusters using average weight and kernel K-means, using $\mathbf{K} = \mathbf{M} + \mathbf{I}$.

   (c) Cluster the graph using the MCL algorithm with inflation parameters $r = 2$ and $r = 2.5$.

Table 16.3. Data for Q7

	X_1	X_2	X_3
$\mathbf{x}_1^T$	0.4	0.9	0.6
$\mathbf{x}_2^T$	0.5	0.1	0.6
$\mathbf{x}_3^T$	0.6	0.3	0.6
$\mathbf{x}_4^T$	0.4	0.8	0.5

Q7. Consider Table 16.3. Assuming these four points are are nodes in a graph, define the weighted adjacency matrix $\mathbf{A}$ using the linear kernel

$$\mathbf{A}(i, j) = 1 + \mathbf{x}_i^T \mathbf{x}_j$$

Cluster the data into two groups using the modularity objective.

CHAPTER 17

Clustering Validation

There exist many different clustering methods, depending on the type of clusters sought and on the inherent data characteristics. Given the diversity of clustering algorithms and their parameters it is important to develop objective approaches to assess clustering results. Cluster validation and assessment encompasses three main tasks: *clustering evaluation* seeks to assess the goodness or quality of the clustering, *clustering stability* seeks to understand the sensitivity of the clustering result to various algorithmic parameters, for example, the number of clusters, and *clustering tendency* assesses the suitability of applying clustering in the first place, that is, whether the data has any inherent grouping structure. There are a number of validity measures and statistics that have been proposed for each of the aforementioned tasks, which can be divided into three main types:

External: External validation measures employ criteria that are not inherent to the dataset. This can be in form of prior or expert-specified knowledge about the clusters, for example, class labels for each point.

Internal: Internal validation measures employ criteria that are derived from the data itself. For instance, we can use intracluster and intercluster distances to obtain measures of cluster compactness (e.g., how similar are the points in the same cluster?) and separation (e.g., how far apart are the points in different clusters?).

Relative: Relative validation measures aim to directly compare different clusterings, usually those obtained via different parameter settings for the same algorithm.

In this chapter we study some of the main techniques for clustering validation and assessment spanning all three types of measures.

17.1 EXTERNAL MEASURES

As the name implies, external measures assume that the correct or ground-truth clustering is known *a priori*. The true cluster labels play the role of external information that is used to evaluate a given clustering. In general, we would not know the correct clustering; however, external measures can serve as way to test and validate different methods. For instance, classification datasets that specify the class for each point can be used to evaluate the quality of a clustering. Likewise, synthetic datasets with known cluster structure can be created to evaluate various clustering algorithms by quantifying the extent to which they can recover the known groupings.

Let $\mathbf{D}$ be a dataset consisting of n points $\mathbf{x}_i$ in a d-dimensional space, partitioned into k clusters. Let $y_i \in \{1, 2, \ldots, k\}$ denote the ground-truth cluster membership or label information for each point. The ground-truth clustering is given as $\mathcal{T} = \{T_1, T_2, \ldots, T_k\}$, where the cluster T_j consists of all the points with label j, i.e., $T_j = \{\mathbf{x}_i \in \mathbf{D} | y_i = j\}$. Also, let $\mathcal{C} = \{C_1, \ldots, C_r\}$ denote a clustering of the same dataset into r clusters, obtained via some clustering algorithm, and let $\hat{y}_i \in \{1, 2, \ldots, r\}$ denote the cluster label for $\mathbf{x}_i$. For clarity, henceforth, we will refer to $\mathcal{T}$ as the ground-truth *partitioning*, and to each T_i as a *partition*. We will call $\mathcal{C}$ a clustering, with each C_i referred to as a cluster. Because the ground truth is assumed to be known, typically clustering methods will be run with the correct number of clusters, that is, with $r = k$. However, to keep the discussion more general, we allow r to be different from k.

External evaluation measures try capture the extent to which points from the same partition appear in the same cluster, and the extent to which points from different partitions are grouped in different clusters. There is usually a trade-off between these two goals, which is either explicitly captured by a measure or is implicit in its computation. All of the external measures rely on the $r \times k$ *contingency table* $\mathbf{N}$ that is induced by a clustering $\mathcal{C}$ and the ground-truth partitioning $\mathcal{T}$, defined as follows

$$\mathbf{N}(i, j) = n_{ij} = |C_i \cap T_j|$$

In other words, the count n_{ij} denotes the number of points that are common to cluster C_i and ground-truth partition T_j. Further, for clarity, let $n_i = |C_i|$ denote the number of points in cluster C_i, and let $m_j = |T_j|$ denote the number of points in partition T_j. The contingency table can be computed from $\mathcal{T}$ and $\mathcal{C}$ in $O(n)$ time by examining the partition and cluster labels, y_i and $\hat{y}_i$, for each point $\mathbf{x}_i \in \mathbf{D}$ and incrementing the corresponding count $n_{y_i \hat{y}_i}$.

17.1.1 Matching Based Measures

Purity
Purity quantifies the extent to which a cluster C_i contains entities from only one partition. In other words, it measures how "pure" each cluster is. The purity of cluster C_i is defined as

$$purity_i = \frac{1}{n_i} \max_{j=1}^{k} \{n_{ij}\}$$

The purity of clustering $\mathcal{C}$ is defined as the weighted sum of the clusterwise purity values:

$$purity = \sum_{i=1}^{r} \frac{n_i}{n} purity_i = \frac{1}{n} \sum_{i=1}^{r} \max_{j=1}^{k} \{n_{ij}\} \tag{17.1}$$

where the ratio $\frac{n_i}{n}$ denotes the fraction of points in cluster C_i. The larger the purity of $\mathcal{C}$, the better the agreement with the groundtruth. The maximum value of purity is 1, when each cluster comprises points from only one partition. When $r = k$, a purity value of 1 indicates a perfect clustering, with a one-to-one correspondence between the clusters and partitions. However, purity can be 1 even for $r > k$, when each of the clusters is a subset of a ground-truth partition. When $r < k$, purity can never be 1, because at least one cluster must contain points from more than one partition.

Maximum Matching

The maximum matching measure selects the mapping between clusters and partitions, such that the sum of the number of common points (n_{ij}) is maximized, provided that only one cluster can match with a given partition. This is unlike purity, where two different clusters may share the same majority partition.

Formally, we treat the contingency table as a complete weighted bipartite graph $G = (V, E)$, where each partition and cluster is a node, that is, $V = \mathcal{C} \cup \mathcal{T}$, and there exists an edge $(C_i, T_j) \in E$, with weight $w(C_i, T_j) = n_{ij}$, for all $C_i \in \mathcal{C}$ and $T_j \in \mathcal{T}$. A *matching* M in G is a subset of E, such that the edges in M are pairwise nonadjacent, that is, they do not have a common vertex. The maximum matching measure is defined as the *maximum weight matching* in G:

$$match = \underset{M}{\arg\max} \left\{ \frac{w(M)}{n} \right\}$$

where the weight of a matching M is simply the sum of all the edge weights in M, given as $w(M) = \sum_{e \in M} w(e)$. The maximum matching can be computed in time $O(|V|^2 \cdot |E|) = O((r+k)^2 rk)$, which is equivalent to $O(k^4)$ if $r = O(k)$.

F-Measure

Given cluster C_i, let j_i denote the partition that contains the maximum number of points from C_i, that is, $j_i = \max_{j=1}^{k}\{n_{ij}\}$. The *precision* of a cluster C_i is the same as its purity:

$$prec_i = \frac{1}{n_i} \max_{j=1}^{k} \{n_{ij}\} = \frac{n_{ij_i}}{n_i} \tag{17.2}$$

It measures the fraction of points in C_i from the majority partition T_{j_i}.

The *recall* of cluster C_i is defined as

$$recall_i = \frac{n_{ij_i}}{|T_{j_i}|} = \frac{n_{ij_i}}{m_{j_i}} \tag{17.3}$$

where $m_{j_i} = |T_{j_i}|$. It measures the fraction of point in partition T_{j_i} shared in common with cluster C_i.

The F-measure is the harmonic mean of the precision and recall values for each cluster. The F-measure for cluster C_i is therefore given as

$$F_i = \frac{2}{\frac{1}{prec_i} + \frac{1}{recall_i}} = \frac{2 \cdot prec_i \cdot recall_i}{prec_i + recall_i} = \frac{2\,n_{ij_i}}{n_i + m_{j_i}} \qquad (17.4)$$

The F-measure for the clustering C is the mean of clusterwise F-measure values:

$$F = \frac{1}{r} \sum_{i=1}^{r} F_i$$

F-measure thus tries to balance the precision and recall values across all the clusters. For a perfect clustering, when $r = k$, the maximum value of the F-measure is 1.

Example 17.1. Figure 17.1 shows two different clusterings obtained via the K-means algorithm on the Iris dataset, using the first two principal components as the two dimensions. Here $n = 150$, and $k = 3$. Visual inspection confirms that Figure 17.1(a) is a better clustering than that in Figure 17.1(b). We now examine how the different contingency table based measures can be used to evaluate these two clusterings.

Consider the clustering in Figure 17.1(a). The three clusters are illustrated with different symbols; the gray points are in the correct partition, whereas the white ones are wrongly clustered compared to the ground-truth Iris types. For instance, C_3 mainly corresponds to partition T_3 (Iris-virginica), but it has three points (the white triangles) from T_2. The complete contingency table is as follows:

	iris-setosa	iris-versicolor	iris-virginica	
	T_1	T_2	T_3	n_i
C_1(squares)	0	47	14	61
C_2(circles)	50	0	0	50
C_3(triangles)	0	3	36	39
m_j	50	50	50	$n = 150$

To compute purity, we first note for each cluster the partition with the maximum overlap. We have the correspondence (C_1, T_2), (C_2, T_1), and (C_3, T_3). Thus, purity is given as

$$purity = \frac{1}{150}(47 + 50 + 36) = \frac{133}{150} = 0.887$$

For this contingency table, the maximum matching measure gives the same result, as the correspondence above is in fact a maximum weight matching. Thus, $match = 0.887$.

The cluster C_1 contains $n_1 = 47 + 14 = 61$ points, whereas its corresponding partition T_2 contains $m_2 = 47 + 3 = 50$ points. Thus, the precision and recall for C_1 are given as

$$prec_1 = \tfrac{47}{61} = 0.77$$

$$recall_1 = \tfrac{47}{50} = 0.94$$

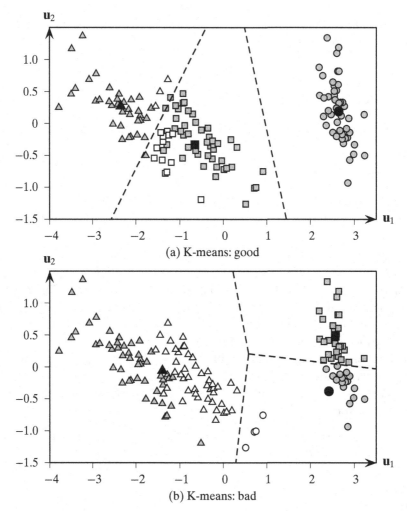

Figure 17.1. K-means: Iris principal components dataset.

The F-measure for C_1 is therefore

$$F_1 = \frac{2 \cdot 0.77 \cdot 0.94}{0.77 + 0.94} = \tfrac{1.45}{1.71} = 0.85$$

We can also directly compute F_1 using Eq. (17.4)

$$F_1 = \tfrac{2 \cdot n_{12}}{n_1 + m_2} = \frac{2 \cdot 47}{61 + 50} = \frac{94}{111} = 0.85$$

Likewise, we obtain $F_2 = 1.0$ and $F_3 = 0.81$. Thus, the F-measure value for the clustering is given as

$$F = \frac{1}{3}(F_1 + F_2 + F_3) = \frac{2.66}{3} = 0.88$$

For the clustering in Figure 17.1(b), we have the following contingency table:

	iris-setosa T_1	iris-versicolor T_2	iris-virginica T_3	n_i
C_1	30	0	0	30
C_2	20	4	0	24
C_3	0	46	50	96
m_j	50	50	50	$n = 150$

For the purity measure, the partition with which each cluster shares the most points is given as (C_1, T_1), (C_2, T_1), and (C_3, T_3). Thus, the purity value for this clustering is

$$purity = \frac{1}{150}(30 + 20 + 50) = \frac{100}{150} = 0.67$$

We can see that both C_1 and C_2 choose partition T_1 as the maximum overlapping partition. However, the maximum weight matching is different; it yields the correspondence (C_1, T_1), (C_2, T_2), and (C_3, T_3), and thus

$$match = \frac{1}{150}(30 + 4 + 50) = \frac{84}{150} = 0.56$$

The table below compares the different contingency based measures for the two clusterings shown in Figure 17.1.

	purity	match	F
(a) Good	0.887	0.887	0.885
(b) Bad	0.667	0.560	0.658

As expected, the good clustering in Figure 17.1(a) has higher scores for the purity, maximum matching, and F-measure.

17.1.2 Entropy-based Measures

Conditional Entropy
The entropy of a clustering $\mathcal{C}$ is defined as

$$H(\mathcal{C}) = -\sum_{i=1}^{r} p_{C_i} \log p_{C_i}$$

where $p_{C_i} = \frac{n_i}{n}$ is the probability of cluster C_i. Likewise, the entropy of the partitioning $\mathcal{T}$ is defined as

$$H(\mathcal{T}) = -\sum_{j=1}^{k} p_{T_j} \log p_{T_j}$$

where $p_{T_j} = \frac{m_j}{n}$ is the probability of partition T_j.

The cluster-specific entropy of $\mathcal{T}$, that is, the conditional entropy of $\mathcal{T}$ with respect to cluster C_i is defined as

$$H(\mathcal{T}|C_i) = -\sum_{j=1}^{k} \left(\frac{n_{ij}}{n_i} \right) \log \left(\frac{n_{ij}}{n_i} \right)$$

The conditional entropy of $\mathcal{T}$ given clustering $\mathcal{C}$ is then defined as the weighted sum:

$$H(\mathcal{T}|\mathcal{C}) = \sum_{i=1}^{r} \frac{n_i}{n} H(\mathcal{T}|C_i) = -\sum_{i=1}^{r} \sum_{j=1}^{k} \frac{n_{ij}}{n} \log \left(\frac{n_{ij}}{n_i} \right)$$

$$= -\sum_{i=1}^{r} \sum_{j=1}^{k} p_{ij} \log \left(\frac{p_{ij}}{p_{C_i}} \right) \tag{17.5}$$

where $p_{ij} = \frac{n_{ij}}{n}$ is the probability that a point in cluster i also belongs to partition j. The more a cluster's members are split into different partitions, the higher the conditional entropy. For a perfect clustering, the conditional entropy value is zero, whereas the worst possible conditional entropy value is $\log k$. Further, expanding Eq. (17.5), we can see that

$$H(\mathcal{T}|\mathcal{C}) = -\sum_{i=1}^{r} \sum_{j=1}^{k} p_{ij} \left(\log p_{ij} - \log p_{C_i} \right)$$

$$= -\left(\sum_{i=1}^{r} \sum_{j=1}^{k} p_{ij} \log p_{ij} \right) + \sum_{i=1}^{r} \left(\log p_{C_i} \sum_{j=1}^{k} p_{ij} \right)$$

$$= -\sum_{i=1}^{r} \sum_{j=1}^{k} p_{ij} \log p_{ij} + \sum_{i=1}^{r} p_{C_i} \log p_{C_i}$$

$$= H(\mathcal{C}, \mathcal{T}) - H(\mathcal{C}) \tag{17.6}$$

where $H(\mathcal{C}, \mathcal{T}) = -\sum_{i=1}^{r} \sum_{j=1}^{k} p_{ij} \log p_{ij}$ is the joint entropy of $\mathcal{C}$ and $\mathcal{T}$. The conditional entropy $H(\mathcal{T}|\mathcal{C})$ thus measures the remaining entropy of $\mathcal{T}$ given the clustering $\mathcal{C}$. In particular, $H(\mathcal{T}|\mathcal{C}) = 0$ if and only if $\mathcal{T}$ is completely determined by $\mathcal{C}$, corresponding to the ideal clustering. On the other hand, if $\mathcal{C}$ and $\mathcal{T}$ are independent of each other, then $H(\mathcal{T}|\mathcal{C}) = H(\mathcal{T})$, which means that $\mathcal{C}$ provides no information about $\mathcal{T}$.

Normalized Mutual Information

The *mutual information* tries to quantify the amount of shared information between the clustering $\mathcal{C}$ and partitioning $\mathcal{T}$, and it is defined as

$$I(\mathcal{C}, \mathcal{T}) = \sum_{i=1}^{r} \sum_{j=1}^{k} p_{ij} \log \left(\frac{p_{ij}}{p_{C_i} \cdot p_{T_j}} \right) \tag{17.7}$$

It measures the dependence between the observed joint probability p_{ij} of $\mathcal{C}$ and $\mathcal{T}$, and the expected joint probability $p_{C_i} \cdot p_{T_j}$ under the independence assumption. When $\mathcal{C}$

and $\mathcal{T}$ are independent then $p_{ij} = p_{C_i} \cdot p_{T_j}$, and thus $I(\mathcal{C}, \mathcal{T}) = 0$. However, there is no upper bound on the mutual information.

Expanding Eq. (17.7) we observe that $I(\mathcal{C}, \mathcal{T}) = H(\mathcal{C}) + H(\mathcal{T}) - H(\mathcal{C}, \mathcal{T})$. Using Eq. (17.6), we obtain the two equivalent expressions:

$$I(\mathcal{C}, \mathcal{T}) = H(\mathcal{T}) - H(\mathcal{T}|\mathcal{C})$$
$$I(\mathcal{C}, \mathcal{T}) = H(\mathcal{C}) - H(\mathcal{C}|\mathcal{T})$$

Finally, because $H(\mathcal{C}|\mathcal{T}) \geq 0$ and $H(\mathcal{T}|\mathcal{C}) \geq 0$, we have the inequalities $I(\mathcal{C}, \mathcal{T}) \leq H(\mathcal{C})$ and $I(\mathcal{C}, \mathcal{T}) \leq H(\mathcal{T})$. We can obtain a normalized version of mutual information by considering the ratios $I(\mathcal{C}, \mathcal{T})/H(\mathcal{C})$ and $I(\mathcal{C}, \mathcal{T})/H(\mathcal{T})$, both of which can beat most one. The *normalized mutual information* (NMI) is defined as the geometric mean of these two ratios:

$$NMI(\mathcal{C}, \mathcal{T}) = \sqrt{\frac{I(\mathcal{C}, \mathcal{T})}{H(\mathcal{C})} \cdot \frac{I(\mathcal{C}, \mathcal{T})}{H(\mathcal{T})}} = \frac{I(\mathcal{C}, \mathcal{T})}{\sqrt{H(\mathcal{C}) \cdot H(\mathcal{T})}} \qquad (17.8)$$

The NMI value lies in the range $[0, 1]$. Values close to 1 indicate a good clustering.

Variation of Information

This criterion is based on the mutual information between the clustering $\mathcal{C}$ and the ground-truth partitioning $\mathcal{T}$, and their entropy; it is defined as

$$VI(\mathcal{C}, \mathcal{T}) = (H(\mathcal{T}) - I(\mathcal{C}, \mathcal{T})) + (H(\mathcal{C}) - I(\mathcal{C}, \mathcal{T}))$$
$$= H(\mathcal{T}) + H(\mathcal{C}) - 2I(\mathcal{C}, \mathcal{T}) \qquad (17.9)$$

Variation of information (VI) is zero only when $\mathcal{C}$ and $\mathcal{T}$ are identical. Thus, the lower the VI value the better the clustering $\mathcal{C}$.

Using the equivalence $I(\mathcal{C}, \mathcal{T}) = H(\mathcal{T}) - H(\mathcal{T}|\mathcal{C}) = H(\mathcal{C}) - H(\mathcal{C}|\mathcal{T})$, we can also express Eq. (17.9) as

$$VI(\mathcal{C}, \mathcal{T}) = H(\mathcal{T}|\mathcal{C}) + H(\mathcal{C}|\mathcal{T})$$

Finally, noting that $H(\mathcal{T}|\mathcal{C}) = H(\mathcal{T}, \mathcal{C}) - H(\mathcal{C})$, another expression for VI is given as

$$VI(\mathcal{C}, \mathcal{T}) = 2H(\mathcal{T}, \mathcal{C}) - H(\mathcal{T}) - H(\mathcal{C}) \qquad (17.10)$$

Example 17.2. We continue with Example 1, which compares the two clusterings shown in Figure 17.1. For the entropy-based measures, we use base 2 for the logarithms; the formulas are valid for any base as such.

For the clustering in Figure 17.1(a), we have the following contingency table:

	iris-setosa T_1	iris-versicolor T_2	iris-virginica T_3	n_i
C_1	0	47	14	61
C_2	50	0	0	50
C_3	0	3	36	39
m_j	50	50	50	$n = 100$

Consider the conditional entropy for cluster C_1:

$$H(\mathcal{T}|C_1) = -\frac{0}{61}\log_2\left(\frac{0}{61}\right) - \frac{47}{61}\log_2\left(\frac{47}{61}\right) - \frac{14}{61}\log_2\left(\frac{14}{61}\right)$$

$$= -0 - 0.77\log_2(0.77) - 0.23\log_2(0.23) = 0.29 + 0.49 = 0.78$$

In a similar manner, we obtain $H(\mathcal{T}|C_2) = 0$ and $H(\mathcal{T}|C_3) = 0.39$. The conditional entropy for the clustering $\mathcal{C}$ is then given as

$$H(\mathcal{T}|\mathcal{C}) = \frac{61}{150}\cdot 0.78 + \frac{50}{150}\cdot 0 + \frac{39}{150}\cdot 0.39 = 0.32 + 0 + 0.10 = 0.42$$

To compute the normalized mutual information, note that

$$H(\mathcal{T}) = -3\left(\frac{50}{150}\log_2\left(\frac{50}{150}\right)\right) = 1.585$$

$$H(\mathcal{C}) = -\left(\frac{61}{150}\log_2\left(\frac{61}{150}\right) + \frac{50}{150}\log_2\left(\frac{50}{150}\right) + \frac{39}{150}\log_2\left(\frac{39}{150}\right)\right)$$

$$= 0.528 + 0.528 + 0.505 = 1.561$$

$$I(\mathcal{C},\mathcal{T}) = \frac{47}{150}\log_2\left(\frac{47\cdot 150}{61\cdot 50}\right) + \frac{14}{150}\log_2\left(\frac{14\cdot 150}{61\cdot 50}\right) + \frac{50}{150}\log_2\left(\frac{50\cdot 150}{50\cdot 50}\right)$$

$$+ \frac{3}{150}\left(\log_2\frac{3\cdot 150}{39\cdot 50}\right) + \frac{36}{150}\log_2\left(\frac{36\cdot 150}{39\cdot 50}\right)$$

$$= 0.379 - 0.05 + 0.528 - 0.042 + 0.353 = 1.167$$

Thus, the NMI and VI values are

$$NMI(\mathcal{C},\mathcal{T}) = \frac{I(\mathcal{C},\mathcal{T})}{\sqrt{H(\mathcal{T})\cdot H(\mathcal{C})}} = \frac{1.167}{\sqrt{1.585\times 1.561}} = 0.742$$

$$VI(\mathcal{C},\mathcal{T}) = H(\mathcal{T}) + H(\mathcal{C}) - 2I(\mathcal{C},\mathcal{T}) = 1.585 + 1.561 - 2\cdot 1.167 = 0.812$$

We can likewise compute these measures for the other clustering in Figure 17.1(b), whose contingency table is shown in Example 1.

The table below compares the entropy based measures for the two clusterings shown in Figure 17.1.

	$H(\mathcal{T}|\mathcal{C})$	NMI	VI
(a) Good	0.418	0.742	0.812
(b) Bad	0.743	0.587	1.200

As expected, the good clustering in Figure 17.1(a) has a higher score for normalized mutual information, and lower scores for conditional entropy and variation of information.

17.1.3 Pairwise Measures

Given clustering $\mathcal{C}$ and ground-truth partitioning $\mathcal{T}$, the pairwise measures utilize the partition and cluster label information over all pairs of points. Let $\mathbf{x}_i, \mathbf{x}_j \in \mathbf{D}$ be any two points, with $i \neq j$. Let y_i denote the true partition label and let $\hat{y}_i$ denote the cluster label for point $\mathbf{x}_i$. If both $\mathbf{x}_i$ and $\mathbf{x}_j$ belong to the same cluster, that is, $\hat{y}_i = \hat{y}_j$, we call it a *positive* event, and if they do not belong to the same cluster, that is, $\hat{y}_i \neq \hat{y}_j$, we call that a *negative* event. Depending on whether there is agreement between the cluster labels and partition labels, there are four possibilities to consider:

- *True Positives:* $\mathbf{x}_i$ and $\mathbf{x}_j$ belong to the same partition in $\mathcal{T}$, and they are also in the same cluster in $\mathcal{C}$. This is a true positive pair because the positive event, $\hat{y}_i = \hat{y}_j$, corresponds to the ground truth, $y_i = y_j$. The number of true positive pairs is given as

$$TP = \big|\{(\mathbf{x}_i, \mathbf{x}_j) : y_i = y_j \text{ and } \hat{y}_i = \hat{y}_j\}\big| \qquad (17.11)$$

- *False Negatives:* $\mathbf{x}_i$ and $\mathbf{x}_j$ belong to the same partition in $\mathcal{T}$, but they do not belong to the same cluster in $\mathcal{C}$. That is, the negative event, $\hat{y}_i \neq \hat{y}_j$, does not correspond to the truth, $y_i = y_j$. This pair is thus a false negative, and the number of all false negative pairs is given as

$$FN = \big|\{(\mathbf{x}_i, \mathbf{x}_j) : y_i = y_j \text{ and } \hat{y}_i \neq \hat{y}_j\}\big| \qquad (17.12)$$

- *False Positives:* $\mathbf{x}_i$ and $\mathbf{x}_j$ do not belong to the same partition in $\mathcal{T}$, but they do belong to the same cluster in $\mathcal{C}$. This pair is a false positive because the positive event, $\hat{y}_i = \hat{y}_j$, is actually false, that is, it does not agree with the ground-truth partitioning, which indicates that $y_i \neq y_j$. The number of false positive pairs is given as

$$FP = \big|\{(\mathbf{x}_i, \mathbf{x}_j) : y_i \neq y_j \text{ and } \hat{y}_i = \hat{y}_j\}\big| \qquad (17.13)$$

- *True Negatives:* $\mathbf{x}_i$ and $\mathbf{x}_j$ neither belong to the same partition in $\mathcal{T}$, nor do they belong to the same cluster in $\mathcal{C}$. This pair is thus a true negative, that is, $\hat{y}_i \neq \hat{y}_j$ and $y_i \neq y_j$. The number of such true negative pairs is given as

$$TN = \big|\{(\mathbf{x}_i, \mathbf{x}_j) : y_i \neq y_j \text{ and } \hat{y}_i \neq \hat{y}_j\}\big| \qquad (17.14)$$

Because there are $N = \binom{n}{2} = \frac{n(n-1)}{2}$ pairs of points, we have the following identity:

$$N = TP + FN + FP + TN \qquad (17.15)$$

A naive computation of the preceding four cases requires $O(n^2)$ time. However, they can be computed more efficiently using the contingency table $\mathbf{N} = \{n_{ij}\}$, with $1 \leq i \leq r$ and $1 \leq j \leq k$. The number of true positives is given as

$$
TP = \sum_{i=1}^{r} \sum_{j=1}^{k} \binom{n_{ij}}{2} = \sum_{i=1}^{r} \sum_{j=1}^{k} \frac{n_{ij}(n_{ij}-1)}{2} = \frac{1}{2} \left(\sum_{i=1}^{r} \sum_{j=1}^{k} n_{ij}^2 - \sum_{i=1}^{r} \sum_{j=1}^{k} n_{ij} \right)
$$
$$
= \frac{1}{2} \left(\left(\sum_{i=1}^{r} \sum_{j=1}^{k} n_{ij}^2 \right) - n \right) \tag{17.16}
$$

This follows from the fact that each pair of points among the n_{ij} share the same cluster label (i) and the same partition label (j). The last step follows from the fact that the sum of all the entries in the contingency table must add to n, that is, $\sum_{i=1}^{r} \sum_{j=1}^{k} n_{ij} = n$.

To compute the total number of false negatives, we remove the number of true positives from the number of pairs that belong to the same partition. Because two points $\mathbf{x}_i$ and $\mathbf{x}_j$ that belong to the same partition have $y_i = y_j$, if we remove the true positives, that is, pairs with $\hat{y}_i = \hat{y}_j$, we are left with pairs for whom $\hat{y}_i \neq \hat{y}_j$, that is, the false negatives. We thus have

$$
FN = \sum_{j=1}^{k} \binom{m_j}{2} - TP = \frac{1}{2} \left(\sum_{j=1}^{k} m_j^2 - \sum_{j=1}^{k} m_j - \sum_{i=1}^{r} \sum_{j=1}^{k} n_{ij}^2 + n \right)
$$
$$
= \frac{1}{2} \left(\sum_{j=1}^{k} m_j^2 - \sum_{i=1}^{r} \sum_{j=1}^{k} n_{ij}^2 \right) \tag{17.17}
$$

The last step follows from the fact that $\sum_{j=1}^{k} m_j = n$.

The number of false positives can be obtained in a similar manner by subtracting the number of true positives from the number of point pairs that are in the same cluster:

$$
FP = \sum_{i=1}^{r} \binom{n_i}{2} - TP = \frac{1}{2} \left(\sum_{i=1}^{r} n_i^2 - \sum_{i=1}^{r} \sum_{j=1}^{k} n_{ij}^2 \right) \tag{17.18}
$$

Finally, the number of true negatives can be obtained via Eq. (17.15) as follows:

$$
TN = N - (TP + FN + FP) = \frac{1}{2} \left(n^2 - \sum_{i=1}^{r} n_i^2 - \sum_{j=1}^{k} m_j^2 + \sum_{i=1}^{r} \sum_{j=1}^{k} n_{ij}^2 \right) \tag{17.19}
$$

Each of the four values can be computed in $O(rk)$ time. Because the contingency table can be obtained in linear time, the total time to compute the four values is $O(n+rk)$, which is much better than the naive $O(n^2)$ bound. We next consider pairwise assessment measures based on these four values.

Jaccard Coefficient

The Jaccard Coefficient measures the fraction of true positive point pairs, but after ignoring the true negatives. It is defined as follows:

$$
Jaccard = \frac{TP}{TP + FN + FP} \tag{17.20}
$$

For a perfect clustering $\mathcal{C}$ (i.e., total agreement with the partitioning $\mathcal{T}$), the Jaccard Coefficient has value 1, as in that case there are no false positives or false negatives. The Jaccard coefficient is asymmetric in terms of the true positives and negatives because it ignores the true negatives. In other words, it emphasizes the similarity in terms of the point pairs that belong together in both the clustering and ground-truth partitioning, but it discounts the point pairs that do not belong together.

Rand Statistic

The Rand statistic measures the fraction of true positives and true negatives over all point pairs; it is defined as

$$Rand = \frac{TP + TN}{N} \tag{17.21}$$

The Rand statistic, which is symmetric, measures the fraction of point pairs where both $\mathcal{C}$ and $\mathcal{T}$ agree. A prefect clustering has a value of 1 for the statistic.

Fowlkes–Mallows Measure

Define the overall *pairwise precision* and *pairwise recall* values for a clustering $\mathcal{C}$, as follows:

$$prec = \frac{TP}{TP + FP} \qquad\qquad recall = \frac{TP}{TP + FN}$$

Precision measures the fraction of true or correctly clustered point pairs compared to all the point pairs in the same cluster. On the other hand, recall measures the fraction of correctly labeled points pairs compared to all the point pairs in the same partition.

The Fowlkes–Mallows (FM) measure is defined as the geometric mean of the pairwise precision and recall

$$FM = \sqrt{prec \cdot recall} = \frac{TP}{\sqrt{(TP + FN)(TP + FP)}} \tag{17.22}$$

The FM measure is also asymmetric in terms of the true positives and negatives because it ignores the true negatives. Its highest value is also 1, achieved when there are no false positives or negatives.

Example 17.3. Let us continue with Example 1. Consider again the contingency table for the clustering in Figure 17.1(a):

	iris-setosa T_1	iris-versicolor T_2	iris-virginica T_3
C_1	0	47	14
C_2	50	0	0
C_3	0	3	36

Using Eq. (17.16), we can obtain the number of true positives as follows:

$$TP = \binom{47}{2} + \binom{14}{2} + \binom{50}{2} + \binom{3}{2} + \binom{36}{2}$$

$$= 1081 + 91 + 1225 + 3 + 630 = 3030$$

Using Eqs. (17.17), (17.18), and (17.19), we obtain

$$FN = 645 \qquad\qquad FP = 766 \qquad\qquad TN = 6734$$

Note that there are a total of $N = \binom{150}{2} = 11175$ point pairs.

We can now compute the different pairwise measures for clustering evaluation. The Jaccard coefficient [Eq. (17.20)], Rand statistic [Eq. (17.21)], and Fowlkes–Mallows measure [Eq. (17.22)], are given as

$$Jaccard = \frac{3030}{3030 + 645 + 766} = \frac{3030}{4441} = 0.68$$

$$Rand = \frac{3030 + 6734}{11175} = \frac{9764}{11175} = 0.87$$

$$FM = \frac{3030}{\sqrt{3675 \cdot 3796}} = \frac{3030}{3735} = 0.81$$

Using the contingency table for the clustering in Figure 17.1(b) from Example 1, we obtain

$$TP = 2891 \qquad FN = 784 \qquad FP = 2380 \qquad TN = 5120$$

The table below compares the different contingency based measures on the two clusterings in Figure 17.1.

	Jaccard	Rand	FM
(a) Good	0.682	0.873	0.811
(b) Bad	0.477	0.717	0.657

As expected, the clustering in Figure 17.1(a) has higher scores for all three measures.

17.1.4 Correlation Measures

Let $\mathbf{X}$ and $\mathbf{Y}$ be two symmetric $n \times n$ matrices, and let $N = \binom{n}{2}$. Let $\mathbf{x}, \mathbf{y} \in \mathbb{R}^N$ denote the vectors obtained by linearizing the upper triangular elements (excluding the main diagonal) of $\mathbf{X}$ and $\mathbf{Y}$ (e.g., in a row-wise manner), respectively. Let μ_X denote the element-wise mean of $\mathbf{x}$, given as

$$\mu_X = \frac{1}{N} \sum_{i=1}^{n-1} \sum_{j=i+1}^{n} \mathbf{X}(i,j) = \frac{1}{N} \mathbf{x}^T \mathbf{x}$$

and let $\bar{\mathbf{x}}$ denote the centered $\mathbf{x}$ vector, defined as

$$\bar{\mathbf{x}} = \mathbf{x} - \mathbf{1} \cdot \mu_X$$

where $\mathbf{1} \in \mathbb{R}^N$ is the vector of all ones. Likewise, let μ_Y be the element-wise mean of $\mathbf{y}$, and $\bar{\mathbf{y}}$ the centered $\mathbf{y}$ vector.

The Hubert statistic is defined as the averaged element-wise product between $\mathbf{X}$ and $\mathbf{Y}$

$$\Gamma = \frac{1}{N} \sum_{i=1}^{n-1} \sum_{j=i+1}^{n} \mathbf{X}(i,j) \cdot \mathbf{Y}(i,j) = \frac{1}{N} \mathbf{x}^T \mathbf{y} \qquad (17.23)$$

The normalized Hubert statistic is defined as the element-wise correlation between $\mathbf{X}$ and $\mathbf{Y}$

$$\Gamma_n = \frac{\sum_{i=1}^{n-1} \sum_{j=i+1}^{n} \big(\mathbf{X}(i,j) - \mu_X\big)\big(\cdot\mathbf{Y}(i,j) - \mu_Y\big)}{\sqrt{\sum_{i=1}^{n-1} \sum_{j=i+1}^{n} \big(\mathbf{X}(i,j) - \mu_X\big)^2 \quad \sum_{i=1}^{n-1} \sum_{j=i+1}^{n} \big(\mathbf{Y}[i] - \mu_Y\big)^2}} = \frac{\sigma_{XY}}{\sqrt{\sigma_X^2 \sigma_Y^2}}$$

where σ_X^2 and σ_Y^2 are the variances, and σ_{XY} the covariance, for the vectors $\mathbf{x}$ and $\mathbf{y}$, defined as

$$\sigma_X^2 = \frac{1}{N} \sum_{i=1}^{n-1} \sum_{j=i+1}^{n} \big(\mathbf{X}(i,j) - \mu_X\big)^2 = \frac{1}{N} \bar{\mathbf{x}}^T \bar{\mathbf{x}} = \frac{1}{N} \|\bar{\mathbf{x}}\|^2$$

$$\sigma_Y^2 = \frac{1}{N} \sum_{i=1}^{n-1} \sum_{j=i+1}^{n} \big(\mathbf{Y}(i,j) - \mu_Y\big)^2 = \frac{1}{N} \bar{\mathbf{y}}^T \bar{\mathbf{y}} = \frac{1}{N} \|\bar{\mathbf{y}}\|^2$$

$$\sigma_{XY} = \frac{1}{N} \sum_{i=1}^{n-1} \sum_{j=i+1}^{n} \big(\mathbf{X}(i,j) - \mu_X\big)\big(\mathbf{Y}(i,j) - \mu_Y\big) = \frac{1}{N} \bar{\mathbf{x}}^T \bar{\mathbf{y}}$$

Thus, the normalized Hubert statistic can be rewritten as

$$\Gamma_n = \frac{\bar{\mathbf{x}}^T \bar{\mathbf{y}}}{\|\bar{\mathbf{x}}\| \cdot \|\bar{\mathbf{y}}\|} = \cos\theta \qquad (17.24)$$

where θ is the angle between the two centered vectors $\bar{\mathbf{x}}$ and $\bar{\mathbf{y}}$. It follows immediately that Γ_n ranges from -1 to $+1$.

When $\mathbf{X}$ and $\mathbf{Y}$ are arbitrary $n \times n$ matrices the above expressions can be easily modified to range over all the n^2 elements of the two matrices. The (normalized) Hubert statistic can be used as an external evaluation measure, with appropriately defined matrices $\mathbf{X}$ and $\mathbf{Y}$, as described next.

Discretized Hubert Statistic

Let $\mathbf{T}$ and $\mathbf{C}$ be the $n \times n$ matrices defined as

$$\mathbf{T}(i,j) = \begin{cases} 1 & \text{if } y_i = y_j, i \neq j \\ 0 & \text{otherwise} \end{cases} \qquad \mathbf{C}(i,j) = \begin{cases} 1 & \text{if } \hat{y}_i = \hat{y}_j, i \neq j \\ 0 & \text{otherwise} \end{cases}$$

Also, let $\mathbf{t}, \mathbf{c} \in \mathbb{R}^N$ denote the N-dimensional vectors comprising the upper triangular elements (excluding the diagonal) of $\mathbf{T}$ and $\mathbf{C}$, respectively, where $N = \binom{n}{2}$ denotes the number of distinct point pairs. Finally, let $\bar{\mathbf{t}}$ and $\bar{\mathbf{c}}$ denote the centered $\mathbf{t}$ and $\mathbf{c}$ vectors.

The discretized Hubert statistic is computed via Eq. (17.23), by setting $\mathbf{x} = \mathbf{t}$ and $\mathbf{y} = \mathbf{c}$:

$$\Gamma = \frac{1}{N}\mathbf{t}^T\mathbf{c} = \frac{TP}{N} \tag{17.25}$$

Because the ith element of $\mathbf{t}$ is 1 only when the ith pair of points belongs to the same partition, and, likewise, the ith element of $\mathbf{c}$ is 1 only when the ith pair of points also belongs to the same cluster, the dot product $\mathbf{t}^T\mathbf{c}$ is simply the number of true positives, and thus the Γ value is equivalent to the fraction of all pairs that are true positives. It follows that the higher the agreement between the ground-truth partitioning $\mathcal{T}$ and clustering $\mathcal{C}$, the higher the Γ value.

Normalized Discretized Hubert Statistic

The normalized version of the discretized Hubert statistic is simply the correlation between $\mathbf{t}$ and $\mathbf{c}$ [Eq. (17.24)]:

$$\Gamma_n = \frac{\bar{\mathbf{t}}^T\bar{\mathbf{c}}}{\|\bar{\mathbf{t}}\| \cdot \|\bar{\mathbf{c}}\|} = \cos\theta \tag{17.26}$$

Note that $\mu_T = \frac{1}{N}\mathbf{t}^T\mathbf{t}$ is the fraction of point pairs that belong to the same partition, that is, with $y_i = y_j$, regardless of whether $\hat{y}_i$ matches $\hat{y}_j$ or not. Thus, we have

$$\mu_T = \frac{\mathbf{t}^T\mathbf{t}}{N} = \frac{TP+FN}{N}$$

Similarly, $\mu_C = \frac{1}{N}\mathbf{c}^T\mathbf{c}$ is the fraction of point pairs that belong to the same cluster, that is, with $\hat{y}_i = \hat{y}_j$, regardless of whether y_i matches y_j or not, so that

$$\mu_C = \frac{\mathbf{c}^T\mathbf{c}}{N} = \frac{TP+FP}{N}$$

Substituting these into the numerator in Eq. (17.26), we get

$$\begin{aligned}
\bar{\mathbf{t}}^T\bar{\mathbf{c}} &= (\mathbf{t} - \mathbf{1} \cdot \mu_T)^T(\mathbf{c} - \mathbf{1} \cdot \mu_C) \\
&= \mathbf{t}^T\mathbf{c} - \mu_C\mathbf{t}^T\mathbf{1} - \mu_T\mathbf{c}^T\mathbf{1} + \mathbf{1}^T\mathbf{1}\mu_T\mu_C \\
&= \mathbf{t}^T\mathbf{c} - N\mu_C\mu_T - N\mu_T\mu_C + N\mu_T\mu_C \\
&= \mathbf{t}^T\mathbf{c} - N\mu_T\mu_C \\
&= TP - N\mu_T\mu_C
\end{aligned} \tag{17.27}$$

where $\mathbf{1} \in \mathbb{R}^N$ is the vector of all 1's. We also made use of identities $\mathbf{t}^T\mathbf{1} = \mathbf{t}^T\mathbf{t}$ and $\mathbf{c}^T\mathbf{1} = \mathbf{c}^T\mathbf{c}$. Likewise, we can derive

$$\|\bar{\mathbf{t}}\|^2 = \bar{\mathbf{t}}^T\bar{\mathbf{t}} = \mathbf{t}^T\mathbf{t} - N\mu_T^2 = N\mu_T - N\mu_T^2 = N\mu_T(1 - \mu_T) \tag{17.28}$$

$$\|\bar{\mathbf{c}}\|^2 = \bar{\mathbf{c}}^T\bar{\mathbf{c}} = \mathbf{c}^T\mathbf{c} - N\mu_C^2 = N\mu_C - N\mu_C^2 = N\mu_C(1 - \mu_C) \tag{17.29}$$

Plugging Eqs. (17.27), (17.28), and (17.29) into Eq. (17.26) the normalized, discretized Hubert statistic can be written as

$$\Gamma_n = \frac{\frac{TP}{N} - \mu_T \mu_C}{\sqrt{\mu_T \mu_C (1 - \mu_T)(1 - \mu_C)}} \tag{17.30}$$

because $\mu_T = \frac{TP+FN}{N}$ and $\mu_C = \frac{TP+FP}{N}$, the normalized Γ_n statistic can be computed using only the TP, FN, and FP values. The maximum value of $\Gamma_n = +1$ is obtained when there are no false positives or negatives, that is, when $FN = FP = 0$. The minimum value of $\Gamma_n = -1$ is when there are no true positives and negatives, that is, when $TP = TN = 0$.

Example 17.4. Continuing Example 17.3, for the good clustering in Figure 17.1(a), we have

$$TP = 3030 \qquad FN = 645 \qquad FP = 766 \qquad TN = 6734$$

From these values, we obtain

$$\mu_T = \frac{TP + FN}{N} = \frac{3675}{11175} = 0.33$$

$$\mu_C = \frac{TP + FP}{N} = \frac{3796}{11175} = 0.34$$

Using Eqs. (17.25) and (17.30) the Hubert statistic values are

$$\Gamma = \frac{3030}{11175} = 0.271$$

$$\Gamma_n = \frac{0.27 - 0.33 \cdot 0.34}{\sqrt{0.33 \cdot 0.34 \cdot (1 - 0.33) \cdot (1 - 0.34)}} = \frac{0.159}{0.222} = 0.717$$

Likewise, for the bad clustering in Figure 17.1(b), we have

$$TP = 2891 \qquad FN = 784 \qquad FP = 2380 \qquad TN = 5120$$

and the values for the discretized Hubert statistic are given as

$$\Gamma = 0.258 \qquad\qquad \Gamma_n = 0.442$$

We observe that the good clustering has higher values, though the normalized statistic is more discerning than the unnormalized version, that is, the good clustering has a much higher value of Γ_n than the bad clustering, whereas the difference in Γ for the two clusterings is not that high.

17.2 INTERNAL MEASURES

Internal evaluation measures do not have recourse to the ground-truth partitioning, which is the typical scenario when clustering a dataset. To evaluate the quality of the clustering, internal measures therefore have to utilize notions of intracluster similarity or compactness, contrasted with notions of intercluster separation, with usually a trade-off in maximizing these two aims. The internal measures are based on the $n \times n$ *distance matrix*, also called the *proximity matrix*, of all pairwise distances among the n points:

$$\mathbf{W} = \left\{ \|\mathbf{x}_i - \mathbf{x}_j\| \right\}_{i,j=1}^{n} \tag{17.31}$$

where $\|\mathbf{x}_i - \mathbf{x}_j\|$ is the Euclidean distance between $\mathbf{x}_i, \mathbf{x}_j \in \mathbf{D}$, although other distance metrics can also be used. Because $\mathbf{W}$ is symmetric and distance of a point to itself is zero, usually only the upper triangular elements of $\mathbf{W}$ (excluding the diagonal) are used in the internal measures.

The proximity matrix $\mathbf{W}$ can also be considered as the adjacency matrix of the weighted complete graph G over the n points, that is, with nodes $V = \{\mathbf{x}_i \mid \mathbf{x}_i \in \mathbf{D}\}$, edges $E = \{(\mathbf{x}_i, \mathbf{x}_j) \mid \mathbf{x}_i, \mathbf{x}_j \in \mathbf{D}\}$, and edge weights $w_{ij} = \mathbf{W}(i, j)$ for all $\mathbf{x}_i, \mathbf{x}_j \in \mathbf{D}$. There is thus a close connection between the internal evaluation measures and the graph clustering objectives we examined in Chapter 16.

For internal measures, we assume that we do not have access to a ground-truth partitioning. Instead, we assume that we are given a clustering $\mathcal{C} = \{C_1, \dots, C_k\}$ comprising $r = k$ clusters, with cluster C_i containing $n_i = |C_i|$ points. Let $\hat{y}_i \in \{1, 2, \dots, k\}$ denote the cluster label for point $\mathbf{x}_i$. The clustering $\mathcal{C}$ can be considered as a k-way cut in G because $C_i \neq \emptyset$ for all i, $C_i \cap C_j = \emptyset$ for all i, j, and $\bigcup_i C_i = V$. Given any subsets $S, R \subset V$, define $W(S, R)$ as the sum of the weights on all edges with one vertex in S and the other in R, given as

$$W(S, R) = \sum_{\mathbf{x}_i \in S} \sum_{\mathbf{x}_j \in R} w_{ij}$$

Also, given $S \subseteq V$, we denote by $\overline{S}$ the complementary set of vertices, that is, $\overline{S} = V - S$.

The internal measures are based on various functions over the intracluster and intercluster weights. In particular, note that the sum of all the intracluster weights over all clusters is given as

$$W_{in} = \frac{1}{2} \sum_{i=1}^{k} W(C_i, C_i) \tag{17.32}$$

We divide by 2 because each edge within C_i is counted twice in the summation given by $W(C_i, C_i)$. Also note that the sum of all intercluster weights is given as

$$W_{out} = \frac{1}{2} \sum_{i=1}^{k} W(C_i, \overline{C_i}) = \sum_{i=1}^{k-1} \sum_{j>i} W(C_i, C_j) \tag{17.33}$$

Here too we divide by 2 because each edge is counted twice in the summation across clusters. The number of distinct intracluster edges, denoted N_{in}, and intercluster edges, denoted N_{out}, are given as

$$N_{in} = \sum_{i=1}^{k} \binom{n_i}{2} = \frac{1}{2} \sum_{i=1}^{k} n_i (n_i - 1)$$

$$N_{out} = \sum_{i=1}^{k-1} \sum_{j=i+1}^{k} n_i \cdot n_j = \frac{1}{2} \sum_{i=1}^{k} \sum_{\substack{j=1 \\ j \neq i}}^{k} n_i \cdot n_j$$

Note that the total number of distinct pairs of points N satisfies the identity

$$N = N_{in} + N_{out} = \binom{n}{2} = \frac{1}{2} n (n - 1)$$

Example 17.5. Figure 17.2 shows the graphs corresponding to the two K-means clusterings shown in Figure 17.1. Here, each vertex corresponds to a point $\mathbf{x}_i \in \mathbf{D}$,

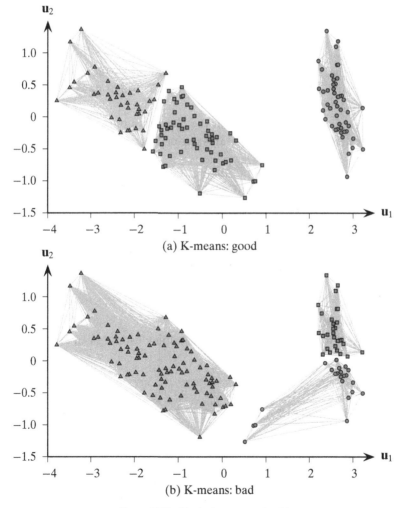

(a) K-means: good

(b) K-means: bad

Figure 17.2. Clusterings as graphs: Iris.

and an edge $(\mathbf{x}_i, \mathbf{x}_j)$ exists between each pair of points. However, only the intracluster edges are shown (with intercluster edges omitted) to avoid clutter. Because internal measures do not have access to a ground truth labeling, the goodness of a clustering is measured based on intracluster and intercluster statistics.

BetaCV Measure

The BetaCV measure is the ratio of the mean intracluster distance to the mean intercluster distance:

$$BetaCV = \frac{W_{in}/N_{in}}{W_{out}/N_{out}} = \frac{N_{out}}{N_{in}} \cdot \frac{W_{in}}{W_{out}} = \frac{N_{out}}{N_{in}} \frac{\sum_{i=1}^{k} W(C_i, C_i)}{\sum_{i=1}^{k} W(C_i, \overline{C_i})} \qquad (17.34)$$

The smaller the BetaCV ratio, the better the clustering, as it indicates that intracluster distances are on average smaller than intercluster distances.

C-index

Let $W_{\min}(N_{in})$ be the sum of the smallest N_{in} distances in the proximity matrix $\mathbf{W}$, where N_{in} is the total number of intracluster edges, or point pairs. Let $W_{\max}(N_{in})$ be the sum of the largest N_{in} distances in $\mathbf{W}$.

The C-index measures to what extent the clustering puts together the N_{in} points that are the closest across the k clusters. It is defined as

$$C\text{-}index = \frac{W_{in} - W_{\min}(N_{in})}{W_{\max}(N_{in}) - W_{\min}(N_{in})} \qquad (17.35)$$

where W_{in} is the sum of all the intracluster distances [Eq. (17.32)]. The C-index lies in the range $[0, 1]$. The smaller the C-index, the better the clustering, as it indicates more compact clusters with relatively smaller distances within clusters rather than between clusters.

Normalized Cut Measure

The normalized cut objective [Eq. (16.21)] for graph clustering can also be used as an internal clustering evaluation measure:

$$NC = \sum_{i=1}^{k} \frac{W(C_i, \overline{C_i})}{vol(C_i)} = \sum_{i=1}^{k} \frac{W(C_i, \overline{C_i})}{W(C_i, V)} \qquad (17.36)$$

where $vol(C_i) = W(C_i, V)$ is the volume of cluster C_i, that is, the total weights on edges with at least one end in the cluster. However, because we are using the proximity or distance matrix $\mathbf{W}$, instead of the affinity or similarity matrix $\mathbf{A}$, the higher the normalized cut value the better.

To see this, we make use of the observation that $W(C_i, V) = W(C_i, C_i) + W(C_i, \overline{C_i})$, so that

$$NC = \sum_{i=1}^{k} \frac{W(C_i, \overline{C_i})}{W(C_i, C_i) + W(C_i, \overline{C_i})} = \sum_{i=1}^{k} \frac{1}{\frac{W(C_i, C_i)}{W(C_i, \overline{C_i})} + 1}$$

We can see that NC is maximized when the ratios $\frac{W(C_i, C_i)}{W(C_i, \overline{C_i})}$ (across the k clusters) are as small as possible, which happens when the intracluster distances are much smaller compared to intercluster distances, that is, when the clustering is good. The maximum possible value of NC is k.

Modularity

The modularity objective for graph clustering [Eq. (16.30)] can also be used as an internal measure:

$$Q = \sum_{i=1}^{k} \left(\frac{W(C_i, C_i)}{W(V, V)} - \left(\frac{W(C_i, V)}{W(V, V)} \right)^2 \right) \tag{17.37}$$

where

$$W(V, V) = \sum_{i=1}^{k} W(C_i, V) \tag{17.38}$$

$$= \sum_{i=1}^{k} W(C_i, C_i) + \sum_{i=1}^{k} W(C_i, \overline{C_i}) \tag{17.39}$$

$$= 2(W_{in} + W_{out}) \tag{17.40}$$

The last step follows from Eqs. (17.32) and (17.33). Modularity measures the difference between the observed and expected fraction of weights on edges within the clusters. Since we are using the distance matrix, the smaller the modularity measure the better the clustering, which indicates that the intracluster distances are lower than expected.

Dunn Index

The Dunn index is defined as the ratio between the minimum distance between point pairs from different clusters and the maximum distance between point pairs from the same cluster. More formally, we have

$$Dunn = \frac{W_{out}^{min}}{W_{in}^{max}} \tag{17.41}$$

where W_{out}^{min} is the minimum intercluster distance:

$$W_{out}^{min} = \min_{i,j > i} \left\{ w_{ab} | \mathbf{x}_a \in C_i, \mathbf{x}_b \in C_j \right\}$$

and W_{in}^{max} is the maximum intracluster distance:

$$W_{in}^{max} = \max_i \left\{ w_{ab} | \mathbf{x}_a, \mathbf{x}_b \in C_i \right\}$$

The larger the Dunn index the better the clustering because it means even the closest distance between points in different clusters is much larger than the farthest distance between points in the same cluster. However, the Dunn index may be insensitive because the minimum intercluster and maximum intracluster distances do not capture all the information about a clustering.

Davies–Bouldin Index

Let μ_i denote the cluster mean, given as

$$\boldsymbol{\mu}_i = \frac{1}{n_i} \sum_{\mathbf{x}_j \in C_i} \mathbf{x}_j \tag{17.42}$$

Further, let σ_{μ_i} denote the dispersion or spread of the points around the cluster mean, given as

$$\sigma_{\mu_i} = \sqrt{\frac{\sum_{\mathbf{x}_j \in C_i} \|\mathbf{x}_j - \boldsymbol{\mu}_i\|^2}{n_i}} = \sqrt{\text{var}(C_i)}$$

where $\text{var}(C_i)$ is the total variance [Eq. (1.8)] of cluster C_i.

The Davies–Bouldin measure for a pair of clusters C_i and C_j is defined as the ratio

$$DB_{ij} = \frac{\sigma_{\mu_i} + \sigma_{\mu_j}}{\|\boldsymbol{\mu}_i - \boldsymbol{\mu}_j\|} \tag{17.43}$$

DB_{ij} measures how compact the clusters are compared to the distance between the cluster means. The Davies–Bouldin index is then defined as

$$DB = \frac{1}{k} \sum_{i=1}^{k} \max_{j \neq i} \{DB_{ij}\} \tag{17.44}$$

That is, for each cluster C_i, we pick the cluster C_j that yields the largest DB_{ij} ratio. The smaller the DB value the better the clustering, as it means that the clusters are well separated (i.e., the distance between cluster means is large), and each cluster is well represented by its mean (i.e., has a small spread).

Silhouette Coefficient

The silhouette coefficient is a measure of both cohesion and separation of clusters, and is based on the difference between the average distance to points in the closest cluster and to points in the same cluster. For each point $\mathbf{x}_i$ we calculate its silhouette coefficient s_i as

$$s_i = \frac{\mu_{out}^{min}(\mathbf{x}_i) - \mu_{in}(\mathbf{x}_i)}{\max\left\{\mu_{out}^{min}(\mathbf{x}_i), \mu_{in}(\mathbf{x}_i)\right\}} \tag{17.45}$$

where $\mu_{in}(\mathbf{x}_i)$ is the mean distance from $\mathbf{x}_i$ to points in its own cluster $\hat{y}_i$:

$$\mu_{in}(\mathbf{x}_i) = \frac{\sum_{\mathbf{x}_j \in C_{\hat{y}_i}, j \neq i} \|\mathbf{x}_i - \mathbf{x}_j\|}{n_{\hat{y}_i} - 1}$$

and $\mu_{out}^{min}(\mathbf{x}_i)$ is the mean of the distances from $\mathbf{x}_i$ to points in the closest cluster:

$$\mu_{out}^{min}(\mathbf{x}_i) = \min_{j \neq \hat{y}_i} \left\{ \frac{\sum_{\mathbf{y} \in C_j} \|\mathbf{x}_i - \mathbf{y}\|}{n_j} \right\}$$

The s_i value of a point lies in the interval $[-1, +1]$. A value close to $+1$ indicates that $\mathbf{x}_i$ is much closer to points in its own cluster and is far from other clusters. A value close to zero indicates that $\mathbf{x}_i$ is close to the boundary between two clusters. Finally, a value close to -1 indicates that $\mathbf{x}_i$ is much closer to another cluster than its own cluster, and therefore, the point may be mis-clustered.

The silhouette coefficient is defined as the mean s_i value across all the points:

$$SC = \frac{1}{n} \sum_{i=1}^{n} s_i \tag{17.46}$$

A value close to $+1$ indicates a good clustering.

Hubert Statistic

The Hubert Γ statistic [Eq. (17.23)], and its normalized version Γ_n [Eq. (17.24)], can both be used as internal evaluation measures by letting $\mathbf{X} = \mathbf{W}$ be the pairwise distance matrix, and by defining $\mathbf{Y}$ as the matrix of distances between the cluster means:

$$\mathbf{Y} = \left\{ \|\mu_i - \mu_j\| \right\}_{i,j=1}^{n} \tag{17.47}$$

where μ_i is the mean for cluster C_i (see Eq. (17.42)). Because both $\mathbf{W}$ and $\mathbf{Y}$ are symmetric, both Γ and Γ_n are computed over their upper triangular elements.

Example 17.6. Consider the two clusterings for the Iris principal components dataset shown in Figure 17.1, along with their corresponding graph representations in Figure 17.2. Let us evaluate these two clusterings using internal measures.

The good clustering shown in Figure 17.1(a) and Figure 17.2(a) has clusters with the following sizes:

$$n_1 = 61 \qquad\qquad n_2 = 50 \qquad\qquad n_3 = 39$$

Thus, the number of intracluster and intercluster edges (i.e., point pairs) is given as

$$N_{in} = \binom{61}{2} + \binom{50}{2} + \binom{31}{2} = 1830 + 1225 + 741 = 3796$$

$$N_{out} = 61 \cdot 50 + 61 \cdot 39 + 50 \cdot 39 = 3050 + 2379 + 1950 = 7379$$

In total there are $N = N_{in} + N_{out} = 3796 + 7379 = 11175$ distinct point pairs.

The weights on edges within each cluster $W(C_i, C_i)$, and those from a cluster to another $W(C_i, C_j)$, are as given in the intercluster weight matrix

$$\begin{pmatrix} W & C_1 & C_2 & C_3 \\ C_1 & 3265.69 & 10402.30 & 4418.62 \\ C_2 & 10402.30 & 1523.10 & 9792.45 \\ C_3 & 4418.62 & 9792.45 & 1252.36 \end{pmatrix} \qquad (17.48)$$

Thus, the sum of all the intracluster and intercluster edge weights is

$$W_{in} = \frac{1}{2}(3265.69 + 1523.10 + 1252.36) = 3020.57$$

$$W_{out} = (10402.30 + 4418.62 + 9792.45) = 24613.37$$

The BetaCV measure can then be computed as

$$BetaCV = \frac{N_{out} \cdot W_{in}}{N_{in} \cdot W_{out}} = \frac{7379 \times 3020.57}{3796 \times 24613.37} = 0.239$$

For the C-index, we first compute the sum of the N_{in} smallest and largest pair-wise distances, given as

$$W_{\min}(N_{in}) = 2535.96 \qquad\qquad W_{\max}(N_{in}) = 16889.57$$

Thus, C-index is given as

$$C\text{-}index = \frac{W_{in} - W_{\min}(N_{in})}{W_{\max}(N_{in}) - W_{\min}(N_{in})} = \frac{3020.57 - 2535.96}{16889.57 - 2535.96} = \frac{484.61}{14535.61} = 0.0338$$

For the normalized cut and modularity measures, we compute $W(C_i, \overline{C_i})$, $W(C_i, V) = \sum_{j=1}^{k} W(C_i, C_j)$ and $W(V, V) = \sum_{i=1}^{k} W(C_i, V)$, using the intercluster weight matrix [Eq. (17.48)]:

$$W(C_1, \overline{C_1}) = 10402.30 + 4418.62 = 14820.91$$

$$W(C_2, \overline{C_2}) = 10402.30 + 9792.45 = 20194.75$$

$$W(C_3, \overline{C_3}) = 4418.62 + 9792.45 = 14211.07$$

$$W(C_1, V) = 3265.69 + W(C_1, \overline{C_1}) = 18086.61$$

$$W(C_2, V) = 1523.10 + W(C_2, \overline{C_2}) = 21717.85$$

$$W(C_3, V) = 1252.36 + W(C_3, \overline{C_3}) = 15463.43$$

$$W(V, V) = W(C_1, V) + W(C_2, V) + W(C_3, V) = 55267.89$$

The normalized cut and modularity values are given as

$$NC = \frac{14820.91}{18086.61} + \frac{20194.75}{21717.85} + \frac{14211.07}{15463.43} = 0.819 + 0.93 + 0.919 = 2.67$$

$$Q = \left(\frac{3265.69}{55267.89} - \left(\frac{18086.61}{55267.89} \right)^2 \right) + \left(\frac{1523.10}{55267.89} - \left(\frac{21717.85}{55267.89} \right)^2 \right)$$

$$+ \left(\frac{1252.36}{55267.89} - \left(\frac{15463.43}{55267.89} \right)^2 \right)$$

$$= -0.048 - 0.1269 - 0.0556 = -0.2305$$

The Dunn index can be computed from the minimum and maximum distances between pairs of points from two clusters C_i and C_j, computed as follows:

$$\left(\begin{array}{c|ccc} W^{\min} & C_1 & C_2 & C_3 \\ \hline C_1 & 0 & 1.62 & 0.198 \\ C_2 & 1.62 & 0 & 3.49 \\ C_3 & 0.198 & 3.49 & 0 \end{array} \right) \qquad \left(\begin{array}{c|ccc} W^{\max} & C_1 & C_2 & C_3 \\ \hline C_1 & 2.50 & 4.85 & 4.81 \\ C_2 & 4.85 & 2.33 & 7.06 \\ C_3 & 4.81 & 7.06 & 2.55 \end{array} \right)$$

The Dunn index value for the clustering is given as

$$Dunn = \frac{W^{\min}_{out}}{W^{\max}_{in}} = \frac{0.198}{2.55} = 0.078$$

To compute the Davies–Bouldin index, we compute the cluster mean and dispersion values:

$$\mu_1 = \begin{pmatrix} -0.664 \\ -0.33 \end{pmatrix} \qquad \mu_2 = \begin{pmatrix} 2.64 \\ 0.19 \end{pmatrix} \qquad \mu_3 = \begin{pmatrix} -2.35 \\ 0.27 \end{pmatrix}$$

$$\sigma_{\mu_1} = 0.723 \qquad\qquad \sigma_{\mu_2} = 0.512 \qquad\qquad \sigma_{\mu_3} = 0.695$$

and the DB_{ij} values for pairs of clusters:

$$\left(\begin{array}{c|ccc} DB_{ij} & C_1 & C_2 & C_3 \\ \hline C_1 & - & 0.369 & 0.794 \\ C_2 & 0.369 & - & 0.242 \\ C_3 & 0.794 & 0.242 & - \end{array} \right)$$

For example, $DB_{12} = \frac{\sigma_{\mu_1} + \sigma_{\mu_2}}{\|\mu_1 - \mu_2\|} = \frac{1.235}{3.346} = 0.369$. Finally, the DB index is given as

$$DB = \frac{1}{3}(0.794 + 0.369 + 0.794) = 0.652$$

The silhouette coefficient [Eq. (17.45)] for a chosen point, say x_1, is given as

$$s_1 = \frac{1.902 - 0.701}{\max\{1.902, 0.701\}} = \frac{1.201}{1.902} = 0.632$$

The average value across all points is $SC = 0.598$

The Hubert statistic can be computed by taking the dot product over the upper triangular elements of the proximity matrix $\mathbf{W}$ [Eq. (17.31)] and the $n \times n$ matrix of distances among cluster means $\mathbf{Y}$ [Eq. (17.47)], and then dividing by the number of distinct point pairs N:

$$\Gamma = \frac{\mathbf{w}^T \mathbf{y}}{N} = \frac{91545.85}{11175} = 8.19$$

where $\mathbf{w}, \mathbf{y} \in \mathbb{R}^N$ are vectors comprising the upper triangular elements of $\mathbf{W}$ and $\mathbf{Y}$. The normalized Hubert statistic can be obtained as the correlation between $\mathbf{w}$ and $\mathbf{y}$ [Eq. (17.24)]:

$$\Gamma_n = \frac{\bar{\mathbf{w}}^T \bar{\mathbf{y}}}{\|\bar{\mathbf{w}}\| \cdot \|\bar{\mathbf{y}}\|} = 0.918$$

where $\bar{\mathbf{w}}, \bar{\mathbf{y}}$ are the centered vectors corresponding to $\mathbf{w}$ and $\mathbf{y}$, respectively.

The following table summarizes the various internal measure values for the good and bad clusterings shown in Figure 17.1 and Figure 17.2.

	Lower better				Higher better				
	BetaCV	*C-index*	*Q*	*DB*	*NC*	*Dunn*	*SC*	*Γ*	*Γ_n*
(a) Good	0.24	0.034	−0.23	0.65	2.67	0.08	0.60	8.19	0.92
(b) Bad	0.33	0.08	−0.20	1.11	2.56	0.03	0.55	7.32	0.83

Despite the fact that these internal measures do not have access to the ground-truth partitioning, we can observe that the good clustering has higher values for normalized cut, Dunn, silhouette coefficient, and the Hubert statistics, and lower values for BetaCV, C-index, modularity, and Davies–Bouldin measures. These measures are thus capable of discerning good versus bad clusterings of the data.

17.3 RELATIVE MEASURES

Relative measures are used to compare different clusterings obtained by varying different parameters for the same algorithm, for example, to choose the number of clusters k.

Silhouette Coefficient

The silhouette coefficient [Eq. (17.45)] for each point s_j, and the average SC value [Eq. (17.46)], can be used to estimate the number of clusters in the data. The approach consists of plotting the s_j values in descending order for each cluster, and to note the overall SC value for a particular value of k, as well as clusterwise SC values:

$$SC_i = \frac{1}{n_i} \sum_{\mathbf{x}_j \in C_i} s_j$$

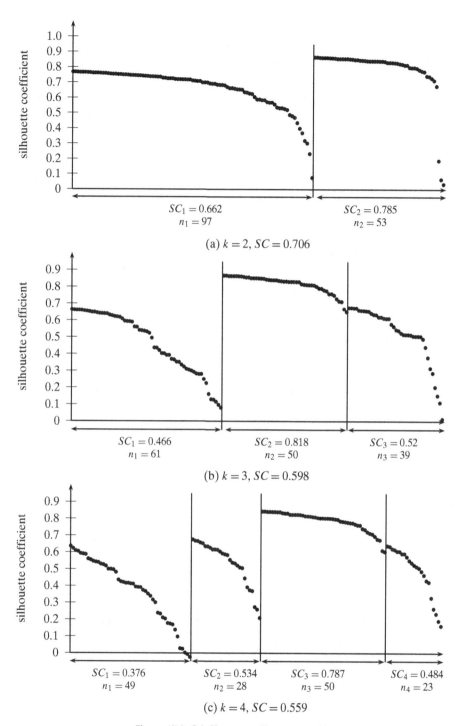

Figure 17.3. Iris K-means: silhouette coefficient plot.

We can then pick the value k that yields the best clustering, with many points having high s_j values within each cluster, as well as high values for SC and SC_i ($1 \le i \le k$).

Example 17.7. Figure 17.3 shows the silhouette coefficient plot for the best clustering results for the K-means algorithm on the Iris principal components dataset for three different values of k, namely $k = 2, 3, 4$. The silhouette coefficient values s_i for points within each cluster are plotted in decreasing order. The overall average (SC) and clusterwise averages (SC_i, for $1 \le i \le k$) are also shown, along with the cluster sizes.

Figure 17.3(a) shows that $k = 2$ has the highest average silhouette coefficient, $SC = 0.706$. It shows two well separated clusters. The points in cluster C_1 start out with high s_i values, which gradually drop as we get to border points. The second cluster C_2 is even better separated, since it has a higher silhouette coefficient and the pointwise scores are all high, except for the last three points, suggesting that almost all the points are well clustered.

The silhouette plot in Figure 17.3(b), with $k = 3$, corresponds to the "good" clustering shown in Figure 17.1(a). We can see that cluster C_1 from Figure 17.3(a) has been split into two clusters for $k = 3$, namely C_1 and C_3. Both of these have many bordering points, whereas C_2 is well separated with high silhouette coefficients across all points.

Finally, the silhouette plot for $k = 4$ is shown in Figure 17.3(c). Here C_3 is the well separated cluster, corresponding to C_2 above, and the remaining clusters are essentially subclusters of C_1 for $k = 2$ (Figure 17.3(a)). Cluster C_1 also has two points with negative s_i values, indicating that they are probably misclustered.

Because $k = 2$ yields the highest silhouette coefficient, and the two clusters are essentially well separated, in the absence of prior knowledge, we would choose $k = 2$ as the best number of clusters for this dataset.

Calinski–Harabasz Index

Given the dataset $\mathbf{D}$ comprising n points $\mathbf{x}_j$, the scatter matrix for $\mathbf{D}$ is given as

$$\mathbf{S} = n\mathbf{\Sigma} = \sum_{j=1}^{n} \left(\mathbf{x}_j - \boldsymbol{\mu}\right)\left(\mathbf{x}_j - \boldsymbol{\mu}\right)^T$$

where $\boldsymbol{\mu} = \frac{1}{n}\sum_{j=1}^{n}\mathbf{x}_j$ is the mean and $\mathbf{\Sigma}$ is the covariance matrix. The scatter matrix can be decomposed into two matrices $\mathbf{S} = \mathbf{S}_W + \mathbf{S}_B$, where $\mathbf{S}_W$ is the within-cluster scatter matrix and $\mathbf{S}_B$ is the between-cluster scatter matrix, given as

$$\mathbf{S}_W = \sum_{i=1}^{k} \sum_{\mathbf{x}_j \in C_i} \left(\mathbf{x}_j - \boldsymbol{\mu}_i\right)\left(\mathbf{x}_j - \boldsymbol{\mu}_i\right)^T$$

$$\mathbf{S}_B = \sum_{i=1}^{k} n_i \left(\boldsymbol{\mu}_i - \boldsymbol{\mu}\right)\left(\boldsymbol{\mu}_i - \boldsymbol{\mu}\right)^T$$

where $\boldsymbol{\mu}_i = \frac{1}{n_i}\sum_{\mathbf{x}_j \in C_i} \mathbf{x}_j$ is the mean for cluster C_i.

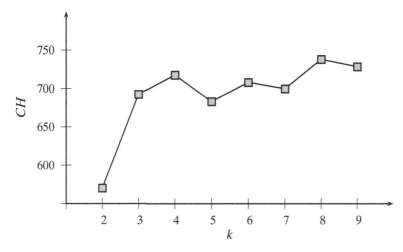

Figure 17.4. Calinski–Harabasz variance ratio criterion.

The Calinski–Harabasz (CH) variance ratio criterion for a given value of k is defined as follows:

$$CH(k) = \frac{tr(\mathbf{S}_B)/(k-1)}{tr(\mathbf{S}_W)/(n-k)} = \frac{n-k}{k-1} \cdot \frac{tr(\mathbf{S}_B)}{tr(\mathbf{S}_W)} \qquad (17.49)$$

where $tr(\mathbf{S}_W)$ and $tr(\mathbf{S}_B)$ are the traces (the sum of the diagonal elements) of the within-cluster and between-cluster scatter matrices.

For a good value of k, we expect the within-cluster scatter to be smaller relative to the between-cluster scatter, which should result in a higher $CH(k)$ value. On the other hand, we do not desire a very large value of k; thus the term $\frac{n-k}{k-1}$ penalizes larger values of k. We could choose a value of k that maximizes $CH(k)$. Alternatively, we can plot the CH values and look for a large increase in the value followed by little or no gain. For instance, we can choose the value $k > 3$ that minimizes the term

$$\Delta(k) = \Big(CH(k+1) - CH(k)\Big) - \Big(CH(k) - CH(k-1)\Big)$$

The intuition is that we want to find the value of k for which $CH(k)$ is much higher than $CH(k-1)$ and there is only a little improvement or a decrease in the $CH(k+1)$ value.

Example 17.8. Figure 17.4 shows the CH ratio for various values of k on the Iris principal components dataset, using the K-means algorithm, with the best results chosen from 200 runs.

For $k = 3$, the within-cluster and between-cluster scatter matrices are given as

$$\mathbf{S}_W = \begin{pmatrix} 39.14 & -13.62 \\ -13.62 & 24.73 \end{pmatrix} \qquad \mathbf{S}_B = \begin{pmatrix} 590.36 & 13.62 \\ 13.62 & 11.36 \end{pmatrix}$$

Thus, we have

$$CH(3) = \frac{(150-3)}{(3-1)} \cdot \frac{(590.36+11.36)}{(39.14+24.73)} = (147/2) \cdot \frac{601.72}{63.87} = 73.5 \cdot 9.42 = 692.4$$

The successive $CH(k)$ and $\Delta(k)$ values are as follows:

k	2	3	4	5	6	7	8	9
$CH(k)$	570.25	692.40	717.79	683.14	708.26	700.17	738.05	728.63
$\Delta(k)$	–	−96.78	−60.03	59.78	−33.22	45.97	−47.30	–

If we choose the first large peak before a decrease we would choose $k = 4$. However, $\Delta(k)$ suggests $k = 3$ as the best (lowest) value, representing the "knee-of-the-curve." One limitation of the $\Delta(k)$ criteria is that values less than $k = 3$ cannot be evaluated, since $\Delta(2)$ depends on $CH(1)$, which is not defined.

Gap Statistic

The gap statistic compares the sum of intracluster weights W_{in} [Eq. (17.32)] for different values of k with their expected values assuming no apparent clustering structure, which forms the null hypothesis.

Let $\mathcal{C}_k$ be the clustering obtained for a specified value of k, using a chosen clustering algorithm. Let $W_{in}^k(\mathbf{D})$ denote the sum of intracluster weights (over all clusters) for $\mathcal{C}_k$ on the input dataset $\mathbf{D}$. We would like to compute the probability of the observed W_{in}^k value under the null hypothesis that the points are randomly placed in the same data space as $\mathbf{D}$. Unfortunately, the sampling distribution of W_{in} is not known. Further, it depends on the number of clusters k, the number of points n, and other characteristics of $\mathbf{D}$.

To obtain an empirical distribution for W_{in}, we resort to Monte Carlo simulations of the sampling process. That is, we generate t random samples comprising n randomly distributed points within the same d-dimensional data space as the input dataset $\mathbf{D}$. That is, for each dimension of $\mathbf{D}$, say X_j, we compute its range $[\min(X_j), \max(X_j)]$ and generate values for the n points (for the jth dimension) uniformly at random within the given range. Let $\mathbf{R}_i \in \mathbb{R}^{n \times d}$, $1 \le i \le t$ denote the ith sample. Let $W_{in}^k(\mathbf{R}_i)$ denote the sum of intracluster weights for a given clustering of $\mathbf{R}_i$ into k clusters. From each sample dataset $\mathbf{R}_i$, we generate clusterings for different values of k using the same algorithm and record the intracluster values $W_{in}^k(\mathbf{R}_i)$. Let $\mu_W(k)$ and $\sigma_W(k)$ denote the mean and standard deviation of these intracluster weights for each value of k, given as

$$\mu_W(k) = \frac{1}{t} \sum_{i=1}^{t} \log W_{in}^k(\mathbf{R}_i)$$

$$\sigma_W(k) = \sqrt{\frac{1}{t} \sum_{i=1}^{t} \left(\log W_{in}^k(\mathbf{R}_i) - \mu_W(k) \right)^2}$$

where we use the logarithm of the W_{in} values, as they can be quite large.

The *gap statistic* for a given k is then defined as

$$gap(k) = \mu_W(k) - \log W_{in}^k(\mathbf{D}) \tag{17.50}$$

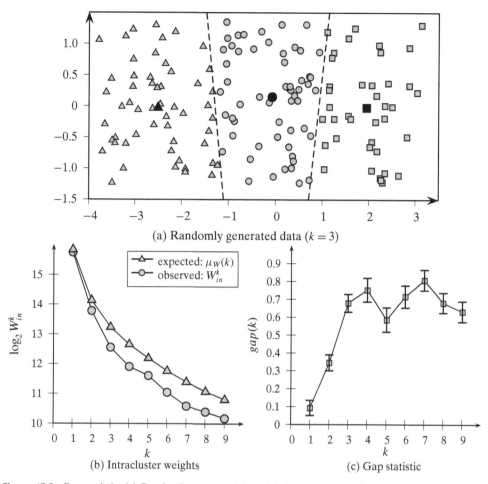

(a) Randomly generated data ($k = 3$)

(b) Intracluster weights

(c) Gap statistic

Figure 17.5. Gap statistic. (a) Randomly generated data. (b) Intracluster weights for different k. (c) Gap statistic as a function of k.

It measures the deviation of the observed W_{in}^k value from its expected value under the null hypothesis. We can select the value of k that yields the largest gap statistic because that indicates a clustering structure far away from the uniform distribution of points. A more robust approach is to choose k as follows:

$$k^* = \arg\min_k \left\{ gap(k) \geq gap(k+1) - \sigma_W(k+1) \right\} \tag{17.51}$$

That is, we select the least value of k such that the gap statistic exceeds one standard deviation of the gap at $k+1$.

Example 17.9. To compute the gap statistic we have to generate t random samples of n points drawn from the same data space as the Iris principal components dataset. A random sample of $n = 150$ points is shown in Figure 17.5(a), which does not have any apparent cluster structure. However, when we run K-means on this dataset it will output some clustering, an example of which is also shown, with $k = 3$. From this clustering, we can compute the $\log_2 W_{in}^k(\mathbf{R}_i)$ value; we use base 2 for all logarithms.

For Monte Carlo sampling, we generate $t = 200$ such random datasets, and compute the mean or expected intracluster weight $\mu_W(k)$ under the null hypothesis, for each value of k. Figure 17.5(b) shows the expected intracluster weights for different values of k. It also shows the observed value of $\log_2 W_{in}^k$ computed from the K-means clustering of the Iris principal components dataset. For the Iris dataset, and each of the uniform random samples, we run K-means 100 times and select the best possible clustering, from which the $W_{in}^k(\mathbf{R}_i)$ values are computed. We can see that the observed $W_{in}^k(\mathbf{D})$ values are smaller than the expected values $\mu_W(k)$.

From these values, we then compute the gap statistic $gap(k)$ for different values of k, which are plotted in Figure 17.5(c). Table 17.1 lists the gap statistic and standard deviation values. The optimal value for the number of clusters is $k = 4$ because

$$gap(4) = 0.753 > gap(5) - \sigma_W(5) = 0.515$$

However, if we had relaxed the gap test to be within two standard deviations, then the optimal value would have been $k = 3$ because

$$gap(3) = 0.679 > gap(4) - 2\sigma_W(4) = 0.753 - 2 \cdot 0.0701 = 0.613$$

Essentially, there is still some subjectivity in selecting the right number of clusters, but the gap statistic plot can help in this task.

17.3.1 Cluster Stability

The main idea behind cluster stability is that the clusterings obtained from several datasets sampled from the same underlying distribution as $\mathbf{D}$ should be similar or "stable." The cluster stability approach can be used to find good parameter values for a given clustering algorithm; we will focus on the task of finding a good value for k, the correct number of clusters.

The joint probability distribution for $\mathbf{D}$ is typically unknown. Therefore, to sample a dataset from the same distribution we can try a variety of methods, including random perturbations, subsampling, or bootstrap resampling. Let us consider the bootstrapping approach; we generate t samples of size n by sampling from $\mathbf{D}$ with replacement, which allows the same point to be chosen possibly multiple times, and thus each sample $\mathbf{D}_i$ will be different. Next, for each sample $\mathbf{D}_i$ we run the same clustering algorithm with different cluster values k ranging from 2 to k^{max}.

Let $\mathcal{C}_k(\mathbf{D}_i)$ denote the clustering obtained from sample $\mathbf{D}_i$, for a given value of k. Next, the method compares the distance between all pairs of clusterings $\mathcal{C}_k(\mathbf{D}_i)$ and $\mathcal{C}_k(\mathbf{D}_j)$ via some distance function. Several of the external cluster evaluation measures can be used as distance measures, by setting, for example, $\mathcal{C} = \mathcal{C}_k(\mathbf{D}_i)$ and $\mathcal{T} = \mathcal{C}_k(\mathbf{D}_j)$, or vice versa. From these values we compute the expected pairwise distance for each value of k. Finally, the value k^* that exhibits the least deviation between the clusterings obtained from the resampled datasets is the best choice for k because it exhibits the most stability.

Table 17.1. Gap statistic values as a function of k

k	$gap(k)$	$\sigma_W(k)$	$gap(k) - \sigma_W(k)$
1	0.093	0.0456	0.047
2	0.346	0.0486	0.297
3	0.679	0.0529	0.626
4	0.753	0.0701	0.682
5	0.586	0.0711	0.515
6	0.715	0.0654	0.650
7	0.808	0.0611	0.746
8	0.680	0.0597	0.620
9	0.632	0.0606	0.571

There is, however, one complication when evaluating the distance between a pair of clusterings $C_k(\mathbf{D}_i)$ and $C_k(\mathbf{D}_j)$, namely that the underlying datasets $\mathbf{D}_i$ and $\mathbf{D}_j$ are different. That is, the set of points being clustered is different because each sample $\mathbf{D}_i$ is different. Before computing the distance between the two clusterings, we have to restrict the clusterings only to the points common to both $\mathbf{D}_i$ and $\mathbf{D}_j$, denoted as $\mathbf{D}_{ij}$. Because sampling with replacement allows multiple instances of the same point, we also have to account for this when creating $\mathbf{D}_{ij}$. For each point $\mathbf{x}_a$ in the input dataset $\mathbf{D}$, let m_i^a and m_j^a denote the number of occurrences of $\mathbf{x}_a$ in $\mathbf{D}_i$ and $\mathbf{D}_j$, respectively. Define

$$\mathbf{D}_{ij} = \mathbf{D}_i \cap \mathbf{D}_j = \left\{ m^a \text{ instances of } \mathbf{x}_a \mid \mathbf{x}_a \in \mathbf{D}, m^a = \min\{m_i^a, m_j^a\} \right\} \qquad (17.52)$$

That is, the common dataset $\mathbf{D}_{ij}$ is created by selecting the minimum number of instances of the point $\mathbf{x}_a$ in $\mathbf{D}_i$ or $\mathbf{D}_j$.

Algorithm 17.1 shows the pseudo-code for the clustering stability method for choosing the best k value. It takes as input the clustering algorithm A, the number of samples t, the maximum number of clusters $k^{\max}$, and the input dataset $\mathbf{D}$. It first generates the t bootstrap samples and clusters them using algorithm A. Next, it computes the distance between the clusterings for each pair of datasets $\mathbf{D}_i$ and $\mathbf{D}_j$, for each value of k. Finally, the method computes the expected pairwise distance $\mu_d(k)$ in line 12. We assume that the clustering distance function d is symmetric. If d is not symmetric, then the expected difference should be computed over all ordered pairs, that is, $\mu_d(k) = \frac{1}{t(t-1)} \sum_{i=1}^{r} \sum_{j \neq i} d_{ij}(k)$.

Instead of a distance function d, we can also evaluate clustering stability via a similarity measure, in which case, after computing the average similarity between pairs of clusterings for a given k, we can choose the best value k^* as the one that maximizes the expected similarity $\mu_s(k)$. In general, those external measures that yield lower values for better agreement between $C_k(\mathbf{D}_i)$ and $C_k(\mathbf{D}_j)$ can be used as distance functions, whereas those that yield higher values for better agreement can be used as similarity functions. Examples of distance functions include normalized mutual information, variation of information, and conditional entropy (which is asymmetric). Examples of similarity functions include Jaccard, Fowlkes–Mallows, Hubert Γ statistic, and so on.

Algorithm 17.1: Clustering Stability Algorithm for Choosing k

---

CLUSTERINGSTABILITY ($A, t, k^{\max}, \mathbf{D}$):

1   $n \leftarrow |\mathbf{D}|$

    // Generate t samples

2   **for** $i = 1, 2, \ldots, t$ **do**

3     $\mathbf{D}_i \leftarrow$ sample n points from $\mathbf{D}$ with replacement

    // Generate clusterings for different values of k

4   **for** $i = 1, 2, \ldots, t$ **do**

5   **for** $k = 2, 3, \ldots, k^{\max}$ **do**

6       $\mathcal{C}_k(\mathbf{D}_i) \leftarrow$ cluster $\mathbf{D}_i$ into k clusters using algorithm A

    // Compute mean difference between clusterings for each k

7   **foreach** *pair* $\mathbf{D}_i, \mathbf{D}_j$ *with* $j > i$ **do**

8     $\mathbf{D}_{ij} \leftarrow \mathbf{D}_i \cap \mathbf{D}_j$ // create common dataset using Eq. (17.52)

9   **for** $k = 2, 3, \ldots, k^{\max}$ **do**

10       $d_{ij}(k) \leftarrow d\big(\mathcal{C}_k(\mathbf{D}_i), \mathcal{C}_k(\mathbf{D}_j), \mathbf{D}_{ij}\big)$ // distance between
        clusterings

11   **for** $k = 2, 3, \ldots, k^{\max}$ **do**

12     $\mu_d(k) \leftarrow \frac{2}{t(t-1)} \sum_{i=1}^{t} \sum_{j>i} d_{ij}(k)$ // expected pairwise distance

    // Choose best k

13   $k^* \leftarrow \arg\min_k \{\mu_d(k)\}$

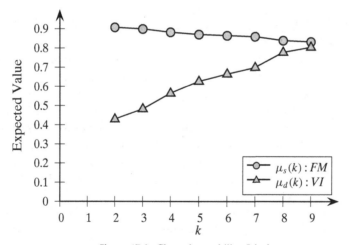

Figure 17.6. Clustering stability: Iris dataset.

Example 17.10. We study the clustering stability for the Iris principal components dataset, with $n = 150$, using the K-means algorithm. We use $t = 500$ bootstrap samples. For each dataset $\mathbf{D}_i$, and each value of k, we run K-means with 100 initial starting configurations, and select the best clustering.

For the distance function, we used the variation of information [Eq. (17.9)] between each pair of clusterings. We also used the Fowlkes–Mallows measure [Eq. (17.22)] as an example of a similarity measure. The expected values of the pairwise distance $\mu_d(k)$ for the VI measure, and the pairwise similarity $\mu_s(k)$ for the FM measure are plotted in Figure 17.6. Both the measures indicate that $k = 2$ is the best value, as for the VI measure this leads to the least expected distance between pairs of clusterings, and for the FM measure this choice leads to the most expected similarity between clusterings.

17.3.2 Clustering Tendency

Clustering tendency or clusterability aims to determine whether the dataset $\mathbf{D}$ has any meaningful groups to begin with. This is usually a hard task given the different definitions of what it means to be a cluster, for example, partitional, hierarchical, density-based, graph-based and so on. Even if we fix the cluster type, it is still a hard task to define the appropriate null model (e.g., the one without any clustering structure) for a given dataset $\mathbf{D}$. Furthermore, if we do determine that the data is clusterable, then we are still faced with the question of how many clusters there are. Nevertheless, it is still worthwhile to assess the clusterability of a dataset; we look at some approaches to answer the question whether the data is clusterable or not.

Spatial Histogram

One simple approach is to contrast the d-dimensional spatial histogram of the input dataset $\mathbf{D}$ with the histogram from samples generated randomly in the same data space. Let $X_1, X_2, \ldots, X_d$ denote the d dimensions. Given b, the number of bins for each dimension, we divide each dimension X_j into b equi-width bins, and simply count how many points lie in each of the b^d d-dimensional cells. From this spatial histogram, we can obtain the empirical joint probability mass function (EPMF) for the dataset $\mathbf{D}$, which is an approximation of the unknown joint probability density function. The EPMF is given as

$$f(\mathbf{i}) = P(\mathbf{x}_j \in \text{cell } \mathbf{i}) = \frac{\left|\{\mathbf{x}_j \in \text{cell } \mathbf{i}\}\right|}{n}$$

where $\mathbf{i} = (i_1, i_2, \ldots, i_d)$ denotes a cell index, with i_j denoting the bin index along dimension X_j.

Next, we generate t random samples, each comprising n points within the same d-dimensional space as the input dataset $\mathbf{D}$. That is, for each dimension X_j, we compute its range $[\min(X_j), \max(X_j)]$, and generate values uniformly at random within the given range. Let $\mathbf{R}_j$ denote the jth such random sample. We can then compute the corresponding EPMF $g_j(\mathbf{i})$ for each $\mathbf{R}_j$, $1 \le j \le t$.

Finally, we can compute how much the distribution f differs from g_j (for $j = 1, \ldots, t$), using the Kullback–Leibler (KL) divergence from f to g_j, defined as

$$KL(f|g_j) = \sum_{\mathbf{i}} f(\mathbf{i}) \log\left(\frac{f(\mathbf{i})}{g_j(\mathbf{i})}\right) \tag{17.53}$$

The KL divergence is zero only when f and g_j are the same distributions. Using these divergence values, we can compute how much the dataset $\mathbf{D}$ differs from a random dataset.

The main limitation of this approach is that as dimensionality increases, the number of cells (b^d) increases exponentially, and with a fixed sample size n, most of the cells will be empty, or will have only one point, making it hard to estimate the divergence. The method is also sensitive to the choice of parameter b. Instead of histograms, and the corresponding EPMF, we can also use density estimation methods (see Section 15.2) to determine the joint probability density function (PDF) for the dataset $\mathbf{D}$, and see how it differs from the PDF for the random datasets. However, the curse of dimensionality also causes problems for density estimation.

Example 17.11. Figure 17.7(c) shows the empirical joint probability mass function for the Iris principal components dataset that has $n = 150$ points in $d = 2$ dimensions. It also shows the EPMF for one of the datasets generated uniformly at random in the same data space. Both EPMFs were computed using $b = 5$ bins in each dimension, for a total of 25 spatial cells. The spatial grids/cells for the Iris dataset $\mathbf{D}$, and the random sample $\mathbf{R}$, are shown in Figures 17.7(a) and 17.7(b), respectively. The cells are numbered starting from 0, from bottom to top, and then left to right. Thus, the bottom left cell is 0, top left is 4, bottom right is 19, and top right is 24. These indices are used along the x-axis in the EPMF plot in Figure 17.7(c).

We generated $t = 500$ random samples from the null distribution, and computed the KL divergence from f to g_j for each $1 \leq j \leq t$ (using logarithm with base 2). The distribution of the KL values is plotted in Figure 17.7(d). The mean KL value was $\mu_{KL} = 1.17$, with a standard deviation of $\sigma_{KL} = 0.18$, indicating that the Iris data is indeed far from the randomly generated data, and thus is clusterable.

Distance Distribution

Instead of trying to estimate the density, another approach to determine clusterability is to compare the pairwise point distances from $\mathbf{D}$, with those from the randomly generated samples $\mathbf{R}_i$ from the null distribution. That is, we create the EPMF from the proximity matrix $\mathbf{W}$ for $\mathbf{D}$ [Eq. (17.31)] by binning the distances into b bins:

$$f(i) = P(w_{pq} \in \text{bin } i \mid \mathbf{x}_p, \mathbf{x}_q \in \mathbf{D}, p < q) = \frac{\left|\{w_{pq} \in \text{bin } i\}\right|}{n(n-1)/2}$$

Likewise, for each of the samples $\mathbf{R}_j$, we can determine the EPMF for the pairwise distances, denoted g_j. Finally, we can compute the KL divergences between f and g_j using Eq. (17.53). The expected divergence indicates the extent to which $\mathbf{D}$ differs from the null (random) distribution.

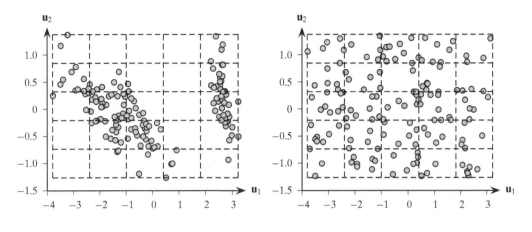

(a) Iris: spatial cells   (b) Uniform: spatial cells

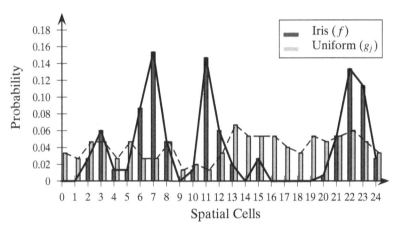

(c) Empirical probability mass function

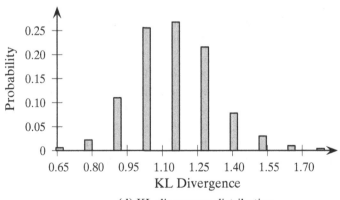

(d) KL-divergence distribution

Figure 17.7. Iris dataset: spatial histogram.

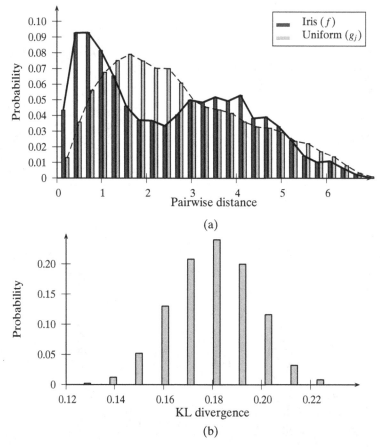

Figure 17.8. Iris dataset: distance distribution.

Example 17.12. Figure 17.8(a) shows the distance distribution for the Iris principal components dataset $\mathbf{D}$ and the random sample $\mathbf{R}_j$ from Figure 17.7(b). The distance distribution is obtained by binning the edge weights between all pairs of points using $b = 25$ bins.

We then compute the KL divergence from $\mathbf{D}$ to each $\mathbf{R}_j$, over $t = 500$ samples. The distribution of the KL divergences (using logarithm with base 2) is shown in Figure 17.8(b). The mean divergence is $\mu_{KL} = 0.18$, with standard deviation $\sigma_{KL} = 0.017$. Even though the Iris dataset has a good clustering tendency, the KL divergence is not very large. We conclude that, at least for the Iris dataset, the distance distribution is not as discriminative as the spatial histogram approach for clusterability analysis.

Hopkins Statistic

The Hopkins statistic is a sparse sampling test for spatial randomness. Given a dataset $\mathbf{D}$ comprising n points, we generate t random subsamples $\mathbf{R}_i$ of m points each, where

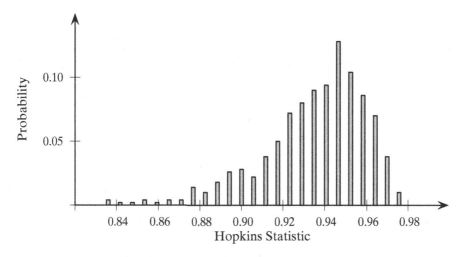

Figure 17.9. Iris dataset: Hopkins statistic distribution.

$m \ll n$. These samples are drawn from the same data space as $\mathbf{D}$, generated uniformly at random along each dimension. Further, we also generate t subsamples of m points directly from $\mathbf{D}$, using sampling without replacement. Let $\mathbf{D}_i$ denote the ith direct subsample. Next, we compute the minimum distance between each point $\mathbf{x}_j \in \mathbf{D}_i$ and points in $\mathbf{D}$

$$\delta_{\min}(\mathbf{x}_j) = \min_{\mathbf{x}_i \in \mathbf{D}, \mathbf{x}_i \neq \mathbf{x}_j} \left\{ \|\mathbf{x}_j - \mathbf{x}_i\| \right\}$$

Likewise, we compute the minimum distance $\delta_{\min}(\mathbf{y}_j)$ between a point $\mathbf{y}_j \in \mathbf{R}_i$ and points in $\mathbf{D}$.

The Hopkins statistic (in d dimensions) for the ith pair of samples $\mathbf{R}_i$ and $\mathbf{D}_i$ is then defined as

$$HS_i = \frac{\sum_{\mathbf{y}_j \in \mathbf{R}_i} \left(\delta_{\min}(\mathbf{y}_j) \right)^d}{\sum_{\mathbf{y}_j \in \mathbf{R}_i} \left(\delta_{\min}(\mathbf{y}_j) \right)^d + \sum_{\mathbf{x}_j \in \mathbf{D}_i} \left(\delta_{\min}(\mathbf{x}_j) \right)^d}$$

This statistic compares the nearest-neighbor distribution of randomly generated points to the same distribution for random subsets of points from $\mathbf{D}$. If the data is well clustered we expect $\delta_{\min}(\mathbf{x}_j)$ values to be smaller compared to the $\delta_{\min}(\mathbf{y}_j)$ values, and in this case HS_i tends to 1. If both nearest-neighbor distances are similar, then HS_i takes on values close to 0.5, which indicates that the data is essentially random, and there is no apparent clustering. Finally, if $\delta_{\min}(\mathbf{x}_j)$ values are larger compared to $\delta_{\min}(\mathbf{y}_j)$ values, then HS_i tends to 0, and it indicates point repulsion, with no clustering. From the t different values of HS_i we may then compute the mean and variance of the statistic to determine whether $\mathbf{D}$ is clusterable or not.

Example 17.13. Figure 17.9 plots the distribution of the Hopkins statistic values over $t = 500$ pairs of samples: $\mathbf{R}_j$ generated uniformly at random, and $\mathbf{D}_j$ subsampled from the input dataset $\mathbf{D}$. The subsample size was set as $m = 30$, using 20% of the points in **D**, that is, the Iris principal components dataset, which has $n = 150$ points in $d = 2$ dimensions. The mean of the Hopkins statistic is $\mu_{HS} = 0.935$, with a standard deviation of $\sigma_{HS} = 0.025$. Given the high value of the statistic, we conclude that the Iris dataset has a good clustering tendency.

17.4 FURTHER READING

For an excellent introduction to clustering validation see Jain and Dubes (1988); the book describes many of the external, internal, and relative measures discussed in this chapter, including clustering tendency. Other good reviews appear in Halkidi, Batistakis, and Vazirgiannis (2001) and Theodoridis and Koutroumbas (2008). For recent work on formal properties for comparing clusterings via external measures see Amigó et al. (2009) and Meilă (2007). For the silhouette plot see Rousseeuw (1987), and for gap statistic see Tibshirani, Walther, and Hastie (2001). For an overview of cluster stability methods see Luxburg (2009). A recent review of clusterability appears in Ackerman and Ben-David (2009). Overall reviews of clustering methods appear in Xu and Wunsch (2005) and Jain, Murty, and Flynn (1999). See Kriegel, Kröger, and Zimek (2009) for a review of subspace clustering methods.

Ackerman, M. and Ben-David, S. (2009). Clusterability: A theoretical study. *Proceedings of 12th International Conference on Artificial Intelligence and Statistics*, pp. 1–8.

Amigó, E., Gonzalo, J., Artiles, J., and Verdejo, F. (2009). A comparison of extrinsic clustering evaluation metrics based on formal constraints. *Information Retrieval*, 12 (4), 461–486.

Halkidi, M., Batistakis, Y., and Vazirgiannis, M. (2001). On clustering validation techniques. *Journal of Intelligent Information Systems*, 17 (2-3), 107–145.

Jain, A. K. and Dubes, R. C. (1988). *Algorithms for Clustering Data*. Upper Saddle River, NJ: Prentice-Hall.

Jain, A. K., Murty, M. N., and Flynn, P. J. (1999). Data clustering: a review. *ACM computing surveys*, 31 (3), 264–323.

Kriegel, H.-P., Kröger, P., and Zimek, A. (2009). Clustering high-dimensional data: A survey on subspace clustering, pattern-based clustering, and correlation clustering. *ACM Transactions on Knowledge Discovery from Data (TKDD)*, 3 (1), 1.

Luxburg, U. von (2009). Clustering stability: An overview. *Foundations and Trends in Machine Learning*, 2 (3), 235–274.

Meilă, M. (2007). Comparing clusterings – an information based distance. *Journal of Multivariate Analysis*, 98 (5), 873–895.

Rousseeuw, P. J. (1987). Silhouettes: A graphical aid to the interpretation and validation of cluster analysis. *Journal of Computational and Applied Mathematics*, 20, 53–65.

Theodoridis, S. and Koutroumbas, K. (2008). *Pattern Recognition*. 4th ed. San Diego: Academic Press.

Tibshirani, R., Walther, G., and Hastie, T. (2001). Estimating the number of clusters in a dataset via the Gap statistic. *Journal of the Royal Statistical Society Series B*, 63, 411–423.

Xu, R., Wunsch, D., et al. (2005). Survey of clustering algorithms. *IEEE Transactions on Neural Networks*, 16 (3), 645–678.

17.5 EXERCISES

Q1. Prove that the maximum value of the entropy measure in Eq. (17.5) is $\log k$.

Q2. Show that if $\mathcal{C}$ and $\mathcal{T}$ are independent of each other then $H(\mathcal{T}|\mathcal{C}) = H(\mathcal{T})$, and further that $H(\mathcal{C}, \mathcal{T}) = H(\mathcal{C}) + H(\mathcal{T})$.
$\mathcal{T}$ is completely determined by $\mathcal{C}$.

Q3. Show that $I(\mathcal{C}, \mathcal{T}) = H(\mathcal{C}) + H(\mathcal{T}) - H(\mathcal{T}, \mathcal{C})$.

Q4. Show that normalized mutual information in Eq. (17.8) lies in the range $[0, 1]$.

Q5. Show that the variation of information is 0 only when $\mathcal{C}$ and $\mathcal{T}$ are identical.

Q6. Prove that the maximum value of the normalized discretized Hubert statistic in Eq. (17.30) is obtained when $FN = FP = 0$, and the minimum value is obtained when $TP = TN = 0$.

Q7. Show that the Fowlkes–Mallows measure can be considered as the correlation between the pairwise indicator matrices for $\mathcal{C}$ and $\mathcal{T}$, respectively. Define $\mathbf{C}(i, j) = 1$ if $\mathbf{x}_i$ and $\mathbf{x}_j$ (with $i \neq j$) are in the same cluster, and 0 otherwise. Define $\mathbf{T}$ similarly for the ground-truth partitions. Define $\langle \mathbf{C}, \mathbf{T} \rangle = \sum_{i,j=1}^{n} \mathbf{C}_{ij} \mathbf{T}_{ij}$. Show that $FM = \frac{\langle \mathbf{C}, \mathbf{T} \rangle}{\sqrt{\langle \mathbf{T}, \mathbf{T} \rangle \langle \mathbf{C}, \mathbf{C} \rangle}}$

Q8. Show that the silhouette coefficient of a point lies in the interval $[-1, +1]$.

Q9. Show that the scatter matrix can be decomposed as $\mathbf{S} = \mathbf{S}_W + \mathbf{S}_B$, where $\mathbf{S}_W$ and $\mathbf{S}_B$ are the within-cluster and between-cluster scatter matrices.

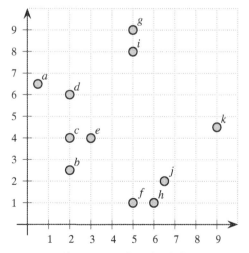

Figure 17.10. Data for Q10 .

Q10. Consider the dataset in Figure 17.10. Compute the silhouette coefficient for the point labeled c. Assume that the clusters are: $C_1 = \{a, b, c, d, e\}, C_2 = \{g, i\}, C_3 = \{f, h, j\}, C_4 = \{k\}$.

Q11. Describe how one may apply the gap statistic methodology for determining the parameters of density-based clustering algorithms, such as DBSCAN and DEN-CLUE (see Chapter 15).

PART FOUR   CLASSIFICATION

The classification task is to predict the label or class for a given unlabeled point. Formally, a classifier is a model or function M that predicts the class label $\hat{y}$ for a given input example $\mathbf{x}$, that is, $\hat{y} = M(\mathbf{x})$, where $\hat{y} \in \{c_1, c_2, \ldots, c_k\}$ and each c_i is a class label (a categorical attribute value). Classification is a *supervised learning* approach, since learning the model requires a set of points with their correct class labels, which is called a *training set*. After learning the model M, we can automatically predict the class for any new point.

This part starts with the powerful Bayes classifier, which is an example of the probabilistic classification approach (Chapter 18). It uses the Bayes theorem to predict the class as the one that maximizes the posterior probability $P(c_i|\mathbf{x})$. The main task is to estimate the joint probability density function $f(\mathbf{x})$ for each class, which is modeled via a multivariate normal distribution. One limitation of the Bayes approach is the number of parameters to be estimated which scales as $O(d^2)$. The naive Bayes classifier makes the simplifying assumption that all attributes are independent, which requires the estimation of only $O(d)$ parameters. It is, however, surprisingly effective for many datasets.

In Chapter 19, we consider the popular decision tree classifier, one of whose strengths is that it yields models that are easier to understand compared to other methods. A decision tree recursively partitions the data space into "pure" regions that contain data points from only one class, with relatively few exceptions. Next, in Chapter 20, we consider the task of finding an optimal direction that separates the points from two classes via linear discriminant analysis. It can be considered as a dimensionality reduction method that also takes the class labels into account, unlike PCA, which does not consider the class attribute. We also describe the generalization of linear to kernel discriminant analysis, which allows us to find nonlinear directions via the kernel trick.

In Chapter 21, we describe the support vector machine (SVM) approach in detail, which is one of the most effective classifiers for many different problem domains. The goal of SVMs is to find the optimal hyperplane that maximizes the *margin* between the classes. Via the kernel trick, SVMs can be used to find nonlinear boundaries, which nevertheless correspond to some linear hyperplane in some high-dimensional "nonlinear" space.

One of the important tasks in classification is to assess how good the models are. We conclude this part with Chapter 22, which presents the various methodologies for assessing classification models. We define various classification performance measures, including ROC analysis. We then describe the bootstrap and cross-validation approaches for classifier evaluation. Finally, we discuss the bias–variance tradeoff in classification, and how ensemble classifiers can help improve the variance or the bias of a classifier.

CHAPTER 18 Probabilistic Classification

Classification refers to the task of predicting a class label for a given unlabeled point. In this chapter we consider three examples of the probabilistic classification approach. The (full) Bayes classifier uses the Bayes theorem to predict the class as the one that maximizes the posterior probability. The main task is to estimate the joint probability density function for each class, which is modeled via a multivariate normal distribution. The naive Bayes classifier assumes that attributes are independent, but it is still surprisingly powerful for many applications. We also describe the nearest neighbors classifier, which uses a non-parametric approach to estimate the density.

18.1 BAYES CLASSIFIER

Let the training dataset $\mathbf{D}$ consist of n points $\mathbf{x}_i$ in a d-dimensional space, and let y_i denote the class for each point, with $y_i \in \{c_1, c_2, \ldots, c_k\}$. The Bayes classifier directly uses the Bayes theorem to predict the class for a new test instance, $\mathbf{x}$. It estimates the posterior probability $P(c_i|\mathbf{x})$ for each class c_i, and chooses the class that has the largest probability. The predicted class for $\mathbf{x}$ is given as

$$\hat{y} = \arg\max_{c_i}\{P(c_i|\mathbf{x})\} \tag{18.1}$$

The Bayes theorem allows us to invert the posterior probability in terms of the likelihood and prior probability, as follows:

$$P(c_i|\mathbf{x}) = \frac{P(\mathbf{x}|c_i) \cdot P(c_i)}{P(\mathbf{x})} \tag{18.2}$$

where $P(\mathbf{x}|c_i)$ is the *likelihood*, defined as the probability of observing $\mathbf{x}$ assuming that the true class is c_i, $P(c_i)$ is the *prior probability* of class c_i, and $P(\mathbf{x})$ is the probability of observing $\mathbf{x}$ from any of the k classes, given as

$$P(\mathbf{x}) = \sum_{j=1}^{k} P(\mathbf{x}|c_j) \cdot P(c_j)$$

Because $P(\mathbf{x})$ is fixed for a given point, Bayes rule [Eq. (18.1)] can be rewritten as

$$\hat{y} = \underset{c_i}{\arg\max}\{P(c_i|\mathbf{x})\} = \underset{c_i}{\arg\max}\left\{\frac{P(\mathbf{x}|c_i)P(c_i)}{P(\mathbf{x})}\right\}$$

$$\boxed{= \underset{c_i}{\arg\max}\big\{P(\mathbf{x}|c_i)P(c_i)\big\}} \tag{18.3}$$

In other words, the predicted class essentially depends on the likelihood of that class taking its prior probability into account.

18.1.1 Estimating the Prior Probability

To classify points, we have to estimate the likelihood and prior probabilities directly from the training dataset $\mathbf{D}$. Let $\mathbf{D}_i$ denote the subset of points in $\mathbf{D}$ that are labeled with class c_i:

$$\mathbf{D}_i = \big\{\mathbf{x}_j^T \mid \mathbf{x}_j \text{ has class } y_j = c_i\big\}$$

Let the size of the dataset $\mathbf{D}$ be given as $|\mathbf{D}| = n$, and let the size of each class-specific subset $\mathbf{D}_i$ be given as $|\mathbf{D}_i| = n_i$. The prior probability for class c_i can be estimated as follows:

$$\boxed{\hat{P}(c_i) = \frac{n_i}{n}} \tag{18.4}$$

18.1.2 Estimating the Likelihood

To estimate the likelihood $P(\mathbf{x}|c_i)$, we have to estimate the joint probability of $\mathbf{x}$ across all the d dimensions, that is, we have to estimate $P\big(\mathbf{x} = (x_1, x_2, \ldots, x_d)|c_i\big)$.

Numeric Attributes

Assuming all dimensions are numeric, we can estimate the joint probability of $\mathbf{x}$ via either a nonparametric or a parametric approach. We consider the non-parametric approach in Section 18.3.

In the parametric approach we typically assume that each class c_i is normally distributed around some mean $\boldsymbol{\mu}_i$ with a corresponding covariance matrix $\boldsymbol{\Sigma}_i$, both of which are estimated from $\mathbf{D}_i$. For class c_i, the probability density at $\mathbf{x}$ is thus given as

$$\boxed{f_i(\mathbf{x}) = f(\mathbf{x}|\boldsymbol{\mu}_i, \boldsymbol{\Sigma}_i) = \frac{1}{(\sqrt{2\pi})^d\sqrt{|\boldsymbol{\Sigma}_i|}}\exp\left\{-\frac{(\mathbf{x}-\boldsymbol{\mu}_i)^T\boldsymbol{\Sigma}_i^{-1}(\mathbf{x}-\boldsymbol{\mu}_i)}{2}\right\}} \tag{18.5}$$

Because c_i is characterized by a continuous distribution, the probability of any given point must be zero, i.e., $P(\mathbf{x}|c_i) = 0$. However, we can compute the likelihood by considering a small interval $\epsilon > 0$ centered at $\mathbf{x}$:

$$P(\mathbf{x}|c_i) = 2\epsilon \cdot f_i(\mathbf{x})$$

The posterior probability is then given as

$$P(c_i|\mathbf{x}) = \frac{2\epsilon \cdot f_i(\mathbf{x})P(c_i)}{\sum_{j=1}^{k} 2\epsilon \cdot f_j(\mathbf{x})P(c_j)} = \frac{f_i(\mathbf{x})P(c_i)}{\sum_{j=1}^{k} f_j(\mathbf{x})P(c_j)} \tag{18.6}$$

Further, because $\sum_{j=1}^{k} f_j(\mathbf{x})P(c_j)$ remains fixed for $\mathbf{x}$, we can predict the class for $\mathbf{x}$ by modifying Eq. (18.3) as follows:

$$\hat{y} = \underset{c_i}{\arg\max}\left\{ f_i(\mathbf{x})P(c_i) \right\}$$

To classify a numeric test point $\mathbf{x}$, the Bayes classifier estimates the parameters via the sample mean and sample covariance matrix. The sample mean for the class c_i can be estimated as

$$\hat{\boldsymbol{\mu}}_i = \frac{1}{n_i} \sum_{\mathbf{x}_j \in \mathbf{D}_i} \mathbf{x}_j$$

and the sample covariance matrix for each class can be estimated using Eq. (2.38), as follows

$$\widehat{\boldsymbol{\Sigma}}_i = \frac{1}{n_i} \overline{\mathbf{D}}_i^T \, \overline{\mathbf{D}}_i$$

where $\overline{\mathbf{D}}_i$ is the centered data matrix for class c_i given as $\overline{\mathbf{D}}_i = \mathbf{D}_i - \mathbf{1} \cdot \hat{\boldsymbol{\mu}}_i^T$. These values can be used to estimate the probability density in Eq. (18.5) as $\hat{f}_i(\mathbf{x}) = f(\mathbf{x}|\hat{\boldsymbol{\mu}}_i, \widehat{\boldsymbol{\Sigma}}_i)$.

Algorithm 18.1 shows the pseudo-code for the Bayes classifier. Given an input dataset $\mathbf{D}$, the method estimates the prior probability, mean and covariance matrix for each class. For testing, given a test point $\mathbf{x}$, it simply returns the class with the maximum posterior probability. The cost of training is dominated by the covariance matrix computation step which takes $O(nd^2)$ time.

Algorithm 18.1: Bayes Classifier

BAYESCLASSIFIER (D):

1 **for** $i = 1, \ldots, k$ **do**

2      $\mathbf{D}_i \leftarrow \left\{ \mathbf{x}_j^T \mid y_j = c_i, j = 1, \ldots, n \right\}$ // class-specific subsets

3      $n_i \leftarrow |\mathbf{D}_i|$ // cardinality

4      $\hat{P}(c_i) \leftarrow n_i/n$ // prior probability

5      $\hat{\boldsymbol{\mu}}_i \leftarrow \frac{1}{n_i} \sum_{\mathbf{x}_j \in \mathbf{D}_i} \mathbf{x}_j$ // mean

6      $\overline{\mathbf{D}}_i \leftarrow \mathbf{D}_i - \mathbf{1}_{n_i} \hat{\boldsymbol{\mu}}_i^T$ // centered data

7      $\widehat{\boldsymbol{\Sigma}}_i \leftarrow \frac{1}{n_i} \overline{\mathbf{D}}_i^T \, \overline{\mathbf{D}}_i$ // covariance matrix

8 **return** $\hat{P}(c_i), \hat{\boldsymbol{\mu}}_i, \widehat{\boldsymbol{\Sigma}}_i$ *for all* $i = 1, \ldots, k$

TESTING ($\mathbf{x}$ **and** $\hat{P}(c_i), \hat{\boldsymbol{\mu}}_i, \widehat{\boldsymbol{\Sigma}}_i$, **for all** $i \in [1, k]$):

9 $\hat{y} \leftarrow \underset{c_i}{\arg\max}\left\{ f(\mathbf{x}|\hat{\boldsymbol{\mu}}_i, \widehat{\boldsymbol{\Sigma}}_i) \cdot P(c_i) \right\}$

10 **return** $\hat{y}$

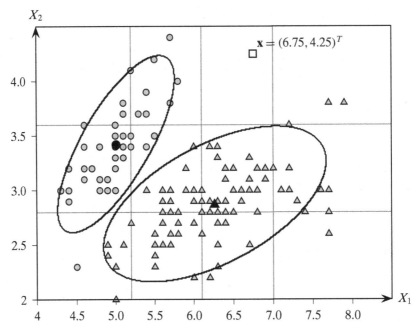

Figure 18.1. Iris data: X_1:sepal length versus X_2:sepal width. The class means are show in black; the density contours are also shown. The square represents a test point labeled **x**.

Example 18.1 (Bayes Classifier). Consider the 2-dimensional Iris data, with attributes sepal length and sepal width, shown in Figure 18.1. Class c_1, which corresponds to iris-setosa (shown as circles), has $n_1 = 50$ points, whereas the other class c_2 (shown as triangles) has $n_2 = 100$ points. The prior probabilities for the two classes are

$$\hat{P}(c_1) = \frac{n_1}{n} = \frac{50}{150} = 0.33 \qquad \hat{P}(c_2) = \frac{n_2}{n} = \frac{100}{150} = 0.67$$

The means for c_1 and c_2 (shown as black circle and triangle) are given as

$$\hat{\mu}_1 = \begin{pmatrix} 5.006 \\ 3.418 \end{pmatrix} \qquad \hat{\mu}_2 = \begin{pmatrix} 6.262 \\ 2.872 \end{pmatrix}$$

and the corresponding covariance matrices are as follows:

$$\hat{\Sigma}_1 = \begin{pmatrix} 0.1218 & 0.0983 \\ 0.0983 & 0.1423 \end{pmatrix} \qquad \hat{\Sigma}_2 = \begin{pmatrix} 0.435 & 0.1209 \\ 0.1209 & 0.1096 \end{pmatrix}$$

Figure 18.1 shows the contour or level curve (corresponding to 1% of the peak density) for the multivariate normal distribution modeling the probability density for both classes.

Let $\mathbf{x} = (6.75, 4.25)^T$ be a test point (shown as white square). The posterior probabilities for c_1 and c_2 can be computed using Eq. (18.6):

$$\hat{P}(c_1|\mathbf{x}) \propto \hat{f}(\mathbf{x}|\hat{\mu}_1, \hat{\Sigma}_1)\hat{P}(c_1) = (4.951 \times 10^{-7}) \times 0.33 = 1.634 \times 10^{-7}$$

$$\hat{P}(c_2|\mathbf{x}) \propto \hat{f}(\mathbf{x}|\hat{\mu}_2, \hat{\Sigma}_2)\hat{P}(c_2) = (2.589 \times 10^{-5}) \times 0.67 = 1.735 \times 10^{-5}$$

Because $\hat{P}(c_2|\mathbf{x}) > \hat{P}(c_1|\mathbf{x})$ the class for $\mathbf{x}$ is predicted as $\hat{y} = c_2$.

Categorical Attributes

If the attributes are categorical, the likelihood can be computed using the categorical data modeling approach presented in Chapter 3. Formally, let X_j be a categorical attribute over the domain $dom(X_j) = \{a_{j1}, a_{j2}, \ldots, a_{jm_j}\}$, that is, attribute X_j can take on m_j distinct categorical values. Each categorical attribute X_j is modeled as an m_j-dimensional multivariate Bernoulli random variable $\mathbf{X}_j$ that takes on m_j distinct vector values $\mathbf{e}_{j1}, \mathbf{e}_{j2}, \ldots, \mathbf{e}_{jm_j}$, where $\mathbf{e}_{jr}$ is the rth standard basis vector in $\mathbb{R}^{m_j}$ and corresponds to the rth value or symbol $a_{jr} \in dom(X_j)$. The entire d-dimensional dataset is modeled as the vector random variable $\mathbf{X} = (\mathbf{X}_1, \mathbf{X}_2, \ldots, \mathbf{X}_d)^T$. Let $d' = \sum_{j=1}^{d} m_j$; a categorical point $\mathbf{x} = (x_1, x_2, \ldots, x_d)^T$ is therefore represented as the d'-dimensional binary vector

$$\mathbf{v} = \begin{pmatrix} \mathbf{v}_1 \\ \vdots \\ \mathbf{v}_d \end{pmatrix} = \begin{pmatrix} \mathbf{e}_{1r_1} \\ \vdots \\ \mathbf{e}_{dr_d} \end{pmatrix}$$

where $\mathbf{v}_j = \mathbf{e}_{jr_j}$ provided $x_j = a_{jr_j}$ is the r_jth value in the domain of X_j. The probability of the categorical point $\mathbf{x}$ is obtained from the joint probability mass function (PMF) for the vector random variable $\mathbf{X}$:

$$P(\mathbf{x}|c_i) = f(\mathbf{v}|c_i) = f\left(\mathbf{X}_1 = \mathbf{e}_{1r_1}, \ldots, \mathbf{X}_d = \mathbf{e}_{dr_d} \mid c_i\right) \qquad (18.7)$$

The above joint PMF can be estimated directly from the data $\mathbf{D}_i$ for each class c_i as follows:

$$\hat{f}(\mathbf{v}|c_i) = \frac{n_i(\mathbf{v})}{n_i}$$

where $n_i(\mathbf{v})$ is the number of times the value $\mathbf{v}$ occurs in class c_i. Unfortunately, if the probability mass at the point $\mathbf{v}$ is zero for one or both classes, it would lead to a zero value for the posterior probability. To avoid zero probabilities, one approach is to introduce a small prior probability for all the possible values of the vector random variable $\mathbf{X}$. One simple approach is to assume a *pseudo-count* of 1 for each value, that is, to assume that each value of $\mathbf{X}$ occurs at least one time, and to augment this base count of 1 with the actual number of occurrences of the observed value $\mathbf{v}$ in class c_i. The adjusted probability mass at $\mathbf{v}$ is then given as

$$\hat{f}(\mathbf{v}|c_i) = \frac{n_i(\mathbf{v}) + 1}{n_i + \prod_{j=1}^{d} m_j} \qquad (18.8)$$

where $\prod_{j=1}^{d} m_j$ gives the number of possible values of $\mathbf{X}$. Extending the code in Algorithm 18.1 to incorporate categorical attributes is relatively straightforward; all that is required is to compute the joint PMF for each class using Eq. (18.8).

Example 18.2 (Bayes Classifier: Categorical Attributes). Assume that the sepal length and sepal width attributes in the Iris dataset have been discretized as shown

Table 18.1. Discretized sepal length and sepal width attributes

Bins	Domain
[4.3, 5.2]	Very Short (a_{11})
(5.2, 6.1]	Short (a_{12})
(6.1, 7.0]	Long (a_{13})
(7.0, 7.9]	Very Long (a_{14})

(a) Discretized sepal length

Bins	Domain
[2.0, 2.8]	Short (a_{21})
(2.8, 3.6]	Medium (a_{22})
(3.6, 4.4]	Long (a_{23})

(b) Discretized sepal width

Table 18.2. Class-specific empirical (joint) probability mass function

Class: c_1		X_2 Short ($\mathbf{e}_{21}$)	X_2 Medium ($\mathbf{e}_{22}$)	X_2 Long ($\mathbf{e}_{23}$)	$\hat{f}_{X_1}$
X_1	Very Short ($\mathbf{e}_{11}$)	1/50	33/50	5/50	39/50
	Short ($\mathbf{e}_{12}$)	0	3/50	8/50	11/50
	Long ($\mathbf{e}_{13}$)	0	0	0	0
	Very Long ($\mathbf{e}_{14}$)	0	0	0	0
	$\hat{f}_{X_2}$	1/50	36/50	13/50	

Class: c_2		X_2 Short ($\mathbf{e}_{21}$)	X_2 Medium ($\mathbf{e}_{22}$)	X_2 Long ($\mathbf{e}_{23}$)	$\hat{f}_{X_1}$
X_1	Very Short ($\mathbf{e}_{11}$)	6/100	0	0	6/100
	Short ($\mathbf{e}_{12}$)	24/100	15/100	0	39/100
	Long ($\mathbf{e}_{13}$)	13/100	30/100	0	43/100
	Very Long ($\mathbf{e}_{14}$)	3/100	7/100	2/100	12/100
	$\hat{f}_{X_2}$	46/100	52/100	2/100	

in Table 18.1(a) and Table 18.1(b), respectively. We have $|dom(X_1)| = m_1 = 4$ and $|dom(X_2)| = m_2 = 3$. These intervals are also illustrated in Figure 18.1: via the gray grid lines. Table 18.2 shows the empirical joint PMF for both the classes. Also, as in Example 18.1, the prior probabilities of the classes are given as $\hat{P}(c_1) = 0.33$ and $\hat{P}(c_2) = 0.67$.

Consider a test point $\mathbf{x} = (5.3, 3.0)^T$ corresponding to the categorical point (Short, Medium), which is represented as $\mathbf{v} = \left(\mathbf{e}_{12}^T \ \ \mathbf{e}_{22}^T \right)^T$. The likelihood and posterior probability for each class is given as

$$\hat{P}(\mathbf{x}|c_1) = \hat{f}(\mathbf{v}|c_1) = 3/50 = 0.06$$

$$\hat{P}(\mathbf{x}|c_2) = \hat{f}(\mathbf{v}|c_2) = 15/100 = 0.15$$

$$\hat{P}(c_1|\mathbf{x}) \propto 0.06 \times 0.33 = 0.0198$$

$$\hat{P}(c_2|\mathbf{x}) \propto 0.15 \times 0.67 = 0.1005$$

In this case the predicted class is $\hat{y} = c_2$.

On the other hand, the test point $\mathbf{x} = (6.75, 4.25)^T$ corresponding to the categorical point (Long, Long) is represented as $\mathbf{v} = \left(\mathbf{e}_{13}^T \ \ \mathbf{e}_{23}^T \right)^T$. Unfortunately the probability mass at $\mathbf{v}$ is zero for both classes. We adjust the PMF via pseudo-counts

[Eq. (18.8)]; note that the number of possible values are $m_1 \times m_2 = 4 \times 3 = 12$. The likelihood and prior probability can then be computed as

$$\hat{P}(\mathbf{x}|c_1) = \hat{f}(\mathbf{v}|c_1) = \frac{0+1}{50+12} = 1.61 \times 10^{-2}$$

$$\hat{P}(\mathbf{x}|c_2) = \hat{f}(\mathbf{v}|c_2) = \frac{0+1}{100+12} = 8.93 \times 10^{-3}$$

$$\hat{P}(c_1|\mathbf{x}) \propto (1.61 \times 10^{-2}) \times 0.33 = 5.32 \times 10^{-3}$$

$$\hat{P}(c_2|\mathbf{x}) \propto (8.93 \times 10^{-3}) \times 0.67 = 5.98 \times 10^{-3}$$

Thus, the predicted class is $\hat{y} = c_2$.

Challenges

The main problem with the Bayes classifier is the lack of enough data to reliably estimate the joint probability density or mass function, especially for high-dimensional data. For instance, for numeric attributes we have to estimate $O(d^2)$ covariances, and as the dimensionality increases, this requires us to estimate too many parameters. For categorical attributes we have to estimate the joint probability for all the possible values of $\mathbf{v}$, given as $\prod_j |\text{dom}(X_j)|$. Even if each categorical attribute has only two values, we would need to estimate the probability for 2^d values. However, because there can be at most n distinct values for $\mathbf{v}$, most of the counts will be zero. To address some of these concerns we can use reduced set of parameters in practice, as described next.

18.2 NAIVE BAYES CLASSIFIER

We saw earlier that the full Bayes approach is fraught with estimation related problems, especially with large number of dimensions. The naive Bayes approach makes the simple assumption that all the attributes are independent. This leads to a much simpler, though surprisingly effective classifier in practice. The independence assumption immediately implies that the likelihood can be decomposed into a product of dimension-wise probabilities:

$$P(\mathbf{x}|c_i) = P(x_1, x_2, \ldots, x_d|c_i) = \prod_{j=1}^{d} P(x_j|c_i) \tag{18.9}$$

Numeric Attributes

For numeric attributes we make the default assumption that each of them is normally distributed for each class c_i. Let μ_{ij} and σ_{ij}^2 denote the mean and variance for attribute

X_j, for class c_i. The likelihood for class c_i, for dimension X_j, is given as

$$P(x_j|c_i) \propto f(x_j|\mu_{ij}, \sigma_{ij}^2) = \frac{1}{\sqrt{2\pi}\sigma_{ij}} \exp\left\{-\frac{(x_j - \mu_{ij})^2}{2\sigma_{ij}^2}\right\}$$

Incidentally, the naive assumption corresponds to setting all the covariances to zero in $\mathbf{\Sigma}_i$, that is,

$$\mathbf{\Sigma}_i = \begin{pmatrix} \sigma_{i1}^2 & 0 & \cdots & 0 \\ 0 & \sigma_{i2}^2 & \cdots & 0 \\ \vdots & \vdots & \ddots & \\ 0 & 0 & \cdots & \sigma_{id}^2 \end{pmatrix}$$

This yields

$$|\mathbf{\Sigma}_i| = \det(\mathbf{\Sigma}_i) = \sigma_{i1}^2 \sigma_{i2}^2 \cdots \sigma_{id}^2 = \prod_{j=1}^{d} \sigma_{ij}^2$$

Also, we have

$$\mathbf{\Sigma}_i^{-1} = \begin{pmatrix} \frac{1}{\sigma_{i1}^2} & 0 & \cdots & 0 \\ 0 & \frac{1}{\sigma_{i2}^2} & \cdots & 0 \\ \vdots & \vdots & \ddots & \\ 0 & 0 & \cdots & \frac{1}{\sigma_{id}^2} \end{pmatrix}$$

assuming that $\sigma_{ij}^2 \neq 0$ for all j. Finally,

$$(\mathbf{x} - \boldsymbol{\mu}_i)^T \mathbf{\Sigma}_i^{-1} (\mathbf{x} - \boldsymbol{\mu}_i) = \sum_{j=1}^{d} \frac{(x_j - \mu_{ij})^2}{\sigma_{ij}^2}$$

Plugging these into Eq. (18.5) gives us

$$P(\mathbf{x}|c_i) = \frac{1}{(\sqrt{2\pi})^d \sqrt{\prod_{j=1}^{d} \sigma_{ij}^2}} \exp\left\{-\sum_{j=1}^{d} \frac{(x_j - \mu_{ij})^2}{2\sigma_{ij}^2}\right\}$$

$$= \prod_{j=1}^{d} \left(\frac{1}{\sqrt{2\pi}\sigma_{ij}} \exp\left\{-\frac{(x_j - \mu_{ij})^2}{2\sigma_{ij}^2}\right\}\right)$$

$$= \prod_{j=1}^{d} P(x_j|c_i)$$

which is equivalent to Eq. (18.9). In other words, the joint probability has been decomposed into a product of the probability along each dimension, as required by the independence assumption.

The naive Bayes classifier uses the sample mean $\hat{\boldsymbol{\mu}}_i = (\hat{\mu}_{i1}, \ldots, \hat{\mu}_{id})^T$ and a *diagonal* sample covariance matrix $\widehat{\mathbf{\Sigma}}_i = diag(\sigma_{i1}^2, \ldots, \sigma_{id}^2)$ for each class c_i. Thus, in total $2d$

Algorithm 18.2: Naive Bayes Classifier

NAIVEBAYES (D):

1 **for** $i = 1, \ldots, k$ **do**
2     $\mathbf{D}_i \leftarrow \left\{ \mathbf{x}_j^T \mid y_j = c_i, j = 1, \ldots, n \right\}$ // class-specific subsets
3     $n_i \leftarrow |\mathbf{D}_i|$ // cardinality
4     $\hat{P}(c_i) \leftarrow n_i / n$ // prior probability
5     $\hat{\boldsymbol{\mu}}_i \leftarrow \frac{1}{n_i} \sum_{\mathbf{x}_j \in \mathbf{D}_i} \mathbf{x}_j$ // mean
6     $\overline{\mathbf{D}}_i = \mathbf{D}_i - \mathbf{1} \cdot \hat{\boldsymbol{\mu}}_i^T$ // centered data for class c_i
7   **for** $j = 1, .., d$ **do** // class-specific var for jth attribute
8        $\hat{\sigma}_{ij}^2 \leftarrow \frac{1}{n_i} (\overline{X}_j^i)^T (\overline{X}_j^i)$ // variance
9     $\hat{\boldsymbol{\sigma}}_i \leftarrow \left(\hat{\sigma}_{i1}^2, \ldots, \hat{\sigma}_{id}^2 \right)^T$ // class-specific attribute variances
10 **return** $\hat{P}(c_i), \hat{\boldsymbol{\mu}}_i, \hat{\boldsymbol{\sigma}}_i$ for all $i = 1, \ldots, k$

TESTING (**x** and $\hat{P}(c_i), \hat{\boldsymbol{\mu}}_i, \hat{\boldsymbol{\sigma}}_i$, for all $i \in [1, k]$):

11 $\hat{y} \leftarrow \underset{c_i}{\arg\max} \left\{ \hat{P}(c_i) \prod_{j=1}^{d} f(x_j \mid \hat{\mu}_{ij}, \hat{\sigma}_{ij}^2) \right\}$

12 **return** $\hat{y}$

---

parameters have to be estimated, corresponding to the sample mean and sample variance for each dimension X_j.

Algorithm 18.2 shows the pseudo-code for the naive Bayes classifier. Given an input dataset **D**, the method estimates the prior probability and mean for each class. Next, it computes the variance $\hat{\sigma}_{ij}^2$ for each of the attributes X_j, with all the d variances for class c_i stored in the vector $\hat{\boldsymbol{\sigma}}_i$. The variance for attribute X_j is obtained by first centering the data for class $\mathbf{D}_i$ via $\overline{\mathbf{D}}_i = \mathbf{D}_i - \mathbf{1} \cdot \hat{\boldsymbol{\mu}}_i^T$. We denote by $\overline{X}_j^i$ the centered data for class c_i corresponding to attribute X_j. The variance is then given as $\hat{\sigma}^2 = \frac{1}{n_i} (\overline{X}_j^i)^T (\overline{X}_j^i)$.

Training the naive Bayes classifier is very fast, with $O(nd)$ computational complexity. For testing, given a test point **x**, it simply returns the class with the maximum posterior probability obtained as a product of the likelihood for each dimension and the class prior probability.

Example 18.3 (Naive Bayes). Consider Example 18.1. In the naive Bayes approach the prior probabilities $\hat{P}(c_i)$ and means $\hat{\boldsymbol{\mu}}_i$ remain unchanged. The key difference is that the covariance matrices are assumed to be diagonal, as follows:

$$\widehat{\boldsymbol{\Sigma}}_1 = \begin{pmatrix} 0.1218 & 0 \\ 0 & 0.1423 \end{pmatrix} \qquad \widehat{\boldsymbol{\Sigma}}_2 = \begin{pmatrix} 0.435 & 0 \\ 0 & 0.1096 \end{pmatrix}$$

Figure 18.2 shows the contour or level curve (corresponding to 1% of the peak density) of the multivariate normal distribution for both classes. One can see that the diagonal assumption leads to contours that are axis-parallel ellipses; contrast these with the contours in Figure 18.1 for the full Bayes classifier.

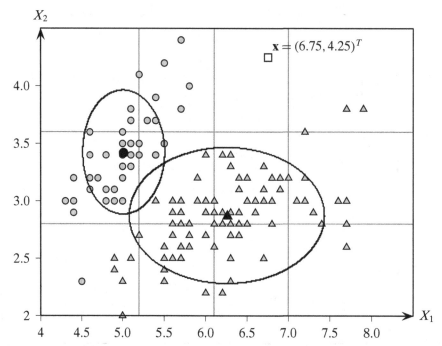

Figure 18.2. Naive Bayes: X_1:sepal length versus X_2:sepal width. The class means are shown in black; the density contours are also shown. The square represents a test point labeled **x**.

For the test point $\mathbf{x} = (6.75, 4.25)^T$, the posterior probabilities for c_1 and c_2 are as follows:

$$\hat{P}(c_1|\mathbf{x}) \propto \hat{f}(\mathbf{x}|\hat{\boldsymbol{\mu}}_1, \widehat{\boldsymbol{\Sigma}}_1) \hat{P}(c_1) = (4.014 \times 10^{-7}) \times 0.33 = 1.325 \times 10^{-7}$$

$$\hat{P}(c_2|\mathbf{x}) \propto \hat{f}(\mathbf{x}|\hat{\boldsymbol{\mu}}_2, \widehat{\boldsymbol{\Sigma}}_2) \hat{P}(c_2) = (9.585 \times 10^{-5}) \times 0.67 = 6.422 \times 10^{-5}$$

Because $\hat{P}(c_2|\mathbf{x}) > \hat{P}(c_1|\mathbf{x})$ the class for **x** is predicted as $\hat{y} = c_2$.

Categorical Attributes

The independence assumption leads to a simplification of the joint probability mass function in Eq. (18.7), which can be rewritten as

$$P(\mathbf{x}|c_i) = \prod_{j=1}^{d} P(x_j|c_i) = \prod_{j=1}^{d} f\left(\mathbf{X}_j = \mathbf{e}_{jr_j} \mid c_i\right)$$

where $f(\mathbf{X}_j = \mathbf{e}_{jr_j}|c_i)$ is the probability mass function for $\mathbf{X}_j$, which can be estimated from $\mathbf{D}_i$ as follows:

$$\hat{f}(\mathbf{v}_j|c_i) = \frac{n_i(\mathbf{v}_j)}{n_i}$$

where $n_i(\mathbf{v}_j)$ is the observed frequency of the value $\mathbf{v}_j = \mathbf{e}_j r_j$ corresponding to the r_jth categorical value a_{jr_j} for the attribute X_j for class c_i. As in the full Bayes case, if the count is zero, we can use the pseudo-count method to obtain a prior probability. The adjusted estimates with pseudo-counts are given as

$$\hat{f}(\mathbf{v}_j | c_i) = \frac{n_i(\mathbf{v}_j) + 1}{n_i + m_j}$$

where $m_j = |dom(X_j)|$. Extending the code in Algorithm 18.2 to incorporate categorical attributes is straightforward.

Example 18.4. Continuing Example 18.2, the class-specific PMF for each discretized attribute is shown in Table 18.2. In particular, these correspond to the row and column marginal probabilities $\hat{f}_{X_1}$ and $\hat{f}_{X_2}$, respectively.

The test point $\mathbf{x} = (6.75, 4.25)$, corresponding to (Long, Long) or $\mathbf{v} = (\mathbf{e}_{13}, \mathbf{e}_{23})$, is classified as follows:

$$\hat{P}(\mathbf{v}|c_1) = \hat{P}(\mathbf{e}_{13}|c_1) \cdot \hat{P}(\mathbf{e}_{23}|c_1) = \left(\frac{0+1}{50+4}\right) \cdot \left(\frac{13}{50}\right) = 4.81 \times 10^{-3}$$

$$\hat{P}(\mathbf{v}|c_2) = \hat{P}(\mathbf{e}_{13}|c_2) \cdot \hat{P}(\mathbf{e}_{23}|c_2) = \left(\frac{43}{100}\right) \cdot \left(\frac{2}{100}\right) = 8.60 \times 10^{-3}$$

$$\hat{P}(c_1|\mathbf{v}) \propto (4.81 \times 10^{-3}) \times 0.33 = 1.59 \times 10^{-3}$$

$$\hat{P}(c_2|\mathbf{v}) \propto (8.6 \times 10^{-3}) \times 0.67 = 5.76 \times 10^{-3}$$

Thus, the predicted class is $\hat{y} = c_2$.

18.3 *K* NEAREST NEIGHBORS CLASSIFIER

In the preceding sections we considered a parametric approach for estimating the likelihood $P(\mathbf{x}|c_i)$. In this section, we consider a non-parametric approach, which does not make any assumptions about the underlying joint probability density function. Instead, it directly uses the data sample to estimate the density, for example, using the density estimation methods from Chapter 15. We illustrate the non-parametric approach using nearest neighbors density estimation from Section 15.2.3, which leads to the *K nearest neighbors* (KNN) classifier.

Let $\mathbf{D}$ be a training dataset comprising n points $\mathbf{x}_i \in \mathbb{R}^d$, and let $\mathbf{D}_i$ denote the subset of points in $\mathbf{D}$ that are labeled with class c_i, with $n_i = |\mathbf{D}_i|$. Given a test point $\mathbf{x} \in \mathbb{R}^d$, and K, the number of neighbors to consider, let r denote the distance from $\mathbf{x}$ to its Kth nearest neighbor in $\mathbf{D}$.

Consider the d-dimensional hyperball of radius r around the test point $\mathbf{x}$, defined as

$$B_d(\mathbf{x}, r) = \left\{ \mathbf{x}_i \in \mathbf{D} \mid \|\mathbf{x} - \mathbf{x}_i\| \leq r \right\}$$

Here $\|\mathbf{x} - \mathbf{x}_i\|$ is the Euclidean distance between $\mathbf{x}$ and $\mathbf{x}_i$. However, other distance metrics can also be used. We assume that $|B_d(\mathbf{x}, r)| = K$.

Let K_i denote the number of points among the K nearest neighbors of $\mathbf{x}$ that are labeled with class c_i, that is

$$K_i = \{\mathbf{x}_j \in B_d(\mathbf{x}, r) \mid y_j = c_i\}$$

The class conditional probability density at $\mathbf{x}$ can be estimated as the fraction of points from class c_i that lie within the hyperball divided by its volume, that is

$$\hat{f}(\mathbf{x}|c_i) = \frac{K_i/n_i}{V} = \frac{K_i}{n_i V} \tag{18.10}$$

where $V = \text{vol}(B_d(\mathbf{x}, r))$ is the volume of the d-dimensional hyperball [Eq. (6.10)].

Using Eq. (18.6), the posterior probability $P(c_i|\mathbf{x})$ can be estimated as

$$P(c_i|\mathbf{x}) = \frac{\hat{f}(\mathbf{x}|c_i)\hat{P}(c_i)}{\sum_{j=1}^{k} \hat{f}(\mathbf{x}|c_j)\hat{P}(c_j)}$$

However, because $\hat{P}(c_i) = \frac{n_i}{n}$, we have

$$\hat{f}(\mathbf{x}|c_i)\hat{P}(c_i) = \frac{K_i}{n_i V} \cdot \frac{n_i}{n} = \frac{K_i}{nV}$$

Thus the posterior probability is given as

$$P(c_i|\mathbf{x}) = \frac{\frac{K_i}{nV}}{\sum_{j=1}^{k} \frac{K_j}{nV}} = \frac{K_i}{K}$$

Finally, the predicted class for $\mathbf{x}$ is

$$\hat{y} = \arg\max_{c_i}\{P(c_i|\mathbf{x})\} = \arg\max_{c_i}\left\{\frac{K_i}{K}\right\} = \arg\max_{c_i}\{K_i\} \tag{18.11}$$

Because K is fixed, the KNN classifier predicts the class of $\mathbf{x}$ as the majority class among its K nearest neighbors.

Example 18.5. Consider the 2D Iris dataset shown in Figure 18.3. The two classes are: c_1 (circles) with $n_1 = 50$ points and c_2 (triangles) with $n_2 = 100$ points.

Let us classify the test point $\mathbf{x} = (6.75, 4.25)^T$ using its $K = 5$ nearest neighbors. The distance from $\mathbf{x}$ to its 5th nearest neighbor, namely $(6.2, 3.4)^T$, is given as $r = \sqrt{1.025} = 1.012$. The enclosing ball or circle of radius r is shown in the figure. It encompasses $K_1 = 1$ point from class c_1 and $K_2 = 4$ points from class c_2. Therefore, the predicted class for $\mathbf{x}$ is $\hat{y} = c_2$.

18.4 FURTHER READING

The naive Bayes classifier is surprisingly effective even though the independence assumption is usually violated in real datasets. Comparison of the naive Bayes

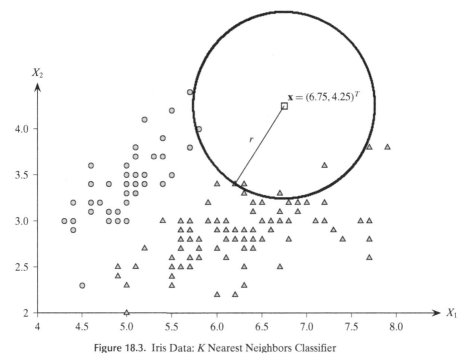

Figure 18.3. Iris Data: *K* Nearest Neighbors Classifier

classifier against other classification approaches and reasons for why is works well have appeared in Langley, Iba, and Thompson (1992), Domingos and Pazzani (1997), Zhang (2005), and Hand and Yu (2001) and Rish (2001). For the long history of naive Bayes in information retrieval see Lewis (1998). The *K* nearest neighbor classification approach was first proposed in Fix and Hodges (1951).

Domingos, P. and Pazzani, M. (1997). On the optimality of the simple Bayesian classifier under zero-one loss. *Machine Learning*, 29 (2-3), 103–130.

Fix, E. and Hodges Jr., J. L. (1951). Discriminatory analysis–Nonparametric discrimination: Consistency properties. *USAF School of Aviation Medicine, Randolph Field, TX, Project 21-49-004, Report 4, Contract AF41(128)-31.*

Hand, D. J. and Yu, K. (2001). Idiot's Bayes-not so stupid after all? *International Statistical Review*, 69 (3), 385–398.

Langley, P., Iba, W., and Thompson, K. (1992). An analysis of Bayesian classifiers. *Proceedings of the National Conference on Artificial Intelligence*. Palo Alto, CA: AAAI Press, pp. 223–228.

Lewis, D. D. (1998). Naive (Bayes) at forty: The independence assumption in information retrieval. *Proceedings of the 10th European Conference on Machine Learning*. New York: Springer Science + Business Media, pp. 4–15.

Rish, I. (2001). An empirical study of the naive Bayes classifier. *Proceedings of the IJCAI Workshop on Empirical Methods in Artificial Intelligence*, pp. 41–46.

Zhang, H. (2005). Exploring conditions for the optimality of naive Bayes. *International Journal of Pattern Recognition and Artificial Intelligence*, 19 (02), 183–198.

18.5 EXERCISES

Q1. Consider the dataset in Table 18.3. Classify the new point: (Age=23, Car=truck) via the full and naive Bayes approach. You may assume that the domain of Car is given as {sports, vintage, suv, truck}.

Table 18.3. Data for Q1

	X_1: Age	X_2: Car	Y: Class
$\mathbf{x}_1^T$	25	sports	L
$\mathbf{x}_2^T$	20	vintage	H
$\mathbf{x}_3^T$	25	sports	L
$\mathbf{x}_4^T$	45	suv	H
$\mathbf{x}_5^T$	20	sports	H
$\mathbf{x}_6^T$	25	suv	H

Table 18.4. Data for Q2

	a_1	a_2	a_3	Class
$\mathbf{x}_1^T$	T	T	5.0	Y
$\mathbf{x}_2^T$	T	T	7.0	Y
$\mathbf{x}_3^T$	T	F	8.0	N
$\mathbf{x}_4^T$	F	F	3.0	Y
$\mathbf{x}_5^T$	F	T	7.0	N
$\mathbf{x}_6^T$	F	T	4.0	N
$\mathbf{x}_7^T$	F	F	5.0	N
$\mathbf{x}_8^T$	T	F	6.0	Y
$\mathbf{x}_9^T$	F	T	1.0	N

Q2. Given the dataset in Table 18.4, use the naive Bayes classifier to classify the new point $(T, F, 1.0)$.

Q3. Consider the class means and covariance matrices for classes c_1 and c_2:

$$\boldsymbol{\mu}_1 = (1, 3) \qquad\qquad\qquad \boldsymbol{\mu}_2 = (5, 5)$$

$$\boldsymbol{\Sigma}_1 = \begin{pmatrix} 5 & 3 \\ 3 & 2 \end{pmatrix} \qquad\qquad\qquad \boldsymbol{\Sigma}_2 = \begin{pmatrix} 2 & 0 \\ 0 & 1 \end{pmatrix}$$

Classify the point $(3, 4)^T$ via the (full) Bayesian approach, assuming normally distributed classes, and $P(c_1) = P(c_2) = 0.5$. Show all steps. Recall that the inverse of a 2×2 matrix $A = \begin{pmatrix} a & b \\ c & d \end{pmatrix}$ is given as $A^{-1} = \frac{1}{\det(A)} \begin{pmatrix} d & -b \\ -c & a \end{pmatrix}$.

CHAPTER 19

Decision Tree Classifier

Let the training dataset $\mathbf{D}$ consist of n points $\mathbf{x}_i$ in a d-dimensional space, with y_i being the corresponding class label. We assume that the dimensions or the attributes X_j are numeric or categorical, and that there are k distinct classes, so that $y_i \in \{c_1, c_2, \ldots, c_k\}$. A decision tree classifier is a recursive, partition-based tree model that predicts the class $\hat{y}_i$ for each point $\mathbf{x}_i$. Let $\mathcal{R}$ denote the data space that encompasses the set of input points $\mathbf{D}$. A decision tree uses an axis-parallel hyperplane to split the data space $\mathcal{R}$ into two resulting half-spaces or regions, say $\mathcal{R}_1$ and $\mathcal{R}_2$, which also induces a partition of the input points into $\mathbf{D}_1$ and $\mathbf{D}_2$, respectively. Each of these regions is recursively split via axis-parallel hyperplanes until the points within an induced partition are relatively pure in terms of their class labels, that is, most of the points belong to the same class. The resulting hierarchy of split decisions constitutes the decision tree model, with the leaf nodes labeled with the majority class among points in those regions. To classify a new *test* point we have to recursively evaluate which half-space it belongs to until we reach a leaf node in the decision tree, at which point we predict its class as the label of the leaf.

Example 19.1. Consider the Iris dataset shown in Figure 19.1(a), which plots the attributes sepal length (X_1) and sepal width (X_2). The classification task is to discriminate between c_1, corresponding to iris-setosa (in circles), and c_2, corresponding to the other two types of Irises (in triangles). The input dataset $\mathbf{D}$ has $n = 150$ points that lie in the data space which is given as the rectangle, $\mathcal{R} = range(X_1) \times range(X_2) = [4.3, 7.9] \times [2.0, 4.4]$.

The recursive partitioning of the space $\mathcal{R}$ via axis-parallel hyperplanes is illustrated in Figure 19.1a. In two dimensions a hyperplane is simply a line. The first split corresponds to hyperplane h_0 shown as a black line. The resulting left and right half-spaces are further split via hyperplanes h_2 and h_3, respectively (shown as gray lines). The bottom half-space for h_2 is further split via h_4, and the top half-space for h_3 is split via h_5; these third level hyperplanes, h_4 and h_5, are shown as dashed lines. The set of hyperplanes and the set of six leaf regions, namely $\mathcal{R}_1, \ldots, \mathcal{R}_6$, constitute the decision tree model. Note also the induced partitioning of the input points into these six regions.

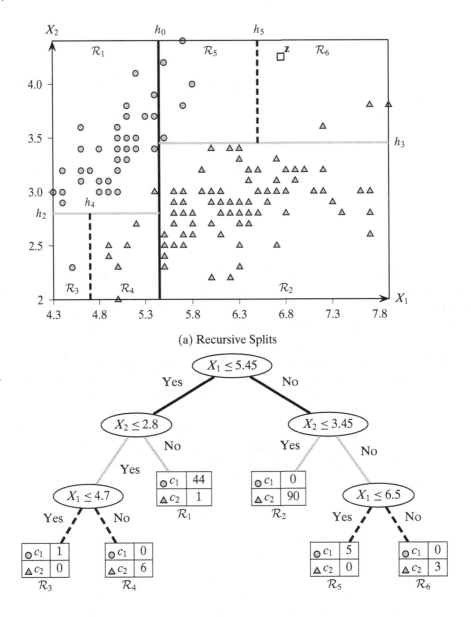

(a) Recursive Splits

(b) Decision Tree

Figure 19.1. Decision trees: recursive partitioning via axis-parallel hyperplanes.

Consider the test point $\mathbf{z} = (6.75, 4.25)^T$ (shown as a white square). To predict its class, the decision tree first checks which side of h_0 it lies in. Because the point lies in the right half-space, the decision tree next checks h_3 to determine that $\mathbf{z}$ is in the top half-space. Finally, we check and find that $\mathbf{z}$ is in the right half-space of h_5, and we reach the leaf region $\mathcal{R}_6$. The predicted class is c_2, as that leaf region has all points (three of them) with class c_2 (triangles).

19.1 DECISION TREES

A decision tree consists of internal nodes that represent the decisions corresponding to the hyperplanes or split points (i.e., which half-space a given point lies in), and leaf nodes that represent regions or partitions of the data space, which are labeled with the majority class. A region is characterized by the subset of data points that lie in that region.

Axis-Parallel Hyperplanes

A hyperplane $h(\mathbf{x})$ is defined as the set of all points $\mathbf{x}$ that satisfy the following equation

$$h(\mathbf{x}): \mathbf{w}^T\mathbf{x} + b = 0 \tag{19.1}$$

Here $\mathbf{w} \in \mathbb{R}^d$ is a *weight vector* that is normal to the hyperplane, and b is the offset of the hyperplane from the origin. A decision tree considers only *axis-parallel hyperplanes*, that is, the weight vector must be parallel to one of the original dimensions or axes X_j. Put differently, the weight vector $\mathbf{w}$ is restricted *a priori* to one of the standard basis vectors $\{\mathbf{e}_1, \mathbf{e}_2, \ldots, \mathbf{e}_d\}$, where $\mathbf{e}_i \in \mathbb{R}^d$ has a 1 for the jth dimension, and 0 for all other dimensions. If $\mathbf{x} = (x_1, x_2, \ldots, x_d)^T$ and assuming $\mathbf{w} = \mathbf{e}_j$, we can rewrite Eq. (19.1) as

$$h(\mathbf{x}): \mathbf{e}_j^T\mathbf{x} + b = 0, \text{ which implies that}$$

$$h(\mathbf{x}): x_j + b = 0$$

where the choice of the offset b yields different hyperplanes along dimension X_j.

Split Points

A hyperplane specifies a decision or *split point* because it splits the data space $\mathcal{R}$ into two half-spaces. All points $\mathbf{x}$ such that $h(\mathbf{x}) \le 0$ are on the hyperplane or to one side of the hyperplane, whereas all points such that $h(\mathbf{x}) > 0$ are on the other side. The split point associated with an axis-parallel hyperplane can be written as $h(\mathbf{x}) \le 0$, which implies that $x_i + b \le 0$, or $x_i \le -b$. Because x_i is some value from dimension X_j and the offset b can be chosen to be any value, the generic form of a split point for a numeric attribute X_j is given as

$$X_j \le v$$

where $v = -b$ is some value in the domain of attribute X_j. The decision or split point $X_j \le v$ thus splits the input data space $\mathcal{R}$ into two regions $\mathcal{R}_Y$ and $\mathcal{R}_N$, which denote the set of *all possible points* that satisfy the decision and those that do not.

Data Partition

Each split of $\mathcal{R}$ into $\mathcal{R}_Y$ and $\mathcal{R}_N$ also induces a binary partition of the corresponding input data points $\mathbf{D}$. That is, a split point of the form $X_j \le v$ induces the data partition

$$\mathbf{D}_Y = \{\mathbf{x}^T \mid \mathbf{x} \in \mathbf{D}, x_j \le v\}$$

$$\mathbf{D}_N = \{\mathbf{x}^T \mid \mathbf{x} \in \mathbf{D}, x_j > v\}$$

where $\mathbf{D}_Y$ is the subset of data points that lie in region $\mathcal{R}_Y$ and $\mathbf{D}_N$ is the subset of input points that line in $\mathcal{R}_N$.

Purity

The purity of a region $\mathcal{R}_j$ is defined in terms of the mixture of classes for points in the corresponding data partition $\mathbf{D}_j$. Formally, purity is the fraction of points with the majority label in $\mathbf{D}_j$, that is,

$$
purity(\mathbf{D}_j) = \max_i \left\{ \frac{n_{ji}}{n_j} \right\} \tag{19.2}
$$

where $n_j = |\mathbf{D}_j|$ is the total number of data points in the region $\mathcal{R}_j$, and n_{ji} is the number of points in $\mathbf{D}_j$ with class label c_i.

Example 19.2. Figure 19.1(b) shows the resulting decision tree that corresponds to the recursive partitioning of the space via axis-parallel hyperplanes illustrated in Figure 19.1(a). The recursive splitting terminates when appropriate stopping conditions are met, usually taking into account the size and purity of the regions. In this example, we use a size threshold of 5 and a purity threshold of 0.95. That is, a region will be split further only if the number of points is more than five and the purity is less than 0.95.

The very first hyperplane to be considered is $h_1(\mathbf{x}): x_1 - 5.45 = 0$ which corresponds to the decision

$$X_1 \le 5.45$$

at the root of the decision tree. The two resulting half-spaces are recursively split into smaller half-spaces.

For example, the region $X_1 \le 5.45$ is further split using the hyperplane $h_2(\mathbf{x})$: $x_2 - 2.8 = 0$ corresponding to the decision

$$X_2 \le 2.8$$

which forms the left child of the root. Notice how this hyperplane is restricted only to the region $X_1 \le 5.45$. This is because each region is considered independently after the split, as if it were a separate dataset. There are seven points that satisfy the condition $X_2 \le 2.8$, out of which one is from class c_1 (circle) and six are from class c_2 (triangles). The purity of this region is therefore $6/7 = 0.857$. Because the region has more than five points, and its purity is less than 0.95, it is further split via the hyperplane $h_4(\mathbf{x}): x_1 - 4.7 = 0$ yielding the left-most decision node

$$X_1 \le 4.7$$

in the decision tree shown in Figure 19.1(b).

Returning back to the right half-space corresponding to h_2, namely the region $X_2 > 2.8$, it has 45 points, of which only one is a triangle. The size of the region is 45, but the purity is $44/45 = 0.98$. Because the region exceeds the purity threshold it is not split further. Instead, it becomes a leaf node in the decision tree, and the entire region ($\mathcal{R}_1$) is labeled with the majority class c_1. The frequency for each class is also noted at a leaf node so that the potential error rate for that leaf can be computed. For example, we can expect that the probability of misclassification in region $\mathcal{R}_1$ is $1/45 = 0.022$, which is the error rate for that leaf.

Categorical Attributes

In addition to numeric attributes, a decision tree can also handle categorical data. For a categorical attribute X_j, the split points or decisions are of the $X_j \in V$, where $V \subset dom(X_j)$, and $dom(X_j)$ denotes the domain for X_j. Intuitively, this split can be considered to be the categorical analog of a hyperplane. It results in two "half-spaces," one region $\mathcal{R}_Y$ consisting of points $\mathbf{x}$ that satisfy the condition $x_i \in V$, and the other region $\mathcal{R}_N$ comprising points that satisfy the condition $x_i \notin V$.

Decision Rules

One of the advantages of decision trees is that they produce models that are relatively easy to interpret. In particular, a tree can be read as set of decision rules, with each rule's antecedent comprising the decisions on the internal nodes along a path to a leaf, and its consequent being the label of the leaf node. Further, because the regions are all disjoint and cover the entire space, the set of rules can be interpreted as a set of alternatives or disjunctions.

Example 19.3. Consider the decision tree in Figure 19.1(b). It can be interpreted as the following set of disjunctive rules, one per leaf region $\mathcal{R}_i$

$\mathcal{R}_3$: If $X_1 \leq 5.45$ and $X_2 \leq 2.8$ and $X_1 \leq 4.7$, then class is c_1, or

$\mathcal{R}_4$: If $X_1 \leq 5.45$ and $X_2 \leq 2.8$ and $X_1 > 4.7$, then class is c_2, or

$\mathcal{R}_1$: If $X_1 \leq 5.45$ and $X_2 > 2.8$, then class is c_1, or

$\mathcal{R}_2$: If $X_1 > 5.45$ and $X_2 \leq 3.45$, then class is c_2, or

$\mathcal{R}_5$: If $X_1 > 5.45$ and $X_2 > 3.45$ and $X_1 \leq 6.5$, then class is c_1, or

$\mathcal{R}_6$: If $X_1 > 5.45$ and $X_2 > 3.45$ and $X_1 > 6.5$, then class is c_2

19.2 DECISION TREE ALGORITHM

The pseudo-code for decision tree model construction is shown in Algorithm 19.1. It takes as input a training dataset $\mathbf{D}$, and two parameters η and π, where η is the leaf size and π the leaf purity threshold. Different split points are evaluated for each attribute in $\mathbf{D}$. Numeric decisions are of the form $X_j \leq v$ for some value v in the value range for attribute X_j, and categorical decisions are of the form $X_j \in V$ for some subset of values in the domain of X_j. The best split point is chosen to partition the data into two subsets, $\mathbf{D}_Y$ and $\mathbf{D}_N$, where $\mathbf{D}_Y$ corresponds to all points $\mathbf{x} \in \mathbf{D}$ that satisfy the

---

Algorithm 19.1: Decision Tree Algorithm

DECISIONTREE ($\mathbf{D}, \eta, \pi$):

1 $n \leftarrow |\mathbf{D}|$ // partition size
2 $n_i \leftarrow |\{\mathbf{x}_j | \mathbf{x}_j \in \mathbf{D}, y_j = c_i\}|$ // size of class c_i
3 $purity(\mathbf{D}) \leftarrow \max_i \left\{ \frac{n_i}{n} \right\}$
4 **if** $n \leq \eta$ *or* $purity(\mathbf{D}) \geq \pi$ **then** // stopping condition
5 $\quad \mid \quad c^* \leftarrow \arg\max_{c_i} \left\{ \frac{n_i}{n} \right\}$ // majority class
6 $\quad \mid \quad$ create leaf node, and label it with class c^*
7 $\quad \mid \quad$ **return**

8 $(split\ point^*, score^*) \leftarrow (\emptyset, 0)$ // initialize best split point
9 **foreach** *(attribute X_j)* **do**
10 $\quad \mid \quad$ **if** *(X_j is numeric)* **then**
11 $\quad \mid \quad \quad \mid \quad (v, score) \leftarrow$ EVALUATE-NUMERIC-ATTRIBUTE$(\mathbf{D}, X_j)$
12 $\quad \mid \quad \quad \mid \quad$ **if** $score > score^*$ **then** $(split\ point^*, score^*) \leftarrow (X_j \leq v, score)$
13 $\quad \mid \quad$ **else if** *(X_j is categorical)* **then**
14 $\quad \mid \quad \quad \mid \quad (V, score) \leftarrow$ EVALUATE-CATEGORICAL-ATTRIBUTE$(\mathbf{D}, X_j)$
15 $\quad \mid \quad \quad \mid \quad$ **if** $score > score^*$ **then** $(split\ point^*, score^*) \leftarrow (X_j \in V, score)$

   // partition $\mathbf{D}$ into $\mathbf{D}_Y$ and $\mathbf{D}_N$ using *split point**, and call
   recursively
16 $\mathbf{D}_Y \leftarrow \{\mathbf{x}^T \mid \mathbf{x} \in \mathbf{D}$ satisfies *split point**$\}$
17 $\mathbf{D}_N \leftarrow \{\mathbf{x}^T \mid \mathbf{x} \in \mathbf{D}$ does not satisfy *split point**$\}$
18 create internal node *split point**, with two child nodes, $\mathbf{D}_Y$ and $\mathbf{D}_N$
19 DECISIONTREE$(\mathbf{D}_Y)$; DECISIONTREE$(\mathbf{D}_N)$

---

split decision, and $\mathbf{D}_N$ corresponds to all points that do not satisfy the split decision. The decision tree method is then called recursively on $\mathbf{D}_Y$ and $\mathbf{D}_N$. A number of stopping conditions can be used to stop the recursive partitioning process. The simplest condition is based on the size of the partition $\mathbf{D}$. If the number of points n in $\mathbf{D}$ drops below the user-specified size threshold η, then we stop the partitioning process and make $\mathbf{D}$ a leaf. This condition prevents over-fitting the model to the training set, by avoiding to model very small subsets of the data. Size alone is not sufficient because if the partition is already pure then it does not make sense to split it further. Thus, the recursive partitioning is also terminated if the purity of $\mathbf{D}$ is above the purity threshold π. Details of how the split points are evaluated and chosen are given next.

19.2.1 Split Point Evaluation Measures

Given a split point of the form $X_j \leq v$ or $X_j \in V$ for a numeric or categorical attribute, respectively, we need an objective criterion for scoring the split point. Intuitively, we want to select a split point that gives the best separation or discrimination between the different class labels.

Entropy

Entropy, in general, measures the amount of disorder or uncertainty in a system. In the classification setting, a partition has lower entropy (or low disorder) if it is relatively pure, that is, if most of the points have the same label. On the other hand, a partition has higher entropy (or more disorder) if the class labels are mixed, and there is no majority class as such.

The entropy of a set of labeled points $\mathbf{D}$ is defined as follows:

$$H(\mathbf{D}) = -\sum_{i=1}^{k} P(c_i|\mathbf{D}) \log_2 P(c_i|\mathbf{D}) \tag{19.3}$$

where $P(c_i|\mathbf{D})$ is the probability of class c_i in $\mathbf{D}$, and k is the number of classes. If a region is pure, that is, has points from the same class, then the entropy is zero. On the other hand, if the classes are all mixed up, and each appears with equal probability $P(c_i|\mathbf{D}) = \frac{1}{k}$, then the entropy has the highest value, $H(\mathbf{D}) = \log_2 k$.

Assume that a split point partitions $\mathbf{D}$ into $\mathbf{D}_Y$ and $\mathbf{D}_N$. Define the *split entropy* as the weighted entropy of each of the resulting partitions, given as

$$H(\mathbf{D}_Y, \mathbf{D}_N) = \frac{n_Y}{n} H(\mathbf{D}_Y) + \frac{n_N}{n} H(\mathbf{D}_N) \tag{19.4}$$

where $n = |\mathbf{D}|$ is the number of points in $\mathbf{D}$, and $n_Y = |\mathbf{D}_Y|$ and $n_N = |\mathbf{D}_N|$ are the number of points in $\mathbf{D}_Y$ and $\mathbf{D}_N$.

To see if the split point results in a reduced overall entropy, we define the *information gain* for a given split point as follows:

$$Gain(\mathbf{D}, \mathbf{D}_Y, \mathbf{D}_N) = H(\mathbf{D}) - H(\mathbf{D}_Y, \mathbf{D}_N) \tag{19.5}$$

The higher the information gain, the more the reduction in entropy, and the better the split point. Thus, given split points and their corresponding partitions, we can score each split point and choose the one that gives the highest information gain.

Gini Index

Another common measure to gauge the purity of a split point is the *Gini index*, defined as follows:

$$G(\mathbf{D}) = 1 - \sum_{i=1}^{k} P(c_i|\mathbf{D})^2 \tag{19.6}$$

If the partition is pure, then the probability of the majority class is 1 and the probability of all other classes is 0, and thus, the Gini index is 0. On the other hand, when each class is equally represented, with probability $P(c_i|\mathbf{D}) = \frac{1}{k}$, then the Gini index has value $\frac{k-1}{k}$. Thus, higher values of the Gini index indicate more disorder, and lower values indicate more order in terms of the class labels.

We can compute the weighted Gini index of a split point as follows:

$$G(\mathbf{D}_Y, \mathbf{D}_N) = \frac{n_Y}{n} G(\mathbf{D}_Y) + \frac{n_N}{n} G(\mathbf{D}_N)$$

where n, n_Y, and n_N denote the number of points in regions $\mathbf{D}$, $\mathbf{D}_Y$, and $\mathbf{D}_N$, respectively. The lower the Gini index value, the better the split point.

Other measures can also be used instead of entropy and Gini index to evaluate the splits. For example, the Classification And Regression Trees (CART) measure is given as

$$CART(\mathbf{D}_Y, \mathbf{D}_N) = 2\frac{n_Y}{n}\frac{n_N}{n}\sum_{i=1}^{k}\left|P(c_i|\mathbf{D}_Y) - P(c_i|\mathbf{D}_N)\right| \tag{19.7}$$

This measure thus prefers a split point that maximizes the difference between the class probability mass function for the two partitions; the higher the CART measure, the better the split point.

19.2.2 Evaluating Split Points

All of the split point evaluation measures, such as entropy [Eq. (19.3)], Gini-index [Eq. (19.6)], and CART [Eq. (19.7)], considered in the preceding section depend on the class probability mass function (PMF) for $\mathbf{D}$, namely, $P(c_i|\mathbf{D})$, and the class PMFs for the resulting partitions $\mathbf{D}_Y$ and $\mathbf{D}_N$, namely $P(c_i|\mathbf{D}_Y)$ and $P(c_i|\mathbf{D}_N)$. Note that we have to compute the class PMFs for all possible split points; scoring each of them independently would result in significant computational overhead. Instead, one can incrementally compute the PMFs as described in the following paragraphs.

Numeric Attributes
If X is a numeric attribute, we have to evaluate split points of the form $X \le v$. Even if we restrict v to lie within the value range of attribute X, there are still an infinite number of choices for v. One reasonable approach is to consider only the midpoints between two successive distinct values for X in the sample $\mathbf{D}$. This is because split points of the form $X \le v$, for $v \in [x_a, x_b)$, where x_a and x_b are two successive distinct values of X in $\mathbf{D}$, produce the same partitioning of $\mathbf{D}$ into $\mathbf{D}_Y$ and $\mathbf{D}_N$, and thus yield the same scores. Because there can be at most n distinct values for X, there are at most $n-1$ midpoint values to consider.

Let $\{v_1, \ldots, v_m\}$ denote the set of all such midpoints, such that $v_1 < v_2 < \cdots < v_m$. For each split point $X \le v$, we have to estimate the class PMFs:

$$\hat{P}(c_i|\mathbf{D}_Y) = \hat{P}(c_i|X \le v) \tag{19.8}$$

$$\hat{P}(c_i|\mathbf{D}_N) = \hat{P}(c_i|X > v) \tag{19.9}$$

Let $I()$ be an indicator variable that takes on the value 1 only when its argument is true, and is 0 otherwise. Using the Bayes theorem, we have

$$\hat{P}(c_i|X \le v) = \frac{\hat{P}(X \le v|c_i)\hat{P}(c_i)}{\hat{P}(X \le v)} = \frac{\hat{P}(X \le v|c_i)\hat{P}(c_i)}{\sum_{j=1}^{k}\hat{P}(X \le v|c_j)\hat{P}(c_j)} \tag{19.10}$$

The prior probability for each class in $\mathbf{D}$ can be estimated as follows:

$$\hat{P}(c_i) = \frac{1}{n}\sum_{j=1}^{n}I(y_j = c_i) = \frac{n_i}{n} \tag{19.11}$$

where y_j is the class for point $\mathbf{x}_j$, $n = |\mathbf{D}|$ is the total number of points, and n_i is the number of points in $\mathbf{D}$ with class c_i. Define N_{vi} as the number of points $x_j \le v$ with class c_i, where x_j is the value of data point $\mathbf{x}_j$ for the attribute X, given as

$$N_{vi} = \sum_{j=1}^{n} I(x_j \le v \text{ and } y_j = c_i) \tag{19.12}$$

We can then estimate $P(X \le v | c_i)$ as follows:

$$\hat{P}(X \le v | c_i) = \frac{\hat{P}(X \le v \text{ and } c_i)}{\hat{P}(c_i)} = \left(\frac{1}{n} \sum_{j=1}^{n} I(x_j \le v \text{ and } y_j = c_i) \right) \Big/ (n_i / n)$$

$$= \frac{N_{vi}}{n_i} \tag{19.13}$$

Plugging Eqs. (19.11) and (19.13) into Eq. (19.10), and using Eq. (19.8), we have

$$\hat{P}(c_i | \mathbf{D}_Y) = \hat{P}(c_i | X \le v) = \frac{N_{vi}}{\sum_{j=1}^{k} N_{vj}} \tag{19.14}$$

We can estimate $\hat{P}(X > v | c_i)$ as follows:

$$\hat{P}(X > v | c_i) = 1 - \hat{P}(X \le v | c_i) = 1 - \frac{N_{vi}}{n_i} = \frac{n_i - N_{vi}}{n_i} \tag{19.15}$$

Using Eqs. (19.11) and (19.15), the class PMF $\hat{P}(c_i | \mathbf{D}_N)$ is given as

$$\hat{P}(c_i | \mathbf{D}_N) = \hat{P}(c_i | X > v) = \frac{\hat{P}(X > v | c_i) \hat{P}(c_i)}{\sum_{j=1}^{k} \hat{P}(X > v | c_j) \hat{P}(c_j)} = \frac{n_i - N_{vi}}{\sum_{j=1}^{k} (n_j - N_{vj})} \tag{19.16}$$

Algorithm 19.2 shows the split point evaluation method for numeric attributes. The for loop on line 4 iterates through all the points and computes the midpoint values v and the number of points N_{vi} from class c_i such that $x_j \le v$. The for loop on line 12 enumerates all possible split points of the form $X \le v$, one for each midpoint v, and scores them using the gain criterion [Eq. (19.5)]; the best split point and score are recorded and returned. Any of the other evaluation measures can also be used. However, for Gini index and CART a lower score is better unlike for gain where a higher score is better.

In terms of computational complexity, the initial sorting of values of X (line 1) takes time $O(n \log n)$. The cost of computing the midpoints and the class-specific counts N_{vi} takes time $O(nk)$ (for loop on line 4). The cost of computing the score is also bounded by $O(nk)$, because the total number of midpoints v can be at most n (for loop on line 12). The total cost of evaluating a numeric attribute is therefore $O(n \log n + nk)$. Ignoring k, because it is usually a small constant, the total cost of numeric split point evaluation is $O(n \log n)$.

Example 19.4 (Numeric Attributes). Consider the 2-dimensional Iris dataset shown in Figure 19.1(a). In the initial invocation of Algorithm 19.1, the entire dataset $\mathbf{D}$ with

---

Algorithm 19.2: Evaluate Numeric Attribute (Using Gain)

EVALUATE-NUMERIC-ATTRIBUTE ($\mathbf{D}, X$):

1 sort $\mathbf{D}$ on attribute X, so that $x_j \leq x_{j+1}, \forall j = 1, \ldots, n-1$

2 $\mathcal{M} \leftarrow \emptyset$ // set of midpoints

3 **for** $i = 1, \ldots, k$ **do** $n_i \leftarrow 0$

4 **for** $j = 1, \ldots, n-1$ **do**

5   **if** $y_j = c_i$ **then** $n_i \leftarrow n_i + 1$
         // running count for class c_i

6   **if** $x_{j+1} \neq x_j$ **then**

7          $v \leftarrow \frac{x_{j+1} + x_j}{2}$; $\mathcal{M} \leftarrow \mathcal{M} \cup \{v\}$ // midpoints

8   **for** $i = 1, \ldots, k$ **do**

9              $N_{vi} \leftarrow n_i$ // Number of points such that $x_j \leq v$ and
             $y_j = c_i$

10 **if** $y_n = c_i$ **then** $n_i \leftarrow n_i + 1$
     // evaluate split points of the form $X \leq v$

11 $v^* \leftarrow \emptyset$; $score^* \leftarrow 0$ // initialize best split point

12 **forall** $v \in \mathcal{M}$ **do**

13   **for** $i = 1, \ldots, k$ **do**

14          $\hat{P}(c_i | \mathbf{D}_Y) \leftarrow \frac{N_{vi}}{\sum_{j=1}^{k} N_{vj}}$

15          $\hat{P}(c_i | \mathbf{D}_N) \leftarrow \frac{n_i - N_{vi}}{\sum_{j=1}^{k} n_j - N_{vj}}$

16      $score(X \leq v) \leftarrow Gain(\mathbf{D}, \mathbf{D}_Y, \mathbf{D}_N)$ // use Eq. (19.5)

17   **if** $score(X \leq v) > score^*$ **then**

18          $v^* \leftarrow v$; $score^* \leftarrow score(X \leq v)$

19 **return** $(v^*, score^*)$

$n = 150$ points is considered at the root of the decision tree. The task is to find the best split point considering both the attributes, X_1 (sepal length) and X_2 (sepal width). Because there are $n_1 = 50$ points labeled c_1 (iris-setosa), the other class c_2 has $n_2 = 100$ points. We thus have

$$\hat{P}(c_1) = 50/150 = 1/3$$
$$\hat{P}(c_2) = 100/150 = 2/3$$

The entropy [Eq. (19.3)] of the dataset $\mathbf{D}$ is therefore

$$H(\mathbf{D}) = -\left(\frac{1}{3} \log_2 \frac{1}{3} + \frac{2}{3} \log_2 \frac{2}{3} \right) = 0.918$$

Consider split points for attribute X_1. To evaluate the splits we first compute the frequencies N_{vi} using Eq. (19.12), which are plotted in Figure 19.2 for both the classes. For example, consider the split point $X_1 \leq 5.45$. From Figure 19.2, we see that

$$N_{v1} = 45 \qquad\qquad N_{v2} = 7$$

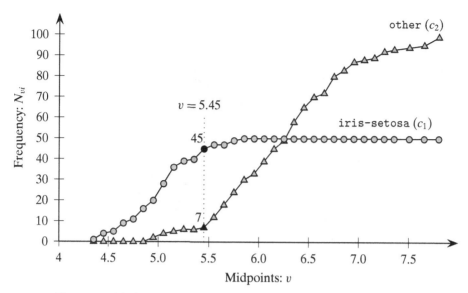

Figure 19.2. Iris: frequencies N_{vi} for classes c_1 and c_2 for attribute sepal length.

Plugging in these values into Eq. (19.14) we get

$$\hat{P}(c_1 | \mathbf{D}_Y) = \frac{N_{v1}}{N_{v1} + N_{v2}} = \frac{45}{45 + 7} = 0.865$$

$$\hat{P}(c_2 | \mathbf{D}_Y) = \frac{N_{v2}}{N_{v1} + N_{v2}} = \frac{7}{45 + 7} = 0.135$$

and using Eq. (19.16), we obtain

$$\hat{P}(c_1 | \mathbf{D}_N) = \frac{n_1 - N_{v1}}{(n_1 - N_{v1}) + (n_2 - N_{v2})} = \frac{50 - 45}{(50 - 45) + (100 - 7)} = 0.051$$

$$\hat{P}(c_2 | \mathbf{D}_N) = \frac{n_2 - N_{v2}}{(n_1 - N_{v1}) + (n_2 - N_{v2})} = \frac{(100 - 7)}{(50 - 45) + (100 - 7)} = 0.949$$

We can now compute the entropy of the partitions $\mathbf{D}_Y$ and $\mathbf{D}_N$ as follows:

$$H(\mathbf{D}_Y) = -(0.865 \log_2 0.865 + 0.135 \log_2 0.135) = 0.571$$

$$H(\mathbf{D}_N) = -(0.051 \log_2 0.051 + 0.949 \log_2 0.949) = 0.291$$

The entropy of the split point $X \le 5.45$ is given via Eq. (19.4)

$$H(\mathbf{D}_Y, \mathbf{D}_N) = \frac{52}{150} H(\mathbf{D}_Y) + \frac{98}{150} H(\mathbf{D}_N) = 0.388$$

where $n_Y = |\mathbf{D}_Y| = 52$ and $n_N = |\mathbf{D}_N| = 98$. The information gain for the split point is therefore

$$Gain = H(\mathbf{D}) - H(\mathbf{D}_Y, \mathbf{D}_N) = 0.918 - 0.388 = 0.53$$

In a similar manner, we can evaluate all of the split points for both attributes X_1 and X_2. Figure 19.3 plots the gain values for the different split points for the two

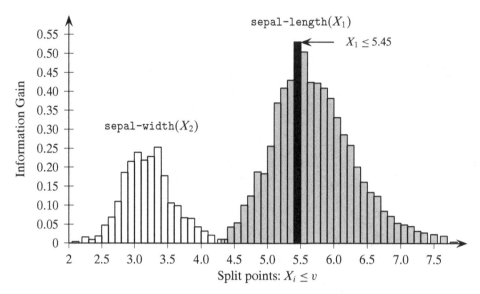

Figure 19.3. Iris: gain for different split points, for sepal length and sepal width.

attributes. We can observe that $X \leq 5.45$ is the best split point and it is thus chosen as the root of the decision tree in Figure 19.1(b).

The recursive tree growth process continues and yields the final decision tree and the split points as shown in Figure 19.1(b). In this example, we use a leaf size threshold of 5 and a purity threshold of 0.95.

Categorical Attributes

If X is a categorical attribute we evaluate split points of the form $X \in V$, where $V \subset dom(X)$ and $V \neq \emptyset$. In words, all distinct partitions of the set of values of X are considered. Because the split point $X \in V$ yields the same partition as $X \in \overline{V}$, where $\overline{V} = dom(X) \setminus V$ is the complement of V, the total number of distinct partitions is given as

$$\sum_{i=1}^{\lfloor m/2 \rfloor} \binom{m}{i} = O(2^{m-1}) \tag{19.17}$$

where m is the number of values in the domain of X, that is, $m = |dom(X)|$. The number of possible split points to consider is therefore exponential in m, which can pose problems if m is large. One simplification is to restrict V to be of size one, so that there are only m split points of the form $X_j \in \{v\}$, where $v \in dom(X_j)$.

To evaluate a given split point $X \in V$ we have to compute the following class probability mass functions:

$$P(c_i | \mathbf{D}_Y) = P(c_i | X \in V) \qquad\qquad P(c_i | \mathbf{D}_N) = P(c_i | X \notin V)$$

Making use of the Bayes theorem, we have

$$P(c_i|X \in V) = \frac{P(X \in V|c_i)P(c_i)}{P(X \in V)} = \frac{P(X \in V|c_i)P(c_i)}{\sum_{j=1}^{k} P(X \in V|c_j)P(c_j)}$$

However, note that a given point $\mathbf{x}$ can take on only one value in the domain of X, and thus the values $v \in dom(X)$ are mutually exclusive. Therefore, we have

$$P(X \in V|c_i) = \sum_{v \in V} P(X = v|c_i)$$

and we can rewrite $P(c_i|\mathbf{D}_Y)$ as

$$P(c_i|\mathbf{D}_Y) = \frac{\sum_{v \in V} P(X = v|c_i)P(c_i)}{\sum_{j=1}^{k} \sum_{v \in V} P(X = v|c_j)P(c_j)} \tag{19.18}$$

Define n_{vi} as the number of points $\mathbf{x}_j \in \mathbf{D}$, with value $x_j = v$ for attribute X and having class $y_j = c_i$:

$$n_{vi} = \sum_{j=1}^{n} I(x_j = v \text{ and } y_j = c_i) \tag{19.19}$$

The class conditional empirical PMF for X is then given as

$$
\begin{aligned}
\hat{P}(X = v|c_i) &= \frac{\hat{P}(X = v \text{ and } c_i)}{\hat{P}(c_i)} \\
&= \left(\frac{1}{n} \sum_{j=1}^{n} I(x_j = v \text{ and } y_j = c_i) \right) \Big/ (n_i/n) \\
&= \frac{n_{vi}}{n_i} \tag{19.20}
\end{aligned}
$$

Note that the class prior probabilities can be estimated using Eq. (19.11) as discussed earlier, that is, $\hat{P}(c_i) = n_i/n$. Thus, substituting Eq. (19.20) in Eq. (19.18), the class PMF for the partition $\mathbf{D}_Y$ for the split point $X \in V$ is given as

$$\hat{P}(c_i|\mathbf{D}_Y) = \frac{\sum_{v \in V} \hat{P}(X = v|c_i)\hat{P}(c_i)}{\sum_{j=1}^{k} \sum_{v \in V} \hat{P}(X = v|c_j)\hat{P}(c_j)} = \frac{\sum_{v \in V} n_{vi}}{\sum_{j=1}^{k} \sum_{v \in V} n_{vj}} \tag{19.21}$$

In a similar manner, the class PMF for the partition $\mathbf{D}_N$ is given as

$$\hat{P}(c_i|\mathbf{D}_N) = \hat{P}(c_i|X \notin V) = \frac{\sum_{v \notin V} n_{vi}}{\sum_{j=1}^{k} \sum_{v \notin V} n_{vj}} \tag{19.22}$$

Algorithm 19.3 shows the split point evaluation method for categorical attributes. The for loop on line 4 iterates through all the points and computes n_{vi}, that is, the number of points having value $v \in dom(X)$ and class c_i. The for loop on line 7 enumerates all possible split points of the form $X \in V$ for $V \subset dom(X)$, such that $|V| \leq l$, where l is a user specified parameter denoting the maximum cardinality of V. For

---

Algorithm 19.3: Evaluate Categorical Attribute (Using Gain)

EVALUATE-CATEGORICAL-ATTRIBUTE ($\mathbf{D}, X, l$):

1 **for** $i = 1, \ldots, k$ **do**
2    $n_i \leftarrow 0$
3   **forall** $v \in dom(X)$ **do** $n_{vi} \leftarrow 0$

4 **for** $j = 1, \ldots, n$ **do**
5   **if** $x_j = v$ *and* $y_j = c_i$ **then** $n_{vi} \leftarrow n_{vi} + 1$ // frequency statistics

   // evaluate split points of the form $X \in V$
6 $V^* \leftarrow \emptyset; score^* \leftarrow 0$ // initialize best split point
7 **forall** $V \subset dom(X)$, *such that* $1 \leq |V| \leq l$ **do**
8   **for** $i = 1, \ldots, k$ **do**
9     $\hat{P}(c_i | \mathbf{D}_Y) \leftarrow \dfrac{\sum_{v \in V} n_{vi}}{\sum_{j=1}^{k} \sum_{v \in V} n_{vj}}$
10    $\hat{P}(c_i | \mathbf{D}_N) \leftarrow \dfrac{\sum_{v \notin V} n_{vi}}{\sum_{j=1}^{k} \sum_{v \notin V} n_{vj}}$
11   $score(X \in V) \leftarrow Gain(\mathbf{D}, \mathbf{D}_Y, \mathbf{D}_N)$ // use Eq. (19.5)
12   **if** $score(X \in V) > score^*$ **then**
13    $V^* \leftarrow V; score^* \leftarrow score(X \in V)$

14 **return** $(V^*, score^*)$

---

example, to control the number of split points, we can also restrict V to be a single item, that is, $l = 1$, so that splits are of the form $V \in \{v\}$, with $v \in dom(X)$. If $l = \lfloor m/2 \rfloor$, we have to consider all possible distinct partitions V. Given a split point $X \in V$, the method scores it using information gain [Eq. (19.5)], although any of the other scoring criteria can also be used. The best split point and score are recorded and returned.

In terms of computational complexity the class-specific counts for each value n_{vi} takes $O(n)$ time (for loop on line 4). With $m = |dom(X)|$, the maximum number of partitions V is $O(2^{m-1})$, and because each split point can be evaluated in time $O(mk)$, the for loop in line 7 takes time $O(mk2^{m-1})$. The total cost for categorical attributes is therefore $O(n + mk2^{m-1})$. If we make the assumption that $2^{m-1} = O(n)$, that is, if we bound the maximum size of V to $l = O(\log n)$, then the cost of categorical splits is bounded as $O(n \log n)$, ignoring k.

Example 19.5 (Categorical Attributes). Consider the 2-dimensional Iris dataset comprising the sepal length and sepal width attributes. Let us assume that sepal length has been discretized as shown in Table 19.1. The class frequencies n_{vi} are also shown. For instance $n_{a_1 2} = 6$ denotes the fact that there are 6 points in $\mathbf{D}$ with value $v = a_1$ and class c_2.

Consider the split point $X_1 \in \{a_1, a_3\}$. From Table 19.1 we can compute the class PMF for partition $\mathbf{D}_Y$ using Eq. (19.21)

$$\hat{P}(c_1 | \mathbf{D}_Y) = \frac{n_{a_1 1} + n_{a_3 1}}{(n_{a_1 1} + n_{a_3 1}) + (n_{a_1 2} + n_{a_3 2})} = \frac{39 + 0}{(39 + 0) + (6 + 43)} = 0.443$$

Table 19.1. Discretized `sepal length` attribute: class frequencies

Bins	v: values	Class frequencies (n_{vi})	
		c_1:`iris-setosa`	c_2:`other`
[4.3, 5.2]	Very Short (a_1)	39	6
(5.2, 6.1]	Short (a_2)	11	39
(6.1, 7.0]	Long (a_3)	0	43
(7.0, 7.9]	Very Long (a_4)	0	12

$$\hat{P}(c_2|\mathbf{D}_Y) = 1 - \hat{P}(c_1|\mathbf{D}_Y) = 0.557$$

with the entropy given as

$$H(\mathbf{D}_Y) = -(0.443\log_2 0.443 + 0.557\log_2 0.557) = 0.991$$

To compute the class PMF for $\mathbf{D}_N$ [Eq. (19.22)], we sum up the frequencies over values $v \notin V = \{a_1, a_3\}$, that is, we sum over $v = a_2$ and $v = a_4$, as follows:

$$\hat{P}(c_1|\mathbf{D}_N) = \frac{n_{a_2 1} + n_{a_4 1}}{(n_{a_2 1} + n_{a_4 1}) + (n_{a_2 2} + n_{a_4 2})} = \frac{11 + 0}{(11 + 0) + (39 + 12)} = 0.177$$

$$\hat{P}(c_2|\mathbf{D}_N) = 1 - \hat{P}(c_1|\mathbf{D}_N) = 0.823$$

with the entropy given as

$$H(\mathbf{D}_N) = -(0.177\log_2 0.177 + 0.823\log_2 0.823) = 0.673$$

We can see from Table 19.1 that $V \in \{a_1, a_3\}$ splits the input data $\mathbf{D}$ into partitions of size $|\mathbf{D}_Y| = 39 + 6 + 43 = 88$, and $\mathbf{D}_N = 150 - 88 = 62$. The entropy of the split is therefore given as

$$H(\mathbf{D}_Y, \mathbf{D}_N) = \frac{88}{150}H(\mathbf{D}_Y) + \frac{62}{150}H(\mathbf{D}_N) = 0.86$$

As noted in Example 19.4, the entropy of the whole dataset $\mathbf{D}$ is $H(\mathbf{D}) = 0.918$. The gain is then given as

$$Gain = H(\mathbf{D}) - H(\mathbf{D}_Y, \mathbf{D}_N) = 0.918 - 0.86 = 0.058$$

The split entropy and gain values for all the categorical split points are given in Table 19.2. We can see that $X_1 \in \{a_1\}$ is the best split point on the discretized attribute X_1.

19.2.3 Computational Complexity

To analyze the computational complexity of the decision tree method in Algorithm 19.1, we assume that the cost of evaluating all the split points for a numeric or categorical attribute is $O(n \log n)$, where $n = |\mathbf{D}|$ is the size of the dataset. Given $\mathbf{D}$, the decision

Table 19.2. Categorical split points for sepal length

V	Split entropy	Info. gain
$\{a_1\}$	0.509	0.410
$\{a_2\}$	0.897	0.217
$\{a_3\}$	0.711	0.207
$\{a_4\}$	0.869	0.049
$\{a_1, a_2\}$	0.632	0.286
$\{a_1, a_3\}$	0.860	0.058
$\{a_1, a_4\}$	0.667	0.251
$\{a_2, a_3\}$	0.667	0.251
$\{a_2, a_4\}$	0.860	0.058
$\{a_3, a_4\}$	0.632	0.286

tree algorithm evaluates all d attributes, with cost $(dn \log n)$. The total cost depends on the depth of the decision tree. In the worst case, the tree can have depth n, and thus the total cost is $O(dn^2 \log n)$.

19.3 FURTHER READING

Among the earliest works on decision trees are Hunt, Marin, and Stone (1966); Breiman et al. (1984); and Quinlan (1986). The description in this chapter is largely based on the C4.5 method described in Quinlan (1993), which is an excellent reference for further details, such as how to prune decision trees to prevent overfitting, how to handle missing attribute values, and other implementation issues. A survey of methods for simplifying decision trees appears in Breslow and Aha (1997). Scalable implementation techniques are described in Mehta, Agrawal, and Rissanen (1996) and Gehrke et al. (1999).

Breiman, L., Friedman, J., Stone, C., and Olshen, R. (1984). *Classification and Regression Trees*. Boca Raton, FL: Chapman and Hall/CRC Press.

Breslow, L. A. and Aha, D. W. (1997). Simplifying decision trees: A survey. *Knowledge Engineering Review*, 12 (1), 1–40.

Gehrke, J., Ganti, V., Ramakrishnan, R., and Loh, W.-Y. (1999). BOAT–Optimistic decision tree construction. *ACM SIGMOD Record*, 28 (2), 169–180.

Hunt, E. B., Marin, J., and Stone, P. J. (1966). *Experiments in Induction*. New York: Academic Press.

Mehta, M., Agrawal, R., and Rissanen, J. (1996). SLIQ: A fast scalable classifier for data mining. *Proceedings of the International Conference on Extending Database Technology*. New York: Springer-Verlag, pp. 18–32.

Quinlan, J. R. (1986). Induction of decision trees. *Machine Learning*, 1 (1), 81–106.

Quinlan, J. R. (1993). *C4.5: Programs for Machine Learning*. New York: Morgan Kaufmann.

19.4 EXERCISES

Q1. True or False:

    (a) High entropy means that the partitions in classification are "pure."

    (b) Multiway split of a categorical attribute generally results in more pure partitions than a binary split.

Q2. Given Table 19.3, construct a decision tree using a purity threshold of 100%. Use information gain as the split point evaluation measure. Next, classify the point (Age=27,Car=Vintage).

Table 19.3. Data for Q2: Age is numeric and Car is categorical. Risk gives the class label for each point: high (H) or low (L)

	Age	Car	**Risk**
$\mathbf{x}_1^T$	25	Sports	L
$\mathbf{x}_2^T$	20	Vintage	H
$\mathbf{x}_3^T$	25	Sports	L
$\mathbf{x}_4^T$	45	SUV	H
$\mathbf{x}_5^T$	20	Sports	H
$\mathbf{x}_6^T$	25	SUV	H

Table 19.4. Data for Q4

Instance	a_1	a_2	a_3	Class
1	T	T	5.0	Y
2	T	T	7.0	Y
3	T	F	8.0	N
4	F	F	3.0	Y
5	F	T	7.0	N
6	F	T	4.0	N
7	F	F	5.0	N
8	T	F	6.0	Y
9	F	T	1.0	N

Q3. What is the maximum and minimum value of the CART measure [Eq. (19.7)] and under what conditions?

Q4. Given the dataset in Table 19.4. Answer the following questions:

    (a) Show which decision will be chosen at the root of the decision tree using information gain [Eq. (19.5)], Gini index [Eq. (19.6)], and CART [Eq. (19.7)] measures. Show all split points for all attributes.

    (b) What happens to the purity if we use Instance as another attribute? Do you think this attribute should be used for a decision in the tree?

Q5. Consider Table 19.5. Let us make a nonlinear split instead of an axis parallel split, given as follows: $AB - B^2 \leq 0$. Compute the information gain of this split based on entropy (use $\log_2$, i.e., log to the base 2).

Table 19.5. Data for Q5

	A	B	Class
$\mathbf{x}_1^T$	3.5	4	H
$\mathbf{x}_2^T$	2	4	H
$\mathbf{x}_3^T$	9.1	4.5	L
$\mathbf{x}_4^T$	2	6	H
$\mathbf{x}_5^T$	1.5	7	H
$\mathbf{x}_6^T$	7	6.5	H
$\mathbf{x}_7^T$	2.1	2.5	L
$\mathbf{x}_8^T$	8	4	L

CHAPTER 20

Linear Discriminant Analysis

Given labeled data consisting of d-dimensional points $\mathbf{x}_i$ along with their classes y_i, the goal of linear discriminant analysis (LDA) is to find a vector $\mathbf{w}$ that maximizes the separation between the classes after projection onto $\mathbf{w}$. Recall from Chapter 7 that the first principal component is the vector that maximizes the projected variance of the points. The key difference between principal component analysis and LDA is that the former deals with unlabeled data and tries to maximize variance, whereas the latter deals with labeled data and tries to maximize the discrimination between the classes.

20.1 OPTIMAL LINEAR DISCRIMINANT

Let us assume that the dataset $\mathbf{D}$ consists of n point $\mathbf{x}_i \in \mathbb{R}^d$, with the corresponding class label $y_i \in \{c_1, c_2, \ldots, c_k\}$. Let $\mathbf{D}_i$ denote the subset of points labeled with class c_i, i.e., $\mathbf{D}_i = \{\mathbf{x}_j^T | y_j = c_i\}$, and let $|\mathbf{D}_i| = n_i$ denote the number of points with class c_i. We assume that there are only $k = 2$ classes. Thus, the dataset $\mathbf{D}$ can be partitioned into $\mathbf{D}_1$ and $\mathbf{D}_2$.

Let $\mathbf{w}$ be a unit vector, that is, $\mathbf{w}^T\mathbf{w} = 1$. By Eq. (1.11), the projection of any d-dimensional point $\mathbf{x}_i$ onto the vector $\mathbf{w}$ is given as

$$\mathbf{x}_i' = \left(\frac{\mathbf{w}^T\mathbf{x}_i}{\mathbf{w}^T\mathbf{w}}\right)\mathbf{w} = \left(\mathbf{w}^T\mathbf{x}_i\right)\mathbf{w} = a_i\mathbf{w}$$

where a_i is the offset or scalar projection (Eq. (1.12)) of $\mathbf{x}_i$ on the line $\mathbf{w}$:

$$a_i = \mathbf{w}^T\mathbf{x}_i$$

We also call a_i a *projected point*. Thus, the set of n projected points $\{a_1, a_2, \ldots, a_n\}$ represents a mapping from $\mathbb{R}^d$ to $\mathbb{R}$, that is, from the original d-dimensional space to a 1-dimensional space of offsets along $\mathbf{w}$.

Example 20.1. Consider Figure 20.1, which shows the 2-dimensional Iris dataset with sepal length and sepal width as the attributes, and iris-setosa as class c_1 (circles), and the other two Iris types as class c_2 (triangles). There are $n_1 = 50$ points in

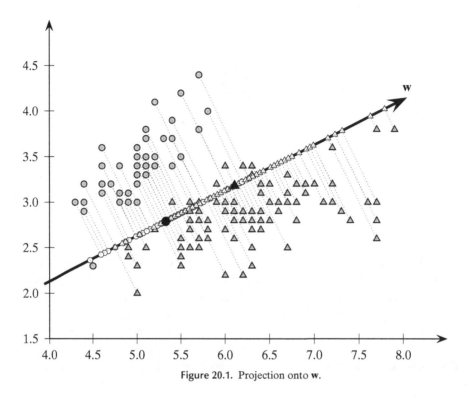

Figure 20.1. Projection onto **w**.

c_1 and $n_2 = 100$ points in c_2. One possible vector **w** is shown, along with the projection of all the points onto **w**. The projected means of the two classes are shown in black. Here **w** has been translated so that it passes through the mean of the entire data. One can observe that **w** is not very good in discriminating between the two classes because the projection of the points onto **w** are all mixed up in terms of their class labels. The optimal linear discriminant direction is shown in Figure 20.2.

Each projected point a_i has associated with it the original class label y_i, and thus we can compute, for each of the two classes, the mean of the projected points, called the *projected mean*, as follows:

$$m_1 = \frac{1}{n_1} \sum_{\mathbf{x}_i \in \mathbf{D}_1} a_i$$

$$= \frac{1}{n_1} \sum_{\mathbf{x}_i \in \mathbf{D}_1} \mathbf{w}^T \mathbf{x}_i$$

$$= \mathbf{w}^T \left(\frac{1}{n_1} \sum_{\mathbf{x}_i \in \mathbf{D}_1} \mathbf{x}_i \right)$$

$$= \mathbf{w}^T \boldsymbol{\mu}_1$$

where $\boldsymbol{\mu}_1$ is the mean of all point in $\mathbf{D}_1$. Likewise, we can obtain

$$m_2 = \mathbf{w}^T \boldsymbol{\mu}_2$$

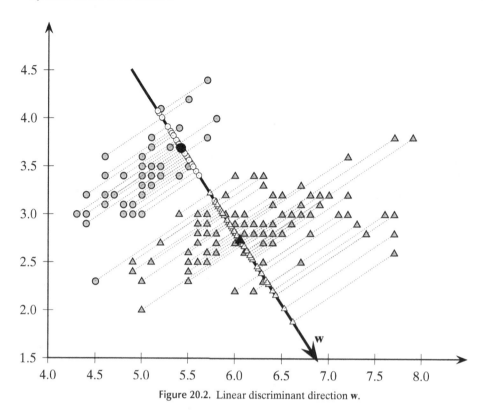

Figure 20.2. Linear discriminant direction **w**.

In other words, the mean of the projected points is the same as the scalar projection of the mean.

To maximize the separation between the classes, it seems reasonable to maximize the difference between the projected means, $|m_1 - m_2|$. However, this is not enough. For good separation, the variance of the projected points for each class should also not be too large. A large variance would lead to possible overlaps among the points of the two classes due to the large spread of the points, and thus we may fail to have a good separation. LDA maximizes the separation by ensuring that the *scatter* s_i^2 for the projected points within each class is small, where scatter is defined as

$$s_i^2 = \sum_{\mathbf{x}_j \in \mathbf{D}_i} (a_j - m_i)^2$$

Scatter is the total squared deviation from the mean, as opposed to the variance, which is the average deviation from mean. In other words

$$s_i^2 = n_i \sigma_i^2$$

where $n_i = |\mathbf{D}_i|$ is the size, and σ_i^2 is the variance, for class c_i.

We can incorporate the two LDA criteria, namely, maximizing the distance between projected means and minimizing the sum of projected scatter, into a single maximization criterion called the *Fisher LDA objective*:

$$\max_{\mathbf{w}} \ J(\mathbf{w}) = \frac{(m_1 - m_2)^2}{s_1^2 + s_2^2} \tag{20.1}$$

The goal of LDA is to find the vector $\mathbf{w}$ that maximizes $J(\mathbf{w})$, that is, the direction that maximizes the separation between the two means m_1 and m_2, and minimizes the total scatter $s_1^2 + s_2^2$ of the two classes. The vector $\mathbf{w}$ is also called the *optimal linear discriminant (LD)*. The optimization objective [Eq. (20.1)] is in the projected space. To solve it, we have to rewrite it in terms of the input data, as described next.

Note that we can rewrite $(m_1 - m_2)^2$ as follows:

$$\begin{aligned}
(m_1 - m_2)^2 &= \left(\mathbf{w}^T(\boldsymbol{\mu}_1 - \boldsymbol{\mu}_2)\right)^2 \\
&= \mathbf{w}^T \left((\boldsymbol{\mu}_1 - \boldsymbol{\mu}_2)(\boldsymbol{\mu}_1 - \boldsymbol{\mu}_2)^T\right) \mathbf{w} \\
&= \mathbf{w}^T \mathbf{B} \mathbf{w}
\end{aligned} \tag{20.2}$$

where $\mathbf{B} = (\boldsymbol{\mu}_1 - \boldsymbol{\mu}_2)(\boldsymbol{\mu}_1 - \boldsymbol{\mu}_2)^T$ is a $d \times d$ rank-one matrix called the *between-class scatter matrix*.

As for the projected scatter for class c_1, we can compute it as follows:

$$\begin{aligned}
s_1^2 &= \sum_{\mathbf{x}_i \in \mathbf{D}_1} (a_i - m_1)^2 \\
&= \sum_{\mathbf{x}_i \in \mathbf{D}_1} (\mathbf{w}^T \mathbf{x}_i - \mathbf{w}^T \boldsymbol{\mu}_1)^2 \\
&= \sum_{\mathbf{x}_i \in \mathbf{D}_1} \left(\mathbf{w}^T(\mathbf{x}_i - \boldsymbol{\mu}_1)\right)^2 \\
&= \mathbf{w}^T \left(\sum_{\mathbf{x}_i \in \mathbf{D}_1} (\mathbf{x}_i - \boldsymbol{\mu}_1)(\mathbf{x}_i - \boldsymbol{\mu}_1)^T\right) \mathbf{w} \\
&= \mathbf{w}^T \mathbf{S}_1 \mathbf{w}
\end{aligned} \tag{20.3}$$

where $\mathbf{S}_1$ is the *scatter matrix* for $\mathbf{D}_1$. Likewise, we can obtain

$$s_2^2 = \mathbf{w}^T \mathbf{S}_2 \mathbf{w} \tag{20.4}$$

Notice again that the scatter matrix is essentially the same as the covariance matrix, but instead of recording the average deviation from the mean, it records the total deviation, that is,

$$\mathbf{S}_i = n_i \boldsymbol{\Sigma}_i \tag{20.5}$$

Combining Eqs. (20.3) and (20.4), the denominator in Eq. (20.1) can be rewritten as

$$s_1^2 + s_2^2 = \mathbf{w}^T \mathbf{S}_1 \mathbf{w} + \mathbf{w}^T \mathbf{S}_2 \mathbf{w} = \mathbf{w}^T(\mathbf{S}_1 + \mathbf{S}_2)\mathbf{w} = \mathbf{w}^T \mathbf{S} \mathbf{w} \tag{20.6}$$

where $\mathbf{S} = \mathbf{S}_1 + \mathbf{S}_2$ denotes the *within-class scatter matrix* for the pooled data. Because both $\mathbf{S}_1$ and $\mathbf{S}_2$ are $d \times d$ symmetric positive semidefinite matrices, $\mathbf{S}$ has the same properties.

Using Eqs. (20.2) and (20.6), we write the LDA objective function [Eq. (20.1)] as follows:

$$\max_{\mathbf{w}} \ J(\mathbf{w}) = \frac{\mathbf{w}^T\mathbf{B}\mathbf{w}}{\mathbf{w}^T\mathbf{S}\mathbf{w}} \tag{20.7}$$

To solve for the best direction $\mathbf{w}$, we differentiate the objective function with respect to $\mathbf{w}$, and set the result to zero. We do not explicitly have to deal with the constraint that $\mathbf{w}^T\mathbf{w} = 1$ because in Eq. (20.7) the terms related to the magnitude of $\mathbf{w}$ cancel out in the numerator and the denominator.

Recall that if $f(x)$ and $g(x)$ are two functions then we have

$$\frac{d}{dx}\left(\frac{f(x)}{g(x)}\right) = \frac{f'(x)g(x) - g'(x)f(x)}{g(x)^2}$$

where $f'(x)$ denotes the derivative of $f(x)$. Taking the derivative of Eq. (20.7) with respect to the vector $\mathbf{w}$, and setting the result to the zero vector, gives us

$$\frac{d}{d\mathbf{w}}J(\mathbf{w}) = \frac{2\mathbf{B}\mathbf{w}(\mathbf{w}^T\mathbf{S}\mathbf{w}) - 2\mathbf{S}\mathbf{w}(\mathbf{w}^T\mathbf{B}\mathbf{w})}{(\mathbf{w}^T\mathbf{S}\mathbf{w})^2} = \mathbf{0}$$

which yields

$$\mathbf{B}\,\mathbf{w}(\mathbf{w}^T\mathbf{S}\mathbf{w}) = \mathbf{S}\,\mathbf{w}(\mathbf{w}^T\mathbf{B}\mathbf{w})$$

$$\mathbf{B}\,\mathbf{w} = \mathbf{S}\,\mathbf{w}\left(\frac{\mathbf{w}^T\mathbf{B}\mathbf{w}}{\mathbf{w}^T\mathbf{S}\mathbf{w}}\right)$$

$$\mathbf{B}\,\mathbf{w} = J(\mathbf{w})\mathbf{S}\mathbf{w}$$

$$\mathbf{B}\mathbf{w} = \lambda\mathbf{S}\mathbf{w} \tag{20.8}$$

where $\lambda = J(\mathbf{w})$. Eq. (20.8) represents a *generalized eigenvalue problem* where λ is a generalized eigenvalue of $\mathbf{B}$ and $\mathbf{S}$; the eigenvalue λ satisfies the equation $\det(\mathbf{B} - \lambda\mathbf{S}) = 0$. Because the goal is to maximize the objective [Eq. (20.7)], $J(\mathbf{w}) = \lambda$ should be chosen to be the largest generalized eigenvalue, and $\mathbf{w}$ to be the corresponding eigenvector. If $\mathbf{S}$ is *nonsingular*, that is, if $\mathbf{S}^{-1}$ exists, then Eq. (20.8) leads to the regular eigenvalue–eigenvector equation, as

$$\mathbf{B}\mathbf{w} = \lambda\mathbf{S}\mathbf{w}$$

$$\mathbf{S}^{-1}\mathbf{B}\mathbf{w} = \lambda\mathbf{S}^{-1}\mathbf{S}\mathbf{w}$$

which implies

$$(\mathbf{S}^{-1}\mathbf{B})\mathbf{w} = \lambda\mathbf{w} \tag{20.9}$$

Thus, if $\mathbf{S}^{-1}$ exists, then $\lambda = J(\mathbf{w})$ is an eigenvalue, and $\mathbf{w}$ is an eigenvector of the matrix $\mathbf{S}^{-1}\mathbf{B}$. To maximize $J(\mathbf{w})$ we look for the largest eigenvalue λ, and the corresponding dominant eigenvector $\mathbf{w}$ specifies the best linear discriminant vector.

Algorithm 20.1: Linear Discriminant Analysis

LINEARDISCRIMINANT (D):

1 $\mathbf{D}_i \leftarrow \left\{ \mathbf{x}_j^T \mid y_j = c_i, j = 1, \ldots, n \right\}, i = 1, 2$ // class-specific subsets
2 $\boldsymbol{\mu}_i \leftarrow \text{mean}(\mathbf{D}_i), i = 1, 2$ // class means
3 $\mathbf{B} \leftarrow (\boldsymbol{\mu}_1 - \boldsymbol{\mu}_2)(\boldsymbol{\mu}_1 - \boldsymbol{\mu}_2)^T$ // between-class scatter matrix
4 $\overline{\mathbf{D}}_i \leftarrow \mathbf{D}_i - \mathbf{1}_{n_i} \boldsymbol{\mu}_i^T, i = 1, 2$ // center class matrices
5 $\mathbf{S}_i \leftarrow \overline{\mathbf{D}}_i^T \overline{\mathbf{D}}_i, i = 1, 2$ // class scatter matrices
6 $\mathbf{S} \leftarrow \mathbf{S}_1 + \mathbf{S}_2$ // within-class scatter matrix
7 $\lambda_1, \mathbf{w} \leftarrow \text{eigen}(\mathbf{S}^{-1}\mathbf{B})$ // compute dominant eigenvector

---

Algorithm 20.1 shows the pseudo-code for linear discriminant analysis. Here, we assume that there are two classes, and that $\mathbf{S}$ is nonsingular (i.e., $\mathbf{S}^{-1}$ exists). The vector $\mathbf{1}_{n_i}$ is the vector of all ones, with the appropriate dimension for each class, i.e., $\mathbf{1}_{n_i} \in \mathbb{R}^{n_i}$ for class $i = 1, 2$. After dividing $\mathbf{D}$ into the two groups $\mathbf{D}_1$ and $\mathbf{D}_2$, LDA proceeds to compute the between-class and within-class scatter matrices, $\mathbf{B}$ and $\mathbf{S}$. The optimal LD vector is obtained as the dominant eigenvector of $\mathbf{S}^{-1}\mathbf{B}$. In terms of computational complexity, computing $\mathbf{S}$ takes $O(nd^2)$ time, and computing the dominant eigenvalue-eigenvector pair takes $O(d^3)$ time in the worst case. Thus, the total time is $O(d^3 + nd^2)$.

Example 20.2 (Linear Discriminant Analysis). Consider the 2-dimensional Iris data (with attributes sepal length and sepal width) shown in Example 20.1. Class c_1, corresponding to iris-setosa, has $n_1 = 50$ points, whereas the other class c_2 has $n_2 = 100$ points. The means for the two classes c_1 and c_2, and their difference is given as

$$\boldsymbol{\mu}_1 = \begin{pmatrix} 5.01 \\ 3.42 \end{pmatrix} \qquad \boldsymbol{\mu}_2 = \begin{pmatrix} 6.26 \\ 2.87 \end{pmatrix} \qquad \boldsymbol{\mu}_1 - \boldsymbol{\mu}_2 = \begin{pmatrix} -1.256 \\ 0.546 \end{pmatrix}$$

The between-class scatter matrix is

$$\mathbf{B} = (\boldsymbol{\mu}_1 - \boldsymbol{\mu}_2)(\boldsymbol{\mu}_1 - \boldsymbol{\mu}_2)^T = \begin{pmatrix} -1.256 \\ 0.546 \end{pmatrix} \begin{pmatrix} -1.256 & 0.546 \end{pmatrix} = \begin{pmatrix} 1.587 & -0.693 \\ -0.693 & 0.303 \end{pmatrix}$$

and the within-class scatter matrix is

$$\mathbf{S}_1 = \begin{pmatrix} 6.09 & 4.91 \\ 4.91 & 7.11 \end{pmatrix} \quad \mathbf{S}_2 = \begin{pmatrix} 43.5 & 12.09 \\ 12.09 & 10.96 \end{pmatrix} \quad \mathbf{S} = \mathbf{S}_1 + \mathbf{S}_2 = \begin{pmatrix} 49.58 & 17.01 \\ 17.01 & 18.08 \end{pmatrix}$$

$\mathbf{S}$ is nonsingular, with its inverse given as

$$\mathbf{S}^{-1} = \begin{pmatrix} 0.0298 & -0.028 \\ -0.028 & 0.0817 \end{pmatrix}$$

Therefore, we have

$$\mathbf{S}^{-1}\mathbf{B} = \begin{pmatrix} 0.0298 & -0.028 \\ -0.028 & 0.0817 \end{pmatrix} \begin{pmatrix} 1.587 & -0.693 \\ -0.693 & 0.303 \end{pmatrix} = \begin{pmatrix} 0.066 & -0.029 \\ -0.100 & 0.044 \end{pmatrix}$$

The direction of most separation between c_1 and c_2 is the dominant eigenvector corresponding to the largest eigenvalue of the matrix $\mathbf{S}^{-1}\mathbf{B}$. The solution is

$$J(\mathbf{w}) = \lambda_1 = 0.11$$

$$\mathbf{w} = \begin{pmatrix} 0.551 \\ -0.834 \end{pmatrix}$$

Figure 20.2 plots the optimal linear discriminant direction $\mathbf{w}$, translated to the mean of the data. The projected means for the two classes are shown in black. We can clearly observe that along $\mathbf{w}$ the circles appear together as a group, and are quite well separated from the triangles. Except for one outlying circle corresponding to the point $(4.5, 2.3)^T$, all points in c_1 are perfectly separated from points in c_2.

For the two class scenario, if $\mathbf{S}$ is nonsingular, we can directly solve for $\mathbf{w}$ without computing the eigenvalues and eigenvectors. Note that $\mathbf{B} = (\mu_1 - \mu_2)(\mu_1 - \mu_2)^T$ is a $d \times d$ rank-one matrix, and thus $\mathbf{B}\mathbf{w}$ must point in the same direction as $(\mu_1 - \mu_2)$ because

$$\mathbf{B}\mathbf{w} = \left((\mu_1 - \mu_2)(\mu_1 - \mu_2)^T \right)\mathbf{w}$$

$$= (\mu_1 - \mu_2)\left((\mu_1 - \mu_2)^T\mathbf{w} \right)$$

$$= b(\mu_1 - \mu_2)$$

where $b = (\mu_1 - \mu_2)^T\mathbf{w}$ is just a scalar multiplier.

We can then rewrite Eq. (20.9) as

$$\mathbf{B}\mathbf{w} = \lambda\mathbf{S}\mathbf{w}$$

$$b(\mu_1 - \mu_2) = \lambda\mathbf{S}\mathbf{w}$$

$$\mathbf{w} = \frac{b}{\lambda}\mathbf{S}^{-1}(\mu_1 - \mu_2)$$

Because $\frac{b}{\lambda}$ is just a scalar, we can solve for the best linear discriminant as

$$\boxed{\mathbf{w} = \mathbf{S}^{-1}(\mu_1 - \mu_2)} \qquad (20.10)$$

Once the direction $\mathbf{w}$ has been found we can normalize it to be a unit vector. Thus, instead of solving for the eigenvalue/eigenvector, in the two class case, we immediately obtain the direction $\mathbf{w}$ using Eq. (20.10). Intuitively, the direction that maximizes the separation between the classes can be viewed as a linear transformation (by $\mathbf{S}^{-1}$) of the vector joining the two class means $(\mu_1 - \mu_2)$.

Example 20.3. Continuing Example 20.2, we can directly compute $\mathbf{w}$ as follows:

$$\mathbf{w} = \mathbf{S}^{-1}(\boldsymbol{\mu}_1 - \boldsymbol{\mu}_2)$$

$$= \begin{pmatrix} 0.066 & -0.029 \\ -0.100 & 0.044 \end{pmatrix} \begin{pmatrix} -1.246 \\ 0.546 \end{pmatrix} = \begin{pmatrix} -0.0527 \\ 0.0798 \end{pmatrix}$$

After normalizing, we have

$$\mathbf{w} = \frac{\mathbf{w}}{\|\mathbf{w}\|} = \frac{1}{0.0956} \begin{pmatrix} -0.0527 \\ 0.0798 \end{pmatrix} = \begin{pmatrix} -0.551 \\ 0.834 \end{pmatrix}$$

Note that even though the sign is reversed for $\mathbf{w}$, compared to that in Example 20.2, they represent the same direction; only the scalar multiplier is different.

20.2 KERNEL DISCRIMINANT ANALYSIS

Kernel discriminant analysis, like linear discriminant analysis, tries to find a direction that maximizes the separation between the classes. However, it does so in *feature space* via the use of kernel functions.

Given a dataset $\mathbf{D}$ comprising n points $\mathbf{x}_i$ in the input space with $y_i \in \{c_1, c_2\}$ being the class label, let $\mathbf{D}_i = \{\mathbf{x}_j^T | y_j = c_i\}$ denote the data subset restricted to class c_i, and let $n_i = |\mathbf{D}_i|$. Further, let $\phi(\mathbf{x}_i)$ denote the corresponding point in feature space, and let K be a kernel function.

The goal of kernel LDA is to find the direction vector $\mathbf{w}$ in feature space that maximizes

$$\max_{\mathbf{w}} \; J(\mathbf{w}) = \frac{(m_1 - m_2)^2}{s_1^2 + s_2^2} \tag{20.11}$$

where m_1 and m_2 are the projected means, and s_1^2 and s_2^2 are projected scatter values in feature space. We first show that $\mathbf{w}$ can be expressed as a linear combination of the points in feature space, and then we transform the LDA objective in terms of the kernel matrix.

Optimal LD: Linear Combination of Feature Points
The mean for class c_i in feature space is given as

$$\boldsymbol{\mu}_i^\phi = \frac{1}{n_i} \sum_{\mathbf{x}_j \in \mathbf{D}_i} \phi(\mathbf{x}_j) \tag{20.12}$$

and the covariance matrix for class c_i in feature space is

$$\boldsymbol{\Sigma}_i^\phi = \frac{1}{n_i} \sum_{\mathbf{x}_j \in \mathbf{D}_i} \left(\phi(\mathbf{x}_j) - \boldsymbol{\mu}_i^\phi \right) \left(\phi(\mathbf{x}_j) - \boldsymbol{\mu}_i^\phi \right)^T$$

Using a derivation similar to Eq. (20.2) we obtain an expression for the between-class scatter matrix in feature space

$$\mathbf{B}_\phi = \left(\boldsymbol{\mu}_1^\phi - \boldsymbol{\mu}_2^\phi\right)\left(\boldsymbol{\mu}_1^\phi - \boldsymbol{\mu}_2^\phi\right)^T = \mathbf{d}_\phi \mathbf{d}_\phi^T \qquad (20.13)$$

where $\mathbf{d}_\phi = \boldsymbol{\mu}_1^\phi - \boldsymbol{\mu}_2^\phi$ is the difference between the two class mean vectors. Likewise, using Eqs. (20.5) and (20.6) the within-class scatter matrix in feature space is given as

$$\mathbf{S}_\phi = n_1 \boldsymbol{\Sigma}_1^\phi + n_2 \boldsymbol{\Sigma}_2^\phi$$

$\mathbf{S}_\phi$ is a $d \times d$ symmetric, positive semidefinite matrix, where d is the dimensionality of the feature space. From Eq. (20.9), we conclude that the best linear discriminant vector $\mathbf{w}$ in feature space is the dominant eigenvector, which satisfies the expression

$$\boxed{(\mathbf{S}_\phi^{-1}\mathbf{B}_\phi)\,\mathbf{w} = \lambda \mathbf{w}} \qquad (20.14)$$

where we assume that $\mathbf{S}_\phi$ is non-singular. Let δ_i denote the ith eigenvalue and $\mathbf{u}_i$ the ith eigenvector of $\mathbf{S}_\phi$, for $i = 1, \ldots, d$. The eigen-decomposition of $\mathbf{S}_\phi$ yields $\mathbf{S}_\phi = \mathbf{U} \boldsymbol{\Delta} \mathbf{U}^T$, with the inverse of $\mathbf{S}_\phi$ given as $\mathbf{S}_\phi^{-1} = \mathbf{U} \boldsymbol{\Delta}^{-1} \mathbf{U}^T$. Here $\mathbf{U}$ is the matrix whose columns are the eigenvectors of $\mathbf{S}_\phi$ and $\boldsymbol{\Delta}$ is the diagonal matrix of eigenvalues of $\mathbf{S}_\phi$. The inverse $\mathbf{S}_\phi^{-1}$ can thus be expressed as the spectral sum

$$\mathbf{S}_\phi^{-1} = \sum_{r=1}^{d} \frac{1}{\delta_r} \mathbf{u}_r \mathbf{u}_r^T \qquad (20.15)$$

Plugging Eqs. (20.13) and (20.15) into Eq. (20.14), we obtain

$$\lambda \mathbf{w} = \left(\sum_{r=1}^{d} \frac{1}{\delta_r} \mathbf{u}_r \mathbf{u}_r^T\right) \mathbf{d}_\phi \mathbf{d}_\phi^T \mathbf{w} = \sum_{r=1}^{d} \frac{1}{\delta_r}\left(\mathbf{u}_r (\mathbf{u}_r^T \mathbf{d}_\phi)(\mathbf{d}_\phi^T \mathbf{w})\right) = \sum_{r=1}^{d} b_r \mathbf{u}_r$$

where $b_r = \frac{1}{\delta_r}(\mathbf{u}_r^T \mathbf{d}_\phi)(\mathbf{d}_\phi^T \mathbf{w})$ is a scalar value. Using a derivation similar to that in Eq. (7.38), the rth eigenvector of $\mathbf{S}_\phi$ can be expressed as a linear combination of the feature points, say $\mathbf{u}_r = \sum_{j=1}^{n} c_{rj} \phi(\mathbf{x}_j)$, where c_{rj} is a scalar coefficient. Thus, we can rewrite $\mathbf{w}$ as

$$\mathbf{w} = \frac{1}{\lambda} \sum_{r=1}^{d} b_r \left(\sum_{j=1}^{n} c_{rj} \phi(\mathbf{x}_j)\right)$$

$$= \sum_{j=1}^{n} \phi(\mathbf{x}_j) \left(\sum_{r=1}^{d} \frac{b_r c_{rj}}{\lambda}\right)$$

$$= \sum_{j=1}^{n} a_j \phi(\mathbf{x}_j)$$

where $a_j = \sum_{r=1}^{d} b_r c_{rj}/\lambda$ is a scalar value for the feature point $\phi(\mathbf{x}_j)$. Therefore, the direction vector $\mathbf{w}$ can be expressed as a linear combination of the points in feature space.

LDA Objective via Kernel Matrix

We now rewrite the kernel LDA objective [Eq. (20.11)] in terms of the kernel matrix. Projecting the mean for class c_i given in Eq. (20.12) onto the LD direction $\mathbf{w}$, we have

$$
\begin{aligned}
m_i = \mathbf{w}^T \boldsymbol{\mu}_i^\phi &= \left(\sum_{j=1}^n a_j\, \phi(\mathbf{x}_j) \right)^T \left(\frac{1}{n_i} \sum_{\mathbf{x}_k \in \mathbf{D}_i} \phi(\mathbf{x}_k) \right) \\
&= \frac{1}{n_i} \sum_{j=1}^n \sum_{\mathbf{x}_k \in \mathbf{D}_i} a_j\, \phi(\mathbf{x}_j)^T \phi(\mathbf{x}_k) \\
&= \frac{1}{n_i} \sum_{j=1}^n \sum_{\mathbf{x}_k \in \mathbf{D}_i} a_j\, K(\mathbf{x}_j, \mathbf{x}_k) \\
&= \mathbf{a}^T \mathbf{m}_i
\end{aligned}
\tag{20.16}
$$

where $\mathbf{a} = (a_1, a_2, \ldots, a_n)^T$ is the weight vector, and

$$
\mathbf{m}_i = \frac{1}{n_i}
\begin{pmatrix}
\sum_{\mathbf{x}_k \in \mathbf{D}_i} K(\mathbf{x}_1, \mathbf{x}_k) \\
\sum_{\mathbf{x}_k \in \mathbf{D}_i} K(\mathbf{x}_2, \mathbf{x}_k) \\
\vdots \\
\sum_{\mathbf{x}_k \in \mathbf{D}_i} K(\mathbf{x}_n, \mathbf{x}_k)
\end{pmatrix}
= \frac{1}{n_i} \mathbf{K}^{c_i} \mathbf{1}_{n_i}
\tag{20.17}
$$

where $\mathbf{K}^{c_i}$ is the $n \times n_i$ subset of the kernel matrix, restricted to columns belonging to points only in $\mathbf{D}_i$, and $\mathbf{1}_{n_i}$ is the n_i-dimensional vector all of whose entries are one. The n-length vector $\mathbf{m}_i$ thus stores for each point in $\mathbf{D}$ its average kernel value with respect to the points in $\mathbf{D}_i$.

We can rewrite the separation between the projected means in feature space as follows:

$$
\begin{aligned}
(m_1 - m_2)^2 &= \left(\mathbf{w}^T \boldsymbol{\mu}_1^\phi - \mathbf{w}^T \boldsymbol{\mu}_2^\phi \right)^2 \\
&= \left(\mathbf{a}^T \mathbf{m}_1 - \mathbf{a}^T \mathbf{m}_2 \right)^2 \\
&= \mathbf{a}^T (\mathbf{m}_1 - \mathbf{m}_2)(\mathbf{m}_1 - \mathbf{m}_2)^T \mathbf{a} \\
&= \mathbf{a}^T \mathbf{M} \mathbf{a}
\end{aligned}
\tag{20.18}
$$

where $\mathbf{M} = (\mathbf{m}_1 - \mathbf{m}_2)(\mathbf{m}_1 - \mathbf{m}_2)^T$ is the between-class scatter matrix.

We can also compute the projected scatter for each class, s_1^2 and s_2^2, purely in terms of the kernel function, as

$$
\begin{aligned}
s_1^2 &= \sum_{\mathbf{x}_i \in \mathbf{D}_1} \| \mathbf{w}^T \phi(\mathbf{x}_i) - \mathbf{w}^T \boldsymbol{\mu}_1^\phi \|^2 \\
&= \sum_{\mathbf{x}_i \in \mathbf{D}_1} \| \mathbf{w}^T \phi(\mathbf{x}_i) \|^2 - 2 \sum_{\mathbf{x}_i \in \mathbf{D}_1} \mathbf{w}^T \phi(\mathbf{x}_i) \cdot \mathbf{w}^T \boldsymbol{\mu}_1^\phi + \sum_{\mathbf{x}_i \in \mathbf{D}_1} \| \mathbf{w}^T \boldsymbol{\mu}_1^\phi \|^2 \\
&= \left(\sum_{\mathbf{x}_i \in \mathbf{D}_1} \left\| \sum_{j=1}^n a_j \phi(\mathbf{x}_j)^T \phi(\mathbf{x}_i) \right\|^2 \right) - 2 \cdot n_1 \cdot \left\| \mathbf{w}^T \boldsymbol{\mu}_1^\phi \right\|^2 + n_1 \cdot \left\| \mathbf{w}^T \boldsymbol{\mu}_1^\phi \right\|^2
\end{aligned}
$$

$$= \left(\sum_{\mathbf{x}_i \in \mathbf{D}_1} \mathbf{a}^T \mathbf{K}_i \mathbf{K}_i^T \mathbf{a} \right) - n_1 \cdot \mathbf{a}^T \mathbf{m}_1 \mathbf{m}_1^T \mathbf{a} \qquad \text{by using Eq. (20.16)}$$

$$= \mathbf{a}^T \left(\left(\sum_{\mathbf{x}_i \in \mathbf{D}_1} \mathbf{K}_i \mathbf{K}_i^T \right) - n_1 \mathbf{m}_1 \mathbf{m}_1^T \right) \mathbf{a}$$

$$= \mathbf{a}^T \mathbf{N}_1 \mathbf{a}$$

where $\mathbf{K}_i$ is the ith column of the kernel matrix, and $\mathbf{N}_1$ is the class scatter matrix for c_1. Let $K(\mathbf{x}_i, \mathbf{x}_j) = K_{ij}$. We can express $\mathbf{N}_1$ more compactly in matrix notation as follows:

$$\mathbf{N}_1 = \left(\sum_{\mathbf{x}_i \in \mathbf{D}_1} \mathbf{K}_i \mathbf{K}_i^T \right) - n_1 \mathbf{m}_1 \mathbf{m}_1^T$$

$$= (\mathbf{K}^{c_1}) \left(\mathbf{I}_{n_1} - \frac{1}{n_1} \mathbf{1}_{n_1 \times n_1} \right) (\mathbf{K}^{c_1})^T \qquad (20.19)$$

where $\mathbf{I}_{n_1}$ is the $n_1 \times n_1$ identity matrix and $\mathbf{1}_{n_1 \times n_1}$ is the $n_1 \times n_1$ matrix, all of whose entries are 1's.

In a similar manner we get $s_2^2 = \mathbf{a}^T \mathbf{N}_2 \mathbf{a}$, where

$$\mathbf{N}_2 = (\mathbf{K}^{c_2}) \left(\mathbf{I}_{n_2} - \frac{1}{n_2} \mathbf{1}_{n_2 \times n_2} \right) (\mathbf{K}^{c_2})^T$$

where $\mathbf{I}_{n_2}$ is the $n_2 \times n_2$ identity matrix and $\mathbf{1}_{n_2 \times n_2}$ is the $n_2 \times n_2$ matrix, all of whose entries are 1's.

The sum of projected scatter values is then given as

$$s_1^2 + s_2^2 = \mathbf{a}^T (\mathbf{N}_1 + \mathbf{N}_2) \mathbf{a} = \mathbf{a}^T \mathbf{N} \mathbf{a} \qquad (20.20)$$

where $\mathbf{N}$ is the $n \times n$ within-class scatter matrix.

Substituting Eqs. (20.18) and (20.20) in Eq. (20.11), we obtain the kernel LDA maximization condition

$$\boxed{\max_{\mathbf{w}} J(\mathbf{w}) = \max_{\mathbf{a}} J(\mathbf{a}) = \frac{\mathbf{a}^T \mathbf{M} \mathbf{a}}{\mathbf{a}^T \mathbf{N} \mathbf{a}}} \qquad (20.21)$$

Notice how all the terms in the expression above involve only kernel functions. The weight vector $\mathbf{a}$ is the eigenvector corresponding to the largest eigenvalue of the generalized eigenvalue problem:

$$\mathbf{M} \mathbf{a} = \lambda_1 \mathbf{N} \mathbf{a} \qquad (20.22)$$

If $\mathbf{N}$ is nonsingular, $\mathbf{a}$ is the dominant eigenvector corresponding to the largest eigenvalue for the system

$$(\mathbf{N}^{-1} \mathbf{M}) \mathbf{a} = \lambda_1 \mathbf{a}$$

As in the case of linear discriminant analysis [Eq. (20.10)], when there are only two classes we do not have to solve for the eigenvector because $\mathbf{a}$ can be obtained directly:

$$\mathbf{a} = \mathbf{N}^{-1} (\mathbf{m}_1 - \mathbf{m}_2)$$

Algorithm 20.2: Kernel Discriminant Analysis

KERNELDISCRIMINANT (D, K):

1 $\mathbf{K} \leftarrow \big\{ K(\mathbf{x}_i, \mathbf{x}_j) \big\}_{i,j=1,\dots,n}$ // compute $n \times n$ `kernel matrix`

2 $\mathbf{K}^{c_i} \leftarrow \big\{ \mathbf{K}(j,k) \mid y_k = c_i, 1 \le j, k \le n \big\}, i = 1, 2$ // `class kernel matrix`

3 $\mathbf{m}_i \leftarrow \frac{1}{n_i} \mathbf{K}^{c_i} \mathbf{1}_{n_i}, i = 1, 2$ // `class means`

4 $\mathbf{M} \leftarrow (\mathbf{m}_1 - \mathbf{m}_2)(\mathbf{m}_1 - \mathbf{m}_2)^T$ // `between-class scatter matrix`

5 $\mathbf{N}_i \leftarrow \mathbf{K}^{c_i}(\mathbf{I}_{n_i} - \frac{1}{n_i}\mathbf{1}_{n_i \times n_i})(\mathbf{K}^{c_i})^T, i = 1, 2$ // `class scatter matrices`

6 $\mathbf{N} \leftarrow \mathbf{N}_1 + \mathbf{N}_2$ // `within-class scatter matrix`

7 $\lambda_1, \mathbf{a} \leftarrow \text{eigen}(\mathbf{N}^{-1}\mathbf{M})$ // `compute weight vector`

8 $\mathbf{a} \leftarrow \frac{\mathbf{a}}{\sqrt{\mathbf{a}^T \mathbf{Ka}}}$ // `normalize` **w** `to be unit vector`

Once **a** has been obtained, we can normalize **w** to be a unit vector by ensuring that

$$\mathbf{w}^T\mathbf{w} = 1, \text{ which implies that}$$

$$\sum_{i=1}^{n} \sum_{j=1}^{n} a_i a_j \phi(\mathbf{x}_i)^T \phi(\mathbf{x}_j) = 1, \text{ or}$$

$$\mathbf{a}^T \mathbf{Ka} = 1$$

Put differently, we can ensure that **w** is a unit vector if we scale **a** by $\frac{1}{\sqrt{\mathbf{a}^T \mathbf{Ka}}}$.

Finally, we can project any point **x** onto the discriminant direction, as follows:

$$\mathbf{w}^T \phi(\mathbf{x}) = \sum_{j=1}^{n} a_j \phi(\mathbf{x}_j)^T \phi(\mathbf{x}) = \sum_{j=1}^{n} a_j K(\mathbf{x}_j, \mathbf{x}) \qquad (20.23)$$

Algorithm 20.2 shows the pseudo-code for kernel discriminant analysis. The method proceeds by computing the $n \times n$ kernel matrix **K**, and the $n \times n_i$ class specific kernel matrices $\mathbf{K}^{c_i}$ for each class c_i. After computing the between-class and within-class scatter matrices **M** and **N**, the weight vector **a** is obtained as the dominant eigenvector of $\mathbf{N}^{-1}\mathbf{M}$. The last step scales **a** so that **w** will be normalized to be unit length. The complexity of kernel discriminant analysis is $O(n^3)$, with the dominant steps being the computation of **N** and solving for the dominant eigenvector of $\mathbf{N}^{-1}\mathbf{M}$, both of which take $O(n^3)$ time.

Example 20.4 (Kernel Discriminant Analysis). Consider the 2-dimensional Iris dataset comprising the sepal length and sepal width attributes. Figure 20.3(a) shows the points projected onto the first two principal components. The points have been divided into two classes: c_1 (circles) corresponds to Iris-versicolor and c_2 (triangles) corresponds to the other two Iris types. Here $n_1 = 50$ and $n_2 = 100$, with a total of $n = 150$ points.

Because c_1 is surrounded by points in c_2 a good linear discriminant will not be found. Instead, we apply kernel discriminant analysis using the homogeneous

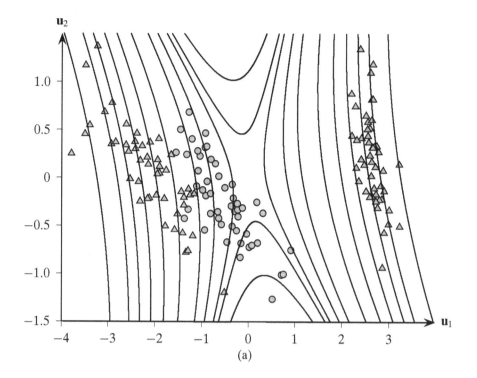

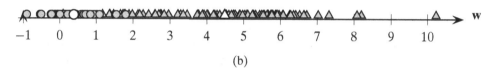

Figure 20.3. Kernel discriminant analysis: quadratic homogeneous kernel.

quadratic kernel

$$K(\mathbf{x}_i, \mathbf{x}_j) = (\mathbf{x}_i^T \mathbf{x}_j)^2$$

Solving for $\mathbf{a}$ via Eq. (20.22) yields

$$\lambda_1 = 0.0511$$

However, we do not show $\mathbf{a}$ because it lies in $\mathbb{R}^{150}$. Figure 20.3(a) shows the contours of constant projections onto the best kernel discriminant. The contours are obtained by solving Eq. (20.23), that is, by solving $\mathbf{w}^T \phi(\mathbf{x}) = \sum_{j=1}^{n} a_j K(\mathbf{x}_j, \mathbf{x}) = c$ for different values of the scalars c. The contours are hyperbolic, and thus form pairs starting from the center. For instance, the first curve on the left and right of the origin $(0, 0)^T$ forms the same contour, that is, points along both the curves have the same value when projected onto $\mathbf{w}$. We can see that contours or pairs of curves starting with the fourth curve (on the left and right) from the center all relate to class c_2, whereas the first three contours deal mainly with class c_1, indicating good discrimination with the homogeneous quadratic kernel.

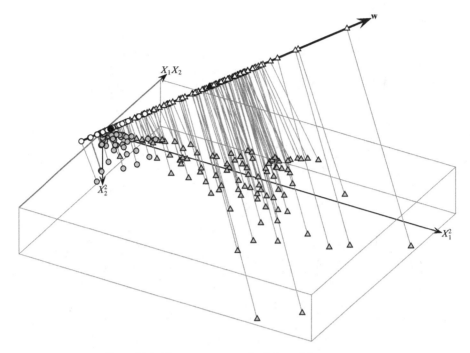

Figure 20.4. Homogeneous quadratic kernel feature space.

A better picture emerges when we plot the coordinates of all the points $\mathbf{x}_i \in \mathbf{D}$ when projected onto $\mathbf{w}$, as shown in Figure 20.3(b). We can observe that $\mathbf{w}$ is able to separate the two classes reasonably well; all the circles (c_1) are concentrated on the left, whereas the triangles (c_2) are spread out on the right. The projected means are shown in white. The projected scatters and means for both classes are as follows:

$$m_1 = 0.338 \qquad\qquad\qquad m_2 = 4.476$$
$$s_1^2 = 13.862 \qquad\qquad\qquad s_2^2 = 320.934$$

The value of $J(\mathbf{w})$ is given as

$$J(\mathbf{w}) = \frac{(m_1 - m_2)^2}{s_1^2 + s_2^2} = \frac{(0.338 - 4.476)^2}{13.862 + 320.934} = \frac{17.123}{334.796} = 0.0511$$

which, as expected, matches $\lambda_1 = 0.0511$ from above.

In general, it is not desirable or possible to obtain an explicit discriminant vector $\mathbf{w}$, since it lies in feature space. However, because each point $\mathbf{x} = (x_1, x_2)^T \in \mathbb{R}^2$ in input space is mapped to the point $\phi(\mathbf{x}) = (\sqrt{2}x_1x_2, x_1^2, x_2^2)^T \in \mathbb{R}^3$ in feature space via the homogeneous quadratic kernel, for our example it is possible to visualize the feature space, as illustrated in Figure 20.4. The projection of each point $\phi(\mathbf{x}_i)$ onto the discriminant vector $\mathbf{w}$ is also shown, where

$$\mathbf{w} = 0.511x_1x_2 + 0.761x_1^2 - 0.4x_2^2$$

The projections onto $\mathbf{w}$ are identical to those shown in Figure 20.3(b).

20.3 FURTHER READING

Linear discriminant analysis was introduced in Fisher (1936). Its extension to kernel discriminant analysis was proposed in Mika et al. (1999). The 2-class LDA approach can be generalized to $k > 2$ classes by finding the optimal $(k-1)$-dimensional subspace projection that best discriminates between the k classes; see Duda, Hart, and Stork (2012) for details.

Duda, R. O., Hart, P. E., and Stork, D. G. (2012). *Pattern Classification*. New York: Wiley-Interscience.

Fisher, R. A. (1936). The use of multiple measurements in taxonomic problems. *Annals of Eugenics*, 7 (2), 179–188.

Mika, S., Ratsch, G., Weston, J., Scholkopf, B., and Mullers, K. (1999). Fisher discriminant analysis with kernels. *Proceedings of the IEEE Neural Networks for Signal Processing Workshop*. IEEE, pp. 41–48.

20.4 EXERCISES

Q1. Consider the data shown in Table 20.1. Answer the following questions:
  (a) Compute μ_{+1} and μ_{-1}, and **B**, the between-class scatter matrix.
  (b) Compute S_{+1} and S_{-1}, and **S**, the within-class scatter matrix.
  (c) Find the best direction **w** that discriminates between the classes. Use the fact that the inverse of the matrix $\mathbf{A} = \begin{pmatrix} a & b \\ c & d \end{pmatrix}$ is given as $\mathbf{A}^{-1} = \frac{1}{\det(\mathbf{A})} \begin{pmatrix} d & -b \\ -c & a \end{pmatrix}$.
  (d) Having found the direction **w**, find the point on **w** that best separates the two classes.

Table 20.1. Dataset for Q1

i	$\mathbf{x}_i^T$	y_i
$\mathbf{x}_1^T$	(4,2.9)	1
$\mathbf{x}_2^T$	(3.5,4)	1
$\mathbf{x}_3^T$	(2.5,1)	−1
$\mathbf{x}_4^T$	(2,2.1)	−1

Q2. Given the labeled points (from two classes) shown in Figure 20.5, and given that the inverse of the within-class scatter matrix is

$$\begin{pmatrix} 0.056 & -0.029 \\ -0.029 & 0.052 \end{pmatrix}$$

Find the best linear discriminant line **w**, and sketch it.

Q3. Maximize the objective in Eq. (20.7) by explicitly considering the constraint $\mathbf{w}^T\mathbf{w} = 1$, that is, by using a Lagrange multiplier for that constraint.

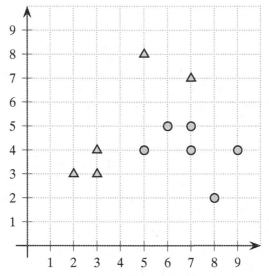

Figure 20.5. Dataset for Q2.

Q4. Prove the equality in Eq. (20.19). That is, show that

$$\mathbf{N}_1 = \left(\sum_{\mathbf{x}_i \in \mathbf{D}_1} \mathbf{K}_i \mathbf{K}_i^T \right) - n_1 \mathbf{m}_1 \mathbf{m}_1^T = (\mathbf{K}^{c_1}) \left(\mathbf{I}_{n_1} - \frac{1}{n_1} \mathbf{1}_{n_1 \times n_1} \right) (\mathbf{K}^{c_1})^T$$

CHAPTER 21

Support Vector Machines

In this chapter we describe Support Vector Machines (SVMs), a classification method based on maximum margin linear discriminants, that is, the goal is to find the optimal hyperplane that maximizes the gap or margin between the classes. Further, we can use the kernel trick to find the optimal nonlinear decision boundary between classes, which corresponds to a hyperplane in some high-dimensional "nonlinear" space.

21.1 SUPPORT VECTORS AND MARGINS

Let $\mathbf{D}$ be a classification dataset, with n points $\mathbf{x}_i$ in a d-dimensional space. Further, let us assume that there are only two class labels, that is, $y_i \in \{+1, -1\}$, denoting the positive and negative classes.

Hyperplanes

Recall from Section 6.1 that a hyperplane in d dimensions is given as the set of all points $\mathbf{x} \in \mathbb{R}^d$ that satisfy the equation $h(\mathbf{x}) = 0$, where $h(\mathbf{x})$ is the *hyperplane function*, defined as follows:

$$h(\mathbf{x}) = \mathbf{w}^T \mathbf{x} + b = w_1 x_1 + w_2 x_2 + \cdots + w_d x_d + b \tag{21.1}$$

Here, $\mathbf{w}$ is a d dimensional *weight vector* and b is a scalar, called the *bias*. For points that lie on the hyperplane, we have

$$h(\mathbf{x}) = \mathbf{w}^T \mathbf{x} + b = 0 \tag{21.2}$$

The hyperplane is thus defined as the set of all points such that $\mathbf{w}^T \mathbf{x} = -b$.

Recall further that the weight vector $\mathbf{w}$ is orthogonal or *normal* to the hyperplane, whereas $-\frac{b}{w_i}$ specifies the offset where the hyperplane intersects the ith dimension (provided $w_i \neq 0$). In other words, the weight vector $\mathbf{w}$ specifies the direction that is normal to the hyperplane, which fixes the orientation of the hyperplane, whereas the bias b fixes the offset of the hyperplane in the d-dimensional space.

Separating Hyperplane

A hyperplane splits the original d-dimensional space into two *half-spaces*. A dataset is said to be *linearly separable* if each half-space has points only from a single class. If the input dataset is linearly separable, then we can find a *separating* hyperplane $h(\mathbf{x}) = 0$, such that for all points labeled $y_i = -1$, we have $h(\mathbf{x}_i) < 0$, and for all points labeled $y_i = +1$, we have $h(\mathbf{x}_i) > 0$. In fact, the hyperplane function $h(\mathbf{x})$ serves as a linear classifier or a linear discriminant, which predicts the class y for any given point $\mathbf{x}$, according to the decision rule:

$$y = \begin{cases} +1 & \text{if } h(\mathbf{x}) > 0 \\ -1 & \text{if } h(\mathbf{x}) < 0 \end{cases} \tag{21.3}$$

Note that because both $\mathbf{w}$ and $-\mathbf{w}$ are normal to the hyperplane, we remove this ambiguity by requiring that $h(\mathbf{x}_i) > 0$ when $y_i = 1$, and $h(\mathbf{x}_i) < 0$ when $y_i = -1$.

Distance of a Point to the Hyperplane

Consider a point $\mathbf{x} \in \mathbb{R}^d$, such that $\mathbf{x}$ does not lie on the hyperplane. Let $\mathbf{x}_p$ be the orthogonal projection of $\mathbf{x}$ on the hyperplane, and let $\mathbf{r} = \mathbf{x} - \mathbf{x}_p$, then as shown in Figure 21.1 we can write $\mathbf{x}$ as

$$\mathbf{x} = \mathbf{x}_p + \mathbf{r}$$
$$\mathbf{x} = \mathbf{x}_p + r \frac{\mathbf{w}}{\|\mathbf{w}\|} \tag{21.4}$$

where r is the *directed distance* of the point $\mathbf{x}$ from $\mathbf{x}_p$, that is, r gives the offset of $\mathbf{x}$ from $\mathbf{x}_p$ in terms of the unit weight vector $\frac{\mathbf{w}}{\|\mathbf{w}\|}$. The offset r is positive if $\mathbf{r}$ is in the same direction as $\mathbf{w}$, and r is negative if $\mathbf{r}$ is in a direction opposite to $\mathbf{w}$.

Plugging Eq. (21.4) into the hyperplane function [Eq. (21.1)], we get

$$h(\mathbf{x}) = h\left(\mathbf{x}_p + r \frac{\mathbf{w}}{\|\mathbf{w}\|}\right)$$
$$= \mathbf{w}^T \left(\mathbf{x}_p + r \frac{\mathbf{w}}{\|\mathbf{w}\|}\right) + b$$
$$= \underbrace{\mathbf{w}^T \mathbf{x}_p + b}_{h(\mathbf{x}_p)} + r \frac{\mathbf{w}^T \mathbf{w}}{\|\mathbf{w}\|}$$
$$= \underbrace{h(\mathbf{x}_p)}_{0} + r \|\mathbf{w}\|$$
$$= r \|\mathbf{w}\|$$

The last step follows from the fact that $h(\mathbf{x}_p) = 0$ because $\mathbf{x}_p$ lies on the hyperplane. Using the result above, we obtain an expression for the directed distance of a point to the hyperplane:

$$r = \frac{h(\mathbf{x})}{\|\mathbf{w}\|}$$

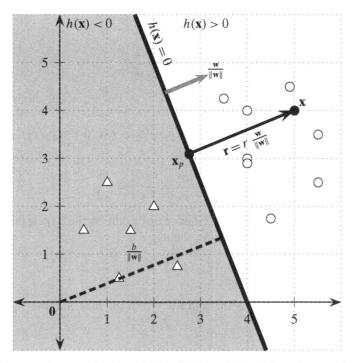

Figure 21.1. Geometry of a separating hyperplane in 2D. Points labeled $+1$ are shown as circles, and those labeled -1 are shown as triangles. The hyperplane $h(\mathbf{x}) = 0$ divides the space into two half-spaces. The shaded region comprises all points $\mathbf{x}$ satisfying $h(\mathbf{x}) < 0$, whereas the unshaded region consists of all points satisfying $h(\mathbf{x}) > 0$. The unit weight vector $\frac{\mathbf{w}}{\|\mathbf{w}\|}$ (in gray) is orthogonal to the hyperplane. The directed distance of the origin to the hyperplane is $\frac{b}{\|\mathbf{w}\|}$.

To obtain distance, which must be non-negative, we can conveniently multiply r by the class label y of the point because when $h(\mathbf{x}) < 0$, the class is -1, and when $h(\mathbf{x}) > 0$ the class is $+1$. The distance of a point $\mathbf{x}$ from the hyperplane $h(\mathbf{x}) = 0$ is thus given as

$$\delta = y\,r = \frac{y\,h(\mathbf{x})}{\|\mathbf{w}\|} \tag{21.5}$$

In particular, for the origin $\mathbf{x} = \mathbf{0}$, the directed distance is

$$r = \frac{h(\mathbf{0})}{\|\mathbf{w}\|} = \frac{\mathbf{w}^T\mathbf{0} + b}{\|\mathbf{w}\|} = \frac{b}{\|\mathbf{w}\|}$$

as illustrated in Figure 21.1.

Example 21.1. Consider the example shown in Figure 21.1. In this 2-dimensional example, the hyperplane is just a line, defined as the set of all points $\mathbf{x} = (x_1, x_2)^T$ that satisfy the following equation:

$$h(\mathbf{x}) = \mathbf{w}^T\mathbf{x} + b = w_1x_1 + w_2x_2 + b = 0$$

Rearranging the terms we get

$$x_2 = -\frac{w_1}{w_2}x_1 - \frac{b}{w_2}$$

where $-\frac{w_1}{w_2}$ is the slope of the line, and $-\frac{b}{w_2}$ is the intercept along the second dimension.

Consider any two points on the hyperplane, say $\mathbf{p} = (p_1, p_2) = (4, 0)$, and $\mathbf{q} = (q_1, q_2) = (2, 5)$. The slope is given as

$$-\frac{w_1}{w_2} = \frac{q_2 - p_2}{q_1 - p_1} = \frac{5 - 0}{2 - 4} = -\frac{5}{2}$$

which implies that $w_1 = 5$ and $w_2 = 2$. Given any point on the hyperplane, say $(4, 0)$, we can compute the offset b directly as follows:

$$b = -5x_1 - 2x_2 = -5 \cdot 4 - 2 \cdot 0 = -20$$

Thus, $\mathbf{w} = \begin{pmatrix} 5 \\ 2 \end{pmatrix}$ is the weight vector, and $b = -20$ is the bias, and the equation of the hyperplane is given as

$$h(\mathbf{x}) = \mathbf{w}^T\mathbf{x} + b = \begin{pmatrix} 5 & 2 \end{pmatrix} \begin{pmatrix} x_1 \\ x_2 \end{pmatrix} - 20 = 0$$

One can verify that the distance of the origin $\mathbf{0}$ from the hyperplane is given as

$$\delta = y\,r = -1\,r = \frac{-b}{\|\mathbf{w}\|} = \frac{-(-20)}{\sqrt{29}} = 3.71$$

Margin and Support Vectors of a Hyperplane

Given a training dataset $\mathbf{D}$ of n labeled points $\mathbf{x}_i$, with $y_i \in \{+1, -1\}$, and given a separating hyperplane $h(\mathbf{x}) = 0$, for each point $\mathbf{x}_i$ we can find its distance to the hyperplane by Eq. (21.5):

$$\delta_i = \frac{y_i\,h(\mathbf{x}_i)}{\|\mathbf{w}\|} = \frac{y_i(\mathbf{w}^T\mathbf{x}_i + b)}{\|\mathbf{w}\|}$$

Over all the n points, we define the *margin* of the linear classifier as the minimum distance of a point from the separating hyperplane, given as

$$\delta^* = \min_{\mathbf{x}_i} \left\{ \frac{y_i(\mathbf{w}^T\mathbf{x}_i + b)}{\|\mathbf{w}\|} \right\} \tag{21.6}$$

Note that $\delta^* \neq 0$, since $h(\mathbf{x})$ is assumed to be a separating hyperplane, and Eq. (21.3) must be satisfied.

All the points (or vectors) that achieve this minimum distance are called *support vectors* for the hyperplane. In other words, a support vector $\mathbf{x}^*$ is a point that lies precisely on the margin of the classifier, and thus satisfies the condition

$$\delta^* = \frac{y^*(\mathbf{w}^T\mathbf{x}^* + b)}{\|\mathbf{w}\|}$$

where y^* is the class label for $\mathbf{x}^*$. The numerator $y^*(\mathbf{w}^T\mathbf{x}^* + b)$ gives the absolute distance of the support vector to the hyperplane, whereas the denominator $\|\mathbf{w}\|$ makes it a relative distance in terms of $\mathbf{w}$.

Canonical Hyperplane

Consider the equation of the hyperplane [Eq. (21.2)]. Multiplying on both sides by some scalar s yields an equivalent hyperplane:

$$s\, h(\mathbf{x}) = s\, \mathbf{w}^T\mathbf{x} + s\, b = (s\mathbf{w})^T\mathbf{x} + (sb) = 0$$

To obtain the unique or *canonical* hyperplane, we choose the scalar s such that the absolute distance of a support vector from the hyperplane is 1. That is,

$$sy^*(\mathbf{w}^T\mathbf{x}^* + b) = 1$$

which implies

$$s = \frac{1}{y^*(\mathbf{w}^T\mathbf{x}^* + b)} = \frac{1}{y^*h(\mathbf{x}^*)} \tag{21.7}$$

Henceforth, we will assume that any separating hyperplane is canonical. That is, it has already been suitably rescaled so that $y^*h(\mathbf{x}^*) = 1$ for a support vector $\mathbf{x}^*$, and the margin is given as

$$\delta^* = \frac{y^*h(\mathbf{x}^*)}{\|\mathbf{w}\|} = \frac{1}{\|\mathbf{w}\|}$$

For the canonical hyperplane, for each support vector $\mathbf{x}_i^*$ (with label y_i^*), we have $y_i^*h(\mathbf{x}_i^*) = 1$, and for any point that is not a support vector we have $y_i h(\mathbf{x}_i) > 1$, because, by definition, it must be farther from the hyperplane than a support vector. Over all the n points in the dataset $\mathbf{D}$, we thus obtain the following set of inequalities:

$$\boxed{y_i\,(\mathbf{w}^T\mathbf{x}_i + b) \geq 1, \text{ for all points } \mathbf{x}_i \in \mathbf{D}} \tag{21.8}$$

Example 21.2. Figure 21.2 gives an illustration of the support vectors and the margin of a hyperplane. The equation of the separating hyperplane is

$$h(\mathbf{x}) = \begin{pmatrix} 5 \\ 2 \end{pmatrix}^T \mathbf{x} - 20 = 0$$

Consider the support vector $\mathbf{x}^* = (2, 2)^T$, with class $y^* = -1$. To find the canonical hyperplane equation, we have to rescale the weight vector and bias by the scalar s, obtained using Eq. (21.7):

$$s = \frac{1}{y^*h(\mathbf{x}^*)} = \frac{1}{-1\left(\begin{pmatrix} 5 \\ 2 \end{pmatrix}^T \begin{pmatrix} 2 \\ 2 \end{pmatrix} - 20\right)} = \frac{1}{6}$$

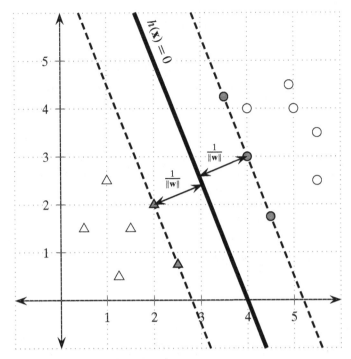

Figure 21.2. Margin of a separating hyperplane: $\frac{1}{\|\mathbf{w}\|}$ is the margin, and the shaded points are the support vectors.

Thus, the rescaled weight vector is

$$\mathbf{w} = \frac{1}{6}\begin{pmatrix} 5 \\ 2 \end{pmatrix} = \begin{pmatrix} 5/6 \\ 2/6 \end{pmatrix}$$

and the rescaled bias is

$$b = \frac{-20}{6}$$

The canonical form of the hyperplane is therefore

$$h(\mathbf{x}) = \begin{pmatrix} 5/6 \\ 2/6 \end{pmatrix}^T \mathbf{x} - 20/6 = \begin{pmatrix} 0.833 \\ 0.333 \end{pmatrix}^T \mathbf{x} - 3.33$$

and the margin of the canonical hyperplane is

$$\delta^* = \frac{y^* h(\mathbf{x}^*)}{\|\mathbf{w}\|} = \frac{1}{\sqrt{\left(\frac{5}{6}\right)^2 + \left(\frac{2}{6}\right)^2}} = \frac{6}{\sqrt{29}} = 1.114$$

In this example there are five support vectors (shown as shaded points), namely, $(2,2)^T$ and $(2.5, 0.75)^T$ with class $y = -1$ (shown as triangles), and $(3.5, 4.25)^T$, $(4,3)^T$, and $(4.5, 1.75)^T$ with class $y = +1$ (shown as circles), as illustrated in Figure 21.2.

21.2 SVM: LINEAR AND SEPARABLE CASE

Given a dataset $\mathbf{D}$ with n points $\mathbf{x}_i \in \mathbb{R}^d$ with labels $y_i \in \{+1, -1\}$, let us assume for the moment that the points are linearly separable, that is, there exists a separating hyperplane that perfectly classifies each point. In other words, all points labeled $y_i = +1$ lie on one side ($h(\mathbf{x}) > 0$) and all points labeled $y_i = -1$ lie on the other side ($h(\mathbf{x}) < 0$) of the hyperplane. It is obvious that in the linearly separable case, there are in fact an infinite number of such separating hyperplanes. Which one should we choose?

Maximum Margin Hyperplane

The fundamental idea behind SVMs is to choose the canonical hyperplane, specified by the weight vector $\mathbf{w}$ and the bias b, that yields the maximum margin among all possible separating hyperplanes. If δ_h^* represents the margin for hyperplane $h(\mathbf{x}) = 0$, then the goal is to find the optimal hyperplane h^*:

$$h^* = \arg\max_{h}\left\{\delta_h^*\right\} = \arg\max_{\mathbf{w},b}\left\{\frac{1}{\|\mathbf{w}\|}\right\}$$

The SVM task is to find the hyperplane that maximizes the margin $\frac{1}{\|\mathbf{w}\|}$, subject to the n constraints given in Eq. (21.8), namely, $y_i (\mathbf{w}^T\mathbf{x}_i + b) \geq 1$, for all points $\mathbf{x}_i \in \mathbf{D}$. Notice that instead of maximizing the margin $\frac{1}{\|\mathbf{w}\|}$, we can minimize $\|\mathbf{w}\|$. In fact, we can obtain an equivalent minimization formulation given as follows:

$$
\boxed{
\begin{array}{l}
\textbf{Objective Function: } \min_{\mathbf{w},b}\left\{\dfrac{\|\mathbf{w}\|^2}{2}\right\} \\[2mm]
\textbf{Linear Constraints: } y_i (\mathbf{w}^T\mathbf{x}_i + b) \geq 1, \ \forall \mathbf{x}_i \in \mathbf{D}
\end{array}
}
\tag{21.9}
$$

We can directly solve the above *primal* convex minimization problem with the n linear constraints using standard optimization algorithms. However, it is more common to solve the *dual* problem, which is obtained via the use of *Lagrange multipliers*. The main idea is to introduce a Lagrange multiplier α_i for each constraint, which satisfies the Karush–Kuhn–Tucker (KKT) conditions at the optimal solution:

$$\alpha_i \left(y_i (\mathbf{w}^T\mathbf{x}_i + b) - 1\right) = 0$$

$$\text{and } \alpha_i \geq 0$$

Incorporating all the n constraints, the new objective function, called the *Lagrangian*, then becomes

$$\min L = \frac{1}{2}\|\mathbf{w}\|^2 - \sum_{i=1}^{n}\alpha_i \left(y_i (\mathbf{w}^T\mathbf{x}_i + b) - 1\right)\tag{21.10}$$

L should be minimized with respect to $\mathbf{w}$ and b, and it should be maximized with respect to α_i.

Taking the derivative of L with respect to $\mathbf{w}$ and b, and setting them to zero, we get

$$\frac{\partial}{\partial \mathbf{w}} L = \mathbf{w} - \sum_{i=1}^{n} \alpha_i y_i \mathbf{x}_i = \mathbf{0} \quad \text{or} \quad \mathbf{w} = \sum_{i=1}^{n} \alpha_i y_i \mathbf{x}_i \tag{21.11}$$

$$\frac{\partial}{\partial b} L = \sum_{i=1}^{n} \alpha_i y_i = 0 \tag{21.12}$$

The above equations give important intuition about the optimal weight vector $\mathbf{w}$. In particular, Eq. (21.11) implies that $\mathbf{w}$ can be expressed as a linear combination of the data points $\mathbf{x}_i$, with the signed Lagrange multipliers, $\alpha_i y_i$, serving as the coefficients. Further, Eq. (21.12) implies that the sum of the signed Lagrange multipliers, $\alpha_i y_i$, must be zero.

Plugging these into Eq. (21.10), we obtain the *dual Lagrangian* objective function, which is specified purely in terms of the Lagrange multipliers:

$$L_{dual} = \frac{1}{2} \mathbf{w}^T \mathbf{w} - \mathbf{w}^T \underbrace{\left(\sum_{i=1}^{n} \alpha_i y_i \mathbf{x}_i \right)}_{\mathbf{w}} - b \underbrace{\sum_{i=1}^{n} \alpha_i y_i}_{0} + \sum_{i=1}^{n} \alpha_i$$

$$= -\frac{1}{2} \mathbf{w}^T \mathbf{w} + \sum_{i=1}^{n} \alpha_i$$

$$= \sum_{i=1}^{n} \alpha_i - \frac{1}{2} \sum_{i=1}^{n} \sum_{j=1}^{n} \alpha_i \alpha_j y_i y_j \mathbf{x}_i^T \mathbf{x}_j$$

The dual objective is thus given as

> **Objective Function:** $\displaystyle \max_{\boldsymbol{\alpha}} \; L_{dual} = \sum_{i=1}^{n} \alpha_i - \frac{1}{2} \sum_{i=1}^{n} \sum_{j=1}^{n} \alpha_i \alpha_j y_i y_j \mathbf{x}_i^T \mathbf{x}_j$
>
> **Linear Constraints:** $\alpha_i \geq 0, \; \forall i \in \mathbf{D}$, and $\displaystyle \sum_{i=1}^{n} \alpha_i y_i = 0$

$$\tag{21.13}$$

where $\boldsymbol{\alpha} = (\alpha_1, \alpha_2, \ldots, \alpha_n)^T$ is the vector comprising the Lagrange multipliers. L_{dual} is a convex quadratic programming problem (note the $\alpha_i \alpha_j$ terms), which can be solved using standard optimization techniques. See Section 21.5 for a gradient-based method for solving the dual formulation.

Weight Vector and Bias

Once we have obtained the α_i values for $i = 1, \ldots, n$, we can solve for the weight vector $\mathbf{w}$ and the bias b. Note that according to the KKT conditions, we have

$$\alpha_i \left(y_i (\mathbf{w}^T \mathbf{x}_i + b) - 1 \right) = 0$$

which gives rise to two cases:

(1) $\alpha_i = 0$, or

(2) $y_i (\mathbf{w}^T \mathbf{x}_i + b) - 1 = 0$, which implies $y_i (\mathbf{w}^T \mathbf{x}_i + b) = 1$

This is a very important result because if $\alpha_i > 0$, then $y_i(\mathbf{w}^T\mathbf{x}_i + b) = 1$, and thus the point $\mathbf{x}_i$ must be a support vector. On the other hand if $y_i(\mathbf{w}^T\mathbf{x}_i + b) > 1$, then $\alpha_i = 0$, that is, if a point is not a support vector, then $\alpha_i = 0$.

Once we know α_i for all points, we can compute the weight vector $\mathbf{w}$ using Eq. (21.11), but by taking the summation only for the support vectors:

$$\mathbf{w} = \sum_{\alpha_i > 0} \alpha_i y_i \mathbf{x}_i \tag{21.14}$$

In other words, $\mathbf{w}$ is obtained as a linear combination of the support vectors, with the $\alpha_i y_i$'s representing the weights. The rest of the points (with $\alpha_i = 0$) are not support vectors and thus do not play a role in determining $\mathbf{w}$.

To compute the bias b, we first compute one solution, denoted b_i, per support vector, as follows:

$$\alpha_i \left(y_i(\mathbf{w}^T\mathbf{x}_i + b_i) - 1 \right) = 0$$

$$y_i(\mathbf{w}^T\mathbf{x}_i + b_i) = 1$$

$$b_i = \frac{1}{y_i} - \mathbf{w}^T\mathbf{x}_i = y_i - \mathbf{w}^T\mathbf{x}_i \tag{21.15}$$

We can then compute b as the average bias value over all the support vectors:

$$b = \operatorname*{avg}_{\alpha_i > 0} \{b_i\} \tag{21.16}$$

SVM Classifier

Given the optimal hyperplane function $h(\mathbf{x}) = \mathbf{w}^T\mathbf{x} + b$, for any new point $\mathbf{z}$, we predict its class as

$$\hat{y} = \operatorname{sign}(h(\mathbf{z})) = \operatorname{sign}(\mathbf{w}^T\mathbf{z} + b) \tag{21.17}$$

where the sign($\cdot$) function returns $+1$ if its argument is positive, and -1 if its argument is negative.

Example 21.3. Let us continue with the example dataset shown in Figure 21.2. The dataset has 14 points as shown in Table 21.1.

Solving the L_{dual} quadratic program yields the following nonzero values for the Lagrangian multipliers, which determine the support vectors

$\mathbf{x}_i^T$	x_{i1}	x_{i2}	y_i	α_i
$\mathbf{x}_1^T$	3.5	4.25	+1	0.0437
$\mathbf{x}_2^T$	4	3	+1	0.2162
$\mathbf{x}_4^T$	4.5	1.75	+1	0.1427
$\mathbf{x}_{13}^T$	2	2	−1	0.3589
$\mathbf{x}_{14}^T$	2.5	0.75	−1	0.0437

Table 21.1. Dataset corresponding to Figure 21.2

$\mathbf{x}_i^T$	x_{i1}	x_{i2}	y_i
$\mathbf{x}_1^T$	3.5	4.25	$+1$
$\mathbf{x}_2^T$	4	3	$+1$
$\mathbf{x}_3^T$	4	4	$+1$
$\mathbf{x}_4^T$	4.5	1.75	$+1$
$\mathbf{x}_5^T$	4.9	4.5	$+1$
$\mathbf{x}_6^T$	5	4	$+1$
$\mathbf{x}_7^T$	5.5	2.5	$+1$
$\mathbf{x}_8^T$	5.5	3.5	$+1$
$\mathbf{x}_9^T$	0.5	1.5	-1
$\mathbf{x}_{10}^T$	1	2.5	-1
$\mathbf{x}_{11}^T$	1.25	0.5	-1
$\mathbf{x}_{12}^T$	1.5	1.5	-1
$\mathbf{x}_{13}^T$	2	2	-1
$\mathbf{x}_{14}^T$	2.5	0.75	-1

All other points have $\alpha_i = 0$ and therefore they are not support vectors. Using Eq. (21.14), we can compute the weight vector for the hyperplane:

$$\mathbf{w} = \sum_{\alpha_i > 0} \alpha_i y_i \mathbf{x}_i$$

$$= 0.0437 \begin{pmatrix} 3.5 \\ 4.25 \end{pmatrix} + 0.2162 \begin{pmatrix} 4 \\ 3 \end{pmatrix} + 0.1427 \begin{pmatrix} 4.5 \\ 1.75 \end{pmatrix} - 0.3589 \begin{pmatrix} 2 \\ 2 \end{pmatrix} - 0.0437 \begin{pmatrix} 2.5 \\ 0.75 \end{pmatrix}$$

$$= \begin{pmatrix} 0.833 \\ 0.334 \end{pmatrix}$$

The final bias is the average of the bias obtained from each support vector using Eq. (21.15):

$\mathbf{x}_i$	$\mathbf{w}^T \mathbf{x}_i$	$b_i = y_i - \mathbf{w}^T \mathbf{x}_i$
$\mathbf{x}_1$	4.332	-3.332
$\mathbf{x}_2$	4.331	-3.331
$\mathbf{x}_4$	4.331	-3.331
$\mathbf{x}_{13}$	2.333	-3.333
$\mathbf{x}_{14}$	2.332	-3.332
$b = \text{avg}\{b_i\}$		-3.332

Thus, the optimal hyperplane is given as follows:

$$h(\mathbf{x}) = \begin{pmatrix} 0.833 \\ 0.334 \end{pmatrix}^T \mathbf{x} - 3.332 = 0$$

which matches the canonical hyperplane in Example 21.2.

21.3 SOFT MARGIN SVM: LINEAR AND NONSEPARABLE CASE

So far we have assumed that the dataset is perfectly linearly separable. Here we consider the case where the classes overlap to some extent so that a perfect separation is not possible, as depicted in Figure 21.3.

Recall that when points are linearly separable we can find a separating hyperplane so that all points satisfy the condition $y_i(\mathbf{w}^T\mathbf{x}_i + b) \geq 1$. SVMs can handle non-separable points by introducing *slack variables* ξ_i in Eq. (21.8), as follows:

$$y_i(\mathbf{w}^T\mathbf{x}_i + b) \geq 1 - \xi_i \qquad (21.18)$$

where $\xi_i \geq 0$ is the slack variable for point $\mathbf{x}_i$, which indicates how much the point violates the separability condition, that is, the point may no longer be at least $1/\|\mathbf{w}\|$ away from the hyperplane. The slack values indicate three types of points. If $\xi_i = 0$, then the corresponding point $\mathbf{x}_i$ is at least $\frac{1}{\|\mathbf{w}\|}$ away from the hyperplane. If $0 < \xi_i < 1$, then the point is within the margin and still correctly classified, that is, it is on the correct side of the hyperplane. However, if $\xi_i \geq 1$ then the point is misclassified and appears on the wrong side of the hyperplane.

In the nonseparable case, also called the *soft margin* case, the goal of SVM classification is to find the hyperplane with maximum margin that also minimizes the

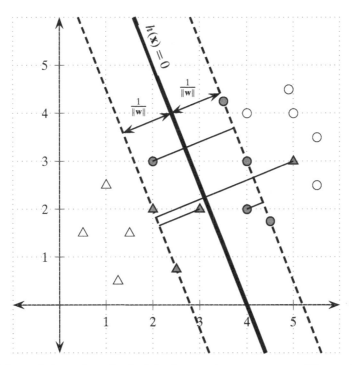

Figure 21.3. Soft margin hyperplane: the shaded points are the support vectors. The margin is $1/\|\mathbf{w}\|$ as illustrated, and points with positive slack values are also shown (thin black line).

slack terms. The new objective function is given as

$$
\begin{aligned}
&\textbf{Objective Function: } \min_{\mathbf{w},b,\xi_i} \left\{ \frac{\|\mathbf{w}\|^2}{2} + C\sum_{i=1}^{n}(\xi_i)^k \right\} \\
&\textbf{Linear Constraints: } y_i\,(\mathbf{w}^T\mathbf{x}_i + b) \geq 1 - \xi_i, \ \ \forall \mathbf{x}_i \in \mathbf{D} \\
&\hspace{9.5em} \xi_i \geq 0 \ \forall \mathbf{x}_i \in \mathbf{D}
\end{aligned}
\tag{21.19}
$$

where C and k are constants that incorporate the cost of misclassification. The term $\sum_{i=1}^{n}(\xi_i)^k$ gives the *loss*, that is, an estimate of the deviation from the separable case. The scalar $C \geq 0$, which is chosen empirically, is a *regularization constant* that controls the trade-off between maximizing the margin (corresponding to minimizing $\|\mathbf{w}\|^2/2$) or minimizing the loss (corresponding to minimizing the sum of the slack terms $\sum_{i=1}^{n}(\xi_i)^k$). For example, if $C \to 0$, then the loss component essentially disappears, and the objective defaults to maximizing the margin. On the other hand, if $C \to \infty$, then the margin ceases to have much effect, and the objective function tries to minimize the loss. The constant $k > 0$ governs the form of the loss. Typically k is set to 1 or 2. When $k = 1$, called *hinge loss*, the goal is to minimize the sum of the slack variables, whereas when $k = 2$, called *quadratic loss*, the goal is to minimize the sum of the squared slack variables.

21.3.1 Hinge Loss

Assuming $k = 1$, we can compute the Lagrangian for the optimization problem in Eq. (21.19) by introducing Lagrange multipliers α_i and β_i that satisfy the following KKT conditions at the optimal solution:

$$
\alpha_i \left(y_i(\mathbf{w}^T\mathbf{x}_i + b) - 1 + \xi_i \right) = 0 \text{ with } \alpha_i \geq 0
$$
$$
\beta_i(\xi_i - 0) = 0 \text{ with } \beta_i \geq 0
\tag{21.20}
$$

The Lagrangian is then given as

$$
L = \frac{1}{2}\|\mathbf{w}\|^2 + C\sum_{i=1}^{n}\xi_i - \sum_{i=1}^{n}\alpha_i \left(y_i(\mathbf{w}^T\mathbf{x}_i + b) - 1 + \xi_i \right) - \sum_{i=1}^{n}\beta_i\xi_i
\tag{21.21}
$$

We turn this into a dual Lagrangian by taking its partial derivative with respect to $\mathbf{w}, b$ and ξ_i, and setting those to zero:

$$
\frac{\partial}{\partial \mathbf{w}}L = \mathbf{w} - \sum_{i=1}^{n}\alpha_i y_i \mathbf{x}_i = \mathbf{0} \quad \text{or} \quad \mathbf{w} = \sum_{i=1}^{n}\alpha_i y_i \mathbf{x}_i
$$

$$
\frac{\partial}{\partial b}L = \sum_{i=1}^{n}\alpha_i y_i = 0
$$

$$
\frac{\partial}{\partial \xi_i}L = C - \alpha_i - \beta_i = 0 \quad \text{or} \quad \beta_i = C - \alpha_i
\tag{21.22}
$$

Plugging these values into Eq. (21.21), we get

$$L_{dual} = \frac{1}{2}\mathbf{w}^T\mathbf{w} - \mathbf{w}^T\underbrace{\left(\sum_{i=1}^{n}\alpha_i y_i \mathbf{x}_i\right)}_{\mathbf{w}} - b\underbrace{\sum_{i=1}^{n}\alpha_i y_i}_{0} + \sum_{i=1}^{n}\alpha_i + \sum_{i=1}^{n}\underbrace{(C - \alpha_i - \beta_i)}_{0}\xi_i$$

$$= \sum_{i=1}^{n}\alpha_i - \frac{1}{2}\sum_{i=1}^{n}\sum_{j=1}^{n}\alpha_i\alpha_j y_i y_j \mathbf{x}_i^T\mathbf{x}_j$$

The dual objective is thus given as

Objective Function: $\displaystyle\max_{\alpha}\ L_{dual} = \sum_{i=1}^{n}\alpha_i - \frac{1}{2}\sum_{i=1}^{n}\sum_{j=1}^{n}\alpha_i\alpha_j y_i y_j \mathbf{x}_i^T\mathbf{x}_j$

(21.23)

Linear Constraints: $0 \le \alpha_i \le C,\ \forall i \in \mathbf{D}$ and $\displaystyle\sum_{i=1}^{n}\alpha_i y_i = 0$

Notice that the objective is the same as the dual Lagrangian in the linearly separable case [Eq. (21.13)]. However, the constraints on α_i's are different because we now require that $\alpha_i + \beta_i = C$ with $\alpha_i \ge 0$ and $\beta_i \ge 0$, which implies that $0 \le \alpha_i \le C$. Section 21.5 describes a gradient ascent approach for solving this dual objective function.

Weight Vector and Bias

Once we solve for α_i, we have the same situation as before, namely, $\alpha_i = 0$ for points that are not support vectors, and $\alpha_i > 0$ only for the support vectors, which comprise all points $\mathbf{x}_i$ for which we have

$$y_i(\mathbf{w}^T\mathbf{x}_i + b) = 1 - \xi_i \tag{21.24}$$

Notice that the support vectors now include all points that are on the margin, which have zero slack ($\xi_i = 0$), as well as all points with positive slack ($\xi_i > 0$).

We can obtain the weight vector from the support vectors as before:

$$\mathbf{w} = \sum_{\alpha_i > 0}\alpha_i y_i \mathbf{x}_i \tag{21.25}$$

We can also solve for the β_i using Eq. (21.22):

$$\beta_i = C - \alpha_i$$

Replacing β_i in the KKT conditions [Eq. (21.20)] with the expression from above we obtain

$$(C - \alpha_i)\xi_i = 0 \tag{21.26}$$

Thus, for the support vectors with $\alpha_i > 0$, we have two cases to consider:

(1) $\xi_i > 0$, which implies that $C - \alpha_i = 0$, that is, $\alpha_i = C$, or

(2) $C - \alpha_i > 0$, that is $\alpha_i < C$. In this case, from Eq. (21.26) we must have $\xi_i = 0$. In other words, these are precisely those support vectors that are on the margin.

Using those support vectors that are on the margin, that is, have $0 < \alpha_i < C$ and $\xi_i = 0$, we can solve for b_i:

$$\alpha_i \left(y_i (\mathbf{w}^T \mathbf{x}_i + b_i) - 1 \right) = 0$$

$$y_i (\mathbf{w}^T \mathbf{x}_i + b_i) = 1$$

$$b_i = \frac{1}{y_i} - \mathbf{w}^T \mathbf{x}_i = y_i - \mathbf{w}^T \mathbf{x}_i \qquad (21.27)$$

To obtain the final bias b, we can take the average over all the b_i values. From Eqs. (21.25) and (21.27), both the weight vector $\mathbf{w}$ and the bias term b can be computed without explicitly computing the slack terms ξ_i for each point.

Once the optimal hyperplane plane has been determined, the SVM model predicts the class for a new point $\mathbf{z}$ as follows:

$$\hat{y} = \text{sign}(h(\mathbf{z})) = \text{sign}(\mathbf{w}^T \mathbf{z} + b)$$

Example 21.4. Let us consider the data points shown in Figure 21.3. There are four new points in addition to the 14 points from Table 21.1 that we considered in Example 21.3; these points are

$\mathbf{x}_i$	x_{i1}	x_{i2}	y_i
$\mathbf{x}_{15}^T$	4	2	+1
$\mathbf{x}_{16}^T$	2	3	+1
$\mathbf{x}_{17}^T$	3	2	−1
$\mathbf{x}_{18}^T$	5	3	−1

Let $k = 1$ and $C = 1$, then solving the L_{dual} yields the following support vectors and Lagrangian values α_i:

$\mathbf{x}_i$	x_{i1}	x_{i2}	y_i	α_i
$\mathbf{x}_1$	3.5	4.25	+1	0.0271
$\mathbf{x}_2$	4	3	+1	0.2162
$\mathbf{x}_4$	4.5	1.75	+1	0.9928
$\mathbf{x}_{13}$	2	2	−1	0.9928
$\mathbf{x}_{14}$	2.5	0.75	−1	0.2434
$\mathbf{x}_{15}$	4	2	+1	1
$\mathbf{x}_{16}$	2	3	+1	1
$\mathbf{x}_{17}$	3	2	−1	1
$\mathbf{x}_{18}$	5	3	−1	1

All other points are not support vectors, having $\alpha_i = 0$. Using Eq. (21.25) we compute the weight vector for the hyperplane:

$$
\begin{aligned}
\mathbf{w} &= \sum_{\alpha_i > 0} \alpha_i y_i \mathbf{x}_i \\
&= 0.0271 \begin{pmatrix} 3.5 \\ 4.25 \end{pmatrix} + 0.2162 \begin{pmatrix} 4 \\ 3 \end{pmatrix} + 0.9928 \begin{pmatrix} 4.5 \\ 1.75 \end{pmatrix} - 0.9928 \begin{pmatrix} 2 \\ 2 \end{pmatrix} \\
&\quad - 0.2434 \begin{pmatrix} 2.5 \\ 0.75 \end{pmatrix} + \begin{pmatrix} 4 \\ 2 \end{pmatrix} + \begin{pmatrix} 2 \\ 3 \end{pmatrix} - \begin{pmatrix} 3 \\ 2 \end{pmatrix} - \begin{pmatrix} 5 \\ 3 \end{pmatrix} \\
&= \begin{pmatrix} 0.834 \\ 0.333 \end{pmatrix}
\end{aligned}
$$

The final bias is the average of the biases obtained from each support vector using Eq. (21.27). Note that we compute the per-point bias only for the support vectors that lie precisely on the margin. These support vectors have $\xi_i = 0$ and have $0 < \alpha_i < C$. Put another way, we do not compute the bias for support vectors with $\alpha_i = C = 1$, which include the points $\mathbf{x}_{15}$, $\mathbf{x}_{16}$, $\mathbf{x}_{17}$, and $\mathbf{x}_{18}$. From the remaining support vectors, we get

$\mathbf{x}_i$	$\mathbf{w}^T \mathbf{x}_i$	$b_i = y_i - \mathbf{w}^T \mathbf{x}_i$
$\mathbf{x}_1$	4.334	−3.334
$\mathbf{x}_2$	4.334	−3.334
$\mathbf{x}_4$	4.334	−3.334
$\mathbf{x}_{13}$	2.334	−3.334
$\mathbf{x}_{14}$	2.334	−3.334
$b = \text{avg}\{b_i\}$		−3.334

Thus, the optimal hyperplane is given as follows:

$$
h(\mathbf{x}) = \begin{pmatrix} 0.834 \\ 0.333 \end{pmatrix}^T \mathbf{x} - 3.334 = 0
$$

One can see that this is essentially the same as the canonical hyperplane we found in Example 21.3.

It is instructive to see what the slack variables are in this case. Note that $\xi_i = 0$ for all points that are not support vectors, and also for those support vectors that are on the margin. So the slack is positive only for the remaining support vectors, for whom the slack can be computed directly from Eq. (21.24), as follows:

$$
\xi_i = 1 - y_i (\mathbf{w}^T \mathbf{x}_i + b)
$$

Thus, for all support vectors not on the margin, we have

$\mathbf{x}_i$	$\mathbf{w}^T\mathbf{x}_i$	$\mathbf{w}^T\mathbf{x}_i + b$	$\xi_i = 1 - y_i(\mathbf{w}^T\mathbf{x}_i + b)$
$\mathbf{x}_{15}$	4.001	0.667	0.333
$\mathbf{x}_{16}$	2.667	-0.667	1.667
$\mathbf{x}_{17}$	3.167	-0.167	0.833
$\mathbf{x}_{18}$	5.168	1.834	2.834

As expected, the slack variable $\xi_i > 1$ for those points that are misclassified (i.e., are on the wrong side of the hyperplane), namely $\mathbf{x}_{16} = (3,3)^T$ and $\mathbf{x}_{18} = (5,3)^T$. The other two points are correctly classified, but lie within the margin, and thus satisfy $0 < \xi_i < 1$. The total slack is given as

$$\sum_i \xi_i = \xi_{15} + \xi_{16} + \xi_{17} + \xi_{18} = 0.333 + 1.667 + 0.833 + 2.834 = 5.667$$

21.3.2 Quadratic Loss

For quadratic loss, we have $k = 2$ in the objective function [Eq. (21.19)]. In this case we can drop the positivity constraint $\xi_i \geq 0$ due to the fact that (1) the sum of the slack terms $\sum_{i=1}^{n} \xi_i^2$ is always positive, and (2) a potential negative value of slack will be ruled out during optimization because a choice of $\xi_i = 0$ leads to a smaller value of the primary objective, and it still satisfies the constraint $y_i(\mathbf{w}^T\mathbf{x}_i + b) \geq 1 - \xi_i$ whenever $\xi_i < 0$. In other words, the optimization process will replace any negative slack variables by zero values. Thus, the SVM objective for quadratic loss is given as

$$\textbf{Objective Function: } \min_{\mathbf{w},b,\xi_i} \left\{ \frac{\|\mathbf{w}\|^2}{2} + C \sum_{i=1}^{n} \xi_i^2 \right\}$$

$$\textbf{Linear Constraints: } y_i(\mathbf{w}^T\mathbf{x}_i + b) \geq 1 - \xi_i, \ \forall \mathbf{x}_i \in \mathbf{D}$$

(21.28)

The Lagrangian is then given as:

$$L = \frac{1}{2}\|\mathbf{w}\|^2 + C\sum_{i=1}^{n} \xi_i^2 - \sum_{i=1}^{n} \alpha_i \left(y_i(\mathbf{w}^T\mathbf{x}_i + b) - 1 + \xi_i \right)$$

(21.29)

Differentiating with respect to $\mathbf{w}$, b, and ξ_i and setting them to zero results in the following conditions, respectively:

$$\mathbf{w} = \sum_{i=1}^{n} \alpha_i y_i \mathbf{x}_i$$

$$\sum_{i=1}^{n} \alpha_i y_i = 0$$

$$\xi_i = \frac{1}{2C}\alpha_i$$

Substituting these back into Eq. (21.29) yields the dual objective

$$L_{dual} = \sum_{i=1}^{n} \alpha_i - \frac{1}{2} \sum_{i=1}^{n} \sum_{j=1}^{n} \alpha_i \alpha_j y_i y_j \mathbf{x}_i^T \mathbf{x}_j - \frac{1}{4C} \sum_{i=1}^{n} \alpha_i^2$$

$$= \sum_{i=1}^{n} \alpha_i - \frac{1}{2} \sum_{i=1}^{n} \sum_{j=1}^{n} \alpha_i \alpha_j y_i y_j \left(\mathbf{x}_i^T \mathbf{x}_j + \frac{1}{2C} \delta_{ij} \right)$$

where δ is the *Kronecker delta* function, defined as $\delta_{ij} = 1$ if $i = j$, and $\delta_{ij} = 0$ otherwise. Thus, the dual objective is given as

$$\max_{\alpha} \; L_{dual} = \sum_{i=1}^{n} \alpha_i - \frac{1}{2} \sum_{i=1}^{n} \sum_{j=1}^{n} \alpha_i \alpha_j y_i y_j \left(\mathbf{x}_i^T \mathbf{x}_j + \frac{1}{2C} \delta_{ij} \right)$$

subject to the constraints $\alpha_i \geq 0, \forall i \in \mathbf{D}$, and $\sum_{i=1}^{n} \alpha_i y_i = 0$

(21.30)

Once we solve for α_i using the method from Section 21.5, we can recover the weight vector and bias as follows:

$$\mathbf{w} = \sum_{\alpha_i > 0} \alpha_i y_i \mathbf{x}_i$$

$$b = \underset{\alpha_i > 0}{\text{avg}} \left\{ y_i - \mathbf{w}^T \mathbf{x}_i \right\}$$

21.4 KERNEL SVM: NONLINEAR CASE

The linear SVM approach can be used for datasets with a nonlinear decision boundary via the kernel trick from Chapter 5. Conceptually, the idea is to map the original d-dimensional points $\mathbf{x}_i$ in the input space to points $\phi(\mathbf{x}_i)$ in a high-dimensional feature space via some nonlinear transformation ϕ. Given the extra flexibility, it is more likely that the points $\phi(\mathbf{x}_i)$ might be linearly separable in the feature space. Note, however, that a linear decision surface in feature space actually corresponds to a nonlinear decision surface in the input space. Further, the kernel trick allows us to carry out all operations via the kernel function computed in input space, rather than having to map the points into feature space.

Example 21.5. Consider the set of points shown in Figure 21.4. There is no linear classifier that can discriminate between the points. However, there exists a perfect quadratic classifier that can separate the two classes. Given the input space over the two dimensions X_1 and X_2, if we transform each point $\mathbf{x} = (x_1, x_2)^T$ into a point in the feature space consisting of the dimensions $(X_1, X_2, X_1^2, X_2^2, X_1 X_2)$, via the transformation $\phi(\mathbf{x}) = (\sqrt{2}x_1, \sqrt{2}x_2, x_1^2, x_2^2, \sqrt{2}x_1 x_2)^T$, then it is possible to find a separating hyperplane in feature space. For this dataset, it is possible to map the hyperplane back to the input space, where it is seen as an ellipse (thick black line)

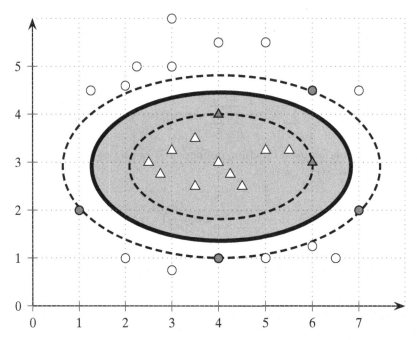

Figure 21.4. Nonlinear SVM: shaded points are the support vectors.

that separates the two classes (circles and triangles). The support vectors are those points (shown in gray) that lie on the margin (dashed ellipses).

To apply the kernel trick for nonlinear SVM classification, we have to show that all operations require only the kernel function:

$$K(\mathbf{x}_i, \mathbf{x}_j) = \phi(\mathbf{x}_i)^T \phi(\mathbf{x}_j)$$

Let $\mathbf{D}$ be the original dataset with n points $\mathbf{x}_i$ and their labels y_i. Applying ϕ to each point, we can obtain the new dataset $\mathbf{D}_\phi$ in the feature space comprising the transformed points $\phi(\mathbf{x}_i)$ along with their labels y_i, for $i = 1, 2, \cdots, n$.

The SVM objective function [Eq. (21.19)] in feature space is given as

$$
\boxed{
\begin{aligned}
&\textbf{Objective Function: } \min_{\mathbf{w}, b, \xi_i} \left\{ \frac{\|\mathbf{w}\|^2}{2} + C \sum_{i=1}^{n} (\xi_i)^k \right\} \\
&\textbf{Linear Constraints: } y_i\,(\mathbf{w}^T \phi(\mathbf{x}_i) + b) \geq 1 - \xi_i, \text{ and } \xi_i \geq 0, \ \forall \mathbf{x}_i \in \mathbf{D}
\end{aligned}
}
\tag{21.31}
$$

where $\mathbf{w}$ is the weight vector, b is the bias, and ξ_i are the slack variables, all in feature space.

Hinge Loss

For hinge loss, the dual Lagrangian [Eq. (21.23)] in feature space is given as

$$\max_{\alpha} L_{dual} = \sum_{i=1}^{n} \alpha_i - \frac{1}{2} \sum_{i=1}^{n} \sum_{j=1}^{n} \alpha_i \alpha_j y_i y_j \phi(\mathbf{x}_i)^T \phi(\mathbf{x}_j)$$

$$= \sum_{i=1}^{n} \alpha_i - \frac{1}{2} \sum_{i=1}^{n} \sum_{j=1}^{n} \alpha_i \alpha_j y_i y_j K(\mathbf{x}_i, \mathbf{x}_j) \tag{21.32}$$

Subject to the constraints that $0 \le \alpha_i \le C$, and $\sum_{i=1}^{n} \alpha_i y_i = 0$. Notice that the dual Lagrangian depends only on the dot product between two vectors in feature space $\phi(\mathbf{x}_i)^T \phi(\mathbf{x}_j) = K(\mathbf{x}_i, \mathbf{x}_j)$, and thus we can solve the optimization problem using the kernel matrix $\mathbf{K} = \{K(\mathbf{x}_i, \mathbf{x}_j)\}_{i,j=1,\ldots,n}$. Section 21.5 describes a stochastic gradient-based approach for solving the dual objective function.

Quadratic Loss

For quadratic loss, the dual Lagrangian [Eq. (21.30)] corresponds to a change of kernel. Define a new kernel function K_q, as follows:

$$K_q(\mathbf{x}_i, \mathbf{x}_j) = \mathbf{x}_i^T \mathbf{x}_j + \frac{1}{2C} \delta_{ij} = K(\mathbf{x}_i, \mathbf{x}_j) + \frac{1}{2C} \delta_{ij}$$

which affects only the diagonal entries of the kernel matrix $\mathbf{K}$, as $\delta_{ij} = 1$ iff $i = j$, and zero otherwise. Thus, the dual Lagrangian is given as

$$\max_{\alpha} L_{dual} = \sum_{i=1}^{n} \alpha_i - \frac{1}{2} \sum_{i=1}^{n} \sum_{j=1}^{n} \alpha_i \alpha_j y_i y_j K_q(\mathbf{x}_i, \mathbf{x}_j) \tag{21.33}$$

subject to the constraints that $\alpha_i \ge 0$, and $\sum_{i=1}^{n} \alpha_i y_i = 0$. The above optimization can be solved using the same approach as for hinge loss, with a simple change of kernel.

Weight Vector and Bias

We can solve for $\mathbf{w}$ in feature space as follows:

$$\mathbf{w} = \sum_{\alpha_i > 0} \alpha_i y_i \phi(\mathbf{x}_i) \tag{21.34}$$

Because $\mathbf{w}$ uses $\phi(\mathbf{x}_i)$ directly, in general, we may not be able or willing to compute $\mathbf{w}$ explicitly. However, as we shall see next, it is not necessary to explicitly compute $\mathbf{w}$ for classifying the points.

Let us now see how to compute the bias via kernel operations for hinge loss. Using Eq. (21.27), we compute b as the average over the support vectors that are on the margin, that is, those with $0 < \alpha_i < C$, and $\xi_i = 0$:

$$b = \operatorname*{avg}_{0 < \alpha_i < C} \{b_i\} = \operatorname*{avg}_{0 < \alpha_i < C} \left\{ y_i - \mathbf{w}^T \phi(\mathbf{x}_i) \right\} \tag{21.35}$$

For quadratic loss, the bias is the average over all support vectors, with $\alpha_i > 0$. Furthermore, substituting $\mathbf{w}$ from Eq. (21.34), we obtain a new expression for b_i as

$$b_i = y_i - \sum_{\alpha_j > 0} \alpha_j y_j \phi(\mathbf{x}_j)^T \phi(\mathbf{x}_i)$$

$$= y_i - \sum_{\alpha_j > 0} \alpha_j y_j K(\mathbf{x}_j, \mathbf{x}_i) \qquad (21.36)$$

Notice that b_i is a function of the dot product between two vectors in feature space and therefore it can be computed via the kernel function in the input space.

Kernel SVM Classifier

We can predict the class for a new point $\mathbf{z}$ as follows:

$$\hat{y} = \text{sign}(\mathbf{w}^T \phi(\mathbf{z}) + b) = \text{sign}\left(\sum_{\alpha_i > 0} \alpha_i y_i \phi(\mathbf{x}_i)^T \phi(\mathbf{z}) + b \right)$$

$$= \boxed{\text{sign}\left(\sum_{\alpha_i > 0} \alpha_i y_i K(\mathbf{x}_i, \mathbf{z}) + b \right)} \qquad (21.37)$$

Once again we see that $\hat{y}$ uses only dot products in feature space.

Based on the above derivations, we can see that, to train and test the SVM classifier, the mapped points $\phi(\mathbf{x}_i)$ are never needed in isolation. Instead, all operations can be carried out in terms of the kernel function $K(\mathbf{x}_i, \mathbf{x}_j) = \phi(\mathbf{x}_i)^T \phi(\mathbf{x}_j)$. Thus, any nonlinear kernel function can be used to do nonlinear classification in the input space. Examples of such nonlinear kernels include the polynomial kernel [Eq. (5.9)], and the gaussian kernel [Eq. (5.10)], among others.

Example 21.6. Let us consider the example dataset shown in Figure 21.4; it has 29 points in total. Although it is generally too expensive or infeasible (depending on the choice of the kernel) to compute an explicit representation of the hyperplane in feature space, and to map it back into input space, we will illustrate the application of SVMs in both input and feature space to aid understanding.

We use an inhomogeneous polynomial kernel [Eq. (5.9)] of degree $q = 2$, that is, we use the kernel:

$$K(\mathbf{x}_i, \mathbf{x}_j) = \phi(\mathbf{x}_i)^T \phi(\mathbf{x}_j) = (1 + \mathbf{x}_i^T \mathbf{x}_j)^2$$

With $C = 4$, solving the L_{dual} quadratic program [Eq. (21.33)] in input space yields the following six support vectors, shown as the shaded (gray) points in Figure 21.4.

$\mathbf{x}_i$	$(x_{i1}, x_{i2})^T$	$\phi(\mathbf{x}_i)$	y_i	α_i
$\mathbf{x}_1$	$(1,2)^T$	$(1, 1.41, 2.83, 1, 4, 2.83)^T$	$+1$	0.6198
$\mathbf{x}_2$	$(4,1)^T$	$(1, 5.66, 1.41, 16, 1, 5.66)^T$	$+1$	2.069
$\mathbf{x}_3$	$(6,4.5)^T$	$(1, 8.49, 6.36, 36, 20.25, 38.18)^T$	$+1$	3.803
$\mathbf{x}_4$	$(7,2)^T$	$(1, 9.90, 2.83, 49, 4, 19.80)^T$	$+1$	0.3182
$\mathbf{x}_5$	$(4,4)^T$	$(1, 5.66, 5.66, 16, 16, 15.91)^T$	-1	2.9598
$\mathbf{x}_6$	$(6,3)^T$	$(1, 8.49, 4.24, 36, 9, 25.46)^T$	-1	3.8502

For the inhomogeneous quadratic kernel, the mapping ϕ maps an input point $\mathbf{x}_i$ into feature space as follows:

$$\phi\left(\mathbf{x} = (x_1, x_2)^T\right) = \left(1, \sqrt{2}x_1, \sqrt{2}x_2, x_1^2, x_2^2, \sqrt{2}x_1x_2\right)^T$$

The table above shows all the mapped points, which reside in feature space. For example, $\mathbf{x}_1 = (1,2)^T$ is transformed into

$$\phi(\mathbf{x}_i) = \left(1, \sqrt{2}\cdot 1, \sqrt{2}\cdot 2, 1^2, 2^2, \sqrt{2}\cdot 1\cdot 2\right)^T = (1, 1.41, 2.83, 1, 2, 2.83)^T$$

We compute the weight vector for the hyperplane using Eq. (21.34):

$$\mathbf{w} = \sum_{\alpha_i > 0} \alpha_i y_i \phi(\mathbf{x}_i) = (0, -1.413, -3.298, 0.256, 0.82, -0.018)^T$$

and the bias is computed using Eq. (21.35), which yields

$$b = -8.841$$

For the quadratic polynomial kernel, the decision boundary in input space corresponds to an ellipse. For our example, the center of the ellipse is given as $(4.046, 2.907)$, and the semimajor axis length is 2.78 and the semiminor axis length is 1.55. The resulting decision boundary is the ellipse shown in Figure 21.4. We emphasize that in this example we explicitly transformed all the points into the feature space just for illustration purposes. The kernel trick allows us to achieve the same goal using only the kernel function.

21.5 SVM TRAINING: STOCHASTIC GRADIENT ASCENT

We now turn our attention to solving the SVM optimization problem via stochastic gradient ascent. Instead of dealing explicitly with the bias b, we map each point $\mathbf{x}_i \in \mathbb{R}^d$ to the *augmented point* $\tilde{\mathbf{x}}_i \in \mathbb{R}^{d+1}$ by adding 1 as an additional column value, so that

$$\tilde{\mathbf{x}}_i = (x_{i1}, \ldots, x_{id}, 1)^T \qquad (21.38)$$

Furthermore, we also map the weight vector $\mathbf{w} \in \mathbb{R}^d$ to an augmented weight vector $\tilde{\mathbf{w}} \in \mathbb{R}^{d+1}$, with $w_{d+1} = b$. That is,

$$\tilde{\mathbf{w}} = (w_1, \ldots, w_d, b)^T \tag{21.39}$$

The equation of the hyperplane [Eq. (21.1)] is then given as follows:

$$h(\tilde{\mathbf{x}}) : \tilde{\mathbf{w}}^T \tilde{\mathbf{x}} = 0$$

$$h(\tilde{\mathbf{x}}) : w_1 x_1 + \cdots + w_d x_d + b = 0$$

In the discussion below we assume that the points and the weight vector have been augmented as per Eqs. (21.38) and (21.39). Thus, the last component of $\tilde{\mathbf{w}}$ yields the bias b. The new set of constraints is given as

$$y_i \tilde{\mathbf{w}}^T \tilde{\mathbf{x}}_i \geq 1 - \xi_i$$

Therefore, the SVM objective is given as

> **Objective Function:** $\min\limits_{\tilde{\mathbf{w}}, \xi_i} \left\{ \dfrac{\|\tilde{\mathbf{w}}\|^2}{2} + C \sum\limits_{i=1}^{n} (\xi_i)^k \right\}$
>
> **Linear Constraints:** $y_i \tilde{\mathbf{w}}^T \tilde{\mathbf{x}}_i \geq 1 - \xi_i$ and $\xi_i \geq 0, \; \forall i = 1, 2, \ldots, n$
>
> $\tag{21.40}$

We consider the Lagrangian only for the hinge loss, when $k = 1$, since quadratic loss corresponds to a change of kernel (with the constraint $\alpha_i \geq 0$) as noted in Eq. (21.33). The Lagrangian for the hinge loss is given as

$$L = \frac{1}{2} \|\tilde{\mathbf{w}}\|^2 + C \sum_{i=1}^{n} \xi_i - \sum_{i=1}^{n} \alpha_i \left(y_i \tilde{\mathbf{w}}^T \tilde{\mathbf{x}}_i - 1 + \xi_i \right) - \sum_{i=1}^{n} \beta_i \xi_i$$

Taking the partial derivative of L with respect to $\tilde{\mathbf{w}}$ and ξ_i, and setting those to zero, we get

$$\frac{\partial}{\partial \tilde{\mathbf{w}}} L = \tilde{\mathbf{w}} - \sum_{i=1}^{n} \alpha_i y_i \tilde{\mathbf{x}}_i = \mathbf{0} \quad \text{or} \quad \tilde{\mathbf{w}} = \sum_{i=1}^{n} \alpha_i y_i \tilde{\mathbf{x}}_i$$

$$\frac{\partial}{\partial \xi_i} L = C - \alpha_i - \beta_i = 0 \quad \text{or} \quad \beta_i = C - \alpha_i$$

Plugging these values into L, we obtain:

$$L_{dual} = \frac{1}{2} \tilde{\mathbf{w}}^T \tilde{\mathbf{w}} - \tilde{\mathbf{w}}^T \underbrace{\left(\sum_{i=1}^{n} \alpha_i y_i \tilde{\mathbf{x}}_i \right)}_{\tilde{\mathbf{w}}} - \sum_{i=1}^{n} \alpha_i + \sum_{i=1}^{n} \underbrace{(C - \alpha_i - \beta_i)}_{0} \xi_i$$

$$= \sum_{i=1}^{n} \alpha_i - \frac{1}{2} \sum_{i=1}^{n} \sum_{j=1}^{n} \alpha_i \alpha_j y_i y_j \tilde{\mathbf{x}}_i^T \tilde{\mathbf{x}}_j$$

Following the discussion in Section 21.4, we can generalize the dual objective to the nonlinear case by replacing $\tilde{\mathbf{x}}_i^T \tilde{\mathbf{x}}_j$ with the augmented kernel value

$$\tilde{K}(\mathbf{x}_i, \mathbf{x}_j) = \tilde{\phi}(\mathbf{x}_i)^T \tilde{\phi}(\mathbf{x}_j)$$

where $\tilde{\phi}(\mathbf{x}_i)$ is the augmented transformed point in feature space, given as

$$\tilde{\phi}(\mathbf{x}_i)^T = \left(\phi(\mathbf{x}_i)^T \ 1\right)$$

That is, $\tilde{\phi}(\mathbf{x}_i)$ has an extra value 1 as the last element. The augmented kernel value is therefore given as

$$\tilde{K}(\mathbf{x}_i, \mathbf{x}_j) = \tilde{\phi}(\mathbf{x}_i)^T \tilde{\phi}(\mathbf{x}_j) = \phi(\mathbf{x}_i)^T \phi(\mathbf{x}_j) + 1 = K(\mathbf{x}_i, \mathbf{x}_j) + 1$$

Using the kernel function, the dual SVM objective is given as

> **Objective Function:** $\displaystyle \max_{\alpha} \ J(\boldsymbol{\alpha}) = \sum_{i=1}^{n} \alpha_i - \frac{1}{2} \sum_{i=1}^{n} \sum_{j=1}^{n} \alpha_i \alpha_j y_i y_j \tilde{K}(\mathbf{x}_i, \mathbf{x}_j)$
>
> **Linear Constraints:** $0 \le \alpha_i \le C, \ \forall i = 1, 2, \ldots, n$

(21.41)

where $\boldsymbol{\alpha} = (\alpha_1, \alpha_2, \cdots, \alpha_n)^T \in \mathbb{R}^n$, and where $\tilde{\mathbf{w}}$ is the augmented weight vector in feature space, with its last element denoting the bias.

An important consequence of mapping the points to $\mathbb{R}^{d+1}$ is that the constraint $\sum_{i=1}^{n} \alpha_i y_i = 0$ does not apply in the SVM dual formulation, as there is no explicit bias term b for the linear constraints in the SVM objective. On the other hand, the constraint $\alpha_i \in [0, C]$ for hinge loss (or $\alpha_i \ge 0$ for quadratic loss) is easy to enforce.

21.5.1 Dual Solution: Stochastic Gradient Ascent

We will now solve for the optimal $\boldsymbol{\alpha}$ vector via the stochastic gradient ascent algorithm. Let us consider the terms in $J(\boldsymbol{\alpha})$ that involve the Lagrange multiplier α_k:

$$J(\alpha_k) = \alpha_k - \frac{1}{2} \alpha_k^2 y_k^2 \tilde{K}(\mathbf{x}_k, \mathbf{x}_k) - \alpha_k y_k \sum_{\substack{i=1 \\ i \ne k}}^{n} \alpha_i y_i \tilde{K}(\mathbf{x}_i, \mathbf{x}_k)$$

The gradient or the rate of change in the objective function at $\boldsymbol{\alpha}$ is given as the partial derivative of $J(\boldsymbol{\alpha})$ with respect to $\boldsymbol{\alpha}$, that is, with respect to each α_k:

$$\nabla J(\boldsymbol{\alpha}) = \left(\frac{\partial J(\boldsymbol{\alpha})}{\partial \alpha_1}, \frac{\partial J(\boldsymbol{\alpha})}{\partial \alpha_2}, \ldots, \frac{\partial J(\boldsymbol{\alpha})}{\partial \alpha_n}\right)^T$$

where the kth component of the gradient is obtained by differentiating $J(\alpha_k)$ with respect to α_k:

$$\frac{\partial J(\boldsymbol{\alpha})}{\partial \alpha_k} = \frac{\partial J(\alpha_k)}{\partial \alpha_k} = 1 - y_k \left(\sum_{i=1}^{n} \alpha_i y_i \tilde{K}(\mathbf{x}_i, \mathbf{x}_k)\right)$$

(21.42)

Because we want to maximize the objective function $J(\boldsymbol{\alpha})$, we should move in the direction of the gradient $\nabla J(\boldsymbol{\alpha})$. Starting from an initial $\boldsymbol{\alpha}$, the gradient ascent approach successively updates it as follows:

$$\boldsymbol{\alpha}_{t+1} = \boldsymbol{\alpha}_t + \eta_t \nabla J(\boldsymbol{\alpha}_t)$$

where $\boldsymbol{\alpha}_t$ is the estimate at the tth step, and η_t is the step size.

Algorithm 21.1: Dual SVM Algorithm: Stochastic Gradient Ascent

---

SVM-DUAL $(\mathbf{D}, K, loss, C, \epsilon)$:

1 **if** $loss$ = hinge **then**
2 $\quad$ $\mathbf{K} \leftarrow \{K(\mathbf{x}_i, \mathbf{x}_j)\}_{i,j=1,...,n}$ // kernel matrix, hinge loss
3 **else if** $loss$ = quadratic **then**
4 $\quad$ $\mathbf{K} \leftarrow \{K(\mathbf{x}_i, \mathbf{x}_j) + \frac{1}{2C}\delta_{ij}\}_{i,j=1,...,n}$ // kernel matrix, quadratic loss
5 $\tilde{\mathbf{K}} \leftarrow \mathbf{K} + 1$// augmented kernel matrix
6 **for** $k = 1, \ldots, n$ **do** $\eta_k \leftarrow 1/\tilde{K}(\mathbf{x}_k, \mathbf{x}_k)$ // set step size
7 $t \leftarrow 0$
8 $\boldsymbol{\alpha}_0 \leftarrow (0, \ldots, 0)^T$
9 **repeat**
10 $\quad$ $\boldsymbol{\alpha} \leftarrow \boldsymbol{\alpha}_t$
11 $\quad$ **for** $k = 1$ *to* n **do**
    $\quad\quad$ // update kth component of $\boldsymbol{\alpha}$
12 $\quad\quad$ $\alpha_k \leftarrow \alpha_k + \eta_k\left(1 - y_k \sum_{i=1}^{n} \alpha_i y_i \tilde{K}(\mathbf{x}_i, \mathbf{x}_k)\right)$
13 $\quad\quad$ **if** $\alpha_k < 0$ **then** $\alpha_k \leftarrow 0$
14 $\quad\quad$ **if** $loss$ = hinge **and** $\alpha_k > C$ **then** $\alpha_k \leftarrow C$
15 $\quad$ $\boldsymbol{\alpha}_{t+1} \leftarrow \boldsymbol{\alpha}$
16 $\quad$ $t \leftarrow t + 1$
17 **until** $\|\boldsymbol{\alpha}_t - \boldsymbol{\alpha}_{t-1}\| \leq \epsilon$

Instead of updating the entire $\boldsymbol{\alpha}$ vector in each step, in the stochastic gradient ascent approach, we update each component α_k independently and immediately use the new value to update other components. This can result in faster convergence. The update rule for the kth component is given as

$$\alpha_k = \alpha_k + \eta_k \frac{\partial J(\boldsymbol{\alpha})}{\partial \alpha_k} = \alpha_k + \eta_k\left(1 - y_k \sum_{i=1}^{n} \alpha_i y_i \tilde{K}(\mathbf{x}_i, \mathbf{x}_k)\right) \tag{21.43}$$

where η_k is the step size. We also have to ensure that the constraints $\alpha_k \in [0, C]$ are satisfied. Thus, in the update step above, if $\alpha_k < 0$ we reset it to $\alpha_k = 0$, and if $\alpha_k > C$ we reset it to $\alpha_k = C$. The pseudo-code for stochastic gradient ascent is given in Algorithm 21.1.

To determine the step size η_k, ideally, we would like to choose it so that the gradient at α_k goes to zero, which happens when

$$\eta_k = \frac{1}{\tilde{K}(\mathbf{x}_k, \mathbf{x}_k)} \tag{21.44}$$

To see why, note that when only α_k is updated, the other α_i do not change. Thus, the new $\boldsymbol{\alpha}$ has a change only in α_k, and from Eq. (21.42) we get

$$\frac{\partial J(\boldsymbol{\alpha})}{\partial \alpha_k} = \left(1 - y_k \sum_{i \neq k} \alpha_i y_i \tilde{K}(\mathbf{x}_i, \mathbf{x}_k)\right) - y_k \alpha_k y_k \tilde{K}(\mathbf{x}_k, \mathbf{x}_k)$$

Plugging in the value of α_k from Eq. (21.43), we have

$$\frac{\partial J(\boldsymbol{\alpha})}{\partial \alpha_k} = \left(1 - y_k \sum_{i \neq k} \alpha_i y_i \tilde{K}(\mathbf{x}_i, \mathbf{x}_k)\right) - \left(\alpha_k + \eta_k \left(1 - y_k \sum_{i=1}^{n} \alpha_i y_i \tilde{K}(\mathbf{x}_i, \mathbf{x}_k)\right)\right) \tilde{K}(\mathbf{x}_k, \mathbf{x}_k)$$

$$= \left(1 - y_k \sum_{i=1}^{n} \alpha_i y_i \tilde{K}(\mathbf{x}_i, \mathbf{x}_k)\right) - \eta_k K(\tilde{\mathbf{x}}_k, \tilde{\mathbf{x}}_k) \left(1 - y_k \sum_{i=1}^{n} \alpha_i y_i \tilde{K}(\mathbf{x}_i, \mathbf{x}_k)\right)$$

$$= \left(1 - \eta_k \tilde{K}(\mathbf{x}_k, \mathbf{x}_k)\right) \left(1 - y_k \sum_{i=1}^{n} \alpha_i y_i \tilde{K}(\mathbf{x}_i, \mathbf{x}_k)\right)$$

Substituting η_k from Eq. (21.44), we have

$$\frac{\partial J(\boldsymbol{\alpha})}{\partial a_k} = \left(1 - \frac{1}{\tilde{K}(\mathbf{x}_k, \mathbf{x}_k)} \tilde{K}(\mathbf{x}_k, \mathbf{x}_k)\right) \left(1 - y_k \sum_{i=1}^{n} \alpha_i y_i \tilde{K}(\mathbf{x}_i, \mathbf{x}_k)\right) = 0$$

In Algorithm 21.1, for better convergence, we thus choose η_k according to Eq. (21.44). The method successively updates $\boldsymbol{\alpha}$ and stops when the change falls below a given threshold ϵ. The computational complexity of the method is $O(n^2)$ per iteration.

Testing

Note that once we obtain the final $\boldsymbol{\alpha}$, we classify a new (augmented) point $\mathbf{z} \in \mathbb{R}^d$ as follows:

$$\hat{y} = \text{sign}\left(h(\tilde{\phi}(\mathbf{z}))\right) = \text{sign}\left(\tilde{\mathbf{w}}^T \tilde{\phi}(\mathbf{z})\right) = \text{sign}\left(\sum_{\alpha_i > 0} \alpha_i y_i \tilde{K}(\mathbf{x}_i, \mathbf{z})\right) \qquad (21.45)$$

Example 21.7 (Dual SVM: Linear Kernel). Figure 21.5 shows the $n = 150$ points from the Iris dataset, using sepal length and sepal width as the two attributes. The goal is to discriminate between Iris-setosa (shown as circles) and other types of Iris flowers (shown as triangles). Algorithm 21.1 was used to train the SVM classifier with a linear kernel $\tilde{K}(\mathbf{x}_i, \mathbf{x}_j) = \mathbf{x}_i^T \mathbf{x}_j + 1$ and convergence threshold $\epsilon = 0.0001$, with hinge loss. Two different values of C were used; hyperplane h_{10} is obtained by using $C = 10$, whereas h_{1000} uses $C = 1000$; the hyperplanes are given as follows:

$$h_{10}(\mathbf{x}): \quad 2.74x_1 - 3.74x_2 - 3.09 = 0$$

$$h_{1000}(\mathbf{x}): \quad 8.56x_1 - 7.14x_2 - 23.12 = 0$$

The hyperplane h_{10} has a larger margin, but it has a larger slack; it misclassifies one of the circles. On the other hand, the hyperplane h_{1000} has a smaller margin, but it minimizes the slack; it is a separating hyperplane. This example illustrates the fact that the higher the value of C the more the emphasis on minimizing the slack.

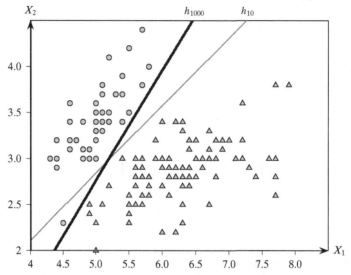

Figure 21.5. SVM dual algorithm with linear kernel.

Example 21.8 (Dual SVM: Different Kernels). Figure 21.6 shows the $n = 150$ points from the Iris dataset projected on the first two principal components. The task is to separate Iris-versicolor (in circles) from the other two types of Irises (in triangles).

Figures 21.6(a) and 21.6(b) plot the decision boundaries obtained when using a linear kernel $\tilde{K}(\mathbf{x}_i, \mathbf{x}_j) = \mathbf{x}_i^T \mathbf{x}_j + 1$, and an inhomogeneous quadratic kernel $\tilde{K}(\mathbf{x}_i, \mathbf{x}_j) = (c + \mathbf{x}_i^T \mathbf{x}_j)^2 + 1$, with $c = 1$. The optimal hyperplane in both cases was found via the gradient ascent approach in Algorithm 21.1, with $C = 10$, $\epsilon = 0.0001$ and using hinge loss.

The optimal hyperplane h_l (shown in Figure 21.6(a)) for the linear kernel is given as

$$h_l(\mathbf{x}) : 0.16x_1 + 1.9x_2 + 0.8 = 0$$

As expected, h_l is unable to separate the classes. It misclassifies 42 points, and therefore its error rate is given as

$$\frac{\# \text{misclassified}}{n} = \frac{42}{150} = 0.28$$

On the other hand, the optimal hyperplane h_q (shown in Figure 21.6(b)) for the quadratic kernel is given as

$$h_q(\mathbf{x}) : \tilde{\mathbf{w}}^T \phi(\tilde{\mathbf{x}}) = 1.78x_1^2 + 1.37x_1x_2 - 0.53x_1 + 0.91x_2^2 - 1.79x_2 - 4.03 = 0$$

where

$$\tilde{\mathbf{w}} = (1.78, 0.97, -0.37, 0.91, -1.26, -2.013, -2.013)^T$$

$$\tilde{\phi}(\mathbf{x}) = \left(x_1^2, \sqrt{2}x_1x_2, \sqrt{2}x_1, x_2^2, \sqrt{2}x_2, 1, 1 \right)^T$$

The hyperplane h_q is able to separate the two classes quite well. It misclassifies only 4 points, for an error rate of 0.027. Here we explicitly reconstructed $\tilde{\mathbf{w}}$ for illustration

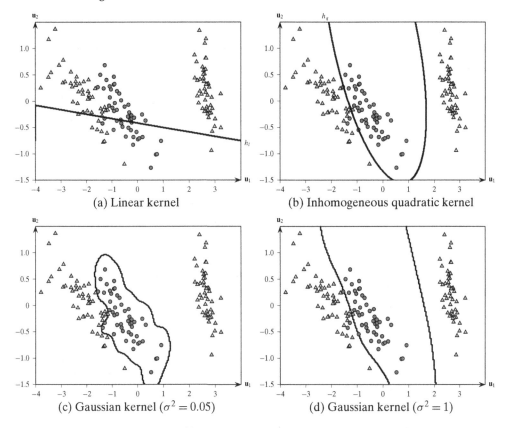

Figure 21.6. SVM dual algorithm: linear, inhomogeneous quadratic, and gaussian kernels.

purposes. However, note that, since we are using an inhomogeneous quadratic kernel with $c = 1$, the last two elements together determine the final bias, which is given as $b = 2 \times -2.013 = -4.03$.

Finally, Figures 21.6(c) and 21.6(d) show the decision boundary using a gaussian kernel $\tilde{K}(\mathbf{x}_i, \mathbf{x}_j) = \exp\left\{-\frac{\|\mathbf{x}_i - \mathbf{x}_j\|^2}{2\sigma^2}\right\} + 1$, with spread $\sigma^2 = 0.05$ and $\sigma^2 = 1.0$, respectively (with the same values of C and ϵ given above, with hinge loss). The small value of spread ($\sigma = 0.05$) results in overfitting, as observed from the "tight" decision boundary; whereas it makes no errors on the training set, it is unlikely to have a similarly good performance on the testing set. We can avoid overfitting by choosing a spread value like $\sigma^2 = 1$, which results in an error rate of 0.027 (4 misclassified points), but is expected to generalize better for unseen test cases, since it has a larger "margin" between classes.

21.6 FURTHER READING

The origins of support vector machines can be found in V. N. Vapnik (1982). In particular, it introduced the generalized portrait approach for constructing an optimal separating hyperplane. The use of the kernel trick for SVMs was introduced in Boser,

Guyon, and V. N. Vapnik (1992), and the soft margin SVM approach for nonseparable data was proposed in Cortes and V. Vapnik (1995). For a good introduction to support vector machines, including implementation techniques, see Cristianini and Shawe-Taylor (2000) and Schölkopf and Smola (2002).

Boser, B. E., Guyon, I. M., and Vapnik, V. N. (1992). A training algorithm for optimal margin classifiers. *Proceedings of the 5th Annual Workshop on Computational Learning Theory*. ACM, pp. 144–152.

Cortes, C. and Vapnik, V. (1995). Support-vector networks. *Machine Learning*, 20 (3), 273–297.

Cristianini, N. and Shawe-Taylor, J. (2000). *An Introduction to Support Vector Machines and Other Kernel-Based Learning Methods*. Cambridge University Press.

Schölkopf, B. and Smola, A. J. (2002). *Learning with Kernels: Support Vector Machines, Regularization, Optimization and Beyond*. Cambridge, MA: MIT Press.

Vapnik, V. N. (1982). *Estimation of Dependences Based on Empirical Data*. Vol. 40. New York: Springer-Verlag.

21.7 EXERCISES

Q1. Consider the dataset in Figure 21.7, which has points from two classes c_1 (triangles) and c_2 (circles). Answer the questions below.

    (a) Find the equations for the two hyperplanes h_1 and h_2.

    (b) Show all the support vectors for h_1 and h_2.

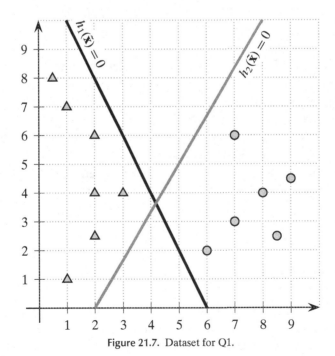

Figure 21.7. Dataset for Q1.

Table 21.2. Dataset for Q2

i	x_{i1}	x_{i2}	y_i	α_i
$\mathbf{x}_1^T$	4	2.9	1	0.414
$\mathbf{x}_2^T$	4	4	1	0
$\mathbf{x}_3^T$	1	2.5	−1	0
$\mathbf{x}_4^T$	2.5	1	−1	0.018
$\mathbf{x}_5^T$	4.9	4.5	1	0
$\mathbf{x}_6^T$	1.9	1.9	−1	0
$\mathbf{x}_7^T$	3.5	4	1	0.018
$\mathbf{x}_8^T$	0.5	1.5	−1	0
$\mathbf{x}_9^T$	2	2.1	−1	0.414
$\mathbf{x}_{10}^T$	4.5	2.5	1	0

(c) Which of the two hyperplanes is better at separating the two classes based on the margin computation?

(d) Find the equation of the best separating hyperplane for this dataset, and show the corresponding support vectors. You can do this witout having to solve the Lagrangian by considering the convex hull of each class and the possible hyperplanes at the boundary of the two classes.

Q2. Given the 10 points in Table 21.2, along with their classes and their Lagranian multipliers (α_i), answer the following questions:

(a) What is the equation of the SVM hyperplane $h(\mathbf{x})$?

(b) What is the distance of $\mathbf{x}_6$ from the hyperplane? Is it within the margin of the classifier?

(c) Classify the point $\mathbf{z} = (3, 3)^T$ using $h(\mathbf{x})$ from above.

CHAPTER 22

Classification Assessment

We have seen different classifiers in the preceding chapters, such as decision trees, full and naive Bayes classifiers, nearest neighbors classifier, support vector machines, and so on. In general, we may think of the classifier as a model or function M that predicts the class label $\hat{y}$ for a given input example $\mathbf{x}$:

$$\hat{y} = M(\mathbf{x})$$

where $\mathbf{x} = (x_1, x_2, \ldots, x_d)^T \in \mathbb{R}^d$ is a point in d-dimensional space and $\hat{y} \in \{c_1, c_2, \ldots, c_k\}$ is its predicted class.

To build the classification model M we need a *training set* of points along with their known classes. Different classifiers are obtained depending on the assumptions used to build the model M. For instance, support vector machines use the maximum margin hyperplane to construct M. On the other hand, the Bayes classifier directly computes the posterior probability $P(c_j|\mathbf{x})$ for each class c_j, and predicts the class of $\mathbf{x}$ as the one with the maximum posterior probability, $\hat{y} = \mathrm{argmax}_{c_j} \{P(c_j|\mathbf{x})\}$. Once the model M has been trained, we assess its performance over a separate *testing set* of points for which we know the true classes. Finally, the model can be deployed to predict the class for future points whose class we typically do not know.

In this chapter we look at methods to assess a classifier, and to compare multiple classifiers. We start by defining metrics of classifier accuracy. We then discuss how to determine bounds, to assess the performance of classifiers and to compare them. Finally, we discuss the ensemble methods, which combine several classifiers exploiting the advantages of each one.

22.1 CLASSIFICATION PERFORMANCE MEASURES

Let $\mathbf{D}$ be the testing set comprising n points in a d dimensional space, let $\{c_1, c_2, \ldots, c_k\}$ denote the set of k class labels, and let M be a classifier. For $\mathbf{x}_i \in \mathbf{D}$, let y_i denote its true class, and let $\hat{y}_i = M(\mathbf{x}_i)$ denote its predicted class.

Error Rate

The error rate is the fraction of incorrect predictions for the classifier over the testing set, defined as

$$Error\ Rate = \frac{1}{n}\sum_{i=1}^{n} I(y_i \neq \hat{y}_i) \qquad (22.1)$$

where I is an indicator function that has the value 1 when its argument is true, and 0 otherwise. Error rate is an estimate of the probability of misclassification. The lower the error rate the better the classifier.

Accuracy

The accuracy of a classifier is the fraction of correct predictions over the testing set:

$$Accuracy = \frac{1}{n}\sum_{i=1}^{n} I(y_i = \hat{y}_i) = 1 - Error\ Rate \qquad (22.2)$$

Accuracy gives an estimate of the probability of a correct prediction; thus, the higher the accuracy, the better the classifier.

Example 22.1. Figure 22.1 shows the 2-dimensional Iris dataset, with the two attributes being sepal length and sepal width. It has 150 points, and has three equal-sized classes: Iris-setosa (c_1; circles), Iris-versicolor (c_2; squares) and

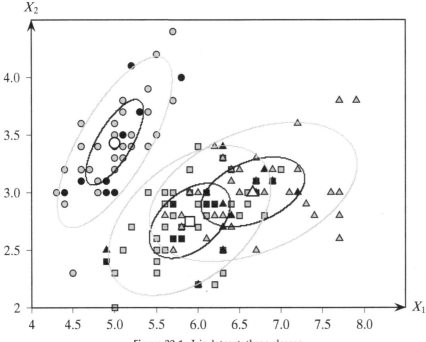

Figure 22.1. Iris dataset: three classes.

Iris-virginica (c_3; triangles). The dataset is partitioned into training and testing sets, in the ratio 80:20. Thus, the training set has 120 points (shown in light gray), and the testing set **D** has $n = 30$ points (shown in black). One can see that whereas c_1 is well separated from the other classes, c_2 and c_3 are not easy to separate. In fact, some points are labeled as both c_2 and c_3 (e.g., the point $(6, 2.2)^T$ appears twice, labeled as c_2 and c_3).

We classify the test points using the full Bayes classifier (see Chapter 18). Each class is modeled using a single normal distribution, whose mean (in white) and density contours (corresponding to one and two standard deviations) are also plotted in Figure 22.1. The classifier misclassifies 8 out of the 30 test cases. Thus, we have

$$Error\ Rate = 8/30 = 0.267$$

$$Accuracy = 22/30 = 0.733$$

22.1.1 Contingency Table–based Measures

The error rate (and, thus also the accuracy) is a global measure in that it does not explicitly consider the classes that contribute to the error. More informative measures can be obtained by tabulating the class specific agreement and disagreement between the true and predicted labels over the testing set. Let $\mathcal{D} = \{\mathbf{D}_1, \mathbf{D}_2, \ldots, \mathbf{D}_k\}$ denote a partitioning of the testing points based on their true class labels, where

$$\mathbf{D}_j = \left\{\mathbf{x}_i^T \mid y_i = c_j\right\} \qquad \text{and} \qquad n_i = |\mathbf{D}_i|$$

Here $n_i = |\mathbf{D}_i|$ denotes the size of true class c_i.

Let $\mathcal{R} = \{\mathbf{R}_1, \mathbf{R}_2, \ldots, \mathbf{R}_k\}$ denote a partitioning of the testing points based on the predicted labels, that is,

$$\mathbf{R}_j = \left\{\mathbf{x}_i^T \mid \hat{y}_i = c_j\right\} \qquad \text{and} \qquad m_j = |\mathbf{R}_j|$$

Here $m_j = |\mathbf{R}_j|$ denotes the size of the predicted class c_j.

The partitionings $\mathcal{R}$ and $\mathcal{D}$ induce a $k \times k$ contingency table **N**, also called a *confusion matrix*, defined as follows:

$$\mathbf{N}(i, j) = n_{ij} = \left|\mathbf{R}_i \cap \mathbf{D}_j\right| = \left|\left\{\mathbf{x}_a \in \mathbf{D} \mid \hat{y}_a = c_i \text{ and } y_a = c_j\right\}\right|$$

where $1 \leq i, j \leq k$. The count n_{ij} denotes the number of points with predicted class c_i whose true label is c_j. Thus, n_{ii} (for $1 \leq i \leq k$) denotes the number of cases where the classifier agrees on the true label c_i. The remaining counts n_{ij}, with $i \neq j$, are cases where the classifier and true labels disagree.

Accuracy/Precision

The class-specific *accuracy* or *precision* of the classifier M for class c_i is given as the fraction of correct predictions over all points predicted to be in class c_i

$$acc_i = prec_i = \frac{n_{ii}}{m_i} \tag{22.3}$$

where m_i is the number of examples predicted as c_i by classifier M. The higher the accuracy on class c_i the better the classifier.

The overall precision or accuracy of the classifier is the weighted average of the class-specific accuracy:

$$Accuracy = Precision = \sum_{i=1}^{k} \left(\frac{m_i}{n}\right) acc_i = \frac{1}{n}\sum_{i=1}^{k} n_{ii} \qquad (22.4)$$

This is identical to the expression in Eq. (22.2).

Coverage/Recall

The class-specific *coverage* or *recall* of M for class c_i is the fraction of correct predictions over all points in class c_i:

$$coverage_i = recall_i = \frac{n_{ii}}{n_i} \qquad (22.5)$$

where n_i is the number of points in class c_i. The higher the coverage the better the classifier.

F-measure

Often there is a trade-off between the precision and recall of a classifier. For example, it is easy to make $recall_i = 1$, by predicting all testing points to be in class c_i. However, in this case $prec_i$ will be low. On the other hand, we can make $prec_i$ very high by predicting only a few points as c_i, for instance, for those predictions where M has the most confidence, but in this case $recall_i$ will be low. Ideally, we would like both precision and recall to be high.

The *class-specific F-measure* tries to balance the precision and recall values, by computing their harmonic mean for class c_i:

$$F_i = \frac{2}{\frac{1}{prec_i} + \frac{1}{recall_i}} = \frac{2 \cdot prec_i \cdot recall_i}{prec_i + recall_i} = \frac{2\,n_{ii}}{n_i + m_i} \qquad (22.6)$$

The higher the F_i value the better the classifier.

The overall *F-measure* for the classifier M is the mean of the class-specific values:

$$F = \frac{1}{k}\sum_{i=1}^{r} F_i \qquad (22.7)$$

For a perfect classifier, the maximum value of the F-measure is 1.

Example 22.2. Consider the 2-dimensional Iris dataset shown in Figure 22.1. In Example 22.1 we saw that the error rate was 26.7%. However, the error rate measure does not give much information about the classes or instances that are more difficult to classify. From the class-specific normal distribution in the figure, it is clear that the Bayes classifier should perform well for c_1, but it is likely to have problems discriminating some test cases that lie close to the decision boundary between c_2 and c_3. This information is better captured by the confusion matrix obtained on the testing set, as shown in Table 22.1. We can observe that all 10 points in c_1 are classified correctly. However, only 7 out of the 10 for c_2 and 5 out of the 10 for c_3 are classified correctly.

From the confusion matrix we can compute the class-specific precision (or accuracy) values:

$$prec_1 = \frac{n_{11}}{m_1} = 10/10 = 1.0$$

$$prec_2 = \frac{n_{22}}{m_2} = 7/12 = 0.583$$

$$prec_3 = \frac{n_{33}}{m_3} = 5/8 = 0.625$$

The overall accuracy tallies with that reported in Example 22.1:

$$Accuracy = \frac{(n_{11} + n_{22} + n_{33})}{n} = \frac{(10 + 7 + 5)}{30} = 22/30 = 0.733$$

The class-specific recall (or coverage) values are given as

$$recall_1 = \frac{n_{11}}{n_1} = 10/10 = 1.0$$

$$recall_2 = \frac{n_{22}}{n_2} = 7/10 = 0.7$$

$$recall_3 = \frac{n_{33}}{n_3} = 5/10 = 0.5$$

From these we can compute the class-specific F-measure values:

$$F_1 = \frac{2 \cdot n_{11}}{(n_1 + m_1)} = 20/20 = 1.0$$

$$F_2 = \frac{2 \cdot n_{22}}{(n_2 + m_2)} = 14/22 = 0.636$$

$$F_3 = \frac{2 \cdot n_{33}}{(n_3 + m_3)} = 10/18 = 0.556$$

Thus, the overall F-measure for the classifier is

$$F = \frac{1}{3}(1.0 + 0.636 + 0.556) = \frac{2.192}{3} = 0.731$$

Table 22.1. Contingency table for Iris dataset: testing set

Predicted	True Iris-setosa (c_1)	Iris-versicolor (c_2)	Iris-virginica(c_3)	
Iris-setosa (c_1)	10	0	0	$m_1 = 10$
Iris-versicolor (c_2)	0	7	5	$m_2 = 12$
Iris-virginica (c_3)	0	3	5	$m_3 = 8$
	$n_1 = 10$	$n_2 = 10$	$n_3 = 10$	$n = 30$

Table 22.2. Confusion matrix for two classes

Predicted Class	True Class Positive (c_1)	Negative (c_2)
Positive (c_1)	True Positive (*TP*)	False Positive (*FP*)
Negative (c_2)	False Negative (*FN*)	True Negative (*TN*)

22.1.2 Binary Classification: Positive and Negative Class

When there are only $k = 2$ classes, we call class c_1 the positive class and c_2 the negative class. The entries of the resulting 2×2 confusion matrix, shown in Table 22.2, are given special names, as follows:

- *True Positives (TP):* The number of points that the classifier correctly predicts as positive:

$$TP = n_{11} = \left| \{\mathbf{x}_i \mid \hat{y}_i = y_i = c_1\} \right|$$

- *False Positives (FP):* The number of points the classifier predicts to be positive, which in fact belong to the negative class:

$$FP = n_{12} = \left| \{\mathbf{x}_i \mid \hat{y}_i = c_1 \text{ and } y_i = c_2\} \right|$$

- *False Negatives (FN):* The number of points the classifier predicts to be in the negative class, which in fact belong to the positive class:

$$FN = n_{21} = \left| \{\mathbf{x}_i \mid \hat{y}_i = c_2 \text{ and } y_i = c_1\} \right|$$

- *True Negatives (TN):* The number of points that the classifier correctly predicts as negative:

$$TN = n_{22} = \left| \{\mathbf{x}_i \mid \hat{y}_i = y_i = c_2\} \right|$$

Error Rate
The error rate [Eq. (22.1)] for the binary classification case is given as the fraction of mistakes (or false predictions):

$$Error\ Rate = \frac{FP + FN}{n} \tag{22.8}$$

Accuracy

The accuracy [Eq. (22.2)] is the fraction of correct predictions:

$$Accuracy = \frac{TP + TN}{n} \tag{22.9}$$

The above are global measures of classifier performance. We can obtain class-specific measures as follows.

Class-specific Precision

The precision for the positive and negative class is given as

$$prec_P = \frac{TP}{TP + FP} = \frac{TP}{m_1} \tag{22.10}$$

$$prec_N = \frac{TN}{TN + FN} = \frac{TN}{m_2} \tag{22.11}$$

where $m_i = |\mathbf{R}_i|$ is the number of points predicted by M as having class c_i.

Sensitivity: True Positive Rate

The true positive rate, also called *sensitivity*, is the fraction of correct predictions with respect to all points in the positive class, that is, it is simply the recall for the positive class

$$TPR = recall_P = \frac{TP}{TP + FN} = \frac{TP}{n_1} \tag{22.12}$$

where n_1 is the size of the positive class.

Specificity: True Negative Rate

The true negative rate, also called *specificity*, is simply the recall for the negative class:

$$TNR = specificity = recall_N = \frac{TN}{FP + TN} = \frac{TN}{n_2} \tag{22.13}$$

where n_2 is the size of the negative class.

False Negative Rate

The false negative rate is defined as

$$FNR = \frac{FN}{TP + FN} = \frac{FN}{n_1} = 1 - sensitivity \tag{22.14}$$

False Positive Rate

The false positive rate is defined as

$$FPR = \frac{FP}{FP + TN} = \frac{FP}{n_2} = 1 - specificity \tag{22.15}$$

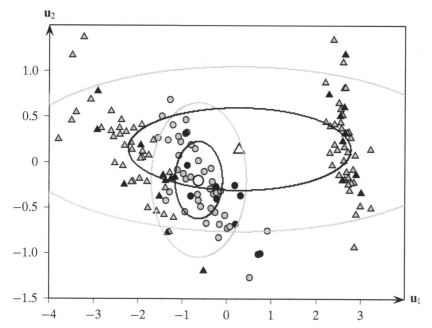

Figure 22.2. Iris principal component dataset: training and testing sets.

Example 22.3. Consider the Iris dataset projected onto its first two principal components, as shown in Figure 22.2. The task is to separate `Iris-versicolor` (class c_1; in circles) from the other two Irises (class c_2; in triangles). The points from class c_1 lie in-between the points from class c_2, making this is a hard problem for (linear) classification. The dataset has been randomly split into 80% training (in gray) and 20% testing points (in black). Thus, the training set has 120 points and the testing set has $n = 30$ points.

Applying the naive Bayes classifier (with one normal per class) on the training set yields the following estimates for the mean, covariance matrix and prior probability for each class:

$$\hat{P}(c_1) = 40/120 = 0.33 \qquad\qquad \hat{P}(c_2) = 80/120 = 0.67$$

$$\hat{\mu}_1 = \begin{pmatrix} -0.641 & -0.204 \end{pmatrix}^T \qquad\qquad \hat{\mu}_2 = \begin{pmatrix} 0.27 & 0.14 \end{pmatrix}^T$$

$$\widehat{\Sigma}_1 = \begin{pmatrix} 0.29 & 0 \\ 0 & 0.18 \end{pmatrix} \qquad\qquad \widehat{\Sigma}_2 = \begin{pmatrix} 6.14 & 0 \\ 0 & 0.206 \end{pmatrix}$$

The mean (in white) and the contour plot of the normal distribution for each class are also shown in the figure; the contours are shown for one and two standard deviations along each axis.

For each of the 30 testing points, we classify them using the above parameter estimates (see Chapter 18). The naive Bayes classifier misclassified 10 out of the 30 test instances, resulting in an error rate and accuracy of

$$Error\ Rate = 10/30 = 0.33$$

$$Accuracy = 20/30 = 0.67$$

Table 22.3. Iris PC dataset: contingency table for binary classification

Predicted	True		
	Positive (c_1)	Negative (c_2)	
Positive (c_1)	$TP = 7$	$FP = 7$	$m_1 = 14$
Negative (c_2)	$FN = 3$	$TN = 13$	$m_2 = 16$
	$n_1 = 10$	$n_2 = 20$	$n = 30$

The confusion matrix for this binary classification problem is shown in Table 22.3. From this table, we can compute the various performance measures:

$$prec_P = \frac{TP}{TP + FP} = \frac{7}{14} = 0.5$$

$$prec_N = \frac{TN}{TN + FN} = \frac{13}{16} = 0.8125$$

$$recall_P = sensitivity = TPR = \frac{TP}{TP + FN} = \frac{7}{10} = 0.7$$

$$recall_N = specificity = TNR = \frac{TN}{TN + FP} = \frac{13}{20} = 0.65$$

$$FNR = 1 - sensitivity = 1 - 0.7 = 0.3$$

$$FPR = 1 - specificity = 1 - 0.65 = 0.35$$

We can observe that the precision for the positive class is rather low. The true positive rate is also low, and the false positive rate is relatively high. Thus, the naive Bayes classifier is not particularly effective on this testing dataset.

22.1.3 ROC Analysis

Receiver Operating Characteristic (ROC) analysis is a popular strategy for assessing the performance of classifiers when there are two classes. ROC analysis requires that a classifier output a score value for the positive class for each point in the testing set. These scores can then be used to order points in decreasing order. For instance, we can use the posterior probability $P(c_1|\mathbf{x}_i)$ as the score, for example, for the Bayes classifiers. For SVM classifiers, we can use the signed distance from the hyperplane as the score because large positive distances are high confidence predictions for c_1, and large negative distances are very low confidence predictions for c_1 (they are, in fact, high confidence predictions for the negative class c_2).

Typically, a binary classifier chooses some positive score threshold ρ, and classifies all points with score above ρ as positive, with the remaining points classified as negative. However, such a threshold is likely to be somewhat arbitrary. Instead, ROC analysis plots the performance of the classifier over all possible values of the threshold parameter ρ. In particular, for each value of ρ, it plots the false positive rate

Table 22.4. Different cases for 2×2 confusion matrix

	True	
Predicted	Pos	Neg
Pos	0	0
Neg	FN	TN

(a) Initial: all negative

	True	
Predicted	Pos	Neg
Pos	TP	FP
Neg	0	0

(b) Final: all positive

	True	
Predicted	Pos	Neg
Pos	TP	0
Neg	0	TN

(c) Ideal classifier

(1-specificity) on the x-axis versus the true positive rate (sensitivity) on the y-axis. The resulting plot is called the *ROC curve* or *ROC plot* for the classifier.

Let $S(\mathbf{x}_i)$ denote the real-valued score for the positive class output by a classifier M for the point $\mathbf{x}_i$. Let the maximum and minimum score thresholds observed on testing dataset $\mathbf{D}$ be as follows:

$$\rho^{\min} = \min_i \{S(\mathbf{x}_i)\} \qquad\qquad \rho^{\max} = \max_i \{S(\mathbf{x}_i)\}$$

Initially, we classify all points as negative. Both TP and FP are thus initially zero (as shown in Table 22.4(a), resulting in TPR and FPR rates of zero, which correspond to the point $(0, 0)$ at the lower left corner in the ROC plot. Next, for each distinct value of ρ in the range $[\rho^{\min}, \rho^{\max}]$, we tabulate the set of positive points:

$$\mathbf{R}_1(\rho) = \{\mathbf{x}_i \in \mathbf{D} : S(\mathbf{x}_i) > \rho\}$$

and we compute the corresponding true and false positive rates, to obtain a new point in the ROC plot. Finally, in the last step, we classify all points as positive. Both FN and TN are thus zero (as shown in Table 22.4(b), resulting in TPR and FPR values of 1. This results in the point $(1, 1)$ at the top right-hand corner in the ROC plot. An ideal classifier corresponds to the top left point $(0, 1)$, which corresponds to the case $FPR = 0$ and $TPR = 1$, that is, the classifier has no false positives, and identifies all true positives (as a consequence, it also correctly predicts all the points in the negative class). This case is shown in Table 22.4(c). As such, a ROC curve indicates the extent to which the classifier ranks positive instances higher than the negative instances. An ideal classifier should score all positive points higher than any negative point. Thus, a classifier with a curve closer to the ideal case, that is, closer to the upper left corner, is a better classifier.

Area Under ROC Curve

The area under the ROC curve (AUC) can be used as a measure of classifier performance. Because the total area of the plot is 1, the AUC lies in the interval $[0, 1]$ – the higher the better. The AUC value is essentially the probability that the classifier will rank a random positive test case higher than a random negative test instance.

ROC/AUC Algorithm

Algorithm 22.1 shows the steps for plotting a ROC curve, and for computing the area under the curve. It takes as input the testing set $\mathbf{D}$, and the classifier M. The first step is to predict the score $S(\mathbf{x}_i)$ for the positive class (c_1) for each test point $\mathbf{x}_i \in \mathbf{D}$. Next, we sort the $(S(\mathbf{x}_i), y_i)$ pairs, that is, the score and the true class pairs, in decreasing order

---

Algorithm 22.1: ROC Curve and Area under the Curve

ROC-CURVE(D, M):

1 $n_1 \leftarrow \big|\{\mathbf{x}_i \in \mathbf{D} \,|\, y_i = c_1\}\big|$ // size of positive class
2 $n_2 \leftarrow \big|\{\mathbf{x}_i \in \mathbf{D} \,|\, y_i = c_2\}\big|$ // size of negative class
   // classify, score, and sort all test points
3 $L \leftarrow$ sort the set $\big\{(S(\mathbf{x}_i), y_i): \mathbf{x}_i \in \mathbf{D}\big\}$ by decreasing scores
4 $FP \leftarrow TP \leftarrow 0$
5 $FP_{prev} \leftarrow TP_{prev} \leftarrow 0$
6 $AUC \leftarrow 0$
7 $\rho \leftarrow \infty$
8 **foreach** $(S(\mathbf{x}_i), y_i) \in L$ **do**
9   **if** $\rho > S(\mathbf{x}_i)$ **then**
10   plot point $\left(\frac{FP}{n_2}, \frac{TP}{n_1}\right)$
11       $AUC \leftarrow AUC + \text{TRAPEZOID-AREA}\left(\left(\frac{FP_{prev}}{n_2}, \frac{TP_{prev}}{n_1}\right), \left(\frac{FP}{n_2}, \frac{TP}{n_1}\right)\right)$
12       $\rho \leftarrow S(\mathbf{x}_i)$
13       $FP_{prev} \leftarrow FP$
14       $TP_{prev} \leftarrow TP$
15   **if** $y_i = c_1$ **then** $TP \leftarrow TP + 1$
16   **else** $FP \leftarrow FP + 1$
17 plot point $\left(\frac{FP}{n_2}, \frac{TP}{n_1}\right)$
18 $AUC \leftarrow AUC + \text{TRAPEZOID-AREA}\left(\left(\frac{FP_{prev}}{n_2}, \frac{TP_{prev}}{n_1}\right), \left(\frac{FP}{n_2}, \frac{TP}{n_1}\right)\right)$

TRAPEZOID-AREA$((x_1, y_1), (x_2, y_2))$:

19 $b \leftarrow |x_2 - x_1|$ // base of trapezoid
20 $h \leftarrow \frac{1}{2}(y_2 + y_1)$ // average height of trapezoid
21 **return** $(b \cdot h)$

---

of the scores (line 3). Initially, we set the positive score threshold $\rho = \infty$ (line 7). The **foreach** loop (line 8) examines each pair $(S(\mathbf{x}_i), y_i)$ in sorted order, and for each distinct value of the score, it sets $\rho = S(\mathbf{x}_i)$ and plots the point

$$(FPR, TPR) = \left(\frac{FP}{n_2}, \frac{TP}{n_1}\right)$$

As each test point is examined, the true and false positive values are adjusted based on the true class y_i for the test point $\mathbf{x}_i$. If $y_1 = c_1$, we increment the true positives, otherwise, we increment the false positives (lines 15-16). At the end of the **foreach** loop we plot the final point in the ROC curve (line 17).

The AUC value is computed as each new point is added to the ROC plot. The algorithm maintains the previous values of the false and true positives, FP_{prev} and TP_{prev}, for the previous score threshold ρ. Given the current FP and TP values, we

Table 22.5. Sorted scores and true classes

$S(\mathbf{x}_i)$	0.93	0.82	0.80	0.77	0.74	0.71	0.69	0.67	0.66	0.61
y_i	c_2	c_1	c_2	c_1	c_1	c_1	c_2	c_1	c_2	c_2

$S(\mathbf{x}_i)$	0.59	0.55	0.55	0.53	0.47	0.30	0.26	0.11	0.04	2.97e-03
y_i	c_2	c_2	c_1	c_1	c_1	c_1	c_1	c_2	c_2	c_2

$S(\mathbf{x}_i)$	1.28e-03	2.55e-07	6.99e-08	3.11e-08	3.109e-08
y_i	c_2	c_2	c_2	c_2	c_2

$S(\mathbf{x}_i)$	1.53e-08	9.76e-09	2.08e-09	1.95e-09	7.83e-10
y_i	c_2	c_2	c_2	c_2	c_2

compute the area under the curve defined by the four points

$$(x_1, y_1) = \left(\frac{FP_{prev}}{n_2}, \frac{TP_{prev}}{n_1} \right) \qquad (x_2, y_2) = \left(\frac{FP}{n_2}, \frac{TP}{n_1} \right)$$

$$(x_1, 0) = \left(\frac{FP_{prev}}{n_2}, 0 \right) \qquad (x_2, 0) = \left(\frac{FP}{n_2}, 0 \right)$$

These four points define a trapezoid, whenever $x_2 > x_1$ and $y_2 > y_1$, otherwise, they define a rectangle (which may be degenerate, with zero area). The function TRAPEZOID-AREA computes the area under the trapezoid, which is given as $b \cdot h$, where $b = |x_2 - x_1|$ is the length of the base of the trapezoid and $h = \frac{1}{2}(y_2 + y_1)$ is the average height of the trapezoid.

Example 22.4. Consider the binary classification problem from Example 22.3 for the Iris principal components dataset. The test dataset $\mathbf{D}$ has $n = 30$ points, with $n_1 = 10$ points in the positive class and $n_2 = 20$ points in the negative class.

We use the naive Bayes classifier to compute the probability that each test point belongs to the positive class (c_1; iris-versicolor). The score of the classifier for test point $\mathbf{x}_i$ is therefore $S(\mathbf{x}_i) = P(c_1|\mathbf{x}_i)$. The sorted scores (in decreasing order) along with the true class labels are shown in Table 22.5.

The ROC curve for the test dataset is shown in Figure 22.3. Consider the positive score threshold $\rho = 0.71$. If we classify all points with a score above this value as positive, then we have the following counts for the true and false positives:

$$TP = 3 \qquad\qquad FP = 2$$

The false positive rate is therefore $\frac{FP}{n_2} = 2/20 = 0.1$, and the true positive rate is $\frac{TP}{n_1} = 3/10 = 0.3$. This corresponds to the point $(0.1, 0.3)$ in the ROC curve. Other points on the ROC curve are obtained in a similar manner as shown in Figure 22.3. The total area under the curve is 0.775.

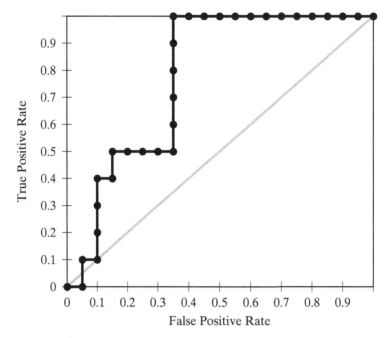

Figure 22.3. ROC plot for Iris principal components dataset. The ROC curves for the naive Bayes (black) and random (gray) classifiers are shown.

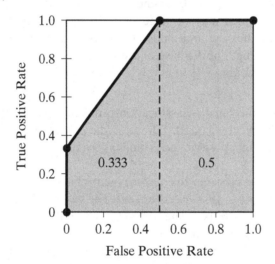

Figure 22.4. ROC plot and AUC: trapezoid region.

Example 22.5 (AUC). To see why we need to account for trapezoids when computing the AUC, consider the following sorted scores, along with the true class, for some testing dataset with $n = 5$, $n_1 = 3$ and $n_2 = 2$.

$$(0.9, c_1), (0.8, c_2), (0.8, c_1), (0.8, c_1), (0.1, c_2)$$

Algorithm 22.1 yields the following points that are added to the ROC plot, along with the running AUC:

ρ	FP	TP	(FPR, TPR)	AUC
∞	0	0	(0, 0)	0
0.9	0	1	(0, 0.333)	0
0.8	1	3	(0.5, 1)	0.333
0.1	2	3	(1, 1)	0.833

Figure 22.4 shows the ROC plot, with the shaded region representing the AUC. We can observe that a trapezoid is obtained whenever there is at least one positive and one negative point with the same score. The total AUC is 0.833, obtained as the sum of the trapezoidal region on the left (0.333) and the rectangular region on the right (0.5).

Random Classifier

It is interesting to note that a random classifier corresponds to a diagonal line in the ROC plot. To see this think of a classifier that randomly guesses the class of a point as positive half the time, and negative the other half. We then expect that half of the true positives and true negatives will be identified correctly, resulting in the point $(TPR, FPR) = (0.5, 0.5)$ for the ROC plot. If, on the other hand, the classifier guesses the class of a point as positive 90% of the time and as negative 10% of the time, then we expect 90% of the true positives and 10% of the true negatives to be labeled correctly, resulting in $TPR = 0.9$ and $FPR = 1 - TNR = 1 - 0.1 = 0.9$, that is, we get the point $(0.9, 0.9)$ in the ROC plot. In general, any fixed probability of prediction, say r, for the positive class, yields the point (r, r) in ROC space. The diagonal line thus represents the performance of a random classifier, over all possible positive class prediction thresholds r. It follows that if the ROC curve for any classifier is below the diagonal, it indicates performance worse than random guessing. For such cases, inverting the class assignment will produce a better classifier. As a consequence of the diagonal ROC curve, the AUC value for a random classifier is 0.5. Thus, if any classifier has an AUC value less than 0.5, that also indicates performance worse than random.

Example 22.6. In addition to the ROC curve for the naive Bayes classifier, Figure 22.3 also shows the ROC plot for the random classifier (the diagonal line in gray). We can see that the ROC curve for the naive Bayes classifier is much better than random. Its AUC value is 0.775, which is much better than the 0.5 AUC for a random classifier. However, at the very beginning, naive Bayes performs worse than the random classifier because the highest scored point is from the negative class. As such, the ROC curve should be considered as a discrete approximation of a smooth curve that would be obtained for a very large (infinite) testing dataset.

Class Imbalance

It is worth remarking that ROC curves are insensitive to class skew. This is because the *TPR*, interpreted as the probability of predicting a positive point as positive, and the *FPR*, interpreted as the probability of predicting a negative point as positive, do not depend on the ratio of the positive to negative class size. This is a desirable property, since the ROC curve will essentially remain the same whether the classes are balanced (have relatively the same number of points) or skewed (when one class has many more points than the other).

22.2 CLASSIFIER EVALUATION

In this section we discuss how to evaluate a classifier M using some performance measure θ. Typically, the input dataset $\mathbf{D}$ is randomly split into a disjoint training set and testing set. The training set is used to learn the model M, and the testing set is used to evaluate the measure θ. However, how confident can we be about the classification performance? The results may be due to an artifact of the random split, for example, by random chance the testing set may have particularly easy (or hard) to classify points, leading to good (or poor) classifier performance. As such, a fixed, pre-defined partitioning of the dataset is not a good strategy for evaluating classifiers. Also note that, in general, $\mathbf{D}$ is itself a d-dimensional multivariate random sample drawn from the true (unknown) joint probability density function $f(\mathbf{x})$ that represents the population of interest. Ideally, we would like to know the expected value $E[\theta]$ of the performance measure over all possible testing sets drawn from f. However, because f is unknown, we have to estimate $E[\theta]$ from $\mathbf{D}$. Cross-validation and resampling are two common approaches to compute the expected value and variance of a given performance measure; we discuss these methods in the following sections.

22.2.1 K-fold Cross-Validation

Cross-validation divides the dataset $\mathbf{D}$ into K equal-sized parts, called *folds*, namely $\mathbf{D}_1, \mathbf{D}_2, \ldots, \mathbf{D}_K$. Each fold $\mathbf{D}_i$ is, in turn, treated as the testing set, with the remaining folds comprising the training set $\mathbf{D} \setminus \mathbf{D}_i = \bigcup_{j \neq i} \mathbf{D}_j$. After training the model M_i on $\mathbf{D} \setminus \mathbf{D}_i$, we assess its performance on the testing set $\mathbf{D}_i$ to obtain the ith estimate θ_i. The expected value of the performance measure can then be estimated as

$$\hat{\mu}_\theta = E[\theta] = \frac{1}{K} \sum_{i=1}^{K} \theta_i \tag{22.16}$$

and its variance as

$$\hat{\sigma}_\theta^2 = \frac{1}{K} \sum_{i=1}^{K} (\theta_i - \hat{\mu}_\theta)^2 \tag{22.17}$$

Algorithm 22.2 shows the pseudo-code for K-fold cross-validation. After randomly shuffling the dataset $\mathbf{D}$, we partition it into K equal folds (except for possibly the last one). Next, each fold $\mathbf{D}_i$ is used as the testing set on which we assess the

---

Algorithm 22.2: K-fold Cross-Validation

CROSS-VALIDATION(K, **D**):
1 **D** ← randomly shuffle **D**
2 $\{\mathbf{D}_1, \mathbf{D}_2, \ldots, \mathbf{D}_K\}$ ← partition **D** in K equal parts
3 **for** $i \in [1, K]$ **do**
4 $\quad$ M_i ← train classifier on $\mathbf{D} \setminus \mathbf{D}_i$
5 $\quad$ θ_i ← assess M_i on $\mathbf{D}_i$
6 $\hat{\mu}_\theta = \frac{1}{K} \sum_{i=1}^{K} \theta_i$
7 $\hat{\sigma}_\theta^2 = \frac{1}{K} \sum_{i=1}^{K} (\theta_i - \hat{\mu}_\theta)^2$
8 **return** $\hat{\mu}_\theta, \hat{\sigma}_\theta^2$

---

performance θ_i of the classifier M_i trained on $\mathbf{D} \setminus \mathbf{D}_i$. The estimated mean and variance of θ can then be reported. Note that the K-fold cross-validation can be repeated multiple times; the initial random shuffling ensures that the folds are different each time.

Usually K is chosen to be 5 or 10. The special case, when $K = n$, is called *leave-one-out* cross-validation, where the testing set comprises a single point and the remaining data is used for training purposes.

Example 22.7. Consider the 2-dimensional Iris dataset from Example 22.1 with $k = 3$ classes. We assess the error rate of the full Bayes classifier via five-fold cross-validation, obtaining the following error rates when testing on each fold:

$$\theta_1 = 0.267 \qquad \theta_2 = 0.133 \qquad \theta_3 = 0.233 \qquad \theta_4 = 0.367 \qquad \theta_5 = 0.167$$

Using Eqs. (22.16) and (22.17), the mean and variance for the error rate are as follows:

$$\hat{\mu}_\theta = \frac{1.167}{5} = 0.233 \qquad\qquad \hat{\sigma}_\theta^2 = 0.00833$$

We can repeat the whole cross-validation approach multiple times, with a different permutation of the input points, and then we can compute the mean of the average error rate, and mean of the variance. Performing ten five-fold cross-validation runs for the Iris dataset results in the mean of the expected error rate as 0.232, and the mean of the variance as 0.00521, with the variance in both these estimates being less than 10^{-3}.

22.2.2 Bootstrap Resampling

Another approach to estimate the expected performance of a classifier is to use the bootstrap resampling method. Instead of partitioning the input dataset **D** into disjoint folds, the bootstrap method draws K random samples of size n *with replacement* from **D**. Each sample $\mathbf{D}_i$ is thus the same size as **D**, and has several repeated points. Consider the probability that a point $\mathbf{x}_j \in \mathbf{D}$ is not selected for the ith bootstrap sample $\mathbf{D}_i$. Due

---

Algorithm 22.3: Bootstrap Resampling Method

BOOTSTRAP-RESAMPLING(K, D):

1 **for** $i \in [1, K]$ **do**
2 | $\mathbf{D}_i \leftarrow$ sample of size n with replacement from $\mathbf{D}$
3 | $M_i \leftarrow$ train classifier on $\mathbf{D}_i$
4 | $\theta_i \leftarrow$ assess M_i on $\mathbf{D}$
5 $\hat{\mu}_\theta = \frac{1}{K} \sum_{i=1}^{K} \theta_i$
6 $\hat{\sigma}_\theta^2 = \frac{1}{K} \sum_{i=1}^{K} (\theta_i - \hat{\mu}_\theta)^2$
7 **return** $\hat{\mu}_\theta, \hat{\sigma}_\theta^2$

---

to sampling with replacement, the probability that a given point is selected is given as $p = \frac{1}{n}$, and thus the probability that it is not selected is

$$q = 1 - p = \left(1 - \frac{1}{n}\right)$$

Because $\mathbf{D}_i$ has n points, the probability that $\mathbf{x}_j$ is not selected even after n tries is given as

$$P(\mathbf{x}_j \notin \mathbf{D}_i) = q^n = \left(1 - \frac{1}{n}\right)^n \simeq e^{-1} = 0.368$$

On the other hand, the probability that $\mathbf{x}_j \in \mathbf{D}_i$ is given as

$$P(\mathbf{x}_j \in \mathbf{D}_i) = 1 - P(\mathbf{x}_j \notin \mathbf{D}_i) = 1 - 0.368 = 0.632$$

This means that each bootstrap sample contains approximately 63.2% of the points from $\mathbf{D}$.

The bootstrap samples can be used to evaluate the classifier by training it on each of samples $\mathbf{D}_i$ and then using the full input dataset $\mathbf{D}$ as the testing set, as shown in Algorithm 22.3. The expected value and variance of the performance measure θ can be obtained using Eqs. (22.16) and (22.17). However, it should be borne in mind that the estimates will be somewhat optimistic owing to the fairly large overlap between the training and testing datasets (63.2%). The cross-validation approach does not suffer from this limitation because it keeps the training and testing sets disjoint.

Example 22.8. We continue with the Iris dataset from Example 22.7. However, we now apply bootstrap sampling to estimate the error rate for the full Bayes classifier, using $K = 50$ samples. The sampling distribution of error rates is shown in Figure 22.5. The expected value and variance of the error rate are

$$\hat{\mu}_\theta = 0.213$$

$$\hat{\sigma}_\theta^2 = 4.815 \times 10^{-4}$$

Due to the overlap between the training and testing sets, the estimates are more optimistic (i.e., lower) compared to those obtained via cross-validation in Example 22.7, where we had $\hat{\mu}_\theta = 0.233$ and $\hat{\sigma}_\theta^2 = 0.00833$.

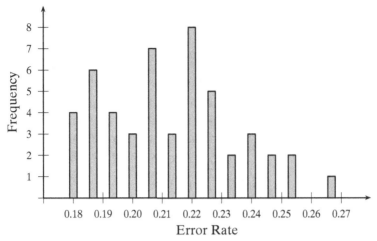

Figure 22.5. Sampling distribution of error rates.

22.2.3 Confidence Intervals

Having estimated the expected value and variance for a chosen performance measure, we would like to derive confidence bounds on how much the estimate may deviate from the true value.

To answer this question we make use of the central limit theorem, which states that the sum of a large number of independent and identically distributed (IID) random variables has approximately a normal distribution, regardless of the distribution of the individual random variables. More formally, let $\theta_1, \theta_2, \ldots, \theta_K$ be a sequence of IID random variables, representing, for example, the error rate or some other performance measure over the K-folds in cross-validation or K bootstrap samples. Assume that each θ_i has a finite mean $E[\theta_i] = \mu$ and finite variance $var(\theta_i) = \sigma^2$.

Let $\hat{\mu}$ denote the sample mean:

$$\hat{\mu} = \frac{1}{K}(\theta_1 + \theta_2 + \cdots + \theta_K)$$

By linearity of expectation, we have

$$E[\hat{\mu}] = E\left[\frac{1}{K}(\theta_1 + \theta_2 + \cdots + \theta_K)\right] = \frac{1}{K}\sum_{i=1}^{K} E[\theta_i] = \frac{1}{K}(K\mu) = \mu$$

Utilizing the linearity of variance for independent random variables, and noting that $var(aX) = a^2 \cdot var(X)$ for $a \in \mathbb{R}$, the variance of $\hat{\mu}$ is given as

$$var(\hat{\mu}) = var\left(\frac{1}{K}(\theta_1 + \theta_2 + \cdots + \theta_K)\right) = \frac{1}{K^2}\sum_{i=1}^{K} var(\theta_i) = \frac{1}{K^2}(K\sigma^2) = \frac{\sigma^2}{K}$$

Thus, the standard deviation of $\hat{\mu}$ is given as

$$std(\hat{\mu}) = \sqrt{var(\hat{\mu})} = \frac{\sigma}{\sqrt{K}}$$

We are interested in the distribution of the z-score of $\hat{\mu}$, which is itself a random variable

$$Z_K = \frac{\hat{\mu} - E[\hat{\mu}]}{std(\hat{\mu})} = \frac{\hat{\mu} - \mu}{\frac{\sigma}{\sqrt{K}}} = \sqrt{K}\left(\frac{\hat{\mu} - \mu}{\sigma}\right)$$

Z_K specifies the deviation of the estimated mean from the true mean in terms of its standard deviation. The central limit theorem states that, as the sample size increases, the random variable Z_K *converges in distribution* to the standard normal distribution (which has mean 0 and variance 1). That is, as $K \to \infty$, for any $x \in \mathbb{R}$, we have

$$\lim_{K \to \infty} P(Z_K \leq x) = \Phi(x)$$

where $\Phi(x)$ is the cumulative distribution function for the standard normal density function $f(x|0, 1)$. Given significance level $\alpha \in (0, 1)$, let $z_{\alpha/2}$ denote the critical z-score value for the standard normal distribution that encompasses $\alpha/2$ of the probability mass in the right tail, defined as

$$P(Z_K \geq z_{\alpha/2}) = \tfrac{\alpha}{2}, \text{ or equivalently } \Phi(z_{\alpha/2}) = P(Z_K \leq z_{\alpha/2}) = 1 - \tfrac{\alpha}{2}$$

Also, because the normal distribution is symmetric about the mean, we have

$$P(Z_K \geq -z_{\alpha/2}) = 1 - \tfrac{\alpha}{2}, \text{ or equivalently } \Phi(-z_{\alpha/2}) = \tfrac{\alpha}{2}$$

Thus, given confidence level $1 - \alpha$ (or significance level α), we can find the lower and upper critical z-score values, so as to encompass $1 - \alpha$ fraction of the probability mass, which is given as

$$P\left(-z_{\alpha/2} \leq Z_K \leq z_{\alpha/2}\right) = \Phi(z_{\alpha/2}) - \Phi(-z_{\alpha/2}) = 1 - \tfrac{\alpha}{2} - \tfrac{\alpha}{2} = 1 - \alpha \qquad (22.18)$$

Note that

$$-z_{\alpha/2} \leq Z_K \leq z_{\alpha/2} \implies -z_{\alpha/2} \leq \sqrt{K}\left(\frac{\hat{\mu} - \mu}{\sigma}\right) \leq z_{\alpha/2}$$

$$\implies -z_{\alpha/2}\frac{\sigma}{\sqrt{K}} \leq \hat{\mu} - \mu \leq z_{\alpha/2}\frac{\sigma}{\sqrt{K}}$$

$$\implies \left(\hat{\mu} - z_{\alpha/2}\frac{\sigma}{\sqrt{K}}\right) \leq \mu \leq \left(\hat{\mu} + z_{\alpha/2}\frac{\sigma}{\sqrt{K}}\right)$$

Substituting the above into Eq. (22.18) we obtain bounds on the value of the true mean μ in terms of the estimated value $\hat{\mu}$, that is,

$$P\left(\hat{\mu} - z_{\alpha/2}\frac{\sigma}{\sqrt{K}} \leq \mu \leq \hat{\mu} + z_{\alpha/2}\frac{\sigma}{\sqrt{K}}\right) = 1 - \alpha \qquad (22.19)$$

Thus, for any given level of confidence $1 - \alpha$, we can compute the corresponding $100(1-\alpha)\%$ confidence interval $\left(\hat{\mu} - z_{\alpha/2}\frac{\sigma}{\sqrt{K}}, \hat{\mu} + z_{\alpha/2}\frac{\sigma}{\sqrt{K}}\right)$. In other words, even though we do not know the true mean μ, we can obtain a high-confidence estimate of the interval within which it must lie (e.g., by setting $1 - \alpha = 0.95$ or $1 - \alpha = 0.99$).

Unknown Variance

The analysis above assumes that we know the true variance σ^2, which is generally not the case. However, we can replace σ^2 by the sample variance

$$\hat{\sigma}^2 = \frac{1}{K}\sum_{i=1}^{K}(\theta_i - \hat{\mu})^2 \tag{22.20}$$

because $\hat{\sigma}^2$ is a *consistent* estimator for σ^2, that is, as $K \to \infty$, $\hat{\sigma}^2$ converges with probability 1, also called *converges almost surely*, to σ^2. The central limit theorem then states that the random variable Z_K^* defined below converges in distribution to the standard normal distribution:

$$Z_K^* = \sqrt{K}\left(\frac{\hat{\mu} - \mu}{\hat{\sigma}}\right) \tag{22.21}$$

and, thus, we have

$$\lim_{K \to \infty} P\left(\hat{\mu} - z_{\alpha/2}\frac{\hat{\sigma}}{\sqrt{K}} \le \mu \le \hat{\mu} + z_{\alpha/2}\frac{\hat{\sigma}}{\sqrt{K}}\right) = 1 - \alpha \tag{22.22}$$

In other words, we say that $\left(\hat{\mu} - z_{\alpha/2}\frac{\hat{\sigma}}{\sqrt{K}}, \hat{\mu} + z_{\alpha/2}\frac{\hat{\sigma}}{\sqrt{K}}\right)$ is the $100(1 - \alpha)\%$ confidence interval for μ.

Example 22.9. Consider Example 22.7, where we applied five-fold cross-validation ($K = 5$) to assess the error rate of the full Bayes classifier. The estimated expected value and variance for the error rate were as follows:

$$\hat{\mu}_\theta = 0.233 \qquad \hat{\sigma}_\theta^2 = 0.00833 \qquad \hat{\sigma}_\theta = \sqrt{0.00833} = 0.0913$$

Let $1 - \alpha = 0.95$ be the confidence level, so that $\alpha = 0.05$ is he significance level. It is known that the standard normal distribution has 95% of the probability density within $z_{\alpha/2} = 1.96$ standard deviations from the mean. Thus, in the limit of large sample size, we have

$$P\left(\mu \in \left(\hat{\mu}_\theta - z_{\alpha/2}\frac{\hat{\sigma}_\theta}{\sqrt{K}}, \hat{\mu}_\theta + z_{\alpha/2}\frac{\hat{\sigma}_\theta}{\sqrt{K}}\right)\right) = 0.95$$

Because $z_{\alpha/2}\frac{\hat{\sigma}_\theta}{\sqrt{K}} = \frac{1.96 \times 0.0913}{\sqrt{5}} = 0.08$, we have

$$P\left(\mu \in (0.233 - 0.08, 0.233 + 0.08)\right) = P\left(\mu \in (0.153, 0.313)\right) = 0.95$$

Put differently, with 95% confidence, the true expected error rate lies in the interval $(0.153, 0.313)$.

If we want greater confidence, for example, for $1 - \alpha = 0.99$ (or $\alpha = 0.01$), then the corresponding z-score value is $z_{\alpha/2} = 2.58$, and thus $z_{\alpha/2}\frac{\hat{\sigma}_\theta}{\sqrt{K}} = \frac{2.58 \times 0.0913}{\sqrt{5}} = 0.105$. The 99% confidence interval for μ is therefore wider: $(0.128, 0.338)$.

Nevertheless, $K = 5$ is not a large sample size, and thus the above confidence intervals are not that reliable.

Small Sample Size

The confidence interval in Eq. (22.22) applies only when the sample size $K \to \infty$. We would like to obtain more precise confidence intervals for small samples. Consider the random variables V_i, for $i = 1, \ldots, K$, defined as

$$V_i = \frac{\theta_i - \hat{\mu}}{\sigma}$$

Further, consider the sum of their squares:

$$S = \sum_{i=1}^{K} V_i^2 = \sum_{i=1}^{K} \left(\frac{\theta_i - \hat{\mu}}{\sigma} \right)^2 = \frac{1}{\sigma^2} \sum_{i=1}^{K} (\theta_i - \hat{\mu})^2 = \frac{K\hat{\sigma}^2}{\sigma^2} \tag{22.23}$$

The last step follows from the definition of sample variance in Eq. (22.20).

If we assume that the V_i's are IID with the standard normal distribution, then the sum S follows a chi-squared distribution with $K - 1$ degrees of freedom, denoted $\chi^2(K - 1)$, since S is the sum of the squares of K random variables V_i. There are only $K - 1$ degrees of freedom because each V_i depends on $\hat{\mu}$ and the sum of the θ_i's is thus fixed.

Consider the random variable Z_K^* in Eq. (22.21). We have,

$$Z_K^* = \sqrt{K} \left(\frac{\hat{\mu} - \mu}{\hat{\sigma}} \right) = \left(\frac{\hat{\mu} - \mu}{\hat{\sigma}/\sqrt{K}} \right)$$

Dividing the numerator and denominator in the expression above by $\sigma/\sqrt{K}$, we get

$$Z_K^* = \left(\frac{\hat{\mu} - \mu}{\sigma/\sqrt{K}} \middle/ \frac{\hat{\sigma}/\sqrt{K}}{\sigma/\sqrt{K}} \right) = \left(\frac{\frac{\hat{\mu} - \mu}{\sigma/\sqrt{K}}}{\hat{\sigma}/\sigma} \right) = \frac{Z_K}{\sqrt{S/K}} \tag{22.24}$$

The last step follows from Eq. (22.23) because

$$S = \frac{K\hat{\sigma}^2}{\sigma^2} \text{ implies that } \frac{\hat{\sigma}}{\sigma} = \sqrt{S/K}$$

Assuming that Z_K follows a standard normal distribution, and noting that S follows a chi-squared distribution with $K - 1$ degrees of freedom, then the distribution of Z_K^* is precisely the Student's t distribution with $K - 1$ degrees of freedom. Thus, in the small sample case, instead of using the standard normal density to derive the confidence interval, we use the t distribution. In particular, given confidence level $1 - \alpha$ (or significance level α) we choose the critical value $t_{\alpha/2}$ such that the cumulative t distribution function with $K-1$ degrees of freedom encompasses $\alpha/2$ of the probability mass in the right tail. That is,

$$P(Z_K^* \geq t_{\alpha/2}) = 1 - T_{K-1}(t_{\alpha/2}) = \alpha/2$$

where T_{K-1} is the cumulative distribution function for the Student's t distribution with $K - 1$ degrees of freedom. Because the t distribution is symmetric about the mean, we have

$$P\left(\hat{\mu} - t_{\alpha/2} \frac{\hat{\sigma}}{\sqrt{K}} \leq \mu \leq \hat{\mu} + t_{\alpha/2} \frac{\hat{\sigma}}{\sqrt{K}} \right) = 1 - \alpha \tag{22.25}$$

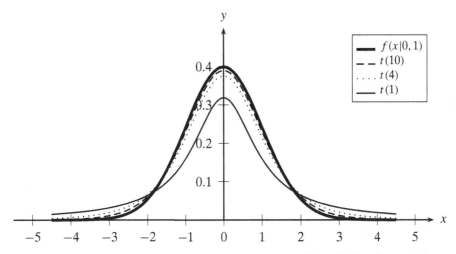

Figure 22.6. Student's t distribution: K degrees of freedom. The thick solid line is standard normal distribution.

The $100(1-\alpha)\%$ confidence interval for the true mean μ is thus

$$\left(\hat{\mu} - t_{\alpha/2}\frac{\hat{\sigma}}{\sqrt{K}} \le \mu \le \hat{\mu} + t_{\alpha/2}\frac{\hat{\sigma}}{\sqrt{K}} \right) \tag{22.26}$$

Note the dependence of the interval on both α and the sample size K.

Figure 22.6 shows the t distribution density function for different values of K. It also shows the standard normal density function. We can observe that the t distribution has more probability concentrated in its tails compared to the standard normal distribution. Further, as K increases, the t distribution very rapidly converges in distribution to the standard normal distribution, consistent with the large sample case. Thus, for large samples, we may use the usual $z_{\alpha/2}$ threshold.

Example 22.10. Consider Example 22.9. For five-fold cross-validation, the estimated mean error rate is $\hat{\mu}_\theta = 0.233$, and the estimated variance is $\hat{\sigma}_\theta = 0.0913$.

Due to the small sample size ($K = 5$), we can get a better confidence interval by using the t distribution. For $K - 1 = 4$ degrees of freedom, for $1 - \alpha = 0.95$ (or $\alpha = 0.05$), we use the quantile function for the Student's t-distribution to obtain $t_{\alpha/2} = 2.776$. Thus,

$$t_{\alpha/2}\frac{\hat{\sigma}_\theta}{\sqrt{K}} = 2.776 \times \frac{0.0913}{\sqrt{5}} = 0.113$$

The 95% confidence interval is therefore

$$(0.233 - 0.113, 0.233 + 0.113) = (0.12, 0.346)$$

which is much wider than the overly optimistic confidence interval $(0.153, 0.313)$ obtained for the large sample case in Example 22.9.

For $1 - \alpha = 0.99$, we have $t_{\alpha/2} = 4.604$, and thus

$$t_{\alpha/2}\frac{\hat{\sigma}_\theta}{\sqrt{K}} = 4.604 \times \frac{0.0913}{\sqrt{5}} = 0.188$$

and the 99% confidence interval is

$$(0.233 - 0.188, 0.233 + 0.188) = (0.045, 0.421)$$

This is also much wider than the 99% confidence interval $(0.128, 0.338)$ obtained for the large sample case in Example 22.9.

22.2.4 Comparing Classifiers: Paired t-Test

In this section we look at a method that allows us to test for a significant difference in the classification performance of two alternative classifiers, M^A and M^B. We want to assess which of them has a superior classification performance on a given dataset $\mathbf{D}$. Following the evaluation methodology above, we can apply K-fold cross-validation (or bootstrap resampling) and tabulate their performance over each of the K folds, with identical folds for both classifiers. That is, we perform a *paired test*, with both classifiers trained and tested on the same data. Let $\theta_1^A, \theta_2^A, \ldots, \theta_K^A$ and $\theta_1^B, \theta_2^B, \ldots, \theta_K^B$ denote the performance values for M_A and M_B, respectively. To determine if the two classifiers have different or similar performance, define the random variable δ_i as the difference in their performance on the ith dataset:

$$\delta_i = \theta_i^A - \theta_i^B$$

Now consider the estimates for the expected difference and the variance of the differences:

$$\hat{\mu}_\delta = \frac{1}{K} \sum_{i=1}^{K} \delta_i \qquad\qquad \hat{\sigma}_\delta^2 = \frac{1}{K} \sum_{i=1}^{K} (\delta_i - \hat{\mu}_\delta)^2$$

We can set up a hypothesis testing framework to determine if there is a statistically significant difference between the performance of M^A and M^B. The null hypothesis H_0 is that their performance is the same, that is, the true expected difference is zero, whereas the alternative hypothesis H_a is that they are not the same, that is, the true expected difference μ_δ is not zero:

$$H_0: \quad \mu_\delta = 0 \qquad\qquad H_a: \quad \mu_\delta \neq 0$$

Let us define the z-score random variable for the estimated expected difference as

$$Z_\delta^* = \sqrt{K} \left(\frac{\hat{\mu}_\delta - \mu_\delta}{\hat{\sigma}_\delta} \right)$$

Following a similar argument as in Eq. (22.24), Z_δ^* follows a t distribution with $K - 1$ degrees of freedom. However, under the null hypothesis we have $\mu_\delta = 0$, and thus

$$Z_\delta^* = \frac{\sqrt{K} \hat{\mu}_\delta}{\hat{\sigma}_\delta} \sim t_{K-1} \tag{22.27}$$

Algorithm 22.4: Paired t-Test via Cross-Validation

PAIRED t-TEST$(1 - \alpha, K, \mathbf{D})$:

1 $\mathbf{D} \leftarrow$ randomly shuffle $\mathbf{D}$
2 $\{\mathbf{D}_1, \mathbf{D}_2, \ldots, \mathbf{D}_K\} \leftarrow$ partition $\mathbf{D}$ in K equal parts
3 **for** $i \in [1, K]$ **do**
4 $\quad$ $M_i^A, M_i^B \leftarrow$ train the two different classifiers on $\mathbf{D} \setminus \mathbf{D}_i$
5 $\quad$ $\theta_i^A, \theta_i^B \leftarrow$ assess M_i^A and M_i^B on $\mathbf{D}_i$
6 $\quad$ $\delta_i \leftarrow \theta_i^A - \theta_i^B$
7 $\hat{\mu}_\delta \leftarrow \frac{1}{K} \sum_{i=1}^{K} \delta_i$ // mean
8 $\hat{\sigma}_\delta^2 \leftarrow \frac{1}{K} \sum_{i=1}^{K} (\delta_i - \hat{\mu}_\delta)^2$ // variance
9 $Z_\delta^* \leftarrow \frac{\sqrt{K} \cdot \hat{\mu}_\delta}{\hat{\sigma}_\delta}$ // test statistic value
10 $t_{\alpha/2} \leftarrow T_{K-1}^{-1}(1 - \alpha/2)$ // compute critical value
11 **if** $Z_\delta^* \in \left(-t_{\alpha/2}, t_{\alpha/2}\right)$ **then**
12 $\quad$ Accept H_0; both classifiers have similar performance
13 **else**
14 $\quad$ Reject H_0; classifiers have significantly different performance

---

where the notation $Z_\delta^* \sim t_{K-1}$ means that Z_δ^* follows the t distribution with $K-1$ degrees of freedom.

Given a desired confidence level $1 - \alpha$ (or significance level α), we conclude that

$$P\left(-t_{\alpha/2} \leq Z_\delta^* \leq t_{\alpha/2}\right) = 1 - \alpha$$

Put another way, if $Z_\delta^* \notin \left(-t_{\alpha/2}, t_{\alpha/2}\right)$, then we may reject the null hypothesis with $100(1 - \alpha)\%$ confidence. In this case, we conclude that there is a significant difference between the performance of M^A and M^B. On the other hand, if Z_δ^* does lie in the above confidence interval, then we accept the null hypothesis that both M^A and M^B have essentially the same performance. The pseudo-code for the paired t-test is shown in Algorithm 22.4.

Example 22.11. Consider the 2-dimensional Iris dataset from Example 22.1, with $k = 3$ classes. We compare the naive Bayes (M^A) with the full Bayes (M^B) classifier via cross-validation using $K = 5$ folds. Using error rate as the performance measure, we obtain the following values for the error rates and their difference over each of the K folds:

$$\begin{pmatrix} i & 1 & 2 & 3 & 4 & 5 \\ \hline \theta_i^A & 0.233 & 0.267 & 0.1 & 0.4 & 0.3 \\ \theta_i^B & 0.2 & 0.2 & 0.167 & 0.333 & 0.233 \\ \delta_i & 0.033 & 0.067 & -0.067 & 0.067 & 0.067 \end{pmatrix}$$

The estimated expected difference and variance of the differences are

$$\hat{\mu}_\delta = \frac{0.167}{5} = 0.033 \qquad \hat{\sigma}_\delta^2 = 0.00333 \qquad \hat{\sigma}_\delta = \sqrt{0.00333} = 0.0577$$

The z-score value is given as

$$Z_\delta^* = \frac{\sqrt{K}\hat{\mu}_\delta}{\hat{\sigma}_\delta} = \frac{\sqrt{5} \times 0.033}{0.0577} = 1.28$$

From Example 22.10, for $1 - \alpha = 0.95$ (or $\alpha = 0.05$) and $K - 1 = 4$ degrees of freedom, we have $t_{\alpha/2} = 2.776$. Because

$$Z_\delta^* = 1.28 \in (-2.776, 2.776) = \left(-t_{\alpha/2}, t_{\alpha/2}\right)$$

we cannot reject the null hypothesis. Instead, we accept the null hypothesis that $\mu_\delta = 0$, that is, there is no significant difference between the naive and full Bayes classifier for this dataset.

22.3 BIAS-VARIANCE DECOMPOSITION

Given a training set $\mathbf{D}$ comprising n points $\mathbf{x}_i \in \mathbb{R}^d$, with their corresponding classes y_i, a learned classification model M predicts the class for a given test point $\mathbf{x}$. The various performance measures we described above mainly focus on minimizing the prediction error by tabulating the fraction of misclassified points. However, in many applications, there may be costs associated with making wrong predictions. A *loss function* specifies the cost or penalty of predicting the class to be $\hat{y} = M(\mathbf{x})$, when the true class is y. A commonly used loss function for classification is the *zero-one loss*, defined as

$$L(y, M(\mathbf{x})) = I(M(\mathbf{x}) \neq y) = \begin{cases} 0 & \text{if } M(\mathbf{x}) = y \\ 1 & \text{if } M(\mathbf{x}) \neq y \end{cases}$$

Thus, zero-one loss assigns a cost of zero if the prediction is correct, and one otherwise. Another commonly used loss function is the *squared loss*, defined as

$$L(y, M(\mathbf{x})) = (y - M(\mathbf{x}))^2$$

where we assume that the classes are discrete valued, and not categorical.

Expected Loss
An ideal or optimal classifier is the one that minimizes the loss function. Because the true class is not known for a test case $\mathbf{x}$, the goal of learning a classification model can be cast as minimizing the expected loss:

$$E_y[L(y, M(\mathbf{x})) \,|\, \mathbf{x}] = \sum_y L(y, M(\mathbf{x})) \cdot P(y|\mathbf{x}) \qquad (22.28)$$

where $P(y|\mathbf{x})$ is the conditional probability of class y given test point $\mathbf{x}$, and E_y denotes that the expectation is taken over the different class values y.

Minimizing the expected zero–one loss corresponds to minimizing the error rate. This can be seen by expanding Eq. (22.28) with zero–one loss. Let $M(\mathbf{x}) = c_i$, then we have

$$E_y[L(y, M(\mathbf{x})) \mid \mathbf{x}] = E_y[I(y \neq M(\mathbf{x})) \mid \mathbf{x}]$$

$$= \sum_y I(y \neq c_i) \cdot P(y|\mathbf{x})$$

$$= \sum_{y \neq c_i} P(y|\mathbf{x})$$

$$= 1 - P(c_i|\mathbf{x})$$

Thus, to minimize the expected loss we should choose c_i as the class that maximizes the posterior probability, that is, $c_i = \arg\max_y P(y|\mathbf{x})$. Because by definition [Eq. (22.1)], the error rate is simply an estimate of the expected zero–one loss, this choice also minimizes the error rate.

Bias and Variance

The expected loss for the squared loss function offers important insight into the classification problem because it can be decomposed into bias and variance terms. Intuitively, the *bias* of a classifier refers to the systematic deviation of its predicted decision boundary from the true decision boundary, whereas the *variance* of a classifier refers to the deviation among the learned decision boundaries over different training sets. More formally, because M depends on the training set, given a test point $\mathbf{x}$, we denote its predicted value as $M(\mathbf{x}, \mathbf{D})$. Consider the expected square loss:

$$E_y\Big[L\big(y, M(\mathbf{x}, \mathbf{D})\big) \mid \mathbf{x}, \mathbf{D}\Big]$$

$$= E_y\Big[(y - M(\mathbf{x}, \mathbf{D}))^2 \mid \mathbf{x}, \mathbf{D}\Big]$$

$$= E_y\Big[\big(y \underbrace{- E_y[y|\mathbf{x}] + E_y[y|\mathbf{x}]}_{\text{add and subtract same term}} - M(\mathbf{x}, \mathbf{D})\big)^2 \mid \mathbf{x}, \mathbf{D}\Big]$$

$$= E_y\Big[(y - E_y[y|\mathbf{x}])^2 \mid \mathbf{x}, \mathbf{D}\Big] + E_y\Big[(M(\mathbf{x}, \mathbf{D}) - E_y[y|\mathbf{x}])^2 \mid \mathbf{x}, \mathbf{D}\Big]$$

$$\quad + E_y\Big[2(y - E_y[y|\mathbf{x}]) \cdot (E_y[y|\mathbf{x}] - M(\mathbf{x}, \mathbf{D})) \mid \mathbf{x}, \mathbf{D}\Big]$$

$$= E_y\Big[(y - E_y[y|\mathbf{x}])^2 \mid \mathbf{x}, \mathbf{D}\Big] + (M(\mathbf{x}, \mathbf{D}) - E_y[y|\mathbf{x}])^2$$

$$\quad + 2(E_y[y|\mathbf{x}] - M(\mathbf{x}, \mathbf{D})) \cdot \underbrace{(E_y[y|\mathbf{x}] - E_y[y|\mathbf{x}])}_{0}$$

$$= \underbrace{E_y\Big[(y - E_y[y|\mathbf{x}])^2 \mid \mathbf{x}, \mathbf{D}\Big]}_{\text{var}(y|\mathbf{x})} + \underbrace{\big(M(\mathbf{x}, \mathbf{D}) - E_y[y|\mathbf{x}]\big)^2}_{\text{squared-error}} \quad (22.29)$$

Above, we made use of the fact that for any random variables X and Y, and for any constant a, we have $E[X + Y] = E[X] + E[Y]$, $E[aX] = aE[X]$, and $E[a] = a$. The first term in Eq. (22.29) is simply the variance of y given $\mathbf{x}$. The second term is the squared error between the predicted value $M(\mathbf{x}, \mathbf{D})$ and the expected value $E_y[y|\mathbf{x}]$. Because this term depends on the training set, we can eliminate this dependence by averaging over all possible training tests of size n. The average or expected squared error for a given test point $\mathbf{x}$ over all training sets is then given as

$$E_{\mathbf{D}}\left[\left(M(\mathbf{x},\mathbf{D}) - E_y[y|\mathbf{x}]\right)^2\right]$$

$$= E_{\mathbf{D}}\left[\left(M(\mathbf{x},\mathbf{D}) \underbrace{-E_{\mathbf{D}}[M(\mathbf{x},\mathbf{D})] + E_{\mathbf{D}}[M(\mathbf{x},\mathbf{D})]}_{\text{add and subtract same term}} -E_y[y|\mathbf{x}]\right)^2\right]$$

$$= E_{\mathbf{D}}\left[\left(M(\mathbf{x},\mathbf{D}) - E_{\mathbf{D}}[M(\mathbf{x},\mathbf{D})]\right)^2\right] + E_{\mathbf{D}}\left[\left(E_{\mathbf{D}}[M(\mathbf{x},\mathbf{D})] - E_y[y|\mathbf{x}]\right)^2\right]$$

$$+ 2\left(E_{\mathbf{D}}[M(\mathbf{x},\mathbf{D})] - E_y[y|\mathbf{x}]\right) \cdot \underbrace{\left(E_{\mathbf{D}}[M(\mathbf{x},\mathbf{D})] - E_{\mathbf{D}}[M(\mathbf{x},\mathbf{D})]\right)}_{0}$$

$$= \underbrace{E_{\mathbf{D}}\left[\left(M(\mathbf{x},\mathbf{D}) - E_{\mathbf{D}}[M(\mathbf{x},\mathbf{D})]\right)^2\right]}_{variance} + \underbrace{\left(E_{\mathbf{D}}[M(\mathbf{x},\mathbf{D})] - E_y[y|\mathbf{x}]\right)^2}_{bias} \qquad (22.30)$$

This means that the expected squared error for a given test point can be decomposed into bias and variance terms. Combining Eqs. (22.29) and (22.30) the expected squared loss over all test points $\mathbf{x}$ and over all training sets $\mathbf{D}$ of size n yields the following decomposition into noise, variance and bias terms:

$$E_{\mathbf{x},\mathbf{D},y}\left[\left(y - M(\mathbf{x},\mathbf{D})\right)^2\right]$$

$$= E_{\mathbf{x},\mathbf{D},y}\left[\left(y - E_y[y|\mathbf{x}]\right)^2 |\mathbf{x},\mathbf{D}\right] + E_{\mathbf{x},\mathbf{D}}\left[\left(M(\mathbf{x},\mathbf{D}) - E_y[y|\mathbf{x}]\right)^2\right]$$

$$= \underbrace{E_{\mathbf{x},y}\left[\left(y - E_y[y|\mathbf{x}]\right)^2\right]}_{noise} + \underbrace{E_{\mathbf{x},\mathbf{D}}\left[\left(M(\mathbf{x},\mathbf{D}) - E_{\mathbf{D}}[M(\mathbf{x},\mathbf{D})]\right)^2\right]}_{average\ variance}$$

$$+ \underbrace{E_{\mathbf{x}}\left[\left(E_{\mathbf{D}}[M(\mathbf{x},\mathbf{D})] - E_y[y|\mathbf{x}]\right)^2\right]}_{average\ bias} \qquad (22.31)$$

Thus, the expected square loss over all test points and training sets can be decomposed into three terms: noise, average bias, and average variance. The noise term is the average variance var$(y|\mathbf{x})$ over all test points $\mathbf{x}$. It contributes a fixed cost to the loss independent of the model, and can thus be ignored when comparing different classifiers. The classifier specific loss can then be attributed to the variance and bias terms. In general, bias indicates whether the model M is correct or incorrect. It also reflects our assumptions about the domain in terms of the decision boundary. For example, if the decision boundary is nonlinear, and we use a linear classifier, then it is likely to have high bias, that is, it will be consistently incorrect over different training sets. On the other hand, a nonlinear (or a more complex) classifier is more likely to capture the correct decision boundary, and is thus likely to have a low bias. Nevertheless, this does not necessarily mean that a complex classifier will be a better one, since we also have to consider the variance term, which measures the inconsistency of the classifier decisions. A complex classifier induces a more complex decision boundary and thus may be prone to *overfitting*, that is, it may try to model all

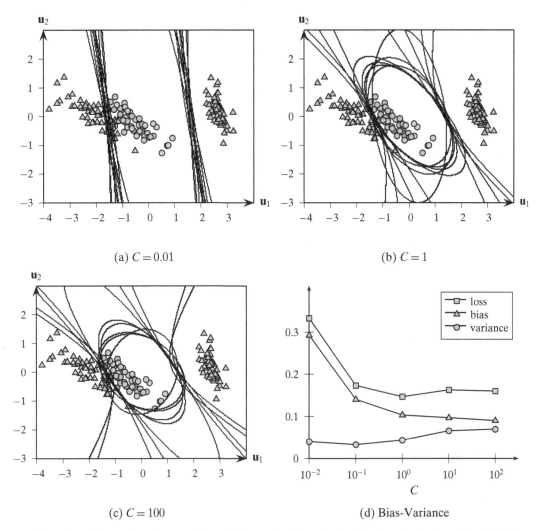

Figure 22.7. Bias-variance decomposition: SVM quadratic kernels. Decision boundaries plotted for $K = 10$ bootstrap samples.

the small nuances in the training data, and thus may be susceptible to small changes in training set, which may result in high variance.

In general, the expected loss can be attributed to high bias or high variance, with typically a trade-off between these two terms. Ideally, we seek a balance between these opposing trends, that is, we prefer a classifier with an acceptable bias (reflecting domain or dataset specific assumptions) and as low a variance as possible.

Example 22.12. Figure 22.7 illustrates the trade-off between bias and variance, using the Iris principal components dataset, which has $n = 150$ points and $k = 2$ classes ($c_1 = +1$, and $c_2 = -1$). We construct $K = 10$ training datasets via bootstrap sampling, and use them to train SVM classifiers using a quadratic (homogeneous) kernel, varying the regularization constant C from 10^{-2} to 10^2.

Recall that C controls the weight placed on the slack variables, as opposed to the margin of the hyperplane (see Section 21.3). A small value of C emphasizes the margin, whereas a large value of C tries to minimize the slack terms. Figures 22.7(a), 22.7(b), and 22.7(c) show that the variance of the SVM model increases as we increase C, as seen from the varying decision boundaries. Figure 22.7(d) plots the average variance and average bias for different values of C, as well as the expected loss. The bias-variance tradeoff is clearly visible, since as the bias reduces, the variance increases. The lowest expected loss is obtained when $C = 1$.

22.4 ENSEMBLE CLASSIFIERS

A classifier is called *unstable* if small perturbations in the training set result in large changes in the prediction or decision boundary. High variance classifiers are inherently unstable, since they tend to overfit the data. On the other hand, high bias methods typically underfit the data, and usually have low variance. In either case, the aim of learning is to reduce classification error by reducing the variance or bias, ideally both. Ensemble methods create a *combined classifier* using the output of multiple *base classifiers*, which are trained on different data subsets. Depending on how the training sets are selected, and on the stability of the base classifiers, ensemble classifiers can help reduce the variance and the bias, leading to a better overall performance.

22.4.1 Bagging

Bagging, which stands for *Bootstrap Aggregation*, is an ensemble classification method that employs multiple bootstrap samples (with replacement) from the input training data $\mathbf{D}$ to create slightly different training sets $\mathbf{D}_t$, $t = 1, 2, \ldots, K$. Different base classifiers M_t are learned, with M_t trained on $\mathbf{D}_t$. Given any test point $\mathbf{x}$, it is first classified using each of the K base classifiers, M_t. Let the number of classifiers that predict the class of $\mathbf{x}$ as c_j be given as

$$v_j(\mathbf{x}) = \left| \left\{ M_t(\mathbf{x}) = c_j \mid t = 1, \ldots, K \right\} \right|$$

The combined classifier, denoted $\mathbf{M}^K$, predicts the class of a test point $\mathbf{x}$ by *majority voting* among the k classes:

$$\mathbf{M}^K(\mathbf{x}) = \arg\max_{c_j} \left\{ v_j(\mathbf{x}) \mid j = 1, \ldots, k \right\}$$

For binary classification, assuming that the classes are given as $\{+1, -1\}$, the combined classifier $\mathbf{M}^K$ can be expressed more simply as

$$\mathbf{M}^K(\mathbf{x}) = \mathrm{sign}\left(\sum_{t=1}^{K} M_t(\mathbf{x}) \right)$$

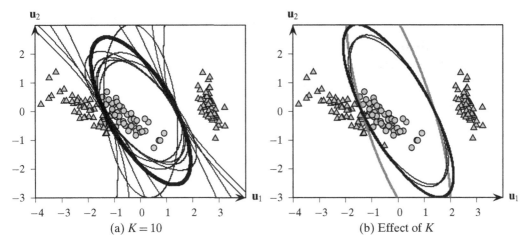

Figure 22.8. Bagging: combined classifiers. (a) uses $K = 10$ bootstrap samples. (b) shows average decision boundary for different values of K.

Bagging can help reduce the variance, especially if the base classifiers are unstable, due to the averaging effect of majority voting. It does not, in general, have much effect on the bias.

Example 22.13. Figure 22.8(a) shows the averaging effect of bagging for the Iris principal components dataset from Example 22.12. The figure shows the SVM decision boundaries for the quadratic kernel using $C = 1$. The base SVM classifiers are trained on $K = 10$ bootstrap samples. The combined (average) classifier is shown in bold.

Figure 22.8(b) shows the combined classifiers obtained for different values of K, keeping $C = 1$. The zero–one and squared loss for selected values of K are shown below

K	Zero–one loss	Squared loss
3	0.047	0.187
5	0.04	0.16
8	0.02	0.10
10	0.027	0.113
15	0.027	0.107

The worst training performance is obtained for $K = 3$ (in thick gray) and the best for $K = 8$ (in thick black).

22.4.2 Random Forest: Bagging Decision Trees

A *random forest* is an ensemble of K classifiers, $M_1, \ldots M_K$, where each classifier is a decision tree created from a different bootstrap sample, as in bagging. However, the key difference from bagging is that the trees are built by sampling a random subset

---

Algorithm 22.5: Random Forest Algorithm

$\textsc{RandomForest}(\mathbf{D}, K, p, \eta, \pi)$:

1 **foreach** $\mathbf{x}_i \in \mathbf{D}$ **do**
2     $\lfloor\ v_j(\mathbf{x}_i) \leftarrow 0$, for all $j = 1, 2, \ldots, k$
3 **for** $t \in [1, K]$ **do**
4     $\mathbf{D}_t \leftarrow$ sample of size n with replacement from $\mathbf{D}$
5     $M_t \leftarrow \textsc{DecisionTree} (\mathbf{D}_t, \eta, \pi, p)$
6   **foreach** $(\mathbf{x}_i, y_i) \in \mathbf{D} \setminus \mathbf{D}_t$ **do** // out-of-bag votes
7         $\hat{y}_i \leftarrow M_t(\mathbf{x}_i)$
8   **if** $\hat{y}_i = c_j$ **then** $v_j(\mathbf{x}_i) = v_j(\mathbf{x}_i) + 1$
9 $\epsilon_{oob} = \frac{1}{n} \cdot \sum_{i=1}^{n} I\Big(y_i \neq \arg\max_{c_j} \{v_j(\mathbf{x}_i) | (\mathbf{x}_i, y_i) \in \mathbf{D}\}\Big)$ // OOB error
10 **return** $\{M_1, M_2, \ldots, M_K\}$

---

of the attributes at each internal node in the decision tree. In general, decision trees can model complex decision boundaries between classes, and therefore have a low bias but high variance. If we simply bag several decision trees, they are likely to be similar to each other, and therefore we will not observe the variance reduction effects of bagging to a great extent. What we require is to have a diversity of trees, so that when we average their decisions, we will see much more of the variance reducing effects of bagging. The random sampling of the attributes results in reducing the correlation between the trees in the ensemble.

Let $\mathbf{D}$ be the training dataset comprising n points $\mathbf{x}_j \in \mathbb{R}^d$ along with the corresponding class y_j. Let $\mathbf{D}_t$ denote the tth bootstrap sample of size n drawn from $\mathbf{D}$ via sampling with replacement. Let $p \leq d$ denote the number of attributes to sample for evaluating the split points (see Section 19.2). The random forest algorithm uses the tth bootstrap sample to learn a decision tree model M_t via the decision tree method (see Algorithm 19.1) with one major change. Instead of evaluating all the d attributes to find the best split point, it samples $p \leq d$ attributes at random, and evaluates split points for only those attributes. A typical value of p is the square root of the number of attributes, i.e., $p = \sqrt{d}$, though this can be tuned for different datasets.

The K decision trees $M_1, M_2, \cdots, M_K$ comprise the random forest model $\mathbf{M}^K$, which predicts the class of a test point $\mathbf{x}$ by majority voting as in bagging:

$$\mathbf{M}^K(\mathbf{x}) = \arg\max_{c_j}\Big\{v_j(\mathbf{x}) \,\big|\, j = 1, \ldots, k\Big\}$$

where v_j is the number of trees that predict the class of $\mathbf{x}$ as c_j. That is,

$$v_j(\mathbf{x}) = \Big|\big\{M_t(\mathbf{x}) = c_j \,\big|\, t = 1, \ldots, K\big\}\Big|$$

Notice that if $p = d$ then the random forest approach is equivalent to bagging over decision tree models.

The pseudo-code for the random forest classifier is shown in Algorithm 22.5. The input parameters include the training data $\mathbf{D}$, the number of trees in the ensemble

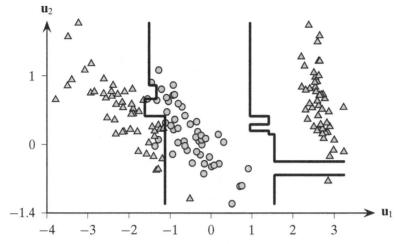

Figure 22.9. Random Forest: Iris principal components dataset ($K = 5$).

K, the number of attributes to sample p, the maximum leaf size η, and the minimum purity level π. The method generates K bootstrap samples $\mathbf{D}_t$ of size n, and constructs the decision tree model M_t using $\mathbf{D}_t$ as the training data. The call to DECISIONTREE refers to Algorithm 19.1 which grows the trees until either the leaf size or purity threshold is met for each leaf node. The only difference is that in line Line 9 instead of trying all attributes X_i, we randomly sample p attributes and evaluate the split points for only those attributes. The random forest classifier comprises the K decision trees $\{M_1, M_2, \cdots, M_K\}$.

Given bootstrap sample $\mathbf{D}_t$, any point in $\mathbf{D} \setminus \mathbf{D}_t$ is called an *out-of-bag* point for classifier M_t, since it was not used to train M_t. One of the side-benefits of the bootstrap approach is that we can compute the *out-of-bag* error rate for the random forest by considering the prediction of each model M_t over its out-of-bag points. Let $v_j(\mathbf{x})$ be the number of votes for class c_j over all decision trees in the ensemble where $\mathbf{x}$ was out-of-bag. We can aggregate these votes after we train each classifier M_t, by incrementing the value $v_j(\mathbf{x})$ if $\hat{y} = M_t(\mathbf{x}) = c_j$ and if $\mathbf{x}$ is out-of-bag for M_t. The out-of-bag (OOB) error for the random forest is given as:

$$\epsilon_{oob} = \frac{1}{n} \cdot \sum_{i=1}^{n} I\left(y_i \neq \arg\max_{c_j} \{ v_j(\mathbf{x}_i) | (\mathbf{x}_i, y_i) \in \mathbf{D} \} \right)$$

Here I is an indicator function that takes on value 1 if its argument is true, and 0 otherwise. In other words, we compute the majority out-of-bag class for each point $\mathbf{x}_i \in \mathbf{D}$ and check whether it matches the true class y_i. The out-of-bag error rate is simply the fraction of points where the out-of-bag majority class does not match the true class y_i. The out-of-bag error rate approximates the cross-validation error rate quite well, and can be used in lieu of k-fold cross-validation to evaluate the random forest model.

Example 22.14 (Random Forest). We illustrate the random forest approach on the Iris principal components dataset comprising $n = 150$ points in 2-dimensional space,

Table 22.6. Random Forest: Iris data, varying K

K	ϵ_{oob}	ϵ
1	0.4333	0.0267
2	0.2933	0.0267
3	0.1867	0.0267
4	0.1200	0.0400
5	0.1133	0.0333
6	0.1067	0.0400
7	0.0733	0.0333
8	0.0600	0.0267
9	0.0467	0.0267
10	0.0467	0.0267

as shown in Figure 22.9. The task is to separate Iris-versicolor (class c_1; in circles) from the other two Irises (class c_2; in triangles). Since there are only two attributes in this dataset, we pick $p = 1$ attribute at random for each split-point evaluation in a decision tree. Each decision tree is grown using $\eta = 3$, that is the maximum leaf size is 3 (with default minimum purity $\pi = 1.0$). We grow $K = 5$ decision trees on different bootstrap samples. The decision boundary of the random forest is shown in bold in the figure. The error rate on the training data is 2.0%. However, the out-of-bag error rate is 49.33%, which is overly pessimistic in this case, since the dataset has only two attributes, and we use only one attribute to evaluate each split point.

Example 22.15 (Random Forest: Varying K). To get a better understanding of the out-of-bag error rate and the number of trees in the random forest, we used the full Iris dataset which has four attributes ($d = 4$), and has three classes ($k = 3$), denoting the three Iris types. We used $p = \sqrt{d} = 2$, so that each decision tree samples only two of the attributes for evaluating each split point. We set $\eta = 3$ and $\pi = 1.0$.

Table 22.6 shows the out-of-bag error ϵ_{oob} and training error ϵ for the random forest model with different number of trees, ranging from $K = 1$ to $K = 10$. Whereas we get low training error rates with only a few trees, we can see that the out-of-bag error decreases rapidly as we increase the number of trees. For this dataset around 9 or 10 trees are sufficient to get low out-of-bag error rates.

22.4.3 Boosting

Boosting is another ensemble technique that trains the base classifiers on different samples. However, the main idea is to carefully select the samples to *boost* the performance on hard to classify instances. Starting from an initial training sample $\mathbf{D}_1$, we train the base classifier M_1, and obtain its training error rate. To construct the next sample $\mathbf{D}_2$, we select the misclassified instances with higher probability, and after training M_2, we obtain its training error rate. To construct $\mathbf{D}_3$, those instances that are hard to classify by M_1 or M_2, have a higher probability of being selected. This process is repeated for K iterations. Thus, unlike bagging that uses independent random samples from the input dataset, boosting employs weighted or biased samples to construct the different training sets, with the current sample depending on the previous ones. Finally, the combined classifier is obtained via weighted voting over the output of the K base classifiers $M_1, M_2, \ldots, M_K$.

Boosting is most beneficial when the base classifiers are *weak*, that is, have an error rate that is slightly less than that for a random classifier. The idea is that whereas M_1 may not be particularly good on all test instances, by design M_2 may help classify some cases where M_1 fails, and M_3 may help classify instances where M_1 and M_2 fail, and so on. Thus, boosting has more of a bias reducing effect. Each of the weak learners is likely to have high bias (it is only slightly better than random guessing), but the final combined classifier can have much lower bias, since different weak learners learn to classify instances in different regions of the input space. Several variants of boosting can be obtained based on how the instance weights are computed for sampling, how the base classifiers are combined, and so on. We discuss *Adaptive Boosting (AdaBoost)*, which is one of the most popular variants.

Adaptive Boosting: AdaBoost

Let $\mathbf{D}$ be the input training set, comprising n points $\mathbf{x}_i \in \mathbb{R}^d$. The boosting process will be repeated K times. Let t denote the iteration and let α_t denote the weight for the tth classifier M_t. Let w_i^t denote the weight for $\mathbf{x}_i$, with $\mathbf{w}^t = (w_1^t, w_2^t, \ldots, w_n^t)^T$ being the weight vector over all the points for the tth iteration. In fact, $\mathbf{w}$ is a probability vector, whose elements sum to one. Initially all points have equal weights, that is,

$$\mathbf{w}^0 = \left(\frac{1}{n}, \frac{1}{n}, \ldots, \frac{1}{n} \right)^T = \frac{1}{n}\mathbf{1}$$

where $\mathbf{1} \in \mathbb{R}^n$ is the n-dimensional vector of all 1's.

The pseudo-code for AdaBoost is shown in Algorithm 22.6. During iteration t, the training sample $\mathbf{D}_t$ is obtained via weighted resampling using the distribution $\mathbf{w}^{t-1}$, that is, we draw a sample of size n with replacement, such that the ith point is chosen according to its probability w_i^{t-1}. Next, we train the classifier M_t using $\mathbf{D}_t$, and compute its weighted error rate ϵ_t on the entire input dataset $\mathbf{D}$:

$$\epsilon_t = \sum_{i=1}^{n} w_i^{t-1} \cdot I\big(M_t(\mathbf{x}_i) \neq y_i\big)$$

where I is an indicator function that is 1 when its argument is true, that is, when M_t misclassifies $\mathbf{x}_i$, and is 0 otherwise.

The weight α_t for the tth classifier is then set as

$$\alpha_t = \ln \left(\frac{1 - \epsilon_t}{\epsilon_t} \right)$$

Algorithm 22.6: Adaptive Boosting Algorithm: AdaBoost

ADABOOST(K, D):

1 $\mathbf{w}^0 \leftarrow \left(\frac{1}{n}\right) \cdot \mathbf{1} \in \mathbb{R}^n$

2 $t \leftarrow 1$

3 **while** $t \leq K$ **do**

4 $\quad$ $\mathbf{D}_t \leftarrow$ weighted resampling with replacement from **D** using $\mathbf{w}^{t-1}$

5 $\quad$ $M_t \leftarrow$ train classifier on $\mathbf{D}_t$

6 $\quad$ $\epsilon_t \leftarrow \sum_{i=1}^{n} w_i^{t-1} \cdot I\left(M_t(\mathbf{x}_i) \neq y_i\right)$ // `weighted error rate on D`

7 $\quad$ **if** $\epsilon_t = 0$ **then break**

8 $\quad$ **else if** $\epsilon_t < 0.5$ **then**

9 $\quad\quad$ $\alpha_t = \ln\left(\frac{1-\epsilon_t}{\epsilon_t}\right)$ // `classifier weight`

10 $\quad\quad$ **for** $i \in [1, n]$ **do**

$\quad\quad\quad$ // `update point weights`

11 $\quad\quad$ $w_i^t = \begin{cases} w_i^{t-1} & \text{if } M_t(\mathbf{x}_i) = y_i \\ w_i^{t-1}\left(\frac{1-\epsilon_t}{\epsilon_t}\right) & \text{if } M_t(\mathbf{x}_i) \neq y_i \end{cases}$

12 $\quad\quad$ $\mathbf{w}^t = \frac{\mathbf{w}^t}{\mathbf{1}^T \mathbf{w}^t}$ // `normalize weights`

13 $\quad\quad$ $t \leftarrow t + 1$

14 **return** $\{M_1, M_2, \ldots, M_K\}$

---

and the weight for each point $\mathbf{x}_i \in \mathbf{D}$ is updated based on whether the point is misclassified or not

$$w_i^t = w_i^{t-1} \cdot \exp\left\{\alpha_t \cdot I\left(M_t(\mathbf{x}_i) \neq y_i\right)\right\}$$

Thus, if the predicted class matches the true class, that is, if $M_t(\mathbf{x}_i) = y_i$, then $I(M_t(\mathbf{x}_i) \neq y_i) = 0$, and the weight for point $\mathbf{x}_i$ remains unchanged. On the other hand, if the point is misclassified, that is, $M_t(\mathbf{x}_i) \neq y_i$, then we have $I(M_t(\mathbf{x}_i) \neq y_i) = 1$, and

$$w_i^t = w_i^{t-1} \cdot \exp\{\alpha_t\} = w_i^{t-1} \exp\left\{\ln\left(\frac{1-\epsilon_t}{\epsilon_t}\right)\right\} = w_i^{t-1}\left(\frac{1}{\epsilon_t} - 1\right)$$

We can observe that if the error rate ϵ_t is small, then there is a greater weight increment for $\mathbf{x}_i$. The intuition is that a point that is misclassified by a good classifier (with a low error rate) should be more likely to be selected for the next training dataset. On the other hand, if the error rate of the base classifier is close to 0.5, then there is only a small change in the weight, since a bad classifier (with a high error rate) is expected to misclassify many instances. Note that for a binary class problem, an error rate of 0.5 corresponds to a random classifier, that is, one that makes a random guess. Thus, we require that a base classifier has an error rate at least slightly better than random guessing, that is, $\epsilon_t < 0.5$. If the error rate $\epsilon_t \geq 0.5$, then the boosting method discards the classifier, and returns to line 4 to try another data sample. Alternatively, one can simply invert the predictions for binary classification. It is worth emphasizing that, for a multiclass problem (with $k > 2$), the requirement that $\epsilon_t < 0.5$ is a significantly stronger requirement than for the binary ($k = 2$) class problem because in the multiclass case a random classifier is expected to have an error rate of $\frac{k-1}{k}$. Note also that if the error rate of the base classifier $\epsilon_t = 0$, then we can stop the boosting iterations.

Once the point weights have been updated, we re-normalize the weights so that $\mathbf{w}^t$ is a probability vector (line 12):

$$\mathbf{w}^t = \frac{\mathbf{w}^t}{\mathbf{1}^T \mathbf{w}^t} = \frac{1}{\sum_{j=1}^n w_j^t} \left(w_1^t, w_2^t, \ldots, w_n^t \right)^T$$

Combined Classifier Given the set of boosted classifiers, $M_1, M_2, \ldots, M_K$, along with their weights $\alpha_1, \alpha_2, \ldots, \alpha_K$, the class for a test case $\mathbf{x}$ is obtained via weighted majority voting. Let $v_j(\mathbf{x})$ denote the weighted vote for class c_j over the K classifiers, given as

$$v_j(\mathbf{x}) = \sum_{t=1}^K \alpha_t \cdot I\big(M_t(\mathbf{x}) = c_j\big)$$

Because $I(M_t(\mathbf{x}) = c_j)$ is 1 only when $M_t(\mathbf{x}) = c_j$, the variable $v_j(\mathbf{x})$ simply obtains the tally for class c_j among the K base classifiers, taking into account the classifier weights. The combined classifier, denoted $\mathbf{M}^K$, then predicts the class for $\mathbf{x}$ as follows:

$$\mathbf{M}^K(\mathbf{x}) = \arg\max_{c_j}\Big\{ v_j(\mathbf{x}) \,\big|\, j = 1, .., k \Big\}$$

In the case of binary classification, with classes $\{+1, -1\}$, the combined classifier $\mathbf{M}^K$ can be expressed more simply as

$$\mathbf{M}^K(\mathbf{x}) = \operatorname{sign}\left(\sum_{t=1}^K \alpha_t M_t(\mathbf{x}) \right)$$

Example 22.16. Figure 22.10(a) illustrates the boosting approach on the Iris principal components dataset, using linear SVMs as the base classifiers. The regularization constant was set to $C = 1$. The hyperplane learned in iteration t is denoted h_t, thus, the classifier model is given as $M_t(\mathbf{x}) = \operatorname{sign}(h_t(\mathbf{x}))$. As such, no individual linear hyperplane can discriminate between the classes very well, as seen from their error rates on the training set:

M_t	h_1	h_2	h_3	h_4
ϵ_t	0.280	0.305	0.174	0.282
α_t	0.944	0.826	1.559	0.935

However, when we combine the decisions from successive hyperplanes weighted by α_t, we observe a marked drop in the error rate for the combined classifier $\mathbf{M}^K(\mathbf{x})$ as K increases:

combined model	$\mathbf{M}^1$	$\mathbf{M}^2$	$\mathbf{M}^3$	$\mathbf{M}^4$
training error rate	0.280	0.253	0.073	0.047

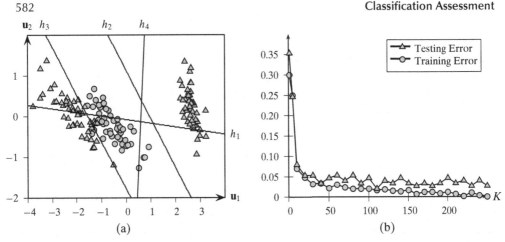

Figure 22.10. (a) Boosting SVMs with linear kernel. (b) Average testing and training error: five-fold cross-validation.

We can see, for example, that the combined classifier $\mathbf{M}^3$, comprising h_1, h_2 and h_3, has already captured the essential features of the nonlinear decision boundary between the two classes, yielding an error rate of 7.3%. Further reduction in the training error is obtained by increasing the number of boosting steps.

To assess the performance of the combined classifier on independent testing data, we employ five-fold cross-validation, and plot the average testing and training error rates as a function of K in Figure 22.10(b). We can see that, as the number of base classifiers K increases, both the training and testing error rates reduce. However, while the training error essentially goes to 0, the testing error does not reduce beyond 0.02, which happens at $K = 110$. This example illustrates the effectiveness of boosting in reducing the bias.

Bagging as a Special Case of AdaBoost: Bagging can be considered as a special case of AdaBoost, where $w^t = \frac{1}{n}\mathbf{1}$, and $\alpha_t = 1$ for all K iterations. In this case, the weighted resampling defaults to regular resampling with replacement, and the predicted class for a test case also defaults to simple majority voting.

22.4.4 Stacking

Stacking or stacked generalization is an ensemble technique where we employ two layers of classifiers. The first layer is composed of K base classifiers which are trained independently on the entire training data $\mathbf{D}$. However, the base classifiers should differ from or be complementary to each other as much as possible so that they perform well on different subsets of the input space. The second layer comprises a combiner classifier C that is trained on the predicted classes from the base classifiers, so that it automatically learns how to combine the outputs of the base classifiers to make the final prediction for a given input. For example, the combiner classifier may learn to ignore the output of a base classifiers for an input that lies in a region of the data space where the base classifier has poor performance. It can also learn to correct the

---

Algorithm 22.7: Stacking Algorithm

STACKING($K, \mathbf{M}, C, \mathbf{D}$):
// Train base classifiers
1 **for** $t \in [1, K]$ **do**
2     $\lfloor$ $M_t \leftarrow$ train tth base classifier on $\mathbf{D}$

    // Train combiner model C on $\mathbf{Z}$
3 $\mathbf{Z} \leftarrow \emptyset$
4 **foreach** $(\mathbf{x}_i, y_i) \in \mathbf{D}$ **do**
5     $\mathbf{z}_i \leftarrow \big(M_1(\mathbf{x}_i), M_2(\mathbf{x}_i), \ldots, M_K(\mathbf{x}_i)\big)^T$
6     $\mathbf{Z} \leftarrow \mathbf{Z} \cup \{(\mathbf{z}_i, y_i)\}$
7 $C \leftarrow$ train combiner classifier on $\mathbf{Z}$
8 **return** $(C, M_1, M_2, \ldots, M_K)$

---

prediction in cases where most base classifiers do not predict the outcome correctly. As such, stacking is a strategy for estimating and correcting the biases of the set of base classifiers.

Algorithm 22.7 presents the pseudo-code for stacking. It takes as input four parameters: K, the number of base classifiers; $\mathbf{M} = \{M_1, M_2, \cdots, M_K\}$, the set of K base classification models; C, the combiner classification model; and $\mathbf{D}$, the training dataset comprising n points $\mathbf{x}_i = (x_{i1}, x_{i2}, \ldots, x_{id})^T$ and their corresponding classes y_i. The algorithm has two main phases: The first phase (lines $1 - 2$) trains each of the base classifiers M_t on the training dataset $\mathbf{D}$. In the second phase (lines $3 - 7$), we train the combiner classifier C. We create the training dataset, $\mathbf{Z}$, for C as follows: For each point $\mathbf{x}_i$ in $\mathbf{D}$, we create the point $\mathbf{z}_i \in \mathbb{R}^K$ that records the predicted class from each of the base classifiers. That is,

$$\mathbf{z}_i = \big(M_1(\mathbf{x}_i), M_2(\mathbf{x}_i), \ldots, M_K(\mathbf{x}_i)\big)^T$$

The pairs $(\mathbf{z}_i, y_i)$ for $i = 1, 2, \cdots, n$ comprise the training dataset $\mathbf{Z}$ used to train C. The algorithm returns both the set of base classifiers and the combiner model.

Example 22.17 (Stacking). We apply stacking on the Iris principal components dataset. We use three base classifiers, namely SVM with a linear kernel (with regularization constant $C = 1$), random forests (with number of trees $K = 5$ and number of random attributes $p = 1$), and naive Bayes. The combiner classifier is an SVM with a Gaussian kernel (with regularization constant $C = 1$ and spread parameter $\sigma^2 = 0.2$).

We trained the data on a random subset of 100 points, and tested on the remaining 50 points. Figure 22.11 shows the decision boundaries for each of the three base classifiers and the combiner model: linear SVM boundary is the line in light gray, naive Bayes boundary is the ellipse comprising the gray squares, random forest boundary is shown via plusses ('+'), and finally the boundary of the stacking classifier is shown as the thicker black lines. The stacked model results in a much better accuracy compared to the base classifiers, as shown in Table 22.7.

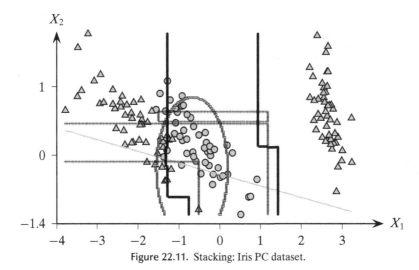

Figure 22.11. Stacking: Iris PC dataset.

Table 22.7. Stacking versus other classifiers

Classifier	Test Accuracy
Linear SVM	0.68
Random Forest	0.82
Naive Bayes	0.74
Stacking	0.92

22.5 FURTHER READING

The application of ROC analysis to classifier performance was introduced in Provost and Fawcett (1997), with an excellent introduction to ROC analysis given in Fawcett (2006). For an in-depth description of the bootstrap, cross-validation, and other methods for assessing classification accuracy, see Efron and Tibshirani (1993). For many datasets simple rules, like one-level decision trees, can yield good classification performance; see Holte (1993) for details. For a recent review and comparison of classifiers over multiple datasets, see Demšar (2006). A discussion of bias, variance, and zero–one loss for classification appears in Friedman (1997), with a unified decomposition of bias and variance for both squared and zero–one loss given in Domingos (2000). For a comprehensive overview on the evaluation of classification algorithms see Japkowicz and Shah (2011). The concept of bagging was proposed in Breiman (1996), and random forests were introduced by Breiman (2001). Adaptive boosting was proposed in Freund and Schapire (1997), and stacking in Wolpert (1992).

Breiman, L. (1996). Bagging predictors. *Machine Learning*, 24 (2), 123–140.

Breiman, L. (2001). Random forests. *Machine Learning*, 45 (1), 5–32.

Demšar, J. (2006). Statistical comparisons of classifiers over multiple data sets. *The Journal of Machine Learning Research*, 7, 1–30.

Domingos, P. (2000). A unified bias-variance decomposition for zero-one and squared loss. *Proceedings of the National Conference on Artificial Intelligence*, pp. 564–569.

Efron, B. and Tibshirani, R. (1993). *An Introduction to the Bootstrap*. Vol. 57. Boca Raton, FL: Chapman & Hall/CRC.

Fawcett, T. (2006). An introduction to ROC analysis. *Pattern Recognition Letters*, 27 (8), 861–874.

Freund, Y. and Schapire, R. E. (1997). A decision-theoretic generalization of on-line learning and an application to boosting. *Journal of Computer and System Sciences*, 55 (1), 119–139.

Friedman, J. H. (1997). On bias, variance, 0/1-loss, and the curse-of-dimensionality. *Data Mining and Knowledge Discovery*, 1 (1), 55–77.

Holte, R. C. (1993). Very simple classification rules perform well on most commonly used datasets. *Machine Learning*, 11 (1), 63–90.

Japkowicz, N. and Shah, M. (2011). *Evaluating Learning Algorithms: A Classification Perspective*. New York: Cambridge University Press.

Provost, F. and Fawcett, T. (1997). Analysis and visualization of classifier performance: Comparison under imprecise class and cost distributions. *Proceedings of the 3rd International Conference on Knowledge Discovery and Data Mining*. Menlo Park, CA: AAAI Press, pp. 43–48.

Wolpert, D. H. (1992). Stacked generalization. *Neural Networks*, 5 (2), 241–259.

22.6 EXERCISES

Q1. True or False:

    (a) A classification model must have 100% accuracy (overall) on the training dataset.

    (b) A classification model must have 100% coverage (overall) on the training dataset.

Table 22.8. Data for Q2

X	Y	Z	Class
15	1	A	1
20	3	B	2
25	2	A	1
30	4	A	1
35	2	B	2
25	4	A	1
15	2	B	2
20	3	B	2

(a) Training

X	Y	Z	Class
10	2	A	2
20	1	B	1
30	3	A	2
40	2	B	2
15	1	B	1

(b) Testing

Q2. Given the training database in Table 22.8(a) and the testing data in Table 22.8(b), answer the following questions:

    (a) Build the complete decision tree using binary splits and Gini index as the evaluation measure (see Chapter 19).

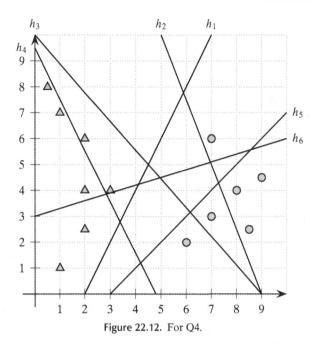

Figure 22.12. For Q4.

(b) Compute the accuracy of the classifier on the test data. Also show the per class accuracy and coverage.

Q3. Show that for binary classification the majority voting for the combined classifier decision in boosting can be expressed as

$$\mathbf{M}^K(\mathbf{x}) = \text{sign}\left(\sum_{t=1}^{K} \alpha_t M_t(\mathbf{x})\right)$$

Q4. Consider the 2-dimensional dataset shown in Figure 22.12, with the labeled points belonging to two classes: c_1 (triangles) and c_2 (circles). Assume that the six hyperplanes were learned from different bootstrap samples. Find the error rate for each of the six hyperplanes on the entire dataset. Then, compute the 95% confidence interval for the expected error rate, using the t-distribution critical values for different degrees of freedom (dof) given in Table 22.9.

Table 22.9. Critical values for t-test

dof	1	2	3	4	5	6
$t_{\alpha/2}$	12.7062	4.3027	3.1824	2.7764	2.5706	2.4469

Q5. Consider the probabilities $P(+1|x_i)$ for the positive class obtained for some classifier, and given the true class labels y_i

	x_1	x_2	x_3	x_4	x_5	x_6	x_7	x_8	x_9	x_{10}
y_i	+1	−1	+1	+1	−1	+1	−1	+1	−1	−1
$P(+1|x_i)$	0.53	0.86	0.25	0.95	0.87	0.86	0.76	0.94	0.44	0.86

Plot the ROC curve for this classifier.

PART FIVE

REGRESSION

The regression task is to predict the value of a (real-valued) dependent variable Y given a set of independent variables $X_1, X_2, \cdots, X_d$. That is, the goal is to learn a function f such that $\hat{y} = f(\mathbf{x})$, where $\hat{y}$ is the predicted response value given the input point $\mathbf{x}$. In contrast to classification, which predicts a categorical response, in regression the response variable is real-valued. Like classification, regression is also a *supervised learning* approach, where we use a *training* dataset, comprising points $\mathbf{x}_i$ along with their true response values y_i, to learn the model parameters. After training, the model can be used to predict the response for new *test* points.

This part begins with linear regression in Chapter 23, which assumes that the regression function f is linear in the parameters, i.e., $\hat{y} = f(\mathbf{x}) = b + \mathbf{w}^T \mathbf{x}$, where b is the bias term, and $\mathbf{w} = (w_1, w_2, \cdots, w_d)$ is the weight vector comprising the *regression coefficients*. We start by presenting bivariate linear regression, where there is only one independent variable X, and then generalize to the multivariate case, where there are d independent attributes $X_1, X_2, \cdots, X_d$. We focus on the geometric interpretation of linear regression, emphasizing the fact that the predicted vector $\widehat{Y}$ is the projection of Y onto the subspace spanned by the d independent attributes and the ones vector. We next consider *ridge regression*, which refers to the regularization of the linear regression model by imposing a penalty on the model parameters using the L_2 or Euclidean norm. We then generalize the regularized model to non-linear regression via kernel ridge regression. Finally, the chapter concludes with the Lasso model, which refers to linear regression with a L_1 penalty on the parameters.

In Chapter 24, we consider logistic regression, which is in fact a classification approach, since it is used to predict a categorical response variable Y. We begin with binary logistic regression where the response variable takes on only two values (e.g., 0 and 1). We use the *maximum likelihood estimation* (MLE) approach to find the model parameters. We then generalize logistic regression to the multiclass scenario, where the response variable can take on K distinct categorical values. We show that the MLE formulation naturally leads to an iterative gradient ascent approach to learn the model.

In Chapter 25, we lay the foundations for neural networks via the multilayer perceptron (MLP) model. We begin with the basic neuron model, and various activation and error functions. We also draw connections to linear and logistic regression, since neural networks can essentially be considered as a multilayered (and/or hierarchical) regression approach. We begin the discussion of neural networks with an MLP with a single hidden layer. We derive the key details of the *backpropagation* algorithm to train neural networks, showing how the gradient descent approach uses the key concept of the derivative of the error function with respect to the net input at a layer — the *net gradient* vector. We show how during learning the error propagates from the output to the hidden, and then from the hidden to the input layer of neurons. Next, we generalize the model to deep MLPs that comprise many hidden layers of neurons. We show how the network is trained using the same general backpropagation approach based on the net gradients.

In Chapter 26, we discuss the details of key deep learning models in detail, namely recurrent neural networks (RNNs), Long Short-term Memory Networks (LSTMs), and convolutional neural networks (CNNs). Recurrent networks generalize the feed-forward architecture of MLPs by introducing feed-back connections between the layers to model sequential data. We show how RNNs can be trained via *backpropagation in time*, which is essentially the same as the MLP backpropagation approach applied to the RNN unfolded in time so that it becomes a deep feed-forward network. We highlight the concepts of *shared parameters*, since RNNs use the same weight matrix and bias vector for the hidden layers for all time points. Unfortunately, deep RNNs are susceptible to the problem of *vanishing* or *exploding* net gradients during backpropagation. Long short-term memory networks alleviate this problem by the use of a novel type of layer, called a *gated layer*, to control what information is used to input, update, and write an internal memory layer. Next, we discuss convolutional neural networks that are essentially deep and sparse MLPs that are designed to hierarchically exploit sequential and spatial relationships in the data. Finally, we also discuss the role of regularization in deep learning, including L_2 regularization and *dropout regularization.*

We end this part with methods to evaluate regression models in Chapter 27, with a focus on linear regression. We consider the questions of how good of a fit is the model to the input data, and how one can derive confidence intervals and perform hypothesis tests for the dependence of the response variable on the independent variables. We especially emphasize the geometric approach to evaluation.

CHAPTER 23

Linear Regression

Given a set of attributes or variables $X_1, X_2, \cdots, X_d$, called the *predictor, explanatory,* or *independent* variables, and given a real-valued attribute of interest Y, called the *response* or *dependent* variable, the aim of *regression* is to predict the response variable based on the independent variables. That is, the goal is to learn a *regression function* f, such that

$$Y = f(X_1, X_2, \cdots, X_d) + \varepsilon = f(\mathbf{X}) + \varepsilon$$

where $\mathbf{X} = (X_1, X_2, \cdots, X_d)^T$ is the multivariate random variable comprising the predictor attributes, and ε is a random *error term* that is assumed to be independent of $\mathbf{X}$. In other words, Y is comprised of two components, one dependent on the observed predictor attributes, and the other, coming from the error term, independent of the predictor attributes. The error term encapsulates inherent uncertainty in Y, as well as, possibly the effect of unobserved, hidden or *latent* variables.

In this chapter we discuss linear regression, where the regression function f is assumed to be a linear function of the parameters of the model. We also discuss regularized linear regression models considering both L_2 (ridge regression) and L_1 (Lasso) regularization. Finally, we use the kernel trick to perform kernel ridge regression that can handle non-linear models.

23.1 LINEAR REGRESSION MODEL

In *linear regression* the function f is assumed to be linear in its parameters, that is

$$f(\mathbf{X}) = \beta + \omega_1 X_1 + \omega_2 X_2 + \cdots + \omega_d X_d = \beta + \sum_{i=1}^{d} \omega_i X_i = \beta + \boldsymbol{\omega}^T \mathbf{X} \qquad (23.1)$$

Here, the parameter β is the true (unknown) *bias* term, the parameter ω_i is the true (unknown) *regression coefficient* or *weight* for attribute X_i, and $\boldsymbol{\omega} = (\omega_1, \omega_2, \cdots, \omega_d)^T$ is the true d-dimensional weight vector. Observe that f specifies a hyperplane in $\mathbb{R}^{d+1}$, where $\boldsymbol{\omega}$ is the the weight vector that is normal or orthogonal to the hyperplane, and β

is the *intercept* or offset term (see Section 6.1). We can see that f is completely specified by the $d+1$ parameters comprising β and ω_i, for $i = 1, \cdots, d$.

The true bias and regression coefficients are unknown. Therefore, we have to estimate them from the training dataset $\mathbf{D}$ comprising n points $\mathbf{x}_i \in \mathbb{R}^d$ in a d-dimensional space, and the corresponding response values $y_i \in \mathbb{R}$, for $i = 1, 2, \cdots, n$. Let b denote the estimated value for the true bias β, and let w_i denote the estimated value for the true regression coefficient ω_i, for $i = 1, 2, \cdots, d$. Let $\mathbf{w} = (w_1, w_2, \cdots, w_d)^T$ denote the vector of estimated weights. Given the estimated bias and weight values, we can predict the response for any given input or test point $\mathbf{x} = (x_1, x_2, \cdots, x_d)^T$, as follows

$$\hat{y} = b + w_1 x_1 + \cdots + w_d x_d = b + \mathbf{w}^T \mathbf{x} \tag{23.2}$$

Due to the random error term, the predicted value $\hat{y}$ will not in general match the observed response y for the given input $\mathbf{x}$. This is true even for the training data. The difference between the observed and predicted response, called the *residual error*, is given as

$$\epsilon = y - \hat{y} = y - b - \mathbf{w}^T \mathbf{x} \tag{23.3}$$

Note that the residual error ϵ is different from the random statistical error ε, which measures the difference between the observed and the (unknown) true response. The residual error ϵ is an estimator of the random error term ε.

A common approach to predicting the bias and regression coefficients is to use the method of *least squares*. That is, given the training data $\mathbf{D}$ with points $\mathbf{x}_i$ and response values y_i (for $i = 1, \cdots, n$), we seek values b and $\mathbf{w}$, so as to minimize the sum of squared residual errors (SSE)

$$SSE = \sum_{i=1}^{n} \epsilon_i^2 = \sum_{i=1}^{n} \left(y_i - \hat{y}_i \right)^2 = \sum_{i=1}^{n} \left(y_i - b - \mathbf{w}^T \mathbf{x}_i \right)^2 \tag{23.4}$$

In the following sections, we will estimate the unknown parameters, by first considering the case of a single predictor variable, and then looking at the general case of multiple predictors.

23.2 BIVARIATE REGRESSION

Let us first consider the case where the input data $\mathbf{D}$ comprises a single predictor attribute, $X = (x_1, x_2, \cdots, x_n)^T$, along with the response variable, $Y = (y_1, y_2, \cdots, y_n)^T$. Since f is linear, we have

$$\hat{y}_i = f(x_i) = b + w \cdot x_i \tag{23.5}$$

Thus, we seek the straight line $f(x)$ with slope w and intercept b that *best fits* the data. The residual error, which is the difference between the predicted value (also called *fitted value*) and the observed value of the response variable, is given as

$$\epsilon_i = y_i - \hat{y}_i \tag{23.6}$$

Note that $|\epsilon_i|$ denotes the vertical distance between the fitted and observed response. The best fitting line minimizes the sum of squared errors

$$\min_{b,w} SSE = \sum_{i=1}^{n} \epsilon_i^2 = \sum_{i=1}^{n} (y_i - \hat{y}_i)^2 = \sum_{i=1}^{n} (y_i - b - w \cdot x_i)^2 \tag{23.7}$$

To solve this objective, we differentiate it with respect to b and set the result to 0, to obtain

$$\frac{\partial}{\partial b} SSE = -2 \sum_{i=1}^{n} (y_i - b - w \cdot x_i) = 0$$

$$\implies \sum_{i=1}^{n} b = \sum_{i=1}^{n} y_i - w \sum_{i=1}^{n} x_i$$

$$\implies b = \frac{1}{n} \sum_{i=1}^{n} y_i - w \cdot \frac{1}{n} \sum_{i=1}^{n} x_i$$

Therefore, we have

$$b = \mu_Y - w \cdot \mu_X \tag{23.8}$$

where μ_Y is the sample mean for the response and μ_X is the sample mean for the predictor attribute. Similarly, differentiating with respect to w, we obtain

$$\frac{\partial}{\partial w} SSE = -2 \sum_{i=1}^{n} x_i (y_i - b - w \cdot x_i) = 0$$

$$\implies \sum_{i=1}^{n} x_i \cdot y_i - b \sum_{i=1}^{n} x_i - w \sum_{i=1}^{n} x_i^2 = 0 \tag{23.9}$$

substituting b from Eq. (23.8), we have

$$\implies \sum_{i=1}^{n} x_i \cdot y_i - \mu_Y \sum_{i=1}^{n} x_i + w \cdot \mu_X \sum_{i=1}^{n} x_i - w \sum_{i=1}^{n} x_i^2 = 0$$

$$\implies w \left(\sum_{i=1}^{n} x_i^2 - n \cdot \mu_X^2 \right) = \left(\sum_{i=1}^{n} x_i \cdot y_i \right) - n \cdot \mu_X \cdot \mu_Y$$

$$\implies w = \frac{\left(\sum_{i=1}^{n} x_i \cdot y_i \right) - n \cdot \mu_X \cdot \mu_Y}{\left(\sum_{i=1}^{n} x_i^2 \right) - n \cdot \mu_X^2} \tag{23.10}$$

The regression coefficient w can also be written as

$$w = \frac{\sum_{i=1}^{n} (x_i - \mu_X)(y_i - \mu_Y)}{\sum_{i=1}^{n} (x_i - \mu_X)^2} = \frac{\sigma_{XY}}{\sigma_X^2} = \frac{\text{cov}(X, Y)}{\text{var}(X)} \tag{23.11}$$

where σ_X^2 is the variance of X and σ_{XY} is the covariance between X and Y. Noting that the correlation between X and Y is given as $\rho_{XY} = \frac{\sigma_{XY}}{\sigma_X \cdot \sigma_Y}$, we can also write w as

$$w = \rho_{XY} \frac{\sigma_Y}{\sigma_X} \tag{23.12}$$

Observe that the fitted line must pass through the mean value of Y and X; plugging in the optimal value of b from Eq. (23.8) into the regression equation [Eq. (23.5)], we have

$$\hat{y}_i = b + w \cdot x_i = \mu_Y - w \cdot \mu_X + w \cdot x_i = \mu_Y + w(x_i - \mu_X)$$

That is, when $x_i = \mu_X$, we have $\hat{y}_i = \mu_Y$. Thus, the point (μ_X, μ_Y) lies on the regression line.

Example 23.1 (Bivariate Regression). Figure 23.1 shows the scatterplot between the two attributes petal length (X; the predictor variable) and petal width (Y; the response variable) in the Iris dataset. There are a total of $n = 150$ data points. The mean values for these two variables are

$$\mu_X = \frac{1}{150} \sum_{i=1}^{150} x_i = \frac{563.8}{150} = 3.7587$$

$$\mu_Y = \frac{1}{150} \sum_{i=1}^{150} y_i = \frac{179.8}{150} = 1.1987$$

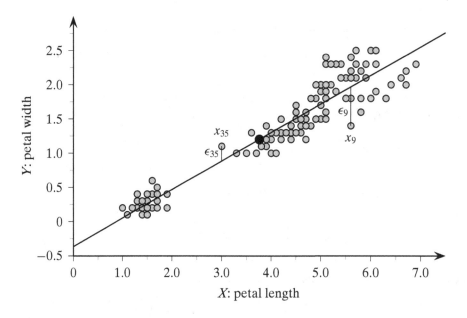

Figure 23.1. Scatterplot: petal length (X) versus petal width (Y). Solid circle (black) shows the mean point; residual error is shown for two sample points: x_9 and x_{35}.

The variance and covariance is given as

$$\sigma_X^2 = \frac{1}{150} \sum_{i=1}^{150} (x_i - \mu_X)^2 = 3.0924$$

$$\sigma_Y^2 = \frac{1}{150} \sum_{i=1}^{150} (y_i - \mu_Y)^2 = 0.5785$$

$$\sigma_{XY} = \frac{1}{150} \sum_{i=1}^{150} (x_i - \mu_X) \cdot (y_i - \mu_Y) = 1.2877$$

Assuming a linear relationship between the response and predictor variables, we use Eq. (23.8) and Eq. (23.10) to obtain the slope and intercept terms as follows

$$w = \frac{\sigma_{XY}}{\sigma_X^2} = \frac{1.2877}{3.0924} = 0.4164$$

$$b = \mu_Y - w \cdot \mu_X = 1.1987 - 0.4164 \cdot 3.7587 = -0.3665$$

Thus, the fitted regression line is

$$\hat{y} = -0.3665 + 0.4164 \cdot x$$

Figure 23.1 plots the best-fitting or regression line; we can observe that the mean point $(\mu_X, \mu_Y) = (3.759, 1.199)$ lies on the line. The figure also shows the residual errors, ϵ_9 and ϵ_{35}, for the points x_9 and x_{35}, respectively.

Finally, we can compute the SSE value (see Eq. (23.4)) as follows:

$$SSE = \sum_{i=1}^{150} \epsilon_i^2 = \sum_{i=1}^{150} (y_i - \hat{y}_i)^2 = 6.343$$

23.2.1 Geometry of Bivariate Regression

We now turn to the attribute-centric view, which provides important geometric insight for bivariate regression. Recall that we are given n equations in two unknowns, namely $\hat{y}_i = b + w \cdot x_i$, for $i = 1, \cdots, n$. Let $X = (x_1, x_2, \cdots, x_n)^T$ be the n-dimensional vector denoting the training data sample, $Y = (y_1, y_2, \cdots, y_n)^T$ the sample vector for the response variable, and $\widehat{Y} = (\hat{y}_1, \hat{y}_2, \cdots, \hat{y}_n)^T$ the vector of predicted values, then we can express the n equations, $y_i = b + w \cdot x_i$ for $i = 1, 2, \cdots, n$, as a single vector equation:

$$\widehat{Y} = b \cdot \mathbf{1} + w \cdot X \tag{23.13}$$

where $\mathbf{1} \in \mathbb{R}^n$ is the n-dimensional vector of all ones. This equation indicates that the predicted vector $\widehat{Y}$ is a linear combination of $\mathbf{1}$ and X, i.e., it must lie in the column space spanned by $\mathbf{1}$ and X, given as span($\{\mathbf{1}, X\}$). On the other hand, the response vector Y will not usually lie in the same column space. In fact, the residual error vector

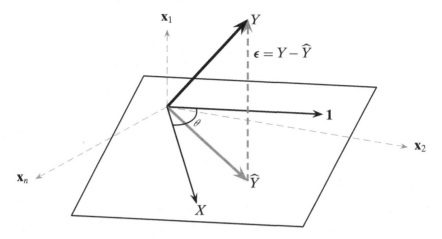

Figure 23.2. Geometry of bivariate regression: non-orthogonal basis. All the vectors conceptually lie in the n-dimensional space spanned by the n data points. The plane illustrates the subspace spanned by $\mathbf{1}$ and X.

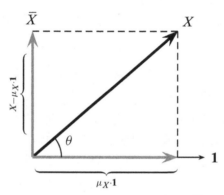

Figure 23.3. Orthogonal decomposition of X into $\bar{X}$ and $\mu_X \cdot \mathbf{1}$.

$\boldsymbol{\epsilon} = (\epsilon_1, \epsilon_2, \cdots, \epsilon_n)^T$ captures the deviation between the response and predicted vectors

$$\boldsymbol{\epsilon} = Y - \widehat{Y}$$

The geometry of the problem, shown in Figure 23.2, makes it clear that the optimal $\widehat{Y}$ that minimizes the error is the orthogonal projection of Y onto the subspace spanned by $\mathbf{1}$ and X. The residual error vector $\boldsymbol{\epsilon}$ is thus *orthogonal* to the subspace spanned by $\mathbf{1}$ and X, and its squared length (or magnitude) equals the SSE value (see Eq. (23.4)), since

$$\|\boldsymbol{\epsilon}\|^2 = \|Y - \widehat{Y}\|^2 = \sum_{i=1}^{n}(y_i - \hat{y}_i)^2 = \sum_{i=1}^{n}\epsilon_i^2 = SSE$$

At this point it is worth noting that even though $\mathbf{1}$ and X are linearly independent and form a basis for the column space, they need not be orthogonal (see Figure 23.2). We can create an orthogonal basis by decomposing X into a component along $\mathbf{1}$ and a component orthogonal to $\mathbf{1}$ as shown in Figure 23.3. Recall that the scalar projection

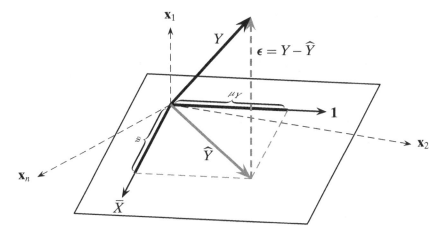

Figure 23.4. Geometry of bivariate regression: orthogonal basis. $\bar{X} = X - \mu_X \cdot \mathbf{1}$ is the centered attribute vector. The plane illustrates the subspace spanned by the orthogonal vectors $\mathbf{1}$ and $\bar{X}$.

of a vector $\mathbf{b}$ onto vector $\mathbf{a}$ (see Eq. (1.12)) is given as

$$\text{proj}_{\mathbf{a}}(\mathbf{b}) = \left(\frac{\mathbf{b}^T \mathbf{a}}{\mathbf{a}^T \mathbf{a}} \right)$$

and the orthogonal projection of $\mathbf{b}$ on $\mathbf{a}$ (see Eq. (1.11)) is given as

$$\text{proj}_{\mathbf{a}}(\mathbf{b}) \cdot \mathbf{a} = \left(\frac{\mathbf{b}^T \mathbf{a}}{\mathbf{a}^T \mathbf{a}} \right) \cdot \mathbf{a}$$

Now, consider the projection of X onto $\mathbf{1}$; we have

$$\text{proj}_{\mathbf{1}}(X) \cdot \mathbf{1} = \left(\frac{X^T \mathbf{1}}{\mathbf{1}^T \mathbf{1}} \right) \cdot \mathbf{1} = \left(\frac{\sum_{i=1}^n x_i}{n} \right) \cdot \mathbf{1} = \mu_X \cdot \mathbf{1}$$

Thus, we can rewrite X as

$$X = \mu_X \cdot \mathbf{1} + (X - \mu_X \cdot \mathbf{1}) = \mu_X \cdot \mathbf{1} + \bar{X}$$

where $\bar{X} = X - \mu_X \cdot \mathbf{1}$ is the centered attribute vector, obtained by subtracting the mean μ_X from all points.

The two vectors $\mathbf{1}$ and $\bar{X}$ form an *orthogonal basis* for the subspace. We can thus obtain the predicted vector $\widehat{Y}$ by projecting Y onto $\mathbf{1}$ and $\bar{X}$, and summing up these two components, as shown in Figure 23.4. That is,

$$\widehat{Y} = \text{proj}_{\mathbf{1}}(Y) \cdot \mathbf{1} + \text{proj}_{\bar{X}}(Y) \cdot \bar{X} = \left(\frac{Y^T \mathbf{1}}{\mathbf{1}^T \mathbf{1}} \right) \mathbf{1} + \left(\frac{Y^T \bar{X}}{\bar{X}^T \bar{X}} \right) \bar{X} = \mu_Y \cdot \mathbf{1} + \left(\frac{Y^T \bar{X}}{\bar{X}^T \bar{X}} \right) \bar{X} \quad (23.14)$$

On the other hand, from Eq. (23.13), we know that

$$\widehat{Y} = b \cdot \mathbf{1} + w \cdot X = b \cdot \mathbf{1} + w \left(\mu_X \cdot \mathbf{1} + \bar{X} \right) = (b + w \cdot \mu_X) \cdot \mathbf{1} + w \cdot \bar{X} \quad (23.15)$$

Since both Eq. (23.14) and Eq. (23.15) are expressions for $\widehat{Y}$, we can equate them to obtain

$$\mu_Y = b + w \cdot \mu_X \quad \text{or} \quad b = \mu_Y - w \cdot \mu_X \qquad\qquad w = \frac{Y^T \bar{X}}{\bar{X}^T \bar{X}}$$

where the bias term $b = \mu_Y - w \cdot \mu_X$ matches Eq. (23.8), and the weight w also matches Eq. (23.10), since

$$w = \frac{Y^T \overline{X}}{\overline{X}^T \overline{X}} = \frac{Y^T \overline{X}}{\|\overline{X}\|^2} = \frac{Y^T(X - \mu_X \cdot \mathbf{1})}{\|X - \mu_X \cdot \mathbf{1}\|^2} = \frac{\left(\sum_{i=1}^n y_i x_i\right) - n \cdot \mu_X \cdot \mu_Y}{\left(\sum_{i=1}^n x_i^2\right) - n \cdot \mu_X^2}$$

Example 23.2 (Geometry of Regression). Let us consider the regression of petal length (X) on petal width (Y) for the Iris dataset, with $n = 150$. First, we center X by subtracting the mean $\mu_X = 3.759$. Next, we compute the scalar projections of Y onto $\mathbf{1}$ and $\overline{X}$, to obtain

$$\mu_Y = \text{proj}_{\mathbf{1}}(Y) = \left(\frac{Y^T \mathbf{1}}{\mathbf{1}^T \mathbf{1}}\right) = \frac{179.8}{150} = 1.1987$$

$$w = \text{proj}_{\overline{X}}(Y) = \left(\frac{Y^T \overline{X}}{\overline{X}^T \overline{X}}\right) = \frac{193.16}{463.86} = 0.4164$$

Thus, the bias term b is given as

$$b = \mu_Y - w \cdot \mu_X = 1.1987 - 0.4164 \cdot 3.7587 = -0.3665$$

These values for b and w match those in Example 23.1. Finally, we can compute the SSE value (see Eq. (23.4)) as the squared length of the residual error vector

$$SSE = \|\boldsymbol{\epsilon}\|^2 = \|Y - \widehat{Y}\|^2 = (Y - \widehat{Y})^T(Y - \widehat{Y}) = 6.343$$

23.3 MULTIPLE REGRESSION

We now consider the more general case called *multiple regression*[1] where we have multiple predictor attributes $X_1, X_2, \cdots, X_d$ and a single response attribute Y. The training data sample $\mathbf{D} \in \mathbb{R}^{n \times d}$ comprises n points $\mathbf{x}_i = (x_{i1}, x_{i2}, \cdots, x_{id})^T$ in a d-dimensional space, along with the corresponding observed response value y_i. The vector $Y = (y_1, y_2, \cdots, y_n)^T$ denotes the observed response vector. The predicted response value for input $\mathbf{x}_i$ is given as

$$\hat{y}_i = b + w_1 x_{i1} + w_2 x_{i2} + \cdots + w_d x_{id} = b + \mathbf{w}^T \mathbf{x}_i \tag{23.16}$$

where $\mathbf{w} = (w_1, w_2, \cdots, w_d)^T$ is the weight vector comprising the regression coefficients or weights w_j along each attribute X_j. Eq. (23.16) defines a hyperplane in $\mathbb{R}^{d+1}$ with bias term b and normal vector $\mathbf{w}$.

Instead of dealing with the bias b separately from the weights w_i for each attribute, we can introduce a new "constant" valued attribute X_0 whose value is always fixed at 1, so that each input point $\mathbf{x}_i = (x_{i1}, x_{i2}, \cdots, x_{id})^T \in \mathbb{R}^d$ is mapped to an augmented

---

[1] We follow the usual terminology and reserve the term *multivariate regression* for the case when there are multiple response attributes $Y_1, Y_2, \cdots, Y_q$ and multiple predictor attributes $X_1, X_2, \cdots, X_d$.

point $\tilde{\mathbf{x}}_i = (x_{i0}, x_{i1}, x_{i2}, \cdots, x_{id})^T \in \mathbb{R}^{d+1}$, where $x_{i0} = 1$. Likewise, the weight vector $\mathbf{w} = (w_1, w_2, \cdots, w_d)^T$ is mapped to an augmented weight vector $\tilde{\mathbf{w}} = (w_0, w_1, w_2, \cdots, w_d)^T$, where $w_0 = b$. The predicted response value for an augmented $(d+1)$ dimensional point $\tilde{\mathbf{x}}_i$ can be written as

$$\hat{y}_i = w_0 x_{i0} + w_1 x_{i1} + w_2 x_{i2} + \cdots + w_d x_{id} = \tilde{\mathbf{w}}^T \tilde{\mathbf{x}}_i \tag{23.17}$$

Since there are n points, in fact we have n such equations, one per point, and there are $(d+1)$ unknowns, namely the elements of the augmented weight vector $\tilde{\mathbf{w}}$. We can compactly write all these n equations as a single matrix equation, given as

$$\widehat{Y} = \tilde{\mathbf{D}} \tilde{\mathbf{w}} \tag{23.18}$$

where $\tilde{\mathbf{D}} \in \mathbb{R}^{n \times (d+1)}$ is the *augmented data matrix*, which includes the constant attribute X_0 in addition to the predictor attributes $X_1, X_2, \cdots, X_d$, and $\widehat{Y} = (\hat{y}_1, \hat{y}_2, \cdots, \hat{y}_n)^T$ is the vector of predicted responses.

The multiple regression task can now be stated as finding the *best fitting hyperplane* defined by the weight vector $\tilde{\mathbf{w}}$ that minimizes the sum of squared errors

$$\begin{aligned}
\min_{\tilde{\mathbf{w}}} SSE &= \sum_{i=1}^{n} \epsilon_i^2 = \|\epsilon\|^2 = \|Y - \widehat{Y}\|^2 \\
&= (Y - \widehat{Y})^T (Y - \widehat{Y}) = Y^T Y - 2 Y^T \widehat{Y} + \widehat{Y}^T \widehat{Y} \\
&= Y^T Y - 2 Y^T (\tilde{\mathbf{D}} \tilde{\mathbf{w}}) + (\tilde{\mathbf{D}} \tilde{\mathbf{w}})^T (\tilde{\mathbf{D}} \tilde{\mathbf{w}}) \\
&= Y^T Y - 2 \tilde{\mathbf{w}}^T (\tilde{\mathbf{D}}^T Y) + \tilde{\mathbf{w}}^T (\tilde{\mathbf{D}}^T \tilde{\mathbf{D}}) \tilde{\mathbf{w}} \tag{23.19}
\end{aligned}$$

where we substituted $\widehat{Y} = \tilde{\mathbf{D}} \tilde{\mathbf{w}}$ from Eq. (23.18), and we used the fact that $Y^T (\tilde{\mathbf{D}} \tilde{\mathbf{w}}) = (\tilde{\mathbf{D}} \tilde{\mathbf{w}})^T Y = \tilde{\mathbf{w}}^T (\tilde{\mathbf{D}}^T Y)$.

To solve the objective, we differentiate the expression in Eq. (23.19) with respect to $\tilde{\mathbf{w}}$ and set the result to $\mathbf{0}$, to obtain

$$\frac{\partial}{\partial \tilde{\mathbf{w}}} SSE = -2 \tilde{\mathbf{D}}^T Y + 2 (\tilde{\mathbf{D}}^T \tilde{\mathbf{D}}) \tilde{\mathbf{w}} = \mathbf{0}$$

$$\implies (\tilde{\mathbf{D}}^T \tilde{\mathbf{D}}) \tilde{\mathbf{w}} = \tilde{\mathbf{D}}^T Y$$

Therefore, the optimal weight vector is given as

$$\tilde{\mathbf{w}} = (\tilde{\mathbf{D}}^T \tilde{\mathbf{D}})^{-1} \tilde{\mathbf{D}}^T Y \tag{23.20}$$

Substituting the optimal value of $\tilde{\mathbf{w}}$ into Eq. (23.18), we get

$$\widehat{Y} = \tilde{\mathbf{D}} \tilde{\mathbf{w}} = \tilde{\mathbf{D}} (\tilde{\mathbf{D}}^T \tilde{\mathbf{D}})^{-1} \tilde{\mathbf{D}}^T Y = \mathbf{H} Y$$

where $\mathbf{H} = \tilde{\mathbf{D}} (\tilde{\mathbf{D}}^T \tilde{\mathbf{D}})^{-1} \tilde{\mathbf{D}}^T$ is called the *hat matrix*, since it puts the "hat" on Y! Notice also that $\tilde{\mathbf{D}}^T \tilde{\mathbf{D}}$ is the uncentered scatter matrix for the training data.

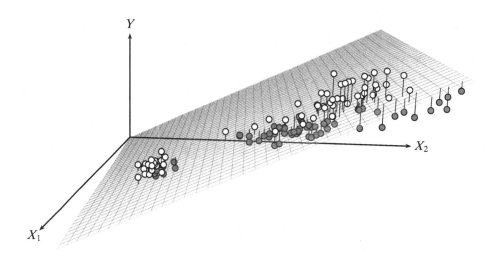

Figure 23.5. Multiple regression: sepal length (X_1) and petal length (X_2) with response attribute petal width (Y). The vertical bars show the residual error for the points. Points in white are above the plane, whereas points in gray are below the plane.

Example 23.3 (Multiple Regression). Figure 23.5 shows the multiple regression of sepal length (X_1) and petal length (X_2) on the response attribute petal width (Y) for the Iris dataset with $n = 150$ points. We first add an extra attribute $X_0 = \mathbf{1}_{150}$, which is a vector of all ones in $\mathbb{R}^{150}$. The augmented dataset $\tilde{\mathbf{D}} \in \mathbb{R}^{150 \times 3}$ comprises $n = 150$ points along three attributes X_0, X_1, and X_2.

Next, we compute the uncentered 3×3 scatter matrix $\tilde{\mathbf{D}}^T \tilde{\mathbf{D}}$ and its inverse

$$\tilde{\mathbf{D}}^T \tilde{\mathbf{D}} = \begin{pmatrix} 150.0 & 876.50 & 563.80 \\ 876.5 & 5223.85 & 3484.25 \\ 563.8 & 3484.25 & 2583.00 \end{pmatrix} \quad (\tilde{\mathbf{D}}^T \tilde{\mathbf{D}})^{-1} = \begin{pmatrix} 0.793 & -0.176 & 0.064 \\ -0.176 & 0.041 & -0.017 \\ 0.064 & -0.017 & 0.009 \end{pmatrix}$$

We also compute $\tilde{\mathbf{D}}^T Y$, given as

$$\tilde{\mathbf{D}}^T Y = \begin{pmatrix} 179.80 \\ 1127.65 \\ 868.97 \end{pmatrix}$$

The augmented weight vector $\tilde{\mathbf{w}}$ is then given as

$$\tilde{\mathbf{w}} = \begin{pmatrix} w_0 \\ w_1 \\ w_2 \end{pmatrix} = (\tilde{\mathbf{D}}^T \tilde{\mathbf{D}})^{-1} \cdot (\tilde{\mathbf{D}}^T Y) = \begin{pmatrix} -0.014 \\ -0.082 \\ 0.45 \end{pmatrix}$$

The bias term is therefore $b = w_0 = -0.014$, and the fitted model is

$$\widehat{Y} = -0.014 - 0.082 \cdot X_1 + 0.45 \cdot X_2$$

Figure 23.5 shows the fitted hyperplane. It also shows the residual error for each point. The white colored points have positive residuals (i.e., $\epsilon_i > 0$ or $\hat{y}_i > y_i$), whereas the gray points have negative residual values (i.e., $\epsilon_i < 0$ or $\hat{y}_i < y$). The SSE value for the model is 6.18.

23.3.1 Geometry of Multiple Regression

Let $\tilde{\mathbf{D}}$ be the augmented data matrix comprising the d independent attributes X_i, along with the new constant attribute $X_0 = \mathbf{1} \in \mathbb{R}^n$, given as

$$\tilde{\mathbf{D}} = \begin{pmatrix} | & | & | & & | \\ X_0 & X_1 & X_2 & \cdots & X_d \\ | & | & | & & | \end{pmatrix}$$

Let $\tilde{\mathbf{w}} = (w_0, w_1, \cdots, w_d)^T \in \mathbb{R}^{(d+1)}$ be the augmented weight vector that incorporates the bias term $b = w_0$. Recall that the predicted response vector is given as

$$\widehat{Y} = b \cdot \mathbf{1} + w_1 \cdot X_1 + w_2 \cdot X_2 + \cdots + w_d \cdot X_d = \sum_{i=0}^{d} w_i \cdot X_i = \tilde{\mathbf{D}}\tilde{\mathbf{w}}$$

This equation makes it clear that the predicted vector must lie in the column space of the augmented data matrix $\tilde{\mathbf{D}}$, denoted $col(\tilde{\mathbf{D}})$, i.e., it must be a linear combination of the attribute vectors $X_i, i = 0, \cdots, d$.

To minimize the error in prediction, $\widehat{Y}$ must be the orthogonal projection of Y onto the subspace $col(\tilde{\mathbf{D}})$. The residual error vector $\epsilon = Y - \widehat{Y}$ is thus orthogonal to the subspace $col(\tilde{\mathbf{D}})$, which means that it is orthogonal to each attribute vector X_i. That is,

$$X_i^T \epsilon = 0$$
$$\implies X_i^T(Y - \widehat{Y}) = 0$$
$$\implies X_i^T \widehat{Y} = X_i^T Y$$
$$\implies X_i^T(\tilde{\mathbf{D}}\tilde{\mathbf{w}}) = X_i^T Y$$
$$\implies w_0 \cdot X_i^T X_0 + w1 \cdot X_i^T X_1 + \cdots + w_d \cdot X_i^T X_d = X_i^T Y$$

We thus have $(d+1)$ equations, called the *normal equations*, in $(d+1)$ unknowns, namely the regression coefficients or weights w_i (including the bias term w_0). The solution to these simultaneous equations yields the weight vector $\tilde{\mathbf{w}} = (w_0, w_1, \cdots, w_d)^T$. The $(d+1)$ normal equations are

$$w_0 \cdot X_0^T X_0 + w1 \cdot X_0^T X_1 + \cdots + w_d \cdot X_0^T X_d = X_0^T Y$$
$$w_0 \cdot X_1^T X_0 + w1 \cdot X_1^T X_1 + \cdots + w_d \cdot X_1^T X_d = X_1^T Y$$
$$\vdots \qquad\qquad = \vdots$$
$$w_0 \cdot X_d^T X_0 + w1 \cdot X_d^T X_1 + \cdots + w_d \cdot X_d^T X_d = X_d^T Y$$

$$(23.21)$$

which can be written compactly in matrix notation to solve for $\tilde{\mathbf{w}}$ as follows

$$\begin{pmatrix} X_0^T X_0 & X_0^T X_1 & \cdots & X_0^T X_d \\ X_1^T X_0 & X_1^T X_1 & \cdots & X_1^T X_d \\ \vdots & \vdots & \cdots & \vdots \\ X_d^T X_0 & X_d^T X_1 & \cdots & X_d^T X_d \end{pmatrix} \tilde{\mathbf{w}} = \tilde{\mathbf{D}}^T Y$$

$$(\tilde{\mathbf{D}}^T \tilde{\mathbf{D}}) \tilde{\mathbf{w}} = \tilde{\mathbf{D}}^T Y$$

$$\tilde{\mathbf{w}} = (\tilde{\mathbf{D}}^T \tilde{\mathbf{D}})^{-1} (\tilde{\mathbf{D}}^T Y) \qquad (23.22)$$

This matches the expression in Eq. (23.20).

More insight can be obtained by noting that the attribute vectors comprising the column space of $\tilde{\mathbf{D}}$ are not necessarily orthogonal, even if we assume they are linearly independent. To obtain the projected vector $\widehat{Y}$, we first need to construct an orthogonal basis for $col(\tilde{\mathbf{D}})$.

Let $U_0, U_1, \cdots, U_d$ denote the set of orthogonal basis vectors for $col(\tilde{\mathbf{D}})$. We can construct these vectors in a step-wise manner via *Gram–Schmidt orthogonalization*, as follows

$$U_0 = X_0$$

$$U_1 = X_1 - p_{10} \cdot U_0$$

$$U_2 = X_2 - p_{20} \cdot U_0 - p_{21} \cdot U_1$$

$$\vdots = \qquad \vdots$$

$$U_d = X_d - p_{d0} \cdot U_0 - p_{d1} \cdot U_1 - \cdots - p_{d,d-1} \cdot U_{d-1}$$

where

$$p_{ji} = \mathrm{proj}_{U_i}(X_j) = \frac{X_j^T U_i}{\|U_i\|^2}$$

denotes the scalar projection of attribute X_j onto the basis vector U_i. Essentially, to obtain U_j, we subtract from vector X_j its scalar projections along all previous basis vectors $U_0, U_1, \cdots, U_{j-1}$.

Rearranging the equations above, so that X_j is on the left hand side, we get

$$X_0 = U_0$$

$$X_1 = p_{10} \cdot U_0 + U_1$$

$$X_2 = p_{20} \cdot U_0 + p_{21} \cdot U_1 + U_2$$

$$\vdots = \qquad \vdots$$

$$X_d = p_{d0} \cdot U_0 + p_{d1} \cdot U_1 + \cdots + p_{d,d-1} \cdot U_{d-1} + U_d$$

The Gram–Schmidt method thus results in the so-called *QR-factorization*[2] of the data matrix, namely $\tilde{\mathbf{D}} = \mathbf{QR}$, where by construction $\mathbf{Q}$ is a $n \times (d+1)$ matrix withi

---

[2] In QR-factorization, the matrix $\mathbf{Q}$ is orthogonal, with orthonormal columns, i.e., with orthogonal columns that are normalized to be unit length. However, we keep the basis vectors un-normalized for ease of presentation.

orthogonal columns

$$\mathbf{Q} = \begin{pmatrix} | & | & | & & | \\ U_0 & U_1 & U_2 & \cdots & U_d \\ | & | & | & & | \end{pmatrix}$$

and $\mathbf{R}$ is the $(d+1) \times (d+1)$ upper-triangular matrix

$$\mathbf{R} = \begin{pmatrix} 1 & p_{10} & p_{20} & \cdots & p_{d0} \\ 0 & 1 & p_{21} & \cdots & p_{d1} \\ 0 & 0 & 1 & \cdots & p_{d2} \\ \vdots & \vdots & \vdots & \ddots & \vdots \\ 0 & 0 & 0 & 1 & p_{d,d-1} \\ 0 & 0 & 0 & 0 & 1 \end{pmatrix}$$

So that, in the column view the QR-factorization of the augmented data matrix is given as:

$$\underbrace{\begin{pmatrix} | & | & | & & | \\ X_0 & X_1 & X_2 & \cdots & X_d \\ | & | & | & & | \end{pmatrix}}_{\tilde{\mathbf{D}}} = \underbrace{\begin{pmatrix} | & | & | & & | \\ U_0 & U_1 & U_2 & \cdots & U_d \\ | & | & | & & | \end{pmatrix}}_{\mathbf{Q}} \cdot \underbrace{\begin{pmatrix} 1 & p_{10} & p_{20} & \cdots & p_{d0} \\ 0 & 1 & p_{21} & \cdots & p_{d1} \\ 0 & 0 & 1 & \cdots & p_{d2} \\ \vdots & \vdots & \vdots & \ddots & \vdots \\ 0 & 0 & 0 & 1 & p_{d,d-1} \\ 0 & 0 & 0 & 0 & 1 \end{pmatrix}}_{\mathbf{R}}$$

Since the new basis vectors $U_0, U_1, \cdots, U_d$ form an orthogonal basis for the column space of $\tilde{\mathbf{D}}$, we can obtain the predicted response vector as a sum of the projections of Y along each new basis vector, given as

$$\widehat{Y} = \mathrm{proj}_{U_0}(Y) \cdot U_0 + \mathrm{proj}_{U_1}(Y) \cdot U_1 + \cdots + \mathrm{proj}_{U_d}(Y) \cdot U_d \qquad (23.23)$$

Bias Term   The geometric approach makes it easy to derive an expression for the bias term b. Note that each of the predictor attributes can be centered by removing its projection along the vector $\mathbf{1}$. Define $\bar{X}_i$ to be the centered attribute vector

$$\bar{X}_i = X_i - \mu_{X_i} \cdot \mathbf{1}$$

All the centered vectors $\bar{X}_i$ lie in the $n - 1$ dimensional space, comprising the orthogonal complement of the span of $\mathbf{1}$.

From the expression of $\widehat{Y}$, we have

$$\begin{aligned} \widehat{Y} &= b \cdot \mathbf{1} + w_1 \cdot X_1 + w_2 \cdot X_2 + \cdots + w_d \cdot X_d \\ &= b \cdot \mathbf{1} + w_1 \cdot \left(\bar{X}_1 + \mu_{X_1} \cdot \mathbf{1} \right) + \cdots + w_d \cdot \left(\bar{X}_d + \mu_{X_d} \cdot \mathbf{1} \right) \\ &= \left(b + w_1 \cdot \mu_{X_1} + \ldots + w_d \cdot \mu_{X_d} \right) \cdot \mathbf{1} + w_1 \cdot \bar{X}_1 + \ldots + w_d \cdot \bar{X}_d \end{aligned} \qquad (23.24)$$

On the other hand, since $\mathbf{1}$ is orthogonal to all $\bar{X}_i$, we can obtain another expression for $\widehat{Y}$ in terms of the projection of Y onto the subspace spanned by the vectors

$\{\mathbf{1}, \bar{X}_1, \cdots, \bar{X}_d\}$. Let the new orthogonal basis for these centered attribute vectors be $\{\bar{U}_0, \bar{U}_1, \cdots, \bar{U}_d\}$, where $\bar{U}_0 = \mathbf{1}$. Thus, $\widehat{Y}$ can also be written as

$$\widehat{Y} = \text{proj}_{\bar{U}_0}(Y) \cdot \bar{U}_0 + \sum_{i=1}^{d} \text{proj}_{\bar{U}_i}(Y) \cdot \bar{U}_i = \text{proj}_{\mathbf{1}}(Y) \cdot \mathbf{1} + \sum_{i=1}^{d} \text{proj}_{\bar{U}_i}(Y) \cdot \bar{U}_i \qquad (23.25)$$

In particular, equating the scalar projections along $\mathbf{1}$ in Eq. (23.24) and Eq. (23.25), we get:

$$\text{proj}_{\mathbf{1}}(Y) = \mu_Y = (b + w_1 \cdot \mu_{X_1} + \ldots + w_d \cdot \mu_{X_d}), \text{ which implies}$$

$$b = \mu_Y - w_1 \cdot \mu_{X_1} - \ldots - w_d \cdot \mu_{X_d} = \mu_Y - \sum_{i=1}^{d} w_i \cdot \mu_{X_i} \qquad (23.26)$$

where we use the fact that the scalar projection of any attribute vector onto $\mathbf{1}$ yields the mean value of that attribute. For example,

$$\text{proj}_{\mathbf{1}}(Y) = \frac{Y^T \mathbf{1}}{\mathbf{1}^T \mathbf{1}} = \frac{1}{n} \sum_{i=1}^{n} y_i = \mu_Y$$

23.3.2 Multiple Regression Algorithm

The pseudo-code for multiple regression is shown in Algorithm 23.1. The algorithm starts by the QR-decomposition of $\tilde{\mathbf{D}} = \mathbf{QR}$, where $\mathbf{Q}$ is a matrix with orthogonal columns that make up an orthogonal basis, and $\mathbf{R}$ is an upper triangular matrix, which can be obtained via Gram–Schmidt orthogonalization. Note that, by construction, the matrix $\mathbf{Q}^T \mathbf{Q}$ is given as

$$\mathbf{Q}^T \mathbf{Q} = \begin{pmatrix} \|U_0\|^2 & 0 & \cdots & 0 \\ 0 & \|U_1\|^2 & \cdots & 0 \\ 0 & 0 & \ddots & 0 \\ 0 & 0 & \cdots & \|U_d\|^2 \end{pmatrix} = \Delta$$

Algorithm 23.1: Multiple Regression Algorithm

MULTIPLE-REGRESSION ($\mathbf{D}$, Y):

1 $\tilde{\mathbf{D}} \leftarrow \begin{pmatrix} \mathbf{1} & \mathbf{D} \end{pmatrix}$ // augmented data with $X_0 = \mathbf{1} \in \mathbb{R}^n$

2 $\{\mathbf{Q}, \mathbf{R}\} \leftarrow$ QR-factorization($\tilde{\mathbf{D}}$) // $\mathbf{Q} = \begin{pmatrix} U_0 & U_1 & \cdots & U_d \end{pmatrix}$

3 $\Delta^{-1} \leftarrow \begin{pmatrix} \frac{1}{\|U_0\|^2} & 0 & \cdots & 0 \\ 0 & \frac{1}{\|U_1\|^2} & \cdots & 0 \\ 0 & 0 & \ddots & 0 \\ 0 & 0 & \cdots & \frac{1}{\|U_d\|^2} \end{pmatrix}$ // reciprocal squared norms

4 $\mathbf{R}w \leftarrow \Delta^{-1} \mathbf{Q}^T Y$ // solve for w by back-substitution

5 $\widehat{Y} \leftarrow \mathbf{Q} \Delta^{-1} \mathbf{Q}^T Y$

We can observe that the matrix $\mathbf{Q}^T\mathbf{Q}$, denoted $\boldsymbol{\Delta}$, is a diagonal matrix that contains the squared norms of the new orthogonal basis vectors $U_0, U_1, \cdots, U_d$.

Recall that the solution to multiple regression is given via the normal equations [Eq. (23.21)], which can be compactly written as $(\tilde{\mathbf{D}}^T\tilde{\mathbf{w}})\tilde{\mathbf{w}} = \tilde{\mathbf{D}}^T Y$ [Eq. (23.22)]; plugging in the QR-decomposition, we get

$$(\tilde{\mathbf{D}}^T\tilde{\mathbf{D}})\tilde{\mathbf{w}} = \tilde{\mathbf{D}}^T Y$$

$$(\mathbf{QR})^T(\mathbf{QR})\tilde{\mathbf{w}} = (\mathbf{QR})^T Y$$

$$\mathbf{R}^T(\mathbf{Q}^T\mathbf{Q})\mathbf{R}\tilde{\mathbf{w}} = \mathbf{R}^T\mathbf{Q}^T Y$$

$$\mathbf{R}^T\boldsymbol{\Delta}\mathbf{R}\tilde{\mathbf{w}} = \mathbf{R}^T\mathbf{Q}^T Y$$

$$\boldsymbol{\Delta}\mathbf{R}\tilde{\mathbf{w}} = \mathbf{Q}^T Y$$

$$\mathbf{R}\tilde{\mathbf{w}} = \boldsymbol{\Delta}^{-1}\mathbf{Q}^T Y$$

Note that $\boldsymbol{\Delta}^{-1}$ is a diagonal matrix that records the reciprocal of the squared norms of the new basis vectors $U_0, U_1, \cdots, U_d$. Furthermore, since $\mathbf{R}$ is upper-triangular, it is straightforward to solve for $\tilde{\mathbf{w}}$ by back-substitution. Note also that we can obtain the predicted vector $\widehat{Y}$ as follows

$$\widehat{Y} = \tilde{\mathbf{D}}\tilde{\mathbf{w}} = \mathbf{QR}\mathbf{R}^{-1}\boldsymbol{\Delta}^{-1}\mathbf{Q}^T Y = \mathbf{Q}(\boldsymbol{\Delta}^{-1}\mathbf{Q}^T Y)$$

It is interesting to note that $\boldsymbol{\Delta}^{-1}\mathbf{Q}^T Y$ gives the vector of scalar projections of Y onto each of the orthogonal basis vectors

$$\boldsymbol{\Delta}^{-1}\mathbf{Q}^T Y = \begin{pmatrix} \text{proj}_{U_0}(Y) \\ \text{proj}_{U_1}(Y) \\ \vdots \\ \text{proj}_{U_d}(Y) \end{pmatrix}$$

Therefore, $\mathbf{Q}(\boldsymbol{\Delta}^{-1}\mathbf{Q}^T Y)$, yields the projection formula in Eq. (23.23)

$$\widehat{Y} = \mathbf{Q} \begin{pmatrix} \text{proj}_{U_0}(Y) \\ \text{proj}_{U_1}(Y) \\ \vdots \\ \text{proj}_{U_d}(Y) \end{pmatrix} = \text{proj}_{U_0}(Y) \cdot U_0 + \text{proj}_{U_1}(Y) \cdot U_1 + \cdots + \text{proj}_{U_d}(Y) \cdot U_d$$

Example 23.4 (Multiple Regression: QR-Factorization and Geometric Approach).
Consider the multiple regression of sepal length (X_1) and petal length (X_2) on the response attribute petal width (Y) for the Iris dataset with $n = 150$ points, as shown in Figure 23.5. The augmented dataset $\tilde{\mathbf{D}} \in \mathbb{R}^{150\times3}$ comprises $n = 150$ points along three attributes X_0, X_1, and X_2, where $X_0 = \mathbf{1}$. The Gram–Schmidt orthogonalization results in the following QR-factorization:

$$\underbrace{\begin{pmatrix} | & | & | \\ X_0 & X_1 & X_2 \\ | & | & | \end{pmatrix}}_{\tilde{\mathbf{D}}} = \underbrace{\begin{pmatrix} | & | & | \\ U_0 & U_1 & U_2 \\ | & | & | \end{pmatrix}}_{\mathbf{Q}} \cdot \underbrace{\begin{pmatrix} 1 & 5.843 & 3.759 \\ 0 & 1 & 1.858 \\ 0 & 0 & 1 \end{pmatrix}}_{\mathbf{R}}$$

Note that $\mathbf{Q} \in \mathbb{R}^{150 \times 3}$ and therefore we do not show the matrix. The matrix $\boldsymbol{\Delta}$, which records the squared norms of the basis vectors, and its inverse matrix, is given as

$$\boldsymbol{\Delta} = \begin{pmatrix} 150 & 0 & 0 \\ 0 & 102.17 & 0 \\ 0 & 0 & 111.35 \end{pmatrix} \qquad \boldsymbol{\Delta}^{-1} = \begin{pmatrix} 0.00667 & 0 & 0 \\ 0 & 0.00979 & 0 \\ 0 & 0 & 0.00898 \end{pmatrix}$$

We can use back-substitution to solve for $\tilde{\mathbf{w}}$, as follows

$$\mathbf{R}\tilde{\mathbf{w}} = \boldsymbol{\Delta}^{-1}\mathbf{Q}^T Y$$

$$\begin{pmatrix} 1 & 5.843 & 3.759 \\ 0 & 1 & 1.858 \\ 0 & 0 & 1 \end{pmatrix} \begin{pmatrix} w_0 \\ w_1 \\ w_2 \end{pmatrix} = \begin{pmatrix} 1.1987 \\ 0.7538 \\ 0.4499 \end{pmatrix}$$

In back-substitution, we start with w_2, which is easy to compute from the equation above; it is simply

$$w_2 = 0.4499$$

Next, w_1 is given as:

$$w_1 + 1.858 \cdot w_2 = 0.7538$$
$$\implies w_1 = 0.7538 - 0.8358 = -0.082$$

Finally, w_0 can be computed as

$$w_0 + 5.843 \cdot w_1 + 3.759 \cdot w_2 = 1.1987$$
$$\implies w_0 = 1.1987 + 0.4786 - 1.6911 = -0.0139$$

Thus, the multiple regression model is given as

$$\widehat{Y} = -0.014 \cdot X_0 - 0.082 \cdot X_1 + 0.45 \cdot X_2 \tag{23.27}$$

which matches the model in Example 23.3.

It is also instructive to construct the new basis vectors $U_0, U_1, \cdots, U_d$ in terms of the original attributes $X_0, X_1, \cdots, X_d$. Since $\tilde{\mathbf{D}} = \mathbf{QR}$, we have $\mathbf{Q} = \tilde{\mathbf{D}}\mathbf{R}^{-1}$. The inverse of $\mathbf{R}$ is also upper-triangular, and is given as

$$\mathbf{R}^{-1} = \begin{pmatrix} 1 & -5.843 & 7.095 \\ 0 & 1 & -1.858 \\ 0 & 0 & 1 \end{pmatrix}$$

Therefore, we can write $\mathbf{Q}$ in terms of the original attributes as

$$\underbrace{\begin{pmatrix} | & | & | \\ U_0 & U_1 & U_2 \\ | & | & | \end{pmatrix}}_{\mathbf{Q}} = \underbrace{\begin{pmatrix} | & | & | \\ X_0 & X_1 & X_2 \\ | & | & | \end{pmatrix}}_{\tilde{\mathbf{D}}} \underbrace{\begin{pmatrix} 1 & -5.843 & 7.095 \\ 0 & 1 & -1.858 \\ 0 & 0 & 1 \end{pmatrix}}_{\mathbf{R}^{-1}}$$

which results in

$$U_0 = X_0$$

$$U_1 = -5.843 \cdot X_0 + X_1$$

$$U_2 = 7.095 \cdot X_0 - 1.858 \cdot X_1 + X_2$$

The scalar projection of the response vector Y onto each of the new basis vectors yields:

$$\text{proj}_{U_0}(Y) = 1.199 \qquad \text{proj}_{U_1}(Y) = 0.754 \qquad \text{proj}_{U_2}(Y) = 0.45$$

Finally, the fitted response vector is given as:

$$\begin{aligned}
\widehat{Y} &= \text{proj}_{U_0}(Y) \cdot U_0 + \text{proj}_{U_1}(Y) \cdot U_1 + \text{proj}_{U_2}(Y) \cdot U_2 \\
&= 1.199 \cdot X_0 + 0.754 \cdot (-5.843 \cdot X_0 + X_1) + 0.45 \cdot (7.095 \cdot X_0 - 1.858 \cdot X_1 + X_2) \\
&= (1.199 - 4.406 + 3.193) \cdot X_0 + (0.754 - 0.836) \cdot X_1 + 0.45 \cdot X_2 \\
&= -0.014 \cdot X_0 - 0.082 \cdot X_1 + 0.45 \cdot X_2
\end{aligned}$$

which matches Eq. (23.27).

23.3.3 Multiple Regression: Stochastic Gradient Descent

Instead of using the QR-factorization approach to exactly solve the multiple regression problem, we can also employ the simpler stochastic gradient algorithm. Consider the SSE objective given in Eq. (23.19) (multiplied by 1/2):

$$\min_{\tilde{\mathbf{w}}} SSE = \frac{1}{2} \left(Y^T Y - 2\tilde{\mathbf{w}}^T (\tilde{\mathbf{D}}^T Y) + \tilde{\mathbf{w}}^T (\tilde{\mathbf{D}}^T \tilde{\mathbf{D}}) \tilde{\mathbf{w}} \right) \tag{23.28}$$

The gradient of the SSE objective is given as

$$\nabla_{\tilde{\mathbf{w}}} = \frac{\partial}{\partial \tilde{\mathbf{w}}} SSE = -\tilde{\mathbf{D}}^T Y + (\tilde{\mathbf{D}}^T \tilde{\mathbf{D}}) \tilde{\mathbf{w}}$$

Using gradient descent, starting from an initial weight vector estimate $\tilde{\mathbf{w}}^0$, we can iteratively update $\tilde{\mathbf{w}}$ as follows

$$\tilde{\mathbf{w}}^{t+1} = \tilde{\mathbf{w}}^t - \eta \cdot \nabla_{\tilde{\mathbf{w}}} = \tilde{\mathbf{w}}^t + \eta \cdot \tilde{\mathbf{D}}^T (Y - \tilde{\mathbf{D}} \cdot \tilde{\mathbf{w}}^t)$$

where $\tilde{\mathbf{w}}^t$ is the estimate of the weight vector at step t.

In stochastic gradient descent (SGD), we update the weight vector by considering only one (random) point at each time. Restricting Eq. (23.28) to a single point $\tilde{\mathbf{x}}_k$ in the training data $\tilde{\mathbf{D}}$, the gradient at the point $\tilde{\mathbf{x}}_k$ is given as

$$\nabla_{\tilde{\mathbf{w}}}(\tilde{\mathbf{x}}_k) = -\tilde{\mathbf{x}}_k y_k + \tilde{\mathbf{x}}_k \tilde{\mathbf{x}}_k^T \tilde{\mathbf{w}} = -(y_k - \tilde{\mathbf{x}}_k^T \tilde{\mathbf{w}}) \tilde{\mathbf{x}}_k$$

Algorithm 23.2: Multiple Regression: Stochastic Gradient Descent

---

MULTIPLE REGRESSION: SGD ($\mathbf{D}, Y, \eta, \epsilon$):

1   $\tilde{\mathbf{D}} \leftarrow \begin{pmatrix} \mathbf{1} & \mathbf{D} \end{pmatrix}$ // augment data

2   $t \leftarrow 0$ // step/iteration counter

3   $\tilde{\mathbf{w}}^t \leftarrow$ random vector in $\mathbb{R}^{d+1}$ // initial weight vector

4 **repeat**

5   **foreach** $k = 1, 2, \cdots, n$ *(in random order)* **do**

6        $\nabla_{\tilde{\mathbf{w}}}(\tilde{\mathbf{x}}_k) \leftarrow -(y_k - \tilde{\mathbf{x}}_k^T \tilde{\mathbf{w}}^t) \cdot \tilde{\mathbf{x}}_k$ // compute gradient at $\tilde{\mathbf{x}}_k$

7        $\tilde{\mathbf{w}}^{t+1} \leftarrow \tilde{\mathbf{w}}^t - \eta \cdot \nabla_{\tilde{\mathbf{w}}}(\tilde{\mathbf{x}}_k)$ // update estimate for $\tilde{\mathbf{w}}$

8     $t \leftarrow t + 1$

9 **until** $\|\mathbf{w}^t - \mathbf{w}^{t-1}\| \leq \epsilon$

Therefore, the stochastic gradient update rule is given as

$$\tilde{\mathbf{w}}^{t+1} = \tilde{\mathbf{w}}^t - \eta \cdot \nabla_{\tilde{\mathbf{w}}}(\tilde{\mathbf{x}}_k)$$
$$= \tilde{\mathbf{w}}^t + \eta \cdot (y_k - \tilde{\mathbf{x}}_k^T \tilde{\mathbf{w}}^t) \cdot \tilde{\mathbf{x}}_k$$

Algorithm 23.2 shows the pseudo-code for the stochastic gradient descent algorithm for multiple regression. After augmenting the data matrix, in each iteration it updates the weight vector by considering the gradient at each point in random order. The method stops when the weight vector converges based on the tolerance ϵ.

Example 23.5 (Multiple Regression: SGD). We continue Example 23.4 for multiple regression of sepal length (X_1) and petal length (X_2) on the response attribute petal width (Y) for the Iris dataset with $n = 150$ points.

Using the exact approach the multiple regression model was given as

$$\widehat{Y} = -0.014 \cdot X_0 - 0.082 \cdot X_1 + 0.45 \cdot X_2$$

Using stochastic gradient descent we obtain the following model with $\eta = 0.001$ and $\epsilon = 0.0001$:

$$\widehat{Y} = -0.031 \cdot X_0 - 0.078 \cdot X_1 + 0.45 \cdot X_2$$

The results from the SGD approach as essentially the same as the exact method, with a slight difference in the bias term. The SSE value for the exact method is 6.179, whereas for SGD it is 6.181.

23.4 RIDGE REGRESSION

We have seen that for linear regression, the predicted response vector $\widehat{Y}$ lies in the span of the column vectors comprising the augmented data matrix $\tilde{\mathbf{D}}$. However, often the data is noisy and uncertain, and therefore instead of fitting the model to the data exactly, it may be better to fit a more robust model. One way to achieve this is via regularization, where we constrain the solution vector $\tilde{\mathbf{w}}$ to have a small norm. In other words, instead of trying to simply minimize the squared residual error $\|Y - \widehat{Y}\|^2$, we add a regularization term involving the squared norm of the weight vector ($\|\tilde{\mathbf{w}}\|^2$) as follows:

$$\min_{\tilde{\mathbf{w}}} \; J(\tilde{\mathbf{w}}) = \|Y - \widehat{Y}\|^2 + \alpha \cdot \|\tilde{\mathbf{w}}\|^2 = \|Y - \tilde{\mathbf{D}}\tilde{\mathbf{w}}\|^2 + \alpha \cdot \|\tilde{\mathbf{w}}\|^2 \qquad (23.29)$$

Here $\alpha \geq 0$ is a regularization constant that controls the tradeoff between minimizing the squared norm of the weight vector and the squared error. Recall that $\|\tilde{\mathbf{w}}\|^2 = \sum_{i=1}^{d} w_i^2$ is the L_2-norm of $\tilde{\mathbf{w}}$. For this reason ridge regression is also called L_2 regularized regression. When $\alpha = 0$, there is no regularization, but as α increases there is more emphasis on minimizing the regression coefficients.

The solve the new regularized objective we differentiate Eq. (23.29) with respect to $\tilde{\mathbf{w}}$ and set the result to $\mathbf{0}$ to obtain

$$\frac{\partial}{\partial \tilde{\mathbf{w}}} J(\tilde{\mathbf{w}}) = \frac{\partial}{\partial \tilde{\mathbf{w}}} \left\{ \|Y - \tilde{\mathbf{D}}\tilde{\mathbf{w}}\|^2 + \alpha \cdot \|\tilde{\mathbf{w}}\|^2 \right\} = \mathbf{0}$$

$$\implies \frac{\partial}{\partial \tilde{\mathbf{w}}} \left\{ Y^T Y - 2\tilde{\mathbf{w}}^T (\tilde{\mathbf{D}}^T Y) + \tilde{\mathbf{w}}^T (\tilde{\mathbf{D}}^T \tilde{\mathbf{D}})\tilde{\mathbf{w}} + \alpha \cdot \tilde{\mathbf{w}}^T \tilde{\mathbf{w}} \right\} = \mathbf{0}$$

$$\implies -2\tilde{\mathbf{D}}^T Y + 2(\tilde{\mathbf{D}}^T \tilde{\mathbf{D}})\tilde{\mathbf{w}} + 2\alpha \cdot \tilde{\mathbf{w}} = \mathbf{0} \qquad (23.30)$$

$$\implies (\tilde{\mathbf{D}}^T \tilde{\mathbf{D}} + \alpha \cdot \mathbf{I})\tilde{\mathbf{w}} = \tilde{\mathbf{D}}^T Y \qquad (23.31)$$

Therefore, the optimal solution is

$$\tilde{\mathbf{w}} = (\tilde{\mathbf{D}}^T \tilde{\mathbf{D}} + \alpha \cdot \mathbf{I})^{-1} \tilde{\mathbf{D}}^T Y \qquad (23.32)$$

where $\mathbf{I} \in \mathbb{R}^{(d+1) \times (d+1)}$ is the identity matrix. The matrix $(\tilde{\mathbf{D}}^T \tilde{\mathbf{D}} + \alpha \cdot \mathbf{I})$ is always invertible (or non-singular) for $\alpha > 0$ even if $\tilde{\mathbf{D}}^T \tilde{\mathbf{D}}$ is not invertible (or singular). This is because if λ_i is an eigenvalue of $\tilde{\mathbf{D}}^T \tilde{\mathbf{D}}$, then $\lambda_i + \alpha$ is an eigenvalue of $(\tilde{\mathbf{D}}^T \tilde{\mathbf{D}} + \alpha \cdot \mathbf{I})$. Since $\tilde{\mathbf{D}}^T \tilde{\mathbf{D}}$ is positive semi-definite it has non-negative eigenvalues. Thus, even if an eigenvalue of $\tilde{\mathbf{D}}^T \tilde{\mathbf{D}}$ is zero, e.g., $\lambda_i = 0$, the corresponding eigenvalue of $(\tilde{\mathbf{D}}^T \tilde{\mathbf{D}} + \alpha \cdot \mathbf{I})$ is $\lambda_i + \alpha = \alpha > 0$.

Regularized regression is also called *ridge regression* since we add a "ridge" along the main diagonal of the $\tilde{\mathbf{D}}^T \tilde{\mathbf{D}}$ matrix, i.e., the optimal solution depends on the regularized matrix $(\tilde{\mathbf{D}}^T \tilde{\mathbf{D}} + \alpha \cdot \mathbf{I})$. Another advantage of regularization is that if we choose a small positive α we are always guaranteed a solution.

Example 23.6 (Ridge Regression). Figure 23.6 shows the scatterplot between the two attributes petal length (X; the predictor variable) and petal width (Y; the response variable) in the Iris dataset. There are a total of $n = 150$ data points. The uncentered scatter matrix is given as

$$\tilde{\mathbf{D}}^T \tilde{\mathbf{D}} = \begin{pmatrix} 150.0 & 563.8 \\ 563.8 & 2583.0 \end{pmatrix}$$

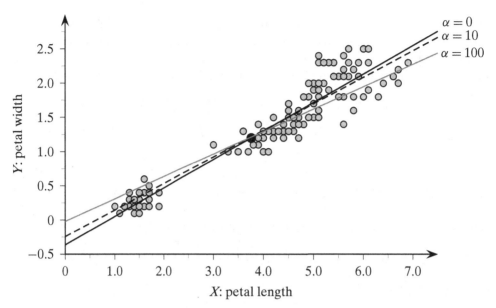

Figure 23.6. Scatterplot: petal length (X) versus petal width (Y). Ridge regression lines for $\alpha = 0, 10, 100$.

Using Eq. (23.32) we obtain different lines of best fit for different values of the regularization constant α:

$$\alpha = 0 : \widehat{Y} = -0.367 + 0.416 \cdot X, \quad \|\tilde{\mathbf{w}}\|^2 = \|(-0.367, 0.416)^T\|^2 = 0.308, \quad SSE = 6.34$$

$$\alpha = 10 : \widehat{Y} = -0.244 + 0.388 \cdot X, \quad \|\tilde{\mathbf{w}}\|^2 = \|(-0.244, 0.388)^T\|^2 = 0.210, \quad SSE = 6.75$$

$$\alpha = 100 : \widehat{Y} = -0.021 + 0.328 \cdot X, \quad \|\tilde{\mathbf{w}}\|^2 = \|(-0.021, 0.328)^T\|^2 = 0.108, \quad SSE = 9.97$$

Figure 23.6 shows these regularized regression lines. We can see that as α increases there is more emphasis on minimizing the squared norm of $\tilde{\mathbf{w}}$. However, since $\|\tilde{\mathbf{w}}\|^2$ is more constrained as α increases, the fit of the model decreases, as seen from the increase in SSE values.

Unpenalized Bias Term   Often in L_2 regularized regression we do not want to penalize the bias term w_0, since it simply provides the intercept information, and there is no real justification to minimize it. To avoid penalizing the bias term, consider the new regularized objective with $\mathbf{w} = (w_1, w_2, \cdots, w_d)^T$, and without w_0, given as

$$\min_{\mathbf{w}} \; J(\mathbf{w}) = \|Y - w_0 \cdot \mathbf{1} - \mathbf{D}\mathbf{w}\|^2 + \alpha \cdot \|\mathbf{w}\|^2 \tag{23.33}$$

$$= \left\| Y - w_0 \cdot \mathbf{1} - \sum_{i=1}^{d} w_i \cdot X_i \right\|^2 + \alpha \cdot \left(\sum_{i=1}^{d} w_i^2 \right)$$

Recall from Eq. (23.26) that the bias $w_0 = b$ is given as

$$w_0 = b = \mu_Y - \sum_{i=1}^{d} w_i \cdot \mu_{X_i} = \mu_Y - \boldsymbol{\mu}^T \mathbf{w}$$

where $\boldsymbol{\mu} = (\mu_{X_1}, \mu_{X_2}, \cdots, \mu_{X_d})^T$ is the multivariate mean of (unaugmented) $\mathbf{D}$. Substituting w_0 into the new L_2 objective in Eq. (23.33), we get

$$\min_{\mathbf{w}} J(\mathbf{w}) = \|Y - w_0 \cdot \mathbf{1} - \mathbf{D}\mathbf{w}\|^2 + \alpha \cdot \|\mathbf{w}\|^2$$

$$= \|Y - (\mu_Y - \boldsymbol{\mu}^T \mathbf{w}) \cdot \mathbf{1} - \mathbf{D}\mathbf{w}\|^2 + \alpha \cdot \|\mathbf{w}\|^2$$

$$= \|(Y - \mu_Y \cdot \mathbf{1}) - (\mathbf{D} - \mathbf{1}\boldsymbol{\mu}^T)\mathbf{w}\|^2 + \alpha \cdot \|\mathbf{w}\|^2$$

Therefore, we have

$$\min_{\mathbf{w}} J(\mathbf{w}) = \|\bar{Y} - \bar{\mathbf{D}}\mathbf{w}\|^2 + \alpha \cdot \|\mathbf{w}\|^2 \qquad (23.34)$$

where $\bar{Y} = Y - \mu_Y \cdot \mathbf{1}$ is the centered response vector, and $\bar{\mathbf{D}} = \mathbf{D} - \mathbf{1}\boldsymbol{\mu}^T$ is the centered data matrix. In other words, we can exclude w_0 from the L_2 regularization objective by simply centering the response vector and the unaugmented data matrix.

Example 23.7 (Ridge Regression: Unpenalized Bias). We continue from Example 23.6. When we do not penalize w_0, we obtain the following lines of best fit for different values of the regularization constant α:

$$\alpha = 0: \widehat{Y} = -0.365 + 0.416 \cdot X \qquad w_0^2 + w_1^2 = 0.307 \qquad SSE = 6.34$$

$$\alpha = 10: \widehat{Y} = -0.333 + 0.408 \cdot X \qquad w_0^2 + w_1^2 = 0.277 \qquad SSE = 6.38$$

$$\alpha = 100: \widehat{Y} = -0.089 + 0.343 \cdot X \qquad w_0^2 + w_1^2 = 0.125 \qquad SSE = 8.87$$

From Example 23.6, we observe that for $\alpha = 10$, when we penalize w_0, we obtain the following model:

$$\alpha = 10: \widehat{Y} = -0.244 + 0.388 \cdot X \qquad w_0^2 + w_1^2 = 0.210 \qquad SSE = 6.75$$

As expected, we obtain a higher bias term when we do not penalize w_0.

23.4.1 Ridge Regression: Stochastic Gradient Descent

Instead of inverting the matrix $(\tilde{\mathbf{D}}^T \tilde{\mathbf{D}} + \alpha \cdot \mathbf{I})$ as called for in the exact ridge regression solution in Eq. (23.32), we can employ the stochastic gradient descent algorithm. Consider the gradient of the regularized objective given in Eq. (23.30), multiplied by 1/2 for convenience; we get:

$$\nabla_{\tilde{\mathbf{w}}} = \frac{\partial}{\partial \tilde{\mathbf{w}}} J(\tilde{\mathbf{w}}) = -\tilde{\mathbf{D}}^T Y + (\tilde{\mathbf{D}}^T \tilde{\mathbf{D}})\tilde{\mathbf{w}} + \alpha \cdot \tilde{\mathbf{w}} \qquad (23.35)$$

Algorithm 23.3: Ridge Regression: Stochastic Gradient Descent

---

RIDGE REGRESSION: SGD (D, Y, η, ϵ):

1 $\tilde{\mathbf{D}} \leftarrow \begin{pmatrix} \mathbf{1} & \mathbf{D} \end{pmatrix}$ // augment data
2 $t \leftarrow 0$ // step/iteration counter
3 $\tilde{\mathbf{w}}^t \leftarrow$ random vector in $\mathbb{R}^{d+1}$ // initial weight vector
4 **repeat**
5 $\quad$ **foreach** $k = 1, 2, \cdots, n$ *(in random order)* **do**
6 $\quad\quad$ $\nabla_{\tilde{\mathbf{w}}}(\tilde{\mathbf{x}}_k) \leftarrow -(y_k - \tilde{\mathbf{x}}_k^T \tilde{\mathbf{w}}^t) \cdot \tilde{\mathbf{x}}_k + \frac{\alpha}{n} \cdot \tilde{\mathbf{w}}$ // compute gradient at $\tilde{\mathbf{x}}_k$
7 $\quad\quad$ $\tilde{\mathbf{w}}^{t+1} \leftarrow \tilde{\mathbf{w}}^t - \eta \cdot \nabla_{\tilde{\mathbf{w}}}(\tilde{\mathbf{x}}_k)$ // update estimate for $\tilde{\mathbf{w}}$
8 $\quad$ $t \leftarrow t+1$
9 **until** $\|\mathbf{w}^t - \mathbf{w}^{t-1}\| \le \epsilon$

Using (batch) gradient descent, we can iteratively compute $\tilde{\mathbf{w}}$ as follows

$$\tilde{\mathbf{w}}^{t+1} = \tilde{\mathbf{w}}^t - \eta \cdot \nabla_{\tilde{\mathbf{w}}} = (1 - \eta \cdot \alpha)\tilde{\mathbf{w}}^t + \eta \cdot \tilde{\mathbf{D}}^T(Y - \tilde{\mathbf{D}} \cdot \tilde{\mathbf{w}}^t)$$

In stochastic gradient descent (SGD), we update the weight vector by considering only one (random) point at each time. Restricting Eq. (23.35) to a single point $\tilde{\mathbf{x}}_k$, the gradient at the point $\tilde{\mathbf{x}}_k$ is given as

$$\nabla_{\tilde{\mathbf{w}}}(\tilde{\mathbf{x}}_k) = -\tilde{\mathbf{x}}_k y_k + \tilde{\mathbf{x}}_k \tilde{\mathbf{x}}_k^T \tilde{\mathbf{w}} + \frac{\alpha}{n}\tilde{\mathbf{w}} = -(y_k - \tilde{\mathbf{x}}_k^T \tilde{\mathbf{w}})\tilde{\mathbf{x}}_k + \frac{\alpha}{n}\tilde{\mathbf{w}} \quad (23.36)$$

Here, we scale the regularization constant α by dividing it by n, the number of points in the training data, since the original ridge value α is for all the n points, whereas we are now considering only one point at a time. Therefore, the stochastic gradient update rule is given as

$$\tilde{\mathbf{w}}^{t+1} = \tilde{\mathbf{w}}^t - \eta \cdot \nabla_{\tilde{\mathbf{w}}}(\tilde{\mathbf{x}}_k) = \left(1 - \frac{\eta \cdot \alpha}{n}\right)\tilde{\mathbf{w}}^t + \eta \cdot (y_k - \tilde{\mathbf{x}}_k^T \tilde{\mathbf{w}}^t) \cdot \tilde{\mathbf{x}}_k$$

Algorithm 23.3 shows the pseudo-code for the stochastic gradient descent algorithm for ridge regression. After augmenting the data matrix, in each iteration it updates the weight vector by considering the gradient at each point in random order. The method stops when the weight vector converges based on the tolerance ϵ. The code is for the penalized bias case. It is easy to adapt it for unpenalized bias by centering the unaugmented data matrix and the response variable.

Example 23.8 (Ridge Regression: SGD). We apply ridge regression on the Iris dataset ($n = 150$), using petal length (X) as the independent attribute, and petal width (Y) as the response variable. Using SGD (with $\eta = 0.001$ and $\epsilon = 0.0001$) we obtain different lines of best fit for different values of the regularization constant α, which essentially match the results from the exact method in Example 23.6:

$$\alpha = 0 : \widehat{Y} = -0.366 + 0.413 \cdot X \qquad\qquad SSE = 6.37$$

$$\alpha = 10 : \widehat{Y} = -0.244 + 0.387 \cdot X \qquad\qquad SSE = 6.76$$

$$\alpha = 100 : \widehat{Y} = -0.022 + 0.327 \cdot X \qquad\qquad SSE = 10.04$$

23.5 KERNEL REGRESSION

We now consider how to generalize linear regression to the non-linear case, i.e., finding a non-linear fit to the data to minimize the squared error, along with regularization. For this we will adopt the kernel trick, i.e., we will show that all relevant operations can be carried out via the kernel matrix in input space.

Let ϕ correspond to a mapping from the input space to the feature space, so that each point $\phi(\mathbf{x}_i)$ in feature space is a mapping for the input point $\mathbf{x}_i$. To avoid explicitly dealing with the bias term, we add the fixed value 1 as the first element of $\phi(\mathbf{x}_i)$ to obtain the *augmented transformed point* $\tilde{\phi}(\mathbf{x}_i)^T = \begin{pmatrix} 1 & \phi(\mathbf{x}_i)^T \end{pmatrix}$. Let $\tilde{\mathbf{D}}_\phi$ denote the *augmented dataset in feature space*, comprising the transformed points $\tilde{\phi}(\mathbf{x}_i)$ for $i = 1, 2, \cdots, n$. The *augmented kernel function* in feature space is given as

$$\tilde{K}(\mathbf{x}_i, \mathbf{x}_j) = \tilde{\phi}(\mathbf{x}_i)^T \tilde{\phi}(\mathbf{x}_j) = 1 + \phi(\mathbf{x}_i)^T \phi(\mathbf{x}_j) = 1 + K(\mathbf{x}_i, \mathbf{x}_j)$$

where $K(\mathbf{x}_i, \mathbf{x}_j)$ is the standard, unaugmented kernel function.

Let Y denote the observed response vector. Following Eq. (23.18), we model the predicted response as

$$\widehat{Y} = \tilde{\mathbf{D}}_\phi \tilde{\mathbf{w}} \tag{23.37}$$

where $\tilde{\mathbf{w}}$ is the augmented weight vector in feature space. The first element of $\tilde{\mathbf{w}}$ denotes the bias in feature space.

For regularized regression, we have to solve the following objective in feature space:

$$\min_{\tilde{\mathbf{w}}} \; J(\tilde{\mathbf{w}}) = \|Y - \widehat{Y}\|^2 + \alpha \cdot \|\tilde{\mathbf{w}}\|^2 = \|Y - \tilde{\mathbf{D}}_\phi \tilde{\mathbf{w}}\|^2 + \alpha \cdot \|\tilde{\mathbf{w}}\|^2 \tag{23.38}$$

where $\alpha \geq 0$ is the regularization constant.

Taking the derivative of $J(\tilde{\mathbf{w}})$ with respect to $\tilde{\mathbf{w}}$ and setting it to the zero vector, we get

$$\frac{\partial}{\partial \tilde{\mathbf{w}}} J(\tilde{\mathbf{w}}) = \frac{\partial}{\partial \tilde{\mathbf{w}}} \left\{ \|Y - \tilde{\mathbf{D}}_\phi \tilde{\mathbf{w}}\|^2 + \alpha \cdot \|\tilde{\mathbf{w}}\|^2 \right\} = \mathbf{0}$$

$$\implies \frac{\partial}{\partial \tilde{\mathbf{w}}} \left\{ Y^T Y - 2\tilde{\mathbf{w}}^T (\tilde{\mathbf{D}}_\phi^T Y) + \tilde{\mathbf{w}}^T (\tilde{\mathbf{D}}_\phi^T \tilde{\mathbf{D}}_\phi) \tilde{\mathbf{w}} + \alpha \cdot \tilde{\mathbf{w}}^T \tilde{\mathbf{w}} \right\} = \mathbf{0}$$

$$\implies -2\tilde{\mathbf{D}}_\phi^T Y + 2(\tilde{\mathbf{D}}_\phi^T \tilde{\mathbf{D}}_\phi) \tilde{\mathbf{w}} + 2\alpha \cdot \tilde{\mathbf{w}} = \mathbf{0}$$

$$\implies \alpha \cdot \tilde{\mathbf{w}} = \tilde{\mathbf{D}}_\phi^T Y - (\tilde{\mathbf{D}}_\phi^T \tilde{\mathbf{D}}_\phi) \tilde{\mathbf{w}}$$

$$\implies \tilde{\mathbf{w}} = \tilde{\mathbf{D}}_\phi^T \left(\frac{1}{\alpha} \left(Y - \tilde{\mathbf{D}}_\phi \tilde{\mathbf{w}} \right) \right)$$

$$\implies \tilde{\mathbf{w}} = \tilde{\mathbf{D}}_\phi^T \mathbf{c} = \sum_{i=1}^{n} c_i \cdot \tilde{\phi}(\mathbf{x}_i) \tag{23.39}$$

where $\mathbf{c} = (c_1, c_2, \cdots, c_n)^T = \frac{1}{\alpha}(Y - \tilde{\mathbf{D}}_\phi \tilde{\mathbf{w}})$. Eq. (23.39) indicates that the weight vector $\tilde{\mathbf{w}}$ is a linear combination of the feature points, with $\mathbf{c}$ specifying the mixture coefficients for the points.

Rearranging the terms in the expression for $\mathbf{c}$, we have

$$\mathbf{c} = \frac{1}{\alpha}(Y - \tilde{\mathbf{D}}_\phi \tilde{\mathbf{w}})$$

$$\alpha \cdot \mathbf{c} = Y - \tilde{\mathbf{D}}_\phi \tilde{\mathbf{w}}$$

Now, plugging in the form of $\tilde{\mathbf{w}}$ from Eq. (23.39) we get

$$\alpha \cdot \mathbf{c} = Y - \tilde{\mathbf{D}}_\phi (\tilde{\mathbf{D}}_\phi^T \mathbf{c})$$

$$(\tilde{\mathbf{D}}_\phi \tilde{\mathbf{D}}_\phi^T + \alpha \cdot \mathbf{I})\mathbf{c} = Y$$

$$\mathbf{c} = (\tilde{\mathbf{D}}_\phi \tilde{\mathbf{D}}_\phi^T + \alpha \cdot \mathbf{I})^{-1} Y$$

$$(23.40)$$

The optimal solution is therefore given as

$$\boxed{\mathbf{c} = (\tilde{\mathbf{K}} + \alpha \cdot \mathbf{I})^{-1} Y} \tag{23.41}$$

where $\mathbf{I} \in \mathbb{R}^{n \times n}$ is the $n \times n$ identity matrix, and $\tilde{\mathbf{D}}_\phi \tilde{\mathbf{D}}_\phi^T$ is the augmented kernel matrix $\tilde{\mathbf{K}}$, since

$$\tilde{\mathbf{D}}_\phi \tilde{\mathbf{D}}_\phi^T = \left\{ \tilde{\phi}(\mathbf{x}_i)^T \tilde{\phi}(\mathbf{x}_j) \right\}_{i,j=1,2,\cdots,n} = \left\{ \tilde{K}(\mathbf{x}_i, \mathbf{x}_j) \right\}_{i,j=1,2,\cdots,n} = \tilde{\mathbf{K}}$$

Putting it all together, we can substitute Eq. (23.41) and Eq. (23.39) into Eq. (23.37) to obtain the expression for the predicted response

$$\begin{aligned}
\widehat{Y} &= \tilde{\mathbf{D}}_\phi \tilde{\mathbf{w}} \\
&= \tilde{\mathbf{D}}_\phi \tilde{\mathbf{D}}_\phi^T \mathbf{c} \\
&= \left(\tilde{\mathbf{D}}_\phi \tilde{\mathbf{D}}_\phi^T \right) \left(\tilde{\mathbf{K}} + \alpha \cdot \mathbf{I} \right)^{-1} Y \\
&= \tilde{\mathbf{K}} \left(\tilde{\mathbf{K}} + \alpha \cdot \mathbf{I} \right)^{-1} Y
\end{aligned} \tag{23.42}$$

where $\tilde{\mathbf{K}}(\tilde{\mathbf{K}} + \alpha \cdot \mathbf{I})^{-1}$ is the *kernel hat matrix*. Notice that using $\alpha > 0$ ensures that the inverse always exists, which is another advantage of using (kernel) ridge regression, in addition to the regularization.

Algorithm 23.4 shows the pseudo-code for kernel regression. The main step is to compute the augmented kernel matrix $\tilde{\mathbf{K}} \in \mathbb{R}^{n \times n}$, and the vector of mixture coefficients $\mathbf{c} \in \mathbb{R}^n$. The predicted response on the training data is then given as $\widehat{Y} = \tilde{\mathbf{K}}\mathbf{c}$. As for prediction for a new test point $\mathbf{z}$, we use Eq. (23.39) to predict the response, which is given as:

$$\begin{aligned}
\hat{y} &= \tilde{\phi}(\mathbf{z})^T \tilde{\mathbf{w}} = \tilde{\phi}(\mathbf{z})^T \left(\tilde{\mathbf{D}}_\phi^T \mathbf{c} \right) = \tilde{\phi}(\mathbf{z})^T \left(\sum_{i=1}^n c_i \cdot \tilde{\phi}(\mathbf{x}_i) \right) \\
&= \sum_{i=1}^n c_i \cdot \tilde{\phi}(\mathbf{z})^T \tilde{\phi}(\mathbf{x}_i) = \sum_{i=1}^n c_i \cdot \tilde{K}(\mathbf{z}, \mathbf{x}_i) = \mathbf{c}^T \tilde{\mathbf{K}}_{\mathbf{z}}
\end{aligned}$$

Algorithm 23.4: Kernel Regression Algorithm

KERNEL-REGRESSION $(\mathbf{D}, Y, K, \alpha)$:

1 $\mathbf{K} \leftarrow \left\{ K(\mathbf{x}_i, \mathbf{x}_j) \right\}_{i,j=1,\dots,n}$ // `standard kernel matrix`

2 $\tilde{\mathbf{K}} \leftarrow \mathbf{K} + 1$ // `augmented kernel matrix`

3 $\mathbf{c} \leftarrow \left(\tilde{\mathbf{K}} + \alpha \cdot \mathbf{I} \right)^{-1} Y$ // `compute mixture coefficients`

4 $\widehat{Y} \leftarrow \tilde{\mathbf{K}} \mathbf{c}$

TESTING $(\mathbf{z}, \mathbf{D}, K, \mathbf{c})$:

5 $\tilde{\mathbf{K}}_{\mathbf{z}} \leftarrow \left\{ 1 + K(\mathbf{z}, \mathbf{x}_i) \right\}_{\forall \mathbf{x}_i \in \mathbf{D}}$

6 $\hat{y} \leftarrow \mathbf{c}^T \tilde{\mathbf{K}}_{\mathbf{z}}$

That is, we compute the vector $\tilde{\mathbf{K}}_{\mathbf{z}}$ comprising the augmented kernel values of $\mathbf{z}$ with respect to all of the data points in $\mathbf{D}$, and take its dot product with the mixture coefficient vector $\mathbf{c}$ to obtain the predicted response.

Example 23.9. Consider the nonlinear Iris dataset shown in Figure 23.7, obtained via a nonlinear transformation applied to the centered Iris data. In particular, the `sepal length` (A_1) and `sepal width` attributes (A_2) were transformed as follows:

$$X = A_2$$
$$Y = 0.2A_1^2 + A_2^2 + 0.1A_1 A_2$$

We treat Y as the response variable and X is the independent attribute. The points show a clear quadratic (nonlinear) relationship between the two variables.

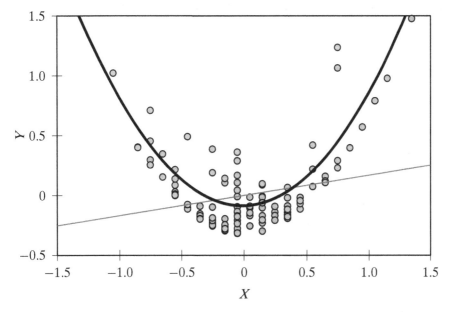

Figure 23.7. Kernel regression on nonlinear Iris dataset.

We find the lines of best fit using both a linear and an inhomogeneous quadratic kernel, with regularization constant $\alpha = 0.1$. The linear kernel yields the following fit

$$\widehat{Y} = 0.168 \cdot X$$

On the other hand, using the quadratic (inhomogeneous) kernel over X comprising constant (1), linear (X), and quadratic terms (X^2), yields the fit

$$\widehat{Y} = -0.086 + 0.026 \cdot X + 0.922 \cdot X^2$$

The linear (in gray) and quadratic (in black) fit are both shown in Figure 23.7. The SSE error, $\|Y - \widehat{Y}\|^2$, is 13.82 for the linear kernel and 4.33 for the quadratic kernel. It is clear that the quadratic kernel (as expected) gives a much better fit to the data.

Example 23.10 (Kernel Ridge Regression). Consider the Iris principal components dataset shown in Figure 23.8. Here X_1 and X_2 denote the first two principal components. The response variable Y is binary, with value 1 corresponding to Iris-virginica (points on the top right, with Y value 1) and 0 corresponding to Iris-setosa and Iris-versicolor (other two groups of points, with Y value 0).

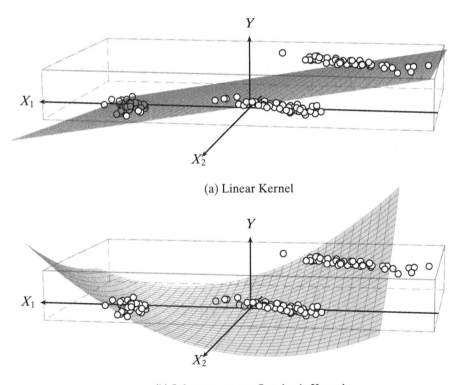

(a) Linear Kernel

(b) Inhomogeneous Quadratic Kernel

Figure 23.8. Kernel ridge regression: linear and (inhomogeneous) quadratic kernels.

Figure 23.8(a) shows the fitted regression plane using a linear kernel with ridge value $\alpha = 0.01$:

$$\widehat{Y} = 0.333 - 0.167 \cdot X_1 + 0.074 \cdot X_2$$

Figure 23.8(b) shows the fitted model when we use an inhomogeneous quadratic kernel with $\alpha = 0.01$:

$$\widehat{Y} = -0.03 - 0.167 \cdot X_1 - 0.186 \cdot X_2 + 0.092 \cdot X_1^2 + 0.1 \cdot X_1 \cdot X_2 + 0.029 \cdot X_2^2$$

The SSE error for the linear model is 15.47, whereas for the quadratic kernel it is 8.44, indicating a better fit for the training data.

23.6 L_1 REGRESSION: LASSO

The *Lasso*, which stands for *least absolute selection and shrinkage operator*, is a regularization method that aims to sparsify the regression weights. Instead of using the L_2 or Euclidean norm for weight regularization as in ridge regression (see Eq. (23.34)), the Lasso formulation uses the L_1 norm for regularization

$$\min_{\mathbf{w}} \ J(\mathbf{w}) = \frac{1}{2} \cdot \left\| \bar{Y} - \bar{\mathbf{D}}\mathbf{w} \right\|^2 + \alpha \cdot \|\mathbf{w}\|_1 \qquad (23.43)$$

where $\alpha \geq 0$ is the regularization constant and

$$\|\mathbf{w}\|_1 = \sum_{i=1}^{d} |w_i|$$

Note that, we have added the factor $\frac{1}{2}$ for convenience; it does not change the objective. Furthermore, we assume that the data comprising the d independent attributes X_1, X_2, ..., X_d, and the response attribute Y, have all been centered. That is, we assume that

$$\bar{\mathbf{D}} = \mathbf{D} - \mathbf{1} \cdot \mu^T$$
$$\bar{Y} = Y - \mu_Y \cdot \mathbf{1}$$

where $\mathbf{1} \in \mathbb{R}^n$ is the vector of all ones, $\mu = (\mu_{X_1}, \mu_{X_2}, \cdots, \mu_{X_d})^T$ is the multivariate mean for the data, and μ_Y is the mean response value. One benefit of centering is that we do not have to explicitly deal with the bias term $b = w_0$, which is important since we usually do not want to penalize b. Once the regression coefficients have been estimated, we can obtain the bias term via Eq. (23.26), as follows:

$$b = w_0 = \mu_Y - \sum_{j=1}^{d} w_j \cdot \mu_{X_j}$$

The main advantage of using the L_1 norm is that it leads to *sparsity* in the solution vector. That is, whereas ridge regression reduces the value of the regression coefficients

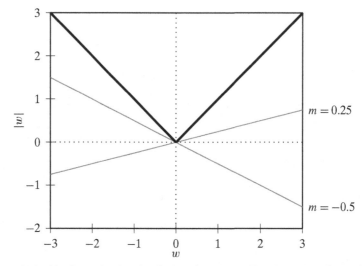

Figure 23.9. Absolute value function (in black) and two of its subgradients (in gray).

w_i, they may remain small but still non-zero. On the other hand, L_1 regression can drive the coefficients to zero, resulting in a more interpretable model, especially when there are many predictor attributes.

The Lasso objective comprises two parts, the squared error term $\|\overline{Y} - \overline{\mathbf{D}}\mathbf{w}\|^2$ which is convex and differentiable, and the L_1 penalty term $\alpha \cdot \|\mathbf{w}\|_1 = \alpha \sum_{i=1}^{d} |w_i|$, which is convex but unfortunately non-differentiable at $w_i = 0$. This means that we cannot simply compute the gradient and set it to zero, as we did in the case of ridge regression. However, these kinds of problems can be solved via the generalized approach of *subgradients*.

23.6.1 Subgradients and Subdifferential

Consider the absolute value function $f : \mathbb{R} \to \mathbb{R}$

$$f(w) = |w|$$

which is plotted in Figure 23.9 (black line).

When $w > 0$, we can see that its derivative is $f'(w) = +1$, and when $w < 0$, its derivative is $f'(w) = -1$. On the other hand, there is a discontinuity at $w = 0$ where the derivative does not exist.

However, we use the concept of a *subgradient* that generalizes the notion of a derivative. For the absolute value function, the slope m of any line that passes through $w = 0$ that remains below or touches the graph of f is called a subgradient of f at $w = 0$. Figure 23.9 shows two such subgradients, namely the slopes $m = -0.5$ and $m = 0.25$. The corresponding lines are shown in gray. The set of all the subgradients at w is called the *subdifferential*, denoted as $\partial|w|$. Thus, the subdifferential at $w = 0$ is given as

$$\partial|w| = [-1, 1]$$

since only lines with slope between -1 and $+1$ remain below or (partially) coincide with the absolute value graph.

Considering all the cases, the subdifferential for the absolute value function is given as:

$$\partial|w| = \begin{cases} 1 & \text{iff } w > 0 \\ -1 & \text{iff } w < 0 \\ [-1, 1] & \text{iff } w = 0 \end{cases} \tag{23.44}$$

We can see that when the derivative exists, the subdifferential is unique and corresponds to the derivative (or gradient), and when the derivative does not exist the subdifferential corresponds to a set of subgradients.

23.6.2 Bivariate L_1 Regression

We first consider bivariate L_1 regression, where we have a single independent attribute $\bar{X}$ and a response attribute $\bar{Y}$ (both centered). The bivariate regression model is given as

$$\hat{y}_i = w \cdot \bar{x}_i$$

The Lasso objective from Eq. (23.43) can then be written as

$$\boxed{\min_w J(w) = \frac{1}{2} \sum_{i=1}^{n} (\bar{y}_i - w \cdot \bar{x}_i)^2 + \alpha \cdot |w|} \tag{23.45}$$

We can compute the subdifferential of this objective as follows:

$$\partial J(w) = \frac{1}{2} \cdot \sum_{i=1}^{n} 2 \cdot (\bar{y}_i - w \cdot \bar{x}_i) \cdot (-\bar{x}_i) + \alpha \cdot \partial|w|$$

$$= -\sum_{i=1}^{n} \bar{x}_i \cdot \bar{y}_i + w \cdot \sum_{i=1}^{n} \bar{x}_i^2 + \alpha \cdot \partial|w|$$

$$= -\bar{X}^T\bar{Y} + w \cdot \|\bar{X}\|^2 + \alpha \cdot \partial|w| \tag{23.46}$$

We can solve for w by setting the subdifferential to zero; we get

$$\partial J(w) = 0$$

$$\implies w \cdot \|\bar{X}\|^2 + \alpha \cdot \partial|w| = \bar{X}^T\bar{Y}$$

$$\implies w + \eta \cdot \alpha \cdot \partial|w| = \eta \cdot \bar{X}^T\bar{Y}$$

where $\eta = 1/\|\bar{X}\|^2 > 0$ is a scaling constant.

Corresponding to the three cases for the subdifferential of the absolute value function in Eq. (23.44), we have three cases to consider:

Case I ($w > 0$ and $\partial|w| = 1$): In this case we get

$$w = \eta \cdot \bar{X}^T\bar{Y} - \eta \cdot \alpha$$

Since $w > 0$, this implies $\eta \cdot \bar{X}^T\bar{Y} > \eta \cdot \alpha$ or $\left|\eta \cdot \bar{X}^T\bar{Y}\right| > \eta \cdot \alpha$.

Case II ($w < 0$ and $\partial|w| = -1$): In this case we have

$$w = \eta \cdot \overline{X}^T\overline{Y} + \eta \cdot \alpha$$

Since $w < 0$, this implies $\eta \cdot \overline{X}^T\overline{Y} < -\eta \cdot \alpha$ or $\left|\eta \cdot \overline{X}^T\overline{Y}\right| > \eta \cdot \alpha$.

Case III ($w = 0$ and $\partial|w| \in [-1, 1]$): In this case, we get

$$w \in \left[\eta \cdot \overline{X}^T\overline{Y} - \eta \cdot \alpha, \; \eta \cdot \overline{X}^T\overline{Y} + \eta \cdot \alpha\right]$$

However, since $w = 0$, this implies $\eta \cdot \overline{X}^T\overline{Y} - \eta \cdot \alpha \leq 0$ and $\eta \cdot \overline{X}^T\overline{Y} + \eta \cdot \alpha \geq 0$. In other words, $\eta \cdot \overline{X}^T\overline{Y} \leq \eta \cdot \alpha$ and $\eta \cdot \overline{X}^T\overline{Y} \geq -\eta \cdot \alpha$. Therefore, $\left|\eta \cdot \overline{X}^T\overline{Y}\right| \leq \eta \cdot \alpha$.

Let $\tau \geq 0$ be some fixed value. Define the *soft-threshold* function $\mathcal{S}_\tau : \mathbb{R} \to \mathbb{R}$ as follows:

$$\mathcal{S}_\tau(z) = \text{sign}(z) \cdot \max\left\{0, \left(|z| - \tau\right)\right\} \tag{23.47}$$

Then the above three cases can be written compactly as:

$$\boxed{w = \mathcal{S}_{\eta \cdot \alpha}(\eta \cdot \overline{X}^T\overline{Y})} \tag{23.48}$$

with $\tau = \eta \cdot \alpha$, where w is the optimal solution to the bivariate L_1 regression problem in Eq. (23.45).

23.6.3 Multiple L_1 Regression

Consider the L_1 regression objective from Eq. (23.43)

$$\min_{\mathbf{w}} \; J(\mathbf{w}) = \frac{1}{2} \cdot \left\|\overline{Y} - \sum_{i=1}^{d} w_i \cdot \overline{X}_i\right\|^2 + \alpha \cdot \|\mathbf{w}\|_1$$

$$= \frac{1}{2} \cdot \left(\overline{Y}^T\overline{Y} - 2\sum_{i=1}^{d} w_i \cdot \overline{X}_i^T\overline{Y} + \sum_{i=1}^{d}\sum_{j=1}^{d} w_i \cdot w_j \cdot \overline{X}_i^T\overline{X}_j\right) + \alpha \cdot \sum_{i=1}^{d} |w_i|$$

We generalize the bivariate solution to the multiple L_1 formulation by optimizing for each w_k individually, via the approach of *cyclical coordinate descent*. We rewrite the L_1 objective by focusing only on the w_k terms, and ignoring all terms not involving w_k, which are assumed to be fixed:

$$\min_{w_k} \; J(w_k) = -w_k \cdot \overline{X}_k^T\overline{Y} + \frac{1}{2}w_k^2 \cdot \|\overline{X}_k\|^2 + w_k \cdot \sum_{j \neq k}^{d} w_j \cdot \overline{X}_k^T\overline{X}_j + \alpha \cdot |w_k| \tag{23.49}$$

Setting the subdifferential of $J(w_k)$ to zero, we get

$$\partial J(w_k) = 0$$

$$\implies w_k \cdot \|\bar{X}_k\|^2 + \alpha \cdot \partial|w_k| = \bar{X}_k^T \bar{Y} - \sum_{j \neq k}^d w_j \cdot \bar{X}_k^T \bar{X}_j$$

$$\implies w_k \cdot \|\bar{X}_k\|^2 + \alpha \cdot \partial|w_k| = \bar{X}_k^T \bar{Y} - \sum_{j=1}^d w_j \cdot \bar{X}_k^T \bar{X}_j + w_k \bar{X}_k^T \bar{X}_k$$

$$\implies w_k \cdot \|\bar{X}_k\|^2 + \alpha \cdot \partial|w_k| = w_k \|\bar{X}_k^T\|^2 + \bar{X}_k^T \left(\bar{Y} - \mathbf{D}\mathbf{w} \right)$$

We can interpret the above equation as specifying an iterative solution for w_k. In essence, we let the w_k on the left hand side be the new estimate for w_k, whereas we treat the w_k on the right hand side as the previous estimate. More concretely, let $\mathbf{w}^t$ represent the weight vector at step t, with w_k^t denoting the estimate for w_k at time t. The new estimate for w_k at step $t+1$ is then given as

$$w_k^{t+1} + \frac{1}{\|\bar{X}_k\|^2} \cdot \alpha \cdot \partial|w_k^{t+1}| = w_k^t + \frac{1}{\|\bar{X}_k\|^2} \cdot \bar{X}_k^T \left(\bar{Y} - \mathbf{D}\mathbf{w}^t \right)$$

$$w_k^{t+1} + \eta \cdot \alpha \cdot \partial|w_k^{t+1}| = w_k^t + \eta \cdot \bar{X}_k^T \left(Y - \mathbf{D}\mathbf{w}^t \right) \tag{23.50}$$

where $\eta = 1/\|\bar{X}_k\|^2 > 0$ is just a scaling constant. Based on the three cases for w_k^{t+1} and the subdifferential $\partial|w_k^{t+1}|$, following a similar approach as in the bivariate case [Eq. (23.48)], the new estimate for w_k can be written compactly as

$$\boxed{w_k^{t+1} = \mathcal{S}_{\eta \cdot \alpha} \left(w_k^t + \eta \cdot \bar{X}_k^T \left(\bar{Y} - \mathbf{D}\mathbf{w}^t \right) \right)} \tag{23.51}$$

The pseudo-code for L_1 regression is shown in Algorithm 23.5. The algorithm starts with a random estimate for $\mathbf{w}$ at step $t = 0$, and then cycles through each dimension to estimate w_k until convergence. Interestingly, the term $-\bar{X}_k^T(\bar{Y} - \mathbf{D}\mathbf{w}^t)$ is in fact the gradient at w_k of the squared error term in the Lasso objective, and thus the update equation is the same as gradient descent with step size η, followed by the soft-threshold operator. Note also that since η is just a positive scaling constant, we make it a parameter of the algorithm, denoting the step size for gradient descent.

Example 23.11 (L_1 Regression). We apply L_1 regression to the full Iris dataset with $n = 150$ points, and four independent attributes, namely sepal-width (X_1), sepal-length (X_2), petal-width (X_3), and petal-length (X_4). The Iris type attribute comprises the response variable Y. There are three Iris types, namely Iris-setosa, Iris-versicolor, and Iris-virginica, which are coded as 0, 1 and 2, respectively.

Algorithm 23.5: L_1 Regression Algorithm: Lasso

L_1-**REGRESSION** $(\mathbf{D}, Y, \alpha, \eta, \epsilon)$:

1 $\mu \leftarrow \text{mean}(\mathbf{D})$ // compute mean
2 $\overline{\mathbf{D}} \leftarrow \mathbf{D} - \mathbf{1} \cdot \mu^T$ // center the data
3 $\overline{Y} \leftarrow Y - \mu_Y \cdot \mathbf{1}$ // center the response
4 $t \leftarrow 0$ // step/iteration counter
5 $\mathbf{w}^t \leftarrow$ random vector in $\mathbb{R}^d$ // initial weight vector
6 **repeat**
7 $\quad$ **foreach** $k = 1, 2, \cdots, d$ **do**
8 $\quad\quad$ $\nabla(w_k^t) \leftarrow -\overline{X}_k^T(Y - \overline{\mathbf{D}}\mathbf{w}^t)$ // compute gradient at w_k
9 $\quad\quad$ $w_k^{t+1} \leftarrow w_k^t - \eta \cdot \nabla(w_k^t)$ // update estimate for w_k
10 $\quad\quad$ $w_k^{t+1} \leftarrow \mathcal{S}_{\eta \cdot \alpha}(w_k^{t+1})$ // apply soft-threshold function
11 $\quad$ $t \leftarrow t + 1$
12 **until** $\|\mathbf{w}^t - \mathbf{w}^{t-1}\| \leq \epsilon$
13 $b \leftarrow \mu_Y - (\mathbf{w}^t)^T \mu$ // compute the bias term

---

The L_1 regression estimates for different values of α (with $\eta = 0.0001$) are shown below:

$\alpha = 0:$ $\widehat{Y} = 0.192 - 0.109 \cdot X_1 - 0.045 \cdot X_2 + 0.226 \cdot X_3 + 0.612 \cdot X_4$ $\quad SSE = 6.96$

$\alpha = 1:$ $\widehat{Y} = -0.077 - 0.076 \cdot X_1 - 0.015 \cdot X_2 + 0.253 \cdot X_3 + 0.516 \cdot X_4$ $\quad SSE = 7.09$

$\alpha = 5:$ $\widehat{Y} = -0.553 + 0.0 \cdot X_1 + 0.0 \cdot X_2 + 0.359 \cdot X_3 + 0.170 \cdot X_4$ $\quad SSE = 8.82$

$\alpha = 10:$ $\widehat{Y} = -0.575 + 0.0 \cdot X_1 + 0.0 \cdot X_2 + 0.419 \cdot X_3 + 0.0 \cdot X_4$ $\quad SSE = 10.15$

The L_1 norm values for the weight vectors (excluding the bias term) are 0.992, 0.86, 0.529, and 0.419, respectively. It is interesting to note the sparsity inducing effect of Lasso, as observed for $\alpha = 5$ and $\alpha = 10$, which drives some of the regression coefficients to zero.

We can contrast the coefficients for L_2 (ridge) and L_1 (Lasso) regression by comparing models with the same level of squared error. For example, for $\alpha = 5$, the L_1 model has $SSE = 8.82$. We adjust the ridge value in L_2 regression, with $\alpha = 35$ resulting in a similar SSE value. The two models are given as follows:

$L_1:$ $\widehat{Y} = -0.553 + 0.0 \cdot X_1 + 0.0 \cdot X_2 + 0.359 \cdot X_3 + 0.170 \cdot X_4$ $\quad \|\mathbf{w}\|_1 = 0.529$

$L_2:$ $\widehat{Y} = -0.394 + 0.019 \cdot X_1 - 0.051 \cdot X_2 + 0.316 \cdot X_3 + 0.212 \cdot X_4$ $\quad \|\mathbf{w}\|_1 = 0.598$

where we exclude the bias term when computing the L_1 norm for the weights. We can observe that for L_2 regression the coefficients for X_1 and X_2 are small, and therefore less important, but they are not zero. On the other hand, for L_1 regression, the coefficients for attributes X_1 and X_2 are exactly zero, leaving only X_3 and X_4; Lasso can thus act as an automatic feature selection approach.

23.7 FURTHER READING

For a geometrical approach to multivariate statistics see Wickens (2014), and Saville and Wood (2012). For a description of the class of generalized linear models, of which linear regression is a special case, see Agresti (2015). An excellent overview of Lasso and sparsity based methods is given in Hastie, Tibshirani, and Wainwright (2015). For a description of cyclical coordinate descent for L_1 regression, and also other approaches for sparse statistical models see Hastie, Tibshirani, and Wainwright (2015).

Agresti, A. (2015). *Foundations of Linear and Generalized Linear Models*. Hoboken, NJ: John Wiley & Sons.

Hastie, T., Tibshirani, R., and Wainwright, M. (2015). *Statistical Learning with Sparsity: The Lasso and Generalizations*. Boca Raton, FL: CRC press.

Saville, D. J. and Wood, G. R. (2012). *Statistical Methods: The Geometric Approach*. New York: Springer Science + Business Media.

Wickens, T. D. (2014). *The Geometry of Multivariate Statistics*. New York: Psychology Press, Taylor & Francis Group.

23.8 EXERCISES

Q1. Consider the data in Table 23.1, with Y as the response variable and X as the independent variable. Answer the following questions:

   (a) Compute the predicted response vector $\widehat{Y}$ for least square regression using the geometric approach.

   (b) Based on the geometric approach extract the value of the bias and slope, and give the equation of the best fitting regression line.

Table 23.1. Data for Q1

X	Y
5	2
0	1
2	1
1	1
2	0

Q2. Given data in Table 23.2, let $\alpha = 0.5$ be the regularization constant. Compute the equation for ridge regression of Y on X, where both the bias and slope are penalized. Use the fact that the inverse of the matrix $\mathbf{A} = \begin{pmatrix} a & b \\ c & d \end{pmatrix}$ is given as

$$\mathbf{A}^{-1} = \tfrac{1}{\det(\mathbf{A})} \begin{pmatrix} d & -b \\ -c & a \end{pmatrix}, \text{ with } \det(\mathbf{A}) = ad - bc.$$

Table 23.2. Data for Q2

X	Y
1	1
2	3
4	4
6	3

Q3. Show that Eq. (23.11) holds, that is

$$w = \frac{\left(\sum_{i=1}^{n} x_i \cdot y_i\right) - n \cdot \mu_X \cdot \mu_Y}{\left(\sum_{i=1}^{n} x_i^2\right) - n \cdot \mu_X^2} = \frac{\sum_{i=1}^{n}(x_i - \mu_X)(y_i - \mu_Y)}{\sum_{i=1}^{n}(x_i - \mu_X)^2}$$

Q4. Derive an expression for the bias term b and the weights $\mathbf{w} = (w_1, w_2, \cdots, w_d)^T$ in multiple regression using Eq. (23.16), without adding the augmented column.

Q5. Show analytically (i.e., without using the geometry) that the bias term in multiple regression, as shown in Eq. (23.26), is given as

$$w_0 = \mu_Y - w_1 \cdot \mu_{X_1} - w_2 \cdot \mu_{X_2} - \cdots - w_d \cdot \mu_{X_d}$$

Q6. Show that $\widehat{Y}^T \epsilon = 0$.

Q7. Prove that $\|\epsilon\|^2 = \|Y\|^2 - \|\widehat{Y}\|^2$.

Q8. Show that if λ_i is an eigenvalue of $\mathbf{D}^T\mathbf{D}$ corresponding to the eigenvector $\mathbf{u}_i$, then $\lambda_i + \alpha$ is an eigenvalue of $(\mathbf{D}^T\mathbf{D} + \alpha \cdot \mathbf{I})$ for the same eigenvector $\mathbf{u}_i$.

Q9. Show that $\mathbf{\Delta}^{-1}\mathbf{Q}^T Y$ gives the vector of scalar projections of Y onto each of the orthogonal basis vectors in multiple regression

$$\mathbf{\Delta}^{-1}\mathbf{Q}^T Y = \begin{pmatrix} \mathrm{proj}_{U_0}(Y) \\ \mathrm{proj}_{U_1}(Y) \\ \vdots \\ \mathrm{proj}_{U_d}(Y) \end{pmatrix}$$

Q10. Formulate a solution to the ridge regression problem via QR-factorization.

Q11. Derive the solution for the weight vector $\mathbf{w} = (w_1, w_2, \cdots, w_d)^T$ and bias $b = w_0$ in ridge regression without subtracting the means from Y and the independent attributes $X_1, X_2, \cdots, X_d$, and without adding the augmented column.

Q12. Show that the solution for ridge regression and kernel ridge regression are exactly the same when we use a linear kernel.

Q13. Show that $w = \mathcal{S}_{\eta \cdot \alpha}(\eta \cdot \overline{X}^T \overline{Y})$ [Eq. (23.48)] is the solution for bivariate L_1 regression.

Q14. Derive the three cases for the subdifferential in Eq. (23.50), and show that they correspond to the soft-threshold update in Eq. (23.51).

Q15. Show that that the gradient at w_k of the SSE term in the L_1 formulation is given as

$$\nabla(w_k) = \frac{\partial}{\partial w_k} \frac{1}{2} \cdot \|\overline{Y} - \overline{\mathbf{D}}\mathbf{w}\|^2 = -\overline{X}_k^T(\overline{Y} - \overline{\mathbf{D}}\mathbf{w})$$

where Y is the response vector, and X_k is the kth predictor vector.

CHAPTER 24

Logistic Regression

Given a set of predictor attributes or independent variables $X_1, X_2, \cdots, X_d$, and given a *categorical* response or dependent variable Y, the aim of *logistic regression* is to predict the probability of the response variable values based on the independent variables. Logistic regression is in fact a classification technique, that given a point $\mathbf{x}_j \in \mathbb{R}^d$ predicts $P(c_i|\mathbf{x}_j)$ for each class c_i in the domain of Y (the set of possible classes or values for the response variable). In this chapter, we first consider the binary class problem, where the response variable takes on one of two classes (0 and 1, or positive and negative, and so on). Next, we consider the multiclass case, where there are K classes for the response variable.

24.1 BINARY LOGISTIC REGRESSION

In logistic regression, we are given a set of d predictor or independent variables $X_1, X_2, \cdots, X_d$, and a *binary* or *Bernoulli* response variable Y that takes on only two values, namely, 0 and 1. Thus, we are given a training dataset $\mathbf{D}$ comprising n points $\mathbf{x}_i \in \mathbb{R}^d$ and the corresponding observed values $y_i \in \{0, 1\}$. As done in Chapter 23, we augment the data matrix $\mathbf{D}$ by adding a new attribute X_0 that is always fixed at the value 1 for each point, so that $\tilde{\mathbf{x}}_i = (1, x_1, x_2, \cdots, x_d)^T \in \mathbb{R}^{d+1}$ denotes the augmented point, and the multivariate random vector $\tilde{\mathbf{X}}$, comprising all the independent attributes is given as $\tilde{\mathbf{X}} = (X_0, X_1, \cdots, X_d)^T$. The augmented training dataset is given as $\tilde{\mathbf{D}}$ comprising the n augmented points $\tilde{\mathbf{x}}_i$ along with the class labels y_i for $i = 1, 2, \cdots, n$.

Since there are only two outcomes for the response variable Y, its probability mass function for $\tilde{\mathbf{X}} = \tilde{\mathbf{x}}$ is given as:

$$P(Y = 1|\tilde{\mathbf{X}} = \tilde{\mathbf{x}}) = \pi(\tilde{\mathbf{x}}) \qquad P(Y = 0|\tilde{\mathbf{X}} = \tilde{\mathbf{x}}) = 1 - \pi(\tilde{\mathbf{x}})$$

where $\pi(\tilde{\mathbf{x}})$ is the unknown true parameter value, denoting the probability of $Y = 1$ given $\tilde{\mathbf{X}} = \tilde{\mathbf{x}}$. Further, note that the expected value of Y given $\tilde{\mathbf{X}} = \tilde{\mathbf{x}}$ is

$$E[Y|\tilde{\mathbf{X}} = \tilde{\mathbf{x}}] = 1 \cdot P(Y = 1|\tilde{\mathbf{X}} = \tilde{\mathbf{x}}) + 0 \cdot P(Y = 0|\tilde{\mathbf{X}} = \tilde{\mathbf{x}})$$

$$= P(Y = 1|\tilde{\mathbf{X}} - \tilde{\mathbf{x}}) = \pi(\tilde{\mathbf{x}})$$

Therefore, in logistic regression, instead of directly predicting the response value, the goal is to learn the probability, $P(Y = 1|\tilde{\mathbf{X}} = \tilde{\mathbf{x}})$, which is also the expected value of Y given $\tilde{\mathbf{X}} = \tilde{\mathbf{x}}$.

Since $P(Y = 1|\tilde{\mathbf{X}} = \tilde{\mathbf{x}})$ is a probability, it is not appropriate to directly use the linear regression model

$$f(\tilde{\mathbf{x}}) = \omega_0 \cdot x_0 + \omega_1 \cdot x_1 + \omega_2 \cdot x_2 + \cdots + \omega_d \cdot x_d = \tilde{\boldsymbol{\omega}}^T \tilde{\mathbf{x}}$$

where $\tilde{\boldsymbol{\omega}} = (\omega_0, \omega_1, \cdots, \omega_d)^T \in \mathbb{R}^{d+1}$ is the true augmented weight vector, with $\omega_0 = \beta$ the true unknown bias term, and ω_i the true unknown regression coefficient or weight for attribute X_i. The reason we cannot simply use $P(Y = 1|\tilde{\mathbf{X}} = \tilde{\mathbf{x}}) = f(\tilde{\mathbf{x}})$ is due to the fact that $f(\tilde{\mathbf{x}})$ can be arbitrarily large or arbitrarily small, whereas for logistic regression, we require that the output represents a probability value, and thus we need a model that results in an output that lies in the interval $[0, 1]$. The name "logistic regression" comes from the *logistic* function (also called the *sigmoid* function) that meets this requirement. It is defined as follows:

$$\theta(z) = \frac{1}{1 + \exp\{-z\}} = \frac{\exp\{z\}}{1 + \exp\{z\}} \tag{24.1}$$

The logistic function "squashes" the output to be between 0 and 1 for any scalar input z (see Figure 24.1). The output $\theta(z)$ can therefore be interpreted as a probability.

Example 24.1 (Logistic Function). Figure 24.1 shows the plot for the logistic function for z ranging from $-\infty$ to $+\infty$. In particular consider what happens when z is $-\infty, +\infty$ and 0; we have

$$\theta(-\infty) = \frac{1}{1 + \exp\{\infty\}} = \frac{1}{\infty} = 0$$

$$\theta(+\infty) = \frac{1}{1 + \exp\{-\infty\}} = \frac{1}{1} = 1$$

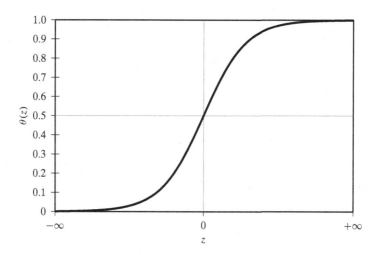

Figure 24.1. Logistic function.

$$\theta(0) = \frac{1}{1 + \exp\{0\}} = \frac{1}{2} = 0.5$$

As desired, $\theta(z)$ lies in the range $[0, 1]$, and $z = 0$ is the "threshold" value in the sense that for $z > 0$ we have $\theta(z) > 0.5$, and for $z < 0$, we have $\theta(z) < 0.5$. Thus, interpreting $\theta(z)$ as a probability, the larger the z value, the higher the probability.

Another interesting property of the logistic function is that

$$1 - \theta(z) = 1 - \frac{\exp\{z\}}{1 + \exp\{z\}} = \frac{1 + \exp\{z\} - \exp\{z\}}{1 + \exp\{z\}} = \frac{1}{1 + \exp\{z\}} = \theta(-z) \quad (24.2)$$

Using the logistic function, we define the logistic regression model as follows:

$$P(Y = 1 | \tilde{\mathbf{X}} = \tilde{\mathbf{x}}) = \pi(\tilde{\mathbf{x}}) = \theta(f(\tilde{\mathbf{x}})) = \theta(\tilde{\omega}^T \tilde{\mathbf{x}}) = \frac{\exp\{\tilde{\omega}^T \tilde{\mathbf{x}}\}}{1 + \exp\{\tilde{\omega}^T \tilde{\mathbf{x}}\}} \quad (24.3)$$

Thus, the probability that the response is $Y = 1$ is the output of the logistic function for the input $\tilde{\omega}^T \tilde{\mathbf{x}}$. On the other hand, the probability for $Y = 0$ is given as

$$P(Y = 0 | \tilde{\mathbf{X}} = \tilde{\mathbf{x}}) = 1 - P(Y = 1 | \tilde{\mathbf{X}} = \tilde{\mathbf{x}}) = \theta(-\tilde{\omega}^T \tilde{\mathbf{x}}) = \frac{1}{1 + \exp\{\tilde{\omega}^T \tilde{\mathbf{x}}\}}$$

where we used Eq. (24.2), that is, $1 - \theta(z) = \theta(-z)$ for $z = \tilde{\omega}^T \tilde{\mathbf{x}}$.

Combining these two cases the full logistic regression model is given as

$$\boxed{P(Y | \tilde{\mathbf{X}} = \tilde{\mathbf{x}}) = \theta(\tilde{\omega}^T \tilde{\mathbf{x}})^Y \cdot \theta(-\tilde{\omega}^T \tilde{\mathbf{x}})^{1-Y}} \quad (24.4)$$

since Y is a Bernoulli random variable that takes on either the value 1 or 0. We can observe that $P(Y | \tilde{\mathbf{X}} = \tilde{\mathbf{x}}) = \theta(\tilde{\omega}^T \tilde{\mathbf{x}})$ when $Y = 1$ and $P(Y | \tilde{\mathbf{X}} = \tilde{\mathbf{x}}) = \theta(-\tilde{\omega}^T \tilde{\mathbf{x}})$ when $Y = 0$, as desired.

Log-Odds Ratio   Define the *odds ratio* for the occurrence of $Y = 1$ as follows:

$$\text{odds}(Y = 1 | \tilde{\mathbf{X}} = \tilde{\mathbf{x}}) = \frac{P(Y = 1 | \tilde{\mathbf{X}} = \tilde{\mathbf{x}})}{P(Y = 0 | \tilde{\mathbf{X}} = \tilde{\mathbf{x}})} = \frac{\theta(\tilde{\omega}^T \tilde{\mathbf{x}})}{\theta(-\tilde{\omega}^T \tilde{\mathbf{x}})}$$

$$= \frac{\exp\{\tilde{\omega}^T \tilde{\mathbf{x}}\}}{1 + \exp\{\tilde{\omega}^T \tilde{\mathbf{x}}\}} \cdot \left(1 + \exp\{\tilde{\omega}^T \tilde{\mathbf{x}}\}\right)$$

$$= \boxed{\exp\{\tilde{\omega}^T \tilde{\mathbf{x}}\}} \quad (24.5)$$

The logarithm of the odds ratio, called the *log-odds ratio*, is therefore given as:

$$\ln\left(\text{odds}(Y = 1 | \tilde{\mathbf{X}} = \tilde{\mathbf{x}})\right) = \ln\left(\frac{P(Y = 1 | \tilde{\mathbf{X}} = \tilde{\mathbf{x}})}{1 - P(Y = 1 | \tilde{\mathbf{X}} = \tilde{\mathbf{x}})}\right) = \ln\left(\exp\{\tilde{\omega}^T \tilde{\mathbf{x}}\}\right) = \tilde{\omega}^T \tilde{\mathbf{x}}$$

$$= \omega_0 \cdot x_0 + \omega_1 \cdot x_1 + \cdots + \omega_d \cdot x_d \quad (24.6)$$

The log-odds ratio function is also called the *logit* function, defined as

$$\text{logit}(z) = \ln\left(\frac{z}{1-z}\right)$$

It is the inverse of the logistic function. We can see that

$$\ln\big(\text{odds}(Y = 1|\tilde{\mathbf{X}} = \tilde{\mathbf{x}})\big) = \text{logit}\big(P(Y = 1|\tilde{\mathbf{X}} = \tilde{\mathbf{x}})\big)$$

The logistic regression model is therefore based on the assumption that the log-odds ratio for $Y = 1$ given $\tilde{\mathbf{X}} = \tilde{\mathbf{x}}$ is a linear function (or a weighted sum) of the independent attributes. In particular, let us consider the effect of attribute X_i by fixing the values for all other attributes in Eq. (24.6); we get

$$\ln(\text{odds}(Y = 1|\tilde{\mathbf{X}} = \tilde{\mathbf{x}})) = \omega_i \cdot x_i + C$$

$$\Longrightarrow \text{odds}(Y = 1|\tilde{\mathbf{X}} = \tilde{\mathbf{x}}) = \exp\{\omega_i \cdot x_i + C\} = \exp\{\omega_i \cdot x_i\} \cdot \exp\{C\} \propto \exp\{\omega_i \cdot x_i\}$$

where C is a constant comprising the fixed attributes. The regression coefficient ω_i can therefore be interpreted as the change in the log-odds ratio for $Y = 1$ for a unit change in X_i, or equivalently the odds ratio for $Y = 1$ increases exponentially per unit change in X_i.

24.1.1 Maximum Likelihood Estimation

Let $\tilde{\mathbf{D}}$ be the augmented training dataset comprising the n augmented points $\tilde{\mathbf{x}}_i$ along with their labels y_i. Let $\tilde{\mathbf{w}} = (w_0, w_1, \cdots, w_d)^T$ be the augmented weight vector for estimating $\tilde{\omega}$. Note that $w_0 = b$ denotes the estimated bias term, and w_i the estimated weight for attribute X_i. We will use the maximum likelihood approach to learn the weight vector $\tilde{\mathbf{w}}$. *Likelihood* is defined as the probability of the observed data given the estimated parameters $\tilde{\mathbf{w}}$. We assume that the binary response variables y_i are all independent. Therefore, the likelihood of the observed responses is given as

$$L(\tilde{\mathbf{w}}) = P(Y|\tilde{\mathbf{w}}) = \prod_{i=1}^{n} P(y_i|\tilde{\mathbf{x}}_i) = \prod_{i=1}^{n} \theta(\tilde{\mathbf{w}}^T\tilde{\mathbf{x}}_i)^{y_i} \cdot \theta(-\tilde{\mathbf{w}}^T\tilde{\mathbf{x}}_i)^{1-y_i}$$

Instead of trying to maximize the likelihood, we can maximize the logarithm of the likelihood, called *log-likelihood*, to convert the product into a summation as follows:

$$\ln\big(L(\tilde{\mathbf{w}})\big) = \sum_{i=1}^{n} y_i \cdot \ln\big(\theta(\tilde{\mathbf{w}}^T\tilde{\mathbf{x}}_i)\big) + (1 - y_i) \cdot \ln\big(\theta(-\tilde{\mathbf{w}}^T\tilde{\mathbf{x}}_i)\big) \qquad (24.7)$$

The negative of the log-likelihood can also be considered as an error function, the *cross-entropy error function*, given as follows:

$$E(\tilde{\mathbf{w}}) = -\ln\big(L(\tilde{\mathbf{w}})\big) = \sum_{i=1}^{n} y_i \cdot \ln\left(\frac{1}{\theta(\tilde{\mathbf{w}}^T\tilde{\mathbf{x}}_i)}\right) + (1 - y_i) \cdot \ln\left(\frac{1}{1 - \theta(\tilde{\mathbf{w}}^T\tilde{\mathbf{x}}_i)}\right) \qquad (24.8)$$

The task of maximizing the log-likelihood is therefore equivalent to minimizing the cross-entropy error.

Typically, to obtain the optimal weight vector $\tilde{\mathbf{w}}$, we would differentiate the log-likelihood function with respect to $\tilde{\mathbf{w}}$, set the result to $\mathbf{0}$, and then solve for $\tilde{\mathbf{w}}$. However, for the log-likelihood formulation in Eq. (24.7) there is no closed form solution to compute the weight vector $\tilde{\mathbf{w}}$. Instead, we use an iterative *gradient ascent* method to compute the optimal value, since Eq. (24.7) is a concave function, and has a unique global optimal.

The gradient ascent method relies on the gradient of the log-likelihood function, which can be obtained by taking its partial derivative with respect to $\tilde{\mathbf{w}}$, as follows:

$$\nabla(\tilde{\mathbf{w}}) = \frac{\partial}{\partial\tilde{\mathbf{w}}}\Big\{\ln\big(L(\tilde{\mathbf{w}})\big)\Big\} = \frac{\partial}{\partial\tilde{\mathbf{w}}}\Big\{\sum_{i=1}^{n} y_i\cdot\ln\big(\theta(z_i)\big) + (1-y_i)\cdot\ln\big(\theta(-z_i)\big)\Big\} \quad (24.9)$$

where $z_i = \tilde{\mathbf{w}}^T\tilde{\mathbf{x}}_i$. We use the chain rule to obtain the derivative of $\ln(\theta(z_i))$ with respect to $\tilde{\mathbf{w}}$. We note the following facts:

$$\frac{\partial}{\partial\theta(z_i)}\Big\{\ln\big(\theta(z_i)\big)\Big\} = \frac{1}{\theta(z_i)}$$

$$\frac{\partial}{\partial\theta(z_i)}\Big\{\ln\big(\theta(-z_i)\big)\Big\} = \frac{\partial}{\partial\theta(z_i)}\Big\{\ln\big(1-\theta(z_i)\big)\Big\} = \frac{-1}{1-\theta(z_i)}$$

$$\frac{\partial\theta(z_i)}{\partial z_i} = \theta(z_i)\cdot(1-\theta(z_i)) = \theta(z_i)\cdot\theta(-z_i)$$

$$\frac{\partial z_i}{\partial\tilde{\mathbf{w}}} = \frac{\partial\tilde{\mathbf{w}}^T\tilde{\mathbf{x}}_i}{\partial\tilde{\mathbf{w}}} = \tilde{\mathbf{x}}_i$$

As per the chain rule, we have

$$\frac{\partial\ln\big(\theta(z_i)\big)}{\partial\tilde{\mathbf{w}}} = \frac{\partial\ln\big(\theta(z_i)\big)}{\partial\theta(z_i)}\cdot\frac{\partial\theta(z_i)}{\partial z_i}\cdot\frac{\partial z_i}{\partial\tilde{\mathbf{w}}}$$

$$= \frac{1}{\theta(z_i)}\cdot\big(\theta(z_i)\cdot\theta(-z_i)\big)\cdot\tilde{\mathbf{x}}_i = \theta(-z_i)\cdot\tilde{\mathbf{x}}_i \quad (24.10)$$

Likewise, using the chain rule, we have

$$\frac{\partial\ln\big(\theta(-z_i)\big)}{\partial\tilde{\mathbf{w}}} = \frac{\partial\ln\big(\theta(-z_i)\big)}{\partial\theta(z_i)}\cdot\frac{\partial\theta(z_i)}{\partial z_i}\cdot\frac{\partial z_i}{\partial\tilde{\mathbf{w}}}$$

$$= \frac{-1}{1-\theta(z_i)}\cdot\big(\theta(z_i)\cdot(1-\theta(z_i))\big)\cdot\tilde{\mathbf{x}}_i = -\theta(z_i)\cdot\tilde{\mathbf{x}}_i$$

Substituting the above into Eq. (24.9) we get

$$\nabla(\tilde{\mathbf{w}}) = \sum_{i=1}^{n} y_i\cdot\theta(-z_i)\cdot\tilde{\mathbf{x}}_i - (1-y_i)\cdot\theta(z_i)\cdot\tilde{\mathbf{x}}_i$$

$$= \sum_{i=1}^{n} y_i\cdot\big(\theta(-z_i)+\theta(z_i)\big)\cdot\tilde{\mathbf{x}}_i - \theta(z_i)\cdot\tilde{\mathbf{x}}_i$$

$$= \sum_{i=1}^{n}\big(y_i - \theta(z_i)\big)\cdot\tilde{\mathbf{x}}_i, \qquad \text{since } \theta(-z_i)+\theta(z_i) = 1$$

$$= \sum_{i=1}^{n}\big(y_i - \theta(\tilde{\mathbf{w}}^T\tilde{\mathbf{x}}_i)\big)\cdot\tilde{\mathbf{x}}_i \quad (24.11)$$

Algorithm 24.1: Logistic Regression: Stochastic Gradient Ascent

---

$\textsc{LogisticRegression-SGA}$ ($\mathbf{D}, \eta, \epsilon$):

1 **foreach** $\mathbf{x}_i \in \mathbf{D}$ **do** $\tilde{\mathbf{x}}_i^T \leftarrow \begin{pmatrix} 1 & \mathbf{x}_i^T \end{pmatrix}$ // map to $\mathbb{R}^{d+1}$

2 $t \leftarrow 0$ // step/iteration counter

3 $\tilde{\mathbf{w}}^0 \leftarrow (0, \ldots, 0)^T \in \mathbb{R}^{d+1}$ // initial weight vector

4 **repeat**

5 $\quad$ $\tilde{\mathbf{w}} \leftarrow \tilde{\mathbf{w}}^t$ // make a copy of $\tilde{\mathbf{w}}^t$

6 $\quad$ **foreach** $\tilde{\mathbf{x}}_i \in \tilde{\mathbf{D}}$ *in random order* **do**

7 $\quad\quad$ $\nabla(\tilde{\mathbf{w}}, \tilde{\mathbf{x}}_i) \leftarrow \left(y_i - \theta(\tilde{\mathbf{w}}^T \tilde{\mathbf{x}}_i)\right) \cdot \tilde{\mathbf{x}}_i$ // compute gradient at $\tilde{\mathbf{x}}_i$

8 $\quad\quad$ $\tilde{\mathbf{w}} \leftarrow \tilde{\mathbf{w}} + \eta \cdot \nabla(\tilde{\mathbf{w}}, \tilde{\mathbf{x}}_i)$ // update estimate for $\tilde{\mathbf{w}}$

9 $\quad$ $\tilde{\mathbf{w}}^{t+1} \leftarrow \tilde{\mathbf{w}}$ // update $\tilde{\mathbf{w}}^{t+1}$

10 $\quad$ $t \leftarrow t + 1$

11 **until** $\|\tilde{\mathbf{w}}^t - \tilde{\mathbf{w}}^{t-1}\| \leq \epsilon$

The gradient ascent method starts at some initial estimate for $\tilde{\mathbf{w}}$, denoted $\tilde{\mathbf{w}}^0$. At each step t, the method moves in the direction of steepest ascent, which is given by the gradient vector. Thus, given the current estimate $\tilde{\mathbf{w}}^t$, we can obtain the next estimate as follows:

$$\tilde{\mathbf{w}}^{t+1} = \tilde{\mathbf{w}}^t + \eta \cdot \nabla(\tilde{\mathbf{w}}^t) \tag{24.12}$$

Here, $\eta > 0$ is a user-specified parameter called the *learning rate*. It should not be too large, otherwise the estimates will vary wildly from one iteration to the next, and it should not be too small, otherwise it will take a long time to converge. At the optimal value of $\tilde{\mathbf{w}}$, the gradient will be zero, i.e., $\nabla(\tilde{\mathbf{w}}) = \mathbf{0}$, as desired.

Stochastic Gradient Ascent

The gradient ascent method computes the gradient by considering all the data points, and it is therefore called *batch* gradient ascent. For large datasets, it is typically much faster to compute the gradient by considering only one (randomly chosen) point at a time. The weight vector is updated after each such partial gradient step, giving rise to *stochastic gradient ascent* (SGA) for computing the optimal weight vector $\tilde{\mathbf{w}}$.

The pseudo-code for SGA based logistic regression is shown in Algorithm 24.1. Given a randomly chosen point $\tilde{\mathbf{x}}_i$, the point-specific gradient (see Eq. (24.11)) is given as

$$\nabla(\tilde{\mathbf{w}}, \tilde{\mathbf{x}}_i) = \left(y_i - \theta(\tilde{\mathbf{w}}^T \tilde{\mathbf{x}}_i)\right) \cdot \tilde{\mathbf{x}}_i \tag{24.13}$$

Unlike batch gradient ascent that updates $\tilde{\mathbf{w}}$ by considering all the points, in stochastic gradient ascent the weight vector is updated after observing each point, and the updated values are used immediately in the next update. Computing the full gradient in the batch approach can be very expensive. In contrast, computing the partial gradient at each point is very fast, and due to the stochastic updates to $\tilde{\mathbf{w}}$, typically SGA is much faster than the batch approach for very large datasets.

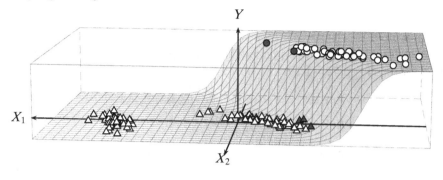

(a) Logistic Regression

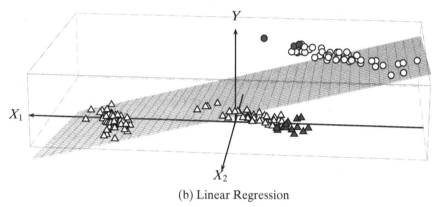

(b) Linear Regression

Figure 24.2. Logistic versus linear regression: Iris principal components data. Misclassified point are shown in dark gray color. Circles denote `Iris-virginica` and triangles denote the other two Iris types.

Once the model has been trained, we can predict the response for any new augmented test point $\tilde{z}$ as follows:

$$\hat{y} = \begin{cases} 1 & \text{if } \theta(\tilde{\mathbf{w}}^T\tilde{\mathbf{z}}) \geq 0.5 \\ 0 & \text{if } \theta(\tilde{\mathbf{w}}^T\tilde{\mathbf{z}}) < 0.5 \end{cases} \tag{24.14}$$

Example 24.2 (Logistic Regression). Figure 24.2(a) shows the output of logistic regression modeling on the Iris principal components data, where the independent attributes X_1 and X_2 represent the first two principal components, and the binary response variable Y represents the type of Iris flower; $Y = 1$ corresponds to `Iris-virginica`, whereas $Y = 0$ corresponds to the two other Iris types, namely `Iris-setosa` and `Iris-versicolor`.

The fitted logistic model is given as

$$\tilde{\mathbf{w}} = (w_0, w_1, w_2)^T = (-6.79, -5.07, -3.29)^T$$

$$P(Y=1|\tilde{\mathbf{x}}) = \theta(\tilde{\mathbf{w}}^T\tilde{\mathbf{x}}) = \frac{1}{1 + \exp\{6.79 + 5.07 \cdot x_1 + 3.29 \cdot x_2\}}$$

Figure 24.2(a) plots $P(Y=1|\tilde{\mathbf{x}})$ for various values of $\tilde{\mathbf{x}}$.

Given $\tilde{\mathbf{x}}$, if $P(Y=1|\tilde{\mathbf{x}}) \geq 0.5$, then we predict $\hat{y} = 1$, otherwise we predict $\hat{y} = 0$. Figure 24.2(a) shows that five points (shown in dark gray) are misclassified. For example, for $\tilde{\mathbf{x}} = (1, -0.52, -1.19)^T$ we have:

$$P(Y=1|\tilde{\mathbf{x}}) = \theta(\tilde{\mathbf{w}}^T\tilde{\mathbf{x}}) = \theta(-0.24) = 0.44$$

$$P(Y=0|\tilde{\mathbf{x}}) = 1 - P(Y=1|\tilde{\mathbf{x}}) = 0.54$$

Thus, the predicted response for $\tilde{\mathbf{x}}$ is $\hat{y} = 0$, whereas the true class is $y = 1$.

Figure 24.2 also contrasts logistic versus linear regression. The plane of best fit in linear regression is shown in Figure 24.2(b), with the weight vector:

$$\tilde{\mathbf{w}} = (0.333, -0.167, 0.074)^T$$

$$\hat{y} = f(\tilde{\mathbf{x}}) = 0.333 - 0.167 \cdot x_1 + 0.074 \cdot x_2$$

Since the response vector Y is binary, we predict the response class as $y = 1$ if $f(\tilde{\mathbf{x}}) \geq 0.5$, and $y = 0$ otherwise. The linear regression model results in 17 points being misclassified (dark gray points), as shown in Figure 24.2(b).

Since there are $n = 150$ points in total, this results in a training set or in-sample accuracy of 88.7% for linear regression. On the other hand, logistic regression misclassifies only 5 points, for an in-sample accuracy of 96.7%, which is a much better fit, as is also apparent in Figure 24.2.

24.2 MULTICLASS LOGISTIC REGRESSION

We now generalize logistic regression to the case when the response variable Y can take on K distinct nominal categorical values called *classes*, i.e., $Y \in \{c_1, c_2, \cdots, c_K\}$. We model Y as a K-dimensional multivariate Bernoulli random variable (see Section 3.1.2). Since Y can assume only one of the K values, we use the *one-hot encoding* approach to map each categorical value c_i to the K-dimensional binary vector

$$\mathbf{e}_i = (\overbrace{0, \ldots, 0}^{i-1}, 1, \overbrace{0, \ldots, 0}^{K-i})^T$$

whose ith element $e_{ii} = 1$, and all other elements $e_{ij} = 0$, so that $\sum_{j=1}^{K} e_{ij} = 1$. Henceforth, we assume that the categorical response variable Y is a multivariate Bernoulli variable $\mathbf{Y} \in \{\mathbf{e}_1, \mathbf{e}_2, \cdots, \mathbf{e}_K\}$, with Y_j referring to the jth component of $\mathbf{Y}$.

The probability mass function for $\mathbf{Y}$ given $\tilde{\mathbf{X}} = \tilde{\mathbf{x}}$ is

$$P(\mathbf{Y} = \mathbf{e}_i|\tilde{\mathbf{X}} = \tilde{\mathbf{x}}) = \pi_i(\tilde{\mathbf{x}}), \text{ for } i = 1, 2, \ldots, K$$

where $\pi_i(\tilde{\mathbf{x}})$ is the (unknown) probability of observing class c_i given $\tilde{\mathbf{X}} = \tilde{\mathbf{x}}$. Thus, there are K unknown parameters, which must satisfy the following constraint:

$$\sum_{i=1}^{K} \pi_i(\tilde{\mathbf{x}}) = \sum_{i=1}^{K} P(\mathbf{Y} = \mathbf{e}_i|\tilde{\mathbf{X}} = \tilde{\mathbf{x}}) = 1$$

Given that only one element of $\mathbf{Y}$ is 1, the probability mass function of $\mathbf{Y}$ can be written compactly as

$$P(\mathbf{Y}|\tilde{\mathbf{X}} = \tilde{\mathbf{x}}) = \prod_{j=1}^{K} \left(\pi_j(\tilde{\mathbf{x}})\right)^{Y_j} \tag{24.15}$$

Note that if $\mathbf{Y} = \mathbf{e}_i$, only $Y_i = 1$ and the rest of the elements $Y_j = 0$ for $j \neq i$.

In multiclass logistic regression, we select one of the values, say c_K, as a reference or base class, and consider the log-odds ratio of the other classes with respect to c_K; we assume that each of these log-odd ratios are linear in $\tilde{\mathbf{X}}$, but with a different augmented weight vector $\tilde{\boldsymbol{\omega}}_i$, for class c_i. That is, the log-odds ratio of class c_i with respect to class c_K is assumed to satisfy

$$\ln(\text{odds}(\mathbf{Y} = \mathbf{e}_i|\tilde{\mathbf{X}} = \tilde{\mathbf{x}})) = \ln\left(\frac{P(\mathbf{Y} = \mathbf{e}_i|\tilde{\mathbf{X}} = \tilde{\mathbf{x}})}{P(\mathbf{Y} = \mathbf{e}_K|\tilde{\mathbf{X}} = \tilde{\mathbf{x}})}\right) = \ln\left(\frac{\pi_i(\tilde{\mathbf{x}})}{\pi_K(\tilde{\mathbf{x}})}\right) = \tilde{\boldsymbol{\omega}}_i^T \tilde{\mathbf{x}}$$

$$= \omega_{i0} \cdot x_0 + \omega_{i1} \cdot x_1 + \cdots + \omega_{id} \cdot x_d$$

where $\omega_{i0} = \beta_i$ is the true bias value for class c_i.

We can rewrite the above set of equations as follows:

$$\frac{\pi_i(\tilde{\mathbf{x}})}{\pi_K(\tilde{\mathbf{x}})} = \exp\{\tilde{\boldsymbol{\omega}}_i^T \tilde{\mathbf{x}}\}$$

$$\Longrightarrow \pi_i(\tilde{\mathbf{x}}) = \exp\{\tilde{\boldsymbol{\omega}}_i^T \tilde{\mathbf{x}}\} \cdot \pi_K(\tilde{\mathbf{x}}) \tag{24.16}$$

Given that $\sum_{j=1}^{K} \pi_j(\tilde{\mathbf{x}}) = 1$, we have

$$\sum_{j=1}^{K} \pi_j(\tilde{\mathbf{x}}) = 1$$

$$\Longrightarrow \left(\sum_{j \neq K} \exp\{\tilde{\boldsymbol{\omega}}_j^T \tilde{\mathbf{x}}\} \cdot \pi_K(\tilde{\mathbf{x}})\right) + \pi_K(\tilde{\mathbf{x}}) = 1$$

$$\Longrightarrow \pi_K(\tilde{\mathbf{x}}) = \frac{1}{1 + \sum_{j \neq K} \exp\{\tilde{\boldsymbol{\omega}}_j^T \tilde{\mathbf{x}}\}}$$

Substituting the above into Eq. (24.16), we have

$$\pi_i(\tilde{\mathbf{x}}) = \exp\{\tilde{\boldsymbol{\omega}}_i^T \tilde{\mathbf{x}}\} \cdot \pi_K(\tilde{\mathbf{x}}) = \frac{\exp\{\tilde{\boldsymbol{\omega}}_i^T \tilde{\mathbf{x}}\}}{1 + \sum_{j \neq K} \exp\{\tilde{\boldsymbol{\omega}}_j^T \tilde{\mathbf{x}}\}}$$

Finally, setting $\tilde{\boldsymbol{\omega}}_K = \mathbf{0}$, we have $\exp\{\tilde{\boldsymbol{\omega}}_K^T \tilde{\mathbf{x}}\} = 1$, and thus we can write the full model for multiclass logistic regression as follows:

$$\pi_i(\tilde{\mathbf{x}}) = \frac{\exp\{\tilde{\boldsymbol{\omega}}_i^T \tilde{\mathbf{x}}\}}{\sum_{j=1}^{K} \exp\{\tilde{\boldsymbol{\omega}}_j^T \tilde{\mathbf{x}}\}}, \qquad \text{for all } i = 1, 2, \cdots, K \tag{24.17}$$

This function is also called the *softmax* function. When $K = 2$, this formulation yields exactly the same model as in binary logistic regression.

It is also interesting to note that the choice of the reference class is not important, since we can derive the log-odds ratio for any two classes c_i and c_j as follows:

$$
\begin{aligned}
\ln\left(\frac{\pi_i(\tilde{\mathbf{x}})}{\pi_j(\tilde{\mathbf{x}})}\right) &= \ln\left(\frac{\pi_i(\tilde{\mathbf{x}})}{\pi_K(\tilde{\mathbf{x}})} \cdot \frac{\pi_K(\tilde{\mathbf{x}})}{\pi_j(\tilde{\mathbf{x}})}\right) \\
&= \ln\left(\frac{\pi_i(\tilde{\mathbf{x}})}{\pi_K(\tilde{\mathbf{x}})}\right) + \ln\left(\frac{\pi_K(\tilde{\mathbf{x}})}{\pi_j(\tilde{\mathbf{x}})}\right) \\
&= \ln\left(\frac{\pi_i(\tilde{\mathbf{x}})}{\pi_K(\tilde{\mathbf{x}})}\right) - \ln\left(\frac{\pi_j(\tilde{\mathbf{x}})}{\pi_K(\tilde{\mathbf{x}})}\right) \\
&= \tilde{\boldsymbol{\omega}}_i^T \tilde{\mathbf{x}} - \tilde{\boldsymbol{\omega}}_j^T \tilde{\mathbf{x}} \\
&= (\tilde{\boldsymbol{\omega}}_i - \tilde{\boldsymbol{\omega}}_j)^T \tilde{\mathbf{x}}
\end{aligned}
$$

That is, the log-odds ratio between any two classes can be computed from the difference of the corresponding weight vectors.

24.2.1 Maximum Likelihood Estimation

Let $\tilde{\mathbf{D}}$ be the augmented dataset comprising n points $\tilde{\mathbf{x}}_i$ and their labels $\mathbf{y}_i$. We assume that $\mathbf{y}_i$ is a one-hot encoded (multivariate Bernoulli) response vector, so that y_{ij} denotes the jth element of $\mathbf{y}_i$. For example, if $\mathbf{y}_i = \mathbf{e}_a$, then $y_{ij} = 1$ for $j = a$, and $y_{ij} = 0$ for all $j \neq a$. We assume that all the $\mathbf{y}_i$'s are independent. Let $\tilde{\mathbf{w}}_i \in \mathbb{R}^{d+1}$ denote the estimated augmented weight vector for class c_i, with $w_{i0} = b_i$ denoting the bias term.

To find the K sets of regression weight vectors $\tilde{\mathbf{w}}_i$, for $i = 1, 2, \cdots, K$, we use the gradient ascent approach to maximize the log-likelihood function. The likelihood of the data is given as

$$
L(\tilde{\mathbf{W}}) = P(\mathbf{Y}|\tilde{\mathbf{W}}) = \prod_{i=1}^{n} P(\mathbf{y}_i|\tilde{\mathbf{X}} = \tilde{\mathbf{x}}_i) = \prod_{i=1}^{n} \prod_{j=1}^{K} \left(\pi_j(\tilde{\mathbf{x}}_i)\right)^{y_{ij}}
$$

where $\tilde{\mathbf{W}} = \{\tilde{\mathbf{w}}_1, \tilde{\mathbf{w}}_2, \cdots, \tilde{\mathbf{w}}_K\}$ is the set of K weight vectors. The log-likelihood is then given as:

$$
\ln\left(L(\tilde{\mathbf{W}})\right) = \sum_{i=1}^{n} \sum_{j=1}^{K} y_{ij} \cdot \ln(\pi_j(\tilde{\mathbf{x}}_i)) = \sum_{i=1}^{n} \sum_{j=1}^{K} y_{ij} \cdot \ln\left(\frac{\exp\{\tilde{\mathbf{w}}_j^T \tilde{\mathbf{x}}_i\}}{\sum_{a=1}^{K} \exp\{\tilde{\mathbf{w}}_a^T \tilde{\mathbf{x}}_i\}}\right) \quad (24.18)
$$

Note that the negative of the log-likelihood function can be regarded as an error function, commonly known as *cross-entropy error*.

We note the following facts:

$$
\frac{\partial}{\partial \pi_j(\tilde{\mathbf{x}}_i)} \ln(\pi_j(\tilde{\mathbf{x}}_i)) = \frac{1}{\pi_j(\tilde{\mathbf{x}}_i)}
$$

$$
\frac{\partial}{\partial \tilde{\mathbf{w}}_a} \pi_j(\tilde{\mathbf{x}}_i) = \begin{cases} \pi_a(\tilde{\mathbf{x}}_i) \cdot (1 - \pi_a(\tilde{\mathbf{x}}_i)) \cdot \tilde{\mathbf{x}}_i & \text{if } j = a \\ -\pi_a(\tilde{\mathbf{x}}_i) \cdot \pi_j(\tilde{\mathbf{x}}_i) \cdot \tilde{\mathbf{x}}_i & \text{if } j \neq a \end{cases}
$$

Let us consider the gradient of the log-likelihood function with respect to the weight vector $\tilde{\mathbf{w}}_a$:

$$\nabla(\tilde{\mathbf{w}}_a) = \frac{\partial}{\partial \tilde{\mathbf{w}}_a}\left\{\ln(L(\tilde{\mathbf{W}}))\right\}$$

$$= \sum_{i=1}^{n}\sum_{j=1}^{K} y_{ij} \cdot \frac{\partial \ln(\pi_j(\tilde{\mathbf{x}}_i))}{\partial \pi_j(\tilde{\mathbf{x}}_i)} \cdot \frac{\partial \pi_j(\tilde{\mathbf{x}}_i)}{\partial \tilde{\mathbf{w}}_a}$$

$$= \sum_{i=1}^{n}\left(y_{ia} \cdot \frac{1}{\pi_a(\tilde{\mathbf{x}}_i)} \cdot \pi_a(\tilde{\mathbf{x}}_i) \cdot (1 - \pi_a(\tilde{\mathbf{x}}_i)) \cdot \tilde{\mathbf{x}}_i + \sum_{j \neq a} y_{ij} \cdot \frac{1}{\pi_j(\tilde{\mathbf{x}}_i)} \cdot (-\pi_a(\tilde{\mathbf{x}}_i) \cdot \pi_j(\tilde{\mathbf{x}}_i)) \cdot \tilde{\mathbf{x}}_i \right)$$

$$= \sum_{i=1}^{n}\left(y_{ia} - y_{ia} \cdot \pi_a(\tilde{\mathbf{x}}_i) - \sum_{j \neq a} y_{ij} \cdot \pi_a(\tilde{\mathbf{x}}_i) \right) \cdot \tilde{\mathbf{x}}_i$$

$$= \sum_{i=1}^{n}\left(y_{ia} - \sum_{j=1}^{K} y_{ij} \cdot \pi_a(\tilde{\mathbf{x}}_i) \right) \cdot \tilde{\mathbf{x}}_i$$

$$= \sum_{i=1}^{n}\left(y_{ia} - \pi_a(\tilde{\mathbf{x}}_i) \right) \cdot \tilde{\mathbf{x}}_i$$

The last step follows from the fact that $\sum_{j=1}^{K} y_{ij} = 1$, since only one element of $\mathbf{y}_i$ can be 1.

For stochastic gradient ascent, we update the weight vectors by considering only one point at a time. The gradient of the log-likelihood function with respect to $\tilde{\mathbf{w}}_j$ at a given point $\tilde{\mathbf{x}}_i$ is given as

$$\nabla(\tilde{\mathbf{w}}_j, \tilde{\mathbf{x}}_i) = \left(y_{ij} - \pi_j(\tilde{\mathbf{x}}_i) \right) \cdot \tilde{\mathbf{x}}_i \tag{24.19}$$

which results in the following update rule for the jth weight vector:

$$\tilde{\mathbf{w}}_j^{t+1} = \tilde{\mathbf{w}}_j^{t} + \eta \cdot \nabla(\tilde{\mathbf{w}}_j^{t}, \tilde{\mathbf{x}}_i) \tag{24.20}$$

where $\tilde{\mathbf{w}}_j^{t}$ denotes the estimate of $\tilde{\mathbf{w}}_j$ at step t, and η is the learning rate. The pseudo-code for the stochastic gradient ascent method for multiclass logistic regression is shown in Algorithm 24.2. Notice that the weight vector for the base class c_K is never updated; it remains $\tilde{\mathbf{w}}_K = \mathbf{0}$, as required.

Once the model has been trained, we can predict the class for any new augmented test point $\tilde{\mathbf{z}}$ as follows:

$$\hat{y} = \arg\max_{c_i}\{\pi_i(\tilde{\mathbf{z}})\} = \arg\max_{c_i}\left\{\frac{\exp\{\tilde{\mathbf{w}}_i^T \tilde{\mathbf{z}}\}}{\sum_{j=1}^{K}\exp\{\tilde{\mathbf{w}}_j^T \tilde{\mathbf{z}}\}}\right\} \tag{24.21}$$

That is, we evelute the softmax function, and then predict the class of $\tilde{\mathbf{z}}$ as the one with the highest probability.

Algorithm 24.2: Multiclass Logistic Regression Algorithm

LOGISTICREGRESSION-MULTICLASS ($\mathbf{D}, \eta, \epsilon$):

1 **foreach** $(\mathbf{x}_i^T, y_i) \in \mathbf{D}$ **do**
2     $\tilde{\mathbf{x}}_i^T \leftarrow \begin{pmatrix} 1 & \mathbf{x}_i^T \end{pmatrix}$ // map to $\mathbb{R}^{d+1}$
3     $\mathbf{y}_i \leftarrow \mathbf{e}_j$ if $y_i = c_j$ // map y_i to K-dimensional Bernoulli vector

4 $t \leftarrow 0$ // step/iteration counter
5 **foreach** $j = 1, 2, \cdots, K$ **do**
6     $\tilde{\mathbf{w}}_j^t \leftarrow (0, \ldots, 0)^T \in \mathbb{R}^{d+1}$ // initial weight vector

7 **repeat**
8   **foreach** $j = 1, 2, \cdots, K-1$ **do**
9        $\tilde{\mathbf{w}}_j \leftarrow \tilde{\mathbf{w}}_j^t$ // make a copy of $\tilde{\mathbf{w}}_j^t$

10   **foreach** $\tilde{\mathbf{x}}_i \in \tilde{\mathbf{D}}$ *in random order* **do**
11   **foreach** $j = 1, 2, \cdots, K-1$ **do**
12          $\pi_j(\tilde{\mathbf{x}}_i) \leftarrow \dfrac{\exp\{\tilde{\mathbf{w}}_j^T \tilde{\mathbf{x}}_i\}}{\sum_{a=1}^{K} \exp\{\tilde{\mathbf{w}}_a^T \tilde{\mathbf{x}}_i\}}$
13          $\nabla(\tilde{\mathbf{w}}_j, \tilde{\mathbf{x}}_i) \leftarrow \big(y_{ij} - \pi_j(\tilde{\mathbf{x}}_i)\big) \cdot \tilde{\mathbf{x}}_i$ // compute gradient at $\tilde{\mathbf{w}}_j$
14          $\tilde{\mathbf{w}}_j \leftarrow \tilde{\mathbf{w}}_j + \eta \cdot \nabla(\tilde{\mathbf{w}}_j, \tilde{\mathbf{x}}_i)$ // update estimate for $\tilde{\mathbf{w}}_j$

15   **foreach** $j = 1, 2, \cdots, K-1$ **do**
16        $\tilde{\mathbf{w}}_j^{t+1} \leftarrow \tilde{\mathbf{w}}_j$ // update $\tilde{\mathbf{w}}_j^{t+1}$

17     $t \leftarrow t + 1$
18 **until** $\sum_{j=1}^{K-1} \|\tilde{\mathbf{w}}_j^t - \tilde{\mathbf{w}}_j^{t-1}\| \leq \epsilon$

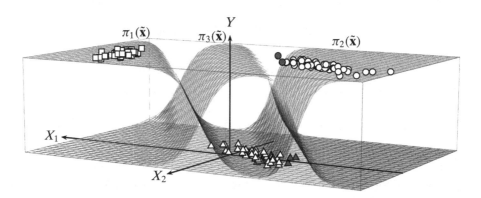

Figure 24.3. Multiclass logistic regression: Iris principal components data. Misclassified point are shown in dark gray color. All the points actually lie in the (X_1, X_2) plane, but c_1 and c_2 are shown displaced along Y with respect to the base class c_3 purely for illustration purposes.

Example 24.3. Consider the Iris dataset, with $n = 150$ points in a 2D space spanned by the first two principal components, as shown in Figure 24.3. Here, the response variable takes on three values: $Y = c_1$ corresponds to Iris-setosa (shown as squares), $Y = c_2$ corresponds to Iris-versicolor (as circles) and $Y = c_3$ corresponds to Iris-virginica (as triangles). Thus, we map $Y = c_1$ to $\mathbf{e}_1 = (1, 0, 0)^T$, $Y = c_2$ to $\mathbf{e}_2 = (0, 1, 0)^T$ and $Y = c_3$ to $\mathbf{e}_3 = (0, 0, 1)^T$.

The multiclass logistic model uses $Y = c_3$ (Iris-virginica; triangles) as the reference or base class. The fitted model is given as:

$$\tilde{\mathbf{w}}_1 = (-3.52, 3.62, 2.61)^T$$

$$\tilde{\mathbf{w}}_2 = (-6.95, -5.18, -3.40)^T$$

$$\tilde{\mathbf{w}}_3 = (0, 0, 0)^T$$

Figure 24.3 plots the decision surfaces corresponding to the softmax functions:

$$\pi_1(\tilde{\mathbf{x}}) = \frac{\exp\{\tilde{\mathbf{w}}_1^T \tilde{\mathbf{x}}\}}{1 + \exp\{\tilde{\mathbf{w}}_1^T \tilde{\mathbf{x}}\} + \exp\{\tilde{\mathbf{w}}_2^T \tilde{\mathbf{x}}\}}$$

$$\pi_2(\tilde{\mathbf{x}}) = \frac{\exp\{\tilde{\mathbf{w}}_2^T \tilde{\mathbf{x}}\}}{1 + \exp\{\tilde{\mathbf{w}}_1^T \tilde{\mathbf{x}}\} + \exp\{\tilde{\mathbf{w}}_2^T \tilde{\mathbf{x}}\}}$$

$$\pi_3(\tilde{\mathbf{x}}) = \frac{1}{1 + \exp\{\tilde{\mathbf{w}}_1^T \tilde{\mathbf{x}}\} + \exp\{\tilde{\mathbf{w}}_2^T \tilde{\mathbf{x}}\}}$$

The surfaces indicate regions where one class dominates over the others. It is important to note that the points for c_1 and c_2 are shown displaced along Y to emphasize the contrast with c_3, which is the reference class.

Overall, the training set accuracy for the multiclass logistic classifier is 96.7%, since it misclassifies only five points (shown in dark gray). For example, for the point $\tilde{\mathbf{x}} = (1, -0.52, -1.19)^T$, we have:

$$\pi_1(\tilde{\mathbf{x}}) = 0 \qquad \pi_2(\tilde{\mathbf{x}}) = 0.448 \qquad \pi_3(\tilde{\mathbf{x}}) = 0.552$$

Thus, the predicted class is $\hat{y} = \arg\max_{c_i}\{\pi_i(\tilde{\mathbf{x}})\} = c_3$, whereas the true class is $y = c_2$.

24.3 FURTHER READING

For a description of the class of generalized linear models, of which logistic regression is a special case, see Agresti (2015).

Agresti, A. (2015). *Foundations of Linear and Generalized Linear Models*. Hoboken, NJ: John Wiley & Sons.

24.4 EXERCISES

Q1. Show that $\frac{\partial \theta(z)}{\partial z} = \theta(z) \cdot \theta(-z)$, where $\theta(\cdot)$ is the logistic function.

Q2. Show that the logit function is the inverse of the logistic function.

Q3. Given the softmax function:

$$\pi_j(\tilde{\mathbf{x}}) = \frac{\exp\{\tilde{\mathbf{w}}_j^T \tilde{\mathbf{x}}\}}{\sum_{i=1}^K \exp\{\tilde{\mathbf{w}}_i^T \tilde{\mathbf{x}}\}}$$

Show that

$$\frac{\partial \pi_j(\tilde{\mathbf{x}})}{\partial \tilde{\mathbf{w}}_a} = \begin{cases} \pi_a(\tilde{\mathbf{x}}) \cdot (1 - \pi_a(\tilde{\mathbf{x}})) \cdot \tilde{\mathbf{x}} & \text{if } j = a \\ -\pi_a(\tilde{\mathbf{x}}) \cdot \pi_j(\tilde{\mathbf{x}}) \cdot \tilde{\mathbf{x}} & \text{if } j \neq a \end{cases}$$

CHAPTER 25

Neural Networks

Artificial neural networks or simply neural networks are inspired by biological neuronal networks. A real biological neuron, or a nerve cell, comprises dendrites, a cell body, and an axon that leads to synaptic terminals. A neuron transmits information via electrochemical signals. When there is enough concentration of ions at the dendrites of a neuron it generates an electric pulse along its axon called an action potential, which in turn activates the synaptic terminals, releasing more ions and thus causing the information to flow to dendrites of other neurons. A human brain has on the order of 100 billion neurons, with each neuron having between 1,000 to 10,000 connections to other neurons. Thus, a human brain is a neuronal network with 100 trillion to a quadrillion (10^{15}) interconnections! Interestingly, as far as we know, learning happens by adjusting the synaptic strengths, since synaptic signals can be either excitatory or inhibitory, making the post-synaptic neuron either more or less likely to generate an action potential, respectively.

Artificial neural networks are comprised of abstract neurons that try to mimic real neurons at a very high level. They can be described via a weighted directed graph $G = (V, E)$, with each node $v_i \in V$ representing a neuron, and each directed edge $(v_i, v_j) \in E$ representing a synaptic to dendritic connection from v_i to v_j. The weight of the edge w_{ij} denotes the synaptic strength. Neural networks are characterized by the type of activation function used to generate an output, and the architecture of the network in terms of how the nodes are interconnected. For example, whether the graph is a directed acyclic graph or has cycles, whether the graph is layered or not, and so on. It is important to note that a neural network is designed to represent and learn information by adjusting the synaptic weights.

25.1 ARTIFICIAL NEURON: ACTIVATION FUNCTIONS

An artificial neuron acts as a processing unit, that first aggregates the incoming signals via a weighted sum, and then applies some function to generate an output. For example, a binary neuron will output a 1 whenever the combined signal exceeds a threshold, or 0 otherwise.

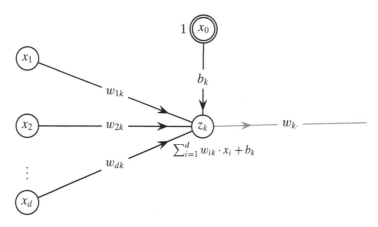

Figure 25.1. Artificial neuron: aggregation and activation.

Figure 25.1 shows the schematic of a neuron z_k that has incoming edges from neurons $x_1, \cdots, x_d$. For simplicity, both the name and the (output) value of a neuron are denoted by the same symbol. Thus, x_i denotes neuron i, and also the value of that neuron. The net input at z_k, denoted net_k, is given as the weighted sum

$$net_k = b_k + \sum_{i=1}^{d} w_{ik} \cdot x_i = b_k + \mathbf{w}^T \mathbf{x} \qquad (25.1)$$

where $\mathbf{w}_k = (w_{1k}, w_{2k}, \cdots, w_{dk})^T \in \mathbb{R}^d$ and $\mathbf{x} = (x_1, x_2, \cdots, x_d)^T \in \mathbb{R}^d$ is an input point. Notice that x_0 is a special *bias neuron* whose value is always fixed at 1, and the weight from x_0 to z_k is b_k, which specifies the bias term for the neuron. Finally, the output value of z_k is given as some *activation function*, $f(\cdot)$, applied to the net input at z_k

$$z_k = f(net_k)$$

The value z_k is then passed along the outgoing edges from z_k to other neurons.

Neurons differ based on the type of activation function used. Some commonly used activation functions, illustrated in Figure 25.2, are:

Linear/Identity Function: Identity is the simplest activation function; it simply returns its argument, and is also called a *linear* activation function:

$$f(net_k) = net_k \qquad (25.2)$$

Figure 25.2(a) plots the identity function. To examine the role of the bias term, note that $net_k > 0$ is equivalent to $\mathbf{w}^T \mathbf{x} > -b_k$. That is, the output transitions from negative to positive when the weighted sum of the inputs exceeds $-b_k$, as shown in Figure 25.2(b).

Step Function: This is a binary activation function, where the neuron outputs a 0 if the net value is negative (or zero), and 1 if the net value is positive (see Figure 25.2(c)).

$$f(net_k) = \begin{cases} 0 & \text{if } net_k \le 0 \\ 1 & \text{if } net_k > 0 \end{cases} \qquad (25.3)$$

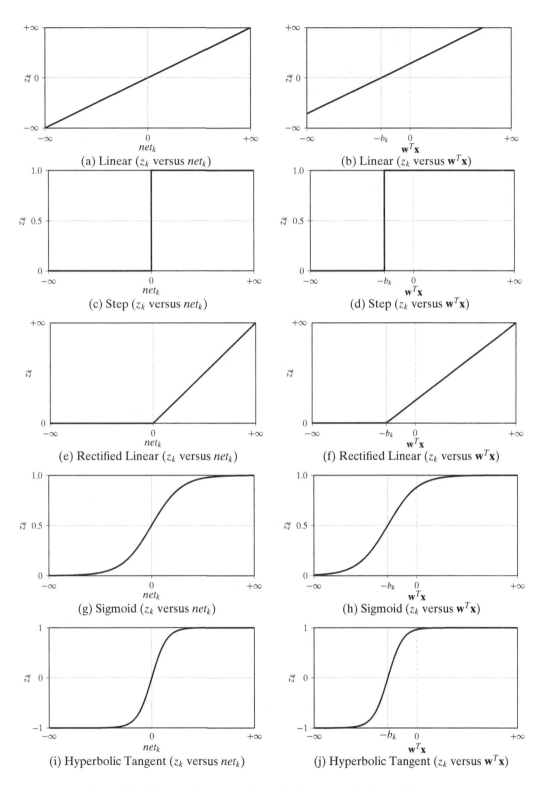

Figure 25.2. Neuron activation functions; also illustrating the effect of bias.

It is interesting to note that the transition from 0 to 1 happens when the weighted sum of the inputs exceeds $-b_k$, as shown in Figure 25.2(d).

Rectified Linear Unit (ReLU): Here, the neuron remains inactive if the net input is less than or equal to zero, and then increases linearly with net_k, as shown in Figure 25.2(e).

$$f(net_k) = \begin{cases} 0 & \text{if } net_k \leq 0 \\ net_k & \text{if } net_k > 0 \end{cases} \tag{25.4}$$

An alternative expression for the ReLU activation is given as $f(net_k) = \max\{0, net_k\}$. The transition from zero to linear output happens when the weighted sum of the inputs exceeds $-b_k$ (see Figure 25.2(f)).

Sigmoid: The sigmoid function, illustrated in Figure 25.2(g) squashes its input so that the output ranges between 0 and 1

$$f(net_k) = \frac{1}{1 + \exp\{-net_k\}} \tag{25.5}$$

When $net_k = 0$, we have $f(net_k) = 0.5$, which implies that the transition point where the output crosses 0.5 happens when the weighted sum of the inputs exceeds $-b_k$ (see Figure 25.2(h)).

Hyperbolic Tangent (tanh): The hyperbolic tangent or tanh function is similar to the sigmoid, but its output ranges between -1 and $+1$ (see Figure 25.2(i)).

$$f(net_k) = \frac{\exp\{net_k\} - \exp\{-net_k\}}{\exp\{net_k\} + \exp\{-net_k\}} = \frac{\exp\{2 \cdot net_k\} - 1}{\exp\{2 \cdot net_k\} + 1} \tag{25.6}$$

When $net_k = 0$, we have $f(net_k) = 0$, which implies that the output transitions from negative to positive when the weighted sum of the inputs exceeds $-b_k$, as shown in Figure 25.2(j).

Softmax: Softmax is a generalization of the sigmoid or logistic activation function. Softmax is mainly used at the output layer in a neural network, and unlike the other functions it depends not only on the net input at neuron k, but it depends on the net signal at all other neurons in the output layer. Thus, given the net input vector,

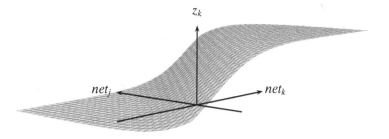

Figure 25.3. Softmax (net_k versus net_j).

$\mathbf{net} = (net_1, net_2, \cdots, net_p)^T$, for all the p output neurons, the output of the softmax function for the kth neuron is given as

$$f(net_k \mid \mathbf{net}) = \frac{\exp\{net_k\}}{\sum_{i=1}^{p} \exp\{net_i\}} \tag{25.7}$$

Figure 25.3 plots the softmax activation for net_k versus the net signal net_j, with all other net values fixed at zero. The output behaves similar to a sigmoid curve for any given value of net_j.

25.1.1 Derivatives for Activation Functions

For learning using a neural network, we need to consider the derivative of an activation function with respect to its argument. The derivatives for the activation functions are given as follows:

Identity/Linear: The identity (or linear) activation function has a derivative of 1 with respect to its argument, giving us:

$$\frac{\partial f(net_j)}{\partial net_j} = 1 \tag{25.8}$$

Step: The step function has a derivative of 0 everywhere except for the discontinuity at 0, where the derivative is ∞.

ReLU: The ReLU function [Eq. (25.4)] is non-differentiable at 0, nevertheless for other values its derivative is 0 if $net_j < 0$ and 1 if $net_j > 0$. At 0, we can set the derivative to be any value in the range $[0, 1]$, a simple choice being 0. Putting it all together, we have

$$\frac{\partial f(net_j)}{\partial net_j} = \begin{cases} 0 & \text{if } net_j \leq 0 \\ 1 & \text{if } net_j > 0 \end{cases} \tag{25.9}$$

Even though ReLU has a discontinuity at 0 it is a popular choice for training deep neural networks.

Sigmoid: The derivative of the sigmoid function [Eq. (25.5)] is given as

$$\frac{\partial f(net_j)}{\partial net_j} = f(net_j) \cdot (1 - f(net_j)) \tag{25.10}$$

Hyperbolic Tangent: The derivative of the tanh function [Eq. (25.6)] is given as

$$\frac{\partial f(net_j)}{\partial net_j} = 1 - f(net_j)^2 \tag{25.11}$$

Softmax: The softmax activation function [Eq. (25.7)] is a vector valued function, which maps a vector input $\mathbf{net} = (net_1, net_2, \cdots, net_p)^T$ to a vector of probability values. Softmax is typically used only for the output layer. The partial derivative of $f(net_j)$ with respect to net_j is given as

$$\frac{\partial f(net_j \mid \mathbf{net})}{\partial net_j} = f(net_j) \cdot (1 - f(net_j))$$

whereas the partial derivative of $f(net_j)$ with respect to net_k, with $k \neq j$ is given as

$$\frac{\partial f(net_j \mid \mathbf{net})}{\partial net_k} = -f(net_k) \cdot f(net_j)$$

Since softmax is used at the output layer, if we denote the ith output neuron as o_i, then $f(net_i) = o_i$, and we can write the derivative as:

$$\frac{\partial f(net_j \mid \mathbf{net})}{\partial net_k} = \frac{\partial o_j}{\partial net_k} = \begin{cases} o_j \cdot (1 - o_j) & \text{if } k = j \\ -o_k \cdot o_j & \text{if } k \neq j \end{cases} \tag{25.12}$$

25.2 NEURAL NETWORKS: REGRESSION AND CLASSIFICATION

Networks of (artificial) neurons are capable of representing and learning arbitrarily complex functions for both regression and classification tasks.

25.2.1 Regression

Consider the multiple (linear) regression problem, where given an input $\mathbf{x}_i \in \mathbb{R}^d$, the goal is to predict the response as follows

$$\hat{y}_i = b + w_1 x_{i1} + w_2 x_{i2} + \cdots + w_d x_{id}$$

Here, b is the bias term, and w_j is the regression coefficient or weight for attribute X_j. Given a training data $\mathbf{D}$ comprising n points $\mathbf{x}_i$ in a d-dimensional space, along with their corresponding true response value y_i, the bias and weights for linear regression are chosen so as to minimize the sum of squared errors between the true and predicted response over all data points

$$SSE = \sum_{i=1}^{n} (y_i - \hat{y}_i)^2$$

As shown in Figure 25.4(a), a neural network with $d+1$ input neurons $x_0, x_1, \cdots, x_d$, including the bias neuron $x_0 = 1$, and a single output neuron o, all with identity activation functions and with $\hat{y} = o$, represents the exact same model as multiple linear regression. Whereas the multiple regression problem has a closed form solution, neural networks learn the bias and weights via a gradient descent approach that minimizes the squared error.

Neural networks can just as easily model the multivariate (linear) regression task, where we have a p-dimensional response vector $\mathbf{y}_i \in \mathbb{R}^p$ instead of a single value y_i. That is, the training data $\mathbf{D}$ comprises n points $\mathbf{x}_i \in \mathbb{R}^d$ and their true response vectors $\mathbf{y}_i \in \mathbb{R}^p$. As shown in Figure 25.4(b), multivariate regression can be modeled by a neural

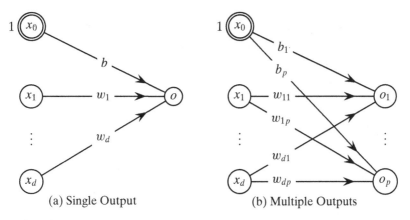

(a) Single Output   (b) Multiple Outputs

Figure 25.4. Linear and logistic regression via neural networks.

network with $d + 1$ input neurons, and p output neurons $o_1, o_2, \cdots, o_p$, with all input and output neurons using the identity activation function. A neural network learns the weights by comparing its predicted output $\hat{\mathbf{y}} = \mathbf{o} = (o_1, o_2, \cdots, o_p)^T$ with the true response vector $\mathbf{y} = (y_1, y_2, \cdots, y_p)^T$. That is, training happens by first computing the *error function* or *loss function* between $\mathbf{o}$ and $\mathbf{y}$. Recall that a loss function assigns a score or penalty for predicting the output to be $\mathbf{o}$ when the desired output is $\mathbf{y}$. When the prediction matches the true output the loss should be zero. The most common loss function for regression is the squared error function

$$\mathcal{E}_{\mathbf{x}} = \frac{1}{2}\|\mathbf{y} - \mathbf{o}\|^2 = \frac{1}{2}\sum_{j=1}^{p}(y_j - o_j)^2$$

where $\mathcal{E}_{\mathbf{x}}$ denotes the error on input $\mathbf{x}$. Across all the points in a dataset, the total sum of squared errors is

$$\mathcal{E} = \sum_{i=1}^{n}\mathcal{E}_{\mathbf{x}_i} = \frac{1}{2}\cdot\sum_{i=1}^{n}\|\mathbf{y}_i - \mathbf{o}_i\|^2$$

Example 25.1 (Neural Networks for Multiple and Multivariate Regression).
Consider the multiple regression of sepal length and petal length on the dependent attribute petal width for the Iris dataset with $n = 150$ points. From Example 23.3 we find that the solution is given as

$$\hat{y} = -0.014 - 0.082 \cdot x_1 + 0.45 \cdot x_2$$

The squared error for this optimal solution is 6.179 on the training data.

Using the neural network in Figure 25.4(a), with linear activation for the output and minimizing the squared error via gradient descent, results in the following learned parameters, $b = 0.0096$, $w_1 = -0.087$ and $w_2 = 0.452$, yielding the regression model

$$o = 0.0096 - 0.087 \cdot x_1 + 0.452 \cdot x_2$$

with a squared error of 6.18, which is very close to the optimal solution.

Multivariate Linear Regression For multivariate regression, we use the neural network architecture in Figure 25.4(b) to learn the weights and bias for the Iris dataset, where we use sepal length and sepal width as the independent attributes, and petal length and petal width as the response or dependent attributes. Therefore, each input point $\mathbf{x}_i$ is 2-dimensional, and the true response vector $\mathbf{y}_i$ is also 2-dimensional. That is, $d = 2$ and $p = 2$ specify the size of the input and output layers. Minimizing the squared error via gradient descent, yields the following parameters:

$$\begin{pmatrix} b_1 & b_2 \\ w_{11} & w_{12} \\ w_{21} & w_{22} \end{pmatrix} = \begin{pmatrix} -1.83 & -1.47 \\ 1.72 & 0.72 \\ -1.46 & -0.50 \end{pmatrix} \qquad \begin{pmatrix} o_1 \\ o_2 \end{pmatrix} = \begin{pmatrix} -1.83 + 1.72 \cdot x_1 - 1.46 \cdot x_2 \\ -1.47 + 0.72 \cdot x_1 - 0.50 \cdot x_2 \end{pmatrix}$$

The squared error on the training set is 84.9. Optimal least squared multivariate regression yields a squared error of 84.16 with the following parameters

$$\begin{pmatrix} \hat{y}_1 \\ \hat{y}_2 \end{pmatrix} = \begin{pmatrix} -2.56 + 1.78 \cdot x_1 - 1.34 \cdot x_2 \\ -1.59 + 0.73 \cdot x_1 - 0.48 \cdot x_2 \end{pmatrix}$$

25.2.2 Classification

Networks of artificial neurons can also learn to classify the inputs. Consider the binary classification problem, where $y = 1$ denotes that the point belongs to the positive class, and $y = 0$ means that it belongs to the negative class. Recall that in logistic regression, we model the probability of the positive class via the logistic (or sigmoid) function:

$$\pi(\mathbf{x}) = P(y = 1 | \mathbf{x}) = \frac{1}{1 + \exp\{-(b + \mathbf{w}^T \mathbf{x})\}}$$

where b is the bias term and $\mathbf{w} = (w_1, w_2, \cdots, w_d)^T$ is the vector of estimated weights or regression coefficients. On the other hand

$$P(y = 0 | \mathbf{x}) = 1 - P(y = 1 | \mathbf{x}) = 1 - \pi(\mathbf{x})$$

A simple change to the neural network shown in Figure 25.4(a) allows it to solve the logistic regression problem. All we have to do is use a sigmoid activation function at the output neuron o, and use the cross-entropy error instead of squared error. Given input $\mathbf{x}$, true response y, and predicted response o, recall that the *cross-entropy error* (see Eq. (24.8)) is defined as

$$\mathcal{E}_{\mathbf{x}} = -\big(y \cdot \ln(o) + (1 - y) \cdot \ln(1 - o)\big)$$

Thus, with sigmoid activation, the output of the neural network in Figure 25.4(a) is given as

$$o = f(net_o) = \text{sigmoid}(b + \mathbf{w}^T \mathbf{x}) = \frac{1}{1 + \exp\{-(b + \mathbf{w}^T \mathbf{x})\}} = \pi(\mathbf{x})$$

which is the same as the logistic regression model.

Multiclass Logistic Regression In a similar manner, the multiple output neural network architecture shown in Figure 25.4(b) can be used for multiclass or nominal logistic regression. For the general classification problem with K classes $\{c_1, c_2, \cdots, c_K\}$, the true response y is encoded as a one-hot vector. Thus, class c_1 is encoded as $\mathbf{e}_1 = (1, 0, \cdots, 0)^T$, class c_2 is encoded as $\mathbf{e}_2 = (0, 1, \cdots, 0)^T$, and so on, with $\mathbf{e}_i \in \{0, 1\}^K$ for $i = 1, 2, \cdots, K$. Thus, we encode y as a multivariate vector $\mathbf{y} \in \{\mathbf{e}_1, \mathbf{e}_2, \cdots, \mathbf{e}_K\}$. Recall that in multiclass logistic regression (see Section 24.2) the task is to estimate the per class bias b_i and weight vector $\mathbf{w}_i \in \mathbb{R}^d$, with the last class c_K used as the base class with fixed bias $b_K = 0$ and fixed weight vector $\mathbf{w}_K = (0, 0, \cdots, 0)^T \in \mathbb{R}^d$. The probability vector across all K classes is modeled via the softmax function (see Eq. (24.17)):

$$\pi_i(\mathbf{x}) = \frac{\exp\{b_i + \mathbf{w}_i^T \mathbf{x}\}}{\sum_{j=1}^{K} \exp\{b_j + \mathbf{w}_j^T \mathbf{x}\}}, \qquad \text{for all } i = 1, 2, \cdots, K$$

Therefore, the neural network shown in Figure 25.4(b) (with $p = K$) can solve the multiclass logistic regression task, provided we use a softmax activation at the outputs, and use the K-way cross-entropy error (see Eq. (24.18)), defined as

$$\mathcal{E}_\mathbf{x} = -\Big(y_1 \cdot \ln(o_1) + \cdots + y_K \cdot \ln(o_K)\Big)$$

where $\mathbf{x}$ is an input vector, $\mathbf{o} = (o_1, o_2, \cdots, o_K)^T$ is the predicted response vector, and $\mathbf{y} = (y_1, y_2, \cdots, y_K)^T$ is the true response vector. Note that only one element of $\mathbf{y}$ is 1, and the rest are 0, due to the one-hot encoding.

With softmax activation, the output of the neural network in Figure 25.4(b) (with $p = K$) is given as

$$o_i = P(\mathbf{y} = \mathbf{e}_i | \mathbf{x}) = f(net_i | \mathbf{net}) = \frac{\exp\{net_i\}}{\sum_{j=1}^{p} \exp\{net_j\}} = \pi_i(\mathbf{x})$$

which matches the multiclass logistic regression task. The only restriction we have to impose on the neural network is that the weights on edges into the last output neuron should be zero to model the base class weights $\mathbf{w}_K$. However, in practice, we can relax this restriction, and just learn a regular weight vector for class c_K.

Example 25.2 (Logistic Regression: Binary and Multiclass). We applied the neural network in Figure 25.4(a), with logistic activation at the output neuron and cross-entropy error function, on the Iris principal components dataset. The output is a binary response indicating Iris-virginica ($Y = 1$) or one of the other Iris types ($Y = 0$). As expected, the neural network learns an identical set of weights and bias as shown for the logistic regression model in Example 24.2, namely:

$$o = -6.79 - 5.07 \cdot x_1 - 3.29 \cdot x_2$$

Next, we we applied the neural network in Figure 25.4(b), using a softmax activation and cross-entropy error function, to the Iris principal components data with three classes: Iris-setosa ($Y = 1$), Iris-versicolor ($Y = 2$) and Iris-virginica ($Y = 3$). Thus, we need $K = 3$ output neurons, o_1, o_2, and o_3. Further, to obtain the same model as in the multiclass logistic regression from Example 24.3,

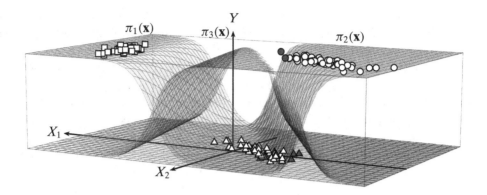

Figure 25.5. Neural networks for multiclass logistic regression: Iris principal components data. Misclassified point are shown in dark gray color. Points in class c_1 and c_2 are shown displaced with respect to the base class c_3 only for illustration.

we fix the incoming weights and bias for output neuron o_3 to be zero. The model is given as

$$o_1 = -3.49 + 3.61 \cdot x_1 + 2.65 \cdot x_2$$
$$o_2 = -6.95 - 5.18 \cdot x_1 - 3.40 \cdot x_2$$
$$o_3 = 0 + 0 \cdot x_1 + 0 \cdot x_2$$

which is essentially the same as in Example 24.3.

If we do not constrain the weights and bias for o_3 we obtain the following model:

$$o_1 = -0.89 + 4.54 \cdot x_1 + 1.96 \cdot x_2$$
$$o_2 = -3.38 - 5.11 \cdot x_1 - 2.88 \cdot x_2$$
$$o_3 = 4.24 + 0.52 \cdot x_1 + 0.92 \cdot x_2$$

The classification decision surface for each class is illustrated in Figure 25.5. The points in class c_1 are shown as squares, c_2 as circles, and c_3 as triangles. This figure should be contrasted with the decision boundaries shown for multiclass logistic regression in Figure 24.3, which has the weights and bias set to 0 for the base class c_3.

25.2.3 Error Functions

Typically, for a regression task, we use squared error as the loss function, whereas for classification, we use the cross-entropy loss function. Furthermore, when learning from neural networks, we will require the partial derivatives of the error function with respect to the output neurons. Thus, the commonly used error functions and their derivatives are listed below:

Squared Error: Given an input vector $\mathbf{x} \in \mathbb{R}^d$, the squared error loss function measures the squared deviation between the predicted output vector $\mathbf{o} \in \mathbb{R}^p$ and the true response $\mathbf{y} \in \mathbb{R}^p$, defined as follows:

$$\mathcal{E}_{\mathbf{x}} = \frac{1}{2}\|\mathbf{y} - \mathbf{o}\|^2 = \frac{1}{2}\sum_{j=1}^{p}(y_j - o_j)^2 \tag{25.13}$$

where $\mathcal{E}_{\mathbf{x}}$ denotes the error on input $\mathbf{x}$.

The partial derivative of the squared error function with respect to a particular output neuron o_j is

$$\frac{\partial \mathcal{E}_{\mathbf{x}}}{\partial o_j} = \frac{1}{2} \cdot 2 \cdot (y_j - o_j) \cdot -1 = o_j - y_j \tag{25.14}$$

Across all the output neurons, we can write this as

$$\frac{\partial \mathcal{E}_{\mathbf{x}}}{\partial \mathbf{o}} = \mathbf{o} - \mathbf{y} \tag{25.15}$$

Cross-Entropy Error: For classification tasks, with K classes $\{c_1, c_2, \cdots, c_K\}$, we usually set the number of output neurons $p = K$, with one output neuron per class. Furthermore, each of the classes is coded as a one-hot vector, with class c_i encoded as the ith standard basis vector $\mathbf{e}_i = (e_{i1}, e_{i2}, \cdots, e_{iK})^T \in \{0, 1\}^K$, with $e_{ii} = 1$ and $e_{ij} = 0$ for all $j \neq i$. Thus, given input $\mathbf{x} \in \mathbb{R}^d$, with the true response $\mathbf{y} = (y_1, y_2, \cdots, y_K)^T$, where $\mathbf{y} \in \{\mathbf{e}_1, \mathbf{e}_2, \cdots, \mathbf{e}_K\}$, the cross-entropy loss is defined as

$$\mathcal{E}_{\mathbf{x}} = -\sum_{i=1}^{K} y_i \cdot \ln(o_i) = -\left(y_1 \cdot \ln(o_1) + \cdots + y_K \cdot \ln(o_K)\right) \tag{25.16}$$

Note that only one element of $\mathbf{y}$ is 1 and the rest are 0 due to the one-hot encoding. That is, if $\mathbf{y} = \mathbf{e}_i$, then only $y_i = 1$, and the other elements $y_j = 0$ for $j \neq i$.

The partial derivative of the cross-entropy error function with respect to a particular output neuron o_j is

$$\frac{\partial \mathcal{E}_{\mathbf{x}}}{\partial o_j} = -\frac{y_j}{o_j} \tag{25.17}$$

The vector of partial derivatives of the error function with respect to the output neurons is therefore given as

$$\frac{\partial \mathcal{E}_{\mathbf{x}}}{\partial \mathbf{o}} = \left(\frac{\partial \mathcal{E}_{\mathbf{x}}}{\partial o_1}, \frac{\partial \mathcal{E}_{\mathbf{x}}}{\partial o_2}, \cdots, \frac{\partial \mathcal{E}_{\mathbf{x}}}{\partial o_K}\right)^T = \left(-\frac{y_1}{o_1}, -\frac{y_2}{o_2}, \cdots, -\frac{y_K}{o_K}\right)^T \tag{25.18}$$

Binary Cross-Entropy Error: For classification tasks with binary classes, it is typical to encode the positive class as 1 and the negative class as 0, as opposed to using a one-hot encoding as in the general K-class case. Given an input $\mathbf{x} \in \mathbb{R}^d$, with true response $y \in \{0, 1\}$, there is only one output neuron o. Therefore, the binary cross-entropy error is defined as

$$\mathcal{E}_{\mathbf{x}} = -\big(y \cdot \ln(o) + (1 - y) \cdot \ln(1 - o)\big) \tag{25.19}$$

Here y is either 1 or 0. The partial derivative of the binary cross-entropy error function with respect to the output neuron o is

$$\begin{aligned}
\frac{\partial \mathcal{E}_{\mathbf{x}}}{\partial o} &= \frac{\partial}{\partial o} \Big\{ -y \cdot \ln(o) - (1 - y) \cdot \ln(1 - o) \Big\} \\
&= -\left(\frac{y}{o} + \frac{1 - y}{1 - o} \cdot -1 \right) = \frac{-y \cdot (1 - o) + (1 - y) \cdot o}{o \cdot (1 - o)} \\
&= \frac{o - y}{o \cdot (1 - o)}
\end{aligned} \tag{25.20}$$

25.3 MULTILAYER PERCEPTRON: ONE HIDDEN LAYER

A multilayer perceptron (MLP) is a neural network that has distinct layers of neurons. The inputs to the neural network comprise the *input layer*, and the final outputs from the MLP comprise the *output layer*. Any intermediate layer is called a *hidden layer*, and an MLP can have one or many hidden layers. Networks with many hidden layers are called *deep neural networks*. An MLP is also a feed-forward network. That is, information flows in the forward direction, and from a layer only to the subsequent layer. Thus, information flows from the input to the first hidden layer, from the first to the second hidden layer, and so on, until it reaches the output layer from the last hidden layer. Typically, MLPs are fully connected between layers. That is, each neuron in the input layer is connected to all the neurons in the first hidden layer, and each neuron in the first hidden layer is connected to all neurons in the second hidden layer, and so on, and finally, each neuron in the last hidden layer is connected to all neurons in the output layer.

For ease of explanation, in this section, we will consider an MLP with only one hidden layer, and we will later generalize the discussion to deep MLPs. For example, Figure 25.6 shows an MLP with one hidden layer. The input layer has d neurons, $x_1, x_2, \cdots, x_d$, and an additional neuron x_0 that specifies the biases for the hidden layer. The hidden layer has m neurons, $z_1, z_2, \cdots, z_m$, and an additional neuron z_0 that specifies the biases for the output neurons. Finally, the output layer has p neurons, $o_1, o_2, \cdots, o_p$. The bias neurons have no incoming edges, since their value is always fixed at 1. Thus, in total there are $d \times m + m \times p$ weight parameters (w_{ij}) and a further $m + p$ bias parameters (b_i) that need to be learned by the neural network. These parameters also correspond to the total number of edges in the MLP.

25.3.1 Feed-forward Phase

Let $\mathbf{D}$ denote the training dataset, comprising n input points $\mathbf{x}_i \in \mathbb{R}^d$ and corresponding true response vectors $\mathbf{y}_i \in \mathbb{R}^p$. For each pair $(\mathbf{x}, \mathbf{y})$ in the data, in the feed-forward phase,

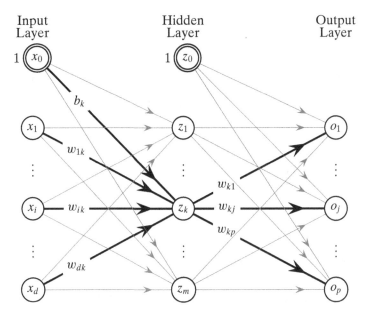

Figure 25.6. Multilayer perceptron with one hidden layer. Input and output links for neuron z_k are shown in bold. Neurons x_0 and z_0 are bias neurons.

the point $\mathbf{x} = (x_1, x_2, \cdots, x_d)^T \in \mathbb{R}^d$ is supplied as an input to the MLP. The input neurons do not use any activation function, and simply pass along the supplied input values as their output value. This is equivalent to saying that the net at input neuron k is $net_k = x_k$, and the activation function is the identity function $f(net_k) = net_k$, so that the output value of neuron k is simply x_k.

Given the input neuron values, we compute the output value for each hidden neuron z_k as follows:

$$z_k = f(net_k) = f\left(b_k + \sum_{i=1}^{d} w_{ik} \cdot x_i\right)$$

where f is some activation function, and w_{ik} denotes the weight between input neuron x_i and hidden neuron z_k. Next, given the hidden neuron values, we compute the value for each output neuron o_j as follows:

$$o_j = f(net_j) = f\left(b_j + \sum_{i=1}^{m} w_{ij} \cdot z_i\right)$$

where w_{ij} denotes the weight between hidden neuron z_i and output neuron o_j.

We can write the feed-forward phase as a series of matrix-vector operations. For this we define the $d \times m$ matrix $\mathbf{W}_h$ comprising the weights between input and hidden layer neurons, and vector $\mathbf{b}_h \in \mathbb{R}^m$ comprising the bias terms for hidden layer neurons, given as

$$\mathbf{W}_h = \begin{pmatrix} w_{11} & w_{12} & \cdots & w_{1m} \\ w_{21} & w_{22} & \cdots & w_{2m} \\ \vdots & \vdots & \cdots & \vdots \\ w_{d1} & w_{d2} & \cdots & w_{dm} \end{pmatrix} \qquad \mathbf{b}_h = \begin{pmatrix} b_1 \\ b_2 \\ \vdots \\ b_m \end{pmatrix} \qquad (25.21)$$

where w_{ij} denotes the weight on the edge between input neuron x_i and hidden neuron z_j, and b_i denotes the bias weight from x_0 to z_i. The net input and the output for all the hidden layer neurons can be computed via a matrix-vector multiplication operation, as follows:

$$\mathbf{net}_h = \mathbf{b}_h + \mathbf{W}_h^T \mathbf{x} \qquad (25.22)$$

$$\mathbf{z} = f(\mathbf{net}_h) = f\left(\mathbf{b}_h + \mathbf{W}_h^T \mathbf{x}\right) \qquad (25.23)$$

Here, $\mathbf{net}_h = (net_1, \cdots, net_m)^T$ denotes the net input at each hidden neuron (excluding the bias neuron z_0 whose value is always fixed at $z_0 = 1$), and $\mathbf{z} = (z_1, z_2, \cdots, z_m)^T$ denotes the vector of hidden neuron values. The activation function $f(\cdot)$ applies to, or distributes over, each element of $\mathbf{net}_h$, i.e., $f(\mathbf{net}_h) = (f(net_1), \cdots, f(net_m))^T \in \mathbb{R}^m$. Typically, all neurons in a given layer use the same activation function, but they can also be different if desired.

Likewise, let $\mathbf{W}_o \in \mathbb{R}^{m \times p}$ denote the weight matrix between the hidden and output layers, and let $\mathbf{b}_o \in \mathbb{R}^p$ be the bias vector for output neurons, given as

$$\mathbf{W}_o = \begin{pmatrix} w_{11} & w_{12} & \cdots & w_{1p} \\ w_{21} & w_{22} & \cdots & w_{2p} \\ \vdots & \vdots & \cdots & \vdots \\ w_{m1} & w_{m2} & \cdots & w_{mp} \end{pmatrix} \qquad \mathbf{b}_o = \begin{pmatrix} b_1 \\ b_2 \\ \vdots \\ b_p \end{pmatrix} \qquad (25.24)$$

where w_{ij} denotes the weight on the edge between hidden neuron z_i and output neuron o_j, and b_i the bias weight between z_0 and output neuron o_i. The output vector can then be computed as follows:

$$\mathbf{net}_o = \mathbf{b}_o + \mathbf{W}_o^T \mathbf{z} \qquad (25.25)$$

$$\mathbf{o} = f(\mathbf{net}_o) = f\left(\mathbf{b}_o + \mathbf{W}_o^T \mathbf{z}\right) \qquad (25.26)$$

To summarize, for a given input $\mathbf{x} \in \mathbf{D}$ with desired response $\mathbf{y}$, an MLP computes the output vector via the feed-forward process, as follows:

$$\mathbf{o} = f\left(\mathbf{b}_o + \mathbf{W}_o^T \mathbf{z}\right) = f\left(\mathbf{b}_o + \mathbf{W}_o^T \cdot f\left(\mathbf{b}_h + \mathbf{W}_h^T \mathbf{x}\right)\right) \qquad (25.27)$$

where, $\mathbf{o} = (o_1, o_2, \cdots, o_p)^T$ is the vector of predicted outputs from the single hidden layer MLP.

25.3.2 Backpropagation Phase

Backpropagation is the algorithm used to learn the weights between successive layers in an MLP. The name comes from the manner in which the *error gradient* is propagated backwards from the output to input layers via the hidden layers. For simplicity of exposition, we will consider backpropagation for an MLP with a single hidden layer with m neurons, with squared error function, and with sigmoid activations for all neurons. We will later generalize to multiple hidden layers, and other error and activation functions.

Let $\mathbf{D}$ denote the training dataset, comprising n input points $\mathbf{x}_i = (x_{i1}, x_{i2}, \cdots, x_{id})^T \in \mathbb{R}^d$ and corresponding true response vectors $\mathbf{y}_i \in \mathbb{R}^p$. Let $\mathbf{W}_h \in \mathbb{R}^{d \times m}$ denote the weight matrix between the input and hidden layer, and $\mathbf{b}_h \in \mathbb{R}^m$ the vector of bias terms for the hidden neurons from Eq. (25.21). Likewise, let $\mathbf{W}_o \in \mathbb{R}^{m \times p}$ denote the weight matrix between the hidden and output layer, and $\mathbf{b}_o \in \mathbb{R}^p$ the bias vector for output neurons from Eq. (25.24).

For a given input pair $(\mathbf{x}, \mathbf{y})$ in the training data, the MLP first computes the output vector $\mathbf{o}$ via the feed-forward step in Eq. (25.27). Next, it computes the error in the predicted output *vis-a-vis* the true response $\mathbf{y}$ using the squared error function

$$\mathcal{E}_{\mathbf{x}} = \frac{1}{2} \|\mathbf{y} - \mathbf{o}\|^2 = \frac{1}{2} \sum_{j=1}^{p} (y_j - o_j)^2 \tag{25.28}$$

The basic idea behind backpropagation is to examine the extent to which an output neuron, say o_j, deviates from the corresponding target response y_j, and to modify the weights w_{ij} between each hidden neuron z_i and o_j as some function of the error – large error should cause a correspondingly large change in the weight, and small error should result in smaller changes. Likewise, the weights between all input and hidden neurons should also be updated as some function of the error at the output, as well as changes already computed for the weights between the hidden and output layers. That is, the error propagates backwards.

The weight update is done via a gradient descent approach to minimize the error. Let $\nabla_{w_{ij}}$ be the gradient of the error function with respect to w_{ij}, or simply the *weight gradient* at w_{ij}. Given the previous weight estimate w_{ij}, a new weight is computed by taking a small step η in a direction that is opposite to the weight gradient at w_{ij}

$$w_{ij} = w_{ij} - \eta \cdot \nabla_{w_{ij}} \tag{25.29}$$

In a similar manner, the bias term b_j is also updated via gradient descent

$$b_j = b_j - \eta \cdot \nabla_{b_j} \tag{25.30}$$

where ∇_{b_j} is the gradient of the error function with respect to b_j, which we call the *bias gradient* at b_j.

Updating Parameters Between Hidden and Output Layer

Consider the weight w_{ij} between hidden neuron z_i and output neuron o_j, and the bias term b_j between z_0 and o_j. Using the chain rule of differentiation, we compute the weight gradient at w_{ij} and bias gradient at b_j, as follows:

$$\begin{aligned}
\nabla_{w_{ij}} &= \frac{\partial \mathcal{E}_{\mathbf{x}}}{\partial w_{ij}} = \frac{\partial \mathcal{E}_{\mathbf{x}}}{\partial net_j} \cdot \frac{\partial net_j}{\partial w_{ij}} = \delta_j \cdot z_i \\
\nabla_{b_j} &= \frac{\partial \mathcal{E}_{\mathbf{x}}}{\partial b_j} = \frac{\partial \mathcal{E}_{\mathbf{x}}}{\partial net_j} \cdot \frac{\partial net_j}{\partial b_j} = \delta_j
\end{aligned} \tag{25.31}$$

where we use the symbol δ_j to denote the partial derivative of the error with respect to net signal at o_j, which we also call the *net gradient* at o_j

$$\delta_j = \frac{\partial \mathcal{E}_{\mathbf{x}}}{\partial net_j} \tag{25.32}$$

Furthermore, the partial derivative of net_j with respect to w_{ij} and b_j is given as

$$\frac{\partial net_j}{\partial w_{ij}} = \frac{\partial}{\partial w_{ij}} \left\{ b_j + \sum_{k=1}^{m} w_{kj} \cdot z_k \right\} = z_i \qquad \frac{\partial net_j}{\partial b_j} = \frac{\partial}{\partial b_j} \left\{ b_j + \sum_{k=1}^{m} w_{kj} \cdot z_k \right\} = 1$$

where we used the fact that b_j and all w_{kj} for $k \neq i$ are constants with respect to w_{ij}.

Next, we need to compute δ_j, the net gradient at o_j. This can also be computed via the chain rule

$$\delta_j = \frac{\partial \mathcal{E}_{\mathbf{x}}}{\partial net_j} = \frac{\partial \mathcal{E}_{\mathbf{x}}}{\partial f(net_j)} \cdot \frac{\partial f(net_j)}{\partial net_j} \tag{25.33}$$

Note that $f(net_j) = o_j$. Thus, δ_j is composed of two terms, namely the partial derivative of the error term with respect to the output or activation function applied to the net signal, and the derivative of the activation function with respect to its argument. Using the squared error function and from Eq. (25.14), for the former, we have

$$\frac{\partial \mathcal{E}_{\mathbf{x}}}{\partial f(net_j)} = \frac{\partial \mathcal{E}_{\mathbf{x}}}{\partial o_j} = \frac{\partial}{\partial o_j} \left\{ \frac{1}{2} \sum_{k=1}^{p} (y_k - o_k)^2 \right\} = (o_j - y_j)$$

where we used the observation that all o_k for $k \neq j$ are constants with respect to o_j. Since we assume a sigmoid activation function, for the latter, we have via Eq. (25.10)

$$\frac{\partial f(net_j)}{\partial net_j} = o_j \cdot (1 - o_j)$$

Putting it all together, we get

$$\delta_j = (o_j - y_j) \cdot o_j \cdot (1 - o_j)$$

Let $\boldsymbol{\delta}_o = (\delta_1, \delta_2, \ldots, \delta_p)^T$ denote the vector of net gradients at each output neuron, which we call the *net gradient vector* for the output layer. We can write $\boldsymbol{\delta}_o$ as

$$\boxed{\boldsymbol{\delta}_o = \mathbf{o} \odot (\mathbf{1} - \mathbf{o}) \odot (\mathbf{o} - \mathbf{y})} \tag{25.34}$$

where $\odot$ denotes the element-wise product (also called the *Hadamard product*) between the vectors, and where $\mathbf{o} = (o_1, o_2, \cdots, o_p)^T$ is the predicted output vector, $\mathbf{y} = (y_1, y_2, \cdots, y_p)^T$ is the (true) response vector, and $\mathbf{1} = (1, \cdots, 1)^T \in \mathbb{R}^p$ is the p-dimensional vector of all ones.

Let $\mathbf{z} = (z_1, z_2, \cdots, z_m)^T$ denote the vector comprising the values of all hidden layer neurons (after applying the activation function). Based on Eq. (25.31), we can compute the gradients $\nabla_{w_{ij}}$ for all hidden to output neuron connections via the outer product of

$\mathbf{z}$ and $\boldsymbol{\delta}_o$:

$$\nabla_{\mathbf{W}_o} = \begin{pmatrix} \nabla_{w_{11}} & \nabla_{w_{12}} & \cdots & \nabla_{w_{1p}} \\ \nabla_{w_{21}} & \nabla_{w_{22}} & \cdots & \nabla_{w_{2p}} \\ \vdots & \vdots & \cdots & \vdots \\ \nabla_{w_{m1}} & \nabla_{w_{m2}} & \cdots & \nabla_{w_{mp}} \end{pmatrix} = \mathbf{z} \cdot \boldsymbol{\delta}_o^T \qquad (25.35)$$

where $\nabla_{\mathbf{W}_o} \in \mathbb{R}^{m \times p}$ is the matrix of weight gradients. The vector of bias gradients is given as:

$$\nabla_{\mathbf{b}_o} = \left(\nabla_{b_1}, \nabla_{b_2}, \cdots, \nabla_{b_p} \right)^T = \boldsymbol{\delta}_o \qquad (25.36)$$

where $\nabla_{\mathbf{b}_o} \in \mathbb{R}^p$.

Once the gradients have been computed, we can update all the weights and biases as follows

$$\begin{aligned} \mathbf{W}_o &= \mathbf{W}_o - \eta \cdot \nabla_{\mathbf{W}_o} \\ \mathbf{b}_o &= \mathbf{b}_o - \eta \cdot \nabla_{\mathbf{b}_o} \end{aligned} \qquad (25.37)$$

where η is the step size (also called the *learning rate*) for gradient descent.

Updating Parameters Between Input and Hidden Layer

Consider the weight w_{ij} between input neuron x_i and hidden neuron z_j, and the bias term between x_0 and z_j. The weight gradient at w_{ij} and bias gradient at b_j is computed similarly to Eq. (25.31)

$$\begin{aligned} \nabla_{w_{ij}} &= \frac{\partial \mathcal{E}_{\mathbf{x}}}{\partial w_{ij}} = \frac{\partial \mathcal{E}_{\mathbf{x}}}{\partial net_j} \cdot \frac{\partial net_j}{\partial w_{ij}} = \delta_j \cdot x_i \\ \nabla_{b_j} &= \frac{\partial \mathcal{E}_{\mathbf{x}}}{\partial b_j} = \frac{\partial \mathcal{E}_{\mathbf{x}}}{\partial net_j} \cdot \frac{\partial net_j}{\partial b_j} = \delta_j \end{aligned} \qquad (25.38)$$

which follows from

$$\frac{\partial net_j}{\partial w_{ij}} = \frac{\partial}{\partial w_{ij}} \left\{ b_j + \sum_{k=1}^{m} w_{kj} \cdot x_k \right\} = x_i \qquad \frac{\partial net_j}{\partial b_j} = \frac{\partial}{\partial b_j} \left\{ b_j + \sum_{k=1}^{m} w_{kj} \cdot x_k \right\} = 1$$

To compute the net gradient δ_j at the hidden neuron z_j we have to consider the error gradients that flow back from all the output neurons to z_j. Applying the chain rule, we get:

$$\delta_j = \frac{\partial \mathcal{E}_{\mathbf{x}}}{\partial net_j} = \sum_{k=1}^{p} \frac{\partial \mathcal{E}_{\mathbf{x}}}{\partial net_k} \cdot \frac{\partial net_k}{\partial z_j} \cdot \frac{\partial z_j}{\partial net_j} = \frac{\partial z_j}{\partial net_j} \cdot \sum_{k=1}^{p} \frac{\partial \mathcal{E}_{\mathbf{x}}}{\partial net_k} \cdot \frac{\partial net_k}{\partial z_j}$$

$$= z_j \cdot (1 - z_j) \cdot \sum_{k=1}^{p} \delta_k \cdot w_{jk}$$

where $\frac{\partial z_j}{\partial net_j} = z_j \cdot (1 - z_j)$, since we assume a sigmoid activation function for the hidden neurons. The chain rule leads to a natural interpretation for backpropagation, namely,

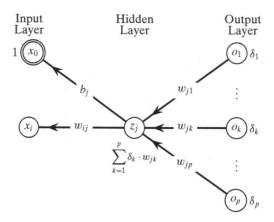

Figure 25.7. Backpropagation of gradients from output to hidden layer.

to find the net gradient at z_j we have to consider the net gradients at each of the output neurons δ_k but weighted by the strength of the connection w_{jk} between z_j and o_k, as illustrated in Figure 25.7. That is, we compute the weighted sum of gradients $\sum_{k=1}^{p} \delta_k \cdot w_{jk}$, which is used to compute δ_j, the net gradient at hidden neuron z_j.

Let $\boldsymbol{\delta}_o = (\delta_1, \delta_2, \ldots, \delta_p)^T$ denote the vector of net gradients at the output neurons, and $\boldsymbol{\delta}_h = (\delta_1, \delta_2, \ldots, \delta_m)^T$ the net gradients at the hidden layer neurons. We can write $\boldsymbol{\delta}_h$ compactly as

$$\boldsymbol{\delta}_h = \mathbf{z} \odot (\mathbf{1} - \mathbf{z}) \odot (\mathbf{W}_o \cdot \boldsymbol{\delta}_o) \tag{25.39}$$

where $\odot$ is the element-wise product, $\mathbf{1} = (1, 1, \cdots, 1) \in \mathbb{R}^m$ is the vector of all ones and $\mathbf{z} = (z_1, z_2, \cdots, z_m)^T$ is the vector of hidden layer outputs. Furthermore, $\mathbf{W}_o \cdot \boldsymbol{\delta}_o \in \mathbb{R}^m$ is the vector of weighted gradients at each hidden neuron, since

$$\mathbf{W}_o \cdot \boldsymbol{\delta}_o = \left(\sum_{k=1}^{p} \delta_k \cdot w_{1k}, \quad \sum_{k=1}^{p} \delta_k \cdot w_{2k}, \quad \cdots, \quad \sum_{k=1}^{p} \delta_k \cdot w_{mk} \right)^T$$

Let $\mathbf{x} = (x_1, x_2, \cdots, x_d)^T$ denote the input vector, then based on Eq. (25.38) we can compute the gradients $\nabla_{w_{ij}}$ for all input to hidden layer connections via the outer product:

$$\nabla_{\mathbf{W}_h} = \begin{pmatrix} \nabla_{w_{11}} & \cdots & \nabla_{w_{1m}} \\ \nabla_{w_{21}} & \cdots & \nabla_{w_{2m}} \\ \vdots & \cdots & \vdots \\ \nabla_{w_{d1}} & \cdots & \nabla_{w_{dm}} \end{pmatrix} = \mathbf{x} \cdot \boldsymbol{\delta}_h^T \tag{25.40}$$

where $\nabla_{\mathbf{W}_h} \in \mathbb{R}^{d \times m}$ is the matrix of weight gradients. The vector of bias gradients is given as:

$$\nabla_{\mathbf{b}_h} = \left(\nabla_{b_1}, \nabla_{b_2}, \cdots, \nabla_{b_m} \right)^T = \boldsymbol{\delta}_h \tag{25.41}$$

where $\nabla_{\mathbf{b}_h} \in \mathbb{R}^m$.

Algorithm 25.1: MLP Training: Stochastic Gradient Descent

MLP-Training $(\mathbf{D}, m, \eta, \texttt{maxiter})$:

// Initialize bias vectors

1 $\mathbf{b}_h \leftarrow$ random m-dimensional vector with small values

2 $\mathbf{b}_o \leftarrow$ random p-dimensional vector with small values

// Initialize weight matrices

3 $\mathbf{W}_h \leftarrow$ random $d \times m$ matrix with small values

4 $\mathbf{W}_o \leftarrow$ random $m \times p$ matrix with small values

5 $t \leftarrow 0$ // iteration counter

6 **repeat**

7 $\quad$ **foreach** $(\mathbf{x}_i, \mathbf{y}_i) \in \mathbf{D}$ *in random order* **do**

$\qquad$ // Feed-forward phase

8 $\qquad$ $\mathbf{z}_i \leftarrow f\left(\mathbf{b}_h + \mathbf{W}_h^T \mathbf{x}_i\right)$

9 $\qquad$ $\mathbf{o}_i \leftarrow f\left(\mathbf{b}_o + \mathbf{W}_o^T \mathbf{z}_i\right)$

$\qquad$ // Backpropagation phase: net gradients

10 $\qquad$ $\boldsymbol{\delta}_o \leftarrow \mathbf{o}_i \odot (\mathbf{1} - \mathbf{o}_i) \odot (\mathbf{o}_i - \mathbf{y}_i)$

11 $\qquad$ $\boldsymbol{\delta}_h \leftarrow \mathbf{z}_i \odot (\mathbf{1} - \mathbf{z}_i) \odot (\mathbf{W}_o \cdot \boldsymbol{\delta}_o)$

$\qquad$ // Gradient descent for bias vectors

12 $\qquad$ $\nabla_{\mathbf{b}_o} \leftarrow \boldsymbol{\delta}_o; \quad \mathbf{b}_o \leftarrow \mathbf{b}_o - \eta \cdot \nabla_{\mathbf{b}_o}$

13 $\qquad$ $\nabla_{\mathbf{b}_h} \leftarrow \boldsymbol{\delta}_h; \quad \mathbf{b}_h \leftarrow \mathbf{b}_h - \eta \cdot \nabla_{\mathbf{b}_h}$

$\qquad$ // Gradient descent for weight matrices

14 $\qquad$ $\nabla_{\mathbf{W}_o} \leftarrow \mathbf{z}_i \cdot \boldsymbol{\delta}_o^T; \quad \mathbf{W}_o \leftarrow \mathbf{W}_o - \eta \cdot \nabla_{\mathbf{W}_o}$

15 $\qquad$ $\nabla_{\mathbf{W}_h} \leftarrow \mathbf{x}_i \cdot \boldsymbol{\delta}_h^T; \quad \mathbf{W}_h \leftarrow \mathbf{W}_h - \eta \cdot \nabla_{\mathbf{W}_h}$

16 $\quad$ $t \leftarrow t + 1$

17 **until** $t \geq \texttt{maxiter}$

Once the gradients have been computed, we can update all the weights and biases as follows

$$\begin{aligned} \mathbf{W}_h &= \mathbf{W}_h - \eta \cdot \nabla_{\mathbf{W}_h} \\ \mathbf{b}_h &= \mathbf{b}_h - \eta \cdot \nabla_{\mathbf{b}_h} \end{aligned} \tag{25.42}$$

where η is the step size (or learning rate).

25.3.3 MLP Training

Algorithm 25.1 shows the pseudo-code for learning the weights considering all of the input points in $\mathbf{D}$ via *stochastic gradient descent*. The code is shown for an MLP with a single hidden layer, using a squared error function, and sigmoid activations for all hidden and output neurons. The approach is called stochastic gradient descent since we compute the weight and bias gradients after observing each training point (in random order).

The MLP algorithm takes as input the dataset $\mathbf{D}$ (with points $\mathbf{x}_i$ and desired responses $\mathbf{y}_i$ for $i = 1, 2, \cdots, n$), the number of hidden layer neurons m, the learning rate

η, and an integer threshold `maxiter` that specifies the maximum number of iterations. The size of the input (d) and output (p) layers is determined automatically from **D**. The MLP first initializes the $d \times m$ input to hidden layer weight matrix $\mathbf{W}_h$, and the $m \times p$ hidden to output layer matrix $\mathbf{W}_o$ to small values, for example, uniformly random in the range $[-0.01, 0.01]$. It is important to note that weights should not be set to 0, otherwise, all hidden neurons will be identical in their values, and so will be the output neurons.

The MLP training takes multiple iterations over the input points. For each input $\mathbf{x}_i$, the MLP computes the output vector $\mathbf{o}_i$ via the feed-forward step. In the backpropagation phase, we compute the error gradient vector $\boldsymbol{\delta}_o$ with respect to the net at output neurons, followed by $\boldsymbol{\delta}_h$ for hidden neurons. In the stochastic gradient descent step, we compute the error gradients with respect to the weights and biases, which are used to update the weight matrices and bias vectors. Thus, for every input vector $\mathbf{x}_i$, all the weights and biases are updated based on the error incurred between the predicted output $\mathbf{o}_i$ and the true response $\mathbf{y}_i$. After each input has been processed, that completes one iteration of training, called an *epoch*. Training stops when the maximum number of iterations, `maxiter`, has been reached. On the other hand, during testing, for any input $\mathbf{x}$, we apply the feed-forward steps and print the predicted output $\mathbf{o}$.

In terms of computational complexity, each iteration of the MLP training algorithm takes $O(dm + mp)$ time for the feed-forward phase, $p + mp + m = O(mp)$ time for the backpropagation of error gradients, and $O(dm + mp)$ time for updating the weight matrices and bias vectors. Thus, the total training time per iteration is $O(dm + mp)$.

Example 25.3 (MLP with one hidden layer). We now illustrate an MLP with a hidden layer using a non-linear activation function to learn the sine curve. Figure 25.8(a) shows the training data (the gray points on the curve), which comprises $n = 25$ points x_i sampled randomly in the range $[-10, 10]$, with $y_i = \sin(x_i)$. The testing data comprises 1000 points sampled uniformly from the same range. The figure also shows the desired output curve (thin line). We used an MLP with one input neuron ($d = 1$), ten hidden neurons ($m = 10$) and one output neuron ($p = 1$). The hidden neurons use tanh activations, whereas the output unit uses an identity activation. The step size is $\eta = 0.005$.

The input to hidden weight matrix $\mathbf{W}_h \in \mathbb{R}^{1 \times 10}$ and the corresponding bias vector $\mathbf{b}_h \in \mathbb{R}^{10 \times 1}$ are given as:

$$\mathbf{W}_h = (-0.68, 0.77, -0.42, -0.72, -0.93, -0.42, -0.66, -0.70, -0.62, -0.50)$$

$$\mathbf{b}_h = (-4.36, 2.43, -0.52, 2.35 - 1.64, 3.98, 0.31, 4.45, 1.03, -4.77)^T$$

The hidden to output weight matrix $\mathbf{W}_o \in \mathbb{R}^{10 \times 1}$ and the bias term $\mathbf{b}_o \in \mathbb{R}$ are given as:

$$\mathbf{W}_o = (-1.82, -1.69, -0.82, 1.37, 0.14, 2.37, -1.64, -1.92, 0.78, 2.17)^T$$

$$\mathbf{b}_o = -0.16$$

Figure 25.8(a) shows the output of the MLP on the test set, after the first iteration of training ($t = 1$). We can see that initially the predicted response deviates

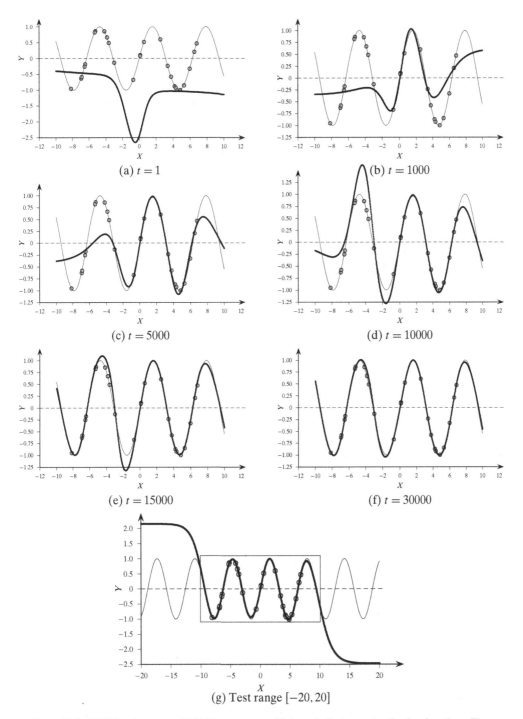

Figure 25.8. MLP for sine curve: 10 hidden neurons with hyperbolic tangent activation functions. The gray dots represent the training data. The bold line is the predicted response, whereas the thin line is the true response. (a)–(f): Predictions after different number of iterations. (g): Testing outside the training range. Good fit within the training range $[-10, 10]$ shown in the box.

significantly from the true sine response. Figure 25.8(a)–(f) show the output from the MLP after different number of training iterations. By $t = 15000$ iterations the output on the test set comes close to the sine curve, but it takes another 15000 iterations to get a closer fit. The final SSE is 1.45 over the 1000 test points.

We can observe that, even with a very small training data of 25 points sampled randomly from the sine curve, the MLP is able to learn the desired function. However, it is also important to recognize that the MLP model has not really learned the sine function; rather, it has learned to approximate it only in the specified range $[-10, 10]$. We can see in Figure 25.8(g) that when we try to predict values outside this range, the MLP does not yield a good fit.

Example 25.4 (MLP for handwritten digit classification). In this example, we apply an MLP with one hidden layer for the task of predicting the correct label for a hand-written digit from the MNIST database, which contains 60,000 training images that span the 10 digit labels, from 0 to 9. Each (grayscale) image is a 28×28 matrix of pixels, with values between 0 and 255. Each pixel is converted to a value in the interval $[0, 1]$ by dividing by 255. Figure 25.9 shows an example of each digit from the MNIST dataset.

Since images are 2-dimensional matrices, we first *flatten* them into a vector $\mathbf{x} \in \mathbb{R}^{784}$ with dimensionality $d = 28 \times 28 = 784$. This is done by simply concatenating all of the rows of the images to obtain one long vector. Next, since the output labels are categorical values that denote the digits from 0 to 9, we need to convert them into binary (numerical) vectors, using *one-hot* encoding. Thus, the label 0 is encoded as $\mathbf{e}_1 = (1, 0, 0, 0, 0, 0, 0, 0, 0, 0)^T \in \mathbb{R}^{10}$, the label 1 as $\mathbf{e}_2 = (0, 1, 0, 0, 0, 0, 0, 0, 0, 0)^T \in \mathbb{R}^{10}$, and so on, and finally the label 9 is encoded as $\mathbf{e}_{10} = (0, 0, 0, 0, 0, 0, 0, 0, 0, 1)^T \in \mathbb{R}^{10}$. That is, each input image vector $\mathbf{x}$ has a corresponding target response vector $\mathbf{y} \in \{\mathbf{e}_1, \mathbf{e}_2, \cdots, \mathbf{e}_{10}\}$. Thus, the input layer for the MLP has $d = 784$ neurons, and the output layer has $p = 10$ neurons.

For the hidden layer, we consider several MLP models, each with a different number of hidden neurons m. We try $m = 0, 7, 49, 98, 196, 392$, to study the effect of increasing the number of hidden neurons, from small to large. For the hidden layer, we use ReLU activation function, and for the output layer, we use softmax activation, since the target response vector has only one neuron with value 1, with the rest being 0. Note that $m = 0$ means that there is no hidden layer – the input layer is directly connected to the output layer, which is equivalent to a multiclass logistic regression model. We train each MLP for $t = 15$ epochs, using step size $\eta = 0.25$.

During training, we plot the number of misclassified images after each epoch, on the separate MNIST test set comprising 10,000 images. Figure 25.10 shows the number of errors from each of the models (with a different number of hidden neurons m), after each epoch. The final test error at the end of training is given as

m	0	7	10	49	98	196	392
errors	1677	901	792	546	495	470	454

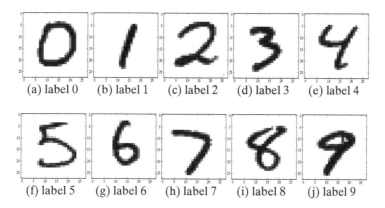

Figure 25.9. MNIST dataset: Sample handwritten digits.

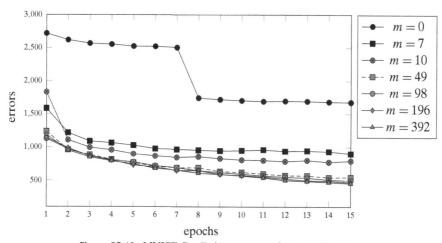

Figure 25.10. MNIST: Prediction error as a function of epochs.

We can observe that adding a hidden layer significantly improves the prediction accuracy. Using even a small number of hidden neurons helps, compared to the logistic regression model ($m = 0$). For example, using $m = 7$ results in 901 errors (or error rate 9.01%) compared to using $m = 0$, which results in 1677 errors (or error rate 16.77%). On the other hand, as we increase the number of hidden neurons, the error rate decreases, though with diminishing returns. Using $m = 196$, the error rate is 4.70%, but even after doubling the number of hidden neurons ($m = 392$), the error rate goes down to only 4.54%. Further increasing m does not reduce the error rate.

25.4 DEEP MULTILAYER PERCEPTRONS

We now generalize the feed-forward and backpropagation steps for many hidden layers, as well as arbitrary error and neuron activation functions.

Consider an MLP with h hidden layers as shown in Figure 25.11. We assume that the input to the MLP comprises n points $\mathbf{x}_i \in \mathbb{R}^d$ with the corresponding true response vector $\mathbf{y}_i \in \mathbb{R}^p$. We denote the input neurons as layer $l = 0$, the first hidden layer as $l = 1$, the last hidden layer as $l = h$, and finally the output layer as layer $l = h+1$. We use n_l to denote the number of neurons in layer l. Since the input points are d-dimensional, this implies $n_0 = d$, and since the true response vector is p-dimensional, we have $n_{h+1} = p$. The hidden layers have n_1 neurons for the first hidden layer, n_2 for the second layer, and n_h for the last hidden layer. The vector of neuron values for layer l (for $l = 0, \cdots, h+1$) is denoted as

$$\mathbf{z}^l = \left(z_1^l, \cdots, z_{n_l}^l \right)^T$$

Each layer except the output layer has one extra bias neuron, which is the neuron at index 0. Thus, the bias neuron for layer l is denoted z_0^l and its value is fixed at $z_0^l = 1$.

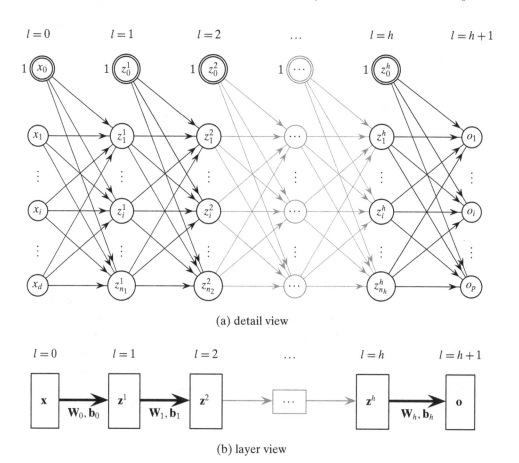

(a) detail view

(b) layer view

Figure 25.11. Deep multilayer perceptron, with h hidden layers.

Figure 25.11(a) displays a detailed view of an MLP with h hidden layers, showing the individual neurons in each layer including the bias neuron. Note that the vector of input neuron values is also written as

$$\mathbf{x} = (x_1, x_2, \cdots, x_d)^T = \left(z_1^0, z_2^0, \cdots, z_d^0\right)^T = \mathbf{z}^0$$

and the vector of output neuron values is also denoted as

$$\mathbf{o} = (o_1, o_2, \cdots, o_p)^T = \left(z_1^{h+1}, z_2^{h+1}, \cdots, z_p^{h+1}\right)^T = \mathbf{z}^{h+1}$$

The weight matrix between layer l and layer $l+1$ neurons is denoted $\mathbf{W}_l \in \mathbb{R}^{n_l \times n_{l+1}}$, and the vector of bias terms from the bias neuron z_0^l to neurons in layer $l+1$ is denoted $\mathbf{b}_l \in \mathbb{R}^{n_{l+1}}$, for $l = 0, 1, \cdots, h$. Thus, $\mathbf{W}_0 \in \mathbb{R}^{d \times n_1}$ is the weight matrix between the input and first hidden layer, $\mathbf{W}_1 \in \mathbb{R}^{n_1 \times n_2}$ is the weight matrix between the first and second hidden layer, and so on; finally, $\mathbf{W}_h \in \mathbb{R}^{n_h \times p}$ is the weight matrix between the last hidden layer and the output layer. For the bias vectors, $\mathbf{b}_0 \in \mathbb{R}^{n_1}$ specifies the biases for neurons in the first hidden layer, $\mathbf{b}_1 \in \mathbb{R}^{n_2}$ the biases for neurons in the second hidden layer, and so on. Thus, $\mathbf{b}_h \in \mathbb{R}^p$ specifies the biases for the output neurons. Figure 25.11(b) shows a layer view for an MLP with h hidden layers. This is a more compact representation that clearly specifies the architecture or topology of the MLP. Each layer l is represented as a rectangular node, and is marked with the vector of neuron values, $\mathbf{z}^l$. The bias neurons are not shown, but are assumed to be present in each layer except the output. An edge between layer l and $l+1$ is labeled with the weight matrix $\mathbf{W}_l$ and bias vector $\mathbf{b}_l$ that specify the parameters between those layers.

For training deep MLPs, we will refer to several partial derivative vectors, described next. Define δ_i^l as the net gradient, i.e., the partial derivative of the error function with respect to the net value at z_i^l

$$\delta_i^l = \frac{\partial \mathcal{E}_{\mathbf{x}}}{\partial net_i} \tag{25.43}$$

and let $\boldsymbol{\delta}^l$ denote the net gradient vector at layer l, for $l = 1, 2, \cdots, h+1$

$$\boldsymbol{\delta}^l = \left(\delta_1^l, \cdots, \delta_{n_l}^l\right)^T \tag{25.44}$$

Let f^l denote the activation function for layer l, for $l = 0, 1, \cdots, h+1$, and further let $\partial \mathbf{f}^l$ denote the vector of the derivatives of the activation function with respect to net_i for all neurons z_i^l in layer l:

$$\partial \mathbf{f}^l = \left(\frac{\partial f^l(net_1)}{\partial net_1}, \cdots, \frac{\partial f^l(net_{n_l})}{\partial net_{n_l}}\right)^T \tag{25.45}$$

Finally, let $\partial \mathcal{E}_{\mathbf{x}}$ denote the vector of partial derivatives of the error function with respect to the values o_i for all output neurons:

$$\partial \mathcal{E}_{\mathbf{x}} = \left(\frac{\partial \mathcal{E}_{\mathbf{x}}}{\partial o_1}, \frac{\partial \mathcal{E}_{\mathbf{x}}}{\partial o_2}, \cdots, \frac{\partial \mathcal{E}_{\mathbf{x}}}{\partial o_p}\right)^T \tag{25.46}$$

25.4.1 Feed-forward Phase

Typically in a deep MLP, the same activation function f^l is used for all neurons in a given layer l. The input layer always uses the identity activation, so f^0 is the identity function. Also, all bias neurons also use the identity function with a fixed value of 1. The output layer typically uses sigmoid or softmax activations for classification tasks, or identity activations for regression tasks. The hidden layers typically use sigmoid, tanh, or ReLU activations. In our discussion, we assume a fixed activation function f^l for all neurons in a given layer. However, it is easy to generalize to a neuron specific activation function f_i^l for neuron z_i^l in layer l.

For a given input pair $(\mathbf{x}, \mathbf{y}) \in \mathbf{D}$, the deep MLP computes the output vector via the feed-forward process:

$$\mathbf{o} = f^{h+1}\left(\mathbf{b}_h + \mathbf{W}_h^T \cdot \mathbf{z}^h\right)$$

$$= f^{h+1}\left(\mathbf{b}_h + \mathbf{W}_h^T \cdot f^h\left(\mathbf{b}_{h-1} + \mathbf{W}_{h-1}^T \cdot \mathbf{z}^{h-1}\right)\right)$$

$$= \quad \vdots$$

$$= f^{h+1}\left(\mathbf{b}_h + \mathbf{W}_h^T \cdot f^h\left(\mathbf{b}_{h-1} + \mathbf{W}_{h-1}^T \cdot f^{h-1}\left(\cdots f^2\left(\mathbf{b}_1 + \mathbf{W}_1^T \cdot f^1\left(\mathbf{b}_0 + \mathbf{W}_0^T \cdot \mathbf{x}\right)\right)\right)\right)\right)$$

Note that each f^l distributes over its argument. That is,

$$f^l\left(\mathbf{b}_{l-1} + \mathbf{W}_{l-1}^T \cdot \mathbf{x}\right) = \left(f^l\left(net_1\right), f^l\left(net_2\right), \cdots, f^l\left(net_{n_l}\right)\right)^T$$

25.4.2 Backpropagation Phase

Consider the weight update between a given layer and another, including between the input and hidden layer, or between two hidden layers, or between the last hidden layer and the output layer. Let z_i^l be a neuron in layer l, and z_j^{l+1} a neuron in the next layer $l+1$. Let w_{ij}^l be the weight between z_i^l and z_j^{l+1}, and let b_j^l denote the bias term between z_0^l and z_j^{l+1}. The weight and bias are updated using the gradient descent approach

$$w_{ij}^l = w_{ij}^l - \eta \cdot \nabla_{w_{ij}^l} \qquad\qquad b_j^l = b_j^l - \eta \cdot \nabla_{b_j^l}$$

where $\nabla_{w_{ij}^l}$ is the weight gradient and $\nabla_{b_j^l}$ is the bias gradient, i.e., the partial derivative of the error function with respect to the weight and bias, respectively:

$$\nabla_{w_{ij}^l} = \frac{\partial \mathcal{E}_\mathbf{x}}{\partial w_{ij}^l} \qquad\qquad \nabla_{b_j^l} = \frac{\partial \mathcal{E}_\mathbf{x}}{\partial b_j^l}$$

As noted earlier in Eq. (25.31), we can use the chain rule to write the weight and bias gradient, as follows

$$\nabla_{w_{ij}^l} = \frac{\partial \mathcal{E}_\mathbf{x}}{\partial w_{ij}^l} = \frac{\partial \mathcal{E}_\mathbf{x}}{\partial net_j} \cdot \frac{\partial net_j}{\partial w_{ij}^l} = \delta_j^{l+1} \cdot z_i^l = z_i^l \cdot \delta_j^{l+1}$$

$$\nabla_{b_j^l} = \frac{\partial \mathcal{E}_\mathbf{x}}{\partial b_j^l} = \frac{\partial \mathcal{E}_\mathbf{x}}{\partial net_j} \cdot \frac{\partial net_j}{\partial b_j^l} = \delta_j^{l+1}$$

where δ_j^{l+1} is the net gradient [Eq. (25.43)], i.e., the partial derivative of the error function with respect to the net value at z_j^{l+1}, and we have

$$\frac{\partial net_j}{\partial w_{ij}^l} = \frac{\partial}{\partial w_{ij}^l}\left\{b_j^l + \sum_{k=0}^{n_l} w_{kj}^l \cdot z_k^l\right\} = z_i^l \qquad \frac{\partial net_j}{\partial b_j^l} = \frac{\partial}{\partial b_j^l}\left\{b_j^l + \sum_{k=0}^{n_l} w_{kj}^l \cdot z_k^l\right\} = 1$$

Given the vector of neuron values at layer l, namely $\mathbf{z}^l = \left(z_1^l, \cdots, z_{n_l}^l\right)^T$, we can compute the entire weight gradient matrix via an outer product operation

$$\nabla_{\mathbf{W}_l} = \mathbf{z}^l \cdot \left(\delta^{l+1}\right)^T \tag{25.47}$$

and the bias gradient vector as:

$$\nabla_{\mathbf{b}_l} = \delta^{l+1} \tag{25.48}$$

with $l = 0, 1, \cdots, h$. Here δ^{l+1} is the net gradient vector at layer $l+1$ [Eq. (25.44)].

This also allows us to update all the weights and biases as follows

$$\begin{aligned} \mathbf{W}_l &= \mathbf{W}_l - \eta \cdot \nabla_{\mathbf{W}_l} \\ \mathbf{b}_l &= \mathbf{b}_l - \eta \cdot \nabla_{\mathbf{b}_l} \end{aligned} \tag{25.49}$$

where η is the step size. However, we observe that to compute the weight and bias gradients for layer l we need to compute the net gradients δ^{l+1} at layer $l+1$.

25.4.3 Net Gradients at Output Layer

Let us consider how to compute the net gradients at the output layer $h+1$. If all of the output neurons are independent (for example, when using linear or sigmoid activations), the net gradient is obtained by differentiating the error function with respect to the net signal at the output neurons. That is,

$$\delta_j^{h+1} = \frac{\partial \mathcal{E}_\mathbf{x}}{\partial net_j} = \frac{\partial \mathcal{E}_\mathbf{x}}{\partial f^{h+1}(net_j)} \cdot \frac{\partial f^{h+1}(net_j)}{\partial net_j} = \frac{\partial \mathcal{E}_\mathbf{x}}{\partial o_j} \cdot \frac{\partial f^{h+1}(net_j)}{\partial net_j}$$

Thus, the gradient depends on two terms, the partial derivative of the error function with respect to the output neuron value, and the derivative of the activation function with respect to its argument. The net gradient vector across all output neurons is given as

$$\delta^{h+1} = \partial \mathbf{f}^{h+1} \odot \partial \mathcal{E}_\mathbf{x} \tag{25.50}$$

where $\odot$ is the element-wise or Hadamard product, $\partial \mathbf{f}^{h+1}$ is the vector of derivatives of the activation function with respect to its argument [Eq. (25.45)] at the output layer $l = h+1$, and $\partial \mathcal{E}_\mathbf{x}$ is the vector of error derivatives with respect to the output neuron values [Eq. (25.46)].

On the other hand, if the output neurons are not independent (for example, when using a softmax activation), then we have to modify the computation of the net gradient at each output neuron as follows:

$$\delta_j^{h+1} = \frac{\partial \mathcal{E}_\mathbf{x}}{\partial net_j} = \sum_{i=1}^{p} \frac{\partial \mathcal{E}_\mathbf{x}}{\partial f^{h+1}(net_i)} \cdot \frac{\partial f^{h+1}(net_i)}{\partial net_j}$$

Across all output neurons, we can write this compactly as follows:

$$\boxed{\delta^{h+1} = \partial \mathbf{F}^{h+1} \cdot \partial \mathcal{E}_\mathbf{x}} \tag{25.51}$$

where $\partial \mathbf{F}^{h+1}$ is the matrix of derivatives of $o_i = f^{h+1}(net_i)$ with respect to net_j for all $i, j = 1, 2, \cdots, p$, given as

$$\partial \mathbf{F}^{h+1} = \begin{pmatrix} \dfrac{\partial o_1}{\partial net_1} & \dfrac{\partial o_1}{\partial net_2} & \cdots & \dfrac{\partial o_1}{\partial net_p} \\ \dfrac{\partial o_2}{\partial net_1} & \dfrac{\partial o_2}{\partial net_2} & \cdots & \dfrac{\partial o_2}{\partial net_p} \\ \vdots & \vdots & \cdots & \vdots \\ \dfrac{\partial o_p}{\partial net_1} & \dfrac{\partial o_p}{\partial net_2} & \cdots & \dfrac{\partial o_p}{\partial net_p} \end{pmatrix}$$

Typically, for regression tasks, we use the squared error function with linear activation function at the output neurons, whereas for logistic regression and classification, we use the cross-entropy error function with a sigmoid activation for binary classes, and softmax activation for multiclass problems. For these common cases, the net gradient vector at the output layer is given as follows:

Squared Error: From Eq. (25.15), the error gradient is given as

$$\partial \mathcal{E}_\mathbf{x} = \frac{\partial \mathcal{E}_\mathbf{x}}{\partial \mathbf{o}} = \mathbf{o} - \mathbf{y}$$

The net gradient at the output layer is given as

$$\delta^{h+1} = \partial \mathbf{f}^{h+1} \odot \partial \mathcal{E}_\mathbf{x}$$

where $\partial \mathbf{f}^{h+1}$ depends on the activation function at the output. Typically, for regression tasks, we use a linear activation at the output neurons. In that case, we have $\partial \mathbf{f}^{h+1} = \mathbf{1}$ (see Eq. (25.8)).

Cross-Entropy Error (binary output, sigmoid activation): Consider the binary case first, with a single output neuron o with sigmoid activation. Recall that the binary cross-entropy error [Eq. (25.19)] is given as

$$\mathcal{E}_\mathbf{x} = -\big(y \cdot \ln(o) + (1 - y) \cdot \ln(1 - o)\big)$$

From Eq. (25.20) we have

$$\partial \mathcal{E}_\mathbf{x} = \frac{\partial \mathcal{E}_\mathbf{x}}{\partial o} = \frac{o - y}{o \cdot (1 - o)}$$

Further, for sigmoid activation, we have

$$\partial \mathbf{f}^{h+1} = \frac{\partial f(net_o)}{\partial net_o} = o \cdot (1 - o)$$

Therefore, the net gradient at the output neuron is

$$\delta^{h+1} = \partial \boldsymbol{\mathcal{E}_x} \cdot \partial \mathbf{f}^{h+1} = \frac{o - y}{o \cdot (1 - o)} \cdot o \cdot (1 - o) = o - y$$

Cross-Entropy Error (K outputs, softmax activation): Recall that the cross-entropy error function [Eq. (25.16)] is given as

$$\mathcal{E}_\mathbf{x} = -\sum_{i=1}^{K} y_i \cdot \ln(o_i) = -\Big(y_1 \cdot \ln(o_1) + \cdots + y_K \cdot \ln(o_K) \Big)$$

Using Eq. (25.17), the vector of error derivatives with respect to the output neurons is given as

$$\partial \boldsymbol{\mathcal{E}_x} = \left(\frac{\partial \mathcal{E}_\mathbf{x}}{\partial o_1}, \frac{\partial \mathcal{E}_\mathbf{x}}{\partial o_2}, \cdots, \frac{\partial \mathcal{E}_\mathbf{x}}{\partial o_K} \right)^T = \left(-\frac{y_1}{o_1}, -\frac{y_2}{o_2}, \cdots, -\frac{y_K}{o_K} \right)^T$$

where $p = K$ is the number of output neurons.

Cross-entropy error is typically used with the softmax activation so that we get a (normalized) probability value for each class. That is,

$$o_j = \text{softmax}(net_j) = \frac{\exp\{net_j\}}{\sum_{i=1}^{K} \exp\{net_i\}}$$

so that the output neuron values sum to one, $\sum_{j=1}^{K} o_j = 1$. Since an output neuron depends on all other output neurons, we need to compute the matrix of derivatives of each output with respect to each of the net signals at the output neurons [see Equations (25.12) and (25.18)]:

$$\partial \mathbf{F}^{h+1} = \begin{pmatrix} \dfrac{\partial o_1}{\partial net_1} & \dfrac{\partial o_1}{\partial net_2} & \cdots & \dfrac{\partial o_1}{\partial net_K} \\ \dfrac{\partial o_2}{\partial net_1} & \dfrac{\partial o_2}{\partial net_2} & \cdots & \dfrac{\partial o_2}{\partial net_K} \\ \vdots & \vdots & \cdots & \vdots \\ \dfrac{\partial o_K}{\partial net_1} & \dfrac{\partial o_K}{\partial net_2} & \cdots & \dfrac{\partial o_K}{\partial net_K} \end{pmatrix} = \begin{pmatrix} o_1 \cdot (1 - o_1) & -o_1 \cdot o_2 & \cdots & -o_1 \cdot o_K \\ -o_1 \cdot o_2 & o_2 \cdot (1 - o_2) & \cdots & -o_2 \cdot o_K \\ \vdots & \vdots & \cdots & \vdots \\ -o_1 \cdot o_K & -o_2 \cdot o_K & \cdots & o_K \cdot (1 - o_K) \end{pmatrix}$$

Therefore, the net gradient vector at the output layer is

$$\delta^{h+1} = \partial \mathbf{F}^{h+1} \cdot \partial \mathcal{E}_{\mathbf{x}} \tag{25.52}$$

$$= \begin{pmatrix} o_1 \cdot (1-o_1) & -o_1 \cdot o_2 & \cdots & -o_1 \cdot o_K \\ -o_1 \cdot o_2 & o_2 \cdot (1-o_2) & \cdots & -o_2 \cdot o_K \\ \vdots & \vdots & \cdots & \vdots \\ -o_1 \cdot o_K & -o_2 \cdot o_K & \cdots & o_K \cdot (1-o_K) \end{pmatrix} \cdot \begin{pmatrix} -\frac{y_1}{o_1} \\ -\frac{y_2}{o_2} \\ \vdots \\ -\frac{y_K}{o_K} \end{pmatrix}$$

$$= \begin{pmatrix} -y_1 + y_1 \cdot o_1 + \sum_{i \neq 1}^{K} y_i \cdot o_1 \\ -y_2 + y_2 \cdot o_2 + \sum_{i \neq 2}^{K} y_i \cdot o_2 \\ \vdots \\ -y_K + y_K \cdot o_K + \sum_{i \neq K}^{K} y_i \cdot o_K \end{pmatrix} = \begin{pmatrix} -y_1 + o_1 \cdot \sum_{i=1}^{K} y_i \\ -y_2 + o_2 \cdot \sum_{i=1}^{K} y_i \\ \vdots \\ -y_K + o_K \cdot \sum_{i=1}^{K} y_i \end{pmatrix}$$

$$= \begin{pmatrix} -y_1 + o_1 \\ -y_2 + o_2 \\ \vdots \\ -y_K + o_K \end{pmatrix}, \text{ since } \sum_{i=1}^{K} y_i = 1$$

$$= \mathbf{o} - \mathbf{y}$$

25.4.4 Net Gradients at Hidden Layers

Let us assume that we have already computed the net gradients at layer $l+1$, namely δ^{l+1}. Since neuron z_j^l in layer l is connected to all of the neurons in layer $l+1$ (except for the bias neuron z_0^{l+1}), to compute the net gradient at z_j^l, we have to account for the error from each neuron in layer $l+1$, as follows:

$$\delta_j^l = \frac{\partial \mathcal{E}_{\mathbf{x}}}{\partial net_j} = \sum_{k=1}^{n_{l+1}} \frac{\partial \mathcal{E}_{\mathbf{x}}}{\partial net_k} \cdot \frac{\partial net_k}{\partial f^l(net_j)} \cdot \frac{\partial f^l(net_j)}{\partial net_j}$$

$$= \frac{\partial f^l(net_j)}{\partial net_j} \cdot \sum_{k=1}^{n_{l+1}} \delta_k^{l+1} \cdot w_{jk}^l$$

So the net gradient at z_j^l in layer l depends on the derivative of the activation function with respect to its net_j, and the weighted sum of the net gradients from all the neurons z_k^{l+1} at the next layer $l+1$.

We can compute the net gradients for all the neurons in level l in one step, as follows:

$$\boxed{\delta^l = \partial \mathbf{f}^l \odot \left(\mathbf{W}_l \cdot \delta^{l+1} \right)} \tag{25.53}$$

where $\odot$ is the element-wise product, and $\partial \mathbf{f}^l$ is the vector of derivatives of the activation function with respect to its argument [Eq. (25.45)] at layer l. For the commonly used activation functions at the hidden layer, using the derivatives from

Section 25.1.1, we have

$$\partial \mathbf{f}^l = \begin{cases} \mathbf{1} & \text{for linear} \\ \mathbf{z}^l(\mathbf{1} - \mathbf{z}^l) & \text{for sigmoid} \\ (\mathbf{1} - \mathbf{z}^l \odot \mathbf{z}^l) & \text{for tanh} \end{cases}$$

For ReLU, we have to apply Eq. (25.9) to each neuron. Note that softmax is generally not used for hidden layers.

The net gradients are computed recursively, starting from the output layer $h + 1$, then hidden layer h, and so on, until we finally compute the net gradients at the first hidden layer $l = 1$. That is,

$$\delta^h = \partial \mathbf{f}^h \odot \left(\mathbf{W}_h \cdot \delta^{h+1} \right)$$

$$\delta^{h-1} = \partial \mathbf{f}^{h-1} \odot \left(\mathbf{W}_{h-1} \cdot \delta^h \right) = \partial \mathbf{f}^{h-1} \odot \left(\mathbf{W}_{h-1} \cdot \left(\partial \mathbf{f}^h \odot \left(\mathbf{W}_h \cdot \delta^{h+1} \right) \right) \right)$$

$$\vdots$$

$$\delta^1 = \partial \mathbf{f}^1 \odot \left(\mathbf{W}_1 \cdot \left(\partial \mathbf{f}^2 \odot \left(\mathbf{W}_2 \cdots \left(\partial \mathbf{f}^h \odot \left(\mathbf{W}_h \cdot \delta^{h+1} \right) \right) \right) \right) \right)$$

25.4.5 Training Deep MLPs

Algorithm 25.2 shows the pseudo-code for learning the weights and biases for a deep MLP. The inputs comprise the dataset $\mathbf{D}$, the number of hidden layers h, the step size or learning rate for gradient descent η, an integer threshold `maxiter` denoting the number of iterations for training, parameters $n_1, n_2, \cdots, n_h$ that denote the number of neurons (excluding bias, which will be added automatically) for each of the hidden layers $l = 1, 2, \cdots, h$, and the type of activation functions $f^1, f^2, \cdots, f^{h+1}$ for each of the layers (other than the input layer that uses identity activations). The size of the input (d) and output (p) layers is determined directly from $\mathbf{D}$.

The MLP first initializes the ($n_l \times n_{l+1}$) weight matrices $\mathbf{W}_l$ between layers l and $l + 1$ with small values chosen uniformly at random, e.g., in the range $[-0.01, 0.01]$. The MLP considers each input pair $(\mathbf{x}_i, \mathbf{y}_i) \in \mathbf{D}$, and computes the predicted response $\mathbf{o}_i$ via the feed-forward process. The backpropagation phase begins by computing the error between $\mathbf{o}_i$ and true response $\mathbf{y}_i$, and computing the net gradient vector δ^{h+1} at the output layer. These net gradients are backpropagated from layer $h + 1$ to layer h, from h to $h - 1$, and so on until we obtain the net gradients at the first hidden layer $l = 1$. These net gradients are used to compute the weight gradient matrix $\nabla_{\mathbf{W}_l}$ at layer l, which can in turn be used to update the weight matrix $\mathbf{W}_l$. Likewise, the net gradients specify the bias gradient vector $\nabla_{\mathbf{b}_l}$ at layer l, which is used to update $\mathbf{b}_l$. After each point has been used to update the weights, that completes one iteration or epoch of training. The training stops when `maxiter` epochs have been reached. On the other hand, during testing, for any input $\mathbf{x}$, we apply the feed-forward steps and print the predicted output $\mathbf{o}$.

It is important to note that Algorithm 25.2 follows a stochastic gradient descent approach, since the points are considered in random order, and the weight and bias gradients are computed after observing each training point. In practice, it is common

---

Algorithm 25.2: Deep MLP Training: Stochastic Gradient Descent

---

DEEP-MLP-TRAINING $(\mathbf{D}, h, \eta, \texttt{maxiter}, n_1, n_2, \cdots, n_h, f^1, f^2, \cdots, f^{h+1})$:

1 $n_0 \leftarrow d$ // input layer size
2 $n_{h+1} \leftarrow p$ // output layer size
  // Initialize weight matrices and bias vectors
3 **for** $l = 0, 1, 2, \cdots, h$ **do**
4      $\mathbf{b}_l \leftarrow$ random n_{l+1} vector with small values
5      $\mathbf{W}_l \leftarrow$ random $n_l \times n_{l+1}$ matrix with small values

6 $t \leftarrow 0$ // iteration counter
7 **repeat**
8   **foreach** $(\mathbf{x}_i, \mathbf{y}_i) \in \mathbf{D}$ *in random order* **do**
           // Feed-Forward Phase
9          $\mathbf{z}^0 \leftarrow \mathbf{x}_i$
10   **for** $l = 0, 1, 2, \ldots, h$ **do**
11              $\mathbf{z}^{l+1} \leftarrow f^{l+1}\left(\mathbf{b}_l + \mathbf{W}_l^T \cdot \mathbf{z}^l\right)$
12          $\mathbf{o}_i \leftarrow \mathbf{z}^{h+1}$
           // Backpropagation Phase
13   **if** *independent outputs* **then**
14              $\delta^{h+1} \leftarrow \partial \mathbf{f}^{h+1} \odot \partial \mathcal{E}_{\mathbf{x}_i}$ // net gradients at output
15   **else**
16              $\delta^{h+1} \leftarrow \partial \mathbf{F}^{h+1} \cdot \partial \mathcal{E}_{\mathbf{x}_i}$ // net gradients at output
17   **for** $l = h, h-1, \cdots, 1$ **do**
18              $\delta^l \leftarrow \partial \mathbf{f}^l \odot \left(\mathbf{W}_l \cdot \delta^{l+1}\right)$ // net gradients at layer l
           // Gradient Descent Step
19   **for** $l = 0, 1, \cdots, h$ **do**
20              $\nabla_{\mathbf{W}_l} \leftarrow \mathbf{z}^l \cdot \left(\delta^{l+1}\right)^T$ // weight gradient matrix at layer l
21              $\nabla_{\mathbf{b}_l} \leftarrow \delta^{l+1}$ // bias gradient vector at layer l
22   **for** $l = 0, 1, \cdots, h$ **do**
23              $\mathbf{W}_l \leftarrow \mathbf{W}_l - \eta \cdot \nabla_{\mathbf{W}_l}$ // update $\mathbf{W}_l$
24              $\mathbf{b}_l \leftarrow \mathbf{b}_l - \eta \cdot \nabla_{\mathbf{b}_l}$ // update $\mathbf{b}_l$

25      $t \leftarrow t + 1$
26 **until** $t \geq \texttt{maxiter}$

---

to update the gradients by considering a fixed sized subset of the training points called a *minibatch* instead of using single points. That is, the training data is divided into minibatches using an additional parameter called *batch size*, and a gradient descent step is performed after computing the bias and weight gradient from each minibatch. This helps better estimate the gradients, and also allows vectorized matrix operations over the minibatch of points, which can lead to faster convergence and substantial speedups in the learning.

One caveat while training very deep MLPs is the problem of vanishing and exploding gradients. In the *vanishing gradient* problem, the norm of the net gradient can decay exponentially with the distance from the output layer, that is, as we backpropagate the gradients from the output layer to the input layer. In this case the network will learn extremely slowly, if at all, since the gradient descent method will make minuscule changes to the weights and biases. On the other hand, in the *exploding gradient* problem, the norm of the net gradient can grow exponentially with the distance from the output layer. In this case, the weights and biases will become exponentially large, resulting in a failure to learn. The gradient explosion problem can be mitigated to some extent by *gradient thresholding*, that is, by resetting the value if it exceeds an upper bound. The vanishing gradients problem is more difficult to address. Typically sigmoid activations are more susceptible to this problem, and one solution is to use alternative activation functions such as ReLU. In general, recurrent neural networks, which are deep neural networks with *feedback* connections, are more prone to vanishing and exploding gradients; we will revisit these issues in Section 26.2.

Example 25.5 (Deep MLP). We now examine deep MLPs for predicting the labels for the MNIST handwritten images dataset that we considered in Example 25.4. Recall that this dataset has $n = 60000$ grayscale images of size 28×28 that we treat as $d = 784$ dimensional vectors. The pixel values between 0 and 255 are converted to the range 0 and 1 by dividing each value by 255. The target response vector is a one-hot encoded vector for class labels $\{0, 1, \ldots, 9\}$. Thus, the input to the MLP $\mathbf{x}_i$ has dimensionality $d = 784$, and the output layer has dimensionality $p = 10$. We use softmax activation for the output layer. We use ReLU activation for the hidden layers, and consider several deep models with different number and sizes of the hidden layers. We use step size $\eta = 0.3$ and train for $t = 15$ epochs. Training was done using minibatches, using batch size of 1000.

During the training of each of the deep MLPs, we evaluate its performance on the separate MNIST test datatset that contains 10,000 images. Figure 25.12 plots the

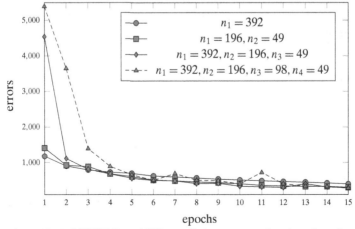

Figure 25.12. MNIST: Deep MLPs; prediction error as a function of epochs.

number of errors after each epoch for the different deep MLP models. The final test error at the end of training is given as

hidden layers	errors
$n_1 = 392$	396
$n_1 = 196, n_2 = 49$	303
$n_1 = 392, n_2 = 196, n_3 = 49$	290
$n_1 = 392, n_2 = 196, n_3 = 98, n_4 = 49$	278

We can observe that as we increase the number of layers, we do get performance improvements. The deep MLP with four hidden layers of sizes $n_1 = 392, n_2 = 196, n_3 = 98, n_4 = 49$ results in an error rate of 2.78% on the training set, whereas the MLP with a single hidden layer of size $n_1 = 392$ has an error rate of 3.96%. Thus, the deeper MLP significantly improves the prediction accuracy. However, adding more layers does not reduce the error rate, and can also lead to performance degradation.

25.5 FURTHER READING

Artificial neural networks have their origin in the work of McCulloch and Pitts (1943). The first application of a single neuron, called a *perceptron*, to supervised learning was by Rosenblatt (1958). Minsky and Papert (1969) pointed out limitations of perceptrons, which were not overcome until the development of the backpropagation algorithm, which was introduced by Rumelhart, Hinton, and Williams (1986) to train general multilayer perceptrons.

McCulloch, W. S. and Pitts, W. (1943). A logical calculus of the ideas immanent in nervous activity. *The Bulletin of Mathematical Biophysics*, 5 (4), 115–133.

Minsky, M. and Papert, S. (1969). *Perceptron: An Introduction to Computational Geometry*. Cambridge, MA: The MIT Press.

Rosenblatt, F. (1958). The perceptron: A probabilistic model for information storage and organization in the brain. *Psychological Review*, 65 (6), 386.

Rumelhart, D. E., Hinton, G. E., and Williams, R. J. (1986). Learning representations by back-propagating errors. *Nature*, 323 (6088), 533.

25.6 EXERCISES

Q1. Consider the neural network in Figure 25.13. Let bias values be fixed at 0, and let the weight matrices between the input and hidden, and hidden and output layers, respectively, be:

$$\mathbf{W} = (w_1, w_2, w_3) = (1, 1, -1) \qquad \mathbf{W'} = (w'_1, w'_2, w'_3)^T = (0.5, 1, 2)^T$$

Assume that the hidden layer uses ReLU, whereas the output layer uses sigmoid activation. Assume SSE error. Answer the following questions, when the input is $x = 4$ and the true response is $y = 0$:

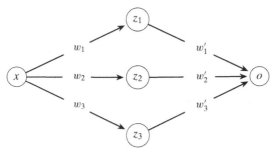

Figure 25.13. Neural network for Q1.

(a) Use forward propagation to compute the predicted output.
(b) What is the loss or error value?
(c) Compute the net gradient vector δ^o for the output layer.
(d) Compute the net gradient vector δ^h for the hidden layer.
(e) Compute the weight gradient matrix $\nabla_{\mathbf{w}'}$ between the hidden and output layers.
(f) Compute the weight gradient matrix $\nabla_{\mathbf{w}}$ between the input and hidden layers.

Q2. Show that the derivative of the sigmoid function [Eq. (25.5)] with respect to its argument is given as

$$\frac{\partial f(z)}{\partial z} = f(z) \cdot (1 - f(z))$$

Q3. Show that the derivative of the hyperbolic tangent function [Eq. (25.6)] with respect to its argument is given as

$$\frac{\partial f(z)}{\partial z} = 1 - f(z)^2$$

Q4. Show that the derivative of the softmax function is given as

$$\frac{\partial f(z_i \mid \mathbf{z})}{\partial z_j} = \begin{cases} f(z_i) \cdot (1 - f(z_i)) & \text{if } j = i \\ -f(z_i) \cdot f(z_j) & \text{if } j \neq i \end{cases}$$

where $\mathbf{z} = \{z_1, z_2, \cdots, z_p\}$.

Q5. Derive an expression for the net gradient vector at the output neurons when using softmax activation with the squared error function.

Q6. Show that if the weight matrix and bias vectors are initialized to zero, then all neurons in a given layer will have identical values in each iteration.

Q7. Prove that with linear activation functions, a multilayered network is equivalent to a single-layered neural network.

Q8. Compute the expression for the net gradient vector at the output layer, δ^{h+1}, assuming cross-entropy error, $\mathcal{E}_{\mathbf{x}} = -\sum_{i=1}^{K} y_i \cdot \ln(o_i)$, with K independent binary output neurons that use sigmoid activation, that is, $o_i = \text{sigmoid}(net_i)$.

Q9. Given an MLP with one hidden layer, derive the equations for δ_h and δ_o using vector derivatives, i.e., by computing $\frac{\partial \mathcal{E}_{\mathbf{x}}}{\partial \mathbf{net}_h}$ and $\frac{\partial \mathcal{E}_{\mathbf{x}}}{\partial \mathbf{net}_o}$, where $\mathbf{net}_h$ and $\mathbf{net}_o$ are the net input vectors at the hidden and output layers.

CHAPTER 26

Deep Learning

In this chapter, we first look at deep neural networks that include feedback from one layer to another. Such network are called *recurrent neural networks* (RNNs), and they can typically be trained by unfolding (or unrolling) the recurrent connections, resulting in deep networks whose parameters can be learned via the backpropagation algorithm. Since RNNs are prone to the vanishing and exploding gradients problem, we next consider *gated RNNs* that introduce a new type of layer that endows the network with the ability to selectively read, store, and write the hidden state via an internal *memory layer*. Gated RNNs are highly effective for prediction tasks on sequence inputs. Finally, we consider *convolutional neural networks* (CNNs) that are deep MLPs that exploit spatial or temporal relationships between different elements of each layer to construct a hierarchy of *features* that can be used for regression or classification tasks. Unlike regular MLPs whose layers are fully connected, CNNs have layers that are localized and sparse. In particular, CNNs are highly effective for image inputs.

26.1 RECURRENT NEURAL NETWORKS

Multilayer perceptrons are feed-forward networks in which the information flows in only one direction, namely from the input layer to the output layer via the hidden layers. In contrast, recurrent neural networks (RNNs) are dynamically driven (e.g., temporal), with a *feedback* loop between two (or more) layers, which makes such networks ideal for learning from sequence data. For example, Figure 26.1 shows a simple RNN where there is a feedback loop from the hidden layer $\mathbf{h}_t$ to itself via a temporal delay of one time unit, denoted by the -1 on the loop.

Let $\mathcal{X} = \langle \mathbf{x}_1, \mathbf{x}_2, \cdots, \mathbf{x}_\tau \rangle$ denote a sequence of vectors, where $\mathbf{x}_t \in \mathbb{R}^d$ is a d-dimensional vector ($t = 1, 2, \cdots, \tau$). Thus, $\mathcal{X}$ is an input sequence of length τ, with $\mathbf{x}_t$ denoting the input at time step t. Let $\mathcal{Y} = \langle \mathbf{y}_1, \mathbf{y}_2, \cdots, \mathbf{y}_\tau \rangle$ denote a sequence of vectors, with $\mathbf{y}_t \in \mathbb{R}^p$ a p-dimensional vector. Here, $\mathcal{Y}$ is the desired target or response sequence, with $\mathbf{y}_t$ denoting the response vector at time t. Finally, let $\mathcal{O} = \langle \mathbf{o}_1, \mathbf{o}_2, \cdots, \mathbf{o}_\tau \rangle$ denote the predicted or output sequence from the RNN. Here $\mathbf{o}_t \in \mathbb{R}^p$ is also a p-dimensional vector to match the corresponding true response $\mathbf{y}_t$. The task of an RNN is to learn a function that predicts the target sequence $\mathcal{Y}$ given the input sequence $\mathcal{X}$. That is, the

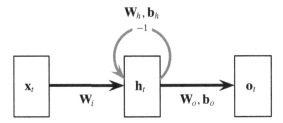

Figure 26.1. Recurrent neural network. Recurrent connection shown in gray.

predicted output $\mathbf{o}_t$ on input $\mathbf{x}_t$ should be similar or close to the target response $\mathbf{y}_t$, for each time point t.

To learn dependencies between elements of the input sequence, an RNN maintains a sequence of m-dimensional hidden state vectors $\mathbf{h}_t \in \mathbb{R}^m$, where $\mathbf{h}_t$ captures the essential features of the input sequences up to time t, as illustrated in Figure 26.1. The hidden vector $\mathbf{h}_t$ at time t depends on the input vector $\mathbf{x}_t$ at time t and the previous hidden state vector $\mathbf{h}_{t-1}$ from time $t-1$, and it is computed as follows:

$$\mathbf{h}_t = f^h(\mathbf{W}_i^T\mathbf{x}_t + \mathbf{W}_h^T\mathbf{h}_{t-1} + \mathbf{b}_h) \tag{26.1}$$

Here, f^h is the hidden state activation function, typically tanh or ReLU. Also, we need an initial hidden state vector $\mathbf{h}_0$ that serves as the prior state to compute $\mathbf{h}_1$. This is usually set to the zero vector, or seeded from a prior RNN prediction step. The matrix $\mathbf{W}_i \in \mathbb{R}^{d \times m}$ specifies the weights between the input vectors and the hidden state vectors. The matrix $\mathbf{W}_h \in \mathbb{R}^{m \times m}$ specifies the weight matrix between the hidden state vectors at time $t-1$ and t, with $\mathbf{b}_h \in \mathbb{R}^m$ specifying the bias terms associated with the hidden states. Note that we need only one bias vector $\mathbf{b}_h$ associated with the hidden state neurons; we do not need a separate bias vector between the input and hidden neurons.

Given the hidden state vector at time t, the output vector $\mathbf{o}_t$ at time t is computed as follows:

$$\mathbf{o}_t = f^o(\mathbf{W}_o^T\mathbf{h}_t + \mathbf{b}_o) \tag{26.2}$$

Here, $\mathbf{W}_o \in \mathbb{R}^{m \times p}$ specifies the weights between the hidden state and output vectors, with bias vector $\mathbf{b}_o$. The output activation function f^o typically uses linear or identity activation, or a softmax activation for one-hot encoded categorical output values.

It is important to note that all the weight matrices and bias vectors are *independent* of the time t. For example, for the hidden layer, the same weight matrix $\mathbf{W}_h$ and bias vector $\mathbf{b}_h$ is used and updated while training the model, over all time steps t. This is an example of *parameter sharing* or *weight tying* between different layers or components of a neural network. Likewise, the input weight matrix $\mathbf{W}_i$, the output weight matrix $\mathbf{W}_o$ and the bias vector $\mathbf{b}_o$ are all shared across time. This greatly reduces the number of parameters that need to be learned by the RNN, but it also relies on the assumption that all relevant sequential features can be captured by the shared parameters.

Figure 26.1 shows an illustration of an RNN, with a recurrent hidden layer $\mathbf{h}_t$, denoted by the feed-back loop with a time delay of -1 noted on the loop. The figure also shows the shared parameters between the layers. Figure 26.2(a) shows the same

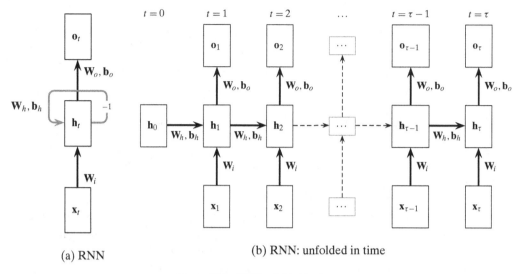

(a) RNN   (b) RNN: unfolded in time

Figure 26.2. RNN unfolded in time.

RNN in vertical format, where the layers are stacked vertically, and Figure 26.2(b) shows the RNN with the layers unfolded in time; it shows the input $(\mathbf{x}_t)$, hidden $(\mathbf{h}_t)$, and output $(\mathbf{o}_t)$ layers at each time step t. We can observe that the feed-back loop has been unfolded for τ time steps, starting with $t = 1$ and ending at $t = \tau$. The time step $t = 0$ is used to denote the previous or initial hidden state $\mathbf{h}_0$. We can also explicitly observe the parameter sharing across time, since all weight matrices and bias vectors are independent of t. Figure 26.2(b) makes it clear that an RNN is a deep neural network with τ layers, where τ is the maximum input sequence length.

The training data for the RNN is given as $\mathbf{D} = \{\mathcal{X}_i, \mathcal{Y}_i\}_{i=1}^n$, comprising n input sequences $\mathcal{X}_i$ and the corresponding target response sequences $\mathcal{Y}_i$, with sequence length τ_i. Given each pair $(\mathcal{X}, \mathcal{Y}) \in \mathbf{D}$, with $\mathcal{X} = \langle \mathbf{x}_1, \mathbf{x}_2, \cdots, \mathbf{x}_\tau \rangle$ and $\mathcal{Y} = \langle \mathbf{y}_1, \mathbf{y}_2, \cdots, \mathbf{y}_\tau \rangle$, the RNN has to update the model parameters $\mathbf{W}_i, \mathbf{W}_h, \mathbf{b}_h, \mathbf{W}_o, \mathbf{b}_o$ for the input, hidden and output layers, to learn the corresponding output sequence $\mathcal{O} = \langle \mathbf{o}_1, \mathbf{o}_2, \cdots, \mathbf{o}_\tau \rangle$. For training the network, we compute the error or *loss* between the predicted and response vectors over all time steps. For example, the squared error loss is given as

$$\mathcal{E}_\mathcal{X} = \sum_{t=1}^\tau \mathcal{E}_{\mathbf{x}_t} = \frac{1}{2} \cdot \sum_{t=1}^\tau \|\mathbf{y}_t - \mathbf{o}_t\|^2$$

On the other hand, if we use a softmax activation at the output layer, then we use the cross-entropy loss, given as

$$\mathcal{E}_\mathcal{X} = \sum_{t=1}^\tau \mathcal{E}_{\mathbf{x}_t} = -\sum_{t=1}^\tau \sum_{i=1}^p y_{ti} \cdot \ln(o_{ti})$$

where $\mathbf{y}_t = (y_{t1}, y_{t2}, \cdots, y_{tp})^T \in \mathbb{R}^p$ and $\mathbf{o}_t = (o_{t1}, o_{t2}, \cdots, o_{tp})^T \in \mathbb{R}^p$. On training input of length τ we first unfold the RNN for τ steps, following which the parameters can be learned via the standard feed-forward and backpropagation steps, keeping in mind the connections between the layers.

26.1.1 Feed-forward in Time

The feed-forward process starts at time $t = 0$, taking as input the initial hidden state vector $\mathbf{h}_0$, which is usually set to $\mathbf{0}$ or it can be user-specified, say from a previous prediction step. Given the current set of parameters, we predict the output $\mathbf{o}_t$ at each time step $t = 1, 2, \cdots, \tau$ via Eq. (26.1) and Eq. (26.2):

$$\mathbf{o}_t = f^o\left(\mathbf{W}_o^T \mathbf{h}_t + \mathbf{b}_o\right)$$

$$= f^o\left(\mathbf{W}_o^T \underbrace{f^h\left(\mathbf{W}_i^T \mathbf{x}_t + \mathbf{W}_h^T \mathbf{h}_{t-1} + \mathbf{b}_h\right)}_{\mathbf{h}_t} + \mathbf{b}_o\right)$$

$$= \qquad \vdots$$

$$= f^o\left(\mathbf{W}_o^T f^h\left(\mathbf{W}_i^T \mathbf{x}_t + \mathbf{W}_h^T f^h\left(\cdots \underbrace{f^h\left(\mathbf{W}_i^T \mathbf{x}_1 + \mathbf{W}_h^T \mathbf{h}_0 + \mathbf{b}_h\right)}_{\mathbf{h}_1} + \cdots\right) + \mathbf{b}_h\right) + \mathbf{b}_o\right)$$

We can observe that the RNN implicitly makes a prediction for every prefix of the input sequence, since $\mathbf{o}_t$ depends on all the previous input vectors $\mathbf{x}_1, \mathbf{x}_2, \cdots, \mathbf{x}_t$, but not on any future inputs $\mathbf{x}_{t+1}, \cdots, \mathbf{x}_\tau$.

26.1.2 Backpropagation in Time

Once the feed-forward phase computes the output sequence $\mathcal{O} = \langle \mathbf{o}_1, \mathbf{o}_2, \cdots, \mathbf{o}_\tau \rangle$, we can compute the error in the predictions using the squared error (or cross-entropy) loss function, which can in turn be used to compute the net gradient vectors that are backpropagated from the output layers to the input layers for each time step.

For the backpropagation step it is easier to view the RNN in terms of the distinct layers based on the dependencies, as opposed to unfolding in time. Figure 26.3(a) shows the RNN unfolded using this layer view as opposed to the time view shown in Figure 26.2(b). The first layer is $l = 0$ comprising the hidden states $\mathbf{h}_0$ and the input vector $\mathbf{x}_1$, both of which are required to compute $\mathbf{h}_1$ in layer $l = 1$, which also includes the input vector $\mathbf{x}_2$. In turn, both $\mathbf{h}_1$ and $\mathbf{x}_2$ are required to compute $\mathbf{h}_2$ in layer $l = 2$, and so on for other layers. Note also that $\mathbf{o}_1$ is not output until layer $l = 2$ since we can compute the output only once $\mathbf{h}_1$ has been computed in the previous layer. The layer view is essentially indexed by the hidden state vector index, except the final layer $l = \tau + 1$ that outputs $\mathbf{o}_\tau$ that depends on $\mathbf{h}_\tau$ from layer $l = \tau$.

Let $\mathcal{E}_{\mathbf{x}_t}$ denote the loss on input vector $\mathbf{x}_t$ from the input sequence $\mathcal{X} = \langle \mathbf{x}_1, \mathbf{x}_2, \cdots, \mathbf{x}_\tau \rangle$. The unfolded feed-forward RNN for $\mathcal{X}$ has $l = \tau + 1$ layers, as shown in Figure 26.3(a). Define $\boldsymbol{\delta}_t^o$ as the net gradient vector for the output vector $\mathbf{o}_t$, i.e., the derivative of the error function $\mathcal{E}_{\mathbf{x}_t}$ with respect to the net value at each neuron in $\mathbf{o}_t$, given as

$$\boldsymbol{\delta}_t^o = \left(\frac{\partial \mathcal{E}_{\mathbf{x}_t}}{\partial net_{t1}^o}, \frac{\partial \mathcal{E}_{\mathbf{x}_t}}{\partial net_{t2}^o}, \cdots, \frac{\partial \mathcal{E}_{\mathbf{x}_t}}{\partial net_{tp}^o}\right)^T$$

where $\mathbf{o}_t = (o_{t1}, o_{t2}, \cdots, o_{tp})^T \in \mathbb{R}^p$ is the p-dimensional output vector at time t, and net_{ti}^o is the net value at output neuron o_{ti} at time t. Likewise, let $\boldsymbol{\delta}_t^h$ denote the net gradient

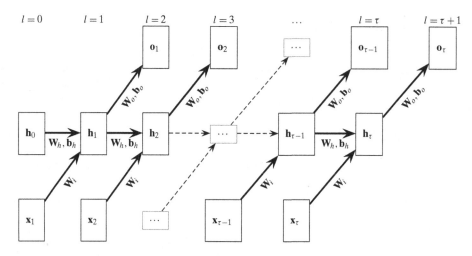

(a) Feed-forward step

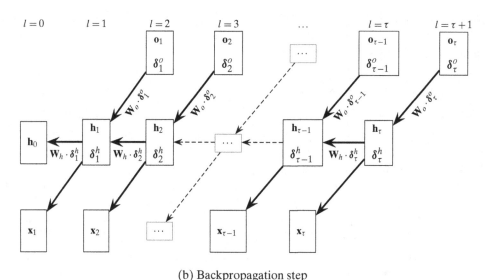

(b) Backpropagation step

Figure 26.3. RNN unfolded as layers.

vector for the hidden state neurons $\mathbf{h}_t$ at time t

$$\delta_t^h = \left(\frac{\partial \mathcal{E}_{\mathbf{x}_t}}{\partial net_{t1}^h}, \frac{\partial \mathcal{E}_{\mathbf{x}_t}}{\partial net_{t2}^h}, \cdots, \frac{\partial \mathcal{E}_{\mathbf{x}_t}}{\partial net_{tm}^h} \right)^T$$

where $\mathbf{h}_t = (h_{t1}, h_{t2}, \cdots, h_{tm})^T \in \mathbb{R}^m$ is the m-dimensional hidden state vector at time t, and net_{ti}^h is the net value at hidden neuron h_{ti} at time t. Let f^h and f^o denote the activation functions for the hidden state and output neurons, and let $\partial\mathbf{f}_t^h$ and $\partial\mathbf{f}_t^o$ denote the vector of the derivatives of the activation function with respect to the net signal (that is, its argument) for the hidden and output neurons at time t, given as

$$\partial\mathbf{f}_t^h = \left(\frac{\partial f^h(net_{t1}^h)}{\partial net_{t1}^h}, \frac{\partial f^h(net_{t2}^h)}{\partial net_{t2}^h}, \cdots, \frac{\partial f^h(net_{tm}^h)}{\partial net_{tm}^h} \right)^T$$

$$\partial \mathbf{f}_t^o = \left(\frac{\partial f^o(net_{t1}^o)}{\partial net_{t1}^o}, \frac{\partial f^o(net_{t2}^o)}{\partial net_{t2}^o}, \cdots, \frac{\partial f^o(net_{tp}^o)}{\partial net_{tp}^o} \right)^T$$

Finally, let $\partial \mathcal{E}_{\mathbf{x}_t}$ denote the vector of partial derivatives of the error function with respect to $\mathbf{o}_t$:

$$\partial \mathcal{E}_{\mathbf{x}_t} = \left(\frac{\partial \mathcal{E}_{\mathbf{x}_t}}{\partial o_{t1}}, \frac{\partial \mathcal{E}_{\mathbf{x}_t}}{\partial o_{t2}}, \cdots, \frac{\partial \mathcal{E}_{\mathbf{x}_t}}{\partial o_{tp}} \right)^T$$

Computing Net Gradients

The key step in backpropagation is to compute the net gradients in reverse order, starting from the output neurons to the input neurons via the hidden neurons. Given the layer view in Figure 26.3(a), the backpropagation step reverses the flow direction for computing the net gradients δ_t^o and δ_t^h, as shown in the backpropagation graph in Figure 26.3(b).

In particular, the net gradient vector at the output $\mathbf{o}_t$ can be computed as follows:

$$\boxed{\delta_t^o = \partial \mathbf{f}_t^o \odot \partial \mathcal{E}_{\mathbf{x}_t}} \tag{26.3}$$

where $\odot$ is the element-wise or Hadamard product, For example, if $\mathcal{E}_{\mathbf{x}_t}$ is the squared error function, and the output layer uses the identity function, then via Eq. (25.8) and Eq. (25.15) we have

$$\delta_t^o = \mathbf{1} \odot (\mathbf{o}_t - \mathbf{y}_t)$$

On the other hand, the net gradients at each of the hidden layers need to account for the incoming net gradients from $\mathbf{o}_t$ and from $\mathbf{h}_{t+1}$ as seen in Figure 26.3(b). Thus, generalizing Eq. (25.53), the net gradient vector for $\mathbf{h}_t$ (for $t = 1, 2, \ldots, \tau - 1$) is given as

$$\boxed{\delta_t^h = \partial \mathbf{f}_t^h \odot \left(\left(\mathbf{W}_o \cdot \delta_t^o \right) + \left(\mathbf{W}_h \cdot \delta_{t+1}^h \right) \right)} \tag{26.4}$$

Note that for $\mathbf{h}_\tau$, it depends only on $\mathbf{o}_\tau$ (see Figure 26.3(b)), therefore

$$\delta_\tau^h = \partial \mathbf{f}_\tau^h \odot \left(\mathbf{W}_o \cdot \delta_\tau^o \right)$$

For the tanh activation, which is commonly used in RNNs, the derivative of the activation function (see Eq. (25.11)) with respect to the net values at $\mathbf{h}_t$ is given as

$$\partial \mathbf{f}_t^h = (\mathbf{1} - \mathbf{h}_t \odot \mathbf{h}_t)$$

Finally, note that the net gradients do not have to be computed for $\mathbf{h}_0$ or for any of the input neurons $\mathbf{x}_t$, since these are leaf nodes in the backpropagation graph, and thus do not backpropagate the gradients beyond those neurons.

Stochastic Gradient Descent

The net gradients for the output δ_t^o and hidden neurons δ_t^h at time t can be used to compute the gradients for the weight matrices and bias vectors at each time point.

However, since an RNN uses parameter sharing across time, the gradients are obtained by summing up all of the contributions from each time step t. Define $\nabla_{\mathbf{W}_o}^t$ and $\nabla_{\mathbf{b}_o}^t$ as the gradients of the weights and biases between the hidden neurons $\mathbf{h}_t$ and output neurons $\mathbf{o}_t$ for time t. Using the backpropagation equations, [Eq. (25.47)] and [Eq. (25.48)], for deep multilayer perceptrons, these gradients are computed as follows:

$$\nabla_{\mathbf{b}_o} = \sum_{t=1}^{\tau} \nabla_{\mathbf{b}_o}^t = \sum_{t=1}^{\tau} \delta_t^o \qquad\qquad \nabla_{\mathbf{W}_o} = \sum_{t=1}^{\tau} \nabla_{\mathbf{W}_o}^t = \sum_{t=1}^{\tau} \mathbf{h}_t \cdot \left(\delta_t^o\right)^T$$

Likewise, the gradients of the other shared parameters between hidden layers $\mathbf{h}_{t-1}$ and $\mathbf{h}_t$, and between the input layer $\mathbf{x}_t$ and hidden layer $\mathbf{h}_t$, are obtained as follows:

$$\nabla_{\mathbf{b}_h} = \sum_{t=1}^{\tau} \nabla_{\mathbf{b}_h}^t = \sum_{t=1}^{\tau} \delta_t^h \qquad\qquad \nabla_{\mathbf{W}_h} = \sum_{t=1}^{\tau} \nabla_{\mathbf{W}_h}^t = \sum_{t=1}^{\tau} \mathbf{h}_{t-1} \cdot \left(\delta_t^h\right)^T$$

$$\nabla_{\mathbf{W}_i} = \sum_{t=1}^{\tau} \nabla_{\mathbf{W}_i}^t = \sum_{t=1}^{\tau} \mathbf{x}_t \cdot \left(\delta_t^h\right)^T$$

where $\nabla_{\mathbf{W}_h}^t$ and $\nabla_{\mathbf{b}_h}^t$ are the gradient contributions from time t for the weights and biases for the hidden neurons, and $\nabla_{\mathbf{W}_i}^t$ the gradient contributions for the weights for the input neurons. Finally, we update all the weight matrices and bias vectors as follows

$$\boxed{\begin{aligned} \mathbf{W}_i &= \mathbf{W}_i - \eta \cdot \nabla_{\mathbf{W}_i} \quad \mathbf{W}_h = \mathbf{W}_h - \eta \cdot \nabla_{\mathbf{W}_h} \quad \mathbf{b}_h = \mathbf{b}_h - \eta \cdot \nabla_{\mathbf{b}_h} \\ \mathbf{W}_o &= \mathbf{W}_o - \eta \cdot \nabla_{\mathbf{W}_o} \quad \mathbf{b}_o = \mathbf{b}_o - \eta \cdot \nabla_{\mathbf{b}_o} \end{aligned}} \qquad (26.5)$$

where η is the gradient step size (or learning rate).

26.1.3 Training RNNs

Algorithm 26.1 shows the pseudo-code for learning the weights and biases for an RNN. The inputs comprise the dataset $\mathbf{D} = \{\mathcal{X}_i, \mathcal{Y}_i\}_{i=1,\cdots,n}$, the step size for gradient descent η, an integer threshold `maxiter` denoting the number of iterations for training, the size of the hidden state vectors m, and the activation functions f^o and f^h for the output and hidden layers. The size of the input (d) and output (p) layers is determined directly from $\mathbf{D}$. For simplicity we assume that all inputs $\mathcal{X}_i$ have the same length τ, which determines the number of layers in the RNN. It is relatively easy to handle variable length input sequences by unrolling the RNN for different input lengths τ_i.

The RNN first initializes the weight matrices and bias vectors with random values drawn uniformly from a small range, e.g., $[-0.01, 0.01]$. The RNN considers each input pair $(\mathcal{X}, \mathcal{Y}) \in \mathbf{D}$, and computes the predicted output $\mathbf{o}_t$ for each time step via the feed-forward process. The backpropagation phase begins by computing the error between $\mathbf{o}_t$ and true response $\mathbf{y}_t$, and then the net gradient vector δ_t^o at the output layer for each time step t. These net gradients are backpropagated from the output layers at time t to the hidden layers at time t, which are in turn used to compute the net gradients δ_t^h at the hidden layers for all time steps $t = 1, 2, \cdots, \tau$. Note that Line 15 shows the case where the output layer neurons are independent; if they are not independent we can replace it by $\partial \mathbf{F}^o \cdot \partial \mathcal{E}_{\mathbf{x}_t}$ (see Eq. (25.51)). Next, we compute the weight gradient

---

Algorithm 26.1: RNN Training: Stochastic Gradient Descent

$\textbf{RNN-Training } (\mathbf{D}, \eta, \texttt{maxiter}, m, f^o, f^h)\textbf{:}$

   // Initialize bias vectors

1 $\mathbf{b}_h \leftarrow$ random m-dimensional vector with small values

2 $\mathbf{b}_o \leftarrow$ random p-dimensional vector with small values

   // Initialize weight matrix

3 $\mathbf{W}_i \leftarrow$ random $d \times m$ matrix with small values

4 $\mathbf{W}_h \leftarrow$ random $m \times m$ matrix with small values

5 $\mathbf{W}_o \leftarrow$ random $m \times p$ matrix with small values

6 $r \leftarrow 0$ // iteration counter

7 **repeat**

8   **foreach** $(\mathcal{X}, \mathcal{Y}) \in \mathbf{D}$ *in random order* **do**

9       $\tau \leftarrow |\mathcal{X}|$ // length of training sequence

        // Feed-Forward Phase

10      $\mathbf{h}_0 \leftarrow \mathbf{0} \in \mathbb{R}^m$ // initialize hidden state

11   **for** $t = 1, 2, \ldots, \tau$ **do**

12         $\mathbf{h}_t \leftarrow f^h(\mathbf{W}_i^T \mathbf{x}_t + \mathbf{W}_h^T \mathbf{h}_{t-1} + \mathbf{b}_h)$

13         $\mathbf{o}_t \leftarrow f^o(\mathbf{W}_o^T \mathbf{h}_t + \mathbf{b}_o)$

        // Backpropagation Phase

14   **for** $t = \tau, \tau - 1, \ldots, 1$ **do**

15         $\boldsymbol{\delta}_t^o \leftarrow \partial \mathbf{f}_t^o \odot \partial \mathcal{E}_{\mathbf{x}_t}$ // net gradients at output

16      $\boldsymbol{\delta}_\tau^h \leftarrow \partial \mathbf{f}_t^h \odot \left(\mathbf{W}_o \cdot \boldsymbol{\delta}_t^o\right)$ // net gradients at $\mathbf{h}_\tau$

17   **for** $t = \tau - 1, \tau - 2, \cdots, 1$ **do**

18         $\boldsymbol{\delta}_t^h \leftarrow \partial \mathbf{f}_t^h \odot \left(\left(\mathbf{W}_o \cdot \boldsymbol{\delta}_t^o\right) + \left(\mathbf{W}_h \cdot \boldsymbol{\delta}_{t+1}^h\right)\right)$ // net gradients at $\mathbf{h}_t$

        // Gradients of weight matrices and bias vectors

19      $\nabla_{\mathbf{b}_o} \leftarrow \sum_{t=1}^\tau \boldsymbol{\delta}_t^o; \quad \nabla_{\mathbf{W}_o} \leftarrow \sum_{t=1}^\tau \mathbf{h}_t \cdot \left(\boldsymbol{\delta}_t^o\right)^T$

20      $\nabla_{\mathbf{b}_h} \leftarrow \sum_{t=1}^\tau \boldsymbol{\delta}_t^h; \quad \nabla_{\mathbf{W}_h} \leftarrow \sum_{t=1}^\tau \mathbf{h}_{t-1} \cdot \left(\boldsymbol{\delta}_t^h\right)^T; \quad \nabla_{\mathbf{W}_i} \leftarrow \sum_{t=1}^\tau \mathbf{x}_t \cdot \left(\boldsymbol{\delta}_t^h\right)^T$

        // Gradient Descent Step

21      $\mathbf{b}_o \leftarrow \mathbf{b}_o - \eta \cdot \nabla_{\mathbf{b}_o}; \quad \mathbf{W}_o \leftarrow \mathbf{W}_o - \eta \cdot \nabla_{\mathbf{W}_o}$

22      $\mathbf{b}_h \leftarrow \mathbf{b}_h - \eta \cdot \nabla_{\mathbf{b}_h}; \quad \mathbf{W}_h \leftarrow \mathbf{W}_h - \eta \cdot \nabla_{\mathbf{W}_h}; \quad \mathbf{W}_i \leftarrow \mathbf{W}_i - \eta \cdot \nabla_{\mathbf{W}_i}$

23    $r \leftarrow r + 1$

24 **until** $r \geq$ maxiter

---

matrices, $\nabla_{\mathbf{W}_i}$, $\nabla_{\mathbf{W}_h}$, and $\nabla_{\mathbf{W}_o}$, and bias gradient vectors, $\nabla_{\mathbf{b}_h}$ and $\nabla_{\mathbf{b}_o}$. These gradients are used to update the weights and biases via stochastic gradient descent. After each point has been used to update the weights, that completes one epoch of training. The training stops when maxiter epochs have been reached.

Note that, whereas Algorithm 26.1 shows the pseudo-code for stochastic gradient descent, in practice, RNNs are trained using subsets or *minibatches* of input sequences instead of single sequences. This helps to speed up the computation and convergence of gradient descent, since minibatches provide better estimates of the bias and weight gradients and allow the use of vectorized operations.

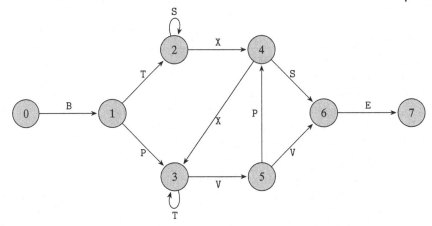

Figure 26.4. Reber grammar automata.

Example 26.1 (RNN). We use an RNN to learn the Reber grammar, which is generated according to the automata shown in Figure 26.4. Let $\Sigma = \{B, E, P, S, T, V, X\}$ denote the alphabet comprising the seven symbols. Further, let $ denote a terminal symbol. Starting from the initial node, we can generate strings that follow the Reber grammar by emitting the symbols on the edges. If there are two transitions out of a node, each one can be chosen with equal probability. The sequence $\langle B, T, S, S, X, X, T, V, V, E \rangle$ is a valid Reber sequence (with the corresponding state sequence $\langle 0, 1, 2, 2, 2, 4, 3, 3, 5, 6, 7 \rangle$). On the other hand, the sequence $\langle B, P, T, X, S, E \rangle$ is not a valid Reber sequence, since there is no edge out of state 3 with the symbol X.

The task of the RNN is to learn to predict the next symbol for each of the positions in a given Reber sequence. For training, we generate Reber sequences from the automata. Let $S_{\mathcal{X}} = \langle s_1, s_2, \cdots, s_\tau \rangle$ be a Reber sequence. The corresponding true output $\mathcal{Y}$ is then given as the set of next symbols from each of the edges leaving the state corresponding to each position in $S_{\mathcal{X}}$. For example, consider the Reber sequence $S_{\mathcal{X}} = \langle B, P, T, V, V, E \rangle$, with the state sequence $\pi = \langle 0, 1, 3, 3, 5, 6, 7 \rangle$. The desired output sequence is then given as $S_{\mathcal{Y}} = \{P|T, T|V, T|V, P|V, E, \$\}$, where $ is the terminal symbol. Here, $P|T$ denotes that the next symbol can be either P or T. We can see that $S_{\mathcal{Y}}$ comprises the sequence of possible next symbols from each of the states in π (excluding the start state 0).

To generate the training data for the RNN, we have to convert the symbolic Reber strings into numeric vectors. We do this via a binary encoding of the symbols, as follows:

B	$(1, 0, 0, 0, 0, 0, 0)^T$
E	$(0, 1, 0, 0, 0, 0, 0)^T$
P	$(0, 0, 1, 0, 0, 0, 0)^T$
S	$(0, 0, 0, 1, 0, 0, 0)^T$
T	$(0, 0, 0, 0, 1, 0, 0)^T$
V	$(0, 0, 0, 0, 0, 1, 0)^T$
X	$(0, 0, 0, 0, 0, 0, 1)^T$
$	$(0, 0, 0, 0, 0, 0, 0)^T$

That is, each symbol is encoded by a 7-dimensional binary vector, with a 1 in the column corresponding to its position in the ordering of symbols in Σ. The terminal symbol $ is not part of the alphabet, and therefore its encoding is all 0's. Finally, to encode the possible next symbols, we follow a similar binary encoding with a 1 in the column corresponding to the allowed symbols. For example, the choice $P|T$ is encoded as $(0, 0, 1, 0, 1, 0, 0)^T$. Thus, the Reber sequence $S_{\mathcal{X}}$ and the desired output sequence $S_{\mathcal{Y}}$ are encoded as:

	$\mathcal{X}$						$\mathcal{Y}$					
	x_1	x_2	x_3	x_4	x_5	x_6	y_1	y_2	y_3	y_4	y_5	y_6
Σ	B	P	T	V	V	E	$P\|T$	$T\|V$	$T\|V$	$P\|V$	E	$
B	1	0	0	0	0	0	0	0	0	0	0	0
E	0	0	0	0	0	1	0	0	0	0	1	0
P	0	1	0	0	0	0	1	0	0	1	0	0
S	0	0	0	0	0	0	0	0	0	0	0	0
T	0	0	1	0	0	0	1	1	1	0	0	0
V	0	0	0	1	1	0	0	1	1	1	0	0
X	0	0	0	0	0	0	0	0	0	0	0	0

For training, we generate $n = 400$ Reber sequences with a minimum length of 30. The maximum sequence length is $\tau = 52$. Each of these Reber sequences is used to create a training pair $(\mathcal{X}, \mathcal{Y})$ as described above. Next, we train an RNN with $m = 4$ hidden neurons using tanh activation. The input and output layer sizes are determined by the dimensionality of the encoding, namely $d = 7$ and $p = 7$. We use a sigmoid activation at the output layer, treating each neuron as independent. We use the binary cross entropy error function. The RNN is trained for $r = 10000$ epochs, using gradient step size $\eta = 1$ and the entire set of 400 input sequences as the batch size. The RNN model learns the training data perfectly, making no errors in the prediction of the set of possible next symbols.

We test the RNN model on 100 previously unseen Reber sequences (with minimum length 30, as before). The RNN makes no errors on the test sequences. On the other hand, we also trained an MLP with a single hidden layer, with size m varying between 4 and 100. Even after $r = 10000$ epochs, the MLP is not able to correctly predict any of the output sequences perfectly. It makes 2.62 mistakes on average per sequence for both the training and testing data. Increasing the number of epochs or the number of hidden layers does not improve the MLP performance.

26.1.4 Bidirectional RNNs

An RNN makes use of a hidden state $\mathbf{h}_t$ that depends on the previous hidden state $\mathbf{h}_{t-1}$ and the current input $\mathbf{x}_t$ at time t. In other words, it only looks at information from the past. A bidirectional RNN (BRNN), as shown in Figure 26.5, extends the RNN model to also include information from the future. In particular, a BRNN maintains a backward hidden state vector $\mathbf{b}_t \in \mathbb{R}^m$ that depends on the next backward hidden state $\mathbf{b}_{t+1}$ and the current input $\mathbf{x}_t$. The output at time t is a function of both $\mathbf{h}_t$ and $\mathbf{b}_t$. In

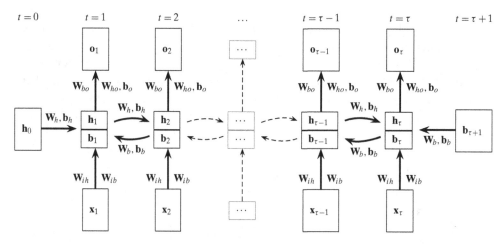

Figure 26.5. Bidirectional RNN: Unfolded in time.

particular, we compute the forward and backward hidden state vectors as follows:

$$
\begin{aligned}
\mathbf{h}_t &= f^h(\mathbf{W}_{ih}^T\mathbf{x}_t + \mathbf{W}_h^T\mathbf{h}_{t-1} + \mathbf{b}_h) \\
\mathbf{b}_t &= f^b(\mathbf{W}_{ib}^T\mathbf{x}_t + \mathbf{W}_b^T\mathbf{b}_{t+1} + \mathbf{b}_b)
\end{aligned}
\tag{26.6}
$$

Also, a BRNN needs two initial state vectors $\mathbf{h}_0$ and $\mathbf{b}_{\tau+1}$ to compute $\mathbf{h}_1$ and $\mathbf{b}_\tau$, respectively. These are usually set to $\mathbf{0} \in \mathbb{R}^m$. The forward and backward hidden states are computed independently, with the forward hidden states computed by considering the input sequence in the forward direction $\mathbf{x}_1, \mathbf{x}_2, \cdots, \mathbf{x}_\tau$, and with the backward hidden states computed by considering the sequence in reverse order $\mathbf{x}_\tau, \mathbf{x}_{\tau-1}, \cdots, \mathbf{x}_1$. The output at time t is computed only when both $\mathbf{h}_t$ and $\mathbf{b}_t$ are available, and is given as

$$
\mathbf{o}_t = f^o(\mathbf{W}_{ho}^T\mathbf{h}_t + \mathbf{W}_{bo}^T\mathbf{b}_t + \mathbf{b}_o)
$$

It is clear that BRNNs need the complete input before they can compute the output. We can also view a BRNN as having two sets of input sequences, namely the forward input sequence $\mathcal{X} = \langle \mathbf{x}_1, \mathbf{x}_2, \cdots, \mathbf{x}_\tau \rangle$ and the reversed input sequence $\mathcal{X}^r = \langle \mathbf{x}_\tau, \mathbf{x}_{\tau-1}, \ldots, \mathbf{x}_1 \rangle$, with the corresponding hidden states $\mathbf{h}_t$ and $\mathbf{b}_t$, which together determine the output $\mathbf{o}_t$. Thus, a BRNN is comprised of two "stacked" RNNs with independent hidden layers that jointly determine the output.

26.2 GATED RNNS: LONG SHORT-TERM MEMORY NETWORKS

One of the problems in training RNNs is their susceptibility to either the *vanishing gradient* or the *exploding gradient* problem. For example, consider the task of computing the net gradient vector $\boldsymbol{\delta}_t^h$ for the hidden layer at time t, given as

$$
\boldsymbol{\delta}_t^h = \partial \mathbf{f}_t^h \odot \left((\mathbf{W}_o \cdot \boldsymbol{\delta}_t^o) + (\mathbf{W}_h \cdot \boldsymbol{\delta}_{t+1}^h) \right)
$$

Assume for simplicity that we use a linear activation function, i.e., $\partial \mathbf{f}_t^h = \mathbf{1}$, and let us ignore the net gradient vector for the output layer, focusing only on the dependence on the hidden layers. Then for an input sequence of length τ, we have

$$\boldsymbol{\delta}_t^h = \mathbf{W}_h \cdot \boldsymbol{\delta}_{t+1}^h = \mathbf{W}_h(\mathbf{W}_h \cdot \boldsymbol{\delta}_{t+2}^h) = \mathbf{W}_h^2 \cdot \boldsymbol{\delta}_{t+2}^h = \cdots = \mathbf{W}_h^{\tau-t} \cdot \boldsymbol{\delta}_\tau^h$$

In particular, for example, at time $t = 1$, we have $\boldsymbol{\delta}_1^h = \mathbf{W}_h^{\tau-1} \cdot \boldsymbol{\delta}_\tau^h$. We can observe that the net gradient from time τ affects the net gradient vector at time t as a function of $\mathbf{W}_h^{\tau-t}$, i.e., as powers of the hidden weight matrix $\mathbf{W}_h$. Let the *spectral radius* of $\mathbf{W}_h$, defined as the absolute value of its largest eigenvalue, be given as $|\lambda_1|$. It turns out that if $|\lambda_1| < 1$, then $\|\mathbf{W}_h^k\| \to 0$ as $k \to \infty$, that is, the gradients vanish as we train on long sequences. On the other hand, if $|\lambda_1| > 1$, then at least one element of $\mathbf{W}_h^k$ becomes unbounded and thus $\|\mathbf{W}_h^k\| \to \infty$ as $k \to \infty$, that is, the gradients explode as we train on long sequences. To see this more clearly, let the eigendecomposition of the square $m \times m$ matrix $\mathbf{W}_h$ be given as

$$\mathbf{W}_h = \mathbf{U} \cdot \begin{pmatrix} \lambda_1 & 0 & \cdots & 0 \\ 0 & \lambda_2 & \cdots & 0 \\ \vdots & \vdots & \ddots & \vdots \\ 0 & 0 & \cdots & \lambda_m \end{pmatrix} \cdot \mathbf{U}^{-1}$$

where $|\lambda_1| \geq |\lambda_2| \geq \cdots \geq |\lambda_m|$ are the eigenvalues of $\mathbf{W}_h$, and $\mathbf{U}$ is the matrix comprising the corresponding eigenvectors, $\mathbf{u}_1, \mathbf{u}_2, \cdots, \mathbf{u}_m$, as columns. Thus, we have

$$\mathbf{W}_h^k = \mathbf{U} \cdot \begin{pmatrix} \lambda_1^k & 0 & \cdots & 0 \\ 0 & \lambda_2^k & \cdots & 0 \\ \vdots & \vdots & \ddots & \vdots \\ 0 & 0 & \cdots & \lambda_m^k \end{pmatrix} \cdot \mathbf{U}^{-1}$$

It is clear that the net gradients scale according to the eigenvalues of $\mathbf{W}_h$. Therefore, if $|\lambda_1| < 1$, then $|\lambda_1|^k \to 0$ as $k \to \infty$, and since $|\lambda_1| \geq |\lambda_i|$ for all $i = 1, 2, \cdots, m$, then necessarily $|\lambda_i|^k \to 0$ as well. That is, the gradients vanish. On the other hand, if $|\lambda_1| > 1$, then $|\lambda_1|^k \to \infty$ as $k \to \infty$, and the gradients explode. Therefore, for the error to neither vanish nor explode, the spectral radius of $\mathbf{W}_h$ should remain 1 or very close to it.

Long short-term memory (LSTM) networks alleviate the vanishing gradients problem by using *gate neurons* to control access to the hidden states. Consider the m-dimensional hidden state vector $\mathbf{h}_t \in \mathbb{R}^m$ at time t. In a regular RNN, we update the hidden state as follows (as per Eq. (26.1)):

$$\mathbf{h}_t = f^h(\mathbf{W}_i^T \mathbf{x}_t + \mathbf{W}_h^T \mathbf{h}_{t-1} + \mathbf{b}_h)$$

Let $\mathbf{g} \in \{0, 1\}^m$ be a binary vector. If we take the element-wise product of $\mathbf{g}$ and $\mathbf{h}_t$, namely, $\mathbf{g} \odot \mathbf{h}_t$, then elements of $\mathbf{g}$ act as gates that either allow the corresponding element of $\mathbf{h}_t$ to be retained or set to zero. The vector $\mathbf{g}$ thus acts as logical gate that allows selected elements of $\mathbf{h}_t$ to be remembered or forgotten. However, for backpropagation we need *differentiable gates*, for which we use sigmoid activation on the gate neurons so that their value lies in the range $[0, 1]$. Like a logical gate, such neurons allow the inputs to be completely remembered if the value is 1, or forgotten if the value is 0. In addition, they allow a weighted memory, allowing partial remembrance of the elements of $\mathbf{h}_t$, for values between 0 and 1.

Example 26.2 (Differentiable Gates). As an example, consider a hidden state vector

$$\mathbf{h}_t = \begin{pmatrix} -0.94 & 1.05 & 0.39 & 0.97 & 0.90 \end{pmatrix}^T$$

First consider a logical gate vector

$$\mathbf{g} = \begin{pmatrix} 0 & 1 & 1 & 0 & 1 \end{pmatrix}^T$$

Their element-wise product gives

$$\mathbf{g} \odot \mathbf{h}_t = \begin{pmatrix} 0 & 1.05 & 0.39 & 0 & 0.90 \end{pmatrix}^T$$

We can see that the first and fourth elements have been "forgotten."

Now consider a differentiable gate vector

$$\mathbf{g} = \begin{pmatrix} 0.1 & 0 & 1 & 0.9 & 0.5 \end{pmatrix}^T$$

The element-wise product of $\mathbf{g}$ and $\mathbf{h}_t$ gives

$$\mathbf{g} \odot \mathbf{h}_t = \begin{pmatrix} -0.094 & 0 & 0.39 & 0.873 & 0.45 \end{pmatrix}^T$$

Now, only a fraction specified by an element of $\mathbf{g}$ is retained as a memory after the element-wise product.

26.2.1 Forget Gate

To see how gated neurons work, we consider an RNN with a *forget gate*. Let $\mathbf{h}_t \in \mathbb{R}^m$ be the hidden state vector, and let $\boldsymbol{\phi}_t \in \mathbb{R}^m$ be a forget gate vector. Both these vectors have the same number of neurons, m.

In a regular RNN, assuming tanh activation, the hidden state vector is updated unconditionally, as follows:

$$\mathbf{h}_t = \tanh\left(\mathbf{W}_i^T \mathbf{x}_t + \mathbf{W}_h^T \mathbf{h}_{t-1} + \mathbf{b}_h\right)$$

Instead of directly updating $\mathbf{h}_t$, we will employ the forget gate neurons to control how much of the previous hidden state vector to forget when computing its new value, and also to control how to update it in light of the new input $\mathbf{x}_t$.

Figure 26.6 shows the architecture of an RNN with a forget gate. Given input $\mathbf{x}_t$ and previous hidden state $\mathbf{h}_{t-1}$, we first compute a candidate update vector $\mathbf{u}_t$, as follows:

$$\mathbf{u}_t = \tanh\left(\mathbf{W}_u^T \mathbf{x}_t + \mathbf{W}_{hu}^T \mathbf{h}_{t-1} + \mathbf{b}_u\right) \tag{26.7}$$

The candidate update vector $\mathbf{u}_t$ is essentially the unmodified hidden state vector, as in a regular RNN.

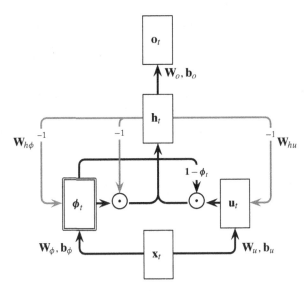

Figure 26.6. RNN with a forget gate ϕ_t. Recurrent connections shown in gray, forget gate shown doublelined. $\odot$ denotes element-wise product.

Using the forget gate, we can compute the new hidden state vector as follows:

$$\mathbf{h}_t = \boldsymbol{\phi}_t \odot \mathbf{h}_{t-1} + (\mathbf{1} - \boldsymbol{\phi}_t) \odot \mathbf{u}_t \tag{26.8}$$

Here $\odot$ is the element-wise product operation. We can see that the new hidden state vector retains a fraction of the previous hidden state values, and a (complementary) fraction of the candidate update values. Observe that if $\boldsymbol{\phi}_t = \mathbf{0}$, i.e., if we want to entirely forget the previous hidden state, then $\mathbf{1} - \boldsymbol{\phi}_t = \mathbf{1}$, which means that the hidden state will be updated completely at each time step just like in a regular RNN. Finally, given the hidden state $\mathbf{h}_t$ we can compute the output vector $\mathbf{o}_t$ as follows

$$\mathbf{o}_t = f^o \left(\mathbf{W}_o^T \mathbf{h}_t + \mathbf{b}_o \right)$$

How should we compute the forget gate vector $\boldsymbol{\phi}_t$? It makes sense to base it on both the previous hidden state and the new input value, so we compute it as follows:

$$\boldsymbol{\phi}_t = \sigma \left(\mathbf{W}_\phi^T \mathbf{x}_t + \mathbf{W}_{h\phi}^T \mathbf{h}_{t-1} + \mathbf{b}_\phi \right) \tag{26.9}$$

where we use a sigmoid activation function, denoted σ, to ensure that all the neuron values are in the range $[0, 1]$, denoting the extent to which the corresponding previous hidden state values should be forgotten.

To summarize, a forget gate vector $\boldsymbol{\phi}_t$ is a layer that depends on the previous hidden state layer $\mathbf{h}_{t-1}$ and the current input layer $\mathbf{x}_t$; these connections are fully connected, and are specified by the corresponding weight matrices $\mathbf{W}_{h\phi}$ and $\mathbf{W}_\phi$, and the bias vector $\mathbf{b}_\phi$. On the other hand, the output of the forget gate layer $\boldsymbol{\phi}_t$ needs to modify the previous hidden state layer $\mathbf{h}_{t-1}$, and therefore, both $\boldsymbol{\phi}_t$ and $\mathbf{h}_{t-1}$ feed into what is essentially a new *element-wise* product layer, denoted by $\odot$ in Figure 26.6.

Finally, the output of this element-wise product layer is used as input to the new hidden layer $\mathbf{h}_t$ that also takes input from another element-wise gate that computes the output from the candidate update vector $\mathbf{u}_t$ and the complemented forget gate, $\mathbf{1} - \boldsymbol{\phi}_t$. Thus, unlike regular layers that are fully connected and have a weight matrix and bias vector between the layers, the connections between $\boldsymbol{\phi}_t$ and $\mathbf{h}_t$ via the element-wise layer are all one-to-one, and the weights are fixed at the value 1 with bias 0. Likewise the connections between $\mathbf{u}_t$ and $\mathbf{h}_t$ via the other element-wise layer are also one-to-one, with weights fixed at 1 and bias at 0.

Example 26.3. Let $m = 5$. Assume that the previous hidden state vector and the candidate update vector are given as follows:

$$\mathbf{h}_{t-1} = \begin{pmatrix} -0.94 & 1.05 & 0.39 & 0.97 & 0.9 \end{pmatrix}^T$$

$$\mathbf{u}_t = \begin{pmatrix} 0.5 & 2.5 & -1.0 & -0.5 & 0.8 \end{pmatrix}^T$$

Let the forget gate and its complement be given as follows:

$$\boldsymbol{\phi}_t = \begin{pmatrix} 0.9 & 1 & 0 & 0.1 & 0.5 \end{pmatrix}^T$$

$$\mathbf{1} - \boldsymbol{\phi}_t = \begin{pmatrix} 0.1 & 0 & 1 & 0.9 & 0.5 \end{pmatrix}^T$$

The new hidden state vector is then computed as the weighted sum of the previous hidden state vector and the candidate update vector:

$$\mathbf{h}_t = \boldsymbol{\phi}_t \odot \mathbf{h}_{t-1} + (\mathbf{1} - \boldsymbol{\phi}_t) \odot \mathbf{u}_t$$

$$= \begin{pmatrix} 0.9 & 1 & 0 & 0.1 & 0.5 \end{pmatrix}^T \odot \begin{pmatrix} -0.94 & 1.05 & 0.39 & 0.97 & 0.9 \end{pmatrix}^T +$$

$$\begin{pmatrix} 0.1 & 0 & 1 & 0.9 & 0.5 \end{pmatrix}^T \odot \begin{pmatrix} 0.5 & 2.5 & -1.0 & -0.5 & 0.8 \end{pmatrix}^T$$

$$= \begin{pmatrix} -0.846 & 1.05 & 0 & 0.097 & 0.45 \end{pmatrix}^T + \begin{pmatrix} 0.05 & 0 & -1.0 & -0.45 & 0.40 \end{pmatrix}^T$$

$$= \begin{pmatrix} -0.796 & 1.05 & -1.0 & -0.353 & 0.85 \end{pmatrix}^T$$

Computing Net Gradients

It is instructive to compute the net gradients for an RNN with a forget gate, since a similar approach is used to compute the net gradients when training an LSTM network. An RNN with a forget gate has the following parameters it needs to learn, namely the weight matrices $\mathbf{W}_u$, $\mathbf{W}_{hu}$, $\mathbf{W}_\phi$, $\mathbf{W}_{h\phi}$, and $\mathbf{W}_o$, and the bias vectors $\mathbf{b}_u$, $\mathbf{b}_\phi$ and $\mathbf{b}_o$. The computation of the hidden state vector $\mathbf{h}_t$ adds together the inputs from the new element-wise layer that multiplies its incoming edges to compute the net input as opposed to computing a weighted sum. We will look at how to account for the element-wise layers during backpropagation.

Figure 26.7 shows a forget gate RNN unfolded in time for two time steps. Let δ_t^o, δ_t^h, δ_t^ϕ, and δ_t^u denote the net gradient vectors at the output, hidden, forget gate, and candidate update layers, respectively. During backpropagation, we need to compute the net gradients at each layer. The net gradients at the outputs are computed by

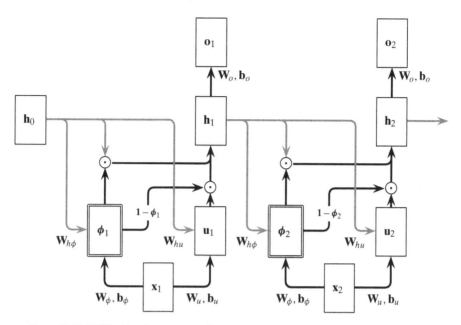

Figure 26.7. RNN with a forget gate unfolded in time (recurrent connections in gray).

considering the partial derivatives of the activation function $(\partial \mathbf{f}_t^o)$ and the error function $(\partial \boldsymbol{\mathcal{E}}_{\mathbf{x}_t})$:

$$\delta_t^o = \partial \mathbf{f}_t^o \odot \partial \boldsymbol{\mathcal{E}}_{\mathbf{x}_t}$$

For the other layers, we can reverse all the arrows to determine the dependencies between the layers. Therefore, to compute the net gradient for the update layer δ_t^u, notice that in backpropagation it has only one incoming edge from $\mathbf{h}_t$ via the element-wise product $(\mathbf{1} - \boldsymbol{\phi}_t) \odot \mathbf{u}_t$. The net gradient δ_{ti}^u at update layer neuron i at time t is given as

$$\delta_{ti}^u = \frac{\partial \boldsymbol{\mathcal{E}}_{\mathbf{x}}}{\partial net_{ti}^u} = \frac{\partial \boldsymbol{\mathcal{E}}_{\mathbf{x}}}{\partial net_{ti}^h} \cdot \frac{\partial net_{ti}^h}{\partial u_{ti}} \cdot \frac{\partial u_{ti}}{\partial net_{ti}^u} = \delta_{ti}^h \cdot (1 - \phi_{ti}) \cdot \left(1 - u_{ti}^2\right)$$

where $\frac{\partial net_{ti}^h}{\partial u_{ti}} = \frac{\partial}{\partial u_{ti}} \left\{ \phi_{ti} \cdot h_{t-1,i} + (1 - \phi_{ti}) \cdot u_{ti} \right\} = 1 - \phi_{ti}$, and we use the fact that the update layer uses a tanh activation function. Across all neurons, we obtain the net gradient at $\mathbf{u}_t$ as follows:

$$\delta_t^u = \delta_t^h \odot (\mathbf{1} - \boldsymbol{\phi}_t) \odot (\mathbf{1} - \mathbf{u}_t \odot \mathbf{u}_t)$$

To compute the net gradient vector for the forget gate, we observe from Figure 26.7 that there are two incoming flows into $\boldsymbol{\phi}_t$ during backpropagation — one from $\mathbf{h}_t$ via the element-wise product $\boldsymbol{\phi}_t \odot \mathbf{h}_{t-1}$, and the other also from $\mathbf{h}_t$ via the element-wise product $(\mathbf{1} - \boldsymbol{\phi}_t) \odot \mathbf{u}_t$. Therefore, the net gradient δ_{ti}^{ϕ} at forget gate neuron i at time t is given as

$$\delta_{ti}^{\phi} = \frac{\partial \boldsymbol{\mathcal{E}}_{\mathbf{x}}}{\partial net_{ti}^{\phi}} = \frac{\partial \boldsymbol{\mathcal{E}}_{\mathbf{x}}}{\partial net_{ti}^h} \cdot \frac{\partial net_{ti}^h}{\partial \phi_{ti}} \cdot \frac{\partial \phi_{ti}}{\partial net_{ti}^{\phi}} = \delta_{ti}^h \cdot (h_{t-1,i} - u_{ti}) \cdot \phi_{ti}(1 - \phi_{ti})$$

where $\frac{\partial net_{ti}^h}{\partial \phi_{ti}} = \frac{\partial}{\partial \phi_{ti}} \left\{ \phi_{ti} \cdot h_{t-1,i} + (1 - \phi_{ti}) \cdot u_{ti} \right\} = h_{t-1,i} - u_{ti}$, and we use the fact that the forget gate uses a sigmoid activation function. Across all neurons, we obtain the net gradient at $\boldsymbol{\phi}_t$ as follows:

$$\boldsymbol{\delta}_t^\phi = \boldsymbol{\delta}_t^h \odot (\mathbf{h}_{t-1} - \mathbf{u}_t) \odot \boldsymbol{\phi}_t \odot (\mathbf{1} - \boldsymbol{\phi}_t)$$

Finally, let us consider how to compute $\boldsymbol{\delta}_t^h$, the net gradient at the hidden layer at time t. In Figure 26.7 we can observe that if we reverse the arrows, $\boldsymbol{\delta}_t^h$ depends on the gradients at the output layer $\mathbf{o}_t$, the forget gate layer $\boldsymbol{\phi}_{t+1}$, the update layer $\mathbf{u}_{t+1}$, and on the hidden layer $\mathbf{h}_{t+1}$ via the element-wise product $\mathbf{h}_{t+1} \odot \boldsymbol{\phi}_{t+1}$. The output, forget and update layers are treated as in a regular RNN. However, due to the element-wise layer, the flow from $\mathbf{h}_{t+1}$ is handled as follows:

$$\frac{\partial \mathcal{E}_{\mathbf{x}_t}}{\partial net_{t+1,i}^h} \cdot \frac{\partial net_{t+1,i}^h}{\partial h_{ti}} \cdot \frac{\partial h_{ti}}{\partial net_{ti}^h} = \delta_{t+1,i}^h \cdot \phi_{t+1,i} \cdot 1 = \delta_{t+1,i}^h \cdot \phi_{t+1,i}$$

where $\frac{\partial net_{t+1,i}^h}{\partial h_{ti}} = \frac{\partial}{\partial h_{ti}} \left\{ \phi_{t+1,i} \cdot h_{ti} + (1 - \phi_{t+1,i}) \cdot u_{t+1,i} \right\} = \phi_{t+1,i}$, and we used the fact that $\mathbf{h}_t$ implicitly uses an identity activation function. Across all the hidden neurons at time t, the net gradient vector component from $\mathbf{h}_{t+1}$ is given as $\boldsymbol{\delta}_{t+1}^h \odot \boldsymbol{\phi}_{t+1}$. Considering all the layers, including the output, forget, update and element-wise layers, the complete net gradient vector at the hidden layer at time t is given as:

$$\boldsymbol{\delta}_t^h = \mathbf{W}_o \boldsymbol{\delta}_t^o + \mathbf{W}_{h\phi} \boldsymbol{\delta}_{t+1}^\phi + \mathbf{W}_{hu} \boldsymbol{\delta}_{t+1}^u + \left(\boldsymbol{\delta}_{t+1}^h \odot \boldsymbol{\phi}_{t+1} \right)$$

Given the net gradients, we can compute the gradients for all the weight matrices and bias vectors in a manner similar to that outlined for a regular RNN in Section 26.1.2. Likewise, stochastic gradient descent can be used to train the network.

26.2.2 Long Short-Term Memory (LSTM) Networks

We now describe LSTMs, which use differentiable gate vectors to control the hidden state vector $\mathbf{h}_t$, as well as another vector $\mathbf{c}_t \in \mathbb{R}^m$ called the *internal memory* vector. In particular, LSTMs utilize three *gate vectors*: an input gate vector $\boldsymbol{\kappa}_t \in \mathbb{R}^m$, a forget gate vector $\boldsymbol{\phi}_t \in \mathbb{R}^m$, and an output gate vector $\boldsymbol{\omega}_t \in \mathbb{R}^m$, as illustrated in Figure 26.8, which shows the architecture of an LSTM network. Like a regular RNN, an LSTM also maintains a hidden state vector for each time step. However, the content of the hidden vector is selectively copied from the internal memory vector via the output gate, with the internal memory being updated via the input gate and parts of it forgotten via the forget gate.

Let $\mathcal{X} = \langle \mathbf{x}_1, \mathbf{x}_2, \cdots, \mathbf{x}_\tau \rangle$ denote a sequence of d-dimensional input vectors of length τ, $\mathcal{Y} = \langle \mathbf{y}_1, \mathbf{y}_2, \cdots, \mathbf{y}_\tau \rangle$ the sequence of p-dimensional response vectors, and $\mathcal{O} = \langle \mathbf{o}_1, \mathbf{o}_2, \cdots, \mathbf{o}_\tau \rangle$ the p-dimensional output sequence from an LSTM. At each time step t, the three gate vectors are updated as follows:

$$
\begin{aligned}
\boldsymbol{\kappa}_t &= \sigma \left(\mathbf{W}_\kappa^T \mathbf{x}_t + \mathbf{W}_{h\kappa}^T \mathbf{h}_{t-1} + \mathbf{b}_\kappa \right) \\
\boldsymbol{\phi}_t &= \sigma \left(\mathbf{W}_\phi^T \mathbf{x}_t + \mathbf{W}_{h\phi}^T \mathbf{h}_{t-1} + \mathbf{b}_\phi \right) \\
\boldsymbol{\omega}_t &= \sigma \left(\mathbf{W}_\omega^T \mathbf{x}_t + \mathbf{W}_{h\omega}^T \mathbf{h}_{t-1} + \mathbf{b}_\omega \right)
\end{aligned}
\tag{26.10}
$$

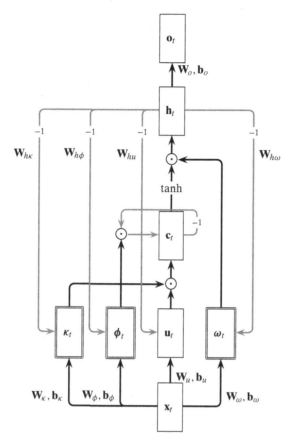

Figure 26.8. LSTM neural network. Recurrent connections shown in gray, gate layers shown doublelined.

Here $\sigma(\cdot)$ denotes the sigmoid activation function. We can observe that each gate is a function of the input vector $\mathbf{x}_t$ at time t, as well as the hidden state $\mathbf{h}_{t-1}$ from the previous time step. Each gate vector has a corresponding weight matrix from the input neurons to the gate neurons, and from the hidden state neurons to the gate neurons, as well as a corresponding bias vector. Each of the gate vectors conceptually plays a different role in an LSTM network. The input gate vector κ_t controls how much of the input vector, via the candidate update vector $\mathbf{u}_t$, is allowed to influence the memory vector $\mathbf{c}_t$. The forget gate vector ϕ_t controls how much of the previous memory vector to forget, and finally the output gate vector ω_t controls how much of the memory state is retained for the hidden state.

Given the current input $\mathbf{x}_t$ and the previous hidden state $\mathbf{h}_{t-1}$, an LSTM first computes a candidate update vector $\mathbf{u}_t$ after applying the tanh activation:

$$\mathbf{u}_t = \tanh\left(\mathbf{W}_u^T \mathbf{x}_t + \mathbf{W}_{hu}^T \mathbf{h}_{t-1} + \mathbf{b}_u\right) \tag{26.11}$$

It then then applies the different gates to compute the internal memory and hidden state vectors:

$$\begin{aligned}\mathbf{c}_t &= \kappa_t \odot \mathbf{u}_t + \phi_t \odot \mathbf{c}_{t-1} \\ \mathbf{h}_t &= \omega_t \odot \tanh(\mathbf{c}_t)\end{aligned} \tag{26.12}$$

The memory vector $\mathbf{c}_t$ at time t depends on the current update vector $\mathbf{u}_t$ and the previous memory $\mathbf{c}_{t-1}$. However, the input gate κ_t controls the extent to which $\mathbf{u}_t$ influences $\mathbf{c}_t$, and the forget gate ϕ_t controls how much of the previous memory is forgotten. On the other hand, the hidden state $\mathbf{h}_t$ depends on a tanh activated internal memory vector $\mathbf{c}_t$, but the output gate ω_t controls how much of the internal memory is reflected in the hidden state. Besides the input vectors $\mathbf{x}_t$, the LSTM also needs an initial hidden state vector $\mathbf{h}_0$ and an initial memory state vector $\mathbf{c}_0$, both typically set to $\mathbf{0} \in \mathbb{R}^m$.

Finally, the output of the network $\mathbf{o}_t$ is obtained by applying the output activation function f^o to an affine combination of the hidden state neuron values:

$$\mathbf{o}_t = f^o(\mathbf{W}_o^T \mathbf{h}_t + \mathbf{b}_o)$$

LSTMs can typically handle long sequences since the net gradients for the internal memory states do not vanish over long time steps. This is because, by design, the memory state $\mathbf{c}_{t-1}$ at time $t-1$ is linked to the memory state $\mathbf{c}_t$ at time t via implicit weights fixed at 1 and biases fixed at 0, with linear activation. This allows the error to flow across time steps without vanishing or exploding.

LSTMs can be trained just like regular RNNs by unfolding the layers in time, as illustrated in Figure 26.9, which shows the unfolded layers for two time steps. The first step in training is to use the feed-forward steps to compute the error, followed by the backpropagation of the gradients as a second step. The latter has to be modified to accommodate the element-wise operations used to update the memory state $\mathbf{c}_t$ and the hidden state $\mathbf{h}_t$. The connections from $\mathbf{c}_{t-1}$ to $\mathbf{c}_t$ starting from $\mathbf{c}_0$ to $\mathbf{c}_\tau$, which can be thought of as using unit weight matrices and zero biases, appear as a straight line in the figure indicating that the internal memory state can flow across longer periods of time without the gradients vanishing or exploding.

26.2.3 Training LSTMs

Consider the unfolded LSTM in Figure 26.9. During backpropagation the net gradient vector at the output layer at time t is computed by considering the partial derivatives of the activation function, $\partial \mathbf{f}_t^o$, and the error function, $\partial \mathcal{E}_{\mathbf{x}_t}$, as follows:

$$\delta_t^o = \partial \mathbf{f}_t^o \odot \partial \mathcal{E}_{\mathbf{x}_t}$$

where we assume that the output neurons are independent.

In backpropagation there are two incoming connections to the internal memory vector $\mathbf{c}_t$, one from $\mathbf{h}_t$ and the other from $\mathbf{c}_{t+1}$. Therefore, the net gradient δ_{ti}^c at the internal memory neuron i at time t is given as

$$\delta_{ti}^c = \frac{\partial \mathcal{E}_{\mathbf{x}}}{\partial net_{ti}^c} = \frac{\partial \mathcal{E}_{\mathbf{x}}}{\partial net_{ti}^h} \cdot \frac{\partial net_{ti}^h}{\partial c_{ti}} \cdot \frac{\partial c_{ti}}{\partial net_{ti}^c} + \frac{\partial \mathcal{E}_{\mathbf{x}}}{\partial net_{t+1,i}^c} \cdot \frac{\partial net_{t+1,i}^c}{\partial c_{ti}} \cdot \frac{\partial c_{ti}}{\partial net_{ti}^c}$$

$$= \delta_{ti}^h \cdot \omega_{ti}(1 - c_{ti}^2) + \delta_{t+1,i}^c \cdot \phi_{t+1,i}$$

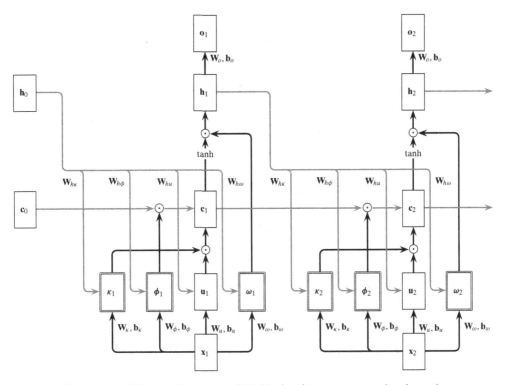

Figure 26.9. LSTM neural network unfolded in time (recurrent connections in gray).

where we use the fact that the internal memory vector implicitly uses an identity activation function, and furthermore

$$\frac{\partial net_{ti}^h}{\partial c_{ti}} = \frac{\partial}{\partial c_{ti}} \{\omega_{ti} \cdot \tanh(c_{ti})\} = \omega_{ti}(1 - c_{ti}^2)$$

$$\frac{\partial net_{t+1,i}^c}{\partial c_{ti}} = \frac{\partial}{\partial c_{ti}} \{\kappa_{t+1,i} \cdot u_{t+1,i} + \phi_{t+1,i} \cdot c_{ti}\} = \phi_{t+1,i}$$

The net gradient vector $\boldsymbol{\delta}_t^c$ at $\mathbf{c}_t$ is therefore given as:

$$\boldsymbol{\delta}_t^c = \boldsymbol{\delta}_t^h \odot \boldsymbol{\omega}_t \odot (\mathbf{1} - \mathbf{c}_t \odot \mathbf{c}_t) + \boldsymbol{\delta}_{t+1}^c \odot \boldsymbol{\phi}_{t+1}$$

The forget gate has only one incoming edge in backpropagation, from $\mathbf{c}_t$, via the element-wise multiplication $\boldsymbol{\phi}_t \odot \mathbf{c}_{t-1}$, with sigmoid activation, therefore the net gradient is:

$$\delta_{ti}^\phi = \frac{\partial \mathcal{E}_\mathbf{x}}{\partial net_{ti}^\phi} = \frac{\partial \mathcal{E}_\mathbf{x}}{\partial net_{ti}^c} \cdot \frac{\partial net_{ti}^c}{\partial \phi_{ti}} \cdot \frac{\partial \phi_{ti}}{\partial net_{ti}^\phi} = \delta_{ti}^c \cdot c_{t-1,i} \cdot \phi_{ti}(1 - \phi_{ti})$$

where we used the fact that the forget gate uses sigmoid activation and

$$\frac{\partial net_{ti}^c}{\partial \phi_{ti}} = \frac{\partial}{\partial \phi_{ti}} \{\kappa_{ti} \cdot u_{ti} + \phi_{ti} \cdot c_{t-1,i}\} = c_{t-1,i}$$

Across all forget gate neurons, the net gradient vector is therefore given as

$$\boldsymbol{\delta}_t^\phi = \boldsymbol{\delta}_t^c \odot \mathbf{c}_{t-1} \odot (\mathbf{1} - \boldsymbol{\phi}_t) \odot \boldsymbol{\phi}_t$$

The input gate also has only one incoming edge in backpropagation, from $\mathbf{c}_t$, via the element-wise multiplication $\kappa_t \odot \mathbf{u}_t$, with sigmoid activation. In a similar manner, as outlined above for δ_t^ϕ, the net gradient δ_t^κ at the input gate κ_t is given as:

$$\delta_t^\kappa = \delta_t^c \odot \mathbf{u}_t \odot (\mathbf{1} - \kappa_t) \odot \kappa_t$$

The same reasoning applies to the update candidate $\mathbf{u}_t$, which also has an incoming edge from $\mathbf{c}_t$ via $\kappa_t \odot \mathbf{u}_t$ and tanh activation, so the net gradient vector δ_t^u at the update layer is

$$\delta_t^u = \delta_t^c \odot \kappa_t \odot (\mathbf{1} - \mathbf{u}_t \odot \mathbf{u}_t)$$

Likewise, in backpropagation, there is one incoming connection to the output gate from $\mathbf{h}_t$ via $\omega_t \odot \tanh(\mathbf{c}_t)$ with sigmoid activation, therefore

$$\delta_t^\omega = \delta_t^h \odot \tanh(\mathbf{c}_t) \odot (\mathbf{1} - \omega_t) \odot \omega_t$$

Finally, to compute the net gradients at the hidden layer, note that gradients flow back to $\mathbf{h}_t$ from the following layers: $\mathbf{u}_{t+1}, \kappa_{t+1}, \phi_{t+1}, \omega_{t+1}$ and $\mathbf{o}_t$. Therefore, the net gradient vector at the hidden state vector δ_t^h is given as

$$\delta_t^h = \mathbf{W}_o \delta_t^o + \mathbf{W}_{h\kappa} \delta_{t+1}^\kappa + \mathbf{W}_{h\phi} \delta_{t+1}^\phi + \mathbf{W}_{h\omega} \delta_{t+1}^\omega + \mathbf{W}_{hu} \delta_{t+1}^u$$

The gradients for the weight matrix and bias vector at the output layer are given as:

$$\nabla_{\mathbf{b}_o} = \sum_{t=1}^\tau \delta_t^o \qquad\qquad \nabla_{\mathbf{W}_o} = \sum_{t=1}^\tau \mathbf{h}_t \cdot \left(\delta_t^o\right)^T$$

Likewise, the gradients for the weight matrices and bias vectors for the other layers are given as follows:

$$\nabla_{\mathbf{b}_\kappa} = \sum_{t=1}^\tau \delta_t^\kappa \qquad \nabla_{\mathbf{W}_\kappa} = \sum_{t=1}^\tau \mathbf{x}_t \cdot \left(\delta_t^\kappa\right)^T \qquad \nabla_{\mathbf{W}_{h\kappa}} = \sum_{t=1}^\tau \mathbf{h}_{t-1} \cdot \left(\delta_t^\kappa\right)^T$$

$$\nabla_{\mathbf{b}_\phi} = \sum_{t=1}^\tau \delta_t^\phi \qquad \nabla_{\mathbf{W}_\phi} = \sum_{t=1}^\tau \mathbf{x}_t \cdot \left(\delta_t^\phi\right)^T \qquad \nabla_{\mathbf{W}_{h\phi}} = \sum_{t=1}^\tau \mathbf{h}_{t-1} \cdot \left(\delta_t^\phi\right)^T$$

$$\nabla_{\mathbf{b}_\omega} = \sum_{t=1}^\tau \delta_t^\omega \qquad \nabla_{\mathbf{W}_\omega} = \sum_{t=1}^\tau \mathbf{x}_t \cdot \left(\delta_t^\omega\right)^T \qquad \nabla_{\mathbf{W}_{h\omega}} = \sum_{t=1}^\tau \mathbf{h}_{t-1} \cdot \left(\delta_t^\omega\right)^T$$

$$\nabla_{\mathbf{b}_u} = \sum_{t=1}^\tau \delta_t^u \qquad \nabla_{\mathbf{W}_u} = \sum_{t=1}^\tau \mathbf{x}_t \cdot \left(\delta_t^u\right)^T \qquad \nabla_{\mathbf{W}_{hu}} = \sum_{t=1}^\tau \mathbf{h}_{t-1} \cdot \left(\delta_t^u\right)^T$$

Given these gradients, we can use the stochastic gradient descent approach to train the network.

Example 26.4 (LSTM). We use an LSTM to learn the embedded Reber grammar, which is generated according to the automata shown in Figure 26.10. This automata has two copies of the Reber automata from Example 26.1. From the state s_1, the top automata is reached by following the edge labeled T, whereas the bottom automata is reached via the edge labeled P. The states of the top automata are labeled as $t_0, t_1, \cdots, t_7$, whereas the states of the bottom automata are labeled as $p_0, p_1, \cdots, p_7$. Finally, note that the state e_0 can be reached from either the top or the bottom

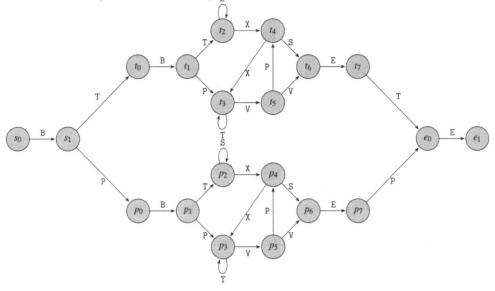

Figure 26.10. Embedded Reber grammar automata.

automata by following the edges labeled T and P, respectively. The first symbol is always B and the last symbol is always E. However, the important point is that the second symbol is always the same as the second last symbol, and thus any sequence learning model has to learn this long range dependency. For example, the following is a valid embedded Reber sequence: $S_X = \langle \text{B, T, B, T, S, S, X, X, T, V, V, E, T, E} \rangle$.

The task of the LSTM is to learn to predict the next symbol for each of the positions in a given embedded Reber sequence. For training, we generate $n = 400$ embedded Reber sequences with a minimum length of 40, and convert them into training pairs $(\mathcal{X}, \mathcal{Y})$ using the binary encoding described in Example 26.1. The maximum sequence length is $\tau = 64$.

Given the long range dependency, we used an LSTM with $m = 20$ hidden neurons (smaller values of m either need more epochs to learn, or have trouble learning the grammar). The input and output layer sizes are determined by the dimensionality of encoding, namely $d = 7$ and $p = 7$. We use sigmoid activation at the output layer, treating each neuron as independent. Finally, we use the binary cross entropy error function. The LSTM is trained for $r = 10000$ epochs (using step size $\eta = 1$ and batch size 400); it learns the training data perfectly, making no errors in the prediction of the set of possible next symbols.

We test the LSTM model on 100 previously unseen embedded Reber sequences (with minimum length 40, as before). The trained LSTM makes no errors on the test sequences. In particular, it is able to learn the long range dependency between the second symbol and the second last symbol, which must always match.

The embedded Reber grammar was chosen since an RNN has trouble learning the long range dependency. Using an RNN with $m = 60$ hidden neurons, using $r = 25000$ epochs with a step size of $\eta = 1$, the RNN can perfectly learn the training sequences. That is, it makes no errors on any of the 400 training sequences. However, on the test data, this RNN makes a mistake in 40 out of the 100 test sequences. In fact, in each of these test sequences it makes exactly one error; it fails to correctly predict the second last symbol. These results suggest that while the RNN is able to "memorize" the long range dependency in the training data, it is not able to generalize completely on unseen test sequences.

26.3 CONVOLUTIONAL NEURAL NETWORKS

A convolutional neural network (CNN) is essentially a *localized* and sparse feedforward MLP that is designed to exploit spatial and/or temporal structure in the input data. In a regular MLP all of the neurons in layer l are connected to all of the neurons in layer $l+1$. In contrast, a CNN connects a contiguous or adjacent subset of neurons in layer l to a single neuron in the next layer $l+1$. Different sliding windows comprising contiguous subsets of neurons in layer l connect to different neurons in layer $l+1$. Furthermore, all of these sliding windows use *parameter sharing*, that is, the same set of weights, called a *filter*, is used for all sliding windows. Finally, different filters are used to automatically extract features from layer l for use by layer $l+1$.

26.3.1 Convolutions

We begin by defining the convolution operation for one-way, two-way and three-way inputs. By one-way we mean data in the form of a single vector, by two-way we mean data in the form of a matrix, and by three-way we mean data in the form of a tensor. We also call them 1D, 2D or 3D inputs where the dimensionality refers to the number of axes in the input data. We will discuss the convolution operation in the context of the input layer and the first hidden layer, but the same approach can be applied to subsequent layers in the network.

1D Convolution

Let $\mathbf{x} = (x_1, x_2, \cdots, x_n)^T$ be an input vector (a one-way or 1D input) with n points. It is assumed that the input points x_i are not independent, but rather, there are dependencies between successive points. Let $\mathbf{w} = (w_1, w_2, \cdots, w_k)^T$ be a vector of weights, called a *1D filter*, with $k \le n$. Here k is also called the *window size*. Let $\mathbf{x}_k(i)$ denote the window of $\mathbf{x}$ of length k starting at position i, given as

$$\mathbf{x}_k(i) = \left(x_i, x_{i+1}, x_{i+2}, \cdots, x_{i+k-1}\right)^T$$

with $1 \le i \le n-k+1$. Given a vector $\mathbf{a} \in \mathbb{R}^k$, define the summation operator as one that adds all the elements of the vector. That is,

$$\text{sum}(\mathbf{a}) = \sum_{i=1}^{k} a_i$$

A *1D convolution* between $\mathbf{x}$ and $\mathbf{w}$, denoted by the asterisk symbol $*$, is defined as

$$\mathbf{x} * \mathbf{w} = \left(\text{sum}(\mathbf{x}_k(1) \odot \mathbf{w}) \quad \cdots \quad \text{sum}(\mathbf{x}_k(n-k+1) \odot \mathbf{w})\right)^T$$

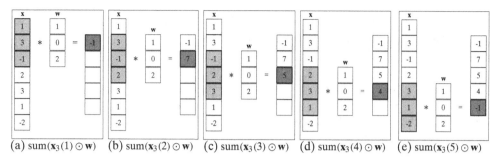

Figure 26.11. 1D Convolution: (a)–(e) show the convolution between different sliding windows of $\mathbf{x}$ and the filter $\mathbf{w}$ (with window size $k = 3$). The final convolution output is shown in (e).

where $\odot$ is the element-wise product, so that

$$\text{sum}(\mathbf{x}_k(i) \odot \mathbf{w}) = \sum_{j=1}^{k} x_{i+j-1} \cdot w_j \qquad (26.13)$$

for $i = 1, 2, \cdots, n - k + 1$. We can see that the convolution of $\mathbf{x} \in \mathbb{R}^n$ and $\mathbf{w} \in \mathbb{R}^k$ results in a vector of length $n - k + 1$.

Example 26.5 (1D Convolution). Figure 26.11 shows a vector $\mathbf{x}$ with $n = 7$ and a filter $\mathbf{w} = (1, 0, 2)^T$ with window size $k = 3$. The first window of $\mathbf{x}$ of size 3 is $\mathbf{x}_3(1) = (1, 3, -1)^T$. Therefore, as seen in Figure 26.11(a), we have

$$\text{sum}(\mathbf{x}_3(1) \odot \mathbf{w}) = \text{sum}\left((1, 3, -1)^T \odot (1, 0, 2)^T\right) = \text{sum}\left((1, 0, -2)^T\right) = -1$$

The convolution steps for different sliding windows of $\mathbf{x}$ with the filter $\mathbf{w}$ are shown in Figure 26.11(a)–(e). The convolution $\mathbf{x} * \mathbf{w}$ has size $n - k + 1 = 7 - 3 + 1 = 5$, and is given as

$$\mathbf{x} * \mathbf{w} = (-1, 7, 5, 4, -1)^T$$

2D Convolution

We can extend the convolution operation to matrix input, for example for images. Let $\mathbf{X}$ be an $n \times n$ input matrix, and let $\mathbf{W}$ be a $k \times k$ matrix of weights, called a *2D filter*, with $k \leq n$. Here k is called the window size. Let $\mathbf{X}_k(i, j)$ denote the $k \times k$ submatrix of $\mathbf{X}$ starting at row i and column j, defined as follows:

$$\mathbf{X}_k(i, j) = \begin{pmatrix} x_{i,j} & x_{i,j+1} & \cdots & x_{i,j+k-1} \\ x_{i+1,j} & x_{i+1,j+1} & \cdots & x_{i+1,j+k-1} \\ \vdots & \vdots & \cdots & \vdots \\ x_{i+k-1,j} & x_{i+k-1,j+1} & \cdots & x_{i+k-1,j+k-1} \end{pmatrix}$$

with $1 \leq i, j \leq n - k + 1$. Given a $k \times k$ matrix $\mathbf{A} \in \mathbb{R}^{k \times k}$, define the summation operator as one that adds all the elements of the matrix. That is,

$$\text{sum}(\mathbf{A}) = \sum_{i=1}^{k} \sum_{j=1}^{k} a_{i,j}$$

where $a_{i,j}$ is the element of $\mathbf{A}$ at row i and column j. The *2D convolution* of $\mathbf{X}$ and $\mathbf{W}$, denoted $\mathbf{X} * \mathbf{W}$, is defined as:

$$\mathbf{X} * \mathbf{W} = \begin{pmatrix} \text{sum}\big(\mathbf{X}_k(1,1) \odot \mathbf{W}\big) & \cdots & \text{sum}\big(\mathbf{X}_k(1, n-k+1) \odot \mathbf{W}\big) \\ \text{sum}\big(\mathbf{X}_k(2,1) \odot \mathbf{W}\big) & \cdots & \text{sum}\big(\mathbf{X}_k(2, n-k+1) \odot \mathbf{W}\big) \\ \vdots & \cdots & \vdots \\ \text{sum}\big(\mathbf{X}_k(n-k+1,1) \odot \mathbf{W}\big) & \cdots & \text{sum}\big(\mathbf{X}_k(n-k+1, n-k+1) \odot \mathbf{W}\big) \end{pmatrix}$$

where $\odot$ is the element-wise product of $\mathbf{X}_k(i, j)$ and $\mathbf{W}$, so that

$$\text{sum}\big(\mathbf{X}_k(i, j) \odot \mathbf{W}\big) = \sum_{a=1}^{k} \sum_{b=1}^{k} x_{i+a-1, j+b-1} \cdot w_{a,b} \tag{26.14}$$

for $i, j = 1, 2, \cdots, n - k + 1$. The convolution of $\mathbf{X} \in \mathbb{R}^{n \times n}$ and $\mathbf{W} \in \mathbb{R}^{k \times k}$ results in a $(n - k + 1) \times (n - k + 1)$ matrix.

Example 26.6 (2D Convolution). Figure 26.12 shows a matrix $\mathbf{X}$ with $n = 4$ and a filter $\mathbf{W}$ with window size $k = 2$. The convolution of the first window of $\mathbf{X}$, namely $\mathbf{X}_2(1,1)$, with $\mathbf{W}$ is given as (see Figure 26.12(a))

$$\text{sum}(\mathbf{X}_2(1,1) \odot \mathbf{W}) = \text{sum}\left(\begin{pmatrix} 1 & 2 \\ 3 & 1 \end{pmatrix} \odot \begin{pmatrix} 1 & 0 \\ 0 & 1 \end{pmatrix} \right) = \text{sum}\left(\begin{pmatrix} 1 & 0 \\ 0 & 1 \end{pmatrix} \right) = 2$$

The convolution steps for different 2×2 sliding windows of $\mathbf{X}$ with the filter $\mathbf{W}$ are shown in Figure 26.12(a)–(i). The convolution $\mathbf{X} * \mathbf{W}$ has size 3×3, since $n - k + 1 = 4 - 2 + 1 = 3$, and is given as

$$\mathbf{X} * \mathbf{W} = \begin{pmatrix} 2 & 6 & 4 \\ 4 & 4 & 8 \\ 4 & 4 & 4 \end{pmatrix}$$

3D Convolution

We now extend the convolution operation to a three-dimensional matrix, which is also called a *3D tensor*. The first dimension comprises the rows, the second the columns, and the third the *channels*. Let $\mathbf{X}$ be an $n \times n \times m$ tensor, with n rows, n columns and m channels. The assumption is that the input $\mathbf{X}$ is a collection of $n \times n$ matrices obtained by applying m *filters*, which specify the m channels. For example, for $n \times n$ image inputs, each channel may correspond to a different color filter — red, green or blue.

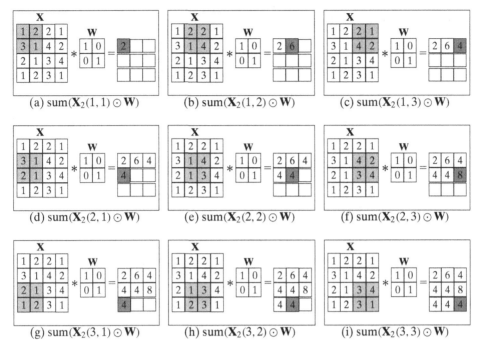

Figure 26.12. 2D Convolution: (a)–(i) show the 2D convolution between different 2×2 sliding windows of $\mathbf{X}$ and the filter $\mathbf{W}$. The final 2D convolution output is shown in (i).

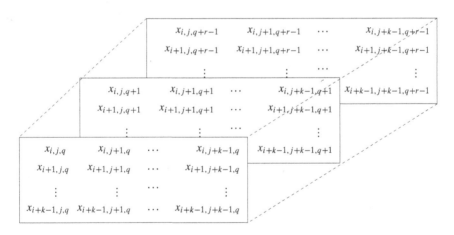

Figure 26.13. 3D subtensor $\mathbf{X}_k(i, j, q)$: $k \times k \times r$ subtensor of $\mathbf{X}$ starting at row i, column j, and channel q.

Let $\mathbf{W}$ be a $k \times k \times r$ tensor of weights, called a *3D filter*, with $k \leq n$ and $r \leq m$. Let $\mathbf{X}_k(i, j, q)$ denote the $k \times k \times r$ subtensor of $\mathbf{X}$ starting at row i, column j and channel q, as illustrated in Figure 26.13, with $1 \leq i, j \leq n - k + 1$, and $1 \leq q \leq m - r + 1$.

Given a $k \times k \times r$ tensor $\mathbf{A} \in \mathbb{R}^{k \times k \times r}$, define the summation operator as one that adds all the elements of the tensor. That is,

$$\text{sum}(\mathbf{A}) = \sum_{i=1}^{k} \sum_{j=1}^{k} \sum_{q=1}^{r} a_{i,j,q}$$

where $a_{i,j,q}$ is the element of $\mathbf{A}$ at row i, column j, and channel q. The *3D convolution* of $\mathbf{X}$ and $\mathbf{W}$, denoted $\mathbf{X} * \mathbf{W}$, is defined as:

$$\mathbf{X} * \mathbf{W} = \begin{pmatrix} \begin{pmatrix} \text{sum}(\mathbf{X}_k(1,1,1) \odot \mathbf{W}) & \cdots & \text{sum}(\mathbf{X}_k(1,n-k+1,1) \odot \mathbf{W}) \\ \text{sum}(\mathbf{X}_k(2,1,1) \odot \mathbf{W}) & \cdots & \text{sum}(\mathbf{X}_k(2,n-k+1,1) \odot \mathbf{W}) \\ \vdots & \cdots & \vdots \\ \text{sum}(\mathbf{X}_k(n-k+1,1,1) \odot \mathbf{W}) & \cdots & \text{sum}(\mathbf{X}_k(n-k+1,n-k+1,1) \odot \mathbf{W}) \end{pmatrix} \\ \begin{pmatrix} \text{sum}(\mathbf{X}_k(1,1,2) \odot \mathbf{W}) & \cdots & \text{sum}(\mathbf{X}_k(1,n-k+1,2) \odot \mathbf{W}) \\ \text{sum}(\mathbf{X}_k(2,1,2) \odot \mathbf{W}) & \cdots & \text{sum}(\mathbf{X}_k(2,n-k+1,2) \odot \mathbf{W}) \\ \vdots & \cdots & \vdots \\ \text{sum}(\mathbf{X}_k(n-k+1,1,2) \odot \mathbf{W}) & \cdots & \text{sum}(\mathbf{X}_k(n-k+1,n-k+1,2) \odot \mathbf{W}) \end{pmatrix} \\ \vdots \qquad\qquad \vdots \qquad\qquad \vdots \\ \begin{pmatrix} \text{sum}(\mathbf{X}_k(1,1,m-r+1) \odot \mathbf{W}) & \cdots & \text{sum}(\mathbf{X}_k(1,n-k+1,m-r+1) \odot \mathbf{W}) \\ \text{sum}(\mathbf{X}_k(2,1,m-r+1) \odot \mathbf{W}) & \cdots & \text{sum}(\mathbf{X}_k(2,n-k+1,m-r+1) \odot \mathbf{W}) \\ \vdots & \cdots & \vdots \\ \text{sum}(\mathbf{X}_k(n-k+1,1,m-r+1) \odot \mathbf{W}) & \cdots & \text{sum}(\mathbf{X}_k(n-k+1,n-k+1,m-r+1) \odot \mathbf{W}) \end{pmatrix} \end{pmatrix}$$

where $\odot$ is the element-wise product of $\mathbf{X}_k(i,j,q)$ and $\mathbf{W}$, so that

$$\text{sum}(\mathbf{X}_k(i,j,q) \odot \mathbf{W}) = \sum_{a=1}^{k} \sum_{b=1}^{k} \sum_{c=1}^{r} x_{i+a-1,j+b-1,q+c-1} \cdot w_{a,b,c} \tag{26.15}$$

for $i,j = 1,2,\cdots,n-k+1$ and $q = 1,2,\cdots,m-r+1$. We can see that the convolution of $\mathbf{X} \in \mathbb{R}^{n \times n \times m}$ and $\mathbf{W} \in \mathbb{R}^{k \times k \times r}$ results in a $(n-k+1) \times (n-k+1) \times (m-r+1)$ tensor.

3D Convolutions in CNNs Typically in CNNs, we use a 3D filter $\mathbf{W}$ of size $k \times k \times m$, with the number of channels $r = m$, the same as the number of channels in $\mathbf{X} \in \mathbb{R}^{n \times n \times m}$. Let $\mathbf{X}_k(i,j)$ be the $k \times k \times m$ subtensor of $\mathbf{X}$ starting at row i and column j. Then the 3D convolution of $\mathbf{X}$ and $\mathbf{W}$ is given as:

$$\mathbf{X} * \mathbf{W} = \begin{pmatrix} \text{sum}(\mathbf{X}_k(1,1) \odot \mathbf{W}) & \cdots & \text{sum}(\mathbf{X}_k(1,n-k+1) \odot \mathbf{W}) \\ \text{sum}(\mathbf{X}_k(2,1) \odot \mathbf{W}) & \cdots & \text{sum}(\mathbf{X}_k(2,n-k+1) \odot \mathbf{W}) \\ \vdots & \cdots & \vdots \\ \text{sum}(\mathbf{X}_k(n-k+1,1) \odot \mathbf{W}) & \cdots & \text{sum}(\mathbf{X}_k(n-k+1,n-k+1) \odot \mathbf{W}) \end{pmatrix}$$

We can see that when $\mathbf{W} \in \mathbb{R}^{k \times k \times m}$, its 3D convolution with $\mathbf{X} \in \mathbb{R}^{n \times n \times m}$ results in a $(n-k+1) \times (n-k+1)$ matrix, since there is no freedom to move in the third dimension. Henceforth, we will always assume that a 3D filter $\mathbf{W} \in \mathbb{R}^{k \times k \times m}$ has the same number of channels as the tensor $\mathbf{X}$ on which it is applied. Since the number of channels is fixed based on $\mathbf{X}$, the only parameter needed to fully specify $\mathbf{W}$ is the window size k.

Example 26.7 (3D Convolution). Figure 26.14 shows a $3 \times 3 \times 3$ tensor $\mathbf{X}$ with $n = 3$ and $m = 3$, and a $2 \times 2 \times 3$ filter $\mathbf{W}$ with window size $k = 2$ and $r = 3$. The convolution

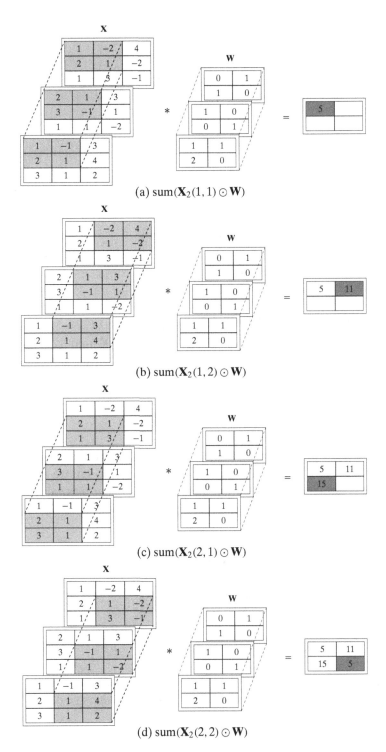

Figure 26.14. 3D Convolution: (a)–(d) Convolution between different $2 \times 2 \times 3$ sliding windows of $\mathbf{X}$, and the filter $\mathbf{W}$. The final 3D convolution output is shown in (d).

of the first window of $\mathbf{X}$, namely $\mathbf{X}_2(1, 1)$, with $\mathbf{W}$ is given as (see Figure 26.14(a))

$$\text{sum}(\mathbf{X}_2(1, 1) \odot \mathbf{W}) = \text{sum}\left(\left(\begin{array}{cc|cc|cc} 1 & -1 & 2 & 1 & 1 & -2 \\ 2 & 1 & 3 & -1 & 2 & 1 \end{array}\right) \odot \left(\begin{array}{cc|cc|cc} 1 & 1 & 1 & 0 & 0 & 1 \\ 2 & 0 & 0 & 1 & 1 & 0 \end{array}\right)\right)$$

$$= \text{sum}\left(\left(\begin{array}{cc|cc|cc} 1 & -1 & 2 & 0 & 0 & -2 \\ 4 & 0 & 0 & -1 & 2 & 0 \end{array}\right)\right) = 5$$

where we stack the different channels horizontally. The convolution steps for different $2 \times 2 \times 3$ sliding windows of $\mathbf{X}$ with the filter $\mathbf{W}$ are shown in Figure 26.14(a)–(d). The convolution $\mathbf{X} * \mathbf{W}$ has size 2×2, since $n - k + 1 = 3 - 2 + 1 = 2$ and $r = m = 3$; it is given as

$$\mathbf{X} * \mathbf{W} = \begin{pmatrix} 5 & 11 \\ 15 & 5 \end{pmatrix}$$

26.3.2 Bias and Activation Functions

We discuss the role of bias neurons and activation functions in the context of a tensor of neurons at layer l. Let $\mathbf{Z}^l$ be an $n_l \times n_l \times m_l$ tensor of neurons at layer l so that $z_{i,j,q}^l$ denotes the value of the neuron at row i, column j and channel q for layer l, with $1 \le i, j \le n_l$ and $1 \le q \le m_l$.

Filter Bias

Let $\mathbf{W}$ be a $k \times k \times m_l$ 3D filter. Recall that when we convolve $\mathbf{Z}^l$ and $\mathbf{W}$, we get a $(n_l - k + 1) \times (n_l - k + 1)$ matrix at layer $l + 1$. However, so far, we have ignored the role of the bias term in the convolution. Let $b \in \mathbb{R}$ be a scalar bias value for $\mathbf{W}$, and let $\mathbf{Z}_k^l(i, j)$ denote the $k \times k \times m_l$ subtensor of $\mathbf{Z}^l$ at position (i, j). Then, the net signal at neuron $z_{i,j}^{l+1}$ in layer $l + 1$ is given as

$$net_{i,j}^{l+1} = \text{sum}\left(\mathbf{Z}_k^l(i, j) \odot \mathbf{W}\right) + b$$

and the value of the neuron $z_{i,j}^{l+1}$ is obtained by applying some activation function f to the net signal

$$z_{i,j}^{l+1} = f\left(\text{sum}(\mathbf{Z}_k^l(i, j) \odot \mathbf{W}) + b\right)$$

The activation function can be any of the ones typically used in neural networks, for example, identity, sigmoid, tanh, ReLU and so on. In the language of convolutions, the values of the neurons in layer $l + 1$ is given as follows

$$\mathbf{Z}^{l+1} = f\left((\mathbf{Z}^l * \mathbf{W}) \oplus b\right)$$

where $\oplus$ indicates that the bias term b is added to each element of the $(n_l - k + 1) \times (n_l - k + 1)$ matrix $\mathbf{Z}^l * \mathbf{W}$.

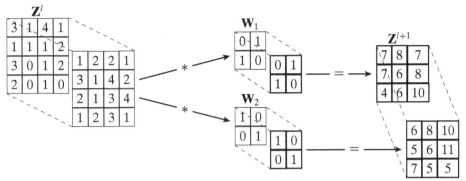

Figure 26.15. Multiple 3D filters.

Multiple 3D Filters

We can observe that one 3D filter $\mathbf{W}$ with a corresponding bias term b results in a $(n_l - k + 1) \times (n_l - k + 1)$ matrix of neurons in layer $l + 1$. Therefore, if we desire m_{l+1} channels in layer $l + 1$, then we need m_{l+1} different $k \times k \times m_l$ filters $\mathbf{W}_q$ with a corresponding bias term b_q, to obtain the $(n_l - k + 1) \times (n_l - k + 1) \times m_{l+1}$ tensor of neuron values at layer $l + 1$, given as

$$\mathbf{Z}^{l+1} = \left\{ z_{i,j,q}^{l+1} = f\left(\text{sum}\left(\mathbf{Z}_k^l(i, j) \odot \mathbf{W}_q\right) + b_q\right) \right\}_{i,j=1,2,\ldots,n_l-k+1 \text{ and } q=1,2,\ldots,m_{l+1}}$$

which can be written more compactly as

$$\mathbf{Z}^{l+1} = f\left(\left(\mathbf{Z}^l * \mathbf{W}_1\right) \oplus b_1, \left(\mathbf{Z}^l * \mathbf{W}_2\right) \oplus b_2, \cdots, \left(\mathbf{Z}^l * \mathbf{W}_{m_{l+1}}\right) \oplus b_{m_{l+1}}\right)$$

where the activation function f distributes over all of its arguments.

In summary, a convolution layer takes as input the $n_l \times n_l \times m_l$ tensor $\mathbf{Z}^l$ of neurons from layer l, and then computes the $n_{l+1} \times n_{l+1} \times m_{l+1}$ tensor $\mathbf{Z}^{l+1}$ of neurons for the next layer $l + 1$ via the convolution of $\mathbf{Z}^l$ with a set of m_{l+1} different 3D filters of size $k \times k \times m_l$, followed by adding the bias and applying some non-linear activation function f. Note that each 3D filter applied to $\mathbf{Z}^l$ results in a new channel in layer $l + 1$. Therefore, m_{l+1} filters are used to yield m_{l+1} channels at layer $l + 1$.

Example 26.8 (Multiple 3D Filters). Figure 26.15 shows how applying different filters yield the channels for the next layer. It shows a $4 \times 4 \times 2$ tensor $\mathbf{Z}^l$ with $n = 4$ and $m = 2$. It also shows two different $2 \times 2 \times 2$ filters $\mathbf{W}_1$ and $\mathbf{W}_2$ with $k = 2$ and $r = 2$. Since $r = m = 2$, the convolution of $\mathbf{Z}^l$ and $\mathbf{W}_i$ (for $i = 1, 2$) results in a 3×3 matrix since $n - k + 1 = 4 - 2 + 1 = 3$. However, $\mathbf{W}_1$ yields one channel and $\mathbf{W}_2$ yields a second channel, so that the tensor for the next layer $\mathbf{Z}^{l+1}$ has size $3 \times 3 \times 2$, with two channels (one per filter).

26.3.3 Padding and Striding

One of the issues with the convolution operation is that the size of the tensors will necessarily decrease in each successive CNN layer. If layer l has size $n_l \times n_l \times m_l$, and

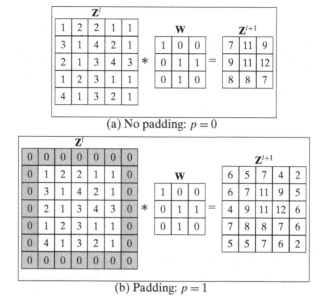

Figure 26.16. Padding: 2D Convolution (a) without padding, and (b) with padding.

we use filters of size $k \times k \times m_l$, then each channel in layer $l + 1$ will have size $(n_l - k + 1) \times (n_l - k + 1)$. That is the number of rows and columns for each successive tensor will shrink by $k - 1$ and that will limit the number of layers the CNN can have.

Padding

To get around this limitation, a simple solution is to pad each tensor along both the rows and columns in each channel by some default value, typically zero. For uniformity, we always pad by adding the same number of rows at the top and at the bottom, and likewise the same number of columns on the left and on the right. That is, assume that we add p rows both on top and bottom, and p columns both on the left and right. With padding p, the implicit size of layer l tensor is then $(n_l + 2p) \times (n_l + 2p) \times m_l$. Assume that each filter is of size $k \times k \times m_l$, and assume there are m_{l+1} filters, then the size of the layer $l + 1$ tensor will be $(n_l + 2p - k + 1) \times (n_l + 2p - k + 1) \times m_{l+1}$. Since we want to preserve the size of the resulting tensor, we need to have

$$n_l + 2p - k + 1 \geq n_l, \text{which implies, } p = \left\lceil \frac{k-1}{2} \right\rceil$$

With padding, we can have arbitrarily deep convolutional layers in a CNN.

Example 26.9 (Padding). Figure 26.16 shows a 2D convolution without and with padding. Figure 26.16(a) shows the convolution of a 5×5 matrix $\mathbf{Z}^l$ ($n = 5$) with a 3×3 filter $\mathbf{W}$ ($k = 3$), which results in a 3×3 matrix since $n - k + 1 = 5 - 3 + 1 = 3$. Thus, the size of the next layer $\mathbf{Z}^{l+1}$ has decreased.

On the other hand, zero padding $\mathbf{Z}^l$ using $p = 1$ results in a 7×7 matrix as shown in Figure 26.16(b). Since $p = 1$, we have an extra row of zeros on the top

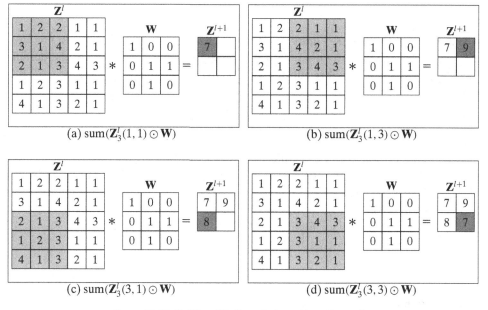

Figure 26.17. Striding: 2D Convolution with stride $s = 2$.

and bottom, and an extra column of zeros on the left and right. The convolution of the zero-padded $\mathbf{X}$ with $\mathbf{W}$ now results in a 5×5 matrix $\mathbf{Z}^{l+1}$ (since $7 - 3 + 1 = 5$), which preserves the size.

If we wanted to apply another convolution layer, we could zero pad the resulting matrix $\mathbf{Z}^{l+1}$ with $p = 1$, which would again yield a 5×5 matrix for the next layer, using a 3×3 filter. This way, we can chain together as many convolution layers as desired, without decrease in the size of the layers.

Striding

Striding is often used to sparsify the number of sliding windows used in the convolutions. That is, instead of considering all possible windows we increment the index along both rows and columns by an integer value $s \geq 1$ called the *stride*. A 3D convolution of $\mathbf{Z}^l$ of size $n_l \times n_l \times m_l$ with a filter $\mathbf{W}$ of size $k \times k \times m_l$, using stride s, is given as:

$$\mathbf{Z}^l * \mathbf{W} = \begin{pmatrix} \text{sum}(\mathbf{Z}_k^l(1,1) \odot \mathbf{W}) & \text{sum}(\mathbf{Z}_k^l(1,1+s) \odot \mathbf{W}) & \cdots & \text{sum}(\mathbf{Z}_k^l(1,1+t\cdot s) \odot \mathbf{W}) \\ \text{sum}(\mathbf{Z}_k^l(1+s,1) \odot \mathbf{W}) & \text{sum}(\mathbf{Z}_k^l(1+s,1+s) \odot \mathbf{W}) & \cdots & \text{sum}(\mathbf{Z}_k^l(1+s,1+t\cdot s) \odot \mathbf{W}) \\ \vdots & \vdots & \cdots & \vdots \\ \text{sum}(\mathbf{Z}_k^l(1+t\cdot s,1) \odot \mathbf{W}) & \text{sum}(\mathbf{Z}_k^l(1+t\cdot s,1+s) \odot \mathbf{W}) & \cdots & \text{sum}(\mathbf{Z}_k^l(1+t\cdot s,1+t\cdot s) \odot \mathbf{W}) \end{pmatrix}$$

where $t = \left\lfloor \frac{n_l - k}{s} \right\rfloor$. We can observe that using stride s, the convolution of $\mathbf{Z}^l \in \mathbb{R}^{n_l \times n_l \times m_l}$ with $\mathbf{W} \in \mathbb{R}^{k \times k \times m_l}$ results in a $(t+1) \times (t+1)$ matrix.

Example 26.10 (Striding). Figure 26.17 shows 2D convolution using stride $s = 2$ on a 5×5 matrix $\mathbf{Z}^l$ ($n_l = 5$) with a filter $\mathbf{W}$ of size 3×3 ($k = 3$). Instead of the default stride of one, which would result in a 3×3 matrix, we get a $(t+1) \times (t+1) = 2 \times 2$ matrix $\mathbf{Z}^{l+1}$, since

$$t = \left\lfloor \frac{n_l - k}{s} \right\rfloor = \left\lfloor \frac{5 - 3}{2} \right\rfloor = 1$$

We can see that the next window index increases by s along the rows and columns. For example, the first window is $\mathbf{Z}_3^l(1, 1)$ and thus the second window is $\mathbf{Z}_3^l(1, 1+s) = \mathbf{Z}_3^l(1, 3)$ (see Figures 26.17(a) and 26.17(b)). Next, we move down by a stride of $s = 2$, so that the third window is $\mathbf{Z}_3^l(1+s, 1) = \mathbf{Z}_3^l(3, 1)$, and the final window is $\mathbf{Z}_3^l(3, 1+s) = \mathbf{Z}_3^l(3, 3)$ (see Figures 26.17(c) and 26.17(d)).

26.3.4 Generalized Aggregation Functions: Pooling

Let $\mathbf{Z}^l$ be a $n_l \times n_l \times m_l$ tensor at layer l. Our discussion of convolutions so far assumes that we sum together all of the elements in the element-wise product of the $k \times k \times r$ subtensor $\mathbf{Z}_k^l(i, j, q)$ and the filter $\mathbf{W}$. In fact, CNNs also use other types of aggregation functions in addition to summation, such as average and maximum.

Avg-Pooling

If we replace the summation with the average value over the element-wise product of $\mathbf{Z}_k^l(i, j, q)$ and $\mathbf{W}$, we get

$$\mathrm{avg}\big(\mathbf{Z}_k^l(i, j, q) \odot \mathbf{W}\big) = \operatorname*{avg}_{\substack{a=1,2,\cdots,k \\ b=1,2,\cdots,k \\ c=1,2,\cdots,r}} \big\{ z_{i+a-1, j+b-1, q+c-1}^l \cdot w_{a,b,c} \big\}$$

$$= \frac{1}{k^2 \cdot r} \cdot \mathrm{sum}\big(\mathbf{Z}_k^l(i, j, q) \odot \mathbf{W}\big)$$

Max-Pooling

If we replace the summation with the maximum value over the element-wise product of $\mathbf{Z}_k^l(i, j, q)$ and $\mathbf{W}$, we get

$$\max\big(\mathbf{Z}_k^l(i, j, q) \odot \mathbf{W}\big) = \operatorname*{max}_{\substack{a=1,2,\cdots,k \\ b=1,2,\cdots,k \\ c=1,2,\cdots,r}} \big\{ z_{i+a-1, j+b-1, q+c-1}^l \cdot w_{a,b,c} \big\} \tag{26.16}$$

The 3D convolution of $\mathbf{Z}^l \in \mathbb{R}^{n_l \times n_l \times m_l}$ with filter $\mathbf{W} \in \mathbb{R}^{k \times k \times r}$ using max-pooling, denoted $\mathbf{Z}^l *_{\max} \mathbf{W}$, results in a $(n_l - k + 1) \times (n_l - k + 1) \times (m_l - r + 1)$ tensor, given as:

$$\mathbf{Z}^l *_{\max} \mathbf{W} = \left(\begin{array}{ccc}
\max\!\big(\mathbf{X}_k(1,1,1)\odot\mathbf{W}\big) & \cdots & \max\!\big(\mathbf{X}_k(1,n-k+1,1)\odot\mathbf{W}\big) \\
\max\!\big(\mathbf{X}_k(2,1,1)\odot\mathbf{W}\big) & \cdots & \max\!\big(\mathbf{X}_k(2,n-k+1,1)\odot\mathbf{W}\big) \\
\vdots & \cdots & \vdots \\
\max\!\big(\mathbf{X}_k(n-k+1,1,1)\odot\mathbf{W}\big) & \cdots & \max\!\big(\mathbf{X}_k(n-k+1,n-k+1,1)\odot\mathbf{W}\big) \\
\hline
\max\!\big(\mathbf{X}_k(1,1,2)\odot\mathbf{W}\big) & \cdots & \max\!\big(\mathbf{X}_k(1,n-k+1,2)\odot\mathbf{W}\big) \\
\max\!\big(\mathbf{X}_k(2,1,2)\odot\mathbf{W}\big) & \cdots & \max\!\big(\mathbf{X}_k(2,n-k+1,2)\odot\mathbf{W}\big) \\
\vdots & \cdots & \vdots \\
\max\!\big(\mathbf{X}_k(n-k+1,1,2)\odot\mathbf{W}\big) & \cdots & \max\!\big(\mathbf{X}_k(n-k+1,n-k+1,2)\odot\mathbf{W}\big) \\
\vdots & \vdots & \vdots \\
\max\!\big(\mathbf{X}_k(1,1,m-r+1)\odot\mathbf{W}\big) & \cdots & \max\!\big(\mathbf{X}_k(1,n-k+1,m-r+1)\odot\mathbf{W}\big) \\
\max\!\big(\mathbf{X}_k(2,1,m-r+1)\odot\mathbf{W}\big) & \cdots & \max\!\big(\mathbf{X}_k(2,n-k+1,m-r+1)\odot\mathbf{W}\big) \\
\vdots & \cdots & \vdots \\
\max\!\big(\mathbf{X}_k(n-k+1,1,m-r+1)\odot\mathbf{W}\big) & \cdots & \max\!\big(\mathbf{X}_k(n-k+1,n-k+1,m-r+1)\odot\mathbf{W}\big)
\end{array}\right)$$

Max-pooling in CNNs   Typically, max-pooling is used more often than avg-pooling. Also, for pooling it is very common to set the stride equal to the filter size ($s = k$), so that the aggregation function is applied over disjoint $k \times k$ windows in each channel in $\mathbf{Z}^l$. More importantly, in pooling, the filter $\mathbf{W}$ is by default taken to be a $k \times k \times 1$ tensor all of whose weights are fixed as 1, so that $\mathbf{W} = \mathbf{1}_{k \times k \times 1}$. In other words, the filter weights are fixed at 1 and are not updated during backpropagation. Further, the filter uses a fixed zero bias (that is, $b = 0$). Finally, note that pooling implicitly uses an identity activation function. As such, the convolution of $\mathbf{Z}^l \in \mathbb{R}^{n_l \times n_l \times m_l}$ with $\mathbf{W} \in \mathbb{R}^{k \times k \times 1}$, using stride $s = k$, results in a tensor $\mathbf{Z}^{l+1}$ of size $\lfloor \frac{n_l}{s} \rfloor \times \lfloor \frac{n_l}{s} \rfloor \times m_l$.

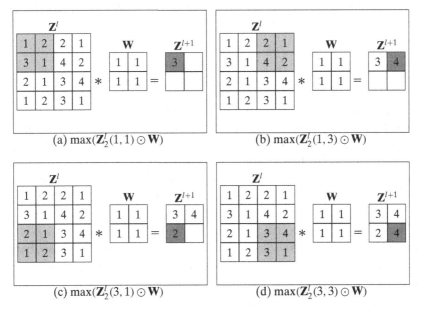

Figure 26.18. Max-pooling: Stride $s = 2$.

Example 26.11 (Max-pooling). Figure 26.18 shows max-pooling on a 4×4 matrix $\mathbf{Z}^l$ ($n_l = 4$), using window size $k = 2$ and stride $s = 2$ that equals the window size. The resulting layer $\mathbf{Z}^{l+1}$ thus has size 2×2, since $\lfloor \frac{n_l}{s} \rfloor = \lfloor \frac{4}{2} \rfloor = 2$. We can see that the filter $\mathbf{W}$ has fixed weights equal to 1.

The convolution of the first window of $\mathbf{Z}^l$, namely $\mathbf{Z}^l_2(1,1)$, with $\mathbf{W}$ is given as (see Figure 26.18(a))

$$\max(\mathbf{Z}^l_2(1,1) \odot \mathbf{W}) = \max\left(\begin{pmatrix} 1 & 2 \\ 3 & 1 \end{pmatrix} \odot \begin{pmatrix} 1 & 1 \\ 1 & 1 \end{pmatrix}\right) = \max\left(\begin{pmatrix} 1 & 2 \\ 3 & 1 \end{pmatrix}\right) = 3$$

The other convolution steps are shown in Figures 26.18(b) to 26.18(d).

26.3.5 Deep CNNs

In a typical CNN architecture, one alternates between a convolution layer (with summation as the aggregation function, and learnable filter weights and bias term) and a pooling layer (say, with max-pooling and fixed filter of ones). The intuition is that, whereas the convolution layer learns the filters to extract informative features, the pooling layer applies an aggregation function like max (or avg) to extract the most important neuron value (or the mean of the neuron values) within each sliding window, in each of the channels.

Starting from the input layer, a deep CNN is comprised of multiple, typically alternating, convolution and pooling layers, followed by one or more fully connected layers, and then the final output layer. For each convolution and pooling layer we need to choose the window size k as well as the stride value s, and whether to use padding p or not. We also have to choose the non-linear activation functions for the convolution layers, and also the number of layers to consider.

26.3.6 Training CNNs

To see how to train CNNs we will consider a network with a single convolution layer and a max-pooling layer, followed by a fully connected layer as shown in Figure 26.19. For simplicity, we assume that there is only one channel for the input $\mathbf{X}$, and further, we use only one filter. Thus, $\mathbf{X}$ denotes the input matrix of size $n_0 \times n_0$. The filter $\mathbf{W}_0$, with bias b_0, for the convolution layer $l = 1$, has size $k_1 \times k_1$, which yields the matrix of neurons $\mathbf{Z}^1$ of size $n_1 \times n_1$, where $n_1 = n_0 - k + 1$ using stride $s_1 = 1$. Since we use only one filter, this results in a single channel at layer $l = 1$, i.e., $m_1 = 1$. The next layer $l = 2$ is a max-pooling layer $\mathbf{Z}^2$ of size $n_2 \times n_2$ obtained by applying a $k_2 \times k_2$ filter with stride $s_2 = k_2$. Implicitly, the max-pooling layer uses a filter of weights fixed at 1, with 0 as the bias, that is $\mathbf{W}_1 = \mathbf{1}_{k_2 \times k_2}$ and $b_1 = 0$. We assume that n_1 is a multiple of k_2 so that $n_2 = \frac{n_1}{k_2}$.

The output of the max-pooling layer $\mathbf{Z}^2$ is recast as a vector $\mathbf{z}^2$ of length $(n_2)^2$, since it is fully connected to the layer $l = 3$. That is, all of the $(n_2)^2$ neurons in $\mathbf{z}^2$ are connected to each of the n_3 neurons in $\mathbf{z}^3$ with the weights specified by the matrix $\mathbf{W}_2$, which has size $(n_2)^2 \times n_3$, and the bias vector $\mathbf{b}_2 \in \mathbb{R}^{n_3}$. Finally, all neurons in $\mathbf{z}^3$ are

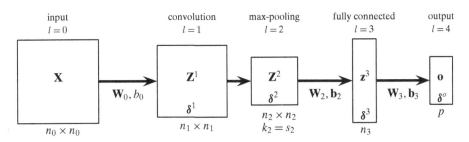

Figure 26.19. Training: Convolutional neural network.

connected to the p output layer neurons $\mathbf{o}$, with the weight matrix $\mathbf{W}_3 \in \mathbb{R}^{n_3 \times p}$ and bias vector $\mathbf{b}_3 \in \mathbb{R}^p$.

Feed-forward Phase

Let $\mathbf{D} = \{\mathbf{X}_i, \mathbf{y}_i\}_{i=1}^n$ denote the training data, comprising n tensors $\mathbf{X}_i \in \mathbb{R}^{n_0 \times n_0 \times m_0}$ (with $m_0 = 1$ for ease of explanation) and the corresponding response vector $\mathbf{y}_i \in \mathbb{R}^p$. Given a training pair $(\mathbf{X}, \mathbf{y}) \in \mathbf{D}$, in the feed-forward phase, the predicted output $\mathbf{o}$ is given via the following equations:

$$\mathbf{Z}^1 = f^1\big((\mathbf{X} * \mathbf{W}_0) + b_0\big)$$
$$\mathbf{Z}^2 = \mathbf{Z}^1 *_{s_2,\max} \mathbf{1}_{k_2 \times k_2}$$
$$\mathbf{z}^3 = f^3\big(\mathbf{W}_2^T \mathbf{z}^2 + \mathbf{b}_2\big)$$
$$\mathbf{o} = f^o\big(\mathbf{W}_o^T \mathbf{z}^3 + \mathbf{b}_o\big)$$

where $*_{s_2,\max}$ denotes max-pooling with stride s_2.

Backpropagation Phase

Given the true response $\mathbf{y}$ and predicted output $\mathbf{o}$, we can use any loss function $\mathcal{E}_\mathbf{X}$ to evaluate the discrepancy between them. The weights and biases are updated by computing the net gradient vector at the output layer, and then backpropagating the net gradients from layer $l = 4$ to $l = 1$. Let $\boldsymbol{\delta}^1, \boldsymbol{\delta}^2$, and $\boldsymbol{\delta}^3$ denote the net gradient vectors at layers $l = 1, 2, 3$, respectively, and let $\boldsymbol{\delta}^o$ denote the net gradient vector at the output layer. The output net gradient vector is obtained in the regular manner by computing the partial derivatives of the loss function ($\partial \mathcal{E}_\mathbf{X}$) and the activation function ($\partial \mathbf{f}^o$):

$$\boldsymbol{\delta}^o = \partial \mathbf{f}^o \odot \partial \mathcal{E}_\mathbf{X}$$

assuming that the output neurons are independent.

Since layer $l = 3$ is fully connected to the output layer, and likewise the max-pooling layer $l = 2$ is fully connected to $\mathbf{Z}^3$, the net gradients at these layers are computed as in a regular MLP

$$\boldsymbol{\delta}^3 = \partial \mathbf{f}^3 \odot \big(\mathbf{W}_o \cdot \boldsymbol{\delta}^o\big)$$
$$\boldsymbol{\delta}^2 = \partial \mathbf{f}^2 \odot \big(\mathbf{W}_2 \cdot \boldsymbol{\delta}^3\big) = \mathbf{W}_2 \cdot \boldsymbol{\delta}^3$$

Let last step follows from the fact that $\partial \mathbf{f}^2 = \mathbf{1}$, since max-pooling implicitly uses an identity activation function. Note that we also implicitly reshape the net gradient vector δ^2, so that its size is $((n_2)^2 \times n_3) \times (n_3 \times 1) = (n_2)^2 \times 1 = n_2 \times n_2$, as desired.

Consider the net gradient δ_{ij}^1 at neuron z_{ij}^1 in layer $l = 1$ where $i, j = 1, 2, \cdots, n_1$. Since we assume that the stride s_2 equals the filter size k_2 for the max-pooling layer, each sliding window in the convolution layer contributes only to one neuron at the max-pooling layer. Given stride $s_2 = k_2$, the $k_2 \times k_2$ sliding window that contains z_{ij}^1 is given as $\mathbf{Z}_{k_2}^1(a, b)$, where

$$a = \left\lceil \frac{i}{s_2} \right\rceil \qquad\qquad b = \left\lceil \frac{j}{s_2} \right\rceil$$

Due to the max aggregation function, the maximum valued element in $\mathbf{Z}_{k_2}^1(a, b)$ specifies the value of neuron z_{ab}^2 in the max-pooling layer $l = 2$. That is,

$$z_{ab}^2 = \max_{i,j=1,2,\ldots,k_2} \left\{ z_{(a-1)\cdot k_2+i,(b-1)\cdot k_2+j}^1 \right\}$$

$$i^*, j^* = \arg\max_{i,j=1,2,\ldots,k_2} \left\{ z_{(a-1)\cdot k_2+i,(b-1)\cdot k_2+j}^1 \right\}$$

where i^*, j^* is the index of the maximum valued neuron in the window $\mathbf{Z}_{k_2}^1(a, b)$.

The net gradient δ_{ij}^1 at neuron z_{ij}^1 is therefore given as

$$\delta_{ij}^1 = \frac{\partial \mathcal{E}_{\mathbf{X}}}{\partial net_{ij}^1} = \frac{\partial \mathcal{E}_{\mathbf{X}}}{\partial net_{ab}^2} \cdot \frac{\partial net_{ab}^2}{\partial z_{ij}^1} \cdot \frac{\partial z_{ij}^1}{\partial net_{ij}^1}$$

$$= \delta_{ab}^2 \cdot \frac{\partial net_{ab}^2}{\partial z_{ij}^1} \cdot \partial f_{ij}^1$$

where net_{ij}^l denotes the net input at neuron z_{ij}^l in layer l. However, since $net_{ab}^2 = z_{i^*,j^*}^1$, the partial derivative $\frac{\partial net_{ab}^2}{\partial z_{ij}^1}$ is either 1 or 0, depending on whether z_{ij}^1 is the maximum element in the window $\mathbf{Z}_{k_2}^1(a, b)$ or not. Putting it all together, we have

$$\delta_{ij}^1 = \begin{cases} \delta_{ab}^2 \cdot \partial f_{ij}^1 & \text{if } i = i^* \text{ and } j = j^* \\ 0 & \text{otherwise} \end{cases}$$

In other words, the net gradient at neuron z_{ij}^1 in the convolution layer is zero if this neuron does not have the maximum value in its window. Otherwise, if it is the maximum, the net gradient backpropagates from the max-pooling layer to this neuron and is then multiplied by the partial derivative of the activation function. The $n_1 \times n_1$ matrix of net gradients δ^1 comprises the net graidents δ_{ij}^1 for all $i, j = 1, 2, \cdots, n_1$.

From the net gradients, we can compute the gradients of the weight matrices and bias parameters. For the fully connected layers, that is, between $l = 2$ and $l = 3$, and $l = 3$ and $l = 4$, we have

$$\nabla_{\mathbf{W}_3} = \mathbf{Z}^3 \cdot (\delta^o)^T \qquad \nabla_{\mathbf{b}_3} = \delta^o \qquad \nabla_{\mathbf{W}_2} = \mathbf{Z}^2 \cdot (\delta^3)^T \qquad \nabla_{\mathbf{b}_2} = \delta^3$$

where we treat $\mathbf{Z}^2$ as a $(n_2)^2 \times 1$ vector.

Note that the weight matrix $\mathbf{W}_1$ is fixed at $\mathbf{1}_{k_2 \times k_2}$ and the bias term b_1 is also fixed at 0, so there are no parameters to learn between the convolution and max-pooling layers. Finally, we compute the weight and bias gradients between the input and convolution layer as follows:

$$\nabla_{\mathbf{W}_0} = \sum_{i=1}^{n_1} \sum_{j=1}^{n_1} \mathbf{X}_{k_1}(i, j) \cdot \delta_{ij}^1 \qquad \nabla_{b_0} = \sum_{i=1}^{n_1} \sum_{j=1}^{n_1} \delta_{ij}^1$$

where we used the fact that the stride is $s_1 = 1$, and that $\mathbf{W}_0$ is a shared filter for all $k_1 \times k_1$ windows of $\mathbf{X}$, with the shared bias value b_0 for all windows. There are $n_1 \times n_1$ such windows, where $n_1 = n_0 - k_1 + 1$, therefore, to compute the weight and bias gradients, we sum over all the windows. Note that if there were multiple filters (that is, if $m_1 > 1$), then the bias and weight gradients for the jth filter would be learned from the corresponding channel j in layer $l = 1$.

Example 26.12 (CNN). Figure 26.20 shows a CNN for handwritten digit recognition. This CNN is trained and tested on the MNIST dataset, that contains 60,000 training images and 10,000 test images. Some examples of handwritten digits from MNIST are shown in Figure 26.21. Each input image is a 28×28 matrix of pixel values between 0 to 255, which are divided by 255, so that each pixel lies in the interval $[0, 1]$. The corresponding (true) output $\mathbf{y}_i$ is a one-hot encoded binary vector that denotes a digit from 0 to 9; the digit 0 is encoded as $\mathbf{e}_1 = (1, 0, 0, 0, 0, 0, 0, 0, 0, 0)^T$, the digit 1 as $\mathbf{e}_2 = (0, 1, 0, 0, 0, 0, 0, 0, 0, 0)^T$, and so on.

In our CNN model, all the convolution layers use stride equal to one, and do not use any padding, whereas all of the max-pooling layers use stride equal to the window size. Since each input is a 28×28 pixels image of a digit with 1 channel (grayscale), we have $n_0 = 28$ and $m_0 = 1$, and therefore, the input $\mathbf{X} = \mathbf{Z}^0$ is a $n_0 \times n_0 \times m_0 = 28 \times 28 \times 1$ tensor. The first convolution layer uses $m_1 = 6$ filters, with $k_1 = 5$ and stride $s_1 = 1$, without padding. Thus, each filter is a $5 \times 5 \times 1$ tensor of weights, and across the six filters the resulting layer $l = 1$ tensor $\mathbf{Z}^1$ has size $24 \times 24 \times 6$, with $n_1 = n_0 - k_1 + 1 = 28 - 5 + 1 = 24$ and $m_1 = 6$. The second hidden layer is a max-pooling layer that uses $k_2 = 2$ with a stride of $s_2 = 2$. Since max-pooling by default uses a fixed filter $\mathbf{W} = \mathbf{1}_{k_2 \times k_2 \times 1}$, the resulting tensor $\mathbf{Z}^2$ has size $12 \times 12 \times 6$, with $n_2 = \lfloor \frac{n_1}{k_2} \rfloor = \lfloor \frac{24}{2} \rfloor = 12$, and $m_2 = 6$. The third layer is a convolution layer with $m_3 = 16$ channels, with a window size of $k_3 = 5$ (and stride $s_3 = 1$), resulting in the tensor $\mathbf{Z}^3$ of size $8 \times 8 \times 16$, where $n_3 = n_2 - k_3 + 1 = 12 - 5 + 1 = 8$. This is followed by another max-pooling

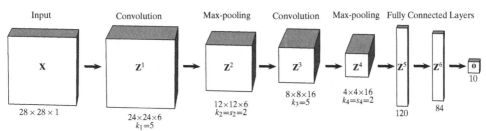

Figure 26.20. Convolutional neural network.

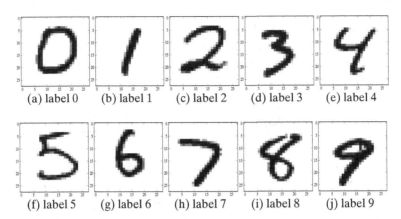

(a) label 0   (b) label 1   (c) label 2   (d) label 3   (e) label 4

(f) label 5   (g) label 6   (h) label 7   (i) label 8   (j) label 9

Figure 26.21. MNIST dataset: Sample handwritten digits.

layer that uses $k_4 = 2$ and $s_4 = 2$, which yields the tensor $\mathbf{Z}^4$ that is $4 \times 4 \times 16$, where $n_4 = \left\lfloor \frac{n_3}{k_4} \right\rfloor = \left\lfloor \frac{8}{2} \right\rfloor = 4$, and $m_4 = 16$.

The next three layers are fully connected as in a regular MLP. All of the $4 \times 4 \times 16 = 256$ neurons in layer $l = 4$ are connected to layer $l = 5$, which has 120 neurons. Thus, $\mathbf{Z}^5$ is simply a vector of length 120, or it can be considered a degenerate tensor of size $120 \times 1 \times 1$. Layer $l = 5$ is also fully connected to layer $l = 6$ with 84 neurons, which is the last hidden layer. Since there are 10 digits, the output layer $\mathbf{o}$ comprises 10 neurons, with softmax activation function. The convolution layers $\mathbf{Z}^1$ and $\mathbf{Z}^3$, and the fully connected layers $\mathbf{Z}^5$ and $\mathbf{Z}^6$, all use ReLU activation.

We train the CNN model on $n = 60000$ training images from the MNIST dataset; we train for 15 epochs using step size $\eta = 0.2$ and using cross-entropy error (since there are 10 classes). Training was done using minibatches, using batch size of 1000. After training the CNN model, we evaluate it on the test dataset of 10,000 images. The CNN model makes 147 errors on the test set, resulting in an error rate of 1.47%. Figure 26.22 shows examples of images that are misclassified by the CNN. We show the true label y for each image and the predicted label o (converted back from the one-hot encoding to the digit label). We show three examples for each of the labels. For example, the first three images on the first row are for the case when the true label is $y = 0$, and the next three examples are for true label $y = 1$, and so on. We can see that several of the misclassified images are noisy, incomplete or erroneous, and would be hard to classify correctly even by a human.

For comparison, we also train a deep MLP with two (fully connected) hidden layers with the same sizes as the two fully connected layers before the output layer in the CNN shown in Figure 26.20. Therefore, the MLP comprises the layers $\mathbf{X}, \mathbf{Z}^5, \mathbf{Z}^6$, and $\mathbf{o}$, with the input 28×28 images viewed as a vector of size $d = 784$. The first hidden layer has size $n_1 = 120$, the second hidden layer has size $n_2 = 84$, and the output layer has size $p = 10$. We use ReLU activation function for all layers, except the output, which uses softmax. We train the MLP model for 15 epochs on the training dataset with $n = 60000$ images, using step size $\eta = 0.5$. On the test dataset, the MLP made 264 errors, for an error rate of 2.64%. Figure 26.23 shows the number of errors on

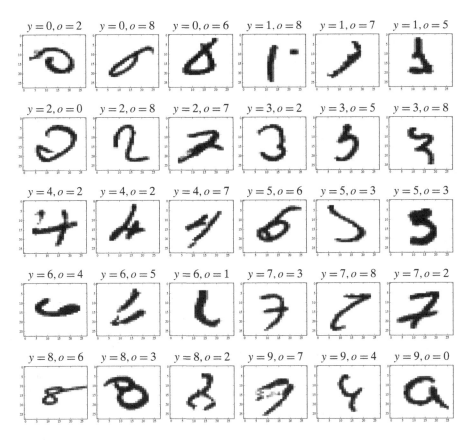

Figure 26.22. MNIST: Incorrect predictions by the CNN model; y is the true label, o is the predicted label.

the test set after each epoch of training for both the CNN and MLP model; the CNN model achieves significantly better accuracy than the MLP.

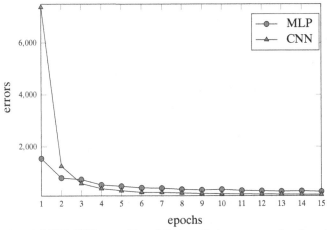

Figure 26.23. MNIST: CNN versus Deep MLP; prediction error as a function of epochs.

26.4 REGULARIZATION

Consider the squared error loss function, given as

$$L(\mathbf{y}, \hat{\mathbf{y}}) = (\mathbf{y} - \hat{\mathbf{y}})^2$$

where $\mathbf{y}$ is the true response and $\hat{\mathbf{y}} = \mathbf{o}$ the predicted response on a given input $\mathbf{x}$. The goal of learning is the minimize the expected loss $E[L(\mathbf{y}, \hat{\mathbf{y}})] = E[(\mathbf{y} - \hat{\mathbf{y}})^2]$.

As described in Section 22.3, the expected loss can be decomposed into three terms: noise, bias, and variance, given as

$$E\left[(\mathbf{y} - \hat{\mathbf{y}})^2\right] = \underbrace{E\left[(\mathbf{y} - E[\mathbf{y}])^2\right]}_{noise} + \underbrace{E\left[(\hat{\mathbf{y}} - E[\hat{\mathbf{y}}])^2\right]}_{average\ variance} + \underbrace{E\left[(E[\hat{\mathbf{y}}] - E[\mathbf{y}])^2\right]}_{average\ bias} \quad (26.17)$$

The noise term is the expected variance of $\mathbf{y}$, since $E[(\mathbf{y} - E[\mathbf{y}])^2] = \text{var}(\mathbf{y})$. It contributes a fixed cost to the loss independent of the model. Since it is the inherent uncertainty or variability of $\mathbf{y}$ it can be ignored when comparing different models. The average bias term indicates how much the model deviates from the true (but unknown) function relating the response to the predictor variables. For example, if the response is a non-linear function of the predictor variables, and we fit a simple linear model, then this model will have a high bias. We can try to fit a more complex non-linear model to reduce the bias, but then we run into the issue of overfitting and high variance, captured by the average variance term, which quantifies the variance of the predicted response $\hat{\mathbf{y}}$, since $E[(\hat{\mathbf{y}} - E[\hat{\mathbf{y}}])^2] = \text{var}(\hat{\mathbf{y}})$. That is, our model may try to fit noise and other artifacts in the data, and will therefore be highly susceptible to small changes in the data, resulting in high variance. In general, there is always a trade-off between reducing bias and reducing variance.

Regularization is an approach whereby we constrain the model parameters to reduce overfitting, by reducing the variance at the cost of increasing the bias slightly. For example, in ridge regression [Eq. (23.29)], we add a constraint on the L_2-norm of the weight parameters as follows

$$\min_{\mathbf{w}} \; J(\mathbf{w}) = \|Y - \widehat{Y}\|^2 + \alpha \cdot \|\mathbf{w}\|^2 = \|Y - \mathbf{D}\mathbf{w}\|^2 + \alpha \cdot \|\mathbf{w}\|^2 \quad (26.18)$$

where Y is the true response vector and $\widehat{Y}$ is the predicted response vector over all training instances. The goal here is to drive the weights to be small, depending on the *hyperparameter* $\alpha \geq 0$ called the *regularization constant*. If $\alpha = 0$, then there is no regularization, and we get a low bias, but possibly high variance model. If $\alpha \to \infty$ then the effect is to drive all weights to be nearly zero, which results in a low variance, but high bias model. An intermediate value of α tries to achieve the right balance between these two conflicting objectives. As another example, in L_1 regression or Lasso [Eq. (23.43)], we minimize the L_1 norm of the weights

$$\min_{\mathbf{w}} \; J(\mathbf{w}) = \|Y - \mathbf{D}\mathbf{w}\|^2 + \alpha \cdot \|\mathbf{w}\|_1$$

where $\|\mathbf{w}\|_1 = \sum_{i=1}^{d} |w_i|$. Compared to L_2 norm, which merely makes the weights small, the use of the L_1 norm *sparsifies* the model by forcing many of the weights to zero, acting as a feature subset selection method.

In general, for any learning model M, if $L(\mathbf{y}, \hat{\mathbf{y}})$ is some loss function for a given input $\mathbf{x}$, and Θ denotes all the model parameters, where $\hat{\mathbf{y}} = M(\mathbf{x}|\Theta)$. The learning objective is to find the parameters that minimize the loss over all instances:

$$\min_{\Theta} J(\Theta) = \sum_{i=1}^{n} L(\mathbf{y}_i, \hat{\mathbf{y}}_i) = \sum_{i=1}^{n} L(\mathbf{y}_i, M(\mathbf{x}_i|\Theta))$$

With regularization, we add a penalty on the parameters Θ, to obtain the regularized objective:

$$\min_{\Theta} J(\Theta) = \sum_{i=1}^{n} L(\mathbf{y}_i, \hat{\mathbf{y}}_i) + \alpha R(\Theta) \qquad (26.19)$$

where $\alpha \geq 0$ is the regularization constant.

Let $\theta \in \Theta$ be a parameter of the regression model. Typical regularization functions include the L_2 norm, the L_1 norm, or even a combination of these, called the elastic-net:

$$R_{L_2}(\theta) = \|\theta\|_2^2 \qquad R_{L_1}(\theta) = \|\theta\|_1 \qquad R_{\text{elastic}}(\theta) = \lambda \cdot \|\theta\|_2^2 + (1 - \lambda) \cdot \|\theta\|_1$$

with $\lambda \in [0, 1]$.

26.4.1 L_2 Regularization for Deep Learning

We now consider approaches for regularizing the deep learning models. We first consider the case of a multilayer perceptron with one hidden layer, and then generalize it to multiple hidden layers. Note that while our discussion of regularization is in the context of MLPs, since RNNs are trained via unfolding, and CNNs are essentially sparse MLPs, the methods described here can easily be generalized for any deep neural network.

MLP with One Hidden Layer
Consider regularization in the context of a feed-forward MLP with a single hidden layer as shown in Figure 26.24. Let the input $\mathbf{x} \in \mathbb{R}^d$, the hidden layer $\mathbf{z} \in \mathbb{R}^m$ and let $\hat{\mathbf{y}} = \mathbf{o} \in \mathbb{R}^p$. The set of all the parameters of the model are

$$\Theta = \{\mathbf{W}_h, \mathbf{b}_h, \mathbf{W}_o, \mathbf{b}_o\}$$

Whereas it makes sense to penalize large weights, we usually do not penalize the bias terms since they are just thresholds that shift the activation function and there is no

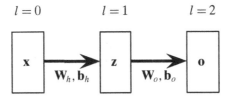

Figure 26.24. Multilayer perceptron with one hidden layer.

need to force them to be small values. The L_2 regularized objective is therefore given
as

$$\min_{\Theta} J(\Theta) = \mathcal{E}_{\mathbf{x}} + \frac{\alpha}{2} \cdot R_{L_2}(\mathbf{W}_o, \mathbf{W}_h) = \mathcal{E}_{\mathbf{x}} + \frac{\alpha}{2} \cdot \left(\|\mathbf{W}_h\|_F^2 + \|\mathbf{W}_o\|_F^2 \right)$$

Here we added the factor $1/2$ to the regularization term for convenience. For the L_2
norm of the weight matrices, we use the *Frobenius norm*, which has the usual sense of
L_2-norm, since for an $n \times m$ matrix $\mathbf{A}$, it is defined as

$$\|\mathbf{A}\|_F^2 = \sum_{i=1}^{n} \sum_{j=1}^{m} a_{ij}^2$$

where a_{ij} is the (i, j)th element of $\mathbf{A}$. The regularized objective tries to minimize the
individual weights for pairs of neurons between the input and hidden, and hidden
and output layers. This has the effect of adding some bias to the model, but possibly
reducing variance, since small weights are more robust to changes in the input data in
terms of the predicted output values.

The regularized objective has two separate terms, one for the loss and the other
for the L_2 norm of the weight matrices. Recall that we have to compute the weight
gradients $\nabla_{w_{ij}}$ and the bias gradients ∇_{b_j} by computing

$$\nabla_{w_{ij}} = \frac{\partial J(\Theta)}{\partial w_{ij}} = \frac{\partial \mathcal{E}_{\mathbf{x}}}{\partial w_{ij}} + \frac{\alpha}{2} \cdot \frac{\partial R_{L_2}(\mathbf{W}_o, \mathbf{W}_h)}{\partial w_{ij}} = \delta_j \cdot z_i + \alpha \cdot w_{ij}$$

$$\nabla_{b_j} = \frac{\partial J(\Theta)}{\partial b_j} = \frac{\partial \mathcal{E}_{\mathbf{x}}}{\partial b_j} + \frac{\alpha}{2} \cdot \frac{\partial R_{L_2}(\mathbf{W}_o, \mathbf{W}_h)}{\partial b_j} = \frac{\partial \mathcal{E}_{\mathbf{x}}}{\partial b_j} = \delta_j$$

where we use Eq. (25.31) to note that $\frac{\partial \mathcal{E}_{\mathbf{x}}}{\partial w_{ij}} = \delta_j \cdot z_i$ and $\frac{\partial \mathcal{E}_{\mathbf{x}}}{\partial b_j} = \delta_j$, and where $\delta_j = \frac{\partial \mathcal{E}_{\mathbf{x}}}{\partial net_j}$ is
the net gradient. Further, since the squared L_2 norm of a weight matrix is simply the
sum of the squared weights, only the term w_{ij}^2 matters, and all other elements are just
constant with respect to the weight w_{ij} between neurons i and j (in $\mathbf{W}_h$ or $\mathbf{W}_o$). Across
all the neuron pairs between the hidden and output layer, we can write the update rule
compactly as follows:

$$\nabla_{\mathbf{W}_o} = \mathbf{z} \cdot \delta_o^T + \alpha \cdot \mathbf{W}_o \qquad\qquad \nabla_{\mathbf{b}_o} = \delta_o$$

where δ_o is the net gradient vector for the output neurons, and $\mathbf{z}$ is the vector of hidden
layer neuron values. The gradient update rule using the regularized weight gradient
matrix is given as

$$\mathbf{W}_o = \mathbf{W}_o - \eta \cdot \nabla_{\mathbf{W}_o} = \mathbf{W}_o - \eta \cdot \left(\mathbf{z} \cdot \delta_o^T + \alpha \cdot \mathbf{W}_o \right) = \mathbf{W}_o - \eta \cdot \alpha \cdot \mathbf{W}_o - \eta \cdot \left(\mathbf{z} \cdot \delta_o^T \right)$$

$$= (1 - \eta \cdot \alpha) \cdot \mathbf{W}_o - \eta \cdot \left(\mathbf{z} \cdot \delta_o^T \right)$$

L_2 regularization is also called *weight decay*, since the updated weight matrix uses
decayed weights from the previous step, using the decay factor $1 - \eta \cdot \alpha$.

In a similar manner we get the weight and bias gradients between the input and
hidden layers:

$$\nabla_{\mathbf{W}_h} = \mathbf{x} \cdot \delta_h^T + \alpha \cdot \mathbf{W}_h \qquad\qquad \nabla_{\mathbf{b}_h} = \delta_h$$

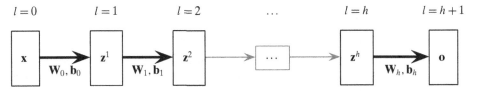

Figure 26.25. Deep multilayer perceptron.

The update rule for the weight matrix between the input and hidden layers is therefore given as

$$\mathbf{W}_h = \mathbf{W}_h - \eta \cdot \nabla_{\mathbf{W}_h} = (1 - \eta \cdot \alpha) \cdot \mathbf{W}_h - \eta \cdot \left(\mathbf{x} \cdot \boldsymbol{\delta}_h^T\right)$$

where $\boldsymbol{\delta}_h$ is the net gradient vector for the hidden neurons, and $\mathbf{x}$ is the input vector.

Deep MLPs

Consider the deep MLP shown in Figure 26.25. We denote the input neurons as layer $l = 0$, the first hidden layer as $l = 1$, the last hidden layer as $l = h$, and the final output layer as $l = h + 1$. The vector of neuron values for layer l (for $l = 0, \cdots, h + 1$) is denoted as

$$\mathbf{z}^l = \left(z_1^l, \cdots, z_{n_l}^l\right)^T$$

where n_l is the number of neurons in layer l. Thus, $\mathbf{x} = \mathbf{z}^0$ and $\mathbf{o} = \mathbf{z}^{h+1}$. The weight matrix between neurons in layer l and layer $l + 1$ is denoted $\mathbf{W}_l \in \mathbb{R}^{n_l \times n_{l+1}}$, and the vector of bias terms from the bias neuron z_0^l to neurons in layer $l + 1$ is denoted $\mathbf{b}_l \in \mathbb{R}^{n_{l+1}}$, for $l = 1, \cdots, h + 1$.

Given the error function $\mathcal{E}_\mathbf{x}$, the L_2 regularized objective function is

$$\min_\Theta J(\Theta) = \mathcal{E}_\mathbf{x} + \frac{\alpha}{2} \cdot R_{L_2}\left(\mathbf{W}_0, \mathbf{W}_1, \ldots, \mathbf{W}_h\right)$$

$$= \mathcal{E}_\mathbf{x} + \frac{\alpha}{2} \cdot \left(\sum_{l=0}^{h} \|\mathbf{W}_l\|_F^2\right)$$

where the set of all the parameters of the model is $\Theta = \{\mathbf{W}_0, \mathbf{b}_0, \mathbf{W}_1, \mathbf{b}_1, \cdots, \mathbf{W}_h, \mathbf{b}_h\}$. Based on the derivation for the one hidden layer MLP from above, the regularized gradient is given as:

$$\nabla_{\mathbf{W}_l} = \mathbf{z}^l \cdot (\boldsymbol{\delta}^{l+1})^T + \alpha \cdot \mathbf{W}_l \qquad (26.20)$$

and the update rule for weight matrices is

$$\mathbf{W}_l = \mathbf{W}_l - \eta \cdot \nabla_{\mathbf{W}_l} = (1 - \eta \cdot \alpha) \cdot \mathbf{W}_l - \eta \cdot \left(\mathbf{z}^l \cdot (\boldsymbol{\delta}^{l+1})^T\right) \qquad (26.21)$$

for $l = 0, 1, \cdots, h$, where where $\boldsymbol{\delta}^l$ is the net gradient vector for the hidden neurons in layer l. We can thus observe that incorporating L_2 regularization within deep MLPs is relatively straightforward. Likewise, it is easy to incorporate L_2 regularization in other models like RNNs, CNNs, and so on. For L_1 regularization, we can apply the subgradient approach outlined for L_1 regression or Lasso in Section 23.6.

26.4.2 Dropout Regularization

The idea behind dropout regularization is to randomly set a certain fraction of the neuron values in a layer to zero during training time. The aim is to make the network more robust and to avoid overfitting at the same time. By dropping random neurons for each training point, the network is forced to not rely on any specific set of edges. From the perspective of a given neuron, since it cannot rely on all its incoming edges to be present, it has the effect of not concentrating the weight on specific input edges, but rather the weight is spread out among the incoming edges. The net effect is similar to L_2 regularization since weight spreading leads to smaller weights on the edges. The resulting model with dropout is therefore more resilient to small perturbations in the input, which can reduce overfitting at a small price in increased bias. However, note that while L_2 regularization directly changes the objective function, dropout regularization is a form of *structural regularization* that does not change the objective function, but instead changes the network topology in terms of which connections are currently active or inactive.

MLP with One Hidden Layer

Consider the one hidden layer MLP in Figure 26.24. Let the input $\mathbf{x} \in \mathbb{R}^d$, the hidden layer $\mathbf{z} \in \mathbb{R}^m$ and let $\hat{\mathbf{y}} = \mathbf{o} \in \mathbb{R}^p$. During the training phase, for each input $\mathbf{x}$, we create a random mask vector to drop a fraction of the hidden neurons. Formally, let $r \in [0, 1]$ be the probability of keeping a neuron, so that the dropout probability is $1 - r$. We create a m-dimensional multivariate Bernoulli vector $\mathbf{u} \in \{0, 1\}^m$, called the *masking vector*, each of whose entries is 0 with dropout probability $1 - r$, and 1 with probability r. Let $\mathbf{u} = (u_1, u_2, \cdots, u_m)^T$, where

$$u_i = \begin{cases} 0 & \text{with probability } 1 - r \\ 1 & \text{with probability } r \end{cases}$$

The feed-forward step is then given as

$$\mathbf{z} = f^h \left(\mathbf{b}_h + \mathbf{W}_h^T \mathbf{x} \right)$$

$$\tilde{\mathbf{z}} = \mathbf{u} \odot \mathbf{z}$$

$$\mathbf{o} = f^o \left(\mathbf{b}_o + \mathbf{W}_o^T \tilde{\mathbf{z}} \right)$$

where $\odot$ is the element-wise multiplication. The net effect is that the masking vector zeros out the ith hidden neuron in $\tilde{\mathbf{z}}$ if $u_i = 0$. Zeroing out also has the effect that during the backpropagation phase the error gradients do not flow back from the zeroed out neurons in the hidden layer. The effect is that any weights on edges adjacent to zeroed out hidden neurons are not updated.

Inverted Dropout There is one complication in the basic dropout approach above, namely, the expected output of hidden layer neurons is different during training and testing, since dropout is not applied during the testing phase (after all, we do not want the predictions to be randomly varying on a given test input). With r as the probability of retaining a hidden neuron, its expected output value is

$$E[z_i] = r \cdot z_i + (1 - r) \cdot 0 = r \cdot z_i$$

On the other hand, since there is no dropout at test time, the outputs of the hidden neurons will be higher at testing time. So one idea is to scale the hidden neuron values by r at testing time. On the other hand, there is a simpler approach called *inverted dropout* that does not need a change at testing time. The idea is to rescale the hidden neurons after the dropout step during the training phase, as follows:

$$\mathbf{z} = f\left(\mathbf{b}_h + \mathbf{W}_h^T \mathbf{x}\right)$$

$$\tilde{\mathbf{z}} = \frac{1}{r} \cdot \left(\mathbf{u} \odot \mathbf{z}\right)$$

$$\mathbf{o} = f\left(\mathbf{b}_o + \mathbf{W}_o^T \tilde{\mathbf{z}}\right)$$

With the scaling factor $1/r$, the expected value of each neuron remains the same as without dropout, since

$$E[z_i] = \frac{1}{r} \cdot \left(r \cdot z_i + (1-r) \cdot 0\right) = z_i$$

Dropout in Deep MLPs

Dropout regularization for deep MLPs is done in a similar manner. Let $r_l \in [0,1]$, for $l = 1, 2, \cdots, h$ denote the probability of retaining a hidden neuron for layer l, so that $1 - r_l$ is the dropout probability. One can also use a single rate r for all the layers by setting $r_l = r$. Define the masking vector for hidden layer l, $\mathbf{u}^l \in \{0,1\}^{n_l}$, as follows:

$$u_i^l = \begin{cases} 0 & \text{with probability } 1 - r_l \\ 1 & \text{with probability } r_l \end{cases}$$

The feed-forward step between layer l and $l+1$ is then given as

$$\boxed{\begin{aligned} \mathbf{z}^l &= f\left(\mathbf{b}_l + \mathbf{W}_l^T \tilde{\mathbf{z}}^{l-1}\right) \\ \tilde{\mathbf{z}}^l &= \frac{1}{r_l} \cdot \left(\mathbf{u}^l \odot \mathbf{z}^l\right) \end{aligned}} \tag{26.22}$$

using inverted dropout. Usually, no masking is done for the input and output layers, so we can set $r^0 = 1$ and $r^{h+1} = 1$. Also note that there is no dropout at testing time. The dropout rates are hyperparameters of the model that have to be tuned on a separate validation dataset.

26.5 FURTHER READING

The backpropagation through time algorithm was introduced by Werbos (1990). Bidirectional RNNs were proposed by Schuster and Paliwal (1997), and LSTMs were proposed by Hochreiter and Schmidhuber (1997), with the forget gate introduced by Gers, Schmidhuber, and Cummins (2000). Convolutional neural networks trained via backpropagation were proposed by LeCun, Bottou, Bengio, and Haffner (1998), with application to handwritten digit recognition. Dropout regularization was introduced by Srivastava, Hinton, Krizhevsky, Sutskever, and Salakhutdinov (2014).

Gers, F. A., Schmidhuber, J., and Cummins, F. (2000). Learning to forget: Continual prediction with LSTM. *Neural Computation*, 12 (10), 2451–2471.

Hochreiter, S. and Schmidhuber, J. (1997). Long short-term memory. *Neural Computation*, 9 (8), 1735–1780.

LeCun, Y., Bottou, L., Bengio, Y., and Haffner, P. (1998). Gradient-based learning applied to document recognition. *Proceedings of the IEEE*, 86 (11), 2278–2324.

Schuster, M. and Paliwal, K. K. (1997). Bidirectional recurrent neural networks. *IEEE Transactions on Signal Processing*, 45 (11), 2673–2681.

Srivastava, N., Hinton, G., Krizhevsky, A., Sutskever, I., and Salakhutdinov, R. (2014). Dropout: A simple way to prevent neural networks from overfitting. *The Journal of Machine Learning Research*, 15 (1), 1929–1958.

Werbos, P. J. (1990). Backpropagation through time: what it does and how to do it. *Proceedings of the IEEE*, 78 (10), 1550–1560.

26.6 EXERCISES

Q1. Consider the RNN architecture in Figure 26.26. Note that an edge labeled -1 indicates dependence on the previous time step, whereas -2 indicates dependence on values from two time steps back. Use f^o and f^h as the activation functions for output and hidden layers. Let τ be the longest sequence length. Answer the following questions:

(a) Unfold the RNN for three steps and show all the connections.

(b) List all the parameters required in this model, including the weight matrices and bias vectors. Next write the forward propagation equations to compute $\mathbf{o}_t$.

(c) Write the equation for the net gradient vector δ_t^o at the output neurons at time t.

(d) Write the equation for the net gradient vector δ_t^h at the hidden neurons at time t.

Q2. Derive the net gradient equations for backpropagation in an RNN with a forget gate using vector derivatives. That is, derive equations for the net gradients at the output δ_t^o, update δ_t^u, forget δ_t^ϕ, and hidden δ_t^h layers by computing the derivative of the error function $\mathcal{E}_{\mathbf{x}_t}$ with respect to $\mathbf{net}_t^o$, $\mathbf{net}_t^u$, $\mathbf{net}_t^\phi$ and $\mathbf{net}_t^h$, the net inputs at the output, update, forget and hidden layers, respectively, at time t.

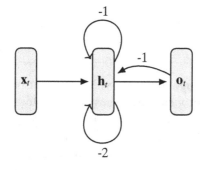

Figure 26.26. RNN architecture for Q1.

Q3. Derive the net gradient equations δ_t^a for backpropagation in an LSTM using vector derivatives of the error function $\mathcal{E}_{\mathbf{x}}$ with respect to $\mathbf{net}_t^a$, where $a \in \{o, h, c, u, \kappa, \phi, \omega\}$. That is, for the output, hidden state, internal memory, and candidate update layers, as well as for the input, forget and output gate layers.

Q4. Show that with stride s, in the convolution of $\mathbf{X} \in \mathbb{R}^{n \times n \times m}$ and $\mathbf{W} \in \mathbb{R}^{k \times k \times m}$, there are $(t+1) \times (t+1)$ possible windows, where $t = \lfloor \frac{n-k}{s} \rfloor$.

Q5. Consider a CNN that takes as input substrings of length 8 over the alphabet $\Sigma = \{A, B, C, D\}$, and predicts whether the class is positive (P) or negative (N). Assume we use two 1D filters with window size $k = 4$ and stride $s = 2$, with weights $\mathbf{w}_1 = (1, 0, 1, 1)^T$ and $\mathbf{w}_2 = (1, 1, 0, 1)^T$, respectively. Assume bias is zero. The 1D convolution is followed by a max-pooling operation with window size $k = 2$ and stride $s = 1$. All of the convolutions use linear activation function, and there is no padding used. Finally, all of the neurons after the max-pooling feed into a single output neuron that uses a sigmoid activation function with bias -15 and all weights set to 1. Given input sequence $ABACABCD$, show the neuron values after the convolution and max-pooling layer, and the final output. Use one-hot encoding for the input alphabet in lexicographic order, and let $P = 1$ and $N = 0$. What is the final output on the given input sequence.

channel 1				
1	1	3	1	1
2	4	4	1	2
2	2	3	1	1
1	2	2	3	1
4	1	1	2	2

channel 2				
1	4	3	3	2
2	2	2	2	2
1	1	4	1	1
1	2	3	1	1
1	4	1	1	2

channel 3				
1	2	4	3	2
2	2	4	2	1
1	1	3	2	4
1	4	3	2	3
1	1	1	4	4

(a) Input tensor: $\mathbf{X}$

channel 1		
1	0	0
0	1	0
0	0	1

channel 2		
0	0	1
0	1	0
1	0	0

channel 3		
1	1	1
1	1	1
1	1	1

(b) 3D filter ($\mathbf{W}$)

Figure 26.27. 3D tensor for Q6.

Q6. Given the 3D tensor in Figure 26.27(a). Using padding $p = 1$ and stride $s = 2$, answer the following questions:
  (a) Compute the convolution of $\mathbf{X}$ with the $3 \times 3 \times 3$ mask $\mathbf{W}$ in Figure 26.27(b).
  (b) Compute the max-pooling output using a $3 \times 3 \times 1$ mask $\mathbf{W}$ of all ones.

CHAPTER 27

Regression Evaluation

Given a set of predictor attributes or independent variables $X_1, X_2, \cdots, X_d$, and given the response attribute Y, the goal of regression is to learn a f, such that

$$Y = f(X_1, X_2, \cdots, X_d) + \varepsilon = f(\mathbf{X}) + \varepsilon$$

where $\mathbf{X} = (X_1, X_2, \cdots, X_d)^T$ is the d-dimensional multivariate random variable comprised of the predictor variables. Here, the random variable ε denotes the inherent *error* in the response that is not explained by the linear model.

When estimating the regression function f, we make assumptions about the form of f, for example, whether f is a linear or some non-linear function of the parameters of the model. For example, in linear regression, we assume that

$$f(\mathbf{X}) = \beta + \omega_1 \cdot X_1 + \ldots + \omega_d \cdot X_d$$

where β is the bias term, and ω_i is the regression coefficient for attribute X_i. The model is *linear*, since $f(\mathbf{X})$ is a linear function of the parameters $\beta, \omega_1, \cdots, \omega_d$.

Once we have estimated the bias and coefficients, we need to formulate a probabilistic model of regression to evaluate the learned model in terms of goodness of fit, confidence intervals for the parameters, and to test for the regression effects, namely whether $\mathbf{X}$ really helps in predicting Y. In particular, we assume that even if the value of $\mathbf{X}$ has been fixed, there can still be uncertainty in the response Y. Further, we will assume that the error ε is independent of $\mathbf{X}$ and follows a normal (or Gaussian) distribution with mean $\mu = 0$ and variance σ^2, that is, we assume that the errors are independent and identically distributed with zero mean and fixed variance.

The probabilistic regression model comprises two components — the *deterministic component* comprising the observed predictor attributes, and the *random error component* comprising the error term, which is assumed to be independent of the predictor attributes. With the assumptions on the form of the regression function f, and the error variable ε, we can answer several interesting questions such as how good of a fit is the estimated model to the input data? How close are the estimated bias and coefficients to the true but unknown parameters, and so on. We consider such questions in this chapter.

27.1 UNIVARIATE REGRESSION

In univariate regression we have one dependent attribute Y and one independent attribute X, and we assume that the true relationship can be modeled as a linear function

$$Y = f(X) + \varepsilon = \beta + \omega \cdot X + \varepsilon$$

where ω is the slope of the best fitting line and β is its intercept, and ε is the random error variable that follows a normal distribution with mean $\mu = 0$ and variance σ^2.

Mean and Variance of Response Variable

Consider a fixed value x for the independent variable X. The expected value of the response variable Y given x is

$$E[Y|X=x] = E[\beta + \omega \cdot x + \varepsilon] = \beta + \omega \cdot x + E[\varepsilon] = \beta + \omega \cdot x$$

The last step follows from our assumption that $E[\varepsilon] = \mu = 0$. Also, since x is assumed to be fixed, and β and ω are constants, the expected value $E[\beta + \omega \cdot x] = \beta + \omega \cdot x$. Next, consider the variance of Y given $X = x$, we have

$$\text{var}(Y|X=x) = \text{var}(\beta + \omega \cdot x + \varepsilon) = \text{var}(\beta + \omega \cdot x) + \text{var}(\varepsilon) = 0 + \sigma^2 = \sigma^2$$

Here $\text{var}(\beta + \omega \cdot x) = 0$, since β, ω and x are all constants. Thus, given $X = x$, the response variable Y follows a normal distribution with mean $E[Y|X=x] = \beta + \omega \cdot x$, and variance $\text{var}(Y|X=x) = \sigma^2$.

Estimated Parameters

The true parameters β, ω and σ^2 are all unknown, and have to be estimated from the training data $\mathbf{D}$ comprising n points x_i and corresponding response values y_i, for $i = 1, 2, \cdots, n$. Let b and w denote the estimated bias and weight terms; we can then make predictions for any given value x_i as follows:

$$\hat{y}_i = b + w \cdot x_i$$

The estimated bias b and weight w are obtained by minimizing the sum of squared errors (SSE), given as

$$SSE = \sum_{i=1}^{n}(y_i - \hat{y}_i)^2 = \sum_{i=1}^{n}(y_i - b - w \cdot x_i)^2$$

with the least squares estimates given as (see Eq. (23.11) and Eq. (23.8))

$$w = \frac{\sigma_{XY}}{\sigma_X^2} \qquad\qquad b = \mu_Y - w \cdot \mu_X$$

27.1.1 Estimating Variance (σ^2)

According to our model, the variance in prediction is entirely due to the random error term ε. We can estimate this variance by considering the predicted value $\hat{y}_i$ and its deviation from the true response y_i, that is, by looking at the residual error

$$\epsilon_i = y_i - \hat{y}_i$$

One of the properties of the estimated values b and w is that the sum of residual errors is zero, since

$$\sum_{i=1}^{n} \epsilon_i = \sum_{i=1}^{n} (y_i - b - w \cdot x_i)$$

$$= \sum_{i=1}^{n} (y_i - \mu_Y + w \cdot \mu_X - w \cdot x_i)$$

$$= \left(\sum_{i=1}^{n} y_i \right) - n \cdot \mu_Y + w \cdot \left(n \mu_X - \sum_{i=1}^{n} x_i \right)$$

$$= n \cdot \mu_Y - n \cdot \mu_Y + w \cdot (n \cdot \mu_X - n \cdot \mu_X) = 0 \tag{27.1}$$

Thus, the expected value of ϵ_i is zero, since $E[\epsilon_i] = \frac{1}{n} \sum_{i=1}^{n} \epsilon_i = 0$. In other words, the sum of the errors above and below the regression line cancel each other.

Next, the estimated variance $\hat{\sigma}^2$ is given as

$$\hat{\sigma}^2 = \text{var}(\epsilon_i) = \frac{1}{n-2} \cdot \sum_{i=1}^{n} (\epsilon_i - E[\epsilon_i])^2 = \frac{1}{n-2} \cdot \sum_{i=1}^{n} \epsilon_i^2 = \frac{1}{n-2} \cdot \sum_{i=1}^{n} (y_i - \hat{y}_i)^2$$

Thus, the estimated variance is

$$\boxed{\hat{\sigma}^2 = \frac{SSE}{n-2}} \tag{27.2}$$

We divide by $n - 2$ to get an unbiased estimate, since $n - 2$ is the number of degrees of freedom for estimating SSE (see Figure 27.2). In other words, out of the n training points, we need to estimate two parameters ω and β, with $n - 2$ remaining degrees of freedom.

The squared root of the variance is called the *standard error of regression*

$$\boxed{\hat{\sigma} = \sqrt{\frac{SSE}{n-2}}} \tag{27.3}$$

27.1.2 Goodness of Fit

The SSE value gives an indication of how much of the variation in Y cannot be explained by our linear model. We can compare this value with the *total scatter*, also called *total sum of squares*, for the dependent variable Y, defined as

$$TSS = \sum_{i=1}^{n} (y_i - \mu_Y)^2$$

Notice that in TSS, we compute the squared deviations of the true response from the true mean for Y, whereas, in SSE we compute the squared deviations of the true response from the predicted response.

The total scatter can be decomposed into two components by adding and subtracting $\hat{y}_i$ as follows

$$TSS = \sum_{i=1}^{n} (y_i - \mu_Y)^2 = \sum_{i=1}^{n} (y_i - \hat{y}_i + \hat{y}_i - \mu_Y)^2$$

$$= \sum_{i=1}^{n} (y_i - \hat{y}_i)^2 + \sum_{i=1}^{n} (\hat{y}_i - \mu_Y)^2 + 2 \sum_{i=1}^{n} (y_i - \hat{y}_i) \cdot (\hat{y}_i - \mu_Y)$$

$$= \sum_{i=1}^{n} (y_i - \hat{y}_i)^2 + \sum_{i=1}^{n} (\hat{y}_i - \mu_Y)^2 = SSE + RSS$$

where we use the fact that $\sum_{i=1}^{n} (y_i - \hat{y}_i) \cdot (\hat{y}_i - \mu_Y) = 0$, and

$$RSS = \sum_{i=1}^{n} (\hat{y}_i - \mu_Y)^2$$

is a new term called *regression sum of squares* that measures the squared deviation of the predictions from the true mean. TSS can thus be decomposed into two parts: SSE, which is the amount of variation not explained by the model, and RSS, which is the amount of variance explained by the model. Therefore, the fraction of the variation left unexplained by the model is given by the ratio $\frac{SSE}{TSS}$. Conversely, the fraction of the variation that is explained by the model, called the *coefficient of determination* or simply the R^2 *statistic*, is given as

$$R^2 = \frac{TSS - SSE}{TSS} = 1 - \frac{SSE}{TSS} = \frac{RSS}{TSS} \tag{27.4}$$

The higher the R^2 statistic the better the estimated model, with $R^2 \in [0, 1]$.

Example 27.1 (Variance and Goodness of Fit). Consider Example 23.1 that shows the regression of petal length (X; the predictor variable) on petal width (Y; the response variable) for the Iris dataset. Figure 27.1 shows the scatterplot between the two attributes. There are a total of $n = 150$ data points. The least squares estimates for the bias and regression coefficients are as follows

$$w = 0.4164 \qquad\qquad b = -0.3665$$

The SSE value is given as

$$SSE = \sum_{i=1}^{150} \epsilon_i^2 = \sum_{i=1}^{150} (y_i - \hat{y}_i)^2 = 6.343$$

Thus, the estimated variance and standard error of regression are given as

$$\hat{\sigma}^2 = \frac{SSE}{n-2} = \frac{6.343}{148} = 4.286 \times 10^{-2}$$

$$\hat{\sigma} = \sqrt{\frac{SSE}{n-2}} = \sqrt{4.286 \times 10^{-2}} = 0.207$$

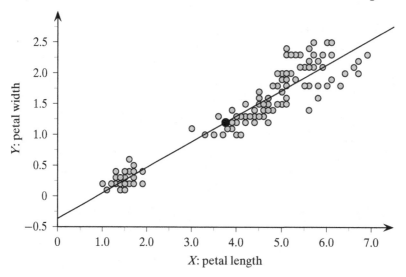

Figure 27.1. Scatterplot: petal length (X) versus petal width (Y). Mean point shown as black circle.

For the bivariate Iris data, the values of TSS and RSS are given as

$$TSS = 86.78 \qquad\qquad RSS = 80.436$$

We can observe that $TSS = SSE + RSS$. The fraction of variance explained by the model, that is, the R^2 value, is given as

$$R^2 = \frac{RSS}{TSS} = \frac{80.436}{86.78} = 0.927$$

This indicates a very good fit of the linear model.

Geometry of Goodness of Fit

Recall that Y can be decomposed into two orthogonal parts as illustrated in Figure 27.2(a).

$$Y = \widehat{Y} + \epsilon$$

where $\widehat{Y}$ is the projection of Y onto the subspace spanned by $\{\mathbf{1}, X\}$. Using the fact that this subspace is the same as that spanned by the orthogonal vectors $\{\mathbf{1}, \bar{X}\}$, with $\bar{X} = X - \mu_X \cdot \mathbf{1}$, we can further decompose $\widehat{Y}$ as follows

$$\widehat{Y} = \text{proj}_{\mathbf{1}}(Y) \cdot \mathbf{1} + \text{proj}_{\bar{X}}(Y) \cdot \bar{X} = \mu_Y \cdot \mathbf{1} + \frac{Y^T \bar{X}}{\bar{X}^T \bar{X}} \cdot \bar{X} = \mu_Y \cdot \mathbf{1} + w \cdot \bar{X} \qquad (27.5)$$

Likewise, the vectors Y and $\widehat{Y}$ can be centered by subtracting their projections along the vector $\mathbf{1}$

$$\bar{Y} = Y - \mu_Y \cdot \mathbf{1} \qquad\qquad \widehat{\bar{Y}} = \widehat{Y} - \mu_Y \cdot \mathbf{1} = w \cdot \bar{X}$$

where the last step follows from Eq. (27.5). The centered vectors $\bar{Y}, \widehat{\bar{Y}}$ and $\bar{X}$ all lie in the $n-1$ dimensional subspace orthogonal to the vector $\mathbf{1}$, as illustrated in Figure 27.2(b).

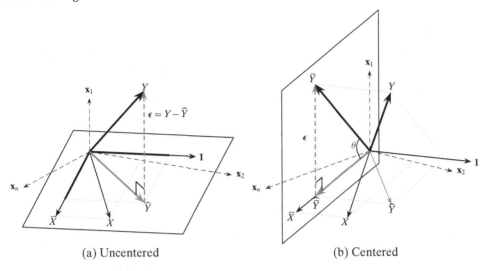

(a) Uncentered   (b) Centered

Figure 27.2. Geometry of univariate regression: uncentered and centered vectors. The vector space that is the complement of $\mathbf{1}$ has dimensionality $n-1$. The error space (containing the vector ϵ) is orthogonal to $\bar{X}$, and has dimensionality $n-2$, which also specifies the degrees of freedom for the estimated variance $\hat{\sigma}^2$.

In this subspace, the centered vectors $\bar{Y}$ and $\widehat{\bar{Y}}$, and the error vector ϵ form a right triangle, since $\widehat{\bar{Y}}$ is the orthogonal projection of $\bar{Y}$ onto the vector $\bar{X}$. Noting that $\epsilon = Y - \widehat{Y} = \bar{Y} - \widehat{\bar{Y}}$, by the Pythagoras theorem, we have

$$\left\|\bar{Y}\right\|^2 = \left\|\widehat{\bar{Y}}\right\|^2 + \left\|\epsilon\right\|^2 = \left\|\widehat{\bar{Y}}\right\|^2 + \left\|Y - \widehat{Y}\right\|^2$$

This equation is equivalent to the decomposition of the total scatter, TSS, into sum of squared errors, SSE, and residual sum of squares, RSS. To see this, note that the total scatter, TSS, is defined as follows:

$$TSS = \sum_{i=1}^{n}(y_i - \mu_Y)^2 = \left\|Y - \mu_Y \cdot \mathbf{1}\right\|^2 = \left\|\bar{Y}\right\|^2$$

The residual sum of squares, RSS, is defined as

$$RSS = \sum_{i=1}^{n}(\hat{y}_i - \mu_Y)^2 = \left\|\widehat{Y} - \mu_Y \cdot \mathbf{1}\right\|^2 = \left\|\widehat{\bar{Y}}\right\|^2$$

Finally, the sum of squared errors, SSE, is defined as

$$SSE = \left\|\epsilon\right\|^2 = \left\|Y - \widehat{Y}\right\|^2$$

Thus, the geometry of univariate regression makes it evident that

$$\left\|\bar{Y}\right\|^2 = \left\|\widehat{\bar{Y}}\right\|^2 + \left\|Y - \widehat{Y}\right\|^2$$

$$\left\|Y - \mu_Y \cdot \mathbf{1}\right\|^2 = \left\|\widehat{Y} - \mu_Y \cdot \mathbf{1}\right\|^2 + \left\|Y - \widehat{Y}\right\|^2$$

$$TSS = RSS + SSE$$

Notice further that since $\overline{Y}, \widehat{\overline{Y}}$ and ϵ form a right triangle, the cosine of the angle between $\overline{Y}$ and $\widehat{\overline{Y}}$ is given as the ratio of the base to the hypotenuse. On the other hand, via Eq. (2.30), the cosine of the angle is also the correlation between Y and $\widehat{Y}$, denoted $\rho_{Y\widehat{Y}}$. Thus, we have:

$$\rho_{Y\widehat{Y}} = \cos\theta = \frac{\|\widehat{\overline{Y}}\|}{\|\overline{Y}\|}$$

We can observe that

$$\|\widehat{\overline{Y}}\| = \rho_{Y\widehat{Y}} \cdot \|\overline{Y}\|$$

Note that, whereas $|\rho_{Y\widehat{Y}}| \leq 1$, due to the projection operation, the angle between Y and $\widehat{Y}$ is always less than or equal to $90°$, which means that $\rho_{Y\widehat{Y}} \in [0, 1]$ for univariate regression. Thus, the predicted response vector $\widehat{\overline{Y}}$ is smaller than the true response vector $\overline{Y}$ by an amount equal to the correlation between them. Furthermore, by Eq. (27.4), the coefficient of determination is the same as the squared correlation between Y and $\widehat{Y}$

$$R^2 = \frac{RSS}{TSS} = \frac{\|\widehat{\overline{Y}}\|^2}{\|\overline{Y}\|^2} = \rho_{Y\widehat{Y}}^2$$

Example 27.2 (Geometry of Goodness of Fit). Continuing Example 27.1, the correlation between Y and $\widehat{Y}$ is given as

$$\rho_{Y\widehat{Y}} = \cos\theta = \frac{\|\widehat{\overline{Y}}\|}{\|\overline{Y}\|} = \frac{\sqrt{RSS}}{\sqrt{TSS}} = \frac{\sqrt{80.436}}{\sqrt{86.78}} = \frac{8.969}{9.316} = 0.963$$

The square of the correlation is equivalent to R^2, since

$$\rho_{Y\widehat{Y}}^2 = (0.963)^2 = 0.927$$

The angle between Y and $\widehat{Y}$ is given as

$$\theta = \cos^{-1}(0.963) = 15.7°$$

The relatively small angle indicates a good linear fit.

27.1.3 Inference about Regression Coefficient and Bias Term

The estimated values of the bias and regression coefficient, b and w, are only point estimates for the true parameters β and ω. To obtain confidence intervals for these parameters, we treat each y_i as a random variable for the response given the corresponding fixed value x_i. These random variables are all independent and identically distributed as Y, with expected value $\beta + \omega \cdot x_i$ and variance σ^2. On the other hand, the x_i values are fixed *a priori* and therefore μ_X and σ_X^2 are also fixed values.

We can now treat b and w as random variables, with

$$b = \mu_Y - w \cdot \mu_X$$

$$w = \frac{\sum_{i=1}^{n}(x_i - \mu_X)(y_i - \mu_Y)}{\sum_{i=1}^{n}(x_i - \mu_X)^2} = \frac{1}{s_X}\sum_{i=1}^{n}(x_i - \mu_X) \cdot y_i = \sum_{i=1}^{n} c_i \cdot y_i$$

where c_i is a constant (since x_i is fixed), given as

$$c_i = \frac{x_i - \mu_X}{s_X} \tag{27.6}$$

and $s_X = \sum_{i=1}^{n}(x_i - \mu_X)^2$ is the total scatter for X, defined as the sum of squared deviations of x_i from its mean μ_X. We also use the fact that

$$\sum_{i=1}^{n}(x_i - \mu_X) \cdot \mu_Y = \mu_Y \cdot \sum_{i=1}^{n}(x_i - \mu_X) = 0$$

Note that

$$\sum_{i=1}^{n} c_i = \frac{1}{s_X}\sum_{i=1}^{n}(x_i - \mu_X) = 0$$

Mean and Variance of Regression Coefficient

The expected value of w is given as

$$E[w] = E\left[\sum_{i=1}^{n} c_i \, y_i\right] = \sum_{i=1}^{n} c_i \cdot E[y_i] = \sum_{i=1}^{n} c_i (\beta + \omega \cdot x_i)$$

$$= \beta \sum_{i=1}^{n} c_i + \omega \cdot \sum_{i=1}^{n} c_i \cdot x_i = \frac{\omega}{s_X} \cdot \sum_{i=1}^{n}(x_i - \mu_X) \cdot x_i = \frac{\omega}{s_X} \cdot s_X = \omega$$

which follows from the observation that $\sum_{i=1}^{n} c_i = 0$, and further

$$s_X = \sum_{i=1}^{n}(x_i - \mu_X)^2 = \left(\sum_{i=1}^{n} x_i^2\right) - n \cdot \mu_X^2 = \sum_{i=1}^{n}(x_i - \mu_X) \cdot x_i$$

Thus, w is an unbiased estimator for the true parameter ω.

Using the fact that the variables y_i are independent and identically distributed as Y, we can compute the variance of w as follows

$$\text{var}(w) = \text{var}\left(\sum_{i=1}^{n} c_i \cdot y_i\right) = \sum_{i=1}^{n} c_i^2 \cdot \text{var}(y_i) = \sigma^2 \cdot \sum_{i=1}^{n} c_i^2 = \frac{\sigma^2}{s_X} \tag{27.7}$$

since c_i is a constant, $\text{var}(y_i) = \sigma^2$, and further

$$\sum_{i=1}^{n} c_i^2 = \frac{1}{s_X^2} \cdot \sum_{i=1}^{n}(x_i - \mu_X)^2 = \frac{s_X}{s_X^2} = \frac{1}{s_X}$$

The standard deviation of w, also called the standard error of w, is given as

$$\boxed{\text{se}(w) = \sqrt{\text{var}(w)} = \frac{\sigma}{\sqrt{s_X}}} \tag{27.8}$$

Mean and Variance of Bias Term

The expected value of b is given as

$$E[b] = E[\mu_Y - w \cdot \mu_X] = E\left[\frac{1}{n}\sum_{i=1}^{n} y_i - w \cdot \mu_X\right]$$

$$= \left(\frac{1}{n} \cdot \sum_{i=1}^{n} E[y_i]\right) - \mu_X \cdot E[w] = \left(\frac{1}{n}\sum_{i=1}^{n}(\beta + \omega \cdot x_i)\right) - \omega \cdot \mu_X$$

$$= \beta + \omega \cdot \mu_X - \omega \cdot \mu_X = \beta$$

Thus, b is an unbiased estimator for the true parameter β.

Using the observation that all y_i are independent, the variance of the bias term can be computed as follows

$$\text{var}(b) = \text{var}(\mu_Y - w \cdot \mu_X)$$

$$= \text{var}\left(\frac{1}{n}\sum_{i=1}^{n} y_i\right) + \text{var}(\mu_X \cdot w)$$

$$= \frac{1}{n^2} \cdot n\sigma^2 + \mu_X^2 \cdot \text{var}(w) = \frac{1}{n} \cdot \sigma^2 + \mu_X^2 \cdot \frac{\sigma^2}{s_X}$$

$$= \left(\frac{1}{n} + \frac{\mu_X^2}{s_X}\right) \cdot \sigma^2$$

where we used the fact that for any two random variables A and B, we have $\text{var}(A - B) = \text{var}(A) + \text{var}(B)$. That is, variances of A and B add, even though we are computing the variance of $A - B$.

The standard deviation of b, also called the standard error of b, is given as

$$\text{se}(b) = \sqrt{\text{var}(b)} = \sigma \cdot \sqrt{\frac{1}{n} + \frac{\mu_X^2}{s_X}} \tag{27.9}$$

Covariance of Regression Coefficient and Bias

We can also compute the covariance of w and b, as follows

$$\text{cov}(w, b) = E[w \cdot b] - E[w] \cdot E[b] = E[(\mu_Y - w \cdot \mu_X) \cdot w] - \omega \cdot \beta$$

$$= \mu_Y \cdot E[w] - \mu_X \cdot E[w^2] - \omega \cdot \beta = \mu_Y \cdot \omega - \mu_X \cdot \left(\text{var}(w) + E[w]^2\right) - \omega \cdot \beta$$

$$= \mu_Y \cdot \omega - \mu_X \cdot \left(\frac{\sigma^2}{s_X} - \omega^2\right) - \omega \cdot \beta = \omega \cdot \underbrace{(\mu_Y - \omega \cdot \mu_X)}_{\beta} - \frac{\mu_X \cdot \sigma^2}{s_X} - \omega \cdot \beta$$

$$= -\frac{\mu_X \cdot \sigma^2}{s_X}$$

where we use the fact that $\text{var}(w) = E[w^2] - E[w]^2$, which implies $E[w^2] = \text{var}(w) + E[w]^2$, and further that $\mu_Y - \omega \cdot \mu_X = \beta$.

Confidence Intervals

Since the y_i variables are all normally distributed, their linear combination also follows a normal distribution. Thus, w follows a normal distribution with mean ω and variance σ^2/s_X. Likewise, b follows a normal distribution with mean β and variance $(1/n + \mu_X^2/s_X) \cdot \sigma^2$.

Since the true variance σ^2 is unknown, we use the estimated variance $\hat{\sigma}^2$ (from Eq. (27.2)), to define the standardized variables Z_w and Z_b as follows

$$Z_w = \frac{w - E[w]}{\text{se}(w)} = \frac{w - \omega}{\frac{\hat{\sigma}}{\sqrt{s_X}}} \qquad Z_b = \frac{b - E[b]}{\text{se}(b)} = \frac{b - \beta}{\hat{\sigma}\sqrt{(1/n + \mu_X^2/s_X)}} \qquad (27.10)$$

These variables follow the Student's t distribution with $n - 2$ degrees of freedom. Let T_{n-2} denote the cumulative t distribution with $n - 2$ degrees of freedom, and let $t_{\alpha/2}$ denote the critical value of T_{n-2} that encompasses $\alpha/2$ of the probability mass in the right tail. That is,

$$P(Z \geq t_{\alpha/2}) = \frac{\alpha}{2} \text{ or equivalently } T_{n-2}(t_{\alpha/2}) = 1 - \frac{\alpha}{2}$$

Since the t distribution is symmetric, we have

$$P(Z \geq -t_{\alpha/2}) = 1 - \frac{\alpha}{2} \text{ or equivalently } T_{n-2}(-t_{\alpha/2}) = \frac{\alpha}{2}$$

Given confidence level $1 - \alpha$, i.e., significance level $\alpha \in (0, 1)$, the $100(1 - \alpha)\%$ confidence interval for the true values, ω and β, are therefore as follows

$$P\left(w - t_{\alpha/2} \cdot \text{se}(w) \leq \omega \leq w + t_{\alpha/2} \cdot \text{se}(w)\right) = 1 - \alpha$$
$$P\left(b - t_{\alpha/2} \cdot \text{se}(b) \leq \beta \leq b + t_{\alpha/2} \cdot \text{se}(b)\right) = 1 - \alpha$$

Example 27.3 (Confidence Intervals). Continuing with Example 27.1, we consider the variance of the bias and regression coefficient, and their covariance. However, since we do not know the true variance σ^2, we use the estimated variance and the standard error for the Iris data

$$\hat{\sigma}^2 = \frac{SSE}{n - 2} = 4.286 \times 10^{-2}$$

$$\hat{\sigma} = \sqrt{4.286 \times 10^{-2}} = 0.207$$

Furthermore, we have

$$\mu_X = 3.7587 \qquad\qquad s_X = 463.864$$

Therefore, the estimated variance and standard error of w is given as

$$\text{var}(w) = \frac{\hat{\sigma}^2}{s_X} = \frac{4.286 \times 10^{-2}}{463.864} = 9.24 \times 10^{-5}$$

$$\text{se}(w) = \sqrt{\text{var}(w)} = \sqrt{9.24 \times 10^{-5}} = 9.613 \times 10^{-3}$$

The estimated variance and standard error of b is

$$\text{var}(b) = \left(\frac{1}{n} + \frac{\mu_X^2}{s_X}\right) \cdot \hat{\sigma}^2$$

$$= \left(\frac{1}{150} + \frac{(3.759)^2}{463.864}\right) \cdot (4.286 \times 10^{-2})$$

$$= (3.712 \times 10^{-2}) \cdot (4.286 \times 10^{-2}) = 1.591 \times 10^{-3}$$

$$\text{se}(b) = \sqrt{\text{var}(b)} = \sqrt{1.591 \times 10^{-3}} = 3.989 \times 10^{-2}$$

and the covariance between b and w is

$$\text{cov}(w, b) = -\frac{\mu_X \cdot \hat{\sigma}^2}{s_X} = -\frac{3.7587 \cdot (4.286 \times 10^{-2})}{463.864} = -3.473 \times 10^{-4}$$

For the confidence interval, we use a confidence level of $1 - \alpha = 0.95$ (or $\alpha = 0.05$). The critical value of the t-distribution, with $n - 2 = 148$ degrees of freedom, that encompasses $\alpha/2 = 0.025$ fraction of the probability mass in the right tail is $t_{\alpha/2} = 1.976$. We have

$$t_{\alpha/2} \cdot \text{se}(w) = 1.976 \cdot (9.613 \times 10^{-3}) = 0.019$$

Therefore, the 95% confidence interval for the true value, ω, of the regression coefficient is given as

$$\left(w - t_{\alpha/2} \cdot \text{se}(w), \ w + t_{\alpha/2} \cdot \text{se}(w)\right) = (0.4164 - 0.019, \ 0.4164 + 0.019)$$

$$= (0.397, 0.435)$$

Likewise, we have:

$$t_{\alpha/2} \cdot \text{se}(b) = 1.976 \cdot (3.989 \times 10^{-2}) = 0.079$$

Therefore, the 95% confidence interval for the true bias term, β, is

$$\left(b - t_{\alpha/2} \cdot \text{se}(b), \ b + t_{\alpha/2} \cdot \text{se}(b)\right) = (-0.3665 - 0.079, \ -0.3665 + 0.079)$$

$$= (-0.446, -0.288)$$

27.1.4 Hypothesis Testing for Regression Effects

One of the key questions in regression is whether X predicts the response Y. In the regression model, Y depends on X through the parameter ω, therefore, we can check for the regression effect by assuming the null hypothesis H_0 that $\omega = 0$, with the alternative hypothesis H_a being $\omega \neq 0$:

$$H_0 : \omega = 0 \qquad\qquad\qquad H_a : \omega \neq 0$$

When $\omega = 0$, the response Y depends only on the bias β and the random error ε. In other words, X provides no information about the response variable Y.

Now consider the standardized variable Z_w from Eq. (27.10). Under the null hypothesis we have $E[w] = \omega = 0$. Thus,

$$Z_w = \frac{w - E[w]}{se(w)} = \frac{w}{\hat{\sigma}/\sqrt{s_X}} \tag{27.11}$$

We can therefore compute the p-value for the Z_w statistic using a two-tailed test via the t distribution with $n - 2$ degrees of freedom. Given significance level α (e.g., $\alpha = 0.01$), we reject the null hypothesis if the p-value is below α. In this case, we accept the alternative hypothesis that the estimated value of the slope parameter is significantly different from zero.

We can also define the f-statistic, which is the ratio of the regression sum of squares, RSS, to the estimated variance, given as

$$f = \frac{RSS}{\hat{\sigma}^2} = \frac{\sum_{i=1}^{n}(\hat{y}_i - \mu_Y)^2}{\sum_{i=1}^{n}(y_i - \hat{y}_i)^2 \Big/ (n - 2)} \tag{27.12}$$

Under the null hypothesis, one can show that

$$E[RSS] = \sigma^2$$

Further, it is also true that

$$E[\hat{\sigma}^2] = \sigma^2$$

Thus, under the null hypothesis the f-statistic has a value close to 1, which indicates that there is no relationship between the predictor and response variables. On the other hand, if the alternative hypothesis is true, then $E[RSS] \geq \sigma^2$, resulting in a larger f value. In fact, the f-statistic follows a F-distribution with $1, (n-2)$ degrees of freedom (for the numerator and denominator, respectively); therefore, we can reject the null hypothesis that $w = 0$ if the p-value of f is less than the significance level α, say 0.01.

Interestingly the f-test is equivalent to the t-test since $Z_w^2 = f$. We can see this as follows:

$$f = \frac{1}{\hat{\sigma}^2} \cdot \sum_{i=1}^{n}(\hat{y}_i - \mu_Y)^2 = \frac{1}{\hat{\sigma}^2} \cdot \sum_{i=1}^{n}(b + w \cdot x_i - \mu_Y)^2$$

$$= \frac{1}{\hat{\sigma}^2} \cdot \sum_{i=1}^{n}(\mu_Y - w \cdot \mu_X + w \cdot x_i - \mu_Y)^2 = \frac{1}{\hat{\sigma}^2} \cdot \sum_{i=1}^{n}(w \cdot (x_i - \mu_X))^2$$

$$= \frac{1}{\hat{\sigma}^2} \cdot w^2 \cdot \sum_{i=1}^{n}(x_i - \mu_X)^2 = \frac{w^2 \cdot s_X}{\hat{\sigma}^2}$$

$$= \frac{w^2}{\hat{\sigma}^2/s_X} = Z_w^2$$

Test for Bias Term
Note that we can also test if the bias value is statistically significant or not by setting up the null hypothesis, $H_0 : \beta = 0$, versus the alternative hypothesis $H_a : \beta \neq 0$. We then

evaluate the Z_b statistic (see Eq. (27.10)) under the null hypothesis:

$$Z_b = \frac{b - E[b]}{se(b)} = \frac{b}{\hat{\sigma} \cdot \sqrt{(1/n + \mu_X^2/s_X)}} \qquad (27.13)$$

since, under the null hypothesis $E[b] = \beta = 0$. Using a two-tailed t-test with $n - 2$ degrees of freedom, we can compute the p-value of Z_b. We reject the null hypothesis if this value is smaller than the significance level α.

Example 27.4 (Hypothesis Testing). We continue with Example 27.3, but now we test for the regression effect. Under the null hypothesis we have $\omega = 0$, further $E[w] = \omega = 0$. Therefore, the standardized variable Z_w is given as

$$Z_w = \frac{w - E[w]}{se(w)} = \frac{w}{se(w)} = \frac{0.4164}{9.613 \times 10^{-3}} = 43.32$$

Using a two-tailed t-test with $n - 2$ degrees of freedom, we find that

$$\text{p-value}(43.32) \simeq 0$$

Since this value is much less than the significance level $\alpha = 0.01$, we conclude that observing such an extreme value of Z_w is unlikely under the null hypothesis. Therefore, we reject the null hypothesis and accept the alternative hypothesis that $\omega \neq 0$.

Now consider the f-statistic, we have

$$f = \frac{RSS}{\hat{\sigma}^2} = \frac{80.436}{4.286 \times 10^{-2}} = 1876.71$$

Using the F-distribution with $(1, n - 2)$ degrees of freedom, we have

$$\text{p-value}(1876.71) \simeq 0$$

In other words, such a large value of the f-statistic is extremely rare, and we can reject the null hypothesis. We conclude that Y does indeed depend on X, since $\omega \neq 0$.

Finally, we test whether the bias term is significant or not. Under the null hypothesis $H_0 : \beta = 0$, we have

$$Z_b = \frac{b}{se(b)} = \frac{-0.3665}{3.989 \times 10^{-2}} = -9.188$$

Using the two-tailed t-test, we find

$$\text{p-value}(-9.188) = 3.35 \times 10^{-16}$$

It is clear that such an extreme Z_b value is highly unlikely under the null hypothesis. Therefore, we accept the alternative hypothesis that $H_a : \beta \neq 0$.

27.1.5 Standardized Residuals

Our assumption about the true errors ε_i is that they are normally distributed with mean $\mu = 0$ and fixed variance σ^2. After fitting the linear model, we can examine how well the residual errors $\epsilon_i = y_i - \hat{y}_i$ satisfy the normality assumption. For this, we need to compute the mean and variance of ϵ_i, by treating it as a random variable.

The mean of ϵ_i is given as

$$E[\epsilon_i] = E[y_i - \hat{y}_i] = E[y_i] - E[\hat{y}_i]$$
$$= \beta + \omega \cdot x_i - E[b + w \cdot x_i] = \beta + \omega \cdot x_i - (\beta + \omega \cdot x_i) = 0$$

which follows from the fact that $E[b] = \beta$ and $E[w] = \omega$.

To compute the variance of ϵ_i, we will express it as a linear combination of the y_j variables, by noting that

$$w = \frac{1}{s_X}\left(\sum_{j=1}^{n} x_j y_j - n \cdot \mu_X \cdot \mu_Y\right) = \frac{1}{s_X}\left(\sum_{j=1}^{n} x_j y_j - \sum_{j=1}^{n} \mu_X \cdot y_j\right) = \sum_{j=1}^{n} \frac{(x_j - \mu_X)}{s_X} \cdot y_j$$

$$b = \mu_Y - w \cdot \mu_X = \left(\sum_{j=1}^{n} \frac{1}{n} \cdot y_j\right) - w \cdot \mu_X$$

Therefore, we can express ϵ_i, as follows

$$\epsilon_i = y_i - \hat{y}_i = y_i - b - w \cdot x_i = y_i - \sum_{j=1}^{n} \frac{1}{n} y_j + w \cdot \mu_X - w \cdot x_i$$

$$= y_i - \sum_{j=1}^{n} \frac{1}{n} y_j - (x_i - \mu_X) \cdot w$$

$$= y_i - \sum_{j=1}^{n} \frac{1}{n} y_j - \sum_{j=1}^{n} \frac{(x_i - \mu_X) \cdot (x_j - \mu_X)}{s_X} \cdot y_j$$

$$= \left(1 - \frac{1}{n} - \frac{(x_i - \mu_X)^2}{s_X}\right) \cdot y_i - \sum_{j \neq i} \left(\frac{1}{n} + \frac{(x_i - \mu_X) \cdot (x_j - \mu_X)}{s_X}\right) \cdot y_j \quad (27.14)$$

where we have separated y_i from the rest of the y_j's, so that all terms in the summation are independent. Define a_j as follows:

$$a_j = \left(\frac{1}{n} + \frac{(x_i - \mu_X) \cdot (x_j - \mu_X)}{s_X}\right) \quad (27.15)$$

Rewriting Eq. (27.14) in terms of a_j, we get

$$\text{var}(\epsilon_i) = \text{var}\left((1 - a_i) \cdot y_i - \sum_{j \neq i} a_j \cdot y_j\right)$$

$$= (1 - a_i)^2 \cdot \text{var}(y_i) + \sum_{j \neq i} a_j^2 \cdot \text{var}(y_j)$$

$$= \sigma^2 \cdot \left(1 - 2a_i + a_i^2 + \sum_{j \neq i} a_j^2\right), \quad \text{since } \text{var}(y_i) = \text{var}(y_j) = \sigma^2$$

$$= \sigma^2 \cdot \left(1 - 2a_i + \sum_{j=1}^{n} a_j^2\right) \tag{27.16}$$

Consider the term $\sum_{j=1}^{n} a_j^2$, we have

$$\sum_{j=1}^{n} a_j^2 = \sum_{j=1}^{n} \left(\frac{1}{n} + \frac{(x_i - \mu_X) \cdot (x_j - \mu_X)}{s_X}\right)^2$$

$$= \sum_{j=1}^{n} \left(\frac{1}{n^2} - \frac{2 \cdot (x_i - \mu_X) \cdot (x_j - \mu_X)}{n \cdot s_X} + \frac{(x_i - \mu_X)^2 \cdot (x_j - \mu_X)^2}{s_X^2}\right)$$

$$= \frac{1}{n} - \frac{2 \cdot (x_i - \mu_X)}{n \cdot s_X} \sum_{j=1}^{n}(x_j - \mu_X) + \frac{(x_i - \mu_X)^2}{s_X^2} \sum_{j=1}^{n}(x_j - \mu_X)^2$$

since $\sum_{j=1}^{n}(x_j - \mu_X) = 0$ and $\sum_{j=1}^{n}(x_j - \mu_X)^2 = s_X$, we get

$$\sum_{j=1}^{n} a_j^2 = \frac{1}{n} + \frac{(x_i - \mu_X)^2}{s_X} \tag{27.17}$$

Plugging Equations (27.15) and (27.17) into Eq. (27.16), we get

$$\text{var}(\epsilon_i) = \sigma^2 \cdot \left(1 - \frac{2}{n} - \frac{2 \cdot (x_i - \mu_X)^2}{s_X} + \frac{1}{n} + \frac{(x_i - \mu_X)^2}{s_X}\right)$$

$$= \sigma^2 \cdot \left(1 - \frac{1}{n} - \frac{(x_i - \mu_X)^2}{s_X}\right)$$

We can now define the *standardized residual* ϵ_i^* by dividing ϵ_i by its standard deviation after replacing σ^2 by its estimated value $\hat{\sigma}^2$. That is,

$$\epsilon_i^* = \frac{\epsilon_i}{\sqrt{\text{var}(\epsilon_i)}} = \frac{\epsilon_i}{\hat{\sigma} \cdot \sqrt{1 - \frac{1}{n} - \frac{(x_i - \mu_X)^2}{s_X}}} \tag{27.18}$$

These standardized residuals should follow a standard normal distribution. We can thus plot the standardized residuals against the quantiles of a standard normal distribution, and check if the normality assumption holds. Significant deviations would indicate that our model assumptions may not be correct.

Example 27.5 (Standardized Residuals). Consider the Iris dataset from Example 27.1, with the predictor variable (petal length) and response variable (petal width), and $n = 150$. Figure 27.3(a) shows the quantile-quantile (QQ) plot. The y-axis is the list of standardized residuals sorted from the smallest to the largest. The x-axis

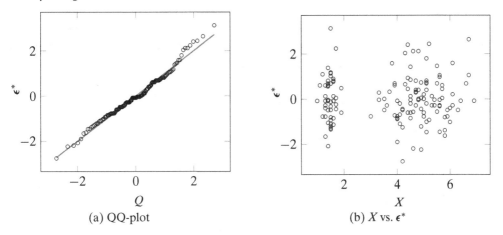

Figure 27.3. Residual plots: (a) Quantile-Quantile scatter plot of normal quantiles versus standardized residuals. (b) Independent variable versus standardized residuals.

is the list of the quantiles of the standard normal distribution for a sample of size n, defined as

$$Q = (q_1, q_2, \ldots, q_n)^T$$

$$q_i = F^{-1}\left(\frac{i - 0.5}{n}\right)$$

where F is the cumulative distribution function (CDF), and F^{-1} is the inverse CDF or quantile function (see Eq. (2.2)) for the normal distribution. Thus, the Q values are also sorted in increasing order from smallest to largest. If the standardized residuals follow a normal distribution, then the QQ plot should follow a straight line. Figure 27.3(a) plots this perfect line for comparison. We can observe that the residuals are essentially normally distributed.

The plot of the independent variable X versus the standardized residuals is also instructive. We can see in Figure 27.3(b) that there is no particular trend or pattern to the residuals, and the residual values are concentrated along the mean value of 0, with the majority of the points being within two standard deviations of the mean, as expected if they were sampled from a normal distribution.

27.2 MULTIPLE REGRESSION

In multiple regression there are multiple independent attributes $X_1, X_2, \cdots, X_d$ and a single dependent or response attribute Y, and we assume that the true relationship can be modeled as a linear function

$$Y = \beta + \omega_1 \cdot X_1 + \omega_2 \cdot X_2 + \ldots + \omega_d \cdot X_d + \varepsilon$$

where β is the intercept or bias term and ω_i is the regression coefficient for attribute X_i. Recall that ω_i denotes the expected increase in Y with a unit increase in the value of X_i, assuming all other variables are held fixed. We assume that ε is a random variable that is normally distributed with mean $\mu = 0$ and variance σ^2. Further, we assume that the errors for different observations are all independent of each other, and consequently the observed responses are also independent.

Mean and Variance of Response Variable

Let $\mathbf{X} = (X_1, X_2, \cdots, X_d)^T \in \mathbb{R}^d$ denote the multivariate random variable comprising the independent attributes. Let $\mathbf{x} = (x_1, x_2, \cdots, x_d)^T$ be some *fixed* value of $\mathbf{X}$, and let $\boldsymbol{\omega} = (\omega_1, \omega_2, \cdots, \omega_d)^T$. The expected response value is then given as

$$E[Y|\mathbf{X} = \mathbf{x}] = E[\beta + \omega_1 \cdot x_1 + \ldots + \omega_d \cdot x_d + \varepsilon] = E\left[\beta + \sum_{i=1}^d \omega_i \cdot x_i\right] + E[\varepsilon]$$

$$= \beta + \omega_1 \cdot x_1 + \ldots + \omega_d \cdot x_d = \beta + \boldsymbol{\omega}^T \mathbf{x}$$

which follows from the assumption that $E[\varepsilon] = 0$. The variance of the response variable is given as

$$\text{var}(Y|\mathbf{X} = \mathbf{x}) = \text{var}\left(\beta + \sum_{i=1}^d \omega_i \cdot x_i + \varepsilon\right) = \text{var}\left(\beta + \sum_{i=1}^d \omega_i \cdot x_i\right) + \text{var}(\varepsilon) = 0 + \sigma^2 = \sigma^2$$

which follows from the assumption that all x_i are fixed *a priori*. Thus, we conclude that Y also follows a normal distribution with mean $E[Y|\mathbf{x}] = \beta + \sum_{i=1}^d \omega_i \cdot x_i = \beta + \boldsymbol{\omega}^T \mathbf{x}$ and variance $\text{var}(Y|\mathbf{x}) = \sigma^2$.

Estimated Parameters

The true parameters $\beta, \omega_1, \omega_2, \cdots, \omega_d$ and σ^2 are all unknown, and have to be estimated from the training data $\mathbf{D}$ comprising n points $\mathbf{x}_i$ and corresponding response values y_i, for $i = 1, 2, \cdots, n$. We augment the data matrix by adding a new column X_0 with all values fixed at 1, that is, $X_0 = \mathbf{1}$. Thus, the augmented data $\tilde{\mathbf{D}} \in \mathbb{R}^{n \times (d+1)}$ comprises the $(d + 1)$ attributes $X_0, X_1, X_2, \cdots, X_d$, and each augmented point is given as $\tilde{\mathbf{x}}_i = (1, x_{i1}, x_{i2}, \cdots, x_{id})^T$.

Let $b = w_0$ denote the estimated bias term, and let w_i denote the estimated regression weights. The augmented vector of estimated weights, including the bias term, is

$$\tilde{\mathbf{w}} = (w_0, w_1, \cdots, w_d)^T$$

We then make predictions for any given point $\mathbf{x}_i$ as follows:

$$\hat{y}_i = b \cdot 1 + w_1 \cdot x_{i1} + \cdots w_d \cdot x_{id} = \tilde{\mathbf{w}}^T \tilde{\mathbf{x}}_i$$

Recall that these estimates are obtained by minimizing the sum of squared errors (SSE), given as

$$SSE = \sum_{i=1}^n (y_i - \hat{y}_i)^2 = \sum_{i=1}^n \left(y_i - b - \sum_{j=1}^d w_j \cdot x_{ij}\right)^2$$

with the least squares estimate [Eq. (23.20)] given as

$$\tilde{\mathbf{w}} = \left(\tilde{\mathbf{D}}^T \tilde{\mathbf{D}}\right)^{-1} \tilde{\mathbf{D}}^T Y$$

The estimated variance $\hat{\sigma}^2$ is then given as

$$\hat{\sigma}^2 = \frac{SSE}{n-(d+1)} = \frac{1}{n-d-1} \cdot \sum_{i=1}^{n} (y_i - \hat{y}_i)^2 \tag{27.19}$$

We divide by $n - (d + 1)$ to get an unbiased estimate, since $n - (d + 1)$ is the number of degrees of freedom for estimating SSE (see Figure 27.5). In other words, out of the n training points, we need to estimate $d + 1$ parameters, β and the ω_i's, with $n - (d + 1)$ remaining degrees of freedom.

Estimated Variance is Unbiased   We now show that $\hat{\sigma}^2$ is an unbiased estimator of the true (but unknown) variance σ^2. Recall from Eq. (23.18) that

$$\widehat{Y} = \tilde{\mathbf{D}}\tilde{\mathbf{w}} = \tilde{\mathbf{D}}(\tilde{\mathbf{D}}^T\tilde{\mathbf{D}})^{-1}\tilde{\mathbf{D}}^T Y = \mathbf{H}Y$$

where $\mathbf{H}$ is the $n \times n$ hat matrix (assuming that $(\tilde{\mathbf{D}}^T\tilde{\mathbf{D}})^{-1}$ exists). Note that $\mathbf{H}$ is an *orthogonal projection matrix*, since it is symmetric ($\mathbf{H}^T = \mathbf{H}$) and idempotent ($\mathbf{H}^2 = \mathbf{H}$). The hat matrix $\mathbf{H}$ is symmetric since

$$\mathbf{H}^T = \left(\tilde{\mathbf{D}}(\tilde{\mathbf{D}}^T\tilde{\mathbf{D}})^{-1}\tilde{\mathbf{D}}^T\right)^T = \left(\tilde{\mathbf{D}}^T\right)^T \left((\tilde{\mathbf{D}}^T\tilde{\mathbf{D}})^T\right)^{-1}\tilde{\mathbf{D}}^T = \mathbf{H}$$

and it is idempotent since

$$\mathbf{H}^2 = \tilde{\mathbf{D}}(\tilde{\mathbf{D}}^T\tilde{\mathbf{D}})^{-1}\tilde{\mathbf{D}}^T\tilde{\mathbf{D}}(\tilde{\mathbf{D}}^T\tilde{\mathbf{D}})^{-1}\tilde{\mathbf{D}}^T = \tilde{\mathbf{D}}(\tilde{\mathbf{D}}^T\tilde{\mathbf{D}})^{-1}\tilde{\mathbf{D}}^T = \mathbf{H}$$

Furthermore, the trace of the hat matrix is given as

$$\text{tr}(\mathbf{H}) = \text{tr}(\tilde{\mathbf{D}}(\tilde{\mathbf{D}}^T\tilde{\mathbf{D}})^{-1}\tilde{\mathbf{D}}^T) = \text{tr}(\tilde{\mathbf{D}}^T\tilde{\mathbf{D}}(\tilde{\mathbf{D}}^T\tilde{\mathbf{D}})^{-1}) = \text{tr}(\mathbf{I}_{(d+1)}) = d + 1$$

where $\mathbf{I}_{(d+1)}$ is the $(d + 1) \times (d + 1)$ identity matrix, and we used the fact that the trace of a product of matrices is invariant under cyclic permutations.

Finally, note that the matrix $\mathbf{I} - \mathbf{H}$ is also symmetric and idempotent, where $\mathbf{I}$ is the $n \times n$ identity matrix, since

$$(\mathbf{I} - \mathbf{H})^T = \mathbf{I}^T - \mathbf{H}^T = \mathbf{I} - \mathbf{H}$$

$$(\mathbf{I} - \mathbf{H})^2 = (\mathbf{I} - \mathbf{H})(\mathbf{I} - \mathbf{H}) = \mathbf{I} - \mathbf{H} - \mathbf{H} + \mathbf{H}^2 = \mathbf{I} - \mathbf{H}$$

Now consider the squared error; we have

$$SSE = \left\| Y - \widehat{Y} \right\|^2 = \left\| Y - \mathbf{H}Y \right\|^2 = \left\| (\mathbf{I} - \mathbf{H})Y \right\|^2$$
$$= Y^T(\mathbf{I} - \mathbf{H})(\mathbf{I} - \mathbf{H})Y = Y^T(\mathbf{I} - \mathbf{H})Y \tag{27.20}$$

However, note that the response vector Y is given as

$$Y = \tilde{\mathbf{D}}\tilde{\omega} + \boldsymbol{\varepsilon}$$

where $\tilde{\omega} = (\omega_0, \omega_1, \cdots, \omega_d)^T$ is the true (augmented) vector of parameters of the model, and $\boldsymbol{\varepsilon} = (\varepsilon_1, \varepsilon_2, \cdots, \varepsilon_n)^T$ is the true error vector, which is assumed to be normally distributed with mean $E[\boldsymbol{\varepsilon}] = \mathbf{0}$ and with fixed variance $\varepsilon_i = \sigma^2$ for each point, so that $\text{cov}(\boldsymbol{\varepsilon}) = \sigma^2 \mathbf{I}$. Plugging the expression of Y into Eq. (27.20), we get

$$SSE = Y^T(\mathbf{I} - \mathbf{H})Y = (\tilde{\mathbf{D}}\tilde{\omega} + \boldsymbol{\varepsilon})^T(\mathbf{I} - \mathbf{H})(\tilde{\mathbf{D}}\tilde{\omega} + \boldsymbol{\varepsilon}) = (\tilde{\mathbf{D}}\tilde{\omega} + \boldsymbol{\varepsilon})^T\big(\underbrace{(\mathbf{I} - \mathbf{H})\tilde{\mathbf{D}}\tilde{\omega}}_{\mathbf{0}} + (\mathbf{I} - \mathbf{H})\boldsymbol{\varepsilon}\big)$$

$$= \big((\mathbf{I} - \mathbf{H})\boldsymbol{\varepsilon}\big)^T(\tilde{\mathbf{D}}\tilde{\omega} + \boldsymbol{\varepsilon}) = \boldsymbol{\varepsilon}^T(\mathbf{I} - \mathbf{H})(\tilde{\mathbf{D}}\tilde{\omega} + \boldsymbol{\varepsilon})$$

$$= \boldsymbol{\varepsilon}^T\underbrace{(\mathbf{I} - \mathbf{H})\tilde{\mathbf{D}}\tilde{\omega}}_{\mathbf{0}} + \boldsymbol{\varepsilon}^T(\mathbf{I} - \mathbf{H})\boldsymbol{\varepsilon} = \boldsymbol{\varepsilon}^T(\mathbf{I} - \mathbf{H})\boldsymbol{\varepsilon}$$

where we use the observation that

$$(\mathbf{I} - \mathbf{H})\tilde{\mathbf{D}}\tilde{\omega} = \tilde{\mathbf{D}}\tilde{\omega} - \mathbf{H}\tilde{\mathbf{D}}\tilde{\omega} = \tilde{\mathbf{D}}\tilde{\omega} - (\tilde{\mathbf{D}}(\tilde{\mathbf{D}}^T\tilde{\mathbf{D}})^{-1}\tilde{\mathbf{D}}^T)\tilde{\mathbf{D}}\tilde{\omega} = \tilde{\mathbf{D}}\tilde{\omega} - \tilde{\mathbf{D}}\tilde{\omega} = \mathbf{0}$$

Let us consider the expected value of SSE; we have

$$E[SSE] = E\big[\boldsymbol{\varepsilon}^T(\mathbf{I} - \mathbf{H})\boldsymbol{\varepsilon}\big]$$

$$= E\left[\sum_{i=1}^n \varepsilon_i^2 - \sum_{i=1}^n\sum_{j=1}^n h_{ij}\varepsilon_i\varepsilon_j\right] = \sum_{i=1}^n E[\varepsilon_i^2] - \sum_{i=1}^n\sum_{j=1}^n h_{ij}E[\varepsilon_i\varepsilon_j]$$

$$= \sum_{i=1}^n (1 - h_{ii})E[\varepsilon_i^2], \text{ since } \varepsilon_i \text{ are independent, and therefore } E[\varepsilon_i\varepsilon_j] = 0$$

$$= \left(n - \sum_{i=1}^n h_{ii}\right)\sigma^2 = (n - \text{tr}(\mathbf{H}))\sigma^2 = (n - d - 1)\cdot\sigma^2$$

where we used the fact that $\sigma^2 = \text{var}(\varepsilon_i) = E[\varepsilon_i^2] - \big(E[\varepsilon_i]\big)^2 = E[\varepsilon_i^2]$, since $E[\varepsilon_i] = 0$. It follows that

$$\hat{\sigma}^2 = E\left[\frac{SSE}{(n - d - 1)}\right] = \frac{1}{(n - d - 1)}E[SSE] = \frac{1}{(n - d - 1)}\cdot(n - d - 1)\cdot\sigma^2 = \sigma^2 \quad (27.21)$$

27.2.1 Goodness of Fit

Following the derivation in Section 27.1.2, the decomposition of the total sum of squares, TSS, into the sum of squared errors, SSE, and the residual sum of squares, RSS, holds true for multiple regression as well:

$$TSS = SSE + RSS$$

$$\sum_{i=1}^n (y_i - \mu_Y)^2 = \sum_{i=1}^n (y_i - \hat{y}_i)^2 + \sum_{i=1}^n (\hat{y}_i - \mu_Y)^2$$

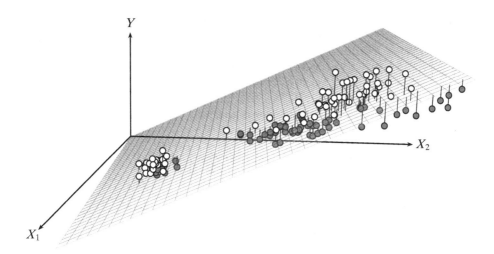

Figure 27.4. Multiple regression: sepal length (X_1) and petal length (X_2) with response attribute petal width (Y). The vertical bars show the residual errors for the points. Points in white are above the plane, whereas points in gray are below the plane.

The *coefficient of multiple determination*, R^2, gives the goodness of fit, measured as the fraction of the variation explained by the linear model:

$$R^2 = 1 - \frac{SSE}{TSS} = \frac{TSS - SSE}{TSS} = \frac{RSS}{TSS} \tag{27.22}$$

One of the potential problems with the R^2 measure is that it is susceptible to increase as the number of attributes increase, even though the additional attributes may be uninformative. To counter this, we can consider the *adjusted coefficient of determination*, which takes into account the degrees of freedom in both TSS and SSE

$$R_a^2 = 1 - \frac{SSE/(n-d-1)}{TSS/(n-1)} = 1 - \frac{(n-1) \cdot SSE}{(n-d-1) \cdot TSS} \tag{27.23}$$

We can observe that the adjusted R_a^2 measure is always less than R^2, since the ratio $\frac{n-1}{n-d-1} > 1$. If there is too much of a difference between R^2 and R_a^2, it might indicate that there are potentially many, possibly irrelevant, attributes being used to fit the model.

Example 27.6 (Multiple Regression: Goodness of Fit). Continuing with multiple regression from Example 23.3, Figure 27.4 shows the multiple regression of sepal length (X_1) and petal length (X_2) on the response attribute petal width (Y) for the Iris dataset with $n = 150$ points. We also add an extra attribute $X_0 = \mathbf{1}_{150}$, which is a vector of all ones in $\mathbb{R}^{150}$. The augmented dataset $\tilde{\mathbf{D}} \in \mathbb{R}^{150 \times 3}$ comprises $n = 150$ points, and three attributes X_0, X_1 and X_2.

The uncentered 3×3 scatter matrix $\tilde{\mathbf{D}}^T\tilde{\mathbf{D}}$ and its inverse are given as

$$\tilde{\mathbf{D}}^T\tilde{\mathbf{D}} = \begin{pmatrix} 150.0 & 876.50 & 563.80 \\ 876.5 & 5223.85 & 3484.25 \\ 563.8 & 3484.25 & 2583.00 \end{pmatrix} \quad (\tilde{\mathbf{D}}^T\tilde{\mathbf{D}})^{-1} = \begin{pmatrix} 0.793 & -0.176 & 0.064 \\ -0.176 & 0.041 & -0.017 \\ 0.064 & -0.017 & 0.009 \end{pmatrix}$$

The augmented estimated weight vector $\tilde{\mathbf{w}}$ is given as

$$\tilde{\mathbf{w}} = \begin{pmatrix} w_0 \\ w_1 \\ w_2 \end{pmatrix} = (\tilde{\mathbf{D}}^T\tilde{\mathbf{D}})^{-1} \cdot (\tilde{\mathbf{D}}^T Y) = \begin{pmatrix} -0.014 \\ -0.082 \\ 0.45 \end{pmatrix}$$

The bias term is therefore $b = w_0 = -0.014$, and the fitted model is

$$\widehat{Y} = -0.014 - 0.082 \cdot X_1 + 0.45 \cdot X_2$$

Figure 27.4 shows the fitted hyperplane. It also shows the residual error for each point. The white colored points have positive residuals (i.e., $\epsilon_i > 0$ or $\hat{y}_i > y_i$), whereas the gray points have negative residual values (i.e., $\epsilon_i < 0$ or $\hat{y}_i < y$).

The SSE value is given as

$$SSE = \sum_{i=1}^{150} \epsilon_i^2 = \sum_{i=1}^{150} (y_i - \hat{y}_i)^2 = 6.179$$

Thus, the estimated variance and standard error of regression are given as

$$\hat{\sigma}^2 = \frac{SSE}{n-d-1} = \frac{6.179}{147} = 4.203 \times 10^{-2}$$

$$\hat{\sigma} = \sqrt{\frac{SSE}{n-d-1}} = \sqrt{4.203 \times 10^{-2}} = 0.205$$

The values of total and residual sum of squares are given as

$$TSS = 86.78 \qquad\qquad\qquad RSS = 80.60$$

We can observe that $TSS = SSE + RSS$. The fraction of variance explained by the model, that is the R^2 value, is given as

$$R^2 = \frac{RSS}{TSS} = \frac{80.60}{86.78} = 0.929$$

This indicates a very good fit of the multiple linear regression model. Nevertheless, it makes sense to also consider the adjusted R_a^2 value

$$R_a^2 = 1 - \frac{(n-1) \cdot SSE}{(n-d-1) \cdot TSS} = 1 - \frac{149 \times 6.179}{147 \times 86.78} = 0.928$$

The adjusted value is almost the same as the R^2 value.

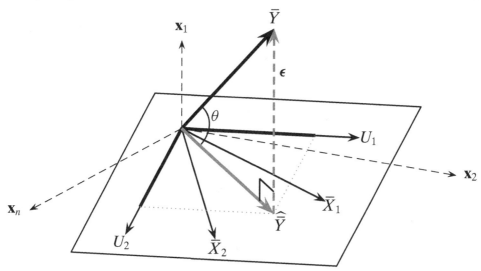

Figure 27.5. Geometry of multiple regression. The figure shows two centered predictor variables $\bar{X}_1$ and $\bar{X}_2$, along with the corresponding orthogonal basis vectors U_1 and U_2. The subspace **1** is not shown. The dimensionality of the error space, containing the vector ϵ, is $n - d - 1$, which also specifies the degrees of freedom for the estimated variance $\hat{\sigma}^2$.

Geometry of Goodness of Fit

In multiple regression there are d predictor attributes $X_1, X_2, \cdots, X_d$. We can center them by subtracting their projection along the vector **1** to obtain the centered predictor vectors $\bar{X}_i$. Likewise, we can center the response vector Y and the predicted vector $\widehat{Y}$. Thus, we have

$$\bar{X}_i = X_i - \mu_{X_i} \cdot \mathbf{1} \qquad \bar{Y} = Y - \mu_Y \cdot \mathbf{1} \qquad \widehat{\bar{Y}} = \widehat{Y} - \mu_Y \cdot \mathbf{1}$$

Once Y, $\widehat{Y}$ and X_i's have been centered, they all lie in the $n - 1$ dimensional subspace orthogonal to the vector **1**. Figure 27.5 shows this $n - 1$ dimensional subspace. In this subspace, we first extract an orthogonal basis $\{U_1, U_2, \cdots, U_d\}$ via the Gram-Schmidt orthogonalization process outlined in Section 23.3.1, and the predicted response vector is the sum of the projections of $\bar{Y}$ onto each of the new basis vectors (see Eq. (23.23)).

The centered vectors $\bar{Y}$ and $\widehat{\bar{Y}}$, and the error vector ϵ form a right triangle, and thus, by the Pythagoras theorem, we have

$$\left\| \bar{Y} \right\|^2 = \left\| \widehat{\bar{Y}} \right\|^2 + \|\epsilon\|^2 = \left\| \widehat{\bar{Y}} \right\|^2 + \left\| Y - \widehat{Y} \right\|^2$$
$$TSS = RSS + SSE \tag{27.24}$$

The correlation between Y and $\widehat{Y}$ is the cosine of the angle between $\bar{Y}$ and $\widehat{\bar{Y}}$, which is also given as the ratio of the base to the hypotenuse

$$\rho_{Y\widehat{Y}} = \cos\theta = \frac{\left\| \widehat{\bar{Y}} \right\|}{\left\| \bar{Y} \right\|}$$

Furthermore, by Eq. (27.4), the coefficient of multiple determination is given as

$$R^2 = \frac{RSS}{TSS} = \frac{\|\widehat{\overline{Y}}\|^2}{\|\overline{Y}\|^2} = \rho_{Y\widehat{Y}}^2$$

Example 27.7 (Geometry of Goodness of Fit). Continuing Example 27.6, the correlation between Y and $\widehat{Y}$ is given as

$$\rho_{Y\widehat{Y}} = \cos\theta = \frac{\|\widehat{\overline{Y}}\|}{\|\overline{Y}\|} = \frac{\sqrt{RSS}}{\sqrt{TSS}} = \frac{\sqrt{80.60}}{\sqrt{86.78}} = 0.964$$

The angle between Y and $\widehat{Y}$ is given as

$$\theta = \cos^{-1}(0.964) = 15.5°$$

The relatively small angle indicates a good linear fit.

27.2.2 Inferences about Regression Coefficients

Let Y be the response vector over all observations. Let $\tilde{\mathbf{w}} = (w_0, w_1, w_2, \cdots, w_d)^T$ be the estimated vector of regression coefficients, computed as

$$\tilde{\mathbf{w}} = \left(\tilde{\mathbf{D}}^T\tilde{\mathbf{D}}\right)^{-1}\tilde{\mathbf{D}}^T Y$$

The expected value of $\tilde{\mathbf{w}}$ is given as follows:

$$E[\tilde{\mathbf{w}}] = E\left[(\tilde{\mathbf{D}}^T\tilde{\mathbf{D}})^{-1}\tilde{\mathbf{D}}^T Y\right] = (\tilde{\mathbf{D}}^T\tilde{\mathbf{D}})^{-1}\tilde{\mathbf{D}}^T \cdot E[Y]$$

$$= (\tilde{\mathbf{D}}^T\tilde{\mathbf{D}})^{-1}\tilde{\mathbf{D}}^T \cdot E[\tilde{\mathbf{D}}\tilde{\omega} + \varepsilon] = (\tilde{\mathbf{D}}^T\tilde{\mathbf{D}})^{-1}(\tilde{\mathbf{D}}^T\tilde{\mathbf{D}})\tilde{\omega} = \tilde{\omega}$$

since $E[\varepsilon] = \mathbf{0}$. Thus, $\tilde{\mathbf{w}}$ is an unbiased estimator for the true regression coefficients vector $\tilde{\omega}$.

Next, we compute the covariance matrix for $\tilde{\mathbf{w}}$, as follows

$$\mathrm{cov}(\tilde{\mathbf{w}}) = \mathrm{cov}\left((\tilde{\mathbf{D}}^T\tilde{\mathbf{D}})^{-1}\tilde{\mathbf{D}}^T Y\right), \text{ letting } \mathbf{A} = (\tilde{\mathbf{D}}^T\tilde{\mathbf{D}})^{-1}\tilde{\mathbf{D}}^T, \text{ we get}$$

$$= \mathrm{cov}(\mathbf{A}Y) = \mathbf{A}\,\mathrm{cov}(Y)\mathbf{A}^T$$

$$= \mathbf{A} \cdot (\sigma^2 \cdot \mathbf{I}) \cdot \mathbf{A}^T$$

$$= (\tilde{\mathbf{D}}^T\tilde{\mathbf{D}})^{-1}\tilde{\mathbf{D}}^T (\sigma^2 \cdot \mathbf{I}) \tilde{\mathbf{D}}(\tilde{\mathbf{D}}^T\tilde{\mathbf{D}})^{-1}$$

$$= \sigma^2 \cdot (\tilde{\mathbf{D}}^T\tilde{\mathbf{D}})^{-1}(\tilde{\mathbf{D}}^T\tilde{\mathbf{D}})(\tilde{\mathbf{D}}^T\tilde{\mathbf{D}})^{-1}$$

$$= \sigma^2(\tilde{\mathbf{D}}^T\tilde{\mathbf{D}})^{-1} \tag{27.25}$$

Here, we made use of the fact that $\mathbf{A} = (\tilde{\mathbf{D}}^T\tilde{\mathbf{D}})^{-1}\tilde{\mathbf{D}}^T$ is a matrix of fixed values, and therefore $\mathrm{cov}(\mathbf{A}Y) = \mathbf{A}\,\mathrm{cov}(Y)\mathbf{A}^T$. Also, we have $\mathrm{cov}(Y) = \sigma^2 \cdot \mathbf{I}$, where $\mathbf{I}$ is the $n \times n$ identity matrix. This follows from the fact that the observed responses y_i's are all independent and have the same variance σ^2.

Note that $\tilde{\mathbf{D}}^T\tilde{\mathbf{D}} \in \mathbb{R}^{(d+1)\times(d+1)}$ is the uncentered scatter matrix for the augmented data. Let $\mathbf{C}$ denote the inverse of $\tilde{\mathbf{D}}^T\tilde{\mathbf{D}}$. That is

$$(\tilde{\mathbf{D}}^T\tilde{\mathbf{D}})^{-1} = \mathbf{C}$$

Therefore, the covariance matrix for $\tilde{\mathbf{w}}$ can be written as

$$\mathrm{cov}(\tilde{\mathbf{w}}) = \sigma^2 \mathbf{C}$$

In particular, the diagonal entries $\sigma^2 \cdot c_{ii}$ give the variance for each of the regression coefficient estimates (including for $b = w_0$), and their squared roots specify the standard errors. That is

$$\mathrm{var}(w_i) = \sigma^2 \cdot c_{ii} \qquad\qquad \mathrm{se}(w_i) = \sqrt{\mathrm{var}(w_i)} = \sigma \cdot \sqrt{c_{ii}}$$

We can now define the standardized variable Z_{w_i} that can be used to derive the confidence intervals for ω_i as follows

$$\boxed{Z_{w_i} = \frac{w_i - E[w_i]}{\mathrm{se}(w_i)} = \frac{w_i - \omega_i}{\hat{\sigma}\sqrt{c_{ii}}}} \qquad (27.26)$$

where we have replaced the unknown true variance σ^2 by $\hat{\sigma}^2$. Each of the variables Z_{w_i} follows a t-distribution with $n - d - 1$ degrees of freedom, from which we can obtain the $100(1 - \alpha)\%$ confidence interval of the true value ω_i as follows:

$$P\left(w_i - t_{\alpha/2} \cdot \mathrm{se}(w_i) \le \omega_i \le w_i + t_{\alpha/2} \cdot \mathrm{se}(w_i)\right) = 1 - \alpha$$

Here, $t_{\alpha/2}$ is the critical value of the t distribution, with $n - d - 1$ degrees of freedom, that encompasses $\alpha/2$ fraction of the probability mass in the right tail, given as

$$P(Z \ge t_{\alpha/2}) = \tfrac{\alpha}{2} \text{ or equivalently } T_{n-d-1}(t_{\alpha/2}) = 1 - \tfrac{\alpha}{2}$$

Example 27.8 (Confidence Intervals). Continuing with multiple regression from Example 27.6, we have

$$\hat{\sigma}^2 = 4.203 \times 10^{-2}$$

$$\mathbf{C} = (\tilde{\mathbf{D}}^T\tilde{\mathbf{D}})^{-1} = \begin{pmatrix} 0.793 & -0.176 & 0.064 \\ -0.176 & 0.041 & -0.017 \\ 0.064 & -0.017 & 0.009 \end{pmatrix}$$

Therefore, the covariance matrix of the estimated regression parameters, including the bias term, is given as

$$\mathrm{cov}(\tilde{\mathbf{w}}) = \hat{\sigma}^2 \cdot \mathbf{C} = \begin{pmatrix} 3.333 \times 10^{-2} & -7.379 \times 10^{-3} & 2.678 \times 10^{-3} \\ -7.379 \times 10^{-3} & 1.714 \times 10^{-3} & -7.012 \times 10^{-4} \\ 2.678 \times 10^{-3} & -7.012 \times 10^{-4} & 3.775 \times 10^{-4} \end{pmatrix}$$

The diagonal entries specify the variances and standard errors of each of the estimated parameters

$$\text{var}(b) = 3.333 \times 10^{-2} \qquad \text{se}(b) = \sqrt{3.333 \times 10^{-2}} = 0.183$$

$$\text{var}(w_1) = 1.714 \times 10^{-3} \qquad \text{se}(w_1) = \sqrt{1.714 \times 10^{-3}} = 0.0414$$

$$\text{var}(w_2) = 3.775 \times 10^{-4} \qquad \text{se}(w_2) = \sqrt{3.775 \times 10^{-4}} = 0.0194$$

where $b = w_0$.

Using confidence level $1 - \alpha = 0.95$ (or significance level $\alpha = 0.05$), the critical value of the t-distribution that encompasses $\frac{\alpha}{2} = 0.025$ fraction of the probability mass in the right tail is given as $t_{\alpha/2} = 1.976$. Thus, the 95% confidence intervals for the true bias term β, and the true regression coefficients ω_1 and ω_2, are:

$$\beta \in \left(b \pm t_{\alpha/2} \cdot \text{se}(b)\right) = (-0.014 - 0.074, -0.014 + 0.074)$$

$$= (-0.088, 0.06)$$

$$\omega_1 \in \left(w_1 \pm t_{\alpha/2} \cdot \text{se}(w_1)\right) = (-0.082 - 0.0168, -0.082 + 0.0168)$$

$$= (-0.099, -0.065)$$

$$\omega_2 \in \left(w_2 \pm t_{\alpha/2} \cdot \text{se}(w_2)\right) = (0.45 - 0.00787, 0.45 + 0.00787)$$

$$= (0.442, 0.458)$$

27.2.3 Hypothesis Testing

Once the parameters have been estimated, it is beneficial to test whether the regression coefficients are close to zero or substantially different. For this we set up the null hypothesis that all the true weights are zero, except for the bias term ($\beta = \omega_0$). We contrast the null hypothesis with the alternative hypothesis that at least one of the weights is not zero

$$H_0: \quad \omega_1 = 0, \omega_2 = 0, \ldots, \omega_d = 0$$

$$H_a: \quad \exists i, \text{ such that } \omega_i \neq 0$$

The null hypothesis can also be written as $H_0 : \boldsymbol{\omega} = \mathbf{0}$, where $\boldsymbol{\omega} = (\omega_1, \omega_2, \cdots, \omega_d)^T$.

We use the F-test that compares the ratio of the adjusted RSS value to the estimated variance $\hat{\sigma}^2$, defined via the f-statistic

$$f = \frac{RSS/d}{\hat{\sigma}^2} = \frac{RSS/d}{SSE/(n - d - 1)} \tag{27.27}$$

Under the null hypothesis, we have

$$E[RSS/d] = \sigma^2$$

To see this, let us examine the regression equations in vector terms, namely

$$\widehat{Y} = b \cdot \mathbf{1} + w_1 \cdot X_1 + \ldots + w_d \cdot X_d$$

$$\widehat{Y} = (\mu_Y - w_1 \mu_{X_1} - \ldots - w_d \mu_{X_d}) \cdot \mathbf{1} + w_1 \cdot X_1 + \ldots + w_d \cdot X_d$$

$$\widehat{Y} - \mu_Y \cdot \mathbf{1} = w_1 (X_1 - \mu_{X_1} \cdot \mathbf{1}) + \ldots + w_d (X_d - \mu_{X_d} \cdot \mathbf{1}), \text{ which implies}$$

$$\widehat{\overline{Y}} = w_1 \overline{X}_1 + w_2 \overline{X}_2 + \ldots + w_d \overline{X}_d = \sum_{i=1}^{d} w_i \overline{X}_i$$

Let us consider the RSS value; we have

$$RSS = \left\| \widehat{Y} - \mu_Y \cdot \mathbf{1} \right\|^2 = \left\| \widehat{\overline{Y}} \right\|^2 = \widehat{\overline{Y}}^T \widehat{\overline{Y}}$$

$$= \left(\sum_{i=1}^{d} w_i \overline{X}_i \right)^T \left(\sum_{j=1}^{d} w_j \overline{X}_j \right) = \sum_{i=1}^{d} \sum_{j=1}^{d} w_i w_j \overline{X}_i^T \overline{X}_j = \mathbf{w}^T (\overline{\mathbf{D}}^T \overline{\mathbf{D}}) \mathbf{w}$$

where $\mathbf{w} = (w_1, w_2, \cdots, w_d)^T$ is the d-dimensional vector of regression coefficients (without the bias term), and $\overline{\mathbf{D}} \in \mathbb{R}^{n \times d}$ is the centered data matrix (without augmentation by the $X_0 = \mathbf{1}$ attribute). The expected value of RSS is thus given as

$$E[RSS] = E \left[\mathbf{w}^T (\overline{\mathbf{D}}^T \overline{\mathbf{D}}) \mathbf{w} \right]$$

$$= \text{tr} \left(E \left[\mathbf{w}^T (\overline{\mathbf{D}}^T \overline{\mathbf{D}}) \mathbf{w} \right] \right), \text{ since, } E \left[\mathbf{w}^T (\overline{\mathbf{D}}^T \overline{\mathbf{D}}) \mathbf{w} \right] \text{ is a scalar}$$

$$= E \left[\text{tr} \left(\mathbf{w}^T (\overline{\mathbf{D}}^T \overline{\mathbf{D}}) \mathbf{w} \right) \right]$$

$$= E \left[\text{tr} \left((\overline{\mathbf{D}}^T \overline{\mathbf{D}}) \mathbf{w} \mathbf{w}^T \right) \right], \text{ since trace is invariant under cyclic permutation}$$

$$= \text{tr} \left((\overline{\mathbf{D}}^T \overline{\mathbf{D}}) \cdot E[\mathbf{w} \mathbf{w}^T] \right)$$

$$= \text{tr} \left((\overline{\mathbf{D}}^T \overline{\mathbf{D}}) \cdot \left(\text{cov}(\mathbf{w}) + E[\mathbf{w}] \cdot E[\mathbf{w}]^T \right) \right) \tag{27.28}$$

$$= \text{tr} \left((\overline{\mathbf{D}}^T \overline{\mathbf{D}}) \cdot \text{cov}(\mathbf{w}) \right), \text{ since under the null hypothesis } E[\mathbf{w}] = \boldsymbol{\omega} = \mathbf{0}$$

$$= \text{tr} \left((\overline{\mathbf{D}}^T \overline{\mathbf{D}}) \cdot \sigma^2 (\overline{\mathbf{D}}^T \overline{\mathbf{D}})^{-1} \right) = \sigma^2 \text{tr} (\mathbf{I}_d) = d \cdot \sigma^2$$

where $\mathbf{I}_d$ is the $d \times d$ identity matrix. We also used the fact that

$$\text{cov}(\mathbf{w}) = E[\mathbf{w} \mathbf{w}^T] - E[\mathbf{w}] \cdot E[\mathbf{w}]^T, \text{ and therefore}$$

$$E[\mathbf{w} \mathbf{w}^T] = \text{cov}(\mathbf{w}) + E[\mathbf{w}] \cdot E[\mathbf{w}]^T$$

Notice that from Eq. (27.25), the covariance matrix for the augmented weight vector $\tilde{\mathbf{w}}$, that includes the bias term, is given as $\sigma^2 (\tilde{\mathbf{D}}^T \tilde{\mathbf{D}})^{-1}$. However, since we are ignoring the bias $b = w_0$ in the hypothesis test, we are interested only in the lower right $d \times d$ submatrix of $(\tilde{\mathbf{D}}^T \tilde{\mathbf{D}})^{-1}$, which excludes the values related to w_0. It can be shown that this submatrix is precisely the inverse of the centered scatter matrix $(\overline{\mathbf{D}}^T \overline{\mathbf{D}})^{-1}$ for the unaugmented data. We used this fact in the derivation above. Therefore, it follows that

$$E \left[\frac{RSS}{d} \right] = \frac{1}{d} E[RSS] = \frac{1}{d} \cdot d \cdot \sigma^2 = \sigma^2$$

Further, as per Eq. (27.21), the estimated variance is an unbiased estimator, so that

$$E[\hat{\sigma}^2] = \sigma^2$$

Thus, under the null hypothesis the f-statistic has a value close to 1, which indicates that there is no relationship between the predictor and response variables. On the other hand, if the alternative hypothesis is true, then $E[RSS/d] \geq \sigma^2$, resulting in a larger f value.

The ratio f follows a F-distribution with $d, (n-d-1)$ degrees of freedom for the numerator and denominator, respectively. Therefore, we can reject the null hypothesis if the p-value is less than the chosen significance level, say $\alpha = 0.01$.

Notice that, since $R^2 = 1 - \frac{SSE}{TSS} = \frac{RSS}{TSS}$, we have

$$SSE = (1 - R^2) \cdot TSS \qquad\qquad RSS = R^2 \cdot TSS$$

Therefore, we can rewrite the f ratio as follows

$$f = \frac{RSS/d}{SSE/(n-d-1)} = \frac{n-d-1}{d} \cdot \frac{R^2}{1-R^2} \tag{27.29}$$

In other words, the F-test compares the adjusted fraction of explained variation to the unexplained variation. If R^2 is high, it means the model can fit the data well, and that is more evidence to reject the null hypothesis.

Hypothesis Testing for Individual Parameters

We can also test whether each independent attribute X_i, contributes significantly for the prediction of Y or not, assuming that all the attributes are still retained in the model.

For attribute X_i, we set up the null hypothesis $H_0 : \omega_i = 0$ and contrast it with the alternative hypothesis $H_a : \omega_i \neq 0$. Using Eq. (27.26), the standardized variable Z_{w_i} under the null hypothesis is given as

$$Z_{w_i} = \frac{w_i - E[w_i]}{\text{se}(w_i)} = \frac{w_i}{\text{se}(w_i)} = \frac{w_i}{\hat{\sigma}\sqrt{c_{ii}}} \tag{27.30}$$

since $E[w_i] = \omega_i = 0$]. Next, using a two-tailed t-test with $n - d - 1$ degrees of freedom, we compute p-value(Z_{w_i}). If this probability is smaller than the significance level α (say 0.01), we can reject the null hypothesis. Otherwise, we accept the null hypothesis, which would imply that X_i does not add significant value in predicting the response in light of other attributes already used to fit the model. The t-test can also be used to test whether the bias term is significantly different from 0 or not.

Example 27.9 (Hypothesis Testing). We continue with Example 27.8, but now we test for the regression effect. Under the null hypothesis that $\omega_1 = \omega_2 = 0$, the expected value of RSS is σ^2. Thus, we expect the f-statistic to be close to 1. Let us check if that is the case; we have

$$f = \frac{RSS/d}{\hat{\sigma}^2} = \frac{80.60/2}{4.203 \times 10^{-2}} = 958.8$$

Using the F-distribution with $(d, n - d - 1) = (2, 147)$ degrees of freedom, we have

$$\text{p-value}(958.8) \simeq 0$$

In other words, such a large value of the f-statistic is extremely rare, and therefore, we can reject the null hypothesis. We conclude that Y does indeed depend on at least one of the predictor attributes X_1 or X_2.

We can also test for each of the regression coefficients individually using the t-test. For example, for ω_1, let the null hypothesis be $H_0 : \omega_1 = 0$, so that the alternative hypothesis is $H_a : \omega_1 \neq 0$. Assuming that the model still has both X_1 and X_2 as the predictor variables, we can compute the t-statistic using Eq. (27.26):

$$Z_{w_1} = \frac{w_1}{\text{se}(w_1)} = \frac{-0.082}{0.0414} = -1.98$$

Using a two-tailed t-test with $n - d - 1 = 147$ degrees of freedom, we find that

$$\text{p-value}(-1.98) = 0.0496$$

Since the p-value is only marginally less than a significance level of $\alpha = 0.05$ (i.e., a 95% confidence level), this means that X_1 is only weakly relevant for predicting Y in the presence of X_2. In fact, if we use the more stringent significance level $\alpha = 0.01$, we would conclude that X_1 is not significantly predictive of Y, given X_2.

On the other hand, individually for ω_2, if we test whether $H_0 : \omega_2 = 0$ versus $H_a : \omega_2 \neq 0$, we have:

$$Z_{w_2} = \frac{w_2}{\text{se}(w_2)} = \frac{0.45}{0.0194} = 23.2$$

Using a two-tailed t-test with $n - d - 1 = 147$ degrees of freedom, we find that

$$\text{p-value}(23.2) \simeq 0$$

This means, that individually X_2 is significantly predictive of Y even in the presence of X_1.

Using the t-test, we can also compute the p-value for the bias term:

$$Z_b = \frac{b}{\text{se}(b)} = \frac{-0.014}{0.183} = -0.077$$

which has a p-value $= 0.94$ for a two-tailed test. This means, we accept the null hypothesis that $\beta = 0$, and reject the alternative hypothesis that $\beta \neq 0$.

Example 27.10 (Centered Scatter Matrix). Here we show that the inverse of the centered scatter matrix $(\overline{\mathbf{D}}^T \overline{\mathbf{D}})^{-1}$ for the unaugmented data is the lower right submatrix of the inverse of the uncentered scatter matrix $(\tilde{\mathbf{D}}^T\tilde{\mathbf{D}})^{-1}$ for the augmented data.

For the augmented data comprising X_0, X_1 and X_2, from Example 27.6, the uncentered 3×3 scatter matrix $\tilde{\mathbf{D}}^T\tilde{\mathbf{D}}$ and its inverse, are given as

$$\tilde{\mathbf{D}}^T\tilde{\mathbf{D}} = \begin{pmatrix} 150.0 & 876.50 & 563.80 \\ 876.5 & 5223.85 & 3484.25 \\ 563.8 & 3484.25 & 2583.00 \end{pmatrix} \quad (\tilde{\mathbf{D}}^T\tilde{\mathbf{D}})^{-1} = \begin{pmatrix} 0.793 & -0.176 & 0.064 \\ -0.176 & 0.041 & -0.017 \\ 0.064 & -0.017 & 0.009 \end{pmatrix}$$

For the unaugmented data comprising only X_1 and X_2, the centered scatter matrix and its inverse are given as:

$$\overline{\mathbf{D}}^T\overline{\mathbf{D}} = \begin{pmatrix} 102.17 & 189.78 \\ 189.78 & 463.86 \end{pmatrix} \quad (\overline{\mathbf{D}}^T\overline{\mathbf{D}})^{-1} = \begin{pmatrix} 0.041 & -0.017 \\ -0.017 & 0.009 \end{pmatrix}$$

We can observe that $(\overline{\mathbf{D}}^T\overline{\mathbf{D}})^{-1}$ is exactly the lower right 2×2 submatrix of $(\tilde{\mathbf{D}}^T\tilde{\mathbf{D}})^{-1}$.

27.2.4 Geometric Approach to Statistical Testing

The geometry of multiple regression provides further insight into the hypothesis testing approach for the regression effect. Let $\overline{X}_i = X_i - \mu_{X_i} \cdot \mathbf{1}$ denote the centered attribute vector, and let $\overline{\mathbf{X}} = (\overline{X}_1, \overline{X}_2, \cdots, \overline{X}_d)^T$ denote the multivariate centered vector of predictor variables. The n-dimensional space over the points is divided into three mutually orthogonal subspaces, namely the 1-dimensional *mean space* $\mathcal{S}_\mu = span(\mathbf{1})$, the d dimensional *centered variable space* $\mathcal{S}_{\overline{X}} = span(\overline{\mathbf{X}})$, and the $n - d - 1$ dimensional *error space* $\mathcal{S}_\epsilon$, which contains the error vector $\boldsymbol{\epsilon}$. The response vector Y can thus be decomposed into three components (see Figures 27.2 and 27.5)

$$Y = \mu_Y \cdot \mathbf{1} + \widehat{\overline{Y}} + \boldsymbol{\epsilon}$$

Recall that the *degrees of freedom* of a random vector is defined as the dimensionality of its enclosing subspace. Since the original dimensionality of the point space is n, we have a total of n degrees of freedom. The mean space has dimensionality $dim(\mathcal{S}_\mu) = 1$, the centered variable space has $dim(\mathcal{S}_{\overline{X}}) = d$, and the error space has $dim(\mathcal{S}_\epsilon) = n - d - 1$, so that we have

$$dim(\mathcal{S}_\mu) + dim(\mathcal{S}_{\overline{X}}) + dim(\mathcal{S}_\epsilon) = 1 + d + (n - d - 1) = n$$

Population Regression Model

Recall that the regression model posits that for a fixed value $\mathbf{x}_i = (x_{i1}, x_{i2}, \cdots, x_{id})^T$, the true response y_i is given as

$$y_i = \beta + \omega_1 \cdot x_{i1} + \ldots + \omega_d \cdot x_{id} + \varepsilon_i$$

where the systematic part of the model $\beta + \sum_{j=1}^d \omega_j \cdot x_{ij}$ is fixed, and the error term ε_i varies randomly, with the assumption that ε_i follows a normal distribution with mean $\mu = 0$ and variance σ^2. We also assume that the ε_i values are all independent of each other.

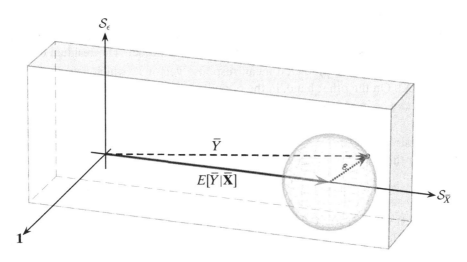

Figure 27.6. Population regression model. The $n-1$ dimensional subspace, comprising $S_{\bar{X}} + S_\epsilon$, orthogonal to $\mathbf{1}$ is shown as a hyperrectangle. The true error vector is a random vector of length $\|\boldsymbol{\varepsilon}\|$; the $(n-1)$-dimensional hypersphere shows the possible orientations of $\boldsymbol{\varepsilon}$ for a fixed length value.

Plugging $\beta = \mu_Y - \sum_{j=1}^{d} \omega_j \cdot \mu_{X_j}$ into the equation above, we obtain

$$y_i = \mu_Y + \omega_1 \cdot (x_{i1} - \mu_{X_1}) + \ldots + \omega_d \cdot (x_{id} - \mu_{X_d}) + \varepsilon_i$$
$$= \mu_Y + \omega_1 \cdot \bar{x}_{i1} + \ldots + \omega_d \cdot \bar{x}_{id} + \varepsilon_i$$

where $\bar{x}_{ij} = x_{ij} - \mu_{X_j}$ is the centered value for attribute X_j. Across all the points, we can rewrite the above equation in vector form

$$Y = \mu_Y \cdot \mathbf{1} + \omega_1 \cdot \bar{X}_1 + \ldots + \omega_d \cdot \bar{X}_d + \boldsymbol{\varepsilon}$$

We can also center the vector Y, so that we obtain a regression model over the centered response and predictor variables, as illustrated in Figure 27.6:

$$\bar{Y} = Y - \mu_Y \cdot \mathbf{1} = \omega_1 \cdot \bar{X}_1 + \omega_2 \cdot \bar{X}_2 + \ldots + \omega_d \cdot \bar{X}_d + \boldsymbol{\varepsilon} = E[\bar{Y}|\mathbf{X}] + \boldsymbol{\varepsilon}$$

In this equation, $\sum_{i=1}^{d} \omega_i \cdot \bar{X}_i$ is a fixed vector that denotes the expected value $E[\bar{Y}|\mathbf{X}]$ and $\boldsymbol{\varepsilon}$ is an n-dimensional random vector that is distributed according to a n-dimensional multivariate normal vector with mean $\boldsymbol{\mu} = \mathbf{0}$, and a fixed variance σ^2 along all dimensions, so that its covariance matrix is $\boldsymbol{\Sigma} = \sigma^2 \cdot \mathbf{I}$. The distribution of $\boldsymbol{\varepsilon}$ is therefore given as

$$f(\boldsymbol{\varepsilon}) = \frac{1}{(\sqrt{2\pi})^n \cdot \sqrt{|\boldsymbol{\Sigma}|}} \cdot \exp\left\{-\frac{\boldsymbol{\varepsilon}^T \boldsymbol{\Sigma}^{-1} \boldsymbol{\varepsilon}}{2}\right\} = \frac{1}{(\sqrt{2\pi})^n \cdot \sigma^n} \cdot \exp\left\{-\frac{\|\boldsymbol{\varepsilon}\|^2}{2 \cdot \sigma^2}\right\}$$

which follows from the fact that $|\boldsymbol{\Sigma}| = \det(\boldsymbol{\Sigma}) = \det(\sigma^2 \mathbf{I}) = (\sigma^2)^n$ and $\boldsymbol{\Sigma}^{-1} = \frac{1}{\sigma^2}\mathbf{I}$.

The density of $\boldsymbol{\varepsilon}$ is thus a function of its squared length $\|\boldsymbol{\varepsilon}\|^2$, independent of its angle. In other words, the vector $\boldsymbol{\varepsilon}$ is distributed uniformly over all angles and is equally likely to point in any direction. Figure 27.6 illustrates the population regression model. The fixed vector $E[\bar{Y}|\mathbf{X}]$ is shown, and one orientation of $\boldsymbol{\varepsilon}$ is shown. It is important to note that the $n-1$ dimensional hypersphere denotes the fact that the random vector $\boldsymbol{\varepsilon}$ can be in any orientation in this hypersphere of radius $\|\boldsymbol{\varepsilon}\|$. Notice how the population regression model differs from the fitted model. The residual error vector $\boldsymbol{\epsilon}$ is orthogonal to the predicted mean response vector $\widehat{\overline{Y}}$, which acts as the estimate for $E[\overline{Y}|\mathbf{X}]$. On the other hand, in the population regression model, the random error vector $\boldsymbol{\varepsilon}$ can be in any orientation compared to $E[\overline{Y}|\mathbf{X}]$.

Hypothesis Testing

Consider the population regression model

$$Y = \mu_Y \cdot \mathbf{1} + \omega_1 \cdot \overline{X}_1 + \ldots + \omega_d \cdot \overline{X}_d + \boldsymbol{\varepsilon} = \mu_Y \cdot \mathbf{1} + E[\overline{Y}|\mathbf{X}] + \boldsymbol{\varepsilon}$$

To test whether $X_1, X_2, \cdots, X_d$ are useful in predicting Y, we consider what would happen if all of the regression coefficients were zero, which forms our null hypothesis

$$H_0 : \quad \omega_1 = 0, \omega_2 = 0, \ldots, \omega_d = 0$$

In this case, we have

$$Y = \mu_Y \cdot \mathbf{1} + \boldsymbol{\varepsilon} \implies Y - \mu_Y \cdot \mathbf{1} = \boldsymbol{\varepsilon} \implies \overline{Y} = \boldsymbol{\varepsilon}$$

Since $\boldsymbol{\varepsilon}$ is normally distributed with mean $\mathbf{0}$ and covariance matrix $\sigma^2 \cdot \mathbf{I}$, under the null hypothesis, the variation in $\overline{Y}$ for a given value of $\mathbf{x}$ will therefore be centered around the origin $\mathbf{0}$.

On the other hand, under the alternative hypothesis H_a that at least one of the ω_i is non-zero, we have

$$\overline{Y} = E[\overline{Y}|\mathbf{X}] + \boldsymbol{\varepsilon}$$

Thus, the variation in $\overline{Y}$ is shifted away from the origin $\mathbf{0}$ in the direction $E[\overline{Y}|\mathbf{X}]$.

In practice, we obviously do not know the true value of $E[\overline{Y}|\mathbf{X}]$, but we can estimate it by projecting the centered observation vector $\overline{Y}$ onto the subspaces $S_{\overline{X}}$ and S_ϵ, as follows

$$\overline{Y} = w_1 \cdot \overline{X}_1 + w_2 \cdot \overline{X}_2 + \ldots + w_d \cdot \overline{X}_d + \boldsymbol{\epsilon} = \widehat{\overline{Y}} + \boldsymbol{\epsilon}$$

Now, under the null hypothesis, the true centered response vector is $\overline{Y} = \boldsymbol{\varepsilon}$, and therefore, $\widehat{\overline{Y}}$ and $\boldsymbol{\epsilon}$ are simply the projections of the random error vector $\boldsymbol{\varepsilon}$ onto the subspaces $S_{\overline{X}}$ and S_ϵ, as shown in Figure 27.7(a). In this case, we also expect the length of $\boldsymbol{\epsilon}$ and $\widehat{\overline{Y}}$ to be roughly comparable. On the other hand, under the alternative hypothesis, we have $\overline{Y} = E[\overline{Y}|\mathbf{X}] + \boldsymbol{\varepsilon}$, and so $\widehat{\overline{Y}}$ will be relatively much longer compared to $\boldsymbol{\epsilon}$, as shown in Figure 27.7(b).

Given that we expect to see a difference between $\widehat{\overline{Y}}$ under the null and alternative hypotheses, this suggests a geometric test based on the relative lengths of $\widehat{\overline{Y}}$ and $\boldsymbol{\epsilon}$ (since we do not know the true $E[\overline{Y}|\mathbf{X}]$ or $\boldsymbol{\varepsilon}$). However, there is one difficulty; we cannot compare their lengths directly, since $\widehat{\overline{Y}}$ lies in a d dimensional space, whereas $\boldsymbol{\epsilon}$ lies in a $n-d-1$ dimensional space. Instead, we can compare their lengths after normalizing

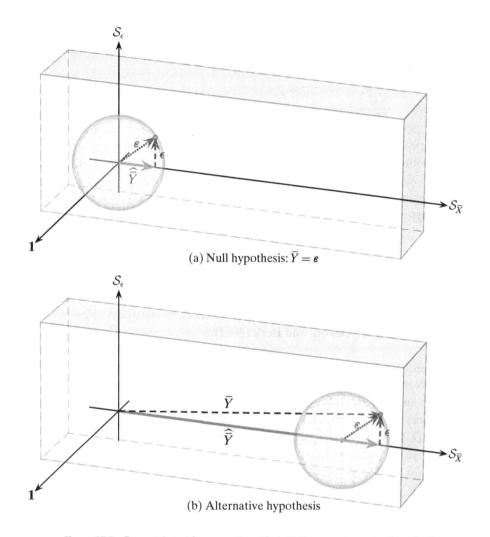

(a) Null hypothesis: $\bar{Y} = \varepsilon$

(b) Alternative hypothesis

Figure 27.7. Geometric test for regression effect: Null versus alternative hypothesis.

by the number of dimensions. Define the mean squared length of per dimension for the two vectors $\widehat{\bar{Y}}$ and ϵ, as follows

$$M\left(\widehat{\bar{Y}}\right) = \frac{\left\|\widehat{\bar{Y}}\right\|^2}{dim(\mathcal{S}_{\bar{X}})} = \frac{\left\|\widehat{\bar{Y}}\right\|^2}{d}$$

$$M(\epsilon) = \frac{\|\epsilon\|^2}{dim(\mathcal{S}_\epsilon)} = \frac{\|\epsilon\|^2}{n-d-1}$$

Thus, the geometric test for the regression effect is the ratio of the normalized mean squared length of $\widehat{\bar{Y}}$ to ϵ, given as

$$\frac{M\left(\widehat{\bar{Y}}\right)}{M(\epsilon)} = \frac{\left\|\widehat{\bar{Y}}\right\|^2 / d}{\|\epsilon\|^2 / (n-d-1)}$$

It is interesting to note that from Eq. (27.24) we have $\left\|\widehat{\overline{Y}}\right\|^2 = RSS$ and $\|\epsilon\|^2 = \left\|Y - \widehat{Y}\right\|^2 = SSE$, and therefore, the geometric ratio test is identical to the F-test in Eq. (27.27), since

$$\frac{M(\widehat{\overline{Y}})}{M(\epsilon)} = \frac{\left\|\widehat{\overline{Y}}\right\|^2/d}{\|\epsilon\|^2/(n-d-1)} = \frac{RSS/d}{SSE/(n-d-1)} = f$$

The geometric approach, illustrated in Figure 27.7, makes it clear that if $f \simeq 1$ then the null hypothesis holds, and we conclude that Y does not depend on the predictor variables $X_1, X_2, \cdots, X_d$. On the other hand, if f is large, with a p-value less than the significance level (say, $\alpha = 0.01$), then we can reject the null hypothesis and accept the alternative hypothesis that Y depends on at least one predictor variable X_i.

27.3 FURTHER READING

For a geometrical approach to multivariate statistics see Wickens (2014), and Saville and Wood (2012). For an excellent treatment of modern statistical inference in the context of regression see Devore and Berk (2012).

Devore, J. and Berk, K. (2012). *Modern Mathematical Statistics with Applications*. 2nd ed. New York: Springer Science+Business Media.

Saville, D. J. and Wood, G. R. (2012). *Statistical Methods: The Geometric Approach*. New York: Springer Science + Business Media.

Wickens, T. D. (2014). *The Geometry of Multivariate Statistics*. New York: Psychology Press, Taylor & Francis Group.

27.4 EXERCISES

Q1. Show that for bivariate regression, we have $\beta = \mu_Y - \omega \cdot \mu_X$, where β and ω are the true model parameters.

Q2. Show that $\sum_{i=1}^{n}(y_i - \hat{y}_i) \cdot (\hat{y}_i - \mu_Y) = 0$.

Q3. Prove that ϵ is orthogonal to $\widehat{Y}$ and $\mathbf{X}$. Show this for bivariate regression and then for multiple regression.

Q4. Show that for bivariate regression, the R^2 statistic is equivalent to the squared correlation between the independent attribute vector X and response vector Y. That is, show that $R^2 = \rho_{XY}^2$.

Q5. Show that $\widehat{\overline{Y}} = \widehat{Y} - \mu_Y \cdot \mathbf{1}$.

Q6. Show that $\|\epsilon\| = \left\|Y - \widehat{Y}\right\| = \left\|\overline{Y} - \widehat{\overline{Y}}\right\|$.

Q7. In bivariate regression, show that under the null hypothesis, $E[RSS] = \sigma^2$.

Q8. In bivariate regression, show that $E[\hat{\sigma}^2] = \sigma^2$.

Q9. Show that $E[RSS/d] \geq \sigma^2$.

Q10. Treating each residual $\epsilon_i = y_i - \hat{y}_i$ as a random variable, show that

$$\text{var}(\epsilon_i) = \sigma^2(1 - h_{ii})$$

where h_{ii} is the ith diagonal of the $(d+1) \times (d+1)$ hat matrix $\mathbf{H}$ for the augmented data $\tilde{\mathbf{D}}$. Next, using the above expression for $\text{var}(\epsilon_i)$, show that for bivariate regression, the variance of the ith residual is given as

$$\text{var}(\epsilon_i) = \sigma^2 \cdot \left(1 - \frac{1}{n} - \frac{1}{s_X} \cdot (x_i - \mu_X)^2\right)$$

Q11. Given data matrix $\mathbf{D}$, let $\overline{\mathbf{D}}$ the centered data matrix, and $\tilde{\mathbf{D}}$ the augmented data matrix (with the extra column $X_0 = \mathbf{1}$). Let $(\tilde{\mathbf{D}}^T\tilde{\mathbf{D}})$ be the uncentered scatter matrix for the augmented data, and let $\overline{\mathbf{D}}^T\overline{\mathbf{D}}$ be the scatter matrix for the centered data. Show that the lower right $d \times d$ submatrix of $(\tilde{\mathbf{D}}^T\tilde{\mathbf{D}})^{-1}$ is $(\overline{\mathbf{D}}^T\overline{\mathbf{D}})^{-1}$.

Index

Printed in the United States
by Baker & Taylor Publisher Services